GREECE

D1603160

THE BLUE GUIDES

ENGLAND
LONDON
SCOTLAND
WALES AND THE MARCHES
IRELAND
CHANNEL ISLANDS
NORTHERN ITALY
ROME AND ENVIRONS
VENICE
SICILY
ATHENS AND ENVIRONS
GREECE
CRETE
CYPRUS
PARIS AND ENVIRONS
LOIRE VALLEY, NORMANDY, BRITTANY
BELGIUM AND LUXEMBOURG
MALTA
SPAIN: The Mainland
MOSCOW AND LENINGRAD

BLUE GUIDE

GREECE

STUART ROSSITER
M.A.

*Atlas of Greece, street atlas of Athens,
and 91 maps and plans*
by JOHN FLOWER

ERNEST BENN LIMITED
LONDON AND TONBRIDGE

RAND McNALLY & COMPANY
CHICAGO, NEW YORK, SAN FRANCISCO

FIRST EDITION 1967
SECOND EDITION 1973
THIRD EDITION 1977
FOURTH EDITION 1981

Published by Ernest Benn Limited
25 New Street Square, London EC4A 3JA
& Sovereign Way · Tonbridge · Kent

Rand McNally & Company
Chicago · New York · San Francisco

© Ernest Benn Limited 1981

Printed in Great Britain

ISBN *Hardcover* 0 510 01642–1 528–84729–5 (USA)
ISBN *Paperback* 0 510 01643–X 528–84728–7 (USA)

WARNING

It seems very likely that many times of opening for museums and sites given hopefully in the text, coupled with the general remarks in the Practical Information section, will be found incorrect. At the time of writing not even official publications would be held responsible for accuracy. The 'Standard Times' has been subject to constant alteration and exceptions, depending on whether the desire of the authorities to open longer hours or of the staffs for shorter hours and higher wages had the upper hand. This has already led to sharp rises in entrance fees and unforeseen failures to open, a situation long familiar in Italy.

PREFACE

This fourth edition of the BLUE GUIDE GREECE follows the very successful pattern set by the previous three. The book has established itself firmly as the accepted guide to the country, not least among students of archaeology, both amateur and professional, though it is designed for any traveller desirous of appreciating more fully whatever he sees.

The development of Greece during the twenty years spanned by work on four successive editions has been rapid, far-reaching, but very uneven. Some changes have been brought about directly by tourism, others are a consequence of large-scale temporary emigration to industrially richer countries, still others stem from government projects to harness natural resources. The effects are complex, sometimes physical and obvious, sometimes cultural and subtle, resulting in changes some of which have been gradual, some sudden.

Individual tourism in the 60s altered the attitude towards strangers from curiosity and welcome to indifferent acceptance of the commonplace. The mass tourism of the 70s brought to selected areas, in the train of improved communications, technical progress and new attitudes, leading at best to greater local comfort and at worst to the understandably ungracious attitude one meets at Olympia. The draining of lowland marshes and the flooding of highland valleys have brought fundamental changes in the landscape itself. The area of irrigated land had trebled, while the use of tractors has increased tenfold. Goats and water-buffalo give way to Friesian herds and on cooperative farms orchards and sugar-beet replace the produce of smallholdings. As fast as improvements come to agriculture, young men desert the land for industrial work in Germany or the sophistication of urban life. The 1981 census is expected to show that nearly a third of the total population has moved into the Attic plain (and strong incentives are already being devised to persuade them out again). The television aerial in the town, the refrigerator, and the motor-cycle carrier in the country have become the symbols of a new consumer era.

Yet in spite of this—and however cynical tourists in Athens may be about the visitor as guest—a country wedding in Arcadia or Epirus or Thrace or Crete remains traditional; folksy brochures notwithstanding, fire rituals and near-eastern musical instruments survive.

During the past two years the author has travelled a further 6000 miles over Greek roads and tracks. Some excursions to mountain areas and remote sites become easier every year as new roads are built or old ones improved. This does not necessarily add to the pleasure of arriving, for half the satisfaction in earlier times was in getting there at all and in noticing things during the slower progress on the way. In the autumn of 1979 plans to visit a number of islands were frustrated by rough seas and an unpleasant day was spent in cloud on the rain-drenched slopes of Pelion.

Once again it has been found difficult to decide which new excavations to mention and which new scholarly theories to adopt—always supposing more than a proportion of these have come to notice. Archaeological sites sometimes remain inaccessible in direct proportion to their importance (as at Vergina), while theories, however well reasoned and attractive, are too frequently contradicted or disproved just as one adopts them.

Though the Blue Guide is probably the most comprehensive single-volume guide to the country available in English, it still leaves large tracts of Greece undescribed. These are there to be discovered by whoever grows to love the country enough to explore beyond the beaten tourist paths. All must be warned, however, that camping except on official camp-sites is now illegal. Except on some of the remoter islands and shores, hotel building has slowed and the industry has settled to a period of consolidation and improvement.

Most of the town plans have been improved by observation on the spot, transferred into visual form by **John Flower,** the original cartographer.

Thanks are rendered once again to friends who have smoothed various paths: to Panayotis ('Peter') Analytis of the National Tourist Organisation of Greece in London, his secretary and staff; to Olympic Airways; to Basil Mantzos of Olympic Holidays; to Basil Iatrides of Astir Hotels for hospitality; to Ted Vassilakis of AutoHellas, the Greek concessionary of Hertz (with particular thanks to his staff in Corfù, Piraeus, and Herakleion for coping at outlandish times of day); to friends at the British School at Athens and the American School of Classical Studies, now too numerous to mention; and to travelling companions and casual acquaintances all through Greece. Particular mention must be made of David Moss who bore the author company on two occasions, driving safely and cheerfully on track and highway from Corfù to Ierapetra through heat and cold, snow and rain, mud and dust, over fields, in cloud, and—not least—in the industrial suburbs of Piraeus and Salonika.

While gratitude is owed to many correspondents who point out the error of the author's topographical ways, long experience has shown that of every ten corrections offered, one at least will be incorrect, being based on a misreading, a misdirection or on a source which has already been rejected in favour of a better. One correspondent was deliberately anonymous leaving no avenue for being corrected in turn. So while freely admitting that most of his/her points were justified and have been gratefully incorporated, one at least was not and he/she should become better acquainted with Philippe, duc de Navailles (1619–84). The readers' continuing assistance is solicited; any constructive suggestions for the correction or improvement of the guide will be most gratefully welcomed.

CONTENTS

III. THE PELOPONNESE

IV. CENTRAL GREECE

MAPS AND PLANS

MAPS

TOWN PLANS

GROUND PLANS OF SITES AND BUILDINGS

EXPLANATIONS

The arrangement of this guide by routes conforms in every way to the past traditions of the series without innovations.

TYPE. The main routes are described in large type. Smaller type is used for branch-routes and excursions, for historical and preliminary paragraphs, and (generally speaking) for descriptions of minor importance.

DISTANCES (placed in front of the place-name) are given cumulatively from the starting-point of the route or sub-route in miles and kilometres; on diversions from a route (placed *after* the place-name), they are specific to that place from the point of divergence from the route. Road distances have been calculated where possible from the km. posts on the roads themselves, otherwise from measurement on official maps; constant realinements make it certain that these distances will vary slightly from those measured by motorists on their milometers. Shorter (walking) distances especially have been given in miles rather than kilometres, in the belief that this still accords with the instinctive preferences of both English and American readers. A Greek asked a walking distance will always give the answer as a walking *time*. Archaeologists, however, invariably use metres and the site plans are accordingly scaled in metres.

HEIGHTS are given in the text in English feet, on the maps in metres.

POPULATIONS are given in round figures according to the Census of 1971.

ASTERISKS indicate points of special interest or excellence.

ABBREVIATIONS. In addition to generally accepted and self-explanatory abbreviations, the following occur in the Guide:

A′, B′	tou Protou (i.e. 'the first'), the second, etc.	Hdt.	Herodotus
		Hesp.	Hesperia
A.J.A.	American Journal of Archaeology	km.	kilometre(s)
		J.H.S.	Journal of Hellenic Studies
Akr.	Akroterion (i.e. Cape)	l.	left
Ay.	Ayios, Ayia, etc. (Saint or Saints)	Leof.	Leoforos (Avenue)
		m.	mile(s)
B.C.H.	Bulletin de Correspondance Hellenique	NR	no restaurant
		N.T.O.	(see below)
B.S.A.	Annual of the British School at Athens	Od.	Odhos (Street)
		Plat.	Plateia (Square)
c.	circa	r.	right
C	century	R.	rooms
DPO	(at least) demi-pension obligatory	Rest.	restaurant
		Rte	route
dr.	drachma(s)	Thuc.	Thucydides
fl.	floruit		

E.O.T. (N.T.O.)	Ἑλληνικός Ὀργανισμός Τουρίσμου (National Tourist Organization).
K.T.E.Λ. (K.T.E.L.)	Κοινόν Ταμείον Εἰσπράξεων Λεωφορείων (Joint Pool of Bus Owners); on plans = Bus Station.
O.T.E.	Ὀργανισμός Τηλεπικοινωνιῶν Ἑλλάδος (Greek Telecommunications Organization); on plans = Telegraph Office.

THE MONUMENTS OF GREECE

by NICOLAS COLDSTREAM

A The Monuments in their Historical Setting

The Stone Age. The earliest vestige of man in Greece—earlier than the emergence of Homo Sapiens himself—consists of a fossilized skull of Neanderthal type found near Salonika. Of the more developed food-gathering culture of Palaeolithic Greece one can now get a clear impression from three cave sites in the Louros valley, Epirus: recent excavations there have revealed occupation going back to c. 40,000 B.C., and a Mousterian flint industry similar to those of Balkan Europe.

The first impulses towards farming, towards the domestication of animals, and towards the foundation of settled villages came to Greece from Anatolia. The oldest farming communities in Greece—and indeed in Europe—were centred round the fertile plains of Thessaly and Macedonia. An Early Neolithic settlement at Nea Nikomedia near Veroia (7th–6th mill. B.C.) shows traces of large rectangular houses, and displays several links with Anatolia in its artefacts. The later stages of Neolithic culture are best represented at Sesklo and Dimini, both near the land-locked gulf of Pagasae. At Sesklo (6th–5th mill. B.C.) the lack of fortifications and the manufacture of elegant painted and burnished pottery bear witness to a peaceful and flourishing agricultural civilization, while the importation of obsidian from the island of Melos proves the existence of trade even at this remote period. The rectangular houses, with walls built of mud brick, were founded on a stone base which remains their only visible memorial to the visitor today. At the neighbouring village of Dimini (founded c. 3400 B.C.) concentric rings of fortification reveal a more turbulent state of affairs; in these unsettled conditions the rise of centralized authority is suggested by the building of a spacious house on the summit of the mound, whose pillared porch, leading into the main hall, foreshadows the Mycenean megaron (p. 23).

The Early Bronze Age (c. 2800–2000 B.C.). In the ensuing centuries, while Thessaly relapsed into provincialism, the centre of civilization moved southward with the arrival of fresh influences from Anatolia (c. 2800 B.C.). The inhabitants learned the use of copper, and spoke a pre-Hellenic language, to which some non-Greek features in Greek place names (such as -nth- and -ss- in Corinth, Knossos) are generally attributed. Most settlements of this period lay on the eastern seaboard of the Peloponnese and of Central Greece, in the Cyclades, and in Crete. On the mainland the most impressive Early Helladic site is at Lerna in the Argolid, where the imposing House of Tiles, evidently an important seat of administrative authority, is the earliest known building of monumental proportions in the Aegean area. Even more progressive was the Early Minoan culture of Crete, perhaps owing to its proximity to the advanced civilizations of the Near East: contact had already been established with the Old Kingdom of Egypt at the very beginning of the Bronze Age. Flourishing settlements grew up in the eastern part of the island, notably at Mochlos, where craftsmen excelled in the production of jewellery and stone vases; at Vasiliki, whose surprisingly elaborate house-plans already look forward to the later palaces; and at Fournou Korifi, where a complete village of c. 2600–2200 B.C. has recently been unearthed. In this period the Cyclades played an active rôle in exchanges with Crete and the mainland: hence come the well-known marble idols.

The Middle and Late Bronze Age: THE PALATIAL CIVILIZATIONS OF CRETE AND MYCENAE (c. 2000–1100 B.C.). Soon after 2000 B.C. the unity of the Aegean world was broken for several centuries. Invaders, usually identified with the first Greeks, swept over the mainland in two waves (c. 2200 and c. 2000 B.C.) destroying the main centres of Early Helladic civilization: meanwhile the Minoans, who suffered no such disruption, gradually extended their influence over the Cyclades.

The focus of Cretan power now moved to the centre of the island, with the foundation of the three palaces at Knossos, Phaestos, and Mallia. The similarity of their layout, and their lack of effective defences suggest the growth of a single organized kingdom, which established a 'pax Minoica' in the Aegean by the exercise of an overwhelming supremacy at sea, unchallenged until the emergence of the Greek mainland as a world power in the 16C B.C.

All three palaces were frequently rebuilt after periodical destructions by earthquake, reaching their most advanced form in the 16C B.C.; yet their basic plan was never radically altered, consisting of a vast network of rooms grouped asymmetrically round a central court, often rising to three stories. This plan was reproduced on a more modest scale in a fourth palace built in c. 1600 B.C. at Kato Zakro on the east coast. On a still smaller scale are the villas of the local gentry, spaced fairly evenly throughout the centre and east of the island (Tylissos, Sklavokampos, Amnisos, Nirou Khani, Myrtos, several near Siteia and especially Gournia where the residence is surrounded by a completely excavated Minoan town). The intricacy of Minoan palaces, which in the impressionable minds of later Greek visitors gave rise to the fanciful legend of the Labyrinth, was demanded by a monarchy that was at once theocratic and bureaucratic: all the reins of authority, whether political, religious, or commercial, were held within the palace walls (although Mallia has also places of public assembly outside the palace). The spaciousness of the state apartments and the secure privacy of the domestic quarters supplied the essential needs of princely dignity. Under the same roof, the most skilful artisans applied their crafts under royal supervision. The magazines, with their ordered rows of earthenware pithoi, stored the royal reserves of oil, wine, corn, and other commodities, whose management required the use of writing: at first a system of hieroglyphs was evolved (c. 2000–1660 B.C.), gradually superseded by a more convenient syllabary script, Linear A (c. 1900–1450 B.C.). Neither of these scripts can yet be read. Finally the presence of small shrines and purificatory areas within the palace reminds us that the Minoan king was also High Priest: the 'Throne Room' at Knossos was perhaps an inner sanctum whither the King could retire to hold converse with his god. Outside the palaces, villas and houses cults were also practised in sanctuaries on mountain peaks and in the numinous atmosphere of caves: in later times their memory was preserved by the association of the caves on Ida and Dicte with the birth and nurture of Zeus, originally the young consort of the Minoan mother-goddess.

By the beginning of the Late Bronze Age (c. 1550 B.C.) the Minoans had attained the summit of their power. Minoan outposts had been planted in the Cyclades (notably at Phylakopi on Melos and at Akrotiri on Thera), on Kythera (Kastri), on Rhodes (Trianda), and at Miletus: Minoan wares had been exported to the markets of Cyprus, Syria, and Egypt: after c. 1500 B.C., Minoan emissaries began to appear in Egyptian tomb paintings of the XVIIIth Dynasty under the name of Keftiu, bearing costly gifts of friendship to the Pharaohs. On the Greek mainland, Minoan influence was probably confined to the artistic sphere; it is first seen in the astounding wealth of gold vessels, jewellery and weapons in the shaft graves at Mycenae (c. 16C B.C.), and continues in the rich offerings of the 15C tombs at Vaphio and in the Pylos area. The Minoan style was frequently adapted to scenes of war and hunting— subjects that were foreign to Minoan taste, but congenial to the martial temper of the mainlanders.

Some time between 1500 and 1450 B.C. the volcanic island of Thera erupted in a truly catastrophic manner, and devastated practically every Cretan site except Knossos. As a result, the mastery of the Aegean world steadily passed from Crete to the rising power of Mycenae— a process that was accelerated by the irretrievable wreckage of the palace at Knossos c. 1380 B.C., whether by human or natural agency: but even before this date some form of mainland control over the Cretan metropolis is clearly indicated by the appearance of a new script in the Knossian archives (Linear B) which has been deciphered as an early form of Greek. Likewise, by the end of the 15C B.C., Mycenean traders had taken over the Minoan overseas outposts, and after this date, the commercial initiative in the Mediterranean from Sicily to Egypt had passed into Mycenean hands.

In the 14–13C B.C. Mycenae became an imperial capital, giving her name to the advanced civilization in which she played the predominant part. Not that impressive memorials of the period are lacking in other parts of Greece: Messenia, Boeotia, Attica, and Laconia were all heavily populated, and it is to Pylos that we turn for the best preserved palace on the mainland (13C B.C.). The Linear B archives from there suggest that the king of each district (*wanax*) stood at the head of his own highly organized feudal system: but we also learn from the Iliad of Homer that these local rulers, in their turn, were obliged to supply contingents for foreign ventures like the Siege of Troy (a historical event of c. 1250 B.C.) under the supreme command of Agamemnon, king of Mycenae, who was regarded as *primus inter pares*.

At Mycenae the pattern of settlement is typical of many other areas. On a low rocky eminence, fortified by a ring of massive Cyclopean masonry, dwelt the king and his court. His palace was smaller than the Cretan prototypes, but more symmetrically designed (p. 14). Not far below, an intricate complex of shrines ('The House with the Idols') also combines Minoan and mainland features. Outside this citadel lived the king's subjects in contiguous villages, each with its own cemetery hewn in the rock: the royal dynasty were buried in the monumental tholos (or 'beehive') tombs, one of the chief glories of the age (p. 23): elsewhere only in Egypt was such veneration paid to the illustrious dead. Far beyond the limits of this lower town, the king's gaze could range over the flourishing settlements of the Argive plain (such as Prosymna, Argos, and Dendra), past the citadel at Tiryns, down to the sea at Nauplia, which, together with the little port at Asine, guarded the entrance to his kingdom from foreign invasion.

About 1200 B.C. the Mycenean world found itself in mortal danger from a quite different direction. Barbarous northerners, equated in Greek tradition with the Dorians, had begun to move from their fastnesses in the Pindus mountains, destroying as they advanced. Energetic measures were taken to meet this new menace: the fortification of the Perseia spring at Mycenae, the galleries at Tiryns, and the stairway to the spring under the Acropolis at Athens, three marvels of military engineering, all belong to this date. Pylos succumbed to the first Dorian onset (c. 1200 B.C.): Mycenae and Tiryns were devastated, and by 1150 B.C., after further assaults, lay in ruins. Significantly for the future course of Greek history, Athens survived the ordeal unscathed. Many of her Ionian kinsmen took refuge on her soil before finding new homes across the Aegean on the western seaboard of Asia Minor (11–10C B.C.). These colonists were the vanguard of a movement which was eventually to spread Hellenic civilization all round the shores of the Mediterranean: but in these pages we cannot follow their fortunes, being concerned exclusively with the monuments of the mother country.

The Hellenic City-State: c. 1100–27 B.C. The Dorian invasions destroyed once again the unity of Aegean civilization, and ushered in a Dark Age (11–9C B.C.). Cut off from the outside world through the loss of their sea power, and isolated from one another by mountain barriers, the inhabitants of Greece were for a time forced to rely on the resources of their own poor soil, whose tillage became easier with the invention of iron tools. This period of poverty saw the birth of the city-state (polis) which remained the normal unit of Greek society for over a thousand years. By about 750 B.C., when prosperity was beginning to return with the revival of seafaring and commerce, the political geography had become reasonably fixed: the Greek world was now divided into several hundreds of these miniature republics, each enjoying complete autonomy. Athens became an exceptionally large state by effecting the union of all Attica, but even so her territory was no larger than an average English county. In the 5C B.C., when all free-born male Athenians possessed the franchise, the citizen roll numbered about 40,000, all of whom were entitled to vote in person at the meetings of the Assembly: among other cities, only a handful could muster more than 10,000. Plato fixed the number at 5040 for his ideal state: Aristotle thought that all citizens should know one another personally.

For the siting of a Hellenic city, three things were indispensable: an effective water-supply, access to arable land, and above all an easily defensible position, since relations between neighbouring states were seldom cordial. At first the acropolis served as a fortress in times of danger: later, whole cities were fortified (p. 18). Athens and Thebes both grew up round typical Mycenean strongholds: in the Peloponnese, where the Dorians tended to avoid the main Mycenean centres, the cities of Corinth and Argos were protected by yet more massive citadels. The Spartans, trusting in their military prowess, dispensed with both natural and artificial defences and chose an exposed site in the Laconian plain. In times of peace, after the disappearance of monarchical rule, the acropolis was usually set apart for the worship of the patron deity.

By the end of the 6C B.C., temples had been built over the ruins of the Bronze Age palaces at Athens, Mycenae, Tiryns, and Knossos: after the sack of the Athenian acropolis by the Persians in 480 B.C., the cult of Athena was glorified by a series of monuments that became the wonder of Greece.

With the rise of democratic and oligarchic governments, the agora became the true centre of public life. Here, in a level square expanse at the very heart of the city, political and commercial business could be conducted; here, too, men could seek congenial company in their idle moments, enjoying the opportunities for free and leisured discussion from which Greek thought derives its originality. All round the square, buildings grew up in a more or less haphazard fashion, depending on the whim of the people and the balance of the treasury at any given time: it was not until the Hellenistic period that the agora was subjected to organized planning. The stoa, or open portico, which offered shelter from the sun and rain, became an essential component in the architecture of the agora: behind the long colonnade, where philosophers did much of their teaching, the interior could be divided into a large number of rooms suitable for shops, offices, banks, or market-stalls. By the 2C B.C., the Athenian agora was virtually surrounded by stoas, of which one, that presented by Attalos II of Pergamon (mid-2C B.C.), has been restored as a museum. Other buildings were devoted to the smooth working of Athenian democracy: the Bouleuterion housed the Council of 500 who prepared the business of the full Assembly of citizens: in the round building known as the Tholos, a standing committee drawn from their numbers (the Prytaneis) remained on duty, in order to deal with any emergency that might arise. The Assembly, too numerous to be accommodated in the Agora, met on the Pnyx, where a bank of earth converted the rocky hill into an artificial theatre. For the same reason, public spectacles were removed from the agora at an early date: hence the construction of theatres, stadia, and gymnasia, usually sited on the outskirts of the city, and sometimes outside its walls.

The nucleus of the Greek theatre was the circular orchestra, or 'dancing-place', since drama had originally evolved from the ritual dances to the God Dionysos at country festivals. For the seating of the spectators, full advantage was taken of natural contours: the auditorium (theatron), with its tiers of stone seats, enclosed the orchestra on three sides, and, if necessary, was banked up at the ends by retaining walls (analemmata). In the 5C B.C., the great age of Attic tragedy and comedy, temporary stages of wood and canvas were thought sufficient: raised stages built of stone were probably an innovation of the Hellenistic period. It was left for Roman architects to bind the stage and the auditorium into a single structure by throwing vaults over the side passages (parodoi) between the two: in the course of this transformation, both the auditorium and the orchestra assumed a semicircular shape (p. 20).

The stadium and gymnasium were designed for athletic contests and athletic practice respectively. The word *stadion* originally meant a unit of distance equivalent to 200 yds, the length of the normal foot-race; where possible (as at Athens and Epidaurus) the course was sited in a long and shallow trough between two hills, and the spectators were placed on the banks either side. The familiar semicircular end (sphendone) and the idea of stone seating were borrowed from the theatre in Hellenistic times: monumental entrances (as at Delphi) were a Roman contribution. The gymnasium usually assumed the form of a large square court, surrounded by colonnades. Besides its original function as an athletic training ground, it inevitably became a social centre, like a miniature agora. The close relation between the physical and spiritual aspects of Greek education (gymnastike and mousike) becomes apparent when we recall that Plato adopted the name of the neighbouring gymnasium (Academia) in naming his own School of philosophy.

In contrast to the splendour of public buildings, private houses were modest and unpretentious. In the islands, walls were constructed entirely of rough stone; on the mainland, the usual material was mud brick, placed on a rubble foundation. A complete town of the 8C B.C., with spacious square rooms, has been recently excavated at Zagora on the island of Andros. For the Archaic period (7–6C B.C.) the steeply-terraced hill-town overlooking the harbour of Emporio on Chios offers the fullest evidence. The excavation of Olynthus has furnished the ground plan of a Classical residential suburb (c. 430–348 B.C.) laid out with streets intersecting at right-angles, under the influence of Hippodamus of Miletus, who first designed cities on a grid system: the houses were approximately 20 yds square, with rooms looking out on to a small central courtyard. A greater degree of comfort is found in the mansions of the wealthy business men of Hellenistic Delos (mainly 2C B.C.) where the courtyard has acquired a handsome peristyle of marble columns, and the floors are often decorated with colourful mosaics: but not until Roman times do houses become really sumptuous.

Among the most permanent and impressive of Hellenic monuments are the walls of fortification, which frequently survive in an excellent state of preservation on sites where little else is to be seen. Full circuits became normal in the 5C B.C., equipped with towers at regular intervals; with the steady improvement in siege engines, rebuilding was often necessary. Exceptionally fine are the walls of Messene, founded in 370 B.C., after the liberation of Messenia from the Spartan yoke. Here the walls were built in their full height and thickness with squared stone blocks, and carefully fitted, as was customary until the Roman period, without any mortar or cement. Such walls were unusually extravagant; the usual practice was to build the parapets and the battlements in mud brick, and to fill the interior with rubble, restricting the fine masonry to the outer surfaces. The fortification of a city was regarded by Aristotle as an essential part of its adornment; and among the rich variety of masonic styles, none is more satisfying to the eye than the polygonal method of walling, which enjoyed an especial vogue before c. 450 B.C., before it became fashionable to lay the blocks in regular courses. At Oiniadai in Akarnania, a complete polygonal circuit (c. 450 B.C.) survives: more accessible are the forts at Eleutherae and Aegosthena, both excellent examples of the regular isodomic style (early 4C B.C.). The visitor to Eleusis will find a good series of fortification and terrace walls, dating from the 8C to the 4C B.C.

THE HELLENIC SANCTUARY. In addition to the temples and shrines within the city, the countryside of ancient Greece abounded in holy places of all kinds, varying in extent from a simple enclosure with an altar to the great Panhellenic sanctuaries of Olympia and Delphi.

Many such shrines give evidence of worship far back into prehistoric times, ultimately owing their sanctity to the awe-inspiring beauty and majesty of their scenery. Sometimes the surroundings reflected the

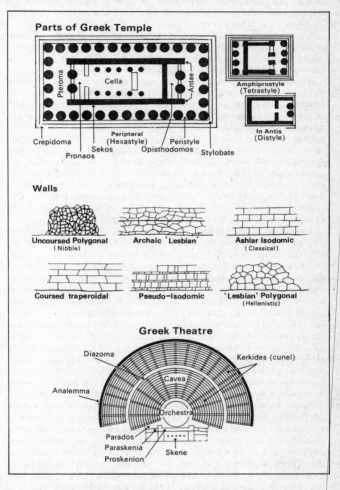

Parts of Greek Temple

Pteroma

Cella

Antae

Amphiprostyle
(Tetrastyle)

In Antis
(Distyle)

Crepidoma

Sekos
Pronaos

Peripteral
(Hexastyle)

Peristyle
Opisthodomos

Stylobate

Walls

Uncoursed Polygonal
(Nibble)

Archaic 'Lesbian'

Ashlar Isodomic
(Classical)

Coursed traperoidal

Pseudo-Isodomic

'Lesbian' Polygonal
(Hellenistic)

Greek Theatre

Diazoma

Kerkides (cunel)

Cavea

Analemma

Orchestra

Parados
Paraskenia
Proskenion

Skene

attributes of the god: thus mountain peaks were sacred to Zeus, while Poseidon was judiciously worshipped on stormy capes.

Since the offering of sacrifices played such a predominant part in the official cult of the Olympian gods, the altar was an indispensable component of even the smallest shrines; set out in the open air and surrounded by a sacred precinct (peribolos), the altar was always the main centre of public veneration. The temple was usually a later addition, whose purpose was to house the image of the god, and not to be a place of congregational worship like the Christian church—here though, an exception is provided by the famous cult of Mysteries at Eleusis, where the secret ceremonies of initiation were confined to the darkness of the Telesterion.

A sanctuary might also acquire a monumental columnar entrance (propylon) and a stoa to provide lodgings for priests, or to house stalls where pilgrims might purchase suitable votive offerings. For local shrines such as the Sanctuary of Aphaia on Aegina, or the Argive Heraeum, no further buildings were necessary. By contrast, the great Panhellenic sanctuaries of Olympia and Delphi, which attracted to their religious festivals thousands of visitors from all over the Greek world, needed many of the administrative buildings found in a large city: a bouleuterion and a prytaneion (town hall) as well as a stadium, a gymnasium, and sometimes a theatre also. Furthermore, the Greek states strove with one another not only for prizes at the quadrennial games, but also in the magnificence of their monumental dedications, which might take the form either of small votive chapels ('treasuries') or of imposing groups of sculpture. Such intense rivalry was always a powerful stimulant to the vitality of Greek art; later, when the Pax Romana put an end to the animosities between the city-states, the Hellenic spirit lost much of its creative impulse.

The Graeco-Roman Period: 27 B.C.–A.D. 330. The political independence of the Greek city-states came to an end in 27 B.C., with the incorporation of the province of Achaea into the Roman Empire. Long before this date, Rome had begun to absorb the civilizing influence of Greek literature, art, and thought: she now repaid her debt by maintaining unbroken peace for the next three centuries. She made little attempt to impose her own way of life on her Greek subjects: not only did Greek remain the official language of the Eastern Mediterranean, but many of the cities of old Greece were allowed to retain their local autonomy, and the responsibility for their own upkeep. In A.D. 160 the traveller Pausanias, whose 'Description of Greece' is a valuable source for the study of Greek monuments, found the main cities and sanctuaries in a flourishing condition, although some of the ancient sites were already desolate. Greece remained a peaceful backwater until the ruinous devastations of the Heruli (267) temporarily shattered her security.

Under Roman rule, Corinth became the administrative capital of the province of Achaea, and today her ruins offer the best impression of a spacious and thriving Graeco-Roman city. Elsewhere in the south, there is a scarcity of typically Roman monuments—of triumphal arches, imperial baths, and amphitheatres: in their stead, Greek magistrates and Greek architects preferred the simplicity of the propylon, the gymnasium, and the old-fashioned theatre, albeit in its Roman form (p. 17: a characteristic example is the Odeum of Herodes Atticus at Athens). But in the north, where Hellenic culture had not penetrated so deep, there is a greater abundance of typically Roman architecture, especially in the later years of the Roman Empire: one may cite the Arch of Galerius at Salonica (c. A.D. 300), the extensive forum of Philippi, and the purely Roman foundation of Nicopolis. A well-appointed Roman town on the island of Cos, where several mural paintings are preserved, has more in common with the sumptuous cities of Asia Minor than with the Greek mainland.

Athens, though shorn of all political power, still played the part of a university town, and remained a great artistic centre. Her sculptors took the lead in attempting to satisfy the insatiable appetite of Roman collectors. Not content with the universal practice of copying famous Classical works Athenian artists specialized in elegant pastiches of the Classical Style of the 5–4C B.C.: especially worthy of note are the lively Neo-Attic reliefs in the Piraeus Museum, and a fine group of Attic sarcophagi in the Salonica Museum (A.D. 2–3C). The more typically Roman work (idealized statues of emperors, and realistic portraits of private individuals) is best represented in the Museums of Corinth and Heraklion.

The Early Christian and Byzantine Age: A.D. 330–1204. Between the foundation of Constantinople and the barbarian incursions of the 6–7C Greece passed through its Early Christian phase to the true beginnings of the Byzantine era. Henceforward her interests were identified with the fortunes of the new imperial capital on the Bosphorus, the brightest beacon of European civilization during the centuries when darkness reigned in the West. Under the protection of Byzantine arms and diplomacy, the Greek peninsula was relatively sheltered from the onslaught of barbarians: while Constantinople bore the brunt of continuous waves of invaders from the north and east, the Slavs and Avars who succeeded in penetrating into the Peloponnese (6C and later) were peacefully absorbed into the local strain. Nevertheless, life was insecure, and the country was greatly depopulated during the period of incessant raids of Arab corsairs, who for a time occupied Crete (810–961). Apart from Salonika, which became the second city of the empire, towns contracted in size: Athens, for long a stronghold of paganism, dwindled to the status of a small provincial town after the attempt to close her philosophical schools by the emperor Justinian in 529.

The finest monuments of this Byzantine age are the churches. In Salonika, always closely in touch with artistic developments in the capital, the visitor may follow the whole progress of Byzantine metropolitan architecture and mosaic decoration from the 4C to the 14C. Elsewhere, the Byzantine churches in smaller towns and villages have a provincial flavour: on the other hand, the three great monasteries at Daphni, Osios Loukas, and Nea Moni (all 11C) form the most impressive memorial to the artistic vitality of the empire during the revival of her prosperity under the Macedonian dynasty (867–1059).

Franks, Venetians, Turks: A.D. 1204–1830. After the sack of Constantinople by the Fourth Crusade in 1204, the Greek mainland fell an easy prey to Frankish barons from Burgundy, Champagne, and Flanders, who carved up the land into feudal states: of these the most important were the Duchy of Athens (ruled from Thebes) and the Principality of Achaea, comprising nearly all the Peloponnese, with its capital at Andravidha (Andréville) in the plains of Elis. Here the ruined Gothic church of St Sophia is all that remains of a once flourishing Latin bishopric. A more impressive relic of Frankish rule is the splendid castle nearby at Chlemoutsi (Clairmont), built in 1220–23 by Geoffrey II de Villehardouin: with its keep and inner court perched upon the summit of a hill, and an outer bailey protecting the most exposed slope, it is typical of the many fortresses set up by the Frankish princes in order to maintain their sway over their Greek subjects. At Nauplia, Argos, and Acrocorinth, Byzantine strongholds were restored and remodelled: new castles were built at Karytaina, Old Navarino, Maina, and Mistra by the Franks.

Their tenancy of Mistra proved to be short-lived. In 1262 the fortress passed into the hands of Michael Palaeologos and became the capital of a Byzantine province (or Despotate) whose vigorous rulers eventually ousted the Franks from the Peloponnese in 1430, one generation before Mistra herself succumbed to the Turkish conquest. The ruins of the Byzantine city on the lower slopes of the hill form the most striking monument of the Later Middle Ages in Greece: here was the scene of a remarkable revival of Byzantine art and learning which may have had some influence on the course of the Renaissance in Italy.

The Venetians, who were largely responsible for the pillage of Constantinople in 1204, were not slow to profit from the temporary eclipse of her rival. With their shrewd commercial instincts, they established themselves in the Aegean islands and in various strategic harbours round the Peloponnesian coast. Long after the mainland had fallen to the Turks, they continued to fight a losing battle against the Ottoman Empire for their possessions in the Levant, until Crete was finally wrested from them in 1669. Among the most typical Venetian monuments are the fortified harbour towns at Naupactus (scene of the great Battle of Lepanto in 1571), Methone, Corone, and above all, Candia in Crete (now Heraklion), which kept a Turkish armament at bay for 23 years. Most of their former strongholds were refortified during their brief reoccupation of Southern Greece from 1690 till 1715: to this period belongs the huge fortress of Palamidi, outside Nauplia (1711–14). In Crete, Monemvasia and the Cyclades (once the medieval Duchy of Naxos) many churches show Venetian features, not least in their picturesque bell-towers.

No survey of Western monuments in Greece would be complete without reference to the medieval city of Rhodes, built by the Knights of St John, whose arrival in that island (1309) gave Christianity one of its strongest bulwarks in the Levant until the city fell to a Turkish armada in 1522.

The Turkish occupation (1460–1830) was for Greece a time of oppression and neglect. Few Moslem monuments now survive intact, except in Western Thrace and in the old city of Rhodes, where Turkish communities have been permitted to remain to this day. In Macedonia a few towns (pre-eminently Kastoria and Kozani) preserve attractive houses of the 17–18C. Elsewhere, many mosques lie in ruins, or have been put to secular uses after the removal of their minarets: however, a fine example in Chalkis, dating from 1470, has recently been restored. The Turkish yoke lay lightest on the smaller islands: the attractive 18C towns on Hydra and Mykonos bear witness to a partial revival of Greek mercantile prosperity at a time when the Ottoman Empire was sinking into an apathetic torpor. On the s. mainland, Nauplia is one of the few towns of any architectural merit to escape destruction during the disastrous ravages of the War of Independence (1821–30).

B The Monuments in their Artistic Aspects

MINOAN AND MYCENEAN ART

I. *Architecture.* In the absence of separate buildings reserved for religious worship, the architectural genius of the Aegean Bronze Age found its fullest expression in royal palaces and royal tombs. The conception of a building as a work of art stems from the older civilizations of Egypt and Syria, whence many of the typical features of Minoan palaces are derived: without going into excessive detail, one may cite the careful dressing of stone into large square blocks, the decorative use of stucco, the elaborate system of drainage through earthenware pipes, and, above all, the grouping of rooms round a central court. Under the fierce Cretan sun, external windows were shunned; instead, diffused light was admitted from the interior through light wells and wooden colonnades. The bright and airy effect of this device may be best appreciated in the domestic quarters at Knossos, where the functional and aesthetic aspects of Minoan architecture are brilliantly combined: it was further exploited on a truly majestic scale at the entrance to the palace at Phaestos, where a monumental flight of steps leads up to two successive porches, lit from beyond by a broad columned patio.

After the circular ossuaries of Early and Middle Minoan times in the Messara plain, the Minoans were normally buried in chambers cut into the soft local rock: the addition of masonry was evidently an honour reserved for royalty. Of the built tombs, the finest is the exceptionally well-preserved Temple Tomb at Knossos, so called because of its upper shrine, reminiscent of a medieval chantry: below, the burial chamber is preceded by a suite of rooms interrupted by an open court—clearly an imitation of a standard house plan.

After the Early Helladic House of Tiles at Lerna (p. 13), the Greek mainland offers no further monumental architecture until the rise of Mycenean civilization. The palaces at Mycenae, Tiryns, and Pylos (14–13C B.C.) all owe much to Crete in the complexity of their plan, but there has been one notable modification: the central position is now occupied by a large suite of state rooms in the form of the ancestral megaron—a type of house whose history can be traced back to the Neolithic period (p. 13), and which was much favoured by the first Greeks who invaded the mainland in c. 2200 and c. 2000 B.C. Its palatial form is as follows: from a relatively small court, a pillared porch (aithousa) leads into an anteroom (prodomos) which in turn gives access to the spacious square throne room (domos) with a low central hearth, round which four wooden columns support the roof. Since all three rooms have the same breadth, and since the doors are all aligned on the same axis, the megaron introduced an element of symmetry lacking in the Minoan prototype, but prophetic of later Greek architecture.

The royal tholos tomb is the most original, and the most distinguished, of Mycenean architectural forms. A monumental passage (dromos) led into a domed funerary chamber, whose masonry rises by corbelled courses, until the gap is closed at the apex: the chamber was then covered by a mound of earth, and the dromos filled in. Among the nine examples at Mycenae, three stages of its development may be followed.

One of the earliest is the 'Tomb of Aegisthus' (early 15C B.C.) whose chamber is nearly all constructed of rubble, except the doorway, which is lined with rather larger masonry and crowned by a massive lintel. The enormous weight of the superstructure led the architects of the second group (of which the Lion Tomb, c. 1450 B.C., is typical) to leave a relieving triangle above the lintel: at the same time some attempt was made to dress the stones of the chamber. The climax of the series is represented by the superb 'Treasury of Atreus' (c. 1300 B.C.): here the whole design is translated into handsome ashlar masonry and the façade is elaborately decorated: the portal was flanked by a tall pair of attached half-columns tapering downwards like their Minoan proto-types; a smaller pair stood at either side of the relieving triangle, which was filled in and covered with friezes of sculptured rosettes and spirals in green and red stone. A close relation exists between the structure of this façade and that of the contemporary Lion Gate, where the walling is also in ashlar technique, and the famous heraldic lions occupy the relieving triangle. Elsewhere the circuit of the citadel is mainly of Cyclopean construction, i.e. composed of roughly dressed boulders, the crevices being filled with small stones.

II. *Painting and Pottery.* Enough has survived of Minoan fresco painting to establish it as one of the major arts of the period. Since the pigments were applied when the plaster was still soft, a rapid and sure touch was essential: where his Egyptian contemporary preferred to linger lovingly over anatomical details, the Minoan artist obtained a lively effect from a few summary, impressionistic strokes. Both the subject and the style of the 'Saffron Gatherer', one of the earliest frescoes (c. 17C B.C.), are typical of the Minoan temperament: the wind-swept crocus blooms reveal a delight in capturing spontaneous move-ment, while the representation of the monkey in a floral setting betrays a profound interest in the world of nature for its own sake, not merely as a background for human activity. Many charming frescoes in the same naturalistic manner have recently been found in the Minoan houses at Akrotiri on Thera, destroyed by earthquake in c. 1500 B.C. This accurate observation of nature reaches its height in the flower landscapes from Ayia Triada (c. 1600 B.C.) one of which shows a cat stalking a pheasant in the undergrowth. At about this time begins the series of frescoes, more monumental in size and in theme, which adorned the walls of the Knossian palace in its final form. Two of these are in painted relief: the vigorous Charging Bull at the North Entrance, and the Priest-King, an idealization of Minoan manhood raised to divine status. On this large scale, human figures tend to receive rather formal treatment, lacking the inner life that is so abundant in the smaller pieces as, for example, the hectic 'Toreador' scene, the delightful and individualistic 'Parisienne' and, above all, the Miniature Frescoes, where animated crowds are portrayed with astonishing economy of detail: here, as elsewhere, the sexes are effectively distinguished by the use of red paint for men, and white for women. However, formalism wins the day with the arrival of the Myceneans, whose taste for symmetry may be re-flected in the heraldic Griffin Fresco in the throne room (late 15C B.C.)—a subject repeated 200 years later in the throne room at Pylos. In general the frescoes of the mainland palaces are less well preserved: typical themes are the Boar Hunt at Tiryns, a battle scene at Pylos, and the long frieze in the megaron at Mycenae showing warriors and horses preparing for battle.

Before the earliest frescoes were painted, Minoan potters had already attained a high peak of excellence in the polychrome Kamares ware, named after the cave-sanctuary high on the eastern flank of Mt Ida where it was first noted. In the best period (19–18C B.C.) the decoration is applied in red and white to a dark ground, and the designs strike a subtle balance between curvilinear abstract ornament and stylized plant motives. Later vases owe much of their decoration to the influence of free painting, although the potter was always guided by the shape of the vase in his choice of ornament. For this reason human figures and animals were avoided, whereas after c. 1550 B.C., when the decoration began to be applied in dark paint on a light ground, flowers and marine subjects could be accommodated in their most naturalistic form; the octopus became a special favourite, since its elastic shape could be adapted to suit any large surface. Such extreme naturalism was short-lived: by the late 15C B.C. the floral and marine motives on the Palace Style jars from the Knossos area began to assume a regular and symmetrical form. After 1400 B.C., when the artistic initiative passed to the mainland, they gradually degenerate into abstract linear patterns.

III. *The Plastic Arts.* No monumental statues survive from either Crete or Mycenae, but small votive figures have a long history. A nude female figure from Lerna, gracefully natural in its pose, shows that even in Neolithic times a lump of clay could be transformed into a thing of beauty: the marble idols of the Cyclades (2500–2000 B.C.), more austerely stylized, belong to the same artistic milieu. The most notable Minoan contribution in this field are the two Faience Goddesses (c. 1600 B.C.) wearing the usual flounced skirt, and the Ivory Acrobat (16C B.C.) leaping over a bull—a fine study in violent movement and meticulous realism, where even the veins and muscles are carefully shown: the missing hair and loincloth were almost certainly added in gold. No less exquisite is an ivory group from Mycenae, portraying two women and a child (15C B.C.), remarkable for its humanity and tenderness. Contemporary work in bronze was crude by comparison, although one may admire the robust expressionism of the Minoan figures of worshippers.

Minoan artists were more consistently successful in the technique of low relief, where their plastic skill could be combined with their innate pictorial talent. Their complete mastery of this medium is displayed in the two magnificent gold cups from the tholos tomb at Vaphio (15C B.C.), both depicting the hunting of wild bulls: with a frame only 4 in. high, full justice has been done to a tense and dramatic theme, and the majesty and ferocity of the animals has been superbly caught. Another consummate masterpiece is the Harvester Vase from Ayia Triada (16–15C B.C.) carved in the soft black stone known as serpentine: in the rollicking procession of revellers returning from the harvest, sometimes marching four abreast, we meet once again the high-spirited humour that informs the Miniature Frescoes. We are also reminded of Minoan free painting by the pictorial use of precious metals in the daggers from the shaft graves at Mycenae, where gold and silver are inlaid in a background of dark niello, and minor details are incised: their free and naturalistic style makes it seem likely that they were the work of Cretan smiths, at a time when the mainland was just beginning to succumb to the spell of Minoan civilization (c. 1550 B.C.).

In the plastic arts both the Minoans and the mainlanders achieved their finest results when working on a small scale. Among their most valuable legacies are their sealstones and gold signet rings, which in a largely illiterate world were used as a means of identification. In the hands of Minoan craftsmen their engraving became a highly developed pictorial art: their subjects vary from intimate studies of animal and bird life to detailed representations of cult scenes, which supply us with our main source of information on the obscure topic of Minoan and Mycenean religion.

HELLENIC ART

I. *Architecture.* The chief glory of Greek architecture is the Doric Temple. Clay models from Perachora (8C B.C.) and the Argive Heraeum (7C B.C.) reveal its embryonic form, which resembled the domestic megaron of prehistoric times (p. 23): a columnar porch (pronaos) led into a long hall (cella) which housed the image of the god: the roof gables were steeply pitched, and must have been thatched. In the earliest temples the roof of the pronaos was already supported by columns, arranged either between the forward continuations of the side walls (in antis) or, less commonly, in a free-standing colonnade across the front (prostyle). Behind these columns a single entrance gave access to the cella, and remained its only source of lighting: if necessary, the wooden beams of the ceiling were supported by one or two rows of internal columns. (The latter arrangement was eventually preferred, since a single row down the centre would interfere with the setting of the cult statue.) Behind the rear wall of the cella, the pronaos was often duplicated by a second porch, the opisthodomos, for the sake of symmetry. Since the walls of the cella were at first built of mud brick on a timber frame, the larger temples from c. 700 B.C. onwards were protected from the rain by a continuous veranda with an outer row of columns all round the building (peripteron).

Both the columns and the superstructure (entablature) were originally constructed of wood, and many of their characteristic features, when later translated into stone, recall the original material. Doric columns were placed directly on the upper foundations (stylobate) without any base, and tapered upwards like tree-trunks, with a pronounced convex curve (entasis): their broad and concave flutes, meeting each other at a sharp angle, might have resulted from the use of a rounded adze to shape a wooden log. Their capitals consist of two parts: a round cushion with a curved profile (echinus), supporting a square abacus. The entablature above the peripteron comprises the plain architrave, the typically Doric frieze where square metopes, sometimes bearing relief sculpture, alternate with grooved triglyphs (representing wooden beam-ends), and the projecting cornice (geison), whose two members, horizontal and sloping, frame the triangular pediments at the façades.

In the Heraion at Olympia (c. 600 B.C.), although the columns and entablature were originally of wood, all these essential elements of the Doric order were already present: the temple had attained a monumental maturity at a time when secular building was still in its infancy. In the next two centuries its proportions were considerably improved, but the basic plan remained unaltered. Soon after, perhaps owing to the

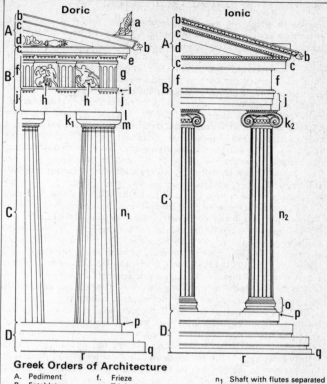

Greek Orders of Architecture

A. Pediment
B. Entablature
C. Column
D. Crepidoma
a. Acroterion
b. Sima
c. Geison or Cornice
d. Tympanum
e. Mutule & Guttae

f. Frieze
g. Triglyphs
h. Metopes
i. Regulae & Guttae
j. Architrave or Epistyle
k_1. Capital (Doric)
k_2. Capital (Ionic) with Volutes
l. Abacus
m. Echinus

n_1 Shaft with flutes separated by sharp arrises.
n_2 Shaft with flutes separated by blunt fillets
o. Bases
p. Stylobate
q. Euthynteria
r. Stereobate

Corinthian Capital

Pergamene Capital

oppressive weight of the newly invented clay roof-tiles, the whole structure was translated into limestone. At first the new medium was treated with caution: the monolithic columns of the temple at Corinth (c. 540 B.C.), the earliest in Greece that still remain standing, are extremely stout and closely bunched: their capitals are as broad as possible, so as to diminish the span of the massive architrave lintels. Further experience brought greater confidence: the columns became progressively taller, thinner, and more widely spaced, the capitals narrower and lighter: both tended to lose their curved profile. Limestone shafts were most conveniently built up in drums, and their appearance was improved by a coat of stucco: but even so they could not vie either in beauty or strength with the marble that the Athenians had begun to quarry from Mt Pentelikon, at the end of the 6C. Thereafter, beginning with her Treasury at Delphi (c. 490 B.C.), Athens used marble for her religious buildings. Further aesthetic progress was made in the 5C with the broadening of the temple's ground plan: the cella was now furnished with increasing elaboration, and the cult statue was often flanked (as at Aegina) by a two-storied colonnade. The splendour of the façades was immeasurably enhanced by the magnificent groups of pedimental sculpture of Aegina (c. 500–480 B.C.) and of the Temple of Zeus of Olympia (c. 460 B.C.). After 200 years of experiment, the Doric style reaches its climax in the Parthenon, finished in 438 B.C. Apart from the superlative excellence of the famous sculptured decorations, a new subtlety is introduced by the rising curves of stylobate and entablature and the inwardly slanting axis of the peripteral columns.

After the perfection of the late 5C, progress on purely Doric lines was hardly possible: but stagnation was happily averted, since mainland architects had begun to interest themselves in other styles. The Ionic order, first evolved across the Aegean in the 6C, had already found mature expression in the grandiose and ebullient temples of Artemis at Ephesus and in the Heraion of Samos, both surrounded by a double peripteron. The Ionic of Attica assumed a more restrained form, illustrated by the Erechtheion and the Temple of Nike (last quarter of 5C): apart from their well-known volute capitals, Ionic columns differ from Doric in their elaborately moulded bases, their slimmer shafts, and their deeper fluting: the architrave is divided into three shallow horizontal slabs, with a continuous frieze above, often bearing sculptured decoration. Doric and Ionic elements were often successfully married, especially by Attic architects: inside the Propylaea tall and graceful Ionic colonnades were happily combined by Mnesikles with a massive Doric exterior; his colleague Iktinos introduced Ionic sculptured friezes outside the cella of the Parthenon, and round the interior of the Temple of Apollo at Bassae (c. 450–420 B.C.). This remote highland sanctuary also preserves the earliest known Corinthian capital: the Corinthian order (which differs from the Ionic only in the acanthus capital) was subsequently much exploited in the interiors of 4C B.C. buildings, reaching great heights of delicacy in the Temple of Athena Alea at Tegea and in the Tholos at Epidaurus. Its use on a gigantic scale in the double peripteron of the Temple of Olympian Zeus at Athens (174 B.C.–A.D. 138) reflects the more flamboyant taste of a later epoch: but even in Hellenistic times the Doric order was never wholly ousted, appearing in extremely attenuated form in the Temple of Isis on Delos. This is one of the few religious buildings of this period which survive to any height: in the secular field, however, the versatility of the Hellenistic architect is attested by many *stoas* (best represented by that of Attalos in Athens, c. 150 B.C.), by the gabled façades of Macedonian built tombs, and by the ingenious octagonal water-clock in Athens, known as the 'Tower of the Winds' (c. 40 B.C.).

II. *Sculpture.* Greek monumental sculpture began under the influence of Egypt in the 7C B.C., when life-size statues of marble and limestone were first made in Crete, in the Peloponnese, and in the Cyclades. Attica entered the field with the kouros from Sounion (c. 600 B.C.), first of a long line of nude male figures offered at tombs or dedicated at local shrines. In this great work, nearly twice life-size, we are inevitably reminded of Egyptian prototypes by the stance (left foot forward), by the rigidity of the arms, by the stylized wig, and by the stiffness of the whole conception: but whereas the Egyptians directed their chief attention to the undulating surfaces of the skin, the sharp transitions of the early Attic statue show a determination to clarify the bone structure underneath. After this ambitious start, the kouroi from Volomandra (c. 560 B.C.), Anavysos (c. 530 B.C.), and Ptoon (c. 510 B.C.), illustrate the gradual progress made by 6C sculptors in defining the anatomy of the human body at rest. With each generation, the transitions at the neck, the hips and the knee-caps are more convincingly rendered and the modelling becomes more rounded and assured. By the time of the Critian Boy (c. 480 B.C.) complete anatomical mastery has been attained: the body has become an organic whole, no longer the sum of its parts. The parallel series of korai (the maiden votaries of Athena dedicated on the Acropolis) reveals another facet of the archaic genius: the power to create harmonious patterns from the gay and elaborate Ionian draperies that came into fashion at the court of the Athenian tyrant Peisistratos and his sons: none, however, is more beautiful than the vivacious Peplos Kore (c. 530 B.C.) who still wears the plainer Doric dress.

Archaic sculptors devoted much of their thought to the decoration of temples and treasuries. Ionic friezes and Doric metopes were both adorned in relief: friezes invited continuous narrative scenes, like the Battle of the Gods and Giants on the Siphnian Treasury at Delphi (c. 525 B.C.) while the square metopes were more suitable for detached episodes, such as the Labours of Herakles, and other single combats. In the triangular pediments, the sculptures were carved in the round and attached to the background by iron dowels: the awkward shape of the field presented a stern challenge to the artist's power of grouping his figures in an effective ensemble, and thus forced him to depart from the rigidly frontal pose of the free-standing statues. Here, too, battle scenes made good compositions. The early 'Hydra' and 'Triton' pedimental groups from the Acropolis (c. 570–560 B.C.) show Herakles engaged with scaly monsters whose tails fit conveniently into the lower angles: more ambitiously, a later group from the Acropolis showing the Battle of Gods and Giants (c. 520 B.C.) and the groups from Aegina (c. 500–480 B.C.) were entirely constructed from human figures, embattled and closely entwined, either striding, falling, kneeling, crouching, or lying wounded in the corners. The Lapiths and Centaurs from the West pediment at Olympia (c. 460 B.C.) bring this spirited tradition to a tempestuous climax.

With such valuable experience behind them, the sculptors of free-standing statues in the Early Classical period (c. 480–450 B.C.) boldly departed from the archaic frontal stance. The Critian Boy (c. 480 B.C.) is allowed to relax, with the weight of the body unevenly divided; in place of the typical archaic smile, the features have assumed the noble severity also found in the Apollo at Olympia, who calmly presides over the struggle between Lapith and Centaur. Other masterpieces of this period are two bronze statues, the Delphic Charioteer (c. 475 B.C.) and the Poseidon of Artemision (c. 460 B.C.): the contrast between the static repose of the charioteer and the dynamic energy of the god emphasizes the tremendous vitality of this versatile generation. In a century when the finest sculptors worked in bronze, it is a tragedy that no other life-size bronze originals of this time survive. For our understanding of the later 5C, the high noon of Greek sculpture and the age of Pheidias and Polykleitos, we are largely dependent on the marble copies—and art critics—of Roman times: however accurate the copies, and however discerning the critics may have been, we can only contemplate the achievement of the great masters through the eyes of a later age. We know that Pheidias superintended the building and the adornment of the Parthenon; yet few, if any, of the existing sculptures can have been chiselled by his own hand, and all would have been considered minor works in comparison with his colossal gold and ivory (chryselephantine) cult images of Athena Parthenos and of Olympian Zeus, both irretrievably lost. Nevertheless we can get some idea of the serene majesty of his style from such Parthenon marbles as still remain in Athens: from the gods and horsemen of the frieze, and from the fine and vigorous metope (Lapith and Centaur) that still remains in position at the s.w. corner of the Temple: although their features are still idealized, the figures are realistically posed, and their drapery falls in natural folds. In the next generation, the Nike of Paionios at Olympia (c. 420 B.C.) and the reliefs from the Nike Balustrade at Athens (c. 410 B.C.) illustrate a novel fashion for windswept diaphanous garments, through which the outlines of the body can be clearly discerned.

In the 4C sculpture lost much of its monumental quality, and began to express the moods of individual human beings. The style of Praxiteles is well-known to us from his Hermes at Olympia (c. 360 B.C.), while a bronze original in Athens, the Marathon Youth, may belong to his school: the softer outlines, the completely relaxed pose, the unprecedented wealth of detail in the modelling, and above all the gentle, dreamy expression of the eyes and mouth are all typical of the new spirit. His contemporary Skopas, to whose hand, or influence, the surviving heads from the Temple at Tegea are attributed, specialized in studies of violent emotion. Lysippos was renowned for the creation of a completely realistic athletic type, less heavily built than before and with a smaller head. These new proportions are embodied in the Agias at Delphi (c. 320 B.C.); more moving, perhaps, is a work of great beauty and pathos which reflects his style: the tombstone (stele) from the Ilissos (Athens, no. 869) showing a father lamenting the death of his son, killed while hunting.

Lysippos was one of the few privileged artists who were commissioned to execute portraits of Alexander the Great, and in the Hellenistic period individualistic portraiture reached a high level of achievement. A fine early example is the brutally realistic bronze bust of the boxer Satyros from Olympia (c. 330 B.C.): later Greek artists found a ready market among the Italian business men on Delos (c. 100 B.C.), whose features they rendered with extreme candour. The scope of themes was vastly enlarged: foreign racial types, childhood, old age, and deformity all came within the sculptor's repertoire. The spirited Boy Jockey from Artemision (c. 220 B.C.), who is clearly not of Hellenic stock, is a typical subject: characteristic, too, is his pose, which offers a satisfactory composition from every viewpoint. Whatever the aesthetic merit of this work, technical virtuosity could hardly be carried further.

III. *Painting and Pottery.* The decoration of clay vases deserves an honourable place in the annals of Greek art for two reasons: first, because the potter's craft preserves the only continuous artistic link between the Mycenean and Hellenic civilizations; secondly, with the loss of almost all free painting of the finest period (6–4C B.C.), the art of vase-painting remains almost the sole witness to the pictorial talent of the Greeks.

After the collapse of Mycenae Athens became the chief source of ceramic ideas. In the Dark Age the decoration of pottery is severely abstract, but always relevant to the shape. On Protogeometric vases (11–10C B.C.) the patterns are mainly confined to neat sets of concentric circles and semicircles derived from the slovenly spirals of the latest Mycenean: in the fully developed Geometric style (9–8C B.C.) the ornament becomes rectilinear in character, and the meander assumes the leading rôle. Representational art is reborn towards the end of the period (c. 750 B.C.) when huge vases, which served as grave markers, bear stylized funerary scenes. Each region has its own local style.

The renewal of contact with the Near East ushered in an Orientalizing phase (7C B.C.) when Greek potters borrowed the fauna and flora of Syro-Phoenician art and adapted them for their own purposes. Corinth seized the initiative in art as well as in commerce, and created a delicate miniature style ('Protocorinthian') based on animal friezes, lotus-flowers, and palmettes: when humans appear, mythical scenes may sometimes be recognized. On small vases the technique known as black-figure was first perfected: figures were first drawn in silhouette (as in Geometric times), and then elaborated with incised detail; and finally touches of colour were added in purple or white. Other Orientalizing figured styles arose in Attica ('Protoattic'), Laconia, the Cyclades, and Rhodes: all could match the vitality of Protocorinthian drawing, but none could excel its purity of line. In each of these regional schools, the details were at first rendered in outline, but by the end of the 7C the black-figure technique had been universally adopted under the influence of Corinth.

In Attica, where the most ambitious potters had cultivated a wild and grandiose style (best illustrated by the ' Polyphemus ' amphora in Eleusis, c. 660 B.C.) the arrival of incision imposed a salutary discipline: on a late Protoattic masterpiece, the Nessos amphora in Athens (c. 610 B.C.), Attic grandeur is tempered by Corinthian refinement; out of this promising union grew the mature Attic Black-figure style of the 6C B.C., when Athens retrieved the artistic and commercial initiative from Corinth, and eventually established a monopoly in the production of fine figured pottery. Animal friezes were now subordinated to scenes of human action, depicting the narratives of Greek mythology: the most popular themes were provided by the cycle of the Trojan war, the Labours of Herakles, and the revels of Dionysus with his attendant rout of satyrs and maenads. Black-figured drawing reached the limits of its potentialities in the work of Exekias (c. 540–525 B.C.), who succeeded in endowing his figures with a new spiritual quality: the calyx-krater in the Agora Museum is a worthy example of his quiet and reflective manner.

The invention of the Red-figure technique (c. 530 B.C.) allowed the painter greater freedom of expression. The colour scheme was now reversed, the figures being left in the orange tone of the clay, while the background was filled in with lustrous black; inner details could be rendered in brown or black paint, depending on the strength of the solution. By c. 500 B.C. the finest artists were using the new technique, and had begun to lay the foundations of European representational drawing. A passionate interest in the structure of the human body led them to vary the pose of their figures: vigorous experiment with three-quarter views and foreshortened limbs introduced for the first time the illusion of a third dimension. At the same time the repertoire of themes became greatly extended, as scenes from daily life took their place beside heroic and dionysiac subjects.

Red-figured vase painting reached its highest level of achievement in the first quarter of the 5C B.C., when the new medium had been fully mastered: the figures on these late archaic vases are drawn with a supple vigour that makes most subsequent work look somewhat staid and academic by contrast. With the rapid advance of sculpture and free painting after c. 475 B.C., the decoration of pottery was gradually reduced to a minor art, which no longer attracted artists of the front rank. A distinguished exception here is the work of the Achilles painter (c. 450–430 B.C.) who specialized in the production of oil-flasks (lekythoi) for funerary use, decorated in subdued matt colours against a white background. His figures, isolated and statuesque, reflect the classical serenity of the Parthenon sculptures, with which they are contemporary, and enable us to visualize something of the grandeur of classical free painting. But in the 4C the figured decoration of pottery became a degenerate art, and in Attica it had died out in c. 320 B.C.

Tantalizing glimpses of figured mural painting in the 4–3C B.C. are offered by the built tombs of western Macedonia. Scenes in the three royal tombs of the Great Tumulus at Vergina represent the late Classical flowering of this monumental art, already enlivened by a daring use of chiaroscuro. On the façade of the Great Tomb at Lefkadhia, the scene of Judgment in Hades, with its four statuesque figures, is a masterpiece of early Hellenistic times. Slighter work of the 3C B.C. may be seen on the Thessalian painted gravestones (stelai) in Volos museum.

On the art of Roman Greece, brief comment has already been made (p. 20). We now pass directly to the next great flowering of the Hellenic genius, in the art and architecture of Byzantine times.

THE ART OF THE ORTHODOX CHURCH

I. *Architecture*. The architects of the earliest churches in Greece followed the prevailing fashion in other Christian lands by adopting the form of the basilica, a standard Roman public hall divided into three aisles by interior colonnades: one or three apses were added at the

Alabastron
Phiale
Rhyton
Askos
Pyxis
Lekythos

Kylix
Kantharos
Aryballos
Skyphos

Krater
Oinochoe
Pelike
Kalpis

Lebes
Amphora
Hydria
Stamnos

Calyx-Krater
Pithos
Loutrophoros
Psykter

Pillar Stele with Sphinx (6th cent.)
Palmette Stele (with Anthemion) (5-4th. cent.)
Memorial Relief (5-4th. cent.)
Naiskos (4th. cent.)

E. end to form the sanctuary, while at the w. a porch (narthex) extended along the whole width of the building. The basilica in its primitive form, best represented by St Demetrius at Salonika (5C, restored after the fire in 1917), was abandoned after the 6C, but the narthex and the apsidal ending were preserved as essential components of later church plans.

The most distinctive feature of the mature Byzantine church is the dome, balanced over a square. The domed rotunda (e.g. St George at Salonika, c. 300, originally a Roman mausoleum) had already been achieved in Roman times, but the transition from a square ground plan to the circular base of a dome posed a more difficult problem. Two solutions were eventually found: the use of pendentives and squinches. The former consist of triangular sections of a dome, springing from the corners of the square and bending inwards to form a circle: the latter were small arches thrown across the corners of the square, transforming it into an octagon. In either case the dome could be easily fitted above, usually superimposed upon a cylindrical drum.

Another church at Salonika, St Sophia (6C), following its more illustrious namesake at Constantinople, shows how a dome could be suspended above a basilical plan. But the most successful shape proved to be the Greek cross, whose four equal arms served admirably to carry the thrust of the dome upon their high barrel vaults, passing it down to the lower vaulted chambers that filled the angles between them: a square ground plan was thereby produced, while in the superstructure the cruciform shape was still apparent. After its first appearance in Greece at Skripou (Orchomenos) in 874, this cross-in-square plan became the classical form. Architecturally, it was entirely self-supporting; no buttresses were needed, as they were with Western Romanesque and Gothic. Furthermore, the curved surfaces of the interior provided the perfect framework for the hierarchy of sacred images (icons) expressed in mural mosaic (see below). The smaller, painted icons, essential to the performance of the liturgy, were exhibited on the iconostasis, a wooden or stone screen which separated the apsidal sanctuary (bema) from the naos, the main body of the church where the congregation assembled.

The cross-in-square type reached maturity in the 10–11C in the large monasteries of Daphni and Osios Loukas, and the smaller churches in and around Athens. No new designs were subsequently evolved, but the old were capable of infinite variety. Subsidiary domes might be added above the corners of the square (Salonika, Church of the Holy Apostles, 1312) or above the narthex: at Mistra, a Greek cross in the superstructure was sometimes imposed upon a basilical ground plan (The Metropolis and Aphentikon, both 14C; the Pantanassa, 15C). All these later churches display a tendency towards taller proportions, and a delight in varying the surface of the exterior with ornate patterns of brickwork. Vigorous experiment with the same architectural forms continued in the monasteries of Mt Athos, where most of the existing churches are subsequent to the Turkish conquest.

II. *Mosaics and fresco paintings*. Byzantine pictorial art found its noblest expression in the mural decoration of church interiors, fashioned for the glory of God and for the instruction of the worshipper. Until the beginning of the 14C, the richer churches were always adorned with mosaics: in poorer and later ones, fresco paintings took their place.

Much of the free naturalism inherent in the later stages of Hellenic art (comp. above) survives into the earliest mosaics: the splendid robed figures in the dome of St George of Salonika (5C) still have a three-dimensional look that recalls the sculpture of late antiquity. Very different are the more formal and two-dimensional figures in the basilica of St Demetrius in the same city (7C); their static, frontal pose, the schematic arrangement of their drapery, and the unrestrained use of gorgeous colours, all represent a strong Near-Eastern element which was blended with the Hellenic manner to form the true Byzantine style. The art of mosaic decoration suffered a temporary setback during the Iconoclastic period (726–843), when figured representation was forbidden: full maturity was not reached until the 10–11C when the fusion of Hellenic and Oriental elements became complete. To this classic phase of Byzantine art belong the magnificent mosaics of the three great monasteries at Osios Loukas, Nea Moni, and Daphni: in the last of these churches, the Hellenic flavour is strong in the evangelic scenes, but single figures never depart from a severely frontal style.

Frontal figures had a special liturgical relevance in the Orthodox church. Sacred representations were icons, venerable images through which the worshipper could communicate with their prototypes: only if they faced the beholder could they receive and convey his worship and veneration. The design of the cross-in-square church (p. 34) gave the images a perfect setting, and allowed them to be arranged in a hierarchic system, whereby the position of each figure depended on its degree of sanctity. The dome, the image of Heaven, portrayed either the Ascension (as in St Sophia, Salonika, late 9C) or the Pantocrator, the all-powerful Christ appearing in glory after the Ascension; the lofty apse received the tall figure of the Virgin. Scenes from the life of Christ in this world occupied the pendentives or squinches, the upper vaults, and the higher expanses of wall; the lowest registers were left for single figures of prophets and saints, decreasing in importance according to their distance from the sanctuary.

Although the Byzantine empire suffered a political decline from 1200 onwards, her artistic vitality remained unimpaired. Indeed, the 14C emerges as one of the great eras in Byzantine pictorial art, now that the cleaning of the mosaics and wall paintings of the Kahrieh Mosque at Constantinople permits us to appreciate them in their full glory: a few mosaics in the same style may also be admired in the church of the Holy Apostles at Salonika (c. 1312). Compared with the older manner, these works are less monumental in character, but are distinguished by a new delicacy and lightness of touch: in place of the stern and impassive features of the earlier style, a note of intimacy and pathos has crept into the rendering of the figures. This new humanism also informs the wall painting at Mistra, where the frescoes in the Peribleptos (1340–60) and the nunnery of the Pantanassa (c. 1428) invite comparison with contemporary work of late Gothic in Italy, in which the influence of Byzantine iconography and technique can be traced.

After the Turkish conquest, the art of mural decoration continued to flourish in the monasteries of Mt Athos in the 16C; vast expanses of wall were covered with narrative cycles in several layers. On a smaller scale, fine painting survives on wooden icons up till the end of the 17C, when the influence of the West began to have a sterilizing effect.

GLOSSARY OF ART TERMS

Types of vases and of funerary monuments are illustrated on p. 33, and their use and development respectively indicated in the text under the National Museum and the Kerameikos. Terms used in classical architecture are explained by illustration of the Orders, etc. on p. 27; for further Byzantine terms, see the Byzantine Museum.

AEGIS. Cuirass or shield with Gorgon's head and ring of snakes.

AGORA. Public square or market-place.

AMAZONOMACHIA. Combat of Greeks and Amazons.

AMBO (pl. *ambones*). Pulpit in a Christian basilica; two pulpits on opposite sides of a church from which the gospel and epistle were read.

ANTHEMION. Flower ornament.

APOTROPAION. A protective symbol to turn away evil.

BEMA. (*Anc.*) Rostrum; (*Byz.*) Chancel.

BRECCIA. A composite rock (pudding-stone).

CHITON. A tunic.

CHLAMYS. Light cloak worn by epheboi.

CHOROS. A hanging circle in metal or wood for the display of icons.

CHTHONIC. Dwelling in or under the ground.

CYMA (recta or reversa). A wave moulding with double curvature.

EPHEBOS. Greek youth under training (military, or university).

EPITAPHIOS. Ceremonial pall.

EROTES. Figures of Eros, god of love.

ESCHARA. Sacred hearth.

EXEDRA. Semicircular recess in a classical or Byzantine building.

GIGANTOMACHIA. Contest of Giants.

GYMNASION (in Mod Gk.). Grammar school.

HERM. Quadrangular pillar, usually adorned with a phallus, and surmounted by a bust.

HEROON. Shrine or chapel of a demigod or mortal.

HIMATION. An oblong cloak thrown over the left shoulder, and fastened over or under the right.

HOPLITE. Heavily armed foot-soldier.

HYPAETHRAL. Open to the sky.

ICONOSTASIS. Screen bearing icons.

KORE. Maiden.

KOUROS. Boy; Archaic male figure.

MEGARON. Hall of a Mycenean palace or house.

NARTHEX. Vestibule of a Christian basilica.

NAUMACHIA. Mock naval combat for which the arena of an amphitheatre was flooded.

NYMPHAION. Sanctuary of the Nymphs.

ODEION. A concert hall, usually in the shape of a Greek theatre, but roofed.

OIKOS. A house.

OMPHALOS. A sacred stone, commemorating the 'centre of the earth' where Zeus' two eagles met.

OPUS ALEXANDRINUM. Mosaic design of black and red geometric figures on a white ground.

PANTOKRATOR. The Almighty.

PARECCLESIA. Chapel added to a Byzantine church.

PEPLOS. A mantle in one piece, worn draped by women.

PERIBOLOS. A precinct, but often archaeologically the circuit round it.

PETASOS. Broad-brimmed felt hat worn by epheboi.

PHIALE. Saucer or bowl.

PINAX. Flat plate, tablet, or panel.

PODIUM. Low wall or continuous pedestal carrying a colonnade or building.

POLYANDREION. Communal tomb.

POROS. A soft, coarse, conchiferous limestone (tufa).

PROPYLON, PROPYLAEA. Entrance gate to a temenos; in plural form when there is more than one door.

PROTHESIS. (*Anc.*) Laying out of a corpse; (*Byz.*) The setting forth of the oblation, or the chamber N. of the sanctuary where this is done.

PUTEAL. Ornamental well-head.

QUADRIGA. Four-horsed chariot.

SIMANTRON. Block of wood or metal bar beaten as a call to divine service.

SPHENDONE. The rounded end of a stadium.

STOA. A porch or portico not attached to a larger building.

TEMENOS. A sacred enclosure.

THEME. (*Byz.*) A province.

THOLOS. A circular building.

THYMELE. Altar set up in a theatre.

TRANSENNA. Openwork grille at the entrance to a Byzantine chapel.

TRILITHON. Gateway made up of two jambs and a lintel.

TRIREME. Greek galley rowed by 3 banks of oars.

XOANON. Wooden image or idol.

PRACTICAL INFORMATION
I. APPROACHES TO GREECE

In view of the distance involved, for the holidaymaker the most practical way of reaching Greece from Britain is by air. A charter flight as part of a 'package' deal can be had at moderate cost. Travellers overland must allow for the return journey six days by rail or about ten days by road. For those who demand comfort even the scheduled air fare may be found cheaper than either the three days' journey by rail or the slightly longer combinations of rail and sea viâ Venice or Bríndisi, where the cost of sleeping-cars, meals on board, porterage, and transport between train and ship, may well double the basic first-class fare. By coach, the journey can be made in four days with hotel lunch and overnight stops. Enterprising individuals, who do not mind the discomfort of three nights without sleeping accommodation and travel second-class, will find the surface route considerably cheaper than scheduled air fares. Reductions are available on application from most shipping companies for students, artists, journalists, and families of more than three people. There is a weekly student train (c. 50% reduction) and various cheap but arduous through buses. Those who can afford both time and money will probably prefer to take ship from Venice down the Dalmatian coast and through the Corinth Canal.

General Information may be obtained gratis from the NATIONAL TOURIST ORGANIZATION OF GREECE (in Gk. EOT), which does *not* book tickets or recommend hotels. It has offices in London (195–197 Regent St., W.1), New York (601 Fifth Avenue), and Los Angeles (627 West Sixth St.). Its booklet 'General Information about Greece' is continually revised, and its regional leaflets well produced.

Among British **Tour Operators** specializing in Greek holidays are *Allsun Holidays* (Olympic Airways), 141 New Bond St., W.1; *Olympos*, 10 Minories, E.C.3; *Olympic Holidays*, 24 Queensway, W.2. Cruises in Greek waters are arranged by *Swans Hellenic Cruises* (Hellenic Travellers' Club), 260 Tottenham Court Rd, W.1; *Fairways & Swinford (Travel) Ltd* (Society for Hellenic Travel), 18 St George St., W.1. 'Flotilla cruises' are arranged by *Yacht Cruising Association*, 9 The Broadway, Crawley, Sussex. Specialists in arranging individual Greek travel with conducted tours are *Gellatly, Hankey, & Co. Ltd.*, 23 Pall Mall, S.W.1; and *Wings Ltd.*, Wings House, Welwyn Garden City, Herts. Seaside holidays of a more than averagely enterprising kind are arranged by *Greek Island Holidays Ltd*, 119 New Bond St., W.1; *Kuoni, Challis, and Benson Ltd*, 133 New Bond St., W.1. Other major operators including Greece in their programmes are *Thomson Holidays* and *Cosmos*.

Travel Agents. There are many accredited members of the *Association of British Travel Agents* who sell travel tickets and book accommodation. The following general travel agents have branches not only in many towns throughout Britain but also in Greece:

Thomas Cook & Son, 45 Berkeley St., W.1 and many branches in Central London; *American Express*, 6 Haymarket, S.W.1, 89 Mount St., W.1.

Regular **Air Services** between London and Athens are maintained

(3–5 times daily) by British Airways and Olympic Airways. Full information may be obtained from *B.A.*, Dorland House, Lower Regent St., London, S.W.1, and from *Olympic Airways*, 141 New Bond St., W.1.

Both Rhodes and Crete (Herakleion) may be reached direct (weekly in winter, twice weekly in summer); also, in summer only, Corfù (twice weekly) and Salonika, (weekly).

Athens, in addition, has direct links with most European capitals, Cyprus-Turkey, New York, Boston, Los Angeles, Montreal, South Africa, and Australia.

Passenger and Car Ferries ply from Ancona, Brindisi, or Bari (also Dubrovnik in summer), direct or viâ Corfù, to Igoumenitsa or Patras, with connecting coaches to Athens, also direct to Piraeus. Services are operated throughout the year by HELLENIC MEDITERRANEAN LINES and ADRIATICA, also by FRAGLINE. From March to October there are many services daily by KARAGEORGIS LINES, EPIRUS LINE, DFDS SEAWAYS, LIBRA MARITIME LTD, and other companies also.

Scheduled **Steamer Services** (limited car-carrying) connect Marseille, Genoa, Naples, and Venice (including car ferries) with Piraeus and Levantine ports. These are operated by the following companies, from which current sailing arrangements should be ascertained: HELLENIC MEDITERRANEAN LINES, ADRIATICA LINES, ITALIA LINES, DENIZCILIK BANKASI T.A.O., LIBRA MARITIME, and BLACK SEA LINES.

Railway Services to Greece from N. European ports are subject to change year by year. The routes are viâ France and Italy, or viâ Belgium/Holland and Germany and Austria, into Yugoslavia. The factors to consider when choosing are: necessity of changing trains; day or night sea crossing (short, viâ Straits of Dover, or long, viâ Ostend or Hook of Holland); availability of couchettes or sleeping cars; convenience of time of departure and arrival. It is unlikely that all these will prove ideal by any route and the latest timetables should be consulted.—A route viâ one of the Adriatic ports of Italy and a ferry to Patras takes least time but involves two sea voyages and usually a change of station in Paris.

The British Railway Travel Centre, Rex House, Lower Regent St., London, S.W.1, provides travel tickets, sleeping berth tickets, seat reservations, etc., on Continental (as well as British) transport services.

Road Routes to Athens are innumerable and include the possibility of various combinations of car-carrier train and ferry. The speediest way of getting a car from England on to Greek soil is viâ the Bríndisi-Igoumenítsa–Patras ferry, using either the shortest route through France and Switzerland and the Autostrada del Sole, or the car-sleeper expresses viâ Milan. In winter snow can be avoided by combining car-sleeper express Paris–Riviera with ship Marseille–Piraeus. The shortest overland route, a drive of c. 1950 m., is viâ Southern Germany, Austria, and Yugoslavia. Comfortably the drive takes about a week; Europabus in late-June–early-Sept (from Victoria Coach Stn) in 4½ days. By car a day may be saved in summer by using the Ostend–Villach car-sleeper express. Cars are easily hired in Greece.

Motorists and motor-cyclists proposing to tour in Greece will save much trouble by joining the *Automobile Association* (Fanum House, Leicester Square, London, W.C.2), the *Royal Automobile Club* (83 Pall Mall, S.W.1) the *Royal Scottish Automobile Club*, or the *American Automobile Association*. These clubs will provide any necessary documents as well as information about rules of the road in force in the countries of transit, advice on routes, and arrangements for spare parts. The Automobile and Touring Club of Greece ('Ελληνική Λέσχη Περιηγήσεων Αὐτοκινήτου), Athens Tower, 2 Mesogeion, affords free assistance to members of affiliated associations. It issues maps, leaflets on parking in Athens, etc.

II. FORMALITIES AND CURRENCY

Passports are necessary for all British and American travellers entering Greece and must bear the photograph of the holder. British passports (£11), valid for ten years, are issued at the Passport Office, Clive House, Petty France, London, S.W.1 (9.30–4.30, Sat. 9.30–12.30), or may be obtained for an additional fee through any tourist agent.

In general passports of the United Kingdom and Crown Colonies, of members of the Commonwealth, of all W. European countries, and the U.S.A. do not require vizas. Nationals of Gr. Britain and Colonies, Ireland, Australia, Canada, New Zealand, or Cyprus wishing to remain in Greece must apply after 3 months (some others, including the U.S.A. and Republic of South Africa, 2 months; a few, including Eire, Hong Kong, 1 month) for a police permit to the nearest police station; in Athens to the Aliens Dept., 9 Khalkokondili.

Health Regulations. Vaccination and inoculation are not required for entry from Europe, Cyprus, Turkey, Canada, or the U.S.A.

Custom House. Except for travellers by air, who have to pass the customs at the airport of arrival, luggage is examined at the frontier or at the first Greek port of call. Normally passengers have to attend in person at the ΤΕΛΩΝΕΙΟΝ (teloníon: custom house), but the luggage of those travelling in international expresses is examined in the train and of those in regular steamers from Italy on the ship.

PRIVATE CARS may be imported for up to 4 months without customs documents, but the formalities may involve recording details in the passport, and the log book should be carried. Trailers and caravans need a customs document. Formalities tend to be simpler and quicker at frontier posts than at ports.

Provided that dutiable articles are declared, bona-fide travellers will find the Greek customs authorities courteous and reasonable. The following are free from duty: books, sporting equipment, camera with a reasonable quantity of film, binoculars, typewriter, record-player with up to 20 records, portable radio, tape-recorder, 250 gr. of tobacco in any form, sweets (up to 10 kg. or 22 lb), 2 packs of playing-cards. Sporting firearms (2 guns and 20 cartridges maximum) must be declared on entry and noted in the passport.

Souvenirs bought in Greece may be exported without licence up to a value of 4500 dr.; the duty-free shops at Athens airport are well stocked and offer very competitive prices. The export of olive-oil is limited to one container not exceeding 18 kg. per person. *The purchase of any work of art dating from before 1830 is strictly prohibited, except from recognized antiquarian shops, and their export totally prohibited except with permission and a special licence.* Infringements are met with confiscation and severe penalties. This applies to potsherds and some coins; licences to cover individual objects may be granted to scholars and institutions.

The duty-free allowance for travellers returning directly to Britain from a country outside the E.E.C., is (in effect) one litre-bottle of spirits (*or* two litre-bottles of fortified wines or aperitifs) *and* two litre-bottles of table wine, 200 cigarettes *or* 50 cigars (or equivalent), a small bottle of perfume *and* a bottle of toilet water, and personal souvenirs to a value of £10. Foreign reprints of copyright English books may be confiscated.

Greece's entry into the E.E.C. is expected to be ratified in 1981, after which E.E.C. regulations will apply.

Currency Regulations. The allowance permitted by the British Government for pleasure travel varies from time to time. In 1980 the regulations had been relaxed completely and no restrictions were in force. Credit cards may be legally used on visits abroad. Not more than 1500 drachmas may be brought into or taken out of Greece in notes. There is no restriction on foreign currency, but sums over $500 or £200 should be declared on arrival. It should be emphasized that it is forbidden in Greece to send abroad by any means whatever, without a Bank of Greece permit, banknotes, *cheques*, payment orders or any other sums in drachmai or *foreign currencies*. This appears, however ludicrously, to include the payment of bills in Britain by a cheque on a British account.

Money. The monetary unit is the drachma (dr.). Bank notes for 50, 100, 500, 1000, and 5000 dr. are issued by the Bank of Greece. There are coins of 20, 10, 5, 2, 1, and ½ dr. Coins from the reigns of Kings Paul and Constantine and of the military dictatorship have recently been demonetized. In 1980 the exchange rate ranged between 80 and 100 dr. to the pound sterling.

Banks. Banking hours, except Sun and holidays, are 8–2. Exchange Bureaux are also available at airports and points of entry into Greece. Certain banks in cities provide currency exchange facilities for much of the day. Personal cheques backed by Eurocards can be cashed.

III. TRANSPORT

Travelling in Greece may be divided into three stages: party travel by cruise ship and coach (well organized but not cheap), providing guided tours of selected antiquities with nights in international hotels, where the traveller is insulated from the local populace, needs no special knowledge of Greece, and will probably acquire none; individual travel by steamer and car or public transport, staying in modest hotels, which can still be inexpensive and, with use of the 'Blue Guide', should produce no problems; and getting off the beaten track, taking accommodation as it is available, for which at least some previous knowledge of Greece and of Greek is advisable.

International **Cruises** in Greek waters are many and varied. From Piraeus cruises to the islands of 2–7 days duration are operated by Chandris, Sun, Epirotiki, Kavounides, Karageorgis, Hellenic Mediterranean and other Lines.—Yachts, caiques, and other craft can be hired from a number of chartering agents. Details from the Greek Yacht Brokers and Consultants Association, 4 Od. Kriezotou, Athens 134. The National Tourist Organization publishes a booklet, giving details of harbour facilities, formalities, and navigational aids.

Coach Tours are organized in Mar–Oct by *A.B.C. Tours*, 47 Stadhiou; *C.H.A.T. Tours*, 4 Stadhiou; *Hellenic Express Travel*, 17 Filellinon; *Key Tours*, 2 Ermou; and *Bell Tours*, 3 Stadhiou (all in central Athens). The tours, lasting one to nine days and including appropriate meals, overnight accommodation, etc., mostly start from Athens and follow similar patterns. Places visited are limited to the popular archaeological sites of Attica and the Peloponnese, Delphi, the Meteora and N. Greece, and Crete. The tours are generally excellent of their kind, with well-informed English speaking guides, and provide an acceptable introduction to Greece for the inexperienced traveller. Short day excursions are available all the year round in Athens and main centres. *Periyitiki Leskhe*, see p. 59.

Individual Travel. Official Timetables are very elusive; invaluable are 'Greek Travel Pages' (GTP) and the 'Key Travel Guide' both published monthly in Athens. Arrangements for internal and external travelling may be made in Athens through experienced local agencies, which are often less crowded than their international counterparts.

Steamers play a large part in Greek transport. Passages on regular services (most of which radiate from Piraeus) can be booked *at the praktoreion of the shipping company concerned*, or in Athens through any travel agent. In summer it is advisable to reserve cabin-berths well in advance; voyages in daylight or travelling 'deck' can be booked at the quayside, but are also more conveniently arranged through agents. Prudent travellers will check sailing times with an official of the line concerned on the day of departure. Travellers should not expect the praktoreion of one company to divulge information about the services of its rivals. The accommodation and food varies greatly from ship to ship, first-class on older boats sometimes not equalling second-class on better vessels. Deck class, cheap, crowded, seldom clean, and often uncomfortably cold at night, can still be preferable in high summer to sharing a small and stuffy cabin with strangers.

Air Services. Domestic services of Olympic Airways link Athens several times daily with *Herakleion; Salonika; Rhodes; Corfù; Mytilene;* and (in summer) *Mykonos*; daily or more frequently with *Khania; Kavalla; Alexandroupolis; Lemnos; Khios; Kalamata; Kos; Samos; Kefallinia; Ioannina; Portokheli; Kithira; Santorini;* and *Skiathos.* Less frequently to *Kozani* (viâ *Volos* or *Larissa*); *Zakynthos.* Direct service (daily in summer; twice weekly in winter) between *Herakleion* and *Rhodes*; also Rhodes to *Kos* and to *Karpathos.*

AIR TAXIS may be hired from Athens airport.

Railways. Greece was the last country in Europe to take up railway development (after 1881) and her railways play only a small part in the country's transport system. The line from Athens to Piraeus was constructed in 1867–69 and electrified in 1904, but the main Piraeus–Athens–Larissa line was built only in 1902–09, and did not reach Salonika until 1916. The first international express (Simplon–Orient) ran in July 1920. The former Peloponnesian Railway is now administratively part of the State Railway system but has a separate terminus in Athens and is of metre gauge only. The services are generally punctual but slow on account of the terrain. For the tourist the Peloponnesian Railway provides a convenient approach to, e.g. Argos, Patras, Olympia, Tripolis, and Kalamata. The State Railways (O.Σ.E.) also operate fast 'pullman' bus services from Athens to Larissa and Salonika, Loutraki, Mycenae and Nauplia, Patras, Zakynthos, and Kefallinia.

Roads. Two 'toll highways' are open from Athens viâ Larissa to Salonika and the Yugoslav frontier, and from Athens viâ Corinth to Patras. Though their alinement and (on the whole) their surface are of motorway standard, neither is equipped with dual carriageways throughout its length, nor free of local crossings or the danger of animals. The tolls are reasonable.

Most main roads and the approaches to places where tourism is fostered are asphalted. Though the condition of these roads is often good, it depends on local upkeep and recent weather conditions; subsidences and potholes can be frequent, particularly through towns and villages, and the edges are often broken. Owing to the general terrain the average speed that can be safely maintained depends on gradients and curves, a fact often forgotten by dwellers in more level lands. Most main roads are marked with km. stones, but everywhere realinements are modifying the distance travelled; our distances must therefore be approximate in some instances. Where road improvements are in progress, long waits for bulldozing or blasting may be experienced.

An increasing proportion of secondary roads but few minor roads are tarred. Unsurfaced or 'dirt' roads are only rarely smooth and, though at their best preferable to deteriorated tarmac, are either dusty or muddy and may be very bad. The fact that a road carries a bus-service does not mean it is fit for a private car, and local advice that the road is good should be treated with caution. On untarred roads the surface (or lack of it) is usually the limiting factor and average speeds can be very low, though, provided the vehicle is robust and the driver experienced, a faster speed can paradoxically give a less uncomfortable ride.

Car Ferries cross various straits and channels at regular intervals. The vessels are mostly landing craft with opening bows, and cars generally have to be skilfully backed on into a confined space. Advance bookings are not made; drivers take their turn on arrival at the embarkation point. Regular bus services always take priority.

RULE OF THE ROAD. In Greece as elsewhere in Europe road traffic keeps to the right. 'Highway-code' rules of overtaking are seldom observed (the horn being the important factor) and giving way by courtesy is almost unknown (and taken as a sign of weakness). The commonest most dangerous infringement is going through traffic lights at red. In 1980 Greece recorded the worst accident rate of any western nation.

Petrol stations are adequately spaced on main roads; on minor roads supplies should not be allowed to run low. Petrol is considerably more expensive than in Britain.

Obedience to changing traffic lights must be immediate and is to be observed equally by pedestrians (who are liable to a fine on the spot for contravention). At main intersections there is often also a duty policeman who can override the lights by use of a whistle. Parking is difficult in the centre of most towns and even movement is often difficult in Athens. Street parking is prohibited in most of central Athens, other than at a few meters. Hotels seldom have garage or parking space of their own.

Motor-buses and a few routes of trolley-buses serve the capital from about 5.30 a.m. to midnight. Though frequent, they are nearly always crowded. Entrance is made at the rear door (marked ΕΙΣΟΔΟΣ) and exit (ΕΞΟΔΟΣ) at the front (visiting buses sometimes marked respectively ΑΝΟΔΟΣ and ΚΑΘΟΔΟΣ). The fare, usually taken at the door, varies slightly by route but is otherwise uniform (10 dr.) within a central area s. of Omonoia Sq.; beyond this area it varies according to distance; to outer suburbs 15 dr. Some recently introduced vehicles (marked ΧΟΡΙΣ ΕΙΣΠΡΑΚΤΟΡΑ) are one-man operated with a slot machine for tickets for which a 10 dr. piece is essential. Similar systems are operated in Salonika and other large towns.

LONG-DISTANCE BUSES are operated by Joint Pools of Bus Owners (Κοινόν Ταμεῖον Εἰσπράξεων Λεωφορείων; K.T.E.L.). These have been further grouped for the operation of two main Terminals, situated in the outskirts of Athens and served by city buses from central points. Each still has its own *Praktoreion* (booking-office). Bookings (preferably well in advance) may be made by telephone; the booking-offices are listed in the telephone directory under TAMEION, or more conveniently topographically in 'The Week in Athens' (comp. above). With a booked seat it is not necessary to appear more than a few minutes before scheduled departure time when luggage is stowed.

Bearing in mind the distances involved buses keep well to schedule. The promoters have strictly-interpreted agreements about the places they serve. A bus from Kalamata may take passengers between that town (or its dependent nome) and any other place along its route to (say) Athens; it may not pick up intermediate passengers beyond Tripolis and Corinth, which, being in different nomes, are the province of other K.T.E.L. The traveller who intends to board a long-distance bus at the roadside needs some knowledge not only of schedules but of the nome boundaries, and should ascertain beforehand the appellation of the K.T.E.L. he wants (this is always prominently displayed on the front of the bus even if the destination sometimes is not). Buses are stopped, as in Britain, by a raised hand.

On important long-distance routes the standard of comfort is reasonable, the buses being built in Sweden, Germany, or Britain. The worst features are now the ubiquitous over-amplified popular music which Mediterranean taste demands, and the high incidence of travel sickness in the local populace.

LOCAL SERVICES. There are few villages not served by buses, but these are mostly *Market Buses* whose function is to get the villagers to their local centre in the morning and back in the evening. They sometimes cover long distances, start very early and are very crowded; their use by strangers generally involves a stay of two nights in the wilds. Mere fullness is seldom a reason for not accepting another passenger. Remote villages often have a communal taxi instead, marked ΑΓΟΡΑΙΟΝ.

Taxicabs (metered) are numerous and cheap in the towns. For excursions a bargain can often be struck in advance.—SELF-DRIVE CARS (international driving licence necessary) may be hired from innumerable firms; *Hertz* (AutoHellas S.A.), *Avis*, and *Hellascars* are the best known and have the advantage of agencies in other principal Greek towns. Prices for a medium-sized car range *from* c. £5 per day plus 3½ p. per kilometre, or from c. £80 per week. Both prices exclude insurance and an 18 per cent luxury tax—and, of course, petrol at 33 dr. per litre.

Walking. The traveller 'me ta podhiá' (on foot) can go almost any-where in safety and will probably find more local transport than he expects. Hazards not met with in England are swarming bees, fierce sheep dogs, and (least dangerous of the three) snakes. The greatest danger is probably of twisted ankles, for which reason it is advisable not to walk alone in mountainous or more remote areas. The walker will everywhere command the respect, and receive the aid, of country people. In this connection it is well to remember that paths used by donkeys and mules nearly always lead from one settlement to another, whereas a path made by goats is likely to peter out on a cliff edge.

Maps. Sheets for Greece are available at 1 : 1,000,000 and 1 : 500,000 in the general World series (published in Britain by G.S.G.S. as series 1301 and 1404 respectively, and stocked by Stanfords' of Long Acre). Tolerable road maps are available in one sheet at a scale of 1 : 1,000,000 (the scale used in this volume), notably the Esso Motor Map. The Automobile and Touring Club of Greece (ΕΛΠΑ) issues a Road Atlas at 10 miles to 1 inch, though it marks some minor roads over which no visitor would wish to take his own car.

Contoured maps at 1 : 200,000 (mostly compiled in the 60s) are available for each nome and can in theory be purchased from the Ethniki Statistiki Yperesia tis Ellados, 14 Likourgou, Athens 112 (and from nowhere else). These are designed mainly to show inhabited localities and communications but those sheets revised and improved in 1972 show ancient sites. They are not (alas) as detailed as the military survey of the Yeografiki Yperesia Stratou at the same scale and of about the same period, which shows ancient sites, isolated churches, tracks and footpaths. Though not technically 'Restricted' this has never been made available to the public. Certain coastal areas, however, are well covered by Greek Naval Charts, which can be bought at the Hydrographic Office. Large-scale maps are, however, still treated with some suspicion and possession of them is not encouraged.

Most larger scale maps are now outdated and out of print. Few commercial maps and town plans will be found to improve on those pro-vided in this book, though maps of a sort are available on the spot at large scales for many islands. Of late the town plans and sectional maps in the N.T.O.G. leaflets have been greatly improved and generally surpass their commercial counterparts.

IV. POSTAL AND OTHER SERVICES

Postal Information. The main Post Office (ΤΑΧΥΔΡΟΜΕΙΟΝ; takhidhromío) in Athens is open from 8 a.m. to midnight, Sindagma office from 7 a.m. to 9 p.m. Postal staff generally speak English or French, and notices are displayed in Greek and French. Letter-boxes (ΓΡΑΜΜΑΤΟΚΙΒΟΤΙΟΝ) are painted yellow and may be marked ΕΣΟΤΕΡΙΚΟΥ (inland) and ΕΞΟΤΕΡΙΚΟΥ (abroad). Postage stamps (γραμματόσημα; grammatósima) are obtainable at kiosks as well as at post offices. A registered letter is ἕνα στημένον γράμμα (éna sistiméno ghrámma).

Letters for most destinations abroad go by air: lowest rate to Britain and Europe 14 dr., N. America 18 dr. Delays are often considerable. Within Greece a letter may well take longer than the visitor spends in the country, and for arranging rendezvous the telephone or telegram are indispensable.

Correspondence marked 'POSTE RESTANTE' (to be called for) may be addressed to any post office and is handed to the addressee on proof of identity (passport preferable). A small fee may be charged. The surname of the addressee, especially the capital letter, should be clearly written, and no 'Esq.' added.

Telephones. The Greek telephone and telegraph services are maintained by a public corporation, the 'Οργανισμός Τηλεπικοινωνιῶν 'Ελλάδος (O.T.E.) separate from the postal authority. All large towns have a central office of the company, with call-boxes and arrangements for making trunk and international calls and sending telegrams. Local calls can be made from subscribers' instruments and from the many instruments available to the public at kiosks and in cafés, bars, etc. Call-box telephones are constructed to take 2 and 5 dr. pieces.

Athens is on the dialling system and local calls include Piraeus numbers. Subscriber Trunk Dialling operates to most large provincial towns and the main islands, to some countries in Europe including Great Britain (dial 0044), and to the U.S.A. (001). For other inter-urban calls dial 151; abroad 161; telegrams 155; police 100; time 141. Transferred-charge calls are accepted.

Outside Athens, especially in rural and island areas the service may not operate for 24 hrs per day. Telephone connections may be slow and indistinct.

Telegrams may be sent from O.T.E. centres or main post offices. Inland rate: 10 words for 35 dr., each additional word, 2 dr.; double on Sun; higher rates for priority. To Great Britain: 7 words (minimum) for 56 dr., 7 dr. each additional word. To New York, 14½ dr. per word. Telegrams, both inland and foreign, may be sent in English and are subject to 8% tax.

In Athens the main and Patissia telegraph offices (Od. Athinas) are always open; that in Od. Stadhiou 8 a.m. to 1 a.m. (Sun to midnight).

PARCELS are not delivered in Greece. They must be collected from the Post Office, where they are subject to handling fees, full customs charges, and often to delay. Dutiable goods sent by letter post are liable to double duty on examination. The bus companies operate an efficient parcels service between their own praktoreia.

V. HOTELS AND RESTAURANTS

Hotels (Ξενοδοχεῖα). The *Hellenic Chamber of Hotels* publishes an annual 'Guide to the Greek Hotels'; lists are also included in the National Tourist Organization's free illustrated pamphlets of the various regions.

There are six official categories: L and A–E. Even in country districts modest but modern hotels are almost everywhere to be found. The de Luxe hotels compare favourably with their counterparts in other countries; almost all have restaurants; their rooms all have private bathrooms and air-conditioning. In all hotels of Class A and most of Class B a proportion of rooms (sometimes all) are equipped with private bath or shower. Class C, at present the most numerous, is the least easy to appraise. Many Greek hotels do not have restaurants. Hotels classed D or E have no public rooms and sometimes only cold water, though their standard of cleanliness and service may well be adequate for a short stay. The existence of an E class hotel is sometimes indicated in the text merely as 'Inn'.

The more modest 'Xenodokheion Ipnou' and guest-houses, without benefit of tourist category, vary from the clean but plain to the verminous and communal. In them a bed not a room may be taken. They are best chosen by recommendation only.

Charges are fixed annually by the Government. Hoteliers may not exceed the maximum permitted figure; the charge appropriate to each room, quoted with service and taxes included (except for Value Added Tax of 7 per cent), is entered in a notice fixed usually to the inside of the door. Central heating or air conditioning is always extra. Considerable reductions can be obtained in Nov–March. In general large hotels in seaside resorts are closed in winter (except where the place is an important town, e.g. Corfù, Nauplia).

The maximum rates which may be charged in the period up to 14 March 1981 are given in the table below:

Cat.	Single Room & Breakfast		Double Room & Breakfast	
	Without bath or shower	With bath or shower	Without bath or shower	With bath or shower
L		from 845*		from 1180*
A		613–946		928–1371
B	334–451	451–730	531–770	611–1068
C	278–379	337–524	410–592	519–700
D	247–310	310–376	397–448	448–578

*Room only

Extras: central heating or air conditioning, add 90 dr., 120 dr.
       stay of less than 3 days, add 10 per cent.
       July, Aug, Sept (to 15th), add 20 per cent.

Despite the official categorization, hotels can still vary widely. As in other countries, this depends very much on individual management: hotels as comfortable in their class as the Rex at Kalamata (B) or the King Otho at Nauplia (D) are rare anywhere. The independent traveller will realize that here as elsewhere, many hotels at popular sites and at beach resorts are geared to package tours and coach groups rather than to the unexpected overnight guest. Furthermore some hotels can legally insist on demi-pension terms, thus tying the visitor to their usually unimaginative restaurants. In the provinces a universal-type basin plug and a stock of toilet paper can still prove an advantage. In seaside resorts, particularly, it is difficult to get single rooms; single occupation of a double room is usually charged at 80% of double price.

Recent experience has shown that out of high season not all the amenities advertised by hotels are always available. In addition, emergency decrees to save fuel or reduce pollution have sometimes resulted in heating and the constant supply of hot water being curtailed.

In this guide hotel charges are not quoted; instead the class is indicated in bold type. In general (but with exceptions where no alternative accommodation is available) hotels have not been included if they insist on prior reservation through agencies, a fixed period stay, or full board being taken; if they are open for short seasons only; or if they have no single rooms. The intention has been to assist the traveller to find a hotel where he has a reasonable chance of getting a comfortable room for the night and the value he has a right to expect from the class concerned. The omission of a name does not imply any adverse judgement; the inclusion equally implies no guarantee of excellence.

Tourist Police, distinguished by their shoulder flashes, will suggest alternative lodging for visitors unable to find their own accommodation. In provincial towns their help is often invaluable in finding keys to locked churches or museums.

Motels, of which there are a growing number, and seaside BUNGALOW-HOTELS partake of the same classification system as hotels.—In regions without hotels the tradition persists of lodging in private houses. Where there is no tourist police office, the traveller is best advised to seek out the local schoolmaster or postmaster. Buses and island boats are usually met by citizens offering 'spiti' (house) or 'domatio' (room).

Youth Hostels. The Greek Youth Hostel Association (4 Odhos Dragatsaniou, Athens) is affiliated to the International Youth Hostels Federation. Its hostels may be used by members of any affiliated association. Accommodation is usually simple and members are obliged to keep early hours; the overnight charge is 30–40 dr.; stay is generally limited to 5 days. There are hostels in Athens, Delphi, Patras, Ioannina, Salonika, Mykonos, Corfù, and Herakleion, also smaller ones elsewhere.—In Athens the Y.W.C.A. (11 Od. Amerikis) and the Y.M.C.A. (28 Od. Omirou) charge 60–150 dr. per day, maximum stay 10 days, meals extra. In July and Aug the Polytechnic School in Athens also accommodates groups of students.

Car-Camping Sites are run by the N.T.O.G. (modest charges) at Voula, Killini, Patras (Ayia), Kamena Vourla, Thessaloniki, Asprovalta, Kavalla, Khalkidiki (Kriopiyi, Paliouri, and Kalandra), Fanarion, Alexandroupolis, and on Mt Olympos (Skotina). Elsewhere there are private camping sites.

Dining Out. In the larger centres a few restaurants and de luxe hotels achieve an international standard of cuisine. The general standard of presentation of Greek foo dhas, however, much improved in late years. Well-prepared Greek dishes are greatly to be preferred to feeble attempts at emulating alien styles. The basic ingredients are usually excellent and, since all Greeks eat out frequently, there is a wide choice of places where Greek food can be enjoyable. Travellers making extended stays in Athens or elsewhere are well advised, unless they must have the reassuring presence of other tourists, to choose an establishment crowded with locals, where the food will be better (and cheaper) and the atmosphere livelier.

Restaurants ('Εστιατόρια). In Athens luncheon is usually taken between 1 and 3 (earlier on Sun) and dinner (generally the more important) between 8 and 11 p.m. (summer 9 p.m. and 1 a.m.), though hotels catering particularly for foreigners conform more nearly to Western times. Outside Athens also hours tend to be earlier. Estiatória display at the entrance a bill of fare, showing their category (L, A–D) and the prices of each dish, both basic and with tax and service included. They can usually provide translations into English and a waiter to interpret. Fixed-price and table d'hôte meals are found only in one special restaurant in Piraeus and in some hotel restaurants. A service charge is added by law so that any small gratuity to the waiter (on the plate) is a recognition of personal service. The wine boy (mikros), however, receives only what is left for him on the *table* (c. 5 per cent).

The distinction between a restaurant proper and a Ταβέρνα is nowadays not clearly definable, but in general the **Taverna** is less formal, patronized for a convivial evening rather than for luncheon, and partly at least out of doors; its fare is uncompromisingly Greek. An EXOKHIKON KENDRON (ΕΞΟΧΙΚΟΝ ΚΕΝΤΡΟΝ) ('rural centre') combines the functions of café and taverna in a country or seaside setting.— The simplest kind of meal, consisting of milk, coffee, bread, butter, honey, etc., can be had in a GALAKTOPOLEION, or dairy. Here in provincial towns the visitor will find the nearest equivalent to breakfast obtainable. A ZAKHAROPLASTEION, or pâtisserie, sells pastries and confectionery, with drinks of all sorts, though larger establishments in the cities serve light meals (generally not cheap). They increasingly resemble the French café, and for younger generations are replacing the traditional Greek kafenion (see below).

Restaurants and taverna meals of comparable standard are now little cheaper than in Britain. The pattern of meals is less stereotyped than in England, the sharing of portions being quite usual; it is essential to order each course separately as several dishes ordered together may arrive together. In tavernas it is by no means unusual to visit the kitchens to choose one's dishes, and in waterside tavernas it is customary to choose one's fish from the ice; this will then be weighed, the price appearing on the menu per kilo. The oily content of most Greek food is too exuberant for northern tastes, and, though the local wine is a good counteragent, travellers will be well advised to keep to grills until they become used to it. Frozen foods (still rare in Greece) must be indicated by law on the menu with the letters KAT.

Good table wines (unresinated, *arrestinato*), both red and white, are obtainable in bottle everywhere and some of the better-known have a nation-wide distribution. Retsina, the resinated white wine characteristic particularly of Attica and the Peloponnese, has lost some of its former popularity in proportion as other wines have improved. It can always be obtained in bottle, but the traditional can or jug from the barrel now has to be sought out. This can still be more refreshing and less soporific in the heat of the day with an al fresco meal. Beer (of Bavarian type) is brewed in Greece and other lagers are brewed under licence or imported. The ordinary water of Athens (as generally in Greece) is safe, but mineral waters from spas such as Loutraki are readily available.

Food and Wine. The favourite Greek apéritif is *ouzo*, a strong colourless drink made from grape-stems and flavoured with aniseed; it is served with *mezé*, snacks consisting of anything from a simple slice of cheese or tomato or an olive to pieces of smoked eel or fried octopus. As in Italy the Greek meal may begin with a foundation course of rice, such as *piláfi sáltsa*, or of pasta (*makarónia*), perhaps baked with minced meat (*pastítsio*), or with *tirópita* (cheese pie). Alternatives are soup or hors d'oeuvre, the latter being particularly good. *Taramosaláta* is a paste made from the roe of grey mullet and olive oil. *Tzatziki* is composed of chopped cucumber in yoghourt heavily flavoured with garlic. The main course may be meat (κρέας, kreas), or fish or a dish on a vegtable base, baked (τοῦ φούρνου, too fournu), boiled (βραστό, vrastó), fried (τηγανιτό, tiganitó), roast (ψητό, psito), or grilled (σχάρας, skáras). The chef's suggestions will be found under ΠΙΑΤΑ ΤΗΣ ΗΜΕΡΑΣ (piáta tis iméras; dishes of the day). *Moussaká* consists of layers of aubergines, minced beef, and cheese, with butter and spices, baked in the oven. Many foreign dishes may appear in transliteration, e.g.: Εσκαλόπ (escalope), Σνίτσελ Χολστάϊν (Schnitzel Holstein), Μπιντόκ άλα Ροῦς (Bitok à la Russe), Κρέμ καραμελέ (crème caramelle), Σαλάτ ντέ φρουί (salade de fruits). Many sweets have Turkish names, and 'shish kebab' is frequently used as a synonym for *souvlakia*, pieces of meat grilled on a skewer. Also cooked in this fashion is *kokoretsi*, which consists of alternate pieces of lamb's liver, kidney, sweetbreads, and heart, wrapped in intestines. When not grilled, meat is often stewed with oil in un-appetizing chunks. Greek cheeses tend to monotony; the ubiquitous *feta* is better eaten—peasant-fashion—with black pepper and oil than on its own. Sweets, however, are elaborate and varied, though more often partaken separately than as a course of a meal. Among the most popular are *baclava*, composed of layered pastry filled with honey and nuts; *kataïfi*, wheat shredded and filled with sweetened nuts; and *galaktoboureko*, pastry filled with vanilla custard.

WINE (κρασί) in Greece is generally of good quality and has greater strength than the wines of France. Wines may be divided into two categories: resinated and unresinated. *Retsína*, flavoured with resin from pine trees, is most characteristic of the south, and to the trained palate varies as much in taste and quality as do unresinated wines. Although a great amount is bottled, retsína is better drunk young from cask. Rosé varieties ('*kokkinelli*') are locally much sought after. There is a large variety of unresinated table wines, white (άσπρο, áspro), red (μαῦρο, mávro, literally 'black'), or rosé (κόκκινο, kókkino, literally 'red'). Excellent draught red wine from *Nemea*, *Rhodos* (Rhodes), or *Corfù* can often be found. Among the wines with nation-wide distribution are the red and white *Hymettos*, bottled at Kamba, and *Demestika*, bottled by the Achaia Klauss Co., based at Patras. Of national status are the excellent *Santa Elena* and *Pallini*, both white and dry, the red *Castel Danielis*, and *Naoussa*, a full-bodied red Macedonian wine not unlike Châteauneuf-du-Pape. The wines from the *Carras* estates are increasingly popular. Equally good but not widely found outside their places of origin are the wines of Crete and Ithaka. Among the best-known dessert wines are *Samos* (golden and sweet) and *Mavrodafni* (approaching the body of port).

The MENU which follows contains a large number of the simpler dishes to be met with:

ΟΡΕΚΤΙΚΑ (orektiká), Hors d'oeuvre
Διάφορα ὀρεκτικά (dhiáfora orektiká), Hors d'oeuvre variés
Ταραμοσαλάτα (táramosaláta), see above
Ντολμάδες Γιαλαντζῆ (dolmádhes Yalantzi), Stuffed vine leaves served hot with egg-lemon sauce
Ντολμαδάκια (dolmadakia), Cold stuffed vine leaves
'Εληὲς (ellies), Olives

ΣΟΥΠΕΣ (soupes), Soups
Σοῦπα αὐγολέμονο (soupa avgholémono), Egg and lemon soup
Σοῦπα ἀπὸ χόρτα (soupa apò hórta), Vegetable soup
Μαγερίτσα (magherítsa), Tripe soup generally with rice (Easter speciality)
Ψαρόσουπα (psarósoupa), Fish soup

ΖΥΜΑΡΙΚΑ (Zimarika) Pasta and Rice dishes
Πιλάφι σάλτσα (piláfi sáltsa), Pilaf
Σπαγέτο σάλτσα μέ τυρί (spagéto sáltsa me tiri), Spaghetti
Μακαρόνια (makarónia), Macaroni

ΨΑΡΙΑ (psária), Fish
Στρείδια (strídhia), Oysters
Συναγρίδα (sinagrídha), Sea bream
Μπαρμπούνια (barboúnia), Red mullet
Μαρίδες (marídhes), Whitebait
'Αστακός (astakós), Lobster
Γαρίδες (garídes), Scampi (Dublin Bay prawns)
Καλαμαράκια (kalamarákia), Baby squids
Κταπόδι (ktapódi), Octopus
Λιθρίνια (lithrínia), Bass

ΛΑΔΕΡΑ (ladhéra), Vegetables or ΧΟΡΤΑ (khorta), Greens
Πατάτες τηγανιτὲς (patátes tiganités), Fried potatoes
Φασολάκια φρ. βουτ. (fasolakia fr. voutiro), Beans in butter
Μπιζέλια (biséllia), Peas
Ντομάτες γεμιστὲς ρῦζι (domátes yemistés rízi), Stuffed tomatoes

AYΓA (avgá) Eggs
'Ομελέτα Ζαμπὸν (Omelétta Jambón), Ham omelette
Αὐγά Μπρουγὲ (avgá 'brouillé'), Scrambled eggs
Αὐγά ἀλά Ροὺς (avgá 'á la Russe'), Eggs with Russian salad

ΕΝΤΡΑΔΕΣ (entrádes), Entrées
Αρνάκι φασολάκια (arnaki fasolakia), Lamb with beans
Μοσχάρι (moskhari), Veal
Σηκοτάκια (sikotakia), Liver
Κοτόπουλο (kotopoulo), Chicken
Χῆνα (khina), Goose
Παπί (papí), Duck
Τζουτζουκάκια (tsoutsoukakia), Meat balls in tomato sauce
Κοτολέτες Χοιρινὲς (kotoléttes khirinés), Pork cutlets

ΣΧΑΡΑΣ (skaras), Grills
Σουβλάκια ἀπὸ φιλὲτο (souvlákia apo filéto), Shish Kebab (see above)
Μπριζόλες μοσχ. (brizóles moskh.), Veal chops
Κεφτέδες σχάρας (keftédes skháras), Grilled meat balls
Γουρουνόπουλο ψητό (gourounópoulo psitó), Roast sucking-pig
Παϊδάκια Χοιρινά (païdhákia khiriná), Pork chops

ΣΑΛΑΤΕΣ (salátes), Salads
Τομάτα σαλάτα (domáta saláta), Tomato salad
Μαοοῦλι (marouli) Lettuce
Ραδίκια (radhíkia), Chicory
Κολοκυθάκια (kolokithákia), Courgettes
'Αγγουράκι (angouráki), Cucumber
'Αγκινάρες (ankináres), Artichokes
Μελιτζάνες (melizánes), Aubergines (eggplants)
Πιπεριές (piperiés), Green peppers
Ρωσσικὴ (Russiki), Russian

ΤΥΡΙΑ (tiría), Cheeses
Φέτα (fetta), Soft white cheese of goat's milk
Κασέρι (kasséri), Hard yellow cheese
Γραβιέρα (graviéra), Greek gruyère
Ροκφὸρ ('Roquefort'), Blue cheeses generally

ΓΛΥΚΑ (glika), Sweets
Χαλβά (halva)
Μπακλαβά (baklava)
Καταϊφι (kataifi)   } see above
Γαλακτομπούρεκκον (galaktoboureko)
'Ρυζόγαλο (rizogalo), Rice pudding
Γιαοῦρτι (yiaourti), Yoghourt

ΦΡΟΥΤΑ (frouta), Fruits
Μῆλο (mílo), Apple
Μπανάνα (banane), Banana
'Αχλάδι (akhládi), Pear
Πορτοκάλι (portokályi), Orange
Κεράσια (kerásia), Cherries
Φράουλες (fráoules), Strawberries
Δαμάσκηνα (damáskina), Plums
Ροδάκινα (rodákina), Peaches
Βερύκοκα (veríkoka), Apricots
Πεπόνι (pepóni), Melon
Καρπούζι (karpouzi), Water-melon

MISCELLANEOUS
Ψωμί (psomi), Bread
Βούτυρο (voútiro), Butter
Αλάτι (aláti), Salt
Πιπέρι (pipéri), Pepper
Μουστάρδα (moustárda), Mustard
Λάδι (ládhi), Oil
Ξείδι (Xídhi), Vinegar
Γάλα (ghála), Milk
Ζάχαρι (zákhari), Sugar
Νερό (neró), Water
Παγωμένο (pagoméno), Iced
Παγωτό (paghotó), Ice cream
Λεμόνι (lemóni), Lemon

The traditional Greek **Café** (ΚΑΦΕΝΕΙΟΝ) of the provinces is an austere establishment usually thronged with male patrons for whom it is both local club and political forum. Casual customers generally occupy tables outside. Coffee (καφὲ) is always served in the 'Turkish' fashion with the grounds. Unless otherwise ordered it is heavily sweetened (*variglikó*). To obtain a less sweetened cup one orders *kafé métrio*, or if desired without sugar *skétto*. Cafés displaying the sign ΚΑΦΕΝΕΙΟΝ-ΜΠΑΡ (Café-Bar) also serve drinks.

VI. GENERAL HINTS

Season. Climatically the best months are April to mid-June and September–October. At more popular places the season extends from March with heavily booked hotels. In July and August beaches are crowded, and the temperature even there may be found excessive (average max. 90° F., min. 72°). During the not infrequent 'heat-waves' shade temperatures may surpass 100° in Athens and 110° in Thessaly. March and November often have surprisingly warm days with long hours of sunshine, but in the earlier part of the year the sea is rarely warm enough for bathing. Equally it can be rainy with chilly evenings until well into April. In winter Athens is subject to very changeable weather, bitter winds and squally rain alternating with dazzling sunny intervals, so that a heavy overcoat and sunglasses may be needed together; but snow (though commonly visible on the surrounding hills) rarely settles in the city. The Aegean islands enjoy milder winters, while the mountainous inland regions of the mainland share the general rigours of the Balkans.

Language. A knowledge of ancient Greek is a useful basis, but no substitute, for the study of modern Greek. Apart from the unfamiliarity of modern pronunciation many of the commonest words (e.g. water, wine, fish) no longer come from the same roots. Fluency in modern Greek will add greatly to the traveller's profit and experience, but those who know no language but English can get along quite comfortably anywhere on the main tourist routes. A knowledge of at least the Greek alphabet is highly desirable, however, since street names, bus destination plates, etc., cannot otherwise be read. A smattering of Greek will often result in the traveller answering more questions than he asks, though it will certainly ensure greater contact with the local populace.

The Greek alphabet now as in later classical times comprises 24 letters:

Α α,   Β β,   Γ γ,   Δ δ,   Ε ε,   Ζ ζ,   Η η,   Θ θ,   Ι ι,   Κ κ,   Λ λ,   Μ μ,   Ν ν,   Ξ ξ,

Ο ο,   Π π,   Ρ ρ,   Σ σ ς,   Τ τ,   Υ υ,   Φ φ,   Χ χ,   Ψ ψ,   Ω ω.

VOWELS. There are five basic vowel sounds in Greek to which even combinations written as diphthongs conform: α is pronounced very short; ε and αι as e in egg (when accented more open, as in the first e in there); η, ι, υ, ει, οι, υι have the sound of ea in eat; ο, ω as the o in dot; ου as English oo in pool. The combinations αυ and ευ are pronounced av and ev when followed by loud consonants (af and ef before mute consonants).

CONSONANTS are pronounced roughly as their English equivalents with the following exceptions: β = v; γ is hard and guttural, before a and o like the English g in hag, before other vowels approaching the y in your; γγ and γκ are usually equivalent to ng; δ = th as in this; θ as th in think; before an i sound λ resembles the lli sound in million; ξ has its full value always, as in ex-king; ρ is always rolled; σ (ς) is a sibilant as in oasis; τ is pronounced half way between t and d; φ = ph or f; χ, akin to the Scottish ch, a guttural h; ψ = ps as in lips. The

English sound b is represented in Greek by the double consonant μπ, d by ντ. All Greek words of two syllables or more have one accent which serves to show the stressed syllable. The classical breathing marks are still written but have no significance in speech. In the termination ον, the n sound tends to disappear in speech and the ν is often omitted in writing.

Manners and Customs. CALENDAR AND TIME: Greece abandoned the Julian calendar only in 1923 so that even 20C dates can be in Old or New Style. All movable festivals are governed by the fixing of Easter according to the Orthodox calendar. Greece uses Eastern European Time (2 hrs ahead of G.M.T.); π.μ.—a.m. and μ.μ.—p.m. When making an appointment it is advisable to confirm that it is an 'English rendez-vous', i.e. one to be kept at the hour stated. The siesta hours after lunch (often late) should not be disturbed by calling or telephoning; an invitation to tea implies the arrival of the guest c. 5.30–6 p.m.

Attention should be paid by travellers to the more formal conventions of Greeks. The handshake at meeting and parting is de rigueur, and inquiry after the health taken seriously. The correct reply to καλῶς ὡρίσατε (kalós orísate: welcome) is καλῶς σᾶς βρήκαμε (kalós sas vríkame: glad to see you). To the inquiry τί κάνετε ; (tí kánete; how do you do?) or πῶς εἶσθε; (pos íste; how are you?) the reply should be καλά, εὐχαριστῶ, καὶ σεῖς (kalà ef kharistó, ke sis): well, thank you—or ἔτσι καί ἔτσι (etsi ke etsi), so-so—*and you?* General greetings are χαίρετε (khérete; greetings, hallo) and Στό καλό (sto kaló; keep well), both useful for greeting strangers on the road. Περαστικά (perastiká) is a useful word of comfort in time of sickness or misfortune meaning 'may things improve'. Except in the centre of Athens it is still customary to greet shopkeepers, the company in cafés, etc., with καλημέρα (kalyméra: good day) or καλησπέρα (kalyispéra: good evening). Σᾶς παρακαλῶ (sas parakaló: please) is used when asking for a favour or for information, but not when ordering something which is to be paid for, when Θά ἤθελα (tha íthela; I should like) is more appropriate. The Greek for yes is ναί (né) or, more formally, μάλιστα (málista); for no, ὄχι (ókhi). 'Αντίο (Addío), goodbye, so long, in Greek has none of the finality of its Italian origin.

In direct contrast to English custom, personal questions (showing interest in a stranger's life), politics, and money are the basis of conversation in Greece, and travellers must not be offended at being asked in the most direct way about their movements, family, occupation, salary, and politics, though they will usually find discussion of the last singularly inconclusive.

By Greek custom the bill for an evening out is invariably paid by the host; the common foreign habit of sharing out payment round the table is looked upon as mean and unconvivial, and visitors valuing their 'face' will do it discreetly elsewhere. A stranger is rarely allowed to play host to a native and may find, if he tries, that the bill has been settled over his head by his Greek 'guest'.

It is not good manners to fill a wine-glass, nor to drain a glass of wine poured for one, the custom being to pour it half full and keep it 'topped up'. Glasses are often touched with the toast εἰς ὑγείαν σᾶς, your health (generally shortened in speech to the familiar yásas or yámas, or, to a single individual, yásou); they are then raised to the light, the bouquet savoured, and the wine sipped before drinking (thus all five senses have been employed in the pleasure).

Entering a Greek house one may formally be offered preserves with coffee and water; this must never be refused. Strictly to conform to custom the water should be drunk first, the preserves eaten and the spoon placed in the glass, and the coffee drunk at leisure. Payment must, of course, never be offered for any service of hospitality. An acceptable way of reducing an obligation is by making a present to a child of the house. Equally hospitality should not be abused; those offering it nearly always have less resources than their foreign guests— even the proverbially poor student.

The 'Volta', or evening parade, universal throughout provincial Greece, has no fixed venue in Athens. Fasting is taken seriously in Lent.

Health. Climate and unfamiliar food alike may cause gastric disorder in all but the strongest stomachs; plain unsweetened lemon-juice can be efficacious. Chemists' advice is generally knowledgeable. Dishes involving reheating and made-up dishes are best avoided. The Greeks are great water-drinkers and the water need not be feared on the mainland; in some islands, however, infective hepatitis (jaundice) is a hazard. Dog bites need immediate treatment.

Public Holidays. Official public holidays in Greece are: New Year's Day; 6 Jan (Epiphany); Kathara Deftera ('Clean Monday'), the Orthodox Shrove Day; 25 March (Independence Day); Orthodox Good Friday, Easter Monday, 1 May; Ascension Day; 15 Aug (Assumption); 28 Oct 'Okhi' day (see below); Christmas Day; and 26 Dec (St Stephen). In addition Athens celebrates the feast of her patron saint, St Dionysios the Areopagite (3 Oct), and some other cities a patronal festival.

Carnival after three weeks' festivities reaches its peak on the Sunday before Clean Monday with processions and student revels. Its manifestations are strong in Patras, Naoussa, and in Athens are centred on Plaka. Procession of shrouded bier on *Good Friday*; 'Christos anesti' (Christ is risen) celebration, with ceremonial lighting of the Paschal candle and release of doves, in front of churches at midnight preceding *Easter Sunday*, followed by candlelight processions and 'open house'. Roasting of Paschal lambs and cracking of Easter eggs on morning of Easter Day. These ceremonies are performed with pomp in the capital.—*Okhi Day*, commemorating the Greek 'no' (ὄχι) to the Italian ultimatum of 1940, is celebrated with remembrance services and military processions, especially in Salonika.

Shops are open in summer 8–1.30 and 5.30–8.30 on Tues, Thurs, & Fri; 8–2.30 or 3 only on Mon, Wed, & Saturday. In winter evening hours are 4–7.30. In large towns chemists take turns to offer a 24 hr service; duty chemists in Athens are listed in 'The Week in Athens', or may be discovered by dialling 173 on the telephone. Characteristic products of genuine rural industries may be sought in monasteries, local bazaars and markets, and in village homes, the best value being in carpets, embroidery, leather-work, and pottery. In Athens such things are best sought through HOMMEH, a national organization for small industries and handicrafts (9 Mitropoleos).

The PERIPTERO (Περίπτερον), or kiosk, developed from a French model, is a characteristic feature of Greek urban life. Selling newspapers, reading matter, postcards, cigarettes, chocolate, toilet articles, roll film, postage stamps, etc., kiosks are open for about 18 hrs a day.

Museums and Archaeological Sites. In places most visited by tourists the way to ancient remains is generally signposted and the sites enclosed, an admission charge being levied varying between 10 and 50 dr. (at the majority 25 dr.). On Sun admission is usually free. The opening hours of museums, and archaeological sites vary according to season, and, in certain cases, to local conditions. At the time of going to press they were more than usually uncertain and erratic. The times given below are the official hours for 1980. Even the official list allows for exceptions. Times in the text show some variants found on the spot. Shortage of staff and new negotiations of conditions of service make further changes inevitable.

STANDARD HOURS for sites, museums, and monuments not rated as exceptional (see below):

	Weekdays	Sundays & Holidays
Spring (1 Apr–15 May)	9–1.30, 4–6	10–4.30
Summer (16 May–15 Sept)	8.30–12.30, 4–6	9–3
Autumn (16 Sept–31 Oct)	9–1, 3.30–5.30	10–4
Winter (1 Nov–31 Mar)	9.30–4	10–4.30

The most popular sites (the Acropolis and Agora, the four main museums of Athens, Corinth, Olympia, Mycenae, Delphi, Mistra, and Epidauros, also Samothrace and the museums at Mytilene, Chios, and Lemnos) do not close in the middle of the day, keep slightly longer hours on weekdays, and are open 10–4.30 on Sun & hol. throughout the year. Museums are closed on Tuesdays; both sites and museums are closed on 1 Jan, 25 March, Good Friday morning, Easter Day, & Christmas Day. On Christmas Eve, New Year's Eve, 2 Jan, 5 Jan, the last Sat of Carnival, Thurs in Holy Week, and Easter Tues, hours are 8–12.30.

Foreign students of art, archaeology, and classical studies can through their institutions acquire a free pass (from the General Directorate of Antiquities and Restoration, Dept. of Museums, 14 Aristidou St., Athens). In general photography (hand cameras) is free on archaeological sites, and may be indulged freely (save where unpublished material is on display) in museums on purchase of a second ticket for the camera. ΑΠΑΓΟΡΕΥΕΤΑΙ (apagorevetai) means forbidden. Set fees (not cheap) are charged for using tripods, etc.

The Greek Antiquities Service treats its visitors' safety as their own responsibility. Travellers should, perhaps, be warned that holes are not generally fenced, nor heights guarded by railings; the very nature of archaeological remains ensures the maximum number of objects that can be tripped over. It is particularly dangerous to move about while reading or sighting a camera.

No guide-book to the whole of Greece has the space to give detailed directions how to reach every remote or minor site. These stand, unfenced and unmarked, often some way from the modern village that has taken upon itself their ancient name (proven or supposed). Assistance beyond that given in the text can usually be canvassed from the locals with the use of the following vocabulary: *yia* (towards) *ta arkhaia* ('ancient things'), *to kastro* (any fortified height), *tis anaskafés* (excavations), *to froúrio* (medieval castle). Country peasants rarely have any idea of periods of chronology, whereas intelligent schoolboys sometimes have a surprising knowledge of their local antiquities. Licensed guides are available in Athens, and on some major sites;

casual offers of guidance are better politely declined in Athens and Piraeus, but can be disinterested and invaluable elsewhere.

Orthodox churches (usually open) may be visited at any reasonable hour; when they are closed inquiry should be made for the key. Women are not permitted to enter the sanctuary.

Equipment. The light in Greece is strong, even in winter, and sun glasses will be needed. Greece is dusty: a clothes brush is essential. Binoculars greatly enhance the pleasure of travel among mountains or islands. An electric torch is useful, especially in the islands. A duffel-coat and a rug are great assets if intending to travel 'deck' on Greek boats.

Swimming. Skin diving and underwater photography are banned in most Greek coastal waters; the local N.T.O.G. or Tourist Police offices should be consulted.

Newspapers. 'Athens Daily News' and 'Athens Daily Post' are published daily in English. Foreign newspapers are régularly obtainable at central street kiosks in Athens on the day of publication at three to five times published price. 'The Athenian', a monthly journal in English, has up-to-date information on entertainment, restaurants, etc.

Weights and Measures. The French metric system of weights and measures adopted in Greece in 1958, is used with the terms substantially unaltered. Thus μέτρο, χιλιόμετρον (khiliómetro), etc. Some liquids are measured by weight (κιλό, etc.), not in litres. The standard unit of land measurement, the *stremma*, is equal to ¼ acre.

NOTE ON TRANSLITERATION

Regarding Greek place-names, Col. Leake wrote 150 years ago 'It is impossible in any manner to avoid inconsistency.' Many recent writers on Greece have tried to make a virtue of 'the avoidance of pedantry', but even pedantry is preferable to chaos, and some measure of consistency must be attempted, even if doomed to incomplete success. Modern Greek is not the same language as ancient Greek, and in any case many modern places in Greece have names derived from Albanian, Turkish, or 'Frankish' roots. The most acceptable compromise is gained by using one set of rules for modern place names, and another for those of ancient times.

Names of modern localities have been transliterated in accordance with the phonetic system codified by the Permanent Committee on Geographical Names, used alike by NATO and by professional and archaeological journals. Though this results sometimes in visual ugliness, and for those with a knowledge of Greek increasing irritation (disguising the familiar apparently unnecessarily: thus Khlóï), it has three merits: a great measure of alphabetical consistency for indexing; easy cross-reference to most official maps and to original excavation reports; and the possibility for non-Greek-speakers of producing a recognizable approximate pronunciation. Where the result has seemed too *outré* to be borne and where there is a recognized and familiar English version (e.g. Rhodes), this has been used at least in all subsidiary references.

Ancient names have been given in the traditional English form used by classical scholars and archaeologists, preferring the purely English form where this exists (e.g. Aristotle, Homer), and the Latin form where this has become accepted everyday English usage: e.g. Boeotia, not Boiotia; Plato, not Platon. In other instances the form nearest to the ancient Greek has generally been preferred (with k for κ, rather than the misleading c), and (e.g) Sounion rather than Sunium.

This duality, though producing inconsistencies between ancient and modern (e.g. respectively ch and kh for χ), highlights the pitfall that the modern place bearing the equivalent of a Classical name is not necessarily in the location of its ancient counterpart. Where they are coincident, some reconciliation may have to be effected: it is well for Christians to remember the Beroea of St Paul, but advisable when journeying there to think of the modern town as Vérria.

It should be pointed out that many place-names have both a *katharevousa* (or formal) and a *demotic* (or spoken) form. Thus Athens is (pedantically but correctly) αἱ Ἀθῆναι in the former, but always in speech ἡ Ἀθήνα. Neither modern form is necessarily the ancient form: thus, Thorikos, anciently ἡ Θόρικος has become ὁ Θορικός. In addition *all* place-names, like other nouns, decline; this often produces a change of stress as well as of inflexion. Some places have their more familiar spoken form in the accusative (given, where thought desirable, in the text), though they appear on maps in the nominative; places ending in -on often drop the 'n' in speech, sometimes the whole syllable. Street names are in the genitive when called after a person, e.g. Ermou (of Hermes), also in the genitive when leading to a place, e.g. Patission (to Patissia). As in English, a church may be spoken of by the name of its saint in the nominative or genitive. In the vexing instance where the Greek name is in itself a transliteration from Roman characters, each example has been treated on its apparent merits. Thus Βερανζέρου (which in Greek pronunciation bears little resemblance to the Fr. *Béranger*) has been rendered Veranzérou; Βύρωνος similarly has been rendered Víronos by sound since Lord Byron properly appears in Greek literary criticism as Μπάυρον. Names of modern Greeks have been rendered where possible as their owners transliterated them or as arbitrary custom has demanded.

No consistency can be attempted in the language or spelling of hotel names, since they are often chosen quite arbitrarily themselves. What is displayed on the building is likely not to correspond with the name listed in the hotel guide—only experience can help in the realization that (e.g.) Ilios, Helios, and Soleil designate the same hotel (Ἥλιος), or that Mont Blanc and Lefkon Oros are one and the same.

In this book, at its first mention, a place-name is given also in Greek capitals, where these have an appearance significantly different to warrant it, as an aid to motorists reading maps or signposts. On main roads Greek signposts are printed in Greek and Roman characters (but, inevitably, not in a consistent transliteration). Accents have been put on transliterated place-names at their main entry since they show pronunciation stress. For the sake of economy they have sometimes been omitted elsewhere.

GREECE

I ATHENS

ATHENS, in official Greek αἱ Ἀθῆναι but popularly ἡ Ἀθήνα, the capital of the Hellenic Republic (Elliniki Dhimokratia), is situated in lat. 37° 58′ N. and long. 23° 43′ E., 4 m. from the sea. The city, which now occupies the greater part of the Attic plain, is surrounded by an amphitheatre of mountains, nowhere far distant, and to the E., in Hymettos, barely 5 m. from the centre. At the 1971 census Greater Athens (Periféria Protevoússis), comprising 37 demes and 19 communes partly in the nome of Attikis and partly in that of Piraios, numbered 2,540,200 inhabitants; of these the city proper, or deme of Athens, accounted for 867,000 and Piraeus for 187,400, while the remainder was distributed between their modern residential and industrial suburbs extending in every direction. Athens has thus engulfed the subordinate and almost isolated group of lesser hills, which more nearly defined the limits of the ancient city.

The northernmost of these hills, which are in reality fragments of the Anchesmos or Tourkovouni range, is Strephis. Immediately s. rises the conical rock of Lykabettos, still called by its classical name. This remarkable hill is to Athens what Vesuvius is to Naples or Arthur's Seat to Edinburgh. From its summit the city is seen as on a map. To the s.w. of Lykabettos are five more hills, all of which were included in ancient Athens. Of these, the nearest is the Acropolis or citadel of Athens, rising abruptly to 512 ft, a little more than half the height of Lykabettos. To the w. of the Acropolis are the Areopagus, the Pnyx, and the Hill of the Nymphs; and to the s.w. is the Mouseion.

Athens, although one of the most easterly cities of Europe and in spite of nearly 400 years of Turkish rule, is almost entirely western in appearance though recent influxes of refugees from the Levant have brought a colourful look in places. A creation of the 19C and 20C, it was planned by the Bavarian architects of King Otho, who laid out a new street plan round the large village that then occupied the N. slope of the Acropolis. Though its approaches are ugly and gimcrack, the centre with squares planted with exotic trees is by no means unattractive; the best of the new buildings achieve a style appropriate to the strong light by successful use of deep balconies and white marble; while the splendour of its ancient monuments grouped about the dominating Acropolis, gives to Athens a distinction enduring time and change.

'Odhos' (Street) is often omitted in addresses; the practice has been followed here, except where the omission might cause confusion; then, for brevity, it has generally been abbreviated to 'Od.'.—**Plan references** refer to the 8-page section between pp. 64–65, the first figure denoting the page, the second the square.

Airport at *Ellinikó*, 6 m. S.E. on the coast, for both international and internal flights (two terminals, separately approached). Free bus between East and West terminals. Direct bus (45 dr.) from East Airport to Amalias, every 20 min. (6 a.m.–midnight); see also suburban buses, below.

Arrival by Sea at Piraeus (see Rte 12); Athens may be reached in 25 min. by the Electric Rly. (5.50 dr.), by bus (10 dr.), or taxi (approx, 100 dr.).

Railway Stations. *Larissa* (2, *1*), in the N.W. of the city, for the standard-gauge line to Thebes, Larissa, Salonika, and Idhoméni (connecting viâ Gevgelija and Belgrade with the European trunk lines). Booking office, 81 Venizelou (opp. University).—*Peloponnisou* (2, *1*), adjoining Larissa to the S.W., for the metre-gauge line to Corinth and the Peloponnese. Booking office, 18 Ay. Konstandinou.—*Omonoia* (3, *3* underground), Omonoia Sq., for the Greek Electric Railway ('Ελληνικοΐ Ἠλέκτρικοι Σιδηρόδρομοι) to Piraeus and Kifisia.

Hotels. Only a proportion of the better-class hotels is given below; there are many others widely spread through the city.

In or near Sindagma Sq.: **Grande Bretagne** (a; 3, *8*), 430 R, **King George** (b; 3, *8*), 150 R, overlooking Sindagma Sq.; **Amalia** (u; 7, *4*), 130 R, with view over National Garden; **King's Palace** (c; 3, *8*), 220 R, 4 Leof. Venizelou; **Athenée Palace** (d; 3, *8*), 130 R, Plat. Kolokotroni, these **L.**—**Olympic Palace** (g; 7, *3*), 130 R, 16 Filellinon; **Attica Palace** (v; 3, *8*), **Astor** (ee; 3, *8*), 130 R, 6 and 16 Karayeoryi Servias; **Electra** (i; 3, *8*), 100 R, 5 Ermou; **Blue House** (pp; 3, *8*), small, RB only, these **A.**—**Pan** (p; 3, *8*), 11 Mitropoleos; **Minerva** (h; 3, *8*), 3 Stadhiou (NR); **Likavittos** (cc; 3, *8*), 6 Valaoritou; **Aretoussa** (ff; 3, *8*), Mitropoleos/Nikis; these **B.**

In Kolonaki/Pankrati or towards the American Embassy: **Athens Hilton** (5, *7*), 480 R, 46 Leof. Vasilissis Sofias; **St George Lycabettus** (f; 4, *6*), 150 R, Plat. Dexameni; **Holiday Inn**, 200 R, 50 Mikhalakopoulou (5, *6*); **Caravel**, 470 R, 2 Vas. Alexandrou (5, *7*), these **L.**—**Golden Age** (ai; 5, *6*), 57 Mikhalakopoulou, **A.**—**Alexandros** (jj; 5, *4*), 8 Timoleondos Vassou; **Stadion** (k; 8, *4*), 38 Leof. Vas. Konstandinou, both **B.**

In Plaka: **Electra Palace** (s; 7, *3*), 18 Nikodhimou, **A.**—**Omiros** (gg; 7, *8*), 15 Apollonos; **Adrian** (nn; 6, *4*), small, 74 Adrianou; **Plaka** (w; 3, *7*) 7 Kapnikareas, these **B.**—**Royal** (q; 3, *7*), 44 Mitropoleos, **C.**

Near the Temple of Olympian Zeus or the Acropolis: **Royal Olympic** (ii; 7, *7*), 125 R, 28 Diakou, **L.**—**Herodion** (ak; 6, *8*), 4 Rovertou Galli; **Parthenon**, 6 Makri (7, *5*); **Divani Zafolia Palace**, 190R, 19 Parthenonos (6, *8*), these **A.**—**Athens Gate** (tt; 7, *5*), 10 Leof. Singrou, **B.**—**Delos** (x; 7, *5*), 12 Makri, **C.**

Between Sindagma and Omonoia, near the University: **Esperia Palace** (m; 3, *5*), 185 R, 22 Stadhiou, **A.**—**Galaxy** (oo; 3, *8*), 100 R, 22 Akadimias; **Titania** (vv; 3, *5*), 400 R, 52 Leof. Venizelou; **Palladion** (n; 3, *5*), 54 Leof. Venizelou (NR); **Academos** (ll; 3, *6*), 100 R, 58 Akadimias; **Metropole** (qq; 3, *5*), 59 Stadhiou (NR), all **B.**

Near Omonoia Sq.: **Ambassadeurs** (j; 2, *4*), 200 R, 67 Sokratous; **King Minos** (rr; 3, *3*), 180 R, 1 Piraios, both **A.**—**Grand** (ab; 3, *3*), 10 Veranzerou; **Dorian Inn** (ak; 2, *6*), 15 Piraios; **El Greco** (z; 3, *5*), 65 Athinas; **Alpha** (r; 3, *3*), **Marmara** (mm; 3, *3*), 17 and 14 Khalkokondili; **Achillion** (aa; 2, *4*), **Ilion** (dd; 2, *4*), 32 and 7 Ay. Konstandinou (both NR), all these **B.**—**Omonoia** (ss; 3, *3*), 260 R, Plat. Omonoias; **Alkistis** (uu; 2, *6*), 120 R, 18 Plat. Theatrou; **Tegea** (ww; 2, *4*), 100 R, 44 Khalkokondili; **Banghion** (hh; 3, *5*), 18b Plat. Omonoias; **Florida** (xx; 2, *6*), 25 Menandrou; **Marina** (yy; 2, *6*), 13 Voulgari; **Pithagorion** (zz; 2, *4*), 28 Ay. Konstandinou (NR), all **C**, and many others.

Near the National Archæological Museum or Pedhion Areos: **Park** (o; 3, *2*), 155 R, 10 Leof. Alexandhras; **Acropole Palace** (e; 3, *1*), 130 R, 51 Ikosiokto Oktovriou, both **L.**—**Divani Zafolia Alexandras** (ac; 4, *2*), 87 Leof. Alexandhras, **A.**—**Cairo City** (y; 3, *1*), 40 and 46 Marnis, both **B.**—**Museum** (ad; 3, *2*), 16 Bouboulinas, **C.**

Near the Rly. Stations: **Minoa** (t; 2, *4*), 12 Karolou; **Candia** (*Iraklion*; ae; 2, *1*), 140 R, 40 Deliyianni; **Stanley** (af; 2, *3*), 270 R, 1 Odisseos; these **B.**—**Nestor** (ag; 2, *4*), 58 Ay. Konstandinou; **Kosmos** (ah; 2, *4*), 16 Psarron, these **C**, and many others.

For hotels in the hills and near the sea, see Rtes 13 and 15.

Flats (apartments), rated as A class hotels, may be rented by the week: **Embassy** (kk; 5, *4*) and **Ariane**, 15 and 22 Timoleontos Vassou; **Kolonaki**, 3 Kapsali; **Egnatia**, 64 Tritis Septemvriou.

Youth Hostels. 1 Ay. Meletiou (200 beds; open always); 87 Alexandhras (220 beds; July–Sept only); 20 Kallipoleos, Viron (80 beds; mid-Apr–mid-Oct).—YMCA, 28 Omirou; YWCA, 13 Amerikis.

Restaurants (lunch usually between 12.30 and 3; dinner between 8.30 and 12). International food and décor (not cheap) at **L** class hotels: *Ta Nissia* (Athens Hilton); *Tudor Hall* (King George); *Templar's Grill* (Royal Olympic); and at the Grande Bretagne. Also: *Balthazar*, 27 Vournazou/Tsoka (evenings, not Sun); *Skorpios*, 1 Evrou, *Prunier*, Ipsilandou (closed July), both near American Embassy; *Ta Papakia*, 5 Iridanou, *Bagatelle*, 9 K. Venturi, *Le Calvados*, 3 Alkmanos, *Flame Steak House*, 9 Khatziyianni Maxi, these near the Hilton; *La Casa*, 22 Anapiron

Polemou, *L'Abreuvoir* (French), *Je Reviens*, 51 and 49 Xenokratous (the last two open also at midday), on S. slope of Lykabettos; *Dionysos*, 42 Rovertou Galli (Mouseion Hill).

Less exclusive: *Floca*, 9 Venizelou; *Corfù*, 6 Kriezotou; *Gerofinikas*, 10 Pindarou; *Delphi*, 15 Nikis; *The Eighteen*, *Europa*, both Tsakalof; *Vassilis*, 14A Voukourestiou; *McMiltons*, 91 Adrianou (Plaka); *Maxim*, off Kanari (Plat. Kolonaki); *Roumeli*, 107 Panormou; modest restaurants and kebab counters in side streets near Omonoia Sq.—*Al Convento* (Italian), 4–6 Anapiron Polemou (Kolonaki); *Stagecoach* (American), 6 Loukianou; *Michiko* (Japanese), 27 Kidatheneon (Plaka); *Pagoda* (Chinese), 2 Bousgou, near Pedhion Areos; *Vladimir*, 12 Aristodimou (Lykabettus), many of these closed Sun.

Tavernas (some open evenings only, 8.30 or 9 to 1) offer excellent food and entertainment of a characteristically Greek kind. They are crowded and convivial; a table once occupied is often kept for the evening. The menu may be in Greek only, but it is not unusual to choose dishes at the kitchen. Many in Plaka cater for tourists; a more local atmosphere may be sought e.g. behind the Hilton or on the slopes of Lykabettus. In summer Athenians tend to dine farther out in Attica. In Plaka: *Xynou*, 4 A. Yeronda; *Vakhos* (Bacchus), Thrassilou; *Erotokritos*, 16 Lissiou; *Zafiris*, 4 Thespidhou; *Epta Adhelfia*, 34 Iperidhou; *Platanos*, 4 Diogenous; *Palea Athena*, 4 Flessa; *Kastro*, 8 Mnesikleous, the last two with music and dancing, and many others. *Pythari*, N. corner of Lykabettos; *Rogdia*, 44 Aristippou. Elsewhere: *Norok*, Kritis, near Larissa Stn; *Svingos*, 41 Ayias Zonis, Patissia. Tavernas with bouzoukia music near Ay. Sostis (Rte 12) and near the racecourse.

Zakharoplastéia, properly speaking, are confectioners. In general now they have the function of a superior type of café or tea-room, serving alcoholic drinks, and the largest also substantial cold dishes. Among the best known are *Zonar's*, 9 Venizelou; *Floca*, 4 Koraï; *Elvetikon*, Venizelou (Omonoia end); *Nouphara Bokolas*, *Nea Lykovrissi*, Plat. Kolonaki; *Petrograd*, 23 Stadhiou.

Cafés are numerous though many serve only Greek ('Turkish') or 'instant' coffee. Those in or near the main squares and avenues cater for tourists, but coffee more nearly approaching western tastes is best sought at the *Brazilian Coffee Stores*, 3 Stadhiou (Stoa Kalliga) and 1 Voukourestiou.

Post Office (3, 5; all services, incl. cables) 100 Aiolou (corner of Omonia Sq.), open Mon–Sat, 7.30 a.m. to 10 p.m.; branch offices: Sindagma, at Othonos/Nikis; Omonoia Sq. (underground); also in Patriarkhou Ioakhim, etc.—O.T.E. CENTRES: 85 Patission, 65 Stadhiou (both open 24 hrs); also 15 Stadhiou: 53 Solonos; 7 Kratinou (these 7 or 8 a.m. to 10 p.m. or midnight).—Police Office (Aliens Dept.), 9 Khalkokondhili.—TOURIST POLICE, 9 Ermou.

Information Bureaux. *National Tourist Office*, 2 Karayeoryi Servias; 4 Stadhiou; in booking hall of Omonoia Underground Stn; and at the Airport; publishes (weekly, free) 'The Week in Athens' in Eng. and French. *Royal National Foundation*, 9 Filellinon.

Travel Agents. *Actravel*, 6 Venizelou; *Alfa*, 6 Skoufou; *Ghiolman Bros.*, *Hellas Travel*, 1 and 14 Filellinon; *American Express*, 15 Venizelou; *Wagons-Lits/Cook*, 8 Ermou; *Agence Générale d'Athènes*, 43 Stadhiou; *Hermès en Grèce*, *C.H.A.T. Tours*, both 4 Stadhiou; *Pausanias*, Akadhimias/Plat. Kaningos; and many others. The *Periyitiki Leskhe*, 28 Leof. Amalias, organizes excursions to many places difficult of access by public transport.

Shipping Offices, mostly in Piraeus (Rte 12), except *United States Lines*, 59B Stadhiou. *Adriatica* has an agency at 2 Karayeoryi Servias, *Hellenic Mediterranean Lines* at 28 Amalias, *Jadrolinija* at 4 Stadhiou.

Airline Offices. *British Airways*, 10 Othonos (Sindagma); *Olympic Airways*, 6 Othonos (all bookings); 96 Singrou (coach terminal); *T.W.A.*, 8 Xenofondos; *P A N A M*, 4 Othonos; *Air France* and *Lufthansa*, 4 Karayeoryi Servias; *Q A N T A S* 5 Mitropoleos.

Taxicabs (ranks in main squares), equipped with taximeters, when disengaged exhibit the sign ΕΛΕΥΘΕΡΟΝ. Hiring charge 10 dr.; then 11.50 dr. per km.; waiting 100 dr. per hour; surcharge 5 dr. if to/from a public transport terminal; also 10 dr. per piece of luggage; surcharge after midnight 5 dr. (1–5 a.m. 10 dr.); minimum total hire 35 dr.; tip by rounding up to nearest 10 dr.—CAR HIRE (chauffeur-driven), 5000 dr. per day (10 hrs; up to 120 km.) plus 300 dr. per extra hour and addit. charge per km.

Electric Railway. Frequent metropolitan service from *Kifissia* vià Omonoia to *Piraeus* in 40 min. Principal intermediate halts (s. of Omonoia): *Monastirion* (2, 8), *Thission* (2, 8), *Kallithea*, *New Phaleron*; N. of Omonoia: *Victoria* and *Patissia*.

City and Suburban Buses (KTEL 1–6 of Athens). Owing to the one-way traffic system their routes through the centre seldom coincide for the return journey; between the Omonoia area and Sindagma Sq. traffic goes N. by Venizelou, s. by either Stadhiou or Akadhimias. Among the most useful routes are:

(*a*) *Within the city.* 1 (trolley). *Larissa Stn*–Omonoia–*Kallithea*; 2 (trolley). *Kipseli*–Amalias–Nat. Museum–*Patission*; 3/7 (trolley or motor-bus). *Patissia*–National Museum–Sofias–*Ampelokipoi*; 5. *Larissa*–Omonoia–Amalias–*Kallithea*; 10. *Votanikos*–Asomaton–Monastiraki–Sindagma–*Ippokratous*; 12 (trolley). *Pankrati*–Olgas–Amalias–Nat. Museum–*Patission*; 14. *Kallithea*–Tsitsifies–*Academy*; 16. *Thon*–Panathenaic Stadium–Sindagma–**Acropolis**–*Thission*; 50. *Marasleion* (Gennadion Library)–*Plat. Kaningos.*

(*b*) *Suburban and Attica.* 1. (bus) *Od. Othonos*–*Edem*–*Kalamaki*–*West Airport*; 25. *Plat. Kaningos*–*Kifissia*; 30. *Olgas*–Singrou–*Glifadha*; 39. *University*–Sofias–*Kaisariani*; 44. *Ay.* Asomáton–Dionisios Areop.–Olgas–Konstandinou–*Paiánia* (Liópesi); 45. as 44, continuing to *Spata*; 46. as 44, continuing to *Koropí*; 47. *Nat. Library*–*Psikhiko*; 60. *Od. Mikhail Voda*–*Parnes*; 62. *Od. Veranzerou*–*Plato's Academy*; 68. *Plat. Eleftherías*–*Elevsis*; 70. *Omonoia*–*Piraeus*; 79. *Demotiki Theatron*–*Glifadha*; 84. *Olgas*–*Ano Voula*; 85. *Olgas*–*Ay.* Nikolaos–*Glifadha*; 88. *Od. Menandhrou*–*Perama* (Salamis); 89. *Olgas*–*Vouliagmeni*; 90. *Olgas*–*Varkiza*; 91. *Demotiki Theatron*–*Vouliagmeni*; 100. *Plat. Eleftherías*–*Dhafni*–*Skaramangas*; 105. *Plat. Kaningos*–*Pal. Pendeli*; 125. *Demot. Theatron*–*Voula*; 137. *Plat. Kaningos*–*Limni Marathónos*; 138. *Plat. Kaningos*–*Varibobi; 163. Academy*–*Neon Faliron*; 165 (EHΣ). *Od. Filellinon*–*Piraeus*; 184. *Amalias*–*East Airport.*

To *Sounion, Lavrion, Porto Rafti, Marathon, Kalamos,* and places in E. Attica, from Odhos Mavromateion. To *Megara* from Kerameikos.

Long-distance Bus Stations. Services to the *Peloponnese, Macedonia, Epirus,* and the *Ionian Is.* from 100 Kifissou (reached in 15 min. by bus 62 from Plat. Ayiou Konstandinou booking office).

Services to *Euboea, Central Greece,* and *Thessaly* from 260 Liossion (reached by bus 63/64 from Leof. Amalias).

Railway Pullman Buses to *Loutraki, Corinth, Patras,* etc. from Peloponnese Stn; and to *Salonika, Edhessa,* and *Alexandroupolis* from Larissa Stn (booking office at 18 Ayiou Konstandinou).

Car Hire (self-drive). *Hertz*, 12 Singrou; *Avis*, 48 Amalias; *Hellascars*, 7 Stadhiou; etc.

Embassies, Legations, and Consulates. *British*, 1 Ploutarkhou (4, *8*); *United States*, Leof. V. Sofias (5, *6*) and (visas) 9 Leof. Venizelou; *Australia*, 15 Mesogeion; *Canada*, 4 Yennadhiou; *Yugoslavia* (visas) 25 Evrou (late mornings only).

English Church, St *Paul's* (7, 5), Odhos Filellinon, Rev. J. Findlow, services on Sun at 8, 9, and 10; special times on Saints' days. American Church (4, 5; St *Andrew's*), 66 Sina; Roman Catholic Church (4, 7; St *Denis*), Leof. Venizelou.

Banks. Head Offices: *Bank of Greece*, 21 Venizelou; *National Bank of Greece*, 86 Aiolou; *Commercial Bank of Greece*, 11 Sofokleous; *Ionian and Popular Bank of Greece*, Pesmazoglou/Venizelou, etc. Normal hours, 8–2.– Of many branches with exchange facilities, several near Sindagma Sq. are open additional hours: *National*, 2 Karayeoryi Servias (Mon–Fri 2–9, Sat & Sun, 8–8); *Ionian and Popular*, 1 Mitropoleos (Mon–Fri 2–5.30, Sat 9–12.30); *Commercial*, 11 Venizelou (Mon–Sat 2–3.30, Sun 9–12).

Learned Institutions. *British School at Athens*, 52 Souedias; *British Council*, 17 Kolonaki Sq., with good library; *American School of Classical Studies*, and *Gennadion Library*, 54 and 61 Souedias; American Library at *Hellenic–American Union*, 22 Massilias; *Greek Archæological Society*, 20 Venizelou; *Direction of Antiquities Services*, Old Palace; *Ecole Française d'Archéologie*, 6 Dhidhotou; *Institut Français d'Athènes*, 29 Sina; *Deutsches Archäologisches Institut*, 1 Fidias; *National Library* see Rte 10; *Municipal Library*, Odhos Kleisthenous; *Parliament Library*, Parliament Building; *Beñakios Library*, 2 Anthimou Gazi; *Royal Research Institute* (Byzantine and Modern Greek studies), 4 Leof. Vas. Sofias; *College of Music*, 35 Piraios; *Foreign Press Service*, 3 Zalokosta.

Clubs. *Automobile and Touring Club of Greece* (E.L.P.A.), Pirgos Athinon, Vas. Sofias/Mesogeion; *Hellenic Alpine Club*, 7 Karayeoryi Servias; *Greek Youth Hostels Assocn.*, 4 Dragatsaniou.

Booksellers. *Eleftheroudakis*, 4 Nikis; *Kaufmann*, 28 Stadhiou, also 11 Voukourestiou; second-hand shops at lower end of Ippokratous.

Theatres. Winter Season (Oct–May): *Ethnikon* (National Theatre Company),

Ay. Konstandinou; *Olympia* (Liriki Skené), 59 Leof. Akadimias, opera and operetta; *Arts* (Tekhnis), Odos Stadhiou; *Rex*, Leof. Venizelou, plays, concerts, and films; *Akropol*, Ippokratous; *Elsa Verghi*, 1 Voukourestiou; *Kava*, Leof. Venizelou; *Athinon*, 10 Voukourestiou; *Dionissia*, 10 Amerikis; *Moussouri*, Plat. Ay. Yeoryiou Karitsi; *Bourneli*, 37 Patission. Summer Season (June–Sept) in the Odeion of Herodes Atticus; *Samartzi*, Karolou; *Poria*, 69 Tritis Septemvriou.— Concerts. Athens State Orchestra (Mon) in winter at Rex, in summer at the Odeion; light orchestral music in winter at Kentrikon (Mon); recitals at Parnassos Hall (Od. Chr. Lada).—Son et Lumière, lighting of the Acropolis viewed from the Pnyx, was suspended in 1980 during repairs.

Cinemas are numerous and cheap. The principal houses (many with films in English) are in Stadhiou and Venizelou.

Baths (Loutra), 26 Veranzerou, and (sea water) at 100 Andromakhis, Kallithea. —Public Lavatories can be found, inadequately marked, in most main squares.

Sport. Tennis at *Athens Tennis Club*, Leof. Olgas; *Panellinios*, Odhos Mavromateion. Swimming, open-air pool Leof. Olgas. Indoor pool, 277 Patission. Golf at Varibopi; also at Glifadha. Sailing (Wed and Sat aft. and Sun) in Phaleron Bay. Racecourse (Wed and Sat) at Phaleron. Motor Racing, *Acropolis Rally* (late May) for touring cars starts and ends in Athens; *Autumn Rally* in Nov.

Festivals. *Athens Festival of Music and Drama*, June–Aug; *Blessing of the Waters* at Epiphany (6 Jan) in Plateia Dexameni after procession from St Dionysios the Areopagite just to the s.; *Feast of St Dionysios* (3 Oct); *Anniversary of 1944 Liberation* (12 Oct), hoisting of National Flag on Acropolis; *Easter* candlelight procession on Lykabettos (other general celebrations, see prefatory pages).— Wine Festival at Daphni (Rte 16) in Sept.

Ancient History. The slopes of the Acropolis have been occupied since Neolithic times. As the early migrations had least effect in Attica, there may be some truth in the classical Athenian claim to be autochthonous. Athens first attained the status of a town in the Middle Helladic period, when the worship of Athena was established on the Acropolis in addition to that of Poseidon Erechtheus; this bears out the traditional date assigned to Kekrops (1581 B.C.), mythical founder of the royal line. The fabled union (synoecism) of several cities into one state under Theseus (1300 B.C.) is doubtful, but an Achaean–Ionian kingdom of Mycenean type does seem to have been based on Athens.

The Dorian invasions are followed by an obscure period, characterized by Geometric pottery, during which the Phoenician alphabet was adopted (? late 9C) to express Greek in writing. Athens begins to emerge for the first time as an artistic centre of Greece; this probably coincides with a historical unification of Attica under Athens (8C B.C.). The 7C is marked by the vigorous 'Protoattic' style of pottery, though sculpture is comparatively little developed. An attempt by Kylon in 632 B.C. to seize power was thwarted; the archon Megakles and the whole Alkmaeonid family in perpetuity were banished for allowing the murder of Kylon while in sanctuary, which led to an unsuccessful war with Megara, his father-in-law's city. At the beginning of the 6C, when the 'Archaic' style of sculpture was already passing from the Cyclades to Athens, Solon reorganized Athenian agriculture and encouraged commerce with more distant parts. He reformed the currency with the state-owned silver mines of Laurion. He inspired the conquest of Salamis from Megara soon after 570 B.C. by Peisistratos, whose triumph enabled him later to seize power. After ten years' exile in Macedonia Peisistratos defeated his opponents at Pallene c. 545. By the acquisition of the Thracian Chersonese and the colonizing of the Hellespont, he and his sons laid the foundations of the Athenian empire. His edition of Homer made Athens the literary centre of Greece, while he instituted the Great Dionysia of the City, the festival from which Attic drama was born. He began the architectural embellishment of the city, and in his reform of the Panathenaic festival (566 B.C.) he gave it a prestige equal to that of the gatherings at Olympia and Delphi. Under Peisistratid autocracy Athenian mature black-figure pottery ousted its Corinthian rival by its masterful technique and art, with an export to Syria and Spain. The reign of Hippias, elder son of Peisistratos, became oppressive after the murder of his brother Hipparchos during the conspiracy of Harmodios and Aristogeiton (514 B.C.). His overthrow was engineered by the Alkmaeonids with the assistance of Kleomenes, king of Sparta. Liberty was thus regained only at the expense of joining the Peloponnesian League, and Hippias retired to plot at the court of Darius, king of Persia. The Athenians aided Plataea against Thebes, and in

506 defeated Chalkis; an expedition against them the same year by Kleomenes failed.

When Aristagoras of Miletus, originator of the Ionian revolt against Darius, appealed for help in 498 B.C. only Athens and Eretria responded. Twenty Athenian ships took part in the burning of Sardis. In revenge Darius despatched a huge army and fleet, accompanied by the aged Hippias, to sack Eretria. Marching on Athens, the Persian army was met at Marathon (Aug or Sept 490) by 9000 Athenians and 1000 Plataeans under Miltiades and decisively defeated. An unsuccessful war against Aegina, at this time supreme at sea, helped to wake Athens to her maritime danger before the Persian storm again broke in 480, when Xerxes came to avenge his father's defeat. The heroism of the Spartans under Leonidas at Thermopylae retarded but did not stop his advance. The Athenians abandoned their city and, guided by Themistocles, trusted themselves to their ships. The Acropolis was sacked, but the power of the Persians was broken in the naval battle of Salamis (20 Sept 480). At Plataea (479) the remnant of the Persian force was defeated on land. With heightened prestige, Athens, led by Kimon and Aristides, assumed the leadership of the naval Confederacy of Delos (478 B.C.) and the Persian danger was finally extinguished at the battle of the Eurymedon in 468. In Aeschylus (fl. 499–458), who fought against the Persians, Greek drama first reaches maturity in Athens.

Members of the Delian League at first contributed ships to a common fleet, an arrangement commuted later to a money tribute to Athens, after which the treasury of the league was moved (454 B.C.) from Delos to the Athenian acropolis. Under Pericles the Athenians put much of the profit towards the aggrandisement of their city, and having defeated Aegina and Corinth, abandoned an unprofitable rivalry on land with Sparta and Thebes for commercial expansion at sea, signing a thirty years' truce in 445. The Periclean vision of a pan-Hellenic congress was nullified by Sparta's refusal to co-operate. The circle of Pericles included some of the greatest names in Athenian arts and letters. Stimulated by Zeno and Anaxagoras, he extended his patronage to the visiting Herodotus; inspired Thucydides; encouraged Attic drama, which attained in his day its completest development in the art of Sophocles (495–406 B.C.); and gave free scope to the genius of Pheidias in the design of the Parthenon. In the foundation of Aegean cleruchies Pericles anticipated the Roman colonial system.

The Peloponnesian War (431–404 B.C.) was the inevitable outcome of rivalry between Sparta and Athens. With the death of Pericles in 429, the now fully-developed democracy lost its only capable leader. The ill-fated Sicilian Expedition (415–414 B.C.), urged on by Alcibiades, was the prelude to the disaster of Aegos-potami in 405. The humiliating conditions of peace forced on Athens in 404 included the destruction of her enceinte. For a brief time even democracy was eclipsed in the *coup d'état* of the Thirty Tyrants, till Thrasyboulos restored the constitution in 403, marring its record by the execution of Socrates (399). The comedies of Aristophanes (fl. 427–387) span these troubled times.

The recovery of Athens was swift. Against Sparta Konon won his great victory at Cnidos in 394 B.C.; and assisted by Thebes Athens re-established her naval hegemony with the Second Maritime League, organized in 378. Art and literature declined but little, and philosophy and oratory reached their apotheosis in the 4C. It was the age of Plato (428–347), Xenophon (c. 430–354), and Isocrates (436–338). A new danger now arose in the person of Philip of Macedon, who conquered Amphipolis in 357, Potidaea in 356, and Methone in 353. Spurred on by the oratory of Demosthenes (383–322), Athens took up the role of champion of Greek liberty, but was finally vanquished at Chaeronea in 338.

The subject city was treated with favour by Alexander the Great, whose Macedonian tutor, Aristotle, taught in the Lyceum. An unsuccessful bid for independence on Alexander's death (323 B.C.) led to the imposition by the usurper Kassander of a collaborating governor, Demetrios of Phaleron (318–307). A brief liberation by Demetrios Poliorketes, claimant to the Macedonian throne, was followed by a period of alternate freedom and subjection to Macedonia; after a defeat by Antigonus Gonatas in the Chremonidean War (266–263), Athens suffered a garrison until 229, although her democratic institutions were respected. Supremacy in science had now passed to Alexandria, but Athens still led in philosophy; in Menander (342–291) comedy reached a new peak. The fall of Perseus in 168 B.C. substituted the Roman for the Macedonian rule, but the city of Athens continued to flourish, retaining many privileges when the province of Achaia was formed out of S. Greece after 146. Having espoused the cause of Mithridates in 86 B.C., it was captured by Sulla, when its fortifications were razed, its treasures looted, and its privileges curtailed. It nevertheless received a free pardon from Julius Caesar for siding with Pompey and from Antony and Augustus after supporting Brutus, who removed here after the Ides of March. Athens continued to be the fashionable seat of learning in the ancient world, attracting the sons of rich Romans, including Cicero and Horace.

St Paul preached 'in the midst of Mars' hill' (Acts, xvii, 22) in A.D. 54. Hadrian (120–128), under whom Plutarch was procurator of Achaia, frequently lived in the city and adorned it with imperial buildings. His example was followed by Herodes Atticus in the time of the Antonines, when the city was visited by Pausanias; and Athens remained the centre of Greek education until the Edict of Justinian in A.D. 529 closed the schools of philosophy.

Later History. The agora suffered in the first Gothic (Herulian) raid of 267, but Alaric's capture of the city in 396 seems to have caused little damage to its monuments. In the reign of Justinian, or earlier, many temples were consecrated to Christian use and modified. Under Byzantine rule Athens dwindled to an unimportant small town. It was sacked c. 580 by the Slavs. Constans II wintered in the city in 662 on his way to Sicily, and Theodore of Tarsus studied here before becoming Abp. of Canterbury (669–690). Basil II, the Bulgar-slayer, celebrated his victories of 1018 in the Parthenon.

After the fall of Constantinople in 1204, the Greek provinces N. of the Isthmus of Corinth fell to the share of Boniface III, Marquis of Montferrat, with the title of King of Thessalonica. Boniface granted Attica and Boeotia to Otho de la Roche, a Burgundian knight, with the title of Grand Seigneur (Megas Kyr; i.e. Μέγας Κύριος) of Athens and Thebes. A century of pacific and prosperous 'Frankish' rule brought some amelioration to the condition of the Athenians but no part in affairs; trading privileges were granted to Genoese and Venetian merchants. Matthew Paris records a visit as a student by Master John of Basingstoke (d. 1252). In 1258 Guy I accepted the title of duke from St Louis of France; the magnificence of the Athenian court of this period is noted by the Catalan chronicler Ramon Muntaner. On the death of Guy II in 1308, the duchy passed to his cousin Walter de Brienne. Walter's designs on Byzantine territories leagued the rulers of Constantinople, Neopatras, and Epirus against him, and he called to his aid the Catalan Company. Being unable later to rid himself of them, he precipitated the disastrous battle of Kopais, where in 1311 the Catalans totally destroyed the power and nobility of Frankish Greece.

The Grand Company now assumed sovereignty of Athens and Thebes, but placed Roger Deslau, one of the two noble survivors of Duke Walter's army, at their head. After pursuing a career of conquest in N. Greece, they approached Frederick of Aragon, king of Sicily in 1326, with the result that his second son Manfred became duke and for sixty years the Duchy of Athens and Neopatras (as it was now styled) was misgoverned from Sicily by avaricious General Commissioners. In 1386 the Siculo-Catalans fell foul of Nerio Acciaioli, governor of Corinth, a member of that family which was "plebian in Florence, potent in Naples, and sovereign in Greece" (Gibbon). Nerio seized Athens, Thebes and Levadia, and in 1394 received the title of duke from Ladislas, king of Naples. Captured by a band of Navarrese troops, he bought his ransom by rifling all the churches in his dominions.

Under his son Antony, Athens, protected by Venice, enjoyed forty years' peace, but Antony's weak cousin and successor, Nerio II (1435–53) held his duchy as a vassal of the Sultan. During his reign Athens was twice visited by Ciriaco de' Pizzicoli (better known as Cyriacus of Ancona), the antiquary. Demetrius Chalcondyles (1424–1511), the Renaissance scholar who published the editio princeps of Homer, was an Athenian. When Nerio's widow and Pietro Almerio, the Venetian governor of Nauplia and her new husband, seized the dukedom, the Athenians complained to the Sultan, who replaced Almerio by Franco Acciaioli, a nephew of Nerio. Franco banished his aunt, the ex-duchess, to Megara and had her murdered there, whereupon Pietro complained to the Porte. Mehmed II ordered Omar, son of Turahan, to seize the Acropolis, and annexed Attica to the Ottoman Empire in 1456. A guide book written by the so-called Vienna Anonymous, describes Athens in 1456–60. A Venetian raid in 1464 achieved nothing but the plunder of the city.

Nearly four hundred years of Turkish rule followed, a peculiar result of which was the rehabilitation of the Orthodox Church, so long dispossessed by Rome. Athens was visited in 1672 by Père Babin, a French Capuchin, who drew the earliest extant plan, and in 1675 by Francis Vernon, who sent back to the Royal Society the first English account of the city. The same year Lord Winchilsea, then ambassador to the Porte, secured some architectural fragments. In 1676 came Spon and Wheler. In 1687 occurred the siege by Francesco Morosini, during which the Parthenon was shattered. Thenceforward until 1821, the condition of Athens under the Turks is picturesquely described by Gibbon, who accuses the Athenians of his day of "walking with supine indifference among the glorious ruins of antiquity". The worst period of tyranny was experienced under Hadji Ali Haseki in 1775–95. After the appearance of Stuart and Revett's 'Antiquities of Athens' (1762), based on a visit of 1750, travellers to Athens became more numerous.

In 1821, soon after the outbreak in Patras of the War of Independence, the Greek general Odysseus seized Athens and the Acropolis. In 1826–27 the Acropolis, besieged by Reshid Pasha, was bravely defended by the klepht Gouras and after his death by the French general Fabvier. Vain attempts to raise the siege were made by Karaïskakis and after his death in 1827 by Adm. Cochrane and Gen. Church. On 27 May 1827, the Acropolis was taken by the Turks and held until 12 April 1833. In 1834 Athens became the capital of liberated Greece.

During the First World War the city was occupied by British and French troops after some opposition by Royalist troops of the pro-German government. The population was greatly increased by the exchange of Greek and Turkish nationals in 1923. On 27 April 1941, German forces entered the capital unopposed after a campaign lasting three weeks, and Athens remained in their hands until Oct 1944. In Dec 1944 open Communist revolution broke out in the Theseion area after a demonstration had been fired on by police earlier the same morning in Sindagma Sq. After bitter street fighting British troops, with reinforcements, landed at Phaleron, eventually restored order and at a conference called by Churchill on Christmas Day an armistice was arranged whereby Abp. Dhamaskinos became regent.

Topography. PREHISTORIC ATHENS. In Early Helladic times groups of settlers had lived within reach of the fortress, and Late Helladic chamber tombs have been found in the N. and W. slopes of the Areopagus hill and in the area which later became the agora. The Mycenean royal city centred on the fortress of the Acropolis, where a 'Cyclopean' wall enclosed the palace complex, Homer's "strong house of Erechtheus", but settlements and shrines extended S. to the Ilissos. At an early date part of the S. and W. slopes of the Acropolis were enclosed by the Pelasgikon wall, but evidence of Sub-Mycenean and Protogeometric graves shows a gradual spread of occupation towards the N.W., where the Kerameikos became the chief necropolis.

THE ARCHAIC CITY. Peisistratid palatial occupation and the siting of a new temple perhaps in 566 B.C. for the Panathenaic festival must have lessened the living space on the Acropolis. The Pnyx and Mouseion hills were already occupied by houses in the 6C, and even before the Peisistratids the popular Kerameikos quarter was becoming the centre of Athenian life. It was the meeting-place of the assembly, the altar of the Twelve Gods was set up there, and the archons had their offices in the vicinity. By the end of the 6C the population seems to have resided wholly in the lower town. No archæological evidence has been found to suggest that any wall was built to replace the Pelasgikon which was slighted under or after the Peisistratids. Since the water supply was now brought by aqueduct and a group of temples existed near the Kallirrhoë spring and the Ilissos, a 7–6C wall now seems unlikely.

CLASSICAL ATHENS. The Acropolis and much of the town outside was laid waste by the Persians in 480. After the battle of Platæa, Themistocles, who had begun to fortify Piraeus as early as 493, began a city wall on a course which endured till the time of Hadrian. Thucydides (I, 93) records its hasty erection with whatever material was at hand. No general plan of the sort adopted in Piraeus was ever made for Athens, and the narrow crooked streets remained. Kimon finished the circuit; and the two Long Walls, connecting Athens with Piraeus, were completed under Pericles. Of the fifteen city gates located, the names of ten are known but not certainly identified. In 450 Kallikrates completed the Phaleric Wall. Much of the monumental greatness of Athens dates from the third quarter of the 5C. The Academy, embellished by Kimon, became a favourite Athenian promenade. In 404 the walls were demolished at the Spartan command, and the Long Walls never rose again. Konon rebuilt the enceinte in 393, and Lycurgus (338–326) completed, rebuilt or embellished much of the city, modifying the Pnyx for the Assembly's use. The walls were shortened about this time by the erection of the Diateichisma, and the city flourished with gradual modifications until the Roman sack of 86 B.C.

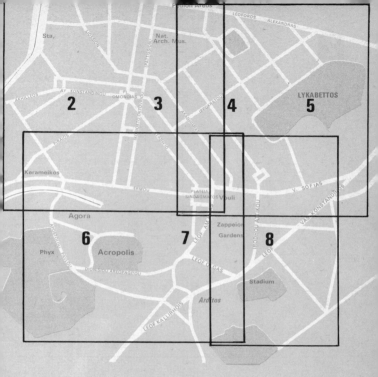

key page
to
Map numbers

0	100	200	300	400 yards
0	100	200	300	400 metres

Pedion Areos

3

IOULIANOU ENIANOS PLAT. AIYIPTOU LEOFOROS THERIANOU

IPIROU IOULIANOU MAVROMMATEON RETHIMNOU METSOVOU BOUBOULINAS ZAIMI NOTARA SPIR. TRIKOUPI KOUNDOURIOTOU SKULITSI FOTILA PLAPOUTA PSELLOU IOUSTINIANOU

MAKEDONIAS Nat. Archeological Mus. *ad* POULKHERIAS

AVEROF *e* TOSITSA LOFOS S

MARNIS POLITEHNIOU Sch. of Fine Arts TSAMADOU KODRINGTONOU ZOSSIMADON KALLIDROMIOU

PATISSION Polytekhnion STOURNARA MELISSINOU

SEPTEMVRIOU SOLOMOU KORASSI SOULTANI THEMISTOKLEOUS BENAKI ARAKHTHOUS DERVENION ERESSOU

KAPODHISTRIOU KANINGOS TZORTZ PL. KANINGOS EM. TZAVELLA METAXA PIRIS MAVROMIKHALI IPPOKRATOUS

HALKOKONDILI *3* *mm* *r* *ab* KOLETI MESSOLOGGIOU TRIKOUPI

TRITIS PATISSION GAMVETA ZALONGGOU ZOODOKHOU KHARILAOU NAVARINOU DHIDHOTOU

ss FIDIOU SOLONOS

PLAT. OMONOIAS French Sch.

hh OTE PO *n* German Sch. *ll* AKADHIMIAS MASSALIAS

LIKOURGOU *z* *vv* LEOFOROS VENIZELOU (PANEPISTIMIOU) SANTAROZA

EFPOLIDOS PLAT. KOTZIA *qq* P. STAVROU Nat. Library SINA

Town Hall ATHINAS KRATINOU Nat. Bank of Greece University OMIROU

ARMODIOU PESMAZOGLOU Hellenic Academy AMERIS

ARISTOGEITONOS Underground Car Park STADHIOU KORAI

POLYTEHNIOU Ay. Theodori ARISTIDOU DRAGATSANIOU PL. KLAFTHMONOS PAPARIGOPOULOU *m* St Denis *oo* VOUKOURESTI

VISSIS KAIRI MILTIADOU PRAMELLOUS American Express LEOFOROS VENIZELOU ELPA *cc* AKADHIMIAS

VDREOU AIOLOU NIKOU LEOKHAROUS Ay. Yeoryios PLAT. KOLOKOTRONI ZALOKOSTA

AG. IRINIS Ay. Irini ATHIN. AIDOS SKOUZE KOLOKOTRONI Pal. Vouli (Nat. Hist. Mus.) *d* *c*

PLOUTONOS Kap. PERIKLEOUS Information Bureau *h* *v* *b* *a*

PANDROSSOU EVANGELISTRIAS *ee* *i* PLATEIA Vouli (Parliament)

Library of Hadrian *w* DEKA ERMOU **7** NIKIS American Express SINDAGMATOS Mem. OTHONOS AMALIAS

q PETRAKI *ff* PO

Cathedral MITROPOLEOS *p*

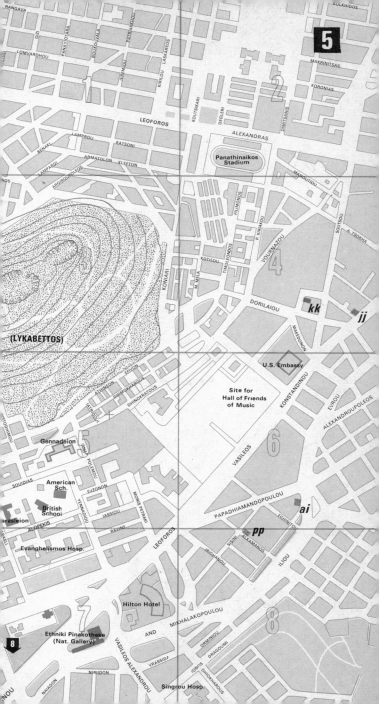

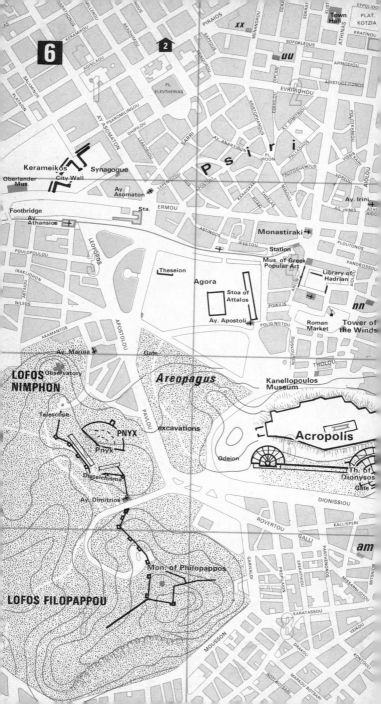

IMPERIAL ATHENS. Archæologists have disagreed whether Hadrian extended the enceinte, but the discovery in 1959 near the Olympieion of a gate which confirms the E. course of the Themistoclean wall suggests that Hadrianopolis was indeed an extension to the E. and not merely the aggrandisement of an older quarter. Here were gymnasia, thermæ, and the usual manifestations of Roman rule. Under Augustus a new market had been built E. of the Agora; Hadrian added a huge library in the same area. He also built a new reservoir on Lykabettos. A generation or so later Herodes Atticus founded his Odeion and reseated the decaying Stadium in marble. After the Herulians had destroyed most of Athens in 267, the Athenians lost confidence in the Roman army and withdrew behind the post-Herulian ('Valerian') wall enclosing the N. slope of the Acropolis.

LATER TOPOGRAPHY. Christian Athens remained round the Acropolis where the Frankish dukes had their palace in the Propylaia. The Turks fortified the S. slope of the Acropolis, Serpentzes turning the Odeion of Herodes Atticus into a redoubt. The later Turkish town was lightly walled by Haseki in 1778–80, using in the N. the ruins of the ancient circuit. The modern city owes its basic inner plan to the Bavarian architects of King Otho and its unplanned suburban development to its rapid growth in 1923.

1   FROM SINDAGMA SQUARE TO THE ACROPOLIS AND THE AGORA

BUS 16/176; by this route the hurried tourist may quickly reach the Acropolis by road while seeing some of the more obvious sights of Athens on the way. For the traveller on foot whose immediate objective is the Acropolis it is more rewarding to approach it from the N. side by plunging directly into the narrow streets of Plaka (Rte 6); the shortest way is by Odhos Apollonos and Odhos Adrianou, whence Odhos Mnesikleous leads to the path under the awe-inspiring cliff crowned by the Erechtheion.

Those on foot who wish to combine the S. slope with the Acropolis itself may avoid the noisiest streets by taking Odhos Nikis and Odhos Kidathenaion to the Monument of Lysikrates. The buildings on the S. slope will, however, be better appreciated after being seen from the Acropolis wall whence their plan is more clearly apparent. This may prove sufficient for the casual visitor while it will stimulate the interest of the antiquary.—For the direct approach to the Agora, see Rte 4.

The centre of the visitors' quarter is **Sindagma Square** (*3, 8*; Πλατεῖα τοῦ Συντάγματος, or *Constitution Sq.*), a busy open space closed on the E. by the palace from whose balcony in 1843 the constitution was proclaimed. The square itself, to the w. and below the level of Amalia Avenue, bustles with the life of its hotels, cafés, and air terminals. The gardens are planted with orange trees, oleanders, and cypresses. The figures in bronze beside its walks are copies, presented by Lord Bute, of antique originals in the museum at Naples. The antique *Stele* in the N.W. corner marked a boundary of the Garden of the Muses (see below). The *Hôtel Grande Bretagne*, enlarged (1958) and refaced in marble, began in 1842–43 as a private house built by Theophilus von Hansen. It was the headquarters of the French School in 1856–74, and of the Greek, German, and British forces in turn during the Second World War. During Christmas eve, 1944, while Churchill was visiting strife-torn Athens, an attempt to blow up the hotel from the sewers was just foiled. Above Amalia Avenue, a paved hollow square, framed by trees, fronts the palace, in the retaining wall of which is placed a *Memorial to the Unknown Soldier* (its removal elsewhere is mooted at intervals).

The bas-relief, depicting a dying Greek, was modelled on a figure from the Temple of Aphaia at Aegina now in the Munich collection; the adjacent texts are from Pericles' funeral oration. On the walls bronze shields celebrate Greek victories since 1821. The guard, drawn in turn from the armed services, is changed on Sun mornings (11.15), and the square is used as a saluting base for national processions. From it a ceremonial marble staircase (1928) leads up to the ex-Royal palace (visitors ascend by the side roads).

Excavations during rebuilding round the square in 1957–61 brought to light 119 graves dating from Classical times when the area, which lay along the Themistoclean wall between the Acharnai and Diocharous gates, was a necropolis.

The *Lykeion*, or Lyceum, dedicated to Apollo, lay beyond the Diocharous gate at the foot of Lykabettos. Its grounds served as a parade-ground for the ephebes; before the time of Solon, the Polemarch had his offices here. Later Aristotle expounded his philosophy here; his disciples were dubbed 'Peripatetics' from their habit of walking as they discoursed. The trees of the Lyceum were cut down by Sulla to make siege-engines. The *Garden of the Muses*, or Mouseion, was given c. 320 B.C. by Demetrios of Phaleron to Theophrastos, Aristotle's heir and successor at the Lyceum, who left it to the school.

The old **Royal Palace** (3, 8; *Pálaion Anáktoron*), since 1935 the seat of the GREEK PARLIAMENT (Βουλή; *Vouli*), is well situated on rising ground E. of the square. Designed by Bavarian court architects, it was built in 1836–42, King Ludwig of Bavaria laying the first stone. It is in the early plain classicizing style and the original interior decoration was in the Pompeian manner. The w. front has a Doric portico of Pentelic marble. The interior was damaged by fire in 1910 and transformed in 1935.

After the senate was abolished in 1862, apart from an unsuccessful attempt in 1927–35 to revive the Upper House, Parliament consisted of one House only. During the military dictatorship of 1967–74 its functions were in abeyance.

LEOFÓROS VASILÍSSIS AMALÍAS (Queen Amalia Av.), a handsome boulevard where many suburban buses terminate, leads s. alongside the ***National Garden*** (*Ethnikós Kípos*; open daily to sunset). Designed by Queen Amalia for the palace and still referred to as the *Royal Gardens*, this is a favourite Athenian retreat from the summer sun. Its sub-tropical trees are irrigated by a channel that succeeds the aqueduct of Peisistratos; peacocks and waterfowl frequent its serpentine walks and ornamental ponds; and nightingales sing here in the spring.

In the garden are busts of the poets Solomos and Valaorites, of Count John Capodistrias, and of Eynard, the Swiss philhellene. Farther N., behind the palace, are some remains of *Roman Baths* with large geometric mosaics, and traces survive of Hadrian's city wall.

Farther along (r.), the **Russian Church** (*St Nicodemus*, properly *Sotíra Likodímou*; 7, 4) overlooks a small square. The church, the largest remaining medieval building in Athens, was founded shortly before 1031 by Stefan Likodemou (d. 1045). Its monastic buildings, ruined by earthquake in 1701, were pulled down in 1780 to provide material for Hadji Ali Haseki's wall. Damaged by shell-fire in 1827, the church remained derelict until restored by the Russian government in 1852–56. The external walls have a terracotta frieze, and the wide dome rests on squinches. The detached belfry is a 19C addition; the great bell was a gift of Tsar Alexander II.

Under the church and square are remains of a Roman bath (2C A.D.); excavations in 1961 suggested its early adaptation as a place of Christian worship. An inscription of the 1C B.C., still near the church where it was found, comes from the Gymnasium of the Lyceum (comp. above), with which this bath is probably to be associated.

Just beyond is the **English Church** (*St Paul's*; 7, 5), designed by C. R. Cockerell in an undistinguished Gothic style in 1840–43. Within on the N. side are a British funerary memorial of 1685, removed here from the Theseion, and a painted window to Sir Richard Church with an inscription by Gladstone. The E. window commemorates the victims of the 'Dilessi murders' (1870). On the opposite side of the avenue open the *Zappeion Gardens*, the s. continuation of the National Garden. To the left of the entrance is a charming marble Pan by Yeoryios Demetriades and in the central avenue a figure of Varvakis, founder of the high school. The **Záppeion** (7, 6), founded by the cousins Zappas as a national exhibition hall, was built by Theophilus von Hansen in 1874–88 and renovated in 1959–60. The semicircular exterior has a handsome porticoed façade and encloses a circular colonnade surrounding an open court. In front are statues of the founders; beyond is a frequented café with an open-air stage (evening cabaret).

The s. side of the Zappeion Gardens is bounded by Leofóros Olgas (see Rte 7) which meets Amalia Avenue in a large open triangle, one of the busiest traffic centres in Athens. On the corner (l.) stands a sentimental 19C group of Byron and Hellas, by Chapu and Falguière. On the far side the **Arch of Hadrian** (7, 5), an isolated gateway in Pentelic marble erected by Hadrian c. A.D. 132 to mark the limit of the ancient city and the beginning of Novæ Athenæ or Hadrianopolis (Rte 7). The façades, otherwise identical, bear differing inscriptions on the frieze: that on the N.W. side towards the Acropolis reads 'This is Athens, the ancient city of Theseus'; that on the s.E. side towards the Olympieion records 'This is the city of Hadrian and not of Theseus'. The gate is some way w. of the line of the Themistoclean Wall; it was incorporated in the 18C Turkish enceinte.

The gate is 59 ft high, 41 ft wide, and 7½ ft thick, with an archway 20 ft across. The piers of the arch were adorned with Corinthian columns, the bases and consoles of which can be traced. Above the archway is an attic consisting of a portico of four Corinthian columns with three bays, the middle one having a pediment.—Behind is the *Olympieion* (Rte 7).

Odhos Lissikrátous leads w. into Plaka (see Rte. 6), passing the church of *Ayia Aikaterini*. The ancient columns that front the palm-shaded garden were probably reused as an earlier church façade in the 6C. At the end of this street ran the STREET OF THE TRIPODS.

It was the custom of the victorious choregi to dedicate to Dionysos the tripods which they had gained in dramatic contests. These tripods were erected either in the precincts of the Theatre or on shrines or columns in a street specially appropriated to them, which led in a semicircle round the E. of the hill from the Prytaneion to the Theatre. The tripods were placed over the works of art, the kettle or cauldron forming a sort of roof. Pausanias singles out for mention the Satyr of Praxiteles, no longer extant (torso of a copy in the Louvre), but ignores the monument of Lysikrates. Such other foundations as were located in 1921 and 1955 (to the number of seven) have been left *in situ* and covered again.

The well-preserved ***Choregic Monument of Lysikrates** is renowned not only for its graceful detail, but as being the earliest building known in which the Corinthian capital is used externally. A square base of Piraeus stone 13 ft high, with a cornice of Eleusinian marble, bears three circular steps of Hymettos marble. On this base six monolithic Corinthian columns are arranged in a circle to support an entablature crowned by a marble dome, wrought with great delicacy from a single block; from the centre of the roof rises an elaborate finial of acanthus-leaf carving, the support for the tripod itself. An inscription on the architrave informs us that "Lysikrates of Kikyna, son of Lysitheides, was choregos; the tribe of Akamantis won the victory with a chorus of boys; Theon played the flute; Lysiades of Athens trained the chorus; Evainetos was archon" (334 B.C.). Round the frieze is represented the story of Dionysos and the Tyrrhenian pirates, whom he turned into dolphins. The whole of the superstructure is in Pentelic marble, except the curved panels (of Hymettian marble), engaged between the columns, that form the central drum. Of these only the three showing a frieze of tripods are original.

The inside of the drum was never intended to be seen for the capitals are un-finished within and there is no provision for light. However, the missing panels were removed during the period (1669–1821) when the monument was incor-porated in the library of a French Capuchin convent. It was then known as the 'Lantern of Demosthenes' from a belief that the orator prepared his speeches in it. Byron, one of many English guests at the convent, is said to have used it as a study; he wrote part of 'Childe Harold' here in 1810–11. On the occupation of Athens by Omer Vrioni the convent was accidentally burned down; the monu-ment was freed and later properly restored in 1892 with French funds. To Monasti-raki and the N. side of the Acropolis, see Rte 6.

The Street of the Tripods curved down to the main Propylaia of the Sanctuary of Dionysos (see below). Inside the curve, just E. of the theatre, stood the **Odeion of Pericles**, built originally before 446 B.C., burnt during the sack of Athens in 86 B.C. by Aristion, a general of Mithridates, who feared that Sulla might use the timbers of the roof for siege engines, and rebuilt in marble on the former plan by Ariobarzanes II, king of Cappadocia (65–52 B.C.). Its site has only recently been expropriated from beneath a jumble of poor houses, but investigations by the Greek Archæological Society in 1914–31 proved it to be rectangular in plan, not circular as had been assumed from classical references to its being modelled on the tent of Xerxes. It was a large hall with interior columns arranged in 9 rows of 10, somewhat similar in plan to the Telesterion at Eleusis, and had a pyramidal roof with a lantern. The scene of the musical contests of the Pan-athenaic Festival, it had the reputation of being the best concert-hall in the Greek world; and rehearsals of the tragedies presented in the Theatre of Dionysos at the Great Dionysiac Festival were held in it.

We continue by the broad Odhos Dionissiou Areopayitou (named after St Paul's convert, Dionysius the Areopagite) to the gate of the **Excavations on the S. slope of the Acropolis** (6, *6*; weekdays 9–1, 3.30–5.30, 25 dr.; Sun & hol., 10–4; Sun free when other entrances are open above and below Theatre of Herodes Atticus). Immediately within the gate we cross the line of the wall that once bounded the TEMENOS OF DIONYSOS ELEUTHERIOS. Traces of the wall survive to the E., but the main entrance to the precinct from the Street of the Tripods (see above) has not been excavated.

The worship of Dionysos Eleutherios was introduced into Athens in the 6C B.C. from the then Boeotian city of Eleutherai. The festival of the Great Dionysia of the City, instituted by Peisistratos, which eclipsed the old festival of the Wine-press (Lenaia) held in the marshes, was characterized by the competing choruses of satyrs, clad in goatskins, who danced round the altar of the god and sang their 'goat songs'. These dithyrambic contests were the forerunners of Attic tragedy.

We pass the breccia foundations of a small 4C *Temple* consisting of pronaos and cella, built to re-house the chryselephantine statue of Dionysos by Alkamenes, seen by Pausanias; the great base on which it was placed remains. Nearer the theatre are scantier remnants of an *Older Temple* dating from the 6C. To the S.E. are foundations repre-senting either the great altar or the base of a large votive dedication.

The **Theatre of Dionysos** was rebuilt in stone by Lycurgus in 342–

326 B.C. to replace an earlier structure in which the masterpieces of Æschylus, Sophocles, Euripides, and Aristophanes were first performed. Extensive modifications in Hellenistic and Roman times involved the re-use of old material so that the existing remains present a puzzling conglomeration of the work of 750 years.

History. Archæologists differ about the dating of much of the structure and historians of the Greek drama have reached no certain conclusions about the superstructure or internal layout of the skene before Roman times. The clearest exposition of the many problems can be found in *A. W. Pickard-Cambridge*: The Theatre of Dionysos in Athens (O.U.P., 1946) and may be supplemented by the reports of further investigations in 1951 and 1963. A meticulous survey was started in 1979. The results, which may modify presently held theories, are intended as a preliminary to restorations.

It is probable that a circular *Orchestra*, or dancing ground, with a central altar, existed here in the 6C B.C. (though traces of a terrace-wall are all that survive from this period) and that by the beginning of the 5C spectators occupied wooden stands. Following an accident (c. 500–470 B.C.) to a stand either here or in the agora, an earthen auditorium (*theatron*) was constructed. Here, against a background of wood and canvas, the great dramas of the Golden Age were performed. About the time of Pericles the auditorium assumed nearly its present shape, when supporting walls were built to the E. and W.; the seats were still probably of wood. The orchestra was moved a little to the N. but remained circular, and a long foundation wall served both to retain the extended terrace and to support a wooden stage set. Immediately behind and slightly below this was built a stoa, connected to the orchestral area by a flight of steps and having an open colonnade on its S. side.

A reconstruction in the 4C was probably finished c. 330 B.C. by Lycurgus, when the theatron was rebuilt in stone in much the form it has today, and a permanent skene in stone, flanked by columned paraskenia, replaced the movable wooden sets. Plays continued to be acted at orchestral level but in Hellenistic times, when attention had passed irrevocably from ritual dancing to dramatic acting, a raised stage was added, supported by a stone proskenion. At the same time the paraskenia were taken back and the parodoi (side entrances) widened to give easier access to the auditorium.

The skene and stage were again rebuilt, possibly by T. Claudius Novius c. A.D. 61. At some time the Roman stage was further extended over the parodoi to meet the auditorium, and a marble barrier erected round the orchestra to protect the audience from gladiatorial exhibitions. At a later period (? A.D. 3C) the Bema of Phædrus was added in front of the Roman proskenion. Still later the reliefs on the bema were truncated and cemented over when the orchestra was turned into a watertight basin for the performance of naumachiæ.

Even in classical times the theatre was used for other purposes than drama. The presentation of crowns to distinguished citizens, the release of orphans from state control on their reaching man's estate, and other ceremonies served as curtain-raisers to the play. The golden crowns presented by independent foreign states and the tribute of subject states were displayed in the theatre. Annual cock-fights, instituted after the Persian wars, took place here. The Assembly, occasionally in the 4C (Thuc. VIII, 93) and regularly after the 3C, met here instead of in the Pnyx. Demetrios Poliorketes after making himself master of Athens (292 B.C.) here overawed the Assembly with a military display.

The AUDITORIUM retains roughly the form it assumed under Lycurgus when, on the W. side, the outer wall of poros was added to the earlier buttressed wall of breccia. At the same time the supporting wall on the E., irregular in contour due to the proximity of the Odeion (see above), was extended to the rock above. Concentric tiers of seats, radiating fanwise from the orchestra, are separated into 13 wedges (kerkides; *Lat.* cunei) by narrow stairways. Some 25 tiers survive in part.

It is generally assumed that there were 64 tiers of stone seats divided by a postulated gangway (*diazoma*) into two sections of 32 rows each. Above this the *Peripatos* (comp. below) formed a second diazoma. An upper section of 14 more rows of seats, hewn from the rock, may have been a later addition; the higher remains are fragmentary. The seating capacity can hardly have exceeded 17,000, far short of Plato's estimate of 30,000 (Symposium).

The seats, made (except for the front row) of Piraeus limestone, are shaped so that one row of spectators did not incommode the next row: each person sat on the flat section in front (probably on a cushion), placing his feet in the trough hollowed behind the seat below. The front row consisted of 67 *Thrones* in Pentelic marble. Sixty remain in the theatre, of which 14 were found in place; the remainder have been restored with some certainty to their original positions. Each bears the name of the priest or dignitary for whom it was reserved; since some of the original inscriptions were replaced with later inscriptions, the thrones have been called replicas of the 1C B.C. However, the style of the relief sculpture and both the design and workmanship of the thrones indicate that the entire front row dates from the time of Lykurgos. Distinguished by its more elaborate shape and fine sculpture is the *Throne of the Priest of Dionysos Eleutherios*, placed in the centre, exactly opposite the thymele, or altar of the god, which stood in the middle of the orchestra.

The throne is a beautifully carved armchair with lion's-claw feet. On the back is delicately carved, in low relief, a representation of two satyrs, supporting on their shoulders a yoke whence hangs a branch of grapes. In front is inscribed the name of the owner; above the inscription is a remarkable relief of two kneeling male figures in Persian costume, each of whom grasps a gryphon by the throat with one hand, lifting with the other a scimitar. On each arm is a beautiful figure in low relief of a winged boy conducting a cock-fight. The Throne of Hadrian occupied the large plinth just behind. The area in front of the seats drains into a channel surrounding the orchestra.—Statues of Roman emperors, tragic and comic poets, orators, statesmen, and philanthropists were numerous; the base of one of Menander, by Kephisodotos and Timarchos (sons of Praxiteles), stands at the N.W. corner of the skene.

The ORCHESTRA preserves today none of its classical appearance. The existing area, in the form of a slightly extended semicircle, represents the orchestra of the Roman rebuilding under Nero. The surface was then paved in marble slabs with a central rhombus made of smaller coloured pieces. Slabs also cover the Lycurgan drainage channel. Both these and the marble barrier protecting the auditorium are pierced with drainage holes, which were later stopped up (and the water channel blocked) when the theatre was used for mock sea-fights.

The so-called *Bema of Phædrus* stands in a mutilated condition for about half its length. This presumably represents the final front of the Roman stage. It takes its name from the dedicatory inscription on the slab that surmounts the uppermost of the four stone steps in the centre. The date of the inscription is doubtful; Phædrus is otherwise unknown; and the stone is not in its original place. The reliefs have been dated to the 2C A.D., and almost certainly came from somewhere near by. They portray scenes in the life of Dionysos, the last (westernmost) relief showing the God installed in his theatre on a gorgeous throne with the Acropolis and Parthenon in the background. The well-preserved crouching sileni were forced into place afterwards. When found in 1862 the figures were still plastered with cement from the waterproofing (see above).

Behind lie the foundations of earlier stage buildings. We may trace the Hellenistic proskenion, flanked by paraskenia, some truncated columns of which survive, and, farther back, the outline of the long stoa of Periclean date; but the remains between are too confused by late masonry, designed merely as support for the Roman skene, to aid any imaginative reconstruction in the mind of a layman, and admit of widely diverging interpretation by experts.

Above the theatre opens the **Panayia Chrysospiliotissa**, or *Chapel of Our Lady of the Cavern*. On the walls are faded Byzantine paintings. Within, every evening, a solitary lamp is lit. Round the mouth of the cave the rock face is cut vertically to form a scarp known as the *Katatomé*. The entrance was masked, until Turkish gunfire destroyed it in 1827, by the *Choregic Monument of Thrasyllos*, erected in 320 B.C. by Thrasyllos, who dedicated the cavern to Dionysos. The monument took the form of a Doric portico raised on two steps. Three marble pilasters supported an architrave bearing the dedication, above which was a frieze adorned with eleven wreaths carved in relief; the tripod stood above the cornice. Fifty years later, when president of the Games (agonothetes), Thrasykles, son of Thrasyllos, added two further dedications commemorating similar victories of his own in choregic contests. The inscriptions may still be seen. A seated figure of Dionysos found above the monument, and now in the British Museum, was a Roman addition.—The two Corinthian *Columns* above the cavern also supported votive tripods; the cuttings for their feet in the triangular capitals may be seen from the top of the wall of Kimon. To the right is a *Sundial* in Pentelic marble, noted in the 15C Vienna Anonymous.

To the w. of the theatre the ancient remains extend along the slope in two terraces. The upper terrace is supported by a massive retaining wall buttressed by a continuous row of arches (some 40 of which now provide from the road the most conspicuous feature of the area), over which ran the PERIPATOS, the main highway, nearly 16 ft wide, round the Acropolis. Steps descend to it from the upper part of the theatre. If we ascend from the orchestra, we see (l.) the rectangular foundations of the *Choregic Monument of Nikias*, erected in 319 B.C. in the form of a prostyle hexastyle and demolished soon after A.D. 267 to provide material for fortifications. The stones were used in the Beulé Gate, where part of the inscription from the architrave may still be seen (comp. Rte 2); the full text read: "Nikias, son of Nikodemos of Xypete, dedicated this monument after a victory as choregos with boys of the tribe of Kekropis; Pantaleon of Sikyon played the flute; the '*Elpenor*' of Timotheos was the song; Neaichmos was archon."

Above the peripatos and to the w. of the theatre extends the **Asklepieion**, or *Sanctuary of Asklepios in the City*, dedicated in 418 B.C. by Telemachos of Acharnai on a site already sacred to a water-god. The 5C sanctuary occupied the w. portion of the terrace; in the 4C a new precinct was built to the E., extending to the theatre wall. Each contained a sacred spring, a temple and an altar, and an abaton or stoa. The most conspicuous remains within the temenos are, however, the walls of a large Byzantine *Church* of the 5C or 6C, where, probably under the patronage of SS Cosmas and Damian, the cure continued under the Christian ægis.

The worship of Asklepios, which spread from Epidauros, was introduced into Athens on the occasion of the plague of 429 B.C. The 'cure' followed a ritual, during which patients washed in the sacred spring, offered sacrifices at an altar, and then retired to the stoa where the mysterious process of incubation (ἐγκοίμησις) was assisted by incense from the altars. This and religious excitement produced dreams, through the medium of which Asklepios was supposed to effect his cure. Many ex-voto tablets to Asklepios and Hygieia have been found showing the portion of the anatomy treated. These were affixed to a wall or inlaid in the columns; larger votive stelai were fixed to the stoa steps (examples in the National Museum).

To the E., somewhat obscured by the Byzantine walls, can be traced the foundations of the later *Abaton*, consisting of a colonnade with 17 Doric columns and two interior galleries separated by another colonnade. The long plinth of Hymettian marble, the back wall to the E. and the intermediate row of bases are all that remain *in situ*, but the stoa probably had two floors, the upper one being the *Enkoimeterion*, or dormitory of the sick. A narrow passage leads from the N. gallery into a circular spring house hewn in the rock. The wonder-working nature of the sacred spring continues, and the ancient spring house is now a chapel which is kept locked.

At the W. end of the stoa, probably under a baldachin roof, was the so-called *Bothros*, perhaps a sacrificial pit where blood was poured to chthonic divinities, but more likely the dwelling of the sacred snakes. In front of the stoa are the foundations of a small *Temple* in antis. In the W. part of the temenos, which is bounded by the Pelasgikon wall, are the foundations of the smaller 5C *Stoa*. The *Old Spring* was contained in a fine 5C rectangular cistern of polygonal masonry, transformed by the Turks. Just to the S. is another huge *Cistern*, probably of Byzantine date.

To the W. of the Asklepieion the sanctuaries enumerated by Pausanias have disappeared beneath the Turkish fortifications. A path follows the general direction of the peripatos through confused remains round the top of the Odeion (see below) to the entrance of the Acropolis.

The arches of the peripatos road were formerly concealed by the so-called **Stoa of Eumenes,** which began c. 30 ft from the Theatre of Dionysos and extended for 535 ft. At its W. end it communicated with the Odeion by two doors. The impressive socle of its back wall is in Hymettian marble. The outer Doric colonnade had 64 columns.

This is assumed to be the colonnade built by Eumenes II, King of Pergamon (197–159 B.C.), who is recorded by Vitruvius (V, 9, 1) as having built a stoa near the theatre to serve as a shelter and promenade. In Roman times it was connected with the much later Odeion of Herodes Atticus and remained in use until the 3C when it was destroyed and the materials used in the Valerian wall. Column drums can be seen at No. 30 Veïkou. The Turks incorporated the remnants in their lower enceinte (Wall of Serpentzes) in 1687.

To the W. of the stoa is the **Odeion of Herodes Atticus,** built in honour of Regilla, wife of Herodes, who died in A.D. 160. It has the typical form of a Roman theatre with a seating capacity of 5000–6000, and was one of the last great public buildings erected in Athens.

The sudden rise to wealth of Julius Atticus, father of Herodes, is wittily related by Gibbon. Julius, who had accidentally found a vast treasure buried in an old house, anticipated the officiousness of informers by reporting his find to the emperor. On being told by Nerva to have no qualms about using—or abusing—fortune's gift, Julius devoted large sums to public works and to educating his son. Herodes, after a distinguished public career, including the consulship at Rome, retired to Athens and continued the munificence of his father, paying for projects in Troas, Delphi, and Corinth, as well as for the stadium and this Odeion in Athens. The Turks converted the Odeion into a redoubt, without, however, injuring its plan. The interior was excavated in 1857–58, when evidence showed that it had been destroyed by a fire. A large quantity of murex shells found at the same time suggest that the Byzantine Greeks had a factory here for Tyrian purple. The theatre is the scene of orchestral and operatic performances during the Athens Festival.

The massive *Façade* stands everywhere to the second story and in places to the third, though the portico that stood in front has disappeared (mosaic excavated and re-covered). Entrance is made to either side through vestibules (traces of mosaics) leading to the parodoi. The stage wall is pierced by three doors and has eight niches for statues. Above are windows. Three steps of the E. stair connecting the stage with the orchestra remain. The steeply-rising *Auditorium*, supported by a thick circular limestone wall, was roofed with cedar. It consists of a cavea, c. 85 yds across, divided by a diazoma, below which are five wedges of seats and ten above. The seating was entirely restored in Pentelic marble in 1950–61, and the *Orchestra* repaved in blue and white slabs.

To the s. of the Odeion, on either side of the modern entrance stairway, are remains (of various dates) including a *Sanctuary of the Nymphe*, excavated by the Greek Archaeological Service in 1955–59 and identified by its boundary stone. Loutrophoroi found date from the mid-7C; these were vessels used for the bridal bath and offered here afterwards as dedications.

Just beyond the Odeion is a busy junction. To the right a drive (no motor vehicles) mounts to the entrance of the Acropolis. Ahead a panoramic avenue circles Mouseion Hill to the Philopappos monument (see Rte 3). Between them Leoforos Apostolou Pavlou continues (½m farther) to the w. entrance of the Agora (Rte 5).

2 THE ACROPOLIS

The Athenian **Acropolis** stands alone in its unique combination of grandeur, beauty, and historical associations. This rocky height, traditionally connected with the Pelasgi, was the original city (πόλις) and the abode of the early kings and their courts. It possessed also an irresistible attraction for the tyrants, Kylon making an abortive, and Peisistratos a successful, attempt to establish it as a fortified residence. After the fall of the Peisistratids, however, the Athenians lived entirely in the Lower City and resigned the Acropolis to their gods. It was sacked by the Persians in 480 B.C. New walls were built by Kimon and Pericles followed by the great era of construction under Pericles, who was responsible for the array of buildings which, despite the vicissitudes of time, remain an inspiration to the world. It is particularly beautiful in the setting sun and by the light of the full moon.

The *Acropolis* is a rock of coarse semi-crystalline limestone and red schist, of very irregular form, measuring c. 350 yds by 140. Its summit (512 ft), to the N.E. of the Parthenon, is 300 ft above the general level of the city. From the summit two ridges run towards the w., the more important of them ending in the bastion of the Temple of Athena Nike, to the s.w. The only accessible slope follows the depression between these two ridges. Elsewhere the hill is precipitous or even overhanging, with inaccessible clefts and caverns in the rock. The sheer descent on the s. side, however, is largely artificial.

History. Natural springs have attracted man to the slopes of the Acropolis since Neolithic times (c. 5000 B.C.) and the site was inhabited continuously throughout the Helladic periods. Towards the end of the Bronze Age (Late Helladic IIIB) the Mycenean settlement was strengthened with a 'Cyclopean' rampart (sometimes loosely called the Pelasgic Wall), consisting of two facing walls of large undressed stones in more or less regular courses, with a core of rubble. It was filled in with clay and its thickness varied from 15 to 22 feet. The surviving fragments show that the wall followed a sinuous course adapted to the contour of the rocky height. A well-preserved section (14 ft high) runs from the Propylaea to the s. circuit wall. To the N. the wall overhung the escarpment of the Long Rocks and is now mostly obscured by later walls; to the s. and E. it kept nearer to the ridge than the later wall of Kimon. The bastion on which the Temple of Athena Nike stands has Mycenean foundations and probably defended a principal w. entrance akin to the Lion Gate at Mycenae. A postern gate to the N.E., approached by narrow steps hewn in a natural cleft, which provided the entrance in Early and Middle Helladic times, was abandoned about this time. Farther w. a secret reservoir, deep underground, was reached by eight flights of stairs, accessible only from the top of the Acropolis, thus securing an unassailable water supply for the Acropolis in time of siege. Explorations, made with great difficulty in 1937–38, showed that the reservoir dated from the latter half of the 13C B.C. and was in use for c. 25 years only. Its existence was quite unknown in Classical times, when the lower flights were buried and the uppermost two flights of stairs were used to provide a secret exit from the Acropolis to the N. slope. The principal Mycenean building was the Royal Palace, Homer's "strong house of Erechtheus", which stood somewhere on the N. side probably in the region of the Old Temple of Athena. The Tomb of Kekrops, founder of the dynasty, was presumably just to the w. A few remains of Mycenean dwellings exist on the N. side, and tombs below.

At some later date a lower wall was constructed on the w. slope to form a precinct similar to that at Tiryns. This wall was known as the Pelasgikon or Pelargikon, perhaps because it was built by the Attic Pelasgi (Hdt. VI, 137), perhaps from the storks which used to nest on the battlements. It was known later as the 'Enneapylon' (nine gates), but no trace of it remains and its course can only be inferred from literary references. Though this was dismantled after the fall of the Peisistratids in 510 B.C. the area enclosed by it remained unoccupied in obedience to the oracle of Delphi until refugees crowded it at the time of the Peloponnesian War.

Little is known of the Acropolis in the five centuries between the Mycenean and Archaic periods, though continuity of the cults of Erechtheus, Kekrops, etc., suggests uninterrupted occupation. The original wall, the Kekropion, and the great altar of Athena seem to have survived until the Persian War. A Geometric temple to Athena is assumed to have stood on the same site as the Peisistratid Temple of Athena which replaced it c. 529 B.C. Numerous fragments of architecture and of pedimental sculpture belonging to a sizable poros limestone temple of the mid-6C B.C. have been found on the s. side of the Acropolis between the Parthenon and the s. wall. This temple has, rightly or wrongly, been identified with the *Hekatompedon* (or 'hundred-footer') to which ancient inscriptions refer. Because the inscriptions clearly name the Parthenon cella 'Hekatompedon' and use the same name for a pre-Parthenon building on the Acropolis, and because the architectural and sculptural remains were found in the immediate vicinity of the Parthenon, many archaeologists equate these remains with the Hekatompedon and consider it a predecessor of the Parthenon built on the Parthenon site. Pedimental sculpture and other members of four small Archaic buildings have been found on the Acropolis; the better preserved fragments are displayed in the museum.

The victory of Marathon (490 B.C.) and the opening of new marble quarries on Mt Pentelikon stimulated a scheme, presumably stemming from Aristides, for an ambitious new temple (usually referred to as the Older or Pre-Parthenon). The surface area of the Acropolis was enlarged by building terraces with retaining walls filled in with debris from the demolished Hekatompedon. The new foundations in poros had been completed and work started on the columns when the Persian sack of 480/79 B.C. reduced the Acropolis to calcined ruins.

Essential cleaning up and patching up were undertaken directly after the battle of Plataea. The gateway was repaired and part of the cella of the Old Temple of Athena may have been restored as a Treasury. In accordance with an oath taken before Plataea, the sanctuaries were left in ruins as reminders of Persian impiety. The Persians had demolished enough of the fortification wall of the 13C B.C. to render it useless, and when the Acropolis north wall was rebuilt the Athenians created a perpetual reminder of Persian barbarism by incorporating remains of both the Old Temple of Athena and of the Older Parthenon near the top of the wall where they can be seen to this day. On the s. side more terrace walls were undertaken and filled in with debris to extend the area of the Acropolis still further. The spoils of the Battle of the Eurymedon (468 B.C.) eventually enabled Kimon to undertake a more ambitious plan whereby a massive s. wall was started. This was completed under Pericles and established the bastion, c. 60 ft high, that still exists.

The decision to rebuild the Acropolis on a monumental scale was taken by Pericles about the time the peace treaty was signed with the Persians at Susa (448 B.C.). The Parthenon was finished in 438 B.C. and the Propylaia immediately begun. The Temple of Athena Nike followed and the Erechtheion. The latter was not finished till 395, and the final demolition of the restored Opisthodomos of the Old Athena Temple in 353 marks the end of the old order. From the time of Pericles till the death of Augustus (A.D. 14) the general appearance of the Acropolis underwent little change. Votive offerings in the form of shields were added to the Parthenon by Alexander the Great, and Antiochus Epiphanes added a gilded Gorgoneion to the s. wall of the Acropolis. The siege of Sulla in 86 B.C. affected only the buildings of the s. slope.

Claudius began the embellishment of the entrance c. A.D. 52 with a monumental staircase (a typical manifestation of Roman grandeur), and Hadrian enriched many shrines. The building of the 'Beulé' Gate in the 3C marked the beginning of the second fortified period presaging damage and deterioration, and the Edict of Theodosius II in A.D. 429 dealt the final blow to pagan worship. Justinian converted the temples to Orthodox Christian churches, restored the military character of the citadel, and provided for the water supply of the garrison. The bronze Athena Promachos of Pheidias was removed to Constantinople before 900 to adorn the Hippodrome.

In 1204 the Acropolis was taken by the Marquess of Montferrat. At the end of the same year it was occupied and plundered by Otho de la Roche. In 1387 Nerio Acciaioli captured the citadel after a long siege. On Nerio's death, the succession was disputed; his son Antony occupied the Acropolis in 1403 after a 17-months siege. During his reign the Propylaia were converted into a Florentine palace. In 1458 Franco, last duke of Athens, surrendered the Acropolis after a two-years defence, to Omar, Attica having been annexed to Turkey in 1456.

To meet the threat of the extended use of cannon, the defences of the Acropolis were remodelled. In 1640 or 1656 a powder magazine in the Propylaia was struck by lightning, causing its first serious injury. About 1684 the Temple of Athena Nike was removed to make way for a new battery. On 21 Sept 1687, the Venetian army under Morosini landed at Piraeus, and on the 23rd two batteries opened fire on the works before the Propylaia. After an explosion in the Parthenon, a fire raged on the Acropolis for 48 hours. On 3 Oct the Turks capitulated, but in April 1688 they reoccupied the citadel and for the next century its ruins were obscured by a maze of little streets. In 1822 the Turkish garrison surrendered to the Greek insurgents; but in June 1827 the Acropolis was recovered after 11 months desultory siege by Reshid Pasha. The Turks now retained possession until after the end of the war when, in 1833, they were succeeded by a Bavarian garrison, which did not quit till 30 March 1835.

In 1801 Lord Elgin, then British Ambassador to the Porte, obtained permission in a firman to fix scaffolding, to excavate, to make casts and drawings, and to take away pieces of stone with inscriptions or figures. Whatever may be the opinion of his action, it should be appreciated that at the time fragments were being reduced to lime in the lime-kilns on the Acropolis; the sculptures which Elgin took away were at least spared the further ravages of time and of successive wars.

Excavations. Demolition of Turkish and Frankish structures began immediately in 1833, not without dissentient voices, one of the regents as early as 1835 opining that "the archæologists would destroy all the picturesque additions of the middle ages in their zeal to lay bare and restore the ancient monuments"; as indeed they have. Restoration and rearrangement of existing fragments continued to 1853, when Beulé uncovered the gate that bears his name. Burnouf discovered the Klepsydra spring in 1874 and Schliemann demolished the Frankish Tower in 1875. In 1876–85 the Greek Archæological Society subsidized excavations by Kavvadias and Kawerau, when the surface of the Acropolis was investigated in many places to bedrock. Restorations and examinations of buildings in detail have gone on almost continuously ever since, with a mass of published reports.

By 1976 continuing damage to the Acropolis had reached unacceptable levels. There were three main causes: internal deterioration of the marble through the use of iron clamps and supports in 19C restoration works; external chemical changes wrought in the surfaces by sulphurous pollution from central heating and vehicle exhausts; and wear to surfaces by visitors' feet. Legislation has already reduced oil pollution. Motor vehicles are no longer permitted on the approaches. Severe restrictions are in force as to where visitors may walk: when new paths have been laid, a channelled round may have to be enforced. The former moonlight openings have ceased. Entry to all buildings is forbidden, except to parts of the Propylaia that are floored. A programme has been started to replace all iron by titanium, to remove much of the remaining original sculpture to controlled museum atmospheres, and replace it with copies (some supplied from British Museum casts of an earlier era). Work on the Erechtheion is expected to be complete by 1983, but for many years visitors will certainly encounter scaffolding and restricted areas.

At a later date it is planned to remove the present museum from the Acropolis to a new site below the Theatre of Dionysos. A design competition to incorporate an existing scheduled 19C building was inaugurated in 1980.

To explore the Acropolis thoroughly is thus almost impossible at present. A superficial tour may be made in 1½–2 hrs by taking a route from the Beulé Gate through the Propylaia, circling the Parthenon, and visiting the Museum; thence viâ the Belvedere and the Erechtheion back to the Beulé Gate. Though visitors will not be able to see everything described hereunder, it is hoped that the text in its present complete form will best serve the changing situation.

Approaches. A paved road, through gardens planned by Queen Amalia, leads up from Odhos Dionissiou Areopayitou (Rte 1). Paths lead from the Agora round the Areopagus, and round the N. slope from Plaka (see Rte 6).—**Admission** 50 dr., Sun free; tickets are taken at the Beulé Gate. Open 8 or 8.30 to sunset. Museum 50 dr.: 9–5 or 7 exc. Tues (closed) and Sun (10–2 or 4.30; free). Rfmts are available below the entrance in summer; food may not be taken on to the Acropolis. There are lavatories in the grove below the ticket office, and by the N.W. corner of the Museum.

A. THE ENTRANCE

In Classical times the Panathenaic Way ended in a ramp going straight up from the level of the tourist post office to the gateway of the Propylaia with an inclination of one in four. On the modern approach we cross first the line of a medieval wall, then the Turkish wall of Serpentzes that ran N. from the retaining wall of the theatre of Herodes Atticus. The ceremonial entrance by which we enter is known as the **Beulé Gate** after the French archæologist who discovered it in 1852. A marble wall between two unequal pylons (the N. one restored) is pierced by a trilithon gateway alined with the central opening of the Propylaia. This had a defensive purpose and was paid for, c. A.D. 280, by F. Septimus Marcellinus. The gate was built of stones from the destroyed **Choregic Monument of Nikias.** The name of Pantaleon of Sikyon the flute-player, may be clearly read above the lintel; the remainder of the inscription is higher up. The inner face of the gate incorporates a grey slab carved with two victor's wreaths.

Within the gate parts of many levels exposed show that the way up was frequently modified. A few courses of polygonal walling lower down on the axis of the Propylaia are all that remains of the N. retaining wall for the late-Archaic ramp of the Panathenaic way; in Pericles' day the ramp was widened to the full width of the central section of the Propylaia; by the time of Pausanias all save a central path for sacrificial animals had been concealed beneath a broad MARBLE STAIRCASE, some 80 yds long, erected within the Propylaia wings in A.D. 52 by Claudius and completed in its lower courses much later.

At the foot of the steps, just to the left of the Beulé Gate, are four fragments of an architrave, with doves, fillets, and an inscription, belonging to the *Shrine of Aphrodite Pandemos*, which stood below the s.w. corner of the hill (confirmed by excavations in 1960).

Half-way up the staircase is a natural landing from which a terrace opens to the N. Partly blocking this is the so-called *Monument of Agrippa*, identified by inscriptions on its face and on the landing below it. The colossal plinth, 29 ft high, has a shaft of Hymettos marble set off by a base moulding and cornice in poros (the foundation steps of conglomerate were not intended to be seen). It bore a quadriga. A partially effaced inscription on the w. side under the Agrippa inscription records the original dedication, probably in 178 B.C., to celebrate a Pergamene chariot victory in the Panathenaic Games. Cuttings in the top show that two chariot groups occupied the plinth at different dates. What happened to the original group depicting Eumenes II is not known. Later, according to Plutarch and Dio Cassius the plinth bore statues of Antony and Cleopatra, which were blown down in 31 B.C. The group to Marcus Agrippa was raised after his third consulship in 27 B.C.

Behind the monument a terrace of the Periclean period extends below the N. wing of the Propylaia. The mound on it consists of marble fragments, many inscribed, dating from the Turkish period. The terrace affords an excellent *View of the Agora and Temple of Hephaistos; the course of the Panathenaic Way along the Wall of Valerian can be traced towards the Klepsydra spring which lies below the bastion. Thither descends the late stairway (inaccessible) that begins from the terrace; emerging from the bastion beneath our feet by a Byzantine doorway, the steps follow a gully and enter a late-Roman well-house.

Klepsydra cannot be visited but can best be understood from this point. The spring, originally called *Empedo*, attracted Neolithic settlers and was early the centre of a cult of Nymphs. It issued from a small natural cave. Within this, c. 460, a well-house with a deep *Draw-Basin* was built, and adjoining it a substantial structure, of which the paved floor and a wall survive. Part of the roof of the well-house fell in the 1C B.C., though the well was still usable in 37 B.C. when Mark Antony set out for Parthia taking (in obedience to an oracle) a bottle of water from Klepsydra. In the reign of Claudius a further fall ruined the building without rendering the water inaccessible. In Roman times a vaulted *Well-House* was built over the fallen roof of the original cave with a shaft driven to water level, and the whole sealed with concrete. The new structure was linked for the first time by a stair to the bastion above and was henceforth accessible only from the acropolis, though the overflow later fed a 6C cistern. At the time the new well-house was built, the court seems to have been abandoned, and later was covered by the Wall of Valerian. The Roman well-house received frescoes during its medieval transformation into a *Church of the Holy Apostles*, perhaps of the same period as the Byzantine door (see above). By 1822 all lay beneath a deposit of earth, though the spring itself bubbled up and served a Turkish fountain lower down the hill. After the Turks on the Acropolis had capitulated in 1822 for lack of water, the Greeks, searching for a water supply, found Klepsydra and repaired it, and in 1826 Gen. Odysseus Androutsos enclosed it in a bastion (demolished 1888). Its water served the Greek garrison throughout the siege of 1827. Excavations by Kavvadias in 1897 uncovered the paved court, but the American investigations of 1936–40 form the basis of modern study. —The remainder of the N. slope is described in Rte 6.

From this point to the Propylaia we mount the modern zigzag ramp that resembles the Mycenean and medieval approaches rather than the classical ramp.

The **Propylaia,** a monumental gateway, designed by Mnesikles to replace an earlier entrance, was planned to extend across the entire width of the Acropolis. Its axis is alined to that of the Parthenon, its width would have equalled the length of the temple, and, like the Parthenon, its proportions are worked out in direct mathematical ratio, thus affording the only certain example before Hellenistic times of designing one building in direct relationship to another. Built in 437–432 B.C., it was left incomplete at the beginning of the Peloponnesian War and the work was never resumed. Except for the foundations, and for certain decorative features in black Eleusinian stone, the construction is wholly of Pentelic marble. Discreet restorations have minimized the ravages of later history and a great part of the building still stands.

History. The Greeks gave the name of Propylon (portico) to the entrance of a sanctuary, palace, or agora. The plural form Propylaia was reserved for more elaborate entrances. Earlier propylaia, probably to be ascribed to Peisistratos, but shown by the re-use of material from the Heraktompedon to date in their later form from 488–480 B.C., were alined differently from the existing structure. The Propylaia of Pericles (the existing edifice), begun upon the completion of the Parthenon, was hampered by political and religious agitation, the original plan of Mnesikles being curtailed on the s. in deference to the prejudices of the priests of the adjoining sanctuaries. The enormous cost (2012 talents) was defrayed by grants from the Treasurers of Athena and Hephaistos, from the sale of old building material, from the rent of houses, and from private subscriptions, as well as by contributions from the Hellenotamiai, but Pericles was accused of squandering the funds of the Delian League on the embellishment of the Acropolis.

The Propylaia remained almost intact down to the 13C, being then used as the Byzantine episcopal palace. The dukes of Athens lived and used it as their chancery. Nerio Acciaioli made the propylaia his palace and erected the so-called Frankish Tower, 90 ft high, on the s. side. The Turks covered the centre vestibule with a cupola and turned it into a magazine, the Aga making it his official residence. In the 17C it was struck by lightning and the magazine exploded with the result that the architraves of the E. portico fell and were broken and two Ionic columns collapsed. The w. facade and the celebrated ceiling were demolished in the Venetian bombardment of 1687. Later on a Turkish bastion was erected between the Bastion of Athena Nike and the s. wing. Some columns were used to make lime. The building suffered again in the siege of 1827. In 1836 Pittakis removed the Frankish and Turkish additions, except the Tower, which was not taken down until 1875 (at the expense of Schliemann). Reconstruction of the central hall was undertaken in 1909–17 and the wings were restored after the Second World War.

The Propylaia comprise a central hall containing the portal and two wings flanking the approach. The CENTRAL HALL forms a rectangle 78 ft long and 60 ft wide, with side walls having antae at each end and Doric hexastyle porticoes facing E. and w. It is divided two-thirds of the way through by the portal itself, to the w. of which is a vestibule screened by an entrance portico. This *West Portico*, 65 ft wide, rests on four high steps, except in the middle, where the steps give place to a continuous ramp (transverse cuts for foothold visible at Roman level). Six sharp-fluted Doric columns are spaced to correspond with the five gateways of the portal. The two end columns stand to their full height (nearly 29 ft) and retain their capitals and portions of their architrave; other parts lie beneath the N. colonnade.

Behind is the *Vestibule*, 45 ft deep, whose coffered ceiling of marble, 39 ft high and painted and gilt, earned the praise of Pausanias. The panels were supported on beams of 18 ft span, each weighing 11 tons, that rested on two rows of blunt-fluted Ionic columns flanking the central carriage way. The beams were reinforced with iron bars set in their upper face. The six Ionic columns were two-thirds the diameter of the Doric columns, and about 10 diameters ($33\frac{1}{2}$ ft) high. One of the beautiful Ionic capitals has been restored to position, with a section of the coffered ceiling. Traces of the paint and star decoration can be seen on a well-preserved panel standing below. The *Portal* stands on a platform at the higher level of the E. portico, and consists of five gateways, graded in size from the centre outwards. The paved ramp continues through the largest gateway in the centre, while the four side gateways are approached from the vestibule by flights of five steps, the topmost of black Eleusinian marble. The entrances had massive wooden gates. Three transverse steps are cut in the rock below the portal but these relics of an earlier entrance are now concealed by wooden planking.

The *East Portico* corresponds to that at the W., having six Doric columns of the same size and arrangement, but reduced in height by nearly a foot; it stands on a simple stylobate. The depth (19 ft) of the portico allowed the ceiling to be supported on beams laid parallel with the axis of the Propylaia, so that no inner colonnade was necessary. Each of the porticoes was surmounted by an entablature of triglyphs and unsculptured metopes supporting a pediment, but though pedimental sculpture was planned it was never started.

The N. and S. wings had Doric porticoes of three columns in antis, facing each other and at right angles to the W. portico of the central hall; but whereas the N. portico screens an important chamber, that to the S. was left with nothing behind it. The wings had hip roofs. The NORTH WING is in a very perfect state. The architrave still has its plain frieze of triglyphs and metopes. The walls of the room at the back still stand; entered by a door and lighted by two windows in the partition wall, this room is called the *Pinakotheke* (picture gallery) from the pictures, many possibly by Polygnotos, that Pausanias saw there. The door and windows are not centred in the wall; scholars have attempted to explain this strange asymmetry with four mutually incompatible theories of varying degrees of implausibility. The rough surface of the walls suggests that the pictures were easel paintings. The joist-sockets of the story added by the dukes of Athens are still visible.

The SOUTH WING appears from the outside to be the counterpart of the N. Wing, but there is no chamber behind the portico, and the area of the portico itself is much smaller. The back wall stops opposite the third column, the W. anta being a sham. At the S.E. corner the wall is slightly chamfered, so as not to interfere with the surviving section of the *Mycenean Wall*, which bounded the Temenos of Artemis Brauronia. The peculiar shape of this wing would make it appear that Mnesikles only temporarily abandoned his design, hoping to overcome the opposition of the priests to its completion.—Above the S. wing later stood the Tower of the Franks.

Mnesikles intended to add two E. halls on the N. and S. sides of the central hall, which would have occupied the entire W. end of the acropolis and given the Propylaia the same length exactly as the Parthenon. The existence of a cornice running round the two walls designed to form inner walls of the N. hall on the S. and W., and of other structural features (comp. below), proves that the N.E. hall was actually started; the S.E. hall, planned as the exact counterpart of its fellow, was abandoned at an early stage, though an anta exists at what would have been its N.E. corner. Both halls would have measured about 70 ft by 40, much more spacious than the Pinakotheke.

The L-shaped foundations between the Mycenean wall and the S. wall of the S. wing (which overlies them) represent a corner of the exedra that flanked the older Propylaia, forming a grandstand for the Panathenaic procession. Here

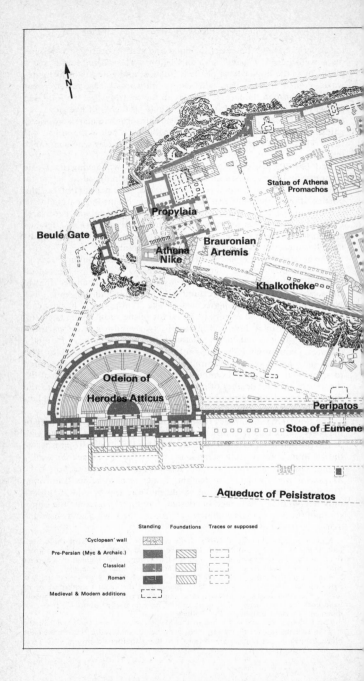

Statue of Athena
Promachos

Propylaia

Beulé Gate

Athena
Nike

Brauronian
Artemis

Khalkotheke

Odeion of
Herodes Atticus

Peripatos

Stoa of Eumene[s]

Aqueduct of Peisistratos

	Standing	Foundations	Traces or supposed
'Cyclopean' wall			
Pre-Persian (Myc & Archaic.)			
Classical			
Roman			
Medieval & Modern additions			

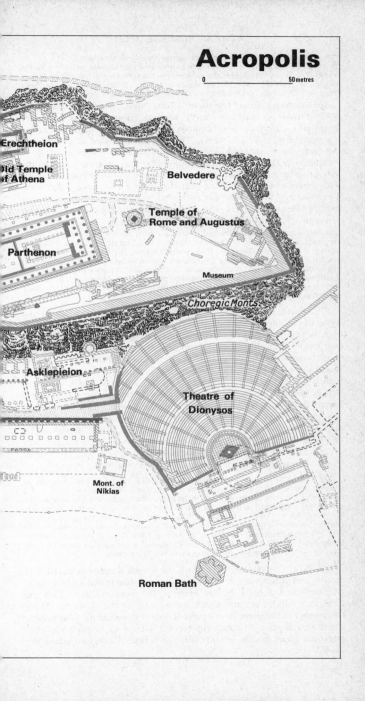

Acropolis

0   50 metres

Erechtheion

Old Temple of Athena

Belvedere

Temple of Rome and Augustus

Parthenon

Museum

Choregic Monts

Asklepieion

Theatre of Dionysos

Mont. of Nikias

Roman Bath

may have stood the well-known 'Hekatompedon Inscription', cut in 485 B.C. on the reverse of an earlier metope, which enumerated prohibitions to visitors to the Acropolis.—The small trapezoidal enclosure to the s. was a precinct of the Graces, associated probably with the worship of Hekate of the Tower, whose triple image by Alkamenes was located hereabouts by Pausanias.

The charming little ***Temple of Athena Nike,** called inaccurately '*of Nike Apteros*' (wingless Victory), reached from the s. wing of the Propylaia, stands on a precipitous platform, 26 ft high, projecting towards the w. (care necessary). The bastion originated as a Mycenean outwork. In Peisistratid times it was consecrated to the worship of Athena Nike, being furnished with an altar and sanctuary, lost in the sack of 480 B.C. In 449 a new temple was planned to celebrate the peace with Persia and the following year the bastion was faced with poros. The design of the temple was entrusted to Kallikrates, but built in a modified form only in 427–424, probably owing to differences of opinion about its structural relationship with the Propylaia.

In the meantime Kallikrates had erected a similar temple by the Ilissos, which survived to be drawn by Stuart and Revett. The Temple of Athena Nike was thrown down by the Turks in 1686 in order to use the bastion as an artillery position, the pieces being used in the construction of another gun emplacement above the Beulé Gate. With the help of Stuart and Revett's drawings of the Ilissos temple, it was reconstructed piece by piece in 1836–42 by Ross, Schaubart, and Hansen, but again dismantled and rebuilt in 1936–40 in order to strengthen the bastion which had become unsafe.

The temple, built entirely of Pentelic marble, stands with its w. front along the w. edge of the bastion on a stylobate of three steps measuring 18 ft by 12. It consists of an almost square cella with an Ionic portico of four columns at either end. The fluted shafts are monolithic and the capitals closely resemble those of the Propylaia. A *Frieze*, 18 in. broad, round the whole exterior of the building, is adorned with sculptures in high relief. It originally consisted of 14 slabs, four of which are in the British Museum (replaced by casts in cement). The genuine slabs, whose correct positions are uncertain, are badly weathered. Divinities (headless) occupy the E. front. Athena may be distinguished by her shield; next to her appears to be Zeus. At the s. corner are Peitho, Aphrodite, and Eros. Of the 22 figures which can be made out, 16 are female. The other sides bear scenes from the Battle of Plataea (479 B.C.); on the w. front Athenians are fighting Boeotians and on the flanks Persians.

The cella housed a marble statue, reproduction of an archaic Xoanon or wooden statue, probably destroyed by the Persians. The goddess held in the right hand a pomegranate, emblem of fertility, which indicated her pacific side, and in her left hand the helmet of the Athena of War. Her correct name was Athena Nike or Athena, bringer of victory. In Greek art the goddess Nike (Victory) was represented as a winged female; common tradition, confusing the two goddesses, supposed the statue of Athena Nike to be a wingless 'Victory' (Nike apteros). The story (retailed by Pausanias) grew up that the Athenians had deprived the Victory of wings to prevent her flying away.

The *Pyrgos*, or platform, on which the temple stands was paved with marble and surrounded by a marble parapet, sculptured in high relief and surmounted by a bronze screen. The grooves into which the slabs were bedded are still visible on the edge of the platform. Many fragments have been recovered and are now in the museum. The reliefs, which date from c. 410 B.C., represented a band of Winged Victories attendant upon Athena, and include the famous Victory adjusting her sandal.

At the top of the small flight of steps that gave access to this temple is a block of Hymettian marble with marks of an equestrian statue and a Greek inscription of c. 457 B.C., recording that it was dedicated by the cavalry and executed by Lykios of Eleutherai, son of Myron. The block appears to have been turned upside down and used for a statue of Germanicus when he visited Athens in A.D. 18. A second inscription (below the block) records this event.

If the air is clear, the platform commands a magnificent view (best at sunset) of Phaleron Bay, Piraeus, Salamis, Acro-Corinth and the mountains beyond it, Aegina, the E. tongue of Argolis, with Idhra behind it, and the coast-line to the left towards Sounion. In the foreground the contour of the Pnyx is clearly seen.—This is the spot where, according to legend Aegeus kept watch for the return of his son Theseus from his expedition against the Minotaur. Theseus, who had promised to hoist a white sail if he was successful instead of his usual black sail, forgot; Aegeus seeing the black sail, thought his son was dead and threw himself over the rock.

B. WALK INSIDE THE WALLS

Few visitors can resist walking straight from the Propylaia to the Parthenon; but they are strongly recommended to make a circuit of the Acropolis before approaching the Parthenon a second time. In Classical times the focus of attention was on the great statue of Athena while the direct approach to the Parthenon was channelled through a propylon; from the Propylaia all but the pediment of the Parthenon was hidden by intervening buildings.

Turning to the left beyond the Propylaia, we pass (l.) the anta or pilaster of the projected N. hall (comp. above). On the open ground to the left stood the chapel of the Frankish dukes, removed in 1860. From here we may observe the beautifully regular but unfinished masonry of the Pinakotheke and the projection at the N.W. corner which is another indication of the unbuilt N. hall. Walking E. we cross an ancient drain, and farther on pass large *Cisterns*, probably built by Justinian c. A.D. 530. We now bear towards the Acropolis wall, and at its next angle observe a flight of steps of Classical date descending from S. to N. This may represent a *Secret Staircase* used annually by the Arrephoroi.

The Arrephoroi were two (or four) girls of noble birth between the ages of seven and eleven, chosen by the King-Archon to perform an obscure service in honour of Athena. Their duties (in addition to the weaving and the carrying of the Peplos) apparently consisted in carrying down by an underground passage to the Sanctuary of Aphrodite in the Gardens (not located) a burden whose contents were unknown. This they exchanged for another mysterious burden, which they brought back.

A platform above the steps affords a fine view towards Piraeus, with the Areopagus in the foreground and the 'Theseion' below. A few yards E. a Turkish staircase, probably on an earlier course, descends from W. to E., turns abruptly under the wall, and enters a cavern. Investigations were started here in 1937 in an attempt to find further evidences of the Arrephoroi; though unsuccessful in this, they unexpectedly uncovered traces (not now accessible) of a secret *Mycenean Stairway*, hewn in the rock, partly in a natural cleft, partly underground, constructed in wood and stone in 8 flights to a depth of 110 ft and leading to a natural spring.

The outer face of the acropolis wall at this point is composed of blocks from the entablature of the Old Temple of Athena: architraves, triglyphs, metopes, and cornices. A row of them is seen directly to the right as we stand at the wall behind the Turkish staircase.

We now pass between a Byzantine cistern, which abuts on the Acropolis wall, and the Erechtheion. Built into the wall on the left are two of the unfinished drums intended for the columns of the Older Parthenon. Farther on are four others in a row. A flight of marble steps leads up to a platform, from which we can view a large section of the N. wall, exposed when the korai, etc., were extracted from the fill. Here unfinished marble column drums and stylobate blocks from the Older Parthenon (490–480) are built into the wall. In the next deep excavation are the remains of the stairway in a rock gully which led down from the *Mycenean Postern*. Beyond the far side of the chasm a few steps farther E. we see poros drums and capitals (reddened by fire) from the Old Temple of Athena, and, to the left of the path farther on, other poros remains from the Old Temple of Athena including an inverted Doric capital with four rings above the fluting.

At the extreme end of the enclosure is the *Belvedere* (*View). By the steps are beautiful fragments of many periods. In the N.E. corner, behind the museum, a capacious Turkish storage jar stands on a well-preserved curving stretch of the Pelasgic wall.

Returning towards the Parthenon, we notice (r.) a large platform in the natural rock, which may have been the *Precinct of Zeus Poleios*. Immediately in front of the Parthenon, the architectural remains of the circular *Monopteros of Rome and Augustus* have been assembled on and around foundations which are still awaiting investigation. The conical roof was supported on nine Ionic columns. The inscribed architrave was recorded by Cyriacus of Ancona.

In front of the museum the parapet above the Wall of Kimon overlooks the Theatre of Dionysos (*View over the Olympieion and Stadium to Hymettos). Hereabouts Attalos I, king of Pergamon, erected four groups of sculpture (probably in bronze), representing the Gigantomachia, the Amazonomachia, the Battle of Marathon, and his own victory (in 230 B.C.) over the Gauls of Asia Minor. Plutarch relates that the statue of Dionysos from the Gigantomachia was blown by a high wind into the theatre below. Marble copies exist in various European museums.

Walking w. along the massive *Wall of Kimon* (restored), we pass a triangular enclosure, where a cross wall of the Ergasterion is visible, and come near the s.w. corner of the Parthenon, to two deep pits revealing earlier walls.

The w. front of the Parthenon is approached by a flight of nine steps cut in the rock, continued upwards by seven more in poros of which fragments survive. These served as a decorative retaining wall for the Parthenon w. terrace and later were used for votive offerings, as is shown by some 38 rock cuttings where the various stelai were fixed. Before the steps at the w. end stood the bull set up by the Council of the Areopagus. Below them was the Periclean *Entrance Court*, conjectured as part of Mnesikles' commission to tidy the Acropolis; rock cuttings suggest that it was entered on the N. by a propylon. The court was closed on the s. side by the *Chalkotheke*, or magazine of bronzes, dating from c. 450 B.C. The foundations show it to have been not quite oblong (c. 45 yds by 15), the E. wall being slightly askew. It was later embellished with a N. portico which encroached upon the steps leading to the Parthenon.

On the inner N. wall are laid five fragments of a long base with inscriptions, from which it appears that they once bore statues by Sthennis and Leocharos (350 B.C.). Roman inscriptions on the S. face show that the bases were afterwards appropriated by Drusus, Tiberius, Augustus, Germanicus, and Trajan. Other pedestals, some detailed by Pausanias, lie hereabouts, and the area is further confused by modern ceiling blocks prepared to protect that part of the Parthenon frieze remaining *in situ* beneath the W. peristyle.

To the W. of the Chalkotheke and the Court lay the **Sanctuary of Artemis Brauronia**, the bear goddess, which took the form of a stoa with two projecting wings. Votive offerings, including a well-carved little Bear, have been found on the site (see Aristophanes, 'Lysistrata', 646). Within the precinct, of which the foundations of the N. and W. walls (4C B.C.) can be easily traced, is the pedestal of a colossal bronze figure of the Trojan Horse by Strongylion. Its two marble blocks, nearly 6 ft long, bearing an inscription, were discovered in 1840; they lie nearly on a line with the E. portico of the Propylaia.

The remnant of Mycenean wall bounded the sanctuary on the W. Behind and below this, in the angle of the Propylaia, foundations remain of one corner of the pre-Periclean propylaia. By the corner column of Mnesikles' propylaia is the round *Pedestal* of a statue to Athena Hygieia, with clear traces of her feet and spear.

Plutarch ('Pericles', 13) tells that during the building of the Propylaia one of the workmen "the quickest and handiest of them all" fell and was badly hurt, Pericles was told by Athena in a dream how to cure him, and in gratitude set up a bronze image of the goddess in her attribute of health-giver. Pliny adds the information that the remedy was the plant parthenion (feverfew), a pleasant punning conceit. Just E. of the pedestal is an *Altar* to Hygieia, which Plutarch records as older than the statue.

In front of the Propylaia the surface of the rock is carefully roughened by transverse grooves, to afford foothold in the ascent to the Parthenon —a rise of c. 40 ft. The numerous rectangular cuttings were occupied by pedestals of statues. On the right are rock-hewn steps ascending to the Sanctuary of Brauronian Artemis. The Sacred Way passed through the entrance court (see above), and along the N. side of the Parthenon, to end at its E. front.

Some 40 paces in front of the Propylaia are some foundations of poros on which stood the colossal bronze *Statue of Athena Promachos* by Pheidias. Blocks of the capping course of its pedestal, with huge egg-and-dart moulding, lie a little to the W. The statue, which Demosthenes calls "the great bronze Athena" was finished c. 458 B.C. as a trophy of Athenian valour in the Persian wars. Details of its form are safely known from the medieval description of Niketas Choniates as well as from contemporary medals. The goddess was represented standing with her right arm leaning on her spear, and holding in her left a shield, with figures in relief (battle of the Lapiths and Centaurs) designed by Parrhasios and wrought by Mys. In later times the epithet Promachos (Champion) was given the statue, to distinguish it from the statues of Virgin Athena in the Parthenon and of Athena Polias in the Erechtheion. It was c. 30 ft high; the spear blade and helmet crest were visible to sailors coming from Sounion as they rounded Cape Zoster. The statue, removed to Constantinople at an uncertain date, was destroyed in a riot in 1203, because the superstitious people believed that her apparently beckoning hand (already lacking the spear) had summoned the invading Crusaders out of the W.

Farther E., opposite the seventh N. column of the Parthenon and protected by a grating, is a rock-carved dedication to Fruit-bearing Earth (Ge Karpophoros). Here stood a personification, rising apparently from the ground, of Earth, praying for rain to Zeus.

C. THE PARTHENON

The **PARTHENON**, or *Temple of Athena Polias*, represents the culmination of the Doric, indeed of the Classical, style of architecture; as a monument it has no equal. The temple was designed to provide a new sanctuary exclusively for Athena Polias, where her statue might be suitably housed and the continually increasing treasure stored, and was erected in 447–438 B.C. as the cardinal feature of Pericles' plan. The loftiest building on the Acropolis, it is situated on its highest part, midway between E. and W. Under the order of Pheidias as 'surveyor-general' were the architect Iktinos and the contractor Kallikrates, who built the Southern Long Wall. The most celebrated sculptors in Athens, rivals or pupils of Pheidias, such as Agorakritos and Alkamenes, worked on the pediments, the frieze, and the metopes. Pheidias supervised, if he did not actually design, the whole of the sculptures, reserving entirely to himself the creation of the chryselephantine statue of Athena. The result is a peerless blend of architecture and sculpture. The Parthenon was regarded, indeed, principally as an artistic masterpiece and as the state treasury, and never replaced the Old Athena Temple or the Erechtheion in the veneration of the Athenians as the holy place sanctified by tradition.

The name Parthenon (Παρθενών), meaning the virgin's apartment, originally applied to one room in the temple. Its first recorded application to the whole building appears in the speeches of Demosthenes. Before this the temple seems to have inherited the sobriquet 'Hekatompedon' from its predecessors on the site. The statue of Athena Polias became popularly though unofficially known as Athena Parthenos.

Save for the roof (which was of wood) the Parthenon is built entirely of Pentelic marble. The whole of the stylobate survives, together with the columns of the peristyle and of the end porticoes, though some are incomplete and some restored. The entablature at the E. and W. ends, most of the W. pediment, fragments of the E. pediment, and considerable portions of the walls of the W. portico and cella still stand.

History. At least four temples were built successively on the Parthenon site. Rooftiles of the late 7C have been attributed to the first archaic temple here. The second temple was the **Hekatompedon.** Enough architecture remains to show that the Hekatompedon was a peripteral temple of the mid 6C B.C. which might be restored as 100 ft long. The interested visitor may get an idea of Hekatompedon architecture by looking at a restoration of the entablature set up behind the museum, outside, at the N. corner. He may then pass round the museum to the S. wall of the Acropolis and stand by the low fence, looking into the area between the S. side of the museum and the S. wall of the Acropolis. There can be seen the mighty grey poros capitals of the Hekatompedon and, behind them, fragments of the columns and other architecture stacked in an oblong.

The scheme to replace the poros Hekatompedon, mooted perhaps after the fall of the Tyrants, seems to have matured under Aristides after the victory of Marathon, just as new marble quarries were opened on Pentelikon. By 488 the Hekatompedon had been demolished and the remains used to build up a new terrace on the W. and S. (comp. above). A massive limestone stereobate 252 ft by 103, was bedded on the rock, from which it rises in places by 22 courses of masonry. The marble stylobate, the lower drums of still unfluted columns (6 × 16), and the first course of the wall of the **Pre-Parthenon** were already *in situ* when in 480 the Persians did their work of destruction. Marks of fire are still visible under the later stylobate (to the W. near the N. angle), as well as on the column-drums built into the acropolis N. wall. Kimon enlarged the terrace on the S. when he built his wall. "The chief interest of this temple is that it initiated marble construction in Attica on a large scale, introduced the use of Ionic elements and the application of delicate refinements in upward curvature and column inclinations, and even contributed much of the material and many of the dimensions for the present Parthenon" (Dinsmoor).

Pericles proposed the erection of a new temple in Pentelic marble with a different columnar arrangement and somewhat wider and shorter than the existing base. It was brought more to the N. and W. so that the old foundations project 14 ft on the E. and 5½ ft on the S., while extra foundation courses were necessary on the N. Work on the **Parthenon** started in 447; in 438, at the Great Panathenaic Festival, the statue of Athena was dedicated in the cella; in 435 the opisthodomos was opened to receive the treasure, and in 434 the first inventories were made; the sculpture was complete by 432. Structurally the Parthenon remained virtually intact for 2000 years. New embellishments were added from time to time, such as the shields of gilded bronze presented by Alexander. In 305 B.C., Demetrios Poliorketes desecrated the temple by turning the W. portion into a residence for himself and his seraglio. In 298 he returned to besiege Lachares, who fled with the golden ornaments of the temple and the precious casing of the statue. The Parthenon was respected by the Romans, except that the statue had disappeared by the 5C A.D. There are grounds for believing that the cult statue of Athena Parthenos was still in place in the 5C A.D. when the Panathenaic festival was still being celebrated.

In the 6C A.D. the Parthenon was turned into a church. Under Justinian the edifice was dedicated at first to Saint Sophia (Holy Wisdom), then to the Virgin Mother of God (Theotokos), and became the metropolitan church of Athens. The entrance was made at the W. end; the opisthodomos became the Byzantine pronaos and the Parthenon proper the narthex. The wall between the Parthenon proper and the cella was pierced with three doorways, two of which gave access to side staircases leading to the womens' galleries, which were erected over a new Byzantine double colonnade replacing the ancient interior Doric colonnade. The walls were covered with frescoes and the ceiling replaced by a barrel-vaulted roof. The pronaos was converted into an apse to receive the altar. Vaults for the interment of the bishops were discovered under the floor in 1910. As the cathedral of the Frankish dukes, it followed the Latin rite in 1208–1458. It was later converted into a mosque, and a Byzantine bell-tower at the S.W. angle of the opisthodomos was converted into a minaret.

Jacques Carrey, a painter in the suite of the Marquis de Nointel, made (in 1674) about 400 drawings (now invaluable) of subsequently destroyed sculptures, and Spon and Wheler (in 1676) were the last travellers to see the Parthenon intact before the disaster of 1687. Carrey's drawings are preserved in the Bibliothèque Nationale in Paris. They include the pediment groups, a large portion of the frieze, and many of the metopes. On 26 Sept 1687, at 7 p.m., a mortar placed by Morosini on the Mouseion Hill was fired by a German lieutenant at the Parthenon, which the Turks were using as a powder magazine. The resulting explosion carried away practically the whole of the cella and its frieze, eight columns on the N. side, and six on the S., together with their entablature; and the temple was cut into two ruinous halves. Morosini added to the damage, on gaining possession of the Acropolis, by attempting to remove from the W. pediment the horses and chariot of Athena: the group fell during the process of removal and was smashed.

By 1766 a small mosque had been built within the ruins. With the revival of antiquarian interest, the Parthenon suffered further damage. The Comte de Choiseul-Gouffier removed to France in 1787 one detached piece of the frieze. His example was followed in 1801 by Lord Elgin, who secured an official permit "to remove some blocks of stone with inscriptions and figures". The artist Lusieri superintended the work of removing the greater part of the frieze, 15 of the metopes from the S. side, the figures from the pediments, etc. In 1816 these 'Elgin Marbles' were placed in the British Museum.

Restoration started in 1834–44. After the earthquake of 1894, Balanos replaced a few pieces of architrave and capitals on the W. façade. In 1921–30, in the face of considerable opposition, he reconstructed the N. peristyle. The new columns were made of Piraeic stone with a covering of concrete; this harmonizes well with the ancient marble yet distinguishes the true from the false. Five missing capitals have, however, been replaced in Pentelic marble. The roofing of the W. portico with copies in Pentelic marble of the original ceiling blocks was planned to protect the remaining section of the cella frieze, which today contrasts sadly with Elgin's casts. Many blocks were made and lie below the W. façade; their erection awaits results of tests to determine whether the structure will now stand their weight.

Exterior. The foundations are best studied on the s. side, where the steps of the earlier temple may still be distinguished beneath the three marble steps that form the *Crepidoma* of the present temple. The Doric *Peristyle* consists of 46 columns (8 by 17), an octastyle arrangement matched only by the earlier Temple G at Selinus in Sicily. The columns, which have a base diameter of $6\frac{1}{4}$ ft, rise to a height of $34\frac{1}{4}$ ft. Each column is formed of 10–12 drums of varying height and has 20 shallow flutings.

A peculiarity of all Greek buildings of the best period, specially remarkable in the Parthenon, is the use of optical refinements executed with great mathematical precision. These include varying the breadth of the intercolumniation throughout the building, thickening the corner columns, and grading the spacing of the triglyphs. Lines that appear horizontal are in fact curved, and lines that appear vertical are slightly inclined. If we stand at one corner and look along the upper step, we notice a perceptible rise in the centre giving to the whole pavement a convex character. The rise is less than 3 in. in 101 ft on the fronts, and $4\frac{5}{16}$ in. in 228 ft on the flanks: the latter giving a radius of curvature of c. $3\frac{1}{2}$ miles. The rising curve is imparted to the entablature. The axes of the columns lean inwards to the extent of nearly $2\frac{1}{2}$ in. in their height. The inclination can be detected by measuring the lowest drum of a corner-column, which will be found shorter on the inside than on the outside. The columns themselves have a convex entasis, or swelling, designed to correct the optical illusion by which straight tapered shafts appear concave.

The deep *Architrave* was adorned at a later date with gilded bronze shields, fourteen on the E. front and eight on the w., between which were inscribed in bronze letters the names of the dedicators; the shields may have been presented by Alexander the Great in 334 B.C. after the battle of the Granicus. An inscription on the E. front, relating to some honour conferred on the Emp. Nero by the Athenian people has been deciphered by means of the marks left by the nails. On the N. and S. sides were bronze nails or pegs for hanging festoons on days of festival. The *Frieze* above was decorated with triglyphs and metopes. The *Cornice* consisted of a slab overlapping the frieze, the projecting ledge of which supported the sculptures of the pediments. On its under side were mutules with guttæ. The upper part was surmounted by a beautiful cyma reversa. The apex of the pediment, 59 ft above the stylobate, was crowned with an immense anthemion, or leaf ornament as acroterion, of which a few fragments have been recovered. The wooden roof had tiles of Pentelic marble, from which the rain water ran off without any channel. At each of the four corners was a lion's head, purely ornamental since the mouth was not pierced, and the eaves were surmounted by palmette antefixes.

Details were brought into relief by polychrome decoration. Many mouldings retain traces of ornaments beautifully drawn; in some of the most protected parts the pigment itself remains. Strong colour seems to have been confined to the parts that were in shade. The intense whiteness of the columns, architraves, and broader surfaces was probably modified by some ochreous colour to such an extent only as to anticipate the rich golden hue produced by time on Pentelic marble. The channels of the triglyphs, or possibly the triglyphs themselves, were painted dark blue, as were also the six guttæ below them. The ceilings were adorned with deep blue panels and gilt stars.—In the British Museum is a coloured reconstruction of the N.W. corner of the Parthenon.

SCULPTURES. *Eastern Pediment.* We know from Pausanias (I, 24, 25) that the subject was the birth of Athena, but there is little left on the pediment, which was ruined when the Byzantine apse was built. Of the various fragments found, some are in the Acropolis Museum, more in the British Museum; a puteal in Madrid is believed to have been copied from the central group. (For recent discussion of the composition in detail, see A.J.A. 1967.)

The *Western Pediment* represented the contest of Athena and Poseidon for the possession of Attica. These sculptures, practically intact when Jacques Carrey made his drawings, were those destroyed by the clumsy avarice of Morosini.

The *Metopes* were originally 92 in number: 14 at either end and 32 on each side. Of these, 41 remain *in situ*, but with rare exceptions they are so battered as to be unintelligible. Their artistic value appears to have been very uneven. Fifteen are in the British Museum and one is in the Louvre. The remaining 35 are, with the exception of some fragments (in the Acropolis Museum, and in the Vatican Museum), entirely destroyed (the greater number in the explosion of 1687) and they are only imperfectly known from Carrey's drawings. The metopes in the British Museum and the Louvre are all from the s. side, and illustrate the contest of the Lapiths and Centaurs at the marriage feast of Peirithoös. Those of the E. front remain in position; they represent a Gigantomachia. The subject of the metopes of the w. front appears to be an Amazonomachia. All the metopes appear to have been deliberately chiselled off in the (?) 6–8C.

The **Interior** has been closed to visitors to protect the structure. Within the peripteral colonnade the ambulatory, 14 ft wide on the flanks and nearly 16 ft at the ends, is equipped with drainage channels. The ceiling was formed of coffered panels of marble, those at the ends supported by marble beams; four of these remain *in situ* at the w. end, where restoration is in progress.

The SEKOS, or temple proper, stands on a socle raised two steps above the stylobate. Unlike the usual Doric temple of three chambers, it was divided by a blank partition wall into two halls, each with a portico of six Doric columns. The ends of the walls forming the sides terminate in antæ facing the portico columns. The Pronaos, or E. portico, opened into the Cella, while the Opisthodomos, facing w., fronted the Parthenon proper. Frieze, see below.

The CELLA or *Hekatompedos Neos* is presumed to have inherited its alternative name from an earlier building; its interior measurements are somewhat less than 100 Attic feet. An inner colonnade, formed (like those at Aegina and Paestum) of two stories separated by an architrave and carried round three sides, supported beams for the roof and ceiling. Some of the circular marks left by the original column-bases are still visible, but the more obvious remains are from slenderer colums of Hellenistic date reused here after a fire. Bronze barriers between the 23 lower columns formed an ambulatory from which privileged visitors (among them Pausanias) could view the great chryselephantine *Statue of Athena Polias*, by Pheidias. Its site is clearly located by an oblong space where the marble floor is economically replaced by plain Piraeic stone; it was placed in position in 432 BC.

Literary references, combined with extant reproductions, provide an accurate account of the work. The statue was of gold plate over an inner wooden frame and stood, with the pedestal, 39 ft high. The face, hands, and feet were of ivory (Plato, Hippias Major). The pupils of the eyes were of precious stones. The goddess stood upright, clad in a dress that reached to her feet; on her breast was the head of Medusa wrought in ivory; in her right hand she held a crowned Victory about four cubits high, and in the other a spear. Her helmet was surmounted by a sphinx, with griffins in relief on either side, representing the winged beasts that fought with the one-eyed Arimaspi for gold (comp. Hdt. III, 116). On her sandals was wrought the battle of the Centaurs and Lapiths. At her feet stood a shield, on the outside of which was represented in relief the battle of the Amazons with the Athenians: in this scene Pheidias introduced figures of himself and Pericles that got him into trouble with pious Athenians (Plutarch, Pericles). On the inside was a representation of the Gigantomachia. Near the base of the spear was a serpent, perhaps Erichthonios. On the pedestal was wrought in relief the birth of Pandora. The dress and other ornaments, all of solid gold and weighing some 40 or 50 talents, were so contrived that the whole could be temporarily removed, in case of national emergency, without injuring the statue (Thuc. II, 13). The whole work was presumably designed to glow softly in semidarkness since the only natural illumination was through the open doorway. It became known (comp. p. 86) as the *Athena Parthenos*.

The w. wall was originally blank. Three doorways were made in it and all the interior columns were removed when the building was converted into a church. Beyond this wall lay the PARTHENON proper, a chamber of the same width as the cella but only 43 ft long, of which three walls still stand. Here four Ionic columns (traces on four square slabs larger than the rest) supported the roof.

Many archæologists have argued that Parthenon means the 'chamber of the maidens' (i.e. of the priestesses of Athena). This is borne out by a recent discovery at Brauron. If it means the 'chamber of the maiden' (Athena herself), the fact that her statue was not placed there needs explanation.

The *Opisthodomos* corresponded to the pronaos in all its details, save that the columns were c. 2 in. thicker; they are probably fashioned from drums cut for the Pre-Parthenon. There are conspicuous traces here on the columns and antæ of the grating which separated the opisthodomos from the ambulatory. A relic of the days when the Parthenon was a mosque is the base of the minaret, below the level of the marble pavement at the s.w. corner, where a rough staircase mounts to the pediment. Some interesting relics are still visible from the time when the opisthodomos served as cathedral narthex: on the left pillar, Byzantine Greek inscriptions; to the right of the doorway, fragmentary wall-paintings. Between the 2nd and 3rd pillars from the N. of the w. peristyle a chequer-board is incised in the pavement.

It is believed that the opisthodomos served as treasury of the Delian League in succession to *the* 'Opisthodomos', part of the Old Temple of Athena.

Right round the outer walls of the sekos, just below the cornice and 39 ft above the stylobate, ran a continuous Ionic **Frieze**. Although much of its sculptural detail was destroyed by the explosion in 1687 and about 45 ft are altogether unrecorded, yet the existing 176 ft in Athens, together with 247 ft in the British Museum, out of a total length of 523½ ft suffice with Carrey's drawings to give a tolerably adequate idea of the whole. Its uniform height is 3 ft 3½ in. and its relief nowhere exceeds 2¼ in. It has generally been taken to represent the procession of celebrants at the Great Panathenaic Festival, though an attempt has recently been made, by equating the number of figures with the number of dead at Marathon, to proclaim the frieze a record of a specific heroizing ceremony.

The *Greater Panathenaia*, traditionally founded by Erichthonios (see below) and renewed by Theseus, was refounded in the archonship of Hippokleides (566/565) and turned into a ceremony of the first rank by Peisistratos. It occurred on every fourth anniversary of the goddess's birthday, in the month of Hekatombaeon (August). Athletic, musical, and equestrian contests were held and the victors received Panathenaic prize amphorae filled with tax-free olive oil from the sacred olive trees. The main feature was the Procession, in which the new embroidered saffron peplos woven to drape an early wooden Xoanon of Athena Polias was borne in state through the streets of Athens on a ship on wheels. The ship was manned by priests and priestesses wearing golden crowns and garlands of flowers (see Philostratus, Vit. Soph. II 1, 7). The chief citizens of Athens, the envoys from the allied states, and even resident aliens had a fixed part to play in the ceremony. The citizens were on this occasion allowed to bear arms without exciting suspicion —at any rate in the time of Hippias (Thuc. VI, 56). The peplos may have been woven by, and was certainly carried (at some part of the procession) by the Arrephoroi, the maids in waiting on Athena. The route of the procession was from the Pompeion in the Kerameikos to the Eleusinion then past the Pelargikon to the Pythion, where the ship was moored. It is probable that the procession halted outside the Parthenon or its predecessor and that the victors in the Pana-thenaic games there received their prize amphorae. The proceedings ended with a sacrifice on the Great Altar and in the depositing of the robe (at any rate latterly) in the Erechtheion.

The entire WEST FRIEZE, with the exception of three figures, remains *in situ*, and in surprisingly good state: the Athenian knights are seen putting on their sandals and cloaks, bridling their horses, mounting, and moving off under the marshals. Viewed from outside the w. front of the building, it gives an excellent idea of the way in which the frieze was intended to be seen between the columns of the peristyle.

Somewhat less than one-third of the N. frieze and five slabs of the S. frieze are in the Acropolis Museum (see below). The remainder is in London, together with all the extant remains of the E. frieze (except for three slabs and sundry fragments in the Acropolis Museum, and eight slabs in the Louvre).

D. THE ERECHTHEION

Looking towards the Erechtheion from the N. colonnade of the Parthenon we see the foundations of a temple, published by Dörpfeld in 1886 and ever since its discovery "the subject of endless controversy as to its identity, its date, its relation to its neighbours, and how long it continued in use" (Ida Thallon Hill). It is now generally called the **Old Temple of Athena** and is believed by Dinsmoor to be of Peisistratid date (529 B.C. is suggested by astronomical calculations from its orientation). Two column bases (once attributed to the Mycenean megaron) are now ascribed to a Geometric predecessor. The temple is the only pre-Persian building in Athens of which complete foundations are extant; to it are ascribed Archaic sculptures (independently dated stylistically to c. 525 B.C.), now in the museum. The building, amphidistyle in antis with a peristyle of 12 columns by 6, was partially destroyed in the Persian sack and poros and marble remains of it were built into the N. wall and used as fill for later terraces. The rear part of it seems to have survived to be rebuilt as a treasury; it may have been the 'Opisthodomos' referred to in the Kallias Decree (439 or 434) and the 'Megaron facing w.' which Herodotus describes with smoke-blackened walls; it was dismantled (says Demosthenes) in 353 B.C.

The ***Erechtheion,** one of the most original specimens of Greek architecture, stands near the N. edge of the rock, about midway between the E. and W. ends. Designed to succeed the Old Temple as the joint shrine of Athena and Poseidon–Erechtheus, it was finished after 395 B.C.

and owes its curious plan to the sacrosanct nature of the associated sanctuaries that preceded it. Like the Parthenon, it became generally known by a name that originally applied only to one of its parts.

The **Legendary History** of the contest between Poseidon and Athena for possession of the Acropolis in the reign of Kekrops occurs in many ancient authors (comp. Hdt. VIII, 55; Apollodorus, Lib. III, xiv). Poseidon produced a 'sea' called Erechtheïs and Athena an olive-tree. Athena was judged the winner but was reconciled with Poseidon and henceforth they were worshipped together. Another myth tells of Erichthonios, born to Hephaistos and Earth, who was placed by his foster-mother Athena in a chest and committed to Pandrosos, daughter of Kekrops. Erichthonios, who had serpent attributes, grew up to expel Amphictyon and become king of Athens; to him is attributed the setting up of the xoanon to Athena and the institution of the Panathenaia. His grandson Erechtheus also became king of Athens. These myths and their dramatis personæ are indissolubly confused, but the sacred tokens (μαρτύρια) venerated in Classical times—Athena's olive-tree and the mark of Poseidon's trident—probably date at least from pre-Homeric times. At some time Poseidon and Erechtheus became identified with one another.

As historical fact we can say that the N. side of the Acropolis became the centre of a group of cults, based on the worship of Athena and Poseidon-Erechtheus, all with elements in common and stemming probably from late Helladic times, since they grew up round the Mycenean megaron. The tokens survived in Roman times and Dionysios of Halicarnassos locates the olive-tree in the *Pandroseion*. Pausanias speaks of Poseidon's well of sea-water within the Erechtheion. The *Kekropion*, or Tomb of Kekrops, was near by, and sacred snakes dwelt in the precinct. No archæological evidence has been found to suggest a combined temple earlier than the Erechtheion as we know it today.

History. The *Erechtheion* formed part of the programme of Pericles. The construction was delayed by the Peloponnesian War, but the evidence of inscription proves that it was nearly ready in 409 B.C. and probably complete a year later. It was damaged by fire in 406 (Xenophon, Hellenica, I, 6, I) and was not rebuilt till 395 or even later. Another fire caused damage in Augustan times, and the reconstruction incorporated some new features. The building was converted into a church about the 6C A.D., and the greater part of the interior destroyed in the successive alterations. The Turks, in 1463, turned it into a harem for the wives of the Commandant of the Acropolis. It suffered from the acquisitiveness of Lord Elgin in 1801 and was damaged during the various sieges of the War of Independence. In 1838 Pittakis cleared some of the wall of rubbish; in 1842–4 Paccard restored the Portico of the Caryatids. A violent storm on 26 Oct 1852 blew down the upper part of the W. façade with its engaged columns. In 1903–09 the exterior was virtually rebuilt by M. Balanos. In 1980 much of it was dismantled or covered in scaffolding.

Curiosities. The temple must have been profoundly interesting to visitors. In addition to the tokens (see above) and the ancient xoanon and its lamp (see below), here also were a wooden Hermes, said to be an offering of Kekrops, a folding chair made by Daedalus, and some Persian spoils from Plataea, including the corselet of Masistius (of gold links) and the sword of Mardonius.

The Erechtheion is unique not only in plan but also in elevation since the foundations of its S. and E. walls stand nearly 9 ft above those on the N. and W. No attempt was made to correct the various levels of the terrain on which it stands, and the exterior is manifestly that of a single building in spite of incorporating existing features at these differing levels. When seen from the E. it has the appearance of an Ionic prostyle temple with a hexastyle portico; behind the façade it is in fact a plain rectangle with a projecting porch on either flank.

The EASTERN PORTICO had six Ionic columns, on a stylobate of three marble steps, supporting a pediment without sculpture. Five columns with their architrave are standing; the sixth (at the N. corner) was carried off by Lord Elgin. They are 22 ft high, including bases and capitals, and 2½ ft in diameter at the base. The back wall of the portico, which had a central doorway and two windows, was pulled down to make way for the Byzantine apse. The s. anta survives, while that to the N., reconstructed in 1909, lacks the capital (in the British Museum).

The INTERIOR is a tangle of late substructures, which have destroyed even the foundations of the Classical building. The modern traveller can only stand at the porches and use his imagination.

The description of Pausanias is unusually ambiguous, and even after considering beddings in the rock together with the original building specifications and progress reports, which survive on marble, archæologists differ widely on their reconstruction of the classical interior. Previous views of the internal arrangement were challenged c. 1970 by John Travlos, but have been questioned in their turn. Some of the argument centres on the route of the profane dog (Philochoros, Fr. 146).

The EASTERN CELLA was at a higher level and separated by a cross-wall from the rest. It is not clear whether this or the WESTERN CELLA was the main cult chamber. In one of them were located three altars: of Poseidon-Erechtheus, of Hephaistos, and of the hero Boutes; also the thrones of their priests (the inscribed thrones of Boutes and Hephaistos are now outside). On the wall, says Pausanias, were portraits of the Boutad family from whom the priests of the cult were drawn. In the other cella was the highly venerated *Statue of Athena Polias*, in olive-wood. This was presumably removed to safety at Salamis in 480 B.C. and housed in a temporary building on the site after Plataea.

The goddess seems to have been represented as standing and armed (Aristophanes, 'Birds', 826–31). She held a round shield on which was the gorgon's head (Euripides, 'Electra', 1254–57). The sacred Peplos, renewed every four years at the Panathenaic Festival, was woven to adorn her shrine. The so-called Dresden statue of Athena is supposed to be a copy of this wooden image. In front of the statue burnt the golden lamp made by the ingenious Kallimachos with an asbestos wick that needed oil only once a year, and a brazen palm-tree to serve as chimney. The lamp was tended by elderly widows; during the siege of Athens by Sulla in 86 B.C. it was allowed by Aristion to go out (Plutarch, 'Sulla', 13).

An enlarged cistern, cut deep into the rock in medieval or Turkish times, has destroyed most of the evidence which might have allowed a positive identification beneath the ante-chamber of the Erechtheïs 'sea' (see above). The visible fragments of brick vault are medieval; the 'sea' or well was presumably covered with marble tiles and seen through a puteal. When the s. wind blew the well gave forth the sound of waves.

To reach the North Porch we descend a modern staircase, replacing an ancient flight. The court enclosed between the stair and the building was paved and probably served a ritual purpose. The **NORTH PORCH** formed a lateral pronaos to the Erechtheion proper, hence its Greek description (πρόστασις ἡ πρὸς τοῦ θυρώματος). Formed of an elegant Ionic colonnade of four columns in front and one at each side, with its architrave, its frieze in dark blue Eleusinian marble, its panelled ceiling, and its richly decorated N. door, this porch is one of the masterpieces of Attic art. The superstructure was restored from fragments that date from a Roman reconstruction. The porch protected the marks left perhaps by a thunderbolt, which are seen through a gap in the tiles as three holes in the rocky bottom of a crypt. A corresponding opening in the roof over this pit was purposely left on the analogy of leaving open to the sky places struck by lightning. By the gap stood the *Altar of the Thyechoös*, a priest important enough to have a place reserved in the theatre. He offered sacrifices of honey-cakes to Zeus Hypatos. An opening leads from the crypt into the basement of the temple. Here perhaps within the adyton surrounding the Tomb of Erechtheus dwelt the serpent guardian of the house (comp. Hdt. VIII, 41, and Plutarch, 'Themistocles' 10), for whom the honey-cakes served as food. The *North Doorway* is celebrated for the magnificent moulding of its Ionic decoration, though much of it consists of exact copies of Augustan date replacing the originals destroyed in a fire; the pierced centres of the rosettes are omitted. The inner linings are Byzantine additions.

From the N. porch, which projects several feet beyond the w. façade of the building, a smaller opening leads down two steps into an outer court of the temple, no longer enclosed. This was the **Pandroseion,** or *Temenos of Pandrosos*, a precinct of uncertain boundaries containing a small temple. Here grew the *Sacred Olive of Athena*. Herodotus tells how it sprouted again after being burnt down by the Persians; the existing tree was planted on 22 February 1917, on Washington's birthday, by Bert Hodge Hill, near a fine ancient copper water-pipe which he excavated, and which he conjectured had been installed to supply water to something of especial importance. More to the s. was a further precinct, the **Kekropion.** The foundations of the Erechtheion were modified at the s.w. corner to avoid disturbing an earlier structure, the presumed *Tomb of Kekrops*, which was spanned by a single huge block, c. 15 ft long and 5 ft deep.

Above rises the WEST FAÇADE of the temple, restored in 1904 (after being blown down in 1852) to the form it acquired in the 1C B.C. It consists of a high basement, upon which were set engaged columns joined by a low solid wall with a parapet. The upper part of the intercolumniation was closed with wooden grilles, except above the Kekropion where it was left open, presumably for some important cult purpose. The original column-bases remain but everything above was renewed after the fire in Roman times to the existing design with three windows; even then, however, the s. opening was left open. The s. block of the entablature is a copy; the original, removed in 1805, has been recovered defaced by Turkish inscriptions. It lies on the ground in front of the w. façade.

The SOUTHERN PORTICO, or *Porch of the Caryatids*, consists of a solid marble wall, rising 6 ft above the peristyle of the Old Temple on which it is founded, surmounted by six statues of maidens (*korai*), rather over life-size, popularly known as Caryatids. The figures stand four in front and two behind, their long Ionic tunics draped like column flutings about their outer legs, on which their weight is thrown. They support an entablature which has capitals of a special decorative form and no frieze. At the close of the War of Independence only three of the caryatids remained in place, all much damaged; the second figure from the w., removed by Lord Elgin, was later replaced by a cast. All surviving originals have been removed to the museum and the porch will be rebuilt with casts having a titanium core. The porch was entered through the E. wall of the podium by narrow steps which seem unlikely to have served the needs of the public. The floor has disappeared, but the flat coffered ceiling is nearly entire. A portal gave access by an awkward descending L-shaped stair to the w. cella.

The idea of using statues in lieu of columns seems to have been borrowed from the Treasuries of the Knidians and Siphnians at Delphi. Vitruvius states that the sculptors took as models the girls of Karyai, in Laconia: whence the name Caryatids. Prof. Dinsmoor suggests that here the figures represent the Arre-phoroi, bearing Athena's burdens on their heads.

The temple was given structural unity by its balancing pediments and by the emphatic nature of the *Frieze*, which, save where the roof of the N. portico interrupted it, extended right round the building above the architrave. Unique in design, it consisted of coarse-grained Pentelic marble figures, cut in high relief and attached by bronze clamps to a ground of dark Eleusinian stone. Two large blocks of the background are still *in situ* above the columns of the E. front; part of the frieze above

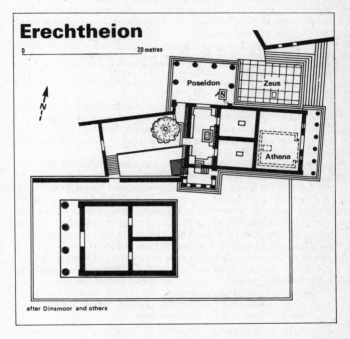

Erechtheion

0   20 metres

Poseidon   Zeus

Athena

after Dinsmoor and others

the N. porch also remains. The holes for fitting the sculptured figures are plainly visible. Of these only 112 small fragments have been re-covered, mostly in bad condition; they are in the Acropolis Museum. The theme of the work is not known.

It must be remembered that here, as in the Parthenon, to the beauty of form was added the attraction of colour. The capitals of the columns were enriched with gilt bronze ornaments, and inlaid with coloured glass 'gems'. The panelled ceilings of the porticoes were painted blue and had gilt bronze stars.

E. THE ACROPOLIS MUSEUM

The *Acropolis Museum, founded in 1878 and reconstructed since the Second World War, was reopened in sections in 1956–61. It occupies the S.E. corner of the Acropolis and is sunk below the surface level of the rock in order not to interfere with the skyline. Started as the repository of finds collected haphazard on the citadel, it was greatly enriched by the systematic excavations of Kavvadias in 1885–90, when the whole of the rock was laid bare. With the exception of the bronzes and the vases (now in the National Museum), it contains all the portable objects discovered since 1834 on the Acropolis. As an education in the development of Attic sculpture, the collection is unique. The arrangement is roughly chronological.

ADMISSION weekdays 9–3.30 or 5, 50 dr.; Sun & hol. 10–2 or 4.30, free; closed Tues. Small charge for photography; cameras must otherwise be left in the vestibule. Concise Guide in English (1965). Students are referred to the 'Catalogue of the Acropolis Museum', 2 vols. (Cambridge), Vol. I (1912) by Guy Dickins, Vol. II (1912) by Stanley Casson, and to 'Archaic Marble Sculpture from the Acropolis' (1939) by Humfry Payne and G. M. Young.

VESTIBULE. 1347. Colossal marble owl; 1338. Panel of a pedestal dedicated by Atarbos to commemorate a victory with his chorus in a Pyrrhic dance, which the youths are executing (late 4C); 1326. Quadrilateral base, with relief of an apobates (a soldier who leaps on and off a chariot at full speed); 2281. Male head.

We turn left. The first three rooms contain **Pedimental Sculpture,** in poros limestone or in imported island marble, from destroyed 6C buildings on the Acropolis. Much shows traces of the bright paint then favoured for accentuating the design and movement of the figures. ROOM I. 552, 554. Fragments of a leopard, in Hymettian marble, perhaps from the metopes of the Hekatompedon; 4572 is notable for its painting; 1. Pediment of a small building (c. 570 B.C.; the oldest known relief from the Acropolis); it shows Herakles and the Hydra, with Iolaos driving his car; on the left is the crab sent by Hera to hamper the hero. 4. Lioness rending a small bull, one of the earliest groups; flanked by serpents (comp. below), it may have formed part of the centre of the w. pediment of the Hekatompedon. 122. Lion's head in Hymettian marble; 701. Archaic head of a running Gorgon, perhaps the acroterion above the E. pediment of the Hekatompedon.

ROOM II. In the doorway, 56. Owl; 41. Serpent's head. Within, 36, 35. Left and right portions of a pediment: l. Herakles and Triton (the head came to light in 1938); r. Typhon, a blue-bearded monster with three human heads and bodies ending in a serpent's tail (traces of vivid colouring). It has been suggested that the lions in the next room should be restored between these two to form the E. pediment of the Hekatompedon. 2, 37, 40. Serpents from a pediment (comp. above). 9. Right half of an early pediment representing the Introduction of Herakles to Olympos; Iris presents him to Zeus who has Hera or Athena beside him. 624. *Moschophoros, a man bearing a calf on his shoulders, in Hymettian marble (c. 570 B.C.), one of the earliest examples of native art in marble, still employing techniques suitable to working in limestone; an inscription on the base bears the name Rhombos. Triglyphs and cornice fragments. In a glass case, terracotta figurines found s. of the

Acropolis in 1955–59. 52. The 'Olive-tree' Pediment, with its remarkable representation of a building: the masonry, roof-tiles, and other architectural details are lovingly rendered. On the left a single olive-tree stands within a walled precinct. Although the figures allow various interpretations, the temptation to recognize Athena's token, the Acropolis olive-tree, is hard to resist. 593. Kore, wearing chiton and Doric peplos (mid-6C); this is one of the earliest of these figures (see below). 575. Small quadriga (fragmentary) in Hymettian marble.

Room III. 3. Part of a colossal group of two lions attacking a bull, a remarkable 6C work which may have been the centre-piece of the E. end of the Hekatompedon (comp. above).

Here also are two primitive korai (677, 619) executed in Naxian marble in the shape of the xoanon; one very stiff, once thought to be of Samian workmanship; the other headless. 618. Lower part of an enthroned female figure (note the modelling of the feet); 620, another, clumsily executed.

In Room IV are displayed the majority of the **Korai**, or maidens, perhaps the chief treasure (because unique as a group) of the museum. These female statues were dedicated as votive offerings to Athena in the course of the 6C B.C. in the precinct of one of her temples. Ruined in the sack of 480 and later scrupulously buried, they were discovered during excavations in 1882–86 mainly to the E. of the Parthenon or N.W. of the Erechtheion. All the statues are clothed and painted, and each kore held an offering in one hand. Under the Peisistratids the Doric dress gradually gave way to the Ionic; we see in the statues the simple symmetry and contour of the woollen Doric peplos and chiton being replaced by the linen Ionic chiton worn with the himation. The new chiton, both thinner and more voluminous, posed new problems in modelling the body, the contour of which was more emphasized in some places by the thinner nature of the material and more covered in others by the increased drapery. The manner of wearing the himation gave a marked diagonal emphasis of line. Parallel to the sartorial changes we notice the developing naturalism of the features, including the losing of the archaic 'smile'. This development was once taken as the ascendency of 'Attic' art over Ionic or island styles; but it seems likely to have been a development common to sculpture in general, more characteristic of a period than of a region. The korai are arranged with other works of their period, but the exact chronology of this period of Attic art and the importance of outside influences ('Ionic' or 'Samian') on it are still the subject of scholarly controversy.

The room divides into three sections. In the first: 1340. Head of a horse in Pentelic marble (? from a 5C votive relief); 581. Worshippers bringing a sacrificial sow to Athena. Grouped together are four works assigned to the same artist, probably called *Phaidimos*: 679. The Peplos Kore (c. 530 B.C.), so called from the girded Dorian peplos she wears over her chiton; it is famous alike for the facial expression and the preservation of the ancient colour. *590. Horseman (c. 560 B.C.); the head is a good cast of the 'Rampin Head' in the Louvre first recognized by Humfry Payne in 1936 as belonging to this figure. This and the second statue (700 below) may be a memorial to Hippias and Hipparchos, the horse-racing sons of Peisistratos. *143. Hound. 69. Lion head, a spout from a cornice. 606. Horseman in Persian or Scythian dress, dedicated by someone with N. interests (? Miltiades), c. 520 B.C.

702. Relief of Hermes, the three Graces, and a boy; 1343. Fragmentary relief of a bearded man, wearing the exomis (singlet); 669. Kore; the hair, the set of the eyes, and the modelling of the ears recall mid-6C styles, but the drapery shows important innovations; this is thought to be the earliest example of the chiton and himation pattern which became standard (? c. 540).

In the second section: 700. Equestrian statue carved in one piece (pre-Persian); of the rider nothing survives above the hips. 665. Kouros (mid-6C), damaged by fire; the muscles are modelled with greater accuracy than usual at this period. 145. Small torso of a warrior, also marked by fire. 594. Kore (headless) of Ionian workmanship; an epiblema (shawl) is thrown over the himation and colours are freely used. 694. Nike, c. 480 B.C. 672. Kore with himation draped unusually on the left shoulder. 675. Kore, preserved with much original colour, having the high forehead and features characteristic of Chiot art; 678. Kore of developed expression but wearing an Ionic himation incorrectly rendered (c. 530 B.C.); 673. Kore, probably by a Chiot artist; 190. Lamp in island marble decorated with four human and four animal heads.

The third part of the room is grouped about a fine selection of korai of the last quarter of the 6C B.C. 682. The hair and dress afford a striking example of late-Peisistratid elaboration (c. 525); the figure is still heavy and stiff. 1342. Chariot relief (comp. 1343, above). Korai: 684. The face is intellectual, the eyes straight, the mouth firm; 674. Shoulders finely modelled; although the head is too large, the face is most delicately rendered (near the end of the 6C); 670. Clad in simple chiton, with features showing a considerable advance in naturalism. 625. Seated Athena (headless), found at the N. foot of the Acropolis, conjecturally identified with that by *Endoios*, seen by Pausanias. The goddess wears the Ionic chiton and appears, from the position of the right foot, to have just sat down—an early example of such mobility. The ægis on her breast was coloured. Korai: 633, 685, and 595 all repay attention; *671. A severe beauty; 696. The 'Polos' kore; note the garment and the simplicity of the hair.

ROOM V. Pedimental figures of the Gigantomachia from the Old Temple of Athena (c. 525 B.C.). These are particularly striking from behind, though presumably never designed to be so seen: 631. Athena, attacking with lance, and aegis snake, newly restored; two terminal kneeling giants. Here also are *681. 'Kore of Antenor', the largest of the Korai, with unusual vertical emphasis of the drapery, and (l.) a base which may or may not belong to it; the base bears the dedication of Nearchos, the donor, and of the sculptor *Antenor* (both Attic work in island marble c. 525 B.C.). 1360. Kore, damaged by fire, but beautiful and elegant.

At the entrance to the alcove, 683 (l.), a curious Kore, disproportionate and heavy; 597 (r.). Youth riding a hippalektryon. 6476 A & B, two terracotta Korai. In the alcove, seven cases of choice pottery and terracottas, mostly from excavations of 1955–59 in the Sanctuary of the Nymphe (p. 73), and archaic *Marble fragments from the Acropolis. Particularly interesting, in addition, are the original cedarwood blocks from the centre holes of column drums.

ROOM VI is devoted to works of the 'severe' style, a stage in the emergence of the Classical style from the Archaic. Most characteristic is *698. The Kritian Boy (c. 480 B.C.); the weight is at last correctly posed and the body liberated from archaic stiffness; the confident modelling and bodily proportions of the early classical style is already felt; it is now proven beyond doubt that head and body belong together. 695. Relief, 'Mourning Athena'; *689. Head of a Kouros, delicately modelled; 697. Forequarters of a horse, in a more developed style than No. 700 (above); 692. Torso of a young boy; 699. Male head (Pheidian school?); 599. Male torso; 688. Kǫre; *686, 609. Kore of Euthydikos (the dedicator) in a fully developed style marking the end of the Archaic period; 302. Torso; 67. Pinax with painting of a warrior running; 690. Nike.

In ROOM VII are arranged the mutilated fragments from the **Parthenon Pediments**: their probable relative positions can be seen from the plaster models constructed in 1896–1904 from the then available evidence: Pausanias' description, the Madrid 'puteal', Carrey's drawings, portions in the British Museum, etc. The composition of the w. pediment is tolerably certain; that of the E. end considerably less so, since the central 40 ft was destroyed in the Christian alterations; most of the figures still extant in Carrey's day are in London (comp. the 'Blue Guide to London').—WEST PEDIMENT. The subject is the contest of Athena and Poseidon. 882. Head of a horse from Athena's team; 1081. Head from Poseidon's team, with hoofs, etc.; 885. Part of torso of Poseidon fitted to a cast of another piece in London; 1735. Seated goddess; 888. Oreithyia (?); 887. Torso and leg from the statue of Ilissos.—EAST PEDIMENT. The birth of Athena. 1202. Two fragments of Hera's robe.

Also in this room are 705. Metope, Centaur carrying off a Lapith woman; 727, 720. Centaurs' heads, from the S. metopes of the Parthenon; 1309. Head of a young girl.

In ROOM VIII, admirably lit and mounted at eye level, is all the detached part of the ****Parthenon Frieze** that remains in Athens. Many of the slabs were blown clear in the explosion and buried, thus escaping Lord Elgin. The slabs have been arranged in correct order; their original positions are indicated on a wall diagram. The subject is the Panathenaic procession.

Since the frieze is displayed on an inside instead of an outside wall for which it was designed the relative positions are reversed: the sculptures from the N. side of the Parthenon are on the S. wall and vice versa. They lead up to the three remaining slabs of the East Frieze on the E. wall. West frieze (*in situ*), see above.

We start at the w. door of the room and proceed along the long S. wall. Here are 13 slabs out of the 42 which composed the *North Frieze*. The beginning of the procession on this side (corner slab and the following 12 pieces) is all in London. *862, 861, 863 (adjoining slabs) portray horses and riders, very spirited; one is turning and apparently being exhorted by a marshal to close up. The next three (872, 859, gap, 781) form a group from the chariot procession (just over half-way along the cella); one chariot has an apobates (comp. p. 96); an official directs. 874. Youth leading horses. Two adjoining slabs (865, 876) depict thallophoroi (bearers of olive branches), and another (875), from farther along, lyre-players. The remaining three slabs are from the head of the procession (alternate slabs are missing): *864. Four epheboi carrying hydriai; the expressions and drapery are exquisite; 860. Four men with rams; 857. Youths leading sacrificial heifers.—The *South Frieze* fragments, five in number, begin opposite by the anta on the N. wall. 866–69. Four slabs from near the w. end, depicting horses and riders; 873. Magistrates and two women. On the adjacent wall to the left of the door follow three slabs (797, 877, *856) from the right side of the *East Frieze* of the Parthenon: nearly all the remaining slabs, which show the ceremony of the peplos, are in London. The third, well-preserved, shows three of the twelve gods attending the Theoxenia, probably Poseidon, Apollo, and Artemis.

In the s.w. corner of the room are displayed the surviving thirteen slabs of the parapet that extended round three sides of the Temple of Athena Nike. This parapet was executed in high relief by a number of artists between 421 and 407 B.C.; the scenes represent winged *VICTORIES at their various tasks, among them the well-known Victory adjusting her sandal.—On the upper part of the central anta are placed fragments of the ERECHTHEION FRIEZE. The marble statues, attached to a background of blue Eleusinian marble, were commissioned at 60 drachmas apiece from a number of sculptors, whose names are known from the building records of 408 B.C. 1075. Presentation of Erichthonios.

In ROOM IX have been placed the surviving Caryatids from the Erechtheion porch; these will be seen through a transparent screen behind which they will have a sterile atmosphere. Also here (but possibly to be moved) are later sculptures, mostly fragmentary. 1339. 'Lenormant' relief of a trireme (c. 400 B.C.), with two finials and a colossal head; 1331. Youthful head (4C), possibly Alexander the Great; 1358. Statue of a woman and child (late 5C; much mutilated), perhaps the Prokne and Itys mentioned by Pausanias as being dedicated by Alkamenes; 1345. Pan and a nymph, found in a cave at the N.W. end of the Acropolis; 1330. Relief (4C) inscribed with a decree appointing a proxenos (consul) for Abydos; 1329. Crowning a victorious athlete; 1348. Votice relief (after 403 B.C.). 1349. Stele with horse in low relief, bearing an inscription dated 372 B.C.; the Alketas mentioned may have been a nephew of Dionysios of Syracuse. 1333. Relief of Athena receiving Hera, symbolizing Samos, with the text of a treaty between Athens and Samos (405 B.C.), defaced under the Thirty Tyrants, and re-engraved two years later when Samos also had meanwhile suffered a change of government.

3 THE AREOPAGUS, MOUSEION, PNYX, AND HILL OF THE NYMPHS

The WEST SLOPE OF THE ACROPOLIS, now covered by ornamental groves, has never been systematically explored, though Dörpfeld unearthed a street and part of the quarter flanking it (see below) in the valley to the w. where Leoforos Apostolou Pavlou now runs. This he took to be the Panathenaic Way; but the agora excavations (Rte 5) have conclusively proved that the processional approach from the Agora to the Acropolis passed to the E. of the Areopagus. The saddle that links the Areopagus spur to the Acropolis, where now extends the car park, may have been the site of the earliest agora of the Archaic period.

A flight of rock-hewn steps mounts to the **Areopagus** (6, *5*; 377 ft), the low hill that gave name to a council of nobles which became at once the senate and the supreme judicial court; with the rise of democracy, it gradually lost its powers.

History. The name, commonly derived (comp. Euripides, 'Elektra', 1258) from the tradition that Ares was tried here by the other Gods for the murder of Halirrhothios, more likely signifies the Hill of Curses (arai). Here Aeschylus placed the camp of the Amazons ('Eumenides', 681–706). The Persians encamped on the hill when they besieged the Acropolis in 480 B.C. (Hdt. VIII, 52). The 7C council of elders, composed entirely of the Eupatridai became known as the *Council of the Areopagus* (ἡ Βουλὴ ἡ ἐξ 'Αρείου πάγου) to distinguish it from later councils. Its original and most important function was the conduct of criminal justice, particularly in cases of murder and manslaughter; but in the aristocratic days it became the governing body of the state. The archons were ex-officio members, or, according to Plutarch (Pericles), became members on quitting office. The Assembly of the people was at this time merely the recording machine for the decisions of the Areopagus. Solon transferred its powers of administration and legislation to the Assembly; but he made the Areopagus the protector of the constitution and the guardian of the laws, with control over the magistrates and the censorship of morals. The institution (c. 488 B.C.) of ostracism deprived it of its guardianship of the constitution. Under Ephialtes (c. 466 B.C.) censorship and control over the magistrates were transferred to the people, and the jurisdiction of the Areopagus limited once again to cases of homicide. Aeschylus, in the Eumenides, 458 B.C., described the trial of Orestes on the Areopagus for the murder of his mother Klytemnestra, and the institution of the Court of the Areopagus—the implication being that this was its proper function and that the restriction of its powers thereto was strictly correct.

In the 4C B.C. the Areopagus dealt also with crimes of treason and corruption, notable cases being the trials of the deserters after Chaeronea in 338, of Demosthenes in 324, and of the courtesan Phryne. It was in existence during the Empire. In A.D. 51 St Paul (Acts xvii, 22–34) delivered "in the midst of Mars' Hill" the sermon on the Unknown God, which converted the senator Dionysius (St Dionysius the Areopagite, patron saint of Athens).

On the artificially levelled summit of the hill are remains of beddings in the rock for the walls of a small edifice, probably connected with the formalities of the tribunal. Bp. Wordsworth started the tradition that these were rock-hewn seats. "The unwrought stones," says Pausanias (I, 28, 5) "on which the accused and accusers stand are named respectively the Stone of Injury (ὕβρις) and the Stone of Ruthlessness" (ἀναιδεία; comp. Euripides, 'Iphigenia in Tauris', 961).

Looking down from the summit we trace the ruins of the 16C church of *St Dionysius the Areopagite* (see above), which stood (as did its predecessors) on a level platform beneath the N. side of the hill. This is believed by Prof. E. Vanderpool to be the site of the court's sessions. Lower down the N.E. slope four ruined *Mycenean Chamber-tombs* (explored in 1939 and 1947; see Agora Mus.) yielded gold rosettes, ivory toilet boxes, swords, etc., suggesting royal burials of the second quarter of the 14C B.C. The N.W. slope has yielded many traces of early occupation, including the foundations of a *Geometric House*, elliptical in plan, recalling the terracotta models from Perachora. The discovery here of a 7C polychrome votive plaque portraying a Chthonic goddess flanked by snakes perhaps locates a *Sanctuary of the Semnai* in a near-by cleft. This accords with tradition, which places the **Cave of the Furies** beneath the N.E. brow of the hill. A spring here was locally credited with medicinal virtues in recent times. Like the Theseion, the precinct of the cave was a recognized sanctuary for murderers and fugitive slaves. Kylon's fellow-conspirators were killed within it in abuse of the right of sanctuary. Persons acquitted by the court of the Areopagus were wont to sacrifice at the cave. Within the enclosure stood

Ancient Athens
(Centre)

0   100 metres

Hadrian's Library

Stoa of Attalos

Agora

'Theseion'

N

Acropolis

Wall of Valerian

THEORIAS

Areopagus

Dörpfeld's
excavations

LEOF: APOSTOLOU PAVLOU

after J. Travlos, with permission of the American School of Classical Studies, Athens.

the Tomb of Oedipus, the possession of which was long regarded as essential to the safety of Athens. The closing scene of the 'Eumenides' of Aeschylus is placed in the cave.

The Areopagus also affords the most illuminating general view of the Agora, and is perhaps the best place from which to appreciate its topographical relationship with the Kerameikos and the Acropolis. A path descends the E. side of the Areopagus past the Cave of the Furies (see above) to join the road bordering the s. gate of the Agora excavations.

From the Areopagus we descend the Acropolis approach road to Leoforos Dionissiou Areopayitou. To the s.w., by the Dionysos Restaurant, paths mount the tree-clad slopes of the **Mouseion** (484 ft), a hill which throughout history has played a strategic role in the fortunes of Athens. A Greco-Roman tradition derives its name from Musæus, the poet-disciple of Orpheus; it was more likely the *Hill of the Muses* who, in their character of Oreades, may have had a shrine here.

The Themistoclean Wall climbed its gentle E. slope, followed the top of its sheer s. face (visible traces), and joined the Southern Long Wall near its w. extremity. The later Diateichisma (see below) ran N.W. from the summit. In 294 B.C. Demetrios Poliorketes built a fort to command the Piraeus road; it changed hands four times in the ensuing struggles. From the hill Morosini bombarded the Acropolis in 1687. At the end of Nov 1916, Greek royalist forces occupied the ground here, and on 1 Dec fired on Allied troops. It was again a scene of activity during the coup of 21 April 1967.

On the summit stands the **Monument of Philopappos,** built in A.D 114–116 by the Athenians in honour of C. Julius Antiochus Philopappus, a prince of Commagene (N. Syria), who had a distinguished career both as an Athenian citizen and as a Roman consul and prætor. The monument, of Pentelic marble, consisted of a rectangular tomb with a slightly concave façade 40 ft high. Intact in 1436 when Cyriacus of Ancona saw it, it later became ruinous. The *Façade*, which faces the Acropolis, is decorated with a frieze showing Philopappus as consul (A.D. 109) driving in his chariot. Above are four Corinthian pilasters which frame three niches. The central niche contains the statue of Philopappus as an Athenian citizen of the Deme of Besa; the left one his grandfather Antiochus IV Epiphanes, last king of Commagene (dethroned by Vespasian); the right one, according to Cyriacus of Ancona, held the statue of Seleukos I Nikator, the Macedonian founder of the dynasty. On the left central pilaster is inscribed in Latin the deceased's cursus honorum at Rome; on the right, in Greek, were his princely titles.—The tomb, traces of which are visible, lay behind the façade.

The *View from the monument, especially at sunset (often windy), is particularly fine, embracing the Parthenon, Hymettus, the Attic Plain with its encircling mountains, and the Saronic Gulf.

A paved path descending directly towards the Observatory (a little w. of N.) along the ridge of the hill follows the **Diateichisma,** the lower courses of which are visible for most of the way. Built to shorten the city's fortifications after the slighting of the Long Walls had made Themistocles' original line untenable, this cross wall was formerly attributed to Kleon on the evidence of Aristophanes ('Knights', 817–8), but is now securely dated on evidence from excavation to the end of the 4C B.C. To it was joined the *Fort of Poliorketes* (comp. above), of which the remains of a tower 33 ft square, can be seen c. 75 yds N. of the Philopappus monument; the foundations of another may be traced at a lower level to the N.E.

The region enclosed by the two diateichismata formed the ancient quarters of *Koile* and *Melite*. It is occupied by a very large number of **Ancient Dwellings**, once thought to represent the region of the Pelasgic *Kranaa*; but archæological evidence does not support any great antiquity. They belong for the most part to the 5C B.C. This quarter, then entirely within the city walls, became over-populated at the time of the Peloponnesian War, when the Athenians flocked from the country into the city (Thuc. II, 14); but it was deserted before the end of the 3C B.C. In the Roman era these old dwellings and cisterns were used as tombs. They lie thick on the ground on both flanks of the hills. The ruins include rooms, niches, terraces, flights of steps, and cisterns. Often two or three walls of the buildings were formed by excavation in the rock. Nearly sixty cisterns, large pear-shaped excavations, may be observed; they vary in depth from 13 to 20 ft. Seven rock-hewn seats, in an elevated spot c. 150 yds W. of the wall, may possibly represent an ancient court of justice. In the bottom of the valley are extensive traces (cart-ruts) of an ancient road that led s.w. from the Ayios Dhimitrios gate (see below).

The path follows the wall down to the modern drive that serves the Philopappos Theatre on the s.w. flank of Mouseion hill. Here on the foundations of the N. tower of the '*Dipylon above the Gates*' (s. tower excavated in 1936 and filled in again) stands the little chapel of *Ayios Dhimitrios* (Rfmts at adjacent Pavilion) with Byzantine paintings. The gate, wrongly identified from a late 4C inscription, is not a dipylon. The so-called *Tomb of Kimon*, which served in later times as the tomb of a certain Zosimianos, is really a rock-dwelling of the 5C B.C. In the cliff-face, a little to the s., is the equally misnamed PRISON OF SOCRATES, another such dwelling having no proven connection whatever with the philosopher. It consists of three rooms, one with a sloping ceiling, and a bottle-shaped cistern once independent of the rest.

Above Ayios Dhimitrios rises the *Hill of the Pnyx* (358 ft), in Classical times popularly called 'The Rocks' (αἱ Πέτραι). On its N.E. slope, 30 yds from the top, is the site of the **Pnyx**, the meeting-place of the Assembly, or Ecclesia (Ἐκκλησία), firmly identified by the discovery in the 19C of its boundary stone (inscribed ΟΡΟΣ ΠΥΚΝΟΣ) and scientifically investigated by Kourouniotes and Homer Thompson between 1930 and 1936. With the establishment of democracy under Kleisthenes the Assembly changed its venue from the Agora to the Pnyx, where its deliberations could not be overlooked; they were thus held, significantly perhaps, above instead of below the Areopagus. Here the great statesmen of the 5C and early 4C, among them Aristides, Themistocles, Pericles and Demosthenes, held their audience.

The word *Pnyx* (ἡ Πνύξ, gen. Πυκνός) means the place where people were tightly packed (πυκνός, compact, dense, crowded). The 'tight-packing' must have had special reference to the single entrance, as there was room inside for four or five times the number of legislators. The Assembly was presided over by the Prytaneis (see the Agora). The citizens, 5000 of whom were needed to form a quorum, were hustled towards the Pnyx by Scythian archers who held across the Agora and neighbouring streets cords daubed with wet red paint in order to hurry up the laggards, and prevent any citizen from 'cutting' a meeting. There was only one entrance. Here the arrivals were scrutinized so that no unauthorized person should slip in. No person not a citizen was allowed to attend without special authority. Citizens marked with the red paint forfeited their allowance.

Three periods of construction have been confirmed. In the first, c. 500 B.C., the seating faced N. and the bema s. towards the sea, a natural adaptation of the configuration of the ground. Under the Thirty Tyrants (403 B.C.) the arrange-

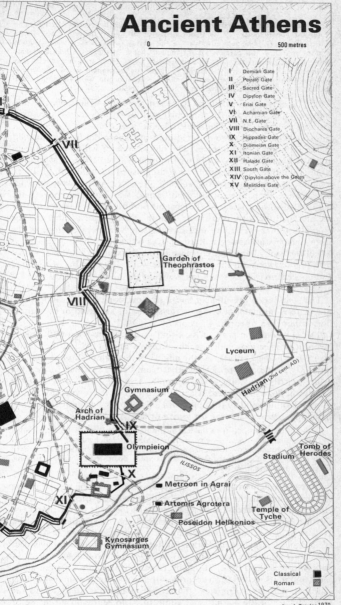

Ancient Athens

0 _____ 500 metres

I	Demian Gate
II	Peiraic Gate
III	Sacred Gate
IV	Dipylon Gate
V	Eriai Gate
VI	Acharnian Gate
VII	N.E. Gate
VIII	Diochares Gate
IX	Hippades Gate
X	Diomeian Gate
XI	Itonian Gate
XII	Halade Gate
XIII	South Gate
XIV	Dipylon above the Gates
XV	Melitides Gate

Garden of Theophrastos

VIII

Lyceum

Hadrian (2nd cent. AD)

Gymnasium

Arch of Hadrian

IX

Olympieion

ILISSOS

Stadium

Tomb of Herodes

X

Metroon in Agrai

Artemis Agrotera

Poseidon Helikonios

Temple of Tyche

XI

Kynosarges Gymnasium

Classical

Roman

after J. Travlos 1970

ments were reversed so that the bema faced to landward because, according to Plutarch ('Themistocles', 19, 4), they thought oligarchy less distasteful to farmers than to mariners. The retaining wall of this period, uncovered in 1930–31, was of poor masonry and carelessly constructed. Most of the extant remains date from the last period; this was first thought to be of Hadrianic date but is now attributed to a comprehensive plan of Lycurgus for the embellishment of the site. The buildings planned to accompany the new auditorium were left unfinished and the Assembly seems to have migrated to the Theatre of Dionysos.

The Pnyx is a huge artificial terrace in the form of a semicircle, the ends of which joined a perpendicular wall of rock, a man-made scarp forming the base-line. The semicircle, 217 yds round, is formed by a colossal *Retaining Wall*, 6 ft thick, built of trapezoidal blocks quarried in the fashioning of the scarp. The blocks, one of which is 13 ft long and 6 ft high, are remarkably well jointed without the use of mortar. About one-third of the wall, now diminished to a height of 15 ft, remains, at the central part of the arc. Its object was to keep in place the gigantic embankment of earth which was built to convert the natural downward slope of the ground into an upward slope, so that the area had the form of a crude theatre. The ravages of time and the mutilation of the retaining wall have restored the natural slope of the earth, which still, however, lies in places 6 ft above the top of what is left of the wall. The single entrance to the Pnyx of the third period was by a flight of steps on the N. side of the wall. The remains of a second and concentric wall exist ten yards within the outer wall below present ground level; this belongs to the second period.

The *Auditorium* presumably had a shallow slope like a scallop-shell, but there is no material evidence for seating of any kind or even for a floor other than of earth.

The perpendicular wall of rock that forms a base-line of 130 yds is hewn in two sections which make an obtuse angle (158°) at the centre, where it is highest (15 ft). At the angle is a three-stepped platform, 3 ft high, 31 ft wide, and projecting 21 ft from the wall, which formed the *Bema* or tribune, from which the orators spoke. The sockets of the balustrade that surrounded it are still visible. It is crowned by a cube of rock 6 ft high and 10 ft square with a flight of five steps at either side. Round its base was a ledge for votive or legislative tablets.

In the wall of rock, 40 ft to the left of the Bema, is a large niche, surrounded by over 50 smaller ones. Twelve marble tablets, found by Lord Aberdeen in 1803 in the ground below them, are now in the British Museum, and others have been recovered since. Most of them are ex-votos dedicated by women to Zeus Hypsistos and date from Roman times.

Above the Bema is a broad terrace levelled from the rock. In the centre, in line with the tribune, is a bedding probably for a monumental *Altar*, flanked by rock-cut benches, perhaps the seats of the prytaneis. Farther back another bedding in the rock may mark the site of the *Heliotropion*, or sundial, erected by the astronomer Meton in 433 B.C. At a higher level are beddings for foundations of two large stoas. The *West Stoa* measures 162 yds by 19½, and would have had 54 columns. The *East Stoa*, 71 yds by 18, was begun on a different aline-ment and in its second form accords with the placing of a smaller central building, perhaps a *Propylon*. These three structures are dated to the third quarter of the 4C B.C. and conjectured to represent a scheme of Lycurgus, c. 330–326 B.C., for the comfort of the Assembly.

They had hardly risen beyond their lowest foundations when a decision was taken to carry the Diateichisma (see above) through the site. The wall did not survive long at this point, being replaced by a parallel wall of white poros with towers, traces of which can be seen to the s. and w. This probably strengthened a weak point in the circuit at the time the Long Walls and the outer diateichisma were finally abandoned as a defensive line (c. 200 B.C.).

To the N. of the Pnyx rises the so-called **Hill of the Nymphs** (340 ft), a modern name borrowed from the dedication to the Nymphs carved on a rock inside the Observatory garden. The garden is open on Tues, 12–1. The slopes of the hill are covered with ancient foundations, in the midst of which stands the little church of *Ayia Marina* and its multi-domed modern successor. On the rock below the church, in a line between the wooden belfry and the Temple of Nike on the Acropolis, is a 6C inscription written from right to left, which marks the limit of the Precinct of Zeus ("Ορος Διός). On the summit of the hill stands the conspicuous *Observatory* (Asteroskopíon), founded by Baron Sinas in 1842, which is open to visitors on the last Sat of the month. A second building, with a large telescope, was added in 1905, and a seismological station in 1957.

Behind the observatory a path leads towards a radio station. To the right (c. 75 yds) is the '*Little Pnyx*', a small rock-cut assembly place. Traces of the *Northern Long Wall* may be seen close by. A long depression to the w., partly filled up, is generally identified with the *Barathron*, the ancient Athenian place of execution.

Returning past the observatory and descending to Leoforos Apostolou Pavlou (comp. below), we face two gates: to the left is the main entrance to the *Agora* excavations (Rte 5); the gate to the right gives access to a tract of ground excavated by Dörpfeld in 1892–97. His contentions that he had discovered here the Temple of Dionysos in the Marshes and the true Enneakrounos were based on topographical suppositions about the location of the Agora which have since been conclusively disproved. DÖRPFELD'S EXCAVATIONS are now largely overgrown, and their identification, though interesting to the scholar, need not delay the ordinary visitor.

An ANCIENT ROAD, c. 13 ft wide, equipped with a gutter and bordered by walls of polygonal masonry, is laid bare for some 250 yards. It was possibly the principal street of the deme of Melite. To the right stood a *Lesche* (club) identified from inscriptions. Farther on is a private house with a record of two mortgages (for 1000 and 210 drachmæ respectively) inscribed on its outer wall in letters of the 4C B.C. On the other side of the ancient road is an early triangular precinct, not the Dionysion in Limnai, but very possibly the *Heroön of Herakles Alexikakos*. The site, which is 6 ft below the level of the road, is covered with later buildings which have no connection with it. In the s. corner is a small *Temple*. In the middle of the adjoining courtyard are the foundations, in poros, of a square base which may have supported the statue of Herakles by Agelades (Scoliast to Aristophanes, Frogs 501). In the N.W. corner is a building formerly identified by Dörpfeld with the *Lenaion*, i.e. the building which enclosed the Sacred Wine Press (Λήναιον). The remains of a wine press were found here. Overlying the Greek remains and extending a little to the E. are the foundations of a Roman basilica, identified from the long inscription (2C A.D.) on a column, which relates to the religious guild of the Iobacchoi, as their clubhouse or *Baccheion*. Farther on, on the same side of the road, are the ruins of the *Amyneion*, a small shrine to the hero Amynos, the assistant of Asklepios, of which Sophocles held the priesthood. Inside are a temple and a well which was fed by a conduit from the main fountain. Opposite are remains of the great WATER SYSTEM OF PEISISTRATOS, which Dörpfeld asserted were those of the Enneakrounos. These are partly beneath the modern avenue and partly on its far side. At the foot of the Pnyx is a small square chamber hewn out of the rock, with a niche from which water still occasionally flows. It feeds a smaller round basin, also rock-hewn, a few feet lower down. This primitive supply, later covered by a Roman well-house, was identified by Dörpfeld with the Fountain of Kallirrhoë (comp. Rte 7). In the time of Solon, the yield was supplemented by cutting connecting channels from neighbouring watercourses on the Acropolis and Mouseion hills. A much more important undertaking, attributed to Peisistratos, was the construction of an *Aqueduct* nearly 3 m. long, which led from the valley of the Ilissos under the present National Garden to the foot of the w. slopes of the Acropolis. It ended in a large square *Cistern*, hewn like the others from the rock, from which pipes lead to a spacious *Square*, where stones belonging to a fountain base have been found.

The ancient road goes on some way farther s. and s.e. along the line of the aqueduct, and then bends n.e. towards the Acropolis. A footpath from the Amyneion leads through the pine-trees to the foot of the Areopagus where we started.

Leoforos Apostolou Pavlou continues n.w. past public gardens to *Ayios Athanasios*, whence a footbridge leads to the entrance gate of the Kerameikos (Rte 4).

4 FROM SINDAGMA SQUARE TO THE AGORA AND THE KERAMEIKOS

Bus No. 10 from opposite the old Palace, viâ Mitropoleos, returning viâ Ermou.

From Sindagma Square the long ODHOS ERMOU (Hermes St.), lined at first with fashion and textile shops, runs straight w. for nearly a mile, dividing the old city in two; as it descends it changes character, being devoted to the furnishing and building trades. In a large square to the s. stands the **Cathedral** (7, 3), built in 1840–55 out of the material of 72 demolished churches and from the designs of four architects. The resultant incongruity is not, therefore, surprising. Since 1864 the Metropolitan Archbishop of Athens has been the chief dignitary of the independent Greek Orthodox Church. To the left of the w. entrance is the tomb of the Patriarch Gregory, transferred from Odessa in 1871, fifty years after his execution at Constantinople. To the s. stands the **Small Metropolis**, or old cathedral, known also as *Panayia Gorgoepikoös* and *Ayios Eleftherios*. In its present form it dates from the 12C, though legend attributes its foundation to the Empress Irene c. 787. Its external dimensions are only 40 ft by 25 ft; the cupola is under 40 ft high. The walls of the church are artfully constructed entirely of ancient architectural blocks and reliefs, some inscribed, and of reliefs from an earlier church or churches of the 6–7C. On the w. side above the arch over the door is a calendar of the Attic state festivals (? 2C A.D.). Each festival is represented by symbolic figures or objects in relief; signs of the zodiac indicate the time sequence. One of the Maltese crosses added by the Christians has blotted out the sole known representation of the Panathenaic ship; its wheels are visible to the right of the second cross from the left.

Outside the s. wall lies a block of grey marble 7 ft long and 2 ft wide, known as the Stone of Cana, with a late Greek inscription recording its use at the Marriage Feast of Cana of Galilee. It was discovered at Elatea, in Phocis.—Behind the Apse: inscriptions and tablets, archaic relief with dancing figures.—N. side: ancient votive tablets.

The modernized church of *St Andrew* at the top of Odhos Filotheis to the s. is now the chapel of the archbishop's palace.

About 500 yds w. of Sindagma Square Odhos Ermou divides to form a little square round the tiny church called *Kapnikarea* (7, 3). The origin of its name is doubtful, as is the inevitable attribution of its foundation to the Empress Irene. The existing cruciform structure, of stone with the usual courses of brick, cannot be older than the 11C; the porch, the exo-narthex and the parecclesion (or N. chapel) were added in the 13C. Saved from demolition in 1834 by Ludwig of Bavaria, the church was carefully restored by the University. The dome is supported by four columns with Roman capitals.

We cross Odhos Aiolou (Rte 8), overshadowed at its s. end by the towering rock of the Acropolis, then skirt the N. side of Monastiraki Square (Rte 6). To the right lies the district of PSIRI, less appealing than Plaka though still maintaining its irregular street plan. In Odhos Ayias Theklas No. 11 (recently burned) was the scene of Byron's ten weeks' stay on his first arrival in Athens in 1809; he later immortalized the 13-year-old daughter of the house, Teresa Makris, as the Maid of Athens. Farther N., on the corner of Evripidhou and Menandrou streets, is the chapel of *Ayios Ioannis stin Kolona*, built round an unfluted Roman column with a Corinthian capital which projects through the roof. The column, probably from a gymnasium dedicated to Apollo, has reputedly the power of curing fevers.

Off the s. side of Odhos Ermou lies the little Plateia Avisinias with the '*Flea Market*' (Sun mornings). The antiquities (especially coins) are not always what they seem. Metal-workers practice their traditional craft in Odhos Ifestou, to the E. Odhos Astingos, its w. continuation, is named after Frank Abney Hastings, the English philhellene who was mortally wounded at Aitoliko. Near by, Ayios Filippos stands above the railway cutting near the N. entrance to the *Agora* (see Rte 5). This may be conveniently visited on the return.

The church of the *Asomaton* (6, 3), freed in 1960 of its 19C additions, closes the N. side of the square fronting Thission Station. Beyond this, Odhos Ermou, here ill-paved, continues alongside the excavations of the Kerameikos. In the street flanking their E. end is a *Synagogue* with a marble 'classical' façade.—On the far side of the railway some traces of the city walls can be seen to the w. of the church of *Ayios Athanasios* (6, 3); the church and adjacent cottages utilize ancient rock-cut foundations.

The **Kerameikos** (6, 1; weekdays 9–3.30 or 5, 25 dr.; Sun and hol., 10–4.30, free; closed Tues) includes the ruins of the Dipylon and Sacred Gates and excavations made outside the walls in the ancient *Cemetery of the Kerameikos*. Here roads from Piraeus, Eleusis, and Boeotia converged upon that from the Academy, so that by this way most ancient travellers entered the city. The brook Eridanos flows from E. to w. across the area, which is frequently waterlogged; frogs abound and tortoises may be seen. The place Kerameikos is said by Pausanias (I, 3, 1) to take its name from the hero Keramos, a supposed son of Dionysos and Ariadne.

Cemeteries existed in the Kerameikos district at least from the 12C B.C. By the 7C a line seems to have been drawn between the Inner Kerameikos, a quarter of potters and smiths, and the *Outer Kerameikos*, but it was the building of the city wall that conclusively separated the two. Few burials later than this are found in the inner area, as thenceforward it became usual (just as later in Rome) to bury the dead outside the enceinte along roads leading from the city gates. The importance of the w. entrance to the city was enhanced by the Dionysiac and Eleusinian processions which passed through it and by that of the Panathenaia which set out from it. In consequence the Academy Road outside the Gate of Thria (later the Dipylon) had already by the 6C become the Demosion Sema, the **Cemetery** *par excellence*, reserved for state tombs and cenotaphs of individuals or polyandreia for groups of battle heroes. Here stood the monuments of Pericles, Thrasyboulos, Konon, Zeno, Harmodios and Aristogeiton, and other worthies. Thucydides tells how "when the remains have been laid in the earth, some man of known ability and high reputation, chosen by the city, delivers a suitable oration over them". From a platform here Pericles delivered the famous oration (Thuc. II, 35–46) on those who died in the first year of the Peloponnesian War. The remainder of the ground was available to all classes, including slaves.

Many tomb monuments removed in the 19C are in the National Archæological Museum. The Greek Archæological Society began excavations in 1863, continuing at intervals until 1913. In 1913–41 the German Archæological Institute conducted excavations directed by A. Brückner and K. Kübler. In 1956 the Greek government requested the Institute to resume responsibility for the Kerameikos site and further intensive work began under the direction of D. Ohly. New excavations have been initiated; the old areas have been reinvestigated, conserved and landscaped; the museum, built with funds donated by Gustav Oberlaender (1867–1936), a German-American silk-stocking manufacturer, has been renovated and expanded. The Academy Road, whose course lies largely beneath modern houses, has not been properly explored, though many casual finds are in the National Archæological Museum. The sector that has been cleared lies s. of the main Kerameikos and consists of an extension to the s.w. made at the beginning of the 4C B.C. Most of its tombs were destroyed for material to repair the city walls after the battle of Chaeronea (338 B.C.), but those remaining were covered by successive layers of earth and later tombs to a depth of 20–30 ft and so were untouched by the extensive siege work of Sulla in 86 B.C.

Half-right inside the entrance on top of a mound is a plan of orientation with a view over the whole site. From it can be clearly identified the Wall of Themistocles with its later outwork and sectional moats. Of the wall the bottom course of masonry only is Themistoclean. On top of this in blue 'acropolis' stone are two courses of Konon's wall, then, in creamy limestone, two courses of a Demosthenian renewal, further courses attributable to Lycurgus, and, to the right, in long and short work, masonry of the period of Justinian.

A path descends to give a closer view of the double **City Walls**, which here occupy a frontage of c. 200 yards, interrupted by the Dipylon and the Sacred Gate. The inner line of wall was built by Themistocles in 479 and rebuilt by Konon in 394. It is only 7–8 ft thick and consists of one course of poros blocks (truly Themistoclean) and two rows of well jointed polygonal blocks of blue limestone (Kononian), interspersed with hastily reused marbles, with a core of rubble. The upper part was of unbaked bricks. The outer breastwork, with moat, was of later date, and may have been contemporary with the Dipylon. It is 14 ft thick and has facings of regularly cut blocks of conglomerate, with an earthen core. To the s.w. of the Sacred Gate both are fairly well preserved, the 'Themistoclean' wall with its later superstructures being 13 ft high in places and the outer wall still higher. Plutarch's contention that Sulla, before he stormed Athens in 86 B.C. razed the whole section of the wall between the Sacred and the Piraeic Gates indicates that earlier socles were by this time below ground level.

The **Sacred Gate** ('Ιερὰ Πύλη) spanned both the Sacred Way to Eleusis and the Eridanos brook. Before the Persian Wars they ran together, with the water probably in a channel of Peisistratid date. In the Themistoclean rebuilding the two were separated by solid masonry and an inner gate was constructed 20 yds inside the circuit wall. The road was protected on the s. by a high wall which joined the enceinte

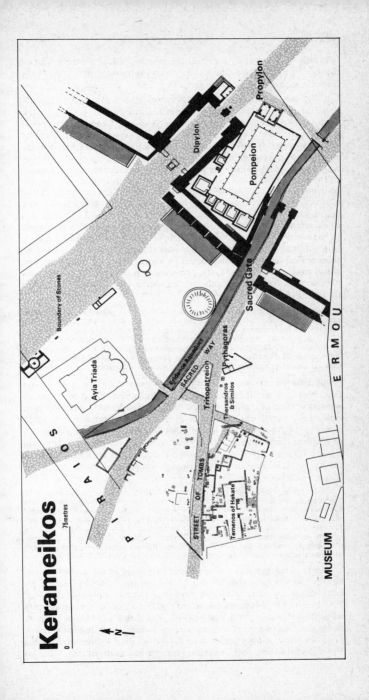

in a massive tower, and a matching tower was added to the E. exit of the gate in the 4C B.C. The water, which presumably bore the sewage from the Agora area, was conveyed in a vaulted channel.

A well-preserved section of the WALL OF KONON, in rusticated polygonal masonry on the Themistoclean line, runs N.E. to the Dipylon Gate. About 8 ft short of the gate is a *Boundary Stone*, inscribed perpendicularly ΟΡΟΣ ΚΕΡΑΜΕΙΚΟΥ; this is one of several found at different points of the Kerameikos boundary. The space between the two gates was occupied by the **Pompeion,** a place of preparation for processions (πομπαί), which served as a storehouse for the heavy vehicles and other paraphernalia used in the Great Eleusinian and Panathenaic festivals. It was adorned with painted portraits of the comic poets and a bronze statue of Socrates by Lysippus, and in emergency served as a centre for distributing corn. The Greek edifice of the 4C B.C. consisted of a court surrounded by a colonnade of six columns by thirteen, known to have been a haunt of Diogenes. The orthostats in Hymettian marble of the E. wall and of part of the s. wall still stand. Off the N. and W. sides project six small dining-rooms. A simple *Propylon* in the E. corner, which gave access from the city, preserves its plan complete. Prominent are the metal clamps joining the marble blocks, wheel-ruts, and the holes for door fittings.

The classical Pompeion was destroyed in Sulla's siege, evidences of which survive in the shape of stone balls from his catapults. A new building occupying the same area was erected on massive concrete foundations in the time of Hadrian. This was basilican in form, divided by two rows of 11 pilasters, and its most prominent remaining features are the buttresses of its s. wall. It was destroyed in turn during the Herulian raid of 267. The plans of both can be best appreciated from an artificial terrace in the S.E. corner of the excavated area.

The **Dipylon** (Δίπυλον, double gateway), was the main gate of the city. Not only was it larger than any of the others, but it received the greatest volume of traffic. A broad thoroughfare known as the Dromos (now built over), bordered with gymnasia and porticoes, ascended direct to the Agora (comp. Rte 5). Outwards, an important avenue led to the Academy, with a branch road to the *Hamaxitos*, the busy old road to Piraeus. This last intersected the *Sacred Way*, which led from the Sacred Gate (see below) to Eleusis, whence high roads ran w. to Megara and N. to Boeotia.

History. The Dipylon was built at the end of the 4C B.C. on the exact plan of its predecessor, the Themistoclean gate of 479 B.C., known as the Thriasian Gate (comp. Plutarch, 'Pericles', 30) which was so-called because it led to Thria, a deme near Eleusis. Known also as the Keramic Gate, it provided the favourite, though not the most direct, way to or from the Piraeus, as it avoided the hills and led straight into the heart of the city. In 200 B.C. Philip V of Macedon, furiously attacking Athens for siding with Pergamon and Rome against him, penetrated into the court and extricated himself with some difficulty (Livy XXXI, 24).

The Dipylon gateway was strategically placed at the end of a deep court c. 44 yds long and 23 broad, open on the w. and protected by flanking towers. A considerable portion of the s.w. tower is preserved. This is nearly 8 yds square and is built of large blocks of conglomerate cased with limestone, very well worked. The *Court* was flanked by thick ramparts. The two gates are separated by a central pier, behind which is a square base supporting a round marble altar dedicated to Zeus Herkeios, Hermes, and Akamas (eponymous hero of the tribe of

Akamantis). To the E. of the entrance was a classical fountain-house behind which are preserved the first few of the steps leading up to the N.E. tower. The *Outer Gate*, added to the defences in the 1C B.C., was set back c. 9 yds from the city wall and was divided vertically by a stone pier c. 12 ft wide; the openings on either side were 11 ft 4 in. wide. The marble base of a monument stands outside the pier.

The Apotheke or dig-house lies beyond (no adm.).

The **Kerameikos Cemetery** lay outside the Dipylon and extended alongside the two principal adjoining roads. Part of the area is being slowly cleared. At present the ACADEMY ROAD offers little on the spot to justify its fame. Beyond the late *Sarcophagus of Philotera*, a *Polyandreion* was found to contain the skeletons of 13 Spartan officers who fell fighting with Thrasyboulos against the Thirty Tyrants in 403. Two of the bodies in the central chamber were named on an inscribed marble slab as Chairon and Thibrachos (mentioned by Xenophon); the third was probably the Olympic victor Lakrates. Here and to the N.W. of the church are two original *Boundary Stones*. Farther on are scanty remains of a *Bath-house* of the 5C B.C., the earliest of its kind yet discovered. Where the road disappears below the modern Odhos Piraios, is an elaborate grave monument, formerly known as the Tomb of Chabrias, of c. 350 B.C., half excavated.

Literary evidences, casual finds, and excavations at intervals to the N. augment our knowledge of the road. Identified post holes are believed to come from the wooden stands erected for spectators of the annual torch races in honour of the dead. Inscriptions have been found from the polyandreia of the battles of Potidaea, the Hellespont, and Corinth. About 200 yds N.W. of the Dipylon lay the *Peribolos of Artemis Kalliste*, identified with walls discovered at No. 11 Odhos Plataion, where votive reliefs came to light in 1922. For the *Academy of Plato* (c. 1 m. N.W. of the Dipylon), see below.

Retracing our steps, keeping the church on our right, we cross the excavations where c. 8000 ostraka (discarded from the Agora in ancient times) came to light in 1966, cross over the Eridanos on an ancient bridge, and reach the *Tritopatreion* in the angle of the SACRED WAY (ΙΕΡΑ ΟΔΟΣ) and the so-called Street of the Tombs. Beyond the excavated area the present-day Iera Odhos follows the line of the ancient Sacred Way all the way to Eleusis. The Tritopatreis were deities connected with ancestor worship and the boundary stone at the N.E. corner of their enclosure warns of their sacred precinct.

Opposite, on the s. side, stand the stelai of Pythagoras, consul (proxenos) of Athens at Selymbria in Thrace (early 5C B.C.) placed on a stepped pyramid of interesting geometrical proportions, and of the Corcyræan envoys, Thersandros and Simylos, who came to Athens at the outbreak of the Peloponnesian War (Thucydides, I, xxii); their tomb furniture in the museum indicates a 5C grave, though the lettering of the stele is 4C.

The **Street of the Tombs** is a planned funerary avenue unique in Greece if we except the usage at the Hieron of Epidauros. It was begun c. 394 B.C. The street, 26 ft wide, has been excavated for 100 yds. On either side of the street the cemetery was divided into plots reserved for wealthy citizens (both Athenian citizens and metics). About 20 of these plots have been discovered, divided into distinct terraces (especially on the s. side).

All types of funerary monument common in the 4C are represented: the plain *stele* with palmette anthemion; more elaborate *stelai* with reliefs enclosed in a frame, culminating in the *nasíkos*, or *ædicula*, where the sculptural frame achieves architectural proportions; the *column* surmounted by a device or animal; and the great marble *lekythoi* (with one handle) and *loutrophoroi* (with two handles; used for unmarried persons), which enjoyed special favour in the 4C. The *sarcophagus* and *pseudo-sarcophagus* do not appear to have become common until Roman times. In 317 B.C. Demetrios of Phaleron limited memorials to a plain *trapeza* (slab) or a *kioniskos* (or cippus; a small undecorated column). A few wells here and there provided the necessary water for the funeral rites.

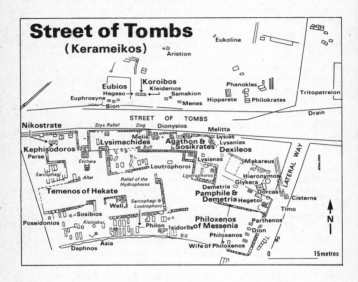

To the left stands the **Memorial of Dexileos**, the 20-year-old son of Lysanias of Thorikos, who was one of the 'five knights' killed in action at Corinth in 394 B.C. On a massive conglomerate base stands a crescent of poros on which the inscribed monument was set off by two sirens. The marble relief (cast *in situ*) represents the young man in the act of despatching a prostrate adversary. The lance, horse, trappings, and bridle were of bronze. The tall stele crowned with a palmette commemorates Lysias and a smaller one Melitta, brother and sister of Dexileos; a trapeza tombstone bears the names of Lysanios, another brother, and his family.

The adjacent plot of the brothers Agathon and Sosikrates of Herakleia contains the *Ædicula of Korallion*, wife of Agathon, as well as the tall *Stele of Agathon and Sosikrates.*—The *Monument of Dionysios of Kollytos* is an ædicula without relief backed by a pillar stele, which supports a conspicuously fine bull, in Pentelic marble.—In the plot of *Lysimachos of Acharnai*, with retaining walls of excellent polygonal masonry, are a Molossian Dog in Hymettian marble and a pudgy Roman sepulchral relief representing a funeral feast on the banks of the Styx, with Charon in attendance. The temenos of Nikostrates and

Kephisodoros occupies the angle of a lateral road mounting to the *Temenos of Artemis Soteira*, a precinct long attributed to the worship of Hekate.

Returning along the NORTH SIDE of the Street of Tombs we see first the concession of Eubios of Potamos, with the *Stele of Euphrosyne* (c. 386), sister of Eubios, and the *Monument of Bion* (his nephew) in the form of a Doric column surmounted by a loutrophoros. The plot of *Koroibos of Melite* contains his own stele, the *Loutrophoros of Kleidemos*, his grandson, and a facsimile of the ædicula of Hegeso, his wife. Beyond are the stelai of *Samakion* and *Menes* (on horseback). Farther over the *Ædicula of Eukoline*, a little girl with her dog; and the *Ædicula of Aristion*, a boy with a pet bird and a slave holding a strigil; below is a mourning siren, supported by kneeling figures. On the side of the mound on which stood the church of Ayia Triada can be seen the small memorial altar that commemorates *Hipparete*, granddaughter of Alcibiades, and the plots of *Phanokles of Leukenoe* and of *Philokrates of Kydathenaion* (slabs, stelai, and columns).

In the LATERAL WAY, to the s., are the graves of two actors, *Makareus* and *Hieronymos*. The plot of Demetria and Pamphile includes the fine *Ædicula of Pamphile* represented as a seated figure beside her mother Demetria, who is standing. Behind is a *Loutrophoros of Hegetor*. Beyond is the reservation of *Philoxenos of Messenia* (statue of the wife of Philoxenos, lekythoi, and tombstones of slaves).

The **Oberlaender Museum** (adm. 25 dr.). ROOM I. SCULPTURE recovered from the Themistoclean Wall: no number, *Dexileos Monument (comp. above); no number, *Stele of Ampharete holding her infant grand-child, with beautifully executed drapery (5C B.C.). I 190, Base of a grave monument (c. 515 B.C.) for the Carian Tymnes, son of Skylax, with three lines in Greek and one in Carian; Skylax may be the famous Carian captain, the earliest explorer of the Indus region and of the coasts of the Indian Ocean and Red Sea. P 105, Sphinx (c. 550 B.C.), acroterion of a grave stele. P 1001, Base (c. 560 B.C.) with four horsemen in relief on the front, found in s. tower of Dipylon, perhaps the base for the famous Discophoros relief in the National Museum. P 1051, Horse and rider (c. 520 B.C.); P 1052, Seated man, grave monument of c. 530 B.C., both found in the Themistoclean Wall. P. 1054, Boxer stele (c. 550 B.C.): head of boxer with cauliflower ear and thongs of glove tied round his wrist. P 1169, Stele of Eupheros (5C B.C.), grave relief of youth with strigil.

ROOM II contains terracotta figures and choice *Vases of all kinds of the Sub-Mycenæan, Protogeometric, Geometric and Protoattic periods (11–7C), part of a most important collection, from which the definitive dating of the period has been largely deduced. Among these are the earliest pictorial representation (a horse: the 'Ur-Pferd') on a pot since Mycenæan times, and a bronze bowl of Phoenician workmanship (late-9C B.C.), 'the earliest confidently dated Near Eastern art object found in Greece' (Akurgal).

ROOMS III AND IV. Grave groups of the Archaic, Classical, and Hellenistic periods, containing black-figured and red-figured pottery of well-known painters (Amasis, Kleophrades), terracotta figurines including 'four exquisite figures attached to a base' (Higgins). Ostraka, from a find of about 9000, naming Themistocles and other famous citizens.— ROOM IV, Selection of sherds from Panathenaic prize amphoræ, found in the area of the Pompeion where prize amphoræ were stored before the awards were made on the Acropolis.

The Academy, made famous by Plato's school of philosophy, was a sacred wood c. 2 stadia in diameter, situated at the end of an avenue (comp. above) 6 stadia from the Diplyon. Pious walkers wishing to follow as nearly as possible the avenue's course should take Odhos Plataion or the parallel Odhos Salaminos (2, 5) and their extensions from the N.W. side of the Kerameikos (1½ m.). The church of Ayios Yeoryios on the corner of Palamidhiou, two-thirds of the way along, stands on the ancient road. *Ayios Trifon*, standing in Kolokinthou off the N. side of the main Corinth road, marks the S. corner of the **Academy of Plato**, whose position was confirmed in 1966 by the discovery *in situ* of a boundary-stone dated to c. 500 B.C. The area is more easily reached by bus No. 62 from Odhos Veranzerou viâ Kolonos.

The hill of *Kolonos Hippios* (184 ft), the refuge of Oedipus, the flowers of which are celebrated by Sophocles' chorus (Oed. Col., 688–719), lies to the E. of Odhos Lenorman, enveloped by the city. On its bare top, above the trees, tombstones commemorate Charles Lenormant (1802–59) and Karl Ottfried Müller (1797–1840), two archaeologists who died in Athens.

The ACADEMY, more correctly the *Hekademeia*, was traditionally founded by Hekademos, who told the Dioscuri where their sister Helen was hidden; hence, in gratitude to Hekademos, the Lacedaemonians always spared it when they invaded Attica (Plutarch, 'Theseus', 32). Twelve sacred olive-trees, supposed to be offshoots of Athena's tree on the Acropolis, grew here. In the 6C B.C. Hipparchos built a wall round the Academy, and excavations have shown that the Kephissos was diverted at about this time. Kimon converted the place "from a bare, dry, and dusty spot into a well-watered grove, with shady walks and racecourses" (Plutarch, 'Kimon', 13). It was a gymnasium in the time of Aristophanes ('Clouds' 1002). Plato taught here from c. 388 B.C., while dwelling between the Academy and the hill of Kolonos; he was buried on his estate. Sulla cut down the Academy trees to make siege engines in 86 B.C., but the damage was immediately made good since Cicero, who visited Athens in 79 B.C., here sets the scene of one of his philosophical dialogues. Funeral games in honour of the dead buried in the Kerameikos were held in the Academy, where also was an Altar of Prometheus, the goal of torch-races from Athens. Excavations, begun in 1929–40 by the Greek architect P. Aristophron, have been continued since 1956 under the patronage of his widow by Ph. Stavropoullos of the Greek Archæological Society. There are now two main areas of excavation some 250 yds apart.

The entrance to one is in Odhos Thenaias near the bus terminus. Here the W. wall of the *Peribolos* (? the Ἱππάρχου Τειχίον) has been laid bare for about 150 yds. During the clearance of debris inside the wall many schoolboys' slates came to light, bearing inscriptions (with the names of Demosthenes and Sophocles) of the late-5C or early-4C B.C. The most surprising discoveries, however, have been of pre-Classical date and outside the wall. An early Helladic dwelling may indeed be the *House of Hekademos*, since a short distance to the S. is a large *Heroön* of the Geometric period (8–7C), extraordinarily preserved since it is built entirely of mud brick, with seven rooms and an eschara nearly 5 ft in diameter, which served presumably for his cult. Unearthed in 1956, this is now protected by a metal roof which did not save it from damage in the storm of Nov 1961. Many fine vases have been found in the area, which is honeycombed with graves from pre-Mycenean times and later cremation burials. A large circular *Well*, of excellent masonry, inscribed round the mouth, has been reconstructed here.

In a second enclosure, to the S.E. near Ay. Trifon, are the excavated remains of a *Gymnasium* of the 5C A.D.

5 THE 'THESEION' AND THE AGORA

ARCHÆOLOGICAL NOTE. The approximate location of the Agora had been demonstrated as early as 1859–62, from the identification of the Stoa of Attalos by the Greek Archæological Society and the interpretation of ancient texts. Haphazard digs were made by Greeks and Germans between 1859 and 1897 where remains showed above the surface, and when the Athens–Piraeus railway was extended through a cutting in 1890–91. In 1931–40 the American School of Classical Studies, with the financial backing of John D. Rockefeller, Jr., undertook systematic excavations under Prof. T. Leslie Shear. They have been continued in 1946–67 under Prof. Homer Thompson and since 1968 under T. Leslie Shear, Jr. The area between the railway and the Acropolis and the Areopagus was declared an archæological zone by law; some 350 dilapidated 19C houses were expropriated and demolished and 300,000 tons of accumulated deposit sifted and removed until the whole area had been excavated to classical, and parts of it to prehistoric, levels. Of the area investigated about two-thirds is now open to the public, the enclosure including the Agora, the buildings bounding its w., s., and E. sides, and the hill of Kolonos Agoraios to the w. Excavations started in 1970 in a further expropriated zone beyond the railway.

Approaches. There are three entrances: at the s.w. corner from Leof. Apostolou Pavlou (Thission terminus of No. 16 bus; comp. Rte 1); from the N. side by bridge over the railway from Od. Adrianou (comp. Rte 4); from the s. side (free days only) near the Church of the Holy Apostles (comp. Rte 3).—ADMISSION 50 dr. (Thurs & Sun free), summer 8–7, winter 9–4; Sun & hol. 10–4.30, incl. entrance to museum (9–4 or 5 only, Sun & hol. 10–2). An excellent 'Guide to the Excavation', published in English by the American School, is available (3rd edn 1976; 180 dr.).

The visitor will be well advised to inquire whether the upper gallery of the Stoa of Attalos is again open to the public; here six plans show the topography of ancient Athens and five stages in the development of the Agora; these are augmented by a model reproducing the agora at its greatest extent (2C A.D.). Having got his bearings, he can begin the visit with either the Theseion or the square itself, reserving the museum till later. Lavatories and iced water are available in the Stoa of Attalos (railway end).

The so-called **'Theseion'** (Agora Pl. 5) that crowns the low knoll of *Kolonos Agoraios* is now certainly identified with the *Temple of Hephaistos and Athena* noted by Pausanias, although the misnomer, applied as early as the Vienna Anonymous MS., is not likely to be easily displaced from popular usage. The ****Hephaisteion**, as it should rightly be called, is the most complete example remaining of a Doric hexastyle temple. Archæological and stylistic grounds alike support the foundation date of 449 B.C. suggested by Prof. Dinsmoor, who assigns the building to the architect of the later temples at Sounion and Rhamnous. It thus opens the great period of reconstruction following the Persian peace.

The temple was mistaken in the Middle Ages, on the evidence of its metopes, for the heroön erected by Kimon c. 475 B.C. to receive the bones of Theseus recovered from Skyros. Excavation has shown that the Hephaisteion stands appropriately amid foundries and metal-workers' shops; sherds have fixed its dates within narrow limits; and its position is unequivocally located by Pausanias. The true Theseion, which ancient sources locate on the Acropolis N. slope, has not yet been found.

The temple, adapted to Christian use probably in the 7C with the addition of an apse, was further modified c. 1300, when it became the *Church of Ay. Yeoryios*, by the construction of a concrete interior vault. A later apse survived till 1835, though in Turkish times the liturgy was celebrated here only once a year, hence its late nickname ἀκαμάτης (the idler). The last services held in it were a Te Deum to celebrate King Otho's arrival in the newly founded capital on 13 Dec 1834, and a centenary Te Deum in 1934. The surroundings of the building were explored in 1936–37 and the cella and peristyle excavated in 1939.

The temple consists of a cella, with pronaos and opisthodomos, both distyle in antis, surrounded by a peristyle of 34 columns (6 by 13). Except for the lowest step of poros it is built entirely of marble, the structure in Pentelic, the sculptured members in Parian. The EXTERIOR lacks only the roof and, save for the sculpture, is excellently preserved. The columns are slighter than those of the Parthenon, though the entablature is heavier; the same optical refinements are incorporated. The pronaos (to the E.) is arranged unusually with the antæ in line with the third columns of the peristyle; the E. pteroma is given special emphasis by the sculptural arrangement. The 10 *Metopes* of the E. front depict nine of the twelve Labours of Herakles: those omitted are the Augean Stables, the Stymphalian Birds, and the Cretan Bull. The metopes above the E. pteroma, four on each flank, show eight exploits of Theseus; the remainder are blank.

The subject of the W. pediment may have been a Centauromachia. That of the E. pediment is not known; in the lower colonnade of the Stoa of Attalos are displayed fragments attributed to this pediment and conjecturally restored as the Apotheosis of Herakles.

INTERIOR. The EAST PTEROMA is still covered by its coffered ceiling. Its importance is emphasized within as without by its sculpture, here an Ionic *Frieze* of heroic combat which extends beyond the antæ to bridge the ambulatory and return above the columns of the peristyle. Since the E. wall was removed and the columns of the *Pronaos* re-erected in 1936–37, the CELLA, with its barrel vault, strikes an uneasy balance between its pagan origin and its dedication to St George. Its proportions were altered during construction, probably under the influence of Iktinos, and a surface treated to take plaster begun inside, presumably in preparation for frescoes, was never completed. The composition of the interior colonnade is still a matter of scholarly controversy. The walls bear sepulchral slabs dating from 896 to 1103, parts of a 'Stone Chronicle' listing events in 1555–1800, graffiti of British visitors (1675), and memorials to others who died in Greece in the 17–19C, when the building seems to have been used as a Protestant cemetery. That of George Watson (d. 1810) bears a defaced Latin epitaph by Byron. The marble floor was ruined in the Middle Ages when graves were dug through it. Two blocks of Eleusinian limestone, which bore the cult statutes by Alkamenes erected c. 420, were recovered from the E. wall in 1936 and restored to position; the clay moulds used to cast the statues themselves came to light 10 yds from the temple.

In the 3C B.C.–1C A.D. a formal garden, planted in sunken flower-pots, bordered the s., w., and N. sides of the temple. It has been replanted as far as knowledge permits with plants known to have been there in antiquity (e.g. pomegranate and myrtle).—To the N. are scanty remains of a large Hellenistic building conjectured to be the *State Arsenal*.

The *AGORA ('Αγορά = assembly), or *Kerameikos Agora*, was the assembly-place *par excellence* where the citizens of Athens met daily in the open air for all purposes of community life. In early days the scene of athletic displays and dramatic competitions, it became the recognized venue for the transaction of business or the discussion of philosophy. In its small compass traders rubbed shoulders with administrators in the shadow of buildings and an ever-increasing number of monuments bearing witness to their past achievements. St Paul disputed in the Agora daily with them that met with him (Acts xvii, 17).

History. The site, which has been occupied since the Protogeometric period, developed slowly in the 6C B.C. as the main square of the city, probably in succession to a site nearer the entrance to the Acropolis. The earliest Council house is known to date from the time of Solon, and the Peisistratid tyrants laid on a water supply. A great drain was built at the order of Kleisthenes, whose constitutional reforms necessitated much reconstruction, most of it swept away in the Persian sack of 480 B.C. The new agora seems to have been well in hand before Pericles' time, since Kimon is known to have embellished it with plane trees. A large addition made by Lycurgus to the E. side of the square was removed in the time of Attalos, king of Pergamon (159–138 B.C.), when the agora was replanned in the more formal style in vogue in Asia Minor. Stoas bounded it on the E. and S. The agora seems to have survived Sulla's sack in 86 B.C. and, with the addition to the centre in the reign of Augustus of an Odeion and a temple, retained its identity with minor changes until the Herulian raid of A.D. 267 laid it waste. For the next century and a half the site lay outside the new fortification, the misnamed Valerian wall, which was largely built of stones from the shattered agora. When the old outer walls were re-established in the 5C part of the site was occupied by a large gymnasium which went out of use in the 6C (possibly to be identified with the University closed down in 529). Abandoned until the 10C, the area was covered by successive dwellings throughout Byzantine, Frankish, and Turkish times, its only public monument of this period being the little church that survives.

Ancient Institutions. The people of Attica belonged to four phylae (tribes), or clans, whose identity survived the union under Athens, while their territory comprised three districts known as the Plain (Pediake), the Coast (Paralia), and the Hill (Diakria). The population was early divided also into three classes, *Eupatridai*, or nobles; *Georgoi* and *Agroikoi*, or farmers (of hill and plain); and *Demiourgoi*, or artisans, all of whom were ipso facto equal members of the *Ekklesia*, or Assembly. The arable land held by free men was immemorially inalienable from their family or clan. A fourth class of freemen without civic rights, known as *Hektemoroi*, included agricultural labourers. At an early date, possibly about the time of the Dorian invasion, the kings of Athens had been overthrown by the Medontid family, who held the hereditary office of *Archon* (regent) for life. Power gradually passed to the *Areopagus*, or Council of Nobles, who supervised the three executive archons elected by the Assembly: the *Basileus*, the *Polemarch*, and the *Eponymos*, whose functions were, broadly speaking, respectively religious, military, and civil. The Archon Eponymos was chief magistrate and nominal head of the polis, or city-state, and after these offices were restricted in 683 B.C. to yearly tenure gave his name to the year. On relinquishing office Archons automatically became life members of the Areopagus. Later their number was increased to nine by the addition of six recording judges (*Thesmothetai*). The aristocracy monopolized political office through after Kylon's unsuccessful attempt to usurp power and the consequent war with Megara, popular discontent extorted Draco's legal code in 621 B.C. The harsh law of property that allowed a debtor's person to be taken in pledge still reduced many peasants to slavery, but a Court of Appeal of 51 judges (*Ephetai*) was instituted to deal with cases of bloodshed.

Towards the end of the century new classes (the *Timocracy*) were emerging, founded on wealth gained in commerce or agriculture, and a new division of the people, based on landed property qualification, was made. The highest class was now the *Pentakosiomedimnoi* (those whose income was equivalent to 500 medimni of corn); next came the *Hippeis* or Knights (300–500 medimni) from whose ranks came wartime cavalry; and below them the *Zeugitai* or Yeomen (those with a pair of oxen) who in war became Hoplites, or infantrymen. The fourth estate of peasants and artisans (*Thetes*) were excluded from the Assembly but paid no taxes. In war they became oarsmen and marines.

Solon, who became Archon Eponymos in 594 B.C., promulgated the Seisachtheia, cancelling all debts involving the person of the debtor. He retained the classes of the Timocracy, limited election to archonship to the highest class, but enfranchised the Thetes. He increased the judicial dignity of the Areopagus while transferring its deliberative functions to the Assembly, and created a new Council of Four Hundred (*Boule*), upon which devolved in effect the transaction of the business of the Assembly. The Thetes were excluded from the Boule. Popular tribunals (*Heliaia* or Heliasts) were enrolled by lot so that justice should be impartial to rich and poor alike. Magistrates were made answerable at the end of their term of office to the Heliaia. Despite Solon's reforms party strife between the clans (including the returned Alkmaeonids) caused thirty years of anarchy, which ended in the constitutional tyranny of the polemarch Peisistratos. Under his benevolent dictatorship the forms of democracy were preserved, and Herodotus (I, 59) acknowledges that he "administered the state according to the established usage and his arrangements were wise and salutary".

After the overthrow of his more despotic son, Hippias, the Alkmaeonid Kleisthenes (c. 508 B.C.) reorganized the tribes. Finding Attica composed of c. 170 *Demes* or parishes, he altered their traditional division into three *Districts*: the City (Ἄστυ), the Coast (Παραλία), and the Inland (Μεσογεία), and to stamp out their old regional rivalries, he regrouped the inhabitants. In each of the Districts the demes were divided into 10 *Trittyes*; three trittyes, one from each district, went to form a new tribe, named after a hero, thus forming 10 new *Tribes* independent of old clannish loyalties. The old Council of 400 became a *Council of 500* composed of 50 deputies from each tribe, elected annually by lot. The deputies of each tribe held office in rotation for about five weeks in the year as *Prytaneis*, or Presidents. They chose one of their number by lot as *Epistates* (Chief President), who with nine *Proedroi* as assistants, and a *Grammateús* (secretary), not of their body, formed the *Prytaneia*, or Presidential Committee. The Prytaneis presided also over the meetings of the Ekklesia, which was the ultimate authority without whose sanction no bill could be passed into law. By the institution of *Ostracism*, a ten years' banishment without loss of rights (used between 487 and 417) the duty of guarding the state against the plots of potential tyrants was transferred from the Areopagus to the sovereign people. Philochoros tells how in such cases "the Agora was fenced with boards, ten entrances being left, through which the citizens entered by tribes to cast their votes; the nine archons and the Boule presided". The classes of the Timocracy were retained; below the rank of citizen were the Metics (Μέτοικοι), or resident aliens, and slaves.

In 487 B.C. the power of the nine archons was reduced by the institution of their election by lot. Before this date the Polemarch had acted as Commander-in-Chief, assisted by the ten tribal generals; henceforward the *Ten Generals* (Strategoi), elected every year one for each tribe, became not only the supreme commanders of the army and navy (one or more being named by the Assembly to lead each expedition), but were also the dominant magistrates in the political field. Pericles was elected general every year from 443 till his death in 429 and to this fact he owed his unique position. To Pericles and his older contemporary Ephialtes is due the completion of Athenian democracy. Nearly all the powers of the Areopagus were transferred to the Assembly. The archonship, no longer confined to the two higher classes, became a paid office, having little political power and pay was also introduced for the Council and the Jurymen. By the time of the Peloponnesian War all property ceased to be entailed.

We descend a path towards the s.w. corner of the excavated area. Near the junction of the two branches of the great drain (see below) stands the **Horos** (Pl. 10), or *Boundary Stone*, inscribed in Attic characters of the 5C B.C. with the legend 'I am the boundary stone of the Agora'. This was necessary because the square was a sacred precinct from which certain classes of convicted persons were barred; citizens entering it performed a purificatory rite. At a higher level immediately to the s. is the stump of a marble pedestal of the 1C A.D., which probably supported a *Perirrhanterion* or holy-water stoup.

The boundary stone is set against a contemporary wall belonging to a row of dwellings or shops. The discovery here of hobnails and of a black glazed cup dating to the third quarter of the 5C B.C. and bearing the name of its owner, Simon, makes it likely that here really was the *Shop of the Cobbler Simon*, where, according to Diogenes Lærtius, Socrates spent much of his time.

The WEST SIDE of the agora was flanked by a group of public buildings. The circular foundations of the **Tholos** (Pl. 5), discovered in 1934 much farther N. than had been expected, provided the first certain fixed point for the topography of the Agora. Built c. 465 B.C., this is the 'Prytanikon', also known from its roof as the *Skias*, or parasol, where, as Aristotle records, the fifty Prytaneis dined daily at the public expense and offered sacrifice before their deliberations. Here their chairman (epistates) and the third of his colleagues who were on duty also slept (Aristotle, 'Constitution of Athens', 44) and the building became the effective headquarters of Athenian government. A set of standard weights and measures were kept here; they are now in the museum.

A porch was added to the original rotunda at the time of Augustus. The six columns that supported the roof (three stumps *in situ*) were cut down during the reign of Hadrian when a single-span roof was substituted. At the same time the floor of mosaic chips (1C A.D.), part of which remains uncovered, was overlaid by marble slabs. The original clay floor is 18 in. below the surface, and, save for a few blocks of poros, the visible outer wall is a restoration. Fragments remain to the N. of a small room that served as a kitchen.

The foundations of the **New Bouleuterion** (Pl. 5), or Council House, lie to the N.W. on a platform cut back into the hill of Kolonos. Here the Boule met under the Prytaneis to prepare legislation for the Assembly. The building apparently replaced its predecessor at the end of the 5C B.C. A formal S. Portico was added by Lycurgus, together with an Ionic *Propylon* facing the agora, the two being connected by a passage along the s. front of the old Bouleuterion. The *Old Bouleuterion*, a square building erected for the Council of 500 soon after its inception by Kleisthenes, replaced a still earlier edifice of the time of Solon. When the council moved to its new chamber, the old building was used to store official documents. Parallel with its N. side was a small archaic *Temple* which was destroyed by the Persians. This is presumed to have been dedicated to the Mother of the Gods, since her worship seems to have survived on this spot until, in the late 2C B.C., a **Metroön** (Pl. 6), consisting of four rooms with a colonnade fronting the square, was built on the site. This had the dual function of *Sanctuary* of the Mother of the Gods (2nd room from the s.) and *Repository of State Archives*, which seems, like the library at Pergamon, to have had quarters (N. end) for a superintendent. The mosaic pavement in the third room from the s. dates from a transformation in the 5C A.D.

In front of the Metroön is a row of foundations for monuments. At its N.E. corner are monument bases carelessly made up in Christian times of reused material. Here has been re-erected a headless *Statue of Hadrian* (A.D 117–138) found in the great drain. It is identified by the decoration of the corselet, which bears a crowned Athena standing upon the wolf suckling Romulus and Remus, a symbol of the captive taking the captor captive. The statue is probably contemporary with the emperor.

The *Great Drain of Kleisthenes*, alined with the Old Bouleuterion, and beautifully constructed of polygonal blocks of limestone, channelled the waters from the hills on the s.w. towards the Eridanos brook to the N. The two branches that flow into it near the boundary stone were dug in the 4C B.C. or later. Beyond the drain, remains of a fenced enclosure round a long base locate the *Peribolos of the Eponymous Heroes*. The 4C base, on which stood statues of the ten legendary heroes chosen for Kleisthenes by the Delphic oracle as 'founders' of his ten tribes, was several times extended after 307 B.C. as additional 'tribes' were created. It bore also two tripods. The sides of the plinth were used as a notice-board for official announcements and for proposed new legislation (comp. Demosthenes, XXIV, 23).

A little to the E. again is an *Altar* (*? Zeus Agoraios*), of 4C workmanship, known by the identifying letters of its parts to have been moved in the mid-1C, presumably from the Pnyx, where a cutting of exactly similar size has been located.

The gap below the Hephaisteion was never completely closed by buildings. Before the Metroön was built, four rows of stone slabs, of which blocks remain, extended N. from the Bouleuterion, serving perhaps as a privileged grandstand from which Councillors could command the square. In early Imperial times a grandiose stairway was erected as an approach to the Hephaisteion.

Beyond the gap stood the *Temple of Apollo Patroös* (Pl. 6), a small structure, tetrastyle in antis, of c. 330 B.C., with conglomerate foundations and walls in the late polygonal style. The two Omphaloi may have stood beneath its porch. The statue of Apollo by Euphranor, that stood within, is probably that found in 1907 and now in the Stoa of Attalos.

Apollo 'Patroös', that is the father of Ion, was specially worshipped by the Athenians who counted themselves of Ionian descent. He was patron deity of state administration; before him magistrates were sworn and citizens registered. A 6C temple on the site was destroyed by the Persians and apparently left derelict in accordance with the Plataean oath for more than a century.

Adjoining are the remains of a slightly earlier cella, identified from the inscription on the altar with the *Temple of Zeus Phratrios and Athena Phratria*, the deities of the ancestral religious brotherhoods, or phratries. The foundations at the E. end supported a porch added to the 4C cella in the mid-2C B.C.

To the N. the poros foundations of the **Stoa of Zeus Eleutherios** extend to the railway, the cutting of which destroyed the N. wing. The portico, which had two projecting wings, was built by unknown architects c. 430 B.C. to honour Zeus as saviour of the Athenians from the Persians. Externally of the Doric order, with marble acroteria on the gables of the wings (flying Nike in the museum), the building had Ionic columns within. It was decorated, according to Pausanias, with paintings by Euphranor. Under its colonnade citizens transacted their private business. Socrates is known to have discussed philosophy here with his friends. An annexe was added behind in the 1C A.D.

The piled marble fragments in front mark the site of superposed altars of the 6C and (?) 3C B.C.

The whole of the NORTH SIDE OF THE AGORA, lying beyond the railway, is to be laid bare, but will only gradually become accessible to the public. At its N.W. angle the *Dromos* (comp. Rte 4), or Panathenaic Way, entered from the Dipylon. The street between the gate and the Agora was lined with porticoes fronted by bronze statues of the famous. Here we may imagine the popular and crowded markets of the day, the money-changers, barbers' shops, and bustle of the most commercial part of the city (comp. Lysias, XXIV, 20; Theophrastos, 'Characters'). Here also lay the *House of Pulytion*, where Alcibiades played the hierophant in the parody of the Eleusinian mysteries (Plut., 'Alcibiades' XIX) before the mutilation of the herms (see below). Between the Pompeion and the Stoa of Zeus lay the *Sanctuary of Demeter, Kore, and Iakchos* with statues of them by Praxiteles (Paus., I, 2, 4); a damaged monumental base, signed by Praxiteles, found built into a wall N. of the railway, is in the museum.

The 1970 excavations immediately uncovered the **Stoa Basileios,** or Royal Portico, where the Archon Basileus held his court. A clear cut identification is provided by the text of Pausanias (I. 3. 1), and the claim to have recognized in the expected spot the 'Lithos'—*'the* Stone' par excellence—on which the archons took their oath of office. A surprisingly small building, with a colonnaded façade of 8 Doric columns, it can be dated c. 500 B.C., perhaps rebuilt on the original lines after the Persian sack of 480 B.C. It survived with alterations until A.D. 400. Two porches were added in the late-5C probably expressly to house the revised statutes of Solon and of Draco. Here occasionally the Council of the Areopagus met—perhaps even when it heard St Paul. A number of sockets for herms may be seen at the N. end, and many herm fragments have been recovered. A base *in situ* records prizewinners in the Epilenaia, a drama festival possibly held in front of the Royal Stoa. To the E.

is the *Leokoreion* near which, while marshalling the Panathenaic procession Hipparchos was assassinated in 514 B.C. by Harmodios and Aristogeiton.

Of the two large groups commemorating the Tyrannicides, only a fragment from an inscribed base has been recovered. The earlier group by Antenor (c. 505 B.C.) was carried off by the Persians. A replacement was fashioned by Kritias and Nesiotes in 476 B.C., and after the original had been returned from Persepolis by Alexander the Great, both groups stood together in the *Orchestra of the Agora*. This early open circle designed for ritual dancing was thus closely related both to the Royal Stoa and the assassination spot, but its exact location is uncertain.

Between the Stoa Basileios and the Stoa Poikile (see below) stood a row of *Herms*, celebrating with epigrams Kimon's great victories over the Persians. On the eve of the Sicilian expedition (415 B.C.) the Athenians were profoundly shocked by the wholesale mutilation of these figures (Thuc. VI, 27–61), and they believed that the outrage was a prelude to an attempt on the constitution. Alcibiades was charged with being the ringleader, recalled from Sicily, and (in his absence) sentenced to death. About 40 fragments listing his personal possessions, confiscated by the state and sold at public auction, have been recovered from the Eleusinion. An inscription naming a 'Stoa of the Herms' was unearthed in 1962.

The most famous of the structures not yet located (probably under the N. side of Adhrianou) was the *Stoa Poikile*, or painted portico, founded c. 460 B.C. by Peisianax (Kimon's brother-in-law), after whom it was sometimes called. Here Zeno taught his disciples, who thus acquire the name Stoics. The building was decorated with battle scenes (Marathon, Troy, etc.), painted by the leading artists of the 5C B.C., including Polygnotos, Mikon, and Panainos, brother of Pheidias. Their work was probably executed on wooden plaques; some blocks fitted with iron spikes (now in the museum) are believed to be from the wall against which they were fixed. The paintings, seen by Pausanias, had disappeared before A.D. 402. In this stoa were also displayed bronze shields captured from the Spartans at Sphakteria in 425 B.C., a fine example of which is displayed in the museum.

Immediately E. of the Altar of Zeus is a late-Roman building, a rectangular structure of unknown purpose on massive concrete foundations. Its N.E. angle lies over the **Peribolos of the Twelve Gods** (Pl. 3), much of which is obscured by the railway, but which has been investigated and firmly identified by an inscription found *in situ*. The *Altar*, was set up by Peisistratos the Younger in 521 B.C. within a fenced enclosure. Situated in the open section of the Agora bordering the Panathenaic Way, it was the 'London Stone' of Athens whence road distances were measured. A recognized place of sanctuary, it may possibly be the '*Altar of Pity*' seen by Pausanias.

The Twelve were not synonymous with the twelve Olympian gods but represent a local Athenian grouping.—Remains of a 6C Eschara, or ground altar, to the S. may mark the *Altar of Aiakos*, mentioned by Herodotus (V, 89).

The site of the TEMPLE OF ARES (Pl. 6) has been marked in gravel. Some architectural fragments have been arranged at its W. extremity and foundation blocks are visible at the E. end. These bear Roman masons' marks showing that the temple, which markedly resembled the Hephaisteion and is ascribed to the same architect, was removed to this site in the Augustan period possibly from Acharnai. Foundations of a large altar can be seen to the E.

To the S. the construction known to 19C archæologists as the '*Stoa of the Giants*' marks the N. limit of two huge interrelated structures, the **Agrippeion** (Pl. 7), or *Odeion of Agrippa*, and a much later *Gymnasium*.

The site may perhaps be equated with the *Perischoinisma*, where some public functions (ostracism, etc.) continued until c. 15 B.C., when an *Odeion*, or concert-hall, was endowed by M. Vipsanius Agrippa, son-in-law of the Emp. Augustus, on the site. Shortly after Pausanias saw it in this form, its roof collapsed, but in

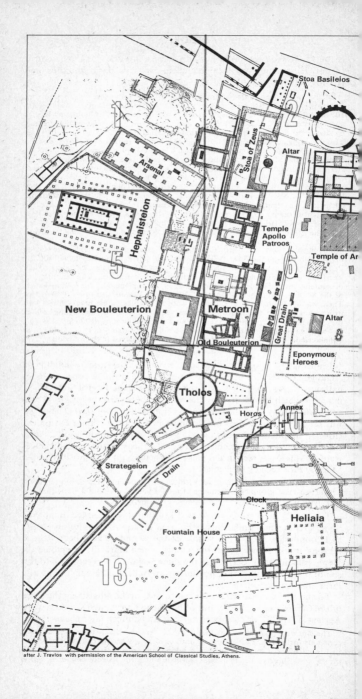

Stoa Basileios

Stoa of Zeus

Altar

Arsenal

Temple Apollo Patroos

Temple of Ar

Hephaisteion

Altar

New Bouleuterion

Metroon

Great Drain

Old Bouleuterion

Eponymous Heroes

Tholos

Horos

Annex

Strategeion

Drain

Clock

Heliaia

Fountain House

after J. Travlos with permission of the American School of Classical Studies, Athens.

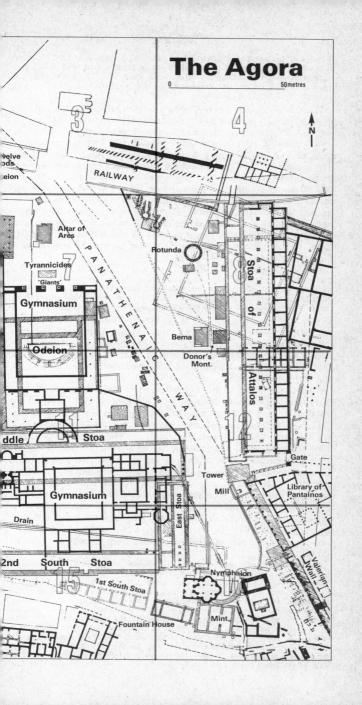

The Agora

0   50 metres

N

3

4

Twelve
Gods
...eion

RAILWAY

Altar of
Ares

Rotunda

Tyrannicides

'Giants'

7

P A N A T H E N A I C

8

Stoa

of

Gymnasium

Odeion

Bema

Donor's
Mont.

Attalos

W A Y

Middle

Stoa

11

12

Gate

Gymnasium

Tower

Mill

Library of
Pantainos

Drain

East Stoa

Valerian
Wall

2nd

South

Stoa

15

1st South Stoa

Nympheion

Fountain House

Mint

the reign of Antoninus Pius (c. A.D. 150) it was rebuilt on a smaller scale, probably as a lecture-hall. This was consumed by fire in the Herulian sack of 267 and much of the masonry used in the 'Valerian' wall. About A.D. 400 a vast *Gymnasium* rose on the site extending well to the S.; this was perhaps the principal seat of the university until its closure in 529.

The ODEION, which was roofed by a single span c. 27 yds wide, was surrounded on three sides by a two-storied portico and entered from the stoa to the S. Traces can be seen of the lower story. Of the *Auditorium*, which seated c. 1000 people, only a few marble seats are preserved, together with some of the polychrome paving of the *Orchestra* floor. The remains of the *Skene* have been buttressed with modern walling. The position of the façade of the Antonine rebuilding is marked by two seated figures (?philosophers) which formed part of its sculptural ornament. The '*Giants*', two of which are in fact Tritons, were reused in the façade of the 5C GYMNASIUM. Copied from figures on the Parthenon pediments, they also belonged originally to the second Odeion, where (being then six in number) they supported the architrave of the remodelled N. façade. The great *Rectangular Court*, behind the gymnasium's façade, can be traced by its rough wall.

To the S., reached by a rectangular lobby and a semicircular corridor, is a *Square Court*, with a *Bath-House* on the W., and on the E. a third *Small Court*, surrounded by well-preserved rooms, which may have served as the administrative offices of the university. The whole of this S. complex lies athwart earlier stoas (see below) now believed to have fulfilled the same function.

We cross the PANATHENAIC WAY, here marked by its stone water channel and lined with bases of unidentified monuments. The processional road crossed diagonally in front of the Stoa of Attalos, where it had a gravel surface, passed in front of the Library of Pantainos (see below), where in later times it was paved, and climbed the slope of the Acropolis on a ramp.

The E. side of the agora is closed by the *Stoa of Attalos** (Pl. 12), dedicated as the **Agora Museum** by King Paul in 1956. Erected by Attalos II, king of Pergamon (159–138 B.C.), as the inscription (recovered in 1861) on the architrave records, it was used for promenades, for watching the Panathenaic Procession and events in the Agora, and for retail trade, and is mentioned by Athenæus alone of classical writers. Pausanias ignores it. The stoa was sacked in A.D. 267, but the ruins were incorporated in the Valerian wall so that the N. end survived throughout the ages to roof height, and sufficient of its plan and members were recovered to make an accurate restoration possible. The building was reconstructed on its old foundations in 1953–56 with materials from the same sources as those originally used, the expense being defrayed by private donors in the United States. The façade is of Pentelic marble, the remainder of creamy limestone from an ancient quarry in Piraeus.

Excavations beneath the foundations uncovered graves of the Mycenean and Protogeometric periods and later wells. The earliest building on the site (late 5C B.C.), consisting of an irregular court surrounded by small rooms, was found to contain bronze voting discs for jurors. It is conjectured to have been the *Parabyston*, or Court of the Eleven, a petty sessions court for offenders taken flagrante delicto. This was superseded as part of the Lycurgan improvements by an edifice c. 65 yds square, which probably served the same function. The Stoa of Attalos survived in part from late-Roman to Turkish times incorporated in a rampart, its rooms being filled with rubble. An oblong tower was built at the N. end, another in the middle of the building. At the S.W. corner stood a gate, the N. tower of which was converted into the chapel of *Panayia Pyrgiotissa* (Our Lady of the Tower), now demolished.

The stoa, a two-storied building 382 ft long and 66 ft wide, has a colonnade of 45 columns, Doric below, double Ionic above, closed by a low balustrade. Within, the portico is divided lengthwise into two aisles by a row of 22 columns, Ionic on the ground floor, Pergamene above. Twenty-one rectangular chambers designed as shops opened from the back of the portico on each floor; each had a door opening on to the inner aisle and a loophole in the back wall. The arrangement has been modified in the reconstruction. The exterior staircase at the N. end has been restored as originally planned; below it an exedra with a marble bench is entered through an arched opening (the earliest known use of a visible arch in an Athenian building). The S. end follows the alterations that were made at the end of the 1C A.D. (comp. below). In front of the centre of the stoa are a *Bema* and the base of the *Donor's Monument*, more than 100 blocks of which have been recovered from the dismantled Valerian wall. It resembled the monument of Agrippa on the Acropolis and bore, about the level of the second story of the stoa, a bronze quadriga. It was later re-dedicated to the Emp. Tiberius. Other statues stood against the terrace wall to the N.

The ancient design has been somewhat modified internally to house c. 65,000 finds from the Agora excavations; the vast majority of these form study collections (available to specialists on application) on the upper floor and in the basement, where there is a unique library of 6700 documents on stone.

The GROUND FLOOR contains a selection of the most notable pieces of the collection. Beneath the portico is displayed **Marble *Sculpture.** AT THE S. END: S 2154, Apollo Citharoedos (350–325 B.C.), conjecturally the cult statue of Apollo Patroös by Euphranor. I 4165, Base for statues of Demeter and Kore: note signature of Praxiteles; the monument was dedicated by Kleiokrateia, daughter of Polyeuktos the Teithrasian (the 41st oration of Demosthenes concerns a lawsuit about Polyeuktos's estate).—ALONG THE WALL: S 2038–39 & I 6628, The Iliad and Odyssey personified and inscribed base for the first, group of the 2C A.D., signed by Jason the Athenian on one of the long lower lappets of the Iliad's cuirass. Odeion stage front restored (model). S 1882, Aphrodite (c. 420 B.C.). S 182, 'Nereid' acroterion (c. 400 B.C.). I 7154, Cave of Pan relief, inscribed (c. 320 B.C.). S 429, Acroterion group of Hephaisteion (c. 415 B.C.), flanked by fragments attrib. to the E. pediment of the temple. S 1232, Torso of Athena (5C B.C.). I 7167, Rider relief (early 4C B.C.), commemorating victory won by the tribe Leontis in the anthippasia, the cavalry contest of the Panathenaic Games. S 676, 679, 870, 1072, Reliefs from the Ares temple frieze (c. 420 B.C.). S 654, Torso of Athena (second half 5C B.C.).—AT THE N. END: S 657, Portrait statue of a magistrate (end 5C A.D.). This elaborate but lifeless piece may be compared with S 312, the Nike acroterion from the S.E. corner of the Stoa of Zeus Eleutherios (c. 400 B.C.), a vivid flamboyant figure with drapery billowing in the wind.—ALONG THE INNER COLONNADE: IG II2 3781, Base of a statue of Karneades, founder of the new Athenian Academy, under whom the dedicators of the statue, the future Attalos II and Ariarathes V, king of Cappadocia, studied as princes. S 270, Roman copy of portrait of Herodotus. S 1654 Nymph with water jar, copy of a famous 5C statue of Aphrodite. S 2354, Head of goddess, faithful replica of a classical original, extraordinarily close to the Nike of Paionios. S 2094, Head of goddess (c. 430 B.C.), by an Attic sculptor of the first rank. *I 6524, Stele inscribed with a law of 336 B.C. against tyranny (the relief represents Democracy crowning the Demos of Athens).

The *EXHIBITION GALLERY (hours, see above), occupying the length of 10 shops, is arranged chronologically and demonstrates the almost unbroken occupation of the site from Neolithic to Turkish times. Representative pottery of all periods is attractively displayed. Case 1. Neolithic vases found in wells on the N. slope of the Acropolis, the earliest evidence of habitation (note the red polished jar of the 4th millennium B.C.). Objects from royal chamber-tombs of the 14C B.C. on the N. slope of the Areopagus: Case 4 (r.) Mycenean bronze sword; Case 5 (l.), BI 511. Ivory *Toilet-box carved with griffins bringing down stags. Burials of various periods, urn, grave, and pithos. Cases 13–18. Pottery of the Geometric period from burials and sacrificial pyres (model chariot, child's boots, etc.). Contents of the grave of a rich Athenian lady of c. 850 B.C. Case 23 (r.) Earthen mould for casting a bronze statue of Apollo (6C B.C.). Heads of Herms. On the right are three inscriptions: I 2729. Rules of the library of Pantainos; I 4809. Dues owed to Athens in 421 B.C. by the tributary cities of the Hellespont; I 4120. List of 6C Eponymous Archons, including the names of Hippias, Kleisthenes, and Miltiades for successive years (525–523 B.C.). I 3872. Fragment of a base belonging to the second group of Tyrannicides. *P 1231. Kneeling boy, terracotta oil flask in the form of an athlete binding his hair with the victor's fillet (540–530 B.C.). To the left (Cases 26–28) standard weights and measures; objects from a court of justice: Bronze voting discs (comp. above); klepsydra, or water clock, in terracotta (5C B.C.), designed to measure the time allowed for pleadings (comp. Aristotle, 'Constitution of Athens'); I3967. Part of a kleroterion for selection by lot using numbered balls.

There follow cases (30–32) of choice black- and red-figured *Vases, attributed to particular vase-painters and potters: P 12628. Alabastron, by *Amasis* (mid-6C); P 24114, P 24110. Two cups assigned to *Epiktetos*. Cups: P 1272. Youth jumping using halteres; P 1273. Youth reclining; P 1274. Youth playing the game of cottabus. P23165, P 24102, P 24116, P 24115. Four cups attributed to *Chairas* (c. 500 B.C.); P24113. Kylix signed by *Gorgos* (c. 510 B.C.; possibly providing the real name of the Berlin Painter?), depicting Achilles and Memnon the Ethiopian in combat; P 24131. Kylix by *Epiktetos*; Calyx-krater (by *Exekias*, c. 530 B.C.), the earliest known example of this form, found in a well on the N. slope of the Acropolis; the paintings show the introduction of Herakles to Olympos and Greeks and Trojans fighting for the body of Patroclus.

*B 30, Bronze Nike head of 430 B.C. The head was originally plated with sheets of gold over silver, which must have been hammered on to the modelled surface of the bronze. Edges of the sheets were bent down in the channels and securely keyed by a packing of solid gold. This may still be seen behind each ear and at the back of the neck.

To the left, B 262. Huge bronze shield, captured by the Athenians from the Spartans at Sphakteria (Pylos), 425 B.C., crudely inscribed ΑΘΗΝΑΙΟΙ ΑΠΟ ΛΑΚΕΔΑΙΜΟΝΙΩΝ ΕΚ ΠΥΛΟ. Child's commode (or 'potty') in terracotta (early 6C B.C.). Case 38 contains Ostraka (sherds used in secret ballots by citizens recommending banishment) of 487–417 B.C. with the names of Aristides the Just, Themistocles, Kimon, and Pericles as candidates for ostracism. Case 39. Household grills and ovens in terracotta. Case 42. A few of the 75,000 coins (mainly 6C B.C. to 6C A.D.) found in the Agora, including four in gold (Persian Daric, 465–425 B.C.; Alexander the Great, 336–323 B.C.; Silvestro Valiero, 1694–1700; and Napoleon III, 1854). BI 236. Statuette in ivory, reconstituted from fragments; this is a replica (2C A.D.) of the Apollo Lykeios of Praxiteles. Among the sculptural fragments to the left is (S 922) a miniature copy of the cult image of the Mother of the Gods by Agorakritos.

The far end of the museum is devoted to Hellenistic pottery, Roman terracottas, including a toy animal on wheels, lamps from the 7C B.C. illustrating a return after 14 centuries of evolution to the crude design of the original, Roman portrait busts; Byzantine and Venetian ceramics (portrait of a Doge). *S 221. Young Satyr in marble, a copy of the 2C A.D. of a Hellenistic prototype. Mosaic pavement from a house of the 5C A.D.

The *Rotunda*, or Monopteros, in front of the N. part of the Stoa may have been an ornamental fountain. The green marble columns probably supported a brick dome.

To the s. of the Stoa of Attalos, the misnamed **'Valerian' Wall** (Pl, p. 103) is a Roman fortification built with stone from buildings partially destroyed in the Herulian sack of A.D. 267 (when the Emp. Valerian was already dead). An inscription attributes it to Claudius Illyrius. The large tower at the N. end of the standing curtain was one of two forming a gate. The wall, which has now been largely dismantled in order to recover the precious earlier inscriptions incorporated in it, followed the line of the façade of the destroyed **Library of Pantainos**, erected before A.D. 102 at the expense of Titus Flavius Pantainos, who dedicated it to Athena Polias and the Emp. Trajan (inscription from the lintel of the main door exposed). A portico of nine Ionic columns faced the road (graffiti suggest youthful readers) and gave on to rooms grouped round a peristyle; the principal rooms lay to the E.

Between the library and the stoa a street led E. towards the Roman market through an *Arch* provided with a small fountain. The construction of this right-of-way necessitated modifications to the s. end of the Stoa of Attalos. A *Public Latrine* behind the arch could be reached from the stoa by a small door from its s. staircase.—Remains of a *Water-Mill* of the 5–6C A.D. and of its well-built conduit can be traced on the outer side of the Valerian wall.

At the s.E. corner of the Agora a temple was erected in Augustan times from materials brought from the Doric temple at Thorikos. Its hexastyle porch was cleared in 1959.

Beyond the fenced enclosure the *Panathenaic Way* continues upward, showing well-preserved paving of the 2C A.D. The site of the *Eleusinion*, about half-way up on the E. side, has been identified by the discovery of reliefs, inscriptions, and cult pottery (kernoi) relating to the worship of Demeter and Kore.

Near the s.E. gate is the pretty **Church of the Holy Apostles** (Pl. 16), stripped in 1954–57 of 19C additions and restored by the American School to its form of c. 1020. Within the narthex are 17C wall-paintings from the demolished church of St Spiridon. Of the four Roman columns that supported the dome, one of the originals remains; the other three are copies.

Beneath and to the E. of the church are the remains of a *Nymphaion*, a fountain-house with a semicircular outer wall, similar to that at Olympia built by Herodes Atticus. Its construction necessitated the demolition of the N. half of a building dated to c. 400 B.C., firmly identified with the *Argyrokopeion*, the mint of Athens, whence came the famous 'Owls' that became the accepted coinage of the E. Mediterranean for 200 years. To the N., bordering the modern road (which retains a course from the Bronze Age), are remains of a *Fountain-House* (the Enneakrounos of Pausanias), probably erected by Peisistratos. This road ran along the back of the *First South Stoa*, which, from the 5C to the 2C B.C., dominated the s. side of the Agora, probably as administrative offices. At its w. end the ground plan has been recovered of a large structure which survived, with alterations, from the mid-6C B.C. to the sack of Sulla. This is tentatively identified as the *Heliaia*. In the 4C B.C. the building had a *Water Clock* attached to its N. side, which probably told the time by means of a float on a column of water. Another *Fountain-House* stands to the s.w.

In the middle of the 2C B.C. the s. side of the Agora was entirely re-modelled. This was achieved by constructing the MIDDLE STOA (Pl. 11) a portico open on both sides and divided lengthwise by a screen wall. Over 150 yds long, it was the largest edifice of the Agora, extending from the Panathenaic Way to the Tholos, in front of which it was raised on a high podium. The red conglomerate foundations are best seen at the w. end (where the floor level is indicated) and members of the poros colon-nade, which had unfluted Doric columns, will be noted at the N.E. corner. The N. terrace of the stoa provided access to the Odeion (comp. above). In Hadrian's time a small annex of the Metroön was built against the podium opposite the Tholos. The *East Stoa* and *Second South Stoa* completed the Hellenistic project, much of which has been obscured by the Roman gymnasium.

To the w. of the Middle Stoa near the Tholos are scanty remains of a large building of the 5C B.C., perhaps the *Strategeion*, headquarters of the Ten Generals.

6 PLAKA

The name **Plaka** seems to be of recent origin and is unsatisfactorily derived either from the Albanian *pliaka* (old), or from a *plaque* said to have marked the crossing of its principal streets (see below). The area it describes has no official boundaries but may be said to comprise that part of the old town extending between Odhos Ermou and the N. and N.E. slopes of the Acropolis, corresponding to the ancient deme of KYDATHENAION and including four small districts once known as *Rizokastro, Brizaki, Alikokou,* and *Anaphiotika*. In Turkish times much of this area was called *Gorgopikos* after the little cathedral. Its narrow undulating lanes have no pattern but follow the configuration of the terrain, rising in steps in the higher sector. The principal streets are Adhrianou and Kidathenaion, which still follow Turkish (perhaps ancient) courses. The houses date for the most part from the mid-19C and despite popular occupation often proclaim their patrician origin. Many of them are occupied by tavernas. The best time for sight-seeing is in the morning; in the evening Plaka is transformed into a tourist area of night-spots where garish lighting and vociferous touting are more in evidence than value for money.

Plateia Monastirakiou, or **Monastiraki Square** (6, 4), opens from the s. side of Odhos Ermou (Rte 5); from the Agora it may be quickly reached by following Odhos Adhrianou (r.; see below) from the N. exit. Here is Monastirion Stn, where the Piraeus railway is still under-ground. In the square stands the church of the *Pantanassa*, or Great Monastery, commonly called MONASTIRAKI because of its smallness. An aisled basilica of the 10C, with an elliptical cupola, it was badly restored in 1911.

At the s.E. corner, dominating the square, is the former **Mosque of Tzistarakis**, built in 1759 by the Voivode Tzistarakis, when a column of the Olympieion was sacrificed in its construction. An open loggia, approached by steps, precedes a plain square building surmounted by a heavy octagon; its minaret was razed after 1821. Used for years as a prison it became a museum in 1918. It was reopened in 1958 under the directorship of Mme. P. Zora as the *Museum of Greek Popular Art* though it now houses only the ceramics of the collection. The rich colours of the surviving *mihrab* (prayer niche) may be noted.

The narrow Odhos Pandrossou, which runs E. towards the cathedral, masking the N. wall of Hadrian's Library, is the principal relic of the Turkish *Bazar*, now occupied by antique dealers and shoemakers; the Albanian tsarouchia (scarlet boots with turned-up toes) are exposed for sale. Ifestou, the other way, runs to the original Flea Market (see Rte 4).

Beyond stands the chief surviving portion of the so-called *Stoa of Hadrian*, a vast forecourt to the Library of Hadrian (see below). The marble w. wall formed the main façade of the building, having at the centre a simple propylon, standing forward of antæ and approached by six steps, the only entrance so far discovered. The left portion survives as far as the jamb of the doorway; the mosaic to the left adorned the little chapel of *Ayios Asomatos sta Skalia* that adjoined the porch until the late 19C. The porch was flanked on either side by seven unfluted columns of Karystos marble standing slightly forward of the wall and supporting on Corinthian capitals an architrave which returns over each column. The finely preserved section N. of the porch remains. —Odhos Areos, lined with booths of workers in old rubber and basketry, continues towards the Acropolis.

A few paces to the left is the *Taxiarkhón* (6, 4), or Church of the Archangels, rebuilt after a fire in 1832, which houses a much venerated ikon, the Panayia Grigorousa. New excavations in Odhos Poikilis (r.) show the Roman way from the new market (see below) to the Agora; a house in this street, described by Chateaubriand as 'a splendid museum', after his reception here by Fauvel, the French consul, in 1806, is now ruinous.

To the left stands the *Gate of Athena Archegetis*, the main entrance to the Roman market (see below), set a little s. of centre in the w. wall. It consists of an outer Doric portico with four columns supporting an entablature and pediment, most of which is still in position. This stood just forward of the main wall, its antæ forming the ends of two side walls which were carried back to the inner colonnade of the market to form a vestibule. Within this a double porch of two columns between antæ formed the gate proper.

A worn inscription on the architrave records the dedication of the building to Athena Archegetis, and states that its erection was due to the generosity of Julius Caesar and of Augustus during the archonship of Nikias. On the central acroterion, as is known from the inscription (lost) that it bore, stood a statue of Lucius Caesar, son of Agrippa and Augustus's daughter Julia, who was adopted by Augustus in 17 B.C. and died in A.D. 2. The gateway was doubtless erected between these dates. On the N. jamb of the doorway is engraved the celebrated edict of Hadrian regulating the sale of oil and the excise duty thereon.

The site of the Roman agora, which is entered from the N.E. corner, was partially excavated in the 19C. Just within the gate (r.) are the foundations of a large *Public Latrine* of the 1C A.D. The *Tower of the Winds (6, 4), properly the *Horologion of Andronikos Kyrrhestes*, stands beyond, just outside the market enclosure. Built in the 1C B.C. by the astronomer Andronikos of Kyrrhos (authorities disagree whether this is the Syrian or the Macedonian town), it served the triple purpose of sundial, water-clock, and weather-vane. The tower, which stands on a base of three steps, takes the form of a marble octagon with a pyramidal roof of marble slabs held together by a round keystone. Each face accurately marks a cardinal point and is adorned with a relief representing the wind blowing from that direction. On the N.E. and N.W. faces were porches of two fluted Corinthian columns with peculiarly simple and graceful capitals. Fragments of the N.W. entablature have been reassembled close by. The tower, according to Vitruvius (I, 6, 4), was originally surmounted by a revolving bronze Triton holding a wand, which pointed out the face corresponding to the prevailing wind.

The eight figures are represented as winged and floating almost horizontally through the air. Beginning at the N. side and proceeding clockwise: N., Boreas, in a thick sleeved mantle, with folds blustering in the air, and high-laced buskins, blows a twisted shell; N.E., Kaikias empties a shield full of hailstones; E., Apeliotes exhibits flowers and fruit; S.E., Euros, with his right arm muffled in his mantle, threatens a hurricane; S., Notos, emptying an urn, is producing a shower; S.W., Lips, driving before him the stern ornament of a ship, promises a rapid voyage; W., Zephyros showers into the air a lapful of flowers; N.W., Skiron bears a bronze vessel of charcoal in his hands, with which he dries up rivers.—Beneath the figures of the winds are traced the lines of eight sundials.

Attached to the S. face is a reservoir in the form of a semicircular turret, from which water could be released in a slow steady stream to run the clock works. Through the doors in the porches can be seen the ancient pavement of white marble, scored with circular channels for a parapet and other channels so far unexplained. It is possible, though unproven, that the building was a gift from Julius Cæsar to the city and that it contained a planetarium. At present miscellaneous finds from all over Athens are stored here, obscuring some of the detail of the interior.

In Turkish times the tower was occupied as a Tekke by dervishes.—The arches of Hymettian marble on a massive base to the S. form the façade of a building dedicated to Athena Archegetis and the Divi Augusti in the 1C A.D. The function of the building, formerly wrongly identified as the Agoranomion (office of the Magistrates of the Market), is not known.

At a lower level to the W. extends the **Roman Market,** the S. half of which is revealed. This was a large rectangle c. 365 ft by 315, bounded by a poros wall (early 1C B.C.), within which, on the S. side at least, a (probably Doric) colonnade flanked central blocks of rooms. Later (? under Hadrian) an Ionic *Peristyle* was added within, having unfluted columns of Hymettian marble with bases, capitals, and epistyle of Pentelic. The central area was bordered by a deep drainage gully and later paved in marble (in places still *in situ*). To reach this we descend the five steps of the *South-East Propylon,* which, though smaller and later, has a similar plan to the W. gate (see above). It is neither, on the central axis of the market, nor at right angles to the wall. Its lower portion is well preserved, though the columns are all broken off 8–10 ft from the pavement. It is flanked by a row of shops, of which five have been explored, when inscriptions were found on the floor or on columns giving the names of the shopkeepers.

The mosque, now used as an archæological workshop, that occupies the corner of the site, dates from the late-15C and is probably the *Fetihie Cami,* or Victory Mosque, built to celebrate the Turkish conquest. From time to time visiting Sheikhs perform their devotions here.

On the corner of Odhos Aiolou all that remains of the *Medresse,* or seminary, is a ruined gate bearing a Turkish inscription that records its foundation by Mehmet Fakri in 1721. Here, a century later, the cadi Haci Khalil dissuaded the Turks from a general massacre of male Greeks in Attica. A few paces along this street is the **Library of Hadrian** (6, 4), closed to the public. The E. wall is buttressed by six Corinthian pilasters and originally presented an unbroken face to the street; the ancient entrance was in the marble W. façade (comp. above). The building consisted of a huge rectangular wall of poros, c. 400 ft by 270, portions of which survive on three sides, which enclosed a cloistered court adorned with a "hundred splendid columns" (Pausanias) of

Phrygian marble (long since vanished). In the N. and S. walks three recesses opened in the outer walls, the central one rectangular, the side ones semicircular. On the E. side the main block of five rooms was ranged along the cloister. The central chamber, which was entered through a porch of four columns, housed the *Library* proper, in the E. wall is a large central niche with four smaller ones on each side, which held the bookshelves—an arrangement similar to that of the library of Pergamon. The rooms on each side were probably (like those in the contemporary library at Alexandria) workrooms and repositories for archives.

The interior of the quadrangle was doubtless laid out as a garden, with a long central reservoir or pool. About A.D. 410 a square building, probably a lecture hall, quatrefoil in plan, was erected by the governor Herculius over the E. end of the pool. Its N.E. angle stands to c. 9 ft and some mosaic fragments of the exedræ survive. This building was replaced in the 6C, by a basilica which, under the Byzantines, became the *Megáli Panayía*, or church of Great St Mary, and survived in a later modification until 1885.—Much of the market site was occupied by a bazar, through which passed Odhos Adhrianou, divided since the excavations into two parts.

We cross the pleasant square opposite, and from Odhos Adhrianou climb the picturesque Odhos Mnesikleous to the little 14C church of the Transfiguration (Μεταμόρφωσις τοῦ Σωτῆρος), known as *Sotiraki*. This stands just beneath the Acropolis but below the level of the ancient *Peripatos*, which here divided the official precincts of the lower slope from the primitive sanctuaries above.

Close by is the **Kanellopoulos Museum** (adm 30 dr.; daily 9–3.30, closed Mon), opened in 1976. The 19C mansion has been tastefully restored and the interior arranged functionally to display the eclectic family *Collection of antiquities of all periods. It is especially rich in everyday objects and jewellery. Upstairs are outstanding Archaic and Classical vases, and downstairs fine ikons and church plate. In the basement are two huge blocks of an ancient building.

Odhos Theorías, a modern road, runs (r.) to the entrance of the Acropolis.

The daunting **North Slope of the Acropolis** (no adm.), occupied in Neolithic times and known in antiquity as the LONG ROCKS, repays inspection from this level. Here were worshipped the primitive deities of vegetation and fertility cults which survived from the remotest times into the Classical period. A decree of 415 B.C., forbidding the erection of altars within the Pelargikon area, may represent an attempt to restrict these rites. Later writers pointedly ignore or mock these survivals of popular belief. The area was investigated by the Greek Archæological Society and the American School in 1931–39, when a mass of black-figured pottery was discovered, together with many objects apparently thrown down from the Acropolis; these included the Erechtheion accounts, the Opisthodomos inventory, the accounts for the Athena Promachos statue, about 200 ostraka inscribed with Themistocles' name, and the calyx-krater of Exekias.

At the w. end, above Klepsydra (comp. Rte 2) are four *Caves*. The first is little more than a niche with rock-cut seats. In the second (B), somewhat larger, have been found a number of tablets (of Roman date) dedicated to Apollo Hypoakraios by archons taking the oath of office. The third (Γ), which is separated from the second only by a spur, has been suggested as the place where the Pythaists watched for the flash of lightning from Mt Parnes before starting the procession to Delphi. The narrow tunnel-like cave (Z), above which later stood a chapel of St Athanasios, is identified with the *Cave of Pan*. Herodotus (VI, 105) tells how the worship of Pan was revived after his appearance to Pheidippides in 490 B.C. This cave is referred to by Euripides ('Ion' 938) and Aristophanes ('Lysistrata' 911). Farther E. cult reliefs with phallic and fertility emblems were discovered as well as fragments of a frieze of Erotes which may have decorated the temenos wall. On a large boulder is inscribed a boundary mark of the Peripatos. The huge *Cave* in the E. face of the Acropolis rock has not been fully explored though much pottery came to light here in 1936.

Just to the N. of the Sotiraki, No. 5 in Odhos Tholou, is the decaying *Old University* (now a taverna), a building dating from the Venetian occupation, used as public offices by the Turks, and rebuilt with a third story by Cleanthes in 1830; here the university functioned in 1837–41. *Ayi Anargyrhi* (6, 6), a little farther E., is by tradition associated with the Athenian orphan who became the Empress Irene (752–803), reigning alone in Byzantium after the death in 797 of Leo IV, her husband. The Sarandapichos family, to which she belonged, is said to have come from this district. The church, remodelled in the 17C, serves the monastery Metokhi tou Panayiou Tafou, a dependency of the Holy Sepulchre at Jerusalem. The Byzantine chapel of *Ayios Nikólaos Rangavás* (7, 5) stands at the corner of Odhos Pritaniou. The site of the Prytaneion itself (the official centre of the city where the sacred flame was kept burning) has not yet been found. Some slight remains to the N. of Od. Kiristou are tentatively identified with the Diogeneum. Overlooking this street, at the corner of Odhos Flessa, are the rooms in which Caroline, Princess of Wales, was entertained in 1816.

We descend to ODHOS ADHRIANOU. No. 96, built under the Turks by the Benizelos archons, is perhaps the oldest surviving house in Athens. The family name survives in Odhos Benizelou, which descends hence to the Cathedral (Rte 4). We follow Adhrianou, where, in a house built c. 1780, lived George Finlay (1799–1875), the historian. The *Demotic School* at the corner of Odhos Flessa occupies the site of the 'Mosque of the Column', which became for Morosini's Lutheran gunners (for a short time in 1687) the first Protestant Church in Greece. The *Hill Memorial School*, at the corner of Thoukididhou and Nikodimou streets, to the N.E., was founded in 1831 by John Henry Hill (d. 1882), an American missionary. We may continue to the Monument of Lysikrates (Rte 1) or turn left into Odhos Kidathenaion, where, at No. 27 (garden) Ludwig of Bavaria stayed in 1835. Many of the neighbouring houses date from this period.

At No. 17 has been installed the **Museum of Greek Popular Art** (daily 9–1, closed Mon; free). The collection of embroidery, ranging from Coptic cloths of the 2C A.D. to local fabrics of the Greek islands, is outstanding. Two magnificent *epitaphioi* (processional palls) date from the 17C. Displayed are gold and silver ware from Asia Minor, ikons, and jewellery of barbaric splendour which emphasises the affinity of Greek medieval art with the Balkans and Near East.

From the little shaded *Plateia* (cafés; 7, 5) we may descend N.E. towards Sindagma Square.

7 FROM THE ARCH OF HADRIAN TO THE BENAKI MUSEUM

Immediately behind the Arch of Hadrian (Rte 1) extends the archæological park (entrance in Leof. Vasilissis Olgas; adm. 8–sunset; fee) surrounding the Temple of Olympian Zeus. To the left we see the remains of a *House* of the 4C B.C.; a cast marks the site where a fine relief (now in the Nat. Mus.) was discovered. A second *House* of the same period, with traces of a pebble mosaic floor, is partly overlaid by **Roman Thermae** of A.D. 124–131, of excellent construction, having four public halls with mosaic floors and the usual three bath chambers off the s. side. It apparently survived into the 7C A.D.

Farther on, excavations at a lower level have revealed part of the *Themistoclean Wall* (c. 479 B.C.), incorporating drums from the Peisistratid Olympieion, with the *Hippades Gate*, a defensive ditch added in the late 4C B.C., and a stretch of ancient road. The ground plan of the *Basilica at the Olympieion*, or St Nicholas of the Columns, a church built of classical fragments in the late 5C, was recovered in 1949 between the baths and the peribolos.

The SANCTUARY OF OLYMPIAN ZEUS occupies an artificial terrace supported by a *Peribolos* of square Piraeic stones buttressed at regular intervals. Except near the propylon and at the S.E. corner, where the buttresses and arched drains date largely from the time of Hadrian, this retaining wall is mostly a work of restoration. It measures 225 yds by 142, making a perimeter (as indicated by Pausanias) of 4 stadia. The ground plan of its principal entrance, a Doric *Propylon*, has been clarified by restoration.

In the centre stand the majestic remains of the **Olympieion**, or *Temple of Olympian Zeus*, the largest temple in Greece. It took 700 years to complete, "a great victory of time," as Philostratus happily describes it. Livy says "it is the only temple on earth of a size adequate to the greatness of the god," though it was in fact exceeded in extent by temples to other gods at Agrigento and Selinus in Sicily, and at Ephesus and Miletus in Asia Minor.

History. Scanty remains of a small early shrine have been discovered with vaults beneath having an exit through a subterranean passage to the Ilissos. This may account for the tradition that a temple was founded here by Deukalion over the chasm through which the waters receded after the flood. Pausanias relates that in commemoration of this event an annual sacrifice of flour mixed with honey was thrown into the cleft. Pesistratos seems to have been the first to undertake the construction of a temple on a grand scale, possibly, as Aristotle suggests ('Politics'), to keep the people too busy to indulge in plots. Work ceased before the stylobate was complete when Hippias went into exile and much of the masonry was used in the Themistoclean wall (comp. above). In 174 B.C. Antiochus Ephiphanes, king of Syria, resumed building to a new design by Cossutius, a Roman architect, who substituted the Corinthian for the Doric order. Work was again interrupted at the entablature stage and put back further in 86 B.C., when Sulla carried off some of the shafts and capitals to Rome for the Capitoline Temple. The honour of its completion was reserved for Hadrian who dedicated the temple on his second visit to Athens c. A.D. 130 and set up a chryselephantine statue of the god within the cella (a copy of that by Pheidias at Olympia), as well as a colossal statue of himself. Cyriacus of Ancona (c. 1450) noted 21 standing columns with their architraves. In 1760 the Turkish governor converted one to lime for the construction of a new mosque; the great storm of 26 Oct 1852 overthrew another.

The **Temple** stands on a stylobate (118 yds by 45) of three steps, the lower two of poros from the original foundation, the upper one of marble (partially restored in 1960–61). The foundations, which were laid by Peisistratos, exhibit the same curvilinear features as those of the Parthenon. Dipteral octastyle in arrangement with an extra row of columns at each end, the temple had 20 columns at each side, making 104 in all. Of these 13 survive in a group with part of the architrave at the s.e., and three farther w. They are of Pentelic marble with 16 blunt flutings. The fallen column, which was blown down in 1852, shows clearly the construction of base, 16 column drums, and capital in two sections. Its base diameter is 5½ ft, and height 56 ft. The capitals are beautifully carved. The original height of the front is estimated at 90 ft. The stones comprising the architrave weigh up to 23 tons; in the middle ages a stylite lived on the architrave that still covers the two w. columns of the s.e. group. The remains are not sufficient to detetermine the plan of the cella, though Vitruvius records it as hypæthral. The ruin is popularly known as *Kolónnaes* (columns); the columns are floodlit in summer.

We leave Leoforos Singrou (Rte 12) on our right and take Odhos Athanassiou Diakou to (5 min.) the *Kallirrhoi Bridge* over the seasonal Ilissos. An older bridge, surviving beneath, is well seen from Kallirrhoi (see below).

The **Ilissos** (Ιλισός) flows from two sources on the slopes of Hymettos, one at Kaisariani, the other at St John Theologos. The united branches, diminished since Classical times and now either underground or canalized, flow on the s. side of the city and, passing to the s. of the Mouseion, descend to the Bay of Phaleron.

The district extending outside the s. wall of the city along the river bank was anciently known as Κεποι, the Gardens. To the s.w. of the Olympieion lay the *Python 'on the Wall'*. Two large fragments (now in the National Museum), found on the right bank of the Ilissos, have been certainly identified with the Altar of Apollo Pythios by their inscription, a dedication by Peisistratos the Younger, which is quoted in full by Thucydides (VI, 54). Further finds in 1965–68 below Od. Iosifton Rogon may locate the site.

Beyond the river lay the district known as Διομεια. Downstream, c. 300 yds below the bridge, is the presumed site (excavated by the British School in 1896–97) of the *Gymnasium of Kynosarges*. An inscription naming Kynosarges has been found near the church of Ay. Pandeleimon.

Just above the bridge somewhat artificially contrived is the *Kallirrhoi*, a shallow fall where the Ilissos flows over a ridge of rock. The traditional name, which dates back at least to Byzantine times, recalls that of the ancient **Kallirrhoë Spring** (8, 5), but the locality has drastically altered since Classical times. In 1896 floods swept away remains of ancient masonry and even altered the contour of the rock. The course of the river has now been irretrievably interfered with and its waters have largely vanished underground. On the s. bank, beyond the modern chapel of Ayía Fotíni, a much eroded figure of Pan adorns a right-angled chamber hewn out of the rock.

Extending towards the Olympieion is the 'ILISSOS AREA' excavated by Threpsiades in 1956–67 during the covering of the Ilissos and the construction of the Arditós highway. The area is traversed by a section of the Valerian Wall, for the building of which most of the ancient structures were quarried. The gate here may be that of Aigeus (comp. Plutarch, 'Theseus', xii). Foundations remain of a temple of late date (mostly under the road) and, between this and the Olympieion temenos wall, of three buildings of some importance amid a confusion of ruins. These are from E. to W.: the *Precinct of Kronos and Rhea*, with prominent foundations of a Doric temple ascribed to the 2C A.D.; a much larger Doric temple of the 5C B.C., which had a peristyle of 13 columns by 6, perhaps to be identified with the *Temple of Apollo Delphinios*; and a civic structure in archaic polygonal masonry believed to be the *Law court of the Delphinion*.

From the S. end of the bridge Odhos Anapafseos mounts to the main gate of the *Proto Nekrotafion Athinon*, the principal Cemetery of Athens. Here, in sumptuous tombs, generally in Classical styles and decorated by the best sculptors of the day, are buried many celebrated Greeks of the 19C and 20C. Among heroes of the War of Independence are the generalissimo, Sir Richard Church (1784–1873), and Kolokotronis (1770–1843), as well as Makriyannis and Androutsos. Writers include Rangavis (1810–92), Panayiotis Soutsos (1800–68) and the statesman-historian Trikoupis (d. 1896). Averoff (see below), Singros (d. 1899), and Antoine Benaki, benefactors of the city, lie here. *The Mausoleum of Heinrich Schliemann* (1822–90), the archæologist, is decorated with Trojan scenes in bas-relief, while the *Tomb of Adolf Furtwängler* (1853–1907) bears a marble copy of a sphinx he unearthed at Aegina.

On the S. side of the Arditós highway, near Od. D. Koutoula, are the remains of the terrace wall of a temple, known to antiquaries as the *Temple by the Ilissos*, which was discovered and drawn by Stuart and Revett in 1751–55 but destroyed in 1778 by the Turks. It appears to have been constructed before the Temple of Athena Nike from the same specifications of Kallikrates, and may be the Temple of Artemis Agrotera. It became an orthodox church but was abandoned after a Roman mass had been said there in 1674.

To avoid the noisier Arditós highway we may return by footpath to LEOFOROS VASILISSIS OLGAS (7, 6), an attractive avenue that skirts the S. side of the Zappeion Gardens (Rte 1). To the right, between the avenues, are the *Tennis Club*, the *Olympic Swimming Pool* (ΟΛΥΜΠΙΑΚΟΝ ΚΟΛΥΜΒΗΤΗΡΙΟΝ), and the *Ethnikos Athletic Club*. The athletic track occupies the site (once an island in the river) where stood the '*Basilica by the Ilissos*' (mosaics in Byz. Mus.). The countryside hereabouts was lyrically described by Plato at the beginning of the 'Phædrus'. The two highways join below the hill of *Arditós*.

On the hill, the former **Ardettos**, or *Helikon*, where the Heliasts came to take their oath, are some scanty foundations (no adm.) assigned to the *Temple of Fortune*, erected by Herodes Atticus. On the opposite height beyond the Stadium some ruins (no adm.) are presumed (from an inscription *in situ* in archaistic letters to the "Marathonian Hero") to be the *Tomb of Herodes*, who died at Marathon but was given a public funeral at Athens.

The **Stadium** (Στάδιον; 8, 5) occupies a natural valley between these two low hills, which is closed at the S. end by an artificial embankment to form the semicircular sphendone. Faithfully restored in 1896–1906 by Anastasios Metaxas, it has the normal plan of a Greek stadium and corresponds to the description of Pausanias, who saw the gleaming Pentelic marble of the first restoration as we see the pristine whiteness of the second. The Plateia tou Stadhiou bears a statue of Averoff (1867–1930), the benefactor who financed the work.

History. Lycurgus constructed the stadium in its original form in 330 B.C. to provide for the contests of the Panathenaic Festival. On the occasion of Hadrian's presidency a thousand wild beasts were baited in the arena. The stadium was reseated in marble by Herodes Atticus for the Games of A.D. 144. In the course of centuries' use as a quarry, the marble all but disappeared. Ernst Ziller cleared the site in 1869–70 at first at his own expense, later with the support of George I of the Hellenes. In 1895, for the forthcoming revival of the Olympic

Games, Yeoryios Averoff, a wealthy Greek of Alexandria, emulating Herodes, undertook to restore the marble. The sphendone was provided with seats in time for the first modern Games of 1896, and the work was completed for the extra 'Olympic' Games, held out of series as a 10th anniversary celebration in 1906 and visited by Edward VII.

The *Arena*, in the form of an elongated horseshoe, measures 223 yds by 36. As restored it comprises a modern running track with provision in the centre for athletic and gymnastic contests. On the E. side a tunnel, c. 10 ft high, admits competitors and officials from the changing-rooms.

In ancient times the course was a straight track measuring one stade of 600 Greek feet, whence the name stadion. The Greek foot varied slightly from place to place, but the Athenian track seems to have measured c. 202 yards. It was divided down the centre by a row of pillars, of which four, in the form of double hermæ, have been recovered. The finishing point was in front of the sphendone, which was surmounted by a Doric stoa to provide shelter for the top corridor. A Corinthian propylon (restored, but since removed) formed a ceremonial entrance at the open end.

The course is enclosed by a low marble parapet, behind which a paved promenade, 9 ft wide, follows the circuit. Rain-water is channelled through gratings in the pavement into an arched drain of brick. A wall, 5¼ ft high, forms the substructure of the first tier of the *Auditorium*, thus affording the spectators a clear view over the parapet. The side tiers are slightly curved to give better visibility. Twenty-nine narrow flights of steps (12 on each side and 5 in the sphendone) lead from the promenade to the seats. These are arranged in 47 tiers, divided into two blocks by a *diazoma*, or gangway, behind the 24th row. The seats are of the same simple pattern as those in the Theatre of Dionysos. The seating capacity is 60,000. A block on the s. side and the front row of the sphendone provide more comfortable accommodation for honoured patrons and royal occasions.

Across the square, at the S.E. entrance to the Zappeion Gardens, stand a bronze statue of a discus thrower (1927) and a huge equestrian figure, also in bronze, of Karaïskakis, by Michael Tombros (1966).

Leoforos Konstantinou continues N.E. to meet Leoforos Vasilissis Sofias (see Rte 10), passing (l.; opp. Stadion Hotel) a monument to Harry S. Truman (1965).

Opposite the stadium Odhos Irodhou Attikou runs between the E. side of the National Garden and the modest former **Palace** (8, *3*), residence of the king after the restoration of 1935 and more recently of the president. The picturesque Evzones have their barracks at the top of the street, which emerges into Leoforos Vasilissis Sofias (Rte 10).

Just opposite in the avenue is the *Benaki Museum (8, *3*; adm. 50 dr.; weekdays in summer, 8.30–2 & 4.30–7.30, winter 9–1 & 3.30–5.30; Sun & hol., summer 8.30–2, winter 10–4; closed Tues), containing the fruits of 35 years eclectic collecting by Antoine Benaki. In 1931, having arranged his collections in the family town-house, Benaki endowed the museum and presented it to the state. Later gifts have been accepted.

Entry is through the garden and by the door facing Vasilissis Sofias. The GROUND FLOOR, recently rearranged to display early objects to better advantage, presents a roughly chronological display of the ancient and medieval arts. We turn left where the first hall is devoted to ancient Greece. Among many notable items: two gold cups of the Copper Age (c. 3000 B.C.) from N. Euboia; Bronze Age finds from Chalcidice and Thessaly; good collection of fibulae; Bronze figure of Herakles from the Ptoion in Boeotia (490–480 B.C.); Macedonian helmets from Dodona; folding mirrors of copper (3C B.C.); Hellenistic jewellery. The front section of the next hall contains Greco-Roman and Coptic cloths and embroidery (3C–8C) from christian Egypt; in this room also are displayed examples of Persian, Byzantine, and Coptic workmanship, mostly objects of daily use, from which the Arabic style evolved. 227 (on the wall). Greco-Roman portrait (2C or 3C A.D.) in water-colour on canvas. 4. Lamp in glass, enamelled and gilded, made for the Mausoleum of Sultan Kuchuk (d. 1341). 5. Goblet. Abbasid and Fatimid glass-ware. A wall-case contains a carved wooden door (9C) from Baghdad.

The back section of the farthest hall is arranged as a Moslem reception hall with original 17C mosaic, etc., from Cairo, and ceramic decorations which include so-called 'Rhodian' ware (16C), which comes in fact from Nicæa in Asia Minor. Ranged against the wall are funerary monuments of the 10–11C bearing Cufic inscriptions. Among objects of fine workmanship displayed in Case 65 (centre) are 17. Box in copper and silver from Mosul (1220); and two Astrolabes: 28. of ivory, signed and dated 1341; 30. of brass, signed Ahmad ibn al-Sarrâj (1328), well-known for his treatises on astronomical instruments. 415 (on pedestal). Turkish helmet from the battlefield of Kopaïs (Boeotia; 1311). Cases 63, 61, and 60 contain 'Rhodes' and 'Damascus' ceramics from Asia Minor. On the walls, Brûsa velvets.

The remaining rooms towards the back contain ecclesiastical furniture of the 17–19C brought from Asia Minor and Thrace by refugees in 1922, and icons.

We ascend to the FIRST FLOOR where three rooms are devoted to historical relics of 19C Greece, in particular of the War of Independence (1821–27). Among objects with British associations may be mentioned: rifles made in London for eastern potentates; ring inscribed *Long live Alfred, King of Greece* recalling the offer of the throne (rejected) to Queen Victoria's second son; bonnet of Theresa Makri, Byron's 'Maid of Athens'; coins of the Ionian Is. under British rule (1815–64); water-colour of the Old Palace, Corfù, by Queen Alexandra.

ROOM K. Italian and Spanish velvets of the 15–18C, including a Venetian tabard. On an easel, 1543. *Dom. Theotokopoulos*, Adoration of the Magi, an ikon of c. 1560 (the earliest known work of the Cretan painter better known as *El Greco*).—The next three rooms contain silks and brocades: ROOM Λ, Persian (17–18C); ROOM M, from Brûsa (16C), also Hispano-Moresque silks; ROOM N, Persian and from Asia Minor. Of greater interest in the last is the collection of *Jewellery, comprising pieces from the late-Bronze Age to the present era, and rich in the Archaic and Hellenistic periods. The diadem and accompanying ornaments of the 3C B.C. found in Thessaly (Case 105, 35–44) might be singled out; also a diamond pendant (Case 107, 27), belonging to Queen Christina of Sweden.

ROOM Ξ is devoted to Chinese ceramics arranged by dynasty and ROOM O to embroidery of the Greek islands, an art that flourished in the 17–18C, but is now almost extinct.—Room Z. Medieval cloths and garments recovered from tombs in Egypt and Mesopotamia; ikons (16–18C).—ROOM ΓΓ. Miscellaneous pottery, medals, and jewellery.

The nine **Basement** rooms are devoted to a unique display of Greek regional *Costume and popular art.

8 FROM MONASTIRAKI TO THE NATIONAL MUSEUM

From Monastiraki (Rte 6) ODHOS ATHINAS strikes N. straight to Omonoia Square. Crowds throng the vegetable and meat markets that line its southern half and extend into the narrow turnings on either side. We take the narrower ODHOS AIOLOU, a popular shopping street, parallel to the E. where excavations in 1961–62 disclosed tombs of c. 500 B.C. On the right is *Ayia Irini* with a colourful market of nurserymen on the N. side.

About 500 yds farther on, beyond Odhos Sofokleous, opens the PLATEIA KOSTA KOTZIA, which, since the demolition in 1937 of the Municipal Theatre, extends to Odhos Athinas. To the left stands a mansion by Ziller which for many years housed the main post office. The severe *Dhimarkhion*, or Town Hall, in Athinas to the W., faces the *National Bank of Greece* (Ethnikí Trápeza tis Elládhos). In the adjacent vacant plot the discovery of extensive remains of the ancient city wall has held up rebuilding. Odhos Aiolou continues N., crosses Stadium St. (Rte 10), and passing E. of Omonoia Sq. becomes Odhos Patission (see below).

Odhos Athinas leads directly to **Omonoia Square** (3. *3*; Πλατεῖα τῆς Ὁμονοίας), the busy centre of commercial Athens, where eight important roads converge. Its name (Concord Sq.) commemorates the reconciliation of two warring 19C political factions. Its fountain, a grandiose but ineffective display of water, is ringed by undistinguished buildings. Escalators lead down to the main station of the Piraeus-Athens-Kifissia Railway (Ε.Η.Σ.), where shops, cafés, a bank, and an information office of the National Tourist Organization surround the concourse.

Immediately to the left the broad ODHOS PIRAIOS begins its straight course to the port of Athens. Many treasures, now in the National Museum, have been found during building operations along its route; but nothing of interest survives above the surface, and the depressing street has been largely superseded as a highway by the boulevards to the S.

To the W., Odhos Ayiou Konstandinou, lined with electrical and record shops, descends to the large modern church of *Ayiou Konstandinou*, in front of which is the booking-office for bus services to the Peloponnese. Opposite stands the *National Theatre*.

Larissa Station of the Greek State Railways and the Peloponnisos Station lie c. ¾ m. N.W.

Odhos Patission (comp. above), alternatively named Odhos Ikosiokto Oktovriou, an uninteresting modern thoroughfare, passes to the W. of PLATEIA KANNINGOS (3. *3*), with a busy local bus terminus, where stands a *Statue of Canning* by Chantrey (1834), erected here in 1931 to honour the British minister's services to Greek independence. The plinth, marked by shrapnel, also celebrates a descendant who fell in Greece in 1941. The street continues N. to the **Polytekhneion** (᾽Εθνικόν Μετσόβιον Πολυτεχνεῖον), designed by Kaftandzoglou and built of Pentelic marble in 1862–80. Two side pavilions in Doric style form propylæa to the main block, where an Ionic upper story is superimposed on the lower Doric. Here the *School of Fine Arts* and the *Polytechnic School* jointly constitute an institution having university status and teaching the practical and artistic subjects not recognized by the Panepistimion.

We pass the **National Archæological Museum** (see below), with its shady garden (café), beyond which (¼ m. from Omonoia) we reach the Plateia Areos at the s.w. corner of the **Pedhion Areos** (3, 2; 'Champ de Mars'). Before the main entrance to this pleasant park stands an equestrian *Statue of Constantine I.* An avenue to the N. of this (running E.–W.) is flanked by busts of heroes and martyrs of the Revolution of 1821.

On the S. side of the park, facing Leoforos Alexandhras, is a *War Memorial* (1952) in Pentelic marble erected "to the memory of soldiers of Britain, Australia, and New Zealand, who fought for the liberty of Greece". Three cenotaphs (each with a bowl for a sacred flame) bear the arms of the three Commonwealth countries; behind, a Greek lion sits on a plinth of steps before a column bearing a statue of Athena. Her left arm holds a shield, the right arm is lacking since the spear it held was struck by lightning. In the park, near the chapel of Ayios Kharalambos is a *Monument to the 'Sacred Battalion'* (Ieros Lokhos), an irregular brigade of students commanded by A. Ypsilanti, which was unnecessarily sacrificed in 1821 in a skirmish at Dragashan in Rumania.—At the N.E. end of the park stands the MILITARY ACADEMY, or Officer Cadets' School, the Sandhurst of Greece, which counts among its former pupils three Greek kings and six prime ministers. In addition to military leaders, it trained naval cadets until 1846 and civil engineers in 1870–87. Founded at Nauplia in 1828 by Capodistrias, the academy was transferred first to Aegina, then in 1837 to Piraeus, before the present building was erected in 1889–94 at the expense of Averoff. Cadets wear a dark blue uniform, with yellow collar and bands, and white gloves. The *Museum of War Memories* (open Sun 11–1 free or by arrangement), in four halls, includes trophies and relics of Greek arms. Before the parade-ground stands a bronze *Statue of a Youth* (1940), by Athanasios Apartis, cast in Paris and since damaged by bullets.

9 THE NATIONAL ARCHÆOLOGICAL MUSEUM

Approaches. Trolley-bus/bus No. 2, 12, or 3/7 from Sindagma Sq. to the museum which is in Odhos Patission (Rte 8), 500 yds N. of Omonoia Sq., and a short walk from Plateia Kanningos. No direct service from the Acropolis.

Admission. Tues–Sat 9–4, 6, or 7; Sun 10–2 or 4.30; closed Mon; 50 dr. (free Sun). A printed catalogue to the Sculpture (1968) and good illustrated souvenir volumes are available in English.

The ****NATIONAL ARCHÆOLOGICAL MUSEUM** (3, 2; 'Εθνικόν 'Αρχαιολογικόν Μουσεῖον) contains an outstanding collection of masterpieces from excavations throughout Greece. All periods of pagan antiquity are included but new finds are now brought here only where no regional museum has a prior claim; Cretan antiquities, for example, are retained in Herakleion and barely represented in Athens. The museum, erected in 1866–89, and extended to the E. with a large new wing in 1925–39, forms a vast rectangle round an inner cross. The façade comprises an Ionic portico flanked by open galleries with plain square pilasters; the wings at either end are marked by plain pediments.

Arrangement. The first collection of antiquities formed in Athens was exhibited at the Theseion, which received sculptures transferred from Aegina in 1834. Both the Tower of the Winds and the Library of Hadrian served as repositories for occasional finds. The systematic excavations undertaken by the Greek Archæological Society and the explorations of the British, French, German, and American Schools at Athens led to the construction of the present building. For safety during the Second World War the collections were scattered. After the war the museum was entirely redecorated, alterations were made to the structure, and a whole new wing was available. For the first time the collections are being arranged as a whole; some rooms will inevitably be found closed, but the final arrangement, which is basically chronological, is predicated by the room numbering. Direct access is not normally allowed from the Prehistoric central halls to the other galleries. From the entrance hall the visitor proceeds by the N. wing to the central gallery, then usually visits whatever is accessible in the new wing. After making the round of the upper floor (pottery galleries open mornings only), he will eventually regain the entrance by the S. wing. Here and there private bequests and donations, or finds from a particular excavation preserved complete, break the sequence. The splendid display, started by the late Dr Christos Karousos (Director 1942–64) and Mrs Semni Karousos, and continued by subsequent directors, is still inadequately labelled even in Greek.

We cross the vestibule and enter the **Hall of Mycenean Antiquities** (R. 4). In this great room are grouped the results of excavations at Mycenae and at other Mycenean sites from 1876 to the present day. Chief among the splendid treasures are the contents of the six shaft graves from the Grave Circle A at Mycenae, five excavated by Schliemann and the sixth by Stamatakis; these are now rivalled in fame by objects from Vaphio and in archæological importance by more recent finds from elsewhere.

The cases are numbered in sequence round the room without regard to content; we follow the logical progression of the room, giving case numbers only for easy identification. Every case merits detailed study; only the outstanding or unique objects are indicated below. The numbers of the objects themselves correspond with the catalogue raisonné of G. Karo, 'Die Schacht-Gräber von Mykenai' (Munich, 1930).

Within the doors (r. and l.), two cases of miscellaneous finds from chamber tombs excavated in 1886–87 and 1892–99 outside the Acropolis of Mycenae. Case 26 (r.) contains an ivory head (T 27) wearing a helmet of boar's tusks (comp. below).—Case 1 (l.): Seal-rings; jewellery; 2947. Small bull in gold; sword-blades and hilts. In the next case (Case 2) similar finds from Wace's excavations of 1921–23: outstanding are the bone objects, especially T 518; seal-stones. Helmet of boar's tusk pieces.—In Case 25, on the right, begins the material from Grave Circle A. Contents of *1st Shaft Grave* (3 women; 1550–1500 B.C.) and of *2nd Shaft Grave* (one man; 1580–1550 B.C.): Gold diadem and cup, arms, fine vases. To left and right of the room are displayed four of the stelai from the grave circle, carved with hunting scenes (of the 17 stelai found, 11 were so decorated). On a central pedestal between them, *Gold mask of a man, bearded and moustached, and a large cup (from the 5th grave). Schliemann claimed, having removed this mask, to "have gazed upon the face of Agamemnon". A pedestal case (l.) contains three bronze **Dagger blades inlaid in gold, silver, and niello with hunting scenes: 394, 395. Lions hunting and being hunted; 765. River scene (? the Nile) with cheetahs retrieving duck.

There follows a group of five cases containing the most valuable objects from the 3rd, 4th, and 5th Shaft Graves. In the centre: Case 27 (*4th Grave*, the richest: 3 men and 2 women; 1580–1550 B.C.) 253, 254, 259. Three portrait masks in gold leaf; 252. Breastplate (plain). *Gold cups of varied designs (note No. 427 behind); **481. Silver rhyton with gold foil rim and handle and repoussé decoration depicting the siege of a maritime town. *412. Gold libation cup with two handles reaching to the foot of the stem and ornamented with falcons (not doves); it recalled to Schliemann Nestor's cup in Homer (Il. XI, 632–5). **Bull's head in silver with gold horns and a gold rosette; Seal rings; 555–70. Symbolic knots moulded in pottery; leg bones with gold ornaments attached.—CASE 24 (r.; same grave): Gold diadems and cups; 388. Base silver rhyton in the form of a stag or reindeer (possibly of Hittite workmanship); 273. Lion-head rhyton in gold; headbands and (263) bracelet in gold; 3 gold pins, one (245) with a spirited reproduction of a goat; golden ornaments in the form of an octopus; three models of temple fronts, in gold, each having an altar surmounted by horns of consecration; on the two corners are doves with outstretched wings. Clasps and buttons; sword-blades and daggers.—Beyond, CASE 23 contains objects from the *3rd Grave* (3 women and 2 children; see also Cases 10 & 11): Gold **Diadems and discs; these may have been affixed to wooden coffins, long since vanished, but more likely were used for personal adornment. Recumbent lions in gold repoussé; pair of scales in gold leaf; three gold seals engraved with a lion fight and a single combat; 116–8. Engraved gems; Gold pin, portraying a goddess of Minoan type, with thick silver shaft.—To the left of the room CASES 3 & 4 are devoted to the *5th Grave* (3 men; 1580–1500 B.C.); Gold mask; breastplate adorned in spirals; swords (one with chased gold hilt); *656. Cup with repoussé lions; *629. Large gold cup; hexagonal wooden box overlaid with gold panels (in a remarkable state of preservation); 829, 854. Vases (in alabaster) of great elegance; sword pommel of alabaster; *Daggers and swords with blades inlaid with gold and silver or patterned with volutes of gold; 828. Ostrich egg adorned with dolphins in alabaster; 812. Sycamore box.

Two low CASES (28 and 29) placed back to back in the centre contain gold objects from the 3rd grave, notably the sheets that covered the bodies of two royal infants; small jugs, boxes, and ornaments; below, Huge bronze bowl.—Lesser objects from the 4th and 6th shaft graves are displayed in CASE 22 (r.): 389. Elaborate vase with three handles of Cretan alabaster; 552. Decorated ostrich egg; metal shield of Minoan type (in miniature: 12 in. high); ceramic vases of fine shape with interesting decoration. Beyond, in CASE 21, are miscellaneous finds from the Acropolis of Mycenae, including elaborately shaped pottery figurines and (2665, 2666) painted plaques; 4573. Blue monkey with cartouche.— On the opposite side of the room (CASES 5 and 6) is a selection of the finds from GRAVE CIRCLE B (1650–1550 B.C.) discovered in 1952–55. These are similar in scope to the foregoing; note, however, the rock-crystal duck vase, the cruder mask, and the differences in the sword-hilt.

Against a red wall (r.) are displayed a female head in limestone, perhaps from a sphinx (13C B.C.); a painted decorative plaque; and a stele originally incised, later covered with plaster and painted. There follow two cases of miscellaneous finds of Late Helladic date (1500–1200 B.C.) from Mycenae: CASE 30 (centre): Four gold vases with dogs' heads on the handles and a gold cup; two large rings or seals, one very elaborate; 991. Small recumbent lion of gold; *Group of two women and a child in ivory; inlaid handles; vases, and alabaster pommels most accurately shaped.—CASE 7 (left): Bronze mirror with an ivory handle; small carved plaques in ivory; bronze pins.—The low central CASE 31

contains ivory *Panels from furniture, boxes, etc., and inscribed clay
tablets from the House of Shields at Mycenae; below is a vase of unusual shape. A case on the opposite wall has been left empty to accommodate new finds. Next to it stands the 'Warrior Vase' found by
Schliemann. This is a large vase (c. 1200 B.C.) painted dark red on light
yellow. On one side is a line of six armed soldiers marching in single
file away from a woman who bids them farewell. On the handles are
modelled animal heads. Beyond the vase are two restored pillars from
the 'Treasury of Atreus'. Other pieces of the pillars are similarly
restored in the British Museum.

The remainder of the room is devoted to other Mycenean sites. On
the left side of the Hall, CASE 8. Finds excavated at Pylos before the
site museum was founded. Two daggers, one (**8340) in a wonderful
state of preservation with repoussé gold hilt and inlaid blade; bronze
mirror with ivory handle; ivory comb, seals, and ornaments. The low
CASE 9, adjacent, contains some of the many calcined clay tablets with
inscriptions in Cretan Linear B script.—Mounted on a partition wall
are fragments of wall-paintings from the old (1350 B.C.) and later (1300–
1200 B.C.) palace at Tiryns. Beyond (l.), two CASES (10 and 11) of
objects from Prosymna are placed either side of a table of large jars
(that with the octopuses on the left has many Minoan parallels at
Heraklion): the smaller pottery in the cases (from chamber-tombs and
Middle Helladic graves) is particularly varied and graceful.

Turning back to the centre of the room we see on two pedestals the
famous **Gold cups (15C B.C.; subject of countless reproductions) from
the beehive tomb at Vaphio dug up in 1889: 1758. Capture of wild bulls
with nets; 1759. Trapping bulls with a decoy cow. Between them, in
CASE 32, are other finds from the same site: engraved gems; shallow
silver cup with gilded rim and bowl. To the right (CASE 19) are miscellaneous objects from Mycenean sites in Attica including Athens,
Brauron, Markopoulo, Salamis, and an interesting vase in the form of a
boot from Voula.

CASE 12 (l.; *Spata*). Ivory comb, tablets, and boar's-tusk helmet (restored).—
CASE 18 (r.). Objects found in the tholos tomb at *Menidi*: musical instruments
in ivory, including a lyre (restored); cylindrical box with sheep carved in relief
on its sides and lid; glass ornaments; engraved gems; stirrup vases.—The last
centre CASE (33) is devoted to gold and silver cups, swords, etc. from *Midea*
(Argolis), while the remaining five cases contain objects from *Nauplia* (13), *Mycenae*
(14; three wall *Paintings), *Tiryns* (15), *Skopelos* (16), and (17) a selection of vase
fragments from Mycenae chosen for their unusual representations of animal and
human figures. CASE 15 includes the 'Tiryns Treasure', the loot of a tomb robber
who had buried it, found in 1915 in a house of the lower town; the objects date from
1500–1100 B.C.: 6208, a huge seal-ring, is especially notable.

To the left and right of the Mycenean Hall are long narrow rooms devoted to
earlier antiquities. In that to the left (R. 5), objects of **Neolithic and Helladic**
cultures from Thessaly (Dimini and Sesklo), from Ayios Kosmas, and from
Poliokhni (Lemnos) showing ceramic affinities with ware from Troy. To the right
(R. 6), **Cycladic** objects from the islands: particularly important are finds from
Phylakopi (Melos) with characteristic painted pottery showing Cretan influence,
and the well-known Flying-fish fresco; vases from Syros; *Statuettes of male
figures playing musical instruments, in Parian marble (2400–2200 B.C.), from Keos;
and the contents of tombs found intact on Naxos.

We return to the vestibule and enter the NORTH WING, where seven
rooms contain **Archaic Sculpture**. Free-standing sculpture of the 7–6C
B.C. has two principal types: the *Kouros* or youth, represented nude

with one leg forward of the other, and the *Kore* or maiden, portrayed draped. The form may derive from the Xoanon, or ancient wooden statue; the stiff position of the arms, held tightly to the body, being dictated in wood-carving by the available shape of the timber. But many of the conventions show marked affinities with Egyptian and Phœnician models.

ROOM 7. In the centre, 804. Huge sepulchral amphora in ripe Geometric style (c. 760 B.C.) found in the Kerameikos area (the like became known from their provenance as 'Dipylos vases'): on it are represented the prothesis (laying-out) and lamentation over the dead. In glass cases behind, 770–79. Geometric pottery and four ivory statuettes from the same grave, one from a Syrian model. 57. Statue of a goddess (?; c. 630 B.C.) found at Ayioryitika near Tripolis. 1. Statue of Artemis found at Delos, the work of a Naxian sculptor (c. 630 B.C.); the inscription on the left side records its dedication by Nikandra of Naxos. 2869. Part of a limestone relief in the 'Dædalic' style, possibly a metope of a temple (Mycenæ; c. 650–630 B.C.), one of the oldest monumental stone reliefs of continental Greece. 56. Grave monument of Kitylos and Dermis, set up by Amphalkes; work of a Boeotian sculptor (mid-6C B.C.), found at Tanagra. In the doorway, 16513. Archaic bronze flautist from Samos (cast solid).—ROOM 8. Kouros figures and fragments. Dominating the room, 2720. Colossal *Kouros* from the earlier Temple of Poseidon at Sounion (c. 600 B.C.), newly restored. 3645. Torso of another. 71. Torso of an Athenian youth (590–580 B.C.) from Kerameikos. 3372. The 'Dipylon Head' from a Kouros funeral monument in the Kerameikos, remarkable Attic work of c. 610 B.C. The hand (3965) in the wall case is from the same work. 353. The 'Piraeus Amphora', funerary vase of 630–620 B.C. (chariot scenes). 15. Head of a kouros from Sanctuary of Ptoan Apollo, of crude Boeotian technique (c. 580 B.C.).

Off R. 8 open three small rooms continuing sculpture of the 6C, with exceptional recent finds. ROOM 9. *1558. Kouros from Melos; 22. Kore; 21. Winged Nike, both from Delos; 10. Kouros from Sanctuary of Apollo at Ptoön; 73. Torso of Kore (Aegina, 570 B.C.); *4889. Myrrhinous Kore (c. 590 B.C.), found in 1972 with a kouros (see below). The lead ring found with it fitted a known base inscribed Phrasikleia and signed by Aristion of Paros.—ROOM 10, beyond. 28. Sphinx (Spata, c. 570); 76. Sphinx (Piraeus, c. 540 B.C.); *38. Fragment of grave stele of a discobolos, of great vitality, executed in Parian marble by an Attic sculptor c. 560 B.C. (Kerameikos); *4890. Myrrhinous Kouros (comp. above). 2687, 2891. Tall stele and crowning sphinx from the Kerameikos; the stele, typical of the 6C style, was hastily chipped back for use in the Themistoclean Wall (the two parts may not belong together).—In Room 10A are *1906. Kouros from Volomandra (Kalivia), a charming Attic work of c. 550 B.C.; 14. Unfinished kouros from Naxos showing tool marks; 18232. Bronze vessel with sculptured handles; 4871. Head of Kouros.

ROOM 11. In the centre, 3686. Kouros from Keos, local work of 530 B.C. Round this are grouped marble sculptures and steles: 8. Kouros from Thera; 3728. Well-preserved Herm from Siphnos (c. 520 B.C.); 1673. Part of pediment, perhaps from the precinct of Pythian Apollo; the other half is in the Metropolitan Museum (N.Y.); 27. Head of a woman with red hair and earrings, from Eleusis; 30. Grave stele of Lyseas erected by his father Semon (c. 500 B.C.) found at Velanideza in 1838: the faded painting is reproduced in the adjacent copy; 26, 25. Ex-voto *Korai* figures from Eleusis, remarkable for their drapery. 31. Lower part of a stele of a horseman with well-preserved painted decoration, found in Aeolus St. (c. 500 B.C.). *29. Funeral stele in Pentelic marble representing the warrior Aristion and signed by Aristokles (Velanideza); this is a typical stele of the period, narrow and crowned with a palmette, bearing a formalized relief of the dead person in a characteristic attitude; the full-length figure retains traces of colour. 3072. Mask of Dionysos; *3071. Grave stele of a hoplite found in Stamata (c. 525 B.C.); 13. Kouros found at Megara (c. 540 B.C.); 93. Marble discus dedicated to Aeneas "the wise and excellent physician" (c. 550 B.C.); 81. Base of a grave monument (c. 550 B.C.) found in Vourva; only the feet of the statue of Phaidimos' daughter survive above the inscription. 41. Crowning member of a grave stele showing the squire of the deceased youth on horseback, carved in very low relief.

We enter ROOM 13, a long hall in which the most striking work stands at the far end before a screen: *3851, the *Anávissos Kouros*, found in 1936; the middle step of the base, found near by in 1938, has the inscription "Stop and lament at the tomb of the dead Kroisos whom furious Ares slew when he was fighting in the forefront". Though in archaic posture, its mobility and modelling suggest a date of c. 520 B.C. Other Kouroi in the room, 12, 20, both from the Sanctuary of Apollo at Ptoön in Boeotia (end of 6C B.C.); 9. A coarse work from Orchomenos; *3938. Sepulchral statue unearthed near Keratea during the German occupation and smuggled to Athens; it represents the young Aristodikos (Attic work of c. 500 B.C.); *16365. Bronze statuette of Apollo from Sparta (end of 6C B.C.). Other fragments include: 32. Sepulchral stele of two youths, Agathon and Aristokrates, from Thespiai (500 B.C.); 1926. Pair of stone halteres (jumping weights) of archaic type from Corinth; 89, 2823, 2826. Slabs decorated with reliefs, probably from a tomb, cut back for use in the Themistoclean wall in 478 B.C. At the far end (r. and behind the screen) are two celebrated bases with reliefs on three sides, found in 1922 in a section of the wall of Themistocles: *3477. In front, six nude epheboi playing a ball game with curved sticks, strongly resembling modern hockey; left and right sides, chariot scenes (c. 490 B.C.). *3476. In front, nude epheboi practising wrestling, jumping, and throwing the javelin; left side, six epheboi playing a ball game; right side, four clothed epheboi starting a fight between a dog and a cat (c. 510 B.C.). To the l. of the far door, 796. Acroterion of stele (Cycladic, c. 440 B.C.). To the r. of door: 36. Fragment of a relief, notable for the finely executed detail of its drapery (Attic, c. 500 B.C.).

ROOM 12 leads off towards the front of the building. SCULPTURE FROM THE TEMPLE OF APHAIA AT AEGINA. 1933–38. Warriors' heads from the first version (c. 500 B.C.) of the E. pediment; for some reason unknown the figures were later replaced by new ones (now in Munich) and the heads buried. 1959. Relief of a running hoplite (end of 6C B.C.) found near the 'Theseion'; 1605. 'The Daphni Torso'; 3711. Seated marble figure, draped; 782. Palmette from a stele of c. 500 B.C.; 3687. 'Kouros of the Ilissos' (early 5C).

5C Sculpture. ROOM 14 is devoted to funerary stelai or GRAVE

MONUMENTS of provincial origin. The period here represented, during which the sculptured stele developed from a single figure to a group composition, is almost entirely lacking in Attica, probably due to a decree of Kleisthenes (c. 509) prohibiting unnecessary expenditure on grave monuments. In the centre: *3990. Fragment of votive medallion of Parian marble, unique in form, found at Melos in 1937; the expressive relief may represent Aphrodite, and is dated stylistically to 460 B.C. 11761. Bronze Warrior, damaged but fine.

Round the walls (l. to r.): 734. Stele of Ekkedamos, found at Larissa (local work of c. 440); 39. Stele, signed by Alxenor of Naxos, found at Orchomenos (Boeotia); 739. Stele of Amphotto, found at Pyri, near Thebes, work of a Boeotian artist c. 440 B.C.; 735. Stele found at Vonitsa (c. 460); 3344. Votive relief of a boy victor crowning himself (Cape Sounion, c. 470); 741. Stele of a youth wearing the petasos and holding a hare, 733. Stele of Polyxena (both local Thessalian work); 4478–9. Ionic capitals from Sounion.

The principal masterpiece of ROOM 15 stands in the centre, admirably displayed before a fawn screen. **15161. *Poseidon*, a powerful bronze of heroic proportions salvaged from the sea off Cape Artemision in 1928. This is an original work of c. 450 B.C. possibly by the sculptor Kalamis; the god held, and is poised to hurl, a trident. It is surrounded by 5C marbles. Within the door (l.) is the famous *Relief from Eleusis* (126) representing Triptolemos receiving the ears of corn from Demeter, while Kore crowns him with a garland. This grand work in very low relief and somewhat hieratic style belongs to the period (c. 440 B.C.) immediately preceding the highest development of Greek sculpture.

742. Grave relief of a youth from Thespiai (Boeotia), work of a local artist influenced by Ionic prototypes (c. 440 B.C.; the inscription shows re-use in Roman times when the hair was probably restyled); 54. Base with sculptured reliefs; 1732. Hebe (mutilated) found near the Temple of Ares in the Agora, probably the central acroterion of the temple. On the other side of the room are various heads; 1825. Stele of a boy; 1385. Relief (fragmentary) of an idealized youth standing behind his horse; 828. Thespian stele (c. 440); the hero, with chlamys flying, rides a galloping horse.

Beyond the great bronze, 332. Head of Hermes, from Piraeus, perhaps by Euphron (440 B.C.). Behind the screen stands (45) the '*Omphalos*' *Apollo*, misnamed from the base (46, in the corner) found with it in the theatre of Dionysos; it is a copy (2C A.D.) of an original bronze by Kalamis. To the left, 1664. Roman copies of Classical statues of Theseus and the Minotaur; to the right, 248. Roman copy in marble of another bronze youth of the school of Kalamis (found in the Olympieion in 1888); 3131. Satyr from a metope (?) in conchiferous limestone; 127. The '*Finlay Crater*', an unfinished marble krater with a relief inspired by the famous group in bronze by Myron (c. 460), which stood on the Acropolis; Marsyas is about to retrieve the double flute, thrown away by Athena.

We enter (ROOM 16) the HALL OF CLASSICAL GRAVE MONUMENTS where are displayed examples of Attic work of the late 5C when Kleisthenes' decree had lapsed.

Attic grave reliefs, starting again c. 440 B.C., continue all the provincial developments. Four main types may be distinguished: narrow stelai, sometimes in the form of a pilaster crowned by palmettes or the like, with a rectangular 'picture' in low relief, often with the addition of rosettes; monuments in the form of a vase ornamented in low relief; broad stelai with sculptured family groups, terminating in a cornice or pediment; lastly the great naïskos monuments (or ædicula) of the 4C (comp. below) with increased emphasis on the temple-like character of the architectural frame.

Opposite the doorway stands (4485) the wonderful *Myrrhine Lekythos*, found in Sindagma Sq. and acquired in 1960 from the Vouros mansion; Hermes Psychopompos leads Myrrhine to the river of Acheron while her living relatives look on (c. 420). Also in the centre are: 14498. Red-figured Pelike by the painter Polion (420–410 B.C.), found on the Sacred Way near the Botanic Garden; it contained a cremation burial. 3709. Stele from the Kerameikos, unusual in having reliefs (lion and lioness) on both sides. 4502. Marble *Base on which stood a lekythos or loutrophoros; the reliefs show Hermes Psychopompos, the dead maiden receiving apples picked by a youth (? Elysian Fields), and a bearded priest with a knife (found in Athens). *715. Tombstone of Pentelic marble (c. 430 B.C., perhaps by Agorakritos), in high relief and surmounted by a superb frieze of palmettes and lilies; the youth bids farewell while his small grieving slave leans sadly on a pillar bearing a (?) cat below a birdcage.

Round the walls: 711. Stele of a woman seated in a high-backed chair, in a severe style probably not Attic (found at Piraeus); 766. Stele of Aristylla, erected by her parents (Piraeus c. 440 B.C.); 716. Later stele from Piraeus, notable for the expressions of grief of the mourners; painted stelai, with names incised but no relief; 714. Early naïskos from Piraeus (c. 390 B.C.); 1858. Upper part of a stele in low relief showing the profile of a young girl; 910. Similar: 3845. Stele of Mnesagora and her little brother Nicochares, erected by their parents (found at Anagyrous, Vari). 713. Stele of Lysander; Chairestrate (? the boy's mother), standing, offers him a bird. 37. Fragment of a striking life-sized figure from Kythnos, by an island sculptor; 880. Two old men shake hands, while a little girl offers her hand too (Piraeus c. 435 B.C.); 712. Attic stele of the family of Iphistiadai, with facing lions on the fronton.

Room 17 displays CLASSICAL VOTIVE SCULPTURE, selected examples of the work of practised sculptors of the 5C. In the centre, *1783. Double relief found near New Phaleron station; on one side the local hero Echelos carrying off his bride Iasile in a chariot, with Hermes in the role of nymphagogos (best man); on the other, Artemis with gods and nymphs; 1500. Offering to Dionysos by actors holding masks (from Piraeus); 254. Attic marble statue of a young athlete from Eleusis (4C B.C.; probably after an original by Polykleitos). 176. Young girl, from Piraeus. Round the walls: 199. Statuette of a young man found at Rhamnous, dedicated by Lysikleides, son of Epandrides; 203–214. Fragments of sculptures from the base of the statue of Nemesis at Rhamnous, by Agorakritos of Paros, pupil of Pheidias (430–420 B.C.). Architectural sculpture from the Heraion at Argos is displayed on two sides of the room: fragmentary metopes, cornice with lion's head spouts, and reliefs of cuckoos, Hera's bird; 1571. Head of Hera, by Argive sculptor of Polykleitan school. 226. Stele of a priestess of Apollo found at Matinea, possibly the famous Diotima of the Symposium of Plato (c. 410 B.C.); 2756. *Relief dedicated by Xenokrateia, showing her leading the little Xeniades to the river-god Kephissos who greets him; to left and right are Apollo and Acheloös (c. 400 B.C., from the same sanctuary as 1783); 1391. Relief of an apobates, from the Amphiareion.

Room 20 leads off from R. 17; in the doorway, 3076. Small relief from Dionisos (Attica). Votive reliefs: 1394. Ephebos with horses, showing influence of the Parthenon frieze (430–420 B.C.); 1329, dedi-

cated to Pan and the Nymphs, from the s. side of the Acropolis; 3572.
Persephone seated with Demeter standing (c. 430 B.C.); 1501. Funeral
banquet, from Piraeus; 223. Small torso of Apollo (copy of 2C B.C.).
The remainder of the room is devoted to copies deriving from works of
Pheidias (and his school), notably the Athena Parthenos: 1612. Torso
of Apollo, Roman copy of a lost original by Pheidias; 200–202.
Statuettes from Eleusis, copies of figures from the w. pediment of
the Parthenon. At the far end, 129. The *Varvakeion Athena,* so
called because discovered near the School of that name in 1880.
This statuette is a reduced copy dating from the 2C or 3C A.D. (at one-
twelfth of the original) of the great chryselephantine statue of Pheidias
though in itself it is disappointing and the workmanship, careful
enough in its way, lacks inspiration. Nearly all the features of the
original seem to be reproduced; Athena's right hand (in which she holds
the winged victory) is here, however, resting on a pillar of no known
order, possibly following a late addition made (after damage ?) to Pheidias' work. 4491. Part of a colossal head of Athena, from the workshop
of Agorakritos; 177. Head of a goddess, copy of another chryselephantine statue of the 5C (found in the Herodes theatre); 128. The *Lenormant
Athena,* an unfinished copy in miniature from the Roman period of
Pheidias' statue; 3718. Athena of the Pnyx; copy (2C A.D.) of the head
of a colossal statue in the style of the master.

R. 19. 3854. Relief of youths (in the Pyrrhic dance); 1811. Aphrodite, copy
(1C A.D.) of a bronze original, perhaps by Kallimachos; 3949. Copy of the cult
statue of Nemesis at Rhamnous by Agorakritos (Roman; found in Athens,
1934); 3569. Head of Aphrodite, a contemporary replica in miniature of an Attic
bronze, c. 420 B.C.; 3043. Acroterion (c. 410 B.C.); 4351. Choregic relief with
masks (5C B.C.) from Dionisos.
Steps lead down from R. 20 to the charming ATRIUM, with a mosaic of Medusa
in the centre. The surrounding colonnade shelters moving 4C grave stelai of
children and Roman sarcophagi, as well as much-eroded marble statuary recovered from the sea off Antikythera (comp. below).

In ROOM 18 are displayed LATE-5C AND EARLY-4C SEPULCHRAL
MONUMENTS. *3624. *Stele of Hegeso,* c. 400 B.C., from the Kerameikos
cemetery, a masterpiece perhaps by Kallimachos himself; Hegeso
seated examines a necklace (originally painted in) from a trinket-box
held by her maid. 3472. Funeral stele of Theano, wife of Ktesileos of
Erythrai (Athens; late 5C B.C.). Two marble lekythoi (835. Rider and
hoplites; the background, perhaps an addition, is delicately sketched in
but unfinished; 2584). Round the walls. 765. Stele of Mika and Dion
from the Kerameikos; 2744, 754. Parts of the War Memorial erected
by the city of Athens in honour of hoplites and cavalry who fell near
Corinth and at Koroneia in 394 B.C., found N.E. of the Dipylon; the
list includes the name of Dexileos. 902. Stele of Tynnias, from Piraeus;
831. Stele of Phrasikleia; 3790. Stele of a young mother, from Psykhiko;
Case of Attic white-ground lekythoi of the same period; 723. Stele of
Polyxene; *717. Stele from the Kerameikos; a young girl bids farewell
to her parents; 752. Stele of Demokleides, son of Demetrios, a hoplite
lost in a naval battle; 718. Grave relief of Ameinokleia from Piraeus
(360–350 B.C.); 724. Stele of Phainarete; 13789. Bronze funeral kalpis
(ash jar; 5C); 1822. Funeral stele of a woman, by a Peloponnesian
Sculptor (420–410 B.C.) found near Omonoia Square.

ROOM 21 (Central Hall). In the centre, *15177. *Horse and Jockey of*

Artemision, a lively masterpiece in bronze of the 2C B.C., found with the statue of Poseidon, and pieced together from many fragments. The jockey is winning a race at full gallop; note, on the horse's right hind leg below the rump, brand markings of ownership. *1826. *Diadumenos*: a good copy of c. 100 B.C. of a lost bronze original by Polykleitos, found at Delos. The support with the false attributes of Apollo is an addition of the copyist. 3622. The 'Matron of Herculaneum', copy of a Greek work attributed to Lysippos; the best known copy of this work was found at Herculaneum. 218. Hermes of Andros, found at Palaiopolis (Andros); copy in Parian marble of an Attid original of the school of Praxiteles. 720. Sepulchral relief of Melite from Piraeus (mid-4C B.C.); 2308. Epikranion; 3964. Stele of Pausimache (Attic, c. 370 B.C.); *3708. Base of a grave stele (early 4C B.C.) with reliefs of a rider fighting a hoplite, found near the Academy of Plato.

Since rearrangement is still proceeding in the New Wing, it is better to see next the rooms that are open there (and at least the Thera frescoes on the upper floor, see below) before continuing to Room 22, even though this breaks the intended sequence.

Beyond the colonnade, ROOM 34, connecting the old museum with the new wing, is arranged to suggest an open-air sanctuary. In the centre, 1495. Altar dedicated by the Boule near the Agora to Aphrodite Hegemone and the Graces. Grouped round it are reliefs of differing provenance and quality. To the left: 303. Triple Hekate, Goddess of the crossroads (late Roman) found at Epidauros; 252. Pan holding the syrinx, from Sparta; another example of the same subject (3534) stands farther on; 4465, 4466. Attic reliefs (4C B.C.) dedicated to the nymphs, found in the Cave of the Nymphs, Mt Pentelikon; 1778. Attic relief dedicated to Zeus Meilichios (3C B.C.), found near the Ilissos. At the end of the room, to either side, 2756, 1783. Two limestone bases (end of 5C B.C.) bearing the inscriptions of the dedicators surmounted by casts of the votive reliefs now in the Classical gallery (see below). Returning along the other side, 227. Torso: copy of the 1C B.C. from the same original as the Aphrodite of Arles now in the Louvre. 1451–52. Reliefs (4C B.C.), Erotes carrying incense-burners, from the sanctuary of Aphrodite and Eros on the N. slope of the Acropolis.

We enter (l.) the NEW WING, where the arrangement is still unfinished. ROOM 36. The **Karapanos Collection,** the fruits of excavations by K. Karapanos in 1875–77 at Dodona and elsewhere, with later finds from the same sites. The original collection, presented to the State in 1902, is particularly rich in small bronze objects, of which we note the most outstanding. On a pedestal in front of the door: 27, 16547. Bronze horseman; the horse was recovered in 1956. *First Case* (r.): Bronze strips with inscriptions of decrees, treaties, manumissions, etc., and Leaden strips with questions asked of the Oracle at Dodona and answers similarly inscribed; the strips were varnished with some preservative. Cheek-shields. The *Second Case* contains votive figures dedicated to the god of the oracle: 22. Satyr; 31. Zeus hurling a thunderbolt; 54. Ram; on the shelf below, 70. Hand holding a dove; 166. Cheek-piece of an ancient bronze helmet, of exquisite hammered work probably Corinthian (early 4C B.C.); bottom shelf, Helmet. On a pedestal, 25. Woman playing the double flute. In the *Third Case* (r.) are delightful animal figures, and (557) Bronze frying-pan. In a *Wall Case*, beyond: Archaic terracotta figures of Artemis from Corfù.—

The *First Case* (*l.*) contains 24. Statuette of a runner, c. 530 B.C.; 36. Horseman. In the *Third Case* is a finely wrought statue of a warrior (550 B.C.). Farther on, mounted on a reconstruction in wood, bronze wheel-hubs and decoration of a Roman state chariot. At the end of the room, 965. Attic gravestone, slave handing open jewel-box to her lady (330 B.C.).

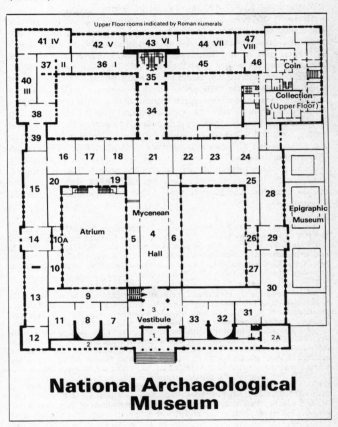

Upper Floor rooms indicated by Roman numerals

National Archaeological Museum

ROOM 37 is the first of the **BRONZE ROOMS to be opened. Here are displayed Geometric and Archaic small bronze objects from Boeotia, Peloponnese, and early excavations on the Athenian Acropolis. Notable are Warriors, depicted helmeted with breast-plate and greaves, in juxtaposition with the helmets themselves. *6440. Head of Zeus from Olympia, in archaic bronze with exquisitely worked hair and beard; 14984. Zeus; 13220. Greave. Incised relief and inscribed tablet from Tegea; helmets of Corinthian type; mirrors from Corinth. Beyond the pillars, bronzes mainly from the Acropolis: *6445. Athlete (c. 500 B.C.), who probably held haltares; 6590. Head of Youth (c. 480 B.C.); *16768. Athena Promachos, from Antikyra (p. 393), early 5C; Wall case, Arrow heads and spearheads from Thermopylae; 6447. Athena Promachos (early 5C), dedicated by Melisso; 13050. Gorgon acroterion (7C); 7146. *Kerykeion (caduceus) with Pan heads (? celebrating the victory of Marathon; comp. Herod. 6. 105 & 9. 100); 6446. Head of a (?) general (life size; c. 490 B.C.).—RR. 38–39 await arrangement.

ROOM 40. Bronzes, mostly 5–4C B.C.: *Athena (second half of 4C), her helmet decorated with griffins and owls, found in Piraeus; *16789. Shepherd carrying a lamb, found at Ambelokipoi; Roman bronze statuettes, part of the associated find. *15118. Ephebos or Hermes dredged from the Bay of Marathon in 1925; Athenian work of the 4C B.C. (the arms altered or restored in Roman times). The eyes are of glass. Case of bronze *Mirrors of varied provenance; *Artemis with a quiver on her shoulder; the superb **'*Piraeus Kouros*', the oldest known hollow-cast bronze statue of large scale, found with the clay filling and iron supports preserved inside; it is believed to represent Apollo, who held a bow, and is from a workshop of the N.E. Peloponnese (530–520 B.C.; ? Kanachos of Sikyon). Behind are an excellent kalpis (7914) from Thebes and a hydria (7913) from Eretria; 7474. Statuette of an athlete from Sikyon; the succeeding case includes an exquisite little dog, locust, mouse, etc.; candelabra; wall lamp-bracket; 16774, 16773. Further statues from the Ambelokipoi find; 15087. Navigational instrument (? astrolabe).

RR. 41–43. GREEK SCULPTURE IN THE HELLENISTIC AND ROMAN PERIODS. Equestrian statue from Melos, of disputed date; an adjacent small votive relief (1401) depicting a horse in similar pose is of the 2C B.C.—R. 42. Portrait heads and herms; also archaizing reliefs of the 1C B.C.–1C A.D., with (3727) the Dionysiac relief from Khalandri (4C B.C.) for comparison.—R. 43. Late Imperial portraits, including Herodes Atticus and Polydeukion (from Kifissia).

First Floor, see below.

We now return to the central hall and continue in the SOUTH WING. ROOM 22. SCULPTURES FROM EPIDAUROS. The display has been remounted since all the fragments formerly at Epidauros were brought together here by Mr. N. Yalouris. Figures from the W. pediment of the Asklepieion at Epidauros (c. 380 B.C.), probably by Timotheus; the positions of the three acroteria are shown; one depicts Penthesilea, queen of the Amazons. The fragments from the E. pediment, which represented the capture of Troy, include the Nike of the central acroterion. In the centre, 254. Attic marble statue of a young athlete from Eleusis (4C B.C.) (probably after an original by Polykleitos).—RR. 23–24. 4C FUNERARY MONUMENTS, notably (in R. 23) *869. 'Stele of the Ilissos', commemorating a young hunter; his father stands at the right, a little slave sits at his master's feet (c. 340 B.C.; possibly by Skopas); *870. Grave relief of two women, Attic work of the mid-4C B.C.; (in R. 24) 823, 824. Scythian archers, probably from the monument of an officer (Kerameikos; ? from the tomb of Lysimachides of Acharnai); 1488. Stele with bilingual inscription in Greek and Phoenician and an unusual theme; 3716. Seated woman (note the drapery; 380 B.C.); 2574. Monument of Alexos of Sounion (c. 320 B.C.).

The L-shaped R. 25 is reached by 23 or 24. This and RR. 26–27, interrupting the sequence, contain DECREE AND VOTIVE RELIEFS of considerable importance as recording treaties and giving insight into cult customs. R. 25. 1861. Funerary stele in Thespian marble, depicting five members of a family (Boeotian; late-5C B.C.); 1879. Satyric scene with Pan, from the Cave of Parnes (4C B.C.); 1950. Votive scene with sacrificial animals (Aegina); 258. 'Asklepios of Munychia' (Piraeus). Of the many votive reliefs from the Athenian Asklepieion, striking is 2565, a tall stele with a vigorous snake surmounted by a votive sandal on which the dedicator, Silon, is represented in relief (360 B.C.).—R. 26. 3369. Relief dedicated by Archinos to Amphiaraos (early 4C B.C.).—R. 27. Bases and reliefs showing funerary feasts; 3246. Votive to the Eumenides, from Argos.

ROOM 28 is devoted to late Classical sculpture. LAST FUNERARY MONUMENTS OF ATTICA comprise the first group: 738. Monument of Aristonautes (c. 310 B.C.), a realistic armed figure depicted in full relief in a deep naiskos; 803, 804. Pair of marble lions from the Kerameikos; *4464. Large relief of a small negro trying to control a spirited horse (c. 300 B.C.) found near Larissa station (Athens) in 1948; 1005. The latest known Attic tomb-relief before the prohibition of 307 B.C., found in the Kerameikos (the drapery is astonishing). In the centre of the room: 13396. **Ephebos of Antikythera (c. 340 B.C.), found in 1900 at the bottom of the sea; this is possibly the Paris of the sculptor *Euphranor*. The eyes are inlaid and the lashes fashioned from bronze plate. The famous bronze is surrounded by originals and later marble copies of works of the same period. 178–80. Boar's and warriors' heads from the Temple of Athena Alea at Tegea (? W. Pediment), by *Skopas* (c. 340 B.C.), almost the only surviving certain work of one of the greatest Greek sculptors. The expression of emotion contrasts with the 5C calm and foreshadows the agonies of the Hellenistic school of Pergamon. 182 (? also by Skopas). Head of Ariadne. 323. Head of Asklepios. *3602. Hygieia from Tegea (by Skopas ?).

ROOM 29, FIRST HELLENISTIC SCULPTURE ROOM. Centre (r.), 247. Fighting Gaul, from Delos (c. 200 B.C.); (l.), 231. Statue of Themis, goddess of Justice, from Rhamnous (by Chairestratos; early 3C B.C.); to the left, 239. Young Satyr (Lamia; 3C B.C.); 215–217. Three reliefs found at Mantineia, representing the musical contest of Apollo and Marsyas, perhaps the bases of a group of Leto and her Children, executed by Praxiteles and noted by Pausanias; 245. Dionysos embracing a Satyr (unfinished; late 4C); 327. Head of Demosthenes, found in 1849 in the Royal Garden, a late copy of a bronze by Polyeuktos; Heads of a colossal group by Damophon from Lykosoura (p. 309).

ROOM 30. *13400. Portrait head of a philosopher, found in the sea off Antikythera (3C B.C.) and other fragments from the statue; 2772. Statuette of Ianiskos playing with a goose (3C B.C.), found at Lilaia. *6439. Portrait of a boxer from Olympia, uncompromisingly naturalistic; possibly the head of a bronze statue of the athlete Satyros by the Athenian sculptor Silanion (c. 340 B.C.); the lips are inlaid. *3266. Portrait head from a statue, from the Stoa of Attalos (c. 150 B.C.); 3556. Ariarathes V (c. 120 B.C.); 235. Poseidon of Melos (of Parian marble; c. 140 B.C.); *14612. Head from Delos, a lifelike portrait of a man torn by doubts, of c. 100 B.C.; *351. Portrait of a (?) Thracian priest, a fine Attic work of the end of the Hellenistic period (1C B.C.); 3485. "The little refugee", a child holding a dog (brought from Asia Minor in 1922); 232. Aristonoe, a priestess of Nemesis, dedicated by her son Hierokles at Rhamnous; 3335. Aphrodite defending her honour from Pan (the so-called 'Slipper Slapper'—well-preserved but inartistic), from the House of the Poseidoniastai at Delos, c. 100 B.C.; 1829. Artemis, also from Delos; 457. Head of a youth (late 1C B.C.); 259, 260. Two relief slabs from the Theatre of Dionysos, depicting (?) Hores, with wind-blown drapery.—R. 31 is devoted to temporary exhibitions illustrating a theme of ancient life (music in 1979).

In R. 32 is displayed the **Hélène Stathatos Collection, presented in 1957, consisting of objects of all periods from the Bronze Age to Byzantine times from Thessaly, Chalcidia, and Macedonia, and a most precious array of ancient *Jewellery and gold ornament. Unique are a breast ornament in gold of the 3C B.C. from Thessaly, consisting of a medallion of Aphrodite in relief surrounded by a network of fine chain; and a naïskos (c. 300 B.C.) in gold, set with precious stones, depicting Dionysos and a Satyr. No finds similar to these have ever been recorded in any scientific excavation. Unique also (Case 6), St. 332 the red-figured ceramic in the shape of an egg. Among small bronzes are (St. 328) an Archaic kriophoros and (St. 316) a graceful doe; and a fine bronze helmet of Illyrian type, with a gold funeral mask, which perhaps belong together.—The display of jewellery will be continued in R. 33.

The FIRST FLOOR, approached from the central hall (comp. above), is devoted to **Pottery,** mainly of post-Mycenean date with a few typical earlier pieces; in general earlier pottery is displayed on the ground floor with other contemporary objects. Classical vase-painting is represented by a daunting array of examples, of all shapes and great mythological interest, and of high average quality; if few rank with the greatest masterpieces now in the major museums of Europe and America, they have the special advantage of being entirely free of foreign admixture. The collection, which is beautifully displayed in chronological sequence, is unique for the ****Early Vases.**

VESTIBULE. Typical pithos, with plain bands in relief, of the Minoan period in Crete, found at Knossos (1878) before systematic excavations were undertaken there; other large storage jars; cast of a votive relief (from the Acropolis), depicting a potter offering two cups to Athena Ergane, goddess of industry.

Here has been mounted a temporary exhibition of recent finds from the **Minoan site of Akrotiri in Thira** (Rte 73); these are eventually to be accommodated on the island. Additional entrance fee. Outstanding are the ****Frescoes,** with colours still fresh and vivid, depicting swallows and lilies, leaping blue monkeys, antelopes, a little priestess, boxing children; fisherboy with a catch of mackerel; and a frieze, 20 ft long, depicting a maritime expedition by galley to a foreign coast (believed by the late Prof. Marinatos to be that of Libya).

We turn right to the vase rooms.

ROOM I. Characteristic pottery of the **Bronze Age** (3rd–2nd millennium B.C.), showing the first attempts at painting in the Aegean, together with Mycenean idols; note the lily and papyrus motives derived from Cretan models and ultimately from Egypt. **Protogeometric and Geometric Pottery** (10–7C).

In the upheaval following the Mycenean downfall, as pottery deteriorated into '*sub-Mycenean*', designs grew more stylized and perfunctory and were reduced to geometric patterns. About 1025 B.C. a new pottery style developed. This *Protogeometric* style, though it involved no change of actual technique and though it made use of the previous shapes and decorative motives, was important because it was the first sign of a new spirit, creative instead of decadent (comp. the works of V. R. Desborough). The style is common to the whole of Greece (disseminated perhaps by Attic seamen?), but Attic invention soon becomes dominant and Athens emerges for the first time as the artistic centre of the Greek world. At the beginning of the period vase-painters use simple decorative motives, circles, and semicircles drawn in dark glaze on the light surface of the clay. Later, in the full *Geometric* style, which brings in new vase types with broad bases, potters begin to cover the greater part of the surface with black glaze; the decoration, at first restricted to zones filled with circles and linear patterns arranged in panels, later covers the whole vase in horizontal bands. In the 8C the human figure begins to take a prominent place in vase decoration, chiefly on large sepulchral amphoræ and kraters. Scenes generally show the prothesis (laying out of the dead), the ekphora (funeral procession), and funeral games, especially chariot racing. This period coincides with the historical unification of Attica under Athens. The leading artist of the age is the so-called 'Dipylon Painter' of the Kerameikos.

To the left of the room, typical examples, standing alone, add emphasis to the general exposition. Against the wall (r.): progression of 10–9C (Protogeometric) vases, at first with simple geometric motives; we see the first appearance of the meander (218) and of the swastika; vases from Nea Ionia and from burials on the Areopagus (219), bearing designs covering a larger area and showing increased mastery of technique; more elaborately decorated pottery from the so-called Tomb of Isis at Eleusis. In the centre, 216. Amphora. To the left, Geometric vases of the 9–8C; 806. Krater from the Kerameikos, with chariot scenes. To the right, free-standing, are two Amphoræ from the Kerameikos, with overall geometric decoration, one with serpents in relief on the handles; in the large case between them; 169, 186, 201–202. Fine examples of the Geometric style (8C), including a bronze tripod that supported a kalpis (cremation urn). Beyond, standing in front of finds from tombs in Odhos Piraios (1891), 811. Oinochoë ornamented with browsing ibexes with a lid surmounted by a bird; the beginnings of Greek sculptural art are foreshadowed in this and in 802. Pyxis with three horses on the lid (in the case behind). In a case on the left wall: vases from excavations (1935) on Mt Hymettos; 192. Oinochoë with a graffito in primitive Greek characters of the 8C, reading "He who dances better than the other dancers will receive this". 17935 (beyond). Painted Geometric amphora with chariot race and helmeted warriors. Case: contemporary bronze and terracotta figurines. Opposite (r.), the farthest case contains finds from graves at Anavissos (last quarter of 8C). Between the pillars, *803. Large late-Geometric amphora of the 'Dipylon' type from the Kerameikos, with typical scenes of prothesis and ekphora (c. 750 B.C.).

Beyond the pillars, in the vestibule to the next room, three huge works in the Ripe Geometric style: 810. Vase in the form of a bowl (frieze of men and four-horse chariot) on an ornamental stand with four bands of painting; 894. Tall amphora with two friezes: chariots with warriors, and procession of warriors.

ROOMS II AND III are devoted to **7C Ceramics** of the style known generally as *Orientalizing* and in its regional application as *Protoattic*.

By the end of the 8C Geometric art becomes perfunctory. The old precision of drawing is neglected but often for the sake of giving the whole composition movement and pictorial coherence. In the 7C Greek colonists penetrated the Black Sea and ranged to Sicily and beyond, making close contacts with both Egyptian and Phœnician culture. Greek potters come under the rejuvenating influence of oriental motives. Linear patterns are replaced by lotus and palmette ornaments, trees, birds, animals (often in hieratic stance), chimæras, gorgons, sphinxes, etc. (comp. the grave monuments of Archaic sculpture). Mythological subjects are increasingly depicted: at first Centaurs and monsters, later heroic myths distortedly reflecting a memory of the great Mycenean days, transmitted in Homeric poetry.

Along the right wall: Empedocleous Bequest (Geometric). Early 7C vases showing the beginning of oriental influences. 313. *Analatos Hydria*, having mixed decoration, Geometric on the neck, Orientalizing on the shoulder, with a choral scene on the body. Amphora painted with scene of a warrior's departure, perhaps Hector and Andromache. Case of Corinthian aryballoi showing (r. to l.) the evolution of the shape. In the centre, 220. Huge amphora from Thebes; metopes depict a bird of prey and Artemis as mistress of the brute creation. Returning along the left wall: Boeotian figurines; 13257. Priest-king seated on a throne. 228. Boeotian stamnos with horse and lion metopes. 15424. Protoattic krater of the earliest Orientalizing style from Phaleron (early 7C). Case of Boeotian and Euboean pottery: note *14481. Clay cart in the form of a horse on wheels carrying six amphoræ (Euboea; ? 9C). To the left as we pass into the next room, 238. Attic louterion from Thebes; the centaurs have human forelegs, an early conception. 14497. The Kynosarges Amphora.

Room III. Four cases in the left-hand corner contain 7C ware from Crete (12509 shows Egyptian influence); from Naxos, Santorin, and Rhodes (12717. Oinochoë decorated with lotus flowers and realistic gazelles); from other Aegean islands; and from Cyprus (17376. Chariot with three figures in pottery). In front are four fine amphoræ from Melos, *911. Two Muses (?) in chariot, accompanied by Apollo and Artemis; on neck, combat of Ajax and Odysseus over the arms of Achilles. *354. On neck, meeting of Hermes and Iole; on body, Herakles mounting chariot in which Iole is accompanied by Eurytos and Antiope, her father and mother; the colouring is rich and the ornamentation elaborate.—We pass into the main body of the room. To the left, Tanagra vases. To the right, Ripe Protoattic pottery: on the middle stand, three kraters from a tomb at Anagyrous, near Vari, probably all by the same painter (c. 620 B.C.) and clearly occupying a position midway between the Orientalizing and Black-figure styles; 16384. Prometheus bound and Herakles shooting the eagle. Opposite stands 221. *The Siren Amphora* (c. 630 B.C.) with black figures on a yellow-grey ground. In the last case to the left: 16391. Amphora, a good example of several showing Chimæra and Bellerophon. At the end of the room, *1002. *The Nessos Amphora*, still a ˙chaic but with many of the techniques brought to perfection in black- and red-figure work; on the neck, the struggle of Herakles with the Centaur, Nessos; below, the three Gorgons (Medusa has already been beheaded by Perseus); from the Kerameikos (c. 600 B.C.).

Room IV. Three cases inside the door (r.) contain miscellaneous finds from the *Heraion of Argos*, both pottery and bronzes, covering many centuries. The large amphora in front comes from a cemetery near the Academy of Plato (c. 570 B.C.). A group of cases opposite the door contains examples of the **Early Black-Figured Style**, several signed by the painter *Sophilos* (590–580 B.C.): 15499. Fragmentary Lebes, representing the funeral games of Patroklos, found near Pharsala; another, similarly signed, Marriage of Thetis and Peleus; others from the Acropolis by the 'Gorgon painter'. 12587. Krater, by *Sophilos*, Herakles and Nereus; in both style and subject it recalls the poros pediment from the Acropolis (p. 96); 991. Loutrophoros from Vourva, by the same; on stand, 1036. Amphora, a late work by *Sophilos* found in the Tumulus at Marathon.

The *Black-Figure* technique, which is first clearly distinguished in Protocorinthian pottery, neglects outline drawing in favour of silhouette. The design is laid on the reddish clay with some addition of incised lines. Later the black is improved to the brilliant Attic glaze, and white (for women's flesh) and dark red paint are added. Decorated patterns are reduced until only the body of the vase has importance, usually adorned with paired subjects on opposing sides.

Continuing clockwise round the room: Vases and terracotta figurines from graves in Boeotia (early 6C). Pottery (of Corinthian workmanship; 7C and 6C) from the Heraion at Perachora (comp. below).

In the last case (l.), ivories from the Temple of Artemis Orthia at Sparta (late 8C or early 7C B.C.) of material imported from Syria or Phœnicia; lead figurines of the same provenance. On the end wall, terracotta metopes from the archaic Temple of Apollo at Thermon in Aetolia, with painted decoration by Corinthian artists (c. 630 B.C.); above, antefixes from the same temple. On the right wall, two cases of Protocorinthian pottery: notable are 295. Bombyle (for pouring a drop at a time) and vases showing Bacchic or Dionysiac scenes; 664 has the earliest known representation of Dionysos (last quarter of the 7C). Model temples in terracotta (8C Geometric) from the Heraion at Perachora. Bronzes and model Archaic house (7C) from the Heraion of Argos. In the centre group of cases: Bronzes from the Sanctuary of the Brazen House, and Ivories from the Temple of Artemis Orthia, both at Sparta. Portions of tempera painting on wood from Corinth (520–500 B.C.).

In ROOM V we are able to compare and contrast works of the mid-6C B.C. from Attica, the Islands, and Asia Minor.

In the course of this century **Attic Black-Figured Vases** win all the markets from Corinth. New shapes (e.g. the kylix) are invented; old shapes are refined as pottery is increasingly demanded for practical household use by the aristocratic society of the Peisistratid period and for export all over the expanding Greek world. A characteristic of technique is the use of incision; mythological scenes are treated with increasing naturalness and humanity; scenes from everyday life become more usual. Known artists of the period include Kleitias (570–560), Phrynos, Nearchos, Lydos, Exekias (540–530), and the 'Amasis Painter'.

Of shapes there was a variety for different uses. To name the most important: at a 6C or 5C banquet wine was mixed in the *krater*, ladled out with the *kyathos*, distributed in the *oinochoë* or *olpe*, and drunk out of a *kylix*, *kantharos*, *kotyle*, *skyphos*, or *rhyton*. A *psykter* served for refrigeration. The *stamnos* and *amphora* were used for storing wine or oil, libations were poured with a *phiale*, scents or oils were carried in a *lekythos*, *alabastron*, or *aryballos*, water in a *hydria*. A *loutrophoros* was used for lustral waters at weddings and funerals.

Inside the door (l.), vases, many with scenes from the myth of Herakles; *404. Lekythos (Rape of Helen), found at Tanagra, by the 'Amasis Painter', c. 530 B.C.; 567. Another with satyr watching a maiden. Beyond is displayed a terracotta model (7C) of a funeral chariot from the Anagyrous necropolis: mourning women surround the bier; the small figure on the pall may represent the spirit of the dead; a rider escorts the procession. On a stand, Attic black-figured lebes, Greeks and Trojans fighting (560 B.C.). In a case of early-6C Corinthian ware, 559. Amphora foreshadowing the Panathenaic type with flute-player and jockey; 521. Olpe, Akamos in chariot; the horses' names are inscribed.

The centre case and the remaining four cases on the left contain Athenian vases of thematic interest: In the first, 445 (kylix). Epheboi with instructors; 493 (lekythos). Sacrifice scene; 1054 (kylix). Monkey on a horse's neck; 1055. Aryballos with inscription "Kealtes painted (it), Mnesikleides gave (it) to Phokis" (c. 550 B.C.). In the third, 1080. Deer scratching; 1085 (oinochoë). Polyphemos in his cave and Odysseus escaping under the ram. In the fifth, 2410–7. Plaques (pinax) by Exekias, part of a frieze from an erection over a tomb. On the right of the far door, black-figured vases and (1044) the sole red-figured vase found in the Marathon Tumulus of 490 B.C. Two Ionian sarcophagi and pottery from Klazomenai (near Smyrna; late and early 6C). Etruscan vases in terracotta or bronze. Finds from the islands, notably 3886. Funeral stele with low relief of a man holding a lance, with inscriptions written in Greek characters but in an unknown language, from Lemnos.

ROOM VI. On the left, Lekythoi from Boeotian workshops: 488. Death of Aktaion; others depict Theseus and the Minotaur, Thetis and Peleus, etc. In the next case, excellent Attic examples of the *Black-figured style: 1134. Dionysos, (Apollo and Hermes; 1124. Theseus slaying the Marathonian bull (?); 550. Peleus bringing the young Achilles to Cheiron. 1045. Oinochoë made by *Xenokles* and painted by *Kleisophos*, Bacchanalian scene (found in the Theatre of Dionysos).

The black-figured ware continues on the right side of the room. In the first case, amid other lekythoi on a yellow ground: 1129. Satyrs torturing Lamia, legendary queen of Libya, realistically violent; 1125. The chariot of Amphiaraos is swallowed up by the earth (490 B.C.). The third case contains *Panathenaic Amphoræ* (prizes given at the Games, which remained by tradition in black-figure to the end), with boxing scenes, etc.

Black-figured decoration reaches its peak c. 500 B.C. and gives way to **Red-Figured Pottery**, in which the decoration is left in the ground colour and the background filled with black (a technique already started by 520). Detail is rendered in thin glazed lines. As complete mastery of draughtmanship is attained, figures lose the archaic stiffness and the art reaches perfection in the time of Pericles. Accessory colours, sparingly used in the 5C, are increasingly added in the 4C. Contemporaneously from c. 460 develops white-ground ware (comp. below), with designs at first in black glaze, later in matt polychromy.

The free-standing *Calyx-Krater (Theseus and the Minotaur; by *Syriskos*, c. 480 B.C.), in the centre of the room, begins the display of RED-FIGURED VASES. The case beyond (l.) shows early examples: 15002. Alabastron signed by *Pasiades*; 1409. Kylix signed by *Pamphaios*; 1628. Kylix (helmeted hoplite), signed by *Phintias*. On the opposite side of the room, a large case contains two vases signed by *Douris*; 15375 (lekythos). Eros whipping a youth; *1666. The 'Trikoupis Kylix'; within, ephebos preparing to pour a libation; on the outside, Theseus and Prokrustes and Herakles and Antaios. Wall-case, Vases found on the Acropolis, mostly dedicated to Athena by the artists themselves (e.g. pyxis by *Makron*).

ROOM VII contains red-figured vases of mature style, to the left mainly of black ground, to the right on white. 9683. Pelike, Herakles killing the attendants of the Egyptian king Busiris, by the '*Pan*' Painter (470 B.C.). Vase, by *Polygnotos*, representing the poetess Sappho and her pupils. Here, continued in ROOM VIII, begins the unrivalled collection of *White Lekythoi, sepulchral vases from Athens and Eretria, with polychrome designs on a white ground.

The commonest subjects are: Offerings at the Tomb; Prothesis, or Lying-in-State; Burial in the Tomb; and Descent into Hades. In the last the deceased is conducted by Hermes to the Styx, where Charon awaits him with his boat. The purest style coincides with the rebuilding of the Acropolis (450–430), after which follows a period of freer design with the addition of red and purple lines. The gems are by the '*Achilles Painter*', a contemporary of Pheidias, and by contemporaries of *Parrhasios* (420–400). The custom of placing white lekythoi on the funeral stele or in the grave stops at the beginning of the 4C. The references in the 'Ecclesiazusae' of Aristophanes (392 B.C.) are contemporary with the 'Triglyph Painter' whose work ends the series.

In ROOM IX are displayed a selection of red-figured vases of various provenance (5C–3C), some of them chosen more for the fascinating themes depicted (Dionysiac, Kabeiroi, etc.) than for fineness of execution. At the far end are a group of mixed red and white figured calyx-kraters; by the door, the 'Niinnion Pinax' from Eleusis.

The unrivalled ***Numismatic Collection** in the s. wing begins with Mycenean bronze talents in a form recalling the double-axe (comp. II. xxiii, 852); hoard of iron spits (used as currency) and a weighing standard found in the Heraion of Argos in 1894, perhaps those dedicated by Pheidon of Argos (according to Herakleides of Pontus) when he introduced his coinage there after the Lydian model. Among c. 400,000 coins (only a few poorly displayed) all the principal types are represented: incuse in electrum with a heraldic design (7C B.C.); in gold and silver, bearing a religious motive (gods, etc.) from the mid-6C; the famous Classical 'Owls' of Athens; tetradrachms of Philip of Macedon and Alexander the Great with inscriptions; and a fine range of later portrait types.

The **Epigraphic Collection** (entered through a courtyard from Odhos Tositsa), a classical library in stone, comprises some of the most important historical records found in excavations, including decrees, laws, building records, inventories, treaties, etc. Among them are the *Troezen Stele*, with a text of Themistocles' decree of 480, ordering the evacuation of Athens and the naval preparations which led to the battle of Salamis.

10 FROM OMONOIA SQUARE TO AMBELOKIPOI

The whole of this route, which comprises the most important thoroughfares of Athens, is followed by trolley-bus No. 3.

From Omonoia Square (Rte 8) as far as Sindagma Square a choice of two routes is offered by Stadium St. and University St., which run parallel in a s.e. direction. Both are one-way streets, the former in the direction we are describing.

ODHOS STADHIOU (in 1945–55 renamed Churchill St.), one side of the triangle of streets laid out by Cleanthes and Schaubert in 1834, takes name from its alinement with the stadium (nowadays hidden by the trees of the National Garden). It is a busy street, commercial at the N. end, with fashionable hotels and cafés farther s. Half-way along it, opposite the wide Odhos Koraï (l.), which affords a sight of the University (see below), the large PLATEIA KLAFTHMÓNOS opens to the right. During rebuilding operations in this square in 1960–61 a large section of the classical *City Wall* was discovered, part of which is visible in an office building on the N.W. side. At the w. corner is the cruciform **Ayii Theodori** (3, 7), the most attractive Byzantine church in Athens. Founded in 1049 or 1065 (inscription in w. wall), it was entirely rebuilt in stone with brick courses and Cufic decoration in the 12C, as an inscription above the w. door records. The belfry is a later addition. The humble two-storied building with the balcony on the s.e. side of the square was *King Otho's Palace*. Off the s. corner of the square is the fashionable modern church of *Ayios Yeoryios*, with the hall of the Parnassos Literary Society opposite.

In the triangular Plateia Kolokotronis, farther on, stands an equestrian *Statue of Kolokotronis*, a copy of that in Nauplia by L. Sokhos; the reliefs on the plinth repay examination. Behind is the PALAIA VOULI, a building designed by Boulanger in 1858 to house the National Assembly and finished (with modifications due to the suppression of the Upper House) in 1874. On its steps Theodoros Deliyannis, three times Prime Minister, was assassinated in 1905. In ten rooms on the ground floor is arranged the **National Historical Museum** (ΕΘΝΙΚΟΝ ΙΣΤΟΡΙΚΟΝ ΜΟΥΣΕΙΟΝ; weekdays, exc. Tues, summer 8.30–12.30 & 4–6; Sun 9–3; winter hours vary slightly; 20 dr.). The display, which is chronological, includes the ceremonial sword of the Emp. Leo V (813–20); helmets (14–16C) found in the castle at Khalkis; and a painting on wood of the Battle of Lépanto, probably by a Kephalonian eye-witness. Among the extensive collection of portraits, arms, and relics of the War of 1821–28 are objects recovered from Navarino Bay and Byron's helmet and sword; *David d'Angers*, Girl weeping for the death of Botzaris; and a splendid series of small watercolours of the first 5 years of Otto's reign by Ludwig Kölnberger. The study of King George I is preserved and royal portraits, photographs, etc. of campaigning monarchs. Temporary exhibitions occupy the upper galleries round the *Chamber*.

Shortly beyond, the street bends to enter the lower side of *Sindagma Square* (Rte 1). Continuation, see below.

If we take the alternative LEOFÓROS ELEFTHERÍOU VENIZÉLOU, formerly and still popularly called *Panepistimíou* (University St.), we pass (r.) the *Arsakeion*, built for a girls' school and training college, founded in 1836 by Apostolos Arsaki (see Rte 15). The classical building by Kaftandzoglou (1848) is now used by the law courts. Farther on an important group of buildings is fronted by formal gardens.

In the centre stands the **University** (Πανεπιστήμιον; 3, 6) built in 1839–42 by the Danish architect Christian Hansen. It is the least disturbing of the neo-Greek buildings, the polychrome decoration having been used with discretion. The handsome Ionic portico is of Pentelic marble; its upper part is frescoed with groups of ancient Greek authors. In front stands a statue of Gladstone, to left and right of the steps are Capodistrias and the philologist Koraï, and before the façade the poet Rhigas and the patriarch Gregory.

The University is modelled on the German system and is governed by a Council (Σύγκλητος) and by a Rector (Πρύτανις), elected annually from among the professors. It comprises five faculties (Σχολάι) of theology, law, medicine, philosophy, and science, each under its Curator (Κοσμήτωρ). The teaching staff of c. 150 consists of Professors (Καθηγηταί), ordinary and extraordinary (Τακτικοὶ and ῎Εκτακτοι), and of Lecturers (Ὑφηγηταί). The Students (Φοιτηταί; c. 7750) mostly read law or medicine. Other faculties are provided by the Polytechnic Institute (p. 142).—Connected with the university are scientific museums (at 33 Akadimias); laboratories and scientific institutes at Goudi (p. 200); a Library (see below); a Botanic Garden (p. 187), several hospitals and clinics, and the Observatory (p. 109).

To the left is the **National Library** (3, 6), planned by Th. von Hansen and built of Pentelic marble in 1887–91 at the expense of P. Vallianos of Kephalonia, whose statue stands in front. The classical style is used with sufficient freedom for the building to look more than a pastiche. Adm. free daily, except holidays, 9–1 & 5–8.

In 1903 the contents of the National Library and the University Library were brought together in this building. It contains c. 500,000 printed books and 3500 MSS. The 700 MSS. from Thessalian convents include two 10C or 11C Gospels, richly illuminated.

On the far side of the University is the **Hellenic Academy** (3, 6), built in 1859, at the expense of Baron Sinas, to the designs of Th. von Hansen. A pastiche in the style of the Erechtheion, it is entirely faced with Pentelic marble, and is adorned with Ionic columns and sculptured pediments. The façade is painted and gilt after the manner of the buildings of classical antiquity, but the effect is 'academic' in every sense of the word.

The colossal figures of Athena and Apollo, which occupy two lofty and unhappy

Ionic columns in front, are by the Greek sculptor Drosos, who was responsible also for the figures in the pediment as well as for the seated statues of Plato and Socrates on each side of the entrance and for the statue of Baron Sinas in the hall.

Just beyond are the *Eye Hospital* ('Οφθαλμιατρεῖον), designed in a Byzantine style (1847–51) by Th. von Hansen, and the *Roman Catholic Church*, a large Italianate basilica (1870) to a design by Klentze, dedicated to 'St Denis', the composite Western version of the Areopagite. Both buildings were completed by Kaftandzoglou; they face the dignified *Bank of Greece*. Beyond the *Archæological Society* (founded 1837), *Schliemann's House* (l.) may be identified by the inscription on the loggia (Iliou Melathron: Palace of Troy); its pleasing Renaissance style (by Ziller; 1878) was castigated by the neo-Greek Kaftandzoglou as "an incurable leprosy". Since 1928 it has housed the Areopagos, or Supreme Court of Appeal, an institution reconstituted in 1834.

At the N.E. corner of Sindagma Square we turn left alongside Parliament House into the aristocratic LEOFÓROS VASILÍSSIS SOFÍAS, lined on the N. with embassies and ministries. Hymettos rises ahead. From the left enters Leofóros Akadimías (once briefly renamed after Roosevelt), a busy avenue that starts at Canning Sq. (Rte 8) and runs parallel to Venizelou. At No. 50, immediately behind the University, is the *Theatre Museum* (adm. 20 dr.; Mon–Fri 9–1, also 5–7.30 on Mon, Wed, & Fri in summer), with collections illustrating the ancient and modern Greek stage. Here are sets for various plays, the reconstructed dressing-room of Katina Paxinou, and a library.

We pass the **Benaki Museum** (Rte 7). To the left the fashionable district of Kolonaki (see below) rises on the s. slope of Lykabettos.

The **Byzantine Museum (4, 8*; adm. 50 dr., weekdays 9–7, Sun & hol. 10–4.30; closed Mon) occupies the *Villa Ilissia*, built in a Florentine style in 1848 by Stamatis Kleanthes for the eccentric Sophie de Marbois, duchesse de Plaisance (1785–1854). Here the circle she received included David d'Angers, Edmond About, and Théophile Gautier. The museum was installed in 1930. Director: E. Chatzidakis.

We cross a large COURT, in the centre of which is a Phiale, a reproduction of a fountain represented in one of the Daphni mosaics. The mosaic before it is of the 4C, and the font came from the church of the Apostoloi in the Agora. The sculptural fragments to the right are from basilicas of the 5–7C, while those to the left came from 9–15C churches. Below the arcades of the wings are (r.) mosaics (Heron killing a snake) from the Basilica by the Ilissos (5C), and (l.) window panels from houses in Tinos and other Cycladic islands. The Right Wing contains a display of ikons arranged regionally and chronologically, a great help to appreciation of the main collection.

VESTIBULE. Characteristic examples of early Christian sculpture of the 4–6C: columns, capitals, etc. The doorway in the centre is from the Church of Ay. Dhimitrios in Salonika. Below, Bust of a Priestess (?; 4C) bearing the inscription ΙΣΒΑΡΔΙΑ. To either side, inscribed fragments of a cornice from the Acropolis. Sculptured remains of tombs.— We turn right. ROOM II reproduces a 5–6C **Basilica** in the form of a rectangle divided into nave and aisles by two rows of columns. The nave ends in an apse separated from the *Naos* by transennae and a central free-standing arch. Round the apse is the *Synthronon* (sedilia) with the *Cathedra* (priest's throne) in the centre. Below the marble

Altar (*Hiera trapeza*, a square table, with a central circular depression, borne on four columns) is a reliquary in the form of a model sarcophagus sunk into a cruciform depression. To the r. of the nave are a plaster copy of an *Ambo* from Salonica and a prothesis table in marble (4C) with sculptured reliefs of animals in a Hellenistic tradition. Round the walls are placed fragments of SCULPTURE from this and other churches. R. Aisle: 72. Christ the Good Shepherd in the guise of a boy (4C; from Old Corinth); 95. Relief of the Nativity, with charming animals; 113. Carved wooden cross. Beneath the arcade: 27. Prothesis table in marble, with reliefs of hunting scenes and Hellenistic heads (4C). L. Aisle: 93. Orpheus surrounded by wild animals; 35. Griffins; epigraphs.

From this aisle opens ROOM III, devoted entirely to **Sculpture** of the main Byzantine period (9–15C). Against the left (w.) wall are three marble ikons of the Virgin: in the centre, 148. Virgin as fountain of life, a stiff and formal creation of the 10C or 11C; to either side, 147. Virgin 'Hodegetria' (13–14C), and 149. Virgin 'Orans' (11–12C), each surmounted by a marble arch (152, 154) with representations of the Descent into Hell (from 13C Franco-Byzantine tombs). Round the lower part of the walls are relief slabs of the 9–12C (from iconostases), showing typical Byzantine motifs influenced strongly by the Orient: 159. Lion devouring a gazelle. Above those on the N. wall are reliefs with mythological subjects, probably used in secular decoration: 176. Hercules and the Erymanthian boar; 177. Gerene, queen of the Pygmies; 178. Centaur playing a lyre. In the centre of the E. wall, 150. Marble plaque with a painting on wax of three apostles, from Moni Vlatadon (Salonika). This is framed in (155) a great arch, surmounted by (251) a slab bearing scenes of the Nativity, both of which formed part of the entrance of a Franco-Byzantine church. Flanking them are two capitals, one (217) bearing monograms referring to Irene, the Athenian empress of Constantinople (A.D. 797–802). The s. wall is devoted to reliefs of the Frankish period: 250. St John the Baptist, from Zante; heads of Venetian doges from Corfù.

ROOM IV reproduces a cruciform **Church**, with a cupola, of 11C Byzantine type. The plan is square with the dome supported on two columns and two pilasters. Between the latter a marble screen (*templon*) separates the nave from the sanctuary. This templon consists of a sculptured architrave (copy of that from the Erechtheion) resting on pillars with capitals, and the lower part is filled in with sculptured panels. In the centre under the dome is a slab with a sculptured eagle (*to omphalion*). The sanctuary floor is decorated in *opus Alexandrinum*. The carvings (of finer workmanship than those in R. III) came from Athenian churches. Above the w. door, fresco of the Virgin and Child (15C). The impression is of simple dignity, good taste, and harmony of proportion.

Hence we enter ROOM V, a reproduction of a **Post-Byzantine Church** in a plain square building (of mosque type) with a flat ceiling. The decoration, mostly 18C, is rococo with marked Turkish influence. The *Iconostasis* is of wood, sculptured and gilded, and panelled with painted ikons; it was reconstructed from pieces from Kephalonia and Ithaca. The bishop's *Throne* was brought by refugees from Asia Minor in 1923. The *Epitaphios*, from Kimolos, was used in the procession of the

Dormition of the Virgin. From the ceiling hangs the *Choros*, a huge circle of sculptured wooden plaques. Round the walls, frescoes from destroyed churches in Atalanta, Delphi, and Athens (Ay. Filothei).

FIRST FLOOR (reached from the portico). The *Vestibule* and the next two rooms contain **Ikons**, the sacred images of the Orthodox religion. Scenes and figures are treated without any concern for natural realism in a formal and hieratic manner. The artist is as far as possible subordinated to an established tradition of representation in an attempt to materialize a spiritual vision of the basic truths of the Christian faith. Thus the ikon itself is believed to embody an inspired truth which can exalt the worshipper. ROOM II (r.) contains the oldest and finest panel paintings, including a number of works of the 14–15C dating from the Palaeologian 'renaissance', as well as three large frescoes.

198. St George (15C) from Asia Minor; 191. Virgin and Child (14C); 157. Double sided: Crucifixion (12C, with 13C additions), backed by Virgin and Child (15C); 100. Mystical Virgin, holding Christ in both hands; 134. Illustration of the hymn, 'For Thee rejoices' surrounded by Passion scenes (Cappadocian; 16C); 89. St George (13C), a painted bas-relief in wood from Kastoria; 176. St Anthony, expressive; 177. Theotokos Hodegetria; *169. Double sided, Crucifixion, fine work of the Palaeologian period; 246. Crucifixion, showing Florentine influence; 145 (mosaic). Theotokos Glykophilousa (14C) from Trilia (Tirilye) on the Sea of Marmara; 2162. Archangel Michael, of the Classical school of Constantinople (14C); 85. St Marina, combining simple composition and spiritual feeling; Chrysobulon of the Emp. Andronikos II conferring privileges on the diocese of Monemvasia (1301); 188. Christ Pantokrator; 185. Wisdom of God, from Salonika. Case by door: Evangile and Cross of Alexis Comnenus of Trebizond. In the centre cases: Liturgical rotuli, bibles, and documents.

ROOM III. Frescoes from vanished churches.—In ROOM IV (MINOR ARTS) are exhibited objects in metal, wood, and ivory, also pottery from the excavation of the basilica of Ay. Dhimitrios at Salonika.—ROOM V. Vestments arranged to show their chronological development, including Coptic work of 5–7C; croziers; *685. Epitaphios of Salonika, magnificent embroidery of the 14C, made, perhaps, in Constantinople.

Adjacent is the imposing **War Museum** (adm. free 9–1, 3.30–5.30, Sun 10–4; closed Tues), erected during the military dictatorship to demonstrate the prowess of Greek arms through the ages. The early galleries are cleverly embellished with reproductions from many Greek museums of sculptured battle scenes, armour, and armaments, as well as helmets and other excavated artefacts and graphic battle plans.—HALL A. Mycenean to Classical periods.—HALL B. Campaigns of Alexander the Great, with excellent explanatory maps.—HALL Γ. Byzantine wars.—HALL Δ. Frankish times and the 'Tourkokratia' (Turkish Occupation) with good prints.—HALL E. The 'Epanastasis' or uprising of 1821–28.—HALL Z. The period 1828–1911 is well documented by contemporary maps.—HALL H. Balkan wars.—HALL Θ. First World War.—HALL I. The Anatolian adventure; Italian War of 1940; and German occupation of 1941.

Greek arms (Middle East, Italy, etc) in the Second World War occupies Galleries of the MEZZANINE FLOOR. Uniforms are displayed in the BASEMENT. On the GROUND FLOOR are cases of medieval and later armour; Turkish weapons; early firearms, and 19C dress armour.—Outside are tanks, and six aircraft, including a restored Farman biplane of 1912 and a 'Spitfire'.

Beyond the next cross-roads (l.) a small public garden fronts the *Evanghelismos Hospital*, founded in 1881. Behind are grouped the

Marasleion, which combines the function of secondary school and teachers' training college, and the British and American Schools (5, 5).

The **British School of Archæology** (opened in 1886), though founded primarily to promote the study of Greek archæology, includes within its province 'research into the language, literature, history, religion, or art of Greece in ancient, mediæval or modern times'. The results of its studies are published in the 'Annual of the British School at Athens'. The school is celebrated for excavations at Knossos, Perachora, and Mycenae. The *Penrose Library* (c. 30,000 vols.) is reserved for members of the school, but applications for reader's tickets (fee per session) from students with a suitable letter of introduction will be considered by the Assistant Director. The **American School of Classical Studies** (1882), adjoining, has similar aims and publishes its findings both in its journal 'Hesperia', and in the 'American Journal of Archæology'. Its most spectacular recent work has been on the Athenian agora, at Corinth, and at Isthmia. The excellent GENNADEION LIBRARY (open free weekdays 9–2 & 5–8; Sat 9–2; closed Sun & hol.), donated to the school by a former Greek minister in London, is housed, a little higher up the s. slope of Lykabettos, in a tasteful building with a central portico of 8 columns in antis and two wings. It was erected by the Carnegie Foundation and opened in 1926.— Close by, to the S.E., is the formerly monastic *Moní Petraki*, founded by a 17C doctor and now, much restored, given over to a theological seminary. The church (14C) has frescoes of 1719 by George Markos of Argos.

The conspicuous *Hilton Hotel* (5, 7), with a huge incised carving by John Moralis, stands at the important junction of Leoforos Vasilissis Sofias with Leoforos Konstandinou. On the corner of the latter street stands the **Ethniki Pinakotheke & Mouseion Alexandrou Soutzou**, or *National Gallery of Greece* (adm. 20 dr., free Wed & Sun; winter 9–5, summer 9–1 & 4–8; Sun 10–2; closed Tues). The pavilion is devoted to well-mounted temporary exhibitions. The main building, behind, displays paintings of all periods, a few imported but mainly the work of Greek artists derived from European models. On the top floor are four paintings attributed to El Greco: Angel Musicians, St Francis, Crucifixion; Christ bearing the Cross.

Nearly ½m. farther out, on the left, are the site of the *Hall of the Friends of Music*, begun in 1976, and the *United States Embassy*, an imposing building in marble and glass attractively landscaped, by Walter Gropius and H. Morse Payne Jr. (1960–61). The road continues to *Ambelokipoi*, where it meets Leoforos Alexandhras, a dual highway from Pedhion Areos (Rte 8). A little farther on below the 'Athens Tower' the road to Marathon and the Mesogeion divides from Kifissia Avenue (Rte 17B).

11 LYKABETTOS

The ascent of Lykabettos, which takes c. 45 min. from Sindagma Square, is best made in the early morning or late afternoon when the superb view is clearest.

Lykabettos (Λυκαβηττός; in modern Greek parlance *Likavittós*; 4, 4) is the highest (910 ft) of the hills of Athens, and the s. termination of the Anchesmos range. Although perhaps the most conspicuous feature of the Athenian landscape, it gets its only classical reference in the 'Clouds' of Aristophanes. Formerly the N.E. surburban limit of the city, it is now an island in a sea of houses. The slopes are wooded, thanks to the Philodasiko Society of Greece, and many pleasant approaches by shady but sometimes steep paths may be made from the s. side.

According to legend, Lykabettos was a rock which Athena was carrying to Athens to form a bulwark for her citadel; in her surprise at hearing that, in defiance of her injunction, Aglauros and Herse had looked into the chest containing Erechtheus, she dropped it.

The N. slopes are readily accessible from any of the turnings leading s. from Odos Asklipiou (Bus 10, 16) and afford the gentler ascent. In Odos Dhidhotou (named after Ambroise Firmin Didot, the French publisher and philhellene) is the École Française d'Athènes, the oldest archæological school in Greece, founded in 1846 and removed to this site in 1874. Edmond About was a student in 1851–53. The French School has explored sites in Asia Minor as well as in Greece where it is perhaps most celebrated for its work at Delphi and Delos. Its journal 'Bulletin de Correspondance Héllenique' is of the first archæological importance. Just behind rises *Skhisti Petra*, a curiously shaped rock (called by the Germans *Frog's Mouth*) easily climbed in a few minutes from its s. side. Behind it ascends a road built to serve a *Wireless Station* of the Royal Hellenic Air Force which occupied the w. slopes of Lykabettos until 1961. In 1941 this was the Operations Centre of the Greek Air Force and formed King George's last H.Q. on the mainland before he retired to Crete in the face of the German advance. Here also are sited the ceremonial cannon used for royal salutes.

A Cable Railway (5 dr.), in a tunnel, 700 ft long, was opened in 1965 from the top of Ploutarkhou, and a Tourist Pavilion (Rfmts) has been hewn from the rock just below the summit.

Visitors are better advised to make on foot the steep approach from the s.w. From the Benaki Museum (Rte 7) the short Odhos Koubári leads to the PLATEIA KOLONAKI, centre of the most fashionable district of Athens. On the right is the *British Council*, with an excellent library (weekdays 8.30–1.30 & 4.30–8.15, closed Wed & Sat afts.) with lending facilities for residents only. From the N.E. corner of the square a short ascent leads to the *Dexameni*, or reservoir of the old Town Aqueduct, a Roman work begun by Hadrian and completed by Antoninus Pius. It was recommissioned in 1840, restored in 1869, and again in 1929, when the ancient aqueduct leading from Tatoi was brought up to date. It is now ancillary to the reservoir on Tourkovouni, served by the Marathon pipeline. Here at Epiphany takes place the ceremony of the Blessing of the Waters. From the top of Odhos Loukianou a zigzag path, passing near the chapel of *St Isidore* (16C), mounts to the little 19C chapel of *Ayios Yeoryios* on the summit, which commands a magnificent *Panorama of Athens and Attica. The Acropolis is however more effectively seen from the steps (café) on the way up, when its matchless marble ruins stand out against the sea.

12 NEW PHALERON AND PIRAEUS

Approaches from Athens. By RAIL, by the Piraeus Electric Railway (E.H.Σ.) from *Omonoia*, 7 m. in 20 min. (5.50 dr.). Trains every 7 min.; intermediate stations: *Monastírion* (2, 8), *Thissíon* (2, 8), *Petrálona, Kallithéa, Moskháton, Néon Fáliron.*—The State Railway lines do not carry local passengers.

By ROAD. The shortest route to Piraeus (5½ m.) is by the old Odhos Piraios, followed by bus No. 70 (from Omonoia Sq.), which traverses the dreary industrial suburbs of Petrálona and Réndis. The EHΣ bus (No. 165 from Sindagma Sq.) takes Leoforos Singrou, then diverges viâ *Kallithéa* to reach Phaleron Bay at Tzitzifies. Leoforos Ilissou follows the course of the Ilissos to link the Stadium with Kallithéa.—The pleasantest route (6¾ m.) is by Leoforos Singrou and Phaleron Bay, described below.

From the Olympieion (Rte 7), two of whose columns dominate the head of the road, LEOFOROS ANDREAS SINGROU (7, 7), an imposing dual highway named after the philanthropist Singros (1830–99) runs straight to the coast. We soon pass the *Fix Brewery*, scene of sharp fighting in 1944, then cross the Ilissos and its boulevard (Rte 7) by a viaduct with

good retrospective views of Philopappos Hill and the Acropolis.—
1½ m. *Ayios Sostis* (l.), a church built by Queen Olga as a thank-offering
after an abortive attempt on the life of George I in 1897. Running
between Kallithea and the large refugee suburb of *Nea Smirni* (New
Smyrna), and passing (l.) the *Athens Chandris Hotel* and the *Planetarium*, the avenue reaches Phaleron Bay at (3¾ m.) the *Racecourse*. We
turn right along the shore, now recovering from former squalour and
pollution by the main sewer outfall from Athens.—4¼ m. *Tzitzifies*
(Sandra, Saronikos **C**) is noted for tavernas with bouzouki music.

PHALERON BAY, a shallow and exposed roadstead, stretches from the peninsula
of Munychia on the w. to the headland of Old Phaleron (Rte 13) on the E. Here
until the beginning of the 5C B.C. the Athenians beached their triremes, and the
gently sloping sands were traditionally held to be the departure place of Theseus
for Crete and of the Athenian contingent to Troy. In 1929–39 flying-boats of
Imperial Airways en route to India and Australia called at a station opposite the
racecourse; an earlier seaplane service of Società Aero-Espresso Italiana from
Brindisi to Istanbul had called since 1926. Warships of the Greek Navy or of
visiting fleets may often be seen anchored offshore.

5 m. **Néon Fáliron**, or *New Phaleron* (*Olympic* **C**, and others), founded
in 1875 as a seaside resort, but spoilt by industrial development, is im-
proving again. It lies along the low sandy shore, anciently marshy and
called *Halipedon*, on either bank of the Kifissos, the position of which is
now marked only by a street name. The *Anglo-French Cemetery*, behind
the Karaïskakis Stadium, N. of the railway station, contains monuments
to sailors who died in Piraeus in 1855–59.—From New Phaleron we may
follow the railway and Odhos Skilitsi to meet the old Athens–Piraeus road
(Pl. 8) or, by Odhos Tzavela and Plat. Ippodamias, reach the central harbour of (6¾ m.) *Piraeus*.

PIRAEUS (Πειραιεύς), in modern parlance *Piraiévs*, is now, as in
classical times, the port of Athens. The town (187,400 inhab.), which
owes its rebirth to the choice of Athens as capital in 1834, is with its
suburbs the third largest in Greece (439,100). It is the seat of a bishop
and an important naval and commercial shipping base. Piraeus
proper occupies a rocky spur-shaped promontory or double peninsula,
joined to the mainland at the N.E. by a stretch of low ground. The s.w.
part of the peninsula, called *Akti*, is joined to the E. part by an isthmus
which separates the Great Harbour (*Kantharos*) from the circular
Pashalimani (anciently *Zea*). Farther E., below the hill of Kastella
(*Munychia*) is the still smaller harbour of Tourkolimano. The spine of
the peninsula divides the modern town into the more fashionable
quarter to the s., and E., well supplied with restaurants and places of
amusement, and a commercial sector surrounding the main harbour.
Beyond this the mainland extensions, including *Dhrapetsona* and *Nikaia*
form the most important manufacturing centre in Greece, with more
than a hundred factories, cotton mills, distilleries, soap works, and
metal foundries.

The modern town follows the rectangular plan of its ancient predecessor, of which visible remains are scanty and, save to the professional
archæologist, unrewarding. The visitor is better employed in a tour of
the harbours, where the interest is equally divided between the seafaring
bustle of a busy Mediterranean port, the considerable remains of
ancient installations, and the varied views of the Saronic Gulf from

the indented coastline. On summer evenings Piraeus is agreeably cooler than Athens.

Arrival by Sea. Customs and passport formalities generally on board; from Greek ports no formalities. On departure for abroad, passports are examined at 53 Akti Miaoulis and baggage at the Custom House on the quay. Taxicabs plying to addresses in Athens are entitled to double fare.

Steamer Quays. Akti Poseidonos (Pl. 3) to Aegina, Poros, Idhra, and Spetsai; **Plateia Karaïskakis** (Pl. 3) to most other Greek destinations; **Akti Miaoulis** (E. end; Pl. 7) to Italy, Turkey, and other ports beyond Greek frontiers; (w. end) for ocean liners.—**Pashalimani** (Pl. 11) for hydroplanes to Idhra and Spetsai.

Railway Stations. ΕΗΣ (Pl. 3), for Athens and Kifissia; ΣΠΑΠ (Pl. 3), for Corinth and the Peloponnesus; ΟΣΕ (Pl. 2) for Salonika.

Hotels. Savoy, 93 Vas. Konstandinou; **Park,** 103 Kolokotroni; **Cavo d'Oro,** 19 Vas. Pavlou (Kastella); **Diogenes** (Pl. b), 27 Vas. Yeoryiou A'; **Homeridon,** 32 Kharilaou Trikoupi; **Noufara,** 45 Vas. Konstandinou; **Triton** (Pl. a), 8 Tsamadhon, these **B. Leriotis,** 294 Akti Themistokleous; **Pheidias** (Pl. c), 189 Koundouriotis; **Delfini** (Pl. d), 7 Leokharous; **Capitol** (Pl. e), Trikoupi/Filonos; **Castella** (Pl. f), 75 Vas. Pavlou; **Glaros** (Pl. g), 4 Trikoupi; **Serifos** (Pl. h), 5 Trikoupi: **Santorini,** 6 Trikoupi, all these C, and others.

Restaurants all along Akti Alex. Koumoudourou, Tourkolímano, including *Kanaris Kokkini Varka,* etc.; *The Landfall, Dhiassimos,* Pashalimani; *Vassilenas,* at corner of Aitolikou and Vitolion, celebrated for its table d'hôte of two dozen courses; many tavernas with bouzouki music.

Post Office (Pl. 7), Odhos Filonos.—TOURIST POLICE at corner of Akti Miaoulis and Filellinon.

Buses. From Electric Rly Stn: **20** (circular) to *Kastella* and *Tourkolimano*; also to *New Phaleron, Custom House, Perama* (for *Salamis*), etc. From Plateia Korai: **165** to *Athens* (Filellinon); **78/158** (circular) to *Akte.* From Leoforos Ethnikis Antistaseos (Pl. 7) to *Athens* (Omonoia; **70**), *Glifadha,* and suburbs.

Shipping Offices. *Adriatica, Greek Line, Italia Line, Turkish Maritime Lines,* all TANPY bldg., 19 Akti Miaoulis; *Kavounides,* 38 Akti Poseidonos; *Efthimiades, Karageorgis,* 10 Akti Kondili; *Epirotiki,* 87 Akti Miaouli; *Hellenic Mediterranean Lines,* Electric Stn Bldg.; *American Export Lines,* 33 Akti Miaouli; *Mediterranean Sun Lines,* 5 Sakhtouri; *Libra Maritime,* 4 Plat. Loudovikou; *Fragline,* 5 Filellinon.

Steamer Services (quays see above). Argossaronikos to *Aegina* (2–3 times per hour), continuing (many times daily) to *Methana* and *Poros,* and (3–4 times daily) to *Idhra, Ermioni,* and *Spetsai*; twice weekly to *Leonidhion.* Also to Aegina by hydroplane (hourly). Aegean services daily (usually exc. Sun) to *Siros, Tinos, Mykonos* (1–3 times), *Samos, Chios, Mytilene, Kos, Rhodes* (1–3 times), and *Crete.* From 2 to 5 times weekly to many other Aegean islands, the *Ionian Is., Brindisi, Venice, Istanbul,* etc.—HYDROPLANES, from Zea to *Poros, Idhra, Spetsai, Leonidhion, Monemvasia,* etc.

Car Hire. *Hertz,* adjacent to Ay. Nikolaos, facing Custom House (Pl. 6).

British Vice-Consulate, 24 Akti Poseidonos.

Theatre. Folk Dancing (Dora Stratou company) in the classical Theatre of Zea, 38 Filellinon (June–Sept).

Festival. *Blessing of the Waters* at Epiphany (6 Jan).

History. *Piraeus,* originally an island, was still isolated in archaic times by the marshes of Halipedon. While Corinth and Aegina remained the principal maritime powers the Athenians kept their triremes on the beach at Phaleron Bay, which was in full view of the city while Piraeus was not. Hippias began to fortify Munychia c. 510 B.C. When Themistocles created an Athenian fleet of 200 ships, he chose Piraeus as its base, beginning in 493 B.C. the ambitious scheme of fortification which was to include the whole of the double peninsula and the approaches from Athens. By the outbreak of the Peloponnesian War (431 B.C.), the three Long Walls (see below) were complete. At its close the Phaleric Wall had fallen into decay, and the conditions of peace offered by Lysander after the defeat of Athens at Aegospotami (405) included the destruction of the remaining Long Walls as well as of the walls of both cities. The population of Piraeus at the zenith of Athenian power consisted largely of Metics (μέτοικοι), or resident aliens, who controlled much of its manufacture and trade, and introduced strange cults, giving the city its cosmopolitan and radical character. Thrasybulos sought the support of the citizens of Piraeus in 403, launching his *coup d'état* against the Thirty from Munychia. Munychia became the chief seat of the Macedonian garrison which controlled Athens in 322–229 save for brief intervals (liberation by Demetrios Poliorketes, 307–294). By 200 B.C., when Philip V of Macedon again attacked Athens, the Long Walls had been abandoned, though Piraeus itself (its walls repaired by Eurykleides and Mikion, c. 306–298) was flourishing as a commercial centre, and the Roman garrison used it as a base. In 86 B.C. Sulla ravaged the city, destroying the arsenal and the docks; but though Strabo dismisses it as an unimportant village, it seems to have revived early in the Imperial era, and could still serve as a base for Constantine's fleet in A.D. 322. After Alaric's raid in 396 it lost all importance. In 1040 Harald Hardrada, the Viking, in the service of the Byzantine emperor, disembarked at Piraeus to suppress an Athenian insurrection. In medieval times the town was known as *Porto Leone* (comp. below) and by the Turks as Aslan-liman. When, in 1834, Athens became the capital of Greece hardly a house stood in Piraeus. Resettled by islanders with the trading instincts of the ancient metics, it grew rapidly through the 19C, playing a large part in the revival of Athens. The population which did not exceed 4000 in 1840, rose from 11,000 in 1870 to 75,000 in 1907. The refugee settlement of 1922 increased it threefold. In 1854–59 Piraeus was occupied by an Anglo-French fleet to prevent Greek nationalists embarrassing Turkey, an allied power in the Crimean War. In the Second World War the port was put out of action and 11 ships sunk on the first night of the German air attack (6 Apr 1941) when the moored 'Clan Fraser' carrying 200 tons of T.N.T., and two other ammunition ships, blew up. Fully restored, it provides a port of call for most steamship lines operating in the E. Mediterranean and is the focus of Greek services to the islands. In 1971 Piraeus handled nearly 21,000 ships (28 million tons) and 3½ million passengers.—The opening scene of Plato's *Republic* is laid in Piraeus, at the house of the aged Kephalos.

Defences of Ancient Piraeus. The LONG WALLS, sometimes called the 'Legs' (τὰ σκέλη), formed part of the original fortification scheme of Themistocles. The *First* or *Northern Long Wall* (4½ m. long) ran from Athens to Piraeus, the *Second* or *Phaleric Long Wall* (4 m. long) from Athens to the E. end of Phaleron Bay. The walls were completed c. 456 B.C. (Thuc. I, 108). A *Third* or *Southern Long Wall*, parallel with the first and of the same length, was built by Kallikrates under the direction of Pericles to guard against the possibility of a surprise landing in Phaleron Bay. The Northern and Southern Long Walls, starting from two points in the outer wall of the Piraeus, converged to within 200 yds of each other and then ran parallel to the region of Pnyx hill (comp. Rte 3). Between them ran a road. A second road, probably the 'carriage-road' (ἁμαξιτός) mentioned by Xenophon (Hellenica II, 4, 10), ran outside the Northern Long Wall. The direct modern road (Odhos Piraios, above) follows the Northern Long Wall for much of its course, the Electric Railway the Southern Long Wall. Sections of both can be seen between the Karaïskakis Stadium and Odhos Piraios (l.) and in front of the Klostoufantourgou School.

The Themistoclean *City Wall* guarded all three harbours; fortified entrances to each, forming part of the circuit, were probably closed by chains. The W. half of Akte was excluded from the defences which crossed the peninsula from N.W. to S.E. On the landward quarter they followed the solid land behind the Halai marsh, and on the side nearest Athens the contour of the ground, making a circuit of 60 stadia (Thucydides II, 13). The rebuilding of the walls is commonly credited to Konon (Xenophon, Hell. IV, 8), though an inscription has shown that this was started before his victory at Knidos, and the work was probably finished only after 346 (Demosthenes XIX, 125). The defences were shortened on the N. side by carrying the wall across the Choma (see below) to Eëtioneia, but the circuit was extended round the whole of Akte.

Under Pericles the *City* itself was laid out by Hippodamos of Miletus on a chessboard plan with a spacious agora at the centre. Special attention was paid to the needs of the fleet, no less than 1000 talents being spent on the construction of *Ship-sheds* and dry docks. Demosthenes considered the ship-sheds of Piraeus worthy of mention in company with the Parthenon and the Propylaea. In 330–322 B.C. they numbered 372, of which 196 were in Zea, 82 in Munychia, and 94 in Kantharos. This corresponds roughly with the strength of the Athenian navy under Lycurgus (c. 400 ships), who completed the work by the construction in the Harbour of Zea of a NAVAL ARSENAL or SKEUOTHEKE (σκευοθήκη), designed by the architect *Philo* in 346–329 B.C.

Odhos Skilitsi and Odhos Ippodamias (comp. above) converge at the PLATEIA IPPODAMOS, with a busy hardware market, whence roads lead w. to the Electric Railway Station and s.w. to the main harbour.

Just off Skilitsi, c. 100 yds E. of Plat. Ippodamos, are the remains of the *Asty Gate*, where the Hamaxitos, or 'carriage-road' (see above), entered the city. Its Themistoclean round towers were later rebuilt on a square plan. Many neighbouring buildings incorporate classical masonry from the Long Walls. A little to the E. are foundations of a second gate and of a sanctuary. Near the Merchant Navy School in Odhos Evanghelistrias, and in Odhos Kodrou, further sections of the defences can be traced.

At the heart of maritime Piraeus at the E. angle of the **Great Harbour** stands the *Dhimarkhion* (Pl. 7), or Town Hall, popularly 'To Roloï', the clock. Immediately in front along Akti Poseidonos moor the small steamers that ply to ports in the Saronic Gulf. To the s.w. along AKTI MIAOULIS extend the liner berths (adm. restricted) with the *Passenger Terminal* and *Custom House* (Pl. 6). Here and in PLATEIA KARAÏSKAKIS (Pl. 3), to the N. beyond the lively Bazar, are situated the offices of shipping companies. From the open quay alongside the square and the mole to the w. depart ships plying to the Peloponnese and the Greek islands, as well as those making calls at Greek ports before continuing to Italy.

The modern harbour corresponds very nearly to the ancient KANTHAROS ('goblet'), which was divided, then as now, between naval and commercial shipping. To the navy was reserved the shore of Eëtioneia (see below) and the N. shore of Akti beyond the custom house (then a temple site); these locations are still favoured by warships. The *Emporion*, or commercial quay, coincided with the modern berths along Akti Miaoulis and Plat. Karaïskakis (comp. above). A jetty, called the *Diazeugma*, divided it into two, roughly where the Passenger Terminal now stands. Five stoas lined the quay, traces of one of which have been found c. 150 yds from the quay s.e. of the custom house; other vestiges of the Emporion are visible in the foundations of the church of *Ayia Triadha* (Pl. 7). The short s. mole projecting from Plat. Karaïskakis corresponds to the ancient *Choma*, the point of assembly where, on the eve of naval expeditions, the trierarchs had to report to the Council of 500 (when the first three to arrive were rewarded). The Trierarchy, instituted by Themistocles, was a form of taxation whereby the state provided the bare hulls of new warships, while the duty of fitting the galley, launching it and training the oarsmen, fell by rotation on the richest citizens. The Trierarch sailed with his ship and was responsible for its upkeep during his term of office.—The ancient harbour was guarded after 337 B.C. by two moles, extending respectively from the s. end of Eëtioneia (still surviving in part) and from the N. shore of Akte, leaving an entrance, 54 yds wide, guarded by towers or lighthouses. Nowadays and *Outer Harbour*, beyond this, formed by the construction of two breakwaters in 1902, shelters naval stores and yards, coal wharves, and a dry dock (comp. below).

NORTH-WESTERN QUARTER. Such vestiges of classical buildings as remain on the peninsula of Eëtioneia are scattered among factories, railway sidings, and somewhat rough popular quarters. Enthusiastic antiquaries may take Akti Kalimasiou from Plat. Karaïskakis (taxi advisable, but driver will need guidance; tram or bus to Larissa Stn) and, leaving on the right the *Stations* of the Piraeus Electric Railway and S.P.A.P., follow the dreary Akti Kondili behind the wharves that line the inner harbour, or *Limin Alon*. Anciently a miry lagoon called the *Halai* or *Kophos Limen* (κωφὸς λιμήν; 'silent ḥarbour'), this is a relic of the marshes that once surrounded Piraeus. The ancient fortifications may at first have run to shoreward of it; later they crossed its entrance. Beyond *Larissa Station* of the State Railway extends the peninsula of Eëtioneia ('Ηετιώνεια), called by Thucydides "the mole of Piraeus". This peninsula was included in the Themistoclean circuit, which enclosed also the inlet of Krommydaron. Theramenes in 411 B.C. gave Eëtioneia separate fortifications but tore them down later owing to a change of policy (comp. Thuc. VIII, 92). The 4C walls enclosed only the peninsula. Railway sidings cross the road (traces, 10–12 ft thick, of the

Wall of Konon) to enter the modern quays which have obliterated the ancient shipbuilding yards (νεώρια) and slipways (νεώσοικοι). Beyond the rails (r.), at the entrance to Odhos Monimon Dexamenon, is a little hill (54 ft) on which are the remains of the 4C *Aphrodision*, a sanctuary dedicated to Aphrodite Euploia, goddess of navigation. This was closely ringed by Konon's wall, of which the *Aphrodision Gate* (excavated by the French School in 1887) can be traced just to the N.W.; its towers are more than 30 ft in diameter. The *Inlet of Krommydaron*, now the Monimai Dexamenai (dry docks), yielded five marble altars in 1866, one with a Phoenician inscription. To the w. are some vestiges of the *Themistoclean Wall*, slighter than that of Konon. Beyond, in the suburb of *Dhrapetsona*, an obelisk in the Anastaseos cemetery commemorates French naval dead of the First World War.

From the Town Hall Leoforos Yeoryiou tou Protou leads shortly to the *Tinan Gardens*, laid out in 1854 by a French admiral. Opposite stands the CATHEDRAL (Pl. 7; *Ayia Triadha*), gutted in 1944 and rebuilt in 1958–62 in its former style. On the corner of Odhos Filonos in July 1959 workmen digging a drain suddenly uncovered a bronze hand; careful excavation brought to light the unique collection of statuary now in the National museum. It is believed that this formed part of Sulla's loot, stored away in 86 B.C. in a commercial stoa for shipment to Rome and overlooked. Farther on in Plateia Koraï is the *Municipal Theatre*. The broad Leoforos Vasileos Konstandinou leads s.w. along the spine of the peninsula, passing between pleasant gardens; streets at right angles lead (r.) to Akti Miaoulis and (l.) to Pashalimani (see below).

At No. 38 Odhos Filellinon (Pl. 6) is the small **Archæological Museum** (closed in 1976; adm., when open, stated as 50 dr.).

Next to the museum are the scanty remains of the **Theatre of Zea**, a Hellenistic edifice of the 2C B.C. which (unusually) was not altered in the Roman period. The rock-hewn cavea was divided by 14 flights of steps. The orchestra, better preserved, is surrounded by a covered channel. Folk-dancing displays are staged here in summer.

We reach **Pashalimani** (Pl. 11), the ancient harbour of ZEA, a land-locked basin connected with the sea by a channel c. 220 yds by 110, lined on either side by the ancient walls, which terminate at the inner end of the channel in two short moles. The port was occupied by 196 *Ship-sheds*, spread fanwise round the bay; many traces of these may be seen, particularly in the basement of a block of flats on the E. side. On the w. side the construction of an outer yacht basin, incorporating the bay to the w., has modified the shore line and narrowed the entrance to Zea.

Excavations in 1885 revealed the plan of the Ship-sheds. The flat beach round the basin was enclosed by a wall, c. 50 ft from the water's edge, which formed the back wall of the sheds. These, with an average breadth of 21 ft, extended at right angles to it; each was separated from its neighbour by plain columns of Piraeic limestone, which supported the roofs (probably of wood). Between the columns the rock was hollowed out to form slipways which descended some way into the water (model in the Naval Museum).

The YACHT BASIN is generally crowded with large sea-going craft. Behind the reclaimed shoreline below Akti Themistokleous a new **Naval Museum of Greece** (ΝΑΥΤΙΚΟΝ ΜΟΥΣΕΙΟΝ ΤΗΣ ΕΛΛΑΔΟΣ) faces a formal garden in which are displayed guns, conning towers, torpedo tubes, etc. The main door is to the right, but entrance more normally to the left (adm. 10 dr.; weekdays in summer 8.30–12.30 & 4–6; in winter 9–1 & 3.30–5.30; Sun & hol. 9–3 or 10–4; closed Tues;

free Fri). Opposite the main entrance the building incorporates part of the Themistoclean wall; to the right, carvings and models of ancient ships, including a fine trireme; representations of the Battle of Salamis and of the Battle of Rion in the Peloponnesian War. Returning, the order is chronological with Byzantine battles and Lepanto explained by drawings and plans. Among interesting documents is a letter from Nelson dated from New York in 1782. In the War of Independence emphasis is placed˜on the careers of admirals Miaoulis, Kanaris, etc. and the Battle of Navarino. Later Greek naval exploits (e.g. the 'Averof' and 'Elli') are celebrated, and the course of Greek naval warfare to the present day shown by relics salvaged from the sea, pictures, uniforms, flags, and ship models.

In the other direction the landing-stage for liberty-boats of visiting fleets continues the harbour's tradition as the *Stratiotiki Limen* (Military Port). Here the shaded PLATEIA KANARIS (Pl. 7) is a favourite promenade. Hereabouts was situated the SKEUOTHEKE, or *Arsenal of Philo*, of which the architect's complete specification was discovered in 1882 (model in the Naval Museum); no trace of the building remains.

The promontory to the S.E. ends in a salient of the fortification where was a series of wells (Φρέατοι). Here was possibly *Phreattys*, where sat the criminal court that tried those charged with homicide committed abroad. The judges sat on the shore while the accused pleaded from a boat in order not to pollute the land.

On the neck of the peninsula is the site of the *Asklepieion*, or Sanctuary of Asklepios Munychios, from which bas-reliefs were recovered in 1886.

The cliff to the E. of the salient is the alleged site of the SERANGEION (σήραγξ, a hollow rock). Here have been found the remains of *Baths* hollowed out of the rock and paved with mosaic: the main bath, with three apses, is connected with the sea by a passage through the rock 13 yds long; to the E. is the cloak room with 18 compartments for the bathers' clothes. The place is now a restaurant.

The road to New Phaleron here quits the shore and passes below *Kastella*, the terraced quarter occupying the slopes of the hill that rises to the left. The HILL OF MUNYCHIA (280 ft; 10 min. walk), the Acropolis of Piraeus, commands all three harbours and *Views of Phaleron Bay and the Saronic Gulf. In 403 B.C. Thrasybulus made it the base of his operations against the Thirty Tyrants, then in possession of Athens. Here in 1827 Karaïskakis was killed during an abortive campaign led by Sir Richard Church, designed to relieve the Greek garrison of the Athenian acropolis. Gen. Thos. Gordon held Munychia from Feb until May, but the defeat of an attempted attack on Athens made from Phaleron Bay put an end to the expedition and the siege. The modern chapel of *Ayios Elias*, near the summit, marks the site not of the Temple of Artemis Munychia but of *Bendis*, a celebrated sanctuary. About 100 yds W. is the upper entrance to a flight of 165 steps, known as the *Cavern of Arethusa*, which leads to the stuccoed subterranean galleries that held the water supply of the citadel (215 ft deep). On the W. slope of the hill (discovered in 1880, but now covered up) was the ancient *Theatre of Dionysos* referred to by Thucydides (VIII, 93).—From Munychia, Leoforos Yeoryiou tou Protou (comp. above) descends to the main harbour. Half-way down stands a charming marble group of Mother and Child (1959).

We keep to the cliffs above the popular bathing beach which faces the rocky islet of *Stalida*, then descend past the *Royal Yacht Club of Greece* (Βασιλικός Ναυτικός ʼΟμιλος ʽΕλλάδος). During its construction in 1935 large unworked blocks belonging to the fortress of Hippias were unearthed and inscribed sherds from (?) the *Temple of Artemis Munychia*. The picturesque yacht basin of *Tourkolimano* (Pl. 12),

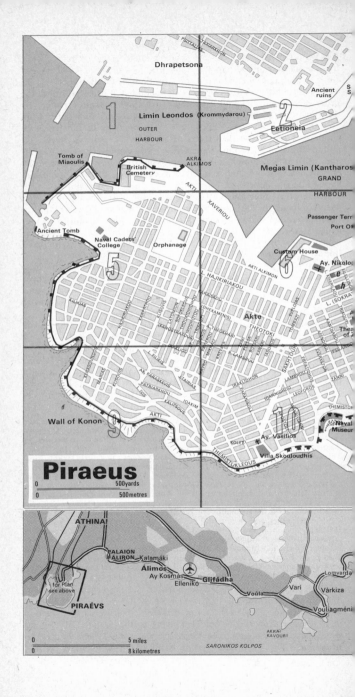

Dhrapetsona

Limin Leondos (Krommydarou)

OUTER
HARBOUR

Ancient
ruins

Eetioneia

Megas Limin (Kantharos

GRAND

HARBOUR

Tomb of
Miaoulis

British
Cemetery

AKRA
ALKIMOS

AKTI

Passenger Terr

Port O

Ancient Tomb

Naval Cadets
College

Orphanage

XAVERIOU

Custom House

Ay. Nikolo

AKTI ALKIMON

L. HAJIKIRIAKOU

Akte

THEOTOKI

Thea
of

Wall of Konon

AKTI

AK. PARASKEVIS

ETAIRAS

IRAKLIDHON

IOANNIDHIOU

LEOFOROS

ZANNI

THEMISTOK

Naval
Museur

KOLETI

THEMISTOKLEOUS

Ay. Vasilios

Villa Skouloudhis

Piraeus

0 ————— 500 yards

0 ————— 500 metres

ATHINAI

PALAION
FALIRON   Kalamáki

Álimos

Ay Kosmás

Ellenikó   Glifádha

for Plan
see above

PIRAÉVS

Voúla

Vari

Várkiza

Lomvarda

Vouliagméni

AKRA
KAVOURI

SARONIKOS KOLPOS

0 ————— 5 miles

0 ————— 8 kilometres

gay with coloured sails and lined with restaurants, retains the form it had as the ancient PORT OF MUNYCHIA. This also was protected by two long moles, each ending in a lighthouse tower, leaving an entrance between them only 40 yds wide. The *N. Mole* affords a good example of ancient marine fortification and bears lower courses of a massive structure of unknown purpose. The harbour had slips for 82 triremes, of which some foundations can be seen under water to the N. and S. The buildings themselves, apparently of wood, have long since vanished and traces only of the surrounding wall exist. The name Tourkolimano seems unlikely to survive a chauvinist campaign to change it to *Mikrolimano*.

The return to either Pashalimani or the Great Harbour can be accomplished by bus No. 20 (circular route).

The rocky and usually deserted S. coast of the **Akte Peninsula** affords a delightful *Walk, especially in the late afternoon when Salamis and the islands of the Saronic Gulf are thrown into relief by the setting sun, which falls full on Hymettos and the coast to the E.

The tour is best made in an anticlockwise direction; the uninteresting popular quarter on the N. side of the peninsula may be avoided by taking bus No. 158/78 (circular route from Plat. Koraī) to the point S. of the Naval School where it emerges on the shore. Thence Pashalimani can be reached on foot in 1 hr.

The W. extremity of the peninsula, once a royal park, is now a restricted naval area whose points of interest can be seen only from offshore. On the most northerly point, the ancient promontory of *Alkimos* (Pl. 1), once stood the great *Marble Lion* (probably from Delos) that was inscribed in runes by Harald Hardrada and gave to Piraeus its alternative names of *Porto Leone* and *Porto Draco*. The lion was removed to Venice by Morosini in 1687. About 300 yds W. of Alkimos are some graves of English soldiers and a *Monument to Andreas Miaoulis* (1769–1835), the admiral. Behind are quarries whence comes the bluish-grey Piraeic stone, and farther on, to seaward of the lighthouse, a rock-hewn grave traditionally known as the Tomb of Themistocles and a poros *Column*, re-erected in 1952, that marked the S. entrance to the harbour.

Leoforos Vasileos Konstandinou (p. 172) is continued to the W. by Leoforos Kiriakou to the *Naval School* (Pl. 5), whence Akti Themistokleous follows the indented S. shore of the peninsula. The **Wall of Konon** is visible in its lower courses for most of the way. Built of local stone (c. 394–391 B.C.) just beyond the reach of the waves and often of blocks cut from the rocks above which it is built, it is closely followed by the road, which is sometimes supported by it. The curtain, 10–11 ft thick, is reinforced at intervals of 50–60 yds by square *Towers*. The bases of many of these now support little wayside tavernas. A short section of the *Wall of Themistocles* survives to the S.E. of the *Signal Station* (185 ft) that crowns the highest point of the peninsula. Beyond the *Villa Skouloudis* (Pl. 10), now the Institute of Hydrology, polygonal masonry at the base of Konon's wall shows where the earlier wall was at first carried some way to the S.W. of the point where it turned across the peninsula.

II ATTICA

The name of **ATTICA** (Ἀττική), the region which surrounds Athens, is probably derived from the word ἀκτή (akte), 'promontory' or 'peninsula', literally 'the place where the waves break'. It became an entity with the amalgamation of the old Mycenean centres during the late-Geometric period. Geographically the region forms a roughly triangular peninsula terminating in Cape Sounion; its base, c. 30 m. wide, is the almost continuous mountain barrier that runs from the bay of Aigosthena, in the w., to the channel of Euboea, in the e. This consists of the ranges of Pateras, Kithairon, and Parnes and the coastal hills of Mavrovouni. The ancient boundary between Attica and Boeotia lay along this barrier, with disputed areas athwart the three ways out: the Megarid, Eleutherai, and Diakria. Possession of Salamis and the Megarid secured the w. approaches, which are effectively cut off from the Peloponnese by the great Yerania range. Athens itself, protected by the inner ring of Aigaleos, Pentelikon, and Hymettos, but connected by easy roads with the plains beyond, is the natural centre of the region. Many of the Attic mountains, in the time of Pausanias crowned by images of the gods, are now surmounted by ugly radar stations, which inhibit access to their summits.

Modern Attica became a separate administrative entity in 1899 when it was detached from Boeotia. The boundaries have been altered several times since. There are now two nomes: Attiki and Piraios. Attiki consists of two eparchies: Attica proper and the Megarid. Piraios has five: Piraeus itself (which, however, includes Salamis and Spetsai); Aegina; Idhra; Kithira; and Troezenia. Greater Athens, comprising part of the eparchy of Attica and part of the eparchy of Piraeus, enjoys special administrative status within its territory.

Among features of interest are the coastal resorts s.e. of Athens; the hill resorts to the N.; Mt Hymettos; the monasteries of Kaisariani and Daphni; the Mesogeia with the remains of Brauron; and Sounion. Archæologically rewarding in addition are Eleusis and Aegina, the new discoveries in the plain of Marathon, and farther away the Amphiareion at Oropos, and Rhamnous. New roads are fast being built and old ones improved, and with a car it is possible to combine two or three places in one day. Bus services are steadily becoming more extensive and frequent to outlying places, though they radiate from central Athens and are little help to those in seaside hotels. In the season there are coach excursions to the main sites. Walkers will find much of Attica within their reach, though expanding towns, military zones, and spreading villa development are ever-increasing obstacles. The countryside is carpeted with flowers in spring, when also the crisp air and clear Attic light are best enjoyed. Dogs are less troublesome than in more distant parts of Greece, but it is still quite easy to get lost on Parnes.

Routes 13–16 are in the nature of excursions which can be made by public transport leaving every few minutes from Central Athens; they can be accomplished at any time of day without advanced planning. The later routes demand a little organization, but except for that to the more distant islands of Rte 23, they can each be made in a single day from Athens. In Rte 19, 20, and 22 the old roads out to the N. are described, in order to indicate what remains of historical interest, every day more hidden in suburbia; a speedier arrival can be gained at the expense of intermediate interest by using the Athens–Salonika Highway.

13   THE ATTIC COAST TO VOULIAGMENI

ROAD, dual carriageway, 15½ m. (25 km.). BUSES every few min. from Sindagma Sq. to Edem; from the Academy, Omonoia Sq., Leof. Olgas, etc. (meeting at the Olympieion) to Glifadha and Vouliagméni, see under Athens. The distances below are measured from Sindagma Sq.

THE WEST COAST OF ATTICA, in classical times a flourishing region with many demes, degenerated into insignificance at an early date, and for centuries lay neglected and difficult of access. The discovery of medicinal springs near Glifadha and Vouliagméni after the First World War led to the foundation of bathing resorts, and in recent years the coast has been developed, under the name of AKTI APOLLON, as the summer playground of Attica. The hinterland, a bare stony tract, is little developed beyond the airport, and still studded with ancient graves, but the coast is very crowded in July–August.

From the Olympieion to (3¾ m.) the *Racecourse*, see Rte 12. We turn left. The rocky headland that closes Phaleron Bay to the E., once identified with Cape Kolias (see below), is more likely the site of ancient

Phaleron itself, which is usually placed near the Chapel of St George. At the bus-stop called Trocadero below the road is the *Marine Biological Institute*.

The ancient deme of *Phaleron*, which was the original port of Athens, was connected with the capital by the Phaleric Long Wall. Scanty remains of this have been found on the hill, and the foundations of a mole have been detected in the sea. In the neighbouring plain were defeated the Spartans who had been tricked by the exiled Alkmaeonids into invading Peisistratid Athens.

4½ m. **Palaión Fáliron** (ΠΑΛΑΙΟΝ ΦΑΛΗΡΟΝ : *Korali*, DPO, *Poseidon*, both B; *Avra* C; *Katina Club Rest.*), or *Old Phaleron*, a pleasant seaside resort (35,100 inhab.) with a water-sports stadium and swimming pool, extends E. along the shore, here broken into tiny creeks. The *Pumping Station* of the Ulen Company on the shore supplies salt water for the Athens fire brigade. We cross the stream of Pikrodaphne. The *Edem Restaurant*, on a small headland, is the terminus of the Edem bus. To the left in the *Phaleron War Cemetery*, stands the Athens memorial, dedicated in May 1961, to 2800 British dead of 1939–45, who have no known grave in Greece or Yugoslavia.—6 m. **Kalamáki** (*Saronis* A; *Venus*, *Rex*, B; *Attica*, *Tropical*, *Hellenikon*, *Galaxy*, all C), with a small yacht basin and good tavernas (*Marida*), affords views of Hymettos.—7 m. *Alimos* (Albatross B) corresponds to the ancient *Halimous*, birthplace of Thucydides (471–c. 400 B.C.), whom Macaulay called "the greatest historian that ever lived". The clay in this area was highly valued by Athenian potters. Trees partly hide a wireless station, beyond which extends the promontory of **Ayios Kosmas,** named after a 19C chapel, whose conventual buildings are now a taverna. The headland probably represents the ancient *Kolias Akra*, where many wrecked Persian ships were washed ashore after the Battle of Salamis.

Excavations by Prof. G. Mylonas in 1930–31 revealed no evidence of ships but proved that the coast has sunk since Classical times. On the E. side of the headland and in the sea below were found remains of two separate occupations, one Early Helladic, the other Late Helladic. Stone walls of houses may be seen. The necropolis along the E. shore, which provided many finds, belongs to the early Bronze Age. The graves show affinities with Cycladic types, suggesting that this was a trading-post to which mariners from the Cyclades brought Melian obsidian. It came to a violent end c. 1900 B.C. In Mycenean times the site was a fortified village, which was abandoned in the 12C B.C. The Classical sanctuary of Aphrodite seen by Pausanias may lie beneath the chapel.

To the right of the road is the *National Athletic Centre;* to the left extends *Athens Airport*, named after (7½ m.) *Ellenikó*. The terminal building, begun in 1961, was one of Eero Saarinen's last works.

10½ m. **Glifadha** (ΓΛΥΦΑΔΑ; *Astir Beach Bungalow Hotel* L, with good restaurant; *Palmyra Beach*, *Congo Palace*, *Bonavista*, A; *Phoenix*, *London*, *Riviera*, *Florida*, *Gripsholm*, *Delfini*, B; *Rial*, *Themis*, C; and many others of every grade; *Rest. Psaropoulos*, *La Bussola*), a flourishing seaside resort (23,400 inhab.) with sandy beaches and an 18-hole golf course, owes its foundation in 1920 to the discovery of medicinal springs. Near the Antonopoulos Hotel are the ruins of an early Christian basilica said to commemorate St Paul's supposed first landing in S. Greece at this spot. We join the old road from Athens.

The old inland road, a trifle shorter, passes S. of the Olympieion, crosses the Ilissos near the Kallirrhoë (8, 5) and turns S. Beyond (2 m.) *Ayios Dimitrios*, a pleasant modern church, Mt. Hymettos, previously hidden by suburbs, is well seen to the left.—5 m. *Trakhones*. The airport (comp. above) can soon be seen (r.) and there is a turning to the West Terminal (Olympic Airways). Farther on is an entrance to the Greek and U.S. Air Force bases, followed immediately by a turning to the East Terminal (foreign airlines). After the airport the main road quits its former direct line to Vouliagmeni (parallel inland) to serve Glifadha, where we may join the coast by Astir Beach.—At the s. end of Hymettos lay ancient *Aixone*, where the Thesmophoria, celebrated by women in the Temple of Demeter, provided Aristophanes with the theme for a play; Aixone has been identified with Glifadha.

From Glifadha, ½ m. beyond Astir Beach, opposite Tiffany's 'discotheque', a road bears left round a hospital and, after passing through an area of suburban development, ascends *Mt Krevati* (951 ft) to an air traffic control building (4 m.; 'No Entry' notice). About 600 yds before the notice, a saddle leads r. to a hill (c. 10 min) on the s. slope of which, not far below the top and overlooking the Bay of Varkiza (Rte 17), is the remarkable stalactite GROTTO OF PAN, APOLLO, AND THE NYMPHS, with its crude sculptures. The mouth is difficult to find and the descent into the cave needs care. A wall of rock divides the grotto into two chambers. The large chamber, in which is a spring of clear water, contains the curious *Relief of Archidamos*, by whom the grotto appears to have been decorated. The figure holds a hammer and chisel, with which it is working at some indefinite object cut in the rock. Likewise cut in the rock are a primitive altar of Apollo Hersos, a headless seated goddess, and a much defaced head of a lion. The cave was excavated by the American School in 1903, when votive reliefs representing Hermes and the Nymphs, Pan playing the syrinx, etc., of the 4–3C B.C. were found as well as coins and deposits proving occupation from c. 600 to 150 B.C. and in the 4C A.D. At the s. foot of the hill, below the cave, a classical farmhouse was explored by the British School in 1966: only the outline is now visible. This is the so-called 'Vari house'. Roads lead from the village of *Vari* to the coast at Voula and at Varkiza.

On the promontory of *Aliki* (r.) late-Mycenean chamber-tombs have been explored.—At (12 m.) **Voula** (*Voula Beach*, DPO, **A**; *Castello Beach, Aktaion, Galini*, DPO, all **B**, and others; *Pamela's Rest.*), a garden city (5600 inhab.) of summer villas, the beach and camping site are controlled by the N.T.O.G. The little church of *Ayios Nikólaos ton Palon* stands just beyond the junction of the Vari road (comp. above), beyond which the main road passes behind (14 m.) *Kavoúri* (Apollo Palace, 285 R, DPO **L**; Kavouri **A**; Pine Hill **B**), crossing the peninsula of *Kaminia* to Vouliagméni. Two wine-trading galleys (of the 4C B.C.) were found in 1960 lying in five fathoms off the islet of *Katramonisi*.

The three-tongued promontory, which forms the seaward end of the Hymettos range, was famous in antiquity as CAPE ZOSTER ('girdle'), strictly the name of the central tongue (now *Cape Lombárda*). Here Leto unloosed her girdle before the birth of Apollo and Artemis (see Paus. I, 31, 1). The 6C *Sanctuary of Apollo Zoster*, unearthed in 1925–26, has been absorbed by a hotel garden; the attendant building of the same period, later enlarged, discovered in 1936, may be the priests' house or a pilgrims' hostel. Herodotus (VIII, 107) tells us that, after the battle of Salamis, the Persians mistook the rocks of the headland for Greek ships. The uninhabited island of *Fleves* (the ancient *Phabra*) lies 1 m. off the cape.

15½ m. **Vouliagméni** (ΒΟΥΛΙΑΓΜΕΝΗ; *Astir Palace*, 240 R., excellent, **L**; *Greek Coast* **A**; *Strand* **B**; and many luxury flats for hire; *Rest. Moorings, Toscana, Lambros, To Limanaki*), the most fashionable seaside resort in Attica (no hotels below class B), has a large yacht marina. It takes its name from a picturesque *Lake* (bathing establishment) of warm, green water enclosed by the sheer limestone rocks of the E. cape of Kaminia. Its brackish, sulphurous waters are beneficial in cases of rheumatism, neuritis, arthritis, and skin diseases. The overflow from the lake runs underground to the sea and bubbles up from the sea bottom, raising its temperature for some distance. The fine sandy beaches (open all year) enclosed by the three headlands have been efficiently equipped by the N.T.O.G. in the international style with good restaurants.

From Vouliagméni to *Sounion*, see Rte 17.

14 KAISARIANÍ AND HYMETTOS

ROAD, 9½ m. viâ Kaisariani, to the Prohibited Area, c. 2 m. before the summit of Hymettos. BUS (No. 39/52 from the University) in 20 min. to the suburb, whence the monastery is 35 min, on foot.

Hymettos ('Υμηττός), in modern Greek pronounced *Imittós*, famous for its sunset glow, its honey, and its marble, is the range of hills, 10 m. long, that shuts in the Attic plain on the S.E., almost reaching the sea at Cape Zoster. It is divided by the Pirnari Glen into the *Great Hymettos* (Μεγάλος 'Υμηττός; 3369 ft) and the *Lesser* or *Waterless Hymettos* (''Ανυδρος 'Υμηττός), of which the highest point is *Mavro Vouni* (2639 ft). The W. slopes reach almost to Athens, the *Kakorrhevma Gorge* extending from below the summit to Zoodhókos Piyí and Pankrati; the abrupter W. side dominates Liópesi. The mountain is almost treeless and the aromatic plants and shrubs which produced the best food for bees are less widespread than in classical times, though terebinth, juniper, thyme, sage, mint, lavender, etc., are still to be found.

The Hymettian bee has migrated to Pentelikon and Tourkovouni. The violet colour which now, as in antiquity, suffuses the mountain at sunset is peculiar to Hymettos (comp. the 'purpureos colles' of Ovid, below). Hymettian marble (so-called Kará marble) was anciently quarried on the W. side of the mountain, close to the Kakorrhevma Gorge and approximately on the site of the ruined *Convent of Karyaes*.—Near the Convent of St John the Hunter (Rte 17B), at the N. end of the ridge, are some modern quarries.

From a little E. of the Hilton Hotel (5, 8) a shrinking pine copse marks the defile of the Ilissos between the suburbs of Zografou and Kaisariani. Leoforos Vasileos Alexandhrou to the S. of the wood is the main approach road to the suburb of *Kaisariani*.—3½ m. *Moni Kaisarianís (1120 ft), an 11C monastery, is closely confined at the end of the ravine amid the welcome shade of cypress, pine, and plane trees. Here since pagan times shrines have marked the source of the Ilissos.

On the brow of the hill just above the monastery is a famous fountain, known in ancient times as *Kyllou Pera*; its waters were supposed to cure sterility. A temple of Aphrodite was adjacent and the spot was made famous by Ovid in the well-known lines of the Ars Amatoria (III, 987) describing the sad legend of Cephalus and Procris. The spring supplied Athens with drinking water before the construction of the Marathon Dam. It feeds a fountain on the outside E. wall of the monastery where the water gushes from a marble ram's head. Fragments built into the walls belong to an earlier Christian basilica, probably of the 5C.

The present structure is first mentioned in the 12C. It has been conjectured that the name derives from Caesarea, whence perhaps came its original ikon. In 1458 when the Sultan Mehmed II visited newly conquered Athens, the Abbot of Kaisariani was chosen to deliver up to him the keys of the city, in recognition of which the convent was exempted from taxation by the Turks. Until 1716 it was independent of the Metropolitan and had a school and a celebrated library (moved to Athens and destroyed in the War of 1821). It was noted also for its honey. Deserted in the 18C, it is now a national monument. During the Second World War the secluded ravine was used by the Germans for the execution of hostages. The monastery was restored in 1956–57; the church is still a goal of pilgrimage on Ascension Day.

The CONVENTUAL BUILDINGS (entered from the far side), grouped round a pretty court, include a *Mill* and *Bakery*, and a *Bath-House*, now restored after use as an oil-press. The *Refectory* has a finely moulded Roman lintel over the door and a domed kitchen. The *Church*, built of stone with brick courses, takes the form of a Greek cross. The dome is supported on Roman columns. The parecclesion (dedicated to *St*

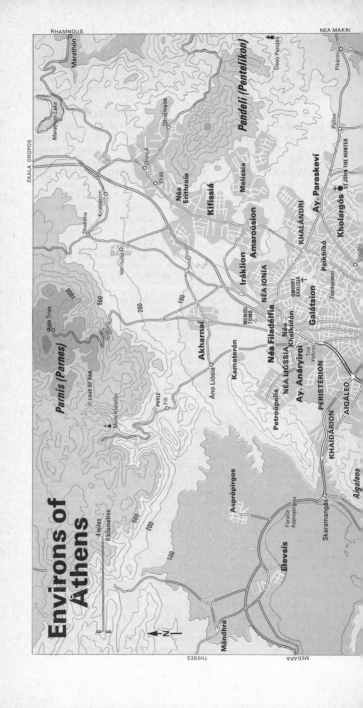

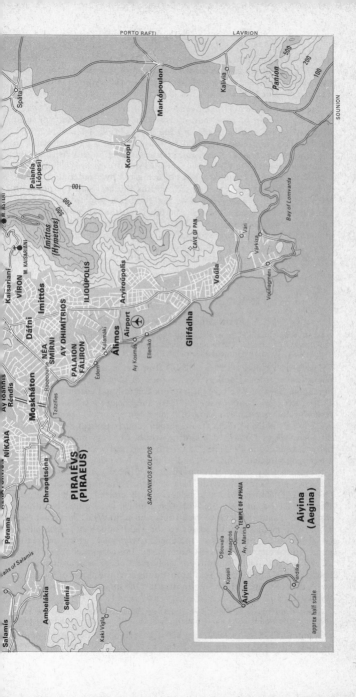

Anthony) was added in the 16C, the narthex in the 17C, and the belfry in the 19C. The frescoes, save for those by Ioannis Ipatos (Peloponnesian, 1682) in the narthex, are in a 17–18C Cretan style. A tomb in the crypt was explored in 1950.

The road crosses a bridge over a gully, then swings left to a saddle below an outcrop of rock that affords a sudden view of the whole of Athens. It then climbs to (5½ m.) the pretty *Moni Asteriou* (1798 ft), another 11C monastery, restored in 1961. Hence a path descends in c. 1 m. to *Ayios Ioannis Theologos*, another Byzantine church above the suburb of Goudí (Rte 17B).—We reach (6¼ m.) *Mávra Brákhia* (2119 ft), a col 2 m. N. of the summit. The col is marred by a radar station, but now that the summit is prohibited, affords the best vantage point on Hymettos, with a wide view over the Mesogeia and to the plain of Marathon. The road climbs s. but the view, though more extensive toward the w., looking across Salamis to the Peloponnese, does not include the E.—At 9½ m. are Stop signs, with a place for turning.

The summit (3369 ft) was crowned in Classical times with a statue of Zeus. Vestiges of an altar were found in 1939, and a cave has yielded Geometric pottery.

15 KIFISSIA AND PENTELIKON

A From Athens to Kifissia and Ekali

ROAD, 9 m. (14 km.). Buses 18 and 49 from Plat. Kanningos every few minutes to Kifissia; 22 to Ekali. The nearer suburbs are served by many local routes.
RAILWAY, 10 m., by Piraeus Electric Railway (E.H.Σ.) from Omonoia Square.

Leoforos Vasilissis Sofias (Rte 10) from Sindagma Sq. and Leoforos Alexandhras from Omonoia Square meet at *Ambelókipoi*, 1¼ m. from Sindagma Square. We take the left fork and follow LEOFOROS KIFISSIAS. To the left rises *Tourkovouni* (1110 ft), the ancient *Anchesmos*, with a reservoir and purification plant of Athens Waterworks. On the E. slope is (3¾ m.) **Psikhikó** (ΨΥΧΙΚΟΝ) a garden suburb. Here at Benaki Hall is installed *Athens College*, a boarding school for boys on an American pattern, founded in 1925; its 225 Greek boys, nearly half from overseas, are taught bilingually in Greek and English. Next to it is the *Arsakeion*, a progressive girls' school removed c. 1930 from a site near the University.—4 m. Turning (r.) to Nea Pendeli, see below.—5 m. *Filothei* (ΦΙΛΟΘΕΗ; Zafiris Rest.), a model suburb erected by the National Bank of Greece in 1930–35, with film studios, is favoured by foreign residents. Roads lead w. to Nea Ionia and E. to Ayia Paraskevi (Rte 17B). The main highway passes to the right of (7½ m.) **Amarousion** (*Anayennisis* C), or *Maroussi*, the ancient *Athmonia*, which derives its name from a temple of Artemis Amarousia. It is celebrated for its bright glazed pottery. Off the old road, *Anávryta College*, a boarding school started in 1947 by Jocelyn Winthrop Young after the model of Gordonstoun, occupies the former Singros estate. One quarter of its boys hold scholarships.

In the main square is a bust, by Tombros (1961), of Spiros Louis, the local shepherd who won the first modern marathon race at the Olympic Games of 1896.

9 m. **KIFISSIA** (ΚΗΦΙΣΙΑ; 880 ft) is an attractive and popular 'garden city' (20,100 inhab.) on the s.w. slopes of Pentelikon. The

summer temperature averages 10° lower than in the city, and the shade of its pine trees affords a welcome relief from the glare of Athens. Menander was a native of Kifissia, and here Herodes Atticus had a villa, a visit to which inspired Aulus Gellius to write his rambling 'Noctes Atticae'. Now, as in Roman times, the town is a favourite retreat of the Athenians in summer. It is also a good place to dine. Here is the seat of the Metropolitan of Attica and Megaris.

Hotels (mainly in the Kefalari area with ample parking space). **Pentelikon,** 66 Deliyianni, L; **Aperyi, Theoxenia,** Kefalari, **Cecil,** Xenias, **Kostis,** 65 Deliyianni, **Attikon** (closed in winter), 12 Pendelis, **Grand Chalet,** 38 Kokkinara, all these DPO and **A. Semiramis,** Kefalari, **Palace** (closed in winter), Kefalari, both A; **Nafsika B,** all the above with restaurant; **Aigli, Plaza,** Plateia Platanou, C, and others, without restaurant.

Restaurants. *Symposium, Ponderossa, Samaldanis, Bokaris,* near station, *Grigoris, Hadzakos,* and others.

Buses direct to coastal resorts in summer.

In Dec 1944 Tatoi aerodrome (occupied by the R.A.F. in Oct) was evacuated in face of the ELAS rising and British air headquarters set up in the Pentelikon and Cecil hotels in Kifissia, already cut off from Athens. ELAS attacked on 18 Dec and forced the garrison to capitulate. On the 20th the survivors (c. 600 officers and men) were subjected to begin a forced march, in company with civilian hostages, largely on foot through Central Greece. R.A.F. aircraft tracked their progress through Thebes, Levadhia, Lamia, and Larissa to Trikkala, dropping supplies wherever possible. At Lazarina (Rte 47c) in the Pindos on 23 Jan an exchange of prisoners was effected and the airmen repatriated from Volos.—At Kifissia died Penelope Delta (1874–1941), the children's writer.

The road enters Plateia Platanou. On the left gardens descend to the station; the road to Kefalari forks right. On this corner (r.) a shelter covers four *Roman Sarcophagi,* with reliefs, perhaps from the family vault of Herodes (busts of Herodes and of Polydeukion, his pupil and cousin, were found in 1961 in a garden near the church of Panayia tis Xidhou, a short way N. of the Plateia). *Kefalari,* a district of villas, gardens, and hotels, takes its name from a small and usually dried up stream, which, after rain, is a source of the Kifissos. The place is fast expanding into the foothills of Pentelikon, and it is possible to walk to Moni Pendeli and the ridge of the mountain.

From the N. end of Kifissia a road branches to the left towards Tatoi and Dekelia (comp. Rte 20).

The main road continues N.E. to *Kastri* (Kastri A), above which (r.) an ancient fort crowns the N.W. spur of Pentelikon, and (12½ m.) **Ekali** (*Ariadne,* B), a pleasant summer resort amid pine woods, which has adopted the name of an ancient deme situated farther N.E.

Immediately N. of Ekali a road diverges (r.) to (2 m.) **Diónisos** (*Chara* C), ancient *Ikaria,* where Dionysos is alleged to have been entertained by Ikarios, and the grateful god of wine instructed his host in the cultivation of the grape.—At 3 m. a turning to the left leads (600 yds) to the Sanctuary of Dionysos (l.) discovered by the American School in 1888.—At 6½ m. *Ayios Petros* (café), view over Marathon Bay.—The road descends to Nea Makri (Rte 21).

B   From Athens to Moní Pendeli

ROAD, 10 m. (16 km). Bus 105 from Plateia Kanningos.

From Athens to (3¾ m.) *Psikhikó,* see above. Shortly beyond we take the right fork to (6¼ m.) **Khalandhri** (XAΛANΔPION; *Olympic, Barbagallos,* **B,** *Acropol, Aiyiptos,* **C;** *Alexandria City* **B,** on the road to the N.), a pleasant suburb occupying the site of *Phyla,* birthplace of Euripides (480–406 B.C.). The ancient orgies of the 'Great Goddess' (probably Mother-Earth) at Phyla antedated the mysteries at Eleusis. About ½ m. s. the chapel of *Panayia Marmariotissa* covers the remains of a Roman tomb.—At 9 m., near a rustic villa (now a taverna) built by the Duchesse de Plaisance, we are joined by a by-road from Amarousion (2½ m., viâ *Melissia*, with film studios).

10 m. *Moní Pendeli*, a monastery founded in 1578 and now one of the richest in Greece, is shaded by a cluster of lofty white poplars. The buildings are modern, but the chapel contains 17C paintings. The road curves round the monastery grounds and ends at a large open space (bus terminus; Achillion C; tavernas): in the centre is the chapel of *Ayia Triadha*, near which traces of terraces mark the site of *Palaia Pendeli*, the ancient deme of Penteli. A little to the s. of the convent (on a by-road towards Stavrós) stands the *Palace of Rododafnis*, built in a Gothic style for the Duchesse de Plaisance by Cleanthes. Here she died (1854) and is buried. It was restored in 1961 as a royal residence.

PENTELIKON (Τὸ Πεντελικόν), the mountainous range enclosing the Attic plain on the N.E., extends for 4½ m. from N.W. to S.E. Its ancient name was *Brilessos* (Βριλησσός), but by Classical times it had come to be called Pentelikon after the township of Pentele where the famous marble quarries lay. The principal summit (*Kokkinaras*; 3640 ft), to the N.W., is, like that of Hymettos, inaccessible since it was crowned by an ugly radar station. *Vayati* (3305 ft), the secondary summit, ¼ m. S.E., can still be attained on foot, as can the little platform between them, the site of the statue of Athena mentioned by Pausanias.

The area beyond the monastery is largely blocked by quarrying, a military hospital, and villa development. However it is still possible to find a way through to the slopes of Pentelikon and the ANCIENT QUARRIES, which lie S.E. of the summit.

No less than 25 of them can be made out, one above the other, at a height of 2300–3300 ft. Their exploitation, though begun c. 570 B.C., was unimportant before the 5C B.C., and became general in Pericles' day. The crystalline rock of Pentelikon yielded the fine white marble which was used for the most important buildings and even in sculpture. It superseded Hymettian marble and poros for architectural purposes, though it never quite ousted Parian marble, which is easier to chisel, for sculpture. The rich golden tint that age gives to Pentelic marble alone is due to the presence of iron oxide. The stone yielded by the modern quarries at Dionisos, on the N. slope of Pentelikon, is less white.

We come first to an ancient *Paved Way*, down which the cut blocks were transported on wooden sledges. The holes on either side held bollards round which steadying ropes were wound. The *Quarry of Spilia* (2300 ft) was worked out by the ancients. In the N.W. corner opens a large *Stalactite Grotto*, where a sculptured column is probably a votive relief of the 4C B.C.; rock-cut inscriptions at the back of the cave indicate an early-Christian shrine; and remains of walls and inscriptions at the entrance mark a monastery of Byzantine date that survived the Frankish period.—From the grotto the climb to the ridge takes 1¼ hr.

The *View, one of the most extensive in Attica, is remarkable for its vast expanse of water, visible in all directions save on the N.W. To the N. rises the pyramidal Dhirfis, while on the E. lie Euboea, Andhros, and Tinos. The Plain of Marathon is partly hidden by an intervening spur. To the S.E. the sea is studded with innumerable islands; across the valley to the S. the ridge of Hymettos runs down to the sea; on the S.W. Athens spreads itself over the plain. Far to the S. are the mountains of Milos, 90 m. distant.

16 FROM ATHENS TO ELEUSIS

ROAD, 14 m. (22 km.), by the Iera Odhos to *Elevsis*, viâ (6¾ m.) *Dhafni*. Buses: No. 68, every 15 min., from Plateia Eleftherias (2, 6) for Dhafni (20 min.) and beyond to Elevsis (45 min.); No. 100 from the same place to intermediate points between Votanikós and Dhafni; No. 10 from Sindagma Sq., etc. to Votanikós; buses also from Piraeus. The first 3 or 4 miles are heavily industrialized and tedious to the pedestrian.

The faster but unrewarding LEOFOROS ATHINON (taken by all long-distance buses), which forms the initial section of the highway to Corinth, runs almost parallel, c. ½ m. to the N. It is reached from Omonoia Sq. by Ayiou Konstandinou and Akhilleos streets (2, 5) and, after crossing Kifissou at a congested roundabout near the Peloponnesian bus station, it joins the Sacred Way just beyond the conspicuous mental hospital at Dhafni.—Beyond Aspropirgos we must take the old road: the Corinth highway now by-passes Elevsis.

BY RAIL TO ELEVSIS (S.P.A.P.), 16¾ m. in 35–45 min. The line strikes N. through haphazard suburban settlements to (6 m.) *Ano Liósia*, where it curves s.w. Beyond a large army transport depot it threads a low defile, passing through a gap in the DEMA (τὸ Δέμα; 'the Link'), or *Aigaleos-Parnes Wall*, a westward-facing rampart that follows an undulating course for 2¾ m. along the watershed. The s. two-thirds are built in various styles of masonry (comp. B.S.A., v. 52, 1957) in 53 short sections separated by 50 sally-ports and two gateways. Farther N. the wall is crude and continuous. Two signal (?) towers command the wall, which is apparently military and may date from the Lycurgan period. A *House*, of the late 5C B.C., disposed round a court, was excavated in 1960 just N. of the railway.—The uninhabited valley between the Aigaleos ridge and the foothills of Parnes is dotted with beehives. Emerging into the Thriasian Plain (see below) at (14¼ m.) *Asprópirgos*, with a huge oil refinery, the line joins the road on the outskirts of (16¾ m.) *Elevsis*.

From Omonoia Square (3, 3) Odhos Piraios leads to (¾ m.) the Kerameikos (Rte 4). The Iera Odhos preserves both the name and very largely the original course of the SACRED WAY ('Ιερὰ ''Οδος) traversed by initiates from Athens to Eleusis, though nowadays few indications remain of the tombs and shrines described at length by Pausanias. From the Kerameikos the narrow road threads the noisy industrial area of *Votanikós*. We pass (1¼ m.; l.) the *Botanic Gardens* (Βοτανικός Κῆπος), with its tall poplars, and the Agricultural School of Athens University. A little farther on, *Plato's Olive-tree* (so called) is one of very few survivors from the famous grove that once bordered the Kifissos from Kolonos to the sea.—2 m. *Ayios Savas* (r.), a medieval church near the conspicuous naval signal station, stands on the site of a Temple of Demeter supposed to commemorate the spot where she rewarded the hospitality of Phytalos by giving him the first fig-tree. Classical and Byzantine marbles are visible in the walls. Farther on, a by-road to the right passes the *Hydrographic Office* of the Greek navy, and joins Leoforos Athinon. We cross Leoforos Kifissou, the extension to Piraeus of the National Highway, with the canalized Kifissos, some way w. of its ancient bed. The country opens out amid sparse olives as we approach the comparatively low ridge of *Aigaleos* (Αἰγάλεως), the w. horn of the natural amphitheatre that surrounds Athens. On the right is the conical hill of *Profitis Ilias* (620 ft), surmounted by a chapel. From this point the traveller from the w. gets the first sudden view of Athens, especially striking at sunset. The new highway (see above) joins the ancient road at (6¾ m.) *Dhafni*.

The **Monastery of Daphni** (or *Dhafni*; adm. 25 dr.; Rfmts at *Tourist Pavilion*; Camping Site), surrounded by a high battlemented wall, stands to the s. of the junction. Both church and walls incorporate ancient materials from a *Sanctuary of Apollo*, on the same site, mentioned by Pausanias but destroyed c. A.D. 395. The convent owes its name to the laurels (δάφναι) sacred to Apollo, which once flourished in the neighbourhood.

History. The monastery, founded in the 5C or 6C, was dedicated to the Virgin Mary. It was rebuilt at the end of the 11C, but sacked by Crusaders in 1205. In 1211 Otho de la Roche gave it to the Cistercians, who held it until 1458. Two Dukes of Athens, Otho himself and Walter de Brienne, were buried here. The convent was reoccupied in the 16C by Orthodox monks until its abandonment in the War of Independence. Restorations were made in 1893 after the building had been used in turn as barracks and lunatic asylum, the structure was strengthened in 1920, and a more elaborate restoration was undertaken after the Second World War.

The fortified enceinte and a few foundations inside near the N.E. corner survive from its earliest Christian period. Of the 11C monastic buildings only some foundations of the great *Refectory* can be seen on the N. side. The pretty *Cloister* (restored), s. of the church, dates from the Cistercian period, with the addition of 16C cells. Round it are displayed sculptural fragments, Classical and Byzantine, but the two sarcophagi, ornamented with fleurs-de-lys and Latin crosses, are doubtfully those of the Frankish dukes.

The *CHURCH is a fine example of Byzantine architecture of c. 1080, with an added exo-narthex, which was restored in 1961 to the later form given it by the Cistercians. The pointed arches and crenellations contrast not unpleasingly with the reused classical pillars. The truncated w. tower on the N. side bore a Gothic belfry. The three-light windows of the church are separated by mullions and surrounded by three orders of brickwork. The lights are closed by perforated alabaster slabs. The drum of the dome has round engaged buttresses between each of its sixteen windows. We enter from the cloister by the s. door. The interior is noted for its *Mosaics, which, though fragmentary in comparison with their original extent, have no rivals in S. Greece; indeed none nearer than Salonika save for those of Osios Loukas in Phocis. Most complete are those on the s. side of the narthex, portraying the Presentation of the Virgin and the Prayer of Joachim and Anna. On the vault of the dome is a celebrated representation, uncompromisingly stern, of Christos Pantokrator, on a gold ground. The frieze, round the drum below, depicts saints and prophets. Finely preserved on the pendentives are the Annunciation, Nativity, Baptism, and Transfiguration. On the w. side of the N. choros, the Entry into Jerusalem shows interesting perspective effects (note the little boys' foreshortened feet). In the bema, or sanctuary, though the Virgin above the apse is fragmentary and the vault is empty, the flanking Archangels are well-preserved. Of the frescoes that once adorned the lower walls of the church, four are still comparatively clear.—The *Crypt* has recently been cleared.

WINE FESTIVAL (Sept–Oct, daily in the evening) in the grounds and pine woods. Entrance fee covers *ad lib.* tasting of 60 or more wines, folk dancing, etc.

Beyond Dhafni the highway has been straightened and nearly trebled in width by blasting away the rock, so that the now intermittent traces of the Sacred Way must be sought first to the left then to the right. A mile beyond the monastery (r.) are the scanty foundations of a *Temple of Aphrodite*.

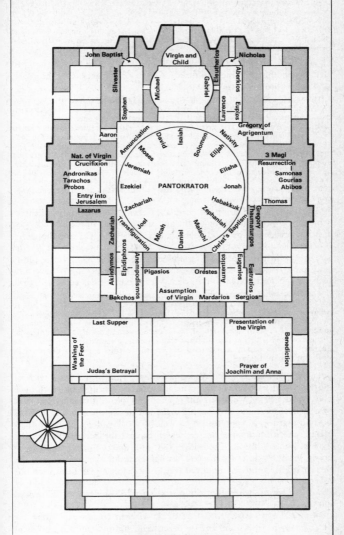

John Baptist · Nicholas

Virgin and Child

Silvester · Stephen · Michael · Gabriel · Eleutherios · Aberkios · Acacius · Euplus

Aaron · Gregory of Agrigentum

Nat. of Virgin
Crucifixion
Andronikas
Tarachos
Probos
Entry into Jerusalem
Lazarus

3 Magi
Resurrection
Samonas
Gourias
Abibos
Thomas

Annunciation · David · Isaiah · Solomon · Nativity

Moses · Elijah

Jeremiah · Elisha

Ezekiel · **PANTOKRATOR** · Jonah

Zachariah · Habakkuk

Joel · Micah · Daniel · Malachi · Zephaniah · Christ's Baptism

Transfiguration · Zachariah · Akindymos · Elpidiphoros · Anempodismos

Gregory Thaumaturgos · Eugenios · Eustratios

Pigasios · Orestes · Auxentios

Bakchos · Assumption of Virgin · Mardarios · Sergios

Last Supper

Presentation of the Virgin

Washing of the Feet

Benediction

Judas's Betrayal

Prayer of Joachim and Anna

Daphni

0   3 metres

In the face of the wall of rock behind are several niches for votive statuettes, with mutilated inscriptions below them. Remains are visible also of "the wall of unwrought stones that is worth seeing" (Pausanias, I, 37, 7). This wall, which was outside the precinct of Aphrodite, at its s.e. corner, was built of rude blocks of stone and was nearly 30 ft thick; it may have been part of an ancient fort. The Sacred Way, laid bare here during the excavation of the temple in 1891–92, ran between the temple and the wall.

We descend towards the Bay of Eleusis, landlocked by the island of Salamis and horribly industrialized. At 9 m. the road reaches the shore, and turns abruptly to the right (N.).

To the left a road leads in 1 m. to **Skaramangas** (*Leto* C, and others), with the *Hellenic Shipyards*, founded in 1956 by Stavros Niarchos, on the site of naval yards destroyed during the Second World War. Here repairs can be effected to any vessel save the largest liners. The three floating docks will accommodate ships up to 72,000 tons and the shipyards, which employ 6500 men, specialize also in the conversion of wartime tankers into dry-cargo freighters of the 22,000-ton class. The first ship to be built here, a 25,000-ton tanker, was launched in 1960. The graving dock, opened in 1970, can accommodate vessels up to 250,000 d.w. tons, and is the largest in the Mediterranean. At the *Naval Training Headquarters* conscripts of the Royal Hellenic Navy receive instruction.—A coastal road continues round the Skaramangas Hills (885 ft; a spur of Aigaleos) to *Perama* (5 m.; p. 205), the starting-point of the ferry to Salamis.

The modern road along the *Paralía Aspropírgou* or Asprópirgos shore, which for a long time occupied the ancient causeway of the Sacred Way, has been widened by land reclamation. On the right are the *Limni Koumoundourou*, now salt marshes and ponds but anciently the *Rheitoi* streams, which formed the fish preserves of the Eleusinian priesthood and marked the boundary between Athens and Eleusis. We are now skirting the Thriasian Plain, so called from the ancient deme of Thria.

The *Thriasian Plain*, extending for c. 9 m. along the Eleusinian Gulf, is usually identified with the Rarian or Rharian Plain, in Greek myth supposedly the first to be sown and the first to bear crops; here Demeter made the ground lie fallow while her daughter remained in the underworld. The plain is now one of the most highly industrialized areas in Greece; its oil tanks, chimneys, and the installation of cargo quays combine with the heavy motor traffic to make the last four miles of the Sacred Way the least romantic road in Greece. Salamis is usually obscured by dust and sulphur fumes.

11¼ m. The *Government Nautical College* (¼ m. l.) trains captains of the merchant navy.—11½ m. Turning (r.) to Asprópirgos (1 m.; see above).—At 13 m. we fork right (signposted 'No toll road') from (and pass under) the main highway. To the left of the old road, c. 200 yds beyond a group of cypresses, by a well ('Kalo Pigadhi'), are four complete arches of a *Roman Bridge*, which carried the Sacred Way across the Eleusinian Kifissos. The bridge, 18 ft wide and c. 50 yds long, built of poros, probably dates from A.D. 124 when Hadrian was initiated into the Eleusinian mysteries. A hundred feet of the Sacred Way have been uncovered to the w. At the entrance to Elevsis is the desecrated chapel of *Ayios Zakharias*, where the famous relief of Demeter and Kore was found.

14 m. (22 km.) **ELEVSIS** (ΕΛΕΥΣΙΣ; *Melissa* C), an expanding industrial town 18,500 inhab.) with cement, petro-chemical, and steel works, is occupied also with shipbuilding and the manufacture of soap and olive oil. The ancient city of **Eleusis**, birthplace of Aeschylus (525–456 B.C.) and home of the Sanctuary of Demeter and of the Eleusinian Mysteries, was situated on the E. slopes of a low rocky hill (207 ft) which runs parallel and close to the shore. The *Sacred Way*, which led direct

to the sanctuary, lies l. of the modern road at the entrance to the town, but the modern approach to the site is signposted from the centre. The extensive excavations of the sanctuary, which had a continuous history from Mycenean to Roman times, are of the greatest interest to antiquaries, but their appreciation is demanding to the lay imagination.

History. The legendary foundation of a city at Eleusis by Eleusis, a son of Ogygos of Thebes, before the 15C is substantiated in date at least by existing remains of houses (Middle Helladic II), dated to the 18–17C B.C. Tradition tells of wars between the Athenians and Eleusinians in heroic times, resulting in the deaths of Erechtheus and of Immarados, son of Eumolpos. Eumolpos was reputed to be the first celebrant of the mysteries of Eleusis. The introduction of the cult of Demeter is ascribed by the Parian Chronicle to the reign of Erechtheus (c. 1409 B.C.) and by Apollodoros to that of Pandion, son of Erichthonios (c. 1462–1423). The first shrine on the sanctuary site is dated by sherds to the Late Helladic II period, though there is nothing concrete to connect it with Demeter. The 'Homeric' Hymn to Demeter (late 7C B.C.) gives the orthodox version of the institution of the mysteries by Demeter herself (comp. below). The city seems to have been a rival of Athens until it came under firm Athenian sway about the time of Solon. Henceforward its cult grew and the sanctuary was constantly enlarged. Its reputation became panhellenic and initiation was opened to non-Athenian Greeks. Peisistratos rebuilt it, enclosing it with a strong wall and doubling its area; but his work fell victim to the Persian invasion. Kimon initiated the reconstruction which was completed under Pericles. His telesterion was to survive with modifications to the end. Eleusis suffered heavily under the Thirty Tyrants, who here established a fortified base against Thrasyboulos, massacring those who opposed them. The sanctuary was extended again in the 4C B.C. The town remained a stronghold throughout the Macedonian period. Under the *pax Romana* the sanctuary was adorned with a new gate. The Imperial transformation of Eleusis probably began under Hadrian. In A.D. 170 the sanctuary was sacked by the Sarmatians, but was immediately restored at the expense of Marcus Aurelius. At his initiation in 176 the Emperor was allowed to enter the anaktoron, the only lay person so honoured in the whole history of Eleusis. The Emperor Julian was initiated, completing his sanctification (according to Gibbon) in Gaul; Valentinian permitted the continuance of the Mysteries, but Theodosius' decrees and Alaric's sack were jointly responsible (c. 395) for their end. The town was abandoned after the Byzantine era and not reoccupied till the 18C.

The Homeric *Hymn to Demeter* sets down the anciently accepted mystique of the cult's divine foundation. While gathering flowers, Persephone (Kore, or the Maiden), Demeter's daughter, was carried off by Hades (Pluto) to the nether regions. Demeter, during her quest for Persephone, came to Eleusis, where she was found resting, disguised as an old woman, by Metaneira, consort of King Keleos. After her first disastrous attempt to reward the king's hospitality by immortalizing his son Demophon, Demeter revealed her identity and commanded Keleos to build a megaron in her honour. To this she retired, vowing that she would neither return to Olympos nor allow crops to grow on earth until Kore was delivered up. Finally Zeus commanded Pluto to return Persephone, but because she had eaten pomegranate seeds while in the underworld she was bound to return there for part of every year. Before leaving Eleusis, Demeter broke the famine and gave to Triptolemos, second son of Keleos, seeds of wheat and a winged chariot, in which he rode over the earth, teaching mankind the use of the plough and the blessings of agriculture.

Candidates for initiation were first admitted to the *Lesser Eleusinia* which were held in the month of Anthesterion (Feb–Mar) at Agrai, in Athens, on the banks of the Ilissos. Being accepted as Mystai (initiates), they were allowed to attend the GREATER ELEUSINIA, which took place in Boëdromion (Sept), and lasted nine days, beginning and ending in Athens. For them a truce was declared throughout Hellas. During the seventh night the qualified Mystai became Epoptai. These annual celebrations (*teletai*) consisted of a public secular display and a secret religious rite. The former, the responsibility of the Archon Basileus and his staff, took the form mainly of a *Procession (pompe)* from Athens to Eleusis. The religious rite was entirely in the hands of the Hierophant and priesthood of Eleusis, hereditary offices of the Eumolpids and the Kerykes. The most important officials included the Dadouchos (torchbearer) and the Hierokeryx (herald). The procession, which took place on the fifth day, was headed by a statue of Iacchos, god associated with the cult, and bore with it the Hiera, or sacred objects, in baskets (*kistai*). During the Peloponnesian War, when no truce was declared, the procession was reduced; for some years after the Spartan occupation of Dekelia the pompe went by sea. In 336 B.C. the news of the destruction of Thebes by Alexander the Great caused the only recorded instance of the procession's cancellation after it had set out.

The fundamental substance of the **Mysteries,** the character of the sacred objects displayed, and the nature of the revelation experienced were never divulged. Alcibiades was condemned to death in absentia for parodying part of the mysteries (though later reprieved); Aeschylus was almost lynched on suspicion of revealing their substance on the stage. It is thought probable that a pageant (dromena) was performed representing the action of the Hymn of Demeter. Initiation carried with it no further obligation, but seems to have afforded spiritual pleasure. Cicero derived great comfort from the experience.

Eleusis attracted the attention of western travellers from Wheler (1676) onwards. E. D. Clarke bore away a statue to Cambridge in 1801. The Propylaea were laid bare in 1812 by the Society of the Dilettanti. Systematic excavations, started by the Greek Archæological Society in 1882, were greatly extended by Konstantinos Kourouniotes in 1917–45, especially after the Rockefeller Institution had provided a grant in 1930. Both the earlier work and that done since the war by G. E. Mylonas, Prof. Orlandos, and John Travlos are admirably summarized in Mylonas: 'Eleusis and the Eleusinian Mysteries' (1962).

A good idea of the layout and complexity of the excavations can be gained from the terrace in front of the prominent 19C chapel. Visitors who are pressed for time can then confine themselves to the forecourt, the two propylaea, the Telesterion, the S.E. walls, and the Museum. A full exploration of the remains takes all day and necessitates a certain amount of scrambling. Care should be taken on the Acropolis, where there are unfenced cisterns.

The Excavations (adm. 25 dr.; weekdays in summer, 8.30–2.30, winter 9–3.30; Sun & hol. 10–4; closed Tues) lie at the foot and on the E. slopes of the Acropolis and comprise the greater part of the **Sanctuary of Demeter and Kore** and its dependencies. This was protected on three sides by the main city wall and separated from the city on the fourth side by a dividing wall. As we pass the entrance gate the *Sacred Way* changes from a modern to an ancient paved road, which ends on the **Great Forecourt** before the city walls. This spacious square formed part of the new monumental entrance planned probably in the reign of Antoninus Pius. Here the mystai gathered in order to perform the necessary acts of purification before entering the sanctuary. From the square the Great Propylaea led directly to the sanctuary; to left and right triumphal arches led towards the main gate of the town and to the visitors' quarter of baths, hotels, and recreation centres.

Numerous marble blocks on the square came from the buildings that defined its limits. To the left are the remains of a *Fountain.* Beyond it stood a *Triumphal Arch*, one of two (comp. above) faithfully copied from the Arch of Hadrian at Athens. The foundations remain; its gable has been reassembled in front; and its inscription (replaced near by) reads 'All the Greeks to the Goddesses and the Emperor'. Close to the N.E. corner of the Great Propylaea is the sacred well that passed throughout classical times for the **Kallíchoron,** or *Well of the Fair Dances.* The well-head, beautifully fashioned in polygonal masonry with clamps, probably dates from the time of Peisistratos. Mylonas has suggested that this is, in fact, the *Parthenion*, or Well of the Maidens, mentioned in the Hymn as the place where Demeter sat to rest. The name Kallichoron may have been transferred to it from the well near the Telesterion after the importance of the Parthenion had been centred on the 'Mirthless Stone' on which she sat (comp. below).

In the centre of the court are the scanty remains of the *Temple of Artemis Propylaia and of Poseidon*, amphiprostyle in form and constructed in marble. It must have been quite new when described by Pausanias. The *Altar* to the E. was presumably dedicated to Artemis, that to the N. probably to Poseidon, while at the N.W. corner is an *Eschara*, constructed in Roman tiles, on remains proving that the sacred nature of the spot goes back to the 6C B.C. The rectangular area that interrupts the pavement beyond the eschara has been identified with the *Temenos of the Hero Dolichos*; beneath the houses outside the enclosure are extensive remains conjectured to be of a *Pompeion*.

The **Great Propylaea,** built in Pentelic marble on a concrete core by Marcus Aurelius or his predecessor, is a close copy of the Propylaea at Athens, both in plan and dimensions. It is approached by six marble steps and faces N.E. Reassembled on the pavement in front are two of the six Doric *Columns* of the façade and the *Pediment* with its central medallion bust of (?) Marcus Aurelius. Parts of the entablature are assembled to the right of the steps. The bases of the six Ionic columns that flanked the central passage are in situ. The transverse wall was pierced by five doorways: the threshold of the small one to the left shows the greatest wear. At some time of danger (? under Valerian) the Doric colonnade was closed by a thick wall; the single door that then gave entrance has left a roller groove in the pavement. Crosses scored on the pavement probably derive from Christian fears of pagan spirits.

The gateway covers a corner tower of the Peisistratid enceinte. To the w. this remained the city's fortification in later times; to the E. a later wall enclosed a Classical extension to the city, while the Peisistratid circuit continued to serve as the peribolos of the sanctuary. Between the two walls are numerous small buildings dating mainly from the time of Kimon. The area between the two propylaea seems to have been a level forecourt in Roman times.

The **Lesser Propylaea,** which face N. and form the entrance to the innermost court, were vowed to the Goddesses by Cicero's friend Appius Claudius Pulcher in his consulship (54 B.C.) and completed after his death by two nephews. The structure consisted of two parallel walls, each 50 ft long, with Ionic attached columns, which enclosed a passage 33 ft wide. This is divided into three at its inner end by two short inner walls (parastadia) parallel to the exterior walls. Forward of the doors, whose supporting rollers have left prominent grooves, extended antae; the bases in front of them supported two Corinthian columns. The inner façade had caryatids instead of columns. Portions of the inscribed architrave and frieze are recomposed at the side. The frieze is composed of triglyphs and metopes, both carved with emblems of the cult.

We now enter the inner **Precinct of Demeter,** for two thousand years an area forbidden to the uninitiated on penalty of death. To the right is the *Plutonion*, a triangular precinct of the 4C B.C., enclosing a cavern sacred to Pluto. A shrine was built at its mouth in the Peisistratid era; the surviving foundations are of a temple completed in 328 B.C. (a dated inscription has been found referring to the purchase of its wooden doors). Following the *Processional Road*, we come next to a rock-cut *Stepped Platform* (Pl. A) which adjoined a small building, perhaps a *Treasury* (Pl. B). The platform may have served as a stand from which the start of a sacred pageant was watched; Mylonas suggests that the '*Mirthless Stone*' (Agelastos Petra) may be identified with the worked piece of rock that here projects above the pavement of the Roman sacred way. The levelled terrace beyond the treasury supported a *Temple* (Pl. C) possibly dedicated to Sabina, wife of Hadrian, on whom the Greeks had conferred the title of New Demeter. Between this and the treasury is a *Thesauros* (offertory box) hewn from a boulder. We ascend to the large square platform on which stood the Hall of the Mysteries.

The first shrine decreed by Demeter 'beneath the citadel and its sheer wall upon a rising hillock above the Kallichoron' occupied a limited site on ground which sloped steeply away. As each enlargement of the sanctuary was undertaken, it became necessary to extend the artificial terrace on which it stood. In consequence each shrine in turn escaped complete destruction by being buried under the next. The result is an archæological palimpsest of rare completeness but, to the layman, of baffling complexity.

The great **Telesterion**, or TEMPLE OF DEMETER, the Hall of Initiation and the Mysteries, is an almost square chamber 175 ft by 170, partly cut out of the rock of the Acropolis and partly built on a terrace. The existing remains appear to be those of the Periclean rebuilding (with the addition of the Portico of Philo), as finally remodelled by Marcus Aurelius. On each of the four sides were eight tiers of seats, partly hewn from the rock and partly built up; these were interrupted at six points only, where two doors on each of the disengaged sides afforded entrance. The hall accommodated 3000. Six rows of seven columns each supported the (? wooden) roof; they were in two tiers separated by an epistyle (possibly with a frieze). The bases of most remain; one of them has as its top course a reused block of the 1C A.D., showing the extent of the Roman restoration. In the centre, on a site it had occupied from the first, was the *Anaktoron*, or holy of holies, a small rectangular room roofed somehow by Xenokles with an Opaion, or lantern, of which no vestige has survived. By the side of the anaktoron stood the throne of the Hierophant. Externally the solid walls, broken only by doorways, must have enhanced the air of mystery. Later the S.E. front was adorned along its whole length by the PORTICO OF PHILO, whose pavement and massive supporting wall (18 courses of masonry) form one of the most prominent features of the site. It was completed, according to Vitruvius, in the reign of Demetrios of Phaleron. The huge prostoön had a colonnade of twelve Doric columns by two, which were left unfluted. An ancient *Well* cut into the rock below may be the original Kallichoron (comp. above).

Excavations have revealed traces of at least six earlier structures on the same site. The *Mycenean Megaron*, traceable in the remains of two walls in the N.E. half of the hall, was a chamber 55 ft square. This was replaced by a Geometric edifice, a Solonian telesterion, and again by the *Telestrion of Peisistratos*, which occupied the N.E. corner of the final structure. This hall had 5 rows of 5 columns each, with a portico on the N.E. front, and was destroyed by the Persians. Kimon incorporated the ruins into a rectangular hall, designed round the old Anaktoron, and having 7 rows of 3 columns each. It was apparently not finished. Pericles probably instigated a grander design by which the building again became square, doubling that of Kimon. This was first entrusted to Iktinos, whose plan to support the roof on only 20 columns (foundations visible) had to be abandoned for technical reasons. The design was replaced by another by Koroibos, which was completed after his death by Metagenes and Xenokles. Lycurgus may have ordered the Portico of Philo. The L-shaped foundations that extend beyond the E. and S. corners show that earlier plans for building a peristyle were started. After the Sarmatian sack, the Romans restored the interior with somewhat makeshift columns and extended the N.W. side another six feet into the rock.

From the Portico of Philo the *Court* of the sanctuary, a level artificial terrace, extended to the E. and S. This had been built up and enlarged with each successive reconstruction, generally using the fortification wall of the previous sanctuary as a retaining wall for the new. The greater part of the late-Classical fill has been removed to show the successive stages, making apparent the steepness of the natural contour. Sections of the *Wall of Peisistratos* are roofed with corrugated iron to preserve their upper part constructed in unbaked bricks. A stretch immediately below the centre of the Portico of Philo shows where Kimon filled the Persian breach in the mud-brick wall with limestone masonry in alternately large and small courses (pseudo-isodomic), based directly on the Peisistratean socle. The inner face is rough and evidently retained a fill of earth. Within this wall parts of an Archaic polygonal terrace wall may be seen. Beyond the Peisistratean corner-tower are the remains of a Kimonian *Gate*. This was later blocked by the Periclean *Siroi*, where the first-fruit offerings were stored; five of its piers are very prominent.

The s. side of the court was bounded in the 5C by the *Periclean Wall*, the function of which was minimized in the following century when the sanctuary was extended to the new *South Wall* of Lycurgus. Against the inside face of this are some remains identified with successive rebuildings in Hellenistic and late-Roman times of a *Bouleuterion*, or chamber of the city council. Outside the Lycurgan *South Gate* is a trapezoidal precinct surrounded by a wall (see below). Within this wall are the foundations of a *Hiera Oikia*, a Geometric house sacred to the memory of a hero; the building was destroyed early in the 7C, but remained a scene of religious rites in the Archaic period. Beyond are some vestiges of a *Mithraeum*. From outside the extreme s. corner of the precinct we get an instructive panorama of contrasted types of ancient wall building.

Looking towards the museum we see the perfectly fitted polygonal masonry (6C) of the peribolos of the Sacred House. To the right is the '*Lycurgan*' *Wall* (? 370–360 B.C.), one of the best preserved examples of ancient fortification, with both a square and a round *Tower*. On four slightly receding courses in pecked Eleusinian stone are set tooled courses in yellow poros; this is probably a conscious matching of the Periclean style. Beyond the corner the wall is masked by ruined Hadrianic cisterns. Farther on, the *Periclean East Wall*, like the Lycurgan, has a separate socle, here rusticated, while the upper part shows traces of bevelling.

On either side of the Telesterion a flight of steps was hewn in Roman times to give access to a wide *Terrace*, 20 ft above the hall floor. We mount the s. steps to the **Museum**, which houses the important but relatively few works of art found in the ruins. Outside the entrance are a Roman sarcophagus (c. A.D. 190) in marble with a well-carved representation of the Kalydonian boar-hunt (the lid does not belong to it); two representations in white marble of torches, c. 8 ft high; a capital from the Lesser Propylaea; and a fine head of a horse.—ROOM I (to the right). Copy of the 'Niinnion Tablet', a red-figured votive pinax now in the Athens museum; the figures are believed to be performing rites from the Mysteries, the only known representation. Reconstruction of one corner of the geison of the Peisistratid telesterion; Archaic kouros (c. 540 B.C.). Running girl from a pediment of c. 485 B.C. In the centre, huge Protoattic *Amphora (7C B.C.), depicting Odysseus blinding Polyphemos and Perseus slaying Medusa. Dedication reliefs: marble stele, Demeter seated with (probably) Hekate (c. 475 B.C.); stele (411 B.C.) depicting a fight between Athenian cavalry and Spartan hoplites. Decree of 421 B.C. concerning the construction of a bridge over the Rheitoi (comp. above), with relief.

ROOM II (entrance-hall) contains a cast of the most famous Eleusinian Relief, now in the Athens museum. Facing the door is a *Statue of Demeter (headless and armless), perhaps by Agorakritos of Paros,

pupil of Pheidias (420 B.C.); behind is the fragmentary Relief of
Lakratides (1C B.C.), showing Triptolemos setting out in his chariot;
the statue of Persephone is of Roman date. Relief: Demeter on the
'Mirthless Stone' approached by votaries.—ROOM III. Heads and
statues, including Asklepios, dedicated by Epikrates (320 B.C.), found in
a field.—ROOM IV displays a model of the site at two stages of its development. Roman statuary; *Antinoos, represented as a youthful

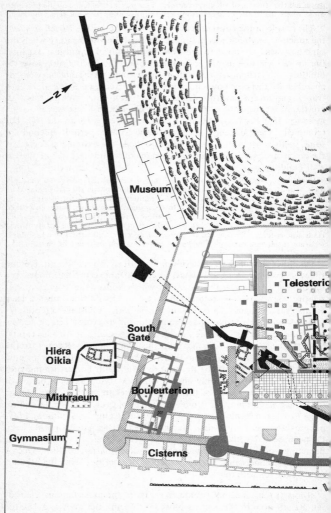

Dionysos standing by the Delphic omphalos; Tiberius as pontifex maximus; small and delicate Herakles.

ROOM V. Caryatid in the form of a kistephore (basket-carrier) from the inner parastade of the Lesser Propylaea (its fellow is in the Fitzwilliam Museum, Cambridge); green stole, in a good state of preservation, from a burial of the 5C B.C. (the only linen cloth surviving from the Classical era); Amphora of c. 610 B.C. from Megara by the Chimaera

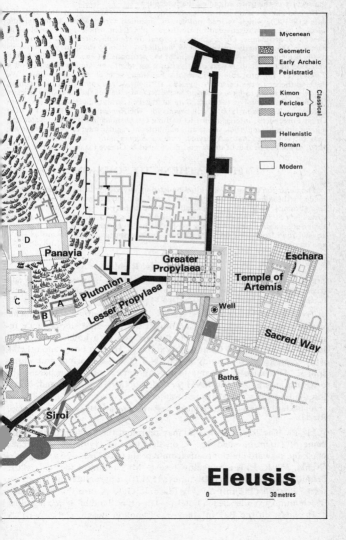

painter; inhumation burials, including that of a boy in a larnax (terra-cotta coffin); decree reliefs.—ROOM VI. Vases of all periods from 1900 B.C. to A.D. 450, including a plain Mycenean vase with a Linear B inscription (? an unidentified Cretan place-name) which recurs on the Knossos tablets; kernoi, the characteristic sacred vessels of the cult.

The tourist may well conclude his visit with the museum. The student of antiquities should continue to visit the Mycenean complex beyond, the Acropolis, and the sectors of the town adjoining the forecourt.

Beyond the museum are some remains of a settlement of Middle Helladic date (18–17C), which yielded pottery of Boeotian type. Many Late Helladic vestiges have been discovered on the ACROPOLIS, from which there is a pleasant view towards Salamis. On the plateau beyond are Hellenistic remains. The Frankish tower that formerly crowned the w. height fell victim to the quarrying activities of the cement factory. At the E. point of the acropolis a *Chapel* (Panayia) with a detached belfry occupies part of a platform on which, in Roman times, stood a *Temple* (Pl. D), probably dedicated to Faustina, wife of Antoninus Pius. We descend thence to the Lesser Propylaea. To the N.W. are some ruins of a Roman house conjectured to have belonged to the Kerykes, one of the hereditary priestly families. Farther off is the *Asty Gate* of the Peisistratid enceinte; its plan, uncovered by Travlos in 1960, is well preserved. The *Roman Quarter* to the E. of the Great Forecourt is interesting for its bathing establishments with piped water and a great drain having brick vaults and manholes at regular intervals.—In the town, near the church of Ayios Yeoryios, another *Roman Bath*, partially excavated in 1959, proved to be one of the largest discovered in Greece (time of Hadrian).

17   FROM ATHENS TO SOUNION

The excursion to Sounion, seldom omitted by any visitor to Athens, is generally made by the coast road. The old inland road, less obviously attractive, nevertheless abounds with interest, especially for the unhurried visitor who can make diversions at will. Much of the E. coast of Attica, c. 5 m. from the road and easily accessible from it by track or footpath, is yet largely unspoilt, though a coastal road from Lavrion to Marathon, already approved, will ensure its rapid spoliation.

A   By the Coast Road

ROAD, 43½ m. (70 km.). Buses from Odhos Mavrommateion c. hourly take passengers for destinations beyond Varkiza. Half-day excursions by coach (C.H.A.T., etc.). Buses for Varkiza depart from Leoforos Olgas.

To (15½ m.) **Vouliagméni**, see Rte 13. The road continues 'en corniche' winding along a rocky *Coast, though the pine-clad slopes, once renowned for game, are fast being interspersed with hotels and bungalows.—19¼ m. *Varkiza* (Glaros A; Varkiza B, DPO at both; and others), with camping sites, a sandy beach (N.T.O.G.), a marina, and watersports. The place gave name to the Agreement of 1945, whereby the organizations ELAS and EAM were demobilized and disarmed, bringing the first Communist rising to an end.

A little farther on a road leads inland to *Vari* (1 m.), a village amid pines (comp. Rte 13).

21½ m. The *Bay of Lomvarda* may represent the harbour of the Attic deme of *Lamptrai*, sited due N. on the slope of Hymettos. Churches mark the seaward ends of roads from Koropi (Rte 17B).—26 m. *Lagonisi* (Xenia, 350 R, L) is a bungalow resort. Mt Panion, to the N.E., is lost behind the Attic *Olimbos* (Olympus; 1594 ft), a pyramidal hill which we skirt. Beyond (28¾ m.) *Saronis* (Saronic Gate A) are the large Eden Beach and Alexander Beach hotels.—The little island of *Arsida* lies close to the coast off the Bay of *Anávissos* (Apollon Beach, Calypso B). A by-road leads left to the hamlet (1 m.), where the celebrated kouros was found, then passes between Olimbos and Panion to Kalivia (10 m.).— Off (37½ m.) *Cape Katafiyi*, which affords a fine panorama of the Saronic Gulf, lies the uninhabited *Gaïdourónisi*, known to Strabo as *Patroklou Charax*, the palisade of Patroclus. Remains may be seen of the 3C fortifications built here by Patroclus, admiral of Ptolemy II, who commanded the Egyptian fleet sent to help the Athenians against Antigonus Gonatas in the Chremonidean War (comp. p. 202).—40 m. *Legrena* (Amphitrite, Minos, B).

43½ m. (70 km.) **Cape Sounion**, known also as *Cape Kolónes* (Κάβο Κολῶνες), is a precipitous rocky headland rising 197 ft from the sea. The low isthmus which joins it to the mainland separates the sandy and exposed *Bay of Sounion* (Aigaion A; Belvedere Park, Cape Sounion Beach, bungalows A; Triton B), a developing bathing resort, from the rocky but sheltered haven to the E., which provides a welcome refuge for mariners unable to weather the cape. On the highest point of the headland, at its end, are the columns of the ruined Temple of Poseidon (see below), which give the headland its alternative name. The visitor wishing to share Byron's experience of "Sunium's marbled steep, Where nothing save the waves and I May hear our mutual murmurs sweep" should visit the site out of season and in the morning. On Sundays and towards sunset it is overrun by coach trippers.

The township of *Sounion* (Σούνιον; Lat. *Sunium*), whose wealth was proverbial in classical times, stood at the head of the bay of the same name, where regattas were held in honour of Poseidon. After the battle of Salamis the Athenians here dedicated a captured Phoenician ship (one of three; Hdt. VIII, 121). Some years before, the Aeginetans had seized the sacred Athenian *Theoris*, the ship that conveyed the sacred envoys (θεωροί) to Delos, while it lay at Sounion (Hdt. VI, 87). The town was a port of call of the corn ships from Euboea to Piraeus. The Athenians fortified it during the Peloponnesian War and, in 413 B.C. (Thuc. VIII, 14), the entire headland was enclosed, the promontory forming the citadel. The inhabitants were noted for harbouring runaway slaves whom they often enfranchised without question. On one occasion a strong gang of slaves seized the fortress and devastated the neighbourhood. Terence mentions Sunium as a haunt of pirates. It was a favourite resort of the corsairs, one of whom, Jaffer Bey, is supposed to have destroyed some of the columns of the temple. One of three of the crew who escaped the foundering of a Levantine trader here was the second mate and poet, William Falconer, who immortalized the incident in 'The Shipwreck' (1762).

The remains of the W. half of the promontory now form an archæological precinct (adm. 25 dr.; 9 or 10 to sunset; opens an hour later Sun morning). The Temple of Poseidon was measured by Revett in 1765 and by the Dilettanti Society in 1812. Byron carved his name on a pillar. The site was excavated by Dörpfeld in 1884 and by the Greek Archæological Society in 1899–1915. In 1906 two colossal kouroi were found in the debris to the E. of the temple. Since 1958 some columns have been re-erected.

The whole Acropolis was enclosed by a double *Fortification Wall*, c. 550 yds long and strengthened at intervals by square towers. It formed a semicircle from the Bay of Sounion on the N.W., where some remains are well preserved, to the s. cliff edge. Its s.E. angle enclosed the TEMENOS OF POSEIDON, a precinct supported on the N. and W. by a terrace wall. This was entered on the N. side by Doric *Propylaea*, built of poros in the 6C and restored in marble in the 5C, the axis of which is alined with the E. front of the temple.

A square room to the w. of the gate, separated it from a *Stoa*, which extended along the peribolos wall. Its foundations have collapsed in the far corner, but five bases remain of six interior columns that divided it lengthwise.

The *Temple of Poseidon, near the edge of the cliff, forms a conspicuous landmark from the sea. From a distance it presents a dazzlingly white appearance that proves illusory at closer view: the columns are of grey-veined marble quarried at *Agrileza* (3 m. N. by an ancient road), where bases of columns of the same dimension can still be seen. The attribution to Poseidon was confirmed by an inscription found in 1898. On stylistic grounds Prof. Dinsmoor ascribes the design of the temple to the architect of the Hephaisteion at Athens, placing it c. 444 B.C. It stands on the foundations of an earlier edifice in poros stone, founded shortly before 490 B.C. and unfinished at the time of the Persian invasion. Some columns were reused for the Doric peristyle having 34 columns (6 by 13), that stands on a stylobate measuring 102 ft by 44. Nine columns remain on the s. side and six (four re-erected in 1958–59) on the N. side, with their architraves. The columns are unusual in having only sixteen instead of the normal twenty flutes. The sculptural arrangement also departed from the normal custom, an Ionic frieze (see below) lining all four sides of the front pteroma (comp. the Hephaisteion), and the external metopes being left blank (perhaps because of the exposed nature of the site); the pediments, which were sculptured, had a raking cornice with a pitch of $12\frac{1}{2}°$ instead of the more usual 15°.

The INTERIOR had the usual arrangement of pronaos, cella, and opisthodomos. Both pronaos and opisthomodos were distyle in antis. There survive only the N. anta of the pronaos, with its adjacent column, and the s. anta, which was reconstructed in 1908.

Thirteen slabs of the frieze, in Parian marble, are protected by wooden shelters to the E. of the approach path. The sculpture, much corroded, is believed to illustrate a contest of Lapiths and Centaurs, the Gigantomachia, and exploits of Theseus.

The *View from the temple over the sea is most striking. To the E. lies Makronisos. About 7 m. s. lies the rocky island of Ay. Yeoryios, the ancient *Belbina*. The nearest islands to the S.E. are *Keos*, *Kithnos*, and *Seriphos*, to the s. of which, on a clear day, even *Melos* can be made out. To the w. is *Aegina*, in the centre of the Saronic Gulf, with the E. coast of the Peloponnese behind it.

Beyond the Tourist Pavilion (Rfmts), on a low hill commanding the isthmus on the N., are the remains of a small *Temple of Athena Sounias*, noted by Vitruvius for the irregularity of its plan. An Ionic colonnade was added before 450 B.C. along the E. and s. sides of an earlier structure, that approximates more to the Mycenean megaron than to the classical Athenian temple. The sekos consisted of a cella 17 ft by $12\frac{1}{2}$, with four columns in the middle arranged in a square. The cult statue stood in the centre.

B   Viâ the Mesogeia

ROAD, 40 m. (64 km.). $7\frac{1}{2}$ m. *Stavrós*.—11 m. *Liópesi*.—15 m. *Koropí*.—$18\frac{1}{2}$ m. Markópoulo.—$24\frac{3}{4}$ m. *Keratea*.—34 m. Lavrion.—40 m. Sounion. Buses from Od. Mavrommateion every hour (more frequently on Sun & hol.) to *Laurion* (45 dr. in $1\frac{1}{2}$ hr.; for Keratea and beyond only; usually continuing after an interval to *Sounion*); also to *Markópoulo* and *Pórto Ráfti*. To *Liópesi* (Paiania; No. 44) and to *Koropí* (No. 46), every 20 min. from Ayia Asomaton (Theseion).

From the centre of the city to ($1\frac{1}{4}$ m.) *Ambelókipoi*, see Rte 11.— We take the right fork. The N. foothills of Hymettos appear intermittently above the suburban development. In trees (r.) stands the *Police College*.—At ($2\frac{1}{2}$ m.) *Goudí* the University of Athens has its Ilissia precinct, with the Botanical Museum (weekdays 8–1, free); the fine

Zoological Museum is still in store. Above stands Ay. Ioannis Theologos (Rte 14).—At (4 m.) *Kholargos*, which bears the name of the native deme of Pericles (c. 490–429 B.C.), we pass (l.) the huge administrative H.Q. of the Greek army. Mt Pentelikon rises behind.—6 m. *Ayía Paraskeví*. The Nuclear Research Centre, designed by a British company and opened in 1961 by King Paul, bears the name of Democritus, the first scientist to propound an atomic theory. A by-road leads (r.; 1¼ m.) to *Moní Ayios Ioánnis Kynigos*, the monastery of St John the Hunter (view); its 12C church has a strangely supported dome and a 17C narthex (festival, 26 July).—At (7½ m.) *Stavrós*, by a radio-telephone station, we round the N. spur of Hymettos, leave the Marathon road, and turn S. into the Mesogeia.

The *Mesogeia* (τὰ, anciently ἡ, Μεσόγεια, 'the inland'), which lies between Hymettos and the Petalion Gulf, is watered by two seasonal rivers: the Valanaris entering the sea S. of Rafina and the Erasinos near Vraona. Its red clay is the most fertile soil in Attica, producing good wine, much of which is flavoured with pine resin to produce the retsina favoured by Athenians. Anciently Brauron was of importance; the modern capital is Koropí. Many of the attractive little churches have frescoes by Yeoryios Markos and his school.

11 m. **Liópesi** (*Kanakis Taverna* in a lemon-grove at the N. end), officially *Paianía*, a straggling village (5030 inhab.) in pleasantly wooded country, has readopted the name of the birthplace of Demosthenes (c. 384–322 B.C.), identified with some remains to the E. A by-road (signposted) leads to the *Koutouki Cave* (daily 10–5.30; 40 dr.).—15 m. **Koropí** (*Old Stables Rest.*), the liveliest village (7860 inhab.) in the Mesogeia, is surrounded by vineyards; the retsina vats are prominent. By-roads lead (r.) to the coast.—18½ m. (30 km.) **Markópoulo**, a busy and prosperous centre (5400 inhab.) is noted for its bread. By its conspicuous *Church*, the interior of which is enlivened with encaustic illustrations of the lives of various saints, diverges the road to Brauron and Pórto Ráfti.

From Markópoulo to Pórto Ráfti, 5 m. by good road (through bus from Athens). 1½ m. By-road to Vraona (see below). About 3 m. S. rises *Mt Mirenda* (2010 ft). Between our road and the mountain near a medieval watch-tower, lay the ancient deme of *Myrrhinous*, where Artemis Kolainis, the Bird Goddess, was worshipped. Inscriptions to Artemis were found on the site in 1960–61, after the Greek Archæological Service had explored 26 tombs, mostly of the 8C B.C., uncovered a section of prehistoric road, and confirmed the existence of a Shrine of Pythian Apollo. From this area in 1972 came also a superb kouros and kore now in Athens Museum.—4 m. Track (r.) to Prasiai (*Aktí C*), see below.

5 m. **Pórto Ráfti** has one of the best natural harbours in Greece, of which little use is made. The beautiful bay is unequally divided by the narrow rocky spit of *Ayios Nikólaos* (Tavernas), off which lies the islet of *Prasonisi*. It is protected on the seaward side by the islets of *Rafti* and *Raftopoula*. On Rafti is a colossal seated marble statue of the Roman period, popularly known as the 'tailor' (ῥάφτης), whence the modern name of the harbour. The statue, which is female, is conjectured to represent Oikoumene and to have served as a beacon-light. Helladic and Byzantine sherds have been noted on the steep slopes of

both islets. From the beach, the last in Attica to remain in Allied hands, 6000 New Zealand troops were evacuated in April 1941. Scholars locate ancient *Prasiai* on the s. slopes of the bay, where 22 Mycenean tombs were found in 1894–95.

From Prasiai the annual Theoria, or sacred embassy, set out to Delos in the ship believed to be that in which Theseus returned triumphant from Knossos. Here Erysichthon, an envoy of Delos, who died on his return journey, was buried, and here came the mysterious first-fruits of the Hyperboreans on their way from central Europe to Delos.

The bay is closed on the s. by the peninsular headland of *Koroni*, anciently *Koroneia*. Its Acropolis and an unbroken Long Wall with nine towers within the isthmus formed a *Fortress*. Excavated in 1960 by the American School, this is proved by coins of Ptolemy II Philadelphus to be an Egyptian encampment of the Chremonidean War (? 265–261 B.C.). In this war the Athenians threw in their lot with Egypt and Sparta in an unsuccessful bid to free themselves from Macedonian domination.—On the N. the bay is dominated by the precipitous *Perati* (1007 ft), with unexplored caves. The road continues beneath the hill past two tavernas to *Ayios Spiridon* (the bus terminus, 1¼ m. from Ayios Nikolaos; Korali C), 10 min. beyond which, above the banks of a stream, has been discovered a huge *Necropolis* of chamber tombs (Late Helladic III). The track continues round the shoreward side of Perati (taverna) to Brauron (c. 5 m.; see below).

From Ay. Spiridon a boat may be hired for the visit to Rafti (see above; rocky disembarkation and stiff climb).

THE BY-ROAD TO VRAÓNA (Brauron), 3½ m. from Markópoulo, diverges from the Pórto Ráfti road (comp. above). A square *Tower* (l.; c. ¾ m. from the road), beyond the fork, is of Frankish date. Farther on (l.) are the interesting remains of an early Christian *Basilica*.

The name Vraóna (Βραώνα) is a medieval corruption of Βραυρῶν, but the ancient name is being readopted as Vravróna.

Brauron (*Vraona Bay*, 230 R & 120 bungalows, A, on the shore), one of the twelve ancient communities antedating the Attic confederation, is situated in the broad and marshy valley of the subterranean Erasínos c. 1 m. from the sea. The district apparently comprised the townships of *Halai Araphenides* (now Loutsa, a little to the N.) and *Philiadai*. Peisistratos had estates in the neighbourhood. The SANCTUARY OF ARTEMIS BRAURONIA (adm. 25 dr.) lies at the foot of a low hill, just below the little late-Byzantine chapel of *Ayios Yeoryios*. To the left of the chapel a small *Shrine* marked the entrance to a cavern, the roof of which fell in the 5C B.C. This seems to have been venerated in Archaic times as the *Tomb of Iphigeneia*. Other tombs probably belong to priestesses of Artemis.

Tradition relates that Iphigeneia brought to Brauron the image of Artemis which she and Orestes stole from Tauris (Euripides, 'Iphigeneia in Tauris', 1446–67). In one version she is virtually identified with the goddess and performs the ritual sacrifice of her brother; in another she herself dies at Brauron. A wooden image was taken by the Persians from Brauron to Susa. In Classical times the savage rites had been moderated, and Artemis was worshipped in her function as protectress of childbirth. The Brauronia was a ceremony held every four years, in which Attic girls between the ages of five and ten, clad in saffron robes, performed rites which included a dance where they were dressed as bears (comp. Aristophanes, 'Lysistrata', 645). The connection between bears, childbirth, and Artemis recalls the legend of ˜allisto, but the purpose of the ritual remains mysterious. In the late 4C B.C. the site suffered from inundations and by the time of Claudius it was deserted, for Pomponius Mela (De situ Orbis, II, 3) exclaims that Thorikos and Brauron, formerly cities, are now but names. Excavations, carried out with difficulty in the waterlogged valley by the Greek Archæological Society under John Papadimitriou in 1946–52 and in 1956–63, show occupation since Middle Helladic times (earliest on hill above).

At a lower level, discovered in 1958, are the remains of a Doric *Temple* of the 5C B.C., measuring c. 66 ft by 33, the foundations of which stand on rock-hewn steps (? the "holy stairs" of Euripides). Here were discovered dedicatory reliefs in coloured terracotta, bronze mirrors, and votive jewellery. Adjoining the temple is a huge Π-shaped *Stoa*, built before 416 B.C., in which have been found inscriptions recording it to be the 'parthenon' of the arktoi, or 'bears'. It had nine dining-rooms. Part of the colonnade and entablature was re-erected in 1962. Just to the W. is a remarkable stone **Bridge* of the same period.

The large well-arranged site MUSEUM (round the next bend of the road; adm. 25 dr.) displays marble statues and heads of little girls and of boys, and beautiful 4C marble reliefs. Preserved by the mud are vases of olive-wood and a wooden statuette of the 5C B.C. unique in Greece. Models reconstruct the appearance of the site. Here also are Geometric finds from Anavyssos and splendid L.H.IIIc *Pottery from Perati.

The main road by-passes (21 m.) **Kalívia** (2300 inhab.), with attractive churches. About 1 m. S.W., on a by-road to Anávissos (10 m.; Rte 17A), is the pretty *Taxiarkhis*, a deserted monastic church. At the 36th km. post a track leads (l.) to *Ayios Yeoryios*, a Byzantine church with reused Ionic capitals. The countryside becomes more hilly. To the left rises Mt Mirenda (see above), to the right the double crest of *Paneion* (2136 ft), known locally as Keratovouni (the horned mountain). Its steep E. summit dominates (24¾ m.) **Keratéa** (*Galini* A), a prosperous village (5600 inhab.), with orchards, vineyards, and good water, where Chateaubriand suffered from sunstroke. Here a track descends to the *Convent of the Palaioimerologitai* (Adherents of the Old Calendar), 5 m. E., above the exposed beach of Kaki Thalassa.—The little mining hamlet of (31 m.) *Plaka* lies below the top of the next ridge (550 ft), from which we look down towards the *Bay of Thorikos*, reached by a zigzag descent. Dominating the bay, between the railway and the sea (1 m. N.E. of the road), is the conical hill of *Velatouri* (480 ft), on which stood the acropolis of **Thorikos**. The ancient town occupied the promontory of Ayios Nikólaos, which divides Portomandhri, to the S., from Frankolimani, a smaller bay to the N., protected by Cape Vrisaki. This deep refuge is halfway between Piraeus and Rhamnous.

A Cretan trading-post. and in the Mycenean age an independent city having dynastic ties with Athens (legend tells of Kephalos, its king, who married Prokris, daughter of Erechtheus), Thorikos was fortified anew in 412 B.C. as a defence outpost of the Laurion mines (comp. Xenophon, Hell. i, 2, i). It was deserted before the 1C A.D. Since 1963 excavations have been conducted by the Belgian Archaeological Mission.

The most significant ruins lie at the s. foot of the hill, which was ringed by a fortification wall. One *Tower* still stands to a height of 12 ft. Higher up is the THEATRE, unique in its irregular plan, which clumsily follows the contour of a natural declivity. An orchestra probably just antedated the 5C but the existing structure is mostly of the late 4C B.C. The *Cavea* forms an irregular ellipse and is divided by two stairways, almost parallel, into three sections, the central one nearly rectangular, those at either end sharply curved. Of the 31 rows of rough-hewn seats, accommodating c. 5000 spectators, nineteen were found in fair preservation. The twenty rows below the diazoma were approached from below; the eleven above were gained by two ramps set against the marble analemma. The w. ramp is pierced by a corbelled passage. The narrow w. parodos is bounded by a small *Temple of Dionysos* in antis, which faces across the rectangular orchestra towards a large *Altar* and a *Store-House* having two rooms.

Of the Mycenean remains, excavated by the Greek Archæological Society in 1890 and 1893, part of the enceinte round the top of the hill can be traced, as well as some walls on the summit that cover still earlier houses (c. 1800 B.C.). On the N.E. side of the hill are three *Tholos Tombs*, and on the S. slope an older oblong tomb has been explored. The maritime fortress of 412 B.C. occupies the isthmus between the two harbours to the w. of the church. A start has been made to excavate the extensive town area, and, N.W. of the theatre, a large industrial complex for processing ore for silver and lead. A hoard of 4–3C tetradrachms was found in 1969.—The remains of a peripteral Doric *Temple of Demeter and Kore* of unusual design, with 7 columns on the fronts and 14 at the sides, unearthed in 1812 c. ½ m. w. of the theatre, have been covered again. Much of its materials were transported to Athens in Augustan times and re-erected in the S.E. corner of the Agora.

About 3 m. offshore lies the island of *Makronisos* (8½ sq. m.), anciently called *Helena*, from a tradition that Helen rested here on her flight with Paris. Used after the civil war of 1946 as a detention centre, it is now uninhabited save by shepherds in summer.

34 m. (54 km.) **Lávrion** (Λαύριον), known in the 19C as *Ergasteria* because of its workshops, is a scattered industrial town of 8300 inhab., which owes its existence to the neighbouring mines and its name to the ancient district of *Laurion*. Its chimneys, placed on the surrounding hills to render the fumes less noisome, are conspicuous from afar. To the possession of the silver mines of Laurion the Athenians owed, in great measure, their commercial and political greatness; the Athenian silver coinage ('Laureot owls') had prestige all over the world.

The mines were probably exploited as early as 1000 B.C.; Aeschylus alludes in the 'Persae' (235) to the θησαυρὸς χθόνος. The decision of the Athenians in 483 B.C. to finance the building of a fleet with the surplus yield of the mines laid the foundations of their naval supremacy, and by the time of Pericles the industry had reached the peak of its prosperity. As a result of the incursion of the Spartans in 413, the mines were closed. Though they were reopened c. 355 thanks to Xenophon's treatise on mines as a neglected source of revenue and lasted another four centuries, they were never again as important. Pausanias refers to them in the past tense and for centuries they lay neglected. Modern exploitation, very largely the result of French initiative, is in the hands of three companies: one French (reconstituted after disputes about government royalties in 1873), one Greek (1860), and one American. The modern mines are concerned principally with the extraction of cadmium and manganese, and, to a less degree, with reworking the ancient slag-heaps for lead. The synthetic textile mills are important.

The best preserved ANCIENT MINES are situated in the Berzeko valley, which runs s. from *Kamáriza*, about 3 m. to the w. A car can be taken as far as the church of Ayia Trias near a huge ruined 19C installation above the valley.

The mines anciently belonged to the State, which granted them on perpetual leases to contractors. They were worked by slave labour. Over 2000 ancient shafts have been found, some perpendicular (60–400 ft deep) and some sloping. The roofs of the galleries (80–150 ft deep) were supported either by artificial piers or by natural ore-bearing pillars left in the rock. The removal of these pillars, which was dangerous, was punishable by death. Ventilation shafts carried off the bad air. Some miners' lamps and other relics have been found. In various places chains of huge *Cisterns* and ore-washeries are to be seen. One in the Agrileza valley was excavated by the British School in 1977–78.

From Lavrion a caïque service plies to the island of *Kea* daily in summer (aft.).

The road continues s. at some distance from the sea. On the w. are moderate wooded hills. Above the coast (*Sun*, 265 R, B) are dotted many summer villas of the Athenians. The columns of the Temple of Poseidon are seen on the skyline as we join the coast road at the approach to (40 m.) *Sounion*.

18 SALAMIS

The crescent-shaped island of **Salamis** (ΣΑΛΑΜΙΣ; 36 sq. m.) lies in the N. of the Saronic Gulf close inshore. Its N.W. coast is less than ½ m. from the coast of Megaris, and its N.E. coast is separated from the mainland of Attica by the Strait of Salamis, scene of the famous battle. The island thus gives to the Bay of Eleusis the character of a lagoon. Salamis with 23,100 inhab., mainly of Albanian descent, forms part of the eparchy of Piraeus. Its soil is dry and rocky and, though a few vineyards and corn fields are found in the plains, the climate is un-healthy. The highest point is *Mavrovouni* (1325 ft). According to Strabo the ancient capital originally lay on the s. coast opposite Aegina; this was moved before Classical times to the E. coast; the modern capital is on the w. side of the island at the head of the Bay of Koulouris. Salamis is famous for its battle and important as a naval base, but it is of run-down appearance and archæological remains are meagre. Military establishments impede a close study of the scene of the battle, the best general view of which is still obtained from Xerxes' vantage-point behind Perama.

History. In Mycenean times *Salamis* seems to have had dynastic connections with both Aegina and Cyprus. The Homeric catalogue records a contribution of twelve ships led by Telamonian Ajax. In the 7C the island was disputed between Athens and Megara. It was annexed to Athens as a cleruchy by Solon, the Athenians going so far as to forge an extra line of Homer in support of their claim. In 480 B.C. the Athenians evacuated Athens and, with Salamis as base, entrusted themselves to their 'wooden walls'. After 318 B.C. Salamis surrendered to the Macedonian Cassander, but in 229 B.C. it was recovered for Athens by Aratos, when the Salaminians were expelled in favour of new colonists.

Approaches. FROM ATHENS in 35 min. by frequent bus No. 88 from Odhos Menandhrou (or from Piraeus by frequent bus) to Pérama on the s. coast of the Skaramangas peninsula. The road traverses the sprawling industrial town of *Níkaia* (86,300 inhab.), which extends N.W. of Piraeus to the Aigaleos hills, and passes below the supposed vantage-point from which Xerxes watched the Battle of Salamis.—9½ m. **Pérama** has shipyards where trawlers, tugs, and coastal steamers are built. The buses terminate at the quay, whence ferries (c. ½ hourly) cross the Strait of Salamis to the island: to *Paloukia* (cars taken), viâ the N. side of the island of Ayios Yeoryios, for the town of *Salamis* (1¼ m.; bus every 10 min.); to *Kamateró*; and to a landing-stage E. of Ambelakia for Selenia. The crossings take c. 15 min. Buses serve all main points on the island.

FROM PIRAEUS by sea (no cars) every ½ hr.

FROM MEGARA, viâ Megalo Pefko (Rte 24) and a by-road to a landing-stage (also called *Pérama*), whence a ferry plies to the N.W. tip of the island.

The STRAIT OF SALAMIS, which averages less than 2 m. in width, forms roughly an S-bend with an island at each turn. From Piraeus the N.–s. channel is divided into two arms by the island of *Lipsoukoutali*, where there are naval installations and a monument to the 'unknown Sailor';

it then turns W. between the Skaramangas peninsula and the long E. promontory of Salamis known as Kynosoura ('the dog's tail'). Beyond the narrowest point (1200 yds), which lies between the Kateró peninsula (site of classical Salamis) and the cape S. of Pérama, the strait bends N. and N.E. The widening corner N. of Kateró is divided into two channels by the islet of *Ayios Yeoryios*, used as a quarantine station. In the narrow confines of this strait the Persian defeat was mainly decided.

The **Battle of Salamis** was fought about 22 Sept. 480 B.C. The tactics of the battle and the fundamental identification of the island of Psyttáleia (Ψυττάλεια) are still the subject of scholarly disagreement. Most commentators identify Psyttáleia with Lipsokoutali, a view excellently argued by A. R. Burn (Persia and the Greeks, 1962) and by Paul W. Wallace (A.J.A., 1969). N. G. L. Hammond (J.H.S., 1956) identifies Psyttáleia with Ayios Yeoryios and Lipsokoutali with Atalanta. This may be thought to accord better with the accounts of Herodotus (VIII, 70–94) and of Aeschylus who fought in the battle and describes it in the 'Persae' performed eight years later. The general strategy of the battle is not in doubt though Athenian tradition seems as usual to have exaggerated the disparity between the opposing forces.

Salamis was a key point in Themistocles' plan of defence against the Persians and in the event a decisive one. While all Athenian woman and children were evacuated to Troezen, Salamis was to receive the old men and exiles (who were ordered to return). An attempt to stem the Persian advance was to be made with half the allied fleet at Artemision while the remaining Athenian triremes with the reserves of the fleets of Sparta, Corinth, and Aegina were to lie off Salamis. Before the action the Persians were in Phaleron Bay. The news that they had despatched an army by land towards the Isthmus alarmed the Peloponnesians who had to be persuaded against retiring on Corinth. Xerxes' first plan to bottle the Athenians in the Skaramangas strait or force them into open water to the E. by building a pontoon boom across the strait itself was foiled by Cretan archers. Themistocles, hoping to force an immediate battle in the narrows, where he would have the advantage, organized a leak of information to Xerxes that the Peloponnesians intended to retreat. Under cover of darkness the Persians put into operation a new plan to encircle the supposedly disunited Greeks: Psyttaleia was occupied; a squadron of 200 Egyptian ships was despatched to block the W. strait between Salamis and Megara; and the remaining ships were drawn up in a line right across the E. exit. The Persian plan seems to have been to surprise the Greeks, while they were still drawn up on the beaches at dawn, and capture their base. Xerxes himself set up a silver throne on Aigaleos, 'the rocky brow that looks o'er sea-born Salamis', whence he could watch the battle. Aristides, the exiled rival of Themistocles, who succeeded in slipping through to the Greek fleet from Aegina, was the first to bring the news of the investment. His statement was confirmed by a Tenean deserter. The forewarned Greeks, who now had no alternative but to fight, embarked before dawn, retired apparently in flight before the advancing enemy and formed up in hiding behind a promontory. When they emerged in battle order the advantage of surprise was with them. With their more manœuverable ships, lower in the water, they made deadly use of the technique of ramming. As Themistocles had foreseen, the Persians became hopelessly confused, Artemisia, queen of Halicarnassos, being noticed to sink one of her allies' ships. 'Their multitude beate their ruin' (Aeschylus). The Corinthian contingent (70 ships) under Adeimantos was later said by Athenian gossip to have taken no part in the battle, perhaps because executing a feint withdrawal or shadowing the Egyptian squadron.

At the critical moment a force under Aristides captured Psyttaleia, making the victory complete. The fleet of Aegina is said to have distinguished itself most, and next the Athenians. Although the battle did not become such a legend to the Athenians as Marathon, it is much more entitled to rank as one of the 'decisive battles' of the world. To the Persians Marathon was merely the defeat of a punitive expedition, Salamis the overthrow of a royal scheme of conquest.

To the N. of *Paloukia* the *Arsenal*, the most important naval station in Greece, extends round the Bay of Arapi, cutting off access to the N.E. part of the island. From Paloukia roads lead S. to *Abalakia*, crossing the base of the *Kateró* peninsula on which stood classical Salamis (few traces) and to *Selinia,* a villa resort; and w. to **Salamis,** or *Koulouri,* the chief town (18,300 inhab.) of the island, at the head of a deep bay on the w. coast. Much of the bay is a rash of bungalows. In the bay, since the laying up in 1959 of ships from Far Eastern waters, the Japanese pearl oyster has been found: attempts to cultivate it are being made at Megalo Pefko.—A road skirts the bay to the straggling village of *Aiandeion;* at the entrance to the village roads lead E. to *Kaki Vigla,* a hamlet on the coast, and s. (rough) over the mountain to (4 m.) *Ag. Nikolaos* and then down to the coast.

Beyond Salamis the road traverses the island's N.W. peninsula.—5 m. The *Moni Faneroméni,* or Convent of the Apparition of the Virgin (Φανερωμένης), has a remarkable fresco of the Last Judgment. It is crowded with pilgrims on 4 Sept. and there are traditional processions in Passion week. Nea Peramos (Rte 24) is seen across Vasiliká Bay.— The road ends at (6 m.) the landing-stage of the Megaris ferry (see above).

To the s. of the road, overlooking St George's Bay just below the ridge, is a long fortification-wall, identified in 1960 by the American School with the fort of *Boudoron,* built by the Athenians in the 5C to keep watch over Megara, and ravaged in 429 B.C. by the Peloponnesian fleet.

19   MOUNT PARNES

Mount Parnes, in Greek *Párnis Oros* (Πάρνης ῎Ορος), the rugged mountain range to the N.W. of Athens, forms the central part of the massif dividing Attica from Boeotia. It is limited at the E. end by the Diakria, or 'Upland', the lowest exit from the Attic plains, and on the w. by the pass between Mt Pastra, its w. extension, and Kithairon. Parnes thus extends some 25 miles from E. to w. Its wildness is well appreciated from the air. Though the disfigurement of radar has come to its summits, it remains sparsely populated, scored by ravines, and, except where its slopes are clothed in forests of pine or oak, exposed to the elements. Wolves and bears, seen in Roman times, are no longer found, but sheep-dogs may be encountered. The mountain is crossed by only one road suitable for wheeled traffic (viâ Dekelia; see Rte 20), though the ancient route to Thebes by way of Phyle and Pyli is still practicable on foot. Walkers intending to make expeditions should take provisions and a compass; prudent travellers will also take a tent, since to the w. of Phyle there is no hotel nearer than Thebes, and, except on the two approaches described below, public transport can be reached only on the Salonika highway or at Avlon Station to the N., or on the Thebes road to the s. The s.E. slopes have been made easily accessible since 1960 and are being developed for winter sports. The w. forts (Panakton, etc.) are more readily visited from the Thebes road (Rte 41).

By car the two routes below may be combined without returning to Athens by using the link road through Akharnai to Ano Liosia.

A   To Ayia Trias and the Summit

ROAD to *Grand Hotel Parnes,* 22 m. (35 km.); bus No. 116 to Ayia Trias from Odhos Favierou (2, 4). Coaches to the hotel from Sindagma Square 4 times daily. ('Parnis' is signposted viâ Odhos Akharnon and the National Highway, quitted after 6 m. to join the road described below c. 1 m. N. of Akharnai.)

From Plateia Vathis, N.W. of Omonoia Sq., Odhos Liossion passes under the National Highway at (3½ m.) *Tris Yéfires* ('Three Bridges'), in the natural 'gap' where the road and two railways cross the Kefissos.— At (5 m.) *Ayioi Anáryiroi* the Filí road diverges left (see below). We bear right and after c. 1¼ m. pass a knoll (l.) marked by some medieval remains; this is possibly the hill occupied by the Peloponnesian army under King Archidamos in 431 B.C., when it ravaged the Athenian Plain. The frustrated Acharnians, prevented by Pericles from defending their lands, were later prominent in opposing the peace party in their desire for revenge (comp. Aristophanes).—7½ m. **Akharnai** (AXAPNAI), or *Menidi*, in modern as in ancient times is a large deme surrounded by vineyards. Its classical inhabitants engaged in charcoal-burning on Parnes. Here in 1932 was found a marble stele of the 4C engraved with the 'Oath of Plataia'. Menidi Tomb, see below. The road climbs gradually at first, then in steep turns, offering wider and wider views over the plain of Attica. At (20½ m.) **Ayia Trias** (*Xenia*, 160 R, June–Sept, DPO, with hotel school, B), a little mountain resort amid pine woods, the bus terminates. The road divides: to the right on a spur with a superb *Panorama is (1½ m. farther) the Grand Hotel Mont Parnes (L; 100 R, cable-car, casino, swimming pool, tennis courts, cinema, etc.); to the left we may reach (1¾ m.) the *Refuge* of the Greek Alpine Club (3822 ft) and the entrance to the radar station (no adm.) that crowns (4½ m.) *Karabola* (4635 ft), the summit of Parnes.

Within a few yards of the top a sacrificial pyre, explored in 1959–60, yielded pottery and 3000 knives of the period 1000–600 B.C. This discovery probably locates one of the two altars to Zeus mentioned by Pausanias.

From the left fork (see above) a track branches (l.) towards the w., then divides. Bearing right, a winding descent may be followed towards the gorge which runs s.w. to the Moní Klistón (see below). At a conspicuous pine tree, a path leads s.w. into the gorge to a spring gushing from a column. Immediately below (easy scramble) is the *Cave of Pan* which forms the locale of Menander's 'Dyskalos'. Across the gorge (s.w.) rises the wooded spur of *Kalamara*, a hump with sheer sides anciently called *Harma* because, when seen from Athens, it resembled a chariot. The Pythiasts watched for lightning to play on its summit as a signal for the departure of the sacred mission to Delphi. A covering of cloud is today taken as a sign of rain.

B   To Phyle

ROAD, 14 m. (22 km.) through the village of Filí (bus No. 64 from Plat. Vathis; 2, 4) and on to Moní Klistón. From Filí on foot to the fortress (c. 2 hrs).

To (5 m.) *Ayioi Anáryiroi*, see above. We bear left in company with the Peloponnese railway, beyond which can be seen a castellated mansion (Pirgos tis Vasilissis), once a model farm of Queen Amalia. Its wine ('Tour la Reine') is celebrated, but the house is now a school for officers of the Boy Scout movement.—7½ m. *Áno Liósia* (railway stn. see Rte 16) stands in the gap between Aigalos and Parnes. We ascend through a defile to (11½ m.) *Fili* (ΦΥΛΗ), a village (formerly Khasiá) in a hollow, which has readopted the ancient name. The road enters the gorge of *Potami Gouras* and then climbs to (14 m.) **Moní Klistón**, correctly Panayia ton Kleiston (Our Lady of the Gorges), an old convent with a 14C church rebuilt in the 17C. There is a school and a terrace with a fine view down into the gorge. A fountain in the court bears the date 1677.

For Phyle we leave the road at the entrance to the gorge and take the valley to the w. which descends towards Eleusis. In 15 min. we come to another torrent in the narrow *Kharadra Fikhti*, which we follow (r.).—1¾ hr. Near the remains of an aqueduct we approach the hill of **Phyle,** whose summit (2 hrs) is crowned by the *Kastro.*

The fortress (2130 ft) crowns a precipitous triangular platform extending forward from a summit some 15 ft higher. It dominated alternative defiles of the ancient direct route from Thebes to Athens (of strategic value only for a comparatively small force) and looks out over the whole Athenian plain. It apparently replaced an earlier fort (see below) in the 4C B.C.; it was garrisoned by Kassander and subsequently dismantled and ceded to the Athenians by Demetrios Poliorketes.

The main entrance is on the E. side. The enclosure has a pentagonal plan. To the w. and s.w. the defences have crumbled, but elsewhere the well-preserved walls stand to the sixth course of squared blocks. Of five towers, four were square and one round. Like Eleutherai and Rhamnous, the fort had no water supply within the walls; in the neighbourhood and also near a spring, 20 min. N.E., are vestiges of houses.

A track continues along an ancient course to the Plateau of Skourta, in which stand *Píli* (15 m. from Fili) and *Pánakton* (Rte 41). From Pili the Skhimatari–Thebes road (Rte 44) can be joined at various points.

About 1 m. to the N.E. of Kastro is another summit, on which are considerable remains of polygonal masonry. These are presumed to mark the post which Thrasybulos captured in 403 B.C. after his expulsion from Athens by the 30 Tyrants and defended with 70 men against 3000. Hence he proceeded to the capture of Piraeus.

20 FROM ATHENS TO TATÓÏ AND SKÁLA OROPÓS

ROAD, 31 m. (50 km.). Poor surface between Tatóï and Malakássa. Local buses (No. 38 from Kanningos) to the inner suburbs; buses to Skála Oropoú (5 times daily), and for Euboea viâ the ferry, start from 4 Michael Voda, but follow the Kifissia road (Rte 15), joining this route at Malakássa. (Skala Oropos can be reached more directly by the National Highway and a new road diverging at 21¼ m.)

We quit central Athens by the Patissia road (Rte 8), passing the National Archaeological Museum.—3 m. **Patíssia** (ΠΑΤΗΣΙΑ) is a favourite suburban resort of the Athenians. It is said to derive its name (*padishah*, Sultan) from the fact that under the Turks the land was crown property.—3½ m. *Alissídha.*

Above *Perissos*, 1½ m. N.E., on the N.W. slope of Tourkovouni, is the *Omorphi Ekklesia*, or 'beautiful church', dedicated to St George in the 12C. It has mural paintings by a Salonican artist of the 14C, when the s. chapel was. added (the narthex is more recent.

We cross the Piraeus Electric Railway, then traverse (4½ m.) *Nea Filadelfia*, a planned refugee suburb. The road divides by a football stadium.

The left fork (Od. Pindou; bus 102/82) leads to Akharnai (3 m.; Rte 19), crossing in turn the old Lavrion railway, the National Highway, and the Kifissos. In *Likótripa* (1½ m.), up the hill beyond the cemetery, to the right of the road, is the tumulus covering the so-called *Menidi Tomb*, a Mycenean tholos tomb dug by the German School in 1879. Its yield is in the National Museum.

We continue N.E. On the hill of Nemesis (l. of road) was the Mycenean settlement to which the Menidi tomb belonged.—Beyond (6½ m.) *Koukouvaounes*, we cross the National Highway, then the Kifissos.— Near (9 m.) *Dekelia Station*, on the State Railway, is *Tatóï Airfield*, a

Hellenic Air Force base and flying school.—12 m. *Varibóbi* (ΒΑΡΥ-
ΜΠΟΜΠΗ; Auberge Tatói L; Varibóbi B) where we join a road from
Kifissia, is noted for its golf course. About 1 m. N.W. are the ruins of
the so-called *Tomb of Sophocles*. We ascend towards the pass.

15 m. **Tatói** (Hibiscus C), known also by its ancient name of *Dekélia*, is
beautifully situated amidst oak-woods in the entrance to the pass of
Klidhi ('key'). To the right the former *Summer Palace* stands in a fine
park, a good example of scientific afforestation on uncongenial soil.
Local antiquities from the royal estate were gathered together into a
small museum by George I; this was destroyed by fire in 1916 but its
surviving objects, together with later finds from the area, have been described by the Princesses Sophia and Irene (1959–60). At Tatói were born
George II (1890) and King Alexander (1893). The *Mausoleum* of George
I and Alexander (d. 1920) stands on the hill called *Palaiokastro* above
the village (l.), where are also the ruins of a Spartan fortress constructed
in 413 B.C. George II and King Paul are also buried at Tatói.

Ancient *Dekelia* (Δεκέλεια) guarded the easternmost of the three passes
over Parnes, the vital route by which food from Euboea reached Athens. By this
pass Mardonius retreated into Boeotia before the battle of Plataia. On the advice
of the renegade Alcibiades, the Spartans captured the pass in 413 B.C. and built a
fortress (see above), initiating the blockade by land which, after the naval victory
of Lysander at Aegospotami, led to the surrender of Athens.—*Hadrian's Aqueduct*,
lengthened and restored by the Ulen company, runs S. from Tatói to a reservoir
below Lykabettos.

The defile passes between the two hills of *Strongyle* (r.) and *Katsimidi*
(2790 ft). On the latter are vestiges of an Athenian fort, built in the 4C
to guard the pass. The wooded uplands resound to the clonking of
sheep bells.—Beyond (20 m.) *Ayios Merkourios*, a chapel with a spring,
the steep zigzag descent commands a superb *View across the Euripos
to Euboea. In the foreground are the railway and the highway to the
north (Rte 44B), which we cross at (23 m.) *Malakassa*. The road winds
through upland scrub, then descends in more wooded country, with
good views of the Strait of Euboea, to (31 m.) **Skála Oropós** (*Alkionis,
Flisvos*, both C; Tavernas), or more correctly *Skála Oropoú* (ΣΚΑΛΑ
ΩΡΩΠΟΥ), on the site of the ancient Oropos. From its shallow bay a
ferry provides the shortest connection between Athens and Euboea.
From the beach King Constantine I embarked in 1917 for Messina on
his way to exile in Switzerland.

Ancient *Oropos* was important to Athens as the nearest accessible place of embarkation affording a short sea passage to Euboea. To it came ships bringing
vital corn supplies and cattle for the capital. According to Dikaiarchos, the
Oropians were rapacious and ill-mannered; their customs officers were especially
notorious. The town fell alternately under Thebes and Athens, with intervals of
independence. Diodoros records that in 402 B.C. the Thebans moved the Oropians
7 stades inland, presumably from Skala to the site of modern Oropós.

The modern village of *Oropós*, 3 m. inland to the S.W., has a 17C church.
Lignite mines are worked in the neighbourhood.

Road from Skala to the *Amphiareion*, see Rte 22. Car Ferry (every 45 min.) to
Nea Psara (comp. Rte 42).

21 FROM ATHENS TO MARATHON. RHAMNOUS

ROAD to Marathon, 26 m. (42 km.). 7½ m. *Stavrós.*—16¼ m. Turning for *Rafína* (1¾ m. r.).—18¼ m. Turning for *Ayios Andréas* (1¼ m. r.).—23½ m. *Marathon Tomb.*—26 m. *Marathón.*—29 m. *Káto Soúli.*—32 m. Turning (r.) to *Ayia Marina* (1½ m.).—36 m. *Rhamnous.*

BUS to *Marathon* from Od. Mavromateion (every 30 min.) in c. 1 hr, continuing 6 times daily to *Grammatikó* (comp. below) or to *Kato Souli* (½ hr more); also 3 times daily to Ayia Marina (best for Rhamnous); also to *Rafína* and to *Spata.*

From Athens to (7½ m.) *Stavrós,* see Rte 17B. We leave the Mesogeion road to our right, cross the old Lavrion railway, and pass a modern church surrounded by cypresses and a cemetery. *Gargetos,* birthplace of Epicurus (341–270 B.C.) lay hereabouts.—9½ m. *Pallíni,* formerly Kharvati and now marked by a radio station, has readopted the name of classical *Pallene,* which had a noted temple of Athena. It was associated with the legendary victory of the Heraklids over Eurystheus and with Theseus' defeat of the Pallantids. Here c. 545 B.C. Peisistratos, returning from exile in Macedonia, defeated an Athenian force to make himself finally master of Athens. The local white wine is noted.

Spáta, a large village, c. 4 m. S.E., in a wine-producing district, has enriched the National Museum with Mycenean finds from chamber-tombs excavated by Stamatakis in 1877. It has been designated the site of a second airport for Athens. Beyond Spáta, on the coast, is the frequented beach of *Loútsa* (Poseidon, June–Sept, D; Tavernas), identified by an inscription as *Halai Araphenides.* Here in 1956 remains were discovered of a Dionysion and a temple of Artemis Tauropolos.

We pass (r.) a tomb of partisans executed in 1942.—13½ m. *Pikérmi* (Pikermi C; Rest. Nea Zoi) is noted for the discovery of fossil remains of the neo-Tertiary period, brought to light by the action of a local torrent; the finds, which included the dinotherium, largest fossil known, are now in the natural history museum of Athens University. The 16C nunnery of Ayia Filothei is now a private house. We now pass through a district rich in vineyards and olive-groves, and the scenery is most attractive. The summit of Pentelikon, which we have been skirting, is hidden behind an intervening spur. Along the road here in April 1941 British troops abandoned their transport before embarking.—Near (15 m.) *Drasesa Bridge,* where the road crosses the Megalo Rhevma, some English tourists, including Lord Muncaster, were captured by brigands in 1870. The scandal attending the subsequent murder of four of them at Dilessi in Boeotia caused energetic steps to be taken to suppress brigandage.—16½ m. Turning (r.) for Rafína.

Rafína (*Bravo, Avra,* C; Rest. *Gallini,* on quay), site of the ancient deme of *Araphen,* is 2 m. away on the sea (bathing). Its small harbour is connected by steamer with Karystos (Euboea) and with Andros and Tinos. A heavy swell hampered evacuation here in 1941. On the height of *Askitarion* (1¼ m. s.) are the remains of an Early Helladic town (explored in 1955).

On the wooded S.E. slope of Pentelikon, to the left, stands the conspicuous sanatorium of the *Moni Daou Pendeli.* The convent, founded in the 10C, was refounded in 1963 after being deserted since 1690. A huge dome, borne on six columns, crowns the church, which shows many Eastern features. The 13C narthex dates from its Frankish period which ended in 1456. The woods are scored by fire lanes. Here, in a *German Military Cemetery* approved in 1962, have been concentrated the German dead of the campaign in Greece (1941–44).

The road approaches within a mile of the shore to cross the ridge where *Xilokeratiá* (880 ft), the last spur of Pentelikon descends to the sea. As we descend behind the attractive shore of *Máti* (Mati, Costa Rica, A;

Attica Beach **B**), the whole Bay of Marathon is seen across the woods that back *Ayios Andréas* (1¼ m. r.), a popular bathing place with tavernas. —20 m. **Néa Mákri** (*Marathon Beach* **B**; *Nereus*, closed Jan–Apr, *Aphrodite* **C**), frequented for bathing, stands at the seaward end of a road that follows the N. slope of Pentelikon from Ekali (Rte 15A). It has an extensive Neolithic settlement and may be the site of *Probalinthos*, whose name betrays an early origin. The road passes between *Mt Agrilíki* and the small marsh of *Brexisa* (comp. below) into the Plain of Marathon.

The PLAIN OF MARATHON claims attention both because of the battle and because of archæological discoveries, particularly those made in 1969–70. Geographically the plain, 6 m. long and 1½–3 m. wide, extends in crescent form round the Bay of Marathon from the *Kynosura Promontory* (with an unidentified acropolis) in the N. to Cape Kavo in the s. On the landward side it is shut in by the stony mountains that "look on Marathon", making up for their moderate height by rising abruptly from the plain. *Stavrokoráki* (1017 ft), the northernmost of these, is separated from *Kotróni* (772 ft) by the torrent bed of the *Kharadra*, which descends from the Marathon Lake past the modern village of Marathon to the sea. Geologists suggest that in the plain it would have been a negligible obstacle in Classical times. Between Kotroni and *Aforismós* (1880 ft) runs the *Valley of Avlona*. The valley is joined at the village of VRANA (possibly the ancient Marathon) by the Rapentosa Gorge. This defile runs N.N.E. from the hamlet of Rapentosa between Aforismos and *Agrilíki* (1825 ft), the mountain forming the southern barrier of the plain. Agriliki has rubble walls that may date from the Mycenean period.

In the N. of the plain the *Great Marsh* (Μεγάλος Βάλτος; nowadays criss-crossed by drainage canals) stretches from Stavrokoraki to the base of the Kynosura Promontory, where it ends in the small salt-water lake of *Drakonéra*. The *Little Marsh* (*Brexisa*) at the s. end is probably a post-Classical formation; it is now partially drained and occupied by a United States forces radio station and the Golden Coast Hotel (240 R, swimming pool, **B**).

Battle of Marathon. After the easy destruction of Eretria (p. 377), the Persians crossed to Attica. Datis, their general, was probably influenced in his choice of the Bay of Marathon by Hippias, whose father had landed here successfully fifty years before. Meanwhile the Athenians, after despatching Pheidippides post haste for Spartan aid, marched to Marathon and encamped in the Sanctuary of Herakles, a strong position astride the mountain track from Athens and commanding the only road. The Persian numbers, not stated by Herodotus and grossly exaggerated by later Athenian tradition, are now thought not to have exceeded two divisions of infantry (? 24,000 men) and a small force of cavalry. The Athenians received unexpected aid from Plataia, which sent its whole available force, perhaps 1000 strong to join the 8000–9000 men of Athens. The command was vested in the Polemarch, Kallimachos, whose staff of ten generals included Miltiades (the traditional architect of the victory), and perhaps Themistocles and Aristides.

Four days passed, the Persians being unwilling to attack the strong Athenian position, the Athenians loth to leave it without the expected Spartan reinforcements. Believing he had failed to lure the Athenian army down into the plain, Datis re-embarked his cavalry to move on Athens by sea, sending a land force forward to cover the operation. Seeing them within striking distance, probably soon after dawn on 12 Sept 490 B.C., Miltiades gave the word for action. He had left his centre weak and strengthened his wings to the utmost: the right wing, the place of honour, was led by Kallimachos; on the left wing were the Plataians. The Greek hoplites advanced rapidly across the mile of No Man's Land before the

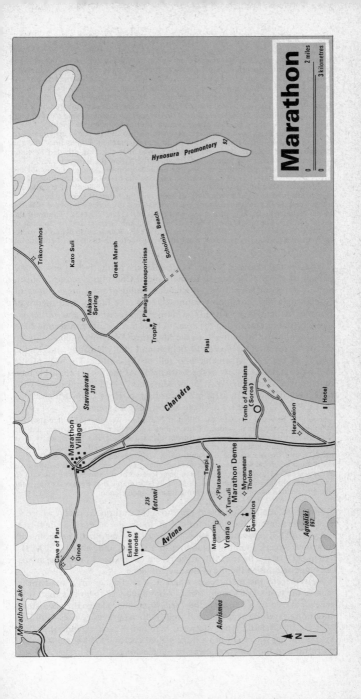

Marathon

0   2 miles

0   3 kilometres

Marathon Lake

Cave of Pan

Oinoe ◇

Alorismos

Kotroni 225

Estate of Herodes ■

Avlona

Museum □

Vrana ○

Tun.uli ◇

St Demetrios ✝

Agrieliki 557

Marathon Village

Stavrokoraki 310

Trikorynthos

Kato Suli

Makaria Spring ○

Great Marsh

Tseplu ◇

'Plataeaans' ◇

Marathon Deme

Mycenaean Tholos ◇

Trophy ■

Panajia Mesosporitissa ✝

Scholnia Beach

Hynosura Promontory 92

Charadra

Plasi

Tomb of Athenians (Soros) ○

Herakleion ◇

Hotel ■

N

surprised Persians could get their archers properly into action, aided possibly by tree cover (Prof. Burn has pointed out the similarity of tactics used at Bannockburn). The Athenian wings were successful, while their weak centre was pierced by the Persians. The wings then enveloped the Persian centre which broke. In the ensuing rout the Persians fled to their ships. Many of them were caught in the Great Marsh. They lost 6400 men, while the Athenian dead numbered only 192, including Kallimachos. All were buried on the spot. A runner is said to have been sent to Athens, where he died of exhaustion after announcing the victory.

The Persian fleet, having lost only seven ships, put out to sea in an attempt to surprise Athens; but Miltiades, by a rapid march, reached Athens first, and the Persians sailed back to Asia. The battle proved that the long-dreaded Persians were vulnerable and was "the victory of which the Athenians were proudest". The Spartan army arrived in time to view the battlefield on the following day. Of the many legends that accrued to Marathon perhaps the best known are those of the ghostly assistance of Theseus and of Pan. The impressive silence of the plain is said to resound at night to the clash of arms and the neigh of steeds (though it is almost certain that no cavalry took part). Unsolved mysteries connected with the battle include the flashing of a shield on Pentelikon (Hdt. VI, 115). The most detailed modern appraisals are by Burn (Persia and the Greeks) and in 'Journal of Hellenic Studies' (vol. 52, 1932), but these and even Kendrick Pritchett's Studies in Ancient Topography II (1969) need to be considered in the light of continuing finds.

THE ARCHÆOLOGICAL SITES. As we enter the plain, there is first a road (r.) across the Brexisa Marsh to the Golden Coast hotel (comp. above), just to the s. of which, on an island of solid ground are vestiges of Roman masonry, commonly supposed to be the family mausoleum of Herodes Atticus (A.D. 101–177, a native of Marathon), and earlier remains have been located in the area. A little farther along, a second road (r.) is signposted 'Monument to the Marathon Warriors' (400 yds; large car park; café). This **Sorós**, 30 ft high and 200 yds round, marks the graves of the 192 Athenians who fell in the battle. The top of the mound commands a view of the battlefield. At the foot is a marble bas-relief, copied from the 'Warrior of Marathon'. The "tombstones with the names of the fallen arranged according to tribes", which Pausanias (I, 32, 3) tells us were set over the Sorós, have disappeared.

Contrary to usual practice, the fallen at Marathon were buried where they fell in token of their signal valour. Excavations undertaken in 1890 confirmed the ancient tradition attaching to the Sorós: ashes and calcined bones, as well as small black-figured lekythoi of the early 5C, were discovered. Obsidian arrow-heads found on the surface by Schliemann six years earlier, which led him to attribute a much earlier date to the mound, may have been used by the Ethiopian archers (Hdt. VII, 69). No graves have been located of the slaves, who are said to have fought for the first time at Marathon. It is probable that Pausanias was right that the Persian dead were merely flung into an open trench.

The Soros road continues to the shore (Marathon C; cafés) where a track leads N. along the beach for c. ½ m. to the site of *Plasi*, a slight rise 200 yds inland, excavated in 1969–70. Here are an Archaic peribolos of polygonal stones, possibly belonging to a shrine, and, near by, a M.H. settlement. In the light of still more recent excavations Prof. Marinatos has suggested this as the site of the ancient deme.

We return to the main road, where c. 1 m. farther on a road forks back to the hamlet of Vrana (2 m.). About 200 yds down this road (r.), largely covered by a hangar is the *Tsepi Vrana* site, a large E.H. cemetery containing carefully arranged and well-built cist graves. Vases found in 1970 are of Cycladic type. Between here and Vrana extends N.W. the Avlona valley, where (1½ m.) a huge walled enclosure is known from an inscription on the ruined gateway to have belonged to Herodes Atticus.

At the entrance to Vrana is (l.) a large tumulus, excavated in 1969–70 and declared to be the TOMB OF THE PLATAIANS who fell at Marathon, which Pausanias records as a separate memorial. The identification is not certain. The mound, constructed entirely of stones, contains two circles of pit graves; skeletons found were mostly of young men, and the pottery in the graves is contemporary with that in the Athenian Soros.—At the far end of Vrana, under a large shelter, are groups of grave circles consisting of paved slabs, each circle containing stone tombs of M.H.–L.H. date. The skeleton of a Przewalski-type horse occupies a separate tomb but this is probably a later intrusion. Another circle stands in the open.

The **Museum** (adm. 25 dr.) has five rooms. We turn right. Room A, Neolithic pottery from the Cave of Pan (comp. below). Room B, case 5, finds from the Early Cycladic cemetery (Tsepi); case 6, from Middle Helladic tumuli (Vrana); case 8, from Geometric graves. Room Γ, vases etc. from the Tombs of the Athenians (case 13) and Plataians (case 10); bronze cinerary urn; boundary stones and inscribed stelai. Room Δ, Classical grave stelai and furnishings; rare bronze mirror with wooden covers; objects from various cemeteries; Panathenaic amphorae. Room E, Hellenistic and Roman finds, including an inscription concerning Herodes Atticus, and an Egyptianizing 'kouros' of 2C A.D.

About ½ m. S.E. of the museum, the small chapel of *Ayios Dhimítrios* stands alone just above the foot of Agriliki: close are the remains of an open-air precinct, 150 yds square, identified in 1954 by Prof. Sotiriades with the celebrated sanctuary of Herakles (comp. above).—On the plain, ½ m. from the chapel, in a small grove of low trees, is a Tholos Tomb (Mycenean II): it yielded a gold cup, and the complete skeletons of two horses were buried beneath the dromos.

The main road continues N. past the Rhamnous turn.—26 m. **Marathón,** a sprawling agricultural village. At the entrance is a marble platform with flag poles, the starting-point for annual marathon races.

FROM MARATHON TO KAPANDRITI, 12½ m. (20 km.), infrequent buses to Grammatikò. Beyond Marathon the road climbs viâ (3 m.) *Ano Souli* to (5 m.) *Grammatikò.* —8½ m. *Varnávas,* on the slope of Mavrovouni.—12½ m. *Kapandriti,* see Rte 22.

A road leads w. from Marathon to (5 m.) Marathon Lake (Rte 22), passing below the site of ancient *Oinoe.* Here in 1957 Papadimitriou discovered the *Cave of Pan and the Nymphs* of Marathon, described by Pausanias and identified by an inscription of 60 B.C. found in situ. The cave (no adm.) seems to have been a place of cult from Neolithic times to the end of the Bronze Age, after which it was deserted until the 5C B.C. Herodotus tells of the resurgence of the worship of Pan following his aid to Pheidippides before the Battle of Marathon.

From the entrance to the village an asphalt road diverges E., following the foot of the hills. At 28½ m. a road diverges (r.) to *Skhoinia,* the narrow strip of solid ground between the marsh and the sea chosen as the venue of the Boy Scouts' 11th World Jamboree in 1963. It is being developed as a bungalow resort.—29 m. *Káto Soúli,* where (l.) are vestiges of the walls (3C A.D.) of ancient *Trikorythos.* We cross a lonely upland valley with barren hills on either side.—32 m. Fork; to the right lies the little seaside hamlet of *Ayía Marína.* We bear left, rise gradually, and join the path from Grammatikò (see below) within sight of (36 m.) *Rhamnous.*

Rhamnous, uninhabited save for the phylax and a few shepherds, is one of the least spoilt sites in Attica, worth visiting more for its romantic isolation and the beauty of its setting than for its archaeological interest.

The headland was famous as early as the 6C B.C. for the worship of Nemesis. Its small cove provided shelter on an otherwise inhospitable coast for ships about to pass the dangerous narrows of Ayia Marina. Later a fortress was built to watch over navigation in the Euripos. This achieved importance in 412 B.C. after the Athenian loss of Dekelia, when Rhamnous became the port of entry for food from Euboea, since it offered the only route wholly on Attic soil that did not involve passing the narrows. The name of the city was derived from the prickly shrub ('ῥάμνος) which still grows in the neighbourhood. In more recent times it was known as *Ovriokastro*, a corruption of 'Ἑβραιὸν κάστρον (Jews' Castle). It was the birthplace of the orator Antiphon (b. 480 B.C.), whose school of rhetoric was attended by Thucydides.—The sanctuary was first described by the Dilettanti Society in 1817; partially excavated by Staïs in 1890–94; and re-examined by Orlandos in 1922–23 (B.C.H., 1924). The fortress was described by J. Pouilloux in 1945.

Nemesis was the compensating goddess, measuring out happiness and misery. She took especial care of the presumptuous, punishing 'hubris', the crime of considering oneself master of one's destiny. She was known also by the surnames of 'Adrastia' ('inescapable') and of Rhamnousia, from her sanctuary at Rhamnous. Associated with the worship of Nemesis was Themis, the goddess who personified law, equity, and custom.

At the head of a glen is an artificial platform, 150 ft wide, constructed of large blocks of local marble laid horizontally. Nine courses are exposed at the N.E. corner; the entrance to the peribolos was at the S.E In the centre of the platform the remains of two temples stand side by side, almost parallel and practically touching, with their N. flank facing the sea. The smaller and earlier TEMPLE OF THEMIS measures only 35 ft by 21, and consists merely of a cella in antis with a Doric portico of two columns. The walls, which stand only to c. 6 ft, are built of large polygonal blocks of white marble. Two marble seats dedicated to Themis and Nemesis and three statues from the cella with inscribed pedestals (found in 1890) are in Athens (pp. 150, 155).

The TEMPLE OF NEMESIS, nearer the sea, was a Doric peripteral building having six columns by twelve, the last of four generally ascribed to the so-called 'Theseum architect'. According to Dinsmoor, it was probably begun on the Festival Day of the Nemesieia (Boedromion 5; i.e. 30 Sept.), 436 B.C., and it is known by an inscription from the East front to have been rededicated to the Empress Livia, probably by Claudius in A.D. 45. The interior had the usual arrangement of cella with pronaos and opisthodomos in antis. The unfinished fluting on the remaining drums of 6 columns (s. side) suggests that the building was never completed.

Among the ruins reliefs from the base as well as a fragment of a colossal head (now in the British Museum) have been found of the *Statue of Nemesis* wrought (c. 421 B.C.) by Agorakritos in Parian marble. Pausanias believed the work was made from the very marble brought by the Persians for use as a victory memorial and attributed its carving incorrectly to Pheidias. Two unfinished seated figures still stand with other fragments before the temple.

Descending the rocky glen towards the sea, we reach in 10 min. an isolated hill girdled with the picturesque but overgrown enceinte (c. ½ m. in circuit) of the ANCIENT TOWN. The lower part of the South Gateway is well preserved, as are short portions (12 ft high in places) of the walls, in ashlar masonry of grey limestone. Nine towers of the fortress can be. made out. Within are some remains of a small *Temple*, a *Gymnasium*, and an inner citadel.

A rocky mule path to the s.w. leads shortly to a bad road which, partly utilising an abandoned mineral railway, comes up from Grammatikò (1½ hrs on foot).

22 FROM ATHENS TO MARATHON LAKE, KALAMOS, AND THE AMPHIAREION

ROAD to the *Amphiareion*, 30½ m. (49 km.); to *Marathon Lake*, 20¼ m. (31 km.).
Buses to *Kalamos* (28 m.; for the Amphiareion) from Odhos Mavromateiou; to
Marathon Lake from Plat. Kaningos.

From central Athens to (12½ m.) *Ekáli*, see Rte 15. We continue N.
passing the road to Diónisos (Rte 15), to (14 m.) *Drosiá* (Dionysos,
Zorbas, C), another upland resort. At *Stamáta* (1¼ m. r.) some ruins
may be identified with ancient *Hekale* where Theseus instituted a festival
to Zeus in memory of the priestess who sheltered him on his way to fight
the Bull of Marathon. *Plotheia* was also hereabouts.—At (15 m.)
Ayios Stefanos a road (r.) leads in 5½ m. to Marathon Lake (Tourist
Pavilion) and on to Marathon (Rte 21).

Marathon Lake (in Gk. *Límni Marathónos*; ΛΙΜΝΗ ΜΑΡΑΘΩΝΟΣ) is an
irregular sheet of water (c. 600 acres) formed by impounding the Charadra and
Varnava torrents. It supplies the needs of Greater Athens, though since the
Second World War its capacity has had to be augmented by artificial inflows from
Parnes and the Boeotian lakes. The *Dam*, built by the Ulen company of New
York in 1925–31, at the S.E. end of the lake, consists of a curved concrete wall
935 ft long, 154 ft wide at the base, and 14 ft wide at the top. It is claimed to be the
only dam in the world faced with marble. A roadway runs across it. It rises 177 ft
above the river bed to an elevation of 745 ft above sea-level. At the downstream
side is a marble replica of the Athenian Treasury at Delphi, which serves as an
entrance to the inspection galleries.

At Ayios Stefanos we can, after ½ m., join the Athens–Salonika highway, leaving it again at the Kapandriti exit. Alternatively we can take
the Marathon Lake turning, then bear left almost immediately in Ayios
Stefanos, rounding the station (*Oion*) on our left and crossing the line,
to continue by the old road running parallel with the highway. Seen to
the left is modern *Áphidnai*, formerly Kiourka; to the right, at the N.
end of Marathon Lake, beyond the new works which control the
entry of waters piped from N. Parnes, is a hill (Kotroni) with some
ancient walls to be identified either with classical Aphidna or with Oion.

Theseus hid Helen at Aphidna after carrying her off from Sparta. Her where-
abouts were divulged by the inhabitants of Dekelia to her brothers, Castor and
Pollux, who laid siege to Aphidna and rescued her. Aphidna was the home of
Kallimachos, polemarch at Marathon.

After (22½ m.) *Kapandríti*, where we join a road from Grammatikò
(Rte 21), the pleasant road winds over tree-clothed hills to (28 m.)
Kálamos, the small centre (1080 ft) of a well-watered and wooded
region above the Gulf of Euboea,

The road continues to (3 m. farther) *Ayioi Apóstoloi* (Kalamos Beach, 170 R, B;
Delfinia, 140 R, Amfiaraïa C; fish restaurants), a fishing village on a fast developing
stretch of the gulf.

From Kalamos a road descends in loops to the *Amphiareion* (2½ m.)
in the Mavrodhilisi ravine. On foot the site can be reached in 25 min.
by the old path, shaded by pines, which crosses the road several times.
The road must be followed for the last 100 yds as the entrance lies
beyond the bridge that crosses the stream.

The *Amphiareion, or *Sanctuary of Amphiaraos*, founded in honour
of the healing god, was at once an oracle and a spa. It occupies a
sheltered and sunny situation, well suited to a resort of invalids, on
the left bank of a wooded glen, watered by a mountain torrent. In
spring anemones carpet the site.

The sanctuary commemorated the elevation to divinity of Amphiaraos, the great seer and warrior of Argos, who fought as one of the seven against Thebes. On the defeat of this expedition he fled, pursued by Periklymenos, but the earth opened and swallowed him up, together with his chariot, near Thebes. His cult was adopted by the Oropians and concentrated here near a spring famed for its healing properties. Mardonius came to consult the oracle before the battle of Plataia. Whoever wished to consult the god sacrificed a ram and lay down for the night, wrapped in its skin, in the portico allotted for the purpose, and there awaited the revelations to be made to him in his dreams. The process of incubation (ἐγκοίμησις) was very similar to that practised in the Asklepieion. The cure did not, however, wholly depend on these miraculous communications, for there were medical baths in the precinct. After his cure, the patient had to throw gold or silver coins into the sacred spring.—The excavations (1927–30) of the Greek Archæological Service were interrupted by the death of Leonardos, the excavator. Restorations have been effected since 1960.

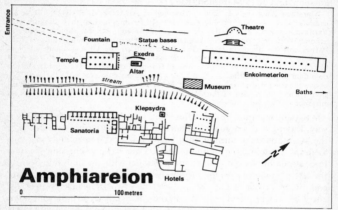

Descending the path parallel to the stream, we see (r.) the little *Temple of Amphiaraos*, a Doric edifice of the 4C, with a pronaos and a cella divided into three by parallel colonnades. The foundations, partly eroded by the stream, have been restored. The base of the cult statue is still in position. The back wall was joined by a porch (door marks in the threshold) to the priests' lodging. Ten yards from the temple is the *Altar*, on which the ram was sacrificed; and below the altar the *Sacred Spring*, into which the coins were thrown. Its waters were drunk from shells, many of which have come to light. Above the altar is a terrace with a line of over 30 inscribed *Pedestals* of statues, mostly Roman. On a line with these are the remains of a long bench. In front is the *Museum*, containing numerous inscriptions, a curious early Herm, torsos, and, in the back court, reassembled architectural members of the temple and stoa. Beyond are the remains of the *Enkoimeterion*, a long stoa, erected c. 387 B.C., having 41 Doric columns on the façade and divided internally into two long galleries by 17 Ionic columns. It had a small room at either end, possibly reserved for women patients. Along the walls ran marble benches, resting on claw feet, on which the patients submitted to the process of incubation. Behind the stoa is a small THEATRE, having a circular orchestra and seating for 300 spectators. Five marble *Thrones* with scroll ornaments are preserved. The *Proskenion* (restored) has 8 Doric columns surmounted by an epistyle with a dedicatory inscription. Beyond the stoa were the *Baths*. On the opposite bank of the stream are some confused remains of the accommodation provided for patients and part of a *Klepsydra*, or water-clock, its bronze plug mechanism visible.

A new road continues to *Skala Oropos* (Rte 20), c. 4 m. N.W.

23 FROM PIRAEUS TO SPETSAI

Motor Vessels of the Argossaronikos Lines from Piraeus (opposite the Dhimarkhion) ply to *Spetsai* in 4–5 hrs, calling at *Aegina* (1¼ hrs), *Methana* (2 hrs), *Poros* (2½ hrs), *Hydra* (3¼ hrs), and *Ermioni* (4¼ hrs). Not every boat calls at every port. In summer 4–5 times daily to Hydra and Spetsai; 10–12 times to Poros; several times per hour to Aegina. Extra services at weekends. Also (by launch) to Ayia Marina (Aegina) direct.

EXPRESS SERVICE ('*Flying Dolphin*' *Hydroplanes*) from Piraeus (Pashalimani; Pl. 11), twice daily to *Poros* (1 hr), *Hydra* (1½ hr), and *Ermioni* (1¾ hr); 4 times to *Hydra*, *Spetsai* (1¾ hr), and *Porto Kheli* (2 hrs); daily to all these ports continuing to *Nauplia* (4 hrs); also service continuing to *Monemvasia* (3¼ hr; see Rte 32), or to *Kithira* (5 hrs) and *Neapolis* (5¼ hrs).—From the main port 10 times daily to *Aegina* in 35 minutes. Transport provided from Athens (4 Akadhimias), whence bookings may be made.

AIR SERVICE in summer to Porto Kheli, whence ferry to *Spetsai*.

BY CAR. Only residents with a special permit may have cars on Spetsai. However the island can be reached by driving to Kosta on the Argolic peninsula (where cars may be left by the landing-stage) and taking the ferry.

To explore the islands and the Argolic peninsula, five or six days are necessary. From Poros (viâ Galata), Ermioni (viâ Kranidi), or Spetsai (viâ Kheli) it is possible to reach *Nauplia* by bus.

Within the day a round cruise (without landing) may be made to Spetsai, or a superficial visit may be made to any one island; organized day trips (C.H.A.T., etc.) briefly visit Aegina, Poros, and Hydra.

A From Piraeus to Aegina

The steamer passes down the centre of the *Great Harbour* of Piraeus with liner berths to the left and commercial wharves to the right. The prominent square building on the Akte peninsula is the Hadjikiriakou Orphanage. We pass between the remains of the ancient moles; from the *Outer Harbour* the w. landmarks of the Akte peninsula (comp. Rte 12) are clearly visible. The channel opens out into the **Saronic Gulf** (*Saronikos Kolpos*), the skyline of which, on a clear day, seems filled by mountains. The long islet of *Lipsokoutali*, with naval installations, is usually taken to be the ancient *Psyttaleia*, though some recent theories about the Battle of Salamis have thrown doubt on this (comp. Rte 18). To the w. rise the scrubby hills of *Salamis*, backed by the higher peaks beyond Megara. Astern the scars of Pentelikon are prominent and the Attic coastline is visible as far as Vouliagmeni and the islet of Fleves. As we draw level with the lighthouse on the s. point of Salamis, we see the sugar-loaf of Acrocorinth backed by the frequently snowy cap of Killini filling the w. end of the Saronic Gulf. Ahead rises Aegina; the temple of Aphaia may be descried high up on the left. The steamer passes E. of *Eleousa* and heads towards the low Akr. Plakakia, the N.W. cape of Aegina (lighthouse). Away to starboard appear the five *Dhiaporioi Nisoi*, the ancient Isles of Pelops. We turn s. into the Strait of Metopi, the shallow channel that separates Aegina from *Angistrion*. The jagged peaks of Methana rise ahead to the right of Moni. A solitary column (see below) marks the promontory guarding (16½ m.) the port of Aegina.

AEGINA or **AIYINA** (Αἴγινα; the stress is on the first syllable), a triangular island of 33 sq. miles occupies the centre of the Saronic Gulf, being almost equidistant from Attica and from Argolis. With Angistrion and the small attendant islets to the w. it forms nowadays an eparchy (10,200 inhab.) of the nome of Piraios. The island is difficult of approach on account of the sunken rocks and reefs that surround it. It relies for its water on wells. Much of the w. part consists of a plain which, though stony, is well cultivated with pistachio nuts and, farther s., with citrus fruits. The interior of the island is mountainous, pine-clad to the N.E., and affords pleasing landscapes, while at the s. corner rises the magnificent conical mountain, *Oros* (1742 ft), the finest natural feature of the island. The climate is delightful and the island is fast developing as a holiday area. The local industries include sponge-fishing and pottery. The two-handled porous water-jars (kanatia), common in Athens, are made here. In addition to pistachio nuts, olives, vines, almonds, and figs are cultivated.

History. Notwithstanding its small size, the key position of *Aegina* in the Saronic Gulf ensured the early importance of the island. The name probably derives from a divinity (Hellenized as Aigáios) imported from Anatolia by Early Helladic invaders speaking a Lycian dialect, but Neolithic finds make it certain that the island was occupied as early as the end of the 4th millennium B.C. About 2000 B.C. the inhabitants were supplanted by a Bronze Age people, probably of Indo-European race, speaking an Aeolian or Arcadian dialect and worshipping Poseidon. Their culture was brought to an end, c. 1400, by an Achaean invasion and a period of Mycenean occupation. Later legend tells of its only hero-king, Aiakos, son of Zeus and Aegina, who afterwards became one of the three judges of the Underworld. His sons Peleus and Telamon had to flee for the murder of their half-brother Phokos; Telamon afterwards became king of Salamis. A Dorian invasion brought the Thessalian cult of Zeus Hellanios. Aphaia seems to have been a variant of the Mother-Goddess from Crete, perhaps imported during the early Iron Age.

Perhaps abandoned for two centuries before 950 B.C., the island was recolonized probably from Epidauros (Herod., VIII, 46). Its infertile soil combined with its geographical situation spurred the inhabitants to maritime enterprise. At the end of the 8C it enjoyed parity with fellow members of the Kalaurian League, and was apparently no longer subject to Argos. By the 7C the Aeginetan marine held first place in the Hellenic world. The island was noted for pottery and especially for the quality of its bronze-founding. The system of coinage introduced in Argos by Pheidon (c. 656 B.C.) was probably borrowed from Aegina (rather than the other way about); indeed coinage very likely first reached Europe by way of the island. Its silver coins became the standard in most of the Dorian states, and in the 6C Aegina was a major centre of Greek art. Aeginetan merchants set up a temple to Zeus at the founding of Naukratis on the Nile; one, Sostratos, according to Herodotus (IV, 152) had also sailed to Spain. Their harbour was crowded with merchant ships (Thuc., V, 53) and the Aeginetan navy grew to a formidable size, exciting the jealousy of Athens. Solon's laws prohibiting the export of corn from Attica were probably directed mainly against Aegina, which henceforward, whatever its alliance, was always anti-Athenian. Aristotle calls it "the eyesore of Piraeus" ('Rhet.', III, 10, 7); Herodotus (V, 82) adduces a mythical feud, and may be historically unreliable about the war between Athens and Aegina (? 488–481) in which the Athenians were worsted.

At Salamis (480 B.C.) the Aeginetans atoned for any previous homage to Persia by distinguishing themselves above all other Greeks, and the battle marked the zenith of their power. As a member of the Spartan League, Aegina was protected from attack until the reversal of Kimon's policy, when the Aeginetans were quickly defeated by the Athenians in two naval battles. In 457 B.C. the city was humiliated after a siege (Thuc., I, 108). At the beginning of the Peloponnesian War the Athenians expelled the inhabitants and established a cleruchy. The scattered remnants were allowed to return in 404 from their exile in Thyrea (where the Spartans had accommodated them), but Aegina never rallied from this blow. It passed with the rest of Greece to Macedon and afterwards to Attalos of Pergamon. In Byzantine times it constituted a joint bishopric with Keos. Paul of Aegina, celebrated for a treatise on medicine and surgery was born here in the 7C A.D. Saracen raids caused the inhabitants to shift the capital inland (comp. below) where it remained until the 19C. After 1204 the island was a personal fief of Venetian and Catalan families until, in 1451 it passed to Venice. Captured and laid waste in 1537 by Khair-ed-Din (Barbarossa), it was repopulated with Albanians. Morosini recaptured it for Venice in 1654, and it became one of the last Venetian strongholds in the E., being ceded to Turkey in 1718. In 1826–28 the city was the temporary capital of partly liberated Greece, and here the first modern Greek coins were minted. Many of the present inhabitants are descended from families who came at this time from the Peloponnese, or from refugees who fled here from Chios and Psara.

The modern town of **Aíyina** (5700 inhab.; *Brown, Avra,* C open all year; *Danae, Nausicaa* B; *Pharos, Klonos,* C, closed in winter; Rest. *Leto* and others on the quay), near the N.W. corner of the island, occupies part of the site of the ancient city, which extended much farther to the N. It still preserves buildings erected during the presidency of Capodistrias, to whose memory a statue stands in the main square. From the sea the most conspicuous features are two churches: Ayios Nikolaos, and the Cathedral on the quay. The modern HARBOUR, oval in shape and crowded with picturesque caïques, corresponds with the ancient *Commercial Harbour.* Its moles were rebuilt by Capodistrias on the ancient foundations. The s. mole marked the s. limit of the ancient city, forming an extension of its walls. The N. mole bears a tiny white chapel of typical Aegean design. Beyond the N. mole remains of rectangular quays of the ancient *Military Harbour* (Κρύπτος Λιμήν) can be seen beneath the surface of a smooth sea.

It was protected on the N. by a low promontory (10 min. from the quay), which formed the citadel, fortified from Neolithic to Christian times. In the Classical period at least it was within the enceinte which was continued seaward from farther N. by a breakwater. Here are the main EXCAVATIONS (adm. 25 dr.), greatly extended w. and s. of the temple in 1969 when an Early Helladic fortified settlement, burnt and then rebuilt, was exposed. Of the *Temple of Apollo* (formerly attributed to Aphrodite), all that remains are a lone column, without its capital, from the opisthodomos, and some scanty poros foundations of polygonal masonry. The temple (Doric, 6 columns by 12), built c. 520–500 B.C., was superseded by a late-Roman fortress, fragments of which survive on the seaward side; the area was quarried during the rebuilding of the harbour.

German excavations by G. Welter in 1924 beneath the temple showed remains of a building about a century earlier, below which again were late-Mycenean houses.
    To the s.e. a square edifice of Archaic date is possibly the *Aiakeion.* To the N.W. of the temple a circular structure is thought to accord with Pausanias' description of the *Tomb of Phokos.* On the extremity of the cape near the water, some scanty Pergamene remains are perhaps those of *Attaleion.*

The Quay has a Tourist Information Office (open only in the season). At its s. end is the *Panayitsa* (1806), cathedral of the Metropolitan of Idhra, Spetsai, and Aegina. Inland from the quay are the Post Office and the museum. The MUSEUM contains sculptural fragments from the Temple of Aphaia (and a reconstruction of its pediments); a statue of Herakles from the Temple of Apollo, a Sphinx of Attic workmanship contemporary with Kalamis, Attic stelai, inscribed anchors, and a selection of local pottery (Neolithic to Archaic) arranged chronologically.

Beyond the Post Office, we reach Odhos Ayiou Nikolaou which leads past the medieval *Markelon Tower* to *Ayios Nikolaos,* a modern church. Behind this are some remains of an early-Christian basilica. A street running N. leads shortly to *Kanaris's House,* once occupied by the hero of Chios. Many of the local houses are given over to the processing of sponges.—In the s. part of the town is the former *Orphanage,* built by Capodistrias for children orphaned by the War of Independence and, since 1854, used successively as barracks and prison. Below the courtyard is an ancient catacomb. Farther on (5 min.) is the *Faneroméni* (18C), with the remains of a basilica over a crypt. On the coast road, opposite the cemetery is the

House of Trikoupis, where both Charilaos Trikoupis (1832–96), the statesman, and Spyridion, his historian father, lived for a short period.—To the left of the road to the temple (see below), about ¼ hr from the town, is the *Omorfi Ekklesia*, a church of 1282 built of antique materials and dedicated to SS Theodore. Its frescoes (somewhat later) are well preserved.

BUSES and taxis to the Temple of Aphaia and elsewhere, from the quay.

THE PRINCIPAL EXCURSION is to the Temple of Aphaia (7½ m.; by Ayia Marina bus). The road runs through pistachio plantations, and vineyards dotted with olive and fig trees.—4 m. **Palaiokhora** (l.), capital of the island from the 9C until 1826. It was rebuilt twice after destruction by Barbarossa (1537) and by the Venetians (1654). Covering the bare hillside are the ruins of more than twenty churches and monasteries, survivors from the 13C and later, some with stone ikonostases and tolerably preserved frescoes. A ruined castle crowns the summit. Below this ghost town is a monastery containing the embalmed body of St Nectarius (Anastasios Kefalas; 1846–1920), Metropolitan of Pentapolis and the first saint to be canonized (1961) by the Orthodox Church in modern times.—5 m. (8 km.) *Mesagros*. From this village a road (unpaved) leads to the N. coast and then through *Souvala* (Ephi, Apr–Oct, C), a pleasant fishing village with radio-active springs, back (paved) to Aiyina.—At 6½ m. the road bears r. and climbs.

7½ m. The *Temple of Aphaia (adm. 25 dr.) stands on a pine-clad hill commanding a splendid view over the Saronic Gulf. Erected at the end of the 6C or in the early years of the 5C on the site of two earlier temples, it has been called "the most perfectly developed of the late Archaic temples in European Hellas". The appearance of its shattered peristyle was enhanced in 1956–60 by the re-erection of fallen columns and the restoration to position of their entablature, though lightning caused damage to the s.w. corner in 1969.

The temple was explored in 1811, when its sculptures were borne off to Munich (comp. below). Bavarian excavations undertaken in 1901–03 by Furtwängler in order to complete these groups proved the dedication to Aphaia, the Aeginetan equivalent of the Cretan goddess Britomartis. The shrine had previously been attributed first to Zeus Panhellenios and later to Athena. Numerous fragments were recovered in 1969 of the earlier Archaic temple's polychrome sculpture.

We pass through the *Outer Peribolos Wall*. To the right are some remains of the living quarters of the priests; three stucco baths served for purification rites. The artificial *Terrace* on which the temple stands is approached by a Propylon of the 5C, having an unusual arrangement of pilasters on the façade. To the E. are the foundations of the latest *Altar*, from the base of which a *Ramp* rises to the *Stereobate* of three steps on which the temple stands. The w. part is well preserved. Adjoining its lower courses are traces of semicircular foundations from a sanctuary of the Geometric period, perhaps an apsidal structure of the 'Perachora house' type, similar to that found at Thermon.

The TEMPLE is a Doric peripteral hexastyle, having twelve columns on the flanks. It was built in local limestone which was coated with a thin layer of stucco and painted. Of the original 32 columns, 24 now stand. They are 3 Doric feet in diameter at the base and axially spaced at 8 feet. The corner columns are thickened for optical effect. All the shafts are monolithic, save for three adjacent columns on the N. flank which are built up of drums, presumably for the purpose of leaving a gap until the last moment to facilitate the erection of the interior. The architrave is extensively preserved and the whole entablature has been restored at the w. end of the N. side by the replacement of the triglyphs, metopes, and cornice. The sekos is divided into a cella with pronaos and opisthodomos in antis. Two columns survive of the *Pronaos*, which once housed figureheads of Samian triremes captured at Kydonia. On the pavement here are traces of red stucco; marks can be seen on the columns where the entrance was closed off with a high grille.

The *Cella*, the walls of which have been partly rebuilt, was divided internally by two colonnades of five columns each; above an epistyle a second row of smaller superposed columns carried a flat ceiling. Seven

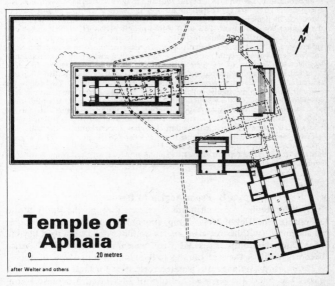

Temple of Aphaia

0   20 metres

after Welter and others

of the interior columns have been restored to place with three of the upper shafts; their taper is continuous throughout. At a later date aisle floors were put in at triforium level, approached presumably by wooden stairs. The position of the cult statue is shown by marks in the floor where a railing stood round it.—The doorway from the opisthodomos is not central and was pierced after a solid cross-wall was started.

The pedimental sculptures were of Parian marble. Seventeen statues found by Cockerell and von Hallerstein in 1811 were acquired by Ludwig I of Bavaria and, after restoration by Thorvaldsen in Rome, sent to Munich, where they remain. The scenes represented two combats before Troy in the presence of Athena. Parts of a third group (now in Athens museum) have since come to light; these are believed to be an earlier group from the E. pediment damaged in a Persian raid and replaced, when their mutilated fragments were erected in the court as a memorial to barbarian impiety.

At the N.E. corner of the terrace is a cistern which caught rainwater from the roof; it connects with a cave below the retaining wall and dates from the Archaic period.

Beyond the temple the road descends to (9½ m.) **Ayia Marina** (*Ammoudia, Oasis*, **C**, open all year; *Apollo* **B**, *Argo, Kyriakakis, Aphaia*,

Marina, Magda, Galini, **C,** all closed in Nov or Dec to Feb), a resort on an attractive bay, used by cruise ships to disembark passengers for Aphaia and served in summer by launches from Piraeus. The road is being extended s. to join the w. coast at Perdika.

From Aiyina to Oros (3 hrs). We take the Perdika road (tarmac; bus), which quits the town by the s. quay and skirts the shore, and follow it as far as (3¾ m.) *Marathon.* Hence a path leads inland to (40 min.) *Pakheia Rakhi.*—1 hr *Ayioi Asómatoi,* a ruined monastic chapel, is built of antique blocks that probably came from the neighbouring ruins known as *Naos.* Here the polygonal terrace walls were repaired in fine Hellenic masonry, of which eight courses remain. From the chapel an arduous path ascends the N. slope of the pyramid to (1¾ hrs) the summit. **Oros** (The Mountain), known also as *Ayios Ilias* and to the ancients as *Panhellenion,* is a conspicuous landmark (1742 ft) from all over the Saronic Gulf. The gathering of clouds on its peak is a sure sign of rain, a phenomenon noted in antiquity. Near the summit is a settlement (13C B.C.) whose people probably introduced the cult of Zeus Hellanios (the rainbearer) from Thessaly and which came to the usual violent end suffered by Mycenean places. It was reoccupied in Geometric times and reached its monumental period in the Pergamene age when the whole mountain was sacred. Remains of this period comprise a great steeped road leading to a rectangular *Terrace* supported by stepped polygonal retaining walls, whence a staircase, 22 ft wide, led to a second area with a hypostyle edifice. Two connected cisterns higher up probably collected sacred waters. The Oros commands a splendid *View;* nearly the whole island is visible, rising apparently from the midst of a vast lake encircled by an almost continuous coastline.—The return may be made by taking a path to the N. past the *Panayia Khrisoleontissa,* an isolated monastery of 1600 whose church, enlarged in 1806, has a remarkable ikonostasis.

From Marathon the road continues to (5½ m.) *Perdika* (Aegina Maris B), whence a track leads to the s. point of the island. Here stands the monastery of *Ayia Trias,* built by St Nectarius (comp. above). The islet of *Moni,* offshore from Perdika, is being developed for holiday use with a camp site and Tourist Pavilion.

B   From Aegina to Poros

Quitting Aegina the boat heads s. to pass through the Vathy Strait. To port (E.) the islet of *Moni* (comp. above) has a prominent lighthouse; to starboard (w.) the tree-clad *Angístrion* hides *Kyra.* We pass beyond Moni and the conspicuous Mt Oros, when the s.E. coast of Attica becomes visible to the E. all the way to Sounion. About 4 m. s. of Aegina is *Petrokáravon,* a dangerous isolated rock, used for target practice. We pass close below the terraced hillsides of MÉTHANA, a peninsula connected by an isthmus only 300 yds across with the mainland of the Peloponnese. The name, properly ἡ Μεθάνα, was corrupted as early as Pausanias to Τὰ Μέθανα. The interior consists of the bare ridges of *Mt Khelona* (2435 ft), an extinct volcano.

Strabo gives an imaginative or derivative account of the seismic disturbance that gave birth to the mountain, which Pausanias places in the reign of Antigonus Gonatas. The peninsula, which was by confusion called *Methone* even in early texts of Thucydides (as Strabo mentions), was fortified by the Athenians as early as 425 B.C. in the Peloponnesian War. The fortifications, traces of which are visible, were strengthened under the Ptolemaic occupation (3C B.C.).

The little port of (27½ m.) **Méthana** (*Saronis* B, *Methanion, American,* **C,** open all year; *Ghionis, Pigae,* **B,** June–Oct, all without Rest.) has the usual attractions of a watering-place. The warm sulphur springs, used in the cure of rheumatic and allied affections, give name to *Vromolímni* ('stinking shore'), the village on the hillside above. *Nisaki,* a rocky islet connected by a causeway with the waterfront, is charmingly planted with pines and oleanders. Both here and on the Thrioni plateau above Vromolimni are traces of antique wall.

A bus (twice daily) follows a coastal road to Galatás, passing close to Troezen. A pretty walk leads viâ (40 min.) *Stenón* on the isthmus to the w. slope of the peninsula where, below the village of *Megalokhóri*, are (2½ hrs) the remains of the acropolis of ancient *Methána*. The *View from *Kaiméni Khóra* ('the burnt village'; 45 min. farther) is delightful: across the Bay of Méthana the majestic Mt Ortholíthi (3655 ft) and Mt Arachnaíon (2910 ft) rise sheer from the water. Above the village is an ancient tower. The tiny chapel of the *Panayía Krasáta*, on the w. point of the peninsula, was erected by a wine merchant saved from shipwreck; wine is said to have been used to mix the mortar.

The steamer threads the narrow right-angled strait dividing Poros from Troezenía and in 2½ hrs from Piraeus reaches the town and port of (32 m.) *Poros*.

POROS, an island about 6 m. long from E. to w., is separated from the mainland by a strait (400 yds across at its narrowest) crossed by a ferry. The name (πόρος) means both strait and ferry. The island was anciently known as *Kalauria*, and was the headquarters of the Kalaurian League. The interior is occupied by low rocky hills wooded with pines. The scenery and climate are delightful and the island is a favourite summer resort of the Athenians.

History. The *Kalaurian League* was a historically shadowy maritime confederation, formed c. 7C B.C. under the aegis of Poseidon. Its members included Athens, Aegina, Epidauros, Troezen, Hermione, Nauplia, and Prasiai (in Attica), together with Boeotian Orchomenos. Under the Turks Poros was practically independent. Here in 1828 were held the conferences of the British, French, and Russian plenipotentiaries entrusted with the task of settling the basis of the Greek kingdom (*Protocol of Poros*). In 1831 the independent islanders, under the leadership of Hydra, took up an attitude of open hostility to the arbitrary government of Capodistrias and established a 'Constitutional Committee'. The national fleet of Greece, including the frigate *Hellas* (flagship) and the steamship *Karteria*, lay in Poros harbour. Capodistrias gave orders for this to be made ready for sea, but *Adm. Miaoulis*, acting under the orders of the Hydriot government, seized the fleet and the arsenal. On 13 Aug. 1831, Miaoulis, rather than hand over the fleet to the Russian Adm. Ricord, blew up the flagship *Hellas* and the corvette *Hydra*.

The town of **Poros** (4050 inhab.; *Latsi, Poros, B; Manessis, Aktaion C*) lies on the strait, opposite the village of Galatá on the Peloponnesian coast. The small volcanic peninsula on which it is built was once the island of *Sphaeria*, named after Sphaeros, the charioteer of Pelops. A low isthmus and bridge now joins it to the island. The first naval arsenal of independent Greece was established here in 1830 and survived until 1877, when it was closed in favour of Salamis. The buildings now house the *Boys' Naval Training School* (Κέντρον Ἐκπαιδεύσεως Ναυτοπαίδων) the Greek Dartmouth. On the shore stands an obelisk to the memory of Frank Abney Hastings, buried in Poros. The boys' training ship, the former cruiser *Averoff*, celebrated for its exploits at Cape Helles in 1912, is the most prominent feature of the bay. The anniversary of the battle (6 Dec.) is marked by parades.

The view across the strait, with its busy small boats, is delightful: Galata (see below) is backed by a long range of green hills. To the left are the *Lemonodásos*, a picturesque spot where lemon groves grow amidst water-mills. The conspicuous fort above was built by forced labour during the German occupation.

From the quay the shore road continues beyond the Naval School (see above), crosses the causeway, and follows the coast to the E., passing (1½ m.) several summer seaside hotels (*Aigli B, Chryssi Avgi C*, etc.).—2½ m. The *Monastery of Zoodokhos Piyi* is beautifully situated in a verdant glen above the Sirene Hotel (120 R, B).— Before the monastery a new road encircling the heights to the E. mounts through the pinewoods to the plateau of *Palatia*, where the ruins of the SANCTUARY

OF POSEIDON are picturesquely situated in a saddle between the highest hills of the island, c. 600 ft above the sea (*View). The ancient city of *Kalauria* was situated near by, and the sanctuary was the headquarters of the Kalaurian League. Excavations in 1894 by the Swedish archæologists Wide and Kjellberg showed that the entire precinct was built in the 6C B.C. on the site of a sanctuary that dates back to Mycenean times. The scanty remains of the *Temple of Poseidon* show it to have been a Doric peripteral hexastyle (6 by 12 columns), built of bluish limestone. Here Demosthenes, seeking sanctuary in 322 B.C., was cornered by Antipater's emissaries and took poison. The inhabitants buried him with honour in the precinct and Pausanias saw his grave. To the S.W. of the temple four *Stoas* formed a quadrangular precinct.

FROM POROS TO TROEZÉN (AND NAUPLIA). FERRY in 5 min. to **Galatás** (*Stella Maris* B; *Galatia, Papasotiriou,* both C) on the mainland; thence ROAD (level walking but little shade) and by-road to (5½ m.) *Damalá* (Troezén).

Buses twice daily to *Damala*; several other services pass (4 m.) *Ayios Yeoryios* on their way to Methana, Lesia, etc., making it possible with a little planning to ride most of the way in both directions. An alternative is to take a small boat to (1 hr) Kelenderis, the ancient mole of Damala in the Bay of Vidi, and to walk thence to Damala in 40 min.—Two buses daily continue beyond Ayios Yeoryios, viâ (13½ m.) *Driópi*, and (25½ m.) *Trakheiá*, to (37½ m.) *Ligourió* (Rte 29), passing close to the Hieron of Epidauros, and thence to (52¾ m.) *Nauplia*.

The road runs W., soon quitting the coast and passing through orange and lemon groves. At 2½ m. a rough mule path (l.), though shorter, affords little saving in time or effort. Near the first cottage of (4 m.) *Ayios Yeoryios* a by-road ascends to (5¼ m.) *Damalá* (Rfmts), a village lying below the N. slope of *Mt Aderes* (2360 ft), the ancient *Phorbantion.* It occupies part of the site of **Troezén** (Τροιζήν), the ancient capital of the small and fertile territory of Troezenia. To the S. between the deep ravines of Ayios Athanasios (E.) and the Yefirion (W.) rises an isolated hill (1027 ft; view), on which a Frankish tower marks the site of the acropolis. The principal ancient ruins, however, lie to the W. of the village.

Troezén appears early in legend as the birthplace of Theseus. Here also Poseidon caused the horses of Hippolytos, his son, to take fright and drag their master to death. Orestes was purified at Troezén after his matricide. In 480 B.C. when the Persians occupied Athens, the Troezenians gave hospitality to Athenian refugees. Here was found the famous stele detailing Themistocles' plan of evacuation. The Athenians captured the city in 457–446. In the Peloponnesian War the Troezenians sided with Sparta. Their city was a member of the Kalaurian League. The Franks here established a barony and a bishopric. At *Damala*, in March 1827, was held the Third Greek National Assembly, at which Capodistrias, the Corfiot foreign minister of Russia, was elected President of Greece. In May 1827, was published the *Constitution of Troezén,* usually known as the charter of the liberties of Greece, though it was put into immediate abeyance at the time. This was the third of the 'constitutions', the others being those of Epidauros (1821) and of Astros (1823).

The proverbial expression 'a bishop of Damala', signifying one whose cupidity has made him overreach himself, springs from the story commemorated in local song of a medieval bishop surprised by a Barbary corsair and sold into slavery while trying to catch fish bigger than some which had been presented to him.

The scanty but scattered remains, exposed by the French School in 1890 and 1899 and re-examined by the German Institute in 1932, lie near three ruined Byzantine chapels incorporating ancient fragments. They have been variously identified without certainty and are best found with local aid. We come first to the so-called *Theseus Stone,* then (10 min.) to the remains of the city walls with a fine *Tower,* 42 ft square and 32 ft high, having a postern and a staircase. The lower half is ancient, the upper medieval. Hence we may follow a path along the course of an ancient aqueduct to the gorge of Yefiraion, spanned by the picturesque single-arched *Devil's Bridge* (Yefira tou Diavolou).

Of the other remains the most interesting (15 min. w. of the tower) is an edifice, 100 ft square, consisting of a colonnaded court surrounded by rooms and, on the w. side, a hall with benches and a channelled floor. This has been identified by Welter as an enkoimeterion and the building may therefore be an *Asklepieion*. Beyond this, the deserted *Palaia Episkopi*, or bishop's palace, is perhaps the site of the *Temple of Aphrodite Kataskopia* ('Peeping Aphrodite'). Pausanias records such a temple built on the spot where the amorous Phaedra used to watch Hippolytos at his manly exercises; their graves were in its precinct.

C Hydra

From Poros the steamer heads s.e. The Strait of Poros is guarded at the e. end by the tiny island of *Bourdzi*, where there are conspicuous remains of a medieval fortress. We round *Cape Skilli*, the ancient Skyllaeon, off which lie the rocky Tselevínia. Ahead extends Idhra, separated from the Argolic peninsula by the sea of Ermione (Ermionis Thalassa).

HYDRA or **IDHRA** (as it is pronounced), the ancient *Hydrea*, is a long narrow island, with inhospitable shores, largely barren of vegetation and short of water. Everywhere mountainous, it rises to 1935 ft in Mt Klimakion. The island, with Dokos, constitutes an eparchy of the nome of Piraios, though all but 160 of the 2540 inhabitants are concentrated in its only town. There are no motor vehicles. Since its discovery as a location for film-making, the island has aspired to become a fashionable artists' colony and retreat of intellectuals and has attracted also a less orthodox fringe of idlers.

Hydrea anciently belonged to the inhabitants of Hermione, who sold it to Samian exiles. They gave it in trust to the Troezenians whilst they went on to Crete. During the centuries of Turkish rule, enterprising refugees from Albania and the Peloponnese settled in Hydra to escape the exactions of the Turkish governors. The Hydriots became practically self-governing, paying no taxes but supplying sailors for the Turkish fleet. Their mercantile marine flourished, carrying corn to France through the British blockade of the French Revolutionary wars, and by 1821 the island had a population of 40,000 and a fleet of 150 merchantmen. After a month's vacillation in 1821, they threw themselves heart and soul into the War of Independence, merchant families, notably that of Koundouriotis, converting their trading vessels at their own expense into men-of-war. Among the many Hydriot naval commanders of the war were Tombazis, Tsamados, Voulgaris, and Miaoulis, the commander-in-ci 'ef. Among their famous descendants are Adm. Paul Koundouriotis (1855–1935), hero of the war of 1912, later regent and president of Greece, and Demetrios Voulgaris (1802–77), Prime minister in 1855. The islanders, however, never recovered from their patriotic efforts in the War of Independence and the commercial centre moved to Syra. The inhabitants now live by fishing for sponges off the N. African coast, and increasingly by tourism.

44½ m. The town of **Idhra** (2380 inhab.; *Miranda* A, *Delfini*, *Hydroussa*, DPO, **B**, open all year; *Leto* **C**, and others all closed in winter; accommodation always difficult; rooms must often be sought in private houses), which is hidden until the last moment from those approaching sea, rises in an amphitheatre on the slopes of the steep hills that enclose its deep natural harbour. It takes character from the imposing mansions, built in the late 18C for the great Hydriot families by Venetian and Genoese architects. They are unusual in Greek island architecture for their individuality, their size, and their sloping tiled roofs. Many retain their ancient doors of cypress and are gaily colour washed. The *Houses of George Koundouriotis* and *Lazaros Koundouriotis*, both with relics of the war of 1821–28, are shown on application, by courtesy of family descendants. A Merchant Navy Training School occupies the *House of Tsamados*; adjacent is a small *Museum* of Hydriot archives. *The House of Tombazis* shelters an international hostel for artists run by the Athens School of Fine Arts. The 17C conventual *Church of the Dormition of the Virgin* (Koimissis Theotokou) has a notable screen; the monastic cells are occupied as municipal offices. Narrow lanes succeeded by paths lead upward past *Ayios Ioannis*, a church with 18C frescoes, to (1 hr) the twin convents of *Ayía Efpraxia* (nuns) and *Profitis Ilias* (monks) just below the summit (1953 ft) dominating the town.

To the E. of the town a coast path leads in 40 min. viâ the village of *Mandraki* (Miramare A, closed in winter), with a deserted naval boatyard, to the dying monastery of *Ayia Triada* (1704). At the E. end of the island (2 hrs more) is the more flourishing *Monastery of Zourvas* (43 monks).—To the W. of the town a mule path follows the N. shore to (¼ hr) *Kamini*, where on Good Friday the epitaphios is borne in procession into the sea. The path continues to (½ hr) *Vlikhos*. A few poor and stony beaches break the rocky inaccessibility of the coast (bathers will do better to hire a boat). A medieval bridge and some offshore islets provide points of interest on the way to (1½ hrs) *Molo*. At (2½ hrs) *Episkopi*, on a plateau, scanty Byzantine remains have been found.

D   From Hydra to Spetsai

From Hydra some boats turn along the N. coast of the island and pass directly through the Petassi Strait, which separates it from Dokos (see below), to Spetsai (59½ m.). Others cross first to (55 m.) **Ermioni** (*Nandia* D), c. 12 m. w. on the mainland where *Petrothalassa*, *Plepi*, and *Saladi* on the neighbouring coast have huge holiday hotels. The little town (2200 inhab.) stands at the base of a spit of land, which separates the two excellent natural anchorages that gave to *Hermione* its ancient importance. At the end of the promontory (good bathing) are some foundations of a *Temple of Poseidon*. A mosaic exposed near the school belonged to a complex of early Christian buildings dependent upon a *Basilica* of the 6C.

A chasm in the neighbourhood was supposed in ancient times to be a short cut to Hades, avoiding the Styx. The frugal Hermionians accordingly put no passage-money in the mouths of their dead.

Buses connect Ermioni with *Galatas* and with *Kranidi*.

From Ermioni the steamer passes between the sparsely populated island of *Dokos* and the promontory of *Mouzaki* which protects Ermioni on the s. To the s. of Dokos lies the island of *Trikeri*. Rounding Cape Milianos (*Kolyergia*; remains of a temple and a tomb), we drop anchor at Spetsai, capital of the island of the same name.

SPETSAI, a small oval island 4 m. long with 3500 inhab., comes directly under the eparchy of Piraios. The central ridge of the attractive and healthy island rises gently to 955 ft. Spetsai, the ancient *Pityoussa*, or pine-tree island, was the first of the archipelago to revolt from the Turks in April 1821, and her sailors distinguished themselves in the war by their ferocity. The anniversary of the naval engagement of 8 Sept 1822, when Spetsiot brigs and fireships repelled a superior Ottoman force, is celebrated by a regatta.

The clean and tastefully built town of **Spetsai** (*Spetsai, Poseidonia* A; *Roumanis* B; *Star* C, and others) is a fashionable resort, favoured by the Athenians in summer. Transport is provided by carriage or donkey. The DAPIA, or fortified point, just by the jetty, is a historic small square where the main cannon battery was deployed. Cannon still decorate its walls. It now forms the modern *Plateia*, with many cafés. Here the rising of 1821 was planned. The Port Offices on the right occupy the Chancellery of the time. The family mansion of Hadzi-Yiannis Mexis, the first Archon of Spetsai, houses a *Museum* of relics of the war, including a casket containing the bones of Bouboulina, local heroine of the struggle. The house in which she lived is behind the Dapia. The four churches of the town are not without interest. The bishop's seat, once in the church of the *Assumption*, is now in *Ayios Nikolaos*: during the revolution the church was monastic, and Napoleon's brother Paul occupied one of its cells. Outside the town is the *Anarghyrios and Korghialenios School of Spetsai*, founded in 1927; the blue blazers of its pupils, emblazoned A.K.S.S., proclaim the English inspiration of this Greek 'public school'.

To the E. of the town the old harbour of *Limani* is closed by a promontory, on which stands the little chapel of *Panayia Armadas*, built to commemorate a naval victory over the Turks in 1822. Farther on is the nunnery of *Ayioi Pendes*. The beach of *Ayía Paraskeví*, on the S. side of the island, is the scene on 26 July of a panegyric.—*Spetsopoula*, a small island off the S.E. coast of Spetsai, belongs to Stavros Niarchos, the shipowner.

FERRY AND MOTOR BOATS to Kosta and Portokheli on the Peloponnesian coast, whence buses to Kranidi and Nauplia. In summer boats also to Nauplia; excursions to Monemvasia; tour of the island by boat in 2½ hrs.

24   FROM ATHENS TO CORINTH

The ATHENS–CORINTH TOLL HIGHWAY replaces much of the former road following the general course of the railway. The realined road holds a straighter and more level course avoiding level-crossings (a notorious hazard before); but with the dangers have also gone the charming proximity to the sea. The narrow bends of the Kaki Skala (see below) no longer need to be negotiated. We describe the old road.

ROAD, 50¼ m. (81 km.). 14 m. Elevsis. Fork left beyond the town.—26 m. **Mégara.**—39 m. *Ayioi Theodhoroi.*—46¾ m. **Corinth Canal.**—50¼ m. **Corinth.** BUSES hourly from Plateia Ayiou Konstandinou.

RAILWAY (S.P.A.P.), 56½ m. (91 km.), 13 trains daily in 1¾–2 hrs.

From Athens to (14 m.) *Elevsís*, see Rte 16. Beyond the town we bear left from the Thebes road (Rte 41), pass large ammunition factories, and gain the shore. The *Trikérato*, the jagged S.E. end of the Pateras range (known in ancient times as Kerata, 'Horns') formed the ancient boundary between Attica and Megaris. It ends in a small cape, below which are the Eleusis Shipyards. The road crosses the cape and continues en corniche with fine views across the landlocked bay to Salamis. —18 m. *Loutrópirgos* (Akti C, Aronis D) is a pleasant resort with villas.— At (19½ m.) *Megálo Pévko* (Megalo Pevko C) are the Piraïki-Patraïki textile works.—21¾ m. *Néa Péramos* (3600 inhab.) founded as a refugee settlement, has artillery and commando schools. The road now crosses the fertile *Plain of Megaris*, planted with vines and olives. We pass the road to the Salamis ferry, signposted 'Perama'.—26 m. *Mégara* can be by-passed, but its twin hills are seen to the right.

Mégara, chief town of the eparchy of Megaris, with 17,300 inhab., rises on the s. slopes of two moderate hills, *Karia* (E., 885 ft) and *Alkathoos* (W., 941 ft). These heights, the twin citadels of the ancient city, are connected by a long and narrow main street which runs w. from the Plateia (bus station). Of the many buildings described by Pausanias (I, 39–44), only the *Fountain of Theagenes*, in the dip between the hills, survives. It was cleared in 1958; the large reservoir had a roof supported on columns. Many ancient blocks are built into chapels and houses, which are still constructed of the white mussel-stone mentioned by Pausanias. At the crowded fair, held on Easter Tuesday on the open space w. of the town, the beauty of the inhabitants and of their gay costumes is more striking than their monotonous traditional dance ('trata': seine-net).

History. Though the Homeric catalogue treats Attica and Megaris as a whole, in the Geometric period *Megara* was independent. Her woollen industry prospered and she planted colonies as far w. as Megara Hyblaea (728 B.C.) and as far E. as Selymbria, Chalcedon, and Byzantium, founded according to tradition by Byzas c. 685. About 640 B.C. Theagenes, a popular leader, made himself tyrant. Rivalry with Athens for possession of Salamis led to strife with Kylon, his son-in-law, and the island fell c. 570 to Peisistratos. Possibly about the same time Perachora was finally lost to Corinth. The invasion of Megaris by Mardonius marked the w. limit of the Persian advance; 3000 Megarians fought at Plataia. In 461, menaced by Corinth, Megara formed a short-lived alliance with the Athenians, who built Long Walls to protect her access to her port, Nisaea. She soon reversed her policy, encroached on sacred Eleusinian land, and murdered an Athenian envoy. Pericles' decree of 432, excluding Megarians from Attic markets and harbours, was one of the prime causes of the Peloponnesian War. During the war the Athenians invaded Megaris twice yearly until in 427 Nikias seized Minoa, then an island connected to the mainland by a causeway, and established a close blockade not a mile from the city. Though the acropolis of Nisaea and the long walls fell in 424, the city itself was never taken. It has never been of much importance since, Pausanias remarking of the Megarians that "they were the only Greek people whom even the Emp. Hadrian could not make to thrive". Their fortifications nevertheless survived to be repaired in the 5C A.D.—Megara was the birthplace of Theognis (c. 570–485), the elegaic poet, and of the sophist Euklides (450–380), a disciple of Socrates, who founded the Megarian School of philosophy.

The well, still in use 15 min. N. of the town, is doubtless the *Fountain of the Sithnidian Nymphs*.—The chapel of *Ayios Nikolaos*, at the seaward end of Odhos Pakhi, marks the site of the ancient harbour of *Nisaea*. *Palaiokastro*, bearing a Venetian tower, to the W., may represent the acropolis of Nisaea; the hill of *Ayios Yeoryios* (chapel), to the E., with ancient walls, is probably *Minoa*, though some authorities have sought to place this farther E. beyond the modern harbour of *Pakhi*.

A road crosses the isthmus to (10 m.) *Alepokhóri* on the Bay of Aigósthena, where there are impressive remains of *Pagai*, a fort held by the Athenians in 459–445 B.C. The track hence to Aigósthena (Rte 41) provides a strenuous but rewarding walk.—From Megara a road across Yeraneia to Loutraki was constructed during the German occupation. This follows the line of an ancient road (visible in places) but is itself now derelict. From the saddle between the gulfs there is a magnificent *View.

Beyond Megara the YERANIA MTS. (Γεράνεια ''Ορι; 4495 ft), the forest-clad range which stretches from the Gulf of Alkionídhon to the Saronic Gulf, form a natural barrier between Central Greece and the Peloponnese. The road at first runs high above the sea, affording a *Panorama of the Saronic Gulf. From the *Malouris Petra* (near the 48th km. post) Ino leapt into the sea with Melikertes. We descend almost to sea-level by the KAKÍ SKÁLA (Κακἡ Σκάλα: 'Evil Staircase'), a narrow tortuous pass under the vertical cliffs. Above tower the *Skironides Petrai* or Skironian Rocks.

In antiquity the road occupied a ledge high up the cliff. The Megarians attributed its construction to their polemarch, Skiros, one of the first settlers in Salamis. The Athenians told of Skiron, a robber who, after despoiling travellers, kicked them into the sea to be eaten by a turtle; he met a like fate at the hand of Theseus. Hadrian made the road passable for chariots, but the route was as dangerous as ever in the 19C. It could always be blocked in time of emergency. The Peloponnesians obstructed it on receiving news of Thermopylae; a section was blown up in the War of Independence.

We enter a little plain that ranges the sandy coast (good bathing). —39 m. *Ayioi Theodhoroi* (Khanikian Beach, 220 R, B) is noted for its crystallized fruits. The district of *Mulki* occupies the site of *Krommyon* (fl. 8C–3C B.C.), where Theseus slew the wild sow. Out in the gulf lies *Evraiónisi*, an islet fortified by the Franks.—We now cross the Plain of Sousaki, marred by oil refineries but with good views of the Peloponnesian mountains ahead: prominent in the foreground, the jagged N. face of the Onia Mts and the sugar-loaf of Acrocorinth; in the distance the great cone of Killini. The ISTHMUS OF CORINTH, a low, flat, and barren tract of limestone, less than 300 ft at its highest point, connects the Peloponnese with the rest of Greece. It is 10 m. long and barely 4 m. wide at its narrowest point.—45¼ m. *Kalamaki*, a little port (ferry to Isthmia; Rte 25C), on the site of ancient *Schoinous*, lies ¼ m. to the left at the entrance to the Corinth Canal. Soon after the turn we join the main highway just beyond the toll point, pass the turning to Loutraki and Perachora (Rte 25F), and cross the *Corinth Canal* on a bridge only 36 yds long but over 200 ft above the water. The bridge was doubled in 1974 by the addition to the E. of a similar structure supplied by a Stockport company. The railway bridge is close on our right.

The ancients used to drag small ships across the Isthmus by the Diolkos (comp. Rte 25D), but the idea of piercing a canal dates at least from the time of Periander, and was periodically revived by Greek and Roman rulers. Caligula had the isthmus surveyed and Nero actually started operations in A.D. 67, using 6000 Jewish prisoners sent by Vespasian from Judaea. The work was stopped by the insurrection of Vindex in Gaul. Its traces, investigated by the French School (B.C.H., 1884), were obliterated by the building of the modern Canal in 1882–93.

This is nearly 4 m. long, 27 yds wide, and 26 ft deep. It is protected at each end by breakwaters, those at the W. end, 262 yds long, serving to enclose the port of *Poseidonia*. The central portion of the canal runs in a cutting through the rock, 285 ft deep. It is quite straight and there are no locks. A current of 1–3 knots necessitates a cautious passage. The canal can accommodate comparatively large vessels, and shortens the distance from Piraeus to Brindisi by c. 200 miles.— German parachutists captured the bridges over the canal on 26 April 1941, thus severing communications between the retiring British forces.

As we breast a low rise the Bay of Corinth comes into view with the w. end of the canal, Loutraki, and the heights of Perachora. We fork right for Corinth and Argos, avoiding the Patras Highway, and enter (50½ m.) **Corinth** (Rte 25). Those bound direct for Ancient Corinth can avoid the modern town by continuing on the Highway for a further 3 m. and taking a signposted turn before the next toll-point.

III THE PELOPONNESE

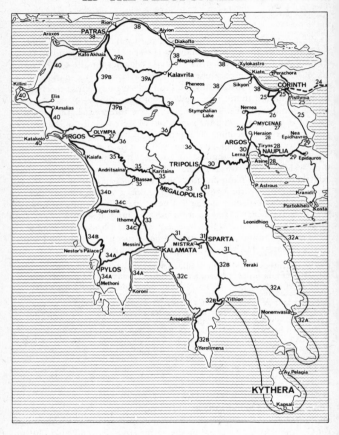

The **PELOPONNESE**, or *Pelopónnisos*, forms the s. extremity of the Balkan peninsula. Joined to the mainland of Greece by an insignificant isthmus, it was known to the ancients as the Island of Pelops (ή Πελοπόννησος); its medieval name, THE MOREA, was probably derived not from a fanciful resemblance to the leaf of the mulberry-tree (μόρον), which it does not resemble in the least, but from the fact that the mulberry flourished in the country. The modern division into the seven nomes of Argolis (E.), Corinthia (N.E.), Achaea (N.), Elis (N.W.), Messenia (S.W.), Laconia (S.E.), and Arcadia (inland, N. centre) roughly corresponds to the ancient regional division. The largest towns are

Patras and Kalamata. The scenery of the Peloponnese is of the rarest grandeur and beauty, and its archaeological interest is unsurpassed.

The N. coast, ending in *Cape Drepanon*, opposite Naupaktos, is separated from the mainland of Greece proper by the long narrow gulf of Corinth, and is comparatively free from indentations. To the S. the peninsula sends out the three long tongues of land, separated by the Messenic and Laconic Gulfs, which give it its characteristic shape. These end (from W. to E.) in *Cape Gallo* (the ancient Akrítas), fringed by the Oenoussae Is.: in *Cape Matapan* (Taínaron), the southernmost point of continental Greece: and in *Cape Maléa*, off which lie the islands of Elaphonisi, Kythera, and Antikythera. A fourth but less obtrusive tongue, fringed with islands and ending in *Cape Skilli* (Skyllaion), stretches S.E. between the Gulf of Nauplia and the Saronic Gulf. Off the N.W. coast lie the Ionian islands of Zante and Kephalonia. The greatest length of the peninsula is 132 m. (from Cape Drepano to Cape Matapan); its greatest width is 134 m. but road distances tend to be longer both in miles and hours than this might indicate, owing to the terrain.

An irregular series of mountains, encircling Arcadia, forms the backbone of the country, with articulations almost reaching to the sea in all directions. The highest peaks of this central group are *Zereia* (the ancient Kyllene; 7800 ft), *Aroania* or Chelmós (7725 ft), and *Olonos* or Erymanthos (7295 ft). These form a natural barrier across the peninsula from E. to W. To the N. of Erymanthos *Mt Voïdià* or Panakhaikon (6330 ft) rises above Patras. Two important chains run S. from the Arcadian group. The long range of *Taiyetos*, with *Ayios Ilias*, the highest mountain in the Peloponnese (7900 ft) separates the Messenian Plain from the Laconian Valley and ends in Cape Matapan. The parallel chain of *Parnon* (6365 ft), continuing the E. mountain wall of Arcadia (culminating in *Artemision*, 5815 ft), closes the Laconian Valley on the E., reaches to Cape Malea, and reappears in the hills of Kythera.

Practically the only low-lying portions are the Isthmus and shores of the Bay of Corinth; the coastal district of Achaia and Elis from Patras to Pirgos, with the vale of Olympia; and the plains or valleys of Messenia, Laconia, and Argos, at the head respectively of the Gulfs of Korone, Laconia, and Nauplia. A feature of Arcadia is the bleak Plain of Tripolis, lying 2000 ft above the sea. The vale of Olympia is watered by the *Alpheios*, the longest and most famous river in the peninsula; the Messenian Plain by the *Pirnatsa* or Pamisos, the most copious stream; the Valley of Laconia by the *Eurotas*; and the Argolic Plain by the seasonal *Panitsa* or Inachos. The *Elean Peneios* flows into the Channel of Zante. The whole of the N. coast is seared by small torrents, generally dry but occasionally sweeping the road into the sea. A feature of the plateaux of the interior is the number of *Katavóthrai* (καταβόθραι), swallow-holes into which the rivers disappear underground; they are common in Arcadia. The only natural lakes are *Pheneos* and *Stymphalos*, both shallow almost to the point of being seasonal, but there are hydroelectric reservoirs behind the Peneios and Ladon dams.

Communications in the main are excellent and it is possible to make a tour of the most famous sites with ease and comfort, either by public transport or by organized coach tour. The 4–5 day tours (from Athens) allow the hurried traveller to see more than would be possible in the time except by private car; even those less pressed, who are satisfied to see the popular highlights of archaeological discovery, may favour this means of transport, arranging longer halts with continuation by a later tour. The Argolid is readily accessible by train, as also is Olympia (viâ Patras). Intending visitors to the s.w. may profitably fly direct to Kalamata. The traveller who wishes to gain more than a superficial acquaintance with antiquities will be greatly rewarded by a more leisurely tour, taking in the remoter areas with their characteristic modes of life, where a few hours' hard travelling brings incommensurate rewards.

History. The Peloponnese was inhabited in Early Helladic times (3rd millennium B.C.), but neither archaeology nor tradition gives any certain answer whence its peoples came or what language they may have spoken. From them perhaps come the non-Hellenic place-names ending in ινθος-, -σσος, and ηνη (e.g. Corinth, Mycenae). They were probably of Asiatic origin. Their implements were of copper and later of bronze; their hand-turned pottery had elongated spouts (the so-called sauce-boat is characteristic) and were painted with brown glaze. Their existence is probably mirrored in the legendary Pelasgoi of Herodotus. Remains of typical sites can be seen at Zygouries and Lerna.

At the beginning of the 2nd millennium opens the period called Middle Helladic. A violent upheaval marks the arrival of new racial groups, of Indo-European stock (perhaps from N. of the Black Sea), presumably the first Greek-speaking people, since their culture develops without a break into the Mycenean civilization now known to have written records in Greek. They were a warrior race, who brought with them a wheel-made grey monochrome pottery ('Minyan') and developed another ware with matt-painted decoration; the latter may represent an assimilation from the earlier race whose culture they absorbed. Their houses were small, but those of the chiefs had a characteristic horseshoe plan, with a hearth in the centre of the largest room and an open porch; the scheme is the prototype of the later megaron. The race understood fortification and developed sculptural carving. Their dead were buried (originally without or with few offerings) in a squatting position in cist graves. Their traditions survive in the hero legends of Perseus, Herakles, etc. Middle Helladic remains have been excavated at Lerna, Asine, and Mycenae. The contents of Grave Circle B, now in Athens, give a good idea of the art of the end of this period of development (c. 1550 B.C.). Thereafter the mainland becomes influenced by Middle Minoan civilization, though developing Cretan ideas in an individual way.

A very rapid development marks the Late Helladic period; a widespread civilization evolves, which Homer knew as Achaean and we call Mycenean because both archaeology and tradition confirm that it reached its apotheosis at Mycenae. The other main centres of the Peloponnese were at Argos and Pylos. No danger seems to have threatened from abroad, quite the reverse if the references to marauders from Ahhiyawa (found on Hittite tablets) indeed refer to the activities of the Achaeans in Asia Minor.

A fresh wave of Greek-speaking people from the N., the so-called Dorian Invasion, brought widespread destruction to the Peloponnese. Classical historians attributed this break to the return of the Herakleidai, descendants of an earlier Mycenean dynasty (which included Herakles) exiled by the Pelopid rulers of Mycenae before the Trojan War. This was a political upheaval of a very violent kind which put back civilization several centuries, but cultural and racial continuity was evidently not affected for Attica seems not to have been occupied by the Dorians and is neither less nor more Greek than the Peloponnese. Arcadia is fabled never to have been subordinated to either Achaeans or Dorians. The dispossessed Achaeans supposedly resettled in the N. in the area which perpetuates their name to the present day.

The recovery of the Peloponnese is associated with the change from the Bronze to the Iron Age, and the slow development of new techniques and more sophisticated arts. ARGOS at first took pride of place, which it held for a long but not very noteworthy period.

The early recorded history of the Peloponnese deals with the rise of SPARTA (comp. Rte 31). From 337 B.C. when the Synedrion of Corinth confirmed Philip of Macedon as leader of the Greek world, the historical centre of the Peloponnese becomes CORINTH (comp. Rte 25). After the sack of Corinth in 146 B.C., the peninsula formed part of the Roman senatorial province of *Achaea*; this was temporarily joined in A.D. 15–44 to Macedonia.

The Peloponnese was ravaged in A.D. 267 and 395 by the Goths and by Alaric. Placed by the Constantinian reorganization in the diocese of Macedonia, the province enjoyed (alone of Eastern provinces) proconsular rank. Ecclesiastically it remained subject to Rome (under the Metropolitan of Thessalonica), sending only one bishop (of Corinth) to Ephesus (431). By 457 the Peloponnese had a number of bishops and Corinth had become a metropolitan see. In 540 the Huns penetrated to the gates and Justinian refortified the Isthmus; the w. shores were attacked by Totila's Ostrogoths in 549; but in the Peloponnese the ancient era survived into the 6C. Widespread earthquakes devasted the peninsula in 522 and 551.

Avar and Slav incursions submerged the Peloponnese c. 587, bringing two centuries of barbarism. Plague wrought havoc in 746–47. In 805 the MOREA (as it was now called) became a Byzantine 'theme', and under the Orthodox church slowly refined and assimilated the Slav elements, although predominantly Slav pockets survived in the Taiyetus region far into Frankish times and the Mani remained aloof as ever. New menaces soon arose in the Saracen corsairs, beaten off in 881, and the Bulgars, who penetrated the Morea in 924–27 and in 996. In general the 11C was a period of reconstruction and prosperity, during which Venetian merchants began to acquire the trading privileges that they developed throughout the 12C.

A year after the fall of Constantinople in 1204 *William de Champlitte* landed in the western Peloponnese. Assisted by *Geoffrey de Villehardouin*, he conquered the Morea and divided it up into 12 fiefs among various barons of France, Flanders, and Burgundy. Geoffrey de Villehardouin, who became in 1210 Prince of Achaea (or Prince of Achaea), governed the country with moderation. In 1261 Michael III Palaeologus regained Monemvasia, the Maina, and Mistra, where he installed a Byzantine 'Despot'. The house of Villehardouin lasted till 1301, when Isabella Villehardouin married Philip of Savoy. Philip became Prince of Morea, sharing his sovereignty with the Marshal of St Omer. In 1318 the principality passed to the Angevin House of Naples, which held it insecurely till 1383. The Venetians occupied Methone, Argos, Nauplia, and Navarino; and Nerio Acciaioli established himself in Corinth, Argolis, and Achaea.

The Byzantine Palaeologi gradually won back the Peloponnese by means of matrimonial and other alliances. In 1453 two rival despots, Demetrius Palaeologus at Mistra, and his brother Thomas at Patras, simultaneously appealed to Turkey for help against the Albanians, who were devastating the country. The Turkish general *Turakhan*, after assisting, proceeded to conquer the two brothers. In 1458 Mehmed II ordered the invasion of the Morea under *Omar*, son of Turakhan. In 1460 the conquest was completed. The Venetian coastal settlements were abandoned in 1573. *Francesco Morosini* reconquered the peninsula in 1685–87, and in 1699 it was ceded to Venice by the Treaty of Carlowitz. In 1715 *Ali Pasha* retook it for Ahmed III, and the Treaty of Passarowitz gave it back to Turkey. In 1770 an insurrection led by Orloff was repressed.

In 1821 the War of Independence was begun in the Peloponnese by the action of *Germanos*, Abp. of Patras. The same year *Peter Mavromichales*, Bey of the Maina, took the field, his example being followed by *Kolokotronis*, a celebrated klepht of the Morea, and by other chieftains. Tripolis fell in Oct 1821. In 1822 Kolokotronis defeated Dramali in the defile of Dervenaki and took Corinth; in 1823 Nauplia fell. The Greeks suffered a set-back in 1825, when *Ibrahim Pasha* invaded the Morea with an Egyptian army; but some months after the battle of *Navarino* (1827) the French landed in the Gulf of Korone, under Gen. Maison, and Ibrahim fled. The Turks evacuated the country in Oct 1828, and the French withdrew soon afterwards. In 1831 an insurrection of the Mainotes, who resented sinking their independence even in liberated Greece, was suppressed by Bavarian troops. In the Second World War the evacuation of British troops was effected at Nauplia, Monemvasia, and Kalamata; a notable naval engagement was fought off Cape Matapan; and Kalavryta suffered one of the more atrocious reprisals of the war.

25 CORINTH AND ITS ENVIRONS

A Corinth

CORINTH (ΚΟΡΙΝΘΟΣ; *Kypselos* B; *Korinthos, Acropolis, Ephyra*, C), or *New Corinth*, capital of the nome of Korinthia and seat of a bishop, is a modern town of 20,800 inhab., situated on the Bay of Corinth, $1\frac{1}{2}$ m. w. of the Corinth Canal. It dates only from the destruction of Old Corinth by earthquake in 1858. The new town was wrecked in its turn in 1928 and rebuilt on antiseismic principles, its low buildings and rectilinear plan giving it a paradoxical air of impermanency. It seems to turn its back on the sea and offers little to the visitor; sea-bathing is best sought to the w. of the town. OLD CORINTH (*Xenia* **A**; good taverna), or *Palaiá Kórinthos*, now a mere village, occupies part of the site of the ancient city. Its little square, with an old plane-tree and a fountain, lies $3\frac{1}{2}$ m. to the s.w. of New Corinth (bus hourly) or may be reached in minutes from the main Patras highway.

The **Ancient City** lay below the N. slopes of the mountain of *Acrocorinth* (1885 ft), its almost impregnable citadel. Its commanding position between two seas early made it a centre of commercial intercourse between Europe and Asia: cautious traders preferred the safe portage of the isthmus to the dangerous voyage round the Peloponnese. In addition, the renowned *Isthmian Games*, which were held every other year in the neighbourhood, further increased its importance. In its most flourishing period Corinth is said to have had a population of 300,000; the number of slaves is put by Athenaeus as high as 460,000. Two important harbours belonged to it: *Lechaion*, on the Bay of Corinth, united to the city by means of Long Walls, and *Kenchreai*, on the Saronic Gulf—hence the epithet 'bimaris' Corinthus. In addition, there was the less important port of *Schoinous*.

The ancient inhabitants, whose worship of Aphrodite was characteristic, were notorious, in an age of licence, for their vices. The Greek proverb, Latinized by Horace "Non cuivis homini contingit adire Corinthum", is usually taken to mean that not everyone could afford to go and join in this reckless profligacy. On this uncongenial soil St Paul founded a church during his eighteen months sojourn in the city. Peculiarly apposite, therefore, is his reminder to the Corinthian citizens that "evil communications corrupt good manners" (I Cor. 15, 33). The First Epistle gives a vivid picture of the internal troubles of the early Church.

Corinth has given its name to an architectural order (the Corinthian capital having been invented according to Vitruvius by Kallimachos in the 4C B.C.; but see Olympia), and in modern times, to the currant (Κορινθιακὴ σταφίς), which was first cultivated in the neighbourhood. In England the 'Corinthian' of the early 19C was a sporting gentleman riding his own horse or sailing his own yacht; today the adjective survives as the name of a yacht club and of a football club.

History. The name *Korinthos* is of pre-Greek origin and the vicinity of Corinth has been occupied with interruptions since the 5th millennium. The longest break seems to have followed a disaster contemporary with the destruction of the House of the Tiles at Lerna (Rte 30; Early Helladic II). The Homeric city of *Ephyra* ('The Lookout'), home of Medea, Sisyphus, and Bellerophon, is probably to be located at Korakou nearer the coast; Mycenaean settlements in Corinthia were subordinate to the Argolid. The site of classical Corinth was refounded by the Dorians. Towards the end of the 8C the historical last king of a semi-mythical line gives place to the oligarchy of the Bacchiadai, under whom Corinth became a mercantile power. Overpopulation may have occasioned the foundation of colonies at Corcyra and Syracuse (c. 734), but Corinthian prowess at sea is attested by the tradition that Ameinokles of Corinth built ships for Samos in 704, by the finding of typical Protocorinthian pottery (aryballoi, alabastra, skyphoi) all over the Mediterranean, and by the naval battle of 664 against her revolting colony Corcyra (at which, according to Thucydides, the trireme was introduced into Greek waters). In the mid-7C the Bacchiads were overthrown by Kypselos, who devoted thirty years to the development of trade and industry.

Under his son Periander, one of the Seven Sages, who reigned for 44 years (629–585), the city reached a level of prosperity that it maintained under Psammetichos, his nephew, and the moderate oligarchy of merchants who overthrew him. New colonies were founded on the Ambracian Gulf, Leukas was occupied, and Corcyra reconquered. The Isthmian Games were founded or reorganized. Trade in bronzes and vases expanded to Egypt and Mesopotamia, to the Black Sea and to Spain. The Corinthians are credited with the invention of the pediment and its decoration.

During the Persian War the city served as Greek headquarters and her forces were represented in the major battles. The increasing commerce of Athens robbed Corinth of her foreign markets. She failed to prevent Athens from annexing Megara (457 B.C.) and for the remainder of the 5C found herself, not always happily, in the Spartan camp. The war in 434 B.C. between Corinth and Corcyra was a cause of the Peloponnesian War, in which Corinth supported the Syracusans against the Sicilian expedition. After the death of Lysander she joined Thebes, Athens, and Argos against her former ally, but fared badly in the ensuing Corinthian War (395–387). At Corinth, after 362, Xenophon wrote the 'Hellenica'. In 346 Timophanes seized power only to be killed by his brother Timoleon, who was later to achieve fame as the saviour of Sicily from the Carthaginians.

Corinth shared in the defeat of Chaironeia (338 B.C.) and received a Macedonian garrison. At the Synedrion of Corinth, the following year, the Greek world ratified the leadership of Philip of Macedon, and after his assassination, of Alexander, in the campaign against Persia. The city flourished under a century of Macedonian rule. To this period belongs the Corinthian painter Euphranor, who practised in Athens c. 336 B.C. The Cynic philosopher Diogenes (412–323) ended his days in Corinth as tutor to the sons of Xeniades. Aratos expelled the Macedonian garrison in 224 B.C. and united Corinth to the resuscitated Achaean League. In 146, after the defeat of the League by the Romans, Corinth was mercilessly razed to the ground by Mummius and his ten legates. It lay desolate until, in 44 B.C., Julius Caesar planted on its site a colony of veterans, the *Colonia Laus Julia Corinthiensis*, which soon achieved splendour and importance as the capital of the province of Achaia. The luxury and dissipation of Corinth again became a byword. St Paul spent 18 months in Corinth in the proconsulship of Gallio (c. A.D. 51–52), plying his trade of tentmaker in company with Aquila and Priscilla (Acts, XVIII, 3). Gallio refused to be judge of complaints about Paul, laid before him by the local Jews. Nero's proclamation of Greek independence at Isthmia was rescinded by Vespasian, but Corinth, embellished by Hadrian (with an aqueduct from Lake Stymphalos) and by Herodes Atticus, became the finest city in Greece.

Though it survived the ravages of the Herulians in 267 and of Alaric in 395, Corinth suffered from disastrous earthquakes in 522 and 551, and its decline set in. After a final period of prosperity in the 11C, it was sacked by the Normans in 1147 and the rest of its history is one of successive captures. Its masters included Villehardouin (1212), the Acciaioli (1358), the Palaeologi (1430), the Turks (1458), the Knights of Malta (1612), and the Venetians (1687). In 1715 it was retaken by the Turks: this siege of Corinth is the one described by Byron. The victory of Kolokotronis over Dramali to the S. opened the way to Corinth, which fell into Greek hands after a short siege; Dramali himself died here and the remnant of the Turks was evacuated by sea.

ANCIENT CORINTH lay on a rocky plateau (200 ft) between its citadel and the sea. Its area was very extensive: the Long Walls started at the top of Acrocorinth, included the city, and ended at the port of Lechaion (see below). The actual length of the city walls does not, however, tally with the measurements of Strabo (viii, 6, 21–22). The principal excavation area lies close to the village cross-roads.

The inspection of the excavations and museum requires at least half a day; with a car it is possible to combine Corinth, Acrocorinth, Lechaion, Isthmia, and the Diolkos in one day's visit, but the unhurried traveller would be well advised to devote two or three days to the region and should on no account omit the visit to Perachora.

Adm. daily, 25 dr. incl. Museum; weekdays 7.30 or 9 to sunset; Sun 10–1 & 2.30–5 or 3–7. Guides to the Excavations and Museum published by the American School are available on the site. There are two entrances: from the open space above the Odeion and from the main street nearer the Plateia. The latter opens directly on to the Lechaion Road and is preferable for a first visit.

The **Lechaion Road** led into the city from its N. port (comp. below). An impressive monument to Roman town planning, 40 ft wide, paved and drained in the 1C A.D., it remained in use for centuries. Steps at its

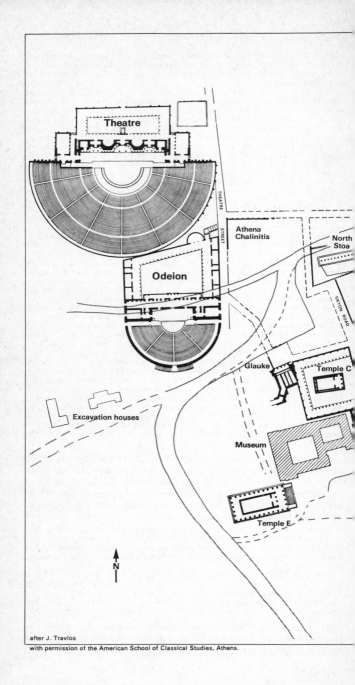

Theatre

Odeion

THEATRE STREET

Athena
Chalinitis

North
Stoa

SIKYON ROAD

Glauke

Temple C

Excavation houses

Museum

Temple E

N

after J. Travlos

with permission of the American School of Classical Studies, Athens.

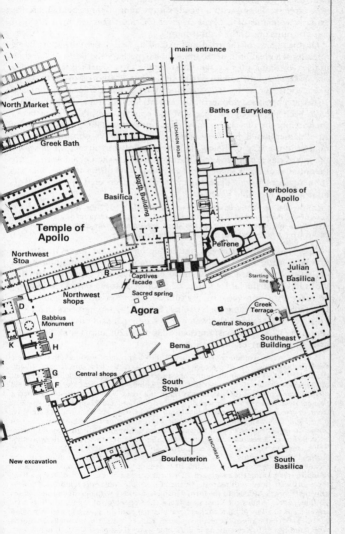

Corinth
Central Area

0   75 metres

main entrance

North Market

Greek Bath

Baths of Eurykles

LECHAON ROAD

Basilica

North Building

Peribolos of Apollo

Temple of Apollo

Northwest Stoa

Peirene

A

Captives facade

Northwest shops

Sacred spring

Agora

Babbius Monument

J

K

H

Starting line

Julian Basilica

Greek Terrace

Central Shops

Central Shops

Bema

Southeast Building

G

F

Central shops

South Stoa

New excavation

KENCHREAI

Bouleuterion

South Basilica

steepest part seem to have precluded use by wheeled traffic. We descend to Roman level and pass on the right a colonnade masking 16 small *Shops*. Their rear wall supported a terrace on which are the foundations in poros of a BASILICA of the 1C B.C., 210 ft by 75, possibly a judgment hall. Deep underneath the basilica, which was later rebuilt in marble on a larger scale and with a façade on the agora (comp. below), are the extensive remains of a *Greek Market* (5C B.C.; reached by a flight of steps through one of the central shops).

On the E. side of the road and extending below the village are some remains of a great bath of the Imperial era, perhaps the *Baths of Eurykles* praised by Pausanias as the finest in the city. Farther S., beyond a *Public Latrine* with some seats in situ, is the PERIBOLOS OF APOLLO, an open court 106 ft by 77, surrounded by a marble Ionic colonnade, 16 ft wide, upon a stylobate of Acrocorinthian limestone. Some columns have been re-erected and parts of the epistyle assembled. The heavy foundations in the centre may have supported the bronze statue of Apollo mentioned by Pausanias. A dyeing works occupied the N.E. quarter in the 5C B.C. Below runs the overflow of Peirene, which served the quarter as a main sewer. On the w. side, by the Lechaion road, are the foundations of a small Greek *Temple* (Pl. A) of the 4C B.C.; this was soon replaced by an open shrine in which a covered statue faced its altar across a pebble pavement.

Off the S. side of the Peribolos is an *Apse*, which has been cut into by the E. apse of the Peirene court. At an earlier level are scanty remains of a Doric hexastyle *Stoa* and, near the foot of the steps ascending to the Peirene court, some basins from the earliest water system of the Tyrants.

The *Fountain of Peirene, the lower one of that name, the upper fountain being on Acrocorinth, is a natural spring of immemorial antiquity, which has been so much elaborated and remodelled that it looks like an artificial fountain. The water is stored in four long reservoirs fed by a transverse supply tunnel. The reservoirs are hidden by a fountain-house, having a six-arched façade, "with chambers made like grottoes, from which the water flows into a basin in the open air" (Paus. II, 3, 3). This basin measures 30 ft by 20, and is sunk below the level of the court of the fountain.

Peirene "was a woman who was turned into a spring of water by the tears she shed in bewailing her son Kenchrias, whom Artemis had unwittingly killed" (Paus, II, 3, 2). The fountain-house has undergone several modifications. In front of the reservoirs are three deep draw-basins, immediately behind the six chambers of the arcade. Before the arcade was built, the front wall of the basins formed a parapet over which the water was originally drawn in jars. Then the clear space in front of the draw-basins was divided into the existing six chambers. Later (3C B.C.) Ionic columns were erected on the old parapet of the draw-basins, which ceased to be accessible. When Corinth was rebuilt by the Romans the old façade was masked by a new two-storied poros façade—the present series of stone arches. Their engaged Doric columns supported an architrave and a second story of engaged Ionic columns. This arrangement was continued at right angles to the façade and made to enclose a court 50 ft square. At the same time the open-air fountain was built in the courtyard. Towards the end of the 1C A.D. the walls of the court were lined with marble. In the 2C A.D. the court was remodelled (probably by Herodes Atticus) to the form which exists today with massive vaulted apses on three sides. About the same time the arched openings of the façade were narrowed so as to allow of blind arches between each of them, giving 11 arches instead of six. The front walls of the chambers were reinforced and the side walls decorated with paintings of fish swimming in dark blue water (best preserved in Chamber 4). Finally, in early Byzantine times a row of columns was built across the façade, and alterations were made to the court. An iron pipe now taps the fountain for the villagers' use.—Corinth was known in verse and to the Delphic oracle as "the city of Peirene". Euripides mentions its "august waters" ('Medea', 68).

At the end of the Lechaion Road, approached by a flight of three steps, followed by a landing and a larger staircase, rose the PROPYLAIA, the gateway to the Agora. Originally a long shallow building, in poros, with a large central arch and two smaller ones on each side, the portal was replaced in the 1C A.D. by a typical Roman triumphal arch in marble, surmounted in the time of Pausanias by two gilt bronze chariots bearing Helios and his son Phaethon. Little remains beyond the foundations of the later arch and a portion of the façade of the earlier one.

Beyond the Propylaia stretches the so-called **Agora,** more accurately the FORUM, since what we see is a Roman market-place. Its vast extent (c. 230 yds by 100) was determined by the existence of the South Stoa (comp. below). The Greek and Hellenistic agora is now being sought elsewhere since no earlier buildings of importance have been found below the area between the temple hill and the South Stoa. This seems to have been occupied by a race-course and various cult places. In a radical Roman replanning the former declivity was transformed into two unequal but more or less level terraces, the upper portion being c. 13 ft higher at the centre. The division between the two was marked at first by a terrace wall; later, shops were erected in front of this.

NORTH SIDE. Just to the w. of the Propylaia stood the *Captives' Façade*, an elaborate two-storied structure of Parian marble. The lower story consisted of Corinthian columns; the upper story had at least four Atlantes of barbarian captives (portions in the Museum). This constituted the final screen of the Basilica flanking the Lechaion road (comp. above), from which it was separated by an open court.

Adjoining is the *Triglyph Wall,* a low terrace wall decorated with a triglyph frieze, originally painted. It bore tripods and statues, and a surviving base of dark Eleusinian limestone has the signature of Lysippos. Of the two openings for stairways which divide the wall into three sections, one leads down to the *Sacred Spring* (closed by a grating; key with the custodian). The spring, which still has its two bronze lion's head spouts (5C B.C.), was originally in the open air, but was transformed into an underground chamber when the surrounding ground level was raised. It apparently ran dry and was unknown to the Romans, being covered by a later basin fed by a conduit. On the terrace to the N. of the Triglyph Wall, and connected with it by an elaborate tunnel, was a small *Oracular Shrine.* The tunnel, entered by a secret door disguised as a metope between the triglyphs, probably housed the 'oracle'—a priest who pronounced through a small hole below the floor of the shrine. The whole of this area was sacred and public access was forbidden; a minatory inscription has been found on its boundary (comp. below).

To the w. stood the colonnade of the 15 *North-West Shops* (3C A.D.). The large central shop, with its stone vault intact, forms the most conspicuous ruin of the Forum; the concrete vaults of the others have fallen. Behind, the *North-West Stoa*, in poros, over 300 ft long, earlier formed the N. boundary of the Forum. The front had Doric columns and the interior Ionic. The front stylobate is well preserved and many columns are still in position (3C B.C.).

On an isolated knoll above stands the **Temple of Apollo**, one of the oldest temples in Greece and the most conspicuous monument on the site. The temple, of the Doric order, had a peristyle of 38 columns (6 by 15). Seven adjacent columns remain standing, five on the w. front and two more on the s. side; the five that form the corner support part of their architrave. Four further columns lie where they fell; foundations remain of four others removed by the Turkish owner in 1830. The shafts are monoliths, 24 ft high and nearly 6 ft in diameter at the base, hewn of rough limestone. The lower side of the fallen columns shows the well-preserved Greek stucco and the thicker plaster of a Roman restoration. They have 20 flutes. Their flat archaic capitals are characteristic of the mid-6C B.C.

The naos had two unequal chambers separated by a wall, with a distyle portico in antis at either end. Two rows of interior columns supported the roof. The foundations of a statue base have been found in the w. chamber, near the partition-wall. In the s.w. corner of the Pronaos was found a rectangular strong-box lined with waterproof cement.—The precinct of the temple has been cleared, exposing slight remnants of an earlier temple (7C).

Below to the N., partly obscured by the modern road, lie the remains of the *North Market*, a rectangular peristyle surrounded by shops. Some mosaic pavements survive. The market was rebuilt and used in Byzantine times. At an earlier date a Greek *Bath-house* stood on the site. Extending to the w. was the long *North Stoa*; some of its coloured terracotta antefixes are in the museum. The gold necklace and hoard of 51 gold staters of Philip and Alexander the Great found here are at the National Archaeological Museum at Athens.

EAST SIDE. We return to the Propylaia and continue to the E. end of the Forum which is closed by the **Julian Basilica.** The well-preserved remains are of a crypto-porticus which formed the base of a Corinthian basilica of the Augustan period. Four imperial portrait statues were found here.

In front of the basilica the Roman pavement has been removed to expose an earlier Greek one. Parallel to the building and 10 ft in front of it is the starting-line of a *Race Course*, preserved in its entire length of 60 ft and having places for sixteen contestants. An earlier starting-line with a different orientation lies beneath it. To the s. is a curved retaining wall which may have supported a judges' grandstand. These remains may be connected with the Hellotia, a Corinthian festival mentioned in the 13th Olympian Ode of Pindar.

Near the corner of the basilica stands a *Circular Pedestal* with a truncated shaft. From this monument, whose function is unknown, a line of buildings extended w., dividing the lower from the upper forum. Its central feature was the **Bema,** a monumental rostrum upon which Roman officials appeared before the public. Since later a Christian church was built above its ruins, this may be the place where Gallio, the Roman governor, refused to act upon Jewish accusations against the Apostle Paul. To right and left of the rostrum extended rows of *Shops*, replaced in Christian times by a flight of steps running the whole length of the forum. In the centre of the lower forum are the foundations of an *Altar* and of an elevated *Grandstand*.

The UPPER FORUM was the administrative centre of the Roman province of Achaea. The *South-East Building* had a marble Ionic colonnade. It was rebuilt three times and may have been the Tabularium, or archive respository of the Roman colony.

Before reaching the South Stoa we cross the line of a low terrace wall below the level of the Roman pavement. Cuttings suggest that this supported over 100 monuments, all probably carried off to Rome during the century following the sack in 146 B.C. Pausanias mentions marble or bronze statues (reproductions perhaps) of Zeus, Athena, Aphrodite, Ephesian Artemis, Apollo, and Hermes, as well as gilded wooden statues of Dionysos with faces painted red. During the period of ruin a cart road passed diagonally across the forum (traces at the E. end of the wall).

The SOUTH SIDE of the forum is closed by the **South Stoa,** the largest classical secular building in Greece, dating originally from the 4C B.C. It had already been reconstructed before 146 B.C. Facing the forum was a double colonnade with 71 Doric columns in front and 34 Ionic columns in the middle. Some columns have been collected and restored to position. The rear of the building was transformed in Imperial times.

In its original form it was divided into a row of 33 shops, each giving on to another room behind. All but two of the front compartments had a well, supplied from the Peirene system. From the number of drinking cups recovered from the wells, it is conjectured that the 'shops' served chiefly as places of refreshment and the wells as refrigerators. A second floor, reached by stairs at either end, probably served as night quarters, and the stoa is believed to have been a huge hostelry built to house delegates to the Panhellenic Union which Philip of Macedon convened at Corinth. The building was restored in Julian times, but in the 1C A.D. most of the rear half was demolished to make way for administrative buildings; the colonnades remained. The Greek form is best observed at the W. end, where at one point Greek walls stand to a height of 9 ft; a section of the roof has been reconstructed from tiles found in the wells.

The Roman administrative buildings begin at the E. end with three halls, the third of which was probably the *Office of the Agonothetes,* who directed the Games at Isthmia. Here (beneath a shed) are preserved a mosaic of a victorious athlete standing before the goddess of good fortune (Eutychia), and the restored roof section (comp. above). Two further mosaics of Dionysiac scenes are preserved farther s. under another shelter. Continuing w. along the stoa we come to the presumed *Office of the Roman Governor,* with an antechamber, floors of marble veneer, and the base of a statue inscribed to a procurator of the Emp. Trajan. The next section of the stoa was turned into a forecourt, through which, by a marble stairway and porch, access was given to the *South Basilica.* This was similar to the Julian Basilica and, like it, once adorned with Imperial statues. To the w. is a beautiful marble *Fountain.* Through the centre of the stoa a paved *Road,* constructed c. A.D. 35, led s. towards Kenchreai. Beyond the road are the elliptical remains of the BOULEUTERION, or council chamber. Its curved stone benches have been replaced in position. Two adjacent shops retained their character in the Roman reconstruction; finds here included a well-preserved head of Serapis in gilded marble, a base inscribed with the full name of the Roman colony, and the remains of a cash-box with coins showing the place to have been destroyed by fire c. 267, perhaps in a Herulian raid. The square hall, to the w., perhaps the *Duovirs' Office,* was later encroached upon by a *Bath-House* (well preserved hypocaust).

From the N.W. corner of the stoa a Roman foundation wall extends at right angles to the building; on it stand archaic columns, taken possibly from the Temple of Apollo, across the top of which a water channel supplied a basin.

The WEST SIDE of the Forum was bounded by a row of *Shops.* An inscription on the entablature of the colonnade relates to a repair after an earthquake in A.D. 375. Set forward of the shops were six **Roman Temples** and a monument, all now so ruined as to mean little to the layman.

From excavation and the description of Pausanias these have been identified from s. to N. as a *Temple of Venus Fortuna* (Pl. F); the *Pantheon* (Pl. G); two

Temples, erected by Commodus, perhaps to *Hercules* (Pl. H) and to *Poseidon* (Pl. J.), the latter replacing the Poseidon fountain seen by Pausanias; the *Babbius Monument*, a rotunda on eight Corinthian columns, of which some members are set up at the side of its square concrete base; the *Temple* (?) *of Clarian Apollo* (Pl. K); and a *Temple of Hermes* (Pl. D).

On the way up to the museum we pass the foundations of *Temple E*, an early Imperial building of imposing proportions, possibly the Capitoleum or the Temple of Octavia. Parts of the entablature are displayed on the platform, which commands a good general view of the forum.

The **Museum,** endowed in 1931 by Ada Small Moore in memory of her father, a Philhellene of Chicago, was extended in 1950. Open winter daily 9–1 & 2.30–5; summer weekdays 8–1 & 3–6, Sun from 10.

In the ENTRANCE COURT: Part of a dolphin from the Fountain of Poseidon.—VESTIBULE. Small marble table (Roman); restored mosaic, Two griffins attacking a horse (c. 400 B.C., one of the earliest known Greek pebble mosaics); Head of Herodes Atticus.—Adjoining (l.) is the PRE-CLASSICAL ROOM, displaying Neolithic, Helladic, and Bronze Age finds from Nemea, Zygouries, and sites in the Isthmus of Corinth, including the only group of Mycenean fragments so far found in the city itself (just E. of the Julian Basilica).

To the right opens the GREEK GALLERY, arranged to show the rise of Corinth from a small settlement to an important manufacturing city-state. Archaic period: Sphinx of limestone (6C B.C.); inscribed stone from the sacred spring reading in archaic Corinthian letters "Sanctuary boundary; do not come down. Fine 8 drachmai"; perirrhanterion (stoup) from the 7C Temple of Poseidon at Isthmia; forepart of a horse (? part of a metope from the Temple of Apollo); small altars, Doric capital, etc., from the Potters' quarter.

The cases contain vases of local manufacture showing the progression of style from Protogeometric (case 8), through Geometric (9–11), to Protocorinthian (cases 12–13; 725–625 B.C.), known throughout the Mediterranean; the aryballos occurs frequently (fine example showing two warriors fighting). Cases 13–20. *Corinthian Pottery (624–550 B.C.) is at its best in the first 25 years, though exquisite late examples can be seen in the krater with a scene of Herakles and the Centaurs (Case 18) and the aryballos (Case 19) with Pyrrhias and his prize-winning choros. For contrast are displayed imported finds of Etruscan bucchero ware, etc.

Head of a fallen Amazon from a fragmentary terracotta group; painted Sphinx; bronze helmet of Corinthian type; Sarcophagus of the 5C B.C. containing the bones and grave furniture of a youth. Cases 21–25. Black-figured ware (550–450 B.C.) in imitation of the Attic style which was capturing all the markets compared with vases imported from Attica (kylix in Case 24 signed by Neandros). The black glaze did not adhere firmly to the local Corinthian clay. Cases 26–27. Imitative Red-figured pottery (500–350 B.C.); and Cases 27–29, 'Conventionalizing' Corinthian to the Roman conquest.

Centre cases: Case 30, misfired pottery; Case 31, Household objects, including an amphoriskos of coloured glass (6C B.C.); Case 32, Pottery of the 8C B.C. with incised inscriptions in the Greek alphabet; Cases 33–34, Figurines and moulds; Cases 35–45, Strigils, lamps, coins, sherds, etc.

Across the vestibule is the ROMAN AND POST-CLASSICAL GALLERY. Statues from the Julian Basilica, representing members of the Gens Julia, including (4) Augustus as Pontifex Maximus (c. A.D. 13); the head (7), thought to be Nero Julius Caesar, son of Germanicus (executed by Tiberius in A.D. 31), is a subtle portrait. Marble statue of Aphrodite. Three mosaics (2C A.D.) from a villa outside the N.W. wall. Roman copies of classical heads from the theatre, probably the Sappho of Silanion (10) and the Doryphoros of Polykleitos (11); also (14) of an Artemis of the 5C, of a Tyche (16), and of an athlete (after Myron or Kalamis). Fragment of a large relief of dancing Maenads (neo-Attic, 1C A.D.). Head of Dionysos (after Praxiteles). Colossal figures from the 'Captives' Façade'. Fragmentary sarcophagus of Hadrian's day with reliefs of the departure of the Seven against Thebes and the death of Opheltes. Heads of Antoninus Pius (33), Caracalla (34) as a youth of eighteen, 35. Woman with her hair in braids. *43. Head, a rare example of its period (4C A.D.). 44–46. Marble statues of emperors or governors (6C A.D.), the third recut from an earlier work. Medieval and modern coins, including a hoard of 30 Byzantine gold pieces. Bronze weight in the likeness of the Emp. Constantine. Bottle of blue glass with painted birds imported from Egypt, used perhaps as a model in the glass factory which flourished in Corinth in the 11C A.D. Sgraffito and incised pottery of the 12C and 'Protomajolica' ware (finds so far paralleled only at Athlit in the Holy Land).

In the CLOISTER. Frieze reliefs from the Theatre (Hadrianic rebuilding), representing the Labours of Herakles and a Gigantomachia; Enyo, goddess of war, seated on a later base inscribed to Regilla (probably the wife of Herodes Atticus); Byzantine decorative carvings; inscription reading Συναγωγή 'Εβραίων (Jewish synagogue; 3C A.D. or later), and a Head of Coptic type, perhaps of Egyptian sandstone and imported in the 4C or 5C A.D.—The *Asklepieion Room* (opened on request) contains finds from the Asklepieion, the site of which (to the N.; comp. below) may be seen from the window. They include typical ex-votos, early Christian gravestones, and a cache of silver and weapons of the early 19C.

As we quit the excavations, we see (r.) a cubic mass of rock, in which are hewn the four large reservoirs that formed the *Fountain of Glauke*, a construction similar to the Peirene fountain (see above). Pausanias (II, 3, 6) attributes its name to Glauke, Jason's second wife, who is supposed to have flung herself into it to obtain relief from the poisoned robe sent her as a wedding-present by Medea. Roman alterations, the decay of the roof in medieval times, and the earthquake of 1928 have all but obliterated its porticoed façade and three drawbasins. The reservoir, which was fed by a small conduit from the base of Acrocorinth, had a storage capacity of 14,000 gallons.—Adjoining the fountain to the E. is a colonnaded precinct, the entrance to which faced the Sikyon road. Within the court stood a somewhat earlier temple (C), perhaps the *Temple of Hera Akraia*, though not (needless to say) that on whose altar the citizens of Corinth slew the children of Medea.

Outside the W. exit across the road lie the remains of two theatres. The **Odeion**, a Roman construction cut largely from the rock, resembles in plan that at Pompeii. It held c. 3000 spectators. Built towards the end of the 1C A.D., it was reconstructed (c. 175) by Herodes Atticus; the interior was totally destroyed by fire and after A.D. 225 was again restored as an arena or beast-pit by cutting away the lowest rows of seats. Even after a further destruction in 375 by earthquake, the building was patched up to serve until Alaric's holocaust. Adjacent to the N. is the **Theatre**, with a similar but even longer history. Founded in the 5C B.C., it ended by presenting naumachiae. Here the multitude acclaimed Aratos of Sikyon after his nocturnal capture of Acrocorinth (243 B.C.). The *Cavea* of the Greek period is well preserved because the Romans filled it in with earth to produce a steeper rake before rebuilding the seating; the central portion has been excavated. When it was dug out in 1925–29 wall-paintings of gladiatorial scenes were found on the late-Roman barrier round the arena; they have since perished. An

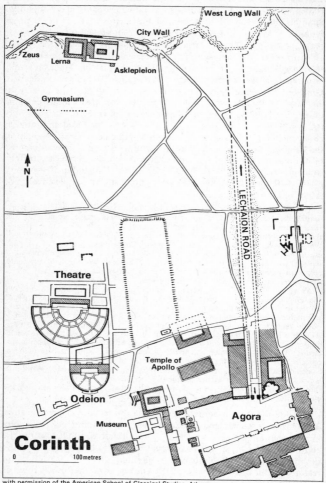

with permission of the American School of Classical Studies, Athens.

inscription, scratched in the plaster, was also found recording the story of Androcles and the lion. In the *Orchestra* several levels of pavement can be distinguished.

To the E. of the stage buildings is a paved square. An inscription on a paving block records that Erastus laid the pavement at his own expense in return for the aedileship. This is probably the Erastus known to St Paul (Romans, xvi, 23).

About ¼ m. N. of the theatre are the remains of the **Asklepieion**, which stood at the edge of the bluff just within the city wall (cars may get close by taking the road which runs immediately below the Xenia Hotel). Rock cuttings show that a small prostyle tetrastyle Doric *Temple* of the 4C B.C. stood in the centre of a colonnaded court. Except on the N. side the spaces within the colonnades are too narrow to have been an ambulatory and probably sheltered the dedications of the cured. Many ex-votos are now in the museum. Near the entrance to the precinct is a stone offertory box in which copper coins were found. Behind and below the w. wall of the sanctuary lies the health centre itself, arranged round a lower court. Off the E. side of its peristyle are three rooms, of which that to the s. preserves its stone benches; they were probably dining rooms. Over them was a great hall, which closed the w. end of the upper court. The s. and w. walks of the peristyle are given access to draw-basins of the FOUNTAIN OF LERNA, fed by four large reservoirs which extend s. into the rock.—Another copious supply of water, 200 yds E., is known as the *Baths of Aphrodite*. Here a Turkish staircase and some fortifications date from the late 17C. (These sites are all individually fenced by barbed wire; however a reasonable view can still be obtained.)

A road leads w. between the Odeion and the Theatre to the site of a *Roman Villa* (1¼ m.), discovered in 1925 and protected by a shelter (key at the Museum). Some of the mosaics from its five rooms have been removed to the museum. More important are the excavations (15 min. on foot farther s.w.) in the KERAMEIKOS, or *Potters' Quarter*, on the w. edge of the plateau. Remains of workshops and store-rooms of the 7–4C lie inside the Archaic city wall (? 7C). Through them run the massive foundations of the Classical *Fortifications*. The later wall with remnants of towers and gates may be traced to the gates of Acrocorinth (see below).

To the E. of the village are some vestiges of an *Amphitheatre* of the 3C A.D., of the *Isthmian Gate*, and of an early Christian *Basilica*, with a martyrium, that existed in various forms from the 5C to Frankish times. This lay just within the *Kenchreai Gate*, whence sections of city wall can be traced.

To the s. of the village, just below the road to Acrocorinth and on its lower slopes, can be seen a *Sanctuary of Demeter*, excavated since 1968 by the American School. The sanctuary dates back to the 7C B.C., and among the finds has been a marble head of the 2C from a cult statue of the goddess.

B Acrocorinth

APPROACH. A motor road mounts from the Museum to the gate, where there is a Tourist Pavilion. On foot the visit requires at least 3 hrs. From the Museum a track leads due s. to a cluster of houses below the *Fountain of Hadji Mustapha*; thence a path winds up to the right round the w. face of the mountain to (1 hr) the outer gate. Adm. free; same hours as main site.

*****Acrocorinth** ('Ακροκόρινθος), the Acropolis of Corinth, the limestone mountain (1885 ft) which rises precipitously to the s. of ancient Corinth, is among the strongest natural fortresses in Europe. The citadel was the goal of all who aspired to the domination of the Peloponnese and it changed hands many times. The summit is enclosed by a wall not less than 1½ m. in circumference and the only approach is defended by a triple line of fortification. To this construction Byzantines, Franks, Venetians, and Turks contributed; but their walls and towers stand mainly on ancient foundations.

In the Frankish invasion Acrocorinth was besieged by William de Champlitte for 3 years (1205–08); its defender, Leo Sgouros, flung himself to his death in 1208, but the citadel continued to resist Geoffrey de Villehardouin and Otho de la Roche until 1210, when Theodore Angelos fled to Argos with the church treasure of Corinth.

We cross a dry moat, once spanned by a drawbridge, to the first of the three gateways which are connected by ramps. The *Outer Gate* is largely Turkish, while the *Middle Gate* is a Venetian rebuilding of a Frankish structure; vestiges of ancient walls can be seen. The *Inner Gate* is flanked by massive square towers, that to the right little altered since the 4C B.C. The gateway incorporates reused Byzantine columns and had a portcullis worked from an upper room. Students of military architecture will not miss the well-preserved *Fortifications* to the N. or the Frankish *Inner Keep* to the right above the gates. Visitors pressed for time may prefer to take the path across more gently rising ground amid an overgrown jumble of ruined Turkish houses, Byzantine chapels, and brick-vaulted cisterns, to the s. circuit wall of the citadel. Here, near ruined Turkish barracks at the s.E. corner, is the UPPER PEIRENE SPRING. The subterranean well-house is covered by a vaulted roof of Hellenistic date (protected above by modern concrete). A stairway leads down to a pedimented entrance screen and continues below water level. The water, which is clear and cold (but *not* safe for drinking), is 12–14 ft deep and has never been known to retreat beyond the screen. The higher of the two summits of Acrocorinth, due N. of Peirene, bore in turn a *Temple of Aphrodite*, a small basilican church, a watch tower, a cloistered mosque, and a paved Venetian belvedere. The worship of Aphrodite, the Syrian Astarte, was accompanied by religious prostitution, and the temple is said to have been served by a thousand sacred courtesans. Little remains now but the *View, one of the finest in all Greece. It was described by Strabo and extends on a clear day from Aegina and the Parthenon in the E. almost to Navpaktos in the w., embracing most of the Saronic Gulf and the whole of the Gulf of Corinth.

The N. horizon is bounded, from E. to w., by Salamis, the hills of Megara, Kithairon, and Yeraneia. The Perachora peninsula is prominent in the foreground, then the distant peaks of Helikon, Parnassos, Ghiona, and the mountains of Aetolia. On the s. side of the Gulf, Killini blocks a more distant prospect to the w.; farther s.w. the sharp point of Artemision is conspicuous; to the s. Mycenae is hidden amid the ranges of Argolis. The tiny Frankish castle of *Pendeskouphi* (Mont-Escorée: bare mountain) boldly crowns the nearest precipitous height of Kastraki.

C   Isthmia and Kenchreai

ROAD, diverging (r.) from the main road to Athens c. halfway between New Corinth and the Canal bridge; coming from Athens the *second* turning (l.) after the canal.—4½ m. *Isthmia.*—7½ m. *Kenchreai.*

The *Ancient Road* ran E. from the agora to Examilia, where it divided, the left branch making directly for Isthmia while the right branch led to Kenchreai.

From New Corinth we follow the Athens road, join the main highway, then fork r. for *Kriás Vrísi*, passing considerable traces of the **Isthmian Wall**, which extends for c. 6 m. across the narrowest part of the Isthmus. The fortification which follows a natural line of low cliffs, can be traced for practically its whole length. The best preserved section is that immediately E. of the Isthmian Sanctuary (see below), where the wall is 23 ft high and 8 ft thick. Most of the visible remains date only from the time of Justinian though a wall is recorded by Herodotus.

We pass through the village to the Isthmian Sanctuary which stands (l.) on a natural terrace between the village and the Isthmian wall.

The **Sanctuary of Poseidon at Isthmia**, one of the four Panhellenic sanctuaries celebrated in the Odes of Pindar, was famous for its games. Like those of Olympia, Nemea, and Delphi, the games appear originally to have honoured the funeral of a particular hero.

Tradition tells of Melikertes, the Phoenician Melkarth, son of Athamos and Ino. When his mother leapt with him into the sea from the Molurian Rock (Rte 24), the drowned boy was landed on the Isthmus by a dolphin. Corinth was undergoing a famine and an oracle declared that this would stop only when the Corin-

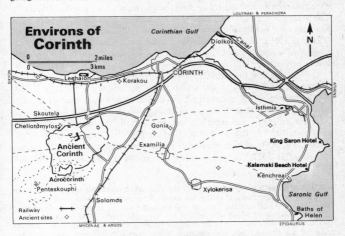

thians gave the boy fitting burial and honoured him with funeral games. His name was changed to Palaimon and the Isthmian Games instituted in his honour. The oracle later declared that, to prevent the famine returning, the games must be perpetual.

It would appear, disregarding legend, which ascribes their foundation to Poseidon, the Sun, or Sisyphos, and Attic tradition, which gives the honour to Theseus, that the games were instituted about the time of Periander, the date of the first Isthmiad usually being given as 582 B.C. They were held in the 2nd and 4th year of each Olympiad. Their organization was in the hands of Corinth until its destruction in 146 B.C., when it passed to Sikyon; the venue of the games may even have been transferred. They reverted to Corinth after the refoundation of the city by Julius Caesar. The Athenians originally had the place of honour while the Eleans were excluded. In 288 B.C. the Romans were allowed to compete. The athletic contests were second only to those at Olympia, which they resembled.

At the games of 336 B.C. Alexander the Great was nominated leader of the Greeks against Persia; at the games of 196 B.C. Flaminius declared the independence of Greece; and here in A.D. 67 the second proclamation of independence was made by Nero. Scientific excavation of the site was begun in 1952 by the University of Chicago under Oscar Broneer.

By the road, at the top of a rise, stands the MUSEUM (adm. 10 dr.; standard hours), so well supplied with explanatory plans and photographs that it is best visited first. The first section is devoted to Isthmia itself: panathenaic amphorae; athletic equipment including haltares (jumping weights); two perirrhanteria (restored); tiles and paintings from the archaic temple (7 × 19 columns). Beyond are finds from Kenchreai, notably panels in opus sectile (glass mosaic) depicting a harbour town (these were found packed in crates and may have been imported from Egypt; they were damaged in an ancient earthquake); wooden doors; sculptured ivory plaques with male seated figures.

The site entrance, just beyond the museum, leads directly to the square foundation in opus incertum of the Roman *Palaimonion*. The temple had a circular open colonnade of eight columns, which is depicted on local coinage of the Antonine period. It is built over an early underground water-conduit, which tradition evidently took to be the tomb of Palaimon. Alongside, beneath the South Stoa, has been laid bare the open end of the *Older Stadium* (perhaps abandoned in 390 B.C.). The triangular pavement, scored with radiating grooves, is part of a *Starting Gate* for sixteen runners of the kind alluded to by Aristophanes (Knights 1159). A starter, standing in the pit, operated traps (balbides) hinged to wooden posts, by means of cords which ran in the grooves under bronze staples.

On level ground immediately to the N. are the remains of the TEMPLE OF POSEIDON, a 5C Doric edifice which had a peristyle of 6 columns by 13. In the words of its excavator "the casual visitor will marvel chiefly, perhaps, at the thoroughness of its destruction" (O. Broneer). An Archaic temple on the same site had been totally destroyed by fire. Another mysterious fire in 394 B.C. damaged the later building (Xen. 'Hell.', IV, v, 4), which was afterwards re-roofed. A colossal statue, unearthed in 1952, formed part of a cult group of Poseidon and Amphitrite.

The sanctuary became derelict after the sack of Corinth and traces of a wagon road can be seen passing across its altar. Reorganization was undertaken by Tiberius. In the 2C A.D. the *Temenos* was extended and the temple area surrounded by stoas, the cost of which was defrayed by the high priest, P. Licinius Priscus.

The *Theatre* was situated in an artificial hollow, now a ploughed field, midway between the precinct and the Isthmian Wall. Virtually nothing remains of the building originally constructed in the early 4C B.C. and several times modified. Its roof tiles are stamped with the name of Poseidon or with a dolphin and trident. Here Nero delivered his speech of liberation.

At present visible only from the fence are the remains of a huge Roman *Baths*, in which excavations since 1975 have uncovered the Great Hall with a superb mosaïc floor, an elaborate hypocaust, and traces of an earlier pool.

On the opposite side of the road, in an obvious gully to the S.E. of the Sanctuary is the *Later Stadium*, larger than the first and orientated at roughly right angles to it. It was in use from c. 390 until 146 B.C. The starting line at the open end was discovered in 1960. On the slope beyond the stadium are traces of a *Cyclopean Wall* of the end of the Mycenean period. This may have been merely the retaining wall of a road.

A prominent feature of the area is a BYZANTINE FORTRESS, constructed of materials pillaged from the sanctuary by Victorinus, a general of Justinian. This irregular enclosure abutting the Peloponnesian side of the wall was taken by early excavators to be the peribolos of the Sanctuary itself. Its identity was established by a British examination in 1933; and full excavation has been undertaken by the Univ. of California since 1967. The South Gate and two adjacent towers have been cleared, and the junctions of the fortress with the Isthmian Wall investigated.

The road continues past by-roads (l.) to the modern hamlet called *Isthmia* (King Saron, 150 R, **A**; Motel Isthmia **B**) at the E. end of the canal. This is served by a minor road direct from the canal bridge. Round a headland (3 m. farther on) lies **Kenchreai.** Here the ancient s.

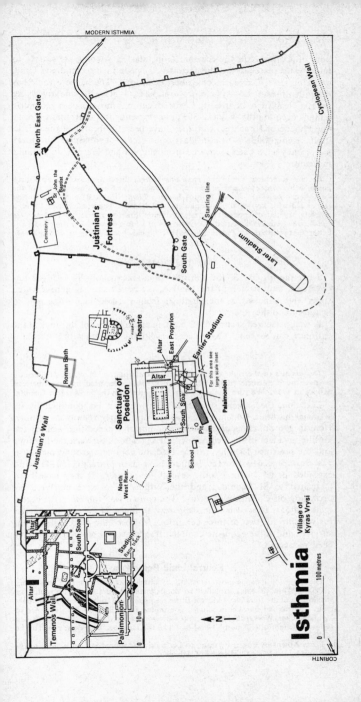

MODERN ISTHMIA

North East Gate

Cyclopean Wall

St John the Baptist

Cemetery

Justinian's Fortress

South Gate

Starting line

Later Stadium

Theatre

Roman Bath

Altar

East Propylon

Earlier Stadium

Altar

Sanctuary of Poseidon

South Stoa

Palaimonion

For this area see large scale inset

Justinian's Wall

West water works

Pit

Museum

North West Resr.

School

Altar

South Stoa

Temenos Wall

Stadium Race Track

Palaimonion

Altar

Isthmia

Village of Kyras Vrysi

CORINTH

N

0   100 metres

10 m

port of Corinth, on the Saronic Gulf, started yielding its secrets to underwater searches and the excavator's spade in 1963 (Indiana Univ. and Univ. of Chicago, under Robert Scranton). The harbour mole has been identified, with a system of warehouses (1–5C A.D.), and, overlying the road leading to it, an early Christian church; mosaics with geometric designs decorate the w. end. St Paul commends to the Romans (16, 1) one Phoebe of Kenchreai who may have been the bearer of the epistle itself. Remarkable panels in glass opus sectile depicting architectural panoramas have been recovered from the sea and are now in Isthmia museum.

Beyond Kenchreai a fine new road providing a direct approach to Epidauros passes below *Stanotopi*, the E. spur of Mt Oneion, with remains of a fort of the 4–3C B.C.—At (8 m. from Corinth) *Loutrón Elénis* (Politi B) a hot sea spring (Helen's Bath), known to Pausanias, is still in use. The road passes through sparsely populated wooded country with views down to the sea. At 20 m. *Nea Epidhavros* (Rte 29) is skirted.—Beyond (24 m.) *Moní Taxiarkhon Agnoundas* the better of two roads to Palaia Epidhavros branches left.—30¼ m. *Ligourió*, see Rte 29.

D The Diolkos

Near the w. end of the Corinth Canal excavations in 1956–62 uncovered a long stretch of the **Diolkos,** the paved slipway across which ships were winched in ancient times from Poseidonia on one gulf to Schoinous on the other.

A well-preserved section (?6C B.C.), including traces of the dock at the entrance, can be seen (l.) by the car ferry linking Corinth with Loutraki.

E Lechaion

The site lies to the right of the Corinth–Patras road, c. 2¼ m. w. of Corinth beyond the prehistoric (E.H.) hill site of *Korakou* excavated by the American School in 1916. We turn right just beyond the turning (l.) for Ancient Corinth.

Lechaion, the ancient N. port of Corinth, can be identified by its artificial harbour, which, though silted up, clearly retains its outline. Here in 396 Stilichon disembarked his punitive expedition against the Gothic invaders of the Peloponnese. Excavations between the harbour and the sea since 1956 have uncovered the complete ground plan of a vast *Basilica*, c. 610 ft by 150, built in the reign of Marcian (450–457) and extended under Justin I some seventy years later. It may have been dedicated to St Leonidas and the Virgins, who were martyred by drowning off Corinth by Decius. The church was ruined in the earthquake of 551, after which the *Baptistery*, to the N. of the narthex, served for worship for two or three centuries. Much of the marble pavement survives and some exquisite fragments of coloured glass have been recovered.

F Loutraki and Perachora

The excursion is made most pleasantly by hired BOAT from Corinth or Sikyon. ROAD, 20½ m. (33 km.), asphalted to Vouliagmene and practicable for motors to within ¼ m. of the *Heraion*.—MOTOR-BUSES frequently to Loutraki, every two hours from Loutraki to Perakhora village, continuing twice daily in high summer to Vouliagmene. Walkers from Loutraki who are willing to swim a few yards can follow a delightful cliff path (3 hrs) direct to the Heraion, keeping seaward of the lake.

From Athens by bus or by train, to Loutraki; occasional Sun excursions to the Heraion by the Periyitiki Leskhe of Athens.

From Corinth we take the Athens road, cross the Canal, and beyond the bridge turn left to (6 m.) **Loutráki** (ΛΟΥΤΡΑΚΙΟΝ; *Apollo*, 275R., *Theoxenia*, *Park*, *Palace*, all **A**; *Marinos*, *Marion*, *Paolo*, *Kondis*, **B**; *Isthmia*, *Possidonion* **C**, these open all year; many others summer only), one of the principal watering-places in Greece, situated at the E. end of the Bay of Corinth and sheltered by the towering Yerania Mts. Like its ancient predecessor *Therma*, the town (5800 inhab.) takes name from the hot springs that issue from the mountainside only a few yards from the sea. Their saline waters (30–31° C.) are used both internally and externally in cases of dyspepsia, arthritis, and liver complaints. The sea-front is attractively laid out with eucalyptus and exotic shrubs.

A long steep climb to the N.W. rises above (7½ m.) *Village Pallas*, a chalet hotel on the shore, with splendid views over the Bay of Corinth. We pass below a monastery and reach a small plain about 1000 ft above the sea, dominated to the N. by a sheer crag.—14 m. *Perakhora* (Anessis, small, **D**) is the village centre (1490 inhab.). From the little museum, a road leads w. through olives, then descends a valley to the Fishing Club (spring) at the N.E. corner of *Lake Vouliagmene*, the ancient *Eschatiotis*, separated from the sea by a narrow spit through which a channel was cut c. 1880. Skirting the N. shore of the lake, we come to a group of tavernas, to the right of which, fed by a catch-pit, is a well-preserved *Cistern* (? 4C B.C.), still in use. Larger cisterns near by, with staircases descending 100 ft into the ground, are more difficult of access. Ancient **Perachora** occupied the greater part of the narrowing *Peninsula to the w. This was anciently called *Peraion* or Πέρα Χώρα, 'the country beyond the sea' (as seen from Corinth), and commands, as even Acrocorinth does not, the entire Gulf. All round jagged rocks tumble towards the sea, save where a valley descends to the sheltered cove which attracted the mariners of the ancient world. The *View extends to the heights behind Naupaktos, 65 m. away, where a bend in the straits gives to the gulf the appearance of a huge lake ringed by mountains. Predominant to the N. are Helikon and Parnassos; to the s., Killini.

History. Only slight traces of occupation have been found from the Middle Helladic and Mycenean periods, at which time, according to Plutarch, Perachora belonged to Megara. In the Geometric period, presumably under Argive influence, a Heraion was founded, but the site flourished as a Corinthian town mainly in the Archaic and Classical periods when Corinth, as an independent city state, dared not allow it to fall into other hands. In the Corinthian War of 391–390 B.C. Agesilaos of Sparta captured the place; Xenophon, who served on the Spartan side, describes the brief campaign ('Hell.', iv, 5). Save for shepherds, the site has been deserted since Roman times, but its remains have suffered from stone robbers from the opposite coast. Perachora was excavated in 1930–33 by Humfry Payne and the British School.

A track winds up to a small plateau from which a path reaches the *Lighthouse*. Polygonal and ashlar retaining walls suggest that there was a fortified acropolis. A second path descends a valley to the little *Harbour*, above which stands the modern chapel of Ayios Ioannis, moved in 1933. In the valley lie the remains of the HERAION, or *Temenos of Hera Limenia*. Foundations are preserved of a *Temple* of the mid-8C B.C., from which came most of the objects now displayed in the National Archaeological Museum, Athens. The prominent cistern, with apsidal ends, farther down, is of Hellenistic date. Grouped round the harbour cove are an L-shaped *Stoa* (4C), an Archaic altar, the foundations of a

Geometric *Temple of Hera Akraia*, and of the narrow 6C *Temple* that replaced it. Beyond this is the small *Agora*.

Bathers from the cove should not venture beyond its mouth (danger of currents and sharks).

26 FROM CORINTH TO MYCENAE, ARGOS, AND NAUPLIA

ROAD, 37¼ m. (60 km.). 11 m. *Khiliomódhion.*—18 m. By-road for **Nemea.**—24½ m. By-road for **Mycenae.**—30 m. **Argos.**—33½ m. **Tiryns.**—37¼ m. **Nauplia.** The former level crossings are being replaced by bridges and the road improved. This route is served by the Athens–Nauplia BUSES, and as far as Argos by other Athens–Peloponnese services; from Corinth to Nauplia in 1½ hr, every 90 min.; frequent local service between Argos and Nauplia.

RAILWAY, S.P.A.P., 6 times daily to *Argos*, 33 m. (53 km.), in 1–1½ hr; through trains from Athens. To *Mycenae*, 27 m. (43 km.), in 50–60 min.

This route traverses the nome of **Argolis**, the easternmost of the divisions of the Peloponnese. Bordered on the N. by Korinthia and on the W. by the mountains of Arcadia, it consists of the Argolic plain (see below) and a mountainous peninsula, the fourth and least conspicuous tongue of the Peloponnese, which separates the Gulf of Nauplia (the ancient Argolic Gulf) from the Saronic Gulf. The modern province corresponds roughly to the ancient Argolid, shorn of the islands off its E. coast (Poros, Hydra, and Spetsai), which nowadays fall under the administration of Attica. The modern capital is Nauplia which provides the most comfortable and convenient centre for exploration. The region is of the highest archaeological importance, including within its borders Mycenae, Tiryns, Argos, and Epidauros as well as many other important (though less visited) sites, both Classical and Mycenean.

From modern Corinth the Argos road runs s.w. through vineyards. On our right rises Acrocorinth. Both road and railway climb the wooded valley between the *Oneia* hills (1847 ft; l.) and *Mt Skiona* (2300 ft).—8 m. *Athikia Station*; in the village, 2½ m. s.E., was found the Apollo of Tenea, now in Munich.—At (11 m.) *Khiliomódhion* (1400 inhab.) a bad road branches left to the *Pass of Ayiónori* (5 m.) with a medieval castle repaired by Morosini. By this road Dramali succeeded in fighting his way out of the plain of Argolis, at the cost of a further 1000 men, two days after his defeat at Dervenaki (see below). The scanty remains of *Tenea* lie near this road at Klénia 1 m. s. of Khiliomódhi.

The inhabitants of Tenea claimed to be Trojans brought captive by the Greeks from Tenedos. Oedipus, who had been exposed as a child by his father, was here brought up by the shepherd Polybos. The town sent out most of the colonists of Syracuse. It sided with Rome in 146 B.C. and so escaped the destruction of Corinth. A man from Asia, contemplating a move to Corinth, asked the oracle's advice, and received the unexpected reply, "Blest is Corinth, but Tenea for me."

The road passes N. of (15½ m.) *Ayios Vasilios*. Above the village (1 m. l.) are the remains of a medieval castle; and a little to the E., off the road to Klénia (comp. above; signposted), the low hill of *Zygouries*, an Early Helladic settlement excavated in 1921–22 by the American School. —To the N.w. is seen the truncated top of *Mt Fokas*, the ancient *Apesas* (2861 ft). We now enter the territory of *Kleonai* the ruins of which lie 2 m. N.w.

'Well-built' *Kleonai* (Iliad, II, 570) was 80 furlongs from Corinth on the prehistoric road over the hills to Argos. Its site (well-fortified, as Strabo remarks) occupies an isolated hill overlooking the valley of the Longos. Off a by-road (r.) a track, initially signposted, leads in the general direction. Ploughed-out blocks and washed-down sherds cover a wide cultivated area, but interpreting what may be found is a matter for experts.

The road becomes increasingly shut in by hills as it reaches its summit-level (1285 ft) near (18¾ m.) *Nemea–Dervenakia Station*. Immediately after we cross the track, a branch road doubles back (l.) to (c. 1 m.) a chapel in a grove beside a spring. Above stands a colossal statue of Kolokotronis, victor in the battle of 1822 (comp. below).

At 19½ m. a road diverges (r.) to modern *Nemea* (6 m.), formerly *Ayios Yeoryios*, situated at the s. end of Trikaranon (2385 ft). Here (1½ m. s.) is the monastery of Vrakhos (1633). The site of ancient **Nemea** is at *Heraklion*, a village only 2½ m. along this road. It lies on a lonely little plateau (1194 ft), 2½ m. long and ¾ m. wide, watered by the river Nemea (or Koutsommati), which flows into the Gulf of Corinth. The valley of Nemea is celebrated for its red wine. Like Olympia, Nemea was a sacred precinct and not a city, though Strabo speaks of the village of Bembina as being close by. Here Herakles slew the Nemean lion. In the long vanished cypress grove surrounding the Temple of Zeus were celebrated biennially the NEMEAN GAMES, one of the four great Pan-hellenic festivals.

According to one legend the Games were instituted by Herakles after he had slain the Nemean lion. They were managed by the people of Kleonai. Kleonai became subject for a short time to Kleisthenes of Sikyon, but with the help of Argos threw off the yoke. In commemoration Argos reinstituted the games in 573, attributing their foundation to their own hero, Adrastus, slayer of the dragon that killed Opheltes. Excavation has suggested there was no occupation between Mycenean times and the 6C.

The French School studied the temple in 1885 and 1912; the site was partly excavated by the American School in 1924–27 and published after further investigation in 1964, but excavations continue. Plastic sheets protecting fragile finds were much in evidence in 1979.

The STADIUM is well seen to the left from the approach road just after the first sight of the temple is obtained. Of embanked earth, it occupies a partly natural hollow. The starting line is in situ and a stone water channel surrounds the course. Foundations of a judges' stand and distance markers are visible. The *Entrance Tunnel* (c. 320 B.C.) has graffiti (boys' names) written by admirers.

The TEMPLE OF NEMEAN ZEUS, a Doric peripteral hexastyle (6 columns by 13), was built between 340 and 320 B.C. of locally quarried stone, on the site of an earlier sanctuary. Its columns are unusually slender; three remain standing, one from the peristyle and two from the pronaos which still support their architrave. The drums of many other columns lie in order as they have fallen, probably as the result of earthquakes in the 4C A.D.; but the roof had already fallen before Pausanias saw it. The lowest course of the cella is sufficiently well preserved to show that it had a pronaos in antis but no opisthodomos. Within the cella fourteen columns enclosed the central space, while to the w., between the colonnade and the wall, and below the floor level, is an *Adyton*, or secret inner chamber, approached by a flight of crude steps.—Parallel to the façade are the foundations of a long narrow *Altar* of unusual type.

To the s.e. of the temple stood a row of nine *Oikoi*, or treasuries, seen by their foundations to be about twice the size of those at Olympia.

Parallel and farther s. is a *Palaestra*, with its *Baths*, protected by a shelter in 1925 but still often waterlogged. Beyond (l.) extends a rectangular edifice, whose central wall, reconstructed in Roman times, preserves a reused pedestal bearing a dedicatory inscription of Aristis, son of Pheidon of Kleonai, who four times won the pankration in the Nemean games. The building, which had five separate entrances from a roadway, is believed to have been a *Xenon* (or hostel). Overlying its middle section is a large Christian *Basilica* (6–8C?) constructed in great blocks taken from the temple, and refloored in terracotta in the 12C. The screen and sanctuary floor are of limestone blocks from a monument of the 4C B.C. The apse and narthex can be traced, and, on the N. side, a baptistery with a large font. The mound which covered these remains had earlier been conjectured to cover the 'Tomb of Opheltes'.

On the hill of *Tsoungiza*, immediately w. of the village, a Helladic settlement has been identified. On the s. slope of this hill a natural cavern, which the locals would accept as the lair of the Nemean lion, yielded much Neolithic material.

From modern Nemea (comp. above) a road continues w. in the triangular plain of *Phliasia* (1000 ft). The site of *Phlious* (r.) is well marked by a small chapel (Panayia Rakhiotissa) on a ridge, round which are scattered the somewhat indeterminate remains, re-examined in 1970 and 1972 by the American School. They include a theatre and a square colonnaded court. The road goes on over two ridges to (20 m.) *Stymphalos* (Rte 38).

The Argos road turns s. into the *Pass of Dervenaki* (Δερβενάκια), the ancient 'Pass of the Tretos', between the twin summits of *Mt Tretos*, the 'perforated' mountain (τρητός), so called because it is honeycombed with caves. Road and railway descend the rocky defile. Near by, on 6 Aug 1822, Kolokotronis caught the army of Dramali, which was retreating from the plain of Argolis. The Turks left 4000 men dead on the field, and though a few cavalry fought their way through to Corinth, Dramali and the remainder retreated to try an alternative route (comp. above). From the s. outlet of the pass we look into the plain of Argos.

The view is generally limited by haze. To the left the bare summits of *Márta*, (2661 ft), *Ayios Ilías* (2460 ft), and *Zára* (1969 ft) overshadow the acropolis of Mycenae. On the right Argos sprawls below its mountain citadel while the E. Arcadian mountains rise behind, *Artemision* reaching 5815 ft, and *Ktenia* 5246 ft. In the centre, beyond the ruins of Tiryns, the battlemented acropolis of Acronauplia rises for a moment above the blue line of the Argolic Gulf.

Near (24 m.) *Fikhtia* are the remains of two ancient watchtowers. Just beyond (l.) are the turning for **Mycenae** (2½ m.; Rte 27) and *Mycenae Station*. The road runs down the middle of the Argolic Plain.

The ARGOLIC PLAIN takes the form of a triangle which extends from a base of c. 12 m. on the Argolic Gulf to an apex at Mt Tretos; to the E. and w. it is hedged in by barren mountains. The plain is watered by the capricious *Panítsa* (the ancient *Inachos*), the *Xerias* (Charadros), and other seasonal streams, their dryness being anciently attributed to the anger of Poseidon because Inachos allotted the country to Hera. Hence Argos is 'very thirsty' in Homer (πολυ-δίψιον Ἄργος). Close to the sea, however, the land is marshy, and between the marshes and the upper part of the plain is the fertile tract of land which was famed for the horses bred in its pastures (Ἄργος ἱππόβοτον, 'Iliad', II, 287; 'aptum equis', Horace, 'Odes', I, 7, 9).

27 m. *Koutsopódhi* lies amid olive-groves, vineyards, and cotton and tobacco fields. We cross the Panítsa and the wide bed of the Xerias.

30 m. (48 km.) **ARGOS** (ΑΡΓΟΣ; *Mikinai*, good, *Telessila*, both **C**), the seat of an eparch, is a prosperous but unexciting town of 18,900 inhab. situated in the centre of the Argolic plain just w. of the Xerias and 5 m. from the sea. Local industries include cattle-breeding and tobacco growing. The modern town occupies the site of the ancient city, at the foot of its two citadels ("duas arces habent Argi", *Livy*). The ancient importance of Argos is reflected in the fact that in Homer 'Argive', like 'Danaan' and 'Achaean', is a synonym for 'Greek'.

Argos is generally ignored by tourists, but if the antiquities are of somewhat specialized interest, the museum is a model of modern display.

History. *Argos*, which traditionally traced its foundation to Pelasgians from another Argos in the north, was occupied from the early Bronze Age. Hither the mythical Danaos fled from his brother Aegyptos. Adrastus of Argos, who led the Seven against Thebes to restore his son-in-law Polyneices to his throne, was the sole survivor of that disastrous expedition. Diomedes, successor of Adrastus and next to Achilles the bravest hero in the Greek army, led the Argive contingent in the Trojan War.

After the Dorian invasions had superseded the power of Mycenae, Argos aspired to the predominant position in the Peloponnese for over four centuries. Her last great king, Pheidon, led an army to the banks of the Alpheios and restored the Olympic Games to Pisa. He was the first to introduce coinage and a new scale of weights and measures into continental Greece. His defeat of the Lacedaemonians at Hysiae (c. 668 B.C.) marked an early round in the long struggle with Sparta for the E. seaboard of Laconia. In 550 Sparta defeated Argos and annexed Argive Thyreatis. An attempt to retrieve this loss was crushed c. 494 B.C. at Sepeia, near Tiryns, when Kleomenes I routed an Argive army. The defence of Argos by the poetess Telesilla is probably legendary. The city took no part in the Persian Wars and resented the participation of Mycenae and Tiryns. A renewal of the struggle against Sparta enabled her to destroy her former dependencies in 468 B.C. Ten years later we find Argos in alliance with Athens and adopting democratic government. During the Peloponnesian War, in 420, Athens, Argos, Elis, and Mantinea formed a league, but the defeat of the allies in 418 by the Lacedaemonians at the First Battle of Mantinea, and an oligarchic rising in Argos effectively put that city out of the war.

Argos was an ally of Corinth in the Corinthian War (395–386). She helped to defeat the Spartans at the Second Battle of Mantinea (362 B.C.). Pyrrhus attacked Argos in 272 B.C.; he was killed in the abortive street-fighting after being felled by a tile thrown by an old woman from a rooftop. In 229 B.C. Argos temporarily joined the Achaean League, and after 146 B.C. was included in the Roman province of Achaia.

The city became a bishopric in the 5C and was elevated to the rank of metropolis in 1088. It withstood the Franks for seven years before surrendering in 1212; thenceforward its history is bound up with that of Nauplia. The Turks ravaged it in 1397. In the War of Independence the seizure of the Larissa by Demetrios Ypsilantis caused the retreat of Dramali (comp. above). At Argos Ypsilantis' 'National Convention' of 1821 met before its removal to Epidauros, and here in 1829 Capodistrias convened the Fourth National Assembly which concentrated power in his hands. The city was sacked by Ibrahim Pasha in 1825 and occupied by the French in 1832 after a fight with armed bands had caused the last bloodshed of the war.

The Argive school of sculpture was famous. Its most renowned member was *Polykleitos* (fl. 452–412). It was commonly held that while Pheidias made the noblest statues of gods, Polykleitos was unsurpassed for his statues of men.

Since the modern town covers much of the area of the ancient city, visible remains are scanty. Systematic explorations outside the town were made in 1902–30 by the Dutch archaeologist, Wilhelm Vollgraff. Since 1952 further excavations have been made on these sites by the French School and new investigations made to the S. of the town.

In the PLATEIA stands *Ayios Petros* (1859), the church of St Peter, patron saint of Argos. Within, the modern woodwork is carved in a traditional style.

To the s.w. is the **Museum** (adm. 10 dr.; closed 1–3), built by the French School. Opposite the door, ROOM I. Middle Helladic, Mycenean, and Protogeometric pottery and bronze objects from tombs.—R. II (r.) Geometric pottery. Bronze *Helmet and cuirass of the late Geometric period; this find and the Mycenean suit, equally unique, in Nauplia have occasioned many scholarly second thoughts on Homeric armour. Krateutai (fire-dogs) in the shape of triremes (bronze); spits; pottery fragment showing Odysseus and Polyphemos (7C B.C.); terracotta figures playing blind man's buff; lyre (6C B.C.; restored) made of the shell of a tortoise and ibex horns.—Upstairs: Roman sculpture including statues from the Baths.—Descending we come to the LERNA ROOM with important pottery finds of Lerna I–VII, excavated by John Caskey since 1952; they extend in time from early Neolithic through all phases of Helladic to Mycenean. Terracotta statuette (c. 3000 B.C.); Early Helladic ceremonial hearth (restored).—On the TERRACE outside are large well-preserved mosaics of the 5C A.D. (Seasons; Bacchus; Hunting scenes).

Beyond the museum extends the animated open *Market*. Hence Odhos Tsokri, the old *Bazaar*, provides the shortest approach to the *Aspis* (see below).

We take the Tripolis road to ($\frac{1}{2}$ m.; l.) the **Agora**. The site is still largely covered by houses, but French excavations have revealed traces of a long *Stoa*, which bounded the area to the s. in the 4C A.D., and of a colonnaded *Hall* of the late 5C B.C., perhaps the Bouleuterion, at the s.w. corner. The 18 temples recorded by Pausanias were probably destroyed by the Goths in 395, for all the excavated buildings were repaired about this period.

In the enclosure opposite, at the s.E. foot of the Larissa are extensive **Roman Baths** of the 2C A.D., restored after the Gothic incursion. The *Frigidarium* was equipped with three plunge-baths and the establishment had three *Calidaria* with marble-faced baths. In the *Crypt* below the apsidal reception hall are three sarcophagi.

Hewn in the side of the hill above is the **Theatre**, which accommodated c. 20,000 spectators and is thus rivalled in size on the Greek mainland only by that at Dodona. It dates from the end of the 4C B.C. or a little later, but was twice remodelled in Roman times.

In the s. parodos is a small relief of the Dioscuri. The *Orchestra*, 28 yds in diameter, was paved in blue and white marble in the 4C A.D. when it was turned into a waterproof basin for the staging of naval contests. The late Roman modifications to the stage have been removed to reveal the foundations of the Greek *Skene*, largely destroyed in the 2C during the Imperial reconstruction. The wings of the *Cavea*, which were built on artificial banking, have disappeared, but 81 rows of seats remain in the rock-hewn centre section. Two (later three) diazomata and seven flights of steps, not placed regularly, divided the seating. The surviving seats of honour in the front row include an imperial *Throne* probably of the time of Gratian. In the theatre two national conventions met in the War of Independence (comp. above).

To the s. are some remains of the *Aqueduct* that brought water for the naumachiae. Fragments of 4C walling here probably upheld a road leading to the theatre. Farther on a Roman *Odeion* of the 1C A.D. (later restored) covers vestiges of a second *Theatre* antedating the larger one farther N. Fourteen curved rows remain of the Roman seating. The straight banks of the Greek structure, originally of some 35 rows, probably constituted the meeting-place of the Argive assembly. To the s. of the Odeion are remnants of an *Aphrodision* which survived from the Archaic period to c. A.D. 405.—From the modern reservoir above the theatres a toilsome zigzag path (better used for the descent) leads up in 45 min. to the *Kastro* (see below), a fortress crowning the ancient Larissa.

Skirting the base of the Larissa we approach the *Deiras*, the ridge joining the Larissa to the Aspis; the ancient road from Argos to Mantinea passed through a gate on this ridge. The convent of *Panayia tou Vrakhou* (Virgin of the Rock; l., above) stands on the site of a *Temple of Hera Akraia*. The rounded hill of *Ayios Ilias* which rises to the N.E. of the ridge is the ancient ASPIS ('Shield'), the original citadel of Argos, which lost its importance when the Larissa was founded. At its s.w. foot Vollgraff discovered a *Mycenean Necropolis*, which was more fully explored in 1955–59. Twenty-six chamber tombs and six shaft graves have come to light as well as a Middle Helladic building of the early 2nd millennium. About 150 yds N.W. the SANCTUARY OF APOLLO AND HERA forms a long rectangle divided into four terraces.

On the w. is a *Great Court* with a stone altar, and bases of tripods and statues. Thence a rock-hewn staircase of 10 steps, 30 yds wide, leads to the central terrace, which contained the *Temple of Pythian Apollo* or *Apollo Deiradiotes* (Apollo of the Ridge) and the *Manteion* or oracle, a rectangular building of unbaked bricks on a stone foundation. A large Byzantine church was built on this spot. To the E., on a lower terrace was a *Round Temple* or Tholos, and on an upper terrace was the *Temple of Athena Oxyderkes* (Sharp-eyed Athena), supposedly dedicated by

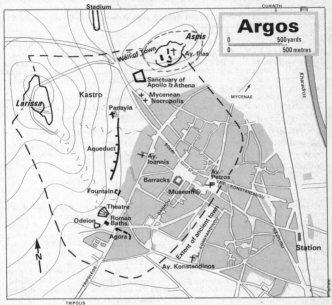

Diomede "because once when he was fighting at Ilium the goddess lifted the darkness from his eyes" (comp. 'Iliad', V, 127). Here also was a large cistern.—The *Stadium* lay farther N. outside the wall.

The summit of the Aspis (328 ft) is crowned by the little chapel of *Ay. Ilias.* Here the Argives had a small ACROPOLIS, built over the remains of an early Bronze Age Settlement (c. 2000 B.C.), discovered by Vollgraff.

The polygonal 6C walls of the Hellenic fortress describe an oval round the chapel. They were everywhere built on the remains of the prehistoric enceinte, except in the N.E. where they formed a triangular salient with 2 square towers and 4 posterns. Within the walls, against the E. wall and round the chapel, are two groups of *Pre-Mycenean Dwellings*, in ashlar bonded with clay. To the S. and W. a group of Macedonian buildings surrounds an Archaic temple. A conspicuous hexagonal *Tower* marks the junction of the Acropolis and City walls.

From the Deiras a road runs W. before climbing steeply to the summit of the **Larissa** (905 ft) the principal citadel of Argos. The ancient citadel was formed of two concentric enceintes, an outer wall of Hellenic masonry (5C) having been added to the polygonal work of the 6C which protected the Archaic acropolis. Sections of antique masonry can be traced in the medieval *KASTRO, which was built largely on the old foundations by the Byzantines and Franks and enlarged by the Venetians and Turks. The 5C wall survives on the N.W. of the outer enceinte, while the polygonal wall is best seen on the N.E. side of the *Keep*. This fine medieval structure incorporates fragments from a *Temple of Zeus Larisaos* and a *Temple of Athena*, the poros foundations of which were excavated in the court by Vollgraff. Traces of Mycenean wall and a votive deposit of the 8C B.C. were also found.

The view embraces the whole Argolid and the Gulf of Nauplia. Far to the E. rises Arachnaion. Immediately to the w. is *Mt Lykone*, crowned by the remains of a small temple of Artemis Orthia; behind rises Artemision. To the N. the flat summit of Mt Fokas is conspicuous.

The descent may be made by one of two paths, neither distinct and both steep. The more westerly passes close to some vestiges of the *Town Walls*, while that to the E. passes a rock-cut relief of a horseman and a snake to reach a rectangular *Terrace* supported by a polygonal wall. At its N.E. corner is a relief of seated divinities. Vollgraff identified the place with the *Kriterion*, or Judgement Place, where Hypermnestra was condemned by her father Danaos for refusing to kill her husband; at a later date it supported a fountain.

From Argos to the *Heraion*, see Rte 28; to *Lerna* and *Tripolis*, see Rte 30.— BUSES every ½ hr to *Nauplia*; many times daily to *Corinth* and *Athens*, to *Tripolis* and *Kalamata*, etc.; also once or twice daily to *Mycenae*, to *Sparta* and *Yithion*, etc.

Road and goods line continue across a fertile plain which supplies the markets of Athens with vegetables.—33½ m. **Tiryns**. The massive walls of the ancient city (Rte 28B) are seen to the left.—37¼ m. (60 km.) **Nauplia**, see Rte 28A.

27   MYCENAE

Approaches. ROAD. From Corinth or Nauplia to *Fikhtia*, see Rte 26. Thence a good by-road (2½ m.) mounts to the Lion Gate. COACH TOURS from Athens, daily mid-Mar–Oct, thrice weekly in winter. TAXIS may be hired at Nauplia or Argos. BUSES from Argos depart from the Museum at 10.30 and return at 3 p.m. affording c. 4 hrs at the site; in summer, however, the lack of shade at the height of the day must be considered.

RAILWAY to *Mycenae Station*, see Rte 26. Thence, on foot (2½ m.), as below. From Fikhtia or the near-by railway station of Mycenae the road leads E. to (1¼ m.) *Kharváti*, the traditional point of departure for Mycenae. The tourist-pavilion (*Xenia A*, not cheap) lies a little to the left c. ½ m. farther on, *La Petite Planète, Agamemnon*, both C, higher up. A huge car-park just below the Lion Gate allows the hasty visitor to approach with the minimum of exertion. Since the citadel has been fenced it is more difficult to appreciate the skilful siting of the fortress and the magnitude of Mycenean conception as a whole. However, out of tourist hours, a better sense of the human scale in comparison with the rugged and difficult terrain can still be obtained by approaching on foot.

ADMISSION 50 dr.; weekdays 8 or 9 to sunset; Sun & hol. 10–4.30.

MYCENAE (Μυκῆναι), in modern pronunciation *Mikínai*, a city known to archaeology as the centre of the great Helladic civilization and to tradition as the capital of Agamemnon, lies 9 m. from the sea, half-hidden in a mountain glen or recess (μυχὸς), between *Mt Ayios Ilías* (2460 ft) on the N. and *Mt Zára* (1969 ft) on the s. Its position commands the landfall in the Gulf of Nauplia and controls the natural roads N. through the mountains to Corinth and the Isthmus. The city, which Homer calls 'rich in gold' (πολύχρυσος) and 'well-built' (ἐϋκτίμενον πτολίεθρον) and 'broad-streeted' was proverbial in classical times for its wealth. At its zenith Mycenae consisted of a fortified administrative centre with inhabited settlements outside the walls. The Acropolis, the residence of its kings (who enclosed within its walls the shrine of their predecessors), stands on an almost isolated hill skirted by two deep ravines which fork from the mouth of the glen, the *Kokoretsa* running w. and the *Khávos* s.w. From the N.w. corner of the Acropolis a long narrow ridge runs s. parallel to the Khávos. In the slopes of this ridge are the tholos or beehive tombs which Pausanias mistook for treasuries, and, in part overlaying these, the less important ruins of Hellenic buildings from the 3C B.C.

Excavations. The earliest systematic excavations, which uncovered the first circle of shaft graves, were initiated in 1874–76 by Heinrich Schliemann, who was succeeded by Stamatakes. In 1886–1902 digging was continued by the Greek Archaeological Society under Tsountas. Extensive excavations in 1920–23 by the British School at Athens under Prof. Alan Wace showed that some of the interim conclusions reached by Evans and Myres about the chronology of Mycenae were ill-founded. Wace resumed excavations in 1950–56; in 1951 work of restoration and preservation was begun on behalf of the Greek government. Since 1952, when Grave Circle B was excavated, the Greek Archaeological Society has been actively engaged at Mycenae. Lord Wm. Taylour directed British excavations after Wace's death, first in collaboration with J. Papadimitriou, then under the general direction of G. Mylonas. Since 1969 the British School has continued studies of material from previous excavations, particularly of pottery (Dr Elizabeth French). These and the decipherment of Linear B tablets found here and elsewhere have advanced knowledge of Mycenean civilization without resolving many of the major chronological problems.

History. Archaeological evidence shows that the site was first occupied by man c. 3000–2800 B.C. and preserved an unremarkable Neolithic and Early Helladic culture to the end of the 3rd millennium. In Middle Helladic times only the summit of the hill, an area slightly larger than that now occupied by the ruins of the palace, was fortified. Scattered settlements existed on the lower slopes, and a large cemetery consisting of groups of cist tombs extended to the w. in the nearest rock soft enough to be dug. In the middle of this area, in the period called Late Helladic I (c. 1600 B.C.), six large shaft graves were dug for a ruling family; a further 14 shaft graves, forming another group farther from the citadel, are slightly earlier.

The earliest of the tholos tombs seems to date from the following century, and this type of interment continues to 1300 B.C., showing a progressive structural development culminating in architecture of a high order. Nine such tombs have been discovered at Mycenae; they are of persons of a royal or ruling class and bear the same relationship to the contemporary chamber tombs as the shaft graves do to the cist tombs. Soon after 1350 B.C. the Cyclopean enceinte, together with the Lion Gate and the Postern Gate, was constructed, and the Palace and most of the buildings within replanned on a more lavish scale. The walls cut through the original cemetery but are aligned so as to include the more important group of royal shaft graves. This, the period of greatest prosperity, was interrupted by violence; the environs were sacked, though the citadel remained untouched. Mycenae recovered from this disaster, but towards the end of the 12C the city was looted and its buildings destroyed by fire; the walls remained virtually intact but were probably not reoccupied until the early Iron Age. A small township developed which sent contingents to fight at Thermopylae and Plataea; this fell to the jealousy of Argos in 468 B.C. and the site was again left waste. Later the walls were repaired and a Hellenistic town spread over the w. ridge. The importance of Mycenae, however, begins c. 1650 B.C. and ceases c. 1100 B.C. with the fall of the civilization to which it gives name.

Mycenean Civilization. Towards the end of the Middle Helladic period a sudden stimulus apparently influences the previously unremarkable mainland culture. There appears at Mycenae (already a dominant centre) evidence in the shaft-graves of a fully developed cult of the dead accompanied by a lavish use of gold. The technique and artistry is highly accomplished. A generation earlier Helladic dead were much less lavishly provided. The theory that Minoan conquerors or colonists were responsible is untenable, the form of burial, the use of gold, and the warlike accoutrements alike being foreign to Minoan custom. Helladic building styles continue unchanged by Cretan influence. A later theory that the riches of these graves were loot from Minoan Crete brought back when Helladic warriors destroyed the Old Palaces must be discarded, since wider exploration has shown that the Cretan sites were more likely ruined in some natural calamity. There is no evidence of gold on this scale in Crete whereas contemporary documents in Egypt record that there it was 'like dust beneath the feet'. The Egyptian pharaohs of the XVIII dynasty paid their commanders in gold. At the time of the shaft-graves (c. 1600 B.C. onwards) the Egyptians were seeking aid from overseas in their struggle against the Hyksos. It is possible that the heavily-armed Achaean warriors fought as mercenaries on the Nile, when they brought back to Mycenae the Egyptian belief in life after death with its attendant technique of embalming, the fashion for golden death-masks, and provision of elaborate grave-goods (comp. the representations of cheetah, and the ostrich eggs, among the finds). Legend attributes an Egyptian origin to the hero Danaos.

Nevertheless, in Late Helladic I (early 16C B.C.), Mycenean culture does assume in addition many Minoan characteristics in its pottery, jewellery, representation of bulls, and the symbols of the double-axe, the sacred pillar and horns of consecration, associated with a cult of the Mother Goddess. A plausible explanation suggests that the Mycenean warriors went to and from Egypt in Minoan ships; this would be natural since the Myceneans at this time were still primarily landsmen while the peaceful Cretans were essentially a maritime race. Relations developed between the two peoples which may have led to dynastic marriages; this would account for the presence in female tombs on the mainland of engraved gold seal-rings of a type exactly paralleled in Crete. For whatever reason, Mycenean craftsmen learned from Minoan masters new techniques.

The following period (L.H. II; 15C B.C.) sees the expansion of Mycenean civilization all over mainland Greece, with considerable trade farther afield. It is uncertain whether or not Knossos itself fell c. 1425 either to mainland aggression or dynastic inheritance (comp. Rte 78A). The graves of this period have mostly been plundered and the architecture obscured by later rebuilding so that less of it is known than of the periods before and after. It is characterized by the earlier tholos tombs and represented artistically by the splendid contents of three such tombs found intact at Vaphio, Midea, and Pylos. The presence of amethyst and amber beads proves that trading relations already existed with Egypt and the Baltic. The vases are better made, their drawing magnificent. The large 'palace-style' vases as well as the beehive tombs typify the insolent exuberance of the age.

The full tide of Mycenean influence (L.H. III) is reached in the 14C. The glory of the latest era was its architecture, so that its remains are more substantial. Houses have basements for storage and several rooms. Royal dwellings, with more than one story and frescoed walls, have become palaces indeed. Accounts are kept in writing, though so far no evidence has come to light of literary composition. The cities are linked by roads and chariots are used.

The ruler of Mycenae seems to have been the overlord of a loose federation of vast extent. Immediately subordinate strongholds in the Argolid included Tiryns, Midea, Asine, and Hermione. The whole of the Peloponnese was under the dominion of Mycenae. Her cultural influence extended to Attica, Aegina, Boeotia, Euboea, Thessaly, the Ionian Is. (except perhaps Corcyra), Aetolia, Phokis, and the islands of the Aegean. Even Crete which had largely inspired the civilization of Mycenae was now subordinated to the younger nation. The principal gates of mainland citadels, which previously faced the hinterland, are rebuilt to face the coast as Mycenean interests of trade or conquest reach out to the confines of the Mediterranean. There was a vigorous export and import trade with Cyprus and on to Egypt. The S. Sporades appear to have had settlers. Mycenean objects have been found in Macedonia and Thrace, in the Troad, and at Boghazkeuy, the Hittité capital. Ugarit on the Syrian coast had a Mycenean trading post.

The almost total eclipse of Mycenean civilization over the whole area has not yet been adequately explained (comp. V. R. d'A. Desborough, 'The Greek Dark Ages', 1972). A surge of defensive building in the 13C, in particular the ensuring of a secret water-supply at Mycenae, Tiryns, and Athens, suggests an external threat. Some great disaster overwhelmed the Greek mainland just before 1200 B.C., followed very shortly afterwards by a second. The majority of smaller settlements are abandoned at this time, except in Achaea, the Ionian Islands, the E. Aegean, and Cyprus, where they increase (presumably reflecting an influx of refugees). Before 1100 B.C. there had been a second wave of disasters throughout the region which effectively ended a whole way of life. The 'Dorian Invasions' of Classical historians, internal risings, famine, pestilence, change of climate, seismic disaster, have all been suggested as the reason, none of them by itself accounting for all the conflicting archaeological evidence. What is indisputable is that the continuity of civic life was disrupted and material progress set back for four centuries.

Homer, Mycenae, and the Trojan War. The visitor to Mycenae can hardly avoid the attempt to fit the Homeric stories into the archaeological setting. The historical trustworthiness of Homer was first questioned by Herodotus and the consistency of the texts by Zoilus of Amphipolis. Quite apart from questions of authorship, date of composition, or unity of the transmitted text, "there remain many anachronisms in language and in social customs, and inconsistencies in the narrative of the poems (whether internal, as between the 'Catalogue of Ships'

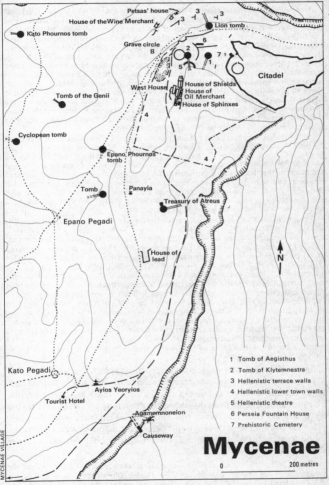

1 Tomb of Aegisthus
2 Tomb of Klytemnestra
3 Hellenistic terrace walls
4 Hellenistic lower town walls
5 Hellenistic theatre
6 Perseia Fountain House
7 Prehistoric Cemetery

Mycenae

0   200 metres

and the rest of the *Iliad*, or external, as between the *Iliad* and the *Odyssey*, or between Homeric and actual geography, as in the description of Ithaca), which have to be accounted for" (A Companion to Homer). Recent finds in Mycenean archaeology, however, have proved the persistence of Mycenean traditions in Homer in matters of armament, social and burial customs, and religion, of which evidence had wholly vanished by Classical times. The deciphering of Linear B tablets found on Mycenean sites has thrown new light on some of the problems.

The Cincinnati expedition to Troy in 1932–38 made it clear that Troy VIIA 'was subjected to siege, capture, and destruction by hostile forces at some time in the general period assigned by Greek tradition' and Prof. Carl Blegen went on to specify a date (agreeing closely with Herodotus) c. 1240 B.C. The pottery of Troy VI shows correlations with that of Mycenae, suggesting that Achaeans and Trojans were of the same stock.

A copy exists of a letter from a Hittite ruler to the king of Ahhiyawa (? Achaea) about events in Lycia; the Homeric letter from the king of Argos to the king of Lycia (*Iliad*, VI, 168–69) may be part of the same correspondence. Myrtilos, the charioteer of Oinomaos, bears a name suggesting that he was a Hittite expert from whom the Greeks learned the art of the chariot. The Attarssyas with a hundred chariots who harried the Hittites in the 13C was perhaps a member of the house of Atreus. Hittite documents record Mycenean activity in Asia Minor amounting to a large-scale expedition. Whether or not this is to be connected with the archaeologically proven sack of Troy VIIA, it implies a fleet and a single leader. The Catalogue of Ships in *Iliad* II reproduces the basic form of Mycenean lists found in Linear B tablets and is taken by some scholars to be a quoted document from the Bronze Age. Aulis, where the ships assembled, has a Mycenean cemetery. It seems, therefore that a historical 13C Mycenean king who led a large expedition to Asia Minor, contributed largely to Homer's Agamemnon.

It is probable, however, that the story of the siege of a maritime town, defended by people whose background is known, belongs to Mycenean tradition as early as the 16C B.C. (comp. the siege rhyton, Athens Mus.). This is confirmed by the discovery on tablets found at Pylos, Knossos and Mycenae, of many names that are given in the 'Iliad' to Trojan warriors. This traditional story was elaborated for generations in the different Mycenean kingdoms, gathering later exploits, with changes of locale and dramatis personae, and sometimes of fashion and armament; it was then given a new eastern setting when Troy VIIA was attacked by an expedition led by a king of Mycenae.

Chronological problems are also raised by the *Odyssey*, the action of which is set after the Trojan War. The correspondence between objects (e.g. Nestor's cup; 'the wrought mixing bowl of solid silver doubled with gold about the rim' given by Menelaus to Telemachus; etc.) described by Homer and those discovered in Mycenean excavations is often exact, though the Homeric object may be more typical of a period before the Trojan War or placed in juxtaposition with an anachronistic object. However, the ascribed provenance of Achaean riches accords with archaeological probability, as when Menelaus mentions his adventures in Egypt and claims to have 'seen Ethiopians in their native haunts'; Polybus of Egyptian Thebes had given him ten talents in gold. It seems that events from several periods of Mycenean adventure may be telescoped in the *Odyssey* into one ancestral epic; the Egyptian expedition, the Trojan War, and the voyages of colonists to the W. Mediterranean. The series of treacheries, improper marriages, and acts of revenge that characterize the Homeric dynasty of Mycenae, and supplied the basis for the embroideries of Classical drama, may actually have happened in the 16C B.C. (comp. below).

From Kharvati the motor-road up to (1¼ m.) the Acropolis of Mycenae runs below an older track which follows some remains of a Turkish aqueduct and overlooks the ravine of the Khávos, or Chaos. The prehistoric road from Mycenae to Prosymna traversed this ravine by a *Bridge* and causeway, the ruins of which may still be seen. We cross the course of this road just below the chapel of *Ayios Yeoryios*, in the cemetery of which is buried Humfry Payne (1902–36), excavator of Perachora.

To the left is the tourist-pavilion (see above), whence the old track follows the ridge back to the village, passing the *Káto Pegádi*, the ancient lower well of the city, 'modernized' in 1940 and still in use. An upper well, *Epáno Pegádi*, lies ¼ m. farther N. between the late-Helladic cemetery of Kalkani and the Panayia Tomb.

The modern road continues to skirt the Atreus Ridge, cutting through a large chamber tomb. Farther on a massive wall of undressed stone supports a wide paved terrace built of packed boulders fronting the so-called ***Treasury of Atreus,** or *Tomb of Agamemnon.* An architectural masterpiece, as well as being the largest and best-preserved of the tholos tombs, this is also one of the latest, being dated from the fineness of its construction to c. 1300 B.C. A connection with Atreus (if the Atreids are indeed historical) is less impossible than has previously been thought: a date of 1300 is only two generations before the most likely date of the Trojan War, and Atreus is said to have been Agamemnon's father. If the tomb was a family vault, there is at least a chance that it was the veritable tomb of Agamemnon.

The THOLOS or BEEHIVE TOMBS, which have given their name to the later dynasty that flourished at Mycenae, are characteristic of the period known as Late Helladic II but extend from L.H. I to L.H. IIIA. Over 100 have been found in widely separated parts of Greece. They are usually composed of two parts, the *Dromos*, or approach, an unroofed passage cut horizontally into the hill, and the *Tholos*, which formed the actual tomb. This was of masonry, built into a circular excavation in the hill, and rising in a cone like a beehive to about the same height as the diameter of the floor. The top of the cone projected above the slope of the hillside and was covered with earth. Occasionally, as in the 'Treasury of Atreus', an additional chamber, rectangular in shape, opened from the tholos; the exact function of this is not certain.

At Mycenae nine such tombs have been discovered, all outside the fortifications. Unlike the shaft-graves on the acropolis they had all been plundered, with the result that less is known about their contents. Architecturally the tholos tombs at Mycenae fall into three groups, showing a progressive structural development, marked in particular by the increased use of dressed stone and the placing of a relieving triangle above the lintel. They may be dated between c. 1520 and 1300 B.C. and the Treasury of Atreus is the finest example of the third group.

By the time of Pausanias the original purpose of these structures had been forgotten and they were taken for underground treasuries. The discovery of six skeletons in the tomb at Menidi placed the question of their purpose beyond all doubt.

The tomb is built into the N. slope of the ridge. From the artificial *Terrace* (see above), we pass through vestiges of the *Enclosing Wall* that barred the entrance. The *Dromos* is 115 ft long and 20 ft wide; its walls, which naturally rise as we penetrate the hillside, are built of great squared blocks of breccia laid in horizontal courses and waterproofed behind with a lining of clay brick. At the end of the approach is a *Doorway* nearly 18 ft high tapering slightly towards the top. The lintel is formed of two large slabs of stone, of which the inner one is 27 ft long, 17 ft wide, and 3 ft 9 in. thick, with an estimated weight of 118 tons. Above, the stone courses are built up obliquely to form a corbelled vault thus lightening the weight borne by the lintel. On either side of the doorway, on a square stepped base (still in position), stood an engaged half-column of dark green limestone. Parts of the shafts and of the carved capitals have been found; a few of these are in Athens Museum, but the greater part is in the British Museum. Above, smaller columns flanked the facing of ornamental coloured bands that masked the 'relieving triangle'; some rosso antico fragments of this façade are also in London. They derive probably from quarries at Kyprianon near Cape Matapan (see B.S.A. 1968). The entrance passage is 17 ft deep; in the middle a stone threshold shows the pivot holes on which the double doors were swung. The bronze nails that held the doorframe and fixed the wood or bronze covering of the threshold are still in place.

The *Tholos* is a circular domed chamber, 43 ft high and 47½ ft in diameter, formed by well-fitting blocks of breccia in 33 concentric courses, joined without mortar and gradually diminishing in height.

The blocks vary from 4 to 7 feet in length. Each course overlaps the one immediately below it, the topmost course being closed by a single block which, unlike the keystone of an arch, could be removed without endangering the stability of the structure. The overlaps have been cut away, so that the interior presents a smooth unbroken surface curved both horizontally and vertically. The floor is of the natural rock. From the third course upwards are rows of holes in regular order, some of them with their original bronze nails; these were bored to receive bronze rosettes as at Orchomenos. The outside of the dome was wedged with smaller stones.

A much smaller doorway, 9½ ft high and 4½ ft wide, similarly surmounted by a triangular opening, leads from the N. side of the beehive chamber into a *Rock-Hewn Chamber*, 27 ft square and 19 ft high. The walls were probably lined and decorated with sculptured slabs. In the centre is a circular depression.

On the thyme-covered ridge to the W. (view) are remains of a settlement of late-Helladic date. The walls are known since the excavations of 1955 to be terrace walls of outlying villas ('House of Lead', 'Lisa's House', etc.), not fortifications; earlier theories of a fortified prehistoric 'lower town' have been abandoned. Just below the conspicuous *Panayia Chapel* is the *Panayia Tomb*, another tholos chamber (of the second group), discovered by Tsountas in 1887; it lacks its upper part. A hundred yards farther N. is a tholos of the first group, known as the *Epano Phournos Tomb*.

We round a corner beyond the Treasury of Atreus and traverse an area of confused Hellenistic ruins surrounded by a wall, the course of which can still be traced. Farther on (r.) are the excavated foundations of several **Houses,** probably the residences of wealthy merchants of the 13C B.C.; all were destroyed by fire. The names given them by the British excavators derive from the objects discovered in them. They are built of rubble packed with clay, which supported a timber frame filled in with brick.

In the *House of Sphinxes* were found ivory plaques depicting sphinxes and nine Linear B tablets which had fallen from an upper room. The *House of the Oil Merchant*, adjoining to the N., contained (N. room) eleven large pithoi and an installation for warming them. Thirty-eight written tablets came to light amid the burnt ruins. Across a narrow lane, the *House of Shields* yielded carved ivories, many in the shape of the figure-of-eight shield.—The *West House*, which adjoins the House of the Oil Merchant, has been excavated by N. Verdelis.

At the N. end of the ridge the road turns E. towards the citadel. On the left is the level *Car Park*; in the angle of the road (r.) lies **Grave Circle B,** discovered by accident in 1951 and excavated in 1952–54 by the late John Papadimitriou.

Though archaeologically one of the most important of recent discoveries at Mycenae the circle affords little of interest to the view. The enclosure, bounded by a wall similar to that of the larger grave circle on the acropolis (see below) and containing 25 graves, 15 of them shaft graves, lay partly beneath the road, while the section to the E. had been overlapped by the vault of the Tomb of Klytemnestra. The bodies had been buried over a period of years with objects of ivory, gold, bronze, and rock crystal, though less sumptuously than the burials of Grave Circle A. The burials are thought to date from c. 1650 B.C. and may represent a rival royal faction to the kings of the larger circle since their resting-place was of sufficient sanctity not to be looted.

In the dip below (r.; footpath) are two tholos tombs. That known as the **Tomb of Klytemnestra** was partially excavated by Mrs Schliemann in 1876 and more fully explored by the Greek Archaeological Society in 1891–92. It is of the normal type without a side-chamber, and is built on the same principle as the Treasury of Atreus, though a little smaller. From the more refined workmanship it is considered to be the latest of the tholos tombs (c. 1300 B.C.). The upper 18 courses of its dome, destroyed probably by Veli Pasha, were restored in 1951. The *Dromos* (214 ft long) contained a circular depression which seems to have been a woman's

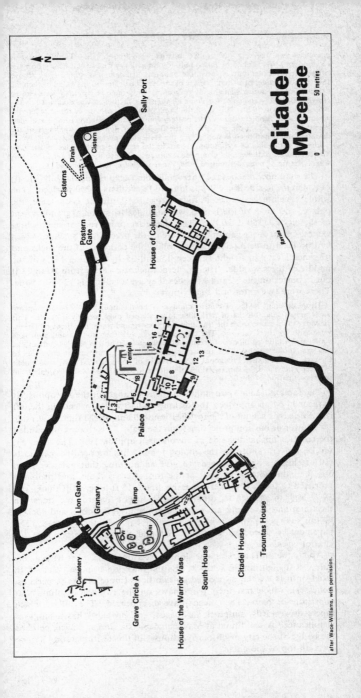

Citadel Mycenae

0   50 metres

N

Sally Port

Cisterns

Drain

Cistern

Postern Gate

House of Columns

Ravine

Temple

Palace

15 16 17

18

5

10 11

4

8

12 13 14

9

Lion Gate

Granary

Ramp

Grave Circle A

Cemetery

House of the Warrior Vase

South House

Citadel House

Tsountas House

after Wace-Williams, with permission.

grave, as gold trinkets and bronze mirrors were found in it. The *Doorway* is recessed and was flanked by fluted half-columns. Here we can see clearly how the ornamental façade that covered the relieving triangle was supported. Above the dromos vestiges of a small *Theatre* of the Hellenistic period show that by then the existence of the tholos was already forgotten. Only one semicircle of seats can be clearly descried.—The so-called **Tomb of Aegisthus**, farther E., was excavated by the British School in 1922. This is on the same plan, but both the manner of its construction with rubble walls and the pottery found within date the tomb in the first group (c. 1470 B.C.); the collapse of the tholos was due to the weakness of the material and it had been looted before the Hellenistic period.

On the other side of the modern road, in the N. slope of the ridge, is the *Lion Tomb*, a tholos of the second group, now ruinous. Over to the left is *Petsas' House*, where a store of over 600 unused pots, ranged in sizes, was unearthed.

The road now reaches the ***Acropolis,** built on a triangular hill (912 ft) of which the N. side is c. 350 yds long and the others c. 200 yds long. The whole enceinte as we see it today, together with the Lion Gate, the palace, and most of the houses within, dates from the aggrandisement of the city c. 1350–1330 B.C. The *Walls* are preserved for their whole extent, except for a gap in the middle of the precipitous s. slope, which had no need to be fortified. They follow the contours of the rocks and in general vary in height between 15 and 35 ft, reaching 56 ft in the middle of the s.w. side. Their general thickness varies from 10 to 23 ft but in places on the N. and S.E. sides they are as much as 33–46 ft wide. There were two gates and a sally-port.

Three different styles of construction may be distinguished. The 'cyclopean' walls are of huge blocks of dark limestone, shaped only roughly if at all. This masonry takes name from the tradition that the original walls, like those of Tiryns, were built by the Cyclopes. The two gateways, with their towers and approach walls, are in squared blocks of breccia, hammer-dressed and in regular courses like the later tholos tombs. This gives extra strength and dignity to the entrances to the city. The so-called Polygonal Tower is built of finely-jointed polygonal blocks of breccia; this and the short sections of wall repaired with similar blocks date from the reoccupation of the 3C B.C.

The famous ***Lion Gate** stands at the N.W. angle of the Acropolis. It is reached by an approach 16 yds long and 10 wide, formed on the left (N.E.) side by a salient of the fortification wall and on the right (s.w.) side by a tower or bastion projecting from the wall. This tower commanded the right or unshielded side of anyone that approached. The gateway, unlike the entrances to the tholos tombs, has monolithic gateposts (10½ ft high) sloping inwards to give an opening that narrows from 10¼ ft at the bottom to 9½ ft at the top. Across these, and probably mortised to them, is placed a massive lintel, 15 ft long, 6½ ft thick, and 3¼ ft high in the centre, diminishing in height towards the sides. In the lintel and threshold are pivot-holes for double doors, and sockets in the side posts show where a wooden bar held them closed. The pavement is scored to give foothold and rutted on either side for chariot-wheels.

Above the lintel a triangular slab of grey limestone, 12 ft wide at the base, 10 ft high, and 2 ft thick, fills the relieving triangle. Carved in relief on it is a pillar supported by two lions (more properly, perhaps, lionesses), which rest their front paws on the two joined altars that constitute its base. Their heads have disappeared. The pillar, which tapers downwards, supports an abacus, and probably has a religious significance. A seal found at Mycenae depicts a similar device, perhaps the badge of the city or of its royal house; in this representation a dove rests on top of the pillar.

Within the gate (r.) is the *Granary*, so-called because pithoi of carbonized wheat were found during its excavation. The building, which was of two stories, may rather have been a guard-house.

From the gate the *Royal Road* climbed by a ramp to the Palace, at first in a s.e. direction, then n. following the line of the wall. Its surface was dug away in Schliemann's excavations, but the massive embanking walls of the ramp remain. The terrace-wall to the n., designed to support the higher ground above, is a modern reconstruction.

To the right is **Grave Circle A,** the ROYAL CEMETERY, a circular enclosure 88 ft in diameter, formed by a double ring of dressed slabs 3–5 ft high and 3 ft apart. The space between the two concentric rings appears to have been filled originally with rubble; the top was covered with horizontal slabs, of which six are in place, showing the mortise-and-tenon joints. The entrance, formed by a well-made opening in the circle, 4 yds wide and lined with slabs, is opposite the Lion Gate. In the centre, all at the same level, were found 10 sepulchral stelai and a small round altar. The stelai, now in the National Museum at Athens, are adorned with crude sculptures in low relief, most of them representing men in chariots fighting or hunting. These are contemporary with the circle and with it represent the final stage of the royal shrine.

Within this enclosure are six SHAFT GRAVES, hewn perpendicularly in the rock at a depth of 25 ft. They vary considerably in size, but all were floored with pebbles and lined with rubble masonry; they appear to have been covered with slabs, which had collapsed beneath the weight of the soil above. In the tombs were found 19 skeletons; the bodies, had been interred in the contracted attitude, not burnt. The burial furnishings, which constitute one of the richest archaeological discoveries ever made, are splendidly displayed in Athens.

Archaeologists date these tombs to the end of the Middle Helladic period, and postulate a 16C royal house, which they call the 'Shaft Grave dynasty'. The cemetery, of which the graves form part, lay outside the early citadel; when the later enceinte was planned the common graves were treated with scant respect and even looted, while this royal group was incorporated within the walls and venerated. The circle was renewed and the entrance moved from the w. to the n. The stelai and altar however were not disturbed and remained facing the original w. entrance.

This is presumably the prehistoric Frogmore pointed out to Pausanias as the graves of Agamemnon and his companions; the local peasants added, following a tradition that goes back to Homer, that the murderers Klytemnestra and Aegisthus were buried outside the walls as they were considered unworthy of burial within. It was Schliemann's unshakeable belief that what he had found was in fact the grave of 'all those who on their return from Ilium were murdered by Aegisthus after a banquet which he gave them'. The belief was fortified by the contents of Grave III, in which were the skeletons of two infants wrapped in sheets of gold together with the remains of three women. Schliemann inferred that these were Cassandra with her two attendants and the twins that she had borne to Agamemnon. For a short time it seemed that Homer might after all be shown to be documentary history.

The grave circle is however undoubtedly centuries earlier than any possible date for the siege of Troy. If the discovery of a second grave circle has confirmed the probability that two rival royal factions did exist in Mycenae, it has strengthened the evidence that any feud between them took place long before the Trojan War. Just as Homer describes customs (e.g. cremation) which are quite foreign to Mycenae at any period, so he seems also to have fused more than one period of Mycenean events into one anachronistic saga. Malory's treatment of the Arthurian legends may be compared. The traveller who here feels himself cheated of the tomb of the legendary hero of Troy may console himself that he has below him the last resting-place of a great king who certainly existed at an age still more remote.

The characteristic shape of the inlaid daggers found here and at other Mycenean sites is curiously echoed in the dagger-shaped marks cut in the trilithons of Stonehenge, the construction of which has elements in common with the final arrangement of the Mycenean shrine; no satisfactory theory yet accounts for these coincidences, especially since a combination of C14 and tree-ring dating techniques now suggest that Stonehenge is *earlier* not later than Mycenae.

To the s. of the royal cemetery two groups of buildings have been uncovered; the remains represent only their basement level, drained and strongly built in stone to support a brick and timber floor above. They were constructed over the plebeian cemetery in the 14C B.C. The first group consists of the *Ramp House*, the *House of the Warrior Vase*, named after the famous vase found here by Schliemann, and *South House*. The farther group is known as *Tsountas' House* from its partial excavation in 1886 by the Greek archaeologist. Further Anglo-Greek investigations were started in 1959 in the adjoining *Citadel House*. Linear B tablets were found in 1960, and excavations by Lord William Taylour in 1968–69 uncovered L.H. IIIB idols and coiled snakes in clay, also a fine ivory head, in three rooms constituting a shrine.

From the ramp a modern path follows the contour of the hill to the domestic entrance of the **Palace**. Two guard rooms (Pl. 1, 2) precede a cobbled court, where the column bases of the *Propylon* are seen. An *Inner Gate* (4) gave access to a long corridor (6) and to the state quarters, the official entrance to which was, however, on the s. side. These centre round the *Great Court* (8). In Mycenean times a *Grand Staircase* (9) led the visitor viâ an *Anteroom* (11) to the *Throne Room* (10). From the E. side of the Great Court a *Porch* (12) and *Vestibule* (13) lead into the MEGARON (14), a room 42 ft by 39, in the centre of which was the sacred *Hearth*. Four wooden pillars supported a roof; three of their bases are still visible. The rooms to the N. are believed to represent the private apartments; a small one (17) with a red stuccoed bath is pointed out as the place of Agamemnon's murder. The topmost point is overlaid by scanty remains of a *Temple* rebuilt in Hellenistic times with material from an earlier structure of the Archaic period. The view comprehends the Argolid with the Larissa of Argos prominent.

In the s.e. angle of the citadel is located the *House of Columns*, or *Little Palace*, a well-drained building with a megaron, store-rooms, and traces of a stair which led to an upper story. On the outer rampart, near by, the so-called *Polygonal Tower*, built of the later and firmly-jointed polygonal blocks, rises to a height of thirty feet. Farther E. is the heavily fortified late extension of the acropolis with a sally-port and a *Secret Cistern*, of the kind now known at both Athens and Tiryns, approached by a passage through the wall and descending stairs. A little to the w. is a *Postern Gate* of the same epoch as the Lion Gate.

28 NAUPLIA, TIRYNS, AND THE ARGIVE HERAION

Quite apart from its own charm, Nauplia is the best centre for excursions in the Argolid. It is possible by hiring a car there to make a superficial tour of Tiryns, Argos, Mycenae, and the Heraion in one day. Visitors who are not pressed for time are recommended to take three days, devoting one to Nauplia and its surroundings, and dividing two between Tiryns, the Heraion, Mycenae and Argos, reserving a fourth for the visit to Epidauros (Rte 29).

A Nauplia

NAUPLIA (ΝΑΥΠΛΙΟΝ, in modern parlance *Návplion*), called by the Venetians *Nápoli di Romania*, is the chief town (9300 inhab.) of an eparchy and the capital of the nome of Argolis. Its delightful situation near the head of the Argolic Gulf and its splendid examples of late-medieval military architecture make it one of the most attractive towns in Greece. Originally walled, the quiet city huddles along the N. slopes of a small rocky peninsula, crowned by the citadel of Its-Kale (279 ft), towards which narrow streets, lined with old houses attractively balconied and shuttered, rise from the quay. On the S.E. the conspicuous fortress of Palamidi (705 ft) dominates the peninsula.

Facing away from the open sea, Nauplia provides the safest harbour on the coast of Argolis, with some trade in tobacco, currants, and cotton. Though the seat of a bishop and a military station, the town has lost the importance it once had as the temporary capital of Greece, and is frequented mainly as a holiday resort.

Hotels. Xenia Palace, on Akronavplion, L; **Amphitryon** (Pl. a), facing N.W. above the sea, with swimming pool; **Xenia** (Pl. c), in a commanding position facing both bays, these **A**; **Agamemnon** (Pl. h) on quay DPO, **B**.—**Victoria** (Pl. d), 8 Farmakopoulou; **Dioskouri** (Pl. f), Zigomala/Vironos; **Amimoni** (Pl. l), Diogenous; **Galini** (Pl. m), Sidiras Merarkhias; **Rex** (Pl. n), Navarinon/Bouboulinas; **Nauplia** (Pl. o), 11 Navarinou; **Park** (Pl. p), Plat. Kolokotronis; **Alkyoni**, on the Argos road, all these **C**.—**Leto** (Pl. i), 28 Zigomala; **King Otho** (Pl. j), 3 Farmakopoulou; **Grande Bretagne** (Pl. e), 1 Akti Miaouli, these **D**, and others.

Restaurants. *Leskhe*, *Ellas*, Plat. Sindagmatos; *Ellenikon*, Od. Emm. Sofroni off main street).—CAFÉS on the quay and in Sindagma Sq.

Tourist Police, Plateia Iatrou.—INFORMATION BUREAU, at the Agamemnon Hotel.

Buses from Plat. Nikitara to *Tiryns* and *Argos* (every ½ hr); to *Corinth* and *Athens* (hourly); from corner of Papanikolaou to *Ligourio* (7 times daily) going on (twice) to *Palaia Epidhavros*, (once) to *Nea Epidhavros*, and (twice) to the *Asklepieion* (Ieron Ligouriou); also (twice daily) to *Kranidhion* (for Ermioni and Spetsai); daily to *Galata* (for Poros).—From Plat. Agoras to *Tolo* (summer ½-hourly; winter morn. hourly, aft. every 2 hrs) for *Asine*; to *Dhrepanon*, etc.

Bathing below the Xenia Hotel, and near the Porporella.

History. In Mycenean times *Nauplia* may have been, as its name suggests, the naval station of Argos. The legend later grew of a mythical founder Nauplios, son of Poseidon by Amymone, daughter of Danaos. A descendant of Nauplios, Palamedes, is said to have invented lighthouses, the art of navigation, measures and scales, and the games of dice and knucklebones, in addition to introducing the letters Y, Φ, X, and Ψ into the alphabet of Cadmus (historically anachronistic). He was slain by his fellow-Greeks in the Trojan War on a false charge of treachery for playing a trick on Odysseus. About 625 B.C. Nauplia, previously a member of the maritime League of Kalauria, fell to Argos. The Nauplians fled to Messenia, where the Lacedaemonians gave them Methone. The town was again deserted in the time of Pausanias, who saw only walls, a sanctuary of Poseidon, the harbour, and the Spring of Kanathos.

Nauplia is mentioned as a trading-post in 11C Venetian annals. After the fall of Constantinople (1204), it remained for a time in Byzantine hands, the governor Leon Sgouros vainly trying to make it the nucleus of a Greek kingdom. In 1210 the town was taken by Geoffrey de Villehardouin, who gave it, with Argos, to Otho de la Roche. It remained an appanage of the Dukes of Athens, but on the fall of Athens to the Catalans in 1311 remained loyal to the Brienne family. In 1388 Nauplia was bought from Marie d'Enghien by the Venetians, whose first task was to recover it from the hands of Theodore Palaeologos of Mistra. It repelled Turkish sieges in 1470, in 1500 when Bayezid II attacked it in person, and for 14 months in 1538–39, but in 1540 it became the Turkish capital of the Morea. Count Königsmark, Morosini's lieutenant, recovered it for Venice in 1686, and until the Turks recaptured it in 1715 it became capital of the kingdom and seat of the Bp. of Corinth. Morosini died within sight of its walls in 1694. After its recapture Ahmed III visited Nauplia in person. As a consequence of a temporary occupation of Nauplia by the Russians in 1770, the capital was removed to Tripolis.

During the War of Independence Nauplia was the most important fortress in the Morea, its two strongholds being regarded as impregnable. The Greeks besieged it for over a year in 1821–22; a few months after the rout of Dramali they seized Palamidi, and the town capitulated. Later the two citadels were for a time in the hands of rival Greek chieftains, who indulged their passion for civil war at the expense of the luckless inhabitants, until Adm. Codrington and Sir Richard Church intervened. The town escaped destruction and hither in 1828 Capodistrias, the regent, moved his provisional seat of government from Aegina. In 1831, Capodistrias was assassinated in the church of St Spiridion. Otho, first king of Greece, disembarked at Nauplia in 1833 after the ratification of his election in 1832 at Pronoia, remaining here till the government was removed to Athens in 1834. The insurrection of the garrison here helped to bring about his abdication in 1862.

At Nauplia on 26 Apr 1941 the British evacuation of 6685 men and 150 nurses was made chaotic in the darkness and many men were lost when the transport 'Ulster Prince' ran aground, blocking the harbour entrance. 'Hyacinth', trying to free her, fouled the tow wire in her screw, and 'Slamat' was sunk by dive bombers. Two destroyers (H.M.S. 'Diamond' and 'Wryneck') were also lost.

The railway station and the bus terminus lie at the N. foot of Palamidi, where three squares divide the suburb of Pronoia from the town. In the E. square stands a vigorous equestrian *Statue of Theodore Kolokotronis* by Lazaros Sochos (1901), and in the central Plateia Dikasterion a marble figure of Capodistrias. We enter the old town by the Plateia Trion Navarkhon, where the *High School*, the first to be founded in liberated Greece, faces the building (now the Institut Français) in which it was installed by King Otho in 1833. In the centre stands a *Monument to Demetrios Ypsilantis*. Odhos Vasileos Konstandinou, the narrow main street, thronged during the evening volta, leads to PLATEIA SINDAGMATOS, the centre of the town. In the s.w. corner is the ex-Mosque of *Vouleftiko*, in which the first Greek parliament met in 1827–34. It is said that this building, the medresse behind it (now the museum store), and the second mosque in the square (now a cinema) were erected by one family in expiation of a crime.

The **Museum** (adm. 25 dr.; standard hours) occupies the upper floors of a dignified Venetian edifice of 1713 once a Naval depôt. FIRST FLOOR. The treasure of the museum is the unique and virtually complete *Suit of Mycenean Armour*, found at Dhendra in 1960. Neolithic pottery from the Frankhthi Cave; *Pottery from Early and Late Helladic sites in the Argolid, showing marked Minoan influences in shape and decoration; psykter, or cooler (E.H.), from Tiryns; stelai from Grave Circle B at Mycenae, one with a bas-relief (perhaps the earliest known from Greece), another with an incised figure of a horseman; hideous idols from Mycenae; mould for gold jewellery from the same; fragments of frescoes from Tiryns and Mycenae; Mycenean lamp from Midea; sherd inscribed in Linear B.—SECOND FLOOR. Sub-Mycenean *Helmet from Tiryns; finds of the Geometric period and later: Voltive discs (7C B.C.) with painted scenes; grotesque masks (8C) from Tiryns and Asine; the 'Tiryns Inscription', sole inscription found at this site until the surprising discoveries of Dec 1962; figurines and votive objects; Panathenaic amphorae; black-glazed krater (4C); Hellenistic terracotta bath.

The QUAY commands a fine view across the bay to the mountains of Argolis. In the Plateia Iatrou in front of the *Custom-House* is the *Monument to the French*, a marble obelisk erected in 1903 in memory of Gen. Fabvier, Adm. de Rigny, and others, who fell in the War of Independence. Akti Miaouli, a wide promenade on the site of the old town walls (demolished 1929–30), leads to the *West Mole*, built on the foundations of the 'porporella', or underwater stone barrier, that once protected the entrance to the harbour. It also ringed the islet of **Bourdzi** (500 yds offshore), on which stands the *Castel Pasqualigo*, erected by the

Bergamasque architect Ant. Gambello in 1471, and many times modified. It was used in the 19C as a retreat of the execrated public executioner. From the w. mole a path follows the *Bastion of the Five Brothers* (Πενταδέλφια), the only surviving part of the circuit wall begun in 1502, to the w. extremity of the peninsula. Here, high up, can be seen a postern gate and a few steps of the way up cut by Morosini's galley-slaves in 1686. We follow the s. side of the peninsula towards the little bay of *Arvanitia* in the neck of the isthmus, now arranged as a bathing place (adm. charge). Above tower the crags of Íts Kalé (Turk. Üç Kalè), the 'three castles' (Greek, Frankish, Venetian) that constituted **Akronavplion**.

A fortress has existed on the site since ancient times. The original walls of polygonal masonry (still visible from below on the N. side) have served as a foundation for each successive rebuilding. The decaying walls were partly restored by the Venetians in 1394–1409 and the lower *Castello del Torrione*, designed by Gambello (see above), added c. 1477–80. This now supports the Xenia Hotel. After the erection of the town wall in 1502 the upper castle was allowed to fall into disrepair until 1701–04 when Dolfin strengthened its entrances. Within, the former untidy but historic ruins have given way to hotels and unfinished tourist installations, but good views can be had from the panoramic road. From the far end long flights of steps within the *Baluardo Dolfin* descend to the *Porta Sagredo* fo 1713, above the main square.

In the lower town Odhos Kapodistriou has surviving Turkish fountains. On its N. side is the charming Venetian portal of the church of *Ay. Spiridon*, built in 1702, outside which Count John Capodistrias was assassinated in 1831 by George and Constantine Mavromichales; the mark of the bullet fired by Constantine is still shown near the entrance. A little higher up the slope, the *Metamorphosis* (Transfiguration), a Venetian conventual church returned by King Otho to the Roman rite after it had served the Turks as a mosque, contains a curious register of Philhellenes.

The **Fortress of Palamidi** (Παλαμήδειον; 705 ft) stands on the summit of a lofty and almost inaccessible rock commanding the whole of the Argolid with a *View of the surrounding mountains. On foot it is reached by a dizzy climb of some thousand steps requiring fortitude even in cool weather; best in the morning. A tourist road has been engineered on the s. side (comp. below). The name preserves the legend of Palamedes, but the difficult terrain seems to have inhibited building here until the governorship of Agost. Sagredo, when, to a design of Ant. Giaxich, a Dalmatian engineer (wounded at Argos, 1695), the fortress was built by Lasalle in 1711–14. The *Caponier*, or covered way, was erected a little earlier to provide a protected retreat from the hill to the city. The complex fortification, entered by a series of gates bearing the Lion of St Mark, consists of outworks and ramparts connecting three independent fortresses, in ascending order named *San Girardo* (the patron saint of the Sagredo), *San Nicolò*, and *Sant'-Agostino* (after the podestà).

Palamidi, inadequately garrisoned, fell after 8 days' siege in 1715. The poet Manthos of Ioannina, who was present, slanderously attributed its fall to the betrayal of its plans by Lasalle. More recently the forts were renamed after Greek heroes and Fort Miltiades (S. Nicolò) served as a convict prison. Kolokotronis was here incarcerated.

The new road up the s.e. slope of Palamidi passes close to a Mycenean cemetery of rock-hewn chamber-tombs.

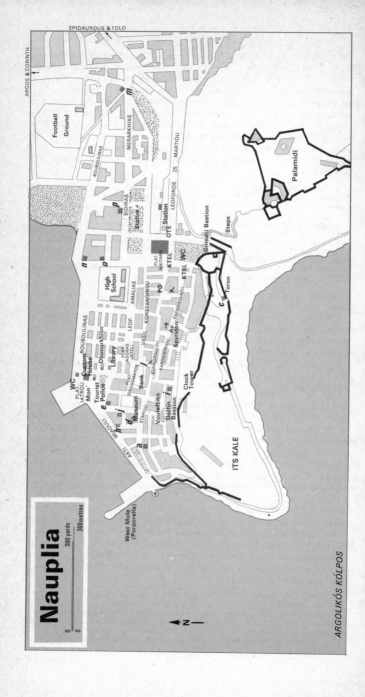

Nauplia

EPIDAUROUS & TOLO

ARGOS & CORINTH

Football
Ground

MERARKHIAS

MARTIOU

BOUBOULINAS

SIDIRAS

Statue

25 LEOFOROS

OTE

m

Station

Grimáni Bastion

Steps

Palamídi

High
School

AMALIAS

LEOF.

VASIL.

KONSTANDINOU

PLAT.
NIKITARA

KTEL

PO

KTEL

WC

Toron

Custom
House

BOUBOULINAS

Dhimarkhíon

Library

PLAT.
IAOMAS
(KTEL)

STAIKOPOULOU

Ay.
Spyridón

PAPANIKOLAOU

Toron

WC

Tourist
Police

PLAT.
IATROÚ
Mon.

Bank

Museum

STAIKOU

Vouleftiko

Dolfin
Bastion

Clock
Tower

ITS KALE

AKTÍ
MIAOÚLI

West Mole
(Porporélla)

N

ARGOLIKÓS KÓLPOS

300 yards
300 metres

THE PRINCIPAL LOCAL EXCURSION is to Tolon (6 m.; bus). We take the Epidauros road. After 300 yards a sign points (r.) to the *Bavarian Lion*. This was carved in the rock by order of Ludwig I of Bavaria to commemorate his soldiers who died in an epidemic at Tiryns in 1833–34. In this suburb of *Prónoia* in 1832 the National Assembly ratified the election of Prince Otho to the throne of Greece.—½ m. Turning (r.) to the *Ayía Moni*, or nunnery of Zoodokhos Piyi, founded by Leo, bp. of Argos; its elegant church dates from 1149. The curious fountain (1836) in the garden, decorated with reliefs and fed by an ancient conduit, is reputed to occupy the site of the Kanathos, a spring in which Hera annually renewed her virginity.—At 2¼ m., beyond the hamlet of *Áreia*, we leave the Epidauros road, turning right.—At 4 m. a tarmac road forks left, passes *Dhrépanon* (Plaka, 120R, C) at the head of a long marshy inlet, then skirts the coast to *Iría* (16½ m.), whose scattered remains attest a Mycenean origin and classical history; this road continues (part unpaved) to join Rte 29.—We keep right, pass through the village of modern *Asini*, then bear left at a fork to arrive at the rocky headland (Kastraki) on which stand the ruins of **Asine**.

Asine was occupied in the Early Helladic period by Anatolian tribes and later by migrants from N. Greece, Dryopians according to Strabo. The inhabitants sided with the Spartans in their invasion of Argos after the First Messenian War, and afterwards fled to Messenia, settling at Korone (Rte 34). The place was deserted until the 2C B.C. when it again became a fortified township.—The Swedish excavations of 1922–30 were the idea of Crown Prince (later King) Gustav Adolf, who himself took part. The results were published in English (Stockholm, 1938). Excavations were resumed in 1970.

The *Lower Town* retains imposing portions of Hellenistic ramparts on the N. side, with a gate and section of paved road. Within were found widespread traces of Early Helladic occupation, foundations of many houses of the Middle Helladic and Late Helladic periods, and of Roman baths, as well as Venetian additions to the fortifications (Morosini landed at Tolo in 1686). Geometric and Hellenistic remains survive on the *Acropolis*. On the s. point are some inscriptions left on a gun position by Italian soldiers in 1942. The wild flowers are varied. A Mycenean necropolis was explored on Mt Barbouna.

Beyond the site, the road turns w., skirting the sandy shore at the foot of Mt Barbouna (300 ft) to (6 m.) *Toló* (Solon, closed Nov–Feb, DPO, B; Epidavria, Tolo, Flivos, Minoa, all open all year, C), a summer resort with camp-sites. The bay is protected by islets. A better beach extends E. of the site.

Among other places accessible by local bus is *Ayios Adhrianos*, 3 m. N.E., where in 1962 a site was located on a hill-top to the N.W. (remains of Cyclopean walls; chapel on temple foundations above a cave), perhaps to be identified with ancient *Lessa* (though this is claimed for each of three other forts on the Ligourio road).

B Tiryns

Approaches. ROAD, *Tiryns* is 2½ m. from Nauplia on the level road to Argos (Rte 26). After 1 m. appear on the right the two limestone hills of *Ayios Ilias* (364 ft and 699 ft), each crowned by a chapel; these hills were used as quarries by the builders of Tiryns. Farther on we reach the penal *Agricultural College* founded by Capodistrias, in a field belonging to which was discovered in 1926 the so-called 'Treasure of Tiryns'. The ruins lie just beyond to the E. of the road. ADMISSION 25 dr.; standard hours.

The citadel of **TIRYNS** (ΤΙΡΥΝΣ) occupies the summit of a low rocky height known inevitably as Palaiokastro (87 ft), the lowest and most westerly of a series of isolated knolls rising like islands from the level plain. It is separated from the sea (now c. 1 m. distant) by reclaimed marshland. The fortress-palace is enclosed by the famous walls the finest specimens known of the military architecture of the Myceneans. Homer speaks of 'wall-girt Tiryns' (Τίρυνθα τειχόεσσαν; 'Iliad', ii, 559); Pindar admires the 'Cyclopean doorways' (κυκλωπία πρόθυρα; Frag. 642); and Pausanias compares the walls of Tiryns with the pyramids of Egypt. The palace within is more elaborate than those at Mycenae and Pylos. The unfortified city lay in the surrounding plain.

History. *Tiryns* was inhabited before the Bronze Age; the earliest people may have been lake-dwellers in the marsh. In one legend Tiryns is the birthplace of Herakles and the base of operations for his labours (Apollodros, II, iv, 12). It was fortified early in Mycenean times and rebuilt in its present form during the 13C B.C. Despite its size and wealth, Tiryns seems always to have been secondary to Argos or Mycenae. Though it continued to be inhabited through Geometric times and sent a contingent to Plataia in 479, the place never again had any importance. It was destroyed by Argos in 468 B.C. The strength of the walls proved an attraction in the Byzantine era when a church was built in the great forecourt. The site was explored by Schliemann and Dörpfeld in 1884–86. Considerable reconstruction of fallen walls was effected in 1962–64; the long-delayed discovery of the water-supply in 1962 by the late N. Verdelis has led to further investigation of the lower enceinte, still continuing.

The fortress is most impressive from below. The summit on which it stands has the form of a waisted oblong 327 yds long and from 65 to 110 ft wide, descending from s. to N. in three terraces. The whole of the area is enclosed by the *WALLS, 750 yds in circuit, which are built of two kinds of limestone, red and grey, in irregular blocks of different sizes, laid as far as possible in horizontal courses. The stones, the largest of which are estimated to weigh 14 tons, are partially hammer-dressed; smaller stones bonded with clay mortar fill the interstices. Round the lower citadel the walls are 23–26 ft thick; round the irregular upper citadel, where their line is broken by towers, salients, and re-entrant angles, they vary in thickness from 16 to 57 ft, in places containing galleries and chambers. They stand to about half their original estimated height of 65 feet.

The main entrance was in the middle of the E. wall. A smaller entrance opened in the great semicircular bastion that projects on the w. side, and there were three posterns in the lower citadel.

Admission is by a new gate from the by-road (E.) to the steep and ruinous *Ramp* (Pl. 1), 15½ ft wide, which formed an approach practicable for chariots. Its disposition exposed the visitor's right or unshielded side to the defenders as at Mycenae and necessitated at the top a sharp turn. The MAIN ENTRANCE (Pl. 2) opened in the outer wall, here 25 ft thick. The original opening of 15½ ft has been reduced to 8 ft by later masonry; there is no trace of a gate. We are now in a long passage running N. and S. between the inner and outer walls. To the right, passing a square niche below an arch (probably a guard post), it leads down to the lower citadel (see below). Fifty yards to the left is the *Outer Gateway* (Pl. 3), similar in dimension to the Lion Gate at Mycenae. In the monolithic threshold may be seen the holes for the pivots of folding doors, and in the rebated gateposts are bolt holes, 6 in. in diameter, allowing a cross-bar to be shot home into the wall. The right gatepost is intact, the left one is broken, and the lintel has disappeared.

Beyond, the passage widens to form a *Barbican* (Pl. 4), narrowing again to a point where an *Inner Gate* (Pl. 5) probably guarded the oblong *Courtyard* (Pl. 6). Here, to the left, in the thickness of the outer wall, is the first of the two series of *GALLERIES AND CHAMBERS for which the

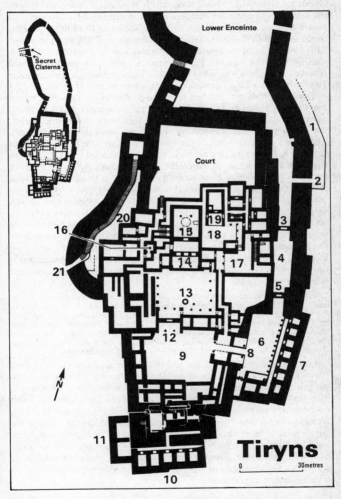

fortress is specially renowned. The *E. Gallery*, fronted by a colonnade, had a corbelled vault and communicated by six doors with six vaulted *Chambers* (Pl. 7), each 11 ft square.

Opposite opens the GREAT PROPYLAIA (Pl. 8), a double porch divided by a wall, in which was a single doorway. Between antae within and without stood wooden columns, the stone bases of which are still in position. The gateway supersedes an earlier one. From the inner porch a narrow passage leads off direct to the smaller megaron (comp. below).

We enter the *Forecourt* (Pl. 9) of the palace, from which remains of a Byzantine church have been removed; it is bounded on three sides by the fortress walls and the complex of *Casemates built into them. We descend by a covered staircase, with a right-angled bend in the middle, to the vaulted *S. Gallery* (66 ft long, 16 ft high, and 5 ft wide) at a level 23 ft below that of the court. The sides narrow to a loophole in the E. wall by which it was lit. Five doorways open from the gallery into rectangular vaulted *Chambers* (Pl. 10).—On the S.W. side a rectangular *Tower* (Pl. 11), with a frontage of 62 ft, enclosed two cisterns.

The **Royal Palace** is reached from the N. side of the forecourt by the *Smaller Propylaia* (Pl. 12). The walls of the palace stand to a height of only 1½–3 ft; above this limestone base they were of sun-dried brick, the whole being then covered by stucco and decorated with frescoes. The huge stone thresholds of the doors remain in situ; the floors are of concrete made of lime and pebbles. In the colonnaded court (Pl. 13) is a round sacrificial altar. A *Porch* (Pl. 14; aithousa), with two columns and elaborate benches, gives access by triple doors to an ante-chamber, and thence through a door (closed in antiquity only by a curtain) to the MEGARON (Pl. 15), or *Great Hall*. In the centre is a circular clay hearth, 11 ft in diameter. The roof was supported by four wooden columns, set on stone bases, which had an open lantern to give light and let out the smoke. The base of the throne is well preserved and the painted floor intact in places. The walls were frescoed with scenes of a boar hunt and a life-size frieze of women. Reached from the ante-chamber is the *Bathroom* (Pl. 16), with a floor composed of one huge limestone monolith 13 ft by 10.

These apartments are duplicated on a smaller scale behind and to the E. (outer court, Pl. 17; inner court, Pl. 18; smaller megaron, Pl. 19; and ancillary buildings), representing, perhaps, the women's quarters. Behind is a large open court separated by the massive inner wall from the LOWER ENCEINTE. This has hitherto been thought to be merely a fortified compound used as a refuge in time of danger, but the area is now being systematically re-explored since the discovery of the secret cisterns (comp. below). Some of their intricacies have been exposed.

From a square tower to the W. of the rear court a well-preserved *Secret Stair* (Pl. 20) winds down within a massive bastion to an inconspicuous corbelled *Postern Gate* (Pl. 21). We pass out of the fortress, turn right, and skirt the outer walls. At the N.W. angle of the lower enceinte two secret passages lead steeply downward through the walls from inside to two *Underground Cisterns* fed by springs. There are comparable arrangements at Mycenae and on the Acropolis at Athens, but the Tiryns passages were discovered by accident only in 1962. Stones covering the cisterns were found (only, unfortunately, after some had been moved) to bear Archaic inscriptions shallowly cut in boustrophedon c. 600 B.C.

C   The Argive Heraion

Approaches. ASPHALT ROAD (bus) from Argos to (4¾ m.) *Khónika*, a village with a 12C church (restored 1963). Passable tracks (landrover or on foot) hither from Mycenae (1 hr). Hence by dirt road (c. 1 m. farther) to the site. Viâ Ayia Trias, see below.—The view is clearest in the evening.

The **Heraion of Argos,** or *Sanctuary of Hera*, dedicated to the tutelary goddess of the Argolid, was common to Argos and Mycenae. An imposing complex of ruins, usually ignored by the present-day traveller, the sanctuary occupies a spur (Palaiókastro; 420 ft) projecting s.w. and commands a fine view over the plain to Argos.

The site was discovered in 1831 by the Philhellene, Gen. Thomas Gordon, who dug here in 1836; its excavation in 1892–95 constituted the first major work of the American School (under Charles Waldstein). Further work was accomplished by Carl Blegen in 1925–28; and a chance discovery led to a short but profitable investigation in 1949 by P. Amandry and J. Caskey ('Hesperia' XXI). The summit of the hill was first occupied in Early Helladic times. Pausanias refers to the area by the name *Prosymna* and in the surrounding slopes Blegen dug many tombs extending in date from Neolithic to Late Mycenean. At the Argive Heraion Agamemnon is fabled to have been chosen leader of the Trojan expedition. Hither from Argos Kleobis and Biton drew the chariot of their mother in the story told by Solon to Croesus (Herod. I, 31). The old temple was burnt down in 423 B.C. by the carelessness of the aged priestess Chryseis.

The Archaic and Classical sanctuary is built on three terraces, above which is the Helladic settlement. A path, to the r., leads to the UPPER TERRACE, supported by a massive retaining wall in conglomerate, which

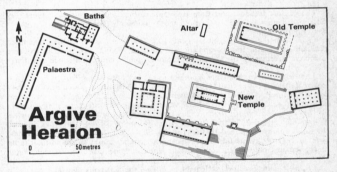

has all the appearances of Mycenean workmanship but is believed to date from the late-Geometric period. The surface of the terrace is paved and remains to this day almost perfectly level. On it may be seen traces of the stylobate of the **Old Temple,** perhaps the earliest peripteral building of the Peloponnese, dated to the first half of the 7C. In the Doric style (6 by 14 columns), its upper structure may have been of wood and unburnt brick.

In the centre of the MIDDLE TERRACE stands the poros stereobate of the **New Temple,** erected c. 420–410 B.C. by Eupolemos of Argos. This was a Doric peripteral building (6 by 12 columns) in which was set up a chryselephantine statue of Hera by Polykleitos, said to have deserved comparison with the Olympian Zeus of Pheidias. Pausanias claims to have seen here also the ancient xoanon in pearwood removed by the Argives from Tiryns in 468 B.C., a bejewelled golden peacock dedicated by Hadrian, and a purple robe offered by Nero.

The buildings bounding this terrace have many unexplained features. Below the wall that supports the upper terrace is the *North Stoa,* believed (on the evidence of surviving capitals which are not known with certainty to belong to it) to date from the 6C B.C. or even earlier. The foundations are of limestone and the blocks forming the rear wall are well squared. In the centre are statue bases and at the w. end a basin, lined with cement, is connected to an elaborate water-supply system. The *North-East Building*, dating from the end of the 7C, was altered at a later date. The *East Building* is a mid-5C rectangular structure in poros with a portico and a triple row of interior columns. The *West Building*, one of the earliest examples known of a peristyle court (late 6C), has three rooms leading off its N. side; it may have been a banqueting place. To the N.W. are further foundations, possibly belonging to a late monumental entrance. Farther w. are a large Roman bathing establishment and a palaestra.

The *South Stoa*, at the third level below the retaining wall of the middle terrace, shows the finest workmanship of any building on the site, and is dated to the mid-5C. It is now suggested that the flights of steps, formerly postulated as leading up to the s. stoa and past it on the E. side to the temple, are in fact Archaic retaining walls of stepped construction (analemma).

The phylax will show a well-preserved tholos tomb c. 200 yds below the main site.

The Middle Helladic and Late Helladic cemeteries of *Prosymna*, explored by Blegen, are in the hillsides to the N.W. at approximately the same contour height as the upper terrace.

From Khonika a road continues N.E. to (5½ m.) *Berbati* (which has readopted the name Prosimni; but comp. above). Here in 1936–37 the Swedish Institute explored a cemetery of Mycenean chamber-tombs and a settlement of Early Helladic II date.

Another road runs s.E. from Khonika to (3½ m.) *Merbaka*, officially *Ayía Triás*, where it meets a better road from Argos (4½ m.). The village, which has an attractive 12C church, is said to derive its name from William of Meerbeke, Latin Abp of Corinth (fl. c. 1280), who translated various Greek medical classics. Turning E. for a further 3 m. by dirt road we may reach **Dhendra** (on foot a more direct track from Khonika avoids Merbaka). Here (on a slope N.W. of the village) the Swedish Institute dug an unrobbed tholos tomb in 1926–27 (L.H. IIIA; finds in Athens) and, in 1937–39, richly furnished Mycenean chamber-tombs surrounding it (gold cups, remains of wooden coffin, etc.). Another tomb dug in 1960 yielded the Mycenean ceremonial armour now in Nauplia museum. The cemetery belongs to the Middle–Late Helladic settlement of *Midea*, the acropolis of which stands 30 min. E. of Dhendra (to the r. of the road to Midia village, from which the ascent is easier); it preserves its cyclopean enceinte.

29 FROM NAUPLIA TO EPIDAUROS AND THE ARGOLIC PENINSULA

ROAD, 19 m. (30 km.) to *Epidauros*; 59 m. (94 km.) to *Kosta*, for Spetsai. Buses, see Rte 28. The Epidauros sanctuary is called locally Ieron Ligouriou and is not at either New or Old Epidauros (comp. below).

On leaving Nauplia we enter the valley separating the slopes of Palamidi, on the s., from the bare waterless range of *Arakhnaíon*, to the N. Its highest point rises to 3935 ft but its most striking peak is the less lofty Mt Arna (3540 ft) above Ligourio. The view is much better on the return journey when the serried ranges of the Peloponnese rise ahead. Just after the 14 km. stone, 50 yds before a modern bridge at a sharp corner, we see above the road (l.) the corbelled arch of a massive *Cyclopean Bridge*, perhaps of the 5C B.C. but probably of Mycenean origin. A little farther on (l.) rises *Kazarma*, a small but precipitous hill (920 ft) with some remains of a citadel of the 5C with walls standing to 20 ft in polygonal masonry. A second fortress of the same period stands conspicuously above the road at (10 m.) *Kastraki* (l.; 1410 ft).—16½ m. The decayed church of *Ayia Marina*, to the left, is built on the site of an Ionic temple of Athena. Near by are the scanty remains of a pyramidal structure of the 4C B.C., believed to be a guard-house capable of accommodating a patrol in emergency.—16½ m. **Ligourió** (ΛΙΓΟΥΡΙΟΝ; *Halcyon, Asklepios*, D; tavernas), with 1730 inhab., has several Byzantine churches, of which the most interesting (on our road, beyond the centre) incorporates small fragments from the Tholos in the Sanctuary (see below).

From Ligourió a road continues N.E. through a defile, then divides. The left branch joins the new road from the Corinth Canal (Rte 25c) just short of *Néa Epídhavros* (8 m.; Epidauros C), where the first 'National Assembly' met on 20 Dec 1821 to declare the independence of Greece ('Constitution of Epidauros'). Above the town (1220 inhab.) are ruins of the Frankish castle of Nicholas de Guise, Constable of the Morea.—The right branch leads to *Palaiá Epídhavros* (5½ m.; Assos, Koronis, C; good taverna), with a little harbour used by ferry services from Piraeus (4 times weekly in summer). The ancient city of *Epidauros* stood on the headland to the S. of the harbour. Cyclopean walls still stand.

Submerged buildings have been identified and a *Theatre of Dionysos excavated in 1972 having 10 kerkides and 18 rows of seats (late 4C B.C.), many inscribed with names of citizens who endowed the seating.

We bear right in Ligourió and 1½ m. farther on left for the Sanctuary of Epidauros. The right branch continues through the peninsula (see below).

19 m. (30 km.) The **Hieron of Epidauros** (Ieron Ligouriou), or *Sanctuary of Asklepios*, is situated in a broad and lonely valley between Mt Velanidhia, the ancient *Titthion* (2815 ft), on the N.E., and Mt Kharani, the ancient *Kynortion*, on the S.E. The place was at once a religious centre and a fashionable spa. In addition to the temples and colonnades devoted to the cult of Asklepios (or Æsculapius) and the cure of his disciples, there were dwellings for the priest-physicians, hospitals for the sick, sanatoria for the convalescent, and hotels and places of amusement for the healthy. In Roman times were added baths, fed by reservoirs which collected water from the local springs.

In extent the Sanctuary compares with Delphi or Olympia, but apart from the Theatre the ruins themselves are interesting only to the specialist, though the pine-clad setting remains charming despite the artificial landscaping and paraphernalia of the festival. The road passes between the Stadium and the fenced part of the site (entrance gate, l.; car park, r.), then enters the main gate (adm. 25 dr.; 8 or 9–sunset; Sun & hol. 10–4.30). Within are (r.) a *Tourist Pavilion* (Rfmts) and the *Xenia Hotel* (B), and (l.) the Museum. The road and paths continue to the Theatre where we start the visit.

History. The worship of Apollo at the Epidaurian sanctuary seems to go back into the mists of time, that of Asklepios being grafted on not earlier than the Archaic period. It superseded that of Apollo by the 4C, by which time Epidauros had become established as the 'birthplace' of Asklepios. The cult seems to have originated in Homeric times in Thessaly, possibly at Trikke, and to have been carried s. viâ Phokis and Boeotia, but first attained prominence at Epidauros in the 6–5C spreading thence to Athens. Kos (Rte 75) always claimed a Trikkan origin for it. Some of the medical as opposed to magical expertise of Asklepios may have filtered through Asia Minor and Kos from Egypt. The Ptolemaic Greeks identified with their own hero-god Asklepios Imhotep (lived c. 2780 B.C.), the Egyptian genius and deified physician, around whose tomb at Sakkara the first healing sanctuary grew up. The fame of the sanctuary at Epidauros reached a peak in the 4C B.C. when, perhaps, magic and faith were giving place to more scientific treatment.

The Hieron belonged to the city of Epidauros (comp. above) and was in charge of an annually elected Priest of Asklepios, assisted by recorders, choristers, police, and other officials. Recovered patients gave costly offering and votive inscriptions. Every four years, nine days after the Isthmian Games, an athletic and dramatic festival known as the *Asklepeia* was celebrated.

Livy and Ovid both tell how Rome, ravaged by an epidemic in 293 B.C., sent for the sacred serpent from Epidauros. The sanctuary was despoiled by Sulla in 86 B.C. and the loot distributed among his soldiers.

The excavations, begun in 1881, became the life's work of P. Kavvadias. The French School also excavated just after the Second World War, and J. Papadimitriou in 1948–51.

The *Theatre, the best preserved of all Greek theatres and one of the best preserved Classical buildings in Greece, dates from the 4C B.C. and seems to have escaped alteration until its judicious restoration in recent years. It is now celebrated as the centre of an annual summer festival of drama. Its acoustics are unusually perfect, the slightest whisper or rustle of paper from the orchestra being clearly audible from any of its 14,000 seats. The *Cavea*, c. 125 yds across, faces N. It has 55 rows of seats, 34 below the diazoma and 21 above. The lower block is divided into 12 wedges by 13 staircases; the upper block has 23 staircases. The seats of honour were of red, the ordinary seats of white limestone. The two flanks of the theatre were supported by poros retaining walls, recently restored. The *Orchestra* is a complete circle 22 yds in diameter, the circumference of which is marked by a ring of limestone flags. The floor was of beaten earth. In the centre is the round base of the *Thymele*, or altar. Between the circle and the front row of seats is a semicircular paved depression, 7 ft wide, placed to collect rainwater. Access to the theatre is by two *Parodoi*, passing through double doorways (restored) having pilasters embellished with Corinthian capitals. The foundations of the *Stage* can be seen when they are not covered by temporary wooden scenery.

Above the theatre, but now not easily accessible owing to the fences, is (15 min.) the *Sanctuary of Apollo Maleatas*, in which excavations have continued since 1974. This is dated to the mid-7C B.C. and consisted at that date merely of an altar, a temple being added in the 4C. A Mycenean settlement has been identified and the 7C altar is on Mycenean foundations.

The **Museum** may conveniently be visited before the excavations. To right and left of the entrance are two Corinthian columns from the interior colonnade of the Tholos and two Ionic columns from the Abaton.—ROOM I. Inscriptions recording miraculous cures; Roman statuary; surgical instruments; building stele with accounts for the Tholos and Temple of Asklepios.—ROOM II. Sculpture (mostly casts) from pediments; reconstruction of the entablature of the Propylaia.— ROOM III. Reconstructions: part of the Temple of Asklepios (380–375). Pavement of the Tholos, a curious building of which two different conjectural versions are illustrated by drawings; it was built c. 360 B.C. possibly by Polykleitos the Younger. Corinthian capital, section of circular wall, ornate ceiling, and decorated doorway, all from the same building and finally a reconstruction of its entablature.

The **Excavations** lie to the N.W. We come first to the remains of a vast square building, probably the *Katagogion*, a hotel to be compared with the Leonidaion at Olympia. It had four cloistered courts from each of which opened 18 rooms. The polygonal walls stand to a height of 2 ft and most of the threshold blocks are in place.—To the w. are the ruined Greek *Baths*.—The GYMNASIUM, a huge colonnaded court, with exedrae and other rooms off it, survives only in one course of the outer walls. The Romans built an *Odeion* in the court, of which considerable portions of the brick-built auditorium and stage buildings survive. The whole base of the *Great Propylaia* of the Gymnasium, at the N.W. corner, is preserved with its pavement and ramp, though its Doric colonnade has vanished.—The indeterminate ruins to the N.E. are of the *Palaestra*, or

Stoa of Kotys, a building originally of unburnt brick that collapsed and was rebuilt (along with other parts of the sanctuary) by a Roman senator Antoninus, probably the Emp. Antoninus Pius.

The most important group of buildings in the Hieron now opens out

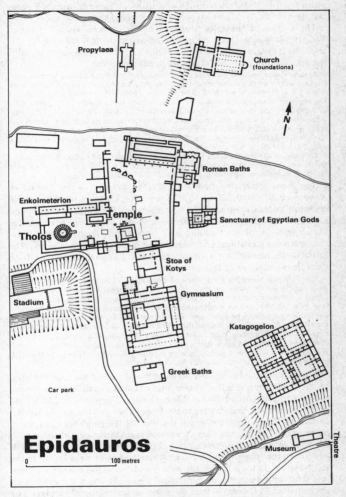

Epidauros

to E. and W.; this was the area that the Byzantines surrounded with walls and converted into a rectangular fortress. At the S.E. corner, immediately N. of the palaestra, is the little Greek *Temple of Themis*, with an unidentified Roman building beyond. Turning to the W., we come to the foundations of the *Temple of Artemis*, a Doric prostyle building with 6 columns on the front (4C B.C.). Almost adjoining on the N. is a large rectangular building which may have been the *Abaton*, where patients slept expecting the visitation of the god and a cure by miraculous dreams. It was replaced in the 4C by another building (see below) and this site altered in Roman times. Various inscribed bases may be seen to the N., which probably bordered the sacred grove.

The **Temple of Asklepios** is approached by a paved road and ramp. The temple was a Doric peripteral hexastyle, with 6 columns by 11, about 80 ft long, and dating from c. 420 B.C. Nothing, however, remains but foundations and the fragments in the museum.

A stele found in 1885 supplies many details of the method and cost of construction. The work was supervised by the architect *Theodotes* and the temple took 4 years and 8½ months to build. The sculptor *Timotheos* supplied the models for the pedimental sculptures, which were executed by other artists. The doors were of ivory and the cult statue in gold and ivory was by *Thrasymedes of Paros*. According to Pausanias Asklepios was represented seated on a throne, grasping a staff in one hand, and holding the other over the head of the serpent; a dog crouched by his side. Two marble reliefs, possibly copies of the statue, were found (now in Athens).

To the s. of the temple is the *Great Altar of Asklepios*, and farther s., crossed by the line of the Byzantine wall, are the foundations of a small building which may be the *Epidoteion*, or sanctuary of the bountiful healers.

The most interesting building after the Theatre is the **Tholos**, or *Rotunda*, built c. 360–320 B.C. by the same Polykleitos, a more florid and elaborate construction than the corresponding buildings at Delphi and Olympia. Nothing is left but the foundations, but a very good idea of the appearance of the building may be obtained from the partial reconstructions, drawings, and plans in the museum (comp. above). The foundations consist of six concentric walls, in conglomerate, with an extreme diameter of 72 ft.

The Rotunda stood on a stylobate of three steps. The three outer foundation walls supported an outer peristyle of 26 Doric columns, in poros, stuccoed and painted; the main circular wall of the building with a large portal flanked on either side by a window; and an interior colonnade of 14 marble columns with beautiful Corinthian capitals. The three inner foundation walls form a miniature labyrinth, the purpose of which, as indeed of the whole building, is obscure. A sacred well or a snake pit are among possibilities. Above the labyrinth rested a spiralling chequered pavement in black and white marble. The ceiling was coffered, carved, and painted. Lion's head gargoyles were regularly placed at the edge of the roof, on the apex of which was a carved floral acroterion.

To the N. of the tholos and forming the N. side of the area enclosed by the Byzantines, is a line of two adjacent stoas, each 32 ft deep, now reduced to their foundations. Their combined length was 232 ft; the w. colonnade was built, owing to the slope of the ground, in two stories, so that its upper floor continued the level of the single story of the E. colonnade. The two together comprised the **Abaton**, or *Enkoimeterion*, the place of incubation. One or two of the benches which lined the walls and joined the columns still survive. A staircase of 14 steps led up to the second story. In the E. colonnade were found tablets (now in the museum) inscribed with accounts of miraculous cures. In the s.E. corner is an ancient *Well*, 55 ft deep; in the s.w. corner an underground passage. The well was sunk in the 6C B.C. and incorporated in the 4C building more, apparently, in piety than for practical use.

Turning N. we leave over on our right a large Roman *Thermal Establishment* fed by water from Mt. Kynortion and reach the main *Propylaea of the Sanctuary* with part of the *Sacred Way* from the town of Epidauros.

The limestone pavement and the ramps leading to the great gate are in good condition. To the s. among the trees are some not very clear remnants of a huge basilican *church* with double aisles and a large atrium. Skirting the boundary fence, to the w., we pass a small *Temple of Aphrodite* and a huge *Cistern* of Hellenic date.

We may leave by the N.W. gate and cross the road to the **Stadium,** arranged in a natural declivity during the 5C B.C., with seats partly hewn from the rock and partly built up in masonry. The starting and finishing lines survive, c. 600 ft apart, and the construction, without sphendone and with an inclined entrance tunnel, has some resemblance to its counterpart at Olympia. A stone water channel with basins at intervals surrounds the track.

To Kosta (for Spetsai), asphalt road. The right branch at (17½ m.) the Epidauros turn (comp. above) runs s. and E.—Beyond (26½ m.) *Trakheiá* an unpaved road branches (l.) to Méthana and Galatás (comp. Rte 23B); while c. 1 m. farther on a by-road (r.; at first unpaved) leads back to Nauplia viâ Íria (see Rte 28A). We continue s., cross the scrub-covered w. flank of Mt Dídima (3525 ft), and from a saddle (1600 ft) have a *View across the Argolic Gulf.—40 m. *Dídima*, which with its mountain preserves an ancient name, lies below in the centre of its circular plain.—47½ m. A road leads (r.) to Koilás (2½ m.), an active fishing and boat-building village. In the *Franchthi Cave*, on the N. side of the bay, has been discovered a stratigraphical sequence going back to the 8th millennium B.C., including, at the bottom of the Mesolithic deposit, the earliest complete skeleton found in Greece. This is thought likely to prove a key site for the study of early and middle Neolithic in Europe.—50 m. (80 km.) **Kranídhi** (Inns) is the market centre (3700 inhab.) of the peninsula. Hither the Greek senate removed in 1823 following their rupture with the executive. Ermioni (Rte 23D) lies 5 m. E. —We continue through fine stone-pines to (54 m.) **Portokhéli** (*Flisvos* D, open all year), on the N. side of an inlet. The remains on the s. side of the harbour have been equated with *Halieis*, settled by refugees from Tiryns after 479 B.C. Here in 1962–68 the American School explored part of the acropolis and traced the N. line of the walls beneath the sea.

Many huge summer hotel complexes (*PLM Porto Kheli* A; *Ververoda, Galaxy, Thermissia,* B, and others) have been built on the adjacent coasts; there is a ferry twice daily to Spetsai (40 min.) and, in the season, an air service from Athens.

We turn left round the E. side of the bay, and reach (57½ m.) **Kósta** (*Cap d'Or*, Apr–Oct, *Lido*, both B), also undergoing holiday development. Ferry to Spetsai (6 times daily in 15 min.); also (more expensive) constant motor boats.

30 FROM ARGOS TO TRIPOLIS

ROAD, 38 m. (61 km.), one of the best in the Peloponnese, with good mountain scenery.—6½ m. **Lerna.**—18 m. (29 km.) *Akhladókambos.*—38 m. **Tripolis.** Buses from the square (originating from Athens; 8 times daily in 4 hrs).

RAILWAY, 43 m. (69½ km.), 6 trains daily in 1½–1¾ hr, all starting from Athens (add 2½–3 hrs; comp. Rtes 24, 26).

Leaving Argos by the avenue that passes the theatre (p. 257), the road turns s., skirting the hills that hem the Argolic plain.—3 m. By-road (r.) to *Kefalári* (1½ m. w.), a shaded village at the foot of the precipitous Mt. Khaon, where the Kephalari, the ancient *Erasinos,* issues from the rocks. The ancients thought that the waters came underground from Lake Stymphalos (32 m. N.W.; Rte 38). The spring (Kefalóvrisi) forms a pool, above which open two caverns, dedicated to Pan and Dionysos. The larger resembles an acute Gothic arch and extends 65 yds into the mountain; the smaller one has been converted into the chapel of the Panayia Kefalarítissa. The ancient festival of *tyrbe* (disorder) is recalled by the modern festival on 18 April.

About 1¼ m. S.W. (accessible by unpaved road) on a hillock stands the ruined PYRAMID OF KENKREAI, the more complete of the two pyramids in the Argolid. The interesting structure is of hard local limestone, laid roughly in courses, having both squared and polygonal blocks. A corbelled arch, at the S.E. corner, gives access by a blind corridor to an inner rectangular room. The pyramid was excavated in 1901 by Wiegand who concluded that it was not, as Pausanias believed the polyandrion of the Argives who fell at Hysiae. Louis Lord re-examined it (Hesperia 1938) and takes it to be a late-4C B.C. guard house used by patrols.

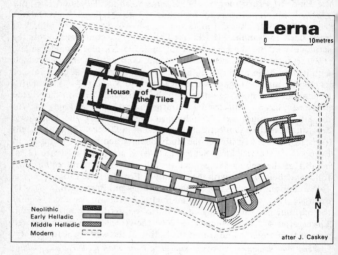

To the right *Mt Ktenias*, the ancient *Kreopolon*, rises to 5245 ft; *Mt Pontinos*, its easternmost spur, closes the Argolic Plain, extending to within 300 yds of the sea. On its summit rise the ruins of a Frankish castle, occupying the site of a house of Hippomedon and a temple of Athena Saïtis.

The vigorous defence of the narrow gap below on 25 June 1825 by Demetrios Ypsilanti with 227 men against a much larger force of Egyptians checked the advance of Ibrahim Pasha on Nauplia after his capture of Tripolis. From the shore here in 1941 Gen. Maitland Wilson, C.-in-C. Greece, departed by flying-boat to reorganize the continuing struggle in Crete. The Germans added three forts to defend the gap.

6½ m. (10½ km.) *Míloi* (ΜΥΛΟΙ, the mills) lies between Mt Pontinos and the sea, on the site of ancient **Lerna**. Here in a sacred grove of plane-trees were celebrated the Lernaean mysteries in honour of Demeter, and here Herakles slew the Hydra. At the s. end of the village, to seaward of the road on a mound fortified by the Germans in 1943, stands the conspicuous concrete shelter protecting the EXCAVATIONS (adm. 10 dr.)

made by the American School under John Caskey in 1952–58. The site was occupied from the 4th millennium B.C. to the close of the Mycenean age, and is one of the most important in Greece for remains of the Early Helladic period. The *Fortifications* are virtually unique for their period. The HOUSE OF THE TILES, so-called from the extensive remains of its rectangular terracotta roof tiles, is the most elaborate E. H. building yet found. A palace, or administrative centre, it is 83 ft long and 40 ft wide and had two stories. It was destroyed by fire at the end of E.H. II, so helping to preserve its mud-brick walls. The E.H. III level yielded pottery from Troy, whereas the Middle Helladic settlement, which here seems to follow without any violent upheaval, has pottery imports from near Niš (Balkan) as well as from Crete and the Cyclades. Two Mycenean royal shaft graves (robbed in antiquity) cut through the house of the Tiles.

We leave on our left a road to Astros (12½ m. s.).

Ástros (Anthini D), an agricultural centre (2550 inhab.), grows olives and fruit, being especially noted for peaches. It belongs to Kynouria, an eparchy of Arcadia. Here in 1823 was held the Second National Assembly called by various Klepht leaders of the insurrection to revise the constitution of 1821. The *Moní Loukoús* 2½ m. away) has a church of 1100. *Parálion Ástros* (Chrissi Akti D, good) is pleasantly situated on the sea, 3 m. to the E. A moderate dirt-road continues viâ *Áyios Andréas* along the precipitous coast to *Leonídhion*(Rte 32; 50 m. from Argos).

The road turns W., climbing *Merovítsa*, the s. spur of Mt Ktenias, by steep, but well-engineered and protected, hairpin bends, which afford splendid retrospective *Views of the Argolic Gulf. The railway runs farther s. in the red gorge of Kivéri, into which we cross by (13 m.) a saddle c. 2000 ft high (*View; café c. 2 m. farther on). The valley opens out as we descend by sharp hairpin bends (springs).

The road passes between (18 m.) *Akhladókambos* (AXΛAΔO-KAMΠOΣ; 1705 ft), a village (960 inhab.) on the hillside, and its railway station (895 ft) in the fertile valley below. The place takes name from the wild pear (αχλαδιά) which once grew on the mountain slopes.

On a ridge nearer the railway are the ruins of *Hysiai*, where the Argives defeated the Lacedaimonians in 669–668 B.C. The town lay on the frontier between Argos and Tegea, and was destroyed by the Lacedaimonians in 417 B.C. Its acropolis is marked by good polygonal walling.

We cross the railway twice on level ground, then ascend towards the head of the valley; the vegetation becomes scrubby and alpine. On a hill near the road summit (2560 ft) are the ruins of *Moukhli*, a Byzantine fortress used by the Franks and destroyed in 1460.—We enter Arcadia.

At (31 m.) *Ayioryítika* (AΓIΩPΓITIKA) we rejoin the railway after its tortuous detour (far to the s.) round *Parthenion* (3985 ft), now on our left. On Parthenion's slope a sanctuary once marked the spot where Pan promised the runner Pheidippides that he would aid the Athenians at Marathon.—32½ m. *Stenón*, watered by the Sarandapotamos, lies amid rolling cornfields of the Plain of Tripolis.

The PLAIN OF TRIPOLIS, a monotonous plateau enclosed by an amphitheatre of barren mountains, really consists of two adjoining level tracts, the *Plain of Tegea* in the s. and the *Plain of Mantinea* in the N. About 20 m. long from N. to S. and with an extreme width of 10 m., it averages 2150 ft above sea-level and suffers extremes of temperature with violent hail and thunderstorms in summer. Vines, wheat, and barley are grown, but, apart from the mulberry, the plateau is now almost treeless. There are several marshes, but few rivers or streams; such as exist mostly disappear into swallow-holes (katavothrae). The plain was famous in antiquity for the three Arcadian cities of Mantinea, Tegea, and Pallantion.

38 m. (61 km.) **TRIPOLIS** (ΤΡΙΠΟΛΙΣ; *Mainalon* A; *Arkadia, Semiramis*, B; *Galaxy, Artemis, Anaktorikon, Alex*, these C), the capital (20,200 inhab.) and only large town of the nome of Arcadia, is the chief centre of communications in the Peloponnese. It lies in a bleak situation at the s. foot of Mt Apáno Krépa (5115 ft), a peak of the Mainalon range. A modern manufacturing town, with hollow-ware and carpet factories, tanneries, and a flourishing wine production, it is also the seat of a bishop.

History. Tripolis was founded, under the name of *Droboglitza* or *Hydropolitza* about the 14C to take the place of the three derelict cities of the plain (comp. above) and the eparchy to which it belongs still keeps the name of Mantineia. Later it was called *Tripolitza* (in Turkish *Tarabolussa*) and became in 1770 the fortified capital of the Pasha of the Morea. It was taken in 1821 by Kolokotronis, when the Turkish population was massacred, and retaken in 1824 by Ibrahim Pasha, who completely destroyed it in the retreat of 1828. It revived after 1834.

The most attractive features of the town are the three squares, with animated cafés beneath their trees, and the saddlery and harness shops in the streets joining them.

Buses of KTEL 6 Arkadias ply from Plat. Ay. Konstandinou every hour to (5 m.) *Alea* (no rfmts), formerly Piali, the site of ancient Tegea **Tegea**, one of the oldest and most important cities in Arcadia, occupied a large area and its few remains are scattered.

The largest city in the plain, Tegea waged a long war with Sparta until beaten into submission c. 560 B.C. as a vassal-state. The Tegeans sent 500 men to Thermopylae and 1500 to Plataia, and after the Persian wars tried unsuccessfully to throw off the yoke of Sparta with Argive aid. In the Peloponnesian War the Tegeans sided with Sparta. In 370 B.C., after the battle of Leuktra, Tegea joined the Arcadian League, and at the second battle of Mantinea (362 B.C.) she fought on the side of Thebes against Sparta. In 222 B.C. Tegea became an unwilling member of the Achaean League. Still a flourishing city in the time of Strabo and in the time of Pausanias, Tegea was destroyed by Alaric in the 5C A.D. It was refounded by the Byzantines, and under the name of *Nikli* it became one of the most important cities in the Morea. In 1209 Geoffrey de Villehardouin here established a barony.— Tegea was the birthplace of *Atalanta*, the fleetest runner of the age and the heroine of the Calydonian boar-hunt.

The site was excavated by the French School in 1889–90, 1902, and 1910 and by the Greek Archaeological Service in 1965.

In the village the bus stops outside a well-arranged little Museum reconstructed in 1967, containing finds from the site. *Central Room* Marble thrones from the theatre; Hellenistic female statues.—*Room to left*. Sculpture from the Temple of Athena Alea, from the workshop of Skopas: Head of Telephos or Herakles; helmeted head; two torsos of Nike Apteros (not Atalanta); cast of 'Hygieia' (original now in Athens) torsos of Heroes from the pediments; architectonic decoration from the temple.—*Room to right*. Six herms conjoined; Head of Herakles Relief from a sarcophagus, depicting Achilles and the corpse of Hector Reliefs: Lion, lioness; funeral feast. In cases: Prehistoric and Classical vases; terracotta and bronze statuettes.—*Inner Room*, beyond, in cases Geometric bronzes from Asea; fragment of Daedalic relief; terracotta votives and plaques; Geometric and Archaic bronzes, both in the round and repoussé; Early Helladic pots.

In 3 min. we reach (near the church of Ayios Nikolaos) the Temple of Athena Alea, excavated in 1889 and 1902. It was one of the most famous sanctuaries in Greece; here two kings of Sparta, Leotychides and Pausanias, took refuge, as well as Chryseis, the careless priestess of the Argive Heraion. An Archaic temple was burnt down in 395 B.C and the rebuilding entrusted to Skopas of Paros. The new Temple had a Doric peristyle of 6 columns by 14, and an internal colonnade of Corinthian half-columns, with Ionic above. The substructure is virtually complete; many fragments of fallen column survive. The pediments were decorated with sculpture (? by Skopas), fragments of which survive in the local museum and in the National Museum at Athens. The E. pediment represented the Hunt of the Calydonian Boar, with figures of Meleager, Theseus, Atalanta, and Ankaios. The w. pediment depicted the Fight of Telephos and Achilles on the banks of the Kaikos in Mysia.

We continue to *Palaia Episkopi* (20 min; tavernas), where a huge church of 1888 replaces the Byzantine basilica of Nikli (fragments are rebuilt into the walls, and ancient mosaic ikons are venerated); a hotel has been provided for pilgrims. Under the triple apse is the semicircular retaining wall of the *Theatre*, rebuilt in marble by Antiochus IV Epiphanes (175–164 B.C.). In the great park to the w. are fragments of the *Agora*. To the N.E. stands part of the medieval wall.—A long avenue leads directly to the main Tripolis–Sparta road at *Kerasítsa* (see below), where we may regain the bus.

The marble for the Tegea temple sculptures came from *Doliauá*, c. 6 m. S.E. as the crow flies. A bus from Tripolis (3 times weekly; very early) plies to *Vérvena*, a roundabout climb of c. 20 m., where the phylax may be found. Thence it is 40 min. on foot to the Quarry, where a ruined 6C Temple of Artemis commands a *View over Arcadia.

FROM TRIPOLIS TO MANTINEA, 9 m. The Kapsia road runs N.N.E. across the plain. To the left is the long range of Maenalos with the village of *Merkovouni* on the hillside. The cornfields give place to vineyards producing a celebrated non-resinated red wine. We approach the narrow gap (1 m. wide) between projecting spurs of Maenalos and Mt Ktenias that marked the ancient frontier between Tegea and Mantinea. On a shoulder of (4 m.) *Mytika* (l.) are the ruins of a square watchtower of polygonal masonry doubtfully identified as the *Skopí* ('lookout') from which the dying Epaminondas watched the Second Battle of Mantinea. This district, once covered by an oak wood, was called *Pelagos* ('the sea'), thus satisfying the oracle's prediction that Epaminondas should beware of the sea. Here were fought several great battles (comp. below).

A by-road descends into the *Plain of Mantinea*, where are grown the marella cherries used in the manufacture of 'Vissinadha', a popular soft drink. The road passes through the **Ruins of Mantinea**, marked by an eccentric church (1972), a Minoan-Classical-Byzantine folly.

Mantinéa, anciently perhaps more correctly Mantíneia (2065 ft), one of the most important Arcadian city-states, was the inveterate rival of Tegea, and its whole history is coloured by this mutual antagonism based probably on disputes over water-supply. The earliest settlement was ½ m. N. on the hill of *Gortsoúli*, known to the ancients as *Ptolis*. Its existence from Geometric to Classical times was confirmed by excavation in 1962. In the Peloponnesian War the Mantineans were generally allies of Athens, the Tegeans being on the side of Sparta. After the Peace of Nikias in 421 B.C. Mantinea joined Athens, Argos, and Elis in the quadruple alliance that led up to the *First Battle of Mantinea* (418 B.C.), described by Thuc. 5. 64–74.

In 385 B.C. King Agesipolis, at the head of the Lacedaemonian army, besieged and took Mantinea after undermining the mud-brick fortification walls with the help of the dammed-up waters of the Ophis. He razed most of the city to the ground and dispersed the population. After the battle of Leuktra the Mantineans, with the help of Thebes, returned to their city, and built the extensive fortifications whose ruins we see today. They rearranged the course of the Ophis so that it became a protection instead of a danger. The foundation in 370 B.C. of the Arcadian League was due to the efforts of *Lykomedes*, a native of Mantinea, but six years later the Mantineans themselves seceded from it and openly joined the Spartans.

At the *Second Battle of Mantinea* (362 B.C.) Tegea, hitherto the age-long ally of Sparta, fought on the side of Thebes, while Mantinea shared in the defeat of her former enemy, Sparta (Xen. Hell., 7. 5. 18–27). Epaminondas was mortally wounded in the moment of triumph and the battle marked the end of the fourth and last Theban invasion of the Peloponnese. Joining the Achaean League the following century the Mantineans fought against Agis IV and helped to defeat Kleomenes III at Sellasia. Revolting against Macedonian dominance of the Achaean League, the city was captured in 222 B.C. by Antigonos Doson, who changed its name to *Antigoneia*, a name it kept until Hadrian's time. In 208 B.C. occurred another 'Battle of Mantinea', in which the Achaeans under Philopoemen defeated the Lacedaemonians, Philopoemen killing the tyrant Machanidas with his own hand (see Polybius, 11.11). An excellent exegesis of the three battles is in Pritchett, *Studies in Ancient Topography* II.

The WALLS of Mantinea, though no longer standing to any height, are among the best examples of Greek period fortification. They are contemporary with the walls of Messene (c. 370 B.C.), and may have been built by the same Theban architects. The circuit is almost entire, elliptical in form, with a perimeter of nearly 2½ miles. The walls, encircled by the diverted *Ophis*, are built of large square or polygonal blocks; up to four courses are still standing. The curtain wall was 14 ft thick. There were over 120 square towers, placed about 28 yds apart, and 10 gates, defended in various ways.

Within the walls are the remains of the *Theatre*, of Roman date, and, immediately to the E., of the *Agora* and *Council House*.

FROM TRÍPOLIS TO VITÍNA VIÂ ALONÍSTAINA, 23 m. (36 km.). The unpaved road quits Tripolis to the W., passing (3¼ m.) within ½ m. of *Selimna*, where the Russo-Greek forces gathered in the 1770 insurrection. We continue N.W. below the sullen slopes of Mainalon.—9¼ m. *Daviá*. A local 'Palaiókastro' marks the site of ancient *Mainalos*, with a medieval fortress. The road divides (left, see Rte 36); the right branch continues round Mainalon to (17 m.) *Alonístaina*, a pretty mountain village founded c. 1300 amid wooded crags.—23 m. *Vitína*, see Rte 36).

31 FROM TRIPOLIS TO SPARTA. MISTRA

ROAD to Sparta, 39 m. (63 km.) with views of wild grandeur, and thence to *Mistra*, 3¾ m. farther. —BUSES from Athens, viâ Tripolis, to Sparta, 8 times daily; from Sparta to Mistra, see below.

A straight road runs across the plain of Tegea.—3 m. *Áyios Sóstis*, on the old road to the left, occupies the acropolis of Tegea; the main ruins (Rte 30) of the ancient city lie to the left at (5 m.) *Kerasítsa*. The road climbs into rocky hills with views back to the marshy *Lake Taka*, drained by swallow-holes.—8½ m. *Manthiréa* (2560 ft; formerly Kamári) has adopted the new name from Manthyrea, one of the nine original townships of Tegea.—12 m. Petrol Station (Restaurant; 2800 ft). We cross an intermittently cultivated upland plain, then descend s. to the *Kleisoura Pass*, the long defile that provides the best approach to Laconia, though we have already entered the modern nome. At the s. end is a *Memorial* to 118 Spartans of the resistance movement who were killed by the Germans on 26 Nov 1943. We climb out of the defile to (26 m.) the summit (2725 ft) of the pass crowned by a modern defence post. The road descends a ridge with *Views of the Taiyetos and Parnon ranges.

At 30½ m. the site of ancient *Sellasia* appears (r.) on a hill now crowned by a chapel of Ayios Konstandinos. At the BATTLE OF SELLASIA in 221 B.C. Antigonos Doson routed the Spartan forces of Kleomenes III. The young Philipoemen of Megalopolis distinguished himself in the allied Achaian force.—The twisting descent reaches (36½ m.) *Kladhás*, where the tributary Oenous is crossed. Shortly after, a long iron bridge carries the road across the Eurotas into (39 m.) Sparta.

SPARTA (735 ft), in Greek **Spárti** (ΣΠΑΡΤΗ), the capital of Laconia, seat of the Metropolitan of Sparta and Monemvasia, and the agricultural centre (10,500 inhab.) of the Eurotas valley, dates only from 1834. Laid out with broad streets on the Diktynnaion Hill (comp. below), the town enjoys a striking situation at the foot of Taiyetos and is protected on the E. by the more distant Parnon. Cool breezes blow, especially in the early evening when the sun disappears behind the mountains. The olive and orange groves which produce its main livelihood are nowhere far distant; and if its buildings lack architectural merit, they are not so high as to spoil the spectacular mountain views.

ANCIENT SPARTA, or *Lakedaimon*, occupied a vast triangular area on the right bank of the Eurotas including six low hills: the *Kolona*, the *Acropolis*, the *Hill of Argive Hera*, the *Issorion*, the *Diktynnaion*, and the *Hill of Armed Aphrodite*. During the period of its greatness the city remained unwalled, since the natural strength of its position and the bravery of its soldiers were considered sufficient protection. The inhabitants dwelt in a group of five scattered townships, separated by gardens and plantations. Sparta had few of the magnificent public buildings that adorned other Greek cities and its scanty remains—as Thucydides foretold—reflect little of its ancient renown.

Hotels. Menelaion (Pl. b), 65 Palaiologou, Leda (Pl. h), Atreidon, B; Dioskouroi (Pl. e), 94 Lykourghou; Maniatis (Pl. d), 60 Palaiologou; Apollon (Pl. a), Vasilissis Frederikis/Thermopilon; Laconia (Pl. f), 61 Palaiologou, these C; Cecil (Pl. g), 1 Stadhiou, D.

Restaurants. *Diethnes*, on the Plateia; *Semiramis*, Palaiologou.—TAVERNAS at Ayios Ioannis and Parori, villages to the s.w.

Buses from street opp. Hotel Menelaion to *Tripolis* and *Athens*; from the same street to *Yithion* and *Monemvasia*; from the square to *Mistra*; to *Yeraki*; and to other Laconian villages.

History and Institutions. Though some traces of L.H. IIIB occupation have been found on the acropolis, Homeric *Sparta* seems to have been elsewhere, perhaps at *Therapnai* near the Menelaion (p. 295), while *Kouphovouno*, to the s.w., was occupied from Neolithic times. The only site so far discovered to be comparable in extent to Mycenae or Pylos is at *Amyklai* (p. 295). *Lakedaimon* was a Dorian foundation and developed in its later history those traditions and customs least suited to urban progress. These fossilized into a constitution which by classical times was unique among city states. Tradition ascribes it to the reforms of Lycurgus (for whom many dates have been argued in the 9C–7C), but its developed form may not be earlier than the end of the 7C B.C. The inhabitants of Lakedaimonia were divided into three classes: Spartans, or more correctly Spartiates, Perioikoi, and Helots, of whom only Spartiates had citizen rights.

The government of the state was composed of the five *Ephors*, the *Gerousia*, or council of elders, the two *Kings*, and the *Apella*, or assembly of citizens over 30 years old. The Gerousia consisted of 28 citizens over 60 years old and the two kings. They prepared necessary legislation and put it to the assembly. The ephors were elected annually and while in office were the most powerful men in Sparta, although final decisions of war and peace were in the hands of the Gerousia and the Apella. The kings were under the control of the ephors and the only power they retained was command of the army in the field. All citizens could attend the assembly, but its power was limited to accepting or rejecting proposals put to it by the Gerousia.

Our knowledge of the Spartan 'caste' system is limited to its evolved state by the Classical period. The *Spartiates*, whose numbers may never have exceeded 10,000, were the rulers of Lakedaimonia. Each was given an estate of public land which was cultivated by slaves, leaving the Spartiate to spend his whole life in military and public service. From birth he was subject to stern discipline. Weak or deformed children were left to die on Taiyetos. Stronger children remained with their mothers until their seventh birthday. Their education in camps was supervised by young soldiers and discipline enforced by pack leaders; drill exercises and brutal competitive games figured largely. At twenty the Spartiate entered the army proper (perhaps after a period in the *Krypteia*, or secret police, which was at intervals let loose upon the Helots). He was expected to marry but continued to live in barracks and to eat in a mess on prescribed rations supplied from his own estate. He became a full soldier-citizen at the age of thirty.

Perioikoi, or 'dwellers around' lived in a number of villages in Laconia and neighbouring Messenia. They had no citizen rights but were free-men. Their only duty to the state was to serve, when called upon, as hoplites. The *Helots* were serfs and completely under the control of the Spartiates, whom they always greatly outnumbered. They consisted of the descendants of former inhabitants of Laconia and of surviving Messenians who were enslaved. They were obliged to cultivate the Spartiate's estates and to deliver the required produce from them.

Though the system itself had all the characteristics least acceptable to the 'democratic' ideal, either ancient or modern, the Spartan régime seems to develop its ruthlessly illiberal and wholly militaristic nature only about the time of the Persian wars. From the Geometric period to the 6C, Spartan arts flourish; pottery, sculpture in bronze, and essential architecture, though never opulent, keep pace with those of other cities. The music and dancing of her festivals are famed. In the 7C poetry flourishes with the native Kinaithon, Terpander of Lesbos, and Tyrtaios. By the 5C every setback—the numerical inadequacy of the ruling caste, the earthquake of 464 B.C., the chronic Messenian discontent—is countered only by greater austerity. This policy was superficially successful while the war machine functioned and the quality of Spartan troops made up for their dwindling numbers, but did nothing in the long run to stave off the inevitable effects of depopulation and an outmoded economy.

Spartan expansion began near the end of the 8C with the attack on the fertile territory of Messenia. This conquest was later followed by a long revolt of Messenians (685–668). After the region had been subdued Sparta began to increase her power in the Peloponnese. A long war with Tegea (c. 600–560) showed that expansion was possible only by dominating vassal allies not by annexation. By the end of the century Tegea and Thyreatis were subdued and the *Peloponnesian League* instituted with Sparta at its head. Argos, the only neighbouring state that could hope to defy Sparta, was decisively defeated at Sepeia c. 494.

Sparta took no part in repelling the first Persian expedition, but in 480–479 added to her prestige by the exploit of Leonidas at Thermopylae and the victory of Plataia under Pausanias. The later intrigues of Pausanias in Byzantium and the campaign of Leotychides in Thessaly, both opposed by Athens, showed Sparta that better policy lay in maintaining strength in the Peloponnese; control of the Aegean was left to Athens. In 464 the Helots revolted and only outside aid saved the state from destruction. The imperialism of Athens in the second half of the 5C forced the Greeks to turn to Sparta as their champion.

The Peloponnesian War ended with the defeat of Athens, leaving Sparta the most powerful state not only of the mainland, but also in the Aegean, where she waged an unsuccessful war with Persia. The Greeks were already finding Sparta a worse master than Athens and in 395 she was attacked by a coalition led by Athens, Thebes, Corinth, and Argos. Although Sparta triumphed on land (at Corinth), her fleet was defeated at Knidos in 394 and all hopes of an overseas empire were abandoned. With the peace of 386, Sparta kept her position by forcing the Persian terms on the rest of the cities. A powerful new enemy soon arose in Thebes; Theban hoplites, using new tactics, at Leuktra in Boeotia (371 B.C.) broke for ever the legend of Spartan invincibility. Epaminondas of Thebes invaded Laconia and reached the outskirts of Sparta itself. To keep Sparta powerless Messenia was revived as an independent state, the Arcadian League was formed, and a chain of fortresses was founded encircling Sparta's N. frontier.

The Achaian League and the Macedonians continued the campaign against Sparta. In 295 B.C. Demetrios Poliorketes all but captured the city, and in 272 Pyrrhus could easily have taken it after defeating the Spartans in the field. Kleomenes III abolished the ephorate and ruled as a tyrant in a vain attempt to restore

Spartan hegemony, but was utterly defeated at Sellasia. Sparta became a dependency of Macedon, regaining momentary independence only under the tyrants Machanidas (207 B.C.) and Nabis (195–192). After Nabis' assassination Philopoemen forced Sparta to join the Achaian League, razed the city walls, and repealed the laws of Lycurgus.

Under the Romans Laconia had a period of prosperity in the 2C A.D. as a province of Achaia and under Septimius Severus was even allowed to revert to a

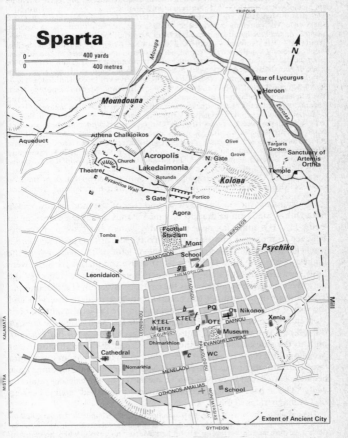

Lycurgan régime. The city was destroyed in A.D. 396 by Alaric and when the Slavs invaded in the 9C the population migrated to the Mani. The Byzantines refounded a town under the name *Lakedaimonia*, but by 1248 it had lost all importance to Mistra and disappears from history until 1834. Excavations were undertaken by the British School in 1906–10 and 1925–29.

The course of the CITY WALLS has been traced for most of the 6 m. circuit. The walls of Sparta were a feature of her decline. The first defences were made in 307–295 B.C. and supplemented when Pyrrhus threatened the city in 272. By 218 walls and gates existed. These were strengthened by Nabis against Flaminius, pulled down by the Achaians in 188 and rebuilt by Appius Claudius Pulcher in 184 B.C.

Sparta centres upon a large flagged and arcaded PLATEIA, scene of the evening volta (unexpectedly elegant). To the E. is the **Museum** (adm. 10 dr; standard hours), containing Laconian sculpture and votive offerings from the sanctuaries.

VESTIBULE. Stelai and inscriptions once bearing inlaid votive sickles of iron, dedicated to Artemis Orthia by boy-victors in ordeal contests; 218. Stele retaining its sickle.—ROOM 1 (r.). Archaic reliefs and statuary. 1. Stele representing (?) Helen and Menelaus; 576. Seated goddess; terracottas from Amyklai.—ROOM 2 (beyond). Votive reliefs dedicated to the Dioscuri, notably those of the Archaic period; mixed Doric and Ionic capitals from Amyklai; marble throne, with reliefs, from the theatre (Roman).—ROOM 3. 326. Statue of Artemis; *Leonidas in marble, upper part of a superb warrior statue, perhaps the memorial raised to Leonidas on his reburial at Sparta (it inspired the modern memorial at Thermopylae); 1030. Stele of Anaxivios (c. 550 B.C.); 440. Stele of Damonon, victor in chariot races, with a long mutilated inscription recording the circumstances of its dedication (5C B.C.); small 5C grave relief from Yeraki; male torso. In cases: Mycenean pottery from the Menelaion, Epidauros Limera, and elsewhere; also Neolithic from Alepotrypa (Mani); votive lamps and plaques, orientalizing pottery (black on yellow).

ROOM 4 (l. of vestibule). Masks in terracotta, lead votive figurines and limestone reliefs from the Sanctuary of Artemis Orthia; kraters and amphorae showing Spartiate warriors in combat; statuary representing Herakles; Archaic bronze *Figurines.—ROOM 5 (beyond). Archaizing and later sculpture: Head of Artemis; Hermes; torso of Asklepios; Dioscuri; wild boar in steatite; 307. Fragmentary relief from a sarcophagus; 717. Triglyph and two metopes from the acropolis. Clay votive model of a Roman galley found in the sea.

*Mosaics survive from Roman villas in the town; the phylax will show these on request. The best known portray Orpheus, Zeus with Europa, and Alcibiades.

The ruins of **Ancient Sparta** lie N. and N.E. of the modern town. We take Odhos Stadhiou at the top of which stands a modern memorial to Leonidas. His tomb lay near the theatre, where the broken statue be-believed to represent him was found. To the left of the sports stadium a track leads through olive-groves to the S. gate of the ACROPOLIS, the highest of the low hills of Sparta (66 ft above the plain). Its walls were built between A.D. 267 and 386 and completed on the E. side after the Slav invasion in the 8C. Here was the centre of Byzantine Lakedaimonia. The contour of the summit has been altered by a modern reservoir and the view is obscured by trees. Immediately inside the gate is a brick-built Roman portico of the 1C A.D. Following the left path along the crest of the hill past two ruined 11C churches, we reach (below; l.) the THEATRE built in the side of the hill in the 2C or 1C B.C. Next to the theatre at Megalopolis it is the largest in Greece, but much of its masonry went into late fortifications or was quarried for Mistra. The stage buildings have been excavated and the cavea can be measured by the existing retaining walls. The E. parodos wall has more than 30 inscribed blocks, bearing lists of magistrates of the 2C A.D.

The terrace to the N. yielded in 1907 remains from the *Temple of Athena Chalkioikos*, a building, lined with bronze plates, legendarily associated with Aristomenes' defiant gesture at the beginning of the first Messenian revolt, when he came by night to hang up a shield with an insulting dedication; and later with the vindictive and sacrilegious treatment accorded to King Pausanias when he sought sanctuary here. Today nothing can be seen.

From the bend in Odhos Tripoleos a path descends to the **Sanctuary of Artemis Orthia**, scene of the endurance tests by flogging that featured in the upbringing of Spartan boys. The sanctuary existed in the 10C B.C., and in Archaic times comprised a walled enclosure with an *Altar* on the E. side and a small *Temple* on the W. In the 2C A.D. the whole complex was rebuilt and a Roman theatre built to accommodate spectators.

There seem in earlier days to have been other contests of milder sort: singing, oratory, and probably not very gentle games for boys of 10 and upward. Farther N. along the Eurotas are a *Heroön* and a huge stone altar.

Excursions may be made to the sites of the Menelaion (3 m.) and the Amyklaion (5 m.). For the first, we cross the Eurotas, turn right on the Yeraki road, and at 2¾ m. take a path to the left (20 min. walk), bearing right at the chapel of *Ayios Ilias*. On a hill of conspicuously red earth are three platforms on which stood the **Menelaion**, or Shrine of Menelaus and Helen. Its ruined masonry is imposing and the view superb. Just below the summit to the N.E. are Mycenean remains uncovered in 1973–74.—From the centre of Sparta the Yithion road leads to modern Amiklia, where we turn left at a sign 'Amyklyon' to *Ayia Kiriakí*, a chapel on the site of the *Amyklaion*, excavated by the German School in 1925. The sanctuary surrounded the Tomb of Hyakinthos, which was crowned by an archaic statue of Apollo seated on a chryselephantine throne. Here took place the great festival of the Hyakinthia in July. The place is firmly identified by an inscription, but the remains are not illuminating. The site however seems to have had continuous occupation since Mycenean times (and Hyakinthos is a pre-Greek deity). The church of *Ayia Paraskevi*, to the S., may occupy the site of the *Sanctuary of Zeus-Agamemnon and Alexandra-Kassandra*, from which a huge Archaic votive deposit with hero-reliefs was unearthed close by in 1956.—**Amyklai**, the ancient capital of the Myceneans in Laconia, probably lay nearby at *Palaiopiryi*, the largest Late Helladic settlement yet discovered in Laconia, and close to the Vaphio tomb (guide necessary). Palaiopiryi has not been excavated.

THE EXCURSION TO MISTRA (5 m. w.) should on no account be missed. Buses, though not infrequent, are irregular with a long mid-morning interval. The road runs w. to the foot of Mt Taiyetos, crossing a luxuriant region, thick with orange, fig, and mulberry trees. The eroded mountain sides are scored with langadhes (deep gorges), each with its torrent. The gorge of *Parori*, the gloomiest and most forbidding ravine, has been identified with the *Apothetai* where the Spartiates used to expose their weakly children. It may also be the *Kaiadas*, or criminal pit, from which Aristomenes made a miraculous escape. To the N. of Parori is the Gorge of Mistra, at the entrance to which is a hill with the ruins of the medieval city. We pass through modern Mistra.

**MISTRA (ΜΥΣΤΡΑΣ), a purely medieval town in its ruin, has been likened to a Byzantine Pompeii, though it has a nearer parallel in Les Baux in Provence. Churches, monasteries, palaces, and houses line the narrow winding streets. The situation alone would make it an enchanting spot, but within its walls are preserved some of the finest examples of 14–15C Byzantine architecture in Greece, and the numerous wall-paintings are among the most characteristic of their kind. Unfortunately they had already reached an advanced stage of decay before reconstruction of the churches provided so much more for the visitor to enjoy (even if its authenticity is sometimes doubtful). An impregnable fortress crowns the summit.

History. On the hill of *Mezythra*, 3 m. from medieval Lakedaimonia, William de Villehardouin built a fortress in 1249 to protect the town from the marauding Slavs of Taiyetos. Mezythra was corrupted by the Franks to *Mistra*, which in the French dialect of the time meant 'mistress'. Villehardouin, taken prisoner in 1259 at Pelagonia by Michael Palaiologos, was forced after 3 years captivity to surrender Mistra, together with Monemvasia and Maina, by way of ransom. The Greeks, using Mistra as a base, drove the Franks into Elis, but were completely defeated in 1265 in the defile of Makriplagi near Gardiki and William returned to Laconia. The inhabitants of Lakedaimonia had meanwhile settled on the hill of Mistra under the protection of the fortress.

After 50 years of strife the Greeks reconquered the greater part of the Morea.

Monemvasia gave way in importance to Mistra and here from 1349 the peninsula was governed by a Despot, either a son or brother of the emperor (often his heir presumptive). The despots were successively Manuel Cantacuzene (1349–80); Matthew, his brother (1380–83); and Demetrios (1383–84). Here after his abdication in 1354 John VI Cantacuzene lived with his sons as the monk Ioasaph Christodulos (d. 1383). The Cantacuzenes were followed by the Palaiologi: Theodore I Palaiologos (1384–1407), who became a monk and was succeeded by his nephew, Theodore II (1407–43); Constantine Dragatses (1443–48) who succeeded to the Imperial throne to be the last Emperor of Byzantium; and Demetrios (1448–60), whose unedifying squabbles with his brothers gave the Turks their opportunity. In 1400–42 Mistra was the home of the philosopher Gemistos

Plethon, the rediscoverer of Plato. Card. Bessarion (1389–1472), the illustrious scholar of Trebizond, attended his lectures in 1423.

Mistra passed to the Turks in 1460, though it was temporarily invested in 1464 by Sigismondo Malatesta of Rimini, then in the service of Venice. From 1687 to 1715 the city was in the hands of the Venetians when it reached its second peak of prosperity. It attained a population of 42,000, whose main industry was silk-worm culture. On the return of the Turks the town rapidly declined. It was burnt in 1770 by Albanian troops after the Mainotes had captured it for Orloff, and again in 1825 by Ibrahim's soldiers. After the refounding of Sparta in 1834 Mistra was virtually abandoned. The French School saved the site from complete ruin in 1896–1910, but it served as a battlefield in 1944 between various partisan forces.

The last 30 families were moved by the Greek Archaeological Service in 1952, and wholesale reconstruction has since been undertaken by Prof. A. Orlandos.

The ruins rise on the N. and E. side of the hill. They are in three parts. The *Kastro* occupies the summit; below to the N. is the walled *Upper Town* (Khora), the houses of which cluster around the Despot's palace; below again extends the *Lower Town* (Katokhora), added somewhat later, which includes the cathedral. The parapets and upper sections of defence walls are generally Turkish refurbishings. A modern motor road ascends the hill to a point above Ayia Sophia (car park), providing the easiest approach to the Kastro. The bus stops at the main gate. About 150 yds farther on is the *Byzantion Hotel* (B).

We enter (adm. 50 dr.; 7.30–dusk) by a restored gate into the LOWER TOWN and turn right.

The CATHEDRAL, or *Metropolitan Church of Ayios Dhimitrios* (Metropolis), built (or perhaps rebuilt) in 1309 by the Metropolitan Nikephoros Moschopoulos, stands in a spacious court in which are an antique sarcophagus and a fountain dated 1802. The basilica was altered in the 15C when the upper part was replaced by five domes after the model of the Aphentiko. As a result the paintings in the nave have been cut in two. The arcade of the marble ikonostasis has remarkable fretwork carving; the cornice above was added in the 15C. The 17C walnut throne is richly carved. In the floor is a two-headed marble eagle that possibly commemorates the coronation here of the Emp. Constantine XII (comp. above). The paintings are ascribed to ten different artists in three periods. Those in the *N. Aisle* (Portraits of saints, Torture and burial of St Demetrios, Sufferers from dropsy and leprosy), are shown by their symmetry and repose to be the earliest works. *S. Aisle*, Prophets, Life of the Virgin, Miracles of Christ, more realistic (14C). *Narthex*, also 14C but by a different hand, Last Judgement.

Adjoining the Cathedral is the **Museum**, formed by Gabriel Millet (d. 1954), who did so much to save Mistra from further ruin. It contains decorative fragments, mostly from the churches. Marble relief of Christ; fragments of a lintel with the monogram and arms of Isabella de Lusignan.—Little survives of the *Episcopal Palace*, part of which gave place to monastic cells in 1754.

Above and to the left stands the 14C *Evangelistria*, a simple mortuary chapel (two ossuaries) with good sculptural detail (notably ikonostasis). We diverge (r.) from the main street for the **Vrontokhion,** a great monastic complex, cultural centre, and burial-place of the Despots. It has two churches, both built by the Archimandrite Pachomios, the first **Ayii Theodori* (c. 1296) being the last in date of the churches in Greece built with a central octagon (comp. Daphni, on a larger scale). It was restored in 1932. Farther on is the attractive APHENTIKO, or *Panayia Hodegetria*, dating from 1310 but much restored since it was largely pulled down in 1863. It was the earliest church at Mistra built to a composite plan, a fusion of the basilica and the cross church with domes, an idea revived from earlier practice. It has four small cupolas and a central dome (rebuilt), with a beautiful bell-tower.

The INTERIOR is remarkable for its proportions, its purity of line, and the carved ornamentation. The marble facings have disappeared. In a side chapel on the N. side of the narthex is the tomb of Theodore II, with (above) frescoed portraits of him in the robes of despot (Aphentis) and the habit of a monk. Here also the tomb of Pachomios. In the corresponding s. chapel the walls bear copies of chrysobuls detailing the foundation, properties, and privileges of the monastery. The **Frescoes*, in bold colour, include the Miracles of Christ (narthex); Group of Martyrs (in N.W. chapel); and a panel of St Gregory, the illuminator of Armenia (in the apse).—The ruined *Cells* and the *Refectory* can be identified.

Beyond the Evangelistria the road passes under a machicolated Gothic archway and higher up divides: the left branch leads to the Pantanassa, which we visit on the descent. By the right branch we enter the UPPER TOWN by the *Monemvasia Gate*, pass below a tall 15C house with arcades and machicolations, skirt a small *Mosque*, and reach the square in front of the Despot's palace.

The **Palace of the Despots** (*Anaktora*), a rare example of a civic Byzantine building, is an extensive ruin dating from various periods. The wing nearest to the mosque may have been erected under the Franks (13C) and had two successive additions under the Cantacuzenes. The Palaiologi added in the 14C the fourth building in the line and in 1400–60 the immense vaulted audience-hall at right angles; its façade was painted and its flamboyant windows are framed in poros mouldings and covered with stucco. The hall was heated by eight chimney-pieces. Behind the palace are other official buildings which extend to the massive *Nauplia Gate*, protected by an external redoubt.

Visitors who are pressed for time should here turn back and make directly for the Pantanassa and Perivleptos.

To the w. of the palace, beyond a small *Turkish Bath* is the church of AYIA SOPHIA, built in 1350 by Manuel Cantacuzene as the katholikon of the Zoodotos monastery. It was used as the palace chapel and here are buried Theodora Tocco, wife of Constantine (d. 1429) and Cleopa Malatesta, wife of Theodore II (d. 1433). There survive remains of the ikonostasis, of the pavement, and of the refectory and cells. The paintings were preserved by Turkish whitewash. A fine view is obtained from the porch.

Hence we continue to ascend, passing under a small aqueduct, to the **Kastro,** built in 1249 by William de Villehardouin and repaired and refortified along existing lines by the Turks, so that the plan remains Frankish even though much of the masonry is later. The *Keep* (1850 ft) commands a magnificent *View, well demonstrating its strategic importance.

On the descent we may pass Ayia Sophia and make our way through ruined houses (r.) to the so-called *Little Palace*, a spacious Byzantine house of early date, then go down steps to *Ayios Nikolaos*, a curious building of the Turkish period with a modern roof.

The **Pantánassa,** the most beautiful of the churches of Mistra, was built in 1365 by Manuel Cantacuzene and enlarged in 1428 by John Frangopoulos, protostrator (minister) of Constantine Palaiologos. It now belongs to a nunnery. In plan the church resembles the Aphentiko, but the proportions are more slender. It is orientated N.–S. A broad flight of steps leads to a picturesque loggia commanding a fine view over the Eurotas valley. Over the narthex is a gallery reached by an external staircase and opening into the Gothic tower (splendid *View). The side galleries are continued over the aisles as far as the apses.

The paintings in the body of the church are late, with the exception of the fine portrait of Manuel Chatsikis (1445) in the narthex. Those in the galleries are more decorative. Under the w. gallery will be observed a happy combination of architectural lines and painted ornament (fine Head of a Prophet on the N.W. pendentive); in the N.W. cupola is a vigorous Patriarch. Note also Palm Sunday, with children playing; Annunciation; and Presentation in the Temple.

We descend a path on the open flank of the hill to the Monastery of the PERIVLEPTOS, named on a plaque over its entrance (1714). The

Church (latter half of the 14C) in stone and brick, with pentagonal apses and an octagonal dome, has the pure style of three centuries earlier. Below the E. end is an unusual little chapel with a tiled pavement. To the S. of the church is a square battlemented tower, richly ornamented on its E. face. The *Frescoes give a good idea of the iconography of a 14C Byzantine church. The dome has retained its Pantokrator. Above the side entrance, Dormition of the Virgin; in the Prothesis chapel to the left, Divine Liturgy, celebrated by Christ and the angels; in the Bema, Ascension; in the vaulting of the S. transept, Nativity; In the w. nave, Transfiguration (observe the silhouette of Christ); in the S. aisle, Childhood of the Virgin.

Returning towards the main gate we pass (r.) the 18C *House of Krevatas*, a vast mass of ruins. The chapel of *Ayios Ioannis* lies outside the walls near the *Marmara Fountain*.

FROM SPARTA TO YERÁKI, 25 m. (40 km.), asphalt and gently undulating through cultivated country; bus. We take the Tripolis road and beyond the bridge turn right. Soon after there is an unpaved turning (l.) to *Khrísafa* (ΧΡΥΣΑΦΑ; 12½ m.), where the churches of the Chrysaphiótissa (1290) and Áyii Pándes (1367) both have wall paintings. Ayios Dhimitrios dates from 1641, and the Moní Prodrómou from 1625.—We continue along the left bank of the Eurotas. At *Skoúra* we turn E.—Beyond (15 m.) *Goritsá* we get a distant view towards Yeraki across a wide valley.—25 m. **Yeráki** (ΓΕΡΑΚΙ), a large village (1590 inhab.), almost unknown to tourists, occupies the site of ancient *Geronthrai*. Its imposing acropolis (1940 ft) has walls in the cyclopean style, best preserved on the N. and E. They were investigated in 1905 by the British School and certainly date from Mycenean times; they may even have Middle Helladic origins. A small *Museum* contains local finds. About ⅓ hr S.E. by bad road (4-wheel drive advisable) on a long detached ridge of Parnon stands medieval *Geraki*, one of the original 12 Frankish baronies, with remains of fifteen small medieval churches. The KASTRO, at the N. end of the ridge (easy path in 20 min. to summit), was built by Jehan de Nivelet in 1254. It commands fine views of Parnon and Taiyetos. *Ayios Yeoryios*, the basilican castle chapel (13C), has a florid Gothic shrine recalling South Italian work. The w. door of the *Zoodokhos Piyi* (1431), and the shrine in *Ayia Paraskevi*, both lower down the slope, show rude incised and sculptured decoration in a local Gothic idiom. During cleaning 13C frescoes were found in the *Evanghelistria* in 1964; *Ayios Athanasios* has been over-restored (dome rebuilt). The church at the extreme S. end of the ridge has a mural painting representing Joshua attacking a city of the Amorites.

FROM SPARTA TO KALAMATA, 37½ m. (60 km.) over the *LANGADA PASS. The road is steep with hairpin bends and affords marvellous views of the Taiyetos and into Messenia on the W. The road is asphalt but the safety of the crossing depends on weather conditions. A bus climbs twice daily from each side to Artemisia, there exchanging passengers.— 3½ m. Superb view of Mistra (l.). At 4½ m. we start to climb, and at (5½ m.) *Trípi* (Keadas D, rest.) enter the Langada Gorge. To the r. is one of the places claimed as that where the Spartans exposed weakly children. After 10 m. we pass into Messenia amid fir forests. There are superb views of the Taiyetos peaks, often snow-capped.—15 m. *Pens. Taiyetos* B, and taverna (summer only). At the summit (5000 ft), a little farther on, is a Tourist Pavilion.—22 m. *Artemísia*. We descend a gorge but, at 30 m., climb a steep zigzag to a col, from the top of which fine view down to Kalamata. The road enters Kalamata by the Frourion; for the centre we keep the river on our right.

32 SOUTHERN LACONIA

The predominantly mountainous region s. of Sparta is seldom visited by foreign tourists and little more by the Greeks themselves. With the exception of the road from Sparta to Yithion (recently extended to give access to the Diros caves), roads are generally poor, unsurfaced, and badly signposted. In the Taíyetos and Parnon ranges the mule is still the only means of transport; haste is impossible, accommodation limited and often primitive. The unhurried visitor who is willing to travel light will, however, be rewarded by superb scenery and unexpected traces of the past. Byzantinists will not willingly miss seeing Monemvasia, best approached by sea. Yithion is a quiet and pleasant enough seaside town. Like Cornwall, southern Laconia is ethnically several invasions behind the rest of the country. The Maniots claim never to have been conquered by Slav or Turk, the Tzakonians to have survived from remoter times still; but claims by either to be indigenous are exaggerated or at best unproven. Certainly both peoples display characteristics of their own and are very resistant to change. Tourism, however, is now being officially fostered to offset depopulation caused by lack of opportunity. The local wines are often heavily resinated.

A From Piraeus by Sea

STEAMER weekly to *Monemvasia* in 6–8¾ hrs, continuing either to Kithira and Andikithira direct, or viâ Neapolis and Kithira to *Yithion* (in 22¾ hrs) as described below. HYDROPLANE four times weekly on similar route (3½ hrs to Monemvasia) as far as Neapolis.

· Quitting Piraeus harbour the ship steams due s. for Cape Skillaion, passing E. of Aegina and between Hydra and the mainland of Argolis (comp. Rte 23). We leave Trikkeri and Spetsopoula to starboard, then head w. across the open sea.

4 hrs. *Skála* is the landfall for **Leonídhion** (ΛΕΩΝΙΔΙΟΝ) the chief town (3200 inhab.) of Kynouria, an Arcadian eparchy which is virtually cut off from the hinterland by the abrupt ranges of Mt Parnon. It relies on sea communication and depends for its livelihood largely on the success of its merchants abroad. Though high mule-paths exist, there is little overland connection with the Laconian villages beyond MT PARNON, a long and sparsely populated range rising to 6350 ft, without low passes. Wolves still have their habitat here. A large wooded tract was designated as a game reserve in 1961.

6½ hrs. *Kiparíssi* (ΚΥΠΑΡΙΣΣΙΟΝ), a charming village, occupies an olive-planted plateau above its picturesque little harbour (*Paralía*) at one of the few points where the forbidding Laconian coast does not rise sheer from the sea.—We follow the rugged and lonely seaboard. The white *Evanghelistria Monastery* is backed by a hill crowned with three round fortress towers.—7¾ hrs. *Limín Iérakos*, known also as Kastrí or Yéraka, the harbour of *Iérax*, a mountain village, is enchantingly situated in a narrow fjord. Dominating the entrance from the N., on a flat rock, is an extensive and unexplored acropolis of (?) Mycenean date (*Zarax*).

8¾ hrs. **MONEMVASIA** (ΜΟΝΕΜΒΑΣΙΑ), aptly described as the Gibraltar of Greece, owes its name to the single entrance (μονὴ 'ἔμβασις) by which it is reached from the landward side. Called by our old writers *Malmsey*, by the Venetians *Napoli di Malvasia*, and by the French *Malvoisie*, it was once famous for its export of wine. Situated at the seaward end of a forbidding rocky promontory, the decayed Byzantine town (*G.H.*), melancholy and evocative (especially by night) now shelters only about 30 of the 445 inhab., the majority of whom live in *Yéfira* (Hot. Monemvasia B; Minoa C; Akroyiali E; Post Office), the mainland settlement. The two are linked by a succession of causeway, bridge (renewed 1889), and roadway round the s. side of the rock. The ship anchors in the bay and landing is made near the causeway.

History. The promontory was anciently called *Minoa*, a name that suggests but by no means proves Cretan influence. After the Slav invasion it became a refuge for the Greeks of Laconia, and, under the name of *Monemvasia*, it developed into an important fortress and flourishing port. In 1147 it repulsed an attack by the Normans of Sicily and thereafter was nearly always the last outpost of the Morea to fall to succeeding waves of conquerors. In 1249 William de Villehardouin took it after a siege of 3 years, but he had to give it up in 1262, with Mistra and the Maina, to Michael Palaiologos, in payment of his ransom. It became the tenth see in the empire, the commercial capital of the Byzantine Morea, and enjoyed special exemptions and trading privileges. The town later came into the hands of the Pope (1460–64), of the Venetians (1464–1540 and 1690–1715), and of the Turks (1540–1690 and 1715–1821). In 1564 the Turks repelled an attack of the Knights of Malta. Monemvasia was the scene in April 1821 of a particularly odious massacre of the surrendered Turkish garrison. Hence in 1941 c. 4000 men of the 6th N.Z. brigade were successfully evacuated.—Malmsey, or Vin de Malvoisie, was originally the name of the celebrated red and white wines shipped from Monemvasia, though produced in Tinos and other Aegean islands.

The end of the approach road (20 min.) is barred by the impressive w. wall with towers and bastions, which descends directly from the castle to the sea. A tiny gate admits pedestrians and their donkeys. Within, the houses are piled upon one another and intersected by steep, narrow, and intricate streets. In the LOWER TOWN four churches survive of an original forty. The CATHEDRAL of the diocese, the largest medieval church in Laconia, dedicated to *Elkomenos Christos* (Christ in chains), dates from the reign of Andronikos II, who in 1293 elevated the see to metropolitan rank. The portal was rebuilt of Byzantine fragments in 1697. Massive piers with pointed arches support the heavy barrel-vaulted nave and aisles. Opposite, *Ayios Pavlos*, built in 956 and transformed by the Turks, serves as a *Museum* of marble fragments, including a Frankish tombstone of 1245 and a 16C font. Just above stands the decayed *Myrtidiotissa*, and farther on, nearer the sea, the 16C *Panayia Chrysaphitissa*, attractively restored and whitewashed.

We wind up a fortified zigzag to the KASTRO, or *Goulá*, entered by a tunnel that still retains iron-bound gates. The ruins, extensive but indeterminate, have been fenced round. On the edge of a vertiginous cliff (*View of wild grandeur at sunset) stands **Ayia Sophia,** a splendid Byzantine church founded by Andronikos II, on a plan similar to that at Daphni (p. 189), well restored in 1958. The exo-narthex is a Venetian addition. The five doorways have sculptured marble lintels. Four frescoed medallions survive in the squinches, above which a 16-sided drum of impressive proportions supports the dome.

On the cliffs, 3 m. N. of the town, *Palaiá Monemvasía* occupies the site of *Epidauros Limera*, a colony from Epidauros and one of the free-Laconian cities. The walls of the acropolis are traceable all round; in some places they retain more than half their original height. The town was divided into three by cross walls.

FROM MONEMVASIA TO SPARTA. ROAD, 59 m. (95 km.), mostly poor and feature-less. Motor-bus daily from the w. gate (long wait in Yefíra) to *Molaoi* (poor connection thence to Sparta in c. 6 hrs; by changing again at Tarapsa, it is possible to reach Yithion in c. 7 hrs and even the Mani the same day); through bus c. 3 times monthly to Sparta and Athens.

From Monemvasia a bad road runs N. along the sandy shore of *Ayia Kiriakí*, turning inland short of Epidauros Limera (comp. above) into a stony valley of scrub.—At 7½ m. we are joined by a road from Velies and Neapolis (25½ m.). —10½ m. *Sikéa* (1130 inhab.) stands (l.) on a hill above the road. We cross a plain cultivated with olives, leaving on the left a turning for Papadhianika and Plitra. —13¾ m. *Moláoi* (Inns), a well-watered market town (2500 inhab.) below a ravine on the E. slope of an isolated hill (3000 ft), preserves remnants of a fortress and of a Byzantine church.

Among low stony hills we pass below the *Monastéri tis Kanganiás* (½ m. l.) and leave (22 m.) a turning for *Apidéa* (5 m. r.), which preserves a 14C church and traces of the walls of ancient *Kome*.—28 m. *Vlakhióti* (ΒΛΑΧΙΩΤΗΣ; Inn), a depressing village (1760 inhab.), is connected by road with Yeraki (10½ m.). Among rice and cotton fields (2 m. l.) lie vestiges of *Helos*, by tradition the first town to be enslaved by the Spartans, providing an etymology for the word 'Helot'. Many traces of prehistoric occupation have also been noted near *Astéri*, to the s. We pass the old church of Paniyíristra and cross the Eurotas.—29¼ m. *Skála* (Inns) is the modern market (2500 inhab.) of the plain.—38½ m. *Krokeaí* (1600 inhab; Hellas D) was famed in antiquity for its stone quarries (Lapis Lacedaemonius). The ancient town lay to the S.E. of its modern counterpart and the quarries beyond.— At (44½ m.) *Kháni Tárapsa* (Rfmts) we join the main Sparta–Yithion road (Rte 32B).—59 m. Sparta, see Rte 31.

The steamer next passes Cape Kamíli, a low narrow promontory, beyond which rises *Cape Maléa*, the s. extremity of Laconia. The cape, the 'Formidatum Maleae caput' of Statius, was dreaded by mariners.— Doubling the cape, we come to (11 hrs) *Neápolis* (Inns), a small town (2200 inhab.) on the Voiátic Gulf. This and the peninsula take name from the free-Laconian town of *Boiai*, some remains of which can be seen near the shore to the s. A museum is destined to house finds from the Pavlopetri site (M.H.–L.H.), to the N., investigated by Cambridge University in 1967–68, mostly underwater. The gulf is closed on the w. opposite Pavlopetri by *Elafónisos*, anciently a promontory named Onugnathos (ass's jaw) and now separated from the mainland by a strait c. 400 yds wide. After calling at (11¾ hrs) its little port, the steamer heads s. to Kithira.

Kíthira (ΚΥΘΗΡΑ), or *Kythera*, known to the Venetians as *Cerigo*, and historically one of the Ionian Islands (comp. Rte 56), has more recently been administered as an eparchy of Piraios. It is connected with Athens by air (3–6 times weekly in Apr–Oct). With Andikithira (see below) it has 4100 inhabitants. Kithira, 20 m. long by 12 m. broad, is separated from Elafonisos by a channel 5 m. wide. The surface of the island is rocky but the hills do not exceed 1650 ft. It is mostly uncultivated, but some parts produce corn, wine, and olive-oil. The honey is much esteemed.

History. In remote antiquity *Kythera* is said to have been called *Porphyrousa* from its abundant murex. The Phoenicians may have developed its purple industry and introduced the worship of Syrian Aphrodite, but in the first half of the 2nd millennium B.C. it was a Minoan colony. In the Iliad Amphidamas and Lykophron are native to Kythera. In the Peloponnesian War the island guarded the s. seaboard of Lakedaimonia until subdued by Athens in 424. After the Fourth Crusade it suffered many invasions, the inhabitants being sold into slavery by Barbarossa in 1537. It became a Venetian possession in 1717 and thereafter shared the fortunes of the Ionian Is. (comp. Rte 56) until 1864. The Greek island, at first linked with Laconia, is now administered by Attica. Its population has halved in the last century and its economy is now tied to migrants in Australia. Some 850 British troops got away viâ Kithira in 1941 after the mainland was completely in German hands.

Its two weekly steamers from Piraeus call first at *Ayia Pelayía* (11–13 hrs) in the N.E., then at Kapsáli at the S. end of the island. Landing by small boat, 10 dr.

13–15 hrs. *Kapsáli* is joined by road (2 m.) with **Khóra**, or *Kíthira*, the chief place (680 inhab.), which stands on a narrow ridge 500 yds long, terminating at the S.E. end in a precipitous rock crowned by a medieval *Kastro* with a museum. There is a small *Inn*, and communal accommodation may be sought at *Moni Myrtidion* (200 beds), *Ayia Moni* (125 beds), or *Ayia Elessa* (50 beds) at various points of the island.

The principal curiosities of Kithira are its stalactite caverns and the Minoan colony site of Kastri, near *Avlémonas* on the wide E. bay. It was occupied as a trading post c. 2000–1450 B.C.; the British School excavation here in 1964 also showed Neolithic occupation. Palaiokastro, farther inland, is believed to be the site of ancient Kythera. Here the church of Ayios Kosmas incorporates Doric capitals traditionally associated with a sanctuary of Aphrodite.

About 23 m. to the S.E. of Kithira and nearly half-way to Crete is the little island of ANDIKITHIRA (ΑΝΤΙΚΥΘΗΡΑ), or *Cerigotto* (14 hrs from Piraeus, once weekly), known as *Lious* to its 140 inhabitants. Like Crete it has undergone upheaval in recent times: along the entire coastline runs a dark band, rising to a height of c. 9 ft above the present sea-level, and exhibiting furrows formed by a dozen successive sea levels. The chief place is the hamlet of *Potamos*, 1 m. N.E. of which, on the headland of Palaiokastro, are the walls (5–3C B.C.) of *Aigilia*, chief place of classical Antikythera.

In the channel between Kithira and Andikithira are the remains of a wreck of the 1C B.C. which has yielded bronzes and marbles now in the National Museum.

The steamer makes three calls on the E. side of the Mani peninsula on the way N. to Yithion.—19¾ hrs. *Portokáyio*, the name of which is a corruption of the Venetian Quaglio (quails), has an imposing late-medieval castle and is 3 m. N. of CAPE MATAPAN, the ancient *Tainaron* (688 ft). Here the Asomaton chapel occupies the site of the famous Temple of Poseidon where the free-Laconians had their headquarters. Exploration has shown that extensive remains include pebble mosaics. The cape has much the same latitude as Gibraltar and is thus the second most southerly place (to Cape Tarifa) on the European mainland. Off Cape Matapan on 28 March 1941 was fought one of the battles that reduced the Italian navy's enthusiasm for the war: three battleships, an aircraft carrier, 4 cruisers, and 13 destroyers, under the command of Adm. Cunningham, engaged the Italian battleship 'Vittorio Veneto', with 9 cruisers and 11 destroyers. The 'Veneto' was damaged, 'Pola' and 'Fiume' sunk, and the 'Zara' crippled; there were no British losses.— At (20¼ hrs) *Kiprianon* before the First World War an Italian company exploited the ancient quarries of rosso antico (Taenarian marble), 2 m. inland.—21 hrs. *Soloteri*, a little farther N. is linked by bus with Yithion.—22¾ hrs. *Yithion*, see below.

B   From Sparta to Yithion and the Mani

ROAD, 60¼ m. (97 km.), excellent to Yithion (bus several times daily), and Areopolis (bus 3 times daily), continuing asphalt to Diros, but poor beyond (bus once daily). 15¼ m. *Khâni Tárapsa.*—28 m. *Yithion.*—44 m. *Areópolis.*—48 m. *Pirgos Dirou.*—60¼ m. *Yeroliména.*

Sparta, see Rte 31. The road runs S. through orange groves, crossing one tributary of the Eurotas after another. We pass, before and after (3½ m.) *Sklavokhori*, the hills of Ayia Kiriaki and Palaiopiryi, both to the left, from whose ruins the village has readopted the name of Amyklai (comp. Rte 31).—5 m. Turning (r.) for the climbers' refuge inaugurated in 1962 at *Ayia Varvara* (c. 17 m.) on Taïyetos. From the refuge (4590 ft) the summit of *Taíyetos* (7874 ft; *Profitis Ilias*) may be climbed.

We continue through olive groves and mulberry plantations.—8½ m. Turning to *Xirokambi* (2 m.; r.) where the torrent is spanned by a single-arched bridge in polygonal masonry of the Hellenistic era.

The road ascends the low Vardounokhoria Hills, which extend E. from the Taïyetos. We pass (r.) the village of Tarapsa, just before (15¼ m.) *Kháni Tárapsa* (Rfmts), where the road divides. The left branch forms the main road to Monemvasia (Rte 32A). Our road continues to ascend through wooded country. From the summit (985ft) there are fine views of the Helos Plain and the Laconic Gulf. On the descent we pass (22 m.) the ruins of *Aegeiai*, which had a temple to Poseidon by a lake. We thread a wooded defile.

28 m. (45 km.) **Yíthion** (ΓΥΘΕΙΟΝ; *Lakonis* A, not cheap; *Actaeon* D), or *Gytheion*, the ancient and modern port of Sparta, is the second largest town (4900 inhab.) in Laconia and the seat of an eparchy. Olives, oil, and valonia are its chief exports. It has a pleasant promenade and is connected by steamer with Piraeus (comp. Rte 32A).

The inhabitants of *Gytheion* claimed Herakles and Apollo as joint founders; classical tradition speaks of Minyan colonists and Phoenician traders in purple-dye. The town became the naval arsenal and port of Sparta, and was sacked by the Athenian admiral Tolmides in 455 B.C. Epaminondas besieged it in vain. Nabis rebuilt and fortified it. Gytheion was the most important city of the free-Laconian League.

The modern town behind the waterfront is largely on reclaimed land. The ANCIENT CITY was situated on low hills, now ½ m. from the shore. The diminutive *Theatre* was excavated in 1891. Above the town is a ruined *Castle*. The *Museum* contains a few local antiquities. The island of MARATHONISI, the ancient *Kranaë*, is a low rocky islet (connected by causeway) crowned by a folly (Pírgo tón Grigorákidon). Here were probably the most ancient settlements.

The remainder of this route lies through the highland region known as the **Mani** (MANH), or *Maina*, compromising the last 30 m. of the Taïyetos range as far as Cape Matapan. The mountains are treeless and almost barren, though olives thrive and the ground is laboriously cultivated wherever a terrace can be contrived. The population is distributed in small villages, often perched on apparently inaccessible mountain ledges. The Outer Mani is described in Rte 32C. Inner or Deep Mani lies beyond Areopolis.

From the very earliest days the inhabitants have been uncooperative with their northern neighbours. In the decline of Sparta they organized their 24 towns into the Confederation of Free-Laconians, whose independence was recognized even by Augustus while the rest of the Peloponnese was subject to Rome. Their descendants acquired the name of Mainotes and continued the same independent spirit. They clung to paganism until the reign of the Emp. Basil I (867–886). Reinforced by refugees during the Slav invasions, they lived in clans commanded by chieftains and did not welcome strangers. Blood-feuds were common and families built towers of refuge. The Turks failed to subdue the area, recognizing its principal chieftain as 'Bey of the Maina' owing nominal allegiance to the Porte. The Mainotes eagerly joined in the Orloff rising and in the War of Independence, when the family of Mavromichales produced one of its most famous generals (Petrobey) and two of its more celebrated assassins. In 1834, however, the Mainotes strongly resented merging their independence in the new kingdom and were with difficulty subdued.

Beyond Yithion the road at first runs s.w. along the coast affording views across the Laconic Gulf to Kythera.—After *Mavrovouni*, by the 5th km. stone from Yithion, there rises (r.) a prominent sandy hill (Skina) with Mycenean chamber tombs. We cross the fertile and marshy plain of Passava and then turn inland through woodland. On many of the hills stand medieval towers.—33 m. The road passes below a hill surmounted by the ruined Frankish CASTLE OF PASSAVA, built in 1254, and incorporating fragments of ancient Greek masonry. The fine enceinte is best reached by a short climb from the w. This was probably the site of Classical *Las*, but no Mycenean remains have so far come to light to justify identification with Laas of the Iliad.—Beyond (35 m.) *Karioupolis*, we pass through a picturesque defile to emerge high above *Limenion*, the harbour of Areopolis, and join the road from Oitilo on the bare grey slopes of Profitis Ilias (2667 ft).—44 m. (77 km.) **Areópolis** (ΑΡΕΟΠΟΛΙΣ; Inn), a constricted village (675 inhab.) of tower houses, is the chief centre of the Mani. The church (*Taxiarkhis*), dating from 1798, has primitive reliefs of martial saints.

To the s. of Areopolis the landscape is dotted with tower-houses and primitive barrel-vaulted chapels (probably 9C); the domed Byzantine churches date mainly from the 11C and 12C.—48 m. *Pírgos Diroú* has a small Tourist Pavilion, whence a road (2½ m.) leads to the Bay of **Diros** (Rfmts; bathing). Here two spectacular *Caverns Vlykhada* (or Glifadha; adm. daily 8.30–3.30, 5, or 7.30; 110 dr., incl. boat on underground lake) and *Alepotrypa* ('fox-hole'; closed in 1980 during further examination) were opened to the public in 1963; both have stalactites and stalagmites and are lit by electricity. Proper study of the Neolithic burials found has been undertaken since 1970. At *Glézou*, 1 m. s.e. of Pirgos, the church of the Taxiarkhai dates from the 11C (façade rebuilt). —At (52 m.) *Vámvaka*, e. of the road, the church of Ayios Theodoros is dated by inscription to 1075. *Mézapos* lies on the coast. On the promontory of Tigani, w. of the same bay, stands the CASTLE OF MAINA, the Frankish fortress erected by William II de Villehardouin in 1248. An earlier wall with three towers on this promontory may be Mycenean and the site has been conjectured to be that of Homeric *Messe*, a distinction also claimed by (57 m.) *Koíta*, where the decayed 10C church has a carved marble iconostasis.—Just above (59 m.) *Káto Boularioí* is the 12C church of Ay. Strategos.—60¼ m. **Yerolimín** (ΓΕΡΟΛΙΜΗΝ; *Inns*) is a tiny port-of-call for Laconian coasting vessels. *Váthia*, a village of tower-houses, stands on a hill farther on. The coast beyond towards Cape Matapan is spectacular. A road is under survey round the Cape to Solotéri, whence a boat or bus can occasionally be caught to Yithion.

C From Kalamata to Areopolis

ROAD, 47½ m. (76 km.), asphalt. No road in Greece offers more spectacular coastal scenery. The greater part of this route lies in Messinian territory. BUS daily to Areopolis.

Kalamata, see Rte 34. We quit the town by the e. suburb of *Yiannits-ánika*.—4½ m. *Almirón* (Messinian Bay **B**), villa resort of Kalamata, and *Káto Sélitsa*, where Mt Kalafi rises steeply from the sea, both form part of the commune of Vérga. The narrow gap was blocked by a wall, the '*Mandra tis Verghas*', in 1826 and the Mani successfully defended against Ibrahim's ravaging army. The road now climbs inland with many turns (*Views first over Cape Kitries to the Messenian Gulf, then inland to the Taïyetos). *Avía*, on the shore (Taygetos Beach **C**), may be the *Hire* of the Iliad.—The road passes below *Sotiriánika*, whose castle is conspicuous from Kalamata but seen only in retrospect from the road. A concrete arch over the wild wooded *Koskaras Defile* replaces an old packhorse bridge, best seen from the steep hairpin bends on the far side.

12½ m. (20 km.) **Kámbos** (580 inhab.), with a conspicuous church, a tholos tomb (dug in 1888), and vestiges of an ancient temple, is dominated by the CASTLE OF ZARNATA, a huge Frankish enceinte (before 1427) with a Turkish keep built by Achmet Kiuprili in 1670. It was captured by stratagem in 1685 by Morosini. The kastro rests on polygonal foundations, perhaps of *Gerenia*. The s. wall was torn down during the disturbances of 1943–49 and further damage done by earthquake in 1947. The Byzantine church of *Zoodokhos Piyi* has a carved wooden templon. Farther on, the square battlemented *Tower of Koumoundouraki* crowns a second height.

Beyond the next summit, the descent affords a tremendous *View right down the Mani: Kardhamili in its little plain of olives is seen below as from the air. Venetiko I., off Cape Akritas, is clearly descried across the Gulf.—22½ m. (36 km.) **Kardhamíli** (ΚΑΡΔΑΜΥΛΗ; *Dioskouri, small*, **D**), a seaside village of 310 inhab., perpetuates the name of *Kardamyle*, one of the seven cities that Agamemnon offered to Achilles to appease his wrath. It was transferred by Augustus from Messenia to Laconia. The medieval *Castle* has an 18C church and ancient foundations. The acropolis has rock-cuttings of probably Mycenean date. Offshore is a fortified islet.

The road, hewn from the rock, clings perilously to the coast. It passes below *Proasteion*, where the church of Ayioi Theodoroi has 13C paintings.—25¼ m. *Stoúpa* or *Lévktron*. Ancient Leuktra, a free. Laconian city, may have occupied the curious table-top hill below the village. The acropolis became Castle Beaufort in the middle ages.—28½ m. *Selínitsa* (Inn), or Áyios Nikólaos, by the seaside, has a prominent war memorial. At Áyios Dhimítrios, to the s., is a stalactite cave. Beyond *Rínglia* the road crosses a ravine and climbs continuously. *Plátsa* and the succeeding villages have little Byzantine churches and arcaded foundations incorporating ancient fragments. The isolated church of Áyios Dhimitrios, on a spur above Platsa, commands a superb view to the N. *Koutifári* is proposed as the site of ancient Thalamai.—The tower-houses of (35 m.) *Langádha* rise in terraces. *Trakhíla*, with a cave, is seen on the coast below. We pass into Laconia, Areopolis appears across the Limenion Gulf and the wilder ranges of Inner Mani rise ahead.—43½ m. **Oítilo** (ΟΙΤΥΛΟΝ), or *Vitylo*, a village making a potent unresinated wine, was the capital of the Mani before Areopolis. Its name survives unchanged from Homeric times. Here Napoleon I put in on his way to Egypt. The village is divided by the Ravine of Milolangadho, the boundary between Outer and Inner Mani, from *Kelefá*, where stands the huge walled frontier-post, erected by the Turks in the 17C to control the Maniotes. The road continues with superb views viâ *Limenion* to (47½ m.) *Areopolis*.

33 FROM TRIPOLIS TO KALAMATA

ROAD, 59 m. (95 km.), bus in 2¼ hrs.—21¼ m. *Megalopolis*.—59 m. *Kalamata*.
RAILWAY, 76½ m. in 2½–3½ hrs. To *Bilali*, junction for Megalopolis, in 1 hr;
to *Zevgolatio*, junction for Kiparissia, in 2 hrs.

Quitting the central square the Kalamata road runs s.w.—2¾ m.
By-road to *Valtetsi* (4 m. w.) where in 1821 Khurshid Pasha's Turks,
marching to the relief of Tripolis, were defeated by Kolokotronis.—
3½ m. *Makri* crossroads (village ½ m. r.); to the left (c. 2 m.), at the foot
of *Mt Krávari*, the ancient Boreion (3570 ft), are the insignificant ruins
of *Pallantion*, confined to foundations of a temple and traces of the city
walls. The approach is by confusing tracks across fields, only the first
few hundred yards being motorable.

According to legend, sixty years before the Trojan War, King Evander, the son
of Hermes by an Arcadian nymph, founded from *Pallantion* a colony by the river
Tiber. The name of the Palatine hill reflects his native town, and Pallantion was
accordingly regarded as the mother-city of Rome itself. When Megalopolis was
founded, Pallantion dwindled to a village, but Antoninus Pius, in memory of
Evander, restored its civic status and privileges. It was explored by the Italian
School in 1940. Just s.e. of the ruins are the remains of an embankment, of rammed
earth encased with stone, that served both as a dyke against the waters of *Táka
Marsh* and as a frontier barrier against Tegea.

The road now climbs the *Pass of Kaloyerikos* (2657 ft; fine retrospect
of the Plain of Tripolis), and descends into the dreary plain of Asea.
The high range of Taïyetos is seen to the s.—10¼ m. *Aséa* station (2146
ft) lies 1¾ m. below its village, near the springs that form the source of
the Alpheios.

An isolated hill below the modern village, ¾ m. beyond the ruined khan of
Frankovrísi, is the acropolis of ASEA, shown by Swedish excavations in 1936–38
to have had a continuous existence from Neolithic to Middle Helladic times and
to have been reoccupied in the Hellenistic period. The remains have been covered
again.

Beyond Aséa the railway draws away to the s. to pass, after *Marmariá*,
below the site of the ancient *Oresthasion* on the long ridge that runs N.
from *Mt Tsemperon* (4108 ft). The line traverses the hills by a gorge,
then descends by wide loops through Leondári (see below) to Bilali,
junction for the Megalopolis branch.—The road surmounts the ridge
(view) and descends in zigzags to the plain.

THE PLAIN OF MEGALOPOLIS, the great w. plain of Arcadia, is about 18 m. long
from N. to s. and 10 m. wide. With an average altitude of 1400 ft, it enjoys a much
more temperate climate than the Plain of Tripolis. It is pleasantly wooded and well
watered by the Alpheios, while the outlines of the encircling mountains make a
fine background.

21¼ m. (34 km.) **Megalopolis** (ΜΕΓΑΛΟΠΟΛΙΣ; 1401 ft; *Akhillion,
Paris*, both D) comprises a modern small town (3400 inhab.) and, about
¾ m. N., the widespread but unrewarding ruins of the 'Great City', at
once the chief town of the surrounding district and the capital of the
federated states of Arcadia. The city straddles the *Hellison*, one of the
seven tributaries of the Alpheios, the federal capital (*Oresteia*) occupying
the nearer bank while the municipal city lies across the river.

History. When the Pan-Arcadian League was formed after Leuktra, Arcadia
lacked a capital city. Mutual jealousies precluded the choice of any existing city,
and a new site was selected. Its position was determined by Epaminondas of
Thebes in accordance with his concept of a strategic barrier to contain the Spartans,

the other bastions of which were to be Messene, Mantineia, and Argos. The 'Great City' (ἡ Μεγάλη Πόλις) as it was called by the Greeks (Megalopolis being a Roman corruption), was built in 371–368 B.C., and populated by wholesale transplantation from 40 local villages and smaller migrations from Tegea, Mantineia, etc. The League had a federal Council of 50 members and an Assembly called the Ten Thousand, which met in the Thersilion at Megalopolis: the executive power was held by a Strategos who had an army of 500 Eparitoi at his command. The confederation soon broke up; Mantineia withdrew in 364 after the League had tampered with the sacred treasuries at Olympia, and in 362 half the Arcadians fought with the Spartans against Thebes. The inhabitants of Megalopolis had to be prevented from returning to their former homes by Pammenes' Theban soldiers. Spartan attempts to reduce the city were foiled in 353 with Theban aid and again in 331 when Megalopolis sided with Macedon. Having joined the Achaean League in 234, the city again suffered Spartan attack; saved once by a hurricane, it was sacked in 223 B.C. by Kleomenes III. Two-thirds of the population escaped to Messenia under the leadership of Philopoemen (253–183 B.C.), almost the only great man produced by Arcadia, returning two years later after Kleomenes' defeat at Sellasia. Strabo quotes an unknown comic poet to the effect that 'the Great City was a great desert', and Pausanias found it 'mostly in ruins', though under the later emperors it was the seat of a bishop. It finally disappeared in the Slav invasion.—Besides Philopoemen, the only native of note is Polybius (204–122 B.C.), the historian.

Megalopolis was excavated by the British School in 1890–93; ploughing has since wrought havoc with much of the site, which is principally interesting for the theatre. This is reached from the Andritsaina road, which passes through the ancient city, by taking a track to the left just before we reach the bridge over the river.

The THEATRE, which is built up against the N. side of a hillock, 100 yds from the river, was the largest in Greece. It dates, in its original form, from the 4C B.C., but is later than the Thersilion. The *Cavea* is divided by 10 stairways and two diazomai, to make 59 rows of seats for c. 21,000 spectators. The lowest tiers are well preserved. The *Orchestra* is 99 ft in diameter. The place of the w. parodos is taken by a *Skenotheke*, or property room. The portico of the Thersilion seems to have served also as a permanent skene for the theatre. The stone *Stage*, adorned by 14 marble columns between antae, is a Roman addition.

The *Thersilion* is perhaps the most elaborate example known of the square hall. Measuring 172 ft by 218½ ft, it had five concentric rows of columns, set parallel to the outside walls and arranged on radials from a tribune offset from centre. The bases of the columns remaining in situ show that the wooden floor sloped down towards the tribune, above which the roof line was probably broken by a lantern. Facing the theatre and originally separated from the hall only by piers (later by a continuous wall with doorways), was a Doric prostyle portico having 14 columns beneath a single pediment. The building was destroyed in 222 B.C. and not rebuilt.

Beyond the river the *Sanctuary of Zeus Soter* and the *Stoa of Philip*, demarcating the Agora, are now barely identifiable.—For the continuation of the road to Andritsaina, see Rte 35.

A tarmac road runs s. viâ (3 m.) Bilali (comp. above).—7 m. **Leondári** (ΛΕΟΝΤΑΡΙΟΝ), a medieval village, 1 m. s.w. of its station, occupies a commanding position on the top of the hill (1896 ft) forming the N. end of the Taïyetos range and overlooking a narrow pass separating Arcadia from Messenia. The Frankish *Castle* is in ruins. Here Thomas Palaiologos was defeated by the Turks in 1460; the inhabitants fled to Gardiki only to be massacred there. The little two-domed Church of the *Apostoloi* (14C) was converted into a mosque. Near it is the smaller 12C church of *Ayios Athanasios*.—About 1½ m. N.W. of Leondári, on the left bank of the Xerillas, are the scanty vestiges of *Veligosti* (ΒΕΛΙΓΟΣΤΗ), in the Byzantine age an important place. It is reached from the bridle-path that leads in 1¼ hr between the Samara Hills and Mt Ellenitsa to Paradhísia (see below). —Beyond Leondári tracks lead s. to the scattered villages (Dhirrakhi, etc.) on the w. slopes of Taïyetos.

Perhaps the most interesting excursion from Megalopolis (after that to Bassae; Rte 35) is to the finely situated site of **Lykosoura** (8¾ m.). We take the Kalamata road (see below) and just beyond the Alpheios branch right on an unmade road. At the end of the second village (*Apidhítsa*), we again branch right, and at 7 m. left. The museum is visible on a saddle to the left; immediately below, a rough track forks left. The site is fenced; key from hamlet below. The *Museum* contains inscriptions and much of the colossal cult statues by Damophon (casts of heads, which are in Athens). The site is more interesting below the museum. There are considerable remains of a prostyle *Temple* with a side door on the s. of the cella (comp. Bassae). In front is a *Stoa*, and in the hillside (s.) a stepped retaining wall.

Beyond Lykosoura tracks continue viâ *Líkaion* and *Kastanokhórion* to *Ano Kariá* (15½ m.) whence 1 hr on foot will bring us to the Sanctuary of Pan (3920 ft) on the s. side of *Mt. Lykaion* (comp. Rte 35). Tracks go on w. from Ano Kariá to *Figalía.*

From Megalopolis the Kalamata road runs s.w., crossing (22½ m.) the Alpheios; just beyond the bridge (r.) is the by-road to Lykosoura (comp. above).—29¼ m. *Paradhísia* guards the approach to the *Makriplayi Pass* (1970 ft), the main route of communication between Arcadia and Messenia. *Khani Vidi* marks the summit of the pass. Here a by-road diverges (l.) to *Kheirádhes* (2 m.) whence a path continues in 1 hr to '*Kokkala*' on a w. spur of Taïyetos. Here the ruined old fortress on ancient foundations (? *Ampheia*) is the Byzantine and Frankish *Castle of Gardiki*, near which William de Villehardouin and Ancelin de Toucy, marching from Kalamata in 1265 beat the forces of the Great Domestic of the Eastern Empire.—The road winds down with views across the tree-covered Plain of Stenyklaros (Rte 34c); Mt Ithome appears behind Meligalá to the s.w.—At the foot of the descent, turnings (r.) first to Kirparissia and then to Ancient Ithome (Rte 34c), as the road runs straight across the plain through thick olive groves.—The copious springs near (46 m.) *Ayios Floros* were considered by the ancients as the source of the Pamisos proper before it joined the Mavrozoumenos.

51 m. *Palaiókastro* (¾ m. E. of the road) is the site of classical THOURIA, a city destroyed in 464 B.C. by the Spartans and rebuilt by Epaminondas. It was given by Augustus to Laconia to punish the Messenians for siding with Antony. The classical remains are at the N. end of a long ridge in which many Mycenean tombs have been found: this may be the place known to Homer as *Anthea*. Modern *Thouría* is 2 m. farther along the road.

At 55¾ m. we join the road from Messini (Rte 34) and enter (59 m.) **Kalamata** (see below).

34   MESSENIA

Messenia, one of the six ancient countries of the Peloponnese and one of its seven modern nomes, is bounded on the N. by Elis and Arcadia, on the E. by Laconia, and on the S. and W. by the Ionian Sea. The region consists mainly of the s.w. peninsula of the Peloponnese, occupied by the triangular mass of high ground that culminates in Aigaleon. To the E. of this range lies the fertile Messenian Plain watered by the Pamisos, the most considerable river in the S. Peloponnese; to the N. and N.E. are secondary plains; and the natural boundaries lie along Xerovouni and Taïyetos. The capital and principal trading port is Kalamata.

In the Homeric age Messenia belonged to the Neleid princes of Pylos, of whom the most famous was Nestor, while the E. part was included in the joint kingdoms of Agamemnon and Menelaus. In the Dorian invasion Messenia was assigned to Kresphontes. The original inhabitants absorbed their conquerors and their prosperity excited the envy of Sparta. In the *First Messenian War* (? 743–724 B.C.) the Spartans conquered the country, and, notwithstanding the devotion of Aristodemos, the Messenian king, captured the fortress of Ithome, reducing the inhabitants to the condition of Helots. A rebellion known as the *Second Messenian War* (or First Messenian Revolt; ? 685–668 B.C.) was with great difficulty suppressed, when the fort of Eira was captured. The hero of this was Aristomenes, 'the first and greatest glory of the Messenian name'. Many of the Messenians emigrated to Sicily, where, in 493 B.C., their descendant Anaxilas of Rhegium captured Zancle and renamed it Messana (now Messina). *The Third Messenian War* (or Second Messenian Revolt) in 464–455 B.C. had far-reaching consequences. The Athenians, who had sent an expeditionary force to help the Lacedaemonians, were rudely dismissed. After the fall of Ithome they therefore befriended the exiled Messenians, settling them in Naupaktos. It was these Messenians who in 425 B.C. aided the Athenians at the siege of Sphakteria. After the battle of Leuktra in 371 B.C., Epaminondas repatriated the Messenians and founded for them the city of Messene. They remained independent till the Roman conquest in 146 B.C.

The ancient topography has been the subject of intensive study by the Univ. of Minnesota Messenia Expedition since 1958 (published in A.J.A. 1961, 1964, and 1969, and elsewhere).

A From Kalamata to Pylos

ROAD, 31½ m. (51 km.), asphalted. BUS 5 times daily in 1½ hr, some continuing to Khora and Kiparissia.

KALAMATA (ΚΑΛΑΜΑΤΑ), officially **Kalámai**, a manufacturing town and port (39,100 inhab.) amid groves of citrus fruit trees is the best base for expeditions in Messenia. The capital of the nome of Messenia, it is the focus of local communication and has air, rail, and coach services from Athens. The centre stands a long mile from its harbour, once the principal outlet for exports from the Peloponnese. Kalamata olives have a high reputation and figs are dried, processed and packed. Kalamata claims to be the first Greek city to have revolted against the Turks in 1821. In 1941 it was forced to surrender after the Royal Navy had put to sea to meet an Italian threat and 7000 allied troops fell into enemy hands.

Airport at Triodhos (10 m. N.W.), with service to Athens 3 times weekly.

Railway to *Athens* 6 times daily (incl. overnight) in 7–8 hrs; to *Kiparissia*, *Pirgos*, and *Patras*, etc.—CAR PARK in Plat. Venizelou, near Stn.

Hotels. In the town: **Rex** (Pl. a), 47 Aristomenous, DPO, B, good; **Achillion** (Pl. b), 6 Kapetan Kroba, **Galaxy**, 14 Kolokotronis, both C.—Near the beach, c. 1 m. s.: **Philoxenia B**; **Elite, America**, 2 and 37 Navarinou, both C.

Restaurants. *Gallia*, Od. Sfakterias; and by the shore.—ZAKHAROPLASTEION, *Galaxias*, s. end of square.

Post Office, Leof. El. Venizelou.

Buses of KTEL 4 Messenias to *Athens*, viâ Tripolis and Corinth (5 times daily); also to *Koroni* (4 times daily); to *Pylos*, *Khora*, and *Kiparissia* (3–5 times daily). From Plat. Mavromikhali to *Kardamyle*, *Oitilo*, etc.

The centre is the PLATEIA VASILEOU YEORYIOU Β´, the tree-lined broadening of Odhos Aristomenous, the long main street. *Ayioi Apostoloi*, farther N., has a Byzantine core of 1317. Odhos Ipapandis, lined with exotic trees, leads N. to the cathedral church of *Tis Ipapandi* (1859). Steps mount to the **Kastro**, erected by Geoffrey I Villehardouin in 1208 on the acropolis of ancient *Pharai*. Some remnants of walls dating back to Mycenean times have been traced. The castle consists of an outer enceinte, an inner redoubt, and a keep.

A Byzantine double enceinte had already fallen into disuse before 1204, and in 1208 its church was encased within the walls of the new keep. The castle was held by the Villehardouins for nearly a century and here William (1218–78) was born and died. It was captured by the Slavs in 1293 but won back, and passed by mar-

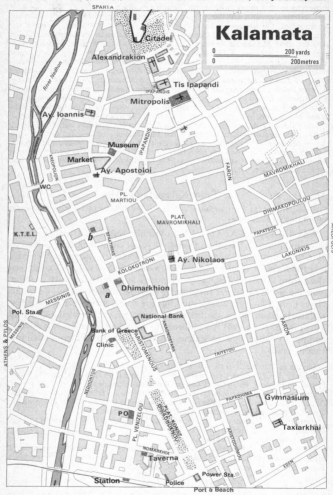

riage to Guy II, Duke of Athens in 1300. Florentines and Angevins held it in turn until it passed to the Palaiologoi in 1425. The Venetians held it during the first Turko-Venetian war (1463–79) and sacked it in a raid in 1659. The Turks blew up part of it in 1685 and the Venetians continued its demolition.

Two fine old houses of the Benaki and Kyriakou families, near the church of Ayios Ioannis, house an *Archaeological Museum* containing a good Roman mosaic, Byzantine icons, and relics of the War of Independence; also the Swedish finds from Malthi.

At *Akovítika*, a hamlet 2 m. due w. of Kalamata, s. of the railway, an E.H. megaraon was unearthed in 1969, representing perhaps a stage of development between that of Troy II and the House of Tiles at Lerna, but larger than either.
From Kalamata to the *Mani*, see Rte 32; to *Sparta*, see Rte 31.

We take the Tripolis road and after 3¼ m. bear left. Beside the branch railway, the road, passing a military air base, crosses the fertile marshes of the Markaria plain and the Pamisos to (5¼ m.) **Messíni** (ΜΕΣΣΗΝΗ; Inn), principal town (6600 inhab.) of its eparchy. A centre of rice production, locally called *Nisí* it should not be confused with the ancient city (Rte 34c) whose name it has adopted. From its vast square buses ply to many Messenian villages.—Olives and figs alternate with vines and fruit-trees. San Agostino Beach Hotel (DPO, B) lies to the s. of (8½ m.) *Análipsis*.—At (12 m.) *Rizómilos* investigations by the Univ. of Minnesota in an eroded hill-top have shown occupation throughout the Bronze Age and later.

A branch road (l.) approaches the Messenian Gulf, with views to the mountains of the Mani.—At (3¼ m.) *Petalídi*, a small port (1230 inhab.) on the w. shore of the Gulf of Kalamata, on 30 Aug 1828, Gen. Maison landed 14,000 French troops, causing Ibrahim Pasha's immediate evacuation of the Morea. Just behind the town rises the acropolis (some remains) of ancient *Aepeia*, renamed by Epimelides (c. 370 B.C.) after Koroneia, his native town in Boeotia, whence the later corruption *Korone*. Its inhabitants migrated farther s. in the middle ages (comp. below) and the town was repopulated in the 19C by Maniots. The whole coast to modern Koroni comes into view, while to the w. rise the pretty cypress-dotted foothills of Mt Likódhimon (3140 ft). The road runs above the sea.—At *Longá*, 1 m. w. of (11 m.) *Ayios Andréas* remains of four successive temples mark the site of a temple of Apollo Korythos.

18 m. **Koroni** (*Flisvos* D), a picturesque medieval town (1530 inhab.), stands on a promontory at the foot of a Venetian castle. The antique remains (breakwater, cisterns, walls, etc.) are of *Asine*, a colony planted by perioikoi from Argive Asine. The derelict site was reoccupied in the middle ages by the inhabitants of Korone (now Petalidi, see above), whence its modern name. This was corrupted by Frankish conquerors into *Coron*. In 1206 after a year's tenure the Franks had to cede it to the Venetians. Coron was attacked from the sea in 1428 by the Turks. In 1500, the inhabitants, demoralized by the news from Methone (comp. below), mutinied and gave in to the Turks only to be banished to Kefalonia. Andrea Doria captured Coron in 1532 for the Holy Roman Empire but, being besieged in turn by Khair-ed-din Barbarossa, was taken off with the inhabitants in a squadron of Sicilian ships, leaving the empty town to the Turks. It fell in 1685 to Morosini who massacred its 1500 defenders. Its final period (1718–1828) under Turkish rule was ended by Gen. Maison.

The principal points of interest in the *Castle* are the reused classical masonry in the outer curtain: the Gothic Entrance Gate; the great talus of the E. scarp moulded to the rocky bluff; the S.E. and S.W. artillery bastions, probably Turkish work; and the Byzantine wall of reused fragments which divides the inner from the outer court.

Messenia ends (7 m. s.w.) in *Cape Gallo*, the ancient *Akritas*, off which lies the rocky uninhabited islet of *Venetiko* or *Theganousa*. Methoni lies 20 m. N.W. by dirt road.

To the w. of Rizómilos the road is crossed by torrents and may be difficult after rain. It closely follows the course of a prehistoric road explored in 1962 and suggested to be that taken by the Homeric heroes between Sparta and Pylos. Beyond (19½ m.) *Kazarma* oak woods clothe the hill slopes.—At 24 m., the road summit (c. 1600 ft) affords a view over Navarino Bay; to the right begins the Venetian aqueduct which feeds a Turkish fountain at Pylos.—We join (30 m.) the Kiparissia road (see below).

31½ m. **PYLOS** (ΠΥΛΟΣ; *Castle, Nestor,* both **B**; *Navarinon* **D**), pronounced Pilos, known locally as *Neókastro,* and more familiar to foreigners as **Navarino,** is the chief town (2260 inhab.) of the eparchy of Pylia. The clean and attractive little town, built with arcaded streets by the French in 1829, rises from the s. shore of Navarino Bay at the foot of a promontory (N. end of *Mt St Nicholas,* 1588 ft) on which a castle guards the s. entrance to the bay. It is the pleasantest centre from which to explore Southern Messenia.

History. This site was not occupied in antiquity. In 1572 the Turks built on Mt St Nicholas a fortress which was called Neokastro to distinguish it from the Palaiokastro to the N. of the bay (see below). The name of *Navarino,* locally obsolete, is probably a Venetian corruption of *Ton Avarinon* (Castle 'of the Avars'), originally given by the Byzantines to the old castle and carried over to the new castle during the Venetian occupation of 1686–1718. In 1825 Ibrahim Pasha made it the centre of his operations in Messenia, which he utterly devastated. The intervention of the powers in 1827, the consequent battle of Navarino (see below), and the imminent arrival of French troops brought about Ibrahim's evacuation of the Morea in Sept. 1828. The town dates from Gen. Maison's occupation and has attracted to itself the classical name of *Pylos,* causing still further confusion (comp. below).

The PLATEIA TRION NAVARKHON, planted with planes and limes, has a memorial (1927) to Admirals Codrington, de Rigny, and von Heyden, who commanded respectively the British, French, and Russians at Navarino. The *Museum* (25 dr.;) contains mementoes of the battle, contents of Hellenistic tombs at Yialova, and Mycenean finds from Koukounara (6 m. N.E.; 1958–59).

The Turko-Venetian fortress of NEOKASTRO is reached in 10 min. by the shore or from the Methoni road, along which are remains of its Turkish aqueduct. The fortress consists of a large crenellated enceinte, enclosing a citadel with 6 bastions, an attractive domed mosque converted into a church, and a small hotel. The outer bastion, to the s.w., with a platform above the sea, affords the best view of the enceinte as a whole and commands the whole bay. The citadel was rebuilt in 1829 by the French and was in use as a prison until recent years; it now shelters Boy Scout headquarters.

BUSES to *Methoni, Kalamata, Gargalianoi,* etc.

NAVARINO BAY forms a magnificent natural harbour, 3½ m. long (N.–S.) and 2 m. wide, with a depth of 12–30 fathoms. Its w. side is formed by Sphakteria (see below). The only practicable entrance, on the s., is 1300 yds wide and divided into unequal channels by the islet of *Pylos* and the *Tsichli-Baba Rocks.* On the islet are a lighthouse and the *French Monument,* erected in 1890 when the remains were transferred here from the mainland cemetery of fallen from Navarino and from the Morea Expedition of 1828–30. In the centre of the harbour a low rock called Khelonaki ('small tortoise') is crowned by the *Memorial to the British Sailors.*

BATTLE OF NAVARINO. The Treaty of London (6 July 1827) provided that Great Britain, France, and Russia should guarantee the autonomy of Greece, under the suzerainty of Turkey, without breaking off friendly relations with the Porte. Their fleets were, without open hostilities or bloodshed, to intimidate Ibrahim Pasha into withdrawing the Turkish and Egyptian fleets from the Morea. A wide discretion was left to the senior admiral (Codrington). The allies called for an armistice; the Greeks promptly accepted but the Turks rejected the demand. On 20 Oct. the allied fleet of 26 sail (11 British, 7 French, 8 Russian), mounting 1270 guns, entered the Bay of Navarino, which sheltered the Turko-Egyptian fleet, numbering 82 warships, 2438 guns, and 16,000 men. After an ultimatum to Ibrahim Pasha demanding his withdrawal from the Morea, a few shots fired by the Turks brought about a general action. At nightfall the Ottoman fleet, reduced to 29 ships, had lost 6000 men. The allies lost 174 killed and 475 wounded, but not a single ship. The news of this unexpected victory was received in England with mixed feelings (being referred to in the King's speech of 1828 as 'an untoward event'), in Russia with ill-concealed satisfaction, and in France with frank delight. Prince Metternich denounced the action as 'an unparalleled outrage'.

The uninhabited island of SPHAKTERIA, or *Sfayia*, which all but closes the bay on the w., is 2¾ m. long and 500 to 1000 yds wide. The uneven interior of the island is covered with thickets. On the harbour side the cliffs, 100–300 ft high, are precipitous. The highest point, Ay. Ilias (550 ft), near the N. end, is partly surrounded by a ruined cyclopean wall—the "ancient wall made of rough stones" (Thuc. iv, 31), where the Spartans made their last stand (see below). In favourable weather we may cross in a small boat from Pylos to the s. end of Sphakteria and cruise up its E. coast. At the s. end of the island is the *Tomb of Capt. Mallet*, a French officer killed in the War of Independence. Farther N. is the *Grotto of Tsamadas*, named after a Greek officer; beside it is the *Monument of Santorre di Santa Rosa* (1783–1824), the Tuscan philhellene. Below the clear waters farther N. the wrecks of Turkish ships can sometimes be seen. We land in the *Bay of Panagoula* in the middle of the E. coast. Here, near a chapel, is the *Monument to the Russian Sailors* with an additional inscription of 1960.

A path ascends in 10 min. to a plateau with two brackish wells. Here for 72 days in the summer of 425 B.C. 420 occupying Spartans held out against an Athenian force under Demosthenes and Kleon. When the 292 survivors eventually surrendered, the myth that Spartans always fought to the death was broken. Thucydides describes the affair in great topographical detail which can easily be related to the terrain.—Sphakteria was long famous as a nest of pirates and it is said to be the scene of Byron's 'Corsair'.

Passing the *Tortori Rocks*, at the N.E. end of Sphakteria, we cross the practically useless Sikia channel, which is only a few feet deep. We land at the foot of the KORYPHASION PROMONTORY, near the remains of an ancient breakwater called *Porte de Junch* (des joncs: 'rushes') by the Franks and 'Zonchio' by the Venetians. A path leads up to the acropolis of 'OLD PYLOS', surmounted by a Venetian Castle. It seems probable that this is in truth to be identified with the harbour town of the Palace of Nestor (comp. below).

Strabo records that some of the inhabitants of Messenian Pylos 'at the foot of Mt Aigaleos' (comp. below) moved to this site, which the Spartans called Koryphasia (Thuc. IV, 3) from κορυφή ('summit'). Its occupation by the Athenians in 425 B.C. was the first act in the drama of Sphakteria.

From the 6C to the 9C A.D. Pylos was the home of a colony of Slavs and Avars: hence its name *Avarinos* or *Navarinon* (comp. above). In 1278 Nicholas II of St Omer built a castle here. In 1353 the Genoese captured a fleet under its walls. In 1381 it was occupied by Gascon and Navarrese adventurers; to the latter is sometimes attributed the origin of the name of Navarino. The castle was purchased by the Venetians in 1423 and fell to the Turks in 1501. After it had been bombarded by Don John of Austria in 1572 it was superseded by the Neokastro and known as *Palaiokastro*. Its capture in 1686 by Morosini and Königsmark ended its utility.

The spacious CASTLE, reached in ½ hr by the path from Porte de Junch, is fairly well preserved. Its crenellated walls and square towers rest partly on 4C foundations. The area enclosed is about 200 yds by 100. There are outer and inner courts. Fragments of ancient walls, both polygonal and cyclopean, may be traced near the middle of the s. wall, on the N.E. side, and on the w. side of the castle. There are also ancient cisterns and staircases hewn in the rock.—Below, to the N., is *Voïdhokoilia* (good bathing) probable site of the Mycenean harbour.

A steep path leads down from the castle to the mouth of the so-called *Grotto of Nestor*, on the N. slope of Koryphasion. The arched entrance is 30 ft wide and 12 ft high. The cave itself is 60 ft long, and 40 ft wide and 40 ft high. Clinging to the walls are stalactites having the shapes of animals and of hanging hides, whence the legend that Neleus and Nestor here kept their cows. The grotto is identified with the cavern of the Homeric *Hymn to Hermes* in which Hermes hid the cattle stolen by him from Apollo and hung up the hides of the two beasts that he had killed. Sherds attest its intensive use in the Mycenean age.

A rough path descends the N. side of Koryphasion in ¾ hr to the Pylos–Kiparissia road (see below).

A road, engineered in 1828–29 by the French army, runs s. to (7½ m.) **Methóni** (ΜΕΘΩΝΗ; *Methoni Beach*, DPO, B; *Alex* C), a small fortress town of 1330 inhab., situated on a promontory opposite the island of *Sapienza*. The harbour is almost sanded up but the imposing fortifications still testify to its medieval importance.

History. *Methoni* or *Mothone*, originally called *Pedasos*, was said to be one of the seven cities which Agamemnon promised to Achilles. In Homer it has the epithet ἀμπελόεσσα (rich in vines). It received a colony of 'perioikoi' from Nauplia about the time of the Second Messenian War. In 431 B.C. an Athenian attack was foiled by the bravery of Brasidas the Spartan. The descendants of the Argive immigrants remained here even after the restoration of the Messenians by Epaminondas. Trajan granted independence to the city. Having become a haunt of pirates, it was razed in 1125 by the Venetians, and after a period of desolation firmly assigned to Venice in 1204. Until 1206, however, Geoffrey de Villehardouin and William de Champlitte used it as a base, establishing a bishopric here. The Venetians fortified it as their main port of call on the way to the Holy Land, to which it sent an annual convoy of pilgrims. The town, known as *Modon*, was noted for its wine and bacon, and had a flourishing silk industry, but although it was a naval station and shared with its neighbour Coron the description 'Oculi capitales communis', its public buildings were never lavish. The Venetian navy, totally defeated at the Battle of Sapienza in 1354 by the Genoese under Andrea Doria, took their revenge in 1403 off Modon, defeating a Genoese fleet commanded by the French marshal, Boucicault. Here on neutral ground in 1366 Count Amadeus VI of Savoy arbitrated in the struggle between Marie de Bourbon and Angelo Acciaiouli, Abp of Patras. In 1500, after resisting a month's bombardment, Methoni fell to Sultan Bayezid II when the defenders prematurely deserted the walls to welcome a relieving force sent from Corfú. An attack by the Knights of Malta in 1551 was unsuccessful, and save for a second brief Venetian period in 1686–1715, following Morosini's conquest, the town remained in Turkish hands until 1828. Chateaubriand made landfall here in 1806, and here Ibrahim Pasha disembarked his army in 1825.—The story of the captive told in 'Don Quixote' may reflect Cervantes' own experience here as a Turkish prisoner.

The Venetian *Fortress-town* occupies a promontory washed on three sides by the sea, except where the sand has built up. Its strongest fortifications on the landward side are separated from the mainland by a great ditch. We cross this on an attractive bridge, rebuilt by the French in 1828, to a Venetian monumental gateway of c. 1700. Within, a covered way leads through a second *Gate* to a third, opening into the area occupied by the medieval town (pulled down by the French when they built the modern area on the mainland). A granite *Column* with a weathered inscription probably commemorates Rector Fr. Bembo (1494). Little remains except a *Turkish Bath*, the ruin of the Latin *Cathedral*, and cisterns. The *Curtain Wall* shows masonry of all periods from Classical (exposed when a section was dynamited in 1943) to 19C. The CITADEL contains many subtleties of Venetian defence, including casemates and underground passages for counter-mining. Numerous lions of St Mark, escutcheons, and dated inscriptions survive. At the s. end of the enceinte an imposing *Sea Gate* and causeway lead to the little islet where the remnant of the Venetian force was massacred in 1500 (fortifications Turkish).

Offshore lie the *Oinoussai Islands*, a group consisting of *Sapienza* (comp. above) and *Schiza* or *Cabrera*, with the tiny islet of *Ayía Mariani* between them. The storms here are very dangerous. The bay between the islands and the mainland was anciently called *Port Phoenikos*.

B From Pylos to Kiparissía

ROAD, 40½ m. (65 km.), asphalt usually in poor state. 13 m. *Khora*.—21½ m. *Gargalianoi*.—30 m. *Filiatrá*.—40½ m. *Kiparissía*. Buses 3 times daily.

From Pylos the road skirts Navarino Bay. The hamlet of *Zounchio* derives its names from the Venetian version of the Porte de Junch (p. 315). At (3 m.) *Yiálova* are shipyards and large warehouses where currants, valonia, etc. are stored while awaiting shipment. A large port with an oil refinery is planned. We skirt the drained *Lagoon of Osman-Aga*, which extended to the foot of Koryphasion; traces of ancient occupation have shown the lagoon to have been a post-Classical formation.—7½ m. Modern *Korifásion*.

The road passes immediately below (10½ m.) the low but abrupt hill of *Epano Englianos* (excavation roof prominent) on which stand the remains of the *Palace of Nestor,** explored in 1939 and excavated since 1952 by Carl Blegen (adm. 25 dr.; excellent illustrated guide-book, to which the numbering of our plan conforms). The site, which had been occupied in the Middle Bronze Age, seems to have been reserved in c. 1300–c. 1200 B.C. for a royal palace, which was destroyed by fire at the end of Mycenean IIIв. The Iliad preserves a tradition of a Neleid dynasty at Messenian Pylos, of whom Nestor ruled for three generations. In the 'Catalogue of Ships' he is credited with the second largest fleet (90 ships against Agamemnon's 100); the palace of Englianos compares in size and richness with that of Mycenae and has dependent tholos burials.

Linear B tablets (the first to be found on the mainland) were unearthed in the room to the left of the entrance within two hours of the first day's digging in 1939, the day Italy invaded Albania. They were stored in a bank vault in Athens throughout the war.

The perimeter seems not to have been fortified in the palace period. The PALACE consisted of two-storied buildings in three main blocks, whose construction somewhat resembled that of Tudor half-timbered buildings, having wooden columns, roofs and ceilings, with the result that the superstructure disappeared during the fire depositing only non-inflammable objects from the upper floor. The exterior walls were faced in squared blocks of limestone; the inner walls were of rubble, faced with plaster and decorated with frescoes, and had wooden wainscots. Most of the walls stand to c. 3 ft above floor level giving a clear ground plan. The upper story had brick walls between the wooden beams.

The MAIN BUILDING was approached across an open court paved in stucco. Jutting out (r.) beyond the entrance stood a *Guard Tower* (Pl. 57). The simple *Propylon* (Pl. 1, 2) had one column in each façade with a single door in the cross-wall between. The stone bases of the columns survive and show that the wooden pillars had 64 flutes. A *Sentry-box* (l.) guarded the palace door and also two small rooms (Pl. 7, 8) beside the gateway, where nearly 100 clay tablets inscribed in Linear B script were found. Here perhaps was the tax collector's office.

A large interior *Court* (Pl. 3), open to the sky, gives access to various sectors of the palace. To the left are a *Pantry* (Pl. 9), its wine jars and cups lying in ruin, and a *Waiting-Room* (Pl. 10) with a stuccoed bench.

A wide *Portico* (Pl. 4), distyle in antis, opened into a *Vestibule* (Pl. 5) and thence by another door into the PRESENCE CHAMBER (Pl. 6), or Megaron proper, 42 ft long by 37 wide. In the centre a great ceremonial hearth of stuccoed clay forms a circle 13 ft across and raised 8 in. above the floor. Round this four great columns, each with 32 flutes, supported a galleried upper story, probably having a lantern above to let light in and smoke out. The floor was divided into patterned

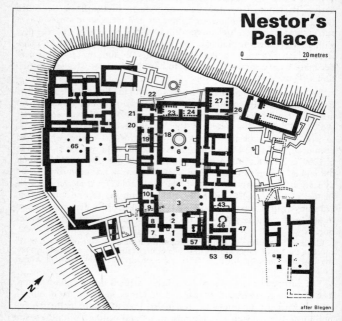

Nestor's Palace

0   20 metres

after Blegen

squares, all abstract in design save for one which bore an octopus. This is directly in front of a depression in the floor against the right-hand wall where almost certainly stood a throne. Beside it in the floor is a hollow from which a channel leads to another hollow, 6 ft away. These may have been used in some libation ceremony performed from the throne. The chamber must be imagined as painted or frescoed, the wall behind the throne being adorned with reclining griffins and lions.

Corridors either side of the Megaron served suites of service rooms and gave access to staircases leading to the upper floor. Five small rooms (Pl. 18–22) filled with thousands of cups and pots of more than 20 types must have formed as much a central depot for issue or sale as the palace pantry. Behind the megaron are magazines (Pl. 23, 24, 27) with larger pithoi fixed in stucco. Tablets were found in one room detailing their contents as olive-oil. Particularly evocative is the *Bathroom* (Pl. 43) with its fixed terracotta tub (larnax) still in situ, together with its pithoi for water and its pouring vessels (kylikes).

On the S.E. side of the court a colonnade (which supported a balcony) gives access to a duplicate but smaller set of apartments (Pl. 45–53) surrounding what appears to be the *Queen's Megaron* (Pl. 46). The suite includes a small room (Pl. 53) with a drain hole, either another bathroom or a lavatory.

The SOUTH-WESTERN BUILDING is conjectured to be an earlier and less sophisticated palace, perhaps turned into a dower house when the new palace was completed. Despite differences in plan (the arrangement is not axial and the storerooms open one from another instead of from corridors) it is a self-contained unit with most of the features of the later construction (megaron, Pl. 65, etc.). Much of its stonework has been robbed through the ages, though parts of the supporting ashlar wall survive.

The NORTH-EASTERN BUILDING may represent the palace *Workshops*, yet it seems to have had an altar in the court. The functions of various workrooms have been divined from fragments found in them and tablet lists; they included a chariot repair-shop and an armoury. Vestiges of an elaborate water-supply system are visible.—Farther to the N. is the WINE MAGAZINE, a separate edifice, in which a large room contains 35 or more great jars. Clay sealings were found marked in Linear B with the character interpreted as 'wine' and indications of its source (or vintage?).

Outside the N.E. gate of the Citadel (100 yds) is a *Tholos Tomb*, excavated by Lord William Taylour in 1953 and restored in 1957 by the Greek Archaeological Service. It is rough in construction compared with those at Mycenae.—Three other tholoi, S. of the palace, excavated in 1912, 1926, and 1939, have been filled in.

The richest finds from Pylos are in the National Museum at Athens; various frescoes, etc., in a small museum at Khora (see below).

13 m. *Khóra* (Nestor B; Galini E), formerly *Ligoúdista*, has a Museum, opened in 1966, containing Mycenean antiquities from Messenia, principally from the Palace of Nestor. The three halls contain objects from tholos and chamber tombs, including swords, and gold cups from one of the Peristeria tholoi; *Frescoes from the palace; Linear B tablets; pottery from the palace 'pantries'. The town (3400 inhab.) lies at the S.W. foot of *Kondovounia*, the ancient AIGALEON, a mountain range which forms the backbone of the peninsula and rises in Ayia Varvára to 4000 ft. We turn N.W. into its foothills.—21½ m. *Gargaliánoi* (970 ft; Ionian View, small, A; Astron D) with 5900 inhab., has a monument to Agras the Macedonian guerilla, who was born here.—30 m. *Filiatrá* (Trifylia D), a well-planned and prosperous town (5900 inhab.) amid currant fields and orchards of citrus fruit. All these towns have been rebuilt since the earthquake of 1886, but their populations are falling by migration to the cities.

Ayía Kiriakí, its little port (2½ m. S.W.), had more important days as *Erane*, as is shown by remains of basilica and baths (5C A.D.) and coins from its Frankish mint.

A poor road climbs S.E. to *Khristianó* (6¼ m.), the *Christianoupolis* of the Byzantines and seat of an archbishop in the 12C. It lost importance in the 14C and the bishopric was transferred in 1837 to Kiparissía. The 12C cathedral of Ayia Sotíra, wrecked in 1886, has been restored.

40½ m. **Kiparissía** (ΚΥΠΑΡΙΣΣΙΑ; *Ionion*, *Vassilikon* C; Restaurants between the plateia and the Rly Stn), the chief town (3900 inhab.) of the eparchy of Messenian Triphylia and the seat of the Bp of Triphylia and Christianoupolis, was called *Arkadiá* in the middle ages. The town, with pleasant broad streets, has expanded from the foot of the acropolis down to its small harbour and beaches, which are backed by groves of trees. The acropolis is a craggy rock 500 ft high connected with Mt Psykhro (3660 ft), the N.E. end of the Aigaleon range. Vestiges of Hellenic masonry survive in the ruinous Byzantine and Frankish *Castle* (*View, including Zante, Kephalonia and the Strophades), which reintroduced the round tower to Greece.

The ancient city of *Kyparissiai* was founded by Epaminondas as the port of Messene. During the Slav invasions it became a refuge of the Arcadians, whence its medieval name. It was taken after a 7-day siege by William de Champlitte in 1205. In 1391–1430 it was held by the Genoese Zaccaria. The town was destroyed by Ibrahim Pasha in 1825 and on its rebuilding resumed the ancient name.

C From Kalamata to Kiparissía

ROAD, 44½ m. (71 km.), asphalted.—13 m. Turning (l.) for ancient Messene (Ithome).—19½ m. *Meligalá*.—21½ m. *Zevgolatió*.—44½ m. *Kiparissía*.

RAILWAY, 41½ m. (67 km.), in 1¾–3½ hr viâ *Zevgolatio* and *Kalonero* where a change is sometimes necessary. To *Valira*, 13 m., for Mavrommati, in ½ hr.

The route traverses the LOWER MESSENIAN PLAIN, known to the ancients as *Makaria* ('Happy Land'), and described by Euripides in a lost play, quoted by Strabo, as a "land of fair fruitage and watered by innumerable streams, abounding in pasturage for cattle and sheep, being neither very wintry in the blasts of winter, nor yet made too hot by the chariot of Helios". Curtius observes: "High hedges of cactus divide the well-tilled fields; the great aloe stands in thick clumps, lemons and oranges flourish plentifully, the date itself ripens under the Messenian sun, and the superabundance of oil and wine is exported from Kalamata". Today, in addition, the banana is successfully grown.—The shorter road, on the E. slope of the valley (15½ m. to Meligalá), is described in Rte 33.

From Kalamata to (5¼ m.) *Messini*, see Rte 34A. On the outskirts of Messini we fork right, then turn N. up the valley of the Pamisos.— At (10 m.) *Tríodhos* roads lead r. to the airport, l. to (2½ m.) Androúsa (ΑΝΔΡΟΥΣΑ; 890 inhab.) the medieval *Druges*, once a bishopric of Frankish Messenia. It is well situated on an elevated terrace overlooking the plain. To the N. of the imposing Frankish *Castle* on the other side of a ravine, is the small Byzantine church of *Áyios Yeoryios*.

Half-an-hour farther w., in a peaceful valley, lies *Ellinoklisiá*, with an elegant church (Samarína), supposedly founded in the 14C by Andronikos II Palaiologos. Its dedication of Zoodokhos Piyi (Source of Life) comes from a spring beneath the church. Built in horizontal layers of brick and stone, it has three apses and a dome supported by ancient marble columns. The narthex supports a square belfry. Within, the mosaic borders, part of the iconostasis, and a mural painting' merit a glance. Some column drums nearby show that an earlier building occupied the site.

13 m. *Khánia Lábaina*. A by-road (signposted *Ithomi*) ascends (l.) in 6 m. to Mavrommati (bus from Kalamata), the pretty well-watered village (1375 ft) that occupies part of the site of ancient Messene. At the far end of the village is a sign to 'Archaeological Site' (footpath).

From the railway the best approach on foot is from Valira station (comp. below), whence we ascend w. for (1¼ hr) the MONASTERY OF VOURKANO (1255 ft), which has long been visible half-way up the N. slope of Mt Eva. The convent is an off-shoot of an older foundation on the summit of Ithome (see below) and accords hospitality. On the 15C entrance gate is displayed the escutcheon of the Knights of St John. The conventual buildings, which date only from 1712, are disposed round a cloistered court, with an earlier *Church* in the centre. The beautiful situation commands a view of S. Messenia and of the Arcadian mountains.—In 20 min. from the monastery we ascend to the saddle between Mts Eva and Ithome and reach the Laconian Gate (see below).

Messene dates from 369 B.C., when Epaminondas restored the Messenians to their country and encouraged them to build a capital. The city was built in a hollow between three hills, Eva on the S.E., Psoriari on the w., and *Ithome* on the N., the acropolis being on the last named which was included in the circuit. The well-preserved *Fortifi-cations are an outstanding example of 4C military architecture.

History. *Messene*, with Megalopolis, Mantineia and Argos, completed the strategic barrier against Sparta organized by Epaminondas after the battle of Leuktra. Diodorus says that the city was built in 85 days. In 214 B.C. Messene was besieged by a Macedonian general, Demetrios of Pharos, who was killed under its walls; in 202 an attack by the Spartan tyrant Nabis was frustrated by Philopoemen. After the demagogue, Dinokrates, had incited the Messenians to revolt against the Achaean League, Philopoemen attacked the rebels, but was taken prisoner by them, thrown into a dungeon in Messene, and forced to take poison. He was avenged by Lykortas, the father of Polybius, who succeeded him.—The sculptor Damophon was a native.

The path crosses walls of still-buried buildings. On the right is the analemma wall of the *Theatre*, pierced, like that at Thorikos, with corbelled archways. Lower down we reach the Hellenistic AGORA, c. 75 yds square, surrounded by a colonnade which had Ionic bases and Corinthian capitals with a winged nike rising from their acanthus leaves. The *Propylaia* occupy the middle of the E. side, between, to the N., a small

Messene

0   400 metres

Theatre (restored) and, to the S., the *Synedrion*, a small council meeting-place.—In the N.E. corner is an oikos. The remainder of the N. side is divided into two equal terraces identified by an inscription as the *Sebasteion*, an area set aside for the worship of the Roman emperors. Its two parts were each reached by a stair and divided by a monumental staircase leading to an upper terrace. Here was found a stone 'standard' for the size of tiles.—Down the w. side are a *Temple of Artemis Orthia*, divided by columns, with three other buildings forming part of the same architectural scheme.—Off the s. side is a square edifice having an inner court, perhaps the Prytaneion.—In the centre of the agora are foundations of a peripteral temple (6 by 12 columns) dedicated to Asklepios and Hygieia.

A little to the s.w. are some remains of the *Stadium* beyond which we approach the line of the walls, here almost disappeared. We may follow their traces w. and then N., or return to the road and follow it past the

Museum (not yet open 1976) to the *Arcadian Gate*, which forms, with the adjoining section of the city wall and the tower to the E., the best-preserved part of the fortifications.

The gateway, through which a road still runs, consists of an outer and an inner entrance, separated by a circular court. The *Outer Entrance* was flanked by square towers, 33 ft apart, the foundations alone of which survive. The gateway is nearly 17 ft wide. The open *Court*, 62 ft in diameter, is remarkable for the perfection of its masonry, laid without mortar on a base of two more massive courses. On either side, near the outer gate, is a niche for statues of the protecting gods, one doubtless the Hermes noted by Pausanias. Under the right niche a worn inscription describes the restorations of Q. Plotius Euphemion. The *Inner Gate* has an enormous mono-lithic doorpost, now half fallen. A short section of *Paved Road* with chariot ruts is visible. Outside the gate is the stepped base of a large monument.

The main road continues w. within the walls towards a line of towers standing to their original height.

The circuit of the *WALLS*, over 5½ m. long, follows the line of the ridge descend-ing from Ithome and was continuous except at various inaccessible points. This vast enceinte, planned to enclose cornfields, doubtless served also as a refuge for the surrounding population in time of danger. The battlemented *Curtain* consists of an outer and inner facing of unmortared squared blocks, with a rubble core; it is 6½–8 ft thick and averaged 15 ft high. The steepness of the escarpment pre-cluded the approach of siege engines. The curtain was flanked at irregular intervals (30–100 yds) by projecting battlemented *Towers*, of which there were at least thirty. These were square or, at the salient angles, semicircular. Seven are still partly extant. They had two stories, the lower with 4 loopholes, the upper with 6 small windows. Of the *Gates*, four have been distinguished.

We may return and on the way up Ithome look at the *Aqueduct* that fed the destroyed Fountain of Klepsydra. Higher up is a small terrace on which are the remains of an Ionic temple (? *Artemis Laphria*), discovered in 1844. The summit of **Ithome** ('Ιθώμη: 'step'; 2630 ft) is really a ridge running S.E. to N.W. Mentioned by Homer, Ithome figured as a refuge in the First and Third Messenian Wars. On the summit stands the small *Monastery of Vourkano*, dating from the 16C, and the mother-convent of the later monastery below (comp above). It was finally abandoned in 1950 and its ikon removed from the ruined Katholikon. A paved threshing floor may have been the scene of the festival of the Ithomaea, which survives to this day in an annual festival of the Panayia. The convent occupies the site of an *Altar-sanctuary of Zeus Ithomatas* where human sacrifice was occasionally offered. To the s. are two large cisterns. The *View* embraces most of Messenia.—We may descend by a branching path to the *Laconian Gate*.

Outside the Arcadian Gate a poor road bears left viâ *Zerbisia* and *Neokhori Ithomis* to Meligalá (see below).—From Mavrommati a track leads s. to *Samári*, where the church of Zoodokhos Piyi has 12C frescoes.

Returning to the main road, we cross the Pamisos.—14¾ m. *Valira*.—At 17½ m. we pass (r.) a short link (1¼ m.) to the Kalamata-Tripolis road.—19½ m. **Meligalá** (ΜΕΛΙΓΑΛΑΣ; Inn), with a prominent clock-tower, is the largest town (1720 inhab.) in the Upper Messenian Plain, or *Plain of Stenyklaros*, the home of the Dorian dynasty of Kresphontes. The site of the royal city is unknown. This beautiful and fertile valley, watered by many streams, enjoys a more temperate climate than is suggested by its vegetation, which includes figs, olives, oranges, mul-berries, cactus, and date palms.

About 1 m. s.w. is the triple **Mavrozoumenos Bridge**, built over the confluence of two rivers. The w. arm spans the *Upper Mavrozoumenos*, the E. arm the *Amphitos*. The N. arm forms a causeway over the apex of land between them which is liable to be flooded. The bridge has seven arches (span 17 ft, height above water 13 ft) and one rectangular opening 7 ft high by 4 wide. The piers are ancient, probably contemporary with Messene; the arches mainly Turkish. English travellers may be reminded of the 14C triangular bridge at Crowland in Lincolnshire. The river below the bridge is called the *Pamisos*.

Beyond the railway junction of *Zevgolatió* we meet the road from Megalopolis and turn W. The road, which is being realined, crosses the *Soulima Plain*, a broad corridor through which flows the Upper Mavrozoumenos.—27 m. *Vasilikó* has a small Museum containing objects from Malthí and a Roman mosaic found near Korone. On the *Malthí Ridge* between Vasilikó and the hamlet of Kokla (l.) is the site doubtfully identified with the Homeric Dorion where Thamyris lost his eyesight. Excavations in 1927–36 by the Swedish archaeologist Natan Valmin disclosed a largely M.H. existence. Two small tholos tombs and a sanctuary containing a bronze double-axe were brought to light.—32½ m. *Káto Kopanáki*, on the watershed between the Arkhadeïka (Aëtos) and the W. tributaries of the Pamisos, lies 3 m. N. of Aëtós, a village on the N. slope of *Mt Sekhi* (4564 ft) where there are cyclopean ruins and remains of a 14C Venetian fort.—39 m. Turning (r; across the railway) for *Sidhirókastro*, a village in the hills to the N.E. On a hill behind it is the 13C castle from which it takes name.

Discoveries in 1960–65 in the region of *Peristeria* by Prof. Sp. Marinatos have shown the area to have had royal tombs of Mycenean date. Three tholos tombs (despite previous plundering) yielded a gold cup and rosettes.

At (40½ m.) *Kaló Neró* we join the coastal road (comp. below) and turn left.—44½ m. **Kiparissía**, see Rte 34B.

D From Kiparissía to Pírgos

ROAD, 36 m. (57 km.).
RAILWAY, 39 m., several times daily in 1½–5 hrs; to *Kaïafa*, 20½ m., in 50 min. (only the slowest trains stop at *Samikó*).

Heading N. from Kiparissía, we meet the main road from the E. at (4 m.) *Kaló Neró*, whence road and railway follow the sandy shore.— 10 m. The *Nedha* river forms the boundary between Messinia and Elis (comp. Rte 40).—12½ m. *Tholon*. A poor road (bus) serves *Strovítsi* (5 m.), on the heights above which are well-preserved walls of ancient *Lepreon*, and *Kato Figalia* (or Zourtsa; 8½ m.), whence bridle-paths wind in 8½ hrs to ancient Phigaleia (Rte 35).—15¾ m. **Kakóvatos** is well-known to archaeologists for the site (15 min. to the N.E. at 'Marmara') identified by Prof. Dörpfeld, following Strabo, as Triphylian Pylos, a place confused until the discoveries at Englianos with the Pylos of Nestor. Three tholos tombs and traces of a palace or sanctuary (L.H. I or II) were excavated in 1909–10, and the position of the lower town was identified in 1961.

Beyond (17½ m.) *Zakháro* (Rex C; 2700 inhab.) we pass between the sea and the LAGOON OF KAÏÁFA, which is 3 m. long and contains valuable fisheries. On the lake-island of Ayía Aikaterini (cross by causeway r. at 20 m.) are the sulphur *Baths of Kaïáfa* (ΛΟΥΤΡΑ ΚΑΙΑΦΑ; Geranion C, May–Oct with annexes).

The waters come from springs in two large sulphurous caverns, the *Cave of the Anigrian Nymphs* and the *Cave of Yeranion* to which the ancients resorted for the cure of skin diseases. The first feeds the baths, the second is used for drinking. Local tradition ascribes the name of the lagoon to Caiaphas, High Priest of Judah, who bathed here after having been shipwrecked. The offensive pungency of the sulphur-laden waters is attributed to him.

The road rounds the w. spur of *Mt Kaïáfa* (2441 ft). On the N. slope of the mountain, immediately above the road and best seen from the N., stands (23½ m.) ancient **Samikon**. The imposing enceinte in developed polygonal masonry of c. 450 B.C. stands in places to 12 courses. Within is a less well preserved and earlier defensive wall to be dated before the 6C B.C. The site has been inhabited since Early Helladic times and a Mycenean burial mound has yielded much pottery. The place was taken by Philip V of Macedon in 219 B.C.

We pass inland of the shallow lagoon of *Agoulínitsa*, itself separated from the sea by a belt of dunes with pines. Roads (r.) lead to Kréstena (whence to Bassae, see Rte 35) and on over the Alpheios Dam to Olympia (8 m.; Rte 36).—31 m. *Epitálion* (1960 inhab.), formerly Agoulínitsa but now probably correctly recording an ancient site, straggles on the hillside, surrounded by cornfields and vineyards. The hill of Ay. Yeoryios has produced L.H. III remains of (?) Homeric *Thryon*. Hence the road runs straight across the alluvial plain, crossing the Alpheios on a bridge 400 yds long that serves also as an irrigation sluice. The railway curves N.E. to cross the river higher up by a long iron bridge and join the branch from Olympia.—39 m. *Pirgos*, see Rte 40.

35   FROM MEGALOPOLIS TO ANDRÍTSAINA (BASSAE) AND PIRGOS

ROAD, 68½ m. (110 km.) affording spectacular scenery. 12½ m. **Karítaina.**—28 m. **Andrítsaina**, turning for **Bassae** (9 m.).—37¼ m. *Zákha.*—56¼ m. *Kréstena.*—68¼ m. **Pirgos**. Bus daily from Megalopolis to Andritsaina; twice daily from Andritsaina to Krestena; more frequently Krestena to Pirgos. Taxis in Megalopolis for Bassae (c. 200 dr.).

Megalopolis, see Rte 33. The road runs through the ancient remains crossing the Helisson. We follow the Alpheios at varying distances from its right bank.—7 m. *Katsímbali*. Here a track diverges (l.) across the river to *Kiparissía*, between which and *Mavriá*, just to the N., are some remains of *Trapezous*.—We see ahead (12½ m.) *Karítaina* (winding ascent for 2 m.) above the junction with the road from Dhimitsana.

Karítaina (KAPYTAINA), a picturesque medieval town, is spectacularly perched on an isolated hill at the N.W. corner of the Plain of Megalopolis above the right bank of the Karitaina (as the Alpheios is called at this point).

Karitaina occupies the site of ancient *Brenthe*, a deserted city which became a refuge for the people of Gortys when they were driven out by the Slavs. The name is, in fact, a corruption of Gortyna. In 1209 the Franks made Karytaina the capital of a barony of 22 fiefs. The castle was built by Hugh de Bruyères in 1254. His son Geoffrey I de Bruyères (d. 1272) was the 'Sire de Caritaine' and the pattern of Peloponnesian chivalry. The castle passed by sale in 1320 to Andronikos II Palaiologos. In the War of Independence, Kolokotronis used the castle as a stronghold from which he defied Ibrahim Pasha.

The churches of the *Panayia* (11C), with a Frankish belfry, and of *Ayios Nikolaos*, merit a visit. A precipitous path climbs in 10 min. to the *CASTLE (1913 ft) which occupies the summit of a high rock, extremely steep and in places overhanging on the river side. The triangular enceinte, adapted for defence by artillery as well as musketry, is a notable example of feudal fortification. In the central court is a large vaulted hall and on the w. the remains of a gallery with large windows and of numerous cisterns (care needed). The *View* is superb.

From Karitaina a bad road leads N. viâ Ipsous (12 m.; Rte 36) to Dhimitsana. The road winds high in the accidented mountain range on the E. side of the gorge down which the clear, green Lousios (or Gortynios) flows to its confluence with the Alpheios. About 6 m. along this road is *Ellinikó*. Before this village a mule-path diverges (l.) to *Atzíkholo* (1½ hr) on the right (w.) bank of the Lousios where the acropolis of **Gortys** occupies the oblong summit of a precipitous height. On all sides except the E., which falls sheer to the river, are remains of walls and towers in trapezoidal masonry of the Macedonian epoch. These were explored in detail by the French School (BCH 1947–48). A smaller walled enclosure borders the ravine at the S.E. corner. Beyond are some foundations of a sanctuary of Asklepios with a Doric temple (explored 1950–52). To the N. of the acropolis (30 min.) near the little chapel of Ayios Andreas are the more interesting remains of a second *Asklepieion* with a thermal establishment (? 4C B.C.), excavated in 1954. Important remains of houses of the same period have also been found. Gortys still gives name to a modern eparchy of Arcadia.

Near by in 1955 were explored three strong-points commanding the ancient route from Megalopolis to Elis: above the village of *Vlakhorafti*, to the w., on the highest point (3090 ft) of the w. chain overlooking the gorge; at *Palaiokastro*, at the w. end of this chain, overlooking the Alpheios (ancient *Bouphagion*); and (smaller but probably of the Archaic period) at Elliniko (see above).

The Andritsaina road crosses the river on a new bridge affording a good view of the *Medieval Bridge*, renovated (as an inscription once recorded) in 1439 by Manuel Raoul Melikes, a member of a noble Turkish family serving the Palaiologi at Mistra.—17 m. *Strongiló*. We climb high along the N. slopes of the barren Mt. Lykaion with views into the Gorge of the Alpheios.

Mt Lykaion (4615 ft) was the centre of a primitive cult of Zeus involving rain-making, human sacrifice, werewolves, and athletic games. Within its precinct neither man nor beast cast a shadow. The sacrificial pyre and precinct were excavated in 1903. The site of the hippodrome can be distinguished. Lykosoura, on the s. flank, see Rte 33.

28 m. (45 km.) **Andritsaina** (ΑΝΔΡΙΤΣΑΙΝΑ; *Theoxenia*, closed in winter, **B**; *Pan* **D**), an attractive ramshackle town (980 inhab.) of wooden houses, was shaken by earthquakes in 1965. It is beautifully situated on elevated ground (2510 ft) facing N.W. and watered by a mountain stream. In the square stands a monument to Panayotis Anagnostopoulos, one of the Philike Etairia who was educated at the local school. The town has an excellent *Library* founded with a bequest in 1840.

A road (9 m.; taxi; no bus), well-engineered but often in bad condition, and not for those nervous of unprotected drops, ascends to the remote Temple of Bassae. The 2½ hrs walk through the valleys is rewarding. Continuation to the coast, see below.

The celebrated *TEMPLE OF APOLLO EPIKOURIOS* at **Bassae** is situated at 3710 ft on a narrow rocky terrace of *Mt Kotilion* (now Paliavlakítsa), whose summit rises above it to the N.E. The mountain is scored with ravines (βάσσαι; vassai) from which the place takes its general name; the temple site is called locally 'the columns' (στοὺς στύλους). The temple, which owes its fine preservation to its inaccessibility, is built of a cold grey local limestone that contributes to, rather than lightens, the melancholy bleakness of the landscape. The immediate surroundings are softened a little by a few oak trees and wild flowers. The only other building is a house belonging to the phylax.

The temple is attributed by Pausanias to Iktinos. Its style makes it almost certainly an earlier work than the Parthenon, and so designed c. 450–447 B.C., though the execution may not have been finished before 425 B.C. The locality was rediscovered in 1765 by Joachim Bocher, a French architect employed by the Venetians in Zante. It was visited in 1805–06 by Leake, Dodwell, and Wm Gell. In 1811–12 the party of British and German antiquaries who had previously stripped the Aegina temple, explored the ruins and removed the sculptures. The 23 marble slabs of the cella frieze were bought by the British Government for £19,000 for the British Museum. In 1902–06 the Greek Archaeological Society replaced some fallen column fragments and restored the cella walls. Additional fragments of the frieze were unearthed in 1961. The foundations have been shown to incorporate reused blocks from an Archaic predecessor which occupied the area immediately to the s.

The temple is a Doric peripteral hexastyle, 125½ ft long and 48 ft wide, longer, therefore, by about one fifth and fractionally wider than the Hephaistaion in Athens. The orientation is unusual, being N. and s. The *Peristyle*, 6 columns by 15, on a stylobate of three steps, is complete save for the s.E. corner column. Most of the architrave blocks are in position, but nothing of the pediments or the roof. The pediments were prepared for sculptured groups which Dinsmoor concludes were taken off in ancient times to Rome: the roof-tiles were of Parian marble. The colonnade had a coffered ceiling of different patterns.

The **Interior** had the conventional pronaos, cella, and opisthodomos, but the arrangement is unusual. The *Pronaos*, 18 ft long, had two columns between antae. It was decorated with a metope frieze, now in a very fragmentary state. A metal barrier, with gates, shut it off from the colonnade. A door led into the cella. The *Opisthodomos*, 13½ ft long, was similarly distyle in antis, open to the colonnade, but cut off by a wall from the cella.

The *Cella*, 55 ft long and 23 ft wide was in two parts. The N. section, 40 ft long, was adorned on either side with a series of 5 semi-columns engaged in buttresses that projected from the side wall, the first four pairs at right angles and the fifth pair (at the s. end) diagonally inward. The semi-columns are most unusually located not opposite the peristyle columns but between the intercolumniations. The first four pairs had bell-shaped bases, resting on a step, 4 in. high, and volutes on three faces of the Ionic capitals. The fifth pair had Corinthian capitals, with between them, a single Corinthian column, in marble, with 20 flutes. Its capital, now lost, is recorded as having acanthus decoration, and thus formed the earliest example of the Corinthian order yet known to us. The height of the interior colonnade (20½ ft) is greater by a foot than that of the peristyle. It supported an Ionic entablature having a frieze, 102 ft long, richly carved in island marble and representing the battles between Greeks and Amazons, and between Lapiths and Centaurs.

The inner *Adyton*, occupying the remaining 15 ft of the cella, is also of unusual design, having a door on the left (E. side). This fact prompted speculation as to whether the cult statue stood against its w. wall, and whether the plan follows that of an earlier sanctuary on the site. It seems clear, however, that the god stood in a more usual position in the cella. Pausanias records that the figure of Apollo in bronze was transferred in 369 B.C. to the agora at Megalopolis and replaced by an acrolithic statue.

To PHIGALEIA AND THE GORGE OF THE NEDHA. From Bassae a road, needing a sturdy vehicle but being improved, descends s. and w. viâ (5 m.) *Dragóni* to (6¾ m.) *Perivólia*, where remains of a Doric temple were found in 1972. Here a track winds s. towards Áno Figália, passing the site of ancient **Phigaleia** (1 hr; inn), an Arcadian city on the borders of Elis and Messenia, which had a reputation for wizardry, witchcraft, and drunkenness. The ruins of its walls and towers occupy a high and uneven plateau with precipitous sides, surrounded by mountains. On the s. the Neda flows far below. The road continues to (8½ m.) *Petrálona*, from which an occasional bus goes down viâ (11½ m.) *Káto Figália* and *Lepreon* (comp. Rte 34D) to (19½ m.) Figália station on the coast.—Alternatively, for those on foot, a difficult but rewarding walk may be made (preferably with a guide from Áno Figália) following the track into the spectacular GORGE OF THE NEDHA to *Aspro Neró*, a superb *Waterfall. Ancient ship-sheds were located lower down the river in 1972.

Beyond Andritsaina the road, asphalt but subject to landslides and subsidences, commands tremendous views across the Alpheios valley towards the N. heights of the Peloponnese. All along this road, which must duplicate the course of an ancient way from Olympia towards Sparta, are remains of classical places, for the most part unexcavated, seldom visited, and not certainly identified (comp. E. Meyer: 'Neue Peloponnesische Wanderungen', Berne, 1957).—We pass through *Miloi* (or Makhalas)— most villages in Arcadia have a Slav or Albanian name and a readopted Greek one—and come to (31½ m.) *Keramídhi* (Kaléntzi).

A little farther on a track leads (r.) to *Alífira*, near which, at *Kastro tis Drósitsas*, A. K. Orlandos excavated in 1932–35 (and published in 1968) the acropolis of ancient *Alipheira*, uncovering foundations of a Doric temple of Athena (6 by 15 columns), founded in the mid-6C, and of a sanctuary of Asklepios (late 4C). A funerary shrine was also located on the course of the ancient road N. to Heraia (p. 330).—Near *Vrestón*, to the s. of our road, a large unidentified site was located in 1955.

37¼ m. (60 km.) **Zákha** (ZAXA), officially *Kallithéa*, a village of 865 inhab. through which the road all but disappears, stands at 1805 ft barely 2½ m. s. of the confluence of the Ladon with the Alpheios (Rte 36). We turn s.w. to *Barakítika*, whence a track goes off (r.) to *Bitzibárdi* (or Tripití) with a Gothic monastery of Notre Dame d'Issova, built by the Franks and burnt by the Byzantines in 1264.

43 m. *Platána*. Above the village to the s. are the walls of ancient **Typaneai**, of splendidly preserved regular isodomic masonry (? 3C B.C.). Their perimeter encloses a narrow ridge, 650 yds long, rising at its w. end to 1965 ft. Within are remains of an antique *Theatre*, cisterns, and two Christian churches. About ¾ m. farther E. are some medieval ruins (Paliakumba) of *Cumba*, a Frankish castle held in 1364 by Marie de Bourbon, widow of Robert of Taranto.—49 m. *Greka*. We pass below a hill (r.) called *Kastro Mundriza*, identified with ancient *Hypana*, and leave on our right a track leading towards another site, perhaps that of Homeric *Aipion*.

56½ m. (91 km.) **Kréstena** (*Inn*) is a large village (2650 inhab.) served by bus from Pirgos. A good road leads viâ Makrisia and over (5 m.) the Alpheios barrage to Olympia (9 m.). *Makrísia* is the site of ancient Skillus. Here the stylobate of a Doric temple has been said by Yalouris

(1954) to be that of Athena Skillountia mentioned by Strabo, rather than that known to have been erected at the cost of the exiled Xenophon on his estate here c. 444–434 B.C.—The road soon joins the Kiparissía–Pírgos road. Hence to (68½ m.) *Pírgos*, see Rte 34.

36 FROM TRIPOLIS TO OLYMPIA AND PYRGOS

ROAD, 96½ m. (156 km.). A well-engineered modern road with fair surface and spectacular mountain scenery, the central section narrow and difficult driving; bus 3 times daily in 4 hrs.—6¼ m. Turning for *Mantinea* (see Rte 30).—16¼ m. *Levídhi.*—21½ m. Turning for Kalavryta and Patras (Rte 39).—28½ m. *Vitína.*—37½ m. *Karkalou*, turning for (8 m.) *Dhimitsana.*—44¾ m. *Langadhia.*—53¼ m. *Stavrodhromi.* —82 m. *Olympia.*—95 m. *Pirgos.*
RAILWAY from Olympia to Pyrgos, 4–5 times daily in 30 min.

From Tripolis to (6¾ m.) the Mantinea turn, see Rte 30. The road follows the w. side of the plain of Mantinea close beneath the foothills of Mainalon, whose triangular summit appears at first to block the broad valley ahead.—Beyond (9 m.) *Kápsia* (740 inhab.) we thread a defile to the small diamond-shaped *Plain of Alkimedon*, immediately below the towering *Mt Ostrakina* (6500 ft), topmost peak of *Mainalon*. A mule track (l.) skirts its s. side to Alonístaina (7 m.; Rte 30). Farther on, a defile (r.) affords a glimpse of (14 m.) *Simiádhes* at the N. end of the Plain of Mantinea.—From the top of the next long rise we descry, crowning the next hill, the campanile of (16¼ m.) *Levídhi* (Inn; 1730 inhab.), native town of Alex. Papanastasiou (1879–1936), republican statesman and prime minister in 1924. A chapel of the Panayia on a low hill to the E. is supposed to mark the site of the sanctuary of Artemis-Hymnia, common to the peoples of Mantinea and Orchomenos. Just beyond the town the road commands a wide view across the plain of Orchomenos (magnificently backed by the.Chelmos range), into which a by-road drops abruptly towards *Kandhíla*. Off this (l.; 3 m.) the hamlet of *Kalpaki* lies at the S.E. foot of the acropolis of Orchomenos on the site of the lower city.

Arcadian **Orchomenos** occupied a strategic position on the midland route between N. and S. Peloponnese. Homer calls it 'rich in sheep' (πολύμηλος; Iliad II, 605). Herodotus tells us that 120 Orchomenian soldiers fought at Thermopylae and 600 at Plataia. Just before the first battle of Mantinea (418 B.C.) the Athenians and Argives besieged and took the city.—The scattered remains excavated in 1913 by the Fr. School (boy as guide helpful) include the foundations of two *Temples* (Apollo and Aphrodite, and, higher up, Artemis Mesopolitis), a stoa of the agora, cisterns, and a small *Theatre*, but the site (save for its situation) is not very interesting. The Acropolis (3070 ft) stands 800 ft above the plain on an almost isolated hill dividing the plain into two halves. On the E. a narrow defile connecting the divided plain is commanded from either side by ruined Venetian watch-towers. The *View is extensive. To the S.W. across the plain towers Mainalon, while farther S.E. we look into the Plain of Mantinea. The fields, under waving corn, present the appearance of a patchwork quilt whose colours change with the passage of clouds. To the N. loom the high peaks round Mt Feneos.

19¾ m. *Vlakhérna* (3280 ft). *Khotoússa*, in the valley to the N. (45 min.), stands close to the scanty remains of Hellenistic and Roman *Caphyae.*—At 21½ m. the road to Patras (Rte 39) drops away in a valley (r.) as we climb round the N. end of the Mainalon range; the village of *Kamenítsa* is seen far below.—28½ m. (46 km.) **Vitína** (BYTINA; *Villa Valos* DPO, **B**, on the Alonistaina road; *Mainalon* C; restaurants; camping), an attractive summer resort (1000 inhab.), stands in a cool and healthy upland situation (3412 ft) amid fir-clad slopes. It has a School of Forestry and a tradition of woodcarving. The town was Kolokotronis' supply-base.—Our road twists through sharp outcrops of rock.—31 m. On a hill to the s. are the scanty remains of *Methydrion*, a town sacrificed in the building of Megalopolis.—33 m. Turning (unpaved) to Magoúliana (2½ m. r.) and Valtesiníkon (8 m.).

Magoúliana, birthplace of Theodore Kolokotronis, the klepht hero of the War of Independence, was a summer residence of the Villehardouin—hence the ruined Frankish fortress (Argyrokastro). *Valtesiníkon* lies just E. of the site of ancient *Glanitsa*, where the French School found a late-Archaic bronze head in 1939.—Tracks go on through the mountains and across the Ladon to Dhafni (Rte 39).

Approaching (37½ m.) *Karkaloú* we descend through pine-woods, with the pleasantly situated Xenia Motel (B), passing a campsite (l.) with a memorial bust in bronze of Dimitri Mitropoulos (1896–1960), the conductor, by Apartis. Some polygonal walls (? *Theisoa*) survive near the village.

From Karkaloú a tarmac road diverges on the left to (5 m.) **Dhimitsána** (ΔΗΜΗΤΣΑΝΑ; *Dimitsana* C), an attractive village (1000 inhab.) in a magnificent situation above the Lousios, on the site of ancient *Teuthis*. An example of cyclopean wall forming part of a modern house may be seen just below the more westerly of the two main churches. Some classical walls also survive, but medieval building predominates. Dhimitsána became a centre of Greek learning after 1764, when its school was founded, and hence of opposition to the Turks; the Patriarch Gregory V and Germanos, Abp of Patras, were both pupils. It became a centre of activity of the Philike Etairia, and an arsenal for the War of Independence with fourteen powder factories. The Museum, Archives, and Library are worth a visit. The *Moní Philosófou* was founded in 963 but not on its present site, 1½ m. s.e., below Zigovisti.

The road continues (unpaved, rough) to (11 m.) **Ipsoús** (ΥΨΟΥΣ; *Trikolonion*), a pleasant country inn, C), a beautiful mountain village (3530 ft) formerly known as *Stemnitsa*, grandly situated against the side of Mt Klinitsa (5080 ft). The Kastro incorporates several little churches: *Ayiou Nikolaou* was repaired in 1589; the *Panayia Baféro* dates probably from 1640. The monastery of *Ay. Ioannou tou Prodromou*, founded by Manuel Comnenos in 1167, lies 2½ m. w. in the Lousios gorge (precipitous path from Dhimitsána road).

Beyond Ipsoús the road forks, the right branch (very bad) for Karítaina and Megalópolis; the left (bad) for (38¾ m.) *Trípolis* viâ Daviá (Rte 30).

Threading rocky gorges in an increasingly barren landscape to a summit of nearly 4000 ft, clothed in ferns, we cross the infant Lousios.—44¾ m. (72 km.) **Langadhia** (ΛΑΓΚΑΔΙΑ; *Langadia* C), native town (1350 inhab.) of the Deliyianni family, appears ahead tumbling vertically down an outcrop of rock above the valley. By a series of sharp downward curves we approach its centre, where a little Plateia (café) forms a superb *Belvedere.

The long descent continues as the tortuous road follows a vertiginous shelf of road a thousand feet above the gorge.—Beyond (49 m.) *Lefkokhóri* it crosses a side valley and, surmounting a ridge, reaches the upland village of (53½ m.) *Stavrodhrómi*.

Here a by-road (r.) leads to *Trópaia* (2½ m; inn), a mountain village. About 1 m. E. of Trópaia are three towers of the Frankish castle of the barony of Akova, and 2 hrs w. some remains of classical *Thelpousa*, another site investigated by the French School in 1939, which had a huge 4C agora.—In Trópaia the road (now unpaved) hairpins right and continues to (6¼ m.) the *Ladon Dam (Fragma Ladonos; ΦΡΑΓΜΑ ΛΑΔΩΝΟΣ), 110 yds long and c. 175 ft high, which has formed a lake, ringed by pine trees, in the upper valley. The waters are fed to hydro-electric works, near the village of Spáthari (comp. below) to the w., by a tunnel, 5 m. long, through a mountain.

The mountains give place to rolling hills as we descend to the broad valley of the *Ladon*, most copious of the seven important tributaries of the Alpheios until its reduction by damming (see above).—59½ m. Turning (r.; 3¾ m.) to the hydro-electric station. We cross the river and descend the right bank.—Beyond (60½ m.) *Bertsia* (café), with its charming wooded stream, the road climbs a ridge commanding the confluence of the Ladon and the Alpheios, where Pausanias' 'Isle of Crows' is seen. On the way up we pass a by-road which returns to the left bank of the Ladon to *Loutrá Iraías*, s. of which, near Ay. Ioannis on the bank of the Alpheios, some remains of ancient *Heraia* were identified by the Greek Archaeological Service in 1931.—A sharp hill and (70 m.) the *Yéfira Koklamá*, a concrete bridge, take us across the Erimanthos and into Elis (comp. Rte 40).—73¾ m. *Vasiláki* (1312 ft) occupies the summit of the ridge of Sauros, a highwayman killed by Herakles. Hence we descend amid lush vegetation to the wide bed of the Alpheios.—77 m. *Mouria.*

The ALPHEIOS or *Alfios*, the largest river in the Peloponnese, rises in south-east Arcadia, close to the source of the Eurotas and flows through Arcadia and Elis, past Olympia, into the Ionian Sea. Pausanias describes it as "a broad and noble stream, fed by seven important rivers". These are the Helisson, Brentheates, Gortynios, Bouphagos, Ladon, Erymanthos, and Kladeos. The Peloponnesians regard the Ladon as the main stream, calling the Alpheios proper the Karytaina above the confluence. In the early part of its course this runs underground. According to legend the river-god Alpheios fell in love with the nymph Arethusa. Spurning his advances she fled to Ortygia, an island off Syracuse in Sicily, and was there changed into a fountain, whereupon Alpheios flowed under the sea to join her. Shelley, celebrating the legend, calls the river a "brackish, Dorian stream". It was the favourite river of Zeus, and on its banks first grew the wild olive, a garland of which was the reward of victors in the Olympic Games.

80 m. *Miráka* (on a by-road; r.) is 15 min. s. of the site of ancient *Pisa.*—Approaching (82 m.) **Olympia** (ΟΛΥΜΠΙΑ; *Olimbía*) we see (r.) the spacious International Olympic Academy, inaugurated in 1961 with the object of maintaining and promoting the Olympic spirit. Annual summer courses are held. Immediately after this (r.) is a stele enclosing the heart of Pierre de Coubertin (1862–1937), who revived the games. We pass between Mt Kronon and the excavations (l.; see Rte 37), cross the Kladeos, and turn into the village, a deme of 700 inhabitants.

Railway Station, ½ m. w. of the village.
Hotels. SPAP, above the site, not cheap, A; **Xenia,** near the Altis; **Neda, DPO; Nea Olympia, Apollon,** the last two closed in winter, all B; **Ilis** C; **Pelops D,** good, and others.
Restaurants. *Karachaliou,* opposite station turning, and at the hotels.
Buses to Athens viâ Pirgos and Patras.

At (85 m.) *Platanos* we join the road from Kalávrita (Rte 39). Most of the villages stand on low hills between successive small tributaries of the Alpheios, and are surrounded by orchards. *Broúma,* on the right beyond (86½ m.) *Krébouki* (officially Pelópion), occupies the site of *Herakleia,* which once had curative springs.—90½ m. The *Eripeus,* now called Lestenítza, was the scene of the myth of Poseidon and Tyro.— 95 m. (153 km.) **Pirgos,** see Rte 40.

37 OLYMPIA

Approaches and hotels, etc., see above.

OLYMPIA, in Greek *Olimbía* (Ολυμπία; 140 ft) is situated in the quietly beautiful valley of the Alpheios in the territory of Pisatis, at its confluence with the Kladeos. The setting, in great contrast with most Greek sites, is pastoral, green, and lush, the ruins being plentifully shaded by evergreen oaks, Aleppo pines, planes, and poplars, as well as by olive-trees. The Kladeos bounds the site on the w. and the Alpheios on the s., while to the N. rises the conical Mt Kronos (405 ft). Olympia was not a city, but a sacred precinct occupied exclusively by temples, dwellings for the priests and officials, and public buildings in connection with the Games, and it became a sanctuary in which were concentrated many of the choicest treasures of Greek art. In the midst was the enclosure known as the *Altis*, dedicated to Zeus, in whose honour were held the quadrennial festival and the games. The best view of the site is from Mt Droúva above the SPAP hotel.

The fame of Olympia rests upon the Olympic Games. Whatever may have been their origin, they remained until they were degraded by specialization and professionalism a great national festival influencing the character and fortunes of the entire Hellenic race. A striking feature of the festival was the proclamation of the *Ekecheiria*, or Olympic Truce; still more surprising was its almost universal observance, a fact sufficient witness in itself to the high prestige of the Olympic festival. During the week of the celebrations the competitors, while not forgetting that they were Athenians, Spartans, Milesians, Syracusans, or whatever, remembered that they were Greeks, and they regarded an Olympic victory as the highest possible honour. The simple reward of a crown of wild olive not only immortalized the victor and his family, but redounded to the glory of his native city.

The Greeks came to use the Olympiads, or periods of four years between festivals, as the basis of their chronology. The Games were held regularly in peace and in war for over 1000 years from 776 B.C. until their suppression in A.D. 393. From the first Olympiad to the time of Hadrian the embellishment of Olympia never ceased. The vitality of the festivals is reflected in the architecture and works of art that have survived.

History. Excavations since 1959 have shown that *Olympia* was already flourishing in Mycenean times. The legendary foundation of the Games and the elaborated later traditions may be found recorded by Pausanias (Bk. V). Homer does not mention them and the official era of the Olympiads started in 776 B.C. The conduct of the games seems at first to have been disputed between Pisa and Elis and ancient authorities differ widely as to the date when the Elians finally prevailed (between 572 and 471 B.C.).

Despite the vicissitudes of fortune and of war, the Olympic Games were held with the utmost regularity, the wealth of the various sanctuaries steadily accumulated, and the prestige of Olympia increased until it reached its zenith in the 5C B.C. The Olympic Truce was strictly observed, with one or two exceptions. In 420 B.C. the Lacedaemonians were excluded from the festival on the ground of truce-breaking (Thuc. V, 49). In 364 B.C., during the invasion of the Pisans and Arcadians, a battle was fought in the Altis in the presence of the crowd that had come to watch the games.

After the age of Hadrian Olympia ceased to have much religious or political significance, but was visited for sentimental reasons or out of curiosity. The games were, however, kept up until A.D. 393, when the edict of Theodosius I, prohibiting all pagan festivals, put an end to them. In 426 Theodosius II ordered the destruction of the temples and the Altis was burnt. Soon afterwards the ruins were quarried to transform the Workshop of Pheidias into a Christian church and to build a fortification against the Vandals. In 522 and 551 the ruins were devastated anew by earthquakes, the Temple of Zeus being partially buried, while a landslip from Mt Kronos destroyed the buildings at its foot. A new settlement was swept away when the Kladeos overflowed and buried all the buildings on the w. side of the precinct deep in sand and mud. Further landslips on Mt Kronos occurred and the Alpheios, changing its bed, carried away the Hippodrome and part of the Stadium, thus completing the ruin of Olympia, which for centuries remained an uninhabited waste covered with a layer of debris 10–12 ft deep.

The first modern traveller to visit Olympia was Dr Chandler, in 1766, though as early as 1713 Montfaucon had suggested excavation. In 1768 Winkelmann planned a restoration of Olympia. In 1811 Stanhope had a plan made of the site. A French expedition in 1829 partially excavated the Temple of Zeus. In 1852 Prof. E. Curtius revived the plan of Winkelmann for the excavation of Olympia and interested the German royal family in the project. At last, in 1874, a convention with Greece was reached, whereby the German government was permitted to carry out excavations. Their work covers three periods: 1875–81, 1936–41, and since 1952. Everything of importance has been housed in the Museum, except for some bronzes (now in the National Museum in Athens). The temples of Zeus and Hera have suffered from exposure since they were uncovered.

ADMINISTRATION. The Altis was reserved for the gods, the dwellings of the priests and officials being outside. The supreme governing body was the *Olympian Senate*, elected from the Elean aristocracy, which met in the Bouleuterion. The senate had control of the revenue and the Olympian officials were responsible to it. The magistrates and priests, Eleans of good family, were elected for the period of each Olympiad. They lived in the Prytaneion. Though each sanctuary had its own staff, a superior hierarchy looked after the administration as a whole and regulated the service of the temples. At its head were three *Theokoloi*, or High Priests, who lived in the Theokoleon and dined at the Prytaneion. Next were three *Spondophoroi*, heralds whose duty it was to travel abroad and proclaim the date of the festival and of the Olympic Truce. Finally the two (later four) hereditary *Soothsayers* interpreted the Oracle. In addition there was a host of minor officials such as the *Kathemerothytes*, or priest of the day, the *Exegetes* (who doubled the role of master of ceremonies with that of cicerone to visitors), the *Epimeletes*, or keeper of the Sanctuary, three *Epispondorchestai*, or dancers, a flute-player, an architect, a doctor, a chef for the Prytaneion, a woodcutter (who provided the wood for the altars), etc.

THE QUADRENNIAL FESTIVALS. The most important of all the festivals at Olympia was the *Festival of Zeus*, accompanied by the Olympic Games. It took place at the time of the second (or possibly first) full moon following the summer solstice, i.e. in August or September. A sacred truce fortified by severe sanctions, universally suspended hostilities during the week of the festival, forbade armed forces to enter the confines of Elis, and proclaimed the inviolability of visitors. The special representatives of the various cities and states were publicly entertained, being housed in buildings adjoining the Altis and fed at the Prytaneion. The *Theoroi* or special ambassadors from foreign states, were sent at their national expense. The crowd of humbler pilgrims were accommodated in tents, or like the competitors slept in blankets on the ground.

THE OLYMPIC OR OLYMPIAN GAMES. The direction of the games (ἀγωνοθεσία) was, with certain interruptions, in the hands of the Eleans. Only men and boys who spoke Greek as their mother-tongue were originally allowed to compete; barbarians were admitted as spectators, but slaves were entirely excluded. No married woman might be present, or even cross the Alpheios while the games were going on, under penalty of being hurled from the Typaeon Rock. Later Romans were admitted.

Ten months before the date of the games the Elean magistrates chose a body of 10 *Hellanodikai*, or umpires, who supervised training and discipline as well as the actual contests. The competitors had to train for the whole 10 months; in addition they were required to undergo a course of exercises in the Gymnasium a month before the festival. They took the oath at the bouleuterion on the Altar of Zeus Horkeios, swearing that they would loyally observe all the regulations of the games, and involving not only their family but their native town in the penalties consequent on any infraction.

The Eleans kept registers of the winners of the foot-race, the oldest event, after the successive winners of which each Olympiad was named; Plutarch, however, questions both their antiquity and authenticity. To the foot-race were added at intervals other competitive events, most notably the Pentathlon (in which jumping, wrestling, and throwing both spear and discus were combined with running), boxing, chariot-racing and horse racing (the 'hippic' as opposed to gymnastic contests at which tyrants and nobles competed, employing professional charioteers and jockeys), and the Pankration (a form of all-in wrestling). An Athenian took the prize for the first time in 696, and in 688 the inaugural boxing contest was won by a man from Smyrna, the first overseas city to claim an Olympic victor. Southern Italy records its first victory in 672. The Spartans were frequent winners. Events for boys were inaugurated in 632 B.C.

The athletic fare was varied by the presence of historians, orators, and sophists, who read their works aloud to the assembled spectators. Herodotus here read extracts from his history. Themistocles attended the 76th Olympiad in celebration of the Persian defeat. The 211th Olympiad was postponed two years to A.D. 69 to allow Nero to compete and win special musical contests and a chariot-race. The records were later expunged.

After each event a herald announced the victor's name and handed him a palm. On the last day the successful competitors (Olympionikai) were each given a garland of wild olive and entertained in the Prytaneion. A victor had the right of erecting a statue in the Altis, which might represent his own features if he had won three events. By the time of the older Pliny the statues had accumulated to the number of 3000. On returning home, the victor was publicly entertained and a lyric composition was recited in his honour. Fourteen of Pindar's odes celebrate olympionikai.

In 1896 a quadrennial international athletic festival, taking the name of the *Olympic Games*, had its inception at the Stadium in Athens, when a Greek won the 'marathon'. The Games are held successively in different countries. There is no modern ekecheiria and the First World War prevented their celebration in 1916, as did the Second in 1940 and 1944. It will not be forgotten that King Constantine II of the Hellenes (when Crown Prince) won a gold medal at the 1960 Games, held in Italy.

To reach the ancient site from the village we take the Tripolis road, pass the museum on a hill (r.), cross the Kladeos, and see (r.) the entrance to the **Excavations** (adm. 25 dr.; Thurs & Sun free; open standard site hours). We visit first the large buildings that lie outside the Altis to the w.

On the right, immediately beyond the entrance, some remains parallel to the path mark the *Xystos*, or covered running track (an Olympic stade long), which formed the E. wing of the **Gymnasion**, a large quadrangle extending to the Kladeos. Its propylon (? 1C B.C.) consisted of a Corinthian portico raised on three steps. Some capitals survive. Adjacent on the s. is the **Palaestra**, or wrestling school, which corresponds closely with Vitruvius' description of such a building. An open court, 45 yds square, is surrounded by a Doric colonnade with 19 columns on each side. Behind the colonnade, on three sides, were rooms of various sizes, entered through Ionic porches or through plain doorways. Some of them retain ancient stone benches set against the wall. On the s. side the colonnade was divided into two long corridors by an inner row of 15 Ionic columns. The main entrances were at the E. and w. ends of the s. side, through porches of two Corinthian columns in antis. The capitals are of unusual design, having parallels in Pompeii and Asia Minor rather than in Greece. The style generally suggests a date in the 3C B.C.

A water channel, entering the Palaestra at its N.E. corner, ran round its four sides. In the N. part of the court is a pavement of grooved and plain tiles, 27 yds by 6 yds; its object is unknown. From the central room in the N. colonnade a plain doorway gave access to the Gymnasium.

To the s. lies the THEOKOLEON, the official residence of the priests. The ruins belong to three periods. The original Greek structure (c. 350 B.C.) consisted of 8 rooms round a central court and covered an area 20 yds square. The foundations and pavement are well preserved. In the court is an ancient well lined with blocks of sandstone. Later three rooms were added on the E. side and a large garden court, with cloisters and rooms, was constructed. The Romans took down the E. half of the extended Greek building and enlarged the garden court. A colonnade was built round it, having 8 columns on each side.

To the w. is a small round *Heroon*, not quite 9 yds in diameter, enclosed within a square. The lower blocks of the circular wall are well preserved; the upper courses were probably of mud brick. Within was found an altar of earth and ashes, coated with stucco.

Adjacent on the s. side is a building, the sandstone walls of which are still standing to a height of 6 ft with later brickwork above. In its later form it was a *Byzantine Church* divided by columns into nave and aisles with an apse on the E. and a narthex on the w. Near the E. end is a ruined ambo (l.) with two flights of three steps, and, beyond it, a perforated marble screen of Byzantine workmanship. The original building was none other than the **Studio of Pheidias**, described by Pausanias. This has been confirmed archaeologically by the discovery of tools and terracotta moulds used in the manufacture of the great chryselephantine statue of Zeus, and finally in 1958 by a cup bearing Pheidias' name. The building has the same measurements as the cella of the temple and a similar orientation; it probably also had similar internal structure, being divided into two compartments having galleries supported on columns.

A long narrow building, to the s., divided by crosswalls into small rooms, is believed to have sheltered his working technicians.

To the w. remains of Roman baths overlie *Baths* of the Archaic period, near the bank of the Kladeos, together with part of a swimming pool of the 5C B.C. This was 25 yds long and c. 5 ft deep.

Farther s., built at a slightly different angle, is the **Leonidaion**, erected by Leonidas the son of Leontas of Naxos in the 4C B.C., possibly as a hostel for distinguished visitors, and adapted in the 2C A.D. as a residence for the Roman governor of Achaia. It stands at the crossing of the roads from Arcadia and Elis outside the processional entrance to the Altis. As originally built it had an open court, 97 ft square, surrounded by Doric colonnades of 12 columns per side, off which rooms opened on all four sides. The principal rooms were on the w. side. Outside ran a continuous colonnade of 138 Ionic columns, the bases of which are almost all in situ, together with many of the capitals. Their bases and capitals were of sandstone, the shafts of shell-limestone; the whole was covered with stucco. In Roman times the rooms were remodelled, and an ornamental garden with elaborate ponds was laid out in the middle of the court. Many fragments of the colonnades were found built into the Byzantine Wall (comp. below) and these, especially those from the terracotta cornice, show great richness of decoration.

The **Altis**, or SACRED PRECINCT OF ZEUS, acquired its name from a corruption of the Greek word ἄλσος meaning 'Sacred Grove'. On the N. it was bounded by Mt Kronos and on the other three sides by walls, the lines of which can still be traced. On the w. side are remains of two parallel walls, the inner one Greek and the outer one Roman. The s. wall is Roman. The original s. wall, now called the South Terrace Wall, was more to the N., the Altis having been enlarged about the time of Nero. The Greek walls seem to have been merely low stone parapets and the precinct was probably not fully enclosed by high boundary walls until the Roman period. Within were the Temple of Zeus, the

Heraion and the small Metroön, besides the Pelopion, or shrine of Pelops, and innumerable altars to Zeus and other divinities. Much of the remaining space was taken up by statues of Olympic victors.

Entering the precinct by the *Processional Entrance*, a small triple opening with an external porch of 4 columns, we see on the right a row of large oblong pedestals, mostly belonging to equestrian statues. On the left are two pedestals bearing respectively the names of *Philonides*, courier of Alexander the Great (Paus. VI, 16, 8) and of *Sophocles*, the sculptor. Turning to the right we pass on the right a wilderness of scattered remains recovered from the Byzantine Wall, but originally forming part of the Leonidaion, Bouleuterion, and many other buildings. Passing between the remains of two unknown Greek buildings with several small partitions, we reach the Bouleuterion.

The BOULEUTERION, or *Council House*, seat of the Olympic Senate, consists of a square hall flanked N. and S. by larger wings of practically equal size and plan. The building was originally quite outside the Altis. On its southward extension, the new S. wall of the precinct was in line with the northernmost wall of the Bouleuterion, which was provided with a special gateway of its own. Each wing consisted of an oblong hall with a central row of 7 Doric (?) columns on separate foundations and a cross-wall cutting off its apse. Each apse was divided into two by a central wall. A triglyph frieze appears to have decorated the exteriors of the wings, whose appearance was further enhanced by the two-stepped basements on which they were raised. On the E. side each wing ended in a screen of three Doric columns in antis. A spacious Ionic portico ran along the whole length of the E. façade, forming the only means of communication between the three parts of the building. This portico had 27 columns on its front and 3 on each side of the narrow sides; only three drums are in situ.

The *Central Hall*, which is much later than the wings and may be contemporary with the Ionic Colonnade (3C B.C.), appears to have had columns on its E. side and blank walls without doors on the other three. A foundation in the middle may have supported the *Statue of Zeus Horkeios*, beside which competitors, their relatives, and their trainers swore that they would be guilty of no foul play in the games. At an earlier date this would have been open to the sky. Of the *N. Wing*, the oldest part of the building (6C B.C.), very little except foundations is left. The *S. Wing* (5C) is the best preserved. The drums of the columns of the Doric porch are still standing; the outer walls are one or two courses high; and some drums of the seven interior columns are in situ. The S. Wing differs from the N. Wing in that its long walls are not straight but form with the apse an elliptical shape recalling ancient structures at Sparta and Thermon: it has been conjectured that it was rebuilt on old foundations.—In front of the connecting portico is an irregular colonnaded court of Roman date, usually called the *Trapezium Court*.

To the S. of the Bouleuterion is the *Southern Stoa*, over 86 yds long, built of tufa and raised on three limestone steps. Gardiner conjecturally identifies this colonnade with the *Proedria* and assigns it to the 3C B.C. It was closed on the N. by a wall, with a narrow passage-way at either end. The other sides were open and had Doric columns. Within it was divided longitudinally (probably in Roman times) by a central row of sandstone Corinthian columns. The Byzantines used the stoa as the S. wall of their fort.

Between the Proedria and the Leonidaion extended the *Agora*, where temporary booths were set up during the festival.

The *Temple of Zeus,* dedicated to the sovereign god of Olympia, is the most important temple in the Altis and one of the largest in mainland Greece. It was built from the spoils of Pisa, after its sack by the Eleans c. 470 B.C., and completed before 456, when an inscribed block (quoted by Pausanias and since found) was let into the E. gable to support a gold shield dedicated by the Spartans in commemoration of their victory at Tanagra. The architect was Libon of Elis. After an earthquake c. 175 B.C. both façades were dismantled and rebuilt and three of the w. pedimental statues replaced. In the early 6C A.D. the edifice was completely shattered by earthquakes.

The building, which is a Doric peripteral hexastyle, stands on a crepidoma of 3 unequal steps, itself borne on a massive platform. The foundations, which are of shell-limestone with inter-spaces filled with earth, are complete. They were sunk 3 ft deep in the soil and rose 10 ft above its natural level. An embankment was raised all round, giving the appearance of an artificial hillock. Access was by a ramp at the E. end. The *stylobate* is made of huge stone blocks averaging 8½ ft in width. Its length, measured on the top step, seems to have been exactly 200 Olympic feet. There is no evidence of optical curvature such as distinguishes the Parthenon.

EXTERIOR. The *Peristyle* had 6 columns at either end and 13 at the sides; these also were made of shell-limestone, but were covered with fine white stucco to give the appearance of marble. Their height was twice the axial spacing. Each of them had the usual 20 flutes and three incised rings round the neck. The echinus of the capitals was similar in outline to those of the Temple of Aphaia on Aegina. Apart from one or two drums in their original positions, none of the columns is standing. On the s. side they lie as they were thrown by the earthquake of the 6C.

Fragments of the entablature lie around. Above the architrave a frieze of triglyphs and plain metopes ran all round the peristyle; 21 gilded shields dedicated by Mummius in 142 B.C. to commemorate his destruction of Corinth were placed on the 10 metopes of the E. front and on the adjacent metopes on the s. side. The marks of attachment can still be seen.

The two pediments were filled with sculptured groups in Parian marble: on the *E. Pediment* the preparations for the chariot race between Pelops and Oinomaos; on the *W. Pediment* the battle of the Lapiths and Centaurs at the wedding of Peirithoos. Pausanias attributed these to Alkamenes and Paionios. The surviving sculptures are in the Museum (see below). At the apex of the E. Pediment was the gold shield dedicated by the Spartans (comp. above), crowned sometime later by a gilt bronze Victory, by Paionios. The corner-acroteria were in the form of gilded bronze tripods.

The roof was of marble tiles, many of which are preserved in the Pelopion. The earliest tiles are of Parian marble, the later ones (replacements of the Augustan era) of Pentelic. There was a continuous marble sima interrupted by 102 lions'-head water-spouts, of which 39 survive (some are crude later replacements). Traces of colour found on the architectural members show that parts at any rate of the temple were painted.

The wide ambulatory surrounding the sekos was occupied by bronze statues and votive offerings. The ceiling was of wood. The pavement was of large blocks of conglomerate covered with river pebbles embedded in mortar. This was replaced in Roman times by a mosaic pavement, traces of which remain.

INTERIOR. The sekos had the usual arrangement of Pronaos, Cella, and Opisthodomos. It was raised one step above the stylobate. The

Pronaos and Opisthodomos each ended in a portico of two Doric columns between antae, surmounted (unusually) by a Doric entablature consisting of an architrave and triglyph frieze. The 12 Parian marble metopes were decorated with sculptures depicting the Labours of Herakles, six at each end. Some were carried off by the French expedition of 1829 and are now in the Louvre; the rest are in the museum.

The *Pronaos* was closed by three folding bronze doors. On the floor are the remains of the earliest known Greek mosaic (now covered) representing a Triton with a boy seated on his tail. Pausanias noticed here the statue of Iphitos being crowned by Ekecheiria (personification of the Olympic truce). Traces of various bases here indicate the former presence of other statues he mentions. A great door, about 16 ft wide, led into the cella.

The CELLA was 94 ft long and 43½ ft wide. It was divided down the middle by two-tiered colonnades of 7 Doric columns to form a nave c. 22 ft wide. This colonnade supported the wooden ceiling and the arrangement of galleries above the aisles from which the public were allowed to view the image of Zeus. The only light came from the doorway.

The *Nave* was divided laterally into four sections. The first, in the nature of a vestibule (open to the public) extended to the second column. On either side, by the first column, was a wooden staircase leading to the galleries. The next two sections were forbidden to the public. The second, closed by a barrier, extended to the base of the statue, and had side screens formed of slabs of conglomerate to divide it from the aisles. A square, the full width of the nave, was paved with black Eleusinian limestone, bordered with a kerb of Pentelic marble, to form a receptacle for the sacred oil used for the anointing of the statue. This probably served two purposes both practical: those of mirroring light from the doorway and providing oil for the wooden core in order to prevent swelling in the damp climate which might have split the ivory. The third section, from the 5th to beyond the 7th column, is entirely occupied by the base of the statue of Zeus. The fourth section is merely a passage 5½ ft wide connecting the two aisles behind the statue.

The similarity in both proportion and decoration with that of the Parthenon makes it certain that the interior arrangement was designed by Pheidias himself. If Pausanias is correct that Pheidias took as model for one of the throne figures the youth Pantarkes, who was victor in the boys' wrestling in 436 B.C., the work at Olympia would seem to have been done in 436–432 after the Athena Polias was finished. This has been recently claimed as confirmed by a study of the moulds for the gold drapery, though C. H. Morgan more persuasively places the Zeus before the Athena (Hesperia, 1952).

The chryselephantine STATUE OF ZEUS, the masterpiece of Pheidias was accounted one of the Seven Wonders of the ancient world.

Apart from one or two Hadrianic coins of Elis, no authenticated copies of the statue exist, and Pausanias alone of ancient writers describes it in detail, and even he devotes more attention to the throne than to the figure. It is believed to have been about 7 times life-size or c. 40 ft high. Pausanias, noting that the measurements had been recorded, says that they did not do justice to the impression made by the image on the spectator. Strabo, on the other hand, tells us that the artist is thought to have missed true proportion as the seated god almost touched the roof, giving the impression that if he rose he would knock the roof off. The ancients on the whole, however, concur in praising the extraordinary majesty and beauty of the statue. Cicero (Orator, II, 8) says that Pheidias made the image, not after any living model, but after that ideal beauty seen with the inward eye alone.

The *Pedestal*, 3 ft high, and decorated with gold reliefs of various divinities, was of blue-black Eleusinian stone, fragments of which have been discovered. Zeus was represented seated on a *Throne* made of ebony and ivory overlaid with gold and precious stones. The four legs of the throne were adorned with carvings and strutted with stretchers which bore golden reliefs of combatants. Some of the great weight was taken by four pillars underneath, hidden by screens on which were paintings by Panainos, and by the footstool which had golden lions and a relief of Theseus fighting the Amazons. The *Figure of Zeus* held in his right hand a chryselephantine *Victory* and in his left a sceptre with an eagle. The undraped parts of the statue—head, feet, hands, and torso— were of ivory. The *Robe* was decorated with figures of animals and lilies.

The care of the statue devolved upon the descendants of Pheidias, who were called the 'Burnishers'. By the 2C B.C., however, the ivory had cracked and had to be repaired by Damophon of Messene. In the time of Julius Caesar it was struck by lightning. The Emp. Caligula wanted to remove it to Rome and to replace the head of Zeus with his own, but every time his agents came near the statue it burst into a loud peal of laughter. It is believed that after the reign of Theodosius II the statue was carried off to Constantinople, where it perished in a fire in A.D. 475.

In 167 B.C. Antiochus IV Epiphanes, King of Syria, dedicated (?) behind the statue, "A woollen curtain, a product of the gay Assyrian looms and dyed with Phoenician purple" (Paus. V, 12, 4). There are grounds for believing this to have been the veil of the temple at Jerusalem which Antiochus carried off (II Macc. VI, 2).

The *Opisthodomos* had no direct communication with the cella. It was reached from the W. peristyle and does not appear to have been enclosed by gratings. It had a long stone bench where people used to meet and talk.

In front of the entrance ramp to the temple are some interesting pedestals of statues detailed by Pausanias. The statues were built into the Byzantine Wall (comp. below).

It was the custom to erect in front of the E. façade of the temple the statues of the Olympionikai and the chariots dedicated by them. The latter included the *Chariot of Gelo*, by Glaukias of Aegina, and the *Chariot of Hiero*, by Kalamis and Onatas of Aegina. Near the large rectangular bases of these is the semicircular base of a group of *Nine Heroes of the Trojan War* dedicated by the Achaean cities and made by Onatas of Aegina; they are represented as drawing lots for the honour of the duel with Hector. Opposite, on a round base, stood *Nestor* shaking the lots in his helmet. Close by is the restored triangular base of the famous *Nike of Paionios*, dedicated by the Dorian Messenians. Adjacent were statues of famous Olympionikai: *Telemachos the Elean* (end of 4C); *Diagoras of Rhodes*, his son *Dorieus*, and other Rhodian athletes. Rather more to the W. are the base of *Praxiteles*, a Mantinean athlete (484–461 B.C.), and the cylindrical plinth of a *Statue of Zeus*, dedicated by the Lacedaemonians in the 6C after the second Messenian revolt. Near the N.E. corner of the ramp are three semicircular moulded plinths which bore statues of the *Elean Women* (1C B.C.). Adjacent are the pedestals of the *Eretrian Bull*, by Philesios (5C B.C.) with an inscription on its E. margin (fragments in the museum); and of the historian Polybius (146 B.C.). These bases and others transferred to the new museum were within the trapezoidal area enclosed by the 6C *Byzantine Wall*, which had as its N. and S. limits the Temple of Zeus and the S. Stoa. The wall, made of ancient blocks from many buildings in the Altis, was demolished by the excavators and the fragments recovered.

Moving S.E. we reach a heap of grey limestone blocks belonging to a pedestal that supported an equestrian group of *Mummius and the Ten Legates*. Close by on the E. are remains of a Roman *Triumphal Arch*, erected for Nero's visit. It was largely built of older materials, including the pedestals of statues, destroyed lest the memory of their prowess should overshadow that of the megalomaniac emperor.

In the S.E. corner of the Altis are foundations of a building with four compartments and faced on all sides but the E. by a 4C Doric colonnade having 19 columns along the front and 8 at each side. It was paved with small pebbles embedded in plaster and may have been the *Hellanodikeon*. It was demolished to make way for the *House of Nero*, hurriedly built for the emperor's visit, the peristyle of which lies farther E. This house has been identified by the discovery of a lead water-pipe inscribed NER. AVG. The Doric columns of the Greek building were broken up into small pieces to form the opus incertum of the walls. Later a large Roman edifice was constructed immediately E. of Nero's house, which was partially sacrificed to the new building. This contained over 30 rooms, one octagonal, and explorations in 1963–64 showed it to have been *Baths*.

Farther E. lay the *Hippodrome*, long since washed completely away by the Alpheios. Here was installed the 'hippaphesis' an ingenious starting gate invented by Cleoitas in the 6C B.C. and described by Pausanias. To the S. of the House of Nero, in 1963 was uncovered the *Altar of Artemis*.

The greater part of the E. side of the Altis is occupied by the foundations of the *Echo Colonnade* or *Stoa Poikile*. The former name is due to its sevenfold echo, the latter to the paintings with which it was decorated. Most of the remains are from the time of Alexander the Great when the stoa was rebuilt, those farther E. from the earlier version of the 5C B.C. Previous to this the stadium extended into the Altis.

In front of the Stoa Poikile are numerous statue bases including a long plinth bearing two Ionic columns, which supported statues of Ptolemy II Philadelphos and Arsinoe, his queen.

We reach the vaulted entrance to the **Stadium,** completely explored in 1958–62 by the German Institute and restored to the form it took in the 4C B.C. The artificial banks never had permanent seats, but could accommodate c. 40,000 people. The track originally extended N.E. from near the Pelopion and was not separated from the Altis until the 5C when the Stoa Poikile was constructed. The embankments were several times enlarged and the German excavators found many older weather-worn votive offerings (helmets, shields, etc.) which had been buried during the alterations as sacred objects not to be profaned by re-use. The starting and finishing lines are in situ, 600 Olympic feet apart. The stone kerb round the track and the water-supply opening at intervals into basins are visible; the paved area for judges on the S. side has been uncovered.

Immediately outside the entrance is a row of twelve pedestals which supported the *Zanes*, bronze images of Zeus erected out of the fines imposed on athletes in the 98th and 112th Olympiads for cheating.

A flight of ancient steps ascends to the **Treasuries** which are arranged roughly in line on a terrace overlooking the Altis at the foot of Mt Kronos, the soil of which is kept back by a substantial retaining wall. These take the form of a small temple, consisting of a single chamber and a distyle portico in antis facing S. They were erected by various cities, all but two outside Greece proper, for the reception of sacrificial vessels used by the theoroi, and possibly for storing weapons and gear used in the games. Little remains but the foundations. The description of Pausanias is not without its difficulties and the proper identification of many of them is not certain. They seem to have been added roughly chronologically from E. to W.

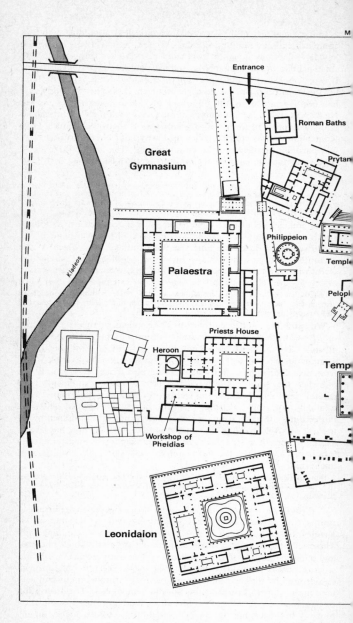

Entrance

Roman Baths

Prytan

Great
Gymnasium

Philippeion

Temple

Palaestra

Pelopi

Priests House

Heroon

Temp

Workshop of
Pheidias

Kladeos

Leonidaion

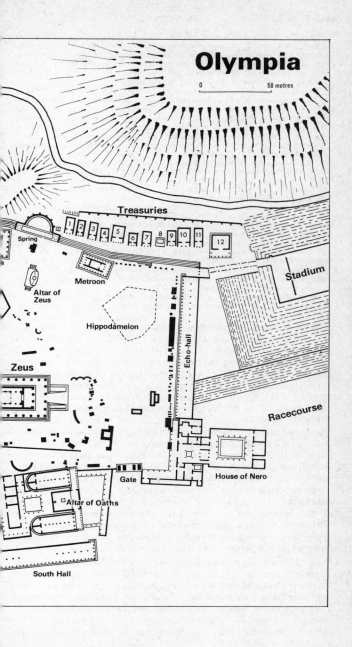

Olympia

0   50 metres

Treasuries

1 2 3 4 5 6 7 8 9 10 11 12

Spring

Metroon

Altar of
Zeus

Hippodàmeion

Stadium

Zeus

Echo-hall

Racecourse

Gate

House of Nero

Altar of Oaths

South Hall

The oldest and largest, built c. 600 B.C. and modernized about a century later, belonged to *Gela* (12). Though constructed of shell-limestone, those parts of the masonry which were most exposed to the weather, e.g. the pediment cornices, were encased in painted terracotta plaques and tiles—a survival from the days when buildings were made of wood. The terracottas were made in Gela and the building was presumably designed by Sicilian architects.

Though little more than the foundations of the Treasury of *Megara* (11) remain in situ, many fragments were recovered from the S. Byzantine wall. It was erected between those of Gela and Metapontum c. 570 B.C. as is shown by the fact that all ornamentation (fluting, mutules, etc.) was omitted where it could not be seen. The pediment may not have received its sculpture until c. 510.—Adjacent are foundations of the *Metapontum* treasury (10), slightly earlier in date. That of *Selinus* (9) is next, squashed in later between existing buildings, then (8) a structure which was probably not a treasury but the *Altar of Gaia*. The next three treasuries, which are very ruinous, are assigned to *Kyrene* (7), to which two sculptured fragments of African limestone probably belong; *Sybaris* (6) which must date before 510 B.C. when that city was destroyed; and *Byzantium* (5).

The architectural remains of the next building (4) belong to the 6C B.C. suggesting that it is more likely that of *Epidamnos* than (as usually attributed) of *Syracuse*. The Syracusan treasury, which contains the spoils of the victory at Himera (480 B.C.) may have been farther along (2), but both this building and that tentatively assigned to *Samos* (3) seem to have been obliterated in Roman times. The Treasury of *Sikyon* (1), by contrast, has well preserved foundations. Many blocks of the superstructure in Sikyonian stone with identifying inscription have been recovered. and were in course of re-erection in 1976. They date from c. 480 B.C. A Sikyonian treasury was dedicated by Myron to celebrate his chariot victory in the 33rd Olympiad, when the two huge bronze shrines also dedicated necessitated a special strengthening of the floor. This must have concerned an earlier building but the existing floor is also strengthened.

Immediately beyond is an *Altar to Herakles* (whether the Idaean Herakles or the famous Herakles Pausanias could not say) and, N. of it, an ancient *Shrine* with a pronaos facing s.

Descending the terrace steps we immediately reach the METROÖN, a small peripteral hexastyle Doric temple of the 4C B.C., dedicated to the Mother of the Gods. It measured only 67 ft by 34. The remains include most of the foundations and a portion of stylobate with the drum of one column and a fragment of another. In Roman times the worship of Cybele gave place to that of Augustus and Rome, and the excavators discovered in the foundations a statue of Claudius and another of Titus.

To the w. of the Metroön six prehistoric houses were uncovered by Dörpfeld, traces of two of which may be seen in front of the EXEDRA OF HERODES ATTICUS. This was the termination of a much-needed supply of pure drinking water brought to Olympia between 157 and 160 by an aqueduct c. 2 m. long. The water was stored in a large semicircular tank from which it flowed through lion's-head spouts into an oblong basin in front. The upper tank was paved with marble and backed by an apse supported by eight buttresses which rose to a half-cupola. The inner side had 15 niches which held statues of the family of Herodes and of their imperial patrons. At each end of the lower tank a small circular Corinthian temple enclosed a statue. A large marble bull bore an inscription recording that Herodes dedicated the reservoir to Zeus in the name of his wife Regilla, who was a priestess of Demeter.

The **Heraion,** the oldest but the best preserved building at Olympia, is situated near the N.W. corner of the Altis. It was originally a joint temple of Zeus and Hera but after the grander temple of Zeus was built was reserved to the goddess alone. The worship of Hera, which played little part in the history of Olympia, may have been introduced by Pheidon of Argos who supposedly usurped control of the festival. The temple is not earlier than the beginning of the 7C, and was originally built of wood, which was gradually replaced by stone. Even in the time of Pausanias columns of wood survived.

The temple, raised on a single step, was a Doric peripteral hexastyle with 16 columns at the sides. Thirty-four of the columns survive in part; two of them were re-erected in 1905 and another in 1970. They vary in diameter, in the height of the drums (while three are monolithic), and in the number and depth of the flutings, while the 18 surviving capitals show by the outlines of their echinus that they belong to every period from the foundation to Roman times. As no trace has been found of the entablature, it is believed to have been of wood. The roof was covered with terracotta tiles.

INTERIOR. The division into three chambers was conventional, though the interior details are unusual. Both Pronaos and Opistho-domos were distyle in antis. The walls of the sekos were nearly 4 ft thick; the four courses forming the inner face are well preserved to a height of 3 ft. The upper part was of mud brick with wooden doorposts. The *Cella*, long in proportion to its breadth, was lighted only by the door. Four internal cross-walls, recalling the structure of the much later temple at Bassae, served to buttress the outside walls and to sup-port the cross-beams of the roof. At a later date the cella was divided longitudinally by two rows of Doric columns, every second one being en-gaged with the corresponding buttress. There was a flat wooden ceiling.

Pausanias tells how, during the repair of the roof, the body of a hoplite was found between the ceiling and the roof. The soldier had apparently fought in the war of 401–399 B.C. between Elis and Sparta, during which a battle had swept over the Altis. Wounded, he had crawled to shelter only to die, remaining un-discovered for 500 years.

At the w. end of the cella stands the pedestal of the archaic group of Zeus and Hera. The head of Hera has been recovered. Of all the other treasures and statues known to have been in the Heraion only the Hermes of Praxiteles has been found. It was lying in front of its pedestal between the second and third columns from the E. on the N. side. Six bases in the Pronaos bore statues of noble Elean women. The opistho-domos is known to have held the cedar-wood *Chest of Kypselos*; the *Disk of Iphitos*, on which was inscribed the Olympic truce; and the gold and ivory *Table of Kolotes*, on which the victor's crowns were displayed.

To the s. of the Heraion is the site of the PELOPION, a grove containing a small eminence and an altar to Pelops, the principal Olympian hero, enclosed by a pentagonal wall. A Doric propylon at its s.w. end, of which foundations remain, appears to date from the 5C B.C. and to have replaced an older entrance. Immense quantities of archaic bronzes and terracottas were recovered in the enclosure as well as roof-tiles from the Temple of Zeus.

Somewhere to the E. must have stood the *Altar of Olympian Zeus*, the most sacred spot in the Altis, where a daily blood sacrifice was made. A heap of stone marks the supposed spot.

As we turn towards the exit we pass, in the N.W. corner of the Altis, the foundations of the **Philippeion**, a circular monument begun by Philip of Macedon after the battle of Chaironeia (338 B.C.) and probably finished by Alexander the Great. Two concentric colonnades stood on a stylobate of three steps, the outer peristyle having 18 Ionic columns, the cella having 12 engaged columns with Corinthian capitals. The roof had marble tiles and a bronze poppy on the roof which held together the rafters. Within was a group of five chryselephantine statues, by Leochares, representing Philip, his mother and father, his wife Olympias, and their son Alexander. Excellently carved fragments of their bases have been recovered.

Beyond stood the PRYTANEION, the official residence of the magistrates, in which Olympic victors were feasted. The remains are scanty. The building, which dates in some form from very early Greek times, was remodelled more than once in Roman times. The later Greek Prytaneion was a square of 108 ft with an entrance on the s. side and a vestibule leading into a central chamber, 22 ft square. Here doubtless was the *Altar of Hestia*, on which burnt perpetual fire. On both sides of the central chamber were open courts. In Roman times a banqueting hall was added to the w.

As we quit the enclosure there are (r.) remains of Roman baths.

Across the road a drive leads to the new ****Museum** (adm. 25 dr.; standard museum hours), opened in 1972. Finds formerly in the old museum and many more previously in store are arranged chronologically. In 1979 the temple pediments were still in the OLD MUSEUM (above the road); their definitive placing in the new hall is not certain and, as there is scholarly controversy about the position and identification of some figures, the description may be only approximate.

In the ENTRANCE HALL, model of the Sacred Altis (a gift of the city of Essen). Statue bases of Olympic victors: Kallias of Athens, by *Mikon*; Euthymos of Lokri Epizephyrii, by *Pythagoras*.

We turn left. GALLERY 1. Neolithic to Geometric, including grave goods from sub-Mycenean chamber-tombs; Mycenean boars' tusk helmet; *Tripods and handles of cauldrons adorned with bronze figures (Telchines); in the centre, large Geometric horse in solid bronze.— GALLERY 2. Geometric and early Archaic bronzes and terracottas; orientalizing bronze plaques, griffins, etc; *Armour and weapons, many richly fashioned, displayed according to type and development: shields and corselets on the wall, cases of greaves, lances, and helmets below; one finely decorated Archaic cuirass recently recovered after being stolen in the First World War; shield bosses; restored pedimental acroterion from the Heraion; colossal Head of Hera, from the same; kouros from Phigaleia.

GALLERY 3. Statuettes and tripods; sculptures and simas from various Treasuries, including the pedimental statuary of the Megarians and a section of polychrome sima from the Gela Treasury; Archaic figures from a perrhiranterion; battering ram; fine vases.—In GALLERY 4 the Classical period is introduced by the arresting and vigorous group of **Zeus carrying off Ganymede*, a late Archaic work executed in terracotta; warrior from a similar group; Persian *Helmet taken by the Athenians at Marathon and dedicated to Zeus; the *Helmet of Miltiades, victor at Marathon; small *Bronzes and pottery; tools.—GALLERY 5. The celebrated *VICTORY (NIKE) OF PAIONIOS. Pedestal and statue are both made of island marble. It bears an inscription recording its erection and dedication to Zeus by the Messenians and Naupactians "as a tithe from their enemies", and the name of its artist, *Paionios* of Mende. The statue was probably erected at the peace of Nikias in 421 B.C. The height of the statue, including the pedestal was c. 30 ft. The face, forearms, hands, and toes, and wings are missing.—Bronze Head of a Boy, from the stadium.

GALLERY 6. The *Hermes* of Praxiteles, a work found in the Temple of Hera in 1877 in the place where it was noted by Pausanias. Its attribution to Praxiteles rests on his summary description; he seems to have considered the work worth no more than the briefest remark. After a period of the greatest artistic adulation, it is no longer necessary to award it uncritical praise. It remains, however, one of the best-preserved Classical statues that have survived to modern times, preserved by the fallen clay of which the upper walls of the temple had been built. The statue is of Parian marble, its original polish scarcely marked by the passage of time, though not quite entire.

Hermes, the messenger of the gods, was charged by Zeus to take his infant son Dionysos out of the reach of the jealous Hera, and to bring him to the nymphs of Mount Nysa, to whose care was entrusted the rearing and education of the child. Hermes is represented as resting on his journey. He stands in an attitude of easy grace, the left knee slightly bent, leaning his left arm on the trunk of a tree. In his left hand was doubtless the caduceus (missing). His cloak is carelessly thrown across his arm and falls in simple graceful folds over the tree trunk. On his left arm sits the ill-proportioned infant Dionysos, reaching up towards an object (a bunch of grapes?) which Hermes holds in his right hand. The form of Hermes, which is entirely nude, presents an ideal combination of grace and strength, not without some danger of the charge of preciosity. The head is slightly turned towards the child. The hair is in short crisp locks, indicated rather than sculptured in detail. Both behind and before can be traced the groove of a metal wreath. Traces of paint have been detected on the hair, lips, and sandal. The date of this masterpiece is usually put between 363 and 343 B.C. though some authorities consider it a Roman copy.

GALLERY 7. Roman sculpture from the Exedra of Herodes Atticus, including a marble bull; beautiful but fragmentary figure (Antinous?).—GALLERY 8. Objects directly concerned with the Olympic Games: dedications of victors; base of statue (by Lysippos) of the Athenian Polydamas; bronze discus; jumping weights (halteres).

The huge CENTRAL HALL will contain the pedimental sculpture from the Temple of Zeus, together with the metopes. The standard work on the sculptures was published by Bernard Ashmole and Nicholas Yalouris in 1967.

The EAST PEDIMENT, attributed by Pausanias to Paionios, represents the start of the chariot-race between Oinomaos and Pelops. All the figures are sculptured in the round except the three inner horses of each team, which are in moderate relief. Not a vestige of either chariot has been found, but the marks of attachment are seen on the horses. The figures, none of which is complete, are $1\frac{1}{2}$ times lifesize and sculptured in the severe style, consistent with a date in the mid-5C.

Oinomaos, King of Pisa, warned by an oracle that he would be killed by a son-in-law, was unwilling to give his daughter Hippodameia in marriage. Aspirants to her hand were challenged to a chariot-race from Olympia to Isthmia and given a start with Hippodameia while Oinomaos sacrificed a ram. By the fleet-footedness of his horses Oinomaos overtook his potential sons-in-law, spearing them in the back. He had thus disposed of 13 suitors when Pelops appeared as claimant. He bribed the charioteer Myrtilos to tamper with the axle-pins of his master's chariot so that Oinomaos was killed when his chariot crashed. Pelops thus won both his bride and her father's kingdom. The unedifying story of cheating and treachery (generally accepted as the root cause of the curse of the Atrides) seems to have provided one legendary version of the founding of the Olympic Games. Alternative versions have omitted Myrtilos' part and attributed Pelops' victory to his magical steeds (a present from Poseidon) and Oinomaos' death to hubris punished by Zeus. The pediment seems to omit Myrtilos and this may have been the Elian version of the story.—NOTE: the terms 'right' and 'left' used below are from the spectator's point of view.

The centre of the composition is the colossal figure of Zeus; to the left (according to the latest of a long series of suggested reconstructions) stand Oinoamaos and his wife, Sterope; to the right Pelops and Hippodameia. Zeus, who is invisible to the contestants, is looking towards Pelops in token of his good will. The identification of Sterope and Hippodameia and their consequent placing l. or r. made by Yalouris has been questioned by Kardara (comp. A.J.A. 1970). On each side of the women is a four-horse chariot, that of Pelops attended by a boy, that of Oinamaos by a girl. Behind the team of Pelops is his charioteer (?; Killas), a seer, and the personified Alpheios. Behind that of Oinomaos, a seer, a boy, and the personified Kladeos.

The WEST PEDIMENT, executed according to Pausanias by Alkamenes, illustrates the fight between the Lapiths and Centaurs at the marriage-feast of Peirithoös. Again none of the figures is complete, though the Apollo is almost perfect.

Peirithoös, King of the Lapiths in Thessaly and a reputed son of Zeus, invited his friend Theseus and the Centaurs to his wedding. The Centaurs had too much to drink and assaulted the women and boys present, one of the Centaurs, Eurytion, attempting to carry off the bride. Peirithoös, assisted by Theseus, defended the attacked, slew many of the Centaurs, and routed the rest.

The central figure is *Apollo, calmly towering above the tumult, who has come to the assistance of the Lapiths. On the right Hippodameia is in Eurytion's clutches; Peirithoös stands ready to strike with his sword. Beyond, a boy is being picked up by a Centaur. Next comes a Lapith woman, her garment torn, trying to tear herself free from a Centaur who has already been transfixed by the sword of a kneeling Lapith. They are watched from the corner by a crouching and a recumbent woman. The left hand side is similar, but even less well preserved. The boy throttling the Centaur is being savagely bitten in the arm and shows his pain in a furrowed brow.

The sculptures are all of Parian marble with the exception of the two old women in the w. pediment, the young woman in its left hand corner, and the arm of the other young woman, which are of Pentelic marble and are thought to be antique restorations. From traces of colour discovered it is clear that all the figures were painted.

On the end walls are the sculptured *METOPES from the cella frieze, illustrating the *Twelve Labours of Herakles*. Each slab measured $5\frac{1}{4}$ by 5 ft, the figures being slightly under life-size. The metopes were originally painted, the brush completing the details of hair, clothes, etc, which the chisel has merely indicated. In delicacy of execution they may be thought superior to the pedimental figures, especially in the moulding of the features.

In a new building in the village is the *Museum of the Olympic Games*, which includes a collection of commemorative stamps.

38 FROM CORINTH TO PATRAS

ROAD, 84 m. (135 km.), mostly near the shore along the Gulf of Corinth.—
13 m. *Kiato*, for *Sikyon* (3 m.).—21 m. *Xilokastro*.—50¼ m. *Dhiakofto*.—58½ m.
Aiyion.—78¾ m. **Rion** (car-ferry to *Andirrion*, for N.W. Greece).—84 m. **Patras.**—
TOLL HIGHWAY, parallel to (and generally inland of) the old road needing great care
in bad weather. BUSES (starting from Athens) approx. hourly (2¼ hrs journey; 3½ hrs
from Athens).
RAILWAY, 81 m. (130 km.), 6 good trains daily in 2¼–3 hrs, all starting from
Athens, whence 1½–2 hrs should be added. To *Xilokastron*, 21 m. (34 km.) in
c. 40 min.; to *Dhiakofto*, 48 m. (77 km.) junction for Kalavryta, in 1½–1¾ hrs;
to *Aiyion*, 56½ m. (91 km.) in 1¾–2 hrs. The railway is seldom out of sight of the
road.

This route follows the S. shore of the GULF OF CORINTH (*Korinthiakós Kólpos*),
which extends for nearly 80 miles from Aigosthena in the E. to the 'Little Dardanelles' in the W. It varies in width between 1¼ and 20 miles, being widest in the
centre and narrowest at the W. The E. end of the gulf is divided by the peninsula of
Perachora into the Gulf of Alkionídhon and the Bay of Corinth, with the entrance
to the Corinth Canal. The N. and S. sides are in remarkable contrast. The alluvial
coast of Achaia, with its innumerable torrents and its currant vineyards fringing
the shore, runs W.N.W. almost in a straight line from Corinth to Cape Drepanon.
The rugged and abrupt coast of Phokis, Lokris, and Aitolia, chiefly forest and
pasture and sparsely inhabited, is broken by the Bay of Aspra Spitia (Andikiron
Kólpos) and the Bay of Salona (Krissaios Kolpos), in addition to several minor
indentations. The encircling mountains are among the highest in Greece so that the
gulf resembles a large inland lake. The fine scenery recalls that of the Italian lakes,
and the storms that spring up are as sudden as those in the Alps.

Corinth, see Rte 25. The road runs W. along the coast. Across the
Bay of Corinth is seen the long low promontory of Perachora; farther E.,
behind Loutraki, rises the great mass of Yeraneia. After 2 m. we pass
the site of *Lechaion* (Rte 25E); on the left towers Acrocorinth.—6 m.
Periyiáli, the first of many villages strung along the road, is situated
amidst currant-vines and fruit trees in the fertile coastal plain of
CORINTHIA, now completely recovered from the earthquake of 1928.
In world production of currants, Greece is second only to the United
States. Corinthian lemons are of the green variety, which are artificially
turned yellow after picking to satisfy foreign demand.—We cross the
Longos (or Rakhiani) near (6¾ m.) *Assos*, a village surrounded by cypress
groves; hereabouts was fought the Spartan victory 'near the Nemea
River' in 394 B.C. Behind, the flat top of *Mt Fokas* (2865 ft; the ancient
Apesas) is prominent.—At (8½ m.) *Vrakhati* (Anessis **D**), a centre for sul-
tanas on the Nemea, is the Kokkoni Holiday Village. Near *Zevgolatió*, 1
m. l., are some remains of a late Roman bath explored in 1954.—Beyond
(11 m.) *Véllo*, where fruit juices are extracted, we cross the Peloponnesian
Asopos, said by classical tradition to be an extension of the Maeander
flowing beneath the sea from near Miletus. The flutes of the presumptuous Marsyas were thrown up on its bank.

13 m. **Kiáto** (*Sikyon*, *Galini*, **C**), or *Sikionia*, with a prominent modern
church, is a flourishing port (7400 inhab.) exporting raisins. Hence the
excursion by boat to Perachora (Rte 25F) may be made. Near the railway
station are some remains of an early Byzantine basilica. The modern
village of *Vasilikó* (c. 3 m. S.W.; bus) has readopted the official name of
Sikyon, the later site of which it occupies.

Sikyon (ΣΙΚΥΩΝ), reputedly one of the oldest of Greek cities, was the capital of Sikyonia, a small district, anciently (as now) renowned for its almonds and olive-oil. In the Classical period the city was a centre of Greek art. Its school of bronze sculpture was made famous by Aristokles, Kanachos, Polykleitos, and Lysippos. Its academy of painting, established by Eupompos, produced Pausias and Pamphilos, the master of Apelles, and endured to Hellenistic times. Sikyonian dress, and in particular the Sikyonian shoe, had a wide reputation. Both the ancient city, which lay in the plain, and the later one founded by Demetrios Poliorketes on the acropolis, lay close to the Asopos.

History. Sikyon ('Cucumber Town' from σικύα, a cucumber) was originally named *Aigialeia*, probably from the Aigialaean ('coast-dwelling') Ionians who founded the city, and later called *Mekone*. The traditional list of its heroic kings includes the Argive Adrastus, the only survivor of the 'seven against Thebes'. The Homeric catalogue makes him commander of the Sikyonian contingent to Troy, and Homer gives to *Sikyon* the epithet εὐρύχορος (wide open). After the Dorian invasions it became subject to Argos. About 660 B.C. Orthagoras, a popular tyrant, established a dynasty lasting a century, during which the city rose to prosperity. Its metal work and pottery were of a high standard and a school of sculpture was founded from Crete. Boutades of Sikyon is credited with inventing the relief. Kleisthenes, greatest of the dynasty and grandfather of the Athenian legislator, joined the Amphictyonic League in the Sacred War (c. 590 B.C.). His destruction of the city of Krisa freed Delphi. After reorganizing the Pythian Games there, he instituted similar games at Sikyon, abolishing the worship of the Argive hero Adrastus. His successor Aeschines was expelled by the Lacedaemonians c. 556, and Sikyon lost its political independence in the Peloponnesian League. It remained a centre of art and industry (comp. above), and its coinage was in widespread use in the 5–3C.

The Sikyonians were loyal allies of Sparta during the Persian invasions, in the Peloponnesian War, and after, on more than one occasion providing a fleet. The city was conquered in 368 B.C. by the Theban Epaminondas, but shortly afterwards a Sikyonian citizen called Euphron achieved a brief local notoriety by seizing the government. In 303 B.C. Demetrios Poliorketes razed the ancient city in the plain and built a new one, temporarily called *Demetrias* in his honour on the ruins of the old acropolis. In 251 B.C. Aratos, son of Kleinias, united the city to the Achaean League, later becoming its leader. During the eclipse of Corinth after 146, Sikyon took over control of the Isthmian Games, but after the refounding of Corinth, gradually declined. Fulvia, wife of Mark Antony, died in exile here in 40 B.C.

The 'new' city of 303 B.C. is admirably situated 2 m. from the sea on an extensive triangular plateau between the gorges of the Asopos and the smaller Helison. Defended on all sides by precipitous cliffs, the plateau is divided by a rocky slope into a lower terrace, the acropolis of the old city, and an upper terrace, forming the apex of the triangle, which became the acropolis of the new. The city walls ran round the edge of the plateau and are least ruined on the w. side. Excavations by the Greek Archaeological Society under Prof. Orlandos have uncovered only a small part of the city, which seems to have been laid out on a rectangular plan.

The modern village stands on the lower level of the plateau. We cross the presumed site of the Agora to (10 min.) the large Roman *Baths*, built in brick in the 2–3C and restored as a MUSEUM (adm. 25 dr.) for the site. In three rooms are displayed Mosaics (? 4C B.C.); bronze mirror; painted terracotta frieze; pieces of sculpture; and pottery models of hedgehogs.

To the left are the foundations of an archaic *Temple*, reconstructed in the Hellenistic epoch; this may be the Temple of Apollo mentioned by Pausanias as being rebuilt by Pythokles. The s. end of the agora was closed by a Hellenistic *Stoa* and the *Bouleuterion*, an almost square hypostyle hall, the ceiling of which was supported by 16 Ionic columns. At a late date it was adapted to other uses. Near it are extensive remains of the GYMNASIUM OF KLEINIAS, built on two levels; on either side of the central stairway linking them is a fountain. The **Theatre**, one of the largest of continental Greece, occupies a natural depression in the slope dividing the upper and lower terraces. It was excavated by the American School in 1889–91 and tidied up in 1951. The building dates from the beginning of the 3C B.C. It is known from Polybius that the Achaean League met here in 168 B.C. The *Cavea* is c. 400 ft across. The lower diazoma could be reached by two vaulted passages as well as by 16 staircases from the parodoi. The fifty-odd tiers of seats, mostly hollowed out of the rock, were divided into 15 wedges, each of which forms one twenty-fifth part of a circle. The front seats have backs, armrests, and sculptured feet. The *Orchestra*, of stamped earth, surrounded by a drain, had a diameter of c. 66 ft. Foundation walls of the stage buildings show that they were twice altered in Roman times. They had as façade a Doric portico of 13 columns in antis.—In a ravine to the w. of the theatre are the remains of the *Stadium*. The straight end had a wall of polygonal masonry, still partly standing. On the upper terrace are scanty ruins of the new *Acropolis*. The dividing slope is honeycombed with subterranean *Aqueducts*. The *View, especially lovely at sunrise and sunset, embraces Helikon, Kithairon, and Parnassos, with a verdant foreground contrasting with the blue of the Gulf.

The old city in the plain and its harbour have left little to mark their sites. The modern road follows the ancient alinement and road-construction in 1966 located a necropolis and mosaics of the old city.

FROM KIATO TO THE STYMPHALIAN LAKE, KASTANIA AND PHENEOS. Road, 42¼ m. (68 km.), asphalted to Souli (8 m.), motor-bus to Goura, more interesting for the landscape than for the remains of antiquity. Skirting the N. side of Mt Botsika (4265 ft), we turn S.W. between it and Kyllini.—21½ m. *Kefalári* (450 inhab.) nestles below the secondary E. summit of Kyllini (see below; the ascent from this side, in 12 hrs, is difficult). At (24 m.) *Kaliáni* diverges a bad road to *Nemea* (20 m.; comp. Rte 26).—Beyond (25½ m.) *Kiónia* (Inn) near the Stymphalian lake we pass (l.) the conspicuous remains of the Frankish church of the Cistercian abbey of Zaraka (13C) next to the ruined Temple of Artemis. The acropolis of *Stymphalos* with Pelasgian walls overlooks the w. end of the lake, while at the F. end are some remains of Hadrian's aqueduct which took the waters to Corinth. In legend Stymphalos was celebrated because its birds provided Herakles with one of his labours.

The road climbs steeply from the w. end of the valley to (32¼ m.) *Kastaniá* (Xenia C, small with rest., at 4270 ft above the village), a mountain resort (2960 ft) on the s. slope of Kyllini below the saddle that separates Stymphalos from Pheneos. It is a good area for walking and for botanists. We descend to the E. side of the *Pedhías Feneoú*, in ancient times a shallow lake or marsh, nowadays more often dry.—From (37 m.) *Mesinón* a path crosses the valley to *Kalívia*, passing the site of *Pheneos*, with remnants of a small Temple of Asklepios and the colossal head and feet of a broken statue. A small museum contains a Classical female statue. The church of Ayios Yeoryios, to the N.W., has frescoes. The road continues between Feneos and Kalivia to (42¼ m.) *Goura*; the modern village of *Feneos* lies on the w. side of the valley, midway between the summits of Kyllini and Chelmos. Here a monument was erected in 1960 to nationalist victims of a communist massacre in 1944. Track across the N. slopes of Kyllini (4 hrs) to Trikkala (see below).

On the N. slopes of Aroánia (Chelmos; 7724 ft), in a lugubrious and eroded valley, is the 'Source of the Styx' (4 hrs w. of Feneos). Make for *Vounariánika*, from which the waterfall is visible and the footpath apparent. Hence Kalavrita

(Rte 39) may be reached in a further 6½ hrs (guide advisable), or, viâ *Sólos*, the descent may be made to the coast (see below).

18 m. *Melissi* (Xylokastro Beach C), with a Mycenean tomb (500 yds s.).—21 m. (34 km.) **Xilókastro** (ΞΥΛΟΚΑΣΤΡΟΝ; *Arion*, DPO; *Apollon*, small, both A; Miramare B; *Periandros*, C; and others) is a popular seaside resort (4600 inhab.), agreeably situated amid luxuriant gardens at the mouth of the Sithas valley. It probably occupies the site of ancient *Aristonautai*, a seaport of Pellene, where the Argonauts put in. Along the sandy E. shore towards Sikia is a pinewood, called *Pefkias*, with a campsite. A *Museum* devoted to the memory of Angelos Sikelianos (1884–1951), the poet, has been established in a villa he once owned. To the s.w. on the mountainside stands *Zemenó* (5 m.), where a wine festival is held in September.

To Trikkala (21 m.) and Mt Killíni. Just w. of Xilokastro a road climbs into the Sithas valley.—7½ m. *Pellíni*. The insignificant ruins of ancient *Pellene*, on the top of the mountain separating the valleys of the Sithas and the Phorissa, command an excellent view.—21 m. **Ano Tríkkala** (3500 ft; *Asteria*, open all year, *Theoxenia*, summer only, C), a winter-sporting resort, stands on the N. slope of *Mt Zíria*, the ancient *Kyllene*, second highest mountain in the Peloponnese (7800 ft). Climbers should obtain keys of the refuges from the Greek Alpine Club in Athens. An easy path climbs in 2½ hrs to *Refuge A* (5400 ft; 50 beds; water), and (30 min. more) to *Refuge B* (5700 ft; 20 beds), whence the w. summit may be reached. The Gymnos summit (7000 ft), to the E. overlooks Kefalari on the Kastaniá road (comp. above).

The mountains come closer to the coast. Parnassos may be seen 30 m. away across the gulf. Above (25 m.) *Kamári*, birthplace of Panayiotis Tsaldaris, opposer of Venizelos, who brought back the monarchy in 1935, rises the pyramidal *Koryphe* (2400 ft) with a nunnery on its summit. We cross the Forissa torrent.—29¾ m. *Likoporiá* (Alkyone C). The conspicuous Cape Avgó, between Petséïka and (32¼ m.) *Stómion*, contends with Koryphe the site of *Donussa*.—35 m. *Dherveni* (Evrostini D), a small town (1230 inhab.) with a long narrow street, has a sandy beach. We enter the nome of Achaia.

Achaia, or Achaea, the mountainous N.W. division of the Peloponnese, marches on the s. with inland Arcadia and maritime Elis. Its capital is Patras. In the Mycenean period the name of the province connoted almost the whole of the Peloponnese. In classical times its meaning was restricted to the N. coastal area. When the Romans conquered the Achaean League they gave the name to the whole peninsula.

The Achaean League was a confederation for mutual defence and protection of the coastal cities of Achaea, which met until 373 B.C. at Helike. It was refounded in 280 B.C. on an anti-Macedonian basis and admitted non-Achaeans. Aratos of Sikyon united Sikyon, Corinth, and other cities to the League, became its general in 245 B.C., and made it the chief political power in Greece. The admission of Megalopolis antagonized Sparta and during the Cleomenic War Aratos allied the League with Antigonus Doson. The League went over to Rome in 198 B.C. under the leadership of Philopoemen (252–183 B.C.) the last great man of free Greece. It lost all power in 146 B.C. The 'twelve cities' of the League were Aigai, Aigeira, Aigion, Boura, Dyme, Kerynea, Olenos, Patrai, Pellene, Pharai, Rhypes, and Tritaia.

36½ m. *Mavra Lithária*. Aigaí (4 m. inland) and (38½ m.) *Aigeira* (Cecil D) perpetuate the names of two of the Achaean twelve cities. Some ruins of Classical Aigeira, including a rock-hewn theatre of horseshoe plan, were excavated in 1915, 1926, and 1972–3 by the Austrians on an isolated hill (Palaiokastro) close to the shore. The city was called *Hyperesia* by Homer (Iliad II, 573). Its inhabitants are said to have frustrated a Sikyonian invasion by collecting goats (ἄιγες) after dark and tying torches to their horns, thus misleading the enemy into believing reinforcements had arrived: hence the later name of the city.— From (40¼ m.) *Akráta Station*, below its village, tracks climb to *Sólos* (6 hrs) providing a possible approach to the Styx (comp. above); its waters feed the *Krathis* which we shortly cross. For some miles the mountains now reach to the sea and the road runs higher with views ahead and across the Culf of Corinth. To the right some striking olive groves and cypresses.

50¼ m. (81 km.) **Dhiakoftó** (ΔΙΑΚΟΠΤΟΝ; Chelmos **D**), in a plain noted for its cherries, is the railway junction for Kalávrita and has a frequent bus connection with Patras. The excursion by train at least as far as Zakhloroú should on no account be missed.

———————

The **Kalávrita Railway** was engineered in 1885–95 by an Italian company in the fantastic, sombre **Gorge down which the Vouraïkós, or Kerynites, tumbles its boulder-strewn course. The partial replacement of the original steam rolling-stock by diesel railcars in 1960–62 has ended the former discomfort and for period enthusiasts much of the romance; but nothing detracts from the awe-inspiring scenery or from the achievement of the engineers. Sometimes pushing, sometimes pulling, the little locomotives (of 75 cm. gauge) proceed partly by adhesion (max. gradient 1 in 28), partly by rack-and-pinion (Abt system; gradient 1 in 7) with frequent halts for water, rising 2300 ft in 14 miles. The line crosses the water several times on bridges and runs in tunnels or on overhung ledges. The sites of ancient *Bura* and *Keryneia* occupy hilltops to E. and W. of the entrance to the gorge. Just below Zakhloroú, where the gorge is only a few feet wide an original tunnel on the E. side suffered a partial collapse and after the Second World War a new tunnel was hewn in the solid cliff on the W. and a new bridge constructed.

7¾ m. *Zakhloroú* (Romantso **D**, on the picturesque station; Rest.). A steep zigzag ascent (mules available; *View towards Kalávrita up the cypress and fir-clad valley) leads E. in 45 min. to the **Moni Megaspeleion** (Ιερά Μονή του Μεγάλου Σπηλαίου), or monastery of the great cavern, built against a vertical and almost smooth cliff. After a disastrous fire in 1934, when a powder magazine (said to date from the War of Independence) exploded, the monastery was courageously rebuilt in an uncompromising 20C style. It has a hostel of 50 beds.

Visitors are shown round by a monk (adm. fee). The *Church* has ancient ikons. The monastic TREASURY has been beautifully arranged as a museum of sacred relics illustrating the history of the convent. Case 1. The miraculous ikon of the Mother of God, supposedly found in the great cavern by the shepherdess Euphrosyne in A.D. 362, and attributed to St Luke. The painting is on waxed wood.—Case 2. Seraphim, carved in wood (c. 1700).—Case 3. Two epitaphioi from Asia Minor, one of Russian workmanship.—Cases 4–6. Gospels on vellum (9–11C), with Byzantine enamel-work covers.—Cases 7–9. Reliquaries containing the left hand of the martyr Charalambos in the attitude of blessing; the heads of the monks Symeon and Theodore, founders of the monastery; hands of the SS. Theodore.—Cases 11–13. Crosses.

Beyond Zakhloroú the valley gradually broadens.—14 m. (22 km.) *Kalávrita*, see Rte 39.

———————

Beyond Dhiakoftó the railway continues near the shore while the road runs farther inland amid olive and cypress groves. The villages become more closely placed.—54 m. *Elíki* (Poseidon Beach B) recalls the name of Classical *Helike* drowned by a tidal wave in the earthquake of 373 B.C. The sanctuary of Helikonian Poseidon was the early meeting-place of the Achaean League. It stood 1½ m. inland. Following a similar seismic disturbance in 1963, underwater investigation was undertaken in 1966, without conspicuous success.—Immediately before we cross the rapid Selinous, or Vostitsa, amid vineyards of currants, a road diverges (l.) for *Ftéri*, or Ptéri (ΠΤΕΡΗ; 12½ m.; Fteres C) a summer hill-resort with a growing local reputation and fine views which have earned it the sobriquet of the 'Balcony of God'.—*Valimítika* (Eliki Beach C) lies E. on the shore.

58½ m. **Aiyion** (AIΓION; Inns), the chief town (18,800 inhab.), of the eparchy of Aigialeia and the seat of a bishop, is a small commercial port. Called *Vostitsa* in the middle ages, it gave name to the finest currants grown in Greece. Currants and olive-oil are exported and there are large paper-mills. It has a ferry to Ay. Nikolaos across the Gulf.

History. According to legend *Aigion* took its name from a local goat (ἄιζ) which suckled the infant Zeus. The city is mentioned in the Homeric Catalogue and sherds attest local occupation from Neolithic to Geometric times. The Achaean League met here in the Homarion and for a time it was the chief city of Achaia. The name *Vostitsa* is of Slav origin. After the division of the Morea in 1209 it was given by Geoffrey de Villehardouin to Hugh de Lille de Charpigny as the barony of La Vostice. After a period under the Acciaioli, it surrendered to the Turks in 1458 and except for a Venetian interlude in 1463–70 remained Turkish until 1821. It was partly destroyed by earthquakes in 1819 and 1888.

The town is built on a cliff 100 ft high above a narrow strip of shore and has several fountains. The Panayia Tripiti stands in an attractive nursery garden. The main square is Ayia Lavra and the attractive smaller *Plateia Psila Alonia*, with a good restaurant, commands a fine view of the Gulf of Corinth.

A pleasant excursion may be made up the Selinous valley to see two monasteries, the Taxiarkhis beyond the river on the right bank, whither it was removed in the 17C from an earlier site, 1 hr farther on, at *Paliomonástiro*.—From the valley a road branches (r.) to mount the foothills of Panakhaïkon (6315 ft), where at *Dhafnai* (7½ m.) are two refuges of the Greek Alpine Club.

The coastal plain is well-watered by torrents descending from Panakhaïkon, and bamboo is grown.—60¼ m. *Rodhodháfni.*—65¼ m. *Selianítika* (Kanelli, Kyani Akti, C)—67 m. *Lambíri* (Galini C), with a Club Méditerranée holiday camp, lies on the semicircular harbour of *Erineos*, founded by earthquake refugees from Boura; here an indecisive battle was fought between the Corinthian and Athenian fleets in 415 B.C. —72½ m. *Psathópirgos* (ΨΑΘΟΠΥΡΓΟΣ, 'thatched tower'; Motel Florida B) lies in the midst of very fine scenery resembling the Italian Riviera, with the additional advantage of a lovely coastline across the Gulf. The mountains, thickly clothed with firs, plane-trees, arbutus, oleander, and a variety of flowering shrubs, run down to the coast, while the road and railway pass immediately above the sea, crossing a number of torrents.—74½ m. *Arakhovítika* (Alexander Beach B). To the right is

Cape Dhrépanon, the northernmost point of the Peloponnese.—At (78¾ m.) *Ayios Yeóryios* is the turning for **Rion** (2 m.; *Averof Grand*, 265 R., A; *Rion Beach* C; ELPA Car Camp) whence a car ferry plies at intervals (½ hr by day; ¾ hr at night) to Andirrion (20 min.; Rte 55) on the N. shore of the Gulf.

The *Castle of the Morea* (no adm.), or 'Kastelli', on the shore, was built by Bayazid II in 1499 before his campaign in the Morea. Parts of its aqueduct still exist by the roadside. Here took place the last stand of the Turks in Oct 1828 when Ibrahim Pasha's troops held out for three weeks against a combined Anglo-French force under Marshal Maison. Its use as a prison and the presence of oil-storage tanks near by make a diversion hardly worth-while though the moated fortress is impressive from the sea.

84 m. (135 km.) **PATRAS**, in the Greek nominative **Pátrai** (ΠΑΤΡΑΙ), the largest town (111,600 inhab.) in the Peloponnese and the third largest in Greece, is the capital of the nome of Achaia, and the seat of a bishop (the historic archiepiscopal see having been degraded in 1899). The ancient city lay some distance inland from its port, to which it was connected by Long Walls. Patras is celebrated in Greek national annals as the see of Abp Germanos, who raised the standard of the Cross at Kalavryta in 1821, and important geographically as the w. gateway to Greece. The modern city was rebuilt on a grid plan with broad arcaded streets by Capodistrias after the Turks had burned the medieval town in 1821. Manufactures include cotton textiles and motor-tyres; among other products shipped from the busy port are currants, olive-oil, valonia, hides, and wine.

Airport at *Araxos*, c. 20 m. s.w. with daily service from Athens.

Hotels. **Astir** (Pl. c), DPO, with swimming pool; **Acropole** (Pl, b). 16 and 32 Ay. Andreou; **Moreas**, Ieroon Polytechniou, these A. **Majestic** (Pl. d), 67 Ay. Andreou; **Galaxy** (Pl. f), 9 Ay. Nikolaou, both B. **Mediterranée** (Pl. e), 18 Ay. Nikolaou; **Esperia** (Pl. g), 10 Zaimi; **Metropolis** (Pl. a), Plat. Trion Simmakhon; **El Greco** (Pl. h), 145 Ay. Andreou, these C; and many more modest.

Restaurants. *Evangelatos*, 9 Ay. Nikolaou; *Markopoulos*, Othonos-Amalias; *Panaretos*, 73 Ay. Andreou; *Elite*, Korinthou; and others; also at the *Majestic* hotel.—TAVERNAS in the upper town.

SUBURBAN. *Koukos*, at Koukali; *Eva*, on shore 2½ m. w.; *Diakou*, Yerokomio; *Daphnes*, Bozaïtika.

Post Office, Ayiou Nikolaou/Ferraiou.—O.T.E. CENTRE, Leof. Gounari.—TOURIST POLICE, 263 Korinthou and on the quay.

Bookseller. *Papakhristou*, 16 Ay. Nikolaou.

Buses to the suburbs from Kolokotronis/Kanakari.—COUNTRY BUSES (terminals being concentrated on the quay E. of the station). KTEL ATHENS, (c. hourly), also railway buses from the station, to *Athens*. To *Aiyion* and *Dhiakofto* (every ½ hr); to *Rion* (every ½ hr); to *Pirgos* (every 1½ hr); to *Varda* (hourly); Kalavrita (twice daily) continuing (once only) to *Tripolis*; to *Mesolonghi* and *Agrinion* (7 times daily); to *Levkas*; to *Arta* and *Ioannina*; to *Navpaktos* (5 times daily); to *Salonika* (twice daily).

Steamers to the Ionian Is. (*Zante*; *Argostoli*; *Sami*; *Paxoi*; *Ithaka*; and *Corfù*); also to *Brindisi* (car ferry), to *Ancona* (car ferry), and to *Venice*.

Festivals. *Carnival* in Feb. (10 days before Lent); *Classical Theatre Season* in Summer; *Procession of St Andrew*, 30 Nov.

Swimming at Itiés, 2½ m. s.w.—*Hellenic Alpine Club*, 184 Kanakari.

History. *Pátrai* was a substantial though not conspicuous member of the Achaean League. The idea of building her long walls came from Alcibiades (Thuc. V, 52). During an invasion of the Gauls the Patraians were the only Achaeans to cross into Phokis to help the Aitolians and they suffered accordingly. After the battle of Actium Augustus settled many of his veterans in the depopulated city which he refounded as the *Colonia Augusta Aroë Patrensis*. Hadrian is dubbed 'Restitutor Achaiae' on coins of Patrai.

St Andrew, the first disciple, preached at Patrai and is said to have been martyred there. The town sent a bishop to the Council of Alexandria in 457 but not to earlier councils. Invading Slavs, assisted by a Saracen fleet, besieged Patras in 805 when the supposed intervention of St Andrew confirmed his veneration as the city's patron saint. The archbishop was raised to metropolitan rank about this time. In 1205 Patras became a Frankish barony and the seat of a Latin archbishop who soon ruled an almost autonomous principality. Carlo Zeno got his early military experience as a canon of Patras when it was besieged by Marie de Bourbon. In 1408 Patras was sold by its abp to Venice, and in 1426 the Pope appointed Pandolfo Malatesta in an attempt to hold it against the brothers Palaiologos. Constantine, however, took it in 1429 and his brother Thomas held it until 1460 when it passed to Mehmed II. It remained the commercial capital of Greece despite the political changes. Here in 1809 Byron first set foot on Greek soil. Both in the abortive rising of 1770 and in 1821 Patras claims to be the first town to have taken up arms. The Turks, however, aware of the intention of Abp Germanos to march on Patras from Kalavryta, occupied the citadel whence the town was bombarded and set on fire. It was not freed till 1828.

Natives of Patras are Kostis Palamas (1859–1943), the national poet; Stylianos Gonatas (1876–1966), revolutionary Prime Minister in 1922–24; and Jean Moreas (1856–1910), the French poet (born Papadiamantopoulos).

The QUAY, with the *Railway Station* and an information bureau, is generally animated. The long mole ending in a lighthouse is a favourite promenade. A little to the E., beyond the busy commercial arcades of Odhos Ay. Andreou, is PLATEIA OLGAS. Here the **Museum** (adm. 5 dr.; standard hours) displays in the Vestibule four good Classical heads. The LOWER ROOM has as centrepiece a *Mosaic*, 18 ft by 8, from a Roman building under Plat. Psila Alonia. Round the walls, Sculpture, mostly Roman, with a Classical Asklepios relief and the head of an Archaic Kore; inscriptions from the Kastro. On the FIRST FLOOR two rooms contain a fine collection of prehistoric, Mycenean, Classical, and Roman pottery (also a Roman marble table); in the 2nd room: Mycenean finds from Kallithea, including unique *Greaves, swords; also (from the tholos tomb near Pharai, Rte 39) a fine dagger blade with dolphins; jewellery, and a superb array of pots.

Odhos Maizonos leads s.w. past the Roman Catholic Church to Od. Ayiou Nikolaou which we mount to the top, continuing up a broad flight of steps (view) to the **Kastro** built on the site of the ancient *Acropolis*. The *Lower Ward* has round and polygonal towers and is planted with flowering shrubs. The N. curtain wall, of early Byzantine date, incorporates Classical drums and blocks; similar elements occur in a flanking tower of the s. curtain, but all periods of Byzantine–Turkish–Venetian rebuilding up to the 17C are represented. The well-preserved *Keep* (no adm.) has square towers but is equally indeterminate in date. The view embraces Zante and Cephalonia, the mountains of the Roumeli coast above Navpaktos, and, to the s., the peaks of Erymanthos.

From opposite the E. gate of the castle a track, skirting below the radio station in the park, passes through two sections of a *Roman Aqueduct*, the first well-preserved, the second (ruinous) standing in places to 100 ft above the valley.

To the s.w. of the Kastro is the **Odeion**, a characteristic Roman theatre of the Imperial epoch, which, when discovered in 1889, had 25 rows of seats (in 4 wedges) nearly entire, made of brick and faced with marble. Much of the marble was later removed by enterprising local builders and the theatre had to be extensively restored in 1960. The cavea faces s.; the orchestra is 31½ ft in diameter. Crossing Plateia Ikosipende Martiou we may take Od. Sisini, passing other Roman

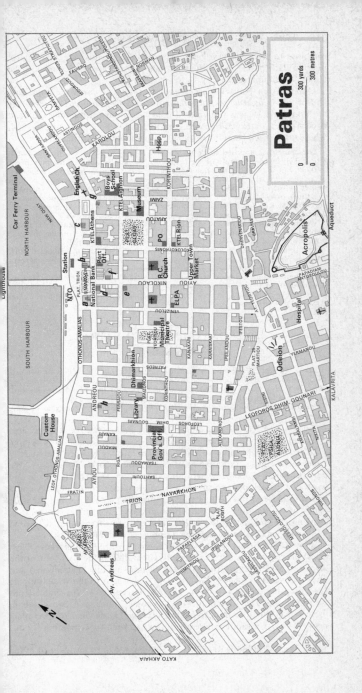

remains, to the PLATEIA PSILÁ ALÓNIA. From this irregular space, planted with palms, a vigorous bronze of Abp Germanos raising the standard dominates the city.

Odhos Trion Navarkhon descends to the w. towards the huge ugly church of *Ayios Andreas*, not yet completed in reinforced concrete by G. Nomikos. Here is venerated a gold *Reliquary containing the head of St Andrew, returned by Pope Paul VI from St Peter's, Rome, in 1964, where it had been since Thomas Palaiologos fled with it in 1460.

The church is supposed to be on the site of the Apostle's crucifixion, but is more likely over a Temple of Demeter. An earlier Byzantine Church suffered in the fire of 1821. An inscription from the Kastro commemorates the restoration of a church by Abp Malatesta in 1426; the composer Dufay is recorded to have written music in the same year for a consecration of his cathedral.—According to a much older tradition the relics of St Andrew had already been removed in the 4C, when St Regulus, or Rule, bp of Patras, fled with the body to Scotland and was wrecked off Muckcross, in Fife, where he founded St Andrews.

We may return viâ Od. Korinthou or Od. Maizonos, passing the not very distinguished public buildings of Patras to PLATEIA YEORYIOU TOU PROTOU, the central square of the city, with the *Theatre*, and thence to the quay.

EXCURSIONS may be made to the Akhaïa-Klauss wine vaults (5 m.), founded 1861, where parties are given conducted tours (7–2, 4–7). The buildings occupy a Mycenean site round which many chamber-tombs have been located.

Climbers wishing to ascend *Mt Panakhaïkon* (6322 ft) should contact the Hellenic Alpine Club in Patras. From *Romanos* (4 m. from Patras) it is 3 hrs on foot to *Psarthi Refuge A* (4900 ft; 50 beds; water; ski-lift), then 45 min. to *Prassondi Refuge B* (5900 ft).

39   FROM TRIPOLIS TO PATRAS
A Viâ Kalávrita

ROAD, 109 m. (175 km.) magnificently scenic, the middle section unsurfaced, the remainder largely reconstructed since 1961, but needing care in the Erymanthos Mts. Bus daily (early morning) in c. 6 hrs (incl. ½ hr in Kalavrita); additional morning bus from Kalavrita to Patras. 36 m. *Káto Klitoría.*—55¾ m. Turning for Kalávrita (1¾ m. r.).—95 m. *Khalandritsa.*—99½ m. Turning for Pirgos.—109 m. Pátras.

Tripolis, see Rte 30; thence to (21½ m.) *Vlakherna*, see Rte 36. Just over ½ m. farther on, at the N. end of Mt Mainalon, we quit the Olympia road and turn right to make a long descent into the wooded and marshy valley of the lesser (s.) affluent of the Ladon.—26 m. *Panayítsa.*—We pass below (28 m.) *Dára*, where Photakos (1798–1878) lived in exile and wrote his history of the war of 1821. The narrow road enters Arcadia and runs close to the rushing stream, threading a defile to join the wide valley of the Ladon below the village of *Sellá*. We turn upstream (N.), crossing (31 m.) the *Aroanios Bridge* (Yéfira tou Aroaníou) to the w. bank, and leaving on the left the Tripótama road (Rte 39B).

36 m. **Káto Klitoría** (Inn), locally known as *Mazéïka*, a market village (1130 inhab.) at the junction of two valleys, lies at the s.w. foot of the Aroania Mts (comp. Rte 38). On a near-by hill (Palaiópolis) are imposing walls of ancient *Kleitor*. The view opens to the w. as we pass (39½ m.) *Áno Klitoría.*—45 m. *Kastélli* lies below us (l.) under iron-bearing hills. The mountain views become immense as we climb in increasingly rough country to (46 m.) *Afkhéna tou Khelmoú* (the 'Aronaia neck'; 3440 ft), a saddle where diverges a bad road to Tripótama (17 m.; see below).

We descend in loops to (47½ m.) *Priólithos* (2620 ft) at the head of the long and pretty valley of the Vouraïkos which gradually broadens. We pass below Ayia Lavra (see below) and reach the Patras–Kalávrita road, 2 m. w. of Kalávrita.—57 m. (92 km.) **Kalávrita** (ΚΑΛΑΒΡΥΤΑ; *Chelmos* B; *Maria* C), chief town (1950 inhab.) of an eparchy and seat of a bishop, is situated at 2480 ft on the Vouraïkos at the foot of Mt Velia. Cool mountain springs and the freshness of the air make it especially attractive in summer.

Kalavryta is the successor to ancient *Kynaithes*, whose inhabitants were distinguished for their independence, wildness, and irreverence. The town was destroyed by the Aetolians in 220 B.C. but revived under Hadrian. After 1205 the fief of *Kalovrate* fell to Otto de Tournai, and in 1301 passed to the barons of Chalandritsa. In modern Greek history it disputes with Kalamata the claim to be the first town liberated in the War of Independence (comp. below). It twice fell into Ibrahim Pasha's hands, in 1826 and 1827. On 13 Dec 1943 German occupying troops here massacred 1436 males over the age of 15 and burnt the town. Since 1962 the German Federal government has re-endowed Kalavritan schools.

The clock on the *Metropolitan Church* stands at 2.34, the hour of the massacre of 1943. Some antique remains may be seen between Ay. Aikaterini and Ay. Yeoryiou and round the Kalavritiní spring, to the s.w. of the town, identified with the classical *Alyssos*. About 1 hr E. of the town on a rocky height stand the ruins of '*Tremola*', or the *Kastro tis Orias*. The first name derives from Humbert de la Trémouille, the second from the beautiful Katherine Palaiologos, daughter of a Chalandritsa baron, who is said to have committed suicide rather than fall into Turkish hands in 1463.

Taxis may be hired for the excursion to (4½ m.) *Ayía Lávra*, the celebrated monastery where Germanos, Abp of Patras, raised the standard of revolt on 21 Mar 1821. A hermitage, started in 961, developed into a monastery many times destroyed and rebuilt. The present edifice, begun in 1839, has suffered by earthquake and fire and in 1943, but, again rebuilt, retains the *Church of the Dormition* from before the sack by Ibrahim in 1826. A little *Museum* contains historical relics and medieval MSS.

From Kalávrita to *Megaspileion* and *Dhiakoftó* (Athens), see Rte 38.

The Patras road heads w. across the valley to enter the winding gap between *Panakhaïkón*, to the N., and *Erímanthos*, to the s., whose jagged peaks are well seen from (66½ m.) *Flámboura*.—70 m. *Boúmbouka* retains a Turkish appearance. The road climbs to nearly 3500 ft before descending to (75¾ m.) *Kato Vlasía* under the N. face of Erímanthos. About 2 m. w. of the road is the site of ancient *Leontion* with a theatre (4C B.C.) excavated by N. Yialouris in 1958. New engineering has removed many loops of the road, which climbs steadily up the N. side of a wild gorge. The dizzy ledge runs along the s. outliers of Panakhaïkón. 84 m. *Plátanos* and *Kálanos* are superbly sited facing *Vistas of epic grandeur extending w. to the sea.—Beyond (85½ m.) *Kalanístra* (*View) the road reaches a further summit (2365 ft) with a magnificent retrospective panorama. A by-road diverges (r.) to *Deméstikha* (5 m.) with vineyards producing well-known wines bottled by Akhaia-Klauss near Patras.—90½ m. *Katarráktis* lies in an enclosed valley above which extensive Mycenean settlements (and, more surprising, traces of Middle Helladic occupation) were located in 1957 in the region of ancient *Pharai*.—95 m. *Khalandrítsa* (1230 inhab.), once a Frankish barony and preserving a fine partly-ruined church, looks over the coastal plain towards Zante. A Mycenean settlement has been located at Ay. Antonios and a tholos tomb at Troumbe, both near by.—We join the road described in Rte 39B.—109 m. (175 km.) **Patras**, see Rte 38.

B Viâ Tripótama

ROAD, 112 m. (179 km.), since its improvement the main link between Arcadia and Achaia.—31 m. *Aroanios Bridge*.—52 m. (83 km.) *Tripótama* (Psophis).—112 m. **Patras**.

From Tripolis to (31 m.) the *Aroanios Bridge*, see Rte 39A. Here a new road diverges w. and, beyond (34½ m.) *Kalívia*, quits the Ladon valley. At 42 m. a bad road ascends to the s. to *Dháfni* (3 m.), a deme of 1720 inhab. in a delightful situation, with a monastery (Evanghelistrias) of the late 17C and many medieval churches. We cross a saddle and join the Seiraíos (Vertsiótiko). To the left the Afrodísion range divides Achaia from Arcadia.—52 m. **Tripótama** (1805 ft), a small village, stands at the confluence of the Seiraíos and the Aroánios (Livartsinó) with the Erímanthos (Nousaïtiko), where the common frontiers of Achaia, Arcadia and Elis meet. Here are extensive but scanty remains of ancient *Psophis*, destroyed by Philip V of Macedon in 219 B.C. The situation, hemmed in by mountains, is subject to extremes of heat and violent winds. The sanctuary of Aphrodite Erykina was identified in 1967–69 at Ayios Petros near by.

Joining a road from Kalávrita (comp. above), we cross the Erimanthos into Elis, rising high above its right bank on the slopes of Mt Lámbeia.—60 m. *Lámbeia* (Inn), a well-watered spot with plane-trees, lies below the Áno Moní Dhívris. As Dhivri, it was the headquarters of the Peloponnesian communist rebels in 1948.

About 3 m. beyond Lambeia a poor road diverges (l.) across the extensive plateau of PHOLÓIS, the watershed between the Alpheios and the Pineios, which ancient legend peopled with Centaurs. Some remains near Koúmanis, off the road (r.) at 5 m., have been identified with Classical *Lasion*.—13½ m. *Lála* (Pandelis D) was of some importance in Turkish times. The road makes a long winding descent to (24 m.) *Platanos* (Rte 36), 2 m. w. of Olympia on the Pirgos road.

The main road descends gradually by twists and turns above a series of ravines, passing into the basin of the Pineios.—At (77½ m.) *Ayía Triádha*, formerly Boukovína, we turn N., crossing the Pineios into Achaia, and run through uplands between Mts Skóllis (w.) and Erímanthos.—89½ m. By-road to *Kaléntzi* (5 m. r.; Xenia B, Apr–Oct), a pleasant mountain base (3198 ft), from which the Ionian Sea. can be seen and the second summit of Erímanthos (6983 ft) climbed. Here was born George Papandreou (1888–1968), prime minister in 1961–65.—At 102 m. the Kalávrita road (Rte 39A) comes in on the right. We pass below *Kallithéa*, with a Late Helladic III cemetery, then descend to the olive-groves in the coastal plain.—112 m. (179 km.) **Patras**, see Rte 38.

40   FROM PATRAS TO PIRGOS

ROAD, 60 m. (96 km.) in flat fertile country.—14¼ m. *Kato Akhaia*.—38½ m. *Lekhaina*, for *Killini* and *Chlemoutsi*.—41 m. *Andravidha*.—45 m. *Gastouni*, for *Loutra Killini*.—52¼ m. *Amalias* (E. of the road.)—60 m. **Pirgos**. Frequent buses.

RAILWAY, 62 m. in c. 2 hrs following the road closely all the way.

The greater part of this route is in Elis, a territory bordered on the N. by Achaia, on the E. by Arcadia, on the S. (for a very short distance) by Messenia, and on the w. by the Ionian Sea. The Channel of Zante separates it from that island, and Kephalonia lies off its N. seaboard. Elis faces w. towards Europe, is remote from the Aegean, and cut off from the rest of the Peloponnese by a mountain barrier intersected by easily guarded ravines.

In antiquity the region was divided into three parts: *Hollow Elis*, or Elis proper, in the N., watered by the Elean Peneios; *Pisatis*, the country of Pisa, on the Alpheios, in the centre (including Olympia; comp. Rtes 36, 37); and *Triphylia*, between the Alpheios and the Neda, in the S. Famous for the grove of Altis and the Temple of Zeus at Olympia and for the Olympic Games, Elis was regarded as a holy land and its neutrality respected from high antiquity until the Peloponnesian War. The country was noted for its horses and especially suited to the growth of fine flax.

Its place-names attest later occupations from the N. and W. by Avars, Slavs, and Albanians. The coastal plain became an important centre of the Frankish occupation and has always supported horses, sheep, goats and cattle. The cultivation of the currant-vine since 1850 has greatly increased its prosperity and importance, though only since the Second World War it has it ceased to be malarial.

The road leaves Patras by an unattractive stretch of shore, backed by untidy factories and workshops, though (3 m.) *Itiés* is the best known beach of Patras.—5 m. *Paralía Proastíou* (Achaïa Beach, Tzaki, with good rest., both **B**). The coast now commands a view across the Gulf of Patras. The plain produces lemons and currants.—7½ m. *Vrakhnéïka*.— At (8 m.) *Tsoukaléïka* a by-road ascends inland to Ano Soudenéïka (7½ m.) whence a poor track continues (3 hrs) to *Sandaméri* a village deriving name from a Frankish Château de Saint-Omer.—We cross the Pirros and enter (14¼ m.) **Káto Akhaïa** (3400 inhab.; *Eupolis* D), the site of ancient *Dyme*. The Chronicle of the Morea is probably incorrect in locating here the landing of Guillaume de Champlitte in 1205.

Here a branch road goes off (r.) to *Araxos* (8 m.), the airfield of Patras, near the marshy lagoons of the N.W. promontory of the Peloponnese. Above the fish-hatcheries rises the 'Kastro tis Kalogrias', a hill with an enceinte of cyclopean walls that stand in places to 30 ft. This is the **Teichos Dymaion** of Polybius. Excavations of the Greek Archaeological Service in 1962–65 have shown occupation in Early, Middle, and Late Helladic times. Most important is that the site has yielded Mycenean IIIc finds showing reoccupation after a destruction c. 1200 B.C. and before a final catastrophic eclipse in the 11C.

As we turn S. from the town green foothills rise ahead with the long stark arête of *Skóllis* (3330 ft), above Sandaméri, farther left.—21¾ m. *Lápas*. We enter the nome of Elis (comp. above).—27 m. *Nea Manoládha*. —29 m. *Várda* lies 1¼ m. E. of *Manoládha*, an estate formerly held by the Crown Prince, scene in 1316 of a battle between Louis of Burgundy and Ferdinand of Majorca in which the latter was slain. It has a 12C church and is noted for water-melons and yoghourt. Beyond Manoládha the by-road continues to *Loutrá Kounoupéli* (6¼ m.; sandy beach) in an area troubled by mosquitoes.—38½ m. *Lekhainá*, a market town of 2600 inhab., is the birthplace of Andrea Karkavitsa (1866–1923), the novelist.—40 m. Turning (r.) for Killini, Chlemoutsi, and Loutra Killini (see below) on the extreme W. projection of the Peloponnese.

The road joins a by-road direct from Lekhaina at (2½ m.) *Mirsíni* and runs w. to (5 m.) *Neokhóri*, where it divides. To the right is (9¾ m.) **Killíni** (ΚΥΛΛΗΝΗ; *Xenia* **A** & **C**; *Ionian* **C**), ferry-boat station for Zante (three times daily in 1½ hr; comp. Rte 56). As *Glarentza* (or Clarence) it was the chief port of Frankish Morea.

Ancient *Kyllene* was the port of Elis, a trading point with Magna Graecia, and in the Peloponnesian War served as a Spartan naval station. Here Alcibiades landed after his fugitive journey from Thurii. Kyllene was captured by Sulpicius in 208 B.C. In the middle ages *Clarence* became the residence of the Villehardouin princes of Achaia, and their Angevin successors here developed the court life described in the Chronicles of the Morea. 'Chiarenza' became the port of transit for Venetian and Genoese galleys from Brindisi or Taranto. In 1428 it passed to Constantine Palaiologos, who systematically destroyed it as soon as he held the last Frankish outpost (Patras).

Scattered foundations of the medieval city remain on the low plateau N.W. of the modern village with a large ruined church similar to that at Andravidha. A medieval castle was dynamited during the German occupation. Earlier remains may be traced near the 12C Byzantine *Moní ton Vlakhernón* (30 min. to the E.), completed by the Franks.

The conspicuous *Castle of Chlemoútsi on the lone height to the S. known to the ancients as *Cape Chelonatas* (from its resemblance when seen from seaward to a tortoise-shell) is reached from Neokhóri (comp. above) by taking the Loutrá Killíni road viâ *Kástro* (5 m.; Killini Golden Beach, 330 R, A). Above the village towers the crenellated enceinte of the best-preserved Frankish monument in the Morea.

Chlemoútsi was built in 1220–23 with revenues confiscated from the Latin clergy by Geoffrey I Villehardouin, who called it *Clairmont*. The Venetians later dubbed it *Castel Tornese* perhaps after the coins (tournois) minted in Glarentza. The castle was held by Ferdinand of Majorca in 1314–16. It fell in 1427 to Constantine Palaiologos, who used it as a base for his campaign against Patras. The Turks refortified it after 1460.—Some traces of Middle Helladic occupation of the hill have been recognized in the castle foundations. On the lower E. slopes of this hill palaeolithic implements came to light in 1960.

The original recessed *Entrance Gate* has been obscured by the Turkish addition built flush with the curtain into the outer passage. Within to the left is a well-preserved 13C construction, but most of the buildings that backed the *Curtain Wall* have disappeared; their fireplaces only remain. The breach made by Ibrahim Pasha's guns in 1825 can be seen near the s.w. angle. The *Keep*, a huge irregular hexagon, consists of a series of vast vaulted galleries arranged round a court. These were divided into two stories either by an intermediate vault (as in the N. and N.W.) or by wooden floors (s. and s.w.). The massive barrel-vaults, in fine ashlar masonry, were strengthened by reinforcing arches; though those have mostly fallen much of the vault has held. The double-arched windows are interesting. The *View commands the Zante channel and the whole plain of Elis.

---

41 m. **Andravídha** (ΑΝΔΡΑΒΙΔΑ), an uninteresting market-town of 3050 inhab., replaces *Andreville*, once the flourishing capital of the Frankish principate of the Morea and seat of a catholic bishop. Of his cathedral church of *Ayia Sophia*, two Gothic bays of the E. end with the apse and E. aisle chapels survive in a ruinous state. Of the Templars' church of St James, where the Villehardouin princes were buried, no vestige remains.—43½ m. *Kavásila* is the railway junction for Killini and Loutra Killini. We cross the Pinios, less copious since its harnessing (comp. below).—45 m. *Gastoúni* (Inns), the livestock market (4200 inhab.) of the plain, takes name from the Frankish fief of Gastogne and under the Turkish occupation was the chief town of Elis.

Here a road diverges w. to *Vartholomió*, another large village (3000 inhab.), where it meets a road from Lekhaina (comp. above), continuing to **Loutra Killini** (10 m.; *Clarence* C; *Ionion* D, both June–Oct; good taverna), a thermal establishment amid pine woods, near the excellent sandy Olympic Beach (holiday camp). By the *Baths* are remains of their Roman predecessors.

In the opposite direction from Gastouni a good road leads N.E. viâ *Boukhióti* (officially Avgeíon) to (7½ m.) **Ancient Elis**, excavated by the Austrian School in 1910–14 and conjointly with the Greek Archaeological Service since 1960. The Apotheke is marked by signposts. A path leads across fields to the *Theatre*, a Hellenistic reconstruction of a Classical edifice, again altered in Roman times. There are remains of parodoi, foundations in poor limestone of the paraskenion, and portions of the analemma. The cavea was banked, probably with radials in stone, but did not have stone seats. Stone 'tickets' were found. An Early Helladic tomb came to light and nine slab-covered graves attributed to the transitional period between sub-Mycenean and protogeometric. The location of the Gymnasium and Palaestra has been found in the N.W. section of the Agora where Doric columns are very similar to those of Olympia. The boundaries of the city have been fixed and two cemeteries explored. The *Acropolis* was on the hill locally called Kaloskopi, a name which gave rise to the erroneous placing here of Beauregard, a lost Frankish castle.—About 3 m. farther up the river near *Kendron* is the huge Pinios irrigation dam, built in 1961–62 by American engineers, forming a large lake. In a series of international 'salvage digs' in the area, the flat-topped hill of Armátova, in the angle of the confluence of the Ladon and Peneios, just N.W. of *Agrapidhokhóri*, upheld its claim to be the site of *Elean Pylos*.

48¼ m. **Savália**. The main road avoids **Amalías** (3¾ m. E.; *Amalia, Ellinis*, C), a modern market town with 14,200 inhab., served by both the railway and the buses. To the right extends the sandy *Paralía tis Kouroútas* (car camping; tavernas, etc.) frequented by Elians in summer. —At (54½ m.) *Khanákia* a by-road runs (r.) to *Skafídhia* (3 m.; Miramare Olympia Beach, 350 R, DPO, A), with a Byzantine monastery. We leave on our right Ayios Ioannis (see below) and enter (60 m.) **Pirgos** (ΠΥΡΓΟΣ; *Letrina, Alcestis, Olympos*, C), a busy but uninteresting market town (20,600 inhab.), occupied with the currant trade (Stafidikó Institouto, etc.)

A branch railway and road run W.—3 m. *Ayios Ioannis* occupies the site of ancient *Letrinoi* which gives to Pirgos its official deme-name.—7 m. Turning (r.) to *Ayios Andreas* (Pheia; see below).—8 m. **Katákolo** (*Delfini* D) is a small port founded for the currant trade in 1857. It is used by cruise ships as a base for the visit to Olympia. *Fia*, on the bay of Ayios Andreas, is a hamlet with a good beach (cafés). Ancient *Pheia*, once the main port of Elis, was partially engulfed by the earthquake that overthrew the Temple of Zeus at Olympia in the 6C A.D. Its low acropolis (Pondikokastro) became the *Beauvoir* of the Villehardouin, and its archaeological traces extend from Neolithic to Hellenistic. The walls can be traced underwater, where the remains were explored by N. Yalouris and John Hall in 1957–60.

To *Olympia*, see Rte 36; *Samikon* and *Kakovatos*, see Rte 34.

IV CENTRAL GREECE

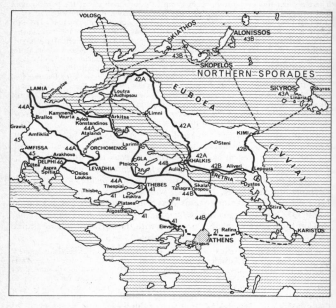

CENTRAL GREECE (*Sterea Ellas*) in modern parlance denotes an administrative grouping comprising seven nomes that extend from Attica to Akarnanía. Of these only Viotía (Boeotia), Évvia (Euboea), Fokís (Phocis), and part of Fthiótis come in this section. In antiquity **Boeotia** (BOIΩTIA; in mod. Gk Viotía) was a district, lying between the Euboean Straits and the Gulf of Corinth, bounded on the N. by Opuntian Locris, and on the S. by Attica and Megaris. The low-lying interior is nearly surrounded by mountains. On the S. is the barrier of Parnes and Kithairon. On the W. are Helikon and Parnassos, and on the N. the Opuntian mountains. The highest summit in Boeotia is Helikon, which rises to 5740 ft. Near the E. coast are more isolated heights, between which the Asopos plain reaches to the sea. The Asopos, rising near Plataiai, flows past Tanagra, and falls into the Euboean Channel N. of Oropos. Its plain is adjoined on the N. by the plain of Thebes, beyond which extend the Boeotian Lakes. The Copaïs, once the largest lake in Greece, is now a fertile plain growing cereals and cotton and grazing pedigree cattle. The Boeotian Kephissos, the other notable river, finds its outlets in swallow-holes. Between Helikon and the coastal ridge to the S. is the plain of Thisbe.

Boeotia had a flourishing existence in prehistoric times with Mycenean centres at 'Minyan' Orchomenos, at Gla, and at 'Cadmeian' Thebes.

The history of the region is summarized with the descriptions of these places. With two sea coasts and good harbours Boeotia was well placed for maritime trade. All land routes between northern and southern Greece pass through it. The soil was fertile. Despite these natural advantages the Boeotians never (save for nine short years under Epaminondas) took the leadership in Greek affairs, because, in the opinion of Strabo, "they belittled the value of learning and of sociability, and cared alone for the military virtues". They had in antiquity a reputation for slow-witted illiteracy and boorish manners, but a certain astuteness is evidenced by their policy towards the Euripos.

Among the many battles fought in Boeotia, three were of vital importance: Plataea, in 479 B.C., which secured the independence of Greece at the end of the Persian wars; Leuktra, in 371, which ended the long-suffered hegemony of Sparta and gave Thebes her nine-years' period of leadership over the rest of Greece; and Chaironeia, in 338, at which city-state democracy was virtually extinguished by the victory of Philip of Macedon.

On account of its Classical interest and sparse modern habitation, Boeotia was one of the earliest regions to attract the archaeologist's spade; it has since been neglected, but is again coming into its own in the study of the Bronze Age. Some of the sites explored by earlier generations, especially those of battles, are quite unrewarding save to the dedicated antiquary, though many of them still enjoy that romantic isolation fast being lost elsewhere. Aigosthena, Gla, and the Museum at Thebes should on no account be missed. Orchomenos is impressive. Places of natural beauty include the valley of the Muses on Mt Helikon and the N. coast of the Gulf of Corinth, the latter accessible with difficulty, but offering a number of impressive fortified sites to the energetic walker. The most populous centres are Thebes and Levadhia, in both of which fair accommodation and good food can be found. Levadhia is the administrative capital of the modern nome. A rash of factories has begun to disfigure the E. plains.

Phocis is a small territory famous for containing the city and oracle of Delphi. In antiquity it was bounded on the N. by Epiknemidian Locris and Opuntian Locris, on the E. by Boeotia, on the W. by Ozolian Locris and Doris, and on the S. by two inlets of the Gulf of Corinth, the Krisaean Gulf (Bay of Itea) and the Antikyran Gulf (Bay of Aspra Spitia). At one time its territory extended across Greece to the port of Daphnous, on the Atalante Channel. The interior is unproductive and mountainous, culminating in Parnassos (8061 ft). None of the 22 Phocian cities was very populous.

41 FROM ATHENS TO THEBES. CENTRAL BOEOTIA

ROAD, 46 m. (74 km.) undulating and sinuous over Mt Kithairon.—To (14 m.) *Elevsis*, see Rte 16. We by-pass the town and fork right.—16¾ m. *Mandhra.*—32 m. Turning for *Aigosthena.*—33 m. **Eleutherai.**—38 m. *Erithrai.*—46 m. **Thebes.**—BUSES from Liossion Terminal hourly in 1½ hr; also, several times daily, to *Villia* and *Aigosthena*.

The RAILWAY, 62 m. (100 km.), to *Thebes* (8 times daily in 1½–2 hrs) runs very close to the Lamia highway described in Rte 44B.

From Athens to the Elevsis turn, see Rte 16. We continue by the main Corinth highway, but at 15m branch right and by-pass *Mándhra* (7400 inhab.) at the base of the stony hills that shut in the plain of Eleusis on the w. The road ascends to (22½ m.) *Ayios Sotír*, the church of the Saviour, the silver-painted dome of which marks the summit of the first ridge. We traverse the mouth of the valley of Palaiokhorion (small Byzantine church), the road undulating across several ridges.—26 m. Restaurant on a col. We descend. An ancient watch-tower marks the entrance to (29½ m.) modern *Oinóï*.

To find the scanty ruins uncertainly identified with ancient *Oinoe*, an important Athenian border fortress, we take the by-road (r.; now signposted to the Kithairon waterworks tunnel) towards Pánakton. They lie r. of the road after c. 2 m., just before a turning (l.) to *Osios Melétios* (2 m. N.), a monastery with an 11C Byzantine church.—At (6 m.) *Pánakton*, a medieval tower on a conical hill commanding the cultivated plateau at the w. end of Parnes marks another fortress, taken by treachery by the Boeotians in 421 B.C. and returned to the Athenians by Demetrios Poliorketes. The identification of both places leaves many historical problems unexplained (comp. J.H.S. 1926). Some scholars would exchange the identities of Panakton and Eleutherai (comp. below). The road goes on to (8 m.) *Pili*, a remote village connected by mule-path with Filí (Rte 19B).

31½ m. Turning (l.) for Aigosthena.

This road runs w. and bypasses (2½ m.) *Víllia* (ΒΙΛΙΑ; *Aktaeon*, Apr–Oct, B; *Cithaeron*, *Kyklamina*, both C, open all year; good tavernas), a chicken-farming village of 1870 inhabitants. Avoiding a military road which goes off right up Kithairon, we continue and at (7½ m.) *Ayios Vasileos* cross the line of an ancient road, explored by N. G. L. Hammond (B.S.A. v. 49, 1954) and claimed by him to be the main highway from Boeotia to the Peloponnese. Near *Vathikhoria*, to the s.w., are the remains of 7 guard-towers of Classical date, two of which stand to almost their original height.—Our road descends (*View) to the sheltered bay of Aigosthena (13½ m.; *Aigosthenion*, Apr–Oct, C; tavernas), the most E. arm of the Gulf of Corinth, known before it readopted the ancient name as *Porto Yermano*. It is thickly planted with olives and shut in to the N. by Kithairon and to the s. by Pateras. **Aigosthena** (ΑΙΓΟΣΘΕΝΑ) belonged to Megara; it was never of great importance, but its *Fortifications are among the most perfect in Greece. The walls enclosed a rectangle c. 600 yds by 200. The E. wall, partly of polygonal masonry, with four square towers in regular ashlar courses, is the best preserved. The tower at the s.E. angle, considered one of the best examples of Greek defensive architecture of the 4C B.C., rises 35 ft above the top of the wall. Joist-holes for wooden floors can be seen in the middle towers. Within the enceinte two little churches locate the remains of late-Byzantine monastic cells; lower down of a larger basilica with floor mosaics. Long Walls descend to the sea.—The Lacedaemonians retreated to Aigosthena after their defeat at Leuktra in 371 B.C.

32½ m. *Khání Káza* lies just within the entrance to the *Pass of Gyphtokástro* between Vordositi (3135 ft), the E. outlier of Kithairón, and the w. spur (3050 ft) of Mt Pástra. It is still argued whether this or the pass farther w. now crossed by a military road represents the ancient *Dryoskephalai*. At the entrance on the right of the road rises a steep and rocky knoll crowned by the *Fortress known as **Eleutherai**, though the identification is questionable (comp. above). Eleutherai, originally Boeotian, went over to Athens in the 6C B.C. The defences, in excellent masonry of the 4C B.C., are nearly entire on the N. side. Eight rectangular towers, 40–50 yds apart, are connected by walls about 12 ft high. Several of the towers cover sally-ports in the adjoining curtain. Each tower had a door giving on to the court and three small openings in the upper story.

In the fields opposite the Aigosthena fork (and well seen from the E. wall of Eleutherai) is the substructure of a temple dating from c. 300 B.C., perhaps that of Dionysos mentioned by Pausanias. Farther E. two early Christian basilicas have been located.

To the w. the heights of *Mt Kithairón* rise to 4625 ft. The mountain, where Oedipus was exposed and where Pentheus was torn to pieces by the Bacchantes, became the frontier between Attica and Boeotia when the Eleutherians cast in their lot with Athens. Its pine-woods are celebrated for their game. At (35½ m.) the summit of the pass, the great Boeotian plain lies at our feet, though Thebes is hidden by an intermediate hillock. In the middle distance the two Boeotian lakes are backed by Mt Ptoön, while farther w. rise the summits of Helikon and Parnassus, and on the N.E. horizon the pyramidal Dírfis in Euboea. The road curves down to (38 m.) *Kriekoúki*, officially *Erithraí* (EPYΘPAI), nowadays an enclave of Attica, with 3300 inhabitants.

At the far end of the town a road leads w. to (3 m.) *Plataiaí*, where just before the village, on both sides of the road, are the widespread ruins of ancient **Plataea**. There is a plan of the battle. The ruined enceinte showing some stretches of excellent 4C ashlar masonry and other, less well-preserved, pieces of polygonal work encompasses foundations of a small temple, and of the *Katagogion*, or hotel, erected for its visitors after the destruction of the town in 426 B.C., neither now visible.

Plataea, a small Boeotian town, near the border with Attica, early turned to Athens in an attempt to maintain its independence of Thebes. In 490 B.C. the Plataeans achieved fame by sending their entire army of 1000 men to support the Athenians at Marathon. During the invasion of Xerxes, they remained staunch to the Athenian cause and their city was destroyed by the Persians and Thebans. A period of peace when Plataea was guaranteed from attack followed the battle of 479 (see below). A Theban attempt in 431 to invest the rebuilt city was foiled, but in 427 after a two years' siege Plataea was razed to the ground by the Spartans and its people slain. Rebuilt after the Peace of Antalcidas (387), it was again destroyed in 373 by the Thebans. After the battle of Chaironeia, Philip, in fulfilment of his policy of humiliating Thebes, refounded the town, but its subsequent history demonstrable archaeologically into Byzantine times is of no importance.

The *Battle of Plataea* is described in detail by Herodotus (IX, 19). In 479, after sacking Athens, Mardonius retired by way of Tanagra to Boeotia, where the terrain was better suited to his cavalry. He encamped before the Asopos near Plataea, facing the foothills of Kithairon over whose passes armies from Attica or the Peloponnese must come. The forces of the Greek league, commanded by the Spartan Pausanias, with Aristides' Athenians on the left wing, took up their first position along the foothills. They were outnumbered three to one and lacked a cavalry arm. For three weeks the opposing generals manoeuvred for favourable positions. The Greeks suffered constant harrying by the Persian cavalry, though a picked force of 300 Athenians succeeded in killing Masistius, the Persian cavalry commander. A Greek attempt to outflank the enemy and cut them off from Thebes miscarried; in the subsequent retreat the Greek forces became split into three. Mardonius attacked the Spartans, whose fighting qualities proved superior, and the Persian general was slain. The Athenians fought a pitched battle with the Boeotians, annihilating the Theban Sacred Band. When the Persian camp was stormed, no quarter was given. The battle clinched the defeat of the Persian campaign, and though its outcome was decided more by the quality of the men than the tactics of their generals, the three weeks' campaign was a notable achievement of Greek unity in the spirit of the oath taken by the League. In honour of the dead the member states instituted a pan-Hellenic festival to Zeus Eleutherios (the Liberator), which survived many centuries.

We cross the tiny Asopos and enter the nome of Boeotia.—46 m. (74 km.) *Thebes*.

THEBES (ΘHBAI; *Dionyssion Melathron*, 7 Ioannis Metaxa, **B**; *Niobe*, 63 Epaminondou, C; Restaurants 'To Tsaki' near the Rly Stn, 'Dhirke' E. side of Epaminondou), in modern parlance *Thívai*, a town (16,000 inhab.) with an extreme climate, has twice been rebuilt after destructive earthquakes in 1853 and 1893. The modern centre is confined to the brow of the ancient acropolis, or *Kadmeia*, a plateau ½ m. long and ¼ m. wide, situated 200 ft above the surrounding plain. The Kadmeia is bounded on either side by rocky gullies, too often filled with rubbish; in recent years haphazard building has spilled into these, further obliterating the scanty pointers to the ancient topography. Beyond, sprawling suburbs occupy part of the area once included in the classical city, which had a circuit of 4–5 miles.

As the birthplace or home of Dionysos, Herakles, Tiresias, and the Labdacidae in the legendary period, and of Pindar, Epaminondas, and Pelopidas in historical times, the 'seven-gated city' is inextricably bound up with Greek myth, literature, and history. The city of Kadmos claimed the invention of the Greek alphabet. The historical city strove to be mistress of Boeotia and, for a very short period in the 4C B.C. led the whole of Greece.

With the exception of the Palace excavations and the contents of the fine museum, there are hardly any visible remains sufficiently important to excite the interest or awaken the enthusiasm of the visitor. Classical scholars may derive satisfaction from topographical detection of the sites of the monuments, streams and fountains that figured so vividly in Greek tragedy and in Greek history.

History. *Thebes* is called Ogygian by many classical poets from the tradition that the land was first inhabited by the Ectenians, whose king was Ogygos. The traditional foundation of the city by Kadmos (or Cadmus; trad. date 1313 B.C.) and the sowing of the dragon's teeth begin a saga of tragedy and bloodshed paralleled at Mycenae. Among the Labidacidae, descendants of Kadmos, was Laios who married Jocasta. Thus Thebes was the scene of the tragic destiny of Oedipus, who slew his own father and became by Jocasta the father of Eteocles, Polyneices, Antigone, and Ismene. Rivalry between Eteocles and Polyneices brought about the intervention of the Argives under Adrastos (father-in-law of Polyneices) and the disastrous war of the Seven against Thebes (trad. date 1213 B.C.). In the reign of Laodamos, son of Eteocles, the Epigonoi (sons of the Seven) took Thebes and razed it to the ground (trad. date 1198 B.C.).

From the earliest times Thebes is represented as a flourishing city, with seven gates. Sixty years after the fall of Troy Thebes is said to have defeated Orchomenos and to have become the capital of a loose federation, later known as the BOEOTIAN LEAGUE. This federation of the greater cities of Boeotia was governed (in the 5C B.C., at any rate) by eleven magistrates called *Boeotarchs*, Thebes supplying two, whereas the other members were allowed only one each. Thebes was a member of the Amphictyonic League.

An inveterate opponent of Athens, Thebes was naturally inclined to favour Athenian enemies. She medised in the Persian Wars. The Spartans are said to have forced some Thebans to help them at Thermopylae, but they deserted at the first opportunity. The fortified city of Thebes was the base of Mardonius before the battle of Plataea (479 B.C.) and his Theban allies shared in his defeat. Shortly before the battle of Tanagra in 457 the Lacedaemonians marched into Boeotia and re-established Thebes at the head of the Boeotian League. At the beginning of the Peloponnesian War Thebes attacked Plataea (431); as an ally of Sparta she helped to bring about the downfall of Athens. In 394, however, she joined a confederacy against Sparta. The seizure of the Kadmeia by the Lacedaemonian Phoebidas in 382 in defiance of the Peace of Antalcidas and its recovery in 379 by the Theban exiles under Pelopidas precipitated war. The battle of Leuktra (371), won by the genius of Epaminondas and the devotion of the Sacred Band, gave Thebes for a brief period of nine years the hegemony in Greece. By restoring Messenia, helping to found Megalopolis, and organizing the Arcadian League, Epaminondas completed the humiliation of Sparta. After his untimely death at Mantinea in 362 the Theban supremacy, which depended entirely on himself, disappeared, and the subsequent history of Thebes is a record of disasters.

Joining her traditional enemy Athens against Philip at the instigation of Demosthenes, Thebes shared in the defeat of Chaironeia in 338, and a revolt shortly after Philip's death was ruthlessly suppressed by Alexander the Great in 336. The city was completely destroyed, with the exception of the temples and Pindar's house; 6000 inhabitants were killed and 30,000 enslaved. In 316 Cassander rebuilt Thebes, but in 290 it was taken by Demetrios Poliorketes. The Thebans sided with Mithridates in his war with Rome, but eventually went over to Sulla. In spite of this the city was finally dismembered in 86 by Sulla, who gave half its territory to the Delphians, by way of compensation for plundering the oracle.

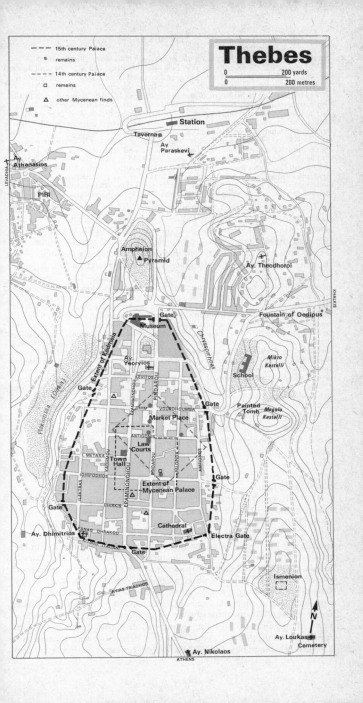

Thebes

	15th century Palace
	remains
	14th century Palace
	remains
△	other Mycenean finds

0   200 yards
0   200 metres

Station

Taverna
Ay. Paraskevi

Ay. Athanasios

LEVADHIA

PIRI

Amphelon
Pyramid

Ay. Theodhoroi

KHALKIS

Fountain of Oedipus

Gate
Museum

Extent of Kadhela

Ay. Yeoryios

KEVITOS

PINDAROU

Chryssorrhoas

Mikro Kastelli

School

Gate

EPAMINONDHOU

THIM

Gate

VOURDHOUMBA

Market Place

Painted Tomb

Megala Kastelli

Plakiotissa (LOPKIS)

ANTIGONIS

Law Courts

METAXA

KADHMOU

PINDAROU

PELOPIDA

AMPHION

Town Hall

EPAMINONDHOU

Gate

CHIPODHOS

Extent of Mycenean Palace

ILLEKTRAS

OHIRKIS

Gate

Cathedral

Ay. Dhimitrios

PANAG. DHRAKOU

Electra Gate

ILIADHI ITALIAN

Gate

AYIAS TRIADHOS

Ismenion

N

Ay. Nikolaos
ATHENS

Ay. Loukas
Cemetery

Strabo (IX) found Thebes hardly the size of a respectable village. In the time of Pausanias (IX, 7, 6) only the Kadmeia was inhabited. In A.D. 248 and again in 396 it was taken by the Goths, being spared (by Alaric) on the second occasion. Thebes enjoyed a second period of renown in the middle ages. From the 9C it was the seat of the Strategos of Byzantine Hellas. In 1040 it surrendered to the Bulgarians after fierce resistance. In 1146 it was sacked by the Normans of Sicily led by their great admiral, George of Antioch. The city was now famous for its silk manufactures, and it was from Thebes that King Roger introduced silk culture into Sicily, whence it reached Lucca a century later, and eventually spread to the rest of Europe. The silks of Thebes, which were worn by the Byzantine emperors, were ultimately supplanted by those of Sicily, and with the decline of the silk trade the prosperity of Thebes departed. In 1205 it was taken by Boniface III of Montferrat, who granted it to Otho de la Roche. Under his house Thebes was the capital of the Duchy of Athens. Half the city subsequently passed by marriage to the family of St-Omer. Under the Turks Thebes degenerated into a wretched village, overshadowed by Levadia, which was made the seat of the pasha.

The plateau is covered by a grid of parallel streets; the main thoroughfare comprises the s. half of Odhos Epaminondhas, a short section of Odhos Antigonis, at right angles, and the N. half of Odhos Pindharou. Beneath the modern streets lie two superposed Mycenean palaces, the extent and positions of which have been tentatively plotted. The **Kadmeion** proper, or *Palace of Kadmos*, was succeeded by a *New Palace*.

The site was identified and partly dug by Keramopoulos in 1906–21; spectacular finds have been made since 1963 by Greek archaeologists mainly during 'rescue digs' on building sites. The archaeological evidence, reappraised, shows that above many earlier levels, the Kadmeion is placed diagonally to the present grid, while the New Palace is set on the N.–S. alinement that the town has followed ever since. The central megaron, the *House of Kadmos* itself, has not yet been located, but may lie below the modern Plateia; annexes of both palaces, including comparable jewellers' workshops, have been explored. The Kadmeion was destroyed by fire about the beginning of L.H. IIIA2 (c. 1375–50); the New Palace, designed for a new orientation and with foundations down to bedrock, was begun immediately but destroyed in its turn at the end of L.H. IIIB1 (c. 1250–40). Linear B tablets found at 28 Pelopidhou were in the context of the earlier palace.— Classical masonry, which overlies parts of the two Mycenean palaces at the junction of Pindharou and Antigonis, and continues under those streets, is identified with the peribolos wall of the *Sanctuary of Demeter Thesmophoros* (which Pausanius placed with the House of Kadmos).

The principal excavations are located on the plan. Not much comprehensible is likely to be visible to the visitor, though the two orientations are obvious in Pindharou, where Keramopoulos' original excavations which produced the stirrup jars with linear B inscriptions are a little N. of a more recent dig where the cylinder seals (comp. below) were found.

The *Museum (adm. 25 dr.; standard hours), at the N. end of Pindhárou, stands within the enceinte of the Frankish castle of Nicholas II de St Omer, largely destroyed in 1311 by the Catalans, below its surviving 13C *Tower*. The pleasant garden and courtyard are strewn with inscriptions of varying dates, sculptural remains including fine Byzantine reliefs, Turkish tombstones, architectural fragments and late Roman mosaics (Seasons). There are five rooms. In the first are a few important inscriptions from different parts of Boeotia, including a stele of the Boeotarch Xenokrates, a colleague of Epaminondas at Leuktra, Nero's proclamatia at the Isthmian games in A.D. 67, and a list of dedications at the Heraion of Khorsiai illustrating an important stage in the development of the alphabet. In the second are displayed Archaic *Kouroi from the Ptoïon; Archaic and 5C funerary stelai from Akraiphnion and Thespiai; Daedalic bust (mid-7C B.C.) from Tanagra; marble torsos and reliefs; Geometric stone tripods from Plataea. Third room in cases, *Pottery, prehistoric from Eutresis and Littarés, Mycenean from Moustapháthos and Thebes (including stirrup jars painted with Linear B characters); 36 *Cylinder seals of lapis lazuli, 14 with cuneiform inscriptions, all from Anatolia, the greater number of them of the Kassite-Babylonian period of the 14C B.C., seemingly confirming the traditional connection of Thebes with Phoenicia; bronze plates and shoulder pieces from a Mycenean corselet; granulated jewellery; carved legs (of a throne or its canopy?), the largest pieces of worked ivory so far found in Greece; Linear B tablets; Archaic Classical and Hellenistic *Vases and *Terracottas found at the Rhitsóna cemetery (including rider and Priapic figure). Fourth room, sepulchral stelai painted and incised, representing Boeotian warriors killed at (?) Delion in 425 B.C. (note the shields adorned with representations of Pegasus, the Chimaera etc.); inscriptions and statues of priestesses from Aulis. Fifth room, Mycenaean painted *Larnakes and other finds (pottery, terracottas, bronzes, etc.) from a large cemetery near Tanagra.

On Kastelli hill, just outside the E. gate, a large frescoed chamber-tomb, approached by two long parallel dromoi, was discovered in 1971.

Other surviving vestiges of ancient Thebes may be sought in clockwise direction beginning from the museum. The Levadhia road descends below the museum through the site of the *Borean Gate*. On the left is a pleasant park on the hillock of the *Ampheion* where recent excavations have revealed a large grave mound of Early Helladic date. We turn right and cross the bed of the Strophia or 'Hollow Road', N. of which extended the *Agora* and, out towards the Railway Station, the *Theatre*. Following the Khalkis road away from the *Proetidian Gate* (where vestiges of the polygonal Kadmeion wall, found in 1915, are partly visible by the road side), we cross the bed of the Ayios Ioannis (anc. *Ismenos*?) by a bridge. On the right of this bridge once gushed the spring of Ayios Theodoros, the ancient *Fountain of Oedipus*, where Oedipus washed off his father's blood (small pleasant park). Following the course of the supposed Ismenos to the S., we pass on our right the wooded hill of *Kastellia* partly occupied by an old People's Home and the Grammar School. Chamber tomb, see above; Christian catacombs are also in evidence. We soon reach to our right the Ismenian Hill, sacred to Apollo, where in 1910 was discovered the *Ismenion* (4C B.C.), the temple where was celebrated the festival of the Daphnophories (laurel-bearers). The foundations are best preserved on the W. There are Mycenean tombs underneath. At the side of the hill in the cemetery chapel of St Luke are fragments of a large marble sarcophagus (3C A.D.), locally venerated as that of the Evangelist, though its three inscriptions refer to the family of a Roman official called Zosimus. The old Athens road returns towards the Kadmeia by the line of the 'Hollow Road' and ends at the *Electra Gate*, the circular foundations of whose two flanking towers in ashlar masonry may be seen on either side of Odhos Amphion. Near the gate was the extensive Sanctuary of Herakles, now probably occupied by the church of *Ayios Nikolaos* (Byzantine lintel in the interior). Crossing the main Athens road, we reach the medieval *Aqueduct* (Kamares) which brought water from the sources on Mt Kithairon to the Kadmeia. The Athens road enters the town through the probable site of the *Onka Gate*. To the N.W. of the centre is a *Necropolis* of the 8C B.C. The stream that flows along the W. foot of the Kadmeia is the *Dirce*.

Excursions from Thebes

To LEUKTRA, 11 m. (18 km.). We take the Athens road and after a mile turn right.—7½ m. *Melissokhórion* (Báltsia).—11 m. *Parapoúngia*, officially Lévktra, is a group of three hamlets on a hill. At *Leuktra* in 371 B.C. the Boeotians under Epaminondas defeated a larger force of Spartans in battle. This was the final blow to the legend of Spartan invincibility and for a short time gave Thebes the hegemony over all Greece. Visible up a valley to the right as we approach Leuktra and signposted at the track is the *Tropaion* (locally 'Marmara'), a monumental trophy erected by the Thebans after the victory and now restored. A circular plinth of triglyphs has a dome-shaped roof of nine stone shields sculptured in relief; it probably supported a warrior figure in bronze.— A dirt road (passable by car in summer) goes on from the village down the right bank of the *Livadóstra* to its mouth on the Gulf of Corinth. Here are some ashlar walls of *Kreusis*, the port of Thespiai, which was occupied by the Spartan Kleombrotos before the battle of Leuktra, and probably saw his retreating embarkation for Aigosthena.

Just under 2 m. N.E. of Leuktra are the foundations of massive walls in polygonal masonry, forming an enclosure 550 yds. square, doubtless the Homeric *Eutresis*. About 300 yds S.E. at the foot of the ridge is the *Arkopódi Fountain*, at the junction of the ancient ways from Thebes to Thisbe and Thespiai to Plataiai. To the E. of the fountain the American School excavated in 1924–27 a series of Early Helladic, Middle Helladic, and Mycenean *Houses*. In 1958 they found traces of Neolithic occupation, including steatopygous clay figurines.

To THESPIAI AND THISBE, 23 m. (37 km.), asphalted. We take the Levadhia road, and after 3 m. diverge left (signposted 'Paralia Beatch') up the cultivated Kanavári valley.—10½ m. The twin villages of *Leondári* and *Thespiaí* (Erimókastro) rise to the right. Below, near the road, are scanty vestiges of ancient **Thespiaí**, excavated by the French School in 1888–91, when they demolished what was left of the walls to recover more than 350 inscriptions. The Thespians honoured Love above all the gods, and here the courtesan Phryne made her home. Her famous marble statue of Love by Praxiteles was still at Thespiaí in the time of Cicero. It was carried off to Rome by Caligula and then (after having been restored to Thespiaí by Claudius) by Nero.

12½ m. Fork. Ahead the shorter road (unpaved) avoids the villages but it is better to bear left through *Ellopía* and (16½ m.) *Xironomí*.

On a disused road running S. from Xironomi to Aliki (comp. below) over the W. shoulder of Mavrovouni are a fine watch-tower and foundations of two fortresses, one a large enclosure dating to the Spartan invasions of Boeotia in the early 4C B.C., and the other small of late Roman date.

22½ m. *Dhómvrena* (officially Koríni), was resettled here after a reprisal destruction in the Second World War. Immediately S. of Kakósi (modern *Thísvi*), its twin village to the N.W., on a low plateau stand the extensive remains of ancient **Thisbe** (ΘΙΣΒΗ), still, as Homer says, "the haunt of doves". A fine length of wall with seven towers of good Classical masonry defends the S. slope. On a hill to the N.W. of modern Thísvi are early polygonal walls.

A rough road leads S.W. from Dhómvrena, crossing the plain by the ancient dyke dividing it into two halves for alternate annual drainage and irrigation. It passes cliffs and an isolated shore to (4 m.) *Áyios Ioánnis* on the Bay of Dhómvrena. A difficult path round the bay leads E. to *Aliki*, dominated by Mt Korombili, on which stand the 4C fortifications of an acropolis identified with the *Siphai* of Thucydides and *Tipha* of Pausanias; other ancient remains are by the shore.

The asphalt road continues beyond Thisvi to (4 m.) *Khóstia* (or *Pródromos*), then descends through rocky outcrops and olive groves to *Paralía*, a hamlet on the Bay of Saranda. A hill site with 4C B.C. walls on the left of the road, 2½ m. from Khóstia, may be *Korsiai*.

To THE VALLEY OF THE MUSES AND MT HELIKON. To Thespiai, see above. We quit the Dhómvrena road and take a poor road W. to (15 m.) *Palaiopanayía*, the farthest point attainable by motor. Here it is advisable to take a guide. On foot or mule-back we rise gently to the N.W. and come in ½ hr to *Palaiopirgos*, a medieval tower possibly on the site of *Keressos*. We cross the stream of Episkopi and see on our right a hill still crowned by the ancient Hellenic tower (Pirgaki) which Pausanias recorded as all that survived of *Askra*. Here was the farm of Hesiod, who called it "a cursed town, bad in winter, unbearable in summer, pleasant at no time".—1¼ hr. We cross the Permessos and reach the **Valley of the Muses.** Here on the site of the chapel of Ayia Triádha (now removed) are the remains taken in 1888–89 to be a temple of the Muses, but reappraised in 1954 as a monumental altar. A little higher up is the *Theatre* (late 3C B.C.) in which were held the contests of the Mouseia. The cavea may be clearly distinguished.

The whole of the upper valley of the Permessos, with its groves and springs, was dedicated to the Muses. Their sanctuary, or *Mouseion*, stood in a sacred grove. The district is now sadly disafforested and the scanty trees that survive scarcely enable the visitor to recapture the charm and mystery of this region; its religious significance appears, however, to have lasted well into the Christian era, for ruined chapels are seen on all sides.

The cult of the *Muses* came originally from Pieria at the foot of Mt Olympos. It was inhabited by Thracian shepherds who worshipped the godesses of the mountains and springs. They came south and founded Askra. In Boeotia Mt Helikon and the fountains of Aganippe and Hippocrene were sacred to the Muses, and in Phocis Parnassos and the Kastalian fountain. Libations of water, milk, and honey were the usual offerings.

The *Mouseia*, or Musean Games, were held every four years and comprised musical and poetic contests, to which were later added dramatic contests. The prize was a wreath of myrtle. In addition there were *Erotica*, or games in honour of Love, which included athletic sports as well as musical competitions. The sanctuary became a fount of poetic inspiration. It was adorned with statues of the Muses by Kephisodotos, Strongylion, and Olympiosthenes; of Dionysos by Lysippus and by Myron; and of the great lyric poets. The sanctuary was despoiled by Constantine the Great.

From the Valley of the Muses to Hippocrene takes about 5 hrs there and back. The route is comparatively easy and most of the distance can be ridden. The fountain is on Mt Zagora, an E. summit of **Mt Helikon**, which comprises a whole range extending W. to the Bay of Aspra Spitia. Its highest point is separated from Mt Zagora by the Pass of Koukoura, and called *Palaiovouni* (5740 ft). From Ayia Triádha we make for a side valley which opens at the foot of the Marandali, an eastern outlier of Zagora. We cross a stream; on the right bank near the chapel of Ayios Nikolaos (1560 ft) and a ruined monastery is a grove with a scanty spring. This may be the *Aganippe Fountain*. After a climb of 2½ hrs we reach a glade (4461 ft) near the top of the N. slope. Here, concealed near the w. angle under rocks and arbutus trees, is seen the mouth of an ancient well, now known as *Krio Pigádhi* ('Cold Water'). This was the HIPPOCRENE ('Fountain of the Horse') which, so tradition tells us, gushed forth from the spot where Pegasus struck his hoofs when he landed from the skies. Here we are ½ hr below the summit of Mt Zagora (5020 ft). From Krio Pigádhi we may descend by the N. slope of the mountain (on foot) direct to Ayia Triádha in 45 minutes.

To *Akraifnion* and the *Ptoion*, to *Khalkis* and *Aulis*, to *Anthedon*, and to *Larimna*, see Rte 44B.

42 EUBOEA

EUBOEA (EYBOIA), in modern Greek *Évvia*, next to Crete the largest Greek island, extends N.W. to S.E. for nearly 100 m. almost parallel to the mainland of Greece (Locris, Boeotia, Attica), from which it is separated by a strait virtually landlocked at either end. Midway along the w. coast the strait contracts to a narrow channel called the Euripos. Here from the 5C B.C. a succession of bridges has joined Euboea to Boeotia. The E. coast is virtually inaccessible by reason of its abrupt and hostile cliffs; it has one port, at Kimi. The other ports are nearly all on the gentler w. coast, chief of these being Khalkis on the Euripos and Karystos, near the S. tip of the island. In antiquity the two principal cities were on the w. coast: Chalkis, looking towards Boeotia, survives as the modern capital; Eretria, though still the ferry terminal from Attica, is a seaside village with no continuous past.

The centre of Euboea is largely occupied by an irregular mountain range, geographically the s.e. continuation of Ossa and Pelion, and broken by valleys. The highest point is Mt Dírfis (5725 ft). In the n. half the mountains are clothed with forests of chestnuts, pines and planes. In the exuberantly fertile plains are grown corn in large quantities, as well as vines, figs, and olives. The most famous of these is the Lelantine Plain between Khalkis and Eretria. The mineral wealth is considerable, lignite and magnesite being exported. The marble and asbestos of Karystos were renowned in antiquity; here was the source of the cipollino extensively used for building in Rome in the Imperial era and later.

Euboea is one of the most delightful regions in Greece. Until recently indifferent roads and the paucity of excavated remains have deterred foreign visitors from its shores, but its equable climate, the wonderful vegetation and the enchanting views, as well as the comparatively undeveloped coastline, are attracting increasing numbers of Athenian motorists, especially at weekends.

History. Euboea was peopled in remote antiquity by colonists from Thessaly who settled in the n. (Ellopians), in the w. (Abantes) and in the s. (Dryopes). According to tradition the early settlers were joined by Ionians from Attica, Aeolians from Phthiotis, and Dorians from the Peloponnesus. The island, also called *Makris* because of its length, was divided between seven independent city-states, of which the most important were Eretria and Chalkis, rivals for the possession of the fertile Lelantine Plain. These two rich and powerful merchant cities founded colonies on the coasts of Thrace, Italy and Sicily, as well as in the islands of the Aegean. After the expulsion of the Peisistratids Chalkis joined Boeotia against Athens. In consequence, in 506 B.C., the Athenians crossed the strait, defeated the Chalcidians and divided their land between 5000 cleruchs. Eretria had assisted in the Ionic revolt against Persia some ten years before the first great Persian invasion of Greece. The Persians, in retaliation, took the city by storm in 490, burned it, and enslaved the inhabitants. Although later rebuilt, Eretria never fully recovered her former power. After the Persian wars the whole of Euboea became subject to Athens. In 446 Euboea revolted, but was reconquered by Pericles. In 411 a second revolt, inspired by the defeat of the Athenian fleet at the hands of the Lacedaemonians, and coming at a time when Athens was weakened by the Sicilian disasters and internal faction, was more successful. The same year the inhabitants of Chalkis, with the cooperation of Boeotia, built a bridge over the Euripos and thereby hampered the maritime trade of Athens (see below). In 378 the Athenians induced most of the Euboean cities to join their new maritime league; but, after the battle of Leuktra (371), the island passed under the suzerainty of Thebes. In 358 it was liberated by Chares, who restored it to the protection of Athens. It was incorporated in Macedonia after the battle of Chaironeia (338). In 194 it was taken from Philip V of Macedon by the Romans, who restored its cities to nominal independence. The island later came under the sway of Byzantium.

In A.D. 1209 Euboea was divided into the three baronies of Chalkis, Karystos and Oreos, which owed allegiance to the king of Salonika. The Venetians held the ports and numerous minor Frankish nobles occupied the interior, which they adorned with their castles. By 1366 the Venetians were masters of almost the whole of Euboea. It was they who gave to the island the name of *Negroponte* ('Black Bridge'), which apparently referred to the bridge over the Euripos (see below). The name is a twofold corruption of Euripos. This had already been corrupted to *Egripo*, and Egripo was turned by the Venetians into Negroponte. Under the Venetians Negroponte ranked as a kingdom, and its standard was one of the three hoisted in St Mark's Square. After the expulsion of the Venetians from Constantinople by the Genoese, Negroponte became the centre of their influence in Romania. In 1470 the island was conquered by the Turks and came under the immediate government of the Capitan Pasha, high admiral of the Ottoman Empire. In 1830, after the War of Independence, Euboea passed to Greece. By special decree, a certain number of Moslems were permitted to remain in the island.

A Khalkis and Northern Euboea

Approaches from Athens. To *Khalkis*, BY ROAD, 50½ m. (81 km.), bus every half-hour in 1½ hr, comp. Rte 44. BY RAILWAY, 51 m. (83 km.), 19 times daily in c. 1½ hr.
—*Loutra Aidipsou* is most easily reached by ferry viâ *Arkitsa* (Rte 44); buses 3 times daily.

KHALKIS (ΧΑΛΚΙΣ; *Lucy* A; *John's, Hilda, Palirria*, all B; *Khara, Manica*, both C; *Rest. Samara*, near the Lucy), attractively situated on the Euripos at its narrowest, is the capital (36,300 inhab.) of the nome of Euboea and the seat of an archbishop. The town carries on an important trade in butter, livestock, and agricultural implements. Its industries include distilleries. It is the centre of bus communications of the island.

Ancient *Chalkis*, of which few vestiges remain, was famous for its manufactures in bronze, exporting arms, vases, and votive tripods; it was the mother-city of many early colonies. The archaic site lay E. of the present town, harbouring on the bay of Áyios Stéfanos, with an acropolis farther E. on the lower height of *Vathrovouniá*. Here polygonal walling probably dates from 377 B.C. In the 4C the city spread over the low hill on which the modern city stands; this may be the classical *Kanethos*.

History. According to the ancients the name of Chalkis (from *chalkos*, bronze) reflected the importance of its chief industry, though modern scholarship has suggested an alternative derivation from *chalke*, the limpet shell yielding purple dye (murex). The site of the Mycenean city of the great-hearted Abantes (Il. II, 540) remains unknown, but the present site was occupied in late-Geometric times. The situation of the city, with two harbours on the Euripos, outlet of a rich island, made for its early development into a commercial and colonizing centre. It was on the trade route between Thessaly (horses and corn), Thrace and Macedonia (gold of Thasos, timber, corn) and Attica and central Greece. In the 8C B.C. Chalkis colonized the Northern Sporades and so many cities (32 in all) in the Macedonian peninsula between the Thermaic and Strymonic gulfs that the whole peninsula was called *Chalkidike*. Later its settlers established themselves in Sicily: Naxos, Messana (now Messina); and in Italy: Rhegion (Reggio) and Cumae.

Chalkis fought many wars with Eretria for possession of the Lelantine Plain, and in the 7C emerged victorious. Its last king Amphidamos, a contemporary of Hesiod, was killed in one of these wars, and the government passed to the aristocracy, who were themselves overthrown when the Athenians overwhelmed the Chalcidians in 506 B.C. Chalkis sent 20 ships in 480 to the Greek fleet and its soldiers took part in the battle of Plataea. Its subsequent history is largely that of Euboea. In 1210 it was seized by the Venetians, who fortified it with walls and made it the capital of the kingdom of Negroponte. When the Turks acquired Euboea in 1470, Chalkis became the headquarters of the Capitan Pasha. Morosini attacked it in 1688 but had to call off his siege after 4000 of his troops and Königsmark, their commander, had died of malaria.

The mainland approach to the Euripos is guarded by **Karababa,** a Turkish fortress of 1686; scanty rock-cuttings suggest an ancient fortress on this site, supposedly a Macedonian fort built c. 334 B.C. The walls afford a wonderful *View of the strait and of the whole town. In the mainland suburb below are (left) the town beach and (right) the *Railway Station* and an information office. The unusual *Bridge* (toll per car crossing to Khalkis) that carries the road over the Euripos opens by a double action: the carriageway descends just sufficiently to allow each half-span to roll on rails under its own approaches.

The **Euripos** is notorious for its alternating currents, which change direction 6 or 7 times a day and on occasion as often as 14 times in 24 hours. The current flows from N. to S. for about 3 hours at a rate which may exceed 6 knots. It then suddenly subsides; then, after a few minutes of quiescence, it begins to flow in the opposite direction. The passage of the channel with the current is dangerous and the bridge is opened only when the direction is favourable. A red ball indicates a N.-S. current; a white ball a S.-N. current. The phenomenon is alluded to by Aeschylus (Agam. 190), as well as by Livy, Cicero, Pliny and Strabo. The cause is complex and still not fully understood. According to a popular tradition, Aristotle, in despair at his failure to solve the problem, flung himself into the Euripos.

The Euripos was first spanned in 411 B.C. In 334 the Chalcidians included the Boeotian fort of Kanethos within the city boundaries. Under Justinian the fixed wooden bridge was replaced by a movable structure. The Turks replaced this with another fixed wooden bridge. In 1856 a wooden swing bridge was erected; in 1896 a Belgian company enlarged the channel, demolished the Venetian fort that had guarded the approach, and built an iron swing bridge. This gave place in 1962 to the existing structure.

The bridge leads to the older part of the town ('Kastro'), S. of Leoforos Venizelou. Here is a *Mosque*, with ancient columns and a truncated polygonal minaret, used as a store (no adm.) for medieval antiquities. In front is a handsome marble *Fountain*. A turning from the square leads to the church of **Ayia Paraskevi**, a basilica with pointed arches, above which runs a second row of large arches, incomplete and without a gallery. The columns are chiefly of cipollino and Hymettian marble, and the capitals are much varied. It was converted by the Crusaders in the 14C into a Gothic cathedral. Note the fine carved boss in the S. choir aisle vault. Near the old Venetian *Governor's Palace*, now a prison, is the arcaded *Turkish Aqueduct*, which supplied Khalkis with water from two springs on Mt Dírfis, 15 m. away.

From the broad ESPLANADE, Leoforos Venizelou leads past the Law Courts to the **Archaeological Museum** (adm. 25 dr.), which contains Mycenean pottery from local tombs and marble sculpture from Chalkis, Eretria, and Karystos. *4. Theseus carrying off Antiope, a fine Archaic group from the pediment of the temple of Apollo Daphnephoros at Eretria; 5. Archaic headless statue of Athena; 3. Male torso; 7. Youth killing a sacrificial animal; 6. Relief of Dionysos with the kantharos; 30. Antinous as Bacchus; 33. Seated woman (4C); three horses from a pedimental quadriga.

AN EXCURSION may be made (viâ Nea Artaki, see below) to (20½ m.) **Steni** (*Steni, Dirfys,* C), the pleasant village below the cone of **Mt Dírfis** that provides the best starting-point for climbing the highest mountain in Euboea (5725 ft). The ancient name *Dirphys* gave the goddess Hera her name 'Dirphya'. Many species of plant are purely local.

THE ASCENT has been simplified by a new road. We continue beyond the village. In ½ m., beyond springs and a large car park, the asphalt ends. An earth road now climbs in zigzags but may be driven in dry weather to a fork just above the tree-line, where a branch (l.) leads in ½ m. to the *Fountain of Liri Refuge* (36 beds; keys from Alpine Club, Khalkis); or it may be quitted ¾ m. before the fork, where a signed path, with painted marks, leads l. to the refuge. A few yards before this path a good, but not motorable, track bears left to a col between the refuge and the summit-ridge, and on the track from the Refuge to the summit (c. 1½ hrs), which is clearly marked in red all the way. The *View is magnificent.

FROM KHALKIS TO LOUTRÁ AIDIPSOU, 94½ m. (153 km.), asphalt. The road runs N., skirting the shore.—5 m. *Artáki* (Motel Bel Air B, Telemachus C). To Steni Dírfios, see above.—From (9½ m.) *Psakhná* (ΨAXNA), a small town (4650 inhab.), can be visited *Kastri*, 1 hr N., a hill surmounted by a Venetian castle. At *Triádha* (4 m. E.) are the house in which was born Nikolaos Kriezoti, the local hero of 1821, and some excavated remains of an early-Christian basilica.—We climb the outlying E. spur of *Kandílion* (4010 ft), the ancient *Makistos*, a long range that now cuts us off from the Euboic Gulf; fine retrospective view to Khalkis and the Euripos.

From the summit (nearly 2000 ft; café), the road descends in bold curves through the *Kleisoura*, a succession of wooded ravines amid scenery of the greatest beauty; there is a magnificent *View across the forests to the islands of Skopelos and Skiathos. We enter a grand defile, in which is the church of Ayios Yeoryios. This gradually opens into a beautiful wide valley, where plane-trees shade a limpid stream.

32 m. *Prokópion* (Inn), renamed after 1923 by refugees from Pro-kopion (Urgüp) in Turkey, has a chapel enshrining the relics of St John the Russian, a Tsarist soldier who died in 1730 as a Turkish slave at Urgüp. He was canonized by the Russian church in 1962 (pilgrimage, 27 May). The place is better known by its former name of **Akhmetaga** for the estate of the Noel-Baker family and for their *North Euboean Founda-tion* which runs a health centre, a veterinary service, and a model farm. The by-road E. traverses fine wooded country to a disappointing shore.—35 m. *Mandoúdhi* (½ m. r. of the road) has magnesite quarries, a brick factory, and a little harbour at *Kimási* on the E. coast (2½ m.).—37 m. *Kirinthos*, where some ramparts of the 6C B.C. are taken for the site of Kerinthos.—At (41 m.) *Strofiliá* the road forks; the left branch crosses the hills to **Limni** (10½ m.; small hotels), a beautiful fishing village of 2400 inhab., served by coasting steamers of the Khalkis–Volos line. Its sands and pine-woods make it beloved of artists. An early Christian basilica came to light in 1960 but little to demonstrate the site of Classical *Aigai*. The hills above are quarried for magnesite. There is a good beach, backed by shady olives, 1½ m. N. on the Roviés road.

From Limni the *Moni Galataki*, to the S.E. beyond *Katoúnia*, may be reached by boat in 1 hr or by road (5½ m.).—*Roviés*, 8 m. N.W. of Limni, was anciently *Orobia*. Hence it is 40 min. walk to the Byzantine monastery of Geronda, with fine frescoes.

Beyond Strofiliá the right branch continues along the E. slopes of Mt Xiron.—After (46½ m.) *Ayía Ánna* we continue climbing, with a view back along the cliffs to the E. coast. We follow a pine-clad ridge (1350 ft), devastated by fire in 1979, to (53 m.) *Pappádhes*, then wind down high above a precipitous valley with views of Skopelos and Skiathos.—60 m. *Vasiliká*.—Just before (68 m.) *Agriovótanon* a signposted track leads in 1¼ m. to **Cape Artemision** and the ruins of a *Temple of Artemis Proseoa*, facing E. from its spur and excavated by the German Institute in 1883. In the straits below in July 480 B.C. took place the first encounter of the Greek fleet with the Persian fleet, based on Trikeri, the peninsula opposite. Neither side could claim the advantage. Near here in 1928 was found the famous bronze Poseidon, now in the National Museum. The countryside is dotted with beehives.

80 m. *Istiaía* (Hermes **D**), or Xerokhóri, with 4100 inhab. the chief town of an eparchy, is beautifully situated in an amphitheatre of hills overlooking the northern plain. This is the only habitat of storks in Euboea. A gravel road runs N.W. to the bathing beach of *Kamatádika* (3½ m.).—84 m. *Oreoi* (Corali **D**), with 1140 inhab., has a small har-bour with remains of an ancient mole. In the village square is a fine Hellenistic bull found in the sea in 1965. The *Kastro* is a Venetian fort

built on the foundations of a Hellenic enceinte, with marble fragments and interior columns, on the site of the maritime acropolis (see below). In the valley between the Kastro and the village are the foundations of a marble temple.

History. The Euboean city of *Histiaia* or *Hestiaia*, colonized by Ellopians of Thessaly, was called by Homer *polystaphylos* ('rich in vines'). It was conquered in 447–446 B.C. by Tolmides and Pericles. The Athenians, having expelled the inhabitants, founded a colony of 2000 cleruchs at *Oreos*, to the W. of the deserted city. After the Peloponnesian War Oreos was subdued by the Lacedaemonians and the cleruchs driven out. The Histiaeans were recalled to their former city, thenceforth known by either name (comp. Strabo X). From now on it was ruled by tyrants until the Macedonian invasion. In 207 it was surprised by Attalos II of Pergamon and the Romans; in 200 it was taken by the Roman fleet under Apustius.—According to Livy, Oreos had two citadels separated by a valley: hence the modern plural *Oreoi*. The maritime acropolis, which dominated the port, was attacked by the Romans; the inland acropolis, now *Oreos Apanos*, was simultaneously attacked by Attalos.

The road now crosses the wooded spurs of *Mt Teléthrion* (4435 ft).— 88 m. Approach road (r.) to the car ferry (6 times daily) from *Ayiokambos* to Glífa in Thessaly.—94½ m. **Loutrá Aidhipsoú** (ΛΟΥΤΡΑ ΑΙΔΗΨΟΥ; *Hermes* B, *Leto*, *Minos*, C, open all year; *Aigli*, *Avra*, A; *Herakleion*, *Kentrikon*, *Thermai Sulla*, all B, and many others, mostly May–Oct only) is a frequented spa well known to the ancients and patronized by Sulla. The sulphur-impregnated springs, with a temperature of 70–160°F., rise near the sea at Cape Therma (hydropathic) at the S. end of the town, in powerful little jets, exhaling steam and leaving alkaline deposits. The ancients believed that they were connected with Thermopylae (Rte 44B). The waters enjoy a high reputation for the cure of stiff joints, gout, rheumatism, sciatica and other related ailments. Near the spring of Ayii Anaryiroi are the ruins of Roman baths.

Car ferry to Arkitsa (Rte 44B; 7 times daily in 45 min.); buses to Athens in 3½ hrs. Caique daily in summer to Khalkis.

A road runs W. from Aidhipsos to Lichas (15 m.) on the W. point of the island, passing *Yialtra* and *Gregolimano* (Roi Soleil A).—A new road along the steep coast to the E. is in construction to Rovies (see above).

B From Khalkís to Kími and Káristos

ROAD to Kimi, 58 m. (93 km.), asphalt; bus. 14½ m. **Erétria**.—28½ m. *Alivéri*.— 33½ m. *Lépoura*, turning for **Káristos** (79 m. from Khalkis).— 58 m. **Kími**.

FROM ATHENS the shortest and quickest approach to *Erétria* is by the car-ferry (½ hr) from Skala Oropos (31 m. from Athens; Rte 20); through buses to Kími.— By public transport *Káristos* is perhaps best reached viâ Ráfina (Rte 21) by boat in 2 hrs.

The road threads the industrial outskirts of Khalkis. On the left rises Vathrovouniá (see above). We cross the LELANTINE PLAIN, the object in the 8–7C B.C. of deadly rivalry between Chalkis and Eretria. In the Hymn to Apollo it is noted as famous for its vineyards, and it is so still.— Beyond (4 m.) *Néa Lámpsakos*, turning (l.) to Mítikas and *Fílla* (4 m.). Between the villages is a hill with two medieval towers. Above Fílla, on the hill of Kastelli conspicuous even from the mainland, a medieval castle stands on an ancient enceinte. A cemetery of the 6C A.D. has been found.—6½ m. *Vasilikó* has a Frankish tower.

A by-road descends in 1¼ m. to *Lefkandi* (Lefkandi C; tavernas), a hamlet, with brickworks, by the sea. The flat headland ('Xeropolis') to the S., was explored in 1965–66 and 1969–70 by the British School and found to be a high occupation mound (no visible remains) with three associated cemeteries. The place seems to have barely survived beyond the Geometric period, but had been occupied from the Early, through the Middle, and Late Helladic periods, and yielded unusually comprehensive and suggestive layers of L.H. IIIc to Protogeometric from which light is being thrown upon the disappearance of Mycenean civilization. Lefkandi has been suggested as the site of *Old Eretria*, the city Homer linked with Chalkis in the Catalogue of Ships.

14½ m. **Erétria**, with 1760 inhab., was founded as *Néa Psará* in 1824 by refugees from the island of Psara. The new town overlies much of the ancient city, the ruins of which are the most considerable in Euboea. *Malakonta Beach*, to the w., has been developed as a holiday resort with large bungalow hotels.

History. *Eretria*, next to Chalkis the most important city in Euboea, was one of the chief maritime states of Greece and is included in the Homeric catalogue. Traces of Mycenean and Protogeometric occupation have been found on the acropolis, and more recently an early Geometric amphoriskos of the mid-9C has come to light. Eretria contributed five ships to the support of Miletus in the revolt from Persia (500 B.C.), a gesture which drew upon it the wrath of the Persians ten years later, when they razed the city to the ground and enslaved the inhabitants. Nevertheless Eretria made a partial recovery, sending contingents to Salamis in 480 and to Plataea in 479. In 377 it joined the Second Athenian Confederacy. In 198 it was plundered by the Romans. After destruction in 87 B.C. in the Mithridatic wars, the city was never in antiquity rebuilt.—A school of philosophy was founded at Eretria in 320 B.C. The ceramics of Eretria, including painted vases and sepulchral lekythoi, rank with the finest; many are exhibited in the National Museum in Athens.

The Swiss Archaeological Mission started a systematic exploration in 1964 and the N.W. quarter has been excavated, but much remains unpublished. On foot a full round of the visible ruins requires at least three hours, but the Museum and lower sites can be cursorily seen more quickly.

On the N.W. outskirts of the village the **Museum** (open standard hours; 25 dr.) contains vessels of bronze, and pottery from the temple of Apollo (sculpture at Khalkis); grave stelai; a loutrophoros supported by griffins; an early Ionic capital; and boustrophedon inscriptions.— Turning towards the acropolis we come first to a large area of recent excavation within the w. fortifications of the city. These comprised a broad moat and a wall. The *West Gate* had a barbican which extended across the moat on a corbelled arch. The masonry on a tightly interlocking trapezoidal system is impressive. Extensive remains of a 4C *Palace*, with a Hellenistic extension, cover an abandoned Heroon of the 7–6C. A well-preserved clay bath remains in situ. To the N.E. are foundations of a *Temple of Dionysos*.

Beyond rises the **Theatre**, excavated by the American School in 1890–95. It retains its seven lower rows of seats, much defaced; the upper tiers, which were exposed to view, have all been carried away, block by block, to build the modern village. A semicircular drainage channel 6 ft wide runs in front of the lowest row. From the orchestra steps descend through a square opening into an underground vaulted passage, leading to the hyposkenion; it was used for the sudden appearance and disappearance of a 'deus ex machina'. The lofty stage is raised on seven or eight courses of masonry. Under its centre is another vaulted passage, probably constituting the public entrance to the orchestra.

Farther E. at the foot of the acropolis is a *Gymnasium*, excavated in 1895 (fenced). Near its w. end was found an inscribed stele set up in honour of a gymnasiarch benefactor. Near the same spot is the pedestal of a statue bearing an inscription within a votive wreath to one who had encouraged boys in athletics. At the E. end is an extensive series of water conduits which supplied the bathing troughs.

On a hill 10 min. w. of the theatre a tumulus encloses a *Macedonian Tomb*. The Dromos, on the N., leads to a square vaulted chamber,

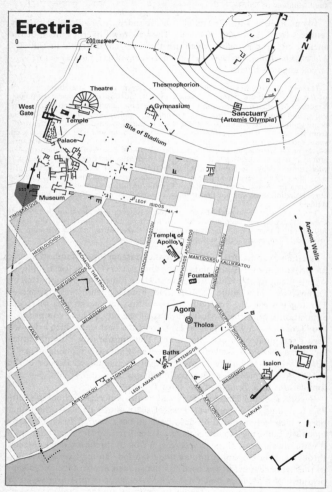

containing two funeral couches in marble, with their pillows and draperies, and two thrones and a table, all picked out in colours.

Above the theatre we climb in 20 min. to the **Acropolis,** with its ashlar walls and towers. It commands a fine *View to the s.w.; on the left and in front, part of Attica, with Pentelikon and Parnes; on the right, Kithairon, with Parnassos in the distance; immediately below, the Lelantine Plain.

On the descent are remains of a *Thesmophoreion* and a Sanctuary of a female deity, perhaps Artemis Olympia. Traversing the town we see bare foundations of the **Temple of Apollo Daphnephoros**, unearthed in 1900 by the Greeks and restudied by the Swiss in 1964, when remains of the Geometric period were found below it, together with potters' workshops near by. Superimposed are the stylobates of a Doric peripteral temple of 6 by 14 columns, having a cella in three equal parts, erected c. 530–520 B.C.; and an Ionic peripteral edifice of c. 670–650, which probably had 6 by 19 columns in wood.

To the E. are some remains of an *Isaion* excavated in 1915 by the Archaeological Society, and beyond them ruins of a *Palaestra*. Close to the sea a mosaic marks an ancient bath site.

19¼ m. *Amárinthos* (2800 inhab.; Blue Beach, 210 R, to the E., **B**; Amarynthos **C**, both closed in winter) has a sandy beach and (on a hill to the E.) two little Byzantine churches. The hills come nearly to the shore.—28½ m. **Alivéri** (Inn), with 4400 inhab., is situated on a hill, the site of ancient *Tamynai*, where the Athenians under Phokion defeated Kallias of Chalkis in 354 B.C. A mineral railway descends from an important lignite mine in the hills to *Káravos*, its little port. Here was probably the landing-place of an ancient ferry. On a knoll above the E. shore of the bay rises a square medieval fortress, with a door 20 ft above the ground; it is a good specimen of the structures common on this coast. At Alivéri taxis may be hired for the visit to Dystos.—32½ m. *Veloúsia* (officially *Vélos*). To the N.W. is a castle and to the s. a square tower.—At (33½ m.) *Lépoura* the road divides.

The visit to ancient **Dystos** is best made by taking the Káristos road through *Kriezá* (1¾ m.); after a further 3 m. (ignore signs to modern Distos) the site can be seen (¾ m. r.; accessible by farm track). The ruins stand on an isolated, overgrown, and snake-infested hill overlooking the E. shore of a marshy lake encircled by swallow-holes. The walls of the 5C city, of polygonal construction, 10 ft high and 6 ft thick, with 11 towers, describe a semicircle eastward from the w. cliff. The main entrance on the E., between two towers, leads to the Agora. On the slopes of the hill, especially on the N., are terraces with remains of *Houses*, almost the only examples surviving from the 5C B.C. They had an entrance passage, an inner court, a living room, two bedrooms, and possibly an upper story. On top of the hill, to the w., is the *Acropolis*, the N. part of which became a Venetian fortress (*View from the shattered tower).

To KARISTOS. From Lépoura the right branch continues S.E.—35¼ m. *Kriezá*.— Near the hamlet of (44 m.) *Zárakes* we pass ruined windmills and some foundations, possibly of *Zaretra*, a place captured by Phokion in 350 B.C.—Between (48 m.) *Almiropótamos* and *Polipótamos* a rocky ridge along the narrowest part of the island affords sea views on both sides. Just beyond the Mesokhória turn a Turkish stone road can be seen below (l.)—60½ m. *Stíra* has a pleasant little square. A Venetian castle crowns probably the acropolis of Homeric *Styra*. *Néa Stíra* (Actaeon, Delfini, open all year; Aegilion, Akti Afroditis, all C), 2½ m. s.w., is a seaside resort, connected by ferry with Rafina. The island of Stíra, offshore, lies almost opposite Rhamnous.—The road winds round the s. end of the *Kliosi Ridge*, on a low spur of which is a small terrace surmounted by three buildings of great antiquity called locally the *Dragon's Houses*. The landscape is reminiscent of Dartmoor with 'tors'.—73¼ m. Turning (r.), viâ Kakagióni, to *Marmári* (Marmari, Galaxy, C), another seaside resort with ancient cipollino quarries.

79 m. **Káristos** (ΚΑΡΥΣΤΟΣ; *Apollon Resort*, DPO, Apr–Sept, **B**; *Louloudhis, Als, Plaza, Karystion,* **C**), an attractive town of 3550 inhab., founded after the War of Independence near the site of ancient *Karystos*, is the seat of a bishop and of an eparch, and a pleasant summer resort on a broad bay facing s. From Attica it is more easily visited by steamer departing from Rafina. The ancient city was famous for its cipollino marble and for asbestos.

At the s.e. end of the esplanade a medieval tower incorporates ancient blocks. From it a road leads inland to *Míli* (2 m.), a hamlet (cafés) in a lush ravine. From the little plateia the left fork climbs to Graviá and by a fine stone bridge across a ravine to *Castel Rosso*, a Venetian fort so called from the reddish colour of its stone, probably the ancient acropolis of Karystos. In the ancient quarries are half-worked columns.

The ASCENT OF MT OKHI can be made from Míli in c. 3 hrs, by a path (difficult to follow) round the s. side to the Refuge (3281 ft) above a chestnut wood. Easier to find is a mule-path to a col (1 hr; goatherds' huts) below the w. summit; this can also be reached from *Melissón* (guide necessary) viâ the Gorge of Kallianou, through magnificent country. Thence the approach is up a ridge round the N. side. The summit consists of a line of tors, of which the w. (Profítis Ilias) is the highest (4610 ft). Below the tors farther E., on the s. side, is a primitive building similar to those at Stira, called the *House of the Dragon*. It may have been a watch-house of the 6C B.C.

About 5 hrs N.E. of Karystos is Kafirévs (Cabo Doro), the ancient *Kaphareus*, where Nauplios, father of Palamedes, is said to have lighted torches to mislead the Greeks on their return from Troy, in revenge for the murder of his son on a false charge of treachery.—About 4 hrs s.E. of Karystos, near the extreme s. point of Euboea, is the site of *Geraistos*, where triglyphs and an inscription have been found from the celebrated sanctuary of Poseidon. The coast facing E. between these two points is probably the 'Hollows' (τὰ κοῖλα) of Herodotus 8. 13, where in 480 a Persian squadron came to grief in a storm.

From Lépoura the Kími road runs N. in a wooded valley between Dhirfis and the hills of the E. coast.—39½ m. *Khania Bouzi*, by two little streams.—40½ m. *Avlonárion* (½ m. r.) stands on the road to *Okhthoniá* (1770 ft), a summer resort, which appears (r.; 4½ m.) massed on its hill, beneath a pretty church and a Frankish tower (2500 ft), built on Roman foundations. The road now enters the attractive valley of the Oxylithos, guarded on all sides by the picturesque Frankish towers so common in Euboea, and sown every mile or so with hamlets and chapels.—45½ m. *Monódri*. We climb with many bends to (47¾ m.) *Dirrévmata*.—49½ m. *Konístrais* has a long main street on a ridge amid rolling olive-clad hills. The road undulates and winds amid lush greenery and small hillside villages.—At (55 m.) *Kalimeriánoi* a new road descends directly to the shore, while the old road threads a pass.

58 m. **Kími** (ΚΥΜΗ; Inns), locally called Koumi, is a cheerful town (2770 inhab.), which owes its prosperity to its vineyards and orchards, and to the lignite mines to the w. It stands at 860 ft on a ridge overlooking the island of Skyros. It is celebrated for figs and honey and for its bold sailors: in 1821 it put to sea a fleet of 55 merchant ships, which earned it a bombardment from the Turks. *Paralía Kímis* (Aktaion **D**), its small port with a merchant navy school, lies 2½ m. away. Its harbour was repaired after 1945 by one Robert Nesbit, as a plaque records.

In the vineyards round Kimi are many graves of the 4–3C B.C. A passable road leads N.E. to the Monastery of the *Sotiros* (1643) which may occupy the site of ancient *Kyme Phyrkontis*. Another road runs N. from Kimi to springs and a café, whence a track climbs round the summit of *Mt Ortári* (2481 ft) to *Cape Kalámi* (splendid cliff scenery from either).

43 THE NORTHERN SPORADES

Grouped near the Thessalian coast are Skiathos, Skopelos, Alonissos, and numerous smaller islands; these together comprise the eparchy of Skopelos, part of the nome of Magnesia. Some way to the E. is Skyros, the largest of all; with its attendant islets, it forms part of the eparchy of Karistia in the nome of Euboea. The whole group is given the geographical designation of **Northern Sporades**, though the islands have very marked individual characteristics. The usual approaches to the islands are given below; these are only part of a complex net of services round the N. Aegean by four ships. Most inter-island journeys can be made most days, the least easy being from Skyros to Skopelos.

A Skyros

APPROACHES. FROM ATHENS by bus to Kími in Euboea (comp. Rte 42), thence by steamer; daily in c. 10 hrs, through booking from Athens.

SKYROS (ΣΚΥΡΟΣ; Skíros) is the most easterly as well as the largest of the Northern Sporades, with a length of c. 17 m. and an area of 79 sq. miles. It is divided into two nearly equal parts by a low-lying isthmus with a natural harbour sheltered by islets in Kolpos Kalamítsas on the s.w., and the exposed little haven of Akhili on the N.E. On the s. coast is another natural harbour, Trís Boúkes. The fertile N. half of the island contains the capital *Skyros* and rises in Mt Olympos to 1312 ft. The mountains of the rugged s. half culminate in Kokhílas (2565 ft) and are covered with forests of oaks, pines, and beeches. Here also are marble quarries, put into production again in 1961 after not having been worked for some years. The Skyrian variegated marble was famed in antiquity. Crayfish are caught in large quantities off the coast. Skyros abounds in water, which affords pasture to a few oxen and to numerous sheep and goats, descendants of the goats that were highly prized in Strabo's time. Wheat, oranges, lemons, honey and wine are among the exports.

Legend and History. Achilles, disguised as a girl, was sent by his mother Thetis to the court of Lykomedes, king of Skyros, to prevent his going to the Trojan War. Her precaution was in vain; for Ulysses lured him to Troy, where he was killed before it fell. Neoptolemos or Pyrrhos, son of Achilles, was brought up in Skyros and thence taken by Ulysses to the Trojan War (Sophocles, *Phil.* 239). It was in Skyros that Lykomedes treacherously killed Theseus, king of Athens, who had sought asylum with him.—In 476 B.C. Kimon conquered the island, enslaved the inhabitants, and planted Athenian settlers (Thucydides I, 98). Kimon discovered the bones of Theseus in the island; he had them taken to Athens and enshrined in the Theseion. In 322 B.C. the Macedonians took Skyros from the Athenians. In 196 the Romans forced Philip V of Macedon to restore the island to the Athenians.

Linariá (Inns), the landing-place, with good fishing, is on the w. coast. About 7 m. away (bus), on the N.E. coast, is the capital **Skyros** (*Xenia*, DPO, **B**, on the beach below to the N.; Rooms to let in the town), situated facing inland on a high terrace at the foot of a precipitous hill, on which is the ruined *Kastro*. The hilltop was the acropolis of the ancient city which Homer calls αἰπύς ('steep'). This may have been Plutarch's 'high cliff' from which Lykomedes pushed Theseus to his death. Remains of ancient walls may be traced in the foundations of the Venetian enceinte; over the gate is a lion of St Mark; within is a decaying convent (St George the Arab), founded in 962, once famous for its miracles. The town has steep narrow and winding streets, and is noted for its little white cubic houses with flat black roofs, furnished with low tables and elaborately carved chairs, ancient and modern embroidery and island pottery. A small *Museum* (9–11) in the Town Hall contains medieval church furniture. Overlooking the sea, on a conspicuous bastion, is an inappropriate *Memorial to Rupert Brooke* in the form of a bronze 'statue of an ideal poet' (1931), by M. Tombros.

The poet Rupert Brooke (1887–1915) was buried on the w. slope of Mt Kokhílas (or Konchylia), in an olive grove about a mile from the shore, during the night of 23 April 1915, having died of septicaemia the same afternoon in the French hospital ship Duguay Trouin. The expeditionary force, of which he was a member, sailed from Skyros at dawn for the Dardanelles. The visit to the grave, restored by the Royal Navy in 1961, is best made by motor-boat from Linariá to *Trís Boúkes*.

B   Skiathos and Skopelos

APPROACHES FROM ATHENS (apply Alkyon Agency, 98 Akadimias). Daily by coach to Ayios Konstandinos (Rte 44), whence by steamer to Skiathos, Glossa, Skopelos, and (twice weekly) Alonnisos.—FROM VOLOS: weekdays to Skiathos and Glossa, continuing most days to Skopelos and Alonnisos.—Occasional caiques also operate locally.

Skiathos has a direct air service from Athens in 45 min.

SKIATHOS (ΣΚΙΑΘΟΣ), nearest of the Northern Sporades to the Thessalian coast, resembles Mt Pelion in its beautiful scenery and thick forests. It is particularly famed for its excellent sandy beaches, with exclusive summer hotels. The island has an area of 30 sq. m. and a friendly population of 3900, all but a handful living in the one town; they are lively and many are occupied in fishing. The fertile but ill-cultivated land yields grape-vines, olives, fruit-trees, and cereals.

At Skiathos in 480 B.C. three Greek guardships of the Artemision fleet were surprised by a Sidonian squadron of Xerxes' fleet (providing Herodotus with one of his most realistic details); Pytheas of Aegina, wounded and captured, was spared for his valour and later rescued at Salamis. Skiathos became a subject-ally of Athens. It was devastated by Philip V of Macedon in 220 B.C. The island was the home of the novelists Alexander Papadiamandis (1851–1911) and Alexander Moraitidis (1851–1929).

Skiathos (*Koukounaries*, *Akti*, C; *Rest. Volos*, on the quay), the only town, lies in a declivity on the S.E. coast, with densely wooded hills rising behind it. This is the site of the ancient city but was deserted in the middle ages (comp. below). The picturesque pine-clad islet of *Bourtzi* (Tourist Pavilion), adorned below the Gymnasion with ancient cannon, is reached by causeway and affords a fine view of the harbour. In the upper town is the *Cathedral* of the Trion Ierakhon.

A road runs s.w. along the shore, passing above (1¾ m.) the pleasant beaches of *Akhladias* (Esperides, Apr–Oct, DPO, A), then crosses the peninsula of *Kalamaki*, a large headland with the Nostos villa hotel. Beyond are the two superb bays (also served by motor-boats in summer) of (4½ m.) *Platania* and (6½ m.) **Koukounaries* (Skiathos Palace L; Xenia B, both Apr–Oct; Neraïda Taverna), said with some justification to have the finest beach in Greece.

In 1538–1829 the inhabitants removed to an almost inaccessible position on the most northerly tip of the island. The *Kastro*, as their deserted town is called, is 3 hrs distant from Skiathos Town. It is built on a rocky peninsula formerly connected to the rest of the island by a drawbridge. Of its ruinous buildings, the *Church of Christ* is the best preserved, with a wooden screen of 1695 and some of its frescoes more or less intact. Once of great importance but now inhabited by only one or two monks, are the *Convent of the Annunciation*, with a fine Byzantine church containing frescoes and a library of MSS, and the *Convent of St Charalambos*, to which the novelist Alexander Moraitidis retired shortly before his death.

SKOPELOS (ΣΚΟΠΕΛΟΣ), the ancient *Peparethos*, separated from Skiathos by the Skopelos Channel, grows grape-vines, olives, almonds, pears, and other fruit. A well-watered island of 47 sq. m., it is more intensively cultivated than Skiathos. Its 4500 inhabitants are more scattered, less seafaring, and more conservative. Local costume may be seen on feast days and pottery is made.

Ancient Peparethos had become *Skopelos* by Ptolemaic times. In the Byzantine era it was used as a place of exile. In Frankish times it was taken by the Brothers Ghizi and attached to the duchy of Naxos. In 1538 Barbarossa slaughtered the entire population.

The capital, **Khora Skopelou** (2500 inhab.; *Xenia*, small **B**; *Aeolus*, May–Oct, **C**), rises imposingly on slopes above a roadstead exposed to the blasts of the Meltemi. The houses have characteristic blue slate roofs quartered by white ridge tiles. Blindingly white in the sun are the many little churches, said to number 123, some of which, notably the *Panayitsa*, stand high on the steep w. scarp of the town. Their ikons and screens (17–18C) are of good local workmanship, notably those in the church of *Khristó*, which has a gilded 'choros' or corona lucis. Pleasant black ware is produced by a local potter. Beyond his workshop, E. of the town, on the shore are vestiges of a Classical building (Asklepieion ?), fast being eroded by the sea. Farther on is *Moní Episkopí*, former seat of the bishopric of Skopelos, suppressed in the last century. Fragments remain of the church of 1078, possibly on the spot where Reginus, first Bp and patron saint of Skopelos, was martyred in 362.

A road (bus twice daily in 45 min.) crosses the island to *Agnónda*, a sheltered harbour on the s. coast where the boats call if the Meltemi blows (in which case a special bus connects). It passes the Bay of Stafilos (Pens. Rigas **B**), said to take name from Staphylos, a Minoan general. A tomb dug here in 1927 was claimed as his. *Glóssa* (1280 inhab.; *Avra* **C**), above the w. coast facing Skiathos, and *Klíma*, a smaller village to the E., are reached from their little port (Kalamaki) at which the steamers call. Glossa has Venetian remains.

A narrow channel, partly occupied by two islets, separates Skopelos from *Khelidhromi*, the ancient *Ikos*, known also as *Liadromia* and officially as **Alónnisos** (ΑΛΟΝΝΗΣΟΣ). It is a hilly wooded island culminating in Mt Kouvoúli (1620 ft). Its main village is *Alónnisos*, or Liadromia, well situated on a hill at the s.w. corner of the island above *Patitíri* (Alonnisos **D**; Galaxy, Marpounta, 100 **R**, at the s. cape, summer only, both **C**,), its little harbour. The other village, *Vótsi*, lies just to the E.

There are several rocky islets to the E. and N.E. of Alónnisos, uninhabited save for a few shepherds and their flocks. They include *Pelagonesi, Gioura, Piperi* ('Peppercorn', so called from its shape), and *Psathoura*, the northernmost of the group, where an extensive ancient city lies submerged. Some authorities consider that Psathoura not modern Alónnisos was the ancient *Halonnesos*, the ownership of which was a bone of contention between Philip of Macedon and the Athenians; one of the surviving orations of Demosthenes is on this subject. A Byzantine wreck off Pelagonesi was examined in 1970. Cargo raised was mainly glazed sgraffito pottery (mid 12C).

44 FROM ATHENS TO LAMIA
A Viâ Levadhia

ROAD, 131½ m. (212 km.). To (46 m.) Thebes, see Rte 41.—74 m. (119 km.)
Levadhia.—77½ m. *Orchomenos* turn.—82 m. *Chaironeia.*—112 m. *Brallos.* Steep
pass.—131½ m. **Lamia.**—BUSES twice daily by this route: more frequently to
Levadhia, and from Levadhia to Lamia.

RAILWAY, viâ Thebes (comp. Rte 44A), beyond which it follows closely the
general course of this road.

From Athens to (46 m.) *Thebes,* see Rte 41. We quit Thebes by a short
curving descent, then pass after 3 m. a road (l.; comp. Rte 41) to Thespiai
and Thisbe.—At 50 m., just beyond a bridge over a torrent bed, a just
motorable track (l.) leads across fields in c. 1 m. to a fold in the hills in
which is the **Kabeirion,** a sanctuary explored in 1887 and more fully
excavated in 1956–69.

The E. end of a *Temple,* showing four architectural styles, forms the skene of a
large *Theatre,* twice rebuilt. A central *Altar,* the focus of both temple and theatre,
shows that the spectacle was a sacred rite. Three circular buildings and two
water basins with pipe connections are of cult significance. Three halls form an
open square at the periphery of the sacred area. Various walls show occupation
from Roman to Archaic times. The site is notable for the amusing Kabeiran
pottery produced at or near it, and apparently exclusively intended for use in it.

The road runs across the Teneric Plain. To our N. *Mt Fagas* (1860 ft),
or *Sphingion,* the reputed haunt of the Sphinx, rises above the *Varikó*
marsh.—From (56½ m.) the low ridge of Kazarma, which separates the
Theban from the Copaic plain, Parnassos may be seen in the distance
ahead. On the ridge stood *Onchestos,* at one time seat of the Amphictyonic League and, in Macedonian times, of the Boeotian Confederation; the Poseidonion and Bouleuterion were identified in 1972. A
medieval watch-tower and grotto lie just off the road (l.). The grotto
produced material from the Old to Middle Stone Age. The road now
follows the margin of the drained **Lake Kopáïs.**

Lake Kopáïs (Copais, Κωπαΐς) is named after the ancient city of Kopai. It
was the largest lake in Greece, measuring 15 m. by 8 m.; Strabo says that it had
a circuit of 380 stadia (42 m.). For most of the year it was a reedy swamp, while
large tracts dried up completely in summer. In the rainy season the surrounding
basin used to be frequently inundated and it is doubtless to some flood of exceptional severity that the tradition of the Ogygian deluge is due. The eels of Copais
were very large and succulent, and the reeds which fringed its shores were the raw
materials of the Greek flute.

The natural outlets of the lake (all on the E. and N.E.) were swallow-holes
(katavothrae). These were not, however, sufficient to cope with a sudden inrush of
water, and from a very early age attempts were made to increase the natural outflow. On the dry bed of the lake traces of prehistoric dikes and canals, attributed
to the Minyans, have been found; they channelled the waters to various katavothrae with such success that the whole basin was reclaimed. Strabo repeats the
tradition that it was dry cultivated ground in the days when it belonged to Orchomenos. Herakles is said, out of enmity to the Orchomenians, to have blocked up
the katavothrae; Strabo explains that the chasms were affected by earthquakes.
After the destruction of the Minyan drainage works and throughout the historic
period the Copaic basin remained a lake.

Attempts were made, however, in historical times to supplement the katavothrae
by means of tunnels. Two artificial emissaries have been discovered. The more
extensive work is the tunnel towards Larimna. This may have been the work of
Krates, engineer to Alexander the Great. The other appears to have anticipated
the modern tunnel from Copais to Likéri. Neither of the ancient tunnels was
completed. A further attempt to control the inflowing rivers was undertaken in
the reign of the Emp. Hadrian. In 1887 Scottish engineers took over from a
French company works started twenty years earlier. A dam was built, two canals

were cut from w. to ᴇ., and the *Melas*, the main affluent, was diverted and canalized. The *Great Central Canal* is 15½ m. long, 25 yds wide, and 6–27 ft deep. The *Outer Canal* (20 m. long), to the s. collects the waters of the affluents from the s. side. The water of the Melas flows down the 'Great Katavothra'. The water of the Outer Canal and the winter overflow is drained through a tunnel into Lake Iliki, and thence to the sea. After reclamation, completed in 1931, the ground was divided between pasture and the cultivation of cereals and cotton. The area under cultivation by the British Lake Kopais Company steadily increased to 70 sq. m. by 1952, when the Greek government acquired the estate by expropriation.

At the *Battle of Lake Kopais*, in 1311, the Catalan Grand Company practically annihilated the chivalry of Frankish Greece. The battle was fought near Orchomenos (Skripou), comp. below.

57½ m. *Aliartos*. Some scanty remains of ancient *Haliartos*, excavated by the British School in 1926, can be seen on a rocky hill (r.), now known as Palaiókastro of *Mazi*. This was one of several fortified places that commanded the road from Orchomenos to Thebes, the only natural highway through Central Greece. To the s. behind (60½ m.) *Petra* rises a jagged row of hills. At *Solinari* (1.) is a site tentatively identified with the Temple of Tilphoussios where the seer Tiresias died.—66½ m. Cross-roads. To the left is modern Koroneia, but off the next turning (l.; to *Ayios Yeoryios*), in a valley 2½ m. s., are some remains (theatre, temple foundations, walls) of ancient *Koroneia*, where in 447 B.C. the Athenians suffered the defeat that lost them control of Boeotia. The Spartans under Agesilaus failed to consolidate a victory here in 394. We turn ɴ. for a short distance with the railway, then quit it to turn w. into the plain of Levadhia.

74 m. (119 km.) **Levadhia** (ΛΕΒΑΔΕΙΑ; *Levadhia* **B**; *Mideia, Helikon*, both **C**; Rest. see below) is a busy town of 15,400 inhab., the capital of the nome of Boeotia, and the seat of a bishop. It is pleasantly situated at the mouth of the gorge of the Erkina (ancient Herkyna) between Mt Lafistios on the ᴇ. and Mt Ayios Ilias on the w. A Frankish castle once protected and still dominates the town. Levadhia is a prosperous industrial centre making gay coloured textiles. The railway station lies 4½ m. ɴ.ᴇ. of the centre.

History. The earliest settlement on the Herkyna was *Mideia*, known to Homer (Il. ii, 507), the citadel of which was possibly on a hill, now called Tripolithári, which rises 1½ m. ɴ. of the modern town, at the point where the gorge opens into the plain. During the classical period *Lebadeia*, built at the foot of Tripolithari, was not of much account. It was sacked by Lysander and later by Archelaus. Pausanias found it "equal in style and splendour to the most flourishing cities in Greece"; its fame and prosperity were chiefly due to the oracle of Trophonios, which was the only one functioning in Boeotia in the time of Plutarch. Having a certain strategic importance *Levadia* prospered in the middle ages. It was the birthplace of St Nicholas Peregrinus (1075–94), a demented youth who, dying in Trani (Apulia), was canonized by the Roman church. In the 13C it passed to the dukes of Athens. In 1311–81 it was the third city of the Catalan duchy of Athens and Neopatras, its military capital, and the seat of a bishop. It withstood a siege by Walter II de Brienne in 1335, but fell by treason to the Navarrese in 1381. The town passed to Nerio Acciaioli in 1385 and Bayezid captured it in 1394. Levadhia gained importance under the Turks and at the War of Independence was still the second city of the Greek mainland.

The most conspicuous feature of the town is the 18C *Clock Tower*. By the riverside are fulling and spinning mills. We make for the s. end of the town where a picturesque *Turkish Bridge* spans the Herkyna just below the **Springs of Trophonios** (Restaurant; tavernas; swimming pool).

The *Oracle of Trophonios* was renowned as far back as the 6C B.C. Among those

who consulted it were Croesus, Mardonius, and the traveller Pausanias, who gives
from personal experience a detailed account of the ritual (see Paus. IX, 39, 5–14).

The visit to the gorge and springs of the Herkyna and to the Kastro
and summit of Mt Ay. Ilias takes about 2 hrs. The river, whose ultimate
source is on Mt Lafistios, is mainly fed by the group of springs which
gush from the foot of the cliff which bears the Kastro. On the left bank
the *Cold Spring* (Kria), whose waters are collected in a reservoir, appears
to correspond to the *Spring of Memory* (Mnemosyne). Above the spring
are votive niches cut in the rock, one of them a chamber 13 ft square and
10 ft high, with benches, a favourite retreat of the Turkish governor.
Below, to the left a narrow passage c. 30 ft long leads to another spring
in the heart of the cliff; this may be the *Spring of Forgetfulness* (Lethe).
On the right bank, opposite, under a clump of plane-trees, is another
group of springs. Higher up the gorge is an extensive *View, including
the Chapel of Jerusalem of the Grotto. At the top of the gorge is a
lonely mountain valley.

The sanctuary and oracle of Trophonios were situated on Mt Ayios Ilias.
The *Temple of Trophonios*, which was surrounded by a sacred grove, may be
sought in the *Chapel of the Panayía*, on the left bank of the Herkyna, where
ancient inscriptions referring to Trophonios have been found and some ancient
blocks have been built into the chapel walls; or on an artificial terrace, now occupied by the Chapel of SS. Anna and Constantine just below the Kastro.

Fifteen minutes above the springs we reach the **Kastro,** the ruined
14C fortress built by the Catalans, partly of ancient blocks. Its custody
was entrusted to the most important Siculo-Catalan families and it
held the precious relic of the head of St George. It was severely damaged by earthquake in 1894 but is impressive in its ruin. Half-an-hour's
climb from the springs brings us to the summit of *Ayios Ilias* (1320 ft),
where a chapel covers the remains of the unfinished Temple of Zeus
seen by Pausanias. To the s.w. are remains of a circular subterranean
construction identified with the *Oracle of Trophonios*, at a late stage
(3C A.D.) of its existence.

From Levadhia to Orchomenos, 7 m. (11 km.). We quit Levadhia
by the Lamia road (comp. below), turning off after 3½ m. to the right
and passing cotton ginneries.—7 m. *Orchomenós*, a town of 5100 inhab.,
combining the former hamlets of Petromagoula and Skripou, lies at the
foot of a desolate rocky ridge, known in antiquity as *Akontion* ('Javelin')
and today as Dourdouvana. The *Church of the former convent of the
Dormition (Koimisis tis Theotokou), admirably restored since its fabric
was split by an earthquake in 1895, was built in 874. Designed in a Bulgar tradition of Byzantine building, it is the unique example of its type in
Greece, though similar in plan to Ayia Sophia at Ohrid. The single squat
cupola rests on solid walls, but the proportions are good. The whole
building consists of column-drums from a Temple (of the Graces) and
blocks from the theatre. The interior, architecturally unadorned, is
frescoed but cluttered by the usual ornate and tasteless furniture.

Ancient **ORCHOMENOS,** occupying a strong position at the E.
end of Akontion, was, as the capital of the Minyans, one of the richest
and most important centres of Mycenean times. Homer compared its
treasures with those of Egyptian Thebes. It appears to have been
inhabited almost continuously from the Neolithic period to the time of
Alexander the Great.

History. The Minyans came from the Thessalian seaboard (or, according to more fanciful theories, direct from Egypt) to Orchomenos and made it their capital. They drained Lake Kopais and built a series of fortresses of which the most remarkable is Gla. Their dominion extended across Boeotia, and Thebes itself came, for a time, under their sway. Minyan Ware, so-called because Schliemann first discovered it at Orchomenos, is a "fine wheel-made ware of well refined, grey clay with a very smooth polished surface which is curiously soapy to the touch". Its origin is a mystery, its period Middle Helladic and it comes also in yellow and other colours.

About 600 B.C. Orchomenos joined the Boeotian League, but did not put its emblem on her coinage until 387 B.C. If she became a member of the Kalaurian League it was in virtue of her authority over the Boeotian coast towns. She took the side of the invader in the Persian Wars. Orchomenos joined Sparta against Thebes in 395 and 394 B.C., and was saved after Leuktra (371) only by the good offices of Epaminondas. In 364 Thebes seized the pretext of a conspiracy to destroy her venerable rival during Epaminondas' absence. Eleven years later the Phocians rebuilt Orchomenos, but it was again destroyed by the Thebans in 349. Under Philip of Macedon and Alexander the Great it was again rebuilt. In 87 Sulla defeated Archelaus, the general of Mithridates, under its walls. The Graces, or Charites, were first worshipped at Orchomenos.

Next to the church excavations in 1970–74 uncovered part of a building of L.H. IIIв date, perhaps a *Mycenean Palace.* Across the road are impressive remains of a *Theatre* of the 4C B.C. About 150 yds s.w. of the church, in a walled enclosure, is the so-called **Treasury of Minyas* (adm. 25 dr.; closed 1–3), a Mycenean tholos tomb recalling the Treasury of Atreus at Mycenae. It was excavated by Schiemann in 1880–86. The stone revetments of the *Dromos* were robbed in 1862 and the roof of the *Tholos* has fallen in, but the gateway still has its lintel of dark grey Levadhia marble and eight courses stand of the tholos itself. The most remarkable features are the remnants of the bronze rosettes, which decorated the walls, and the *Thalamos*, or inner sepulchral chamber hewn out of the rock. In its ceiling are slabs of green schist, carved with spirals interwoven with fan-shaped leaves, and surrounded with a border of rosettes. In the middle of the tholos are remains of a marble pedestal belonging to a funerary monument of the Macedonian period, once erroneously taken for the tomb of Hesiod, which was in the agora.

The *City Walls* of the Archaic period ran along the N. and S. sides of the ridge forming a long triangle, whose apex was the acropolis. Within these walls the excavations of Furtwängler and Bulle in 1903–05 laid bare a series of superimposed settlements.

To the w. and e. of the Treasury of Minyas are the remains of a NEOLITHIC CITY (? 6000–3400 B.C.), consisting of beehive huts built of unburnt brick on bases of masonry. Above this was a second city of Early Helladic date (3000–2000), characterized by deep circular ashpits, 20–26 ft in diameter. Above this again appear the apsidal house and rectangular megaron common in Thessaly and Elis (2000–1750) and yielding the so-called Minyan ware (see above) of Middle Helladic date.

Near the cemetery are the substructions (69 ft by 28) of an *Archaic Temple*, of the 9C or 8C B.C., resting, as at Tiryns and at Mycenae, on a much older settlement. This was a part of the MIDDLE HELLADIC CITY of 1700–1450 B.C. About 400 yds w. of the Cemetery, on an intermediate terrace, are the remains of a *Temple of Asklepios*, measuring 72 ft by 38. Thence we reach the upper terraces, on which was built the *Macedonian City.*

An ancient staircase mounts to the *Acropolis* (1010 ft), in size hardly more than a square keep. The cliffs on the e. and N. formed a natural defence; on the s. and w. the site was protected by massive walls, dating from the 4C B.C. and among the finest extant examples of ancient Greek fortification. The view is extensive including the entire Copaic plain.

From Levadhia to *Arakhova* and *Delphi*, and to *Osios Loukas*, see Rte 45.

The Lamia road turns N. out of Levadhia and rounds the easterly foothills of the Parnassos range to enter the broad valley of the Boeotian

Kefissos.—77½ m. Turning (r.) for *Orchomenos* (comp. above). We now cross the battlefield of Chaironeia at the entrance (l.) of the defile of Kérata.—82 m. *Kápraina* (no rest.) has readopted the old name Khaironia. Ancient **Chaironeia** (ΧΑΙΡΩΝΕΙΑ) cannot be missed since the *Lion* stands at the roadside. It guarded the *Polyandrion*, or common tomb, in which the Thebans buried the members of the Sacred Band killed in the battle of Chaironeia. This remarkable but not very realistic sculpture, which was discovered by a party of English visitors in 1818 almost buried in the ground, was smashed during the War of Independence by the brigand patriot Odysseus Androutsos under the impression that it contained treasure. In 1902–4 the Greek Archaeological Society restored it and replaced it on its ancient plinth. It is built up of three hollow sections of bluish-grey Boeotian marble, and is represented seated on its haunches; its height is 18 ft, or, including the plinth, 28 ft. The ossuary which it adorned was a rectangular enclosure surrounded by a peribolos wall; inside it were found 254 skeletons and various objects now in Athens.

Adjacent is a *Museum* (25 dr.; closed 12–3) containing Neolithic and Protogeometric ware from Chaironeia; neolithic, E.H., and M.H. vessels from Elateia; black-figure vases from Abai; finds from Exarkhos and Ayia Marina (comp. below) and Mycenean remains from Orchomenos, including a fragment of fresco from the palace; vases, terracottas, and arms from the Tumulus of the Macedonians, as well as weapons recovered from the battlefield of 338 B.C.

The BATTLE OF CHAIRONEIA was the outcome of the sabre-rattling policy of Demosthenes, who, by rousing anti-Macedonian feeling in the Athenians and concluding an alliance with Boeotia, provoked Philip of Macedonia to attack Southern Greece. After capturing Amphissa, Philip entered Boeotian territory at the head of 30,000 foot and 2000 horse. He found the allied army, perhaps slightly inferior in numbers, barring his way in the plain to the E. of Chaironeia. The Athenians, attacking on the left wing, gained an initial advantage. The Macedonian cavalry, led by the 18-year old Alexander, overwhelmed the Theban sacred band, who fought on to the death. The Athenians (among them Demosthenes himself), taken in the rear, fled. Philip buried the Macedonian dead in a great tumulus (to be seen near the railway); he burned the Athenian corpses and sent the ashes to Athens. The Thebans were permitted to bury their dead in a common tomb (comp. above). The result of the battle was the unquestioned supremacy of Macedon, crystallized the following year at the Synedrion of Corinth. After the battle Philip treated Thebes with the utmost severity, but was unexpectedly lenient towards Athens.—In the same plain Sulla won his great victory over Archelaus in 86 B.C.

The ancient city, whose chief industry was the distillation of unguents from the lily, rose, narcissus, and iris, was the birthplace of Plutarch (A.D. 46–? 127), who kept a school here, holding a priesthood for life from A.D. 95 at Delphi. The *Acropolis* (885 ft) occupies two summits separated by a saddle. There are remains of Hellenic walls and fragments of earlier walls in polygonal and Cyclopean work. At the N. foot of the hill is a little *Theatre*.

We pass a by-road (l.) to *Áyios Vlásios*, a name disguising St Blaize, above which (l.) stand *Walls of the acropolis of ancient *Panopeos*, the reputed home of Epeios, who built the Trojan Horse. We cross the railway near (85½ m.) *Dhavlía* Station. The village lies 4½ m. w.; and 30 min. s. of the village, in a wooded situation on an abrupt E. spur of Parnassos, the ruins of ancient *Daulis*. Road and railway pass out of Boeotia into Lokris through the *Pass of Belessi*, anciently Pass of Parapotamoi, down which Philip marched to Chaironeia in 338 B.C.—At 87½ m. the road divides by a cotton-mill.

The right branch runs N.E. to *Atalandi* (17½ m.; Rte 44B). At 4½ m. we leave on our left an asphalted by-road to modern *Elátia* (4 m.), formerly Drakhmani, with a small museum and (2 m. farther N. by a dry-weather track) a Neolithic settlement mound. An (uncorrected) Carbon 14 dating of c. 5520 B.C. was obtained for monochrome pottery and of c. 5080 for the earliest painted pottery. The road crosses a ridge between *Mt Khlomón* (r.; 3545 ft) and Mt Varvás, the E. spur of Kallídhromon with a fine view of Parnassos. At (8½ m.) *Kalapódhi*, near the church of Ay. Apostoloi, German excavators have found Byzantine walls and foundations of a large peripteral temple (6 × 14 columns) of early date. A road (l.) leads to *Zéli*, from which in 40 min. may be reached the ruins of *Elateia*, the capital of ancient Phokis and the city of Onomarchos, a noted general in the Sacred War of 357–346 B.C. Philip made Elateia his base for the invasion of Greece. The consternation which seized the Athenians on learning of its capture by Philip in 339 B.C. is described in a famous passage of Demosthenes. In 198 it was taken by the Roman general Flaminius. It was unsuccessfully besieged in 86–85 B.C. by Taxilas, a general of Mithridates, and c. A.D. 176 by the robber horde of the Costobocs (from Hungary). On a hill called *Kastro Lazou* (fine view) are the ruins of a Temple of Athena Kranaia, excavated by the French School in 1886. The temple, which was served by boy-priests, was in the Doric order with 6 columns by 13.—To the E. of Kalopódhi a bridle path leads round Mt Khlomon in 5 m. to *Exarkhos*, passing the remains of *Abai* and *Hyamopolis*.

The main road bears left. The long range of Kallídhromon appears ahead.—At (93 m.) *Kifissokhóri* a by-road runs s.w. to *Velítsa* (4 m.), a tobacco-growing village (1150 inhab.), officially called *Tithorea* after the near-by ancient remains of that city. Its walls, 10 ft thick, and towers are noteworthy. *Ayía Marína*, to the s. has a Neolithic settlement. We traverse a defile between Parnassós and Kallídhromon.— 102 m. **Amfiklia** (ΑΜΦΙΚΛΕΙΑ), or Dadí, with 3000 inhab., the most considerable town in W. Lokris, is piled up the hill in terraces, as was its ancient predecessor to the w. We cross the river and the railway to (105 m.) *Lilaía* Station. The citadel of *Lilaía*, with walls and towers standing to a great height, occupies the precipitous edge of a remote slope of Parnassós, 4½ m. s.w. beyond *Polídhroso*.—We start to climb through increasingly grand scenery.

At (112 m.) **Brállos** (ΜΠΡΑΛΛΟΣ; restaurant) a turning for Amfissa, important as connecting Lamia viâ the Rion ferry with Patras, drops across the valley to enter at *Graviá* a defile on the opposite side (comp. Rte 45). Just below Gravia (2 m. s. of Brallos station) is *Bralo British Military Cemetery* with the graves of 95 allied soldiers who died (mostly of influenza) in the 49th Stationary Hospital, transferred here in 1917. Brallos was the N. end of the overland supply route from Itea for the Macedonian front.—Road and railway now start their arduous passage of the *Pass of Fournataki*, the col connecting Mt Oiti on the w. with Mt Kallídhromon.

The railway threads two long tunnels, between which a long iron viaduct crosses the *Asopos*. Farther on another viaduct traverses the *Gorgopotamos*. Both these bridges were blown up in 1942–43 by British parachutists aided by Greek partisans, exploits which cut for six months a German supply route to North Africa. The Gorgopotamos Bridge was again blown by the retreating Germans and the present bridge was built by U.S. army engineers in 1948. The anniversary of the allied exploit is usually celebrated every Nov; at the commemoration in 1964 an old mine exploded killing 13 people and injuring 51 others.

On the steep ascent the road passes (116 m.) *Elevtherokhóri*, starting-point for (1¼ hr) the refuge-hut on Kallídhromon (organized from Lamia). Just beyond the summit (2030 ft) is (118 m.) the *Khani Karnásou* (Rfmts), overlooking the great plain of Lamia. The descent is one of the steepest and most tortuous in Greece. The region is steeped in legends of Herakles. Some ruins above the gorge of the Asopos (l.) are taken to be *Trachis*, his last residence, whence, suffering torments from the poisoned shirt of Nessus, he ascended to his self-immolation on Mt Oite. During the Persian invasion of 480 B.C. the Persians had their camp at Trachis and from here the Anopaia path, betrayed to them by Ephialtes, led to the rear of the Greek position at Thermopylae.—From the foot of the pass the road drives straight across the plain and the Spercheios to (131½ m.) **Lamia** (Rte 47).

B   Viâ Kammena Vourla

ROAD, ETHNIKI ODHOS 1, 133 m. (214 km.), toll highway.—23¾ m. *Malakassa*.—38 m. (61 km.) Turning for *Khalkis* (12½ m.).—53 m. (85 km.) Turning for **Thebes** (3¾ m.).—68¼ m. *Kastron* (**Gla**).—105 m. Kamena Vourla.—120½ m. Thermopylae.—133 m. **Lamia.**—BUSES 10 times daily in 3½ hrs.

RAILWAY, 136 m. (219 km.), through carriages 7 times daily in 3½–4½ hrs. The line closely follows the highway nearly to *Thebes* (56 m.; comp. below); thence it takes the course of the old road, viâ Livadhia, described in Rte 44A, leaving the main Salonika line at *Lianokladi* (4 m. w. of Lamia).

To reach the National Highway we may leave central Athens by Patission (Rte 20), by Liossion (Rte 19B), or (best) by Akharnon, between the two, to merge beyond *Patissia* with the approach from Piraeus.—At 12½ m. we pass under the railway. A turning (signposted Ay. Stéfanos) branches (r.) for Marathon Lake, which, near the 25 km. post, comes briefly into view.—We recross the railway; here the highway follows a course parallel to the old Kalamos road (Rte 22).—Near (18 m.) *Polidhendhri* (Golden Horse A), road (r.) to the Amphiareion (Rte 22). To the left rises *Béletsi* (2760 ft), the N.E. extremity of Parnes. Road and railway pass through the narrow gap between Béletsi and *Mavrinóra* (2120 ft) in the district known in ancient times as the Diakria.

We by-pass *Malakassa*, standing at the foot of the Dekelia pass, with (23½ m.) the road (r.) to Skala Oropos and the ferry to Euboea. We traverse the gentle rolling country that extends from Parnes to the S. Euboean Gulf.—29¼ m. *Avlon*, with 2500 inhab., lies 1¼ m. l. on the railway. We enter Boeotia and cross the Asopos.—Beyond (33 m.) *Staniátes*, which has readopted the ancient name *Oinófita*, TOLL GATE. The battle of Oenophyta resulted in a victory for the Athenians in 457 B.C.—36½ m. Turning for *Dilessi*, a little coastal village made notorious by the murders of 1870. It probably occupies the site of ancient *Delion*; the Athenian defeat of 425 B.C. is to be placed c. 3 m. to the s. near 'Palaiokhani'.—The road crosses the Khalkis branch line just beyond its junction with the main railway at *Oinoi* (1 m. l.).—38 m. *Skhimatárion* (l.) in a spreading industrial zone has a little Museum containing stelai, figurines, and inscriptions from Tanagra.

Ancient *Tanagra* occupied a nearly circular hill rising from the N. bank of the Asopos, c. 3 m. s. of Skhimatarion and a similar distance from modern Tanagra. The most prominent feature of the plain today is an airfield of the Hellenic Air Force, for which reason identity documents should be carried. Tanagra was the scene of a Spartan victory over the Athenians and Argives in 457 B.C. and (?) birthplace of the poetess Corinna, who defeated Pindar in a musical contest at Thebes. The ruins, not easy of access, include an enceinte of c. 385 B.C. and a visible but still buried theatre. The place owes its fame to the terracotta figurines discovered in the extensive necropolis in 1874. A further series of chamber tombs by modern Tanagra excavated since 1969 has yielded Mycenean larnakes and associated terracotta plaques of most unusual design. A clay larnax can be dated to L.H. IIIB but shows two scenes of Prothesis together with a chariot scene and one of bull-leaping, the first association of two typically Geometric motifs with a Minoan motif in a Mycenean mainland context.

———————

To KHALKIS (50½ m. from Athens). A new road diverges N. to (4½ m.) *Vathy* (Aulis C), with shipyards, a huge radio station, and a station on the Khalkis branch line. The coast roads to the E. are to be avoided. Farther on are some ruins of ancient **Aulis**, famed in the Homeric epic as the place where Agamemnon sacrificed Iphigenia. The long narrow *Temple of Artemis* was discovered during the building of the road in 1941. Its identification is certain from the inscription of a statue base. The site was excavated by Threpsiades in 1956–61. The cella dates from the 5C but was restored in Roman times; it originally had a porch with two columns in antis, which was rebuilt with four columns in Hellenistic times. To the s. of the temple are some remains of *Potters' Establishments*, with a kiln, and a third building, perhaps a hotel. Beyond a cement works we join the old road (see below) and cross the Euripos (Toll).—12½ m. **Khalkis**, see Rte 42A.

In the mainland outskirts of Khalkis a road runs N. to *Khalía* (2½ m.), renamed *Dhrosia*, whence a passable dirt road continues round the coast past the site of (?) *Salganeus* (large mound with E.H. traces) to *Anthedon* (7 m.), excavated by the American School. Here are some well-preserved remains of a quay, now thought to be of Byzantine date, and of two moles (partly submerged). The line of the city walls can be traced round the acropolis, a low hill close to the shore to the E., and around the lower town to the s.w.

———————

At 43¾ m. (70 km.) diverges the old road to Khalkis (11¾ m.).

This road diverges N.E. At the approach to (3 m.) *Ritsona*, now a mere hamlet after its destruction as a reprisal during the German occupation, is the site of ancient *Mykalessos*, mentioned by Homer and bearing a pre-Greek name. Its existence ended in 414 B.C. when a body of Theban mercenaries hired by Athens fell upon the place on their way home and slew every living creature, including the animals and a school of boys just gathered for their morning lesson. The road crosses a tortuous pass (view) between Messapion and *Mt Galatsidheza*, then runs in the flat plain through the industrial mainland development of Khalkis.

We continue very straight with the low grey *Messapion Oros* on our right, rising at its N. end to 3350 ft. The railway diverges towards Thebes. At 53 m. (85 km.) the flyover junction, **Thebes** (2½ m.) is well seen to the left. On the w. side of *Lithares*, the next hill to the right, near the lake shore, excavations in 1971–72 uncovered a large E.H. habitation comparable with Zygouries. The N. side of Mt Fagas crowds in on the left as we approach the **Boeotian Lakes,** reduced to two since the draining of Kopaïs. The road skirts the rocky s.w. shore of Lake Iliki (Motel B; Restaurant), an irregular sheet of water ringed by low steep hills.

Lake Likéri, renamed *Ilíki* ('Υλική), occupies a deep depression 165 ft below the level of the Kopaic plain. After the lake received the waters of Kopais its level rose to 262 ft and the lake spread, submerging a ruined city (? *Hyle*) on the w. shore. In 1958, however, a new aqueduct was opened to supply water from Iliki to Marathon Lake. Iliki is 5 m. long and, at its widest, N.–s. point 2½ m. broad. The ridge of *Mouriki* (272 ft), pierced by a canal, separates Iliki from

Lake Paralimni (Παραλίμνη), which extends to the N.E. towards the sea. Oval in shape, 5 m. long and 1 m. broad, it is enclosed by Mt Ptoon, to the N. and W., and Messapion, on the E. The ridge (312 ft) which separates it from the sea, is pierced by a tunnel which carries off its superfluous waters to the Euboean Channel near Anthedon. Both ridges are seared by ancient cuttings. A recession of Paralimni exposed two sets of remains investigated in 1965–66 and identified with the *Isos* of Strabo at the N.E. end and with the early site of Hyle at the s.w. end.

64 m. (102 km.) *Akraifnion* (1220 inhab.; 1 m. r.), formerly *Kardhitsa*, has readopted a variant name of the ancient ruined city occupying the ridge of Kriaria, 10 min. s.E. of the village beyond a ravine. Here was found the inscription relating to Nero's proclamation of Greek freedom, now in Thebes museum. Vestiges of fortifications (4C B.C.) may be traced. The church of Ayios Yeoryios high above the village bears an inscription of 1311 naming Antoine le Flamenc, one of the survivors of the Battle of Kopais. The village is the starting-point for the Ptoion.

From Akraifnion we take the road towards Kokkino and at its first bend continue straight ahead on a motorable track which soon divides. The right branch crosses the valley in 10 min. towards a quarry, to the left of which on the flat hill of *Kastraki* is an ESPLANADE dedicated to the HERO PTOIOS. Two altars, two buildings, and the bases of 28 tripods suggest that the cult flourished during the two periods when Akraiphion enjoyed relative autonomy (c. 550–480 and 456–446). Above are remains of a 4C *Temple* to an Earth goddess, mother of the hero.—The left track keeps to the N. side of the valley (view back over the esplanade) and leads in ¾ hr to the ravine of *Perdikovrisi* on the slope of Mt Ptoon (2380 ft). Here, below the main summit, was the **Ptoion**, or *Sanctuary of Ptoan Apollo*, seat of an infallible oracle. The ruins were cleaned up in 1963–64 by the French School, but had already suffered greatly from the depredations of men and goats since their excavation in 1885. These yielded statues, bronzes, vases, and inscriptions, now divided between the museums of Athens and Thebes.

The site occupies three terraces below a spring. We pass to the W. of the disused chapel of Ayia Paraskevi and come to the *Lower Terrace*, on which are the ruins of a large CISTERN, with seven compartments, which collected the waters of the upper spring and fed them by a conduit to an ablutionary building just below. Above the cistern extends the *Middle Terrace* mainly occupied by two long parallel stoas. The *Upper Terrace* bears a few courses of the foundations of a TEMPLE of the Doric order that had 6 columns by 13. It was rebuilt in the 3C B.C. over the ruins of a 7C edifice. A little higher up is a CAVERN, perhaps the abode of the oracle. The modern *Fountain* on the path above has taken the place of the ancient one at the foot of the sanctuary. From the s. end of the site, fine view over the Lakes.

The main track mounts in ½ hr to the *Convent of Pelayia*, visible on its plateau (1850 ft).

The Kokkino road can be used as an approach to Larimna. The first col affords a fine view down to Gla (see below), which on foot can be reached from the Ptoion in 1 hr.

We cross the channelled effluents of Lake Copais (see Rte 44), which extends to the left. On a clear day Mt Parnassos is seen ahead. The road sweeps right.—68½ m. *Kástron*, formerly Topólia, rises on a hill to the left, which was once an island; here vestiges of polygonal walling and inscribed stones in the church mark the site of *Kopai*, the city mentioned in the 'Catalogue of Ships' which gave name to the 'Copaic'. To the right, on a low eminence also an island in antiquity, is the Mycenean stronghold of *Gla, a remarkable fortress many times larger than Mycenae or Tiryns, whose very identification is uncertain. The approach road (passable for motors; 25 min. walk) leaves the highway immediately before a large petrol station, and makes a complete circuit of the fortress. The site was partially explored by the French School in 1883. The four gates of the city were cleared in 1956–60 by the Greek Archaeological Service under Threpsiades. They were damaged by fire when the city fell. The FORTIFICATIONS, 1¾ m. in length, run along the edge of a precipitous low cliff. The South or *Royal Gate* had double bronze-faced doors. Hence a road led directly to the vast walled '*Agora*', a space enclosed by long parallel buildings. The best preserved ruins are of a *Palace* on the highest eminence (235 ft above the plain) against the N. wall.

We continue N. and climb through scrub-covered hills.—73¾ m. Turning for *Lárimna*.

A poor road descends viâ (1 m.) *Martínon* to (5 m.) **Lárimna** (*Galini* D), a friendly village on an inlet of the N. Euboean Gulf. On the farther shore of the inlet are the extensive works of the only nickel mine in Europe lying W. of the 'Iron Curtain'. The village, built largely on ancient foundations, fronts two small bays. In the bay to the W. (taverna; bathing) are considerable remains of the port installations of the 4C B.C., when *Larymna* had the most easterly harbour of Locris. Two piers forming the harbour mouth (once guarded by a chain) can be seen underwater with the line of a long protective mole; the quay, of ashlar masonry, was guarded by towers.—At *Ayios Ioannis Theologos*, on the coast farther W. (approach road at top of hill before Proskinas, see below), are the ruins of *Halai* comprising harbour and acropolis excavated by the Americans in the 1910's.

We descend through cultivated country (82 m. Toll Gate) to the Gulf of Atalandi. The little port of (88 m.) *Skala* is connected by steamer with Khalkis. It serves *Atalandi* (Andreas D), 3 m. to the W., the chief town of the eparchy of Lokris with 4600 inhabitants, connected also with the main road from Thebes to Lamia. It brews a popular German beer under licence.—90½ m. *Livanátai*. On a spur to the W. is a military satellite station.—Our road now runs in the cultivated strip between the hills of Lokris and the narrowing North Euboean Gulf (or Atalandi Channel).—93 m. *Arkítsa* (½ m. r.; Calypso, DPO, B) has a car-ferry service 7 times daily to Loutra Aidhipsou in Euboea.—96 m. *Áyios Nikólaos* (Neraïda D) is on the shore. The landscape becomes grander as the *Knimís Mts* (3075 ft) crowd in towards the sea.

Beyond the olive groves of Cape Kálamos is (103½ m.) **Áyios Konstandínos** (*Motel Levendi*, DPO, to the N., A, *Astir* C, and others), a pleasant developing resort on a little bay near the site of *Daphnous*. Steamer services to the Northern Sporades, see Rte 43. On our right is the *Dhiavlos Knimidhos*, the narrow channel partly blocked with islets that separates the W. tip of Euboea from Cape Knimís.

109½ m. (175 km.) **Kaména Voúrla** (*Galini*, DPO, A; *Leto*, B; *Astir*, *Asteria*, *Delfini*, with good Rest., *Pringipikon*, *Bouca*, C, these open all year; also *Sissy*, DPO, *Violetta*, *Rhadion*, B, and many others in summer) is a fashionable thermal resort ringed by olive trees; its salt radio-active waters are recommended to sufferers from rheumatism and arthritis.— 113 m. *Kainoúryion*. The site of ancient *Thronion* is on a hill to the left. For a brief moment distant Parnassos can be glimpsed again behind the foothills of Kallídhromon. We cross several broad torrents.—116¼ m. Modern *Skárfia*, with an earth satellite station, lies r.; the site of ancient Skarpheia is on a hill (l.) just before we by-pass (118 m.) *Mólos*.— 120½ m. *Ayía Triás* (1½ m. r.) lies in the flat alluvial marsh that borders the Maliakos Kolpos; across the gulf are seen the distant slopes of Mt Othrys.—At 124 m. a good gravel road winds back E. to Mendenítsa (6 m.).

Mendenitsa, the site of ancient *Pharygai*, is occupied by the *Castle of Bodonitsa*, seat of the Frankish marquisate of the Pallavicini in 1205–1410. It survived the

Catalan invasion by placing itself under Venetian protection in 1335, but fell to the Turks after a siege. The fortress has a double enceinte, the lower enclosure on ancient foundations; the upper part, better preserved, is approached by a barbican.

We approach the famous PASS OF THERMOPYLAE (Στενά τῶν Θερμοπυλῶν) between the steep N. side of Kallídromon and the sea. The pass will always be remembered for the devotion of Leonidas and his Spartans during the Persian invasion of 480 B.C. The defile, which is just under 4 m. long, ran between precipitous mountains and the sea. It was extremely narrow at both ends, but widened in the middle, where were the hot springs that gave the pass its name. It was in antiquity, for a force of any size, the only practical means of communication on land between Thessaly and S. Greece. To understand the ancient topography, we must imagine the sea on our right hand. Today the silt brought down by the Spercheios has advanced the coast-line by nearly 3 miles, though the plain is still marshy. The modern road coincides with the ancient road for most of the way, except at the critical narrows where it runs N. of the old course; here we must visualise the road nearer to the cliffs with the sea extending to within a few yards of their foot.

History. By the time Xerxes was bridging the Hellespont for his invasion forces, the confederacy gathered at the Isthmus of Corinth was planning a combined forward defence of Greece. The Pass of Tempe, in N. Thessaly, was considered but found impracticable because it could be turned. The next point of defence was Thermopylae, which it was decided to hold. Like Xerxes' invasion, the defence was to be a combined operation on land and sea. While the small Greek army occupied Thermopylae, the Greek fleet lay off *Artemision* (Euboea) to prevent the Persian fleet sailing down the Euboean Gulf in support of their army. Meanwhile the Persian army had reached Trachis and the Persian fleet the coast of Magnesia, at which point the weather came to the aid of the Greek naval forces.

The Greek army was under the command of Leonidas, king of Sparta. He repaired the Wall of the Phocians and took up his main position behind it, in the centre of the pass. The total Greek force was about 7300 men. The Persians are credited by modern historians with 300,000 men, though Herodotus adduces a grand total of more than 5¼ million. The Persians made several unsuccessful and costly assaults on the improvised fortifications of the Greeks. Xerxes had almost given up hope of forcing a passage when the Malian Ephialtes indicated a means of turning the Greek position by a mountain path called the *Anopaia*. Leonidas had posted the 1000 Phocians along it so that there could be no surprise from that quarter. However, Xerxes determined to use the path. Led by Ephialtes, Hydarnes, commander of the Persian 'Immortals', set out in the evening with 2000 men and marched through the night. The next morning they routed the Phocians and reached the E. end of the pass, where they took the defenders in the rear.

Leonidas, foreseeing that he would be crushed between two attacks, had already ordered the withdrawal of the main force, retaining only his 300 Spartans, the 700 Thespians, and the 400 Thebans, who "were kept back as hostages, very much against their will" since the Thebans were suspected of medizing; they deserted in a body to the Persians as soon as opportunity offered. The course of the desperate battle, the death of Leonidas, and the famous 'last stand' of the Spartans on the hillock of Kolonos is told in detail by Herodotus (Bk. VII), and visitors wishing to traverse the ground in detail cannot do better than follow his vivid and dramatic account.

All save two of the 300 Spartans were killed. One atoned for his survival by his valour at Plataia; the other hanged himself on his return to Sparta. The dead were buried where they fell and later commemorated by monuments bearing two celebrated epigrams. On the hillock a stone lion, which survived to the time of Tiberius, was erected to Leonidas. Forty years after the battle his body was taken to Sparta.

Thermopylae was seized by Leosthenes in the Lamian War. The tactics of Xerxes were copied by all who wished to force the Pass of Thermopylae. In 279 Brennus, at the head of his Gauls, finding himself checked by the troops of Kallipos, used the Anopaia path to turn the Greek position; but this time the

Greeks were able to escape to their ships. In 191 Antiochus III, King of Syria, with 10,000 men, tried to deny the pass to the 40,000 legionaries of the Roman consul Manlius Acilius Glabrio and his legate M. Porcius Cato. Antiochus raised a double wall, with trenches, across the defile, and built forts on the slopes of Mt Kallidromos. Cato succeeded in carrying the forts and in taking the position in the rear, while Glabrio made a frontal attack. Antiochus escaped with only 500 men.

In 395 A.D. Alaric entered the pass without opposition. In the 6C "the straits of Thermopylae, which seemed to protect, but which had so often betrayed, the safety of Greece, were diligently strengthened by the labours of Justinian" (Gibbon, *Decline and Fall*). In 1204 Boniface of Montferrat came through unopposed. Retreating British troops began to take up position here in 1941, but evacuation was ordered before the Germans reached the area.

125 m. **Thermopylae** (*Aegli* C), or *Thermópilai*. Here in 1955 King Paul inaugurated the *Memorial* to Leonidas and the Three Hundred, a white marble monument, surmounted by a striking bronze figure of Leonidas. The base bears reliefs of scenes from the battle and records the famous epigrams. It was erected at American expense. On the opposite side of the road is the *Grave Mound*. On the left, just beyond, are hot springs, with a hot waterfall, a frequented hydropathic establishment and a restaurant. The waters (110° F.), which are abundant, are impregnated with carbonic acid, lime, salt, and sulphur, and are said to be efficacious in the cure of sciatica, stiff joints, and glandular complaints. At the w. exit to the defile a hill is probably the site of *Anthela* where the meetings of the Amphictyonic League were held in autumn (in spring they met at Delphi).

We cross the Spercheios. The *Alamánas Bridge* here was heroically defended on 5 May 1821 by Athanasios Diakos and the Bp of Salona, with 700 Greeks, against a superior force led by Omer Vrioni and Mehmet Pasha (monument with mosaic). To the left the solemn mass of Mt Oiti is well seen, and, farther behind us, the zigzag descent from Kallidromon of the road from Amfissa and Livadhia (Rte 44A). Looking up the Specheios valley we see the imposing mass of Mt Timfristos.

133½ m. (215 km.) **Lamia**, see Rte 47. The National Highway turns E., the Lamia by-pass continues straight on; we turn left entering the city from the E. side.

45 FROM (ATHENS) LEVADHIA TO DELPHI AND AMFISSA

ROAD, 117½ m. (189 km.). To *Thebes*, see Rte 41, thence to (74 m.) *Levadhia*, see Rte 44A.—88 m. (141 km.) Turning for **Osios Loukas** (8¾ m.).—97 m. (156 km.) *Arakhova*.—103 m. (166 km.) **Delphi** (Rte 46).—117½ m. **Amfissa**. Extensive widening and realinement has been effected.

From Athens to (46 m.) **Thebes,** see Rte 41; thence to (74 m.) **Levadhia,** see Rte 44A. The road continues w., winding up the N. side of the narrowing valley. The scenery becomes increasingly grand as Parnassos dominates the whole region, though its summit is often hidden in cloud or capped with snow. Korakólithos is now avoided by a tunnel. The road descends before climbing through a defile.—At (88 m.) *Schíste*, or '*Tríodos*' (1390 ft), the meeting-place in antiquity of three roads, from Daulis, Delphi, and Ambrossos, Sophocles laid the scene of Oedipus' murder of his father (Oedipus Tyrannus). Lying in a setting of lonely grandeur between the heights of Bardana and Kastri, it is still a parting of the ways, where diverge roads important alike to industry and tourism.

The branch road leads s. in an open valley to **Dhístomo** (ΔΙΣΤΟΜΟ; 2½ m.; *America, Koutriaris,* D), scene of a Nazi reprisal massacre on 10 June 1944, when 218 villagers were killed (plaques on church façade). In commemoration a community in Atlantic City adopted the name Distomo. The little town occupies the site of *Ambrossos,* few traces of which are visible. Most travellers will here turn left to Osios Loukás (comp. below). Ahead the road zigzags down a further 6½ m. to *Áspra Spítia,* on the Bay of Andikira, a hideous dormitory town built by Aluminium of Greece, whose works were erected in 1962–65 at Ayios Theodoros on the E. side of the bay. Here the Roman and Byzantine remains of *Medeon* were excavated by the French School and Greek Archaeological Service in 1962–63 before they were built over. A huge Mycenean acropolis was also explored and 250 tombs dug. At the w. end of the bay, 1½ m. farther on, is *Andíkira* on the site of the ancient Phocian town of *Antikyra.* Continuation to *Itéa,* see Rte 55c.

Ósios Loukás, the *Monastery of St Luke Stíris,* lies 5 m. E. of Dhístomo by an asphalt road which passes through *Stíris* and then through almond groves. The monastery, one of the most interesting ecclesiastical groups in Greece, stands on the brow of a peaked hill facing s. and commanding wonderful views of Helikon and the surrounding country. Though there are still monks, the place is more ancient monument than retreat (adm. 25 dr.), and is equipped with a small *Xenia* Hotel and Restaurant (**B**).

The monastery is dedicated not to the Evangelist, but to a local beatified hermit, the Blessed Luke (Ósios Loukás) of Stíri. His family fled from Aegina on its invasion by the Saracens and Luke was born in 'Kastorion' (probably Kastri, i.e. Delphi). After many adventures the hermit came to Stíri, where in 953 he died. Already between 941 and 944 a church had been founded, dedicated to St Barbara, but tradition attributes the foundation of the monastery to Romanos II in 961 in recognition of the fulfilment of Luke's prophecy that Crete should be liberated by an emperor named Romanos. Both the existing churches have suffered from earthquakes, and their latest restoration in 1958–60 has reversed former ideas of their chronological sequence. The mosaics are incomplete and parts have been reset, but they remain important and beautiful.

From the flagged terrace we see the rebuilt *Trapeza,* or Refectory, above which rises the s. flank of the *Katholikon* set off by the flowing line of its dome. Dedicated to St Luke and dating from c. 1020, it is comparable with the church at Daphni (Rte 16) and with it coupled by Krautheimer as "probably the most beautiful representatives of the Greek-cross-octagon plan". The foundation walls are of stone with stone and brick above. Columns of cipollino, Hymettian marble, and bigio antico divide the windows, each of which is surmounted by a large impost bearing a Greek cross. The lower parts of the windows are filled with sculptured marble. An inscription in the outer wall records the dedication by Xenocrates and Eumaridas of a *Fountain*; the slab probably came from ancient Stiris.

INTERIOR. The w. door opens into a *Narthex,* which has a vaulted ceiling and is decorated with *Mosaics on a gold ground. Upon the arches are depicted the Apostles; in the lunettes, the Washing of Feet, the Crucifixion, and the Resurrection. On the ceiling are medallions of the Baptist, the Virgin with angels, and saints. On the pavement are slabs of verde antico.

The central domed *Nave* is approached through a vestibule, which, with the two transepts and the Bema, form in plan the arms of the cross enclosed within the external rectangle of the walls. The angles are filled in by twelve groin-vaulted or domed bays, surmounted by a second story of equal height to form a *Matroneum*; this is frescoed (interesting graffiti of medieval ships) and carried over the transepts by open galleries. The piers have polychrome marble revetments. The *Bema* and its flank-

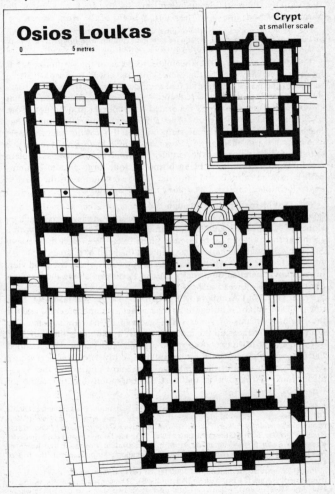

Osios Loukas

0   5 metres

Crypt
at smaller scale

ing chapels are each closed off by a templon, that in the centre forming the ikonostasis, those to left and right open colonnades. There are ikons by Mikhail Damaskinos (16C).

The interplay of light and shade produced by the multiplicity of arches gives an air of solemn mystery, enhanced by reflected light from gold Mosaics. Those in the dome were damaged in 1659 by earthquake and replaced by paintings. The mosaics are most complete in the vestibule and its aisles, and in the N. transept (though these are medallions with busts of saints only). On the squinches supporting the dome mosaics of the Nativity, Presentation and Baptism. In the *Apse*, mosaics of the Virgin and Child; above, in the vault, Descent of the Holy Ghost.

The *Crypt*, once taken to be the original church of St Barbara since it contains St Luke's tomb, is supported by square bevelled columns with imposts. It retains its 11C frescoes. Beneath is a rock-cut refuge with its own water supply.

The smaller church of the **Theotókos**, to the N. of the Katholikon, has recently been shown to be the older, since its S. wall forms part of the N. wall of the larger building; it had previously been assigned to c. 1040, but may be the church of Romanos' foundation. The exterior has elaborate cloisonné masonry decorated with courses of deep dog-tooth brickwork and a cufic frieze. The *Drum*, architecturally clumsy, has marble panels worked in great sculptural detail, recalling Islamic work. The church is preceded by an *Exonarthex* (16C), having a triple portico surmounted by a loggia. The interior beyond the narthex is a plain cross-in-square, the dome being borne on four large granite columns with Byzantine capitals and imposts. The two columns in the narthex have Corinthian capitals. The floor mosaic is notable.

The Delphi road passes through the *Stenopos Zemenous*, the upper ravine of the Platania, between the precipices of Parnassos and the bare slopes of Xerovoúni (5098 ft).—91 m. *Khan of Zimeno* (2296 ft), with a spring at the foot of a large oriental plane tree.—We reach the *Khan of St Athanasius*, with a chapel by a spring, at the head of the pass (2513 ft). At a bend in the road, which winds steeply upwards, there is a good view of Arákhova, perched on a rocky spur of Parnassos above the gorge of the Pleistos. We thread a short tunnel.

97 m. (157 km.) **Arákhova** (ΑΡΑΧΩΒΑ; 3090 ft; Xenia, DPO, **B**), a town of 2800 inhab., is noted for its rugs, wines and embroideries, and for the copious streams of water running down its narrow streets. The houses rise in terraces on the mountain spur; at the top is the church of *St George*. The town may occupy the site of a small classical place called *Petrites*, which succeeded the two prehistoric towns of *Anemoreia* and *Kyparissos*. Vestiges of these may be seen below and above the Katoptirio rock. Arákhova is the best starting-point for the climb of Parnassos.

Parnassos is a complex mountain mass, with two main peaks: hence Ovid's *biceps Parnassus*. The higher summit is called *Lyakoura* or *Lykeri* ('Wolf Mountain', anciently *Lykorea*; 8061 ft) and the lower *Gerontovrachos* ('Old Man's Rock'; 7989 ft). To the Greeks Parnassos was sacred to Dionysos and the Maenads; it was the Latin poets who made it, with the Castalian Fountain, the home of Apollo and the Muses. During the flood, Deucalion's ship rested on the top of Parnassos.

The Ski Centre at *Fterolakkas* (c. 5000 ft; car park) is reached by road (c. 10 m.) from Arakhova viâ (2½ m.) *Kalivia* (Anemolia **B**). The centre is open for skiing in Dec–Apr (Restaurant), when chair-lifts operate in two stages to c. 6500 ft where there are ski slopes (ski-lifts). Higher slopes with lifts and a restaurant at *Kelaria* were planned for 1980. The lower centre functions as an excursion resort in summer. July and August are the only practicable months for climbing to the summit when the paths are free of snow. The climb is best done by spending a night at the Hellenic Alpine Club refuge (*Katafiyion Sarantari*; 6233 ft; 28 beds); a robust vehicle can get to within 15 min walk of the refuge. The guide lives in Arákhova, where contact should be made through the Alpine Club. Only food need be taken to the Refuge. The climb is usually made before dawn and takes about 5 hrs there and back, though fell-walkers would do it in less. It is practicable for a fit climber, who does not mind the heat, to do the whole expedition in the day from Kalivia, ignoring the refuge.

The *View at sunrise, before the mists gather, exceeds in grandeur and interest almost every other prospect in the world. Little by little the map of Greece unfolds. To the N.W. are Timphristos and Pindos; to the N., beyond Kallidromon, are Oite, Othrys, Pelion, Ossa and Olympos. To the N.E. we see the Atlante Channel and the island of Euboea, with the Gulfs of Lamia and Volo, and the Northern Sporades beyond. In the far distance the grey mass of Mount Athos rises from the sea. To the S.E. are Helikon, Attica and the Cyclades; to the S. the Gulf of Corinth, with its isthmus; beyond, the Peloponnesian mountains: Kyllene, Maenalon, Aroania, Erymanthos, and Panachaikon, with Taiyetos in the background. To the W., beyond the vale of Amphissa, the view is masked by the mountains of Locris and Doris, two of which, Kiona (8202 ft) and Vardousi (8186 ft) are higher than Parnassos.

The road now descends gradually, skirting the cliffs of Parnassos on the right and keeping high above the Pleistos, whose ravine is hidden by vineyards. Egyptian vultures may be seen. We pass through one of the ancient cemeteries of Delphi. On the right are the Phaedriades, the precipices that shut in Delphi on the N. We now pass through the centre of **Ancient Delphi** (Rte 46). On the left is Marmaria, with the Sanctuary of Athena. The road bears right and then makes a sharp bend to the left at the Castalian Fountain. To the s. is the Papadia Glen, through which the overflow from the spring flows into the Pleistos. Passing on the right the Pythian Sanctuary and the Museum, we sweep round to the right to enter the modern village.

103 m. (166 km.) **DELPHI** (ΔΕΛΦΟΙ; *Amalia Xenia, Vouzas,* DPO, **A**; *Pythia, Stadion, Iniochos* **C**, these open all year; *Kastalia,* DPO, **B**; *Parnassos, Hermes, Greca* **C**, these closed in winter, and others), in modern Greek *Dhelfi,* at one time called *New Kastri,* is a modern village (1185 inhab.) built since 1892, about ½ m. w. of the former village, *Kastri,* which stood on the ruins of ancient Delphi. By a special convention with the Greek Government in April 1891, the French School obtained a ten-years' lease of the ancient site, bought out the inhabitants, and arranged for their transplantation to the new village, which was supplied with water by means of an aqueduct from the Fountain of Kassotis. In Delphi is an annexe of the School of Fine Arts in Athens, where artists of all nationalities may stay, and here in 1965 was founded an International Cultural Centre sponsored by the Council of Europe.

From Delphi the road descends steeply with many acute bends.— 109 m. *Khrissó* (now just off the road) is the modern equivalent of *Krisa* without the importance of the ancient town. Krisa gave its name to the Krisaean Gulf (Krissaíos Kolpos), on which Itéa stands, and to the plain that extends for c. 11 miles from the head of the bay to Amfissa. The plain, which is divided into two parts by the intrusion above Itéa from W. and from E. of two mountain spurs, is exceptionally fertile in the N. section (the Krisaean Plain proper as opposed to the Kirrhaean Plain), where grows the largest plantation of olives in Greece.—At 111 m. the road divides; to the left the Navpaktos road descends in 4 m. through the olives to *Itéa* (see Rte 55C), our road drives straight for Amfissa.

117½ m. **Amfissa** (ΑΜΦΙΣΣΑ; 590 ft; *Stalion* **C**; *Apollo* **D**), the chief town (6600 inhab.) of the eparchy of Parnassidos and the seat of a bishop, is better remembered by its medieval name of *Salona*. It is well situated at the N.W. end of the Krisaean Plain on the first slopes of the Locrian mountains. In antiquity *Amphissa* was the capital of Ozolian Locris. The ruined Frankish **Castle**, or FROURION (1205), has three enceintes, partly built on the walls of the ancient *Acropolis*. Antique survivals include the remains of walls of Classical quadrangular and Hellenistic polygonal masonry, some reused, and of two towers. There are also a cistern of which the lower part is ancient and the upper part medieval, two ruined churches, and a circular keep. At the s. foot of the castle are a fine arcaded Turkish fountain and the 12C church of the *Sotiros*.

Amphissa was denounced by Aeschines in 339 B.C. for violating the Krisaean Plain. The Amphictyonic League appealed to Philip of Macedon who, making good use of the opportunity, invaded Greece and destroyed Amphissa. The city was rebuilt and furnished 400 hoplites in the war against Brennus in 279 B.C. Destroyed again, by the Bulgars in the middle ages, it was rebuilt by the Franks, who renamed it *Salona*. The Picard Autremencourt barons of Salona were feudatories of the kings of Salonika. In 1311 the Catalan Roger Deslaurs took the title of count, which passed in 1335 to Alfonso Frederichs of Aragon. In 1394 Salona fell to the Turks.

FROM AMFISSA TO LAMIA, 45½ m. (bus), magnificent asphalt road with sharp winding ascent and descent of the *Pass of Gravia* (2855 ft), between Gkiona and Parnassos, celebrated for its heroic defence in 1821 by Odysseus Androutsos with 180 Greeks, against 3000 Turks.—20½ m. *Graviá*, and thence viâ (25½ m.) Brallos to Lamia, see Rte 44A.

To *Návpaktos* and *Mesolongi*, see Rte 55.

46   DELPHI

Approaches and hotels, see Rte 45. A hurried visit to the site can be made in 3 hrs; a reasonably thorough exploration requires at least twice as long. The hilly terrain is tiring though there are good paths. Changes of temperature are frequent and often violent; even in high summer a light woollen garment or wind-cheater is an advisable precaution.

**DELPHI (ΔΕΛΦΟΙ; Dhelfí), transformed by the excavators' skill since it disappointed Byron and Barry, is by common consent the most spectacularly beautiful ancient site in Greece and the one which, even to the uninitiated, most vividly evokes the Classical past. In antiquity Delphi was regarded as the centre of the world ('ομφαλὸς γῆς) and to this and to its oracle the place owed its prestige, which extended far beyond the Greek world. The sacred precinct enjoys a superb situation below the s. slopes of Parnassos within the angle formed by the twin *Phaedriades* ('Shining Rocks', so called because they reflect the light), which constitute a tremendous precipice 800–1000 ft high. The w. rock is called *Rhodini* ('Roseate'), anciently Nauplia; from the E. rock, *Phleboukos* ('Flamboyant', anciently Hyampeia) the Delphians used to hurl those found guilty of sacrilege. The cleft between the two rocks, hollowed out by cascades from the upper plateau is continued on the s. by a line of ravines, by which the waters flow into the Pleistos. To the w. the rocky spur of Mt Ay. Ilias (2297 ft) completes the theatre-like setting. On the s. Delphi is bounded by the ravine of the river Pleistos, in which the pipeline from Lidhoriki is conspicuous; beyond rises the barrier of Mt Kirphys. The site is in a seismic area. On several occasions earthquakes and storms have caused the fall of great fragments of rock from Parnassos and serious landslips endangering the safety of the monuments. The *View down the sacred plain to Itéa, with its myriad olive-trees, is not the least of the delights which make Delphi the goal of countless excursions every day of the year.

History. The natural features of the site, in the 'centre of the world', with its springs, exhalations and crevasses, in a theatre of forbidding precipices, have helped to give Delphi its mysterious and sacred character. In the beginning it was sacred to Mother Earth and Poseidon, and was called *Pytho*, the name by which it is known in Homer (Iliad IX, 405; Odyssey VIII, 80). It had an oracle where the Pythia officiated near the cave of the serpent Python, son of Mother Earth. At an early date Delphi was colonized by settlers from *Lykorea*, which was situated on the plateau above it, but it was in the territory of *Krisa* and was therefore partially subject to that city.

The importation into Krisa from Crete of the cult of Apollo Delphinios, an island deity worshipped in the form of a dolphin, led to the introduction of his cult at Pytho, which then changed its name to *Delphoi*. Henceforward the holy place became the Sanctuary of Pythian Apollo. Later other gods were associated with the sanctuary; these included Dionysos and Athena Pronoia. The Pythian Games, one of the four great national Greek festivals, were instituted in honour of Apollo, Artemis and Leto, and at first were held every eight years (see below). The fame of the oracle, whose efficacy was fostered by its priestly administrators, spread all over the ancient world, and the festival attracted competitors and visitors from far and wide.

After the Dorian Invasion (c. 1100 B.C.) the sanctuary became a centre of an association called the *Amphictyonic League*. This was by false etymology supposed to have been founded by Amphictyon, but really only means the league of the dwellers round a particular locality. The league was composed of twelve tribes, each of which contained various city-states, large and small, all of which had equal status within it, whatever their importance outside. Both Athens and Sparta belonged to the league, but they had in theory no more authority in it than some insignificant states that happened to be members. This rudimentary United Nations included Thessalians, Dorians, Ionians and Achaeans.

The city of Krisa levied dues on all pilgrims to Delphi, many of whom had to disembark at its port of Kirrha. Early in the 6C the pilgrims complained of extortionate charges, and the Delphians appealed to the Amphictyonic League. The league, urged on, it is said, by Athens, declared war against the Krisaeans. The ensuing conflict was known as the *First Sacred War* (c. 595–586 B.C.). Invaluable assistance was given by Kleisthenes of Sikyon, and Krisa, with its port Kirrha, was destroyed. Its territory was confiscated. The Amphictyonic League took the Temple of Apollo at Delphi under its wing, and the state of Delphi was made autonomous. The Krisaean Plain was dedicated to the god and no one was allowed to till it or use it for grazing on pain of excommunication. About this time the Pythian Games were reorganized and, from 582 B.C., like the Olympic Games, were held every four years (see below). Kleisthenes won the first chariot race. He later instituted Pythian Games at Sikyon. Now followed a period of great prosperity. In this century the Treasuries of Corinth, Sikyon and Klazomenai were dedicated. Croesus, last king of Lydia (560–546 B.C.), was a great benefactor of the sanctuary—to no avail in his case. Amasis, king of Egypt, was another. These world-wide benefactions show that, while Olympia may be regarded as an expression of Greek nationalism, the prestige of Delphi rested on its international character. In 548 B.C. the temple was destroyed by fire. The contract to rebuild was let to the exiled Athenian Alkmaeonidae (p. 61), who gained a reputation for munificence by facing the new temple with Parian marble instead of the common stone prescribed in the specifications (Hdt. V, 62).

In the Persian Wars the oracle was inclined to medize. Nevertheless, in 480 B.C., Xerxes sent a detachment to plunder the temple. The soldiers had reached the Sanctuary of Athena Pronoia when thunder was heard and two huge crags rolled down and crushed many of them to death (Hdt. VIII, 35–39; comp. below). After the Persian defeats, trophies, statues, and new treasuries were set up in celebration. Delphi now became involved, despite the prudence of its administrators, in the rivalries of the leading Greek states. The oracle lost much of its prestige because of charges of partiality and corruption; but offerings continued to arrive from the conflicting states and from foreign rulers such as the tyrants of Syracuse.

In 448 B.C. occurred the *Second Sacred War*, in which the Lacedaemonians wrested the temple from the Phocians and handed it over to the Delphians. As soon as they had withdrawn the Athenians recovered the temple and handed it back to the Phocians. The Delphians soon got it back and their possession of it was confirmed in the Peace of Nicias (421 B.C.). In 373 the temple was again destroyed, this time by an earthquake, and it was again rebuilt, by international cooperation. In 356 the Phocians, who had, on the accusation of Thebes, been fined by the Amphictyonic League for having cultivated a portion of the Krisaean Plain, retaliated by seizing Delphi with all its treasures. This precipitated the *Third Sacred War*, during which Phocis temporarily became one of the leading powers in Greece. In 346, when the conflict had been determined by the intervention of Philip of Macedon, the temple was restored to the custody of the Amphictyonic League. In the same year Philip, who had replaced Phocis in the league, was elected president of the Pythian Games. The *Fourth Sacred War* broke out in 339. This time it was the Amphissans who were accused of cultivating the Krisaean Plain. The Amphictyons appealed to Philip, who invaded Greece in 338, won the battle of Chaironeia, and destroyed the city of Amphissa.

The Aetolians succeeded the Macedonians as masters of Delphi. In 279 B.C. Brennus and his Gauls advanced to the attack of Delphi by the same route as the Persians in 480. They were repulsed in the same supernatural manner. Their retreat was disastrous. Some years later their discomfiture was celebrated in the festival of the *Soteria*, organized by the Aetolians. In 189 the Aetolians were driven out by the Romans. Under Roman sway the oracle lost further prestige, as the Romans did not take its utterances very seriously. The precinct was plundered by Sulla in 86 B.C.; by way of compensation, he gave the Delphians half the territory of dismembered Thebes.

In the imperial era the fortunes of the oracle depended on the whim of the ruler for the time being. Augustus reorganized the Amphictyonic League. Nero seized over 500 bronze statues in a fit of rage at the oracle's condemnation of his matricide. Domitian effected some restoration. Pliny counted more than 3000 statues and Pausanias found Delphi still rich in works of art. It was restored by Hadrian and the Antonines to much of its former splendour. Constantine carried off several of its treasures to adorn his new capital. The oracle was consulted by Julian, but was finally abolished by Theodosius about A.D. 385. Long before its extinction its authority, impaired by its strong Doric prejudices, had sadly diminished. Towards the end its utterances were almost entirely concerned with private and domestic matters such as marriages, loans, voyages and sales.—Cyriac of Ancona copied inscriptions here in March 1436, after which the site appears to have been ignored until rediscovered by Wheler and Spon in 1676. Flaubert records finding in 1851 Byron's name on a column of the new destroyed Panayia.

The Oracle. The Delphic oracle was the most famous in Greece. Those who wished to consult it first sacrificed a sheep, goat, boar or other animal, after which (if the omens were favourable) they went into the room adjoining the *Adyton*. There they awaited their turn, which was determined by lot, unless they had received from the Delphians the *Promanteia*, or prior right of consultation. No women were admitted. They handed in questions written on leaden tablets, many of which have been discovered. The *Pythia*, or priestess who delivered the oracle, was a peasant woman over 50 years old. At the height of the oracle's fame there were three of them. After purifying herself in the Castalian Fountain and drinking of the water of the Kassotis, and munching a laurel leaf, she took her seat upon the tripod, which was placed over the chasm in the Adyton. Intoxicated by the exhalations from the chasm, she uttered incoherent sounds, which were interpreted in hexameter verse by a poet in waiting. The interpretation, which was always obscure and frequently equivocal, was handed over to the enquirer, who not seldom returned more mystified than he had come. Even Croesus, the great benefactor of Delphi, was cruelly misled by the oracle on the eve of his war with Persia. All the same, according to Strabo, "of all oracles in the world it had the reputation of being the most truthful".

Festivals. The PYTHIAN GAMES were instituted to commemorate Apollo's slaying of the serpent Python. At first they were held every eight years. Originally they were little more than a religious ceremony taking the form of a hymn in honour of Apollo. After the Amphictyonic League had taken over the control of the temple in the early 6C (see above), the games were reorganized and held every four years. The first Pythiad of the new regime was in 582 B.C. The festival began with sacrifices and a sacred play about the fight of Apollo and the serpent. There followed, in the theatre, musical contests of cithara, flute and song, and hymns of praise in honour of Apollo; later tragedies and comedies were added. Then came athletic competitions in the stadium, and finally chariot races in the Krisaean Plain, the prize for which was a laurel wreath. The Greek states sent *Theoriae*, or sacred embassies, to the games, who were loaded with gifts to the god. The Athenians also sent on occasions not connected with the games a special embassy or *Pythiad* for the purpose of holding a separate festival, which included athletic games and plays. After the repulse of the Gauls in 278 B.C. a special festival called the *Soteria* was held under the aegis of the Aetolians (see above). In the imperial era the interval between the games reverted to eight years.

Excavations. The French architect Laurent examined the site in 1838. He was followed in 1840 by Ottfried Müller, who succumbed to a fever contracted here, and E. Curtius. In 1860–61 Foucart and others did some preliminary work. In 1892 an exhaustive survey was begun by the French School, under the leadership of Th. Homolle. The work went on at high pressure until 1903. Since then it has slowed down but not ceased. The figures on the plan correspond with those of the French excavation reports.

Following Pausanias (X, 8, 6 ff.), we begin our visit with the attractive spot called **Marmaria**, nearly a mile to the E. of the Sanctuary. We descend to it from the Arakhova road by a pathway. Marmaria was the **Sanctuary of Athena,** whom the Delphians worshipped as *Athena Pronaia* (Guardian of the Temple), or, by a play upon words, as *Athena Pronoia* (Providence). Some of the finest sculptures found here are in the Museum. The precinct is roughly rectangular, with the entrance on the E.

An upper terrace N. of the gate supported the small *Precinct of Phylakos*; one of its two buildings was the *Heroon of Phylakos*, who, with Autonoos, routed the Persians in 480 B.C. The other may have been dedicated to the saviours of Delphi at the time of the onset of the Gauls in 279 B.C. An inscription on the retaining wall locates the *Altars of Athena Hygieia* and of *Eileithyia*.

We pass through the gateway, noticing the huge lintel on the ground, into the oldest part of the sanctuary, dedicated to *Athena Hygieia* and *Zosteria*, where the excavations of 1922 revealed the existence of a Mycenean settlement (finds in the Museum). We immediately come upon the remains of the OLD TEMPLE OF ATHENA PRONOIA. This was a Doric peripteral hexastyle in tufa, built at the beginning of the 5C B.C. on the site of a still older edifice (7C) from which capitals survive. The temple was damaged in 480 B.C. by the fall of rocks that routed the Persians and its ruin was completed by the earthquake of 373. Fifteen columns and the stylobate had been brought to light when in 1905 another landslip demolished all but three of the columns.

The centre of the precinct is occupied by three buildings. A *Doric Treasury* (490–460 B.C.), of marble, stood on a lime-stone foundation. The Aeolian *Treasury of Massalia*, in antis, built c. 530 B.C. in Parian marble, was of remarkably fine workmanship, recalling the Treasury of the Siphnians. The third building, a Pentelic marble *Tholos, or Rotunda, of the early 4C, was one of the finest in Delphi. Its dedication and purpose are unknown. It has a circular peristyle of 20 slender Doric columns on a platform of three steps. Three columns with their entablature were re-erected in 1938; the cornice and metopes have been restored in replica from the best surviving fragments. The entrance to the circular cella was on the s. The paved interior was decorated with Corinthian half-columns. To the w. of the Tholos c. 360 B.C. rose the NEW TEMPLE OF ATHENA PRONOIA, a severe prostyle edifice having a portico of six columns of the Doric order. Beyond this temple, and partly built over by it, is an earlier rectangular building (5C), probably a priest's dwelling.

To the N.W. of Marmaria are the remains of the **Gymnasium,** originally dating from the 4C B.C., but rebuilt by the Romans. The slope of the ground necessitated its arrangement on different levels. On the upper level was the *Xystos*, or covered colonnade, where the athletes practised in bad weather, with a parallel track in the open air. The lower terrace was occupied by the *Palaestra*. This is divided into the Palaestra proper, a court 45 ft square surrounded by a colonnade on all four sides, and the *Baths*, comprising a circular (cold) bath 30 ft in diameter and 6 ft deep, and, in the retaining wall at the back, a series of douche baths.—The hot baths, N. of the court, are a Roman addition. A column hereabouts bears the names of Byron and Hobhouse.

We return to the road. A short way farther up, on a sharp bend, opens the ravine separating the two Phaedriades. Here is the celebrated **Castalian Fountain** (1765 ft). By this spring Apollo planted a cutting of the laurel he had brought from Tempe (see Rte 57). The base of a statue of Ge, the goddess of Earth, shows that the spring was an early place of cult-worship.

In this spring all who came to Delphi for any religious object whatever had to purify themselves. The bathing of the hair seems to have been the principal part of the ceremony and is one attributed to the god himself. Murderers, however, bathed the whole body. The fancy which ascribed poetic inspiration to the waters of the Castalian fountain was an invention of the Roman poets. The fountain as we see it today is of Roman or Hellenistic date.

The spring was ornamented with a façade of seven marble pilasters. The four niches seen therein doubtless were for votive offerings; in the largest of them is a column drum once used as the altar of a Byzantine chapel. The water was collected in a long narrow reservoir (30 ft by 3 ft) which fed seven jets (holes still visible). These jets fell into a rectangular court, 30 ft by 10 ft, reached by rock-hewn steps. The overflow from the fountain joins the water of the gorge dividing the Phaedriades, which plunges into a deep rocky glen, to join the Pleistos flowing in the Delphic valley far below. An Archaic square fountain house, discovered in 1957, lies nearer the road.

A wide, paved path leads to the main entrance of the Pythian Sanctuary and Museum. Admission 50 dr. to each; free Sundays. The Sanctuary is open weekdays 8 or 9 to 5, 6, or 7, Sun & hol. 10–4.30 and the Museum on weekdays except Tues, 9 or 9.30 to 4.30, 6, or 7, Sun & hol. 10–4.30. Lavatories at top of first flight of entrance steps.

The **PYTHIAN SANCTUARY**, or *Temenos of Apollo*, like the much more extensive Altis at Olympia, was an enclosure containing many monuments besides the temple. This sacred precinct was situated on the rising ground above the town. It was surrounded by the usual *Peribolos*, or enclosure wall, with several gates. Its shape is that of an irregular quadrangle or trapezium, and it measures about 200 yds by 140. The s. wall is built of squared blocks and dates from the 5C B.C.; the w. and N. walls, which are polygonal, from the 6C; while the splendid E. wall was rebuilt in the 4C. on the old foundations by the architect Agathon. The steepness of the slope necessitated terraces, running E.–W., and the provision of a separate platform for each building. The terraces, some having a gate on either side, were intersected by the *Sacred Way*, which wound up from the main entrance, at the S.E., to the N.W. corner.

From the main entrance modern steps lead to a paved rectangular *Square*, which was enclosed by Roman porticoes and doubtless used as a market-place for the sale of religious objects. Five steps lead up to the *Main Gate*, 12 ft wide, through which we enter the **Sacred Way**. This is 12–16 ft wide, and was paved in the Roman period with slabs taken from near-by buildings. Most of this makeshift pavement is intact. The Sacred Way was adorned on either side with the votive monuments that are a feature of the precinct.

Immediately within the gate, to the right, stood the *Bull of Corcyra*

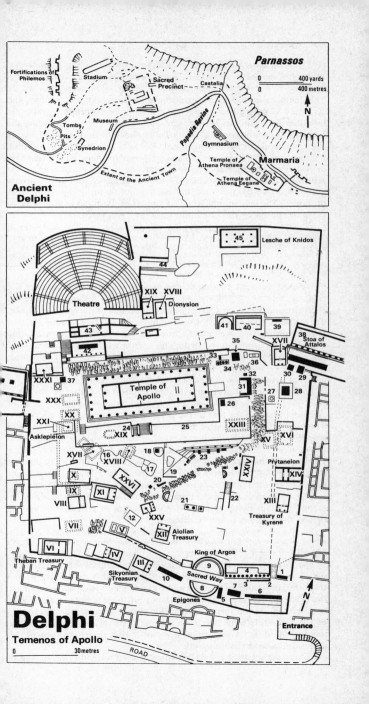

Parnassos

Fortifications of Philemos

Stadium

Sacred Precinct

Castalia

Tombs

Museum

Pits

Synedrion

Papadia Ravine

Extent of the Ancient Town

Gymnasium

Marmaria

Temple of Athena Pronaea

Temple of Athena Eegane

Ancient Delphi

0 — 400 yards
0 — 400 metres

N

Lesche of Knidos

45

44

XIX XVIII Dionysion

Theatre

43

41 40 39

38 Stoa of Attalos

XVII

35

42

33

34 36

30 29

32

31 26

27 28

Temple of Apollo

XXIII

XXXI 37

XXX

XXI XX

XV XVI

XIX

24

XVIII XIX

25

Asklepieion

Phytaneion

XVII

16

18

XIV

XVIII

17

23

XXIV

X

19

20

IX

XI XXVI

22

VIII

21

XIII

VII

12

XXV

Treasury of Kyrene

V

XII Aiolian Treasury

VI

King of Argos

Theban Treasury

9

10

4 1

III

Sacred Way

7 3 2

Sikyonian Treasury

8

5 6

Epigones

Delphi

Temenos of Apollo

0 — 30 metres

ROAD

Entrance

N

(Pl. 1). The base, which we see, supported a bronze bull by Theopropos of Aegina, dedicated c. 480 B.C. from the proceeds of a catch of tunny. Next, beyond a flight of steps, are the *Offerings of the Arcadians* (Pl. 2). The line of bases supported nine bronze statues of Apollo, Victory, and Arcadian heroes. They were erected to commemorate a successful invasion of Laconia in 369 B.C. and placed, out of bravado, facing the Lacedaemonian monument, insult being added to injury by employing the ageing sculptor Antiphanes (comp. below). The *Base* (Pl. 3), beyond, bore a statue of Philopoemen. The grandiose *Monument of the Admirals*, dedicated by the Spartan Lysander in 403 B.C. after he had crushed the Athenians at Aegospotami, held 37 bronze statues of gods and Spartiate admirals, made by nine Peloponnesian sculptors including Antiphanes of Argos. The inscriptions from the statues of Lysander and Arakos, in verse composed by Ion of Samos, have been recovered.

Until 1963 it was commonly accepted that the large rectangular exedra (Pl. 4) behind the Arcadian bases was Lysander's monument though there have been attempts recently to place it on the s. side of the Sacred Way (Pl. 6).—On the s. side also was the *Offering of Marathon*, dedicated by the Athenians 30 years after the battle in honour of Miltiades. The long base supported 16 statues, the original ones by Pheidias, according to Pausanias.

We pass between two semicircular exedrae, both dedicated by the Argives, that to the left erected in honour of the *Epigones* (Pl. 8) the successors of the Seven Champions, likewise out of the spoils of Oinoe. To the right the *Kings of Argos* monument (Pl. 9) was added at the foundation of Messene, and its position near to the Spartan offering would not have gone unnoticed. This exedra was to bear 20 statues of the early kings and heroes of Argos. Ten statues only were finished, filling the w. quadrant; their bases have been restored to place.—The adjacent square niche is covered with personal decrees.

To the left four plinths survive, three of them with inscriptions, from the *Offerings of the Tarentines* (Pl. 10); the statues were by Ageladas of Argos. Beyond is the first of the many TREASURIES we shall encounter. These served much the same purpose as those at Olympia; in them were stored smaller votive offerings, vessels, etc., and here important documents were recorded. The TREASURY OF THE SIKYONIANS (Pl. III), a Doric edifice in antis, was built about the beginning of the 5C in place of those raised by Kleisthenes after the First Sacred War. In the foundations were used remains of two older buildings, a tholos of 13 columns (c. 580 B.C.) and a rectangular monopteros of 14 columns surmounted by a roof, perhaps designed to shelter the chariot of Kleisthenes; to this belong the metopes in the museum.

Opposite, to the right, behind unidentifiable bases, are some confused foundations of an unidentified Aeolian treasury. Another destroyed *Treasury* (Pl. V) was perhaps that of the Megarians.

The TREASURY OF THE SIPHNIANS (Pl. IV) the massive foundations of which we now pass, was built in 526–525 B.C. with a tithe of the profits from the gold-mines of Siphnos and was intended to surpass in opulence the existing treasuries at Delphi. It was an Ionic temple in antis, with two columns in the form of Caryatids between the antae. Fragments of the Caryatids were found on the site (now in the museum). The treasury faced w. A sculptured frieze of Parian marble ran round the four sides (also in the museum).

We have reached the so-called CROSSROADS OF THE TREASURIES. A branch-road,

30 yds long runs to a w. gate. On its s. side was the *Treasury of the Thebans* (Pl. VI) built after Leuktra. At the corner some vestiges may mark the *Treasury of the Boeotians* (Pl. VII). Behind the Treasury of the Athenians (comp. below) are unimportant remains of three further treasuries: that of the Potidaians (Pl. VIII), an older Athenian treasury (?; Pl. IX), and that of the Etruscans (Pl. X).

The Sacred Way, now at an altitude of 1805 ft, describes a semicircle and ascends to the N.E. Prominent on the left is the *Treasury of the Athenians** (Pl. XI), built just after 490 B.C. with a tithe of the spoils of Marathon. The French School, aided by a large grant from the municipality of Athens, re-erected the building in 1904–06. The scattered stones were put back in their proper places (more than four-fifths of them having been found), though the foundations had to be readjusted and the columns supplied. This Doric building is distyle *in antis*, and measures 33 ft by 20. It stands on a terrace ending in a triangular buttress and reached by a staircase from the Sacred Way. The triglyph frieze depicted the exploits of Herakles and of Theseus; the originals are in the Museum, the sculptures *in situ* being casts in arbitrary positions.

The walls are covered with more than 150 inscriptions. Many of them, decorated with crowns, refer to the Athenian Pythaid, or special embassy (comp. p. 77); others include honorific decrees in favour of the Athenians, decrees of the Amphictyons about Dionysiac artists, and two *Hymns to Apollo*, with the musical notation in Greek letters above the text.—On the s. the terrace ended in a triangular space on which were displayed the trophies of Marathon with the dedication "The Athenians dedicate to Apollo the spoils of the Medes after the battle of Marathon". The inscription is a 3C copy of the damaged original.

Just across the Sacred Way must be located the *Treasury of the Syracusans* (Pl. 12), which (true to form) was erected here after the Athenian expedition had come to grief. This part of the sanctuary was dug into by a Christian cemetery, but some surviving foundation blocks mark the spot. Adjacent are the foundations of the *Treasury of the Knidians* (Pl. XXV), built in Parian marble before the capture of Knidos in 544 B.C. by the Persians. A lateral road leads E. to the *Treasury of Cyrene* (Pl. XIII), probably of mid-4C date.

The *Bouleuterion* (Pl. XXVI), seat of the Delphic senate, was a plain rectangular building. Higher up is the SANCTUARY OF EARTH or of GE-THEMIS (Pl. 16), part of which was destroyed to make way for the great retaining wall. This is a circle of rocks surrounding a natural cleft in the ground, and is the site (or one of them) of the primitive oracle of Ge-Themis, guarded by the serpent Python. One of the rocks, supported by modern masonry, was the *Rock of the Sibyl* (Pl. 17) on which, according to ancient local tradition, the sibyl Herophile prophesied. Another rock supported a statue of Leto; on a third was the *Monument of the Naxians* (Pl. 18) dedicated c. 570 B.C. This was an Ionic column with 44 flutings, over 30 ft high, surmounted by a sphinx (now in the museum). The lower part of the column is in situ. An inscription of 322 B.C. on the base renews to the Naxians the right of Promanteia.

A little higher up the Sacred Way crosses the *Threshing Floor* (Halos), a circular place 50 ft in diameter, surrounded by seats. Here was presented every seventh year the Septerion, a morality play celebrating the death of Python. To the N. was the STOA OF THE ATHENIANS (Pl. 23), dedicated after the end of the Persian Wars. A three-stepped limestone basement supported a colonnade, 98 ft long and 13 ft deep, consisting of 8 Ionic columns in Parian marble, set 13 ft apart. The architrave was of wood, as well as the roof, which leaned against the wall of the temple terrace. On the top step of the basement is an Archaic inscription recording the Athenian dedication of cables (from the pontoon bridge thrown by Xerxes across the Hellespont) and figureheads (from Persian ships).

Beneath the Byzantine paving in front of the portico was found a deposit of ivory, gold, and bronze votive objects, which had been damaged in a fire in the mid-5C and deliberately buried.—A lane branches off to the right to a small gate in the peribolos wall. On the right (s.) of this lane is the *Treasury of Corinth* (Pl. XXIV), ascribed by Herodotus to Kypselos. It was not only the oldest but the richest of the buildings of this kind, thanks to the generosity of the kings of Lydia. Opposite (N.) are the remains of two destroyed treasuries (Pl. XV, XVI) and of the *Prytaneion* (Pl. XIV).—Outside the gate, to the N., are Roman baths, with mosaics.

The Sacred Way now describes another curve (to the N.; 1840 ft), below and to the right of the remarkable POLYGONAL WALL, which supports the platform on which stands the Temple of Apollo. It is built in irregular interlocking blocks with curved joints, a style unique to Delphi, having the double practical and aesthetic advantages of strength in seismic shocks without appearing to be a rigid barrier across the sanctuary.

The wall, site of the first excavations at Delphi, follows the irregularities of the ground. Its height varies from 6 to 12 ft, and its total length from E. to W. is c. 270 ft. The dressed face of the wall was covered in the 2C B.C.–1C A.D. with inscriptions of every kind, more than 800 having been found. Along the base the rough-hewn blocks project in their natural condition. The blocks of the upper courses were joined by double T-clamps run with lead.—Towards the S.E. end the inscriptions are particularly numerous. Records, public and private, important and trivial, are all mixed together; they relate above all to the emancipation of slaves, and constitute an invaluable record of Delphic families and events.

The SACRED WAY, here about 20 ft wide and well paved, climbs steeply. On the right is the site of the TRIPOD OF PLATAIA (Pl. 27). The circular pedestal has been re-erected. This offering was dedicated by the Greeks from the spoils of Plataea (Paus. X, 13, 9). On the stone base was a gilt bronze pedestal about 18 ft high, consisting of 3 intertwined serpents, on which were engraved the names of the 31 city-states contributing to the victory. This was carried off by Constantine the Great and still reposes in a mutilated state in the ancient Hippodrome, at Istanbul. The three serpent heads supported a golden tripod, which was seized by the Phocians after 356 B.C.

At the top of the slope we come to the so-called Crossroads of the Tripods, where stand the bases of long vanished votive offerings. The most remarkable were the *Tripods of Gelon and Hiero* (Pl. 36), tyrants of Syracuse, and of their brothers. The offering which commemorated Gelon's victory at Himera over the Carthaginians in 481 B.C., comprised four monuments supporting golden tripods and Victories, weighing 50 talents in all. They were some of the earliest objects to be looted when in 353 B.C. the Phocians needed funds for the Sacred War. The *Stele*, in front, adorned with a bull, bears an honorific decree in favour of a citizen of Kleitor in Arcadia. The base adjoining that of the tripods on the left is that of the *Acanthus Column* with the dancing girls, now in the museum.

Before entering the temple terrace, we may visit a group of buildings to the E. On our right, adjacent to the Plataian Tripod, is the rectangular plinth of a *Chariot of Helios* (Pl. 28), dedicated by the Rhodians. A detailed examination (see B.C.H. 1963) of the cuttings into which the hooves of the quadriga fitted has suggested that the missing horses may be those now adorning St Mark's cathedral, Venice, though these have been derived by other authorities from a similar group made for Alexander the Great and set up at Corinth in 336 B.C. On the left are a ruined Treasury (Acanthians ?), and two enormous bases, which bore statues of *Eumenes* (Pl. 29) and *Attalos* (Pl. 30) of Pergamon. Above, extending across the temenos wall, are the ruins of the *Stoa of Attalos* (Pl. 38).

The Sacred Way turns w. and becomes the upper walk of the temple precinct (1880 ft). In front of the entrance to the E. is the *Great Altar of Apollo* (Pl. 31) a rectangular structure with steps in black and white marble, dedicated by the Chians in gratitude for their deliverance from the Persians. It presumably kept the orientation of its predecessor, which is slightly oblique to the present temple but accorded with that of the temple burnt in 548 B.C. The altar was piously re-erected in 1920 at the expense of the inhabitants of Chios but restored more accurately in 1960.

Between the altar and its temple extends an esplanade bearing bases of other monuments. By the altar stood a golden statue of Eumenes II (Pl. 32). A big square plinth (Pl. 35) bore perhaps the Apollo Sitalcus; there follow the dual column-bases (Pl. 34) of the offering of Aristaineta and the base of the Palm-tree of Eurymedon, dedicated by the Athenians after their victory of 468 B.C. Behind is the restored *Monument of Prusias II* (Pl. 33), king of Bithynia (182–149), which bore an equestrian statue of that devious monarch.

The **Temple of Apollo**, reduced before the restorations of 1939–41 to its bare foundations, rests on its N. side on the living rock, and on the s. side on a huge substructure of irregular courses nearly 200 ft long and 10–15 ft high. The foundations consist of two concentric rectangles, the outer supporting the peristyle and the inner the sekos. The stylobate, on three steps of fine bluish local limestone, has been partially restored and many of the pavement blocks returned to place. One complete column of the 4C façade and portions of the others have been re-erected so that the building, even in its ruin, once again dominates the sanctuary as it should. A stone ramp leads up to the entrance of the temple on the E.

History. Discounting the legendary constructions of laurel, beeswax, and bronze, of which Pausanias gives the traditional account but for which there is no archaeological evidence, the existing building had two predecessors. An edifice of the 7C was burnt in 548 B.C., and replaced by a larger temple, started perhaps in 536, but completed in 513–505 by the Alkmeonids, who were in exile from Athens. Of this archaic temple, which was admired by Aeschylus, Pindar, and Euripides, fragments, including some of the pedimental sculptures by Antenor, have been found (now in the museum). It was ruined in 373 B.C. The existing temple was built in 366–c. 329 by Xenodoros and Agathon on the old foundations. It was fired in 88 B.C. by Thracian invaders, and restored by Domitian after the further ravages of Sulla. The robbing of the metal clamps in the middle ages was the prime cause of its final dismemberment.

The temple was the usual Doric peripteral hexastyle, 197 ft by 72, with 6 stuccoed poros columns at the ends and 15 on the sides. Both pronaos and opisthodomos had 2 columns between antae. The architrave was decorated with shields captured from the Persians at Plataea (E. side) and from the Gauls (w. and s. sides). Some of the spouts and marble tiles have been discovered, but not a fragment of the pediments described by Pausanias. Earthquakes and systematic spoliation have left practically nothing of the sekos, so that we know nothing with certainty about the arrangement of the *Adyton*, or inner shrine. This was an underground chamber, in which were the *Omphalos* and the *Oracular Chasm*.

To the w. of the temple are the foundations of a Roman building (Pl. XX), in which was found the statue of Antinous, now in the museum.—From the s.w. angle of the temple we may descend past the *House of the Pythia* (?; Pl. XXIX) to the s. walk (Pl. 25). In the s.e. corner was probably the *Offering of the Messenians of Naupaktos* (Pl. XXIII), erected to commemorate their victory at Sphakteria. Below the temple ramp was the monument of Aemilius Paullus (Pl. 26).

The Sacred Way was protected above the Temple of Apollo by a retaining wall, called the *Ischegaon*, constructed c. 355 B.C. of reused material from the Alkmaeonid temple. This was examined by the French School during the 1950–57 excavations. At the N.W. angle of the terrace was the *Offering of Polyzalos*, which was buried in some catastrophe (? 373 B.C.) and from which the celebrated Charioteer was recovered. Adjoining on the w. is the *Lion Hunt of Alexander the Great* (Pl. 42), a large rectangular exedra of dressed stones.

An epigram on the back wall has established the identity of this exedra with the monument described by Pliny and Plutarch. It was dedicated in 320 B.C. by Krateros, who had saved the life of Alexander the Great during a lion-hunt near Susa. A bronze group by Lysippos and Leochares represented the incident (comp. also the mosaic at Pella).

We mount a Roman staircase to the *Theatre, one of the best pre-served in Greece, built in the 4C B.C., and restored by Eumenes II in 159 and by the Romans. The Cavea was contained in a parallelogram 165 ft broad. The N. and w. sides of the *Analemma*, or supporting wall, coincide with the line of the peribolos. The 35 tiers of seats were divided into 2 uneven sections by a paved *Diazoma* or landing (28 in the lower section and 7 in the upper). The seats were of white marble from Parnassos. The *Orchestra* was paved with polygonal slabs and measured 60 ft across. It was surrounded by an enclosed conduit. The front of the *Stage* (Pl. 43) was adorned with a frieze in relief depicting the Labours of Herakles (now in the museum). There is a fine *View of the sanctuary from the top of the theatre (1955 ft).

Between the stage buildings and the Alexander exedra a pathway runs E. above the Ischegaon, passing a semicircular exedra (Pl. 41). Beyond is the *Monument of the Thessalians* (Pl. 40), a rectangular exedra, dedicated by Daochos II of Pharsala, who as hieromnemon represented Thessaly in 336–332 at the Amphictyonic League, over which he presided. On a plinth 40 ft long stood statues of his house; the inscriptions remain in situ and five of the statues are in the museum. Beyond is the ruined *Temenos of Neoptolemos* (Pl. 39), beneath which have been excavated remains of a primitive village of the Mycenean period that gradually became superseded as the cult grew in importance. In front is a long base atttributed to the Corcyraeans.

Somewhere N.E. of the theatre was the *Fountain of Kassotis* (1952 ft), the water of which descended into the Adyton. This was an artificial reservoir fed by the *Delphousa* (now *Kerna*), a spring which rises from a rock 75 yds N. The Pythia drank the waters of this spring before prophesying. Two stages of the *Kerna Fountain*, one Classical, the other Archaic, have been uncovered between the theatre and the stadium. Farther E. of the theatre was the *Lesche of the Knidians* (Pl. 45). This was a club-house dedicated by the Knidians c. 450 B.C. The building formed a rectangle 62 ft by 32, with a door in the middle of the s. side. The walls, of unburnt brick, rested on a socle of poros. The wooden roof was held in place by 8 wooden pillars. The club was adorned by Polygnotos with paintings described in detail by Pausanias.

A path winds up from the diazoma of the theatre to (5 min.) the **Stadium.** This was situated in the highest part of the ancient city (2116 ft). The N. side is hewn out of the rock. The s. side was artificially supported, and recent excavations now afford a fine view of the massive supporting blocks of Classical masonry (5C B.C.). Four pillars remain of the Roman *Triumphal Arch* which decorated the s.e. entrance of the final form given it by Herodes Atticus. The *Track* was then established at 600 Roman feet (582 ft). Both starting-point (*Aphesis*) and finishing post (*Terma*) had stone sills with posts separating the 17 or 18 runners.— The N. long side had 12 tiers of seats; 13 staircases divided it into 12 rectangular blocks. A rectangular tribune, on which are benches with backs, was the stand of the *Proedria* or presidents of the games. The W. end or *Sphendone* had the conventional semicircular shape (unlike the Stadia at Olympia and at Epidauros). Here were 6 tiers of seats divided by 3 staircases into 4 *Cunei*. The S. long side had only 6 tiers of seats. There was accommodation for 7000 spectators.

Above the Stadium, to the W., on the slopes of Mt Ayios Ilias (2297 ft), the *Fortress of Philomelos*, the sole fortification of Delphi, was built in 355 B.C. as a defence against the Lokrians of Amphissa. The hill again saw fighting in the Communist civil war.—To the S. of the fortress are threshing-floors and tombs. Here was the *West Necropolis*. Sepulchral relics of every age, from the Mycenean to the Byzantine, have been found in this region. The *Chapel of Ay. Ilias*, on the road between the Sanctuary and the village, stands on a rectangular platform partly built of ancient masonry. This was the site of the *Synedrion* or place of assembly built by Hadrian for the Amphictyonic League. The spot was called *Pylaea*. The name was afterwards given to a suburb which came into existence here in Roman times.—Above the chapel is an interesting *Tomb* and, N. of the tomb, is the *House of the French School*. Below this is a sepulchral crypt.—Just S. is the Museum.

The **Museum** (closed Tues), rebuilt in 1959–61 and splendidly arranged, is especially rich in Archaic sculpture from the site; the free-standing work may be compared with that in the Acropolis museum, while the relief sculpture ranks with the Aegina marbles in Munich.

TERRACE: Sarcophagus of Meleager, discovered by Capodistrias; large panelled mosaic (5C A.D.) depicting animals and birds.—We enter, and ascend the stair (r.) to the LANDING (R. 1), where stands the Omphalos, a sculptured stone found in the S. wall of the Temple of Apollo and anciently believed to mark the point where the eagles of Zeus met at the centre of the known world. Cauldron on marble stand (7C; restored). The poor frieze of the Labours of Herakles (1C A.D.) on the left wall is from the proscenium of the theatre.

ROOM 2 (HALL OF THE BRONZE SHIELDS). On the walls, heavy bronze shields of Cretan or Hittite style; in the centre, small bronze Kouros (Daedalic; c. 650 B.C.); Griffins.

ROOM 3. Two *Kouroi, erected to commemorate Cleobis and Biton, who were called to heaven by the Gods while asleep in the Heraion of Argos as a reward for yoking themselves to their mother's chariot; the statues, which are mentioned by Herodotus, mark the transition between the Daedalic and true Archaic styles (? 582 B.C.). Bronze statuette of Apollo (c. 530 B.C.). Five metopes from the TREASURY OF SIKYON (second quarter of 6C B.C.). These are Sikyonian work, in yellow limestone, very carefully executed but in poor condition.

Left to right: 1. *The Dioscuri and the Argo*. Castor and Pollux, on horseback, appear on the right and left of the ship; in the midst of the warriors in the Argo is Orpheus.—2. *Europa and the Bull*.—3. *The Dioscuri and Idas, Son of Aphareus, on a Cattle-Lifting Raid in Arcadia*. Castor is leading, followed by Idas and Pollux (Lynkeus, brother of Idas, is not shown). The raiders fell out after their expedition and all, except the immortal Pollux, were killed.—4. *Calydonian Boar*. Under its belly is the silhouette of a wounded hound.—5. *Flight of Helle on the Ram with the Golden Fleece*.

In ROOM 4 are displayed the relics recovered in fragments in 1939 from an apothetes, or sacred dump, in front of the Stoa of the Athenians. Archaic *Bull (6C B.C.) of silver sheets, originally attached by silver nails to a copper frame; hooves, horns, and other gold-plated parts are better preserved. *Head of a seated male chryselephantine statue with elements of the gold decoration of the garments, notably two plates with repoussé animal motifs in differing styles (6C B.C.). Another ivory head with its golden diadem. Forearm of a chryselephantine statue. Miniature friezes in ivory from a throne or casket. Ivory statuette of a god with a tame lion (7C B.C.). Bronzes: Athletes (early 5C B.C.); censer held up by an exquisite female figure (c. 460 B.C.).

Room 5. Hall of the Siphnian Treasury. Displayed are the East Pediment, much of the **Frieze, a caryatid with polos capital, and part of the doorway with admirable lotus and palmette decoration. In addition the hall contains the winged *Sphinx of the Naxians (Ionic work of 570–560 B.C.), and another caryatid head with polos, of unknown provenance, once thought to have belonged to the Treasury of Knidos.

The *East Pediment* represents the dispute between Herakles and Apollo over the Delphic tripod.—The *Frieze*, in a mature Archaic style, foreshadows in its rhythmic quality that of the Parthenon nearly a century later. The horses are especially spirited and the fallen corpse almost natural in position. The four sides have no narrative continuity: the *E. Side*, below the pediment, depicts in two panels an Assembly of Gods (supporters of Troy to the left of Zeus, of Greece to the right) who watch Homeric heroes fighting over the body of Patroclus. The *N. Side* shows nine groups of Gods in battle with the Giants, grouped round three chariots. The names were painted at the bottom of the composition after the manner of ancient vases. The chariot of Cybele and the death of Ephialtes are well preserved. The *S. and W. Sides* (believed to be by a different sculptor) are fragmentary.

Room 6 contains 24 surviving metopes (some very fragmentary) out of 30, from the Athenian Treasury. Good authorities place these stylistically (moulding of stomach muscles) in the days of Kleisthenes (510–500 B.C.) or earlier, but the expressive *Heads and fluidity of the figures have been thought to confirm Pausanias' contention that the treasury was dedicated after Marathon. The metopes represent the Labours of Herakles (N. and W. sides), the Exploits of Theseus (S. side) and the Battle of the Amazons (E. side). Note especially Herakles and the Arcadian Stag, Theseus and the Bull of Marathon.

In Rooms 7 and 8 are grouped pedimental statuary from the Archaic Temple of Apollo. All the figures have unfinished backs, with tenons and mortises to fix them to the tympanum. Some traces of colour survive. Lion's head spouts; Nike acroterion, and other fragments; inscriptions. Small bronze of a walking cow.

The Inscriptions concern the history of the temple: lists of subscribers to its rebuilding; re-dedication; repairs by the Emp. Domitian (A.D. 84); also, with musical notation, Hymns to Apollo composed in the 2C B.C.

Room 9. Grave stelai; bronze kalpis (early 4C); fragments of the coffered ceiling from the peristyle of the Tholos; circular altar with reliefs, found in the Tholos; head of Dionysos.—In Room 8 are Metopes and other fragments from the Tholos.

Room 10 contains sculpture of the 4C B.C. Left to right: Fragment of pillar.—Three colossal Dancing Girls, grouped round a column representing an acanthus stalk, probably a monumental support

(30 ft high) for a tripod; the figures were possibly Thyiads, who celebrated feasts in honour of Dionysos.—Five *Statues from the votive offering of Daochos of Thessaly, celebrating the victory of his master Philip in 336 B.C. at Chaironeia. This family monument of nine statues reproduced in marble a group in bronze at Pharsala, of which part at least was by Lysippos. The group, identified from the surviving inscription of the plinth (p. 410), forms a genealogical succession of 7 generations from the 6C B.C. The best-preserved figures are those representative of Agias, great-grandfather of the dedicator (depicted as an athlete), who had not only won an Olympic wreath, but had five victories

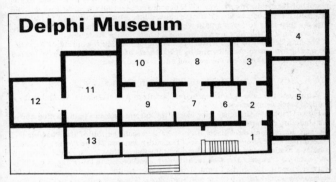

Delphi Museum

at the Nemean, three at the Pythian, and five at the Isthmian Games; and Agelaos, his young brother, who won a track event at Delphi.—Statue of a Philosopher.

ROOM 12, the HALL OF THE CHARIOTEER contains the famous *Charioteer and the few other surviving fragments of the Auriga of Polyzalos, of which it was part. The figure was discovered in 1896 where it had fallen when the remainder was crushed during the earthquake of 373 B.C. The rider, dressed in a long tunic (xystis), is represented life-size. On his head is a victor's fillet. He holds the reins in his right hand. From this calm and formal pose we may infer that he is performing his lap of honour. Taken out of its context, the figure is at first sight less than satisfactory. The disproportion of the body, often criticized, may have been a deliberate attempt to counter optical distortion when seen from below. Similarly the eyes, of magnesium and onyx, wonderfully preserved, are not symmetrical. The work, one of the few great surviving bronzes of the 5C, dates from c. 475 and was dedicated by a Sicilian prince to commemorate a chariot victory in the Pythian Games in 478 or 474 B.C. The sculptor may have been Pythagoras of Samos, who was in exile at this time at Rhegion.

ROOM 13. Small *Bronzes and pottery (case of excellent fragments); *Antinous, in polished Parian marble, particularly good of its genre, with an expression of gentle melancholy; Head, probably of Titus Q. Flaminius, victor of Cynoscephalae (197 B.C.); Head of an unknown philosopher, expressive (Hellenistic); Young girl laughing, reminiscent of the arktoi found at Brauron.

A To the Sybaris Cave and the Gorge of the Pleistos

This excursion takes 3½–4 hrs there and back, or 2½ hrs if the visit to the gorge is omitted. A new earth road descends from the main road E. of Marmaria. The path descends in zigzags, crosses some retaining walls, and reaches an irrigation ditch at the bottom of the gorge. Thence it ascends for c. 100 yds, passes some caves, crosses the stream, passes near a waterfall which works a fulling mill, and ends (1 hr) at a deep well-like hole in the rock full of water in winter. This is called *Zaleska* and was in antiquity the *Spring of Sybaris*. It is dangerous to approach the well over the chaos of slippery rocks that surround it.

The *Cave of Sybaris* is a large cavern in a deep ravine on the hillside beyond the Pleistos. This is known also as *Krypsana* ('Hiding Place') or *Asketario* ('Hermitage', after a hermit who is said to have lived in it). It was used as a refuge by the people of Kastri during the War of Independence.—From the cavern we descend again to the torrent as far as an irrigation ditch, which we follow for 150 yds; then we turn right to reach a path which ascends in ½ hr to the little *Monastery of the Panayia*. On the right are the ruins of a Chapel of the Redeemer.

We may descend to the Pleistos (1½ hrs more), passing the spring of *Kephalovrysi*, which turns some mills, and by the *Chapels of Ayios Vasilios, Ayios Ioannis* and other chapels, near an ancient well and a sacred wood.

B To the Corycian Cave

With a car the cave is more easily reached from Kalivia, above Arákhova, by a marked track (¾ hr walk).

From Delphi the site fence now blocks the ancient rock-cut path starting above the stadium; the modern mule-path swings out in wider zigzags to the W. and is reached direct from the village. In c. 1 hr we reach the top of the **Phaedriades**, known today as *Elafokastro* (4018 ft). The path continues on the *Plateau of Livadi*, used as a pasturage by ancient and modern shepherds alike, as far as the conspicuous watering troughs. Here we turn right (E.) and cross the low ridge. On the E. slope a broad path will be found at the entrance to the forest, leading down the valley (this is marked with red arrows and signs). These are not easy to follow near two small tarns, where we make for the gap between two hills. From this gap a rough path climbs in zigzags. 2½ hrs. We reach (4261 ft) the low arched entrance to the **Corycian Cave**, now called *Sarantavli* ('Forty Rooms'). This cave, which Pausanias thought the finest he had seen (X, 32, 2), was sacred to Pan and the Nymphs (inscriptions). Above it the Dionysiac orgies were celebrated by the Thyiades (Aeschylus, *Eumenides* 22). When the Persians were marching on Delphi, the inhabitants took refuge in the Corycian Cave (Hdt. VIII, 36); it was again used as a refuge during the War of Independence and on other occasions. Within a faint light reveals the pink and green walls of the cave, and the stalactites and stalagmites. Excavations of the French School in 1970 showed the periods of use to be Neolithic, late-Mycenean, and 6–4C.

Ascent of Parnassos, see Rte 45.

V THESSALY

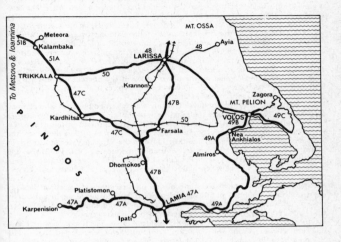

Thessaly, one of the most fertile areas of Greece and, in summer, one of the hottest places in Europe, consists of a vast plain surrounded on all sides by mountains. On the N. the Kamvounian Mts. separate it from Macedonia; on the w. is the Pindos range beyond which is Epirus; to the E. Olympos, Ossa, and Pelion bar the way to its sea coast on the Gulf of Salonika; to the s. Othrys divides it from Aitolia and from Phthiotis and Phocis. In antiquity Thessaly included also the long narrow valley of the Spercheios between Othrys and Mt Oiti, in which is the city of Lamia. In the S.E. the peninsula of Magnesia extends beyond Pelion almost to Euboea, and the Northern Sporades, with the sea encroaching into the Gulf of Volos. Mountain passes give access to Thessaly from outside.

In the Tertiary epoch the whole plain was under water. It is nowadays drained by the Peneios, which rises in the Pindos and, receiving important tributaries, flows through the Vale of Tempe into the Gulf of Salonika. The surrounding mountains are covered with forests of pine, oak, and beech; the plain yields corn, rice, tobacco, and fruit. Unfortunately agricultural labour is so scarce that much of the land is uncultivated. The horses of Thessaly have always been famous; Thessalian cavalry helped the Athenians in the Peloponnesian War. Cattle and sheep thrive on its pastures. In the mountains bears, wolves, and wild boar still roam but are seldom seen; in the plain the fauna include hares, herons, cranes, storks, and wildfowl.

The population includes Albanians and Vlachs, some of whom are still nomadic shepherds. The province has three large towns, Larissa, its political centre, Volos, its chief port, and Trikkala. Thessaly is traversed from s. to N. by the main line of the Greek State Railway, with branches to Volos and Trikkala; the principal towns are linked by good roads with frequent bus services. The archaeological interest of Thessaly is mainly prehistoric. Rural life in the villages is hardly affected by modern changes.

From a very early date Thessaly was divided into four districts or tetrarchies, an organization which subsisted up to the time of the Peloponnesian War. The divisions were *Hestaeotis* (region of Trikkala), in the N.W.; *Thessaliotis* (including Pharsalos, now Farsala), in the S.W.; *Pelasgiotis* (Larissa), in the E. and N.E., in which was Skotoussa, the original home of the Dodona oracle; and *Phthiotis* (Othrys), in the S.E., which included the Homeric city of Phthia and was the country of Deukalion and of Achilles and his Myrmidons. There were also four secondary divisions: *Magnesia*, covering the peninsula of that name (Rte 49); *Dolopia*, S. of Thessaliotis, inhabited by the ancient race of the Dolopians who fought before Troy; *Oetaea*, in the upper valley of the Spercheios (now part of Phthiotis and Phocis); and *Malis*, a district on the shores of the Maliac Gulf (Gulf of Lamia), which extended as far as Thermopylae.

For some time after the conquest Thessaly was governed by kings who claimed descent from Herakles. Later the kingship was abolished and the government in the separate cities became oligarchic, with power concentrated in the hands of a few great families descended from the kings. The most powerful of these were the *Aleuadai*, who ruled at Larissa, and their kinsmen the *Skopadai*, whose seat was at Krannon (c. 15 m. S.W. of Larissa). Pausanias reminds us (VII, 10, 2) that the Aleuadai betrayed Thessaly to the Persians in 480 B.C. The general attitude of these northern oligarchs was never cordial to the rest of Greece, although, says Thucydides (IV, 78), the common people of Thessaly liked the Athenians. As time went on, the rulers formed themselves into a kind of confederation. Each of the four main divisions remained politically independent but, to guard against the contingency of war, a chief magistrate was elected under the name of *Tagos* (Ταγός), who had supreme command. He was generally one of the Aleuadai.

Other cities of importance in antiquity besides Larissa and Krannon were Pharsalos and Pherai. About 374 B.C. Jason, tyrant of Pherai, was elected Tagos. His rule and that of his successor Alexander (d. 357) was so unbearably harsh that the Thessalians solicited aid from the Thebans and threw off their yoke. Twenty years later, Philip of Macedon, similarly invited, annexed the whole country to his own dominions. In 275 Pyrrhus, king of Epirus, after his adventures in Italy, made himself master of Thessaly and Macedonia. In 197, the Romans took Thessaly under their protection, as part of a Roman province (comp. Strabo, XVII). Larissa soon became the political and religious capital of the reorganized confederation, which was surrounded by a number of minor leagues.

In the imperial era Thessaly was united to Macedonia, but in the reign of Diocletian it became a separate province.

In the 12C, after a succession of invaders, Thessaly became the centre of a Bulgar-Vlach kingdom known as *Great Wallachia*. The Turks conquered the country in 1389 and held it for five centuries. The Congress of Berlin (1878) assigned to Greece Thessaly and the District of Arta (Rte 53); three years later Turkey ceded to Greece the whole of Thessaly S. of the Peneios. Greece retained her new acquisition despite the disastrous war of 1897, and after the war of 1912–13 she obtained the remaining area of Thessaly.

47   CENTRAL THESSALY

A   Lamia and the Valley of the Spercheios

LAMIA (ΛΑΜΙΑ; *Delta*, with rest., *Samaras*, *Helena*, *Apollonion*, *Leonidaion*, *Sonia*, all C, and others), the chief town of the nome of Fthiotis and the seat of an archbishop, is a lively but undistinguished town of 37,900 inhab., lying below two wooded hills. It is a market centre for cotton, cereals, and garden produce. A characteristic sight are the storks' nests on the roofs.

History. *Lamia* is remembered for the Lamian War (323–322 B.C.) in which the Athenians attempted to free themselves from Macedonian domination. Leosthenes seized Thermopylae and shut up Antipater, the Macedonian viceroy, in Lamia. After Leosthenes had been killed in a sortie, the command passed to Antiphilos. A Macedonian relief force freed Antipater, and Antiphilos was defeated at Krannon. A stronghold in the middle ages, Lamia was known to the Franks as *Gipton* and to the Catalans as *El Cito*, whence perhaps the Turkish name *Zitouni*. Since 1961 Lamia has had 'sister town' links with Dover, Delaware.

Round the central PLATEIA ELEVTHERIAS are grouped the Nomarkhia, the Cathedral, and several hotels. Odhos Dhiakou leads to *Plateia Dhiakou*, adorned with a characteristic statue of Athanasios Dhiakos, a local patriot. Hence a street ascends in steps the hill of Ayios Loukas (restaurant). Just to the E. of Plateia Elevtherias is the shaded PLATEIA LAOU (good taverna), where the waters of the Gorgopotamos gush from a fountain. Dominating the town on the N.E. is the **Kastro**, a castle of the Catalan Duchy of Neopatras (1319–93). The walls stand on Classical foundations and show masonry of many later epochs (incl. Roman; Catalan; Turkish battlements). They command a fine view both to E. and W.

BUSES from Plateia Laou to *Almiros* and *Volos* (twice daily); to *Pelasgia* (6 times); to *Dhomokos* (8 times); and *Farsala* (5 times). Opposite corner to *Larissa* (5 times), *Trikkala* (4), *Karditsa* (4), and *Kozani* (3); also to *Kastoria* (daily).

FROM LAMIA TO KARPENISION, good road, 51 m. (82 km.). The road runs w. with the railway to (5 m.) *Lianokládi Station*, junction for Lamia, on the main Athens–Salonika line. We cross the railway and gradually ascend in the lush broad valley of the Spercheios. The huge mass of Mt Oiti looms on our left as we continue through the village of (9 m.) *Lianokládi*. Excavation of a mound by the Ipati turn has revealed a M.H. apsidal house.

At the far end of the village a road diverges left across the river to **Loutrá Ipátis** (ΛΟΥΤΡΑ ΥΠΑΤΗΣ; 1¾ m.; *Xenia, Oiti, Pigai*, all A; *Astron, Lamia* C, and others, summer season only), a thermal establishment whose waters (78° F.) are good for skin diseases and bronchial infections. The branch road continues to (5 m.) **Ipáti**, the ancient *Hypata* and the *Neo-Patras* of the Franks and Catalans, finely situated on the N. slope of Mt Oiti. In antiquity it was the capital of the Aenianes, a tribe which migrated s. from Ossa. During the Lamian War it was the centre of the military operations of the confederate Greeks. Some ancient masonry can be seen in the Catalan castle. In the 13C it was the capital of the dominions of John Doukas who with help from Athens here defeated the forces of Michael VIII Palaiologos in 1275. In 1318 it became the second capital of Alfonso's Catalan duchy 'of Athens and Neo-Patras'. The town was taken by the Turks in 1393 and made the seat of a pasha. Here were born Leo the Mathematician (c. 800) and St Athanasios the Meteorite (1305–83). The inhabitants cultivate tobacco and weave linen. Ipáti is the starting-point for the ascent of *Mt Oiti* (Οἴτη) legendary scene of the death of Herakles, whose summit (Pirgos; 7064 ft) may be climbed from the Trapeza refuge of the Greek Alpine Club (3½ hrs from Ipáti). The descent from the refuge may be made in 4 hrs to *Pávliani*, c. 5 m. w. of Brallos (Rte 44A).

14¼ m. *Kastrí* takes name from a ruined fortress with square towers.— 18½ m. *Varibóbi* has readopted the name of *Makrakómi*, a town known to Livy, the ruins of which stand on the hill to the N.E. of the little market town (1970 inhab.). Beyond the Spercheios we see *Sperkheiás* (2800 inhab.), to the E. of which, on the left bank of the tributary Inakhos, is *Ayios Sóstis*, site of ancient *Sosthenis*, mentioned by Ptolemy. About 3 m. to the N. of Makrakómi are the Baths of *Platístomon* (ΛΟΥΤΡΑ ΠΛΑΤΥΣΤΟΜΟΥ; Asklepios D), the waters of which are recommended in cases of dyspepsia, anaemia, disorders of the stomach, and spinal complaints. Another road climbs N. to Smokovon (comp. Rte 47c).

Beyond Makrakómi another road diverges across the river to *Palaiovrákha* on the N. slope of Mt Goulinás (4810 ft; view). Between this village and its neighbour Pteri (or Fteri) are some remains of ancient

Spercheiai.—The vegetation becomes increasingly temperate as the valley narrows to a gorge. Above (29½ m.) *Ayios Yeoryios* the slopes become increasingly wooded and the climb gradually steeper. The valley divides. Just beyond (32¼ m.) *Khani Panétsou* in the Dipotoma valley by-roads lead N.W. to *Merkádha, Mavrilon,* and *Ayia Triás* (21 m.), a beautiful mountain village which upheld a tradition of learning in Turkish times. We climb out of the valley by continuous turns to (37¼ m.) *Timfristós* (2760 ft), known for its cherries. The road now zigzags across the spruce-clad saddle between Pikrovouni (4930 ft; N.) and Kokkália (5645 ft; s.). As we reach the road-summit (c. 4700 ft), on the watershed of the Southern Pindos and the boundary between Phthiotis and Eurytania, there is a fine view of the peak of Mt Timfristós. Along the summit ridge a difficult road runs s. to Kríkello (11 m.) and *Domnista* (16 m.; Xenon Domnistis **B**). Our road winds down to *Ayios Nikólaos* (l. ; ½ m.) in the enclosed valley of the Karpenisiotis. Beyond the Miríki turn, a track leads (r.) to the *Refuge of Diavolotopos* (6036 ft; 40 beds; 2 hrs walk from Karpenisi) on **Mt Timfristos** (TYMΦPHΣTOΣ), or *Veloukhi*, the summit (7594 ft) of which towers above the road.

51 m. **Karpenísion** (KAPΠENHΣION; *Lecadin,* 100R, *Mont Blanc,* both **B**; *Helvetia, Anessis,* **C**, and others; Fthenia Rest.) is the chief and only sizeable place (4400 inhab.) of Evritania, by population the smallest nome of mainland Greece. The town was captured by Communist rebels in Jan 1949 and held for 18 days. Its houses occupy both slopes of a torrent that descends to a small plain, wholly enclosed by mountains and dominated on the N. by the peaks of Timfristos. At present somewhat bleak and without charm, the town is undergoing increasing industrial development. One road leads s. to *Méga Khorío* (9½ m.; Antigone **D**) on the N. slope of *Mt Kalliakoúdha* (6890 ft). Its companion village, *Mikró Khorío,* was overwhelmed on 13 Jan. 1963 by a landslide while most of the 336 inhab. were at a church festival in another village.

From Karpenision to *Agrinion,* see Rte 54.

B From Lamía to Lárissa viâ Fársala

ROAD, 71 m. (114 km.), part of the traditional s.–N. route through Greece, which has been only partly superseded by the new highway to Salonika viâ the coast. 21¾ m. *Dhomokós.*—42¼ m. *Farsala.*—71 m. **Larissa.** BUS several times daily in 3–3½ hrs.

RAILWAY (from Lianokladi), 79 m. (127 km.) in 2–2½ hrs, part of the main line from Athens to Salonika. From Lianokladi the railway climbs at a gradient of 1 in 50 for nearly 22 m. to surmount the barrier of Mt Othrys; its course lies w. of the road. There is a succession of bridges, then follow 27 short tunnels as the line climbs out of the Spercheios valley. It reaches the summit-level (1920 ft) to the E. of Mt Mokhlouka (2925 ft), then descends, crossing the w. end of the drained Lake Xynias.—27 m. *Angeias*; we accompany the river Sofaditikos through a gap in the hills.—Beyond (38 m.) *Thavmakós* (comp. below) the kastro of Dhomokós may be seen. The railway then accompanies the road in the plain to Neon Monastirion (see below).—53 m. **Palaiofarsalos** is the most important junction in Thessaly; branch lines run E. to Volos and w. to Trikkala and Kalabaka (Rte 50). Farsala is c. 8 m. E. The line surmounts a low ridge.—63 m. *Doxará.*—68 m. *Krannón*; the ruins of the ancient city are 6 m. w.—79 m. **Larissa.**

We quit Lamia by Odhos Ipsilandi. The road skirts the E. side of Mt Profitis Ilias, soon joining the by-pass, and begins the gradual ascent of the *Furka Pass* (2790 ft), the main route through the brown w. foothills of Mt Othrys. There are fine views to the left over the Spercheios to Mt Oiti. On the curving descent is (10 m.) the *Khani Dragoman Aga,* now a taverna. We cross the level cultivated plain formed by the draining of Lake Xynias. Some walls of ancient *Xyniai* survive near its s. limit (s. of the modern village, 2 m. w. of our road). We pass chromium mine workings and surmount another ridge.

21¾ m. **Dhomokós** (ΔΟΜΟΚΟΣ; 2000 inhab.), chief town of an eparchy and seat of a bishop, is picturesquely situated ½ m. above the road (l.) on a rocky hill (1705 ft). Its railway station, in the plain to the N., keeps the ancient name, *Thaumakoi*. Some Classical masonry can be seen built into various house on the hill.

The town, which commanded the defile of Koile, was so called because of the astonishment (thauma) of the traveller from the s. who had climbed over rugged hills and had suddenly been confronted with the vast plain of Thessaly. Thaumakoi was vainly besieged by Philip V in 198 B.C. and was taken by Acilius Glabrio in 191. During the Greco-Turkish war of 1897 Dhomokos was the last stage in the retreat of the Greek army under Constantine I (17 May). The advance of the Turks, who reached the Furka pass two days later, was halted only by the intervention of the Powers.

The abrupt descent affords a fine *View of the Thessalian Plain, in which we continue N.—The road to Trikkala (Rte 47c) and Ioannina diverges at (34¾ m.) *Néon Monastírion*. On a hill (r.) some well-preserved walls (known as Yinaikokastro) remain to locate ancient *Proerna*; its Temple of Demeter has been recognized in the village.—After *Vrisiá* we pass between two isolated hills, Plaka (l.) and Griva (r.). Beyond the turning to Stavros is a restaurant.—42½ m. **Fársala** (ΦΑΡΣΑΛΑ; *Akhilleion* D), four-fifths destroyed in the earthquake of 1954, has nothing of interest save its past history and is mainly noted for its 'halva' sweetmeat. Its bishopric was suppressed in 1900 and incorporated in the see of Larissa, but with 7000 inhab., it is still the largest place in its eparchy. It has a station, 2 m. N., on the railway from Volos to Trikkala. The ridge of Fetih-Djami, s.w. of the town, has been occupied since Neolithic times.

The *Battle of Pharsalus* (9 Aug, 48 B.C.), which took place in the plain to the w., decided the issue between Pompey and Caesar and the fate of the Roman world. Pompey, trusting to his overwhelming superiority in cavalry, led by Labienus, planned to turn Caesar's right wing and fall upon his rear. Labienus' cavalry charge was put to flight, panic spread through Pompey's army, and Pompey himself fled with an escort of only four men. His army lost 15,000 and the remainder surrendered next day. Yves Béquignon (B.C.H. 1960) concludes that the battle took place on the left bank of the Enipeus.

We cross the Volos–Trikkala railway and the Enipeus, an important tributary of the Peneios, on a five-arched bridge.—51 m. *Khalkiádes*. Here a by-road leads right to *Áno Skotoússa*, to the E. of which are some remains of ancient *Skotoussa*, the supposed original home of the Dodona oracle.

Above to the N. and E. rise the mountains of Khalkodónion or Kara Dagh, anciently called Kynos Kephalai or Cynoscephalae ('dogs' heads') and famous for two battles. The *First Battle of Cynoscephalae*, in 364 B.C., was between Alexander of Pherai and the combined forces of Thessalians and Thebans. Alexander was defeated but the Theban general Pelopidas was killed. The *Second Battle of Cynoscephalae*, in 197, irreparably weakened the power of Macedonia. The Romans under Flaminius totally defeated Philip V of Macedon, the issue being decided by an elephant charge. An uneasy period followed, ending in the battle of Pydna and complete Macedonian dependence upon Rome.

57 m. *Záppion*. The road continues in the plain through agricultural land, passing the Xenia motel on the way into (71 m.) **Larissa**, see Rte 48.

C From Lamía to Kardhítsa and Tríkkala

ROAD, 73¼ m. (118 km.). 34¾ m. *Néon Monastírion.*—43½ m. *Sofádhes.*—
57 m. **Kardhítsa.**—73¼ m. **Tríkkala.**

To (34¾ m.) *Néon Monastírion*, see Rte 47B. We branch left and run
N.W. through the Thessalian plain, crossing torrents and streams from
the Pindos on our left.—43½ m. *Sofádhes* (ΣΟΦΑΔΕΣ; Inns), an
agricultural centre (4500 inhab.) on the Thessalian railway, is by-passed
to the W. A by-road leads (l.) in 5 m. to the village of *Philia* where an
important pan-Thessalian sanctuary of Athena was located in 1963.
Excavations yielded Geometric and Archaic bronzes, amber and
ivory objects, Hellenistic inscriptions, and architectural remains of
Hellenistic and Roman times. On a prominent hill (600 ft) to the N.,
near the hamlet of Pirgos (2 m.), are some remains identified by an
inscription found at Mataranga (comp. below) as ancient *Kierion*, a
place Stephanus of Byzantium equated with Thessalian *Arne.*—We pass
(l.) remains of an old bridge and (r.) conical mounds. At (52 m.) *Áyios
Theódoros* we join the road from Larissa just w. of Mataránga.

57 m. **KARDHITSA** (ΚΑΡΔΙΤΣΑ; *Astron, Avra,* 42 Karaïskakis, on
way to rly. stn., *Arni,* all **C**; *Rest. Pindos, Ilyssia,* in main square), the
capital of its nome, is an uninteresting town of 25,700 inhab., laid out on
a rectilinear plan in Turkish times. It has no ancient associations. An
important market-town attracting custom from the Thessalian plain and
from the mountainous Agrafa region, it trades in tobacco, cereals,
cotton, silk, and cattle, and is served by the Thessalian railway. Its
buildings are liberally adorned with storks' nests. There is a pleasant
park. Recently methane gas has been discovered in the vicinity.
Kardhítsa was the birthplace of Gen. Nikolaos Plastiras (1883–1953),
leader of the revolution of 1922.

BUSES hourly to *Trikkala*; 5 times daily to *Larissa*; and to surrounding villages.

From Kardhitsa a road runs s.w. to (6½ m.) *Mitrópolis*, then ascends to the hydro-
electric LAKE OF MEGDOVA at (16 m.) *Koróni*. This is formed by the **Tavropos
Barrage** on a tributary of the Acheloos. After serving electrical generators, the
water provides irrigation in the plain and finally discharges into the Peneios.—
About 5 m. along this road, in the foothills of Pindos, are the ruins of ancient
Metropolis, a civic centre made up of several towns, including Ithome (see below).
It formed, with Trikke, Pelinnaion, and Gomphoi, a fortified rectangle protecting
the approach to the Thessalian plain. Within the enclosing walls, circular in plan,
is the citadel. Metropolis was captured in 191 B.C. by Flaminius and occupied by
Caesar before the battle of Pharsalus. To the s. of the modern village (comp. above)
a Mycenean tholos tomb was discovered in 1958. Above, on the mountainside
(3775 ft), are the little fortresses of *Vounesi* and *Portítsa*.

About 21 m. s.E. of Kardhitsa (bus in summer) is **Smokovon Spa** (ΛΟΥΤΡΑ
ΣΜΟΚΟΒΟΥ; *Tembi* B; *Agrafa* C), with alkaline sulphur springs (102–104° F.),
efficacious for nervous, rheumatic, catarrhal, and skin complaints. The spa is
beautifully situated at an altitude of 1475 ft in a shady ravine and is an excursion
centre. Thence a secondary road continues a serpentine course through *Rendína*,
with a fine old monastery (frescoes of 1662), to join the Lamia–Karpenisi road at
Makrakómi (p. 417).

Another road runs w. from Kardhitsa in company with the railway to (7 m.)
Fanarion, a village of 1310 inhab., situated on the w. side of a rocky hill called 'the
Beacon' (Φανάρι). A Hellenic wall and a Byzantine fortress mark the site of 'rugged
Ithome' of the Iliad, one of the towns incorporated in Metropolis (comp. above).
It was 'a heap of stones' in Strabo's day.

From Kardhitsa to *Larissa*, see Rte 50.

The broad level road drives N.W. The local inhabitants may be seen in
the fields wearing bright shades of red, and many fine horses graze.

Prominent to the w. is the castle at Ithome (comp. above).—67 m.
Agnanteró has a local festival on 27 Aug. We cross the Peneios.

73¼ m. (118 km.) **TRIKKALA** (ΤΡΙΚΑΛΑ), the third largest town in
Thessaly, with 34,800 inhab., is attractively situated on both banks of
the Lethaios (locally Trikkalinos), some distance from its confluence
with the Peneios, at the end of a low ridge (Mt Khasia) projecting from
the N. limit of the Thessalian plain. The town is the capital of the nome
of Tríkkala and seat of an archbishop. Its population is increased in

winter by the influx of Vlach shepherds driven from their mountains by
the inclement weather. It has an important market in cereals, rice, silk,
cotton, tobacco, and livestock.

Hotels. *Divani* (Pl. a), 11 Plat. Kitrilaki; *Achillion* (Pl. c), Vironos/Vas. Yeoryios,
both B; **Dina** (Pl. d), Asklipiou/Karanasou; **Palladion** (Pl. b), 4 Vironos; **Rex** (Pl.
e), 1 Apollonos, these C; **Lithaeon**, 10 Othonos, **D**.

Restaurants. *Elleniko, Elatos*, both in Od. Asklipiou.

Buses (KTEL 17 Trikkalon) from Plat. Kitrilaki to *Larissa* (hourly), to *Athens*,
and to local destinations; (KTEL 16 Kardhitsis) from Od. Amalias to *Kardhitsa* and
to *Kalambaka*.

History. Trikkala is the *Trikke* of Homer, the domain of Podaleiros and Ma-
chaon, the two sons of Asklepios, 'cunning leeches' who led the Trikkeans to the
Trojan War ('Iliad', II, 729). It was credited with the earliest of all the temples to
Asklepios and in later times had a medical school of repute. Trikke was one of the
four cities of Hestaiotis forming a defensive quadrilateral (comp. above). The
plain of Trikke produced the finest of the renowned Thessalian horses, the features
of which are reproduced in the frieze of the Parthenon. The name *Trikkala* first
appears in the 12C. Under the Turks Trikkala was the chief town of Thessaly
despite periodical uprisings such as that of Dionysios 'the Skylosophos', its
bishop. After the battle for Athens in 1945, Trikkala became one of the communist guerrilla strongholds.

The road from Kardhitsa passes, close to Ayios Konstandinos, the

Kursum Cami, a mosque built by Sinan Pasha in 1550, with a fine soaring dome supported on four slender columns. It is destined as a museum. The river Lethaios divides the town. On its banks are numerous cafés. The Plateia Riga Ferraiou on the s. bank is connected by bridges with the Plateia Kitrilaki and the large central PLATEIA AMERIKANON, both opening on the N. bank. Odhos Vasileos Konstandinos leads w. to the **Frourion**, a Byzantine fortress on Hellenistic foundations, where the lower ward has a Tourist Pavilion (view) and the great keep (no adm.) a castellated clock tower. To the N.w. are some remains of the *Asklepieion* (?), partly excavated by the Greek Archaeological Service in 1912. The *Bazar*, to the E. of the Frourion, is a picturesque quarter of old Turco-Greek houses. The principal churches lie in this quarter.

A PLEASANT EXCURSION may be made to Gomphoi and the Porta Panayia in the foothills of the Pindos to the s.w. We pass the railway station and drive s.w. across the plain.—4½ m. *Piyí.*—6½ m. *Ligariá* stands above the Portaïkos, a torrent that often floods the plain.—At 7½ m. an unpaved road leads to *Gómfoi* (1 m.), a village on a hill overlooking the Pamisos, 3 m. w. of *Lazarina*. Ancient **Gomphoi**, of considerable importance by reason of its domination of the chief pass from Thessaly into Epirus, was one of the four strongholds forming a square (comp. above). It was fortified by Philip II. In the civil war it supported, to its cost, Pompey against Caesar. On its site the Byzantines founded the city of *Episkope*. Many ancient blocks are incorporated in the houses of the village.—We now see ahead the Stena tis Pórtas with, right, half-way up the mountain, the great monastery of Dousiko (see below).—11¾ m. *Píli* (1760 inhab.) stands at the entrance to the *Stena tis Pórtas*, a beautiful defile through which the Portaïkos emerges from the Pindos. The PORTA PANAYIA, a charming church across the river (bridge) and 1 m. upstream, was founded in 1283. The narthex is later. Within, the mosaic figures of Christ and of the Virgin are striking. On the marble ikonostasis the figure of Christ is on the left, a reversal of customary Orthodox iconography.—A rough road leads (r.) from the village across the bridge and up to the MONASTERY OF DOUSIKO (3½ m.; women not admitted), known locally as *Ai Vessáris*, which stands at 2500 ft above its village on the opposite slope amid chestnuts and limes. It was founded in 1515 by the Blessed Bessarion (later Abp of Larissa), and completed in 1556 by his son. The monastery is on the grand scale with 336 cells, a library of importance and an imposing church having a carved wooden ikonostasis of 1767.— Up the defile, 1½ m. beyond Píli, stands an attractive single-arched *Bridge* built in 1518 by the Blessed Bessarion; a pebble mosaic decorates the rock face on the far side.—12½ m. We cross the river.—At 14 m. the asphalt ends and a difficult route into Epirus continues through wonderful scenery viâ (21 m.) *Eláti* (Pens. Elatos B), high in a valley on the w. side of **Kerkétion** (Kóziaka; comp. Rte 51). Higher up to the right is the *Khatzipetros Refuge* (4100 ft) from which the summit (6235 ft) may be climbed.—30 m. *Pertoúli*, cold even in August at nearly 4000 ft, beyond the watershed, has a forestry station of Salonika University.—36 m. *Neraïdokhóri* stands above the infant Acheloos, down which remote tracks and paths descend to mountain villages to N. and w. The three villages mentioned all have inns.

From Trikkala to *Kalabaka* and the *Meteora*, see Rte 51.

48   LARISSA AND ITS ENVIRONS

LARISSA, or *Lárisa* (ΛΑΡΙΣΑ), the chief town of its nome and capital of the province of Thessaly, with 72,300 inhab., is an important road centre, the headquarters of the Greek First Army, and the seat (since the 7C) of the Metropolitan 'Bishop of the Second Thessaly and Exarch of All Hellas'. Situated in the middle of the Thessalian plain on the right bank of the Peneios, with its spacious squares and busy streets it has more the air of a city than anywhere else in central Greece. Its long history is scarcely apparent, though some vestiges of the Turkish enceinte still survive to the s. of the town. The quality of local ouzo, halva, and ice cream is noted. The bicycle, unusually in Greece, is here a conspicuous feature and the presence of storks on the roofs adds a bizarre touch to the townscape.

Airport, just E. of the town.

Railway Station, ¾ m. s. of the centre, for the main Athens–Salonika line, and for Volos.

Hotels. Divani Palace (Pl. c), 19 Vas. Sofias, A; **Grand** (Pl. s), Plat. Riga Ferraiou, **Astoria** (Pl. d), 4 Protopapadaki, **Melathron** (Pl. a), 20 Kouma, **Xenia,** motel on the Farsala road, c. 5 m. s., DPO, these B. **Metropole** (Pl. e), 8 Roosevelt, **El Greco** (Pl. f), 35 Meg. Alexandhrou/Patroklou, **Ambassadeurs** (Pl. g), 65 Papakiriazou, **Adonis** (Pl. p), 8 Vas. Konstandinou, **Esperia** (Pl. q), 4 Amalias, **Achillion** (Pl. r), 10 Kentavron, **Atlantic** (Pl. h), 1 Vas. Konstandinou, **Dionysos,** 30 Vas. Yeoryiou B′, **Olympion** (Pl. b), 1 Meg. Alexandhrou, old-established, **Acropole** (Pl. k), 142 El. Venizelou, **Anessis** (Pl. 1), 25 Meg Alexandhrou, **Helena** (Pl. m), Kouma/28 Oktovriou, **Doma** (Pl. n), 1 Anthimou Gazi, **Galaxy** (Pl. o), 23 Vas Konstandinou, all C, and others.

Restaurants. Dionysos, Roosevelt; *Elatos,* Filellinon. Zakharoplasteia and Cafés in the main square and in the Alkazar park.

Post Office, Od. Papakiriazi.—O.T.E. CENTRE, Od. Filellinon.

Buses (stations, see plan). To *Athens* (3 times daily); to *Volos* (every 30–45 min.); to *Tríkkala* (hourly), also to *Ioannina* (twice daily); to *Tirnavos* and *Elasson* (c. 10 times daily); to *Kozani* (6 times daily), also to *Karditsa* (5 times daily); to *Farsala* (every 1½ hr) from Od. Irakliou (Plat. Riga Ferraiou).—S.E.K. COACHES from the main square to *Athens* and to *Salonika.*

History. The name *Larissa,* meaning 'citadel', is of pre-Hellenic origin, and a settlement seems to have existed on the site from the earliest times. Palaeolithic remains were discovered in 1960 on the w. outskirts. An early ruler, Aleuas, who claimed descent from Herakles, founded the powerful family of the Aleuadai. The dynasty attracted to their court the poet Pindar, the sophist Gorgias, and the physician Hippocrates, the last two of whom died at Larissa. In 480 B.C. the Aleuadai supported Xerxes; four years later the Spartans attacked them unsuccessfully. At the end of the 5C B.C. their power was weakened by a democratic revolt and by the rise of the tyrants of Pherai, the most formidable of whom was Jason. The last Aleuadai injudiciously invited the aid of Philip of Macedon, who annexed Larissa and the whole of Thessaly. After the second battle of Cynoscephalae (197) the Romans made Larissa the capital of the reorganized Thessalian confederation. In 171 Perseus, king of Macedon, defeated the Romans near Larissa. Pompey passed through the city on his flight after the battle of Pharsalus.

Achilleios, Bp and patron saint of Larissa, was present at the Council of Nicaea (325) and by the 5C the city had metropolitan rank. Larissa fell to the Bulgars in 985. Byzantine rule was restored, and, though the Normans laid siege to the town in 1096, survived till the Frankish occupation of the 4th Crusade, when Thessaly fell to Boniface of Montferrat. Theodore Angelos drove out the Franks and Michael II, his nephew, ruled Thessaly from Arta. Michael's illegitimate son, John Doukas, defied the emperors and his half-brother in Epirus alike. After his death in 1289, his son John II remained the ward and vassal of Guy de la Roche until 1308, when he threw in his lot with Byzantium in time to rid his territories of the Catalan Grand Company, who passed through on their way s. In 1318 John II died without an heir and Thessaly, invaded from all sides, was quarrelled over until Andronikos III restored uneasy Byzantine rule. By bloodless conquest Thessaly fell in 1348 to Stephen Dušan, who installed its conqueror Gregory Preljub, as 'Caesar' in Trikkala. After Dušan's death another period of anarchy in 1355–59 ended when Symeon Uroš established himself as 'Emperor'. His son, John Uroš, turned monk and the Serbs became little more than Byzantine vassals. By 1393 Bayezid's Turks were encamped on the Spercheios and Thessaly remained Turkish until 1881. The Turks renamed Larissa *Yenişehir* ('new town') in contradistinction to the 'old town', of Krannon. It was the headquarters of Mehmed IV during the siege of Candia in 1669 and its military garrison inhibited the participation of Thessaly in the War of Independence. Larissa did not, however, succeed Trikkala as the Turkish capital of Thessaly, until 1870.

The centre of Larissa is a huge square with several names, shaded by limes and orange trees and lively with cafés, patisseries, and cinemas. From its N.W. corner Vasilissis Sofias, where in 1968 was located the late-Hellenistic *Theatre,* leads shortly to the low hill, once the Acropolis of the ancient city, now crowned by a *Clock Tower* (To Rolói). Farther

N.E. is the Byzantine *Frourion*. To the w. are the unfinished new *Cathedral* and some vestiges of a Classical *Temple*, overlooking the new bridge which replaced a medieval bridge of 12 arches across the Peneios. Beyond, along the river, extends the *Alkazár*, a fine shady park (cafés), a favourite promenade in summer.

Returning by Odhos Venizelou, we pass between the *Philharmonic Hall* and the covered *Market*. Opposite a small public garden is a *Mosque* with a conspicuous minaret. Here is housed the **Archaeological Museum**, containing Thessalian antiquities from the nome of Larissa. In the single hall are displayed a menhir from Soufli tumulus (Middle Bronze Age); Archaic temple fragments and funerary stelai from Larissa; later

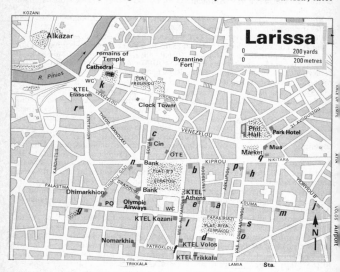

sculpture, displaying the characteristics typical of Thessalian workmanship; late-Imperial stelai depicting mounted warriors (the Greco-Roman antecedents in art of the Byzantine portrayal of St George). Important are the early prehistoric finds (in cases) from the valley of the Peneios, dating from the Palaeolithic epoch to the Neolithic.

The mound (*Magoula*) of *Gremmou*, near Dhendra, 6¼ m. from Larissa off the Kozani road to the left, represents the site of Homeric *Argyssa*, though the principal antiquities dug from the mound since 1955 by the German Institute have belonged to the Neolithic era.

A road leads s.w. to (c. 15 m.) the ruins of **Krannon**, once one of the foremost cities of Thessaly and the seat of the *Skopadai*, kinsmen of the Aleuadai, whose wealth was proverbial. The poet Simonides (556–467 B.C.), who beat Aeschylus in a competition for the best elegy on the fallen at Marathon, lived for a time at Krannon under the patronage of the Skopadai. At Krannon, in 322 B.C., Antipater, the Macedonian regent, defeated the confederate Greeks and so put a stop to the Lamian War. Excavations of the Greek Archaeological Society have laid bare the ruins of a *Temple of Asklepios*, by the side of which flowed and still flows an ancient stream, the waters of which warmed the wine with which it was mixed. Here in 1960 were discovered two tholos tombs of the 5C B.C., showing a remarkable survival in Thessaly of a Mycenean form. The Turks called Krannon

Eskişehir ('Old Town' or 'Old Larissa'), by way of contrast to the 'New Town' of Larissa (see above).

From Larissa an asphalt road runs N.E. via Omorfokhórion to (12½ m.) *Sikoúri*, continuing (unpaved) to *Spiliá* (2580 ft), 5 m. farther on, departure point for the mountain refuge (3 hrs) on *Mt Ossa* (comp. below). A group of Mycenean tholos tombs was identified in 1969 near the village.

FROM LARISSA TO AYIA, 24½ m. (39 km.), bus. We take the Volos road E. across the plain, and at 4 m. branch left.—At (10 m.) *Elevthérion*, a rough by-road goes off left for *Marmáriani* (4 m.) where many tholos tombs were examined in 1903 and there are scanty remains of ancient Lakereia. We pass into the Dotion Plain.— 24½ m. *Ayiá* (Inn), chief place (3200 inhab.) of an eparchy, is situated on the s. slopes of Ossa above the gorge dividing Ossa from Pelion, and c. 7 m. from the sea. It has a 16C monastery with frescoes of 1721. Guides may be hired for expeditions on **Mt Ossa**, or *Kissavos* (6490 ft), a bold isolated mountain commanding a magnificent *View. Mules can be taken almost to the summit, from which Mt Athos and, in clear weather, the Turkish coast may be seen. The Giants, in their war with the Gods, are fabled to have piled Pelion on Ossa in order to reach the summit of Olympos. The w. slopes of Ossa provided Verde antico and Atrax marble (serpentine) for the buildings of ancient Rome.

To the N.W. of Ayia (4½ m.) is *Melívia*, occupying the site of ancient *Meliboias*, native place of Philoktetes.—The royal estate of *Polidhendhri* (c. 10 m. S.E.) was donated by King Paul to the State in 1962 as a training school for Greek farmers.

From Larissa to *Pharsala*, see Rte 47B; to *Volos*, see Rte 50; to *Tirnavos* and *Elasson*, see Rte 58; to the *Vale of Tempe*, see Rte 57; to *Trikkala* and *Meteora*, see Rtes 50 & 51.

49 MAGNESIA

A From Lamia to Volos

ROAD, 69½ m. (111 km.), of which 51 m. by National Highway (toll).—32 m. (51 km.). Exit for *Glifa* car ferry.—54 m. (86 km.) Exit for *Volos*.—55 m. (88 km.) *Mikrothivai* and 58 m. (93 km.) *Nea Ankhialos* (**Phthiotic Thebes**).—69½ m. **Volos**. —Buses from Plateia Laou twice daily to Almiros and Volos, 6 times to Pelasyia.

We quit Lamia on the E. and in 2½ m. join the National Highway. 10 m. *Stilís* (ΣΤΥΛΙΣ; exit), the port of Lamia, is served by coasting steamer. It occupies the site of Thessalian *Phaleron* and its 4400 inhabitants derive their livelihood from olive culture.—Just beyond *Karavómilos* (Stylos Beach, 150R, Apr–Oct, C), at 16¼ m. we see (l.) *Akhinós*, backed by a flat-topped hill (chapel) bearing remains, perhaps to be identified with the *Echinos* referred to in the 'Lysistrata'.—19 m. Exit for *Rákhes* and *Pelasyía* (ΠΕΛΑΣΓΙΑ); about 1½ hr N. on foot from Pelasyía (buses from Lamia and Volos) are the remains of *Larissa Kremaste*.—22½ m. Parking area by the channel (Diavlos Oreon), across which is *Mt Likhás*, the w. promontory of Euboea (comp. Rte 42).— 25 m. Toll Gate.—32 m. (51 km.) Exit: roads to Pelasyía (10½ m.; comp. above), and to *Glifa* (7 m.; car ferry to Ayiókambos in Euboea, comp. Rte 42).

Here we may make a seaward detour (c. 6 m. farther), passing just inland of *Akhílleo*, a popular bathing-place, to *Ftelió* (officially Pteliós), a pleasant village lying inland of the site of Homeric *Pteleon*, marked perhaps by a medieval tower on a height nearer the sea (Mycenean tombs to the N.W.).—Passing *Soúrpi* (ΣΟΥΡΠΗ), a nesting-place of storks, we may rejoin the National Highway by the ruins of ancient Halos (comp. below).

If we stay on the old road, Hellenistic *Halos* lies to the right, the remains of its Archaic predecessor on a hill to the left. The *Moní Xiniás* (6 m. w.) dates from the 17C, when it moved down from a higher site, where there are ruins of the 5–13C.— **Almiros**, 4 m. beyond Halos, is the capital of an eparchy, with 5700 inhab. and a small museum. It has an hourly bus connection (in 45 min) with Volos. Benjamin of Tudela remarks on the presence of numerous Italian and Jewish merchants at Almiros, and the Emp. Alexios III in 1199 granted trading concessions here to the Venetians.

39 m. Toll Gate. To our right is *Mt Khlomon* (2930 ft) which guards the Trikkeri Strait (Diavlos Trikeriou), the landlocked entrance to the gulf of Volos, scene in 480 B.C. of the first encounter between the Greek and Persian fleets (comp. Rte 42).—44 m. (70 km.) Exit for Halos and Almiros, see above.—47½ m. Xirias bridge, followed by the return spur from Almiros.—At 54 m. we take the Volos exit, quitting the Highway which continues N. to join near Velestinon (c. 10 m. on) the line of the old Volos–Larissa road (Rte 50).

We are now following the old road.—55 m. (88 km.) *Mikrothívai* stands below the flat hill of **Phthiotic Thebes,** which is ringed by ruined classical walls with 40 towers and has remains of a temple of Athena, a theatre, and a stoa; the walls may be seen from the road (two fields' lengths away) about a mile beyond Mikrothívai. Finds are in the Volos museum.—58 m. (93 km.) **Néa Ankhíalos,** a village (3300 inhab.) by the sea, founded by refugees in 1906, and occupying the site to which Phthiotic Thebes moved in early-Christian times below the acropolis of ancient *Pyrasos*, its port. In three large areas of excavation along the main road (best to the w.) five important early Christian *Basilicas* having extensive mosaics have been exposed by the Greek Archaeological Society, together with sections of a road, public buildings, and houses of the 4–6C A.D. Some beautiful capitals and other fragments are displayed in the small *Museum*, which stands within the site enclosure on the left of our road.

The road now follows the pretty coast above little bays backed by olive-clad hills. From the summit of the last rise there is a wide panorama over the Gulf, then a fine view down to Volos, with Mt Pelion behind. The sanctuary of *Amphanai* (r.) was located by the German Institute in 1972. In the plain we pass the sites of Pagasai and Demetrias (comp. below) and enter (69½ m.) **Volos.**

B Volos and its Environs

VOLOS (BOΛOΣ), a bustling town of 51,300 inhab., capital of its eparchy and of the nome of Magnesia and constituting a deme still officially called Pagasai, is the seat of an archbishop (Metropolitan of Demetrias) and the chief port of Thessaly. Its harbour dates from 1912, but some form of maritime town has existed hereabouts from the remotest antiquity. It is the main channel of Thessalian exports: cereals, garden produce, cotton, silk, olive-oil, skins, sugar, and soap. With its mills, tanneries, and refineries, it rivalled the industrial potential of Piraeus until stricken by two disastrous earthquakes in 1954 and 1955. The recent start of a rail and road ferry to Syria has given new impetus to a large industrial area on the Larissa road. The town provides no monument of interest; but its attractive site between Mt Pelion and the Gulf and the quality of its hotels and restuarants make it the pleasantest base in Central Greece, and its museum should on no account be missed.

Hotels. Palace (Pl. c), 44 Iasonos, A; Alexandros (Pl. g), 3 Topali; Park (Pl. e), 2 Deliyioryi; Electra (Pl. n), 16 Topali; Nefeli (Pl. h), 6 Koumoundourou; Aigli (Pl. d), 17 Argonavton; Argo (Pl. b), 135 Vas. Konstandinou; Xenia (Pl. a), N. Plastira, DPO, private beach, these B; Kypseli (Pl. f), Galaxy (Pl. j), 1 and 3 Ay. Nikolaou; Avra (Pl. k), 5 Solonos; Admitos (Pl. l), 43 Vas. Konstandinou/Ath. Dhiakon, Sandy (Pl. m), Iasonos/Topali, all these C.

Restaurants. *Socrates,* 33 Argonavton; *Kentrikon,* 24 Argonavton; *Mandra Fani,* 2 Koumoundourou; and others mainly on the quay (good fish).

Post Office, 10 Ipirou (upstairs).—O.T.E. CENTRE, Vasileos Konstandinou.—
TOURIST OFFICE, near the harbour.—TOURIST POLICE, 134 Dhimitriados.

Buses from KTEL Larissa to *Athens*, 5 times daily; to *Larissa*, every ¾ hr; to
Velestino, 7 times daily; to *Almiros*, hourly; to *Pelasyia*, twice daily; to *Loutra
Aidipsou*, twice daily, viâ Arkitsa. From KTEL 29 Magnesias to *Portaria* and
Makrinitsa, c. 10 times daily; to most other villages on *Pelion*, 2–3 times daily; to
Lekhonia, etc.

Steamers from Town Quay to the *Northern Sporades, Euboea.*

Near the Railway Station at the N.W. end of the town, the PLATEIA
RIGA FERRAIOU, a huge triangle behind the *Dhimarkhion*, borders the
picturesque *Fishing Harbour*. Hence Odhos Vasileos Konstandinou, or
Dhimitriados, the uninspiring main street, runs through the chequer-
board town parallel to the waterfront. The bustling quayside leads to
the open space, the social centre of the town, which fronts the *Landing
Stage* (whence boats sail for the Sporades). Here a model of the Argo
forms a graceful monument to the past. The quay is continued s. for
nearly a mile by the ARGONAVTON, a splendid esplanade (venue of the
volta).

The *Museum, at the S.E. extremity of the town, was founded in 1909
by Alexis Athanasakis and, rebuilt after the earthquakes, was reopened
in 1961. Its collection of c. 300 painted stelai is unique. Admission 25
dr.; standard hours.

VESTIBULE. Neolithic pottery and seals from various Thessalian sites; Protogeometric bronze ornaments from Omolion; stelai of Antimachos and of Diodotos,
warrior stele, all from Demetrias.

ROOM A, to the right: *Painted Grave Stelai from Demetrias (Hellenistic); figurines; good model of the site of Demetrias and Pagasai. In the
centre, Hellenistic gold *Jewellery from a tomb in Omolion, found in
tic); Mycenean vases and bead jewellery from various Thessalian sites;
Mycenean and Protogeometric finds from the palace at Iolkos. In doorway, Head of a youth from Meliboia (reminiscent of the Kritian Boy).

ROOM B. Walls: relief grave stelai from Phalanna, Larissa, Pherai,
and Gonnoi (5C B.C.). In cases: Palaeolithic flints and bone implements
from Larissa, Sesklo, etc.; pre-pottery Neolithic tools (7th mill. B.C.),
including a bone and flint saw; Thessalian Neolithic pottery is continued in ROOM Γ, where a wall map, excavation section, and choice pots
demonstrate the sequences of Dimini and Sesklo.

ROOM Δ (left of vestibule): Painted grave stelai are further displayed;
good model of the site of Demetrias and Pagasai. In the centre, good
male torso in marble (?Roman copy of an original of the 5C B.C.). In
cases: Geometric pins and clasps, from Pherai; Archaic fragments,
including a miniature amphora with a (?) 7C inscription; coins, placed
and dated; Hellenistic gold *Jewellery from a tomb in Omolion.

ROOM E (beyond). Offerings from various graves; finds from a
Roman tomb at Trikke; fine case of jewellery.

In ROOM Z are reconstituted burials of all periods from Mycenean to
Classical with the skeletons and grave offerings in place; here also are
later Demetrian grave stelai.

To the E. of the town, on Goritsa hill rising from the Gulf, stands a fortress-
town of the 4C B.C. excavated since 1971 by a Dutch team.

The site of ancient **Iolkos,** also within the periphery of the town, lies to the right of the Larissa road between the railway and a dried-up river bed, perhaps the ancient Anauros. The site was firmly identified in 1956 by the Greek Archaeological Service (D. Theokaris) and occupies a mound (Ayii Theodori), 30 ft high and measuring c. 450 by 350 yds, partly surrounded by a medieval wall. Until expropriation of modern property is completed, the greater part of the area cannot be explored.

Iolkos, famous in legend as the place whence the Argonauts set forth in quest of the Golden Fleece, had a flourishing existence in Early, Middle, and Late Helladic times, and probably continuity of occupation down the ages. With other towns it was depopulated by Demetrios Poliorketes and its inhabitants moved to Demetrias. Excavations since 1958 have shown the existence of two Mycenean palaces which it is tempting to ascribe respectively to King Pelias, uncle of Jason (c. 1400 B.C.) and to Eumelos and Alcestis (palace destroyed by fire c. 1200 B.C.).

A stiff climb (bus) may be made to ANO VOLOS, the medieval town, with houses built on the sides of steep hills rising to 2600 feet. One of the houses has frescoes (1912) by Theophilos. The church of the Metamorfosis on the hill of Episkopi has a 16C ikon.

EXCURSIONS FROM VOLOS

The ruins of the cities that preceded Volos are of considerable archaeological importance. The places described below are within easy reach of the town, and each of the excursions can be made in a day or half-day, though they are not recommended to the casual visitor.

I. TO PAGASAI AND DEMETRIAS. The adjacent remains of the two cities lie 2 m. s. of Volos and can be reached in 10 min. by car or bus, in $\frac{1}{2}$ hr on foot, or in $\frac{1}{2}$ hr by hired boat from Volos quay. We take the Almiros road to the s.w. (Rte 49A). This goes through the middle of ancient **Demetrias** (bus stop by track leading to Theatre) and then passes between **Pagasai** and a pleasant beach (taverna). The site was first explored in 1920–23 and excavations since 1961 by Prof. Milojčić (German Institute) have resulted in a definitive survey. On the ground there is at present little to see and much of the area is fenced.

Pagasai was the port of Iolkos and afterwards of Pherai. The port gave its name to the Pagasitikos Kolpos (Gulf of Volos). The Argo was, by the traditional story, built at Pagasai, which had a famous oracle and an altar of Apollo mentioned by Hesiod. It flourished in the 5C B.C. under the wing of Pherai. It was captured by Philip II of Macedon who separated it from Pherai and incorporated it in Magnesia. When Demetrios Poliorketes founded *Demetrias* just to the N., Pagasai became a dependency of the new city. Demetrias was a favourite resort of its founder and his descendants. It was the base of Philip V but tamely surrendered to the domination of Rome in 196. After the battle of Pydna (168) its fortifications were razed. The great towers of the Hellenistic ramparts were hastily strengthened in c. 50 B.C. with outer lines. Concealed in the stone plinths of these were discovered the painted stelai now in the museum at Volos. These had come from neighbouring cemeteries. In the Byzantine epoch it was joined to the see of Thessaly. Invading Saracens sacked the town in 902.—Off the coast here in 1275 the Euboean Franks were utterly defeated by the forces of Michael VIII Palaiologos.

II. TO DIMINI AND SESKLO, 4 m. and 11$\frac{1}{2}$ m. w. of Volos by road. The two sites lie 2 hours' walk apart to the s. of the main Larissa road (Rte 50). A bus may be taken to either. Though of great importance to archaeologists (comp. p. 13), the sites are not very illuminating to the layman (a visit to Volos museum first is recommended).—We take the Larissa road and then, still in the outskirts of Volos, an asphalted road (l.; signposted) to the village of *Dhimíni* (ΔIMHNION). At the beginning of the village a track (r.; sign) leads to the hill crowned by pre-

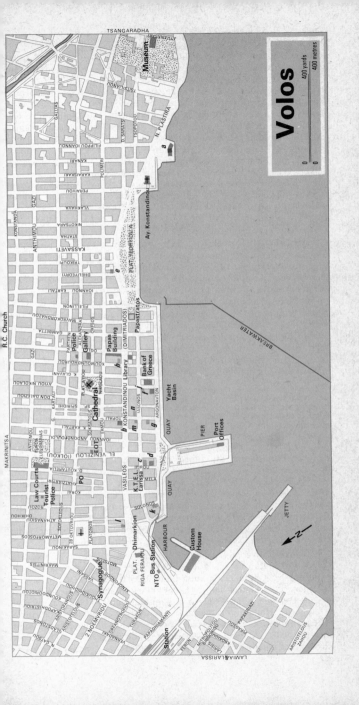

Volos

historic remains of the 4th millennium B.C. that have given the name **'Dimini'** to a culture of the period known more generally as Neolithic B.—To reach **Sésklo** (ΣΕΣΚΛΟΝ) by road we follow the Larissa road for 6½ m., then turn left over a rough railway crossing. Beyond, a tarmac road continues s. towards the village, but after 1¾ m. a further left turn (small sign in Greek) brings us in c. ½ m. to the Acropolis which has given name to a culture of the Neolithic A period; its presence has since been found widely in Thessaly and also elsewhere in Greece. The hill has remains of a large palace with prodromos, megaron having a square hearth, and opisthodomos. Further excavations since 1962, however, have revealed remains of a very much remoter era (? 7th millennium B.C.). The site is fenced, but a partial view can be had from outside if it is shut.—About ¼ hr away is the ruined 'Palaiokastro' which may be *Aisonia*, the city of Jason's father.

C   Mt Pelion

**Mt Pelion (ΠΗΛΙΟΝ; 5415 ft), or *Pílion Oros*, the long mountain range that occupies the greater part of the peninsula enclosing the Pagasitic Gulf, forms one of the most delightful regions of all Greece. Its climate, cool in summer but mild in winter, with abundant streams from the upper slopes, encourages a lush vegetation scarcely found elsewhere on the Greek mainland. It is famed for its fruit, exports chestnuts, and produces attar of roses. From its slopes the sea is rarely hidden from view. The delightful villages, well-watered and shady, have timber-framed houses with balconies; stone-paved mule paths wind between their gardens. The churches are low and wide and have an exo-narthex supported on wooden pillars, which often extends round the N. and S. sides of the nave in the form of a pentise.

The ancients envisaged the Giants piling Pelion on Ossa in the war with the Gods. Pelion was the home of Chiron, wisest of the Centaurs, who taught Achilles the art of music and looked after Jason in his childhood. Here the gods celebrated the nuptials of Peleus and his unwilling bride Thetis. The trees of the mountain supplied timber for the Argo.

I. To PORTARIA AND ZAGORA, 29 m. (47 km.), bus to Zagora twice daily; to Portaria and Makrinitsa 10–11 times daily. We pass (2½ m.) *Ano Volos* (comp. above), climbing steadily. The road winds steeply to (8¾ m.) **Portariá** (ΠΟΡΤΑΡΙΑ; *Xenia* B, double rooms with bath only, DPO; *Kentrikon, Alkistis*, both summer only, C), a beautiful summer resort (730 inhab.) with a magnificent plane-tree and spring in its square. It has excellent cheese and unresinated red wine. The small *Church* (1273) has frescoes of 1581. Portarià is the starting-point for the 3½ hr climb to *Pliasidhi* (5080 ft), one of the main heights of Pelion.

A by-road diverges round the Megarevma ravine to **Makrinítsa** (ΜΑΚΡΥΝΙΤΣΑ; 1¼ m.), a delightful village of 490 inhabitants. Old mansions have been made guest houses (A) by the NTOG. The picturesque little Plateia has a huge hollow plane-tree, a sculptured marble *Fountain*, a small *Church* with apsidal sculptural decoration, and a fine view. Higher up is the formerly monastic church of the *Panayia* (18C) with Greek inscriptions and Roman and Byzantine carvings built into the walls. A small chapel, with a school below, has frescoes. A street name commemorates Charles Ogle (1851–78), special correspondent of the 'Times', who was killed here (it is said in cold blood by order of the Turkish commander) while reporting on a fight between local insurgents and the Turks.

From Portaria the road continues to climb in zigzags, then runs along a high ledge affording enormous views over the Gulf.—15½ m. *Khánia* (3800 ft; Peleus **C**; restaurant), amid beech woods, stands at the head of the pass with a wide panorama in either direction. It has a chair-lift to Pliasídhi. Under the radar-capped crests of Pelion, we descend a tremendous valley through chestnuts, oaks, and planes, joining the road from Tsangaradha (see below) just over a mile short of (29 m.) **Zagorá** (ΖΑΓΟΡΑ; 1600 ft; Inn; Rooms), a large community (2800 inhab.) of four hamlets on the E. slope, facing the Aegean. In the plateia is the church of *Ayios Yeóryios*, a typical Pelionic construction with an 18C ikonostasis. The countryside around is famed for the variety of its fruit (plums, damsons, pears, peaches, fraises de bois, etc.) and its good red wine.

Below Zagora on the coast is *Khorevtó* (4½ m.), with a fine sandy beach, from which motor-boat excursions may be made.

II. To MELIES AND TSANGARÁDHA, 34 m. (55 km.), bus twice daily to Tsangarádha, continuing to Makrirrákhi; 3 times daily to Milées. We quit Volos to the S.E., passing cement works and oil refineries, and skirt the Pagasitic Gulf.—5 m. *Agriá* (3500 inhab.; Barbara **C**) is served by town buses.—6¼ m. *Káto Lekhónia* is the terminus of a bus service (every ¾ hr).—7½ m. *Ano Lekhónia* (tavernas). We pass through orchards.—At (11¾ m.) *Kalá Nerá* (Nirvana **D**) diverges the road to **Milées** (5 m.), birthplace of Anthimos Gazi (1764–1828), who raised the Thessalian revolt in 1821. A charming village, it is a good base for walks in the Magnesian peninsula.—Just beyond (13½ m.) *Korópi* we turn inland, leaving (r.) a by-road to *Afissos* (Actaeon **E**), a small seaside resort on the Gulf. The road climbs; the view is at first obstructed by olive-groves, then, as we reach the pass above (16¾ m.) *Afétai*, or *Niáou*, there is a fine *View over the whole Gulf. We leave on our right the road to *Argalastí* (6¾ m.; Luxe **E**), chief town (1620 inhab.) of Southern Pelion.

Beyond (22½ m.) *Niokhóri* (Inn) we join a by-road from Milées. We cross a deep valley and get our first sight of the Aegean.—28½ m. *Lambinoú*. The road winds vertiginously in and out of the deep clefts that fissure the E. face of Pelion; the *View extends to the island of Skiathos. —34 m. **Tsangarádha** (ΤΣΑΓΚΑΡΑΔΑ; *Ayios Stefanos*, *Galaxy*, open all year, *Xenia*, DPO, Apr–Oct, all **B**), verdantly situated amid oak and plane forests at 1550 ft, enjoys superb views down to the sea. A road (4½ m.) descends to the superb beach at *Milopótamos*.

III. FROM TSANGARÁDHA TO ZAGORA, 14½ m. (23½ km.), one of the most beautiful roads in Greece, a splendid day's *Walk in spring or autumn. The road runs fairly level at c. 1600 ft on the slopes, which are clad with oak forests and plane-trees.—3¾ m. *Moúresi*.—At (7½ m.) *Kissós*, a pretty village, the church of Ayia Marina has frescoes and a pentise 'cloister'. *Ayios Ioánnis* (Aloe, DPO, **B**; Galini, Aigaion, **C**, both Apr–Oct only; Kentrikon, open all year, **D**), its bathing-place, lies below (4½ m. by road).—10¾ m. *Makrirrákhi*, another pleasant hamlet. We join the road from Portariá (comp. above).—14½ m. *Zagorá*.

50 FROM VOLOS TO LARISSA AND TRIKKALA

ROAD, 75¾ m. (122 km.), asphalted and mainly level. 11¾ m. (19 km.) *Velestínon.*
—38 m. (61 km.) *Larissa.*—75¾ m. *Tríkkala.* By bus a change is necessary in
Larissa.

STATE RAILWAY to *Larissa*, 37¼ m. (60 km.) in ¾ hr; through railcars to Athens.
The THESSALIAN RAILWAY from Volos to *Trikkala* (and Kalabaka), viâ Palaiofarsalos, 102 m. (164 km.), follows the road to (11¾ m.) *Velestinon* (comp. below).
It then turns s. to cross two low passes round the E. and s. slopes of Khalko-
donion.—19¼ m. *Aerinon* stands c. 3 m. N. of Phthiotic Thebes (Rte 49) and just N.
of the National Highway.—27½ m. *Rigaion.* About 2 m. S.E. of the station are
Eretria, with chromium mines and a mineral railway, and, on a hill (1670 ft), the
ruins of *Eretria of Phthiotis*, a prehistoric site with a fortified acropolis. This
Eretria, according to Strabo, was one of the cities under the sway of Achilles.—At
(43 m.) *Farsala* the line crosses the Lamia–Larissa road (Rte 47B).—409 m. *Palaiofarsalos*, junction for the main Athens–Salonika line, is near the village of *Stavros*.
The line now follows roughly the course of the Lamia–Karditsa–Tríkkala road
(Rte 47C).—61 m. *Sofádhes.*—70½ m. *Karditsa.*—78 m. *Fanárion.*—88¾ m. *Tríkkala.*
To (102 m.) *Kalabaka*, see Rte 51.

We quit Volos, passing over the railway, and in the next mile or so
leave on our left roads to Almiros and Lamia (Rte 49A) and to Dhimini
(Rte 49B). We follow the railway, ascending the *Defile of Pilav-Tepe*
(450 ft), named ('heap of rice') after a conical tomb of the Hellenic age
(l.) opened in 1899. On the way up we cross the line of the Karla Tunnel
(see below) and see below us the expanding Volos industrial zone. Just
beyond (6 m.) *Latomeion Station*, which serves neighbouring quarries,
we leave on our left the by-road to Sesklo (Rte 49B).—11¾ m. **Velestínon**
(ΒΕΛΕΣΤΙΝΟΝ) is a railway junction of some importance where the
line to Tríkkala (comp. above) parts company with the branch to Larissa.
By the station a by-road leads l. for the town (2700 inhab.), pleasantly
situated amid gardens and fountains in a ravine of Khalkodónion (p.
419.) It was the birthplace of the revolutionary poet Rhigas Pheraios
(1757–98), who was executed by the Turks in Belgrade for working towards a Balkan confederacy.

Velestinon occupies the site of **Pherai**, at one time one of the great cities of
Thessaly; its port was Pagasai. Pherai was the legendary home of Admetus, whose
wife Alcestis sacrificed her life for him, a story that inspired a celebrated tragedy of
Euripides and an opera by Gluck. In the 4C B.C. the rulers of Pherai tried to dominate the whole of Thessaly and to interfere in the Greek world generally. The most
notorious were Jason, elected Tagus of Thessaly in 374 and assassinated in 370, his
successor Alexander who, defeated by the Theban general Pelopidas, died in
357, and Lykophron II, driven out in 352 by Philip of Macedon. Antiochus the
Great (223–187) took Pherai in 191, but it was almost immediately recaptured
by M. Acilius Glabrio.—Some archaeological explorations were made by the Greek
Archaeological Service in 1920 and 1923, and again, in collaboration with the
French School, in 1925–26.

The primitive city was built on a hill about ½ m. S.E. of the historic city, on which
the town of Velestinon was built. The *Acropolis* is on a trapezoidal plateau to the N.
of the Vlach quarter; here are the remains of the Larissan Gate and of a temple of
Hercules. The city proper extended to the S.W.; near the church of the Panayia are
traces of the walls. Walls and towers uncovered on the hill of Ay. Athanasios show
that this too was within the enceinte. Pherai was noted for two fountains, *Hypereia*
and *Messeis*. The former is in the centre of Velestinon; the basin and conduit are
covered with tiles.—On the Larissa road was uncovered a Doric *Temple of Zeus
Thaulios*, rebuilt in the 4C with columns from an earlier temple, which in turn
covered an ancient cemetery. Archaic bronzes were removed to Athens and Geometric pottery to Volos.

We now have a choice of roads, almost equidistant. The faster

National Highway runs slightly above and w. of the plain, with views across it (toll after 15 m.). We describe the more interesting old road.— 14¼ m. *Rizómilos*. To the right was the large marshy LAKE KARLA, the ancient *Boibeïs*, once 15 m. long and 5 wide with a depth of 13– 20 ft. Controlled and drained by a tunnel (comp. above) inaugurated in 1961, which takes surplus water to the Pagasitic Gulf, the lake is now a mere fraction of its former size and cannot be seen from the road. On the reclaimed and irrigated land experiments are being made with various crops, including cotton.

The ruins of several ancient cities are on the original shores: on the E. is *Boibe*; on the N.W. Armenion (comp. below); on the S.E. is *Glaphyrai*, where there are foundations of a temple. The seaward side is fringed by *Mavrovouni* (3565 ft) and the saddle that connects it with Pelion.

20 m. *Armenió*. The site of Homeric *Armenion* is said to lie a little farther w. at Kokkínes, and the huge Mycenean circuit of walls on the hill of Petra, overlooking the lake (r.), is equated with *Kerkinion*. The plain is dotted with mounds showing prehistoric occupation. The modern villages lie mainly to the E. The range of Olympos rises ahead.— 38 m. **Larissa** (Rte 48) may be by-passed.

Beyond Larissa the road runs w. through the plain, which is interrupted ahead by isolated moderate hills culminating in MT DOBROUTSI, the ancient *Titanos* (2515 ft). At (49 m.) *Koutsókheron* the village fountain has been hewn from a large Dóric column drum. To our right, one behind the other, are the twin heights above *Gounitsa* between which, through the impressive *Defile of Kalamaki*, the Peneios emerges into the plain.

About 1 hr s.w. of Koutsókheron, on a spur of Mt Dobroútsi, is the *Palaiokastro of Aléfaka*, the wreck of a Byzantine fortress built on ancient foundations. The ancient remains belong to *Atrax*, once inhabited by the warlike Perrhaebi. One of the city gates, flanked by a fine piece of polygonal wall, survives in part.

Beyond the village we cross the winding Peneios above its entry into the defile. A by-road (r.), affording a view into the defile, leads in 7 m. to Damasion (see Rte 58).—At (53½ m.) *Pineiás* road and river pass between Dobroútsi and the abrupt spur of *Zárkos* (2245 ft), the vertical w. scarp of which looms over the village of *Zárkos*, 2 m. N. of our road. Here was an ancient city, possibly *Phayttos* or *Pharkadon*, which in the Middle Ages became the seat of the Bp of Gardiki (comp. below).—At 58½ m., between modern *Farkadón* (to the N.) and the confluence of the Peneios with its most important tributary, the Enipeus (to the s.), a road diverges s. to Karditsa (17½ m.).

The Karditsa road crosses the Peneios and its affluents. It follows the course of an old Turkish stone road, the fine bridges of which, mostly abandoned, survive on its w. side. Just s. of (5 m.) *Vlokhós* we pass through a line of hills surmounted by ancient citadels, the identity of which is in doubt. That rising prominently above the road (r.) may be *Peirsia*; farther right Kastro of Kourtiki may be *Limnaion*; to the left is Pétrino (? *Phakion*).—6½ m. *Palamá* (5840 inhab.).—At (12½ m.) *Ayios Theodoros* we join a more direct but less interesting road from Larissa and the Lamia–Kardhitsa road (Rte 47C).

62 m. Crossroads. To the right, *Neokhóri* (2 m.), to the N.W. of which, in the foothills of Andikhasia, are some remains of Thessalian *Oichalia*. —Just before (68½ m.) *Petróporos* we pass below the hill of *Palaiogardíki* (r.), the summit of which commands a fine view of the plain of Tríkkala. Near by, the abandoned Byzantine town of *Gardiki*, which gave title to a

bishop (see above), has a ruined church (Ayía Paraskeví), and occupies the site of *Pelinnaion*, of which there survive fragmentary walls, with gates and towers. Pelinnaion was one of four strongholds forming a defensive quadrilateral.—75¾ m. **Tríkkala**, see Rte 47c.

51 THE METEORA AND THE CENTRAL PINDOS

The visit to the Metéora can hardly occupy less than half a day even if confined to the three principal monasteries with the use of a car between them. It is inadvisable to allow less than a full day for the journey thence to Ioannina, though Metsovo can be reached in a long afternoon's drive (c. 3¾ hrs).

A   From Tríkkala to Kalambáka. Metéora

ROAD to Kalambáka, 13 m. (21 km.); motor-bus in ½ hr, continuing to (14¼ m.) *Kastráki* for the Metéora (through service from Larissa every 1½ hr). The tour of the monasteries may be effected by asphalted road, 13 m. round from Kalambaka; on foot the ancient stone paths are shorter but often steep.

RAILWAY to Kalambáka, 13½ m. in 40 min., 6 times daily; through trains from Volos, viâ Farsala and Karditsa (comp. Rte 50).

We quit Tríkkala by the Castle and turn N.W. The road, lined with poplars, drives straight across the plain, accompanied by the railway. To the w. rise the steep slopes of *Kerkétion*, a long range running N. and s. and having its highest point (6235 ft) near its s. end (ascent, see Rte 47). On an isolated foothill, w. of our road (near the village of *Peristéra*), are some ruins to be identified with ancient *Pialeia*.

13 m. **Kalambáka** (ΚΑΛΑΜΠΑΚΑ; *Motel Divani*, 110R, A; *Aeolikos Astir* C, both open all year; *Xenia* A, *Odyssion* C, Apr–Oct only; *Rex* D; Rooms in private houses in the town and in Kastráki; Rest. in the Plateia), an attractive little town of 5500 inhab., spreads fanwise on the green slopes at the foot of the Meteora rocks near the point where the Peneios emerges from the Pindos gorges.

History. Kalambáka is the *Aiginion* of antiquity, a town of the Tymphaei stated by Livy to have been impregnable. Here Caesar joined Cnaeus Domitius before marching on Pharsalus. The Byzantines called the town *Stagoi*, perhaps a corruption of εις τους 'Αγίους and they established here a bishopric in the 10C; the see is now at Trikkala. In 1854 a force of Greeks captured and temporarily held Kalambáka against the Turks.

The CATHEDRAL, dedicated to the Dormition of the Virgin, bears an inscription ascribing its foundation to Manuel I Comnenos (mid-12C). The chrysobull of Andronikos III painted on the N. wall of the narthex concerns the privileges of the diocese not the building of the church. The present edifice, an aisled basilica, stands on even earlier foundations; some mosaics remain beneath the sanctuary floor. The *Synthronon* in the apse as well as the *Ciborium* and centrally placed *Ambo* probably belonged to the earlier building. One wall, next to the sanctuary, preserves 12C paintings. The remaining frescoes were painted by Cretan artists after a reconstruction in 1573, when the narthex and cloisters were added.—The church of *Ayios Ioannis Prodromos* (11–14C) is constructed of Roman materials.

A ROAD from the town centre leads round the w. end of the colossal mass of rock that looms over Kalambaka. Beyond the by-road to *Kastráki* (1240 inhab.) we enter the weird valley of the Metéora. The foot-path is shorter.

The *MÉTÉORA (Τὰ Μετέωρα) comprise a series of monastic build-ings perched on a cluster of detached precipitous rocks. These are com-posed of a stratified conglomerate of iron-grey colour scarred by erosion of wind and streaked by centuries of rainwater. "They rise" (in the words of Dr Henry Holland who visited them in 1812) "from the comparatively flat surface of the valley; a group of isolated masses, cones, and pillars of rock, of great height, and for the most part so perpendicular in their ascent, that each one of their numerous fronts seems to the eye as a vast wall, formed rather by the art of man, than by the more varied and irregular workings of nature. In the deep and winding recesses which form the intervals between these lofty pinnacles, the thick foliage of trees gives a shade and colouring, which, while they enhance the contrast, do not diminish the effect of the great masses of naked rock impending above." Awe-inspiring in the most favourable conditions, the landscape in lowering weather or by the light of the full moon is daunting in the extreme.

History. The earliest monastic community here, the 'Thebaid of Stagoi' at Doúpiani developed before 1336 among the hermits who earlier sought in the caves religious isolation and a secure retreat from the turbulent times. Their Protaton, or communal church, is located by a small chapel (comp. below) on old foundations. Before the end of the century this skete and its protos had been eclipsed by the Meteoron, which, with other communities, was encouraged and endowed by the Orthodox Serbian conquerors of Thessaly. During the Turkish conquest the monasteries became an asylum for refugees. At its greatest extent the community numbered 13 monasteries, all coenobite, and c. 20 smaller settlements, flourishing under Abbot Bessarion in the time of Suleiman the Magnificent, deriving revenues from estates on the Danube granted by the voivodes of Wallachia. The Patriarch Jeremias I (1522–45) raised several of them to the rank of imperial stavropegion. They declined in the 18C, and were already a decaying curiosity to early-19C travellers. They lost their independence to the Bp of Trikkala in 1899. The motor road that now makes the visit a commonplace of tourism has shattered the solitude and isolation. There are now only some ten monks, largely occupied in receiving visitors, and some twenty nuns. However, continuing religious occupation seems assured by the Church's policy of a period of monastic service for its priests.

Access was intentionally difficult, being made either by a series of vertical wooden ladders of vertiginous length (65–130 ft), which could be retracted at night or in emergency, or in a net drawn up by rope and windlass to specially built towers, overhanging the abyss. The old methods, uncomfortable at best and often perilous, gave way in the 1920s to steps cut on the orders of Polykarpos, Bp. of Trikkala, though the rope and windlass is still occasionally used for taking in provisions. The monasteries may be visited daily 8–12, 3–6, but the Gt. Metéora is closed on Wed. There is no guest-house.

Beyond the Kastraki turn the road bends right. On the left stands the *Doúpiani Chapel* (comp. above), rebuilt in 1861. The 'Broad Rock' (l.), on which is seen the Great Meteoron, rises above several lesser pillars: the cleft rock of the *Prodromos* whose scanty ruins, already deserted in 1745, are now inaccessible; on a higher rock *Ayios Nikolaos tou Ana-pavsá* (c. 1388), partly repaired in 1960 when its frescoes, by Theophanes the Cretan (1527), were restored; and the inaccessible *Ayia Moni*, dangerously perched on its slender pinnacle in 1614 and ruined in an earthquake of 1858. We leave Rousanou to the right, take the left fork, pass Barlaam (l.), and arrive at the **Great Meteoron**, or coenobitic *Monastery of the Transfiguration*, the largest and loftiest of the monas-teries, built on the Platys Lithos ('Broad Rock'; 1752 ft).

The Great Meteoron was founded by St Athanasios as the poor community of the Theotokos Meteoritissa. Its privileges were guaranteed in 1362 by the Serbian Emp. Symeon Uroš and under the guidance of John Uroš, his son, who retired here c. 1373 as the monk Ioasaph, it became a rich monastic house. Euthymios, Patriarch of Constantinople (1410–16), made it independent of local jurisdiction, but its head was not officially granted the title of Abbot (hegoumenos) until c. 1482.

The *Katholikon* was reconstructed at his own expense by Ioasaph in 1387–88. His apse and sanctuary, decorated with painting in 1497–98, form the E. extension of the existing church, which was enlarged after an earthquake in 1544. It is a Greek cross in square with a dome set on a drum. The paintings are in good preservation. The *Refectory* (1557), on the N. side of the church, has a vaulted roof set on five pillars.

From the S.E. corner of the monastery (or from the path in the ravine towards Barlaam) there is a striking view of the neighbouring rock. Here among the vultures' nests can be descried two painted ikons and broken lengths of the ladders that once gave access to *Hypselotéra*, highest of the monasteries and dedicated to the 'Highest in the Heavens' ('Υψηλοτέρα τῶν Οὐρανῶν). This convent was founded c. 1390 and disappeared in the 17C, possibly owing to the peril of the ascent.

About 30 min. N. of the Broad Rock is the seldom-visited *Hypapanti*, derelict but still accessible, in a huge cavern. It merits a visit for its brightly painted frescoes and gilded ikonostasis. The inaccessible *Ayios Dhimitrios* stands on top of a nearby rock. It was destroyed by Turkish gunfire in 1809 after having served as headquarters of a local klephtic band.

The monastery of **Barlaam* is approached by bridge from the road. The windlass and rope in the *Tower* (erected in 1536) were much used for materials in 1961–63 when the refectory was reconstructed as a *Museum* (adm. 3 dr.; closed 1–3) for the monastic treasures. The founders in 1517, Nektarios and Theophanes Asparas of Ioannina, reoccupied a site where a 14C anchorite named Barlaam had built a church dedicated to the Three Hierarchs. This they restored and it survives (repaired and frescoed in 1627–37) as a side chapel of the present *Katholikon* erected in 1542–44. This is a good example of the late-Byzantine style with a carved and gilded ikonostasis and frescoes by Frangos Kastellanos and George of Thebes (in the narthex; 1566).

We return to the main fork. **Rousánou**, a small monastery compactly set on a lower hill, is approached by bridges built in 1868. It was founded before 1545 by Maximos and Ioasaph of Ioannina, but by 1614 had decayed to such an extent that it was made subject to Barlaam. It has recently been reoccupied by a convent of nuns. The *Church*, with an octagonal dome, is a smaller version of that of Barlaam, with frescoes of 1560.

Ayía Triádha, the monastery of the Holy Trinity (1 monk), situated on an isolated pillar between two ravines, is entered by 130 steps partly in a tunnel through the rock. Off the passage leading into the courtyard a round chapel carved out of the rock was dedicated to St John the Baptist in 1682. The little *Church* of 1476, ornamented in brick and tile, was not improved by the addition in 1684 of a large and ugly narthex. The conventual buildings are in an attractive half-timbered style with a pretty garden.

The **Moní Ayíou Stefanou,** or nunnery of St Stephen, though the farthest away by road, is the only monastery visible from Kalambaka. It is easy of access since its solitary pinnacle is joined directly to the Kuklióli hill by a bridge. The convent was founded c. 1400 by Antonios Cantacuzene (probably a son of Nikephoros II of Epirus), whose portrait in the *Parecclesion* (the original katholikon) was defaced by Communist rebels in 1949. The *New Katholikon*, rebuilt in 1798, is dedicated to the martyr Charalambos, whose head is the monastery's chief relic.

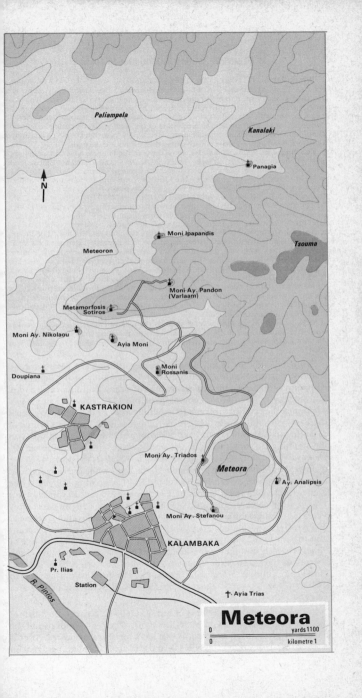

B From (Tríkkala) Kalambáka to Ioannina

ROAD, 94½ m. (152 km.). To (13 m.) **Kalambáka**, see above.—50 m. *Katara Pass.*—57¾ m. **Métsovo** (1¼ m. s.).—94½ m. **Ioannina**. Bus twice daily. This is a mountain road of spectacular grandeur, crossing the highest pass in Greece open to motor traffic. In winter this route is closed by snow; even in early summer the snow-line must be crossed. The road is unsurfaced near the summit and there is some danger of landslides, so that the state of the road and the weather conditions should, if possible, be ascertained before leaving. The crossing should be attempted only in full daylight by drivers with experience of mountain roads.

The **Pindos**, or *Pindus Mountains*, an offshoot of the Dinaric Alps and an integral part of the backbone of Greece, runs from N. to S. and separates Epirus from Thessaly. From its s. end a branch, under the name of OTHRYS, starting from Mt Veluchi (Tymphrestos), runs E. to the Gulf of Volos and bounds the Thessalian plain on the S. The highest of the range's many peaks rise to the E. and S.E. of Ioannina: these include *Kakarditsa* (7612 ft), *Peristeri* (7530 ft) and *Kataphidi* (7851 ft). Farther S. the range divides: the W. branch, culminating in *Tsournata* (7113 ft), is separated by the valley of the Agrapha from the E. branch, the *Agrapha Mountains* (*Dolopia* in antiquity). In classical times the highest peak was called *Lakmon*, a name transferred to Mt Zygos (5102 ft), a peak to the E. of Peristeri. The mountain sides are thickly wooded with trees of beech, oak and pine to within a short distance of the bare crests. Five important rivers have their source in the Pindos: the *Arakthos*, flowing s. through Epirus into the Gulf of Arta; the *Akheloos*, through Epirus, Akarnania, and Aitolia into the Ionian Sea; the *Aoos*, through Epirus and Albania into the Adriatic; the *Aliakmon* and the *Pinios* into the Gulf of Salonika. In many parts of the range the rivers find their way down through deep valleys or gorges. Wolves and wild boar are still common in places; brown bears survive, and, in smaller numbers, the lynx. Of the larger birds Egyptian and Griffon vultures greatly outnumber the Golden Eagle.

Most journeys in the Pindos other than by the Katara Pass or by the Karpenisi-Frangista route in the s. (Rte 54) still need the planning and equipment for a mountain expedition (comp. the trek led in 1963 by Sir John Hunt: *Geog. Jnl.*, Sept 1964).

From Tríkkala to (13 m.) **Kalambáka**, see above. The Metsovo road leads w. past the Xenia motel and ascends the valley of the Peneios in company with the abandoned earthworks of a railway (to Kozani; comp. Rte 58), begun by a Belgian company before 1939.—At (19¼ m.) *Khani Mourgane* the road to Grevena (Rte 62) diverges to the right. We cross the Peneios by a Bailey bridge. A by-road goes off (l.) across a bridge of 11 arches to *Kastaniá* (11 m.) and *Amáranton* (13 m.) in a side valley to the s. Our road now makes height on the slopes of the flat-topped *Mt Orthovoúni* (3630 ft).—At (29 m.) *Orthovoúni* (2230 ft) the peaks of *Notía*, usually snow-covered, are prominent to the s.w., while the ranges ahead fill the horizon in a seemingly level circle. The road continues at the higher level along the s. slopes of *Krátsovon* (5135 ft). Beyond (34 m.) *Trigón*, steep descent. Just after (35½ m.) a Petrol Station, we pass below *Pévki* (r.). Panayia is seen far ahead.—39¾ m. *Koridallós* stands to the E. of a pass into an isolated valley of the Khasia range.—We cross a mountain torrent to (42¼ m.) *Koutsofiani*, a hamlet above the large village of *Panayía* which dominates the junction of the valleys. We now climb sharply in zigzags towards the main watershed between Khásia (r.) and Notía (l.). Turning to *Malakási* (3¾ m., l.). The holm-oak gives place to pine and beech.—48 m. *Kámbos tou Despóti* (Restaurant; petrol) at a height of 4265 ft.

We mount to (50 m.) the **Pass of Katára** (5600 ft; refuge). Just before the summit splendid view in both directions. The road winds round the head of the w. valley, keeping nearly level for some distance. After a mile or two in disappointingly bleak and enclosed surroundings, sudden superb *View of Metsovo backed by a gigantic range of snow-clad peaks. The road makes a great loop, descending amid slopes clothed in fir, beech, and box, affording views of peaks in every direction. Turning to *Vovoúsa* (r.; 22 m.), an isolated village in the Valiakalda range.—At 57¾ m. we leave the main road at a saw-mill and in 1¼ m. reach Metsovo.

Métsovo (ΜΕΤΣΟΒΟ; *Pens. Flokas* **B**; *Olympic, Galaxy,* **C**; *Egnatia* **D**) has the status of deme and eparchy though little more than a large mountain village, having 2800 inhab., many of them Vlachs. The attractive houses are built in terraces on the steep side of a mountain separated from Mt Zygos (5100 ft) by two deep ravines. The town is divided by the chasm of the Metsovitikos into two parts—the 'Prosílio' (exposed to the sun) and the 'Anílio' (away from the sun)—which are connected by a bridge. All the five great rivers in the Pindos have their sources near Metsovo. The views on all sides are wonderful and the air exhilarating. The woollen rugs and local embroidered textiles are very attractive. The *MUSEUM (Mouseio Laïkis Tékhnis; adm. 5 dr.; visit guided), a beautiful display of the handicrafts of the region, occupies the restored 'arkhontikó' of Baron Michael Tositsa (1885–1950).

In the 17C a Turkish vizier, in disgrace with his sultan, sought asylum at Metsovo and was kindly treated. Later returning to favour at court, he repaid the generosity of his hosts when, in 1669, the town was granted special privileges, giving it virtual independence which lasted to the time of Ali Pasha. Many rich Christian families took refuge at Metsovo, which has since had a reputation for its philanthropists, among them George Averoff (1815–99). The monastery of Ayios Nikolaos has frescoes by Eustathios (1702).

BUSES daily to *Athens*, viâ *Trikkala* or viâ *Ioannina*; daily to *Salonika*; twice daily to *Ioannina*.

Above Metsovo we emerge high above the Metsovitikos, longest affluent of the Arachthos, in a wild landscape of sandstone. The road here is subject to falls of rock. We descend the rugged N. side of the gorge, across which, above the gentler forest-clad S. slopes, tower the outlying crags and central mass of *Peristéri* (7530 ft).—At (64½ m.) *Votonósi*, where Tsolakoglou (first Quisling prime minister of Greece) signed an armistice with the Germans in 1941, the vegetation becomes less alpine; judas-trees, walnuts, etc. are seen again. We descend to the swift-flowing river. A by-road to Peristéri crosses the river by a Turkish pack-horse bridge. The road rises higher as the river drops below into a wild boulder-strewn gorge, while Peristéri rises to view again on the left.

We get a splendid *View down the widening river while we climb round the S. side of Mt Dhemati. Across the river on Mt Gradetsi, above *Mikrá Gótista*, is the highest fortified enceinte of antiquity (3C B.C.) yet found in Greece (5126 ft). Ahead rises the streaked, forbidding *Mitsikeli* range (5935 ft) as we descend to (78¼ m.) *Baldoúmas* (café; petrol) and cross the tributary Zagoritikos on a Bailey-bridge. The road now ascends in serpentine loops over the S. part of Mitsikeli, affording retrospective *Vistas of range upon range of the Pindos.—85 m. *Mázia* occupies the saddle between Mitsikeli and Driskos. From the summit a broad well-engineered road descends, with views across Lake Pamvotis. —86¼ m. The Monastery *Panayia Dourahan* is reputed to have been founded in 1434 by Dourahan Pasha as a thanks offering to the Virgin for protecting his night ride across the frozen lake.—90 m. *Stroúni* is a starting-point for climbing Mitsikeli (Refuge 2½ hrs above the village). We descend to (94½ m.) **Ioannina** (Rte 52).

VI NORTH-WESTERN GREECE

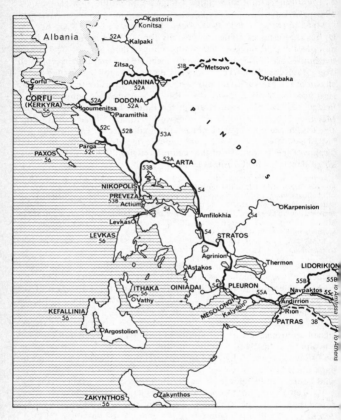

Epirus or *Ipiros* ("Ηπειρος; 'The Mainland'), the N.W. province of Greece, is separated from Albania by an artificial frontier, and from Thessaly by the Pindus range. On the s. it is washed by the Gulf of Arta and on the w. by the Ionian Sea, with the island of Corfù lying opposite the frontier between Greece and Albania. The mountainous character of the interior and the scarcity of communications have always isolated Epirus, whose inhabitants were only partly Hellenic. The few Greek colonies were confined to the coast and to the low-lying region of the s. The province, the most humid in Greece, is well wooded and yields a little corn; it has long been famous for its flocks and pasturage and for its breed of Molossian dogs. Its principal rivers are the Arta (Arachthos), the Kalamas (Thyamis), and the

Mavropotamos (Acheron). Epirus is divided into four nomes: Ioannina, Preveza, Arta, and Thesprotia. The largest towns are Ioannina and Arta, both well inland, and Preveza, on the coast. The main roads are now better than most maps suggest. In antiquity the oracle of Dodona was renowned as the oldest in Greece.

History. Of the 14 tribes inhabiting Epirus, the chief were the Chaones, the Thesproti and the Molossi, which gave their names to the three main divisions of the country. Each tribe was governed by its own prince. The Molossians, who claimed descent from Neoptolemus (Pyrrhus), son of Achilles, later took over the whole country as kings of Epirus. The most famous of these kings was Pyrrhus (318–272 B.C.). In 286 he invaded Macedonia, of which he became king for a brief period. In 280 he accepted the invitation of the Tarentines to join them in their war against Rome. After his victory at Heraclea, he came within 24 miles of Rome. A second Pyrrhic victory, at Asculum (Apulum), in 279, exhausted both sides. After adventures in Sicily helping the Greeks against the Carthaginians, Pyrrhus returned to Italy in 276; his defeat near Beneventum in the following year obliged him to leave Italy for good. But he did not remain idle. In 273 he again invaded Macedonia, becoming king for the second time, again for a short period. Afterwards he turned against Sparta and Argos, where he was ignominiously killed. After his death the kingship of Epirus was abolished, and the country divided between three generals. In the Macedonian wars, Epirus joined the Macedonians, went over to the Romans (198), and then turned against them (170). After the defeat at Pydna in 168 of Perseus, the last king of Macedon, 70 towns in Epirus were destroyed and 150,000 of the inhabitants enslaved, and the country became a Roman province.

In the middle ages Epirus was constantly invaded. After the division of the Byzantine empire the country was divided into *New Epirus*, with Dyrrachium (Durazzo), and *Old Epirus*, with Acarnania. After the capture of Constantinople by the Crusaders in 1204, a despotate of Epirus was set up. The first despot, Michael I, made Ioannina his capital. A later despot, Theodore Angelus, seized the Latin kingdom of Thessalonika in 1223. The dynasty expired at the end of the 13C. In 1318–35 Epirus with Cephalonia came under the domination of the Orsini, returned briefly to Byzantium, fell to the Serbs (1348–86), and returned to Cephalonia under the Tocco. The Turks captured Ioannina in 1431. In the 15C and 16C the Venetians occupied several strong points in the country. Epirus took no part in the War of Independence. In 1881 the District of Arta was freed from Turkish domination. During the Second Balkan War the Greek army took Ioannina (Feb 1913), and occupied all the north of Epirus; but much of the liberated territory was subsequently given to Albania. In the Second World War the Greek army threw back the invading Italians in 1940 and, until the German intervention, reoccupied Northern Epirus.

Aitolia and Akarnania (Αἰτωλακαρνανία), together form the most westerly nome of Central Greece, lying between Epirus and the Gulf of Patras. **Aitolia**, on the E., is divided from Akarnania by the river Acheloos. Its w. half, lying between the Acheloos and the Evenos, was anciently called *Old Aetolia* and included the city of Kalydon, mythologically famous for the boar hunt. *New Aetolia* or *Aitoliá Epiktetos* ('Acquired Aetolia') extended to the E. from the Evenos to the country of the Ozolian Locrians. The interior of Aitolia is roadless, wild and mountainous, with numerous peaks exceeding 6000 ft, and is accessible only to determined travellers.

Aetolia, originally inhabited by the Curetes, derives its name from Aetolos, son of Endymion, who fled hither after having killed Apis. The five cities of Old Aetolia all took part in the Trojan War. The three tribes living in New Aetolia were barbarous, ate raw flesh, and spoke an unintelligible dialect (Thuc. III, 94). Loosely connected by a religious tie, they had a common temple at the sanctuary of Thermon. After the battle of Chaironeia (338 B.C.), they formed the Aetolian League which, at the beginning of the 3C B.C., was strong enough to frustrate the invading armies of the Gaul Brennus. Before the expansion of the rival Achaean League under Aratos, the Aetolians reached the zenith of their power. They acquired or dominated Locris, Phocis, central Akarnania, and Boeotia, as well as numerous cities in the Peloponnesus. In the ruinous War of the Leagues (219–217 B.C.), Philip V of Macedon, with the Achaeans as allies, invaded Aetolia. In 211 the Aetolians allied themselves with Rome, and in 197 they helped the Romans to win the battle of Cynoscephalae. Later they joined Antiochus the Great against the Romans, and in the peace of 188 their federation was virtually dissolved. In 31, after the battle of Actium, Octavian (Augustus) completed the depopulation caused by centuries of warfare by transferring most of the inhabitants to his new city of Nikopolis, on the Epirus side of the Ambracian Gulf. In the War of Independence the Aetolians defeated the Turks at Karpenisi, and Mesolongi endured three sieges.

Akarnania has the sea on three sides. It is bounded on the N. by the Ambracian Gulf; on its W. coast it is joined by a causeway to the island of Levkas, and has two other Ionian Islands—Ithaca and Cephalonia—and numerous islets to the S. A mountain range (over 5000 ft) occupies most of the eparchy of Xiromeros between Astakós, on the S. coast, and Vónitsa, on the Ambracian Gulf.

The Akarnanians emerged from obscurity at the beginning of the Peloponnesian War (431 B.C.). Like the Aetolians, they were uncivilized, living by piracy and robbery, and like them they formed their towns into a league, which first met at Stratos, their chief town. South and central Aetolia are entirely agricultural, but the cultivation is not intensive. Currants are grown near Mesolongi, olives round Aitoliko, and tobacco near Agrinion. The mountain eparchies depend upon the produce of the forests; Xeromeros, in Akarnania, exports valonia, the acorn of the *quercus aegilops*, used for tanning.

52   FROM IGOUMENITSA TO IOANNINA, PARGA AND PREVEZA

A To Ioannina (and Dodona)

ROAD, 63 m. (101 km.), a fine modern *Highway through rugged mountainous country. Buses of KTEL 21 approx. every 3 hrs.

Igoumenítsa (*Xenia Motel*, DPO, Apr–Oct, **B**, *Tourist* **C**, *Actaeon*, *Lux*, **D**), the port of call on the Greek mainland of car ferries from Brindisi and Otranto and the terminus of a local ferry (6–10 times daily; comp. Rte 56) from Corfù, was an insignificant village until, in 1936, it became the seat of the nomarch of Thesprotia. Rebuilt on the ruins left by the occupying troops in 1944, it is now a flourishing transit town (4100 inhab.) with a pleasant sea front.

Through the formerly marshy plain to the N. the Kalamas, the ancient Thyamis, winds its way to the channel separating Corfù from the mainland. A barrage (1962) at the exit of the last defile now controls irrigation, and experiments are being made in rice growing. The small hills which rise above the marsh are considered by some authorities to represent the ancient *Sybota Islands*, near which a naval battle was fought in 433 B.C. between the Corinthians and Corcyraeans (Thuc. I, 45). Their name is now held by a group of islands between Igoumenitsa and Parga to the S.

From Igoumenitsa to *Preveza*, see Rte 52B, 52C; to *Parga*, see Rte 52C.

Climbing out of Igoumenitsa, the Ioannina road enters a level valley enclosed by rugged mountains.—5½ m. Turning to Filiátes and Sayiádha.

This road runs out towards the Albanian frontier and military restrictions may be encountered. The road is unpaved to Elaia, then asphalt.—½ m. We cross the Kalamas (military check at the bridge).—2 m. *Elaia* (the road from Elaia back to the main road near Neraida, marked as good on many maps, is very rough).—5 m. *Filiátes* (ΦΙΛΙΑΤΕΣ; 720 ft) is a lively market town. The former Turkish population dwindled in the plague of 1821 and the town was repopulated by Christian refugees. A cheese factory was built in 1963–65 by United Nations Association volunteers. *Yeroméri*, near by, has a monastery founded in 1285.—8½ m. Turning to *Plaision* (3 m.), a decayed old town with a 17C church, which in the 19C had flourishing tanneries. It was the birthplace of Kyra Vasiliki, consort of Ali Pasha. Besieged by Albanians in 1908–13 and looted and burnt in 1943, it now has only a third of its former population.—14½ m. *Sayiádha*, rebuilt on the coast after the hill town was destroyed in 1940–41, has a jetty opposite Corfù. The old ruins can be seen high above the road.

The main road turns s. to cross a spur and descends again to the river, which here makes a wide loop through a gorge to the N. We follow the right bank below steep hills; the villages lie across the river. The precipitous W. ranges of the Pindus rise ahead. The Paramithiá road (see Rte 52B) diverges ½ m. before (14½ m.) *Menína* (officially *Neráïda*). Our road rises continuously amid scrub, passing a turning to the 16C *Moní Paganion*. Beyond (24 m.) *Plakotí*, it zigzags sharply up to 2000 ft while the river threads another ravine. The view opens out ahead (café) as we descend by continuous turns to rejoin the river at 32½ m.) *Vrosína*, where an old packhorse bridge (left) crosses a tributary. We cross the Tyrias and undulate through cultivated hills.—At (43¼ m.) *Soulópoulo* we cross another affluent of the Kalamas and climb out of the river basin through countryside patterned by stone walls.—Just beyond (49½ m.) *Klimatiá* a poor road diverges N. to *Zitsa* (4 m.; 2230 ft), a picturesque little town (950 inhab.) locally renowned for its somewhat sweet wine. Its prosperity in Turkish times is attested by its stone houses and paved streets. The monasteries of *Profitis Ilias* and *tou Pateron* (14C), fired with nationalist zeal in 1778 by Kosmas Aitolou, fostered Greek schools. Byron sings the charms of the view in Childe Harold (II, xlviii).

53½ m. Turning for *Rodhotópi* (3 m.) with slight remains of ancient *Passaron*, a Molossian town which survived into Roman times. The site of its Sanctuary of Zeus Areios was identified by inscriptions in 1954.—At 57½ m. we join the Kónitsa road in the upland plain N. of Ioannina. Beyond the airport, at the N. end of the lake, the Métsovo road (Rte 51B) comes in from the left.

63 m. (101 km.) **IOANNINA** (Τά Ιωάννινα), a deme (40,100 inhab.) of the eparchy of Dodona, is the capital of the nome of Ioánnina, the seat of the Government-General of Epirus and of an archbishop, and an army headquarters. It occupies a rocky promontory jutting into Lake Pambotis opposite the foot of the precipitous Mt Mitsikeli. The busy and friendly town lies at 1588 ft in the midst of a plain divided between pasture and the cultivation of cereals and tobacco. Local industries include the manufacture of filigree silver jewellery. To the E. and S.E. of the town rise the highest peaks of the Pindus. In summer the temperature is oppressive; winters are long and cold.

Airport, with daily service to Athens viâ Agrinion.

Hotels. **Xenia** (Pl. a), Od. Dodonis; **Palladion** (Pl. c), 1 Skoubourdhi, both B.— Acropole (Pl. b), 3 Leof. Yeoryiou A'; **Alexios**, 14 Od. Pouqueville; **Olympic** (Pl. g), Yerakeri/Angelou; **Galaxy** (Pl. h), Plat. Pirrhou; **Astoria** (Pl. d), 8 Paraskevopoulou; **King Pyrrhos** (Pl. j), 3 Gounari; **Dioni** (Pl. k), 10 Tsirigoti; **Esperia** (Pl. l), 3 Kalpani; **Byzantion**, Plat. Politekhniou; **Tourist** (Pl. e), 18 Koletti; **Egnatia** (Pl. i), 20 Aravanitinou, all C, and others.

Restaurants. *Ellas*, 24 Od. Yeoryiou A'; *Diethnes*, near P.O.; and at the Palladion and Xenia hotels.

Post Office, Od. 28 Oktovriou.—INFORMATION BUREAU (N.T.O), Od. Nap. Zerva.—*Olympic Airways Office* at Olympic Hotel.

Buses from opp. Clock Tower (KTEL 13 Agrinion) 5 times daily to *Arta*, continuing 3 times to *Agrinion, Mesolongi*, and *Patras*; from the Frourion (KTEL 20) to *Athens*, etc.; from KTEL 21, 4 Zosimadhou, to *Perama, Igoumenitsa, Konitsa*, etc.; from Ay Marinis (times not very convenient) to *Dodona*.

History. *Ioannina* is first documented in 1020 and may have taken name and site from a monastery of St John the Baptist. Taken by Bohemond, eldest son of Robert Guiscard, in the 11C, it was visited in 1160 by Benjamin of Tudela. Ioannina dates its importance, however, from the influx of refugees in 1205 from Constantinople and the Morea and its consequent fortification by Michael I Angelos. An archbishopric was established here between 1284 and 1307. In 1345 Ioannina was captured by the Serb Stefan Dušan, proclaimed in the following year Emperor of Serbia and Greece. In 1431 it surrendered to the army of the Sultan Murad II. In 1618, after an abortive rising led by Dionysos 'Skylosophos', the fanatical Bp. of Trikkala, the Christians were expelled from the citadel and their churches destroyed. Nevertheless, Spon in 1666 found the town rich and populous. Its zenith was reached under *Ali Pasha* (born in 1741 at the Albanian village of Tepelini), a brilliant, resourceful, and vindictive adventurer who alternately fought and served the Sultan of Turkey. Having assisted the Turks in their war of 1787 against Austria, he was made Pasha of Trikkala in 1788, in which year he seized Ioannina, then a town of 35,000 inhabitants, and made it his headquarters. In 1797 he allied himself with Napoleon, but the next year he took Preveza from the French. In 1803 he subdued the Suliots. After 1807 his dependence on the Porte was merely nominal. Byron visited Ioannina in 1809, while Col. W. M. Leake, the great topographer of Greece, was British resident, and Henry Holland was Ali Pasha's doctor. In 1817 Ali entered into an alliance with the British, who gave him Parga. At length the Sultan decided to eliminate this daring rebel. He was captured at Ioannina after a siege, and executed there in 1822. Two years before his death, besieged by Ismail Pasha, he had set fire to the town. The Congress of Berlin (1878) assigned Epirus to Greece, but it remained in Turkish hands for over 35 more years. On 21 Feb 1913, the Greek army entered Ioannina.

Ioannina was long famous for its *Schools*, founded by Michael Philanthropinos (1682–1758), Leondati Giouma (1675–1725), and Meletios (1690), later Bp. of Athens and a noted historian and geographer. They were all destroyed in the fire of 1820.

The social life of Ioannina centres on Odhos Yeoryiou tou Protou which connects Plateia Pirrou, a beautiful belvedere laid out in front of the *Municipal Offices* (*View of Mitsikeli), and the Kentriki Plateia with its clock tower (*To Rolói*) farther down the hill. Commanding the central square is the *Merarkhia* (army H.Q.) in front of which the Colours are ceremonially lowered each evening. Behind, the museum and gardens occupy the levelled upper esplanade of the Kastro, which once sheltered the Christian quarter of *Litharitsa*; its walls were demolished by Ali Pasha and the material used to build his palace and outer fortifications of the town. The N. part of the castle has been restored as a café-restaurant.

The *Museum (adm. 25 dr.; standard hours), opened 1970, has five halls, of which the first is the most important. Hall A (r.), cases arranged chronologically from r. to l. Case 1. Stone tools from Cambridge Univ. excavations in Paleolithic caves at Asprokhalikò and Kastritsa; Cases 2 & 3. Neolithic and Bronze Age finds, chiefly from L.H. IIIb–c cist graves (swords, daggers); Case 4. Protogeometric vases from the region of Agrinion.—Cases 5–9, finds from the cemeteries of Vitsa, ranging from 9C Geometric to late-Classical; notable are the small stylized Geometric horse (case 7) and a fine bronze kylix (case 9); two superb bronze beaked *Pitchers (in central cases) are especially attractive with their marbled patina.—Case 10. Vases and terracotta figurines of Persephone from the Necromanteion of Ephyra (see Rte 52c), also the windlass mechanism.—In Case 11 note the finger ring of crystal with a sculptured bull, also elaborate gold earrings, from Ambracia; gilded bronze plaque depicting Klytemnestra and Orestes, small but exquisite.—Case 12. Finds from many sites including heads of Goddesses.

Table cases 13 & 14. Epirote coins. Some of the large bronze *Vessels from the Votonosi hoard discovered in 1939 are displayed in Case 15, while Cases 16–20 and VIII–XI contain *Votive bronzes

(eagle, warriors, boy with dove, lion) and oracular tablets of lead from Dodona.

In the CORRIDOR are inscriptions from Dodona, Ionic capitals from Kassope, and grave goods from Mikhalitsi (model cart from a child burial).—HALL B. Marble sculptures from Mikhalitsi include female heads and an elaborate sarcophagus.—Beyond HALLS C & E, with 19–20C paintings, HALL D shows fine Frankish–Byzantine *Capitals from a church at Gliki and hoards of Venetian coins.

Odhos Averof, lined with silversmiths, descends directly to the **Frourion,** the fortress of the Despots, restored in 1815 by Ali Pasha as his headquarters. The *Walls*, though impressive, preserve very little

Byzantine work. The landward side was protected by the 'Khantáki', a moat (now filled in) joining the two little landing places (comp. below) and crossed by three wooden bridges. Towards the N.w. is the former *Turkish Library*, restored in 1973. Enclosed by a wall in the N.w. corner, overlooking the lake, is the picturesque *Cami of Aslan Pasha, a conventual foundation of 1618. An implausible tradition places here the rape and murder in 1801 of Kyra Phrosyne and her 17 companions. The mosque, which continued in use until 1928, now houses the crowded **Municipal Museum** (adm. 15 dr.; 8.30–12.30, 4–6, or 5–7). On the way up are cannon and piles of balls. Note the recesses for shoes in the vestibule. The Mosque has a well-proportioned dome. Striking among the exhibits are the Epirote costumes and adornments of the 18–19C.

The *Minaret* affords a superb *View of the lake and the surrounding mountains. We look down (S.E.) on the inner citadel of *Its-Kalé* (military; adm. sometimes granted) with the *Fetihie Cami*, or Victory Mosque, a circular *Tower*, the *Tomb of Ali Pasha*, and the restored *Palace* (officers' mess) where the 'Lion of Ioannina' entertained Byron and Hobhouse in Oct 1809.

The shady Leoforos Dionissiou Skilosofou runs by the lakeside beneath the walls. In the cliff is the cave where the Skylosophos was caught and flayed alive in 1611. From the Skala Psaradika, with its quaint fishing boats, we may reach the Cathedral (Ayios Athanasios), rebuilt in 1820, with ornate carved woodwork and the tomb of a local patriot of 1828. We may continue s. below the Kastro to a charming disused *Mosque*, its truncated minaret the haunt of storks, whence the picturesque Odhos Koungiou ascends to Plateia Pirrou (comp. above).

The **Lake of Ioannina,** or *Limni Pambotis*, is fed by torrents from the precipices of Mitsikeli and discharges its waters into swallow-holes. It is 6–7 m. long, averages 2 m. across, and ranges in depth from 30 to 65 ft, with shallow reedy shores. After very wet weather it may form one with the Lapsista marsh to the N. The local boats are similar in design to those on Lake Kastoria. A boat (hourly) plies to the ISLAND (Taverna; crayfish and eels) in the lake, on which are numerous monasteries very prettily situated amid trees and flowers. We first visit the *Monastery of the Prodromos* (St John the Baptist), to the E. of the little island village. Its most ancient parts (13C) are the katholikon and the E. aisle. It was restored in the 16C, the 18C frescoes in the 19C.—In the 16C *Monastery of Pantaleimon*, near by, Ali Pasha was killed on 17 Jan 1822; the bullet marks on the floor witness to his assassination. The katholikon is in the form of a basilica. There is a small *Museum* of prints and costumes. The *Monastery of Ayios Nikolaos Spanos*, or Philanthropini, on a rocky height to the N. of the village, was built in the 13C and rebuilt in the 16C. It has a katholikon with decorated doors and 16C frescoes.

In the *Apse*; Communion of Saints. In the nave vault, the Almighty and the Evangelists; on the walls, Life of Jesus. *Narthex*: In the vault, Annunciation; N. side, the five founders of the monastery kneeling before St Nicholas; above, Head of Christ; N.W. corner, Portraits of Greek philosophers.

The *Monastery of Ayios Nikolaos Dilios*, or Stratigopoulou, is the oldest (11C). It lies to the E. of the Monastery of Spanos. In the katholikon, Fresco (restored in 16C); Judas returning his pieces of silver. In the Narthex, Lives of the Virgin and of St Nicholas, Last Judgment.— To the s. the *Monastery of Ayios Eleouses* takes name from a 15C ikon brought here from the kastro. The katholikon (before 1584) has 18C frescoes.

At the N. end of the lake, on the way to *Perama* (2½ m.; bus) is an isolated hill on which are a spectacular series of *Caverns, discovered by accident when places of refuge were being sought in the Second World War. Their stalagmites and talactites are admirably lit by electricity and well worth a visit; parties are taken through the ½-mile of galleries by guides (8–sunset; 45 dr.).

At the s. end of the lake, on the hill of *Kastrítsa*, near an old monastery, is the site of ancient *Tekmona*. Below this, palaeolithic remains were dug in 1966 by the British School. Kastrítsa (c. 5 m.) is reached by taking the w. lakeshore road out of Ioannina, branching l. for Katsiká, then l. again for Drosokhóri (rough road).

The EXCURSION TO DODONA should on no account be missed. ROAD asphalted), 13½ m. (22 km.), infrequent bus. We take the Arta road, passing the Xenia Hotel and an artillery barracks, and run level through tobacco fields with distant views (l.) of the Pindus.—At 5 m. we turn right and wind over a ridge (fine retrospective views of the lake and the Pindos) into the enclosed valley of Tsarkovitsa at the foot of MT TOMAROS, the long ridge of which rises from the N. end (4370 ft) to two peaks at the s. (Mt Olitsikas; 6475 ft).

The road ends by the *Tourist Pavilion* at the entrance (adm. 25 dr., daily; closed Sun lunchtime) to (13½ m.) the ruins of **Dodona** (Pens. Andromache, small, **B**), beautifully sited facing Mt Tómaros amid fresh and smiling scenery. The modern village of *Dodoni* (ΔΩΔΩNH) stands a little farther w.

The Oracle of Zeus at Dodona, regarded as Pelasgic, was reputedly the oldest in Greece. 'Wintry Dodona' is mentioned in both Iliad and Odyssey. Strabo says that the oracle was moved from Skotoussa, in Thessaly, in obedience to the command of Apollo, but Herodotus tells of the arrival of a dove from Egyptian Thebes, which settled in an oak tree at Dodona. Homer assumes that the servers were men, calling them *selloi*, prophets of Zeus, who did not wash their feet and slept on the ground. In the time of Plato, however, the divine message was given by priestesses in a state of inspired frenzy. According to Herodotus the oracle spoke in the rustling of leaves in the sacred oaks in sounds made by beating a copper vessel with a whip. The Molossian word 'peleiae' seems to have meant both doves and old women; there are trees but no oaks in the vicinity today and the main sound is the tinkling of sheep bells.

The site was identified in 1873 by Constantin Karapanos, who discovered a number of bronze objects now in the museum at Athens. More scientific excavations have been undertaken by the Greek Archaeological Service since 1952 and some judicious restorations made.

We enter along the axis of the *Stadium*, of which part of the Sphendone has been uncovered. The seating rises on the N. side on a bank thrown up against the w. retaining wall of the theatre at the end of the 3C B.C. The superb *Theatre* was judiciously restored in 1960–63 for use at the annual festival of drama. Constructed originally in the time of Pyrrhus (297–272 B.C.), it was destroyed by the Aetolians in 219 B.C. and rebuilt shortly afterwards by Philip V out of the spoils taken from Thermon. It suffered at the hands of the Romans in 168–167 B.C. and was converted into an arena about the time of Augustus when the lowest seating was replaced by a protective wall (comp. below).

The SKENE is built in good isodomic masonry. The outer *Façade* consisted of a stoa of 13 octagonal columns. An *Arch* admitted to the centre of the stage. Double *Gateways*, with Ionic half-columns, lead into either parodos, whence we reach the *Orchestra*. The fine drainage channel in the shape of a horseshoe is well-preserved.

The CAVEA is partly recessed in the side of the Acropolis hill and partly supported by massive retaining walls of excellent rusticated ashlar masonry up to 70 ft high, buttressed by towers. It is divided by two diazomai, the three resulting banks of seats having 21 (reduced later to 15; comp. above), 16, and 21 rows (the lower two banks restored to position). Ten stairways divide the lower banks into 9 kerkides, while the topmost bank has 18 wedges. Two broad staircases added later against the façade lead up to the upper diazoma, while a *Ceremonial Entrance* from the direction of the Acropolis opens into the topmost

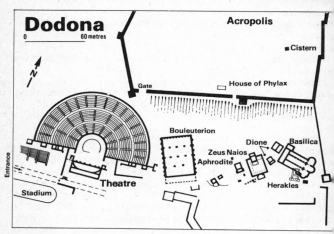

gallery; here cuttings show where a gate fitted. The back retaining wall is largely whole though some wall slabs of the gallery have fallen forward.

Behind the theatre a well-preserved *Gate* leads into the ACROPOLIS. The surrounding wall, 10–15 ft wide, is now less than 10 ft high. The enclosure is roughly quadrilateral with towers on three sides. The fabric is of various periods with Hellenistic predominating.

A path descends to the terrace, E. of the theatre, site of the **Sanctuary**. Only foundations subsist. The large hypostyle hall is shown by inscribed decrees and an inscribed altar to be the *Bouleuterion* of the Epirot confederacy built by Pyrrhus. Beyond is a small, rectangular *Temple of Aphrodite*. The TEMENOS OF ZEUS NAIOS, or *Hiera Oikia*, is a complex ruin in which four stages of growth can be differentiated. At first worship centred upon the sacred oak-tree; fragments of votive tripods of the 8C B.C. have been recovered. A stone temple was not built until the 4C, consisting merely of cella and pronaos. This and the oak were then surrounded by a peribolos wall. The wall was replaced in the time of Pyrrhus by an enclosure of Ionic colonnades facing inwards on three sides with a blind wall on the E. next the tree. After the burning of the sacred groves in 219 B.C. the temple was enlarged with an Ionic portico and an adyton, and the peribolos rebuilt with an Ionic propylon.

Beyond are two successive versions of a *Temple of Dione*, and a *Sanctuary of Herakles*. These are overlain by an early Christian *Basilica*, which incorporates an honorific decree of 180 B.C. Dodona sent a bishop to the Council of Ephesos in A.D. 431, but the basilica is probably of Justinian date.

FROM IOANNINA TO THE VIKOS GORGE, road c. 50 m., a comfortable half-day excursion by car. The Konitsa road (see below) is followed to (11¾ m.) *Kariés*. Beyond the village a by-road (signposted Vitsa) diverges right, climbing the slope of Mitsikeli with wide views over the main road. It soon turns E., running level through a gap into the Zagoria, an upland forested valley extending S.E. Below Asprángeloi and again at a further junction we bear left, following signs for Monodhéndri.—22½ m. *Vítsa*, an old stone-built village, commands wide views of forest-clad mountains. Some indeterminate excavations (l.; finds in Ioannina) are passed just before (25 m.) *Monodhéndrion* (3575 ft.). A difficult cobbled road through the village square leads in ½ m. to the deserted monastery of *Ayía Paraskeví* (1412). perched high on a sheer cliff above the **Vikos Gorge (Farangi Vikou). The cells and frescoed chapel have been restored and vertiginous paths with perilous bridges lead on to caves and hermits' cells. In the lush gorge the river Voïdbomati runs N.W. to Vikos; the beautiful region would repay exploration (strong walking boots and provisions needed).

FROM IOANNINA TO KONITSA AND NEAPOLIS (Kozani or Kastoria). ROAD, 108½ m. (174 km.); some discretion needed in view of proximity of Albanian frontier. Leaving the Metsovo road to the right and that to Igoumenitsa on the left, our road runs N. across the marshy plain of Lapsista at the foot of Mitsikeli.—10½ m. *Asfáka* stands on the E. shore of the seasonal *Lake Miradhia*.—At (11¾ m.) *Kariés*, by-road (r.) to the Vikos Gorge (see above).—20½ m. *Memorial to the Fallen* of 1940–41 and Museum (open summer 9–12, 5–7; winter 10–12, 2–6) at the junction of the by-road to the monastery of *Vella* (1½ m. s.w.). Vella takes its name from a ruined Byzantine town near by; its bishopric was merged with that of Ioannina in 1842.—21¼ m. *Kalpaki* (1968 ft; Inn; police post), a road junction of great strategic importance, commands the chief route into Greece from Albania. Here, on 1–14 Nov 1940, the Greek army fought a stubborn defensive battle against the Italian invaders; their counter-offensive threw the Italians back over the Albanian frontier.

Here diverges a road now effectively serving only the eparchy of Pogonion, but once leading to Argyrokastro (Gjinokastrë in Albania). *Dhelvinákion* (13¾ m.), with 1070 inhab., has superseded *Pogoniani* as chief town of the region. The archbishopric of Pogoniani, perhaps founded by Constantine IV Pogonatos (668–685) and dissolved in 1863, may originally have had its seat at *Molyvdosképastis* (best reached from Konitsa; see below), where the monastery of Koimisis Theotókou dates from his reign and was restored by Andronikos Comnenus c. 1183. The frescoes were restored in 1521 and there is 14C woodwork.

The main road makes a steep ascent with views of Mt Gaméla (r.), the several rugged peaks of which rise to 8135 ft.—After the junction below (28 m.) *Yeroplátanos*, the road descends in loops to the Voïdhomati, crosses the river below the Vikos Gorge (comp. above), and runs through an upland plain growing melons.

40 m. **Kónitsa** commands the road from a hillside above the colossal gorge through which the Aoos emerges from the Pindos. To the N.E. towers *Smolikas* (8640 ft), highest peak of the Pindos; to the S., *Gamela* (see above). The town (3150 inhab.), seat of an eparchy and birthplace of the mother of Ali Pasha, was conquered by the Turks of Murad II in 1440. The Greeks entered the town on 24 Feb 1913. It remains a typical mountain market centre. From 24 Dec 1947 to 15 Jan 1948 its garrison withstood violent attacks of the communist Gen. Markos, who intended to make it his capital. The church of the *Kokkini Panayia* has frescoes.—From Konitsa a road leads w. towards the frontier (12 m.), where the Aoos below its confluence with the Voïdhomati becomes the Vijosë (Viosa) as it flows through Albania into the Adriatic above Valona. The river is crossed by two ancient bridges, *Bourazani* and *Mertzani*, near Molyvdosképastos (comp. above).

From Konitsa a broad new road climbs sharply out of the Aoos valley, then winds amid the w. foothills of Smolikas. It descends to the Sarandáporos and follows its left bank upstream. At 55½ m. the river is crossed.—Beyond (59 m.) *Pirsóyianni*, which is by-passed, a tributary is bridged at the confluence, and the road gradually bears E. We cross the boundary into the nome of Kastoria and quit the river for another tributary.—Beyond (73¾ m.) *Eptakhórion* a steady climb passes a spring and picnic site to a summit of 4735 ft at the boundary of the nome of Kozani. Here is a wide view to the s.—84¼ m. *Pendálofos* (3476 ft), a picturesque mountain village with stone houses that formed the headquarters of the British Mission to the Greek Resistance in the Second World War. The road zigzags down to the gorge of the Pramoritsu, or Koutsomilia, then gradually climbs into more open upland. Beyond (93 m.) *Morfi* it drops down again to the Koutsomilia, crossing the torrent to climb a long windswept ridge with extensive retrospective views near (98 m.) the Omalí turn.—102½ m. *Tsotílion* (2755 ft; Inns), with one of the first colleges founded during the Turkish domination. The road descends to (108½ m.) *Neápolis*, whence to Kastoria or Kozani, see Rte 62.

From Ioannina to *Metsovo* and into Thessaly, see Rte 51B.

B   To Preveza viâ Paramithia

ROAD, 69½ m. (112 km.), asphalt to (36 m.) *Glikí*, then alternating with good gravel.

For the first 15 m. we follow the Ioannina road (Rte 52A), then turn right. The road crosses a ridge.—21 m. (34 km.) **Paramithiá** (ΠΑΡΑ-ΜΥΘΙΑ; *Souli* D), a large village (2700 inhab.), picturesquely scattered on the slopes below the w. scarp of Mt Koríllas, is the chief place of the eparchy of Suli. Its name, which means 'consolation', is variously derived. It was called by the Turks *Aij Donat Kalessi* and by the Venetians *Castel San Donato*, names again variously derived as a corruption of the ancient *Aidonati* or after the 4C Donatos, Bp. of Euroia. In the 18C Paramithia was the capital of one of the three sanjaks of Epirus. About 10 min. above the town is the ruined Venetian *Kastro*, built on Hellenic foundations. The town was temporarily held by British forces in 1941. At *Velianí*, 4 m. S.E., remains of a 7C basilica may mark the see of the Bp. of Photike.—We now continue in the enclosed valley of the Kokkitos below the steep scarps of Paramithiás.— At (25 m.) *Prodrómio* a bad road diverges (r.) to *Mórfion* (see below). —36 m. *Glikí* (ΓΛΥΚΗ), on the Akherontos, is possibly the site of *Euroia*; there are remains of a church of the Despotate, supposed to be the burial place of Bp. Donatos.

The Akherontos, the mystic *Acheron* of mythology, was the river of the nether world. It comes down from the mountains of Suli and flows through a deep and gloomy ravine with precipitous sides, suggesting the terrors of Hades. At Gliki it enters the wide plain of Phanari, where it traverses meres and swamps, never wholly dry even in summer, which were known to the ancients as the *Acherousian Lake*. The river flows past Ephyra (comp. below) and enters the sea at *Ammoudhia* on the Bay of Fanari, S. of Parga.

A track leads through the gorge, and after 1 hr turns N. and enters by a narrow pass into the region of Suli. The scenery is grand and impressive.—1½ hr. The **Castle of Suli** stands on an isolated hill near the ruined village of the same name, 1200 ft above the Acheron. It was one of the strongholds of the Suliots, a tribe of Christian Epirots, mustering about 4000 fighting men and women. Their territory, like Montenegro farther N., was a centre of stubborn resistance to the Moslems. From 1790 they were at war with Ali Pasha until 1803, when at great cost he captured their principal fastnesses, and they retired to the Ionian Islands. At the outbreak of the War of Independence most of the Suliots returned to the mainland where they again engaged the Turks. Among them was Marko Botsaris, defender of Mesolongi. In 1823 Great Britain negotiated their capitulation on favourable terms and they all emigrated to Cephalonia.—A road has been planned to link the area with Ioannina.

We descend to (43 m.) *Skepaston*, beyond which we immediately join Rte 52C.—69½ m. **Preveza**, see Rte 53B.

C To Parga and Preveza

ROAD, 61½ m. (99 km.).—17½ m. *Margaríti.*—23¾ m. *Mórfion,* for **Parga** (7½ m.). —32½ m. *Kastri,* for **Ephyra.**—35 m. *Skepastón.*—61½ m. *Preveza.* This excellent scenic road through rich agricultural country with tidy villages provides the shortest direct route (using the ferries at Preveza and Rion) from Igoumenitsa to Athens (296 m.; bus in 9 hrs).

The road skirts the s. side of Igoumenitsa bay, then rounds the point to (7½ m.) *Platariá,* with a good beach. We turn inland up a broad valley between mountain ranges, then descend through low hills on to a dyke road across marshes.—17½ m. (28 km.) *Margaríti,* (Rest.) despite its size (770 inhab.) controls a tiny eparchy of a few neighbouring villages. The relics of its more important past under Venetians and Turks disappeared when the town was fired during military occupation in 1944, though remains of two fortresses crown neighbouring heights.—23¾ m. (38 km.) *Mórfion* stands at the junction of the road (r.) to *Parga* (7½ m.). From this road also Ephyra (see below) can be reached more directly.

PARGA (*Avra* **C**; *Ayios Nektarios,* good, *Paradeisos,* both **D**; *Tzimas Rest.*; *Lichnos Beach,* in cove 1½ m. E., **B**), a clean and picturesque little seaside town (1690 inhab.) backed by slopes of orange and olive groves, stands opposite the island of Paxos, 12 m. distant. The town spreads across the neck of a roçky headland, crowned by a *Frourion* of Norman origin (its keep is adorned with the Lion of St Mark). The tiny bay has rocks and islets and many cafés along the waterfront. The larger bay of *Khrissoyiali* (Parga Beach **B**), a mile to the w., has a superb sweep of beach, partly occupied by the Club Mediterranée. Tourist development is so far within bounds.

Parga was already important in the 14C. In 1401 it came under the protection of the Venetians, who dominated it until 1797, except for brief intervals in 1452–54 and after 1701 when it fell into Turkish hands. It fell to the French, who left a small fort on the densely wooded islet of the Panayia, enjoyed a brief existence in 1800–07 as an independent state under the aegis of Russia, then at the Treaty of Tilsit passed again to the French. Ali Pasha bought it from the British who had replaced the French in 1814. He drove out its people who sought refuge in the Ionian Is. Some of them later returned, but thenceforward to 1913 Parga was subject to Turkey, when it became Greek.—Constantine Kanaris, the admiral of the War of Independence, was born here in 1790.

For Preveza, we bear left at Mórfion and cross a ridge to the valley of the Acheron, with cotton fields.—32½ m. *Kastri* occupies the site of *Pandosia* whose Classical walls are still imposing. Immediately before the Acheron crossing a turning (r.; signposted) leads in 3 m. by a dyke-road to *Mesopótamo.* Here (road r. in village), on a rocky hill above the confluence of the Kokytos with the Acheron (Periphlegethon), are the *Remains of the **Necromanteion of Ephyra,** oracle of the dead and sanctuary of Persephone and Hades. From the site the extent of the ancient Acherousian Lake is obvious; the river (comp. above) flows on to the sea through willows and poplars. The Acropolis of *Ephyra* rises to the N.

The visit (fee; closed 1–2.30) is guided by the phylax, and an excellent handbook by Prof. Dakaris, the excavator in 1958–64, is available in English.

The Necromanteion is an astonishing construction with labyrinthine corridors and windowless rooms, both above and below ground. The remains, impressively complete in plan with standing arches, are in excellent polygonal masonry, Hellenistic in date, and were ruined by fire in 168 B.C. Their arrangement and purpose recall Homer's description (Od. x, 512) of the visit of Odysseus to the House of Hades and his sacrifice to the spirits of the dead. Remains of a bronze windlass suggest that mechanical trickery may have been employed, after a preparation involving disorientation techniques and hallucinatory drugs, in inducing satisfactory spiritual visitation.

35 m. We join Rte 52B just below *Skepaston*. The road now climbs steeply, then winds s. through a long valley.—At 47 m. a road (signposted Zalonga) climbs (l.) to the village of *Kamarina* (officially *Zálongon* after its mountain), continuing as a dirt road to a footpath (3¼ m.; l.; small sign) leading in 3 min. to **Kassope**. On a plateau facing s. these ruins of the 4C B.C. were discovered in 1951–55; excavations were resumed in 1976. The city was laid out early in the 4C B.C. on the Hippodamian system and protected by a polygonal wall. It was burned by the Romans in 167 B.C. and abandoned when Nikopolis was founded. A *Stoa* and an *Odeion* (damaged by landslide) flank the Agora, above which are the remarkable remains of a Katagogeion built round a central peristyle court. Farther N.W. are the *Theatre* and a 'Macedonian' *Chamber Tomb*. The road climbs a further 500 yds to the *Monastery of Zalonga*, where the Suliot mountaineers took refuge when attacked by Ali Pasha. Sixty women escaped with their children to the summit, whence, after performing their traditional dance, they threw themselves over the precipice. This act is commemorated by a huge sculpture above the monastery (footpath).

Beyond (49½ m.) *Arkhángelos* we emerge on the Bay of Gomares joining a new coastal road, on which (2 m. N.) is *Kastrosikiá* (Preveza Beach, 260 R, **B**).—At 56 m. the ruins of Nikopolis lie to the left.—61½ m. **Preveza,** see below.

53   FROM IOANNINA TO ARTA AND PREVEZA

A   To Arta

ROAD, 48½ m. (78 km.), well engineered section of the main highway to Athens. BUSES (KTEL 13), 5 times daily, continuing (with one exception) to Agrinion and Patras.

From Ioannina to (5 m.) the Dodona turn, see Rte 52. The road continues straight and level with views of the scarred heights of Mt Tómaros (r.). A causeway carries the highway across a marsh-lake. We ascend between *Bizani* (l.) and *Manolassa* (r.), two heights known as battlefields in 1913.—13½ m. *Khání Avgóu* stands on a col (2065 ft), the highest point on the route. The walls of *Phtelia* are visible on an isolated hill (r.) as we descend to the cultivated upper valley of the *Louros*. The road has been realined; on the old loop is (19¼ m.) *Khání Emin Agá*, a police post with a small museum illustrating the campaign of 1912–13; a memorial, opposite, marks the site of Constantine's headquarters during the siege of Ioannina.

We pass the principal springs that feed the infant Louros.—20½ m. *Khánia Teróvou* (Restaurants). At the entrance to the Louros *Gorge the road crosses to the right bank. The river, shaded by great planes,

flows between *Xerovouni* (5295 ft), the long range of mountains to the
E. and *Zarkorakhi* (4370 ft; to the w.). Here and there are remains of
fortifications ancient and modern.—25 m. *Potamiá* (Platanakia Rest.).
—Near (26 m.) *Kleisoura*, the narrowest point and the nome boundary,
we traverse a tunnel.

The valley broadens and bamboo is grown. Soon after Kerasóna
it narrows again, becoming craggy.—34¾ m. *Ayios Yeóryios*, with an
ornamented church, appears ½ m. left on a hill. Just before its turning
is (r.) the *Asprokhalikó* cave which in 1965 proved to contain the first
large stratified deposits of Middle and Upper Palaeolithic date found
in Greece. We reach the artificial lake formed by the LOUROS DAM.
Immediately beyond (r.) is the entrance to a rock-cut conduit, part of a
Roman Aqueduct that fed Nikopolis, over 40 miles away. Some spectacular arches can be seen by the Ay. Yeoryios road (comp. above).
About 1 m. farther down (l.) is a hydro-electric station. We pass (r.) the
Paidopolis Zirou, an orphanage of the Royal Foundation.—40¼ m.
Filippiás (ΦΙΛΙΠΠΙΑΣ; 3200 inhab.) has an excavated 13C church.

A rough by-road crosses the river to *Kambi* (3 m.), continuing amid the s. foothills of Xerovouni to *Kastri* (10 m.; bus daily), the ruins of a classical town destroyed in 167 B.C. (rough path in 10 min.).

Two miles farther on, by an orangeade factory, we leave the road to
Preveza (Rte 53 B), turn left across the Louros, and traverse the orange-
groves of the Ambracian plain. At the approach to the Arakhthos a
road enters on the right from *Salaóra* (11 m.; with fish hatcheries) on
the Ambracian Gulf. Crossing the Arakhthos to enter Arta, we see (l.)
a Turkish packhorse *Bridge: the legend according to which the mason
built his wife into the foundations to strengthen the bridge is enshrined
in a song that has currency with other Balkan peoples.

48½ m. (78 km.) **ARTA** (*Xenia*, pl. a, in the castle, DPO, B; *Cronos*,
pl. b; *Ambrakia*, pl. c; *Anessis*, all C), pleasantly situated in a loop of
the Arakhthos, is a friendly town (19,500 inhab.) interspersed with
orange groves. Remains are coming to light of its ancient past as
Ambracia, capital of Pyrrhus, king of Epirus, and it retains reminders of
its period of greatness as the seat of the Despotate of Epirus.

History. Ambracia was colonized by Corinth c. 625 B.C. and had a grid plan
as early as the 5C B.C. Pausanias found only ruins. After the fall of Constantinople
and of the Morea to the Franks, Michael I Angelos, with the approval of the exiled
Emp. Alexios III, set up the autonomous Despotate of Epirus at Arta, or Narte.
Here Euphrosyne, Alexios' empress, died in exile. The town fell to the Turks in
1449, but soon passed to the Venetians. The French held it for two years after the
Treaty of Campoformio (1797), but, after a period of subjection to Ali Pasha of
Ioannina, it fell again under direct Turkish rule in 1822–1912. Hoca Ishak Efendi
(1774–1834), the accomplished linguist who first introduced western science into
Turkish education, was born at Arta.

The FROURION, a 13C castle occupied by the *Xenia Hotel*, commands
the bend of the river. The restored outer walls, with reused classical
blocks, afford pleasant views northward to Xerovouni. Some scanty
remains of a Classical *Temple* survive near the river bank. To the s.w. off
Od. Pirrhou is *Ayios Vasilios*, a small 14C church with the elaborate brick
and tile decoration characteristic of the area. Farther on is *Ayia Theodora*, properly the church of St George the Martyr, a conventual church
where Theodora, consort of Michael II, took the veil and ended her
days. The domed narthex, perhaps added in her lifetime, has out-

standing brick and tile decoration; within stands a reconstruction of
Theodora's tomb (excavated in 1873), originally erected by Nikephoros
I, her son. The fine capitals are said to derive from Nikopolis.

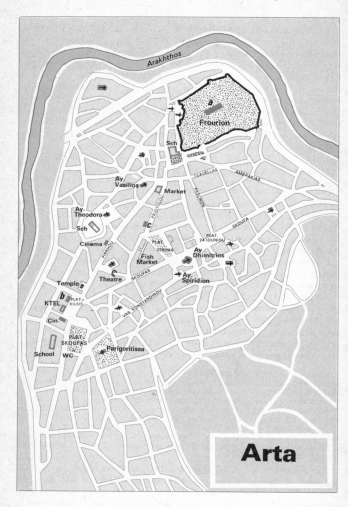

Odhos Pirrhou continues s.w. Below a narrow street (50 yds l.) in
1976 was found the *Bouleuterion*. Farther on (r.) are the foundations
of a large Doric *Temple* of the early 5C B.C., uncovered in 1964–69. Its
tiles were stamped AMBP. The busy PLATEIA KILKIS, the main square
with the bus station, has several restaurants. Beyond is the larger

PLATEIA SKOUFAS dominated by the former metropolitan church of **Panayia Paragoritissa**, a huge square edifice crowned by six domes, erected in 1282–89 by Nikephoros and John, sons of Michael II. The gloomy interior (adm. fee; 9–6), has a certain majesty; the curious substructure of the central dome, borne on antique columns on a primitive cantilever principle, cannot be as unsound as it appears. The mosaics of the Pantocrator and the prophets in the dome (cleaned) belong to the original decoration.

By the river in the s. outskirts of the town is the *Kato Panayia*, a nunnery founded by Michael II whose monogram can be traced on the s. wall of the church. It shelters 20 orphaned girls who weave blankets and carpets (for sale). The Church incorporates prophyry columns perhaps from a Syrian Temple of Aphrodite (classical foundation blocks visible in the terrace). The exterior walls are adorned with bands of cable and meander patterns with decorative motifs worked in red tile. The frescoes within are mainly of the 18C; fragments in the apse date from the 13C.

Among the monasteries for which the region is noted we may visit the *Moni Vlakhernai* (N.E. of the town), transformed into a convent of nuns by Theodore Angelos c. 1225, not many years after its foundation. The church was embellished by Michael II. Fragments of the original marble templon are built into the narthex doorway. Within are two marble tombs, believed from their fragmentary inscriptions to belong to Michael II and to two of his sons.—*Ayios Dhimitrios Katsouri* (3 m. s.w. of Arta), the chapel of a Patriarchal monastery, was built in the 10C and altered in the 13C, when the frescoes were painted. The near-by church of *Ayios Nikolaos tis Rodhias* (12–13C) also retains well-preserved frescoes.—The *Panayia tou Bryoni*, on the Amfilokhia road, was enlarged with a transept and dome during the Patriarchate of Germanos II, perhaps at the time of his visit to Epirus in 1238.—The monastery at *Peta* (3 m. E.) has a 17C epitaphios from the Morea and a monument of 1821.

B   To Preveza

ROAD, 67 m. (108 km.), following the Arta road to (40¼ m.) *Filippiás* (comp. above), then branching right.—62 m. **Nikópolis** —67 m. **Préveza**. BUSES several times daily.

From Ioannina to (42¼ m.) the Fix orangeade factory, see above. The Preveza road turns s.w. and runs roughly parallel with the lower reaches of the Louros. Just beyond (44½ m.) *Néa Kerasoús* we see (l.; easiest access from village side on old road), on a low hill, the extensive ruins of **Rogon**, or *Rogous*, protected by a marshy loop of the river. An excellent polygonal enceinte encloses a medieval citadel, built on ashlar foundations (? 4C B.C.), with a church (defaced frescoes). The place gave its name to a medieval see.—At (49 m.) *Stefáni* at the s. end of the Thesprotiká range, we join a road from *Thesprotikó* (6¼ m. N.), a deme of 2000 inhabitants.—Beyond (51½ m.) *Loúros* (Rfmts.), a large village (1540 inhab.), the road runs straight and level in the lush plain irrigated by the Louros.—At (59 m.) *Mikhalitsi*, off the road to the right, tombs of the 4C B.C. have been explored. The peninsula narrows to an isthmus. On the E. is a marshy lagoon, the haunt of herons and other wildfowl.

The road passes through the extensive and overgrown site of **Nikopolis**, the city founded by Augustus after his victory at Actium. To the w. is the Bay of Gomares where he had concentrated his forces before the battle (p. 458).

History. In commemoration of his victory, Octavian (Augustus) raised the status of Patrai to that of Roman colony and founded the new *Colonia* of *Nikopolis* ('victory city') on his camp site. To populate the new city, he resettled the inhabitants of most of the towns of Aetolia and Akarnania, including Kalydon, Ambracia, and Amphilochian Argos. It was made a member of the Amphictyonic League and to it was transferred the Actian games. St Paul spent a winter (?64) at 'Nicopolis of Macedonia', where he wrote his Epistle to Titus. By A.D. 67 the city was the capital of an Epirot province. The philosopher Epictetus (c. 60–140) had a school here, and the city was the reputed birthplace of Pope St Eleutherios (175–189). Thriving in the time of Strabo, it was plundered by Alaric, Genseric, and Totila. Justinian rebuilt its defences, reducing their compass. At the coming of the Slavs, the Byzantines removed the seat of the theme to Naupaktos and Nikopolis decayed. Here, in 1795, John Sibthorp, the English botanist, fell ill and returned to die in Bath.—The Greek Archaeological Service has excavated at intervals since 1913.

We may visit first the ruined **Theatre,** prominent on the right of the road. The walls of the proscenium still stand, and the auditorium rises to the upper portico, its niches and arcades the haunt of storks. In several places may be seen the holes in which the poles for the velarium, or awning, were fixed. The line of the cunei can be distinguished though the stone seats have mostly vanished.

A dirt road to the left skirts the side of the *Stadium*, which unusually in Greece was rounded at both ends like those of Asia Minor; it leads in 500 yds to the village of *Smyrtoula*, above which are the remains of the commemorative MONUMENT erected by Augustus after the battle of Actium on the site where his tent had been pitched. A massive podium of masonry is preserved in whose face are cuttings, shaped like enormous bass-viols, in which the prows of ships must have been attached. The monument was of the Corinthian order. Numerous fragments of a frieze with a Latin inscription commemorating the victory are lying about. It is beautifully carved in letters a foot high. One fragment bears the letters TUNO, indicating that the monument was dedicated to Neptune.

The road runs s., meeting the road from Parga (Rte 52c) near some ruined *Baths*, then enters the Byzantine enceinte. To the left are the excavated remains of the BASILICA OF ALKYSON, a double-aisled church with tripartite transept, founded by Bp. Alkyson (d. 516). Two heads in mosaic survive from its Christian decoration. Just beyond the basilica a track leads (r.) through a fine *Gate* in Justinian's ***Walls,** here extending for c. 500 yds in a good state of preservation. The path may be followed past the Augustan *Odeion*, restored for use in the annual festival of ancient drama (Aug), to the *Great Gate* in the *City Walls* of the Augustan age. Some remains of the *Aqueduct* that supplied the city with water from the Louros survive to the N.

Continuing along the main road we come to the **Museum,** opened in 1972. On the walls of the Lobby are inscribed stelai bases and gravestones. Two rooms display statues, sarcophagi, Roman portraits (notably Agrippa, Augustus's general at Actium, and Faustina the Younger, wife of Marcus Aurelius) and capitals; in the centre of the first room, grave *Lion (3C B.C.; in the second, huge cylindrical base with Amazonomachia reliefs (reused as the ambo of the Alkyson basilica); large glass cinerary urn; rings and lamps.—In the field near by (phylax will guide) is the **Basilica of Doumetios,** or *Basilica A*, dated from its fine floor mosaics to the second quarter of the 6C. Adjacent is the palace of the archbishops of Epirus Vetus who had their seat here.— Near the s. wall is the smaller *Basilica Γ* and, outside the walls, *Basilica Δ* with a peacock mosaic floor.

67 m. (108 km.) **Preveza** (ΠΡΕΒΕΖΑ; *Dioni, Minos, Almini,* **C**), the unprepossessing chief town (11,400 inhab.) of a small nome, stands on the N. shore of the shallow strait, here only ½ m. wide, through which

the waters of the Ambracian Gulf reach the sea. The waterside esplanade is a favourite evening promenade. A car ferry crosses the strait (half-hourly).

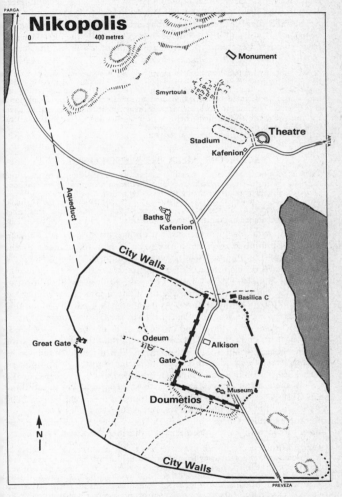

Preveza occupies the site of ancient *Berenikia*, founded c. 290 B.C. by Pyrrhus in honour of his mother-in-law Berenice, queen of Ptolemy Soter. The town was occupied by the Venetians in 1499. Ceded to the Turks by the Treaty of Carlowitz (1699), it was retaken in 1717. In 1797 it passed, with the Ionian Is., to the French, but the next year it was retaken by Ali Pasha in the name of the Sultan of Turkey and remained in Turkish hands until it fell to the Greek army in 1912. In 1881–1912 the Greco-Turkish frontier ran through the strait.

On the s. side of the strait is the sandy promontory of **Aktion** (Latin, *Actium*), sharper in outline than that of Preveza and almost closing the entrance to the Gulf. At the naval BATTLE OF ACTIUM, on 2 Sept 31 B.C., Agrippa, Octavian's commander, with a smaller but more manoevrable fleet, routed the combined navies of Antony and Cleopatra. The royal leaders deserted the army they had massed for an invasion of Italy, and it surrendered a week later. By the ferry landing-place stands a Venetian fort. On the promontory, ½ m. N., are scanty remains of the *Temple of Apollo Aktios*.

A temple, under the protection of neighbouring Anaktorion, existed here in the 5C B.C. From it came two kouroi now in the Louvre. Gymnastic games and horse races were held. After his victory at Actium, Augustus rebuilt the temple and consecrated in special boathouses examples of the vessels captured in the battle. The festival he transferred to his new city of Nikopolis, adding naval and musical events. The '*Actia*', held every five years and declared sacred, thus took rank with the four great Hellenic games.

To *Levkas*, and to *Amfilokhia*, see Rte 54.

54   FROM ARTA TO MESOLONGI

ROAD, 76½ m. (123 km.), traversing the varied countryside of Aitolia and Akarnania with its characteristic lakes and lagoons and impressive monuments. The road, already good, is still being widened and realined, with bypasses of main towns. 26¼ m. *Amfilokhía*.—45 m. *Stratos*.—53 m. (85 km.) **Agrinion**, for *Thermon*.—70¾ m. *Aitolikó*, for *Oiniadai*.—74 m. *Pleuron*.—76½ m. **Mesolongi**. Bus either direct or by changing at Agrinion, several times daily.

We quit Arta and turn s.E. through orange-groves.—7½ m. *Kombóti* 1 m. l.; 2100 inhab.) was the native town of Nik. Skoufa, one of the founders of the Philike Heteiria. As we approach the Ambracian Gulf the road rises on the oak-clad slope of *Makrinóros*, a long mountain ridge parallel to the shore. The pass *en corniche* thus formed, sometimes called the 'Thermopylae of Western Greece', was guarded in antiquity by a string of forts. At its summit is Kastro Palaiokoulia, defended during the War of Independence by the Greek captain Iskos.—11 m. *Meuídhi* marks the N. end of the pass; 17 m. *Anoixiátikon*, the s. end.—Just beyond (21 m.) *Kríkelo* we see (l.) the little church of Ayios Ioannis, behind which (road signposted) rise the insignificant remains of *Amphilochian Argos*, a town of some importance in the Peloponnesian War.—26¾ m. **Amfilokhía** (ΑΜΦΙΛΟΧΙΑ; *Mistral* C) is situated at the head of the Gulf of Karvasará, the farthest inland reach of the Ambracian Gulf. The town (4700 inhab.) was founded by Ali Pasha as a military station; its former name, *Karvasarás*, is supposed to be a corruption of 'caravanserai'. On the hill (620 ft) above are some remains of an ancient town with long walls, perhaps to be identified with *Limnaia*.

FROM AMFILOKHIA TO LEVKAS, 37 m. (59 km.). The road follows the s. verge of the Ambracian Gulf, often away from the shore amid marsh, cotton fields, or low hills. To the left Mt Bergandi rises to 4684 ft; *Thyrion*, on its N. slope, has adopted the ancient name of a place where Cicero, sailing along the Akarnanian coast, spent two hours at the house of his friend Xenomanes.—23 m. (38 km.) **Vónitsa** (*Avra* D), chief town of the eparchy of Vonitsa and Xiromeros, has a small port below a Venetian citadel of 1676. An asphalt road runs w. from Vónitsa to the Aktion–Preveza ferry (7½ m.), passing after 3 m., near the shore, the conspicuous hill-top ruins of *Anaktorion*, a Corinthian colony of 630 B.C.—Our road bears s.w. Coming in to (30½ m.) *Ayios Nikólaos* we meet another road from Aktion (6½ m.) and beyond the village cross the outlet of the marsh-lake Voulkariá to the Ionian Sea. We see (l.) the *Castle of Grivas*, dating from the War of Independence, then cross a long causeway which brings us to the Frankish *Kastro Santa Maura* (comp.

Rte 56), guarding a gap between the mainland and the island of Levkas. The strait is crossed by chain ferry (free), whence another causeway carries the road into (37 m.) *Levkas* (see Rte 56).

We cross a low saddle behind the town between two ranges of hills.—30½ m. *Stános*, on the w. slope, overlooks the N. arm of *Lake Ambrakia*, which we cross on a causeway, continuing along the E. shore.—39¾ m. Poor by-road (r.) to *Astakós* (25½ m.), with 3000 inhab., formerly *Dragomestre*, coastal base of Sir Richard Church's operations in W. Greece in 1828. A little beyond the turning we see in the distance *Lake Ozeros* (r.).

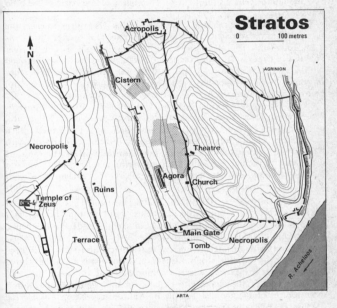

45 m. *Strátos* (ΣΤΡΑΤΟΣ), a melancholy village (l.) stands in the centre of the *Ruins of **Stratos**, the ancient capital and largest city of Akarnania. The walls, dating from before 429 B.C. and particularly well preserved, stand on a low bluff commanding the broad Acheloos. On our road beyond the turning to the village is a small *Xenia Hotel* (B). A folk-dancing festival is held annually in September.

History. The site was occupied in early times but *Stratos* first achieved importance in the 5C B.C. During the Peloponnesian War Knemos of Sparta besieged it vainly in 429 B.C. and in 426 Eurylochos passed below its walls without daring to attack. Agesilaos failed to take it in 391, but it passed to Kassander in 314, and in 263, when Akarnania was partitioned, fell to the Aitolians. After the dissolution of the Aitolian League (188), the Romans held it against Philip V and Perseus of Macedon, but before our era began it had lost all importance. The site was explored by the French School in 1892, 1910–11, and 1924.

The *Walls* embrace four parallel N.–S. ridges with their three intervening depressions. A transverse N.–S. wall divides the city into two parts. With the exception of the *Theatre* (still buried), most of the public buildings seem to have been in the w. sector. In the centre of the s. wall, to the right of the track to the village, is the MAIN GATE, with a defensive interior court. The remains of the *Agora* are scanty. Thence we may follow the central wall up past the ancient quarries to the *Acropolis*, seemingly a fortified rather than a religious place. Curiously placed athwart a projecting section of the w. wall is the Doric TEMPLE OF ZEUS, built on a platform c. 80 yds from E. to W. Peripteral, with 6 columns by 11, and somewhat larger than the Athenian Hephaisteion, it dates from the 4C, probably after 338 B.C. An Ionic colonnade surrounded the cella on three sides. The stylobate and parts of the cella walls survive.

The road passes within the E. wall of Stratos, then turns to cross the ACHELOOS BARRAGE (ΦΡΑΓΜΑ ΑΧΕΛΩΟΥ). The former bridge is 3 m. upstream. The *Acheloos*, or Aspropotamos, is the longest river (135 m.) in Greece. Rising in the Pindus, it forms the boundary between Aitolia and Akarnania, and falls into the sea opposite the Echinades Is. Since 1960 the river has been harnessed to provide power (comp. below) and irrigation. A by-pass to the w. avoids Agrinion.

53 m. (85 km.) **Agrinion** (ΑΓΡΙΝΙΟΝ; *Galaxy, Esperia, Soumelis Motel*, all **B**; *Leto, Aliki*, **C**, and others), a lively town of 31,000 inhab., is the capital of the eparchy of Trikhonidos and the largest place in the nome. It is a tobacco-growing centre, linked by air services with Athens and Ioannina, and a starting-point for the visit to Thermon. It was almost completely rebuilt after an earthquake in 1887. The site of *Ancient Agrinion* has been located above the village of *Megáli Khóra*, 2½ m. N.w. of the town.

FROM AGRINION TO THERMON, 20 m., infrequent bus. A tarred road branches right from the Karpenisi road (comp. below) and traverses the agricultural villages along the N. shore of *Lake Trikhonis. Mt Vlokhos* (2000 ft; l.) affords a wonderful view. At (7 m.) *Paravóla* are some remains of ancient *Boukation* (Classical and 4C with Byzantine towers).—We run along the shore, then climb in turns above orange groves to *Myrtiá*, where is a monastery of 1491.—18 m. *Ayía Sofía* is a long pretty village with gushing streams; its Byzantine church incorporates blocks from a Temple of Aphrodite.—20 m. *Kefalóvrisi*, (Aetolia **D**), officially *Thermon*, has a charming rural square with country inns and restaurants, reminiscent of Mt Pelion. Just over ½ m. s. at 'Palaio Bazari' are the remains of ancient **Thermon**, the spiritual centre of the Aitolians, who here held their elections of magistrates at an annual festival.

The festival was the occasion also for a great fair and for athletic games. Thermon became a Pan-Aitolian sanctuary centred on the temple of Apollo Thermios. Some 2000 of the statues collected here were destroyed by Philip V of Macedon when he sacked the place in 218 B.C. The Greek Archaeological Service excavated the ruins in 1898–1916.

The SANCTUARY, with its E. side against Mt Mega Lakkos, was surrounded by a rectangular peribolos protected by towers dating from the 3C B.C. The largest of three temples, near the N. wall, is the *Temple of Apollo Thermios* (6C B.C.), a narrow peripteral building with five columns at the ends and 15 at the sides. A row of columns down the centre divided the building lengthwise; some column-drums remain in place. The walls may have been made of sun-dried brick. The entablature was of decorated wood; the frieze and acroteria of painted terracotta. At a lower level (not clearly visible) are the foundations of a temple of the Geometric period built with an apsidal peristyle. To the N. and at a still lower level are houses of a prehistoric village, one of them particularly large and well-built with an apsidal end. To the S. is a *Fountain*, still operating, with three spouts, and beyond three *Stoas* locate the agora. Notable in the *Museum* are Archaic terracotta metopes and decorative fragments from the Temple, Middle Bronze Age pottery, part of a Mycenean helmet, and a fine pair of bronze horses mounted on a single base (Geometric).

The return to Agrinion may be made by the S. shore of the lake, making a round of c. 45 m.; or, by another poor road (infrequent bus), *Navpaktos* (Rte 55) may be reached.

FROM AGRINION TO KARPENISI, 72½ m. (116 km.) in course of improvement; a tough but impressive drive over a series of ridges of the Southern Pindus with climbs up to 4000 ft. Bus once daily. The road winds N.E. in the foothills of *Panaitolikón*.—Beyond (15 m.) *Kelanítis* we climb in earnest to reach a saddle affording the first view of Lake Kremaston.—25 m. *Ayios Vlásios* (3800 ft), a scattered mountain village (restaurant). We descend and just after (29 m.) *Khoúni* pass a tarred road to *Kremasta* (4 m., l.), standing just below the confluence of the Acheloos with its two greatest tributaries. Here a great dam, 565 ft high, and a hydro-electric power station have been constructed by an American company.—31¾ m. Fork left for **Lake Kremaston**, the largest artificial lake in Greece, which drowned several villages, rebuilt on the slopes above. The main road veers E. to cross an arm of the lake by a new bridge and regains the line of the former road (which made use of a ferry crossing) near (39 m.) *Ayios Yeóryios*. We zigzag high above the valley to (47 m.) *Frangísta* (ΦΡΑΓΚΙΣΤΑ). The road suddenly reaches a small plane-shaded opening with springs, grass, and a café.—We climb steeply to 3500 ft, then descend to cross the Megdova by (57 m.) the *Markopoulos Bridge* (Restaurant). The road climbs again through firs to a col (c. 4000 ft) in the W. outliers of Timfristós, then descends.—72½ m. *Karpenisi*, and thence to Lamia, see Rte 47A.

Quitting Agrinion we turn S. The route runs straight across the irrigated plain dividing Lakes Trikhonis (l.; comp. above) and Lysimakhia (r.), crosses the canal linking the two lakes, joins the road coming from the S. shore of Lake Trikhonis, then follows the S.E. shore of *Lake Lysimakhia* before turning S. into the hills.—63¼ m. *Frangouléika* lies in the pretty valley that leads into the *Stená tis Kleisoúras*, a long cleft in the sandstone, in which stands the monastery of Ayios Eleousas. At the exit, pleasant prospect of the Aitolikó lagoon.—67 m. Turning (r.) to *Angelókastro* (10 m.) where there are remains of a Byzantine fortress (13C). The coastal plain is planted with olives. The realined road runs well above the older road (and eventually by-passes Mesolongi).—71 m. Turning to *Aitolikó* (4¼ m.) and (9 m. farther) **Oiniadai**.

Aitolikó (ΑΙΤΩΛΙΚΟΝ), a medieval refuge-town of 4800 inhab., stands on an island between its lagoon and the larger seaward Lagoon of Mesolongi, and is joined to the mainland at either end by fine stone bridges. The 15C church of the *Panayia* has wall paintings. William Martin, an English deserter seaman, was one of the 600 who here successfully defied Omer Vrioni's siege in 1823.

From Aitolikó an asphalt road runs W. in very flat arable country. We leave on the right a road to Astakós (28¼ m.; see above), pass through *Neokhóri* (3200 inhab.), cross the Acheloos by a new bridge, and reach *Katokhí* (2850 inhab.) with a ruined medieval tower. In the village we ignore the more important road on our right and beyond the village the road divides (no signpost): either branch (gravel) leads in c. 1 m. to the ruins of **Oiniadai**, that to the right approaching the harbour side, that to the left the Acropolis, a rocky wooded hill known as *Tríkardo Kástro*. The city, explored by the American School in 1901, is heavily overgrown and a wary eye should be kept for snakes and hornets as well as for the dogs of the local vlachs. On all sides, except the S., it is surrounded by the marshes of Lezini, the ancient Lake Melita. On the S. a plain slopes down to the Acheloos. The well-preserved *Fortifications* follow the irregular hill.

Oiniadai, though unhealthily situated and inaccessible in winter, was strategically important as the key to S. Akarnania. It was taken after a siege in 455 B.C. by exiled Messenians established at Naupaktos, and attacked in vain by Pericles in 453. Demosthenes in 424 forced it to join the Athenian alliance. It fell to the Aitolians in 336 and, without bloodshed, to Philip V in 219. The Romans captured it eight years later and handed it over to the Aitolian League. The town was restored to the Akarnanians in 189.

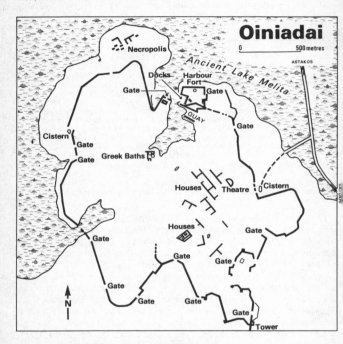

We enter, near a cottage, by the E. wall. The closely jointed polygonal masonry is of the 6C. To the S. are the main *Gate*, one of many with arched openings, a feature unusual in Greek architecture, and the *Acropolis*. In the other direction are the remains of a small *Theatre* having 27 rows of seats; inscriptions on the lowest three rows record the freeing of slaves and date the building (late 3C B.C.). Farther N. are remarkable vestiges of the *Docks* reconstructed by Philip V. Here are a buttressed quay, porticoes surrounding a basin hewn in the rock, berths with traces of the rings to which ships were moored, and their slipways. To the S.W. of the port are some remains of *Baths* of Greek construction.

Beyond Aitolikó the road continues through rice fields. To the right are salt flats.—74 m. Ancient **Pleuron** is conspicuous from the main road but difficult of access owing to a water pipeline and culverts. The two lower hills of Petrovouni and Gyphtokastro have some Archaic remains of an enceinte that probably represents *Old Pleuron*, the city of the Curetes destroyed by Demetrios II, son of Antigonus Gonatas, in 234 B.C. An arduous path ascends to the enceinte of ashlar masonry (Kastro Irinio), the **New Pleuron* built soon afterwards. The splendid WALLS, the most remarkable antiquity in Aitolia, have 36 towers and

7 gates; the circuit is almost complete and stands in places to fifteen courses of Hellenistic masonry.

Within are the ruins of a *Theatre*, perhaps the smallest in Greece. The stage, with the proscenium, backed on to the city wall; a small doorway led through

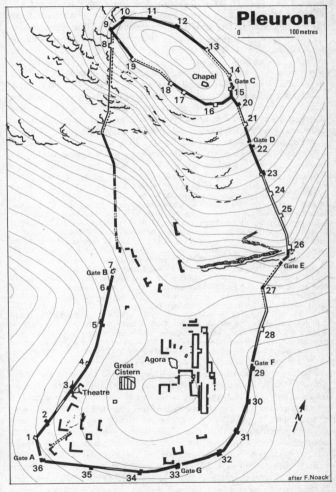

the orchestra to a square tower. In a hollow to the S.E. is a *Cistern*, 100 ft by 65, with a depth of 13 ft, divided into five rectangular basins by four partition walls pierced by triangular openings. Near the E. wall is the *Agora*, a rectangular terrace 160 yds long. It is crowded with the debris of buildings; among them is a portico 66 yds by 11, with enclosing walls still standing to a height of c. 2 ft. There are also exedrae and pedestals. On a hill to the N. is the site of the *Acropolis*, which had square towers. Below the terrace the hill sinks rapidly E. towards the city walls. At the foot of the depression is a fine gateway 5½ ft wide, 9 ft high and 6½ ft thick. The lintel is formed of two large horizontal blocks; in it and in the stone of the threshold are seen the holes for the gatepost.

76½ m. (123 km.) **MESOLONGI** (ΜΕΣΟΛΟΓΓΙΟΝ; *Liberty*; *Theoxenia*, DPO, both B; *Rest. Diethnes, Panorama*), or *Missolonghi*, with 11,600 inhab., is the capital of the nome of Aitolia and Akarnania, and the seat of a bishop. The town is, by repute, more familiar to the English-speaking world than many others in Greece of greater importance, for here Lord Byron (b. 1788) died of fever on 19 April 1824, after ten months of incessant activity in the cause of Greek independence. Mesolongi, now by-passed by the main highway, is situated on the E. shore of a vast lagoon (Limnothalassa) partly given over to fish hatcheries and the haunt of many water-birds. This has always been too shallow to allow the approach of vessels of any size, and a long causeway extends s. to deep water at *Tourlidha*. The local sailing boats have affinities with the Egyptian felucca and the nets are unusual. Drainage and reclamation work is hastening the disappearance of the fishing community and their characteristic reed huts built on piles. In the local cafés the 'mezès' are varied and good.

History *Mesolongi* was the w. centre of resistance against the Turks in the War of Independence, and had to endure three sieges. In 1822 it was defended by Mavrocordato against a force of 10,000 led by Omer Vrioni and Reshid Pasha. In 1823 its commander was the Suliot, Markos Botsaris. In Jan 1824 Lord Byron came to Mesolongi and inspired the defenders with his enthusiasm; he died the following April before the beginning of the final siege. In April 1825 Reshid Pasha appeared before the town with 15,000 troops. The defenders numbered only 5000. Hampered by furious sorties and by a lack of supplies, Reshid Pasha could make no headway for six months. Then Ibrahim Pasha, with 10,000 Egyptians, advanced to his aid from the Peloponnese. After fluctuating struggles for the islands in the lagoon, the enemy closed round the devoted town. At the end of their resources after 12 months of siege, almost the whole population determined to break out. Their attempt (the 'Exodos') was made on the night of 22/23 April 1826. Though they managed to get clear of the town, they were frustrated by the treachery of a Bulgarian deserter, who had forewarned the besiegers. The fugitives, imagining themselves safe, were ambushed by 1000 Albanians on the slopes of Mt Zygos. Out of the 9000 who left Mesolongi—soldiers and civilians—only 1800 made good their escape to Amphissa. Meanwhile those who had stayed behind fired their magazines, overwhelming themselves and their enemies in a common destruction.—In 1828 the Turks surrendered Mesolongi without firing a shot.

The town is entered through the Venetian walls by the 'Gate of the Sortie', rebuilt by King Otho to protect the hastily repaired earthen rampart through which the exodos was made. Within the gate (r.) is a pleasant garden with the *Heroon* (adm. free) commemorating the heroes of the town's three sieges. A large central tumulus contains the bodies of unnamed defenders; to the right is the tomb of Botsaris, and, between the two, a statue of Byron erected in 1881, beneath which is the poet's heart. The centre of the town is the PLATEIA BOTSARI, where the *Dhimarkhion* houses the Museum of the Revolution, with Byron relics and several dramatic pictures of the war. Odhos Trikoupis leads w. and at its end Odhos Levidou brings us to a small square where a *Memorial Garden* occupies the site of the house in which Byron died: the house was destroyed in the Second World War. Continuing round a school we reach the causeway, with a bust of the poet Kostis Palamas and the reconstructed base of the historic *Windmill* blown up by Christos Kapsalis on 11 April 1826.

55 FROM MESOLONGI TO ATHENS
A Viâ Rion

ROAD to (25½ m., 41 km.) *Andirrion*, whence by ferry to *Rion*; from Rion to *Athens* (131 m.), see Rtes 38, 24. Bus 8 times daily in 5½ hrs; also from Mesolongi to Patras.

The road runs E. towards the dark mass of Varásova. To the right are seen the mountains that rise behind Patras.—3 m. Turning (l.) to *Ayios Simeon*, the monastery where the people of Mesolonghi made their last stand after the 'exodos' in 1826.—At 5¼ m. a track (l.; signposted) leads in a few min. to ancient **Kalydon**, celebrated in the heroic age as the home of Oeneus and his sons Tydeus and Meleager. On the neighbouring slopes, culminating in Mt Zygos (3115 ft), took place the hunt of the Kalydonian boar. Though Strabo couples Kalydon with Pleuron as an ornament to Greece, it was historically insignificant. The city received its death blow when Augustus transferred its inhabitants to Nikopolis and most of the public treasures to Patras.

To the right of our path are some remains of a *Heroön*, comprising a number of rooms grouped round a peristyle court with a well and cistern. Under the main room is a sepulchral chamber. The path continues to a farmhouse standing just outside the West Gate (foundations) of the ancient town. A natural spur extends s.w. for c. 350 yds, commanding the plain and the gulf. Here stood the **Sanctuary of Artemis Laphria**, excavated by Danish archaeologists in 1925–32. A massive foundation platform locates the 4C *Temple*, erected on a terrace supported by 6C retaining walls. Remains of metopes were recovered from earlier temples of c. 570 and c. 620 B.C.

We cross the Evinos. The road passes inland of *Mt Varásova* (3005 ft), the ancient Mt Chalkis, by a low pass to emerge *en corniche* above the Gulf of Patras on the barren flanks of *Klókova* (Taphiassos; 3415 ft). The *Views across the gulf comprise Patras itself and the mountains behind as far as the long crest of Erymanthos.—At (20 m.) *Riza* we descend to the narrow coastal plain. Palaiokastro Mamakou (l.) may be ancient *Makynia*. The torrents crossing the Patras–Rion road are conspicuous across the water.—At 23¼ m. our road diverges r. to **Andírrion** (ANTIPPION), where the ferry (car 112 dr.) to *Rion* (Rte 38) across the 'Little Dardanelles' provides the shortest approach from N.W. Greece to **Athens** (131 m. from Rion; comp. Rtes 38, 24).

Andirrion, like Rion, has a picturesque medieval fortress. It is known as the *Castle of Roumeli*.

B Viâ Delphi

ROAD, 216 m. (348 km.), mountainous with splendid scenery, but arduous driving between Navpaktos and Amfissa.—33½ m. Návpaktos.—72 m. *Lidhoríki*.—100 m. Amfissa. Thence, viâ (114 m.) **Delphi** to *Athens*, see Rte 45. BUSES twice daily from Navpaktos to *Amfissa* in 4 hrs; also twice daily from Amfissa to *Delphi*; three times daily from Delphi to *Athens* (poor connections).

From Mesolongi to (23¼ m.) the *Andirrion* turning, see Rte 55A. Beyond Andirrion the road runs a field's length from the sea, and for a brief period affords a long view right down the Gulf of Corinth.

30 m. (48 km.) **Návpaktos** (ΝΑΥΠΑΚΤΟΣ; *Amaryllis*, B; *Akti, New Hellas* C; *Rest. Diethnes*; Y.H.) is a charming little town (8200 inhab.) with a good beach. The picturesque, mainly Venetian, *Castle*, from which ramparts descend to enclose the little *Harbour*, recalls its

medieval past when it was known in the West as *Lépanto*. The plateia, shaded by jacaranda trees, looks across the Gulf to Mt Panakhaïkon.

Here in 1571 the Turkish admiral fitted out before the decisive *Battle of Lepanto*, fought in fact off the Echinades. The allied fleet, under Don John of Austria, natural son of the Emp. Charles V, included contingents from Venice, Genoa, the Papal States, Spain, Sicily, and Naples. The Turks were assisted by the Bey of Alexandria and the Bey of Algiers. The result was the overwhelming victory of Christendom, and Moslem sea-power suffered a blow from which it never recovered. The young Cervantes, creator of 'Don Quixote', here lost the use of his left hand.

Ancient *Naupaktos*, a town of the Ozolian Locrians, was taken in 455 by the Athenians. Here they established a colony of Messenians, who had been dispossessed by their Spartan conquerors. The place played an important part in the Peloponnesian War; it was successfully defended in 429 by Phormion and in 426 by Demosthenes against the Spartans, and became a base for the Sicilian expedition.

A by-road (bus twice daily) leads inland to (30 m.) *Thermon*, see Rte 54.

Quitting Navpaktos, we cross the *Mornos* near its mouth on a five-span bridge. A by-road goes up the w. side of its valley to Paliokhoraki (5½ m.); higher up it flows through a gorge; our road will cross it twice more still higher up its course.—At (36 m.) *Kastráki* a by-road leads (r.) to *Evpálion* and *Monastiráki* (4 m.), a pretty place on the coast where Herodotus located ancient *Erythrai*. The way continues through rolling hills interspersed with orchards and little streams, climbing gradually. Prominent on a bluff, to the right as we climb, is a radar station commanding the Rion strait. The mountains behind Patras become very prominent beyond the Gulf.—46 m. *Kardára* lies hidden (l.) off the road. We reach a col with splendid retrospective views of the Gulf, and descend to (47½ m.) *Goumaíoi* (or Filothei).—48½ m. Turning (l.) for the *Varnákova Monastery* (3 m.), a Byzantine foundation rebuilt by Capodistrias in 1831. Our road turns N., crosses a second col, then follows a ledge high up the mountainside above a side valley of the Mornos. During the gradual descent to the main river the horizon becomes increasingly filled with peaks, those to the N. barren, those to the E. clothed with forests.—54 m. We cross the Mornos, here narrow and swift, at its confluence with the Loufolóreko, entering the valley of the tributary in order to cross it.

A by-road continues up the valley to *Terpsithéa* (8 m.). Off it (l.), at (3 m.) *Limnítsa*, tracks lead into the mountains to *Khrísovo* and *Katafíyio*, once refuges from the Turks.

We climb high above the N. bank of the Mornos. The slopes opposite are cultivated in terraces by scattered smallholders; above extend dark pine forests. We descend again almost to river level to cross a side stream. The valley becomes broader with views ahead towards Mt Giona (8230 ft).—62¾ m. Turning to *Krokíli* (7 m.), native village of Yiannis Makriyiannis, a hero of the 1821 revolt. At (67½ m.) the turning to *Pendayioí* (11 m.) we get an extensive view to the N. up the Kókkino valley towards the Vardoúsia Mts (7995 ft). We cross the Kókkino and leave a by-road to *Dhiakópion* (4½ m.) on our left. Our road skirts a conical hill with ancient remains, below which is (70 m.) the *Mornos Tourist Pavilion*. Next to an old packhorse bridge we cross the Mornos for the last time and turn s. into the valley of the Velá. Higher up, the Mornos is being dammed to provide water for Athens. About 1 m. farther on we pass a stone-arched bridge of an older road.

72 m. **Lidhoríki** (1835 ft; Inn), a pleasant mountain village with

1180 inhab., is the chief market centre of Doris, one of the two eparchies of Phocis. It was known to the Catalans as *Ledorix*, and was one of the three strong-points of the county of Salona. We continue s. in the shallow and comparatively populous valley of the Velá, passing Palaio-kastro, an ancient site.—79 m. Roads branch (l.) to *Malandríno* and (r.) to *Amigdaliá*. Beyond this turn some classical walling is visible (l.). We climb amid scrub to the road summit (2790 ft), passing, near the top, the monastery of *Panayía tis Koutsouriótissas*. We pass (r.) a tarred road to Eratiní (with, after 2 m., a track to Ayioi Pandes), and then a road, mostly unpaved, to Galaxidhi (comp. Rte 55c).

Our road bears N.E. Ahead and right rises the range of Parnassos as we descend to (89 m.) *Vounikhóra* (2495 ft). Beyond the village the *View opens out to the right affording a glimpse of the Bay of Galaxidhi with Khriso and Delphi lying on the Parnassian slopes.— From (94½ m.) *Ayía Evthímia* (1510 ft) tracks descend to Galaxídhi and Itéa. The landscape mellows suddenly as we come into full view of the olive groves which fill the valley, at the head of which stands Amfissa. We descend by turns on the flank of Mt Kokinari to (100 m.) **Amfissa**, whence viâ (114 m.) **Delphi** to (216 m.) **Athens**, see Rte 45.

C Viâ Galaxidhi

ROAD, 195 m. (312 km.), new highway to Itéa along the Gulf of Corinth, thence joining Delphi–Levadhia road.

To (30 m.) *Návpaktos*, see Rte 55B. Just E. of the town the ways part by the Mornos. The new road (r.), crossing the river nearer its mouth, soon approaches the coast, which it then follows most of the way. There are few villages, the place-names being derived from beaches or isolated churches.—36 m. *Káto Marathiás*. Farther on a cluster of hamlets faces the I. of Trizonia.—52½ m. (84 km.) *Ayios Nikólaos* is linked 3 times daily by car ferry with Aighion (1 hr.; Rte 38).—57 m. *Paralía Tolofonos* (Delphi Beach B) and (59 m.) *Eratiní* (Ameriki D) are served by a minor road while the main road passes to landward. Eratiní stands on the bay of *Vitrinitsa* where in 1675 died Sir Giles Eastcourt, one of the first recorded Englishmen to visit Greece. The site of ancient *Tolophon*, with a well-preserved enceinte, lies near (65 m.) *Ayioi Pandes*.

The road now skirts the sheltered inner bays of the w. side of the Gulf of Itea.—71¼ m. (114 km.) **Galaxídhi** (ΓΑΛΑΞΙΔΙ; *Ganymede* C), a well-built old seafaring town with inhabitants in absentia, is picturesquely situated on a wooded bay with a fine view of Parnassos. The church of the *Metamorphosis* was reputedly built by Michael II Angelos in gratitude for his recovery from an illness; it has an exceptionally good altar screen. There is a small maritime museum. The town has sections of ancient wall, which belonged perhaps to ancient *Chaleion*, and two me-dieval towers adorn hills above.

The coast is scarred with quarries and mines, bauxite being loaded by cableway and tip direct into ships. The little Bay of Salona, site of Salona's medieval port, now Órmos Itéas, was also the scene of Frank Abney Hastings' exploit with the steamship 'Karteria' against the Turks in 1827.

82½ m. **Itéa** (*Xenia, Kalafati, Galini*, all B; *Akti* C), with 3400 inhab., the modern harbour of Amfissa, stands round a headland at the head of the Gulf. It is a fresh and pleasant small resort, busy at intervals with cruise ships disembarking their excursions to Delphi.

Until the new road (in construction) to the E. is completed, many travellers may prefer to turn N. to join the Amfissa road W. of Delphi (Rte 55B).

From (84 m.) *Kirra* Delphi can be reached by hilly mule-path. French excavations have shown ancient *Kirrha* to have flourished in Early and Middle Helladic times, though it is best known for its part in the First Sacred War. Those with robust vehicles and a head for heights may essay the narrow precipitous zigzag that climbs 2000 ft up the face of Koútsouras and across its saddle to (96½ m.) *Dhesfína*. The road continues in an enclosed valley.—At (99 m.) the large *Moní Tímíou Prodrómou*, it divides. The right branch makes a steep descent to Andikira (7 m.; Rte 45), while the left branch crosses another ridge to (104¼ m.) *Dhistomo*. Hence to (121 m.) **Levadhía** and viâ Thebes to (195 m.) **Athens,** see Rte 45.

56 THE IONIAN ISLANDS

The **IONIAN ISLANDS,** known also as the *Eptanisos*, from the seven principal islands, lie in the Ionian Sea mainly along the W. coast of Greece. The 'seven islands', from N. to S., are *Corfù* (off the coast of Albania and Epirus); *Paxoi* (off the coast of Epirus); *Levkas* (off Akarnania); *Ithaka, Cephalonia,* and *Zante* (at the entrance to the Gulf of Corinth); and *Kithira* (to the S. of the Vátika Peninsula in the Peloponnese). The smaller islands include the group of the Othonian Islands—*Fano, Merlera,* and *Samothraki*—to the N.W. of Corfù; *Andipaxoi,* S. of Paxoi; *Meganisi* and *Kalamos,* between Levkas and the mainland of Akarnania; the *Echinades* lying E. of Ithaka near the mouth of the Acheloos; and *Andikithira,* S. of Kithira. A claim by Palmerston at the time of the 'Don Pacifico' incident in 1848 that the islets of Sapienza and Cervi, off Messenia, formed part of the Ionian Islands was not sustained. The grouping of the islands is a largely artificial conception of medieval and 19C politics. The group, excluding Kithira (now administered from Piraeus), still remains nominally an administrative region, divided into four nomes, but the frequency of communication between each nome and Athens is greater than between the nomes. The islands are here treated together because of the interest to British travellers of their tenure by Britain in 1815–64 as a protectorate.

The largest of the islands is Cephalonia, which also has the highest mountain, but by far the most important is Corfù, with the most populous city. The scenery combines the lush greenness of the English countryside (together with a rainfall spread through the year) with the characteristic Greek seascape. The high hedges that line the roads are also unusual in Greece. The total population of the four nomes is 184,400.

CLIMATE AND SEASON. The climate of the Ionian Islands is generally temperate, but subject to sudden changes. Their winter is rather rainy and their summer rather too hot, but in spring and autumn they are enchanting. The average temperature ranges from 44° to 91° Fahr.; the annual average of rainy days is as high as 100. The *Scirocco*, which blows from the S.E., is most depressing and disagreeable. Frost is rare, and snow seldom falls except on the tops of the hills. Squalls (*borasche*) are frequent. Earthquakes, especially in Zante, Levkas, and Cephalonia are not uncommon.

History The name Ionian is not easily explained; Herodotus in his account of the Ionian peoples does not refer to the *Ionian Islands* as such. In the Homeric age a maritime people, under the generic name of *Kephallenians*, inhabited the islands at the mouth of the Gulf of Corinth. *Ulysses* or *Odysseus*, King of Ithaca, was the epic personification of this naval realm, which comprised the islands (or cities) of *Ithaca, Doulichion, Same*, and *Zakynthos*, as well as the islets (Od. IX, 21 ff). At the 'extreme end of the earth' was *Scheria* (? Corcyra or Corfù), where dwelt the friendly Phaeaceans. Since classical times authorities have not been agreed as to the modern equivalents. The traditional school identifies Ithaca with Ithaka, Same with Same in Cephalonia, and Zakynthos with Zante; but, echoing the perplexity of the ancients, it is hazy about Doulichion. Strabo (X, 2) insists that it was one of the Echinades. Others place it at Pale, in Cephalonia. The revolutionary views of Dörpfeld, put forward in detail in 1927, that Levkas is ancient Ithaka, modern Ithaka ancient Same, and Cephalonia ancient Doulichion, have not received general support; though the theory removes the problem of the identification of Doulichion (which, since it sent 40 ships to Troy as against 12 from the other three cities, must have been larger than the Echinades), it poses other problems, equally insoluble. Samuel Butler reminds us that we ought not to look for the accuracy of a guide-book in a narrative that tells us of a monster with six heads and three rows of teeth in each; and, remembering that the whole region is particularly prone to seismic disturbances, we must perhaps be resigned to the geographical mysteries of the Odyssey. A thorough archaeological exploration of Cephalonia may one day clarify its position in the Mycenean world and provide new answers. Some lively views have recently been put forward by experienced yachtsmen on the Homeric topography of this area.

After the age of Homer the islands ceased for centuries to have any common bond of union. At the outbreak of the Peloponnesian War (431 B.C.) Corcyra, Kephallenia, and Zakynthos were allies of Athens, and Leucas (Levkas) of Sparta. Both the Corcyreans and the Leucadians provided fleets for their respective leaders.

Towards the end of the 3C B.C. the islands became Roman. In 890 A.D. the Byzantine emperor Leo the Philosopher (886–911) formed all seven into one province; and in this condition they belonged to the Eastern Empire after the disintegration of Italy. In the decline of the Empire they were again divided up, and various Latin princes owned the different islands. They are heard of occasionally in the struggles between the Greek emperors and the Western crusaders. They were desolated by the ravages of corsairs, Christian as well as Mohammedan. After many vicissitudes, the inhabitants of Corfù placed themselves, in 1386, under the sovereignty of Venice, the state which was more than any other to influence the destinies of the islands. During the next two centuries Venice obtained control of most of the other Ionian Islands; but two of them remained independent much longer. Levkas was annexed in 1684. Kythera not till 1717.

The rule of the Venetians, much less severe than in the Archipelago, embodied some of the principles of Machiavelli. The more prominent citizens, instead of being imprisoned or executed, were ennobled. Frequent intermarriages made for a close assimilation of races, and the ascendency of the more cultured partner helped to consolidate the domination of Venice. Education was discouraged and Ionian youths were granted the privilege of purchasing degrees at Italian universities without having to pass examinations. Italian became the official language and the Roman Catholic religion was established. The humbler classes who formed the great bulk of the population, remained faithful to the Greek tongue and to the Orthodox Church.

On the fall of Venice in 1797, the Treaty of Campo Formio transferred the Ionian Islands to the French Republic, and they were occupied by a small French garrison. The French soldiers were driven out in 1798 by a combined Russian and Turkish force. By the provisions of the Treaty of 21 March 1800, between the Tsar, and the Sultan, the Ionian Islands were formed into a separate state, with the high-sounding title of the *Septinsular Republic*. The republic was under the protectorate first of the Porte, later of Russia. This period of quasi-independence (1800–07) proved to be little better than a reign of terror. Within two years all seven islands had risen against their general government and each separate island against its local authorities. Horrors, resembling those of the Corcyrean factions described by Thucydides (III, 81) were of daily occurrence. In 1802, on the change of masters, the principal Ionians sent an envoy to the Tsar, imploring his interference, and as a result the Russian plenipotentiary, Count Mocenigo, a native of Zante, which had become particularly notorious for the number of its assassinations, was empowered to proclaim new forms of administration.

But in 1807, by the Treaty of Tilsit, the islands were given back to France, and incorporated in the province of Illyria. In 1809 Great Britain came on the scene. General Oswald took Cephalonia, Ithaka, Zante, and Kythera that year, and Levkas in 1810. Paxos was reduced in 1814 and after the fall of Napoleon Corfù was surrendered by its French defender, at the command of Louis XVIII, to Sir James Campbell. The Treaty of Paris (1815) made the Ionian Islands an independent state under the protection of the British crown.

Sir Thomas Maitland (1759?–1824) was first Lord High Commissioner. A constitution was drawn up at his direction, and adopted by the Ionian Constituent Assembly in 1817. The administration at Corfù comprised the Lord High Commissioner, the Senate of six members, and the Assembly. The Senate and the Assembly of 42 deputies were ciphers, for the Lord High Commissioner, had the right of veto on all their acts, charge of foreign relations, and the immediate control of the police and health departments. He was represented in each of the other six islands by a British Resident, with local functions similar to his own.

Maitland was not slow to make use of his dictatorial powers and soon acquired the nickname 'King Tom'. Despite the defects of the colonial system, the next thirty years gave the Ionian Islands an era of peace and prosperity unparalleled on the mainland. The administration of justice became impartial. Direct taxation was practically abolished and the revenue, raised chiefly by import and export duties, was freed from peculation. Trade and agriculture were encouraged; educational establishments (including even a short-lived university at Corfù) were founded; and excellent roads, unknown in Greece since Roman times, were built, as well as harbours, quays, and aqueducts. The Greek Church was restored.

Nationalist feeling soon overrode material considerations. The islanders, who had at first welcomed the British particularly resented the measures taken to enforce their neutrality in the Greek struggle for independence. The achievement by Greece in 1830 of her immediate aims increased the discontent with foreign rule. A powerful opposition, headed by Andreas Mustoxidi, agitated for union with Greece. In 1858, Gladstone was sent on a special mission and for a few days exercised the functions of Lord High Commissioner. He vainly attempted to meet the situation by proposing a number of reforms. As late as 1861 he declared that it would be a "crime against the safety of Europe" to give up the islands.

On the change of dynasty in Greece, however, Great Britain voluntarily ceded all rights over the Ionian Islands by the Treaty of London signed in 1864; at the same time their union with Greece was formally recognized. Edward Lear made a tour in 1863, drawing his 'Views in the Seven Ionian Islands'.

A Corfù

Approaches By Air. From *Athens*, 3 times daily in c. 1½ hr. From *London* direct twice weekly.

By Sea. Car Ferry from *Igoumenitsa*, many times daily in 1½ hr; from *Patras*, every other day via *Sami* in 10 hrs; buses from Athens connect at both ports. Through bus from Athens 3 times daily via Rion and Igoumenitsa.

Corfù is a port-of-call also (several times daily in summer; several times weekly in winter) of international Car Ferry services, Patras–Brindisi, Corinth–Brindisi, Patras–Ancona (break of journey at Corfù—no extra charge—must be notified before embarkation); and it is visited by innumerable cruise ships. Passengers without an international ticket travelling between two Greek ports can do so only by Greek shipping lines.

CORFÙ, in Greek **Kérkira** (KEPKYPA), is the best known and most beautiful of the Ionian Islands. With a length of 40 m. and an extreme breadth in the N. of nearly 20 m., it is in area the second largest of the seven islands, but its population (90,700 inhab.) is much greater than that of the more spacious Cephalonia. Its capital is likewise the most important and populous town in the group. The most northerly of the Ionian Islands, situated less than 2 m. off the N. Epirot coast of Albania, and the nearest Greek land to Italy, Corfù has a natural importance as the gateway between East and West. Until the Balkan Wars of 1912–13 extended the Greek frontier, it had long been a Christian outpost on the very verge of Turkish territory.

The land, especially in the long s. peninsula, is well-watered and fertile. Cypress, fig, orange, and lemon trees are found in magnificent profusion, but above all the olive, which here unpruned almost attains the size and dignity of a forest tree. About four million grow in the island, providing a large output of oil. Cactus is common. Vineyards abound, producing good white wine (unresinated) and a rather sweet heavy red wine with a short life. Apples and pears are grown and, more important, tomatoes. The broad N. section is crossed by a range of hills from w. to E., culminating in Pantokrator (3000 ft). In the s. a lesser range is topped by Mt Ayioi Dhéka (1860 ft), a conspicuous landmark.

The effects of the long Venetian domination are still apparent. Italian, once the official language, and strongly tinged with the Venetian dialect, is still commonly spoken and everywhere understood. The place-names are bi-lingual, with a preference for the Italian form. Among the legacies of British rule are cricket and ginger beer. A local speciality is the *kum-kwat*, the crystallized miniature Japanese orange. Except in Corfù town, hotels are mostly closed in winter.

History. The name *Corfù* is an Italian corruption of Koryphó, a Byzantine name derived from the two peaks (Κορυφαί) on which the citadel of the chief town is built. The ancient name *Corcyra* appears first in Herodotus. About 734 B.C. (traditional date, not yet confirmed by pottery found) a colony was planted here by the Corinthians, which soon became rich and powerful enough to found colonies of its own. Corinth soon became jealous and apprehensive, and c. 664 B.C. a battle was fought between their respective fleets, the first Greek sea-fight on record. The Corcyreans took no part in the Persian wars. In 432 B.C. they invoked the help of Athens against the Corinthians. The consequent engagement off the Sybota Is., between the Corcyreans and their mother-city, precipitated the Peloponnesian War. During this struggle the power and importance of Corcyra was irretrievably squandered in the calamitous feuds between the oligarchic and democratic parties. The victory of the democrats in 425 B.C. was signalized by atrocities. Corcyra was chosen by the Athenians for the final review of their fleet in 415 B.C. on the eve of the Sicilian expedition.

Though Corcyra never recovered her former importance, the island was by 373 B.C., according to Xenophon, in a wonderful state of fertility and opulence. After a succession of masters, it became Roman in 229 B.C. Here Octavian assembled his fleet before the battle of Actium, and hither came at various times Tibullus, Cato, and Cicero. In A.D. 67 Corcyra was visited, on his way to Greece by Nero who, according to Suetonius, sang and danced before the altar of Zeus at Kassiope.

During the Crusades, the geographical position of Corfù again brought it into prominence. Robert Guiscard seized the island in 1081 during his wars with the Eastern Empire. Richard I of England landed here on his return from the Holy Land in 1193, on his way to Ragusa and unexpected captivity. Passing from the Venetians to the Genoese and back again (1204–14), Corfù came under Epirus until 1267, then under the Angevins of Naples. Towards the end it suffered greatly at the hands of pirates. In 1386, the inhabitants invoked the aid of Venice, under those sovereignty they remained until her downfall in 1797. Venice made Corfù her principal arsenal in Greece and surrounded the town with extensive fortifications, which set at defiance the whole power of the Ottomans in 1537 and 1570, and, above all, in the celebrated siege of 1716, remarkable as the last great attempt of the Turks to extend their conquests in Christendom. In this siege the personal efforts of the High Admiral of the Ottoman Empire were frustrated by the skill and daring of *Marshal Schulenburg*, a soldier of fortune from Saxony.

The subsequent history of Corfù is largely that of the Ionian Islands as a whole (see above). *Count John Capodistrias*, the first President of independent Greece, was a Corfiot. In 1915–16 the island was used as a base for the reorganization of the Serbian army after its disastrous retreat, until its transfer to the Salonika front. In Aug 1923, in consequence of the murder of Gen. Tellini, the Italian president of the Greco-Albanian Boundary Commission, Italy bombarded Corfù, and subsequently occupied the island, together with Paxos, Antipaxos, Merlera, and Samothraki, until 27 Sept, when the incident was closed by the payment of an idemnity of 50 million lire. As a result, however, Corfù remained a 'frontier region' with special restrictions from 1924 to 1961. In the Second World War the island was occupied in 1941–43 without much unpleasantness by the Italians and later by the Germans. There followed ten days of bombardment and fighting (13–23 Sept) before the city was reduced by the Germans. During this time a quarter of the town was destroyed, including the seat of the Ionian parliament, the magnificent old library of the former university with 70,000 volumes, and 14 churches with their paintings of the Ionian school. In the international channel N.E. of Corfù on 22 Oct 1946 two British destroyers hit an uncharted Albanian minefield, deliberately laid, losing 45 men.

Corfù has a tradition of musical performance dating from 1733. Edward Lear (1812–88), author of the 'Book of Nonsense', lived for some time at Corfù while painting and writing about Greece.

The town of **Corfù** or *Kérkira* (ΚΕΡΚΥΡΑ), situated on an irregular peninsula about the middle of the E. coast, just S. of the islet of *Vido*, is the capital of the island and the largest town in the Ionian Islands. Including the suburbs of *Mandouki* to the W. and *Garitsa* and *Sarokko* to the S., now all contiguous, it has 28,600 inhabitants. Destined by the Venetians to become the headquarters of their Greek possessions, it was strongly fortified, and their fortresses arrest the attention of every new arrival. As a busy port-of-call for steamers plying between Brindisi and Piraeus, for cruise ships, and for naval vessels, it is a favourite resort of visitors. The old town has narrow streets and tall houses, having formerly been enclosed by walls. During the British occupation it was given a good water supply and extended towards the site of the ancient city to the S. The grave damage, caused by the fighting in 1943 between Italians and Germans and worsened in 1944 by Anglo-American bombing, left scars which are slowly disappearing.

Airport, just beyond the suburb of Sarokko.

Hotels (Class B and above all DPO). Corfù **Palace** (Pl. a), Leof. Vas. Konstandinou, with swimming pool, **L. Cavalieri** (Pl. c), 4 Od. Kapodistriou, **A. Astron** (Pl. b), Od. Donzelot; **Alkinoos** (Pl. d), **Olympic** (Pl. e), Leof. Megali Doukissis Marias; all **B. Arkadion** (Pl. f), **Bretagne** (Pl. g), **Ionion** (Pl. h), **Calypso** (Pl. i), **Suisse** (*Elvetia*; Pl. j), all **C**, and others.—At *Anemomylos*, near Mon Repos, **Arion, Marina**, both **B**.—At *Kanoni*, **Corfù Hilton L**; **Corfù Kanoni, Ariti, A**, both summer only; **Royal, Salvos**, both **DPO**, open all year, **C**.

Restaurants. *Aktaion*, on the Spianada; *Rex*, 66 Kapodistriou; *Navtikon*, on the N. plateia; Tavernas near Mon Repos beach, near the Achilleion, at Kanoni, at Perama, etc.

Post Office (Pl. 6), off Leof. M. Doukissis Marias.—O.T.E. CENTRE (Pl. 6), Od. Mantzaros.

Buses from the Spianadha (Pl. 3) to *Mon Repos* and *Kanoni*; from Plat Theotoki (Sarokko; Pl. 6) to *Dasia*, *Ipsos*; to the *Achilleion*, etc.; from the Neon Frourion (Pl. 2) to *Kassiopi*, etc.

Motor-Boats in summer, 3 times daily, from below the Spianada to *Dasia* (out morning; return aft. and early evening).

Amusements. CASINO at the Achilleion, 5½ m. s.; TENNIS CLUB (Pl. 7); DANCING at Club Méditerranée camps, tickets from Town Office; BATHING (nearest) at Mon Repos beach (Pl. 16).—CONCERTS in the Bandstand on Sun.

The modern HARBOUR extends along the N.W. edge of the city, from the Adriatic steamer berths to the W. (Pl. 1) to the drive-on quay of the Igoumenitsa car ferry to the E. (Pl. 2). From the *Custom House* (Pl. 2) we follow the quay E. beneath the untidy lower slopes of the **Néon Froúrion** (Fortezza Nuova), built in 1577–88 by the Venetians. The fortress, having served the French, was given its superstructure by the British and only ceased to be a military post after 1864. Until the Second World War it was used by a police school; during the war its casemates sheltered the Corfiots from air raids; the barrack-block is now occupied by a naval detachment. The bastions, picturesquely overgrown by fig trees and wild flowers, may be explored (free; 9–12 & 3–7) from the E. side entrance. The w. wall above the dry moat has two large Lions of St Mark.

We reach the sun-drenched PLATEIA YEORYIOS B′, with its judas-trees, where even the horses of the hired carriages wear hats. The *Porta Spilia* (16C), incorporated in a later edifice, admits to the main street through the heart of the town (comp. below). From the S.E. corner another narrow passage passes the Nea Yorki hotel and leads by stepped streets (skalinades) into the Kambielo (Campiello) quarter where constricted alleys (kantounia) wind through high tenements; here are an attractive Venetian well-head of 1699 and the church of *Panayia Kremasti* and the *Pandokrator* both with good altar-screens.

In fine weather it is better to follow the sea road, flanked by handsome houses along the line of the old walls, and enjoying good views of the mainland. As we round the point we pass the *Archbishop's Palace*, the former *Nomarkhia* (1835), on the site of Capodistrias' birthplace, and the *Corfù Literary Society*. The point affords also a view of the citadel.

The **Royal Palace** (Pl. 3), a large classical building constructed of Malta stone, has an elegant Doric portico of 32 columns, set forward and linking two gates (of St Michael and St George) in the form of triumphal arches; beyond these the portico curves forward to lateral pavilions. Above the cornice are sculptured seven medallions with the emblems of the Ionian islands. In front stands a bronze statue, by Prosellenti, of Sir Frederic Adam, who organized the water-supply of Corfù.

The palace was designed by Col. (later General Sir George) Whitmore in 1819 to serve as treasury of the newly created Order of St Michael and St George, and as residence for the Lord High Commissioner. A legislative assembly was incorporated. In 1864 the building was handed intact to the King of the Hellenes; it served as a royal residence but fell into disrepair after 1913. After some damage by billeted refugees in the Civil War, the High Commissioner's private apartments were restored for the Greek government for use as a museum, while in 1954, at the instance of Sir Charles Peake, then British ambassador in Athens, the state rooms were restored as a memorial to the British connection with Corfù.

The State Rooms (no adm. at present) comprise the *Throne Room*, meeting-place of the Ionian senate, with the original throne and full-length portraits of High Commissioners; the *Rotunda*, or ballroom, with ceiling motif of the badge of the Order and the original floor; and the *Dining Room*. One wing houses a collection of Chinese and Japanese porcelain and bronzes, presented by Greg. Manos, a former Greek ambassador in the Far East, while in another room are floor mosaics from the Christian Basilica (comp. below); and Ikons by Hieremias Palladhes (16C), Yeoryios Kortezas, Emmanuel Tzanes, and Mikhail Dhamaskinos.

The ***Esplanade** (Pl. 3, 7), or *Spianada*, a huge open space separating the citadel from the town, served the Venetians as parade and exercise ground. It is divided by a central avenue. The N. half of the Esplanade, known as the Plateia, in front of the Palace, forms the 'field' on which in July are played the traditional cricket matches between two local clubs and visiting teams from Britain and Malta. Its former gravel

Custom House STRATIGOU
Paxos Caique Berth

Neon Frourion

St Fran

XENOFONTOS STRATIGOU

h

ABRAMIOU

ZA

Mandouki

EULISSARIOU
SOLOMOU

Jewish
Quarter

Lofos Avrami
(Mt Abraham)

M. Platitera

POLICHRONI KONSTANTA

ARAMIOU
PLAT
(YEORYIOU-THEOTOKI)

THETOKI

YEORYIOU
LEOF.

d
MEG

SAT

MARGARITI

Hospital

DIMOULITSA

IMG. DOUKISSIS MARIAS

English
Cemetery

KOLOKOTRONI

Tomb
Menek

Prison

Garitsa

ALKIN

OATH

MARASLI

Airport

VLACHERNON

Inset map:

Airport

GARITSA BAY

Alkinoos ■East Tower

Roman Baths

Wall

Gate Tower ■

Ayioi Theodoroi

Palaiopolis Ch.

Mon Repos

Hieron

KHALIKIOPOULOS LAGOON

Nausicaa Rest.

Kardaki Temple

ANALIPSIS

Barakka Rest.

Ay. Paraskevi ■

M. Kassopitras

Small Hieron of Artemis

Salvos Rest.

Tourist Pav.

Xenia Hotel

KANONI

Foot causeway

Boat to PONDIKONISI

PERAMA

Airport

500 yds
500 metres

4

AGLIA
IOU **N.T.O**

Archbishop's
Palace —— AKRA AY. NIKOLAOS

Nomarkhía

Corfu Club   Baths

Cathedral   Old Palace

Ay.
Spiridon IOU SPIRIDONOS   Panayía Mandrakína

Ionian Bank   Mandraki

Ay. Panayía
Ioannis

khíon IOU GAREOS   **Spianádha**

RC Cath.   DOUSMANI
of Greece   Schulenburg   **Palaíon Froúrion**
        Statue

Law
Courts PARCHOU
ruins

ament   MOUSTOXIDOU   St George

       Maitland Rotunda

Brit. Vice   Restaurant
Con.
(Ionian Academy)   Nautical Club

AKADIMIAS

8

Museum

VASSILEOS KONSTANTINOU

ouglas Obelisk

11   **12**

GARITSA BAY

15   **16**

VASSILEOS
KONSTANTINOU

ALKIVIADOU DARI

Anemómilos

↑
N

Ay. Iason & Sosipatros   for continuation see inset   Beach surface has given place to turf but a matting wicket is still used. On the w. it is bounded by the 'LISTON', an imposing arcaded row of tall houses designed during the French occupation in 1807–14 in imitation of the Rue de Rivoli; here are many popular cafés. On the grass-sown s. half of the Esplanade (the Spianada proper) rise a bandstand (*Palko*) and an elegant Ionic *Rotunda* in memory of Sir Thomas Maitland, first Lord High Commissioner (1815–23). At the s. end the former Ionian Academy (now a school) faces the Nautical Club whose 'eights' row offshore.

On the central avenue stands a *Statue of Marshal Schulenburg*, erected by the Venetians in his lifetime just after the siege of 1716. Executed by Ant. Corradini in Carrara marble, it was removed here from the citadel by the British. To the N. the glacis of the citadel is occupied by exotic gardens, containing a statue of the eccentric Phil-hellene Lord Guilford (1769–1828), founder of the Ionian Academy. Beyond on the wall stands the chapel of *Panayia Mandrakina* (1700). A bridge flanked by cannon of 1684 crosses the 16C moat, where (l.) motor-boats may be hired and (r.) the local children usually swim. The **Pálaion Froúrion** (Fortezza Vecchia), or *Citadel* (open daily, subject to some restrictions; no cameras), occupies a promontory with two heights, first heard of as '*Korypho*' in 968, which remained through the middle ages the fortified township. The heights are crowned by the 'Castel di Terra' with a semaphore and lighthouse, and the 'Castel de Mar', a Byzantine foundation, formerly the powder magazine. Explo-sions in the 18C destroyed most earlier work, but the w. bastions are substantially as built in 1558 by Savorgnani and Martinengo. Below to the s. is the former *Garrison Church* of St George, with a Doric portico, built by the British (1830). On the N. side are the buildings of the *Military Academy*, which with some ancient Venetian barracks overlook the little harbour of *Mandraki*. On the seaward point once stood a temple of Hera Akraia.

The landward fortress, reached by a curving tunnel, affords a magnificent *View, depending for its greatest effect on its gorgeous colouring. To the E. extends the long mountainous coastline of Albania and Epirus. To the w. the island rises above and beyond the town.

Leoforos Kapodistriou runs along the w. side of the Esplanade behind the Liston. From its N. end we may quickly reach the church of **Ayios Spiridon**, erected in 1589–96. The early-18C ceiling paintings by Panayotis Doxaras were tastelessly refurbished in the 19C. The marble iconostasis (1864; by the Austrian Maurs) takes the form of a complete church façade. Adm. And. Pisani's lamp, near the pulpit, dates from 1711.

Spiridon, Bp. of Cyprus, suffered during the persecution of Diocletian and was a member of the Council of Nicaea in 325. His body was brought to Corfù in 1489 and is preserved in a richly-ornamented silver *Sarcophagus* (1867; Vien-nese) to the right of the high altar. Four times a year (11 Aug; first Sun in Nov; Palm Sunday; Saturday in Holy Week) the remains are carried in solemn proces-sion round parts of the town and esplanade. The routes and rites are different and commemorate miraculous deliverances, respectively from the Turks in 1716, from plague in 1673, from plague in 1630, and from famine (? before 1553). So popular is the saint that nearly half the boys in the island are named after him.

We turn left into Od. Filarmonikis, with its animated vegetable market, and soon meet OD. NIKIFOROU THEOTOKI, the main pedestrian street since Venetian times, which runs through the town from the

Liston to the Old Port. Beyond it we cross, farther on, Od. Voulgareos, the narrow arcaded street that channels traffic from the Esplanade towards Sarokko. On the corner stands the *Dhimarkhion*, built in 1663 as a Venetian loggia; converted (1720) into the Teatro San Giacomo, it became in 1903 the town hall. A mutilated relief of 1691 in the e. façade commemorates Morosini's victories. N. C. Mantzaros (1795–1874), who here directed the opera, is best remembered as composer of the Greek national anthem. In the square, to the s., stands the elegant façade (1658) of the *Latin Cathedral* (St James), remarkably unadorned for Italian work of this period; the church, made a roofless shell in 1943, has been restored. The former Archbishop's Palace (1754; later, Law Courts), opposite, is still in ruins.

In the quarter within the ramparts farther s., the former *Ionian Parliament*, removed here from the palace in 1855, was given after 1869 to the British community as their Anglican church; bombed in the war, it was repaired in 1961 to house a small art gallery.

Leoforos Yeoryiou Theotoki runs s.w. towards the PLATEIA THEOTOKI, the centre of the modern quarter that has evolved from the former suburb of Sarokko (San Rocco). We pass on the way the site of the *Municipal Theatre* of 1902, ruined in 1944. It was the H.Q. of the Serbian army in 1915–16 and here in 1918 was proclaimed the new country of Yugoslavia. A new theatre was designed in 1963 by P. Sakellarios to replace it.

To the w. ($\frac{1}{2}$ m.) of the Plateia Theotoki in the convent church of *Platitera* (Pl. 5) are the tombs of Count John Capodistrias and of Photios Tzavellas (1774–1811), the Suliot klepht, and there are paintings by Clotzas (Last Judgment) and Poulakis (Revelation of St John).—From Sarokko Leof. Alexandhras runs down to the Bay of Garitsa.

From the Spianada Leoforos Vasileos Konstandinou skirts the Bay of Garitsa. Beyond the Corfù Palace Hotel we come to the *Museum (Pl. 11; adm. 5 dr.; June–mid-Oct, daily 8–7; winter, 9–1, 3–5, mid-Mar–May, 8.30–1, 4–6, in both periods closed Sat aft, Sun & hol 10–1). Beneath the colonnade (A): Inscribed statue bases.—GROUND FLOOR HALL (B), Sculpture, mostly Roman copies of Greek originals.

FIRST FLOOR. On the *Landing* (Δ), left, huge Pithos (6C b.c.); tomb monuments from the Garitsa cemetery; vigorous lion-head spouts from the Classical temple of Mon Repos; early Doric capital, with abacus bearing an Archaic inscription; funerary stele with boustrophedon inscription in Homeric hexameters honouring Arniada, a Corcyraean general who died in battle on the Arachthos in Epirus (6C b.c.); (case 1) pottery (7–6C) from tombs.—CORRIDOR ROOM (E): left of door (case 2), Prehistoric finds from Sidari, Ermones, and Aphiona; right of door (case 3), Archaic finds from Garitsa cemetery; along the wall, arranged chronologically, finds from the Hieron at Kerousádhes, from Ródha, and from N. Epirus, as well as from Garitsa: notably Corinthian and Laconian pottery, terracotta antefixes from the Temple at Ródha (5C b.c.), and (case 8) inscribed bronze decrees appointing consuls (4C b.c.; transferred here from the National Museum in 1967); (case 9) Head of Aphrodite (c. 300 b.c.; Praxitelean school); large Protocorinthian olpe decorated with four bands of animals; bronze komast carrying a rhyton (part of a lebes; 570 b.c.).

HALL OF THE GORGON (Z). *Pediment (restored) of the Archaic Temple of Artemis (590–580 b.c.): the central Gorgon is flanked by hybrid 'panthers', the whole composition stiff, formalized, but not lacking in grandeur. Other architectonic fragments of the same temple include triglyphs and metopes, the terracotta sima and antefixes, and those in Parian marble with which they were replaced c. 520 B.C.— NORTH HALL (H). Head of a Corinthian kouros, in Naxian marble. Bronze figures of men and beasts, sculptured terracotta roof tiles, Gorgon's head, lion spout, all from a large temple (of Hera?) excavated in the grounds of Mon Repos in 1962–67. Part of a smaller pediment from Figareto with horizontal figures. Lead plate showing the profile of a frieze. Painted *Sima from a smaller building, reminiscent of the temple fragments at Thermon (p. 461). *Lion of Menekrates, probably the crowning ornament of his tomb; discovered in 1843 (though not on the tomb), its date is disputed between 625 and 550 B.C. Terracotta votive figurines from the Small Hieron of Artemis, near Kanoni. Archaic torso of the type of the Kassel Apollo; head of Menander, good copy of an original by Kephisodotos and Timarchos; head of an unknown philosopher (Roman copy of an original c. 300 B.C.).

An *Obelisk* to Sir Howard Douglas (d. 1841) stands at the seaward end of Leoforos Alexandhras, where a road leads towards a hill crowned by the prison. Here during the demolition of the Venetian fort of San Salvatore in 1843 was discovered an extensive necropolis. The huge circular *Tomb of Menekrates* (in the garden of the police station) (? 7C B.C.) was supposedly crowned by the lion in the museum. Menekrates, according to the inscription, was drowned.

The *English Cemetery*, on the N. side of the Prison, has interesting memorials both civil and military. Here are buried the dead from H.M.S. 'Saumarez' and 'Volagé' (1946).

The pleasant *Promenade, backed with gardens, skirts the suburb of *Garitsa*, or Kastrades, and curves to the left. Keeping straight on in the district called *Anemómilos*, we reach the Byzantine church of *Ayion Iásonos kai Sosipátrou*, a 12C building with bands of cufic decoration and incorporating three antique monolithic columns. SS Jason and Sosipater, according to tradition the disciples of St Paul from Tarsus and Iconium, were the first preachers of christianity in Corcyra and Sosipater was here martyred under Caligula. Two 15C tombs beneath the screen are sometimes optimistically shown as those of the saints.

Here we are within the bounds of 'Palaiópolis' or ancient Corcyra, which occupied the peninsula between the bay of Garitsa (anc. *Alkinoös*) and the lagoon of Khalikiopoulo (anc. Hyllaian Harbour). The ancient city was sacked by the Goths in the 6C and later abandoned. The later Greeks and Venetians used it as a quarry in the erection of the modern town of Corfù. A large tower, forming the S.E. extremity of the harbour of Alkinoös was excavated in 1965 beside the church of Ay. Athanasios.

About 5 min. farther on is the entrance to the royal villa of **Mon Repos** (no adm.), laid out for Sir Frederic Adam in 1824 and successively the summer residence of British Lord High Commissioners and Greek kings. Here in 1921 was born Prince Philip, Duke of Edinburgh. Opposite the gates is the gutted Palaiopolis church of *Ayia Kerkyra*, where an inscription recording its foundation by Bp. Jovian before 450 and reused elements of a Doric temple have survived successive destructions in the 11C by the Saracens, in 1537 by the Turks, and in 1940. A Venetian lion of a 17C rebuilding also survives.

The Basilica, which succeeded a semicircular building of the 2–1C (itself on

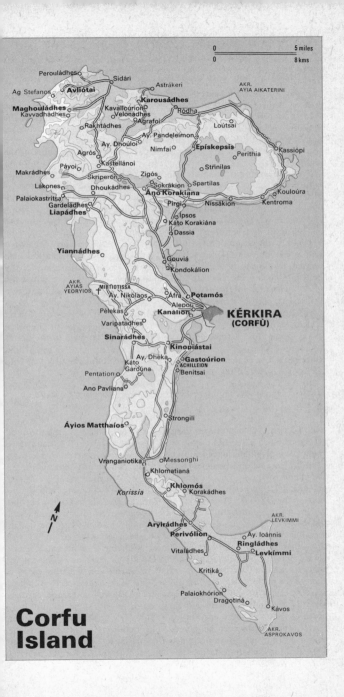

Corfu
Island

foundations of a 6C temple), had double aisles and an exo-narthex and was comparable with Ayios Dhimitrios at Salonika. After its sack by the Goths, it was reconstructed with single aisles using old materials.

A path to the right leads to further remains of the ancient lower city. Just w. of the monastery of Ayioi Theodoroi are vestiges of the Archaic *Altar* and *Temple of Artemis*, from which came the pediments in the museum. The building was peripteral with 8 columns by 17. Another hundred yards to the w. is the ruined chapel of *Nerandzika* built over a section of the ancient city *Walls*; these can be traced to the shore of the lagoon.

To ANALIPSIS AND KANONI. The road (followed by a bus) continues s. to the village of *Analipsis* (⅓ m. farther), on the site of Analipsis of the old city. Here are the meagre remains of the 6C Doric 'Kardaki' temple and of a fountain (used in Venetian times and for watering British ships). The larger Archaic temple of the 7C, which was replaced (c. 400 B.C.) by a Classical building (comp. above) on the same site, lies within the grounds of Mon Repos to the N. Passing the Corfù Hilton we come to (2½ m.) **Kanoni** (Hotels, see above), a semi-circular terrace, fashioned as a gun position by the French and called by the British 'One-gun Battery'. It commands a celebrated *View across the former entrance to the Hyllaian harbour. In the foreground are two little islets, each bearing a monastery. A causeway (reached by a steep path) leads to *Vlakhernai*, gleaming white beneath its red roofs, from which small boats cross to PONDIKONISI (*Mouse Island*) where the monastery peeps from a thick clump of cypresses (pilgrimage to the disappointing 19C chapel on 6 Aug). It was the inspiration of Arnold Boecklin's 'Isle of the Dead', and is one of two claimants to be the ship of Odysseus turned to stone by Poseidon.

The Hyllaian harbour, once guarded by moles and a chain, is now cut off by a causeway across which (on foot only) we may reach Perama (see below).

EXCURSIONS ON THE ISLAND

I. To THE ACHILLEION AND BENITSES, a round of 15 m., asphalt road. We quit Plateia Theotoki on the s.w., pass the airport (Pl. 13) and skirt the lagoon of Khalikiopoulos. At 3 m. *Vrióni* we leave on our left the road for Perama and Benitses (by which we shall return), continuing by the inland road. At 4 m. we leave, on our right, a road for *Ayioi Dhéka* (1¾ m.), starting point for the ascent in 1½ hr of the mountain of the same name (1860 ft; *View).—5¼ m. *Gastoúri* (Achillion C) just beyond which, on the summit of a wooded eminence overlooking the sea and the town of Corfù, stands the **Achilleion**, built in 1890–91 by the Italian architect Cardilo for the empress Elisabeth of Austria. After her assassination it was bought by Kaiser Wilhelm II, who spent every spring here in 1908–14. It passed to the Greek government as enemy property and in Dec 1962 was leased to Baron von Richthoven as a CASINO for roulette and chemin-de-fer. The villa, dedicated to Achilles, favourite hero of the empress, is set in an Italian landscape garden, liberally ornamented with statuary, of Homeric subjects and proportions but mediocre inspiration. The Dying Achilles, by Herter (1884), should however be noted. The mansion, a curious pastiche within of Teutonic fin-de-siècle neo-Classicism, has been restored. The ground floor includes a *Museum* of mementoes of its former owners, including fine portraits of the Emp. Elisabeth by Winterhalter and the saddle-throne from which Wilhelm II dictated despatches.

The best view is obtained from the neighbouring hill of Ayia Kiriaki. Near by is a *French Military Cemetery* (225 graves) of the First World War, when the Achilleion became an allied naval hospital.

Our road drops by steep bends to join the coastal road (comp. above) halfway between Perama and (7½ m.) **Benítses** (*Potomaki*, March–Oct DPO, B; *Avra* D), a pretty fishing village with a small beach. Amid an orange grove, on private land, are some remains of Roman villa baths with mosaic pavements. Continuation to the s., see below. The return to Corfù is made by the *Coastal road. We turn back, leave on our left the road to the Achilleion by which we came, and pass its ruined private landing-place (Kaiser's Bridge Inn).—10 m. *Pérama* (Aeolus Beach Bungalows, Akti Motel, B; Oasis, Aegli, C). About ½ m. farther on, a promontory (Restaurants) commands views of Pontikonisi (comp. above) and Mon Repos. We rejoin the road on which we started out.— 15 m. *Corfù.*

II. To PALAIOKASTRITSA, 15¼ m. (25 km.). This road also starts at Plateia Theotoki and after ½ m. divides (l. to Pelekas, see below). We pass the monastery of Platitera (comp. p. 477) and bear left, rejoining the coast some way outside the town. To the right we see *Lazaretto*, an islet offshore, formerly the quarantine station. We skirt the sheltered roadstead of Gouviá, where some French ships evaded pursuit by Nelson. The bay has large hotels, camping sites, a yacht marina, and a youth hostel.—5 m. *Kondokáli* (Kondokali Palace A) lies at its s. end. On the shore is a roofless Venetian Arsenal, or galley repair shed, of 1716.—Beyond (5½ m.) *Gouviá* (Corcyra Beach A; Galaxy C), we quit the coast road (continuation, see below) and turn inland.—9 m. Turning (signposted XOPIA) to Skriperón and, viâ the col of Ayios Pandeleimon (*View), to *Sidhári* (22 m. from Corfù), where Early Neolithic pottery was unearthed in 1965, and *Perouládhes* (24 m.) at the N.W. corner of the island. The road is tarred to Sidhári, good gravel beyond. Both places have beaches, and good sandy coves can be reached on foot between the two.

Offshore, 7 m. N.W., are three islands (*Epikoússa, Othonoí,* and *Mathráki*), with 1020 seafaring inhab., constituting the final limit of Greek sovereignty in the N.W.

13½ m. By-road for *Lákones* (1½ m.) which commands a lovely panorama of Palaiokastritsa and its surroundings; here the classical student can assess the merits of locating on the coast below the site of Homeric *Scheria*, with the twin ports of the Phaeacians and the gardens of Alkinoös. From Lakones a mule-path climbs to *Angelokastro*, a castle already existing in 1272 when it is referred to in the Neapolitan Angevin archives as Castrum Sancti Angeli. This commands an even finer view, including the citadel of Corfù. We descend to the delightful *Bay of **Palaiokastrítsa** (ΠΑΛΑΙΟΚΑΣΤΡΙΤΣΑ; *Akrotiri Beach* A; *Xenia Pavilion, Palaiokastritsa, Okeanis,* all B; tavernas, good lobsters). The road continues to the gates of the monastery, attractively sited on a promontory (300 ft; view) with terraced gardens. Though founded in 1228, it now has little that dates before the 18C.

III. To Pantokrator and Kassiopi. To (5¼ m.) Gouviá, see above. We continue by the coast road, surmount a wooded promontory (*Astir Palace* L), and descend to the shore of a beautiful bay.—At (8 m.) *Dasiá* (Chandris Corfù, 300R, Chandris Dasia, 250R, both A; Dasia C) is the huge camp of the Club Méditerranée and other camping-sites. To the left a by-road leads to the *Castello Mimbelli* (DPO, L), a hotel occupying a 19C castle in a Venetian Gothic style that once belonged to George II of the Hellenes.—9 m. **Ipsos** (ΥΨΟΣ; *Ipsos Beach* B; *Mega* C). —10 m. *Piryi* (ΠΥΡΓΙ; Emerald C). *Ayios Markhos* (¾ m. w.) has a church (Ay. Mercurios) of 1075 with contemporary frescoes in Cappadocian style, and another (Pantokrator), above the village, with good wall paintings of 1576. The road divides.

The asphalted left branch mounts to *Spartíla* (5 m. farther), whence an unpaved, steep and rocky road leads to the *Pantokrator* monastery (11½ m.), built in 1347 on Mt **Pantokrator** (2972 ft), or *Monte San Salvatore*, the highest point of the island. The summit is spoilt by a radio mast, but the *View is superb. In clear weather the coast of Italy is just visible above the horizon to the n.w. To the e. are the Acroceraunian Mountains, the castle and plain of Butrinto, with its river and two lakes, and villages extending far into the interior of Albania. To the s. the city and whole island of Corfù are stretched out like a, map with Paxoi and Levkas in the distance.

The right branch continues along the n.e. coast with views across the strait to Albania.—12 m. *Barbati* beach is seen below (r.).—14 m. *Nisáki* (Nisaki Beach A, to the e.)—23 m. **Kassiópi**, a charming fishing village, preserves its ancient name and a large Angevin *Castle*, the haunt of owls. The church may occupy the site of the Temple of Zeus visited by Nero. It was rebuilt after 1537 and enlarged in 1590 by successive Venetian admirals. Note the ikon Panayia Cassiopitra by Th. Poulakis (c. 1670) and 17C frescoes. A broad new road continues w. to (33 m.) *Ródha* (Rodha Beach, 360R, B), site of another temple (5C b.c.) explored in 1938 by John Papadimitriou.

IV. The S. of the Island. From (7½ m.) Benitses (see above) a road continues s. along the coast to (12½ m.) *Moraítika* (Miramare Beach, bungalows, L; Delfinia A, both DPO, n. of the village), with fine sands. The road turns inland near the huge Mesongi Beach hotel (510 R) to pass down the middle of the long peninsula. A path leads (r.) to *Gardíki* (2 m.) with remains of a Byzantine castle and of Upper Palaeolithic occupation.—16¾ m. *Vranganiotika*. To the right lies Lake Korission.—21¼ m. *Argirádhes* (1565 inhab.).—27½ m. *Levkímmi*, a decayed town (1750 inhab.), is the centre of a group of villages, of which (31 m.) *Kavos*, near the s.e. tip of the island, has an attractive beach.

From Corfù a road runs w. to (8 m.) *Pélekas*, an attractive cluster of colour-washed houses with a famous belvedere furnished by the Kaiser. Winding by-roads lead n. to *Glifádha* (*Grand Hotel Glyfada A; fine beach), the convent of *Myrtidiótissa*, and *Érmones* (Ermones Beach A), occupied in Neolithic and Bronze Ages; and to the summit of Ayios Yeoryios (1285 ft; view).

Between the Gouviá road and the Pélekas road, a third runs out, viâ Potamos, to The Village, a reconstruction by the Bouas family of a complete community, with church, museum of bygones, local crafts and a good restaurant. The buildings, constructed with old materials, form a living replica of the Venetian era in Corfù.

Near Ermones is the *Corfù Golf Club*.

B Paxoi

APPROACHES. From Corfù, daily ferry in 4 hrs (this leaves Paxoi in the morning, returning in the afternoon). From Patras and Parga in summer, inquiry should be made locally.

Paxos, more correctly **Paxoí** (2250 inhab.), the smallest of the seven chief Ionian Islands, is 5 m. long and only 2 m. broad. It is situated 9 m. s. of Corfù and 8 m. w. of the coast of Epirus off Parga. The island produces little else than olives, almonds, and vines. The highest point is not more than 600 ft above the sea. The principal village is an attractive cluster of houses at *Gáïo* (Paxoi Beach, DPO, **B**, ½ m. s.; San Giorgio **E**) on the E. side. The harbour is curiously formed by a small rocky islet crowned with a fort, and sheltering a little creek which can be entered at both ends. A road (5 m.; bus) links Gáïo with *Lakka*, the second little harbour at the N. end of the island.

Immediately s. of Paxoi, and separated from it by a narrow channel, is the rocky islet of ANDIPAXOI, inhabited by a few shepherds and fishermen and cultivated for garden produce and wine by the Paxians. It is visited by sportsmen in the season for shooting migratory quail, and has two good bathing-beaches.

C Levkas

Approaches. BY ROAD and chain ferry from Akarnania, see Rte 54.

LEVKÁS (ΛΕΥΚΑΣ), more often spoken of in the accusative form and pronounced *Lefkádha*, is an island separated at its N.E. corner from the mainland of Akarnania by a shallow lagoon and a narrow strait, through which runs the Levkas Ship Canal. The name of the island is derived from the white cliff at its southern tip. The island has a length of 20 m. and its breadth varies between 5 and 8 miles; with minor attendant islets, it forms a nome of 24,600 inhabitants. The centre of the island is occupied by a range of limestone mountains, culminating in Mt Elati (3550 ft). The most populous and wooded district is that opposite the mainland, where the valleys, running down to the sea, are sprinkled with small villages. The island exports oil, wine, and salt, of which a considerable quantity is obtained by evaporation in the lagoon.

The TOPOGRAPHY of the N.E. end of the island is peculiar. A long narrow sandy spit (the *Yiro*) runs out from the N. coast, sweeping E. towards the mainland which it virtually joins in an area of marshes. This spit encloses a shallow lagoon which surrounds the modern town of Levkas on three sides and extends s. between the island and the mainland. Much of the lagoon is only 2–5 ft deep, and to the s. there are islands and sandbanks.

The evidence of ancient writers suggests that in antiquity Leukas was joined to the mainland by an isthmus, probably across the narrow strait to the S.E. of the modern town and roughly opposite Ancient Leucas (comp. below). But if, as is also believed, a canal was cut by the Corinthian colonists in the 7C B.C., then Thucydides (III, 81) implies that it was silted up by 427 B.C. when the Peloponnesians "transported their ships over the Leucadian isthmus". The canal was restored, probably about the time of Augustus, and a stone bridge, of which some remains are still visible near Fort Constantine (comp. below), was built from the ancient city to Rouga, on the Akarnanian coast. In the middle ages one of the Latin princes built a fort on the Yiro, midway between Levkas and the mainland and on the landward side of the channel that breaches it. This fort, which acquired the name of FORT SANTA MAURA, from a chapel within its walls so called, gave an alternative name to the whole island. It was remodelled by the Turks, who connected it with Levkas by an aqueduct of 260 arches, serving also as a causeway, 1300 yds long, which divided the lagoon into two. The aqueduct was shattered by earthquake of 1704 but survived as a dangerous causeway till 1825 (ruins in lagoon N. of existing road causeway). The Venetians maintained the canal and the Venetian governor lived initially in the fort, while the town, then called *Amaxikhi*, that developed into modern Levkas grew up at the nearest point on the island.

During the protectorate of Russia *Fort Alexander* and *Fort Constantine*, a few hundred yds N. of it on the Akarnanian shore, were built to guard the S. approach channel. A little farther S. are the remains of a medieval fort. The Anglo-Ionian government constructed a harbour on the spit of sand flanking Fort Santa Maura and protected by a mole ending in a lighthouse. In 1905 the Greek government built the existing LEVKAS SHIP CANAL from Fort Santa Maura southwards past Forts Alexander and Constantine. Its length is 3 m. and it is kept dredged to a depth of c. 15 ft.

History. Leucas was colonized by the Corinthians in 640 B.C., about a century after Corcyra. The Leucadians had three ships at the Battle of Salamis, and they sided with Sparta in the Peloponnesian War. The island was devastated by the Corcyraeans in 436 B.C. and by the Athenians ten years later. In the war between Rome and Philip of Macedon, the Akarnanians, who had made Leucas their capital in 230 B.C., rejected the Roman alliance, and were reduced after a gallant defence vividly described by Livy (XXXIII, 17). Leucas continued to be important under the Romans, its bishop being one of the fathers at the Council of Nicaea in A.D. 325. The island passed in the 13C to Giovanni Orsini as the dowry of his wife Maria, daughter of Nikephoros Comnenus, Bp. of Epirus. The Turks seized it in 1479. Thenceforward the island was alternately Turkish and Venetian until 1718, when it was formally ceded to Venice. It suffered four bad earthquakes in the 18C, when it shared the political fortunes of the other Ionian Islands. Levkas was captured from the French in 1810 by a force under Gen. Oswald that included Richard Church, Hudson Lowe, and Kolokotronis.

Native to Levkas are the writers Aristoteles Valaoritis (1824–79), and Angelos Sikelianos (1884–1951). Here also was born, of an Irish army surgeon and a Kytheran mother, Lafcadio Hearn (1850–1904) who ended his life (as Yakumo Koizumi) a citizen of Japan.

Levkas (*Santa Mavra* C), the capital (6800 inhab.), directly approached by the causeway, was badly damaged by earthquakes in 1867 and 1948 and takes character from the light and temporary nature of its upper stories. The Cathedral (*Pantokrator*) of 1684 has the tomb of Valaoritis. A little *Museum* (ikons and antiquities) is housed below the Library (weekday morn, free). The ceiling paintings of *Ayios Minas* are by Nicolas Doxaras (d. 1761), and *Ayios Dhimitrios* has paintings attributed to Panayiotis Doxaras (d. 1729). The causeway, affording glimpses in the water (l.) of its Turkish predecessor (comp. above), and followed (r.) by the modern deep water canal, leads to the chain ferry. Beyond stands the *Castle of Santa Maura* (adm. free), erected by Orsini in 1300. It passed to Walter de Brienne in 1331 and from the Angevins to the Tocco family after 1362, but the present structure is largely due to Venetian and Turkish repairs.

A good view of the town, with the lagoon, causeway, and canal, may be had from the Convent of *Faneromeni*, high up the hill immediately W. of the town (2 m.; road signposted Tsoukalades, where it peters out).

TOUR OF THE ISLAND, 50 m. (80 km.), bus. Roads are being improved, but asphalt will be found only in stretches. Elsewhere conditions vary between indifferent and bad, but those not minding dust and a rough ride may make a round tour of this attractive and still peaceful island. We bear inland, then soon fork left for the E. coast. On a hill to the right is the site of ancient *Leucas*, where traces of walls remain amid the modern terracing. We reach the shore in sight of Forts Alexander and Constantine, with the medieval Fort of St George, on the opposing shore (comp. above).—10 m. *Nidri* (reached also by caique from Levkas) stands opposite the islet of *Madouri*, the retreat of A. Valaoritis. On the peninsula of Ayia Kiriaki, across the landlocked bay of Vlikho (5 min. by boat), is the house in which lived Wilhelm Dörpfeld (1853–1940) during his long excavations when trying to prove that Levkas, not Ithaki, is the island described as Ithaka by Homer. His tomb is 200 yds from the house. He uncovered Early Bronze Age circular tombs in the plain of Nidri.—13½ m. *Vlikhó.* The village churches in the s. part of the island have 17C and 18C frescoes.—25 m. *Vasiliki* is a pretty fishing village on a deep bay backed by a fertile plain.

A track leads s. along the rocky peninsula to *Ayios Nikolaos Niras*, at the end of a bad road down the w. coast. *Cape Dukato* (5 m.; lighthouse), the ancient *Leukatas*, the point to the s., is the precipitous white cliff (200 ft), which gives the island its name. A few fragments and sherds mark the once famous Temple of Apollo. The place is well-known from the sea by many passing travellers but rarely visited. Here Childe Harold "saw the evening star above Leucadia's far-projecting rock of woe". The rock was the scene in antiquity of leaps or dives into the sea (katapontismos), performed as a trial, a sacrifice, or a cure for un-requited love. The leap was successfully performed in the time of Strabo and of Cicero by having live birds attached to the victim (or performer) and rescue boats handy. Sappho is supposed to have leaped to her death here.

From Vasiliki we may turn N. and return by the w. side of the island (poor road), viâ (29 m.) *Ayios Pétros* and (32 m.) *Komelion.*

D Ithaka and Cephalonia

Approaches. CAR FERRY daily from Patras to Cephalonia (Sami), in c. 4 hrs, continuing (c. 1½ hr.) to Ithaka; also every other day between Sami and Corfù.—AIR service to Cephalonia from Athens in ¾ hr (airport 4 m. s. of Argostóli).

ITHAKA, in Greek **Itháki** (IΘAKH), with an area of 44 sq. m., makes up for being the second smallest of the seven islands by its fame in the Homeric epic. Seventeen miles long and 4 m. wide at its broadest part, it is divided into two unequal peninsulas by a narrow isthmus and everywhere rises in rugged hills, which reach their highest point in the N. peninsula. Ithaka is separated from Cephalonia by the Ithaka Channel, a deep strait hardly 2½ m. across at its narrowest. Its N. extremity, Cape Marmakas, is 7 m. from the s. coast of Levkas. To the N.E. lie the islets of Arkoudi and Atokos. The island's 4160 inhabitants, with 790 more on Kalamos and Kastos, near the Akarnanian coast to the N.E., are administered as an eparchy of the nome of Kefallinia.

The bold and barren outline of the mountains and cliffs is impressive. There is hardly any level ground. The coasts are indented by numerous small harbours and creeks, the λιμένες πάνορμοι of the Odyssey (XIII, 195). Exceptions to the general barrenness are seen in the cultivated declivities of the ridges and in little valleys, where olive and almond trees grow; the upper slopes are clothed with vineyards or with ever-green copses of myrtle, cypress, arbutus, mastic, oleander, and all the aromatic shrubs of the Levant. Here and there among the rocks are little green patches, gay with wild flowers.

The inhabitants, who enjoy a high reputation for hospitality, are industrious and make the best of their scanty soil, tilling their minute holdings. Ithakan wine is reputed the best in the Ionian Islands and the roast hare is noted. The Ithakans have always been first-rate mariners and the depopulation of the island is partly due to their roving disposition. English spoken on the island may have been acquired in Australia or South Africa.

History. Few architectural remains have so far been discovered to confirm the topography of the Odyssey, though Geometric tripods have come to light in circumstances very suggestive of Homer. After the heroic period the island retired into obscurity. By 1504 it was practically depopulated owing to the depredations of corsairs and to the furious wars between Turks and Christians. The Venetians resettled on it Ionians from neighbouring islands.

Vathy (BAΘΥ; *Odysseus* B; Rooms to let), like the island officially called *Itháki*, the chief town (2300 inhab.), lies in the s. peninsula at the end of a deep inlet (Bay of Vathy) opening from the *Gulf of Molo*, which almost separates the island into two halves. The town, which dates only from the 16C, is beautifully situated, extending in one narrow strip of white houses round the s. extremity of the horseshoe deep (βαθύς) from which it takes its name. Comparatively large ships can moor close to the doors of their owners. In the harbour is a chapel, once the *Lazaretto*. The majority of the town has been repaired or rebuilt since 1953. The carved wooden screen in the *Cathedral* is worth a visit. The rebuilt Museum was opened in 1965. Within, owing to the efforts of Miss Sylvia Benton who salvaged the pieces from the earthquake ruins and supervised their mending, are nearly 1000 vases (mainly 8–6C) found by the British School in two shrines at Aetos. The house of Odysseus Androutsos was ruined. An old Venetian town once stood below the cliffs high above the present town.

EXCURSIONS (cars can be hired; a guide is advisable).

I. GROTTO OF THE NYMPHS. About 1½ m. w. of Vathy is the little *Bay of Dexia*, perhaps the harbour of *Phorkys*, in which the sleeping Odysseus was deposited by the Phaeacians. At 630 ft, c. ¾ hr s. of the bay and marked by a copse of cypresses, a stalactite cave, known as *Marmarospilia*, is equated with the *Grotto of the Nymphs* (Od. XIII, 103). A narrow entrance only 6 ft high leads to a cavern 50 ft across. At the s. end there is an opening in the roof, presumably cut to carry off the smoke of the sacrificial fires, 56 ft above the floor.

II. THE S. END OF THE ISLAND. A track runs s. from Vathy through a fertile valley to a col, c. 3 m. from the town. Hence by a cliff path (l.) in 15 min. we may reach the spring of Perapigádi (220 ft). This is identified with Homer's *Fountain of Arethusa*, where the swine of Eumaios were watered. The peasants call the neighbouring cliff *Korax* (Raven rock). On the plateau of *Marathia* to the s. may have been located the pigsties of Eumaios. A path leads down in 40 min. to the Bay of *Ayios Andreas*, where Odysseus landed on his return from Pylos in order to avoid the ambush laid for him by the suitors of Penelope.

III. TO ALALKOMENAI AND PISAETOS. The road passes the Bay of Dexia (comp. above) and at 2½ m. divides. To the left we climb to the chapel of (4 m.) *Ayios Yeoryios* (425 ft). Here on the sides and summit (20 min.) of the rocky hill of Aëtós (1250 ft), which rises from the narrow isthmus connecting the two parts of the island, are situated the remains of **Alalkomenai**, known to the locals as *Kástro tou Odysséos* and wrongly identified by Schliemann in 1878 as the site of the Homeric capital. The walls, of polygonal masonry, date from c. 700 B.C. The view is magnificent. On the slopes the British School uncovered remains of an Archaic temple and a large dump of vases of Geometric and Archaic Corinthian ware. Eagles nest on the heights.—4½ m. *Pisaëtós*, a creek, has a pleasant pebble beach.

FROM VATHY TO STAVROS. The road coincides to (2½ m.) with that to *Pisaetos* (comp. above). We keep right and cross the isthmus with the Gulf of Mólo on our right. Ahead rises *Mt Nírito* (2645 ft) round which, at 7½ m., the road divides. Formerly called Anoyi, the mountain has taken the ancient name, the 'Neritos ardua saxis' of Virgil and Νήριτον εἰνοσίφυλλον of Homer, though its barren slopes (if correctly identified) must since have been greatly disforested. The circuitous route on the E. side passes the monastery of *Katharón* (1825 ft) affording a *View over the Gulf of Vathy, and the village of *Anoyí*. The better road along the w. flank above the Ithaka Channel passes above *Ayios Ioánnis*, a bathing place served by a lower by-road.—9 m. *Levkí* (525 ft). —11 m. **Stavrós** (*Homerikon* E) is the focal point (370 inhab.) of the villages in the N. part of the island, with a restaurant, an unexpectedly Americanized café, and a regular morning taxi service to Vathy (return in the aft.).

A path descends s.w. in 20 min. to the bay of *Polis*, the name of which recalls the Homeric capital. On its N.W. shore opens a Cave-sanctuary (Spilio Louizou), explored in 1930 by the British School. It yielded pottery of all periods from Mycenean to Roman, and 12 Geometric tripods (Il. XIII). A late ex-voto inscribed ΕΥΧΗΝ ΟΔΥΣΣΕΙ ('my vow to Odysseus') suggests that Odysseus was the object of a local hero-cult. About ½ m. N. of Stavros is the Kastro on the hill of **Pelikáta**. Excavations of the British School revealed the ruins of a small settlement of the early Bronze Age which flourished to Mycenean times. Apart from a few Hellenic and Hellenistic tombs, the site was not again occupied until the Venetian period. Part of a circuit wall, which ran just below the flat summit, is preserved with part of a paved road alongside. A small *Museum*, restored in 1957, contains materials from the site and from Polis, including the tripods (comp. above), also other local finds, rescued undamaged in 1953.

Beyond Pelikata we may visit the chapel of *Ayios Athanasios* on the ruins of a tower of the 6C B.C., a spot popularly called the *School of Homer*. Near *Exogi* (to the N.W.) is the spring of Melanidhro.

From Stavrós the road descends E. to *Fríkes*, to the N. of which is a camp of the Club Mediterranée, and *Kióni* (4 m.), attractively sited above the E. coast.

CEPHALONIA, in mod. Greek **Kefallinía** (ΚΕΦΑΛΛΗΝΙΑ), in Italian *Cefalonia*, with 31,800 inhab., is the largest in area of the Ionian Islands. Separated from Ithaka by the Ithaka Channel, it lies between Levkas and Zante, exactly opposite the entrance to the Gulf of Patras. Of very irregular shape the island is rugged and mountainous. A lofty ridge runs from N.W. to S.E., the foothills covering almost the whole island. The chief summit is the highest point of the Ionian Islands. Cephalonia is divided into three eparchies, which together with that of Ithaka, form the nome of Kefallinia. The population has halved in the 20C and is still falling.

The soil is fertile but not at all well watered, there being few constantly flowing streams; and the landscape lacks the luxuriance of Corfù and Zante. Characteristic features of the fine scenery are the noble forests of a local fir-tree (*abies Cephalonensis*) which give the mountain slopes their sombre look; the currant vineyards; and the olive groves. Perfumes are made from the flowers and pines, and there are excellent local wines. About one-sixth of the land belongs to the convents.

History. There were four cities in ancient Kephallenia: *Pale, Kranioi, Same,* and *Pronnoi*. Herodotus mentions that 200 citizens of Pale fought at Plataea. The Athenians, without fighting, gained over the Kephallenians at the outbreak of the Peloponnesian War. In the Roman wars in Greece the island was reduced (189 B.C.); according to Strabo, C. Antonius possessed the whole island as his private estate. It was afterwards given to the Athenians by Hadrian. In the middle ages it was taken from the Normans of Sicily by Robert Guiscard, who died on the island in 1085. Subsequent masters were the Pisans (1099); Margaritone of Brindisi (1185), succeeded by the Orsini (1194) and the Tocchi (1323); the Turks (1485); the Venetians (1500); and the French (1797). A member of the short-lived Septinsular Republic (p. 469), it was taken in 1809 by the British, who held it with the other Ionian Islands until 1864 (see p. 470). *Sir Chas. Napier*, Resident in 1822–30, built roads and did much else for the island. After his day, in 1848, a rising of the inhabitants was checked at the entrance to the town of Argostoli by a section of a British company under a sergeant. The following year another insurrection was as speedily suppressed.

In 1943 the occupying Italian force, comprising 9000 troops of the Alpine 'Acqui' Division, not only refused to cooperate with or surrender to the Germans, but for seven days fought them for possession of the island. Three thousand were forced to surrender and during three ensuing days were shot in cold blood (it is said on Hitler's personal order). Only 34 survived by shamming death. The bodies were taken in 1953 to a cemetery in Bari. Much of the island was destroyed by earthquake in 1953.

The majority of visitors (except those arriving by air) land at **Sami** (*Ionion* C), a pleasant modern anchorage (960 inhab.) on the deep bay that indents the E. coast opposite Ithaka. Here Don John of Austria anchored his fleet before Lepanto. On the two hills of Ayioi Fanentes and Palaiókastro, above the town, are some remains of ancient **Same**, the island's capital in antiquity, ringed by cyclopean and polygonal walling; a walk of c. ½ hr is necessary to reach the remains, but, from the harbour, part of the wall can be seen against the skyline. At the back of the town, c. 200 yds from the harbour, is a Roman building with a mosaic. Sami is in an area of speliological interest (comp. below).

FROM SAMI TO ARGOSTOLI, 15 m. (23 km.), asphalt road, bus. On the outskirts of the town is a turning (r.) to the N. of the island. Near Vlakháta 1½ m. along this road is (l.) the remarkable semi-underground *Lake Melissani* (adm. 8 dr., including short boat trip). An artificial tunnel leads to a small lake of clear turquoise and indigo water; a boat takes the visitor to an inner cavern.—1¼ m. Turning (l.) for Poros (15 m.; summer hotels) and the S.E. of the island.—2¼ m. The *Cave of Drogarati* (adm. 8 dr., 7–12 & 3–6), a large, electrically lit, stalagmitic cavern, lies ¼ m. right of the road.—The road now winds up through maquis to the AGRAPIDIAES PASS (1800 ft). Near the top a road leads (l.) to *Mt Ainos*, climbing first to a radar station on the N. crest, then continuing to a television station on the summit (5310 ft).—9¾ m. Col, with fine view down to Argostóli and across the gulf.

A tarred road descends (l.) to a small plain in which lies *Frangáta*. This village and *Valsamáta*, its neighbour, were built after the earthquake with funds subscribed from Britain. About 1¼ m. beyond Frangáta is the convent of *Ayios Yerásimos* (closed 1–3), with the venerated silver sarcophagus of St Gerasimos, the patron saint of the island, who founded an order of women in 1554 and was beatified in 1622.

As we descend, in the distance (l.) the walls of Ancient Kranioi (see below) can be seen following a low ridge.—13 m. Immediately below the road in a cleft is *Ayia Varvara*, a little cave chapel. We pass turnings (l.) round the Lagoon of Koutavos (see below) and (r.) to Assos and the N. end of the island (see below), then cross a causeway to reach (15 m.) *Argostóli*.

Argostóli (ΑΡΓΟΣΤΟΛΙΟΝ; *Xenia* B, good; *Aenos, Phocas, Tourist, Armonia, Dido,* all C), the capital (7060 inhab.), seat of the nomarch and of an archbishop, has been completely rebuilt since the earthquake of 1953. The *Archaeological Museum* contains a good collection of miscellaneous prehistoric finds: Middle Helladic from Kokkolata, Mycenean from Masakarata, etc, also terracotta revetments from a Doric temple at Miniá (early 6C B.C.) and a good bronze head of the 3C

A.D. The excellent *Public Library* preserves the Venetian archives and has a *Museum* of local interest. The town is delightfully situated some way up the gulf of Argostoli on an inlet so shallow that a causeway and bridge 700 yds long have been thrown across it to shorten the road in from the E. The bridge, with its many arches, was built by the British military commander in 1813. The circuit of the shallow *Lagoon of Koutavos*, thus cut off, makes a pleasant walk (3 m.) and may include a visit to the ruins of *Kranioi*, on a double hill above the modern waterworks. Parts of the ancient walls, nearly 3 m. round, are well preserved, with a section beside the road, and a Temple of Demeter has been identified by an inscribed statue base. (The site may also be reached from the Argostoli–Sami road by a track above Ayia Varvara.) On the E. side of the bay, along the Assos road to the N. of the causeway, is a *British Cemetery* (key with cottage just before, r.).

Another short excursion may be made to the tip of *Lassis* (Mediterranée, 225R, A), the peninsula on which Argostóli stands. 1½ m. N. of the town are the marine katavothrai, where the sea pours endlessly into subterranean tunnels. A team of Austrian scientists has shown that the water reappears at Melissani (comp. above). The flow was used in the 19C to drive mills. It was interrupted by the earthquake but a mill has been put into order again. On the headland of Ay. Theodori a lighthouse ('Sapper' Doric of 1820, rebuilt) commands the entire gulf. We may continue round Telegraph Hill and return (l.) to the town, or go on s. to the well-known beaches of *Makrí Yialós* and *Plati Yialós* (White Rocks, May–Oct, A), with organized facilities for bathing (7 dr.)

A longer excursion (c. 16 m.) to the S. of Argostóli, using minor but tarred roads, comprises several places of interest. We leave by the W. shore of Koutavos. —4 m. *Kastro*, a village on the site of *San Giorgio*, the medieval and Venetian capital of the island, which clustered round the 13C CASTLE OF ST GEORGE. This is perched on an isolated hill, surrounded by considerable remains of houses, churches, and of a convent. The remains of the citadel include a drawbridge, the enceinte, churches, and barracks. The town, which once had 15,000 inhab., was destroyed by an earthquake in 1636 and abandoned for Argostoli in 1757. The *View comprises the peninsula of Paliki on the w., Mt Ainos, and the island of Zante. We turn S.W.—5 m. The necropolis of *Masarakata*, excavated by Kavvadias, yielded 83 Mycenean tombs, one of the tholos type. Another necropolis at Kokkolata, nearer Argostoli, has pre-Mycenean tombs.—At (6 m.) *Metaxata* the house occupied by Lord Byron in 1823–24 was wrecked in 1953 but a plaque on the gate opposite commemorates his still flourishing ivy. Near here have been found graves of the Classical period. We may return viâ LIVATHO, the richest agricultural district of the island. At *Lakithra* (rebuilt by French subscriptions) are antique grain silos hewn from the rock. The model village of *Kourkoumelata*, built after 1953 by Andreas Vergotis, whose body lies in its cemetery, has the look of a prosperous city suburb. Returning N. towards the coast we pass *Miniá* and, by the shore, the *Airport*.

A ferry crosses the gulf several times daily in ½ hr to **Lixoúri** (ΛΕΙΞΟΥΡΙΟΝ; *Ionios Avra* D), the second town (3400 inhab.) of the island, situated on the isolated peninsula of *Paliki* (by poor road 19¼ m.). It is served also by steamer services from Patras and Zante, and occasionally from Piraeus. Here were born Elias Meniates (1669–1714), patriotic writer, and Andreas Lascaratos (1811–1901), satirist and anti-clerical pamphleteer. There is a folk-lore museum. The ancient city of *Pale* was situated close to the sea, c. 1 m. N. of Lixouri, which was probably built in great part from its ruins. Little now remains of the city which once successfully resisted Macedonia, and Lixouri itself has suffered ruin in 1867 and 1953.

The s.e. end of the island, reached by roads passing either flank of Mt Ainos, is thickly sown with hamlets, of which the principal is *Skala*. Here foundations have been found of an Archaic temple (6C B.C.). Beneath the ruined church of Ayios Athanasios has been excavated an extensive Roman villa of the 2C A.D., of which the second room was early converted to Christian use. Mosaics with metrical inscriptions naming Krateros as the artist include an apotropaic representation of Phthonos (Envy being devoured by wild beasts).—At *Markopoulo*, to the s.w., a strange (? migratory) phenomenon occurs c. 6–15 Aug when small harmless snakes invade the church.

From Argostóli to Fiskárdo, 33 m., arduous road, bus daily. From Argostoli it is 18 m. (from Sami 10 m.) to a road-junction (Sinióri) in the valley that lies between the main part of the island and Mt Kalón in the northern Peninsula of Erissos. On the w. side of this peninsula, 6 m. farther n., Assos (*Pens. Myrto* B; restaurant) occupies the most beautiful situation on the island. The ruined Venetian *Castle* (1595) stands on a peninsular headland commanding two anchorages. The cottages and vineyards within the large enclosure are attractive, while the picturesque village on the isthmus below relieves the stern grandeur of the sea and mountains. The main road runs on to Fiskárdo (*Panormos*, June–Sept, B), near the n. end of the island, probably the ancient Panormos. The place takes name from Robert Guiscard, who died here in 1085. One of the few places to suffer no earthquake damage, Fiskárdo still has houses typical of the island before the disaster. The curious *Church* (ruined) on the headland to the n.e. has twin w. towers of Norman type, but nothing is known of its history. There is also a small lighthouse, possibly Venetian. Much of the tiny village is owned by rich expatriates. The ferry from Sami to Paxos and Corfù calls once a week.

E   Zante

Approaches. Car ferry, 2–3 times daily from Killíni (Rte 40) in 1½ hr; through bus from Athens viâ Patras. Car-drivers should obtain a priority ticket for the return from the agent in Zákinthos.—By Air from Athens in 1 hr.

Zante, officially styled by its ancient name of Zakynthos (ZAKYN-ΘΟΣ), in modern transliteration *Zákinthos*, is the southernmost of the four central Ionian Islands. It lies 13 m. w. of the Peloponnesian coast, and is separated from it by the deep Channel of Zante. It is 25 m. long and 12 m. broad (177 sq. m.). The beauty and fertility of Zakynthos and the picturesque situation of its capital on the margin of its semicircular bay have been celebrated in all ages, from Theocritus onwards. Pliny and Strabo describe the richness of its woods and harvests, though Herodotus, who had visited the island, remembers only the pitch wells (IV, 195). The Homeric epithet 'woody' is no longer apposite, as its woods have been mostly replaced by currant vines and olives, the mainstays of the export trade. The potency of its wine merits mention by English travellers as early as 1517. Mandolato is a local brand of nougat.

The island abounds in gardens, and in spring and autumn is carpeted with fragrant wild flowers, whence the Venetian jingle 'Zante, fior di Levante'. In the w. of this volcanic island the land is barren and mountainous (*Mount Yíri*, 2480 ft); the fertile e. half has no height greater than *Mount Skopos* (1590 ft). The island has suffered from periodic earthquakes, one of the worst having occurred in 1820. Those of 1840 and 1893 were less severe, but that of 1953 wrecked the island.

As in Corfù and Cephalonia, there are many Roman Catholic families in Zante, chiefly of Italian origin. A large proportion of its inhabitants are descended from settlers brought by the Venetians from the Peloponnese (comp. Ithaka), from Christians who emigrated from Cyprus and Crete when those islands were conquered by the Turks, and from younger branches of noble Italian families.

History. Homer, both in the Iliad and in the Odyssey calls the island by the name it still officially bears, though Pliny (IV, 54) affirms that it was in the earliest time called *Hyrie*. An ancient tradition quoted by Strabo ascribed to the Zakynthians the foundation of Saguntum in Spain.

According to Thucydides (II, 66), Zakynthos was colonized by Achaeans from the Peloponnese. Herodotus (VI, 70) relates how Demaratos, the exiled King of Sparta, who had taken refuge in Zakynthos, was hospitably sheltered by the inhabitants from the wrath of the pursuing Lacedaemonians and escaped thence to Persia. Not long before the Peloponnesian War the island was reduced by the Athenian general Tolmides. An ally of Athens during that war, it appears to have been subsequently dependent on Sparta. Later it belonged to Philip III of Macedon (Polybius V, 4). During the second Punic War it was occupied by the Romans. It was afterwards restored to Philip, whose deputy Hierocles of Agrigentum sold it to the Achaeans. It again became Roman in 191 B.C.

The part played by Zante since has been insignificant. It was ravaged by the Vandals (in 474), Saracens, and Normans, and depopulated by the Turks (in 1479). It was Venetian from 1489 to 1797. Kolokotronis took refuge in Zante in 1805. Richard Church conducted the landing of a small British force in 1809. During the War of Independence some of the chief families of Zante and Cephalonia distinguished themselves by their efforts on behalf of the national cause, despite official discouragement. Lord Byron, whose enthusiasm for the Greek cause had assured the success of two loans floated in London, banked the first instalment of £40,000 in Zante. Frank Abney Hastings died on Zante in 1828 of tetanus as a result of a wrist wound received the week before at Aitoliko.

Zante was the birthplace of Ugo Foscolo (1778–1827), whose Ionian nationality is generally merged in his Italian reputation; of Andreas Kalvos (d. 1867), the poet, whose remains were returned to his native island in 1960 from Lincolnshire where he lived with his English wife; and of Solomos (1798–1857), the Greek national poet, who, inspired by Dante, forged Demotic Greek into a poetic idiom. Andreas Vesalius (1514–64), the founder of modern anatomy, was shipwrecked off Zante and died on the island, while returning from a pilgrimage to Jerusalem enforced on him by the Inquisition for an experiment in human dissection.

Zakynthos (*Xenia, Strada Marina*, DPO, both **B**; *Phoenix, Diana*, **C**; *Ionion* **D**; also at Argasi, 2½ m. s., see below), the capital (9300 inhab.) of the island nome, faces Loutra Killini on the Peloponnesian coast. The town, which is the seat of an archbishop, stretches along its bay for 1½ m., but extends in depth only at one point, uphill to the castle. It has been almost completely rebuilt since the earthquake of 1953 in the attractive arcaded style for which it was celebrated. A few of the old streets survive. There are two museums. In Plateia Solomos is a small *Museum of Byzantine Art* mainly retrieved from wrecked churches; the local carving of various ikonostases is notable; here also is a sculptured relief by Thorvaldsen from a monument (1820) to Maitland. This museum also contains a fine collection of postByzantine icons. The *Solomos Museum* (closed Sun aft. & Mon), in St Mark's Square a little inland, is installed above the Mausoleum of the two poets, Solomos and Kalvos. The site of Ugo Foscolo's house is now a small garden with a marble monument. Among the reconstructed churches worth a visit are *Ayios Nikólaos tou Molou* (on the quay), and the *Kyria ton Angelon*, beyond the Xenia Hotel. At the N. end of the town is a *British Cemetery*.

Towards the s. end of the town, the *Panayia Faneroméni*, before 1953 the finest church, has been rebuilt. In *Ayios Dhionisios*, farther on, are the relics of the local St Dionysios (d. 1622), the island's patron, brought back in 1716 from the Strophades, also frescoes by Cozzari, a local pupil of Tiepolo. Both churches have conspicuous campanili.

The ruins of the Venetian **Kastro** (350 ft) occupy the flat top of the hill above the town. The *View comprises the w. coast of Greece from the Mesolongi lagoon to Navarino Bay, backed by the lofty mountains of Akarnania, Aitolia, Arcadia, and Messenia. On the headland across the Channel of Zante rises Chlemoutsi (Rte 40). To the w. extend enormous currant vineyards.

Mt SKOPOS (1590 ft), so called from a rock on the top resembling a sentry, may be ascended in 2½ hrs. John Dallam, the English organ-builder, with two companions, climbed it on Easter Sunday 1599 while on the way to deliver an organ to Mehmet III as a gift from Elizabeth I. The road s.e. along the shore is followed for 2 m. whence a path mounts to the right passing the Panayia Skopiotissa. The most striking feature of the view from the top is the gloomy peak of Ainos in Kephalonia rising abruptly from the sea.—Farther s.e. the road runs very prettily viâ *Argasi* (Mimosa Beach, DPO, B; Chrissi Akti C) to (7 m.) *Vasilikó* (Restaurant with rooms) beyond which is *Cape Yeraki*, with quarries of sandstone.

EXCURSIONS FROM ZAKYNTHOS. A. TO THE NORTH, 38 m., asphalt. We round the s. of the Kastro hill, then bear N.w. through currant vineyards to (9½ m.) *Katastári*, the island's largest village (1080 inhab.). Here there is a turn to the saltpans and beach of *Alikes* (1½ m., r.; inn). The roads winds up, with views across to Cephalonia, passes below the *Moní Ayios Ioánnis Pródromos* (16–17C), with a good icon by Th. Poulakis, then turns w. across a cultivated plateau.—17½ m. Road (r.) to *Volímes* (3 m.), whence there is a 6 m. walk to Skinari lighthouse at the N. tip of the island, with another 16C monastery to visit on the way. 18½ m. Road (r.) to *Anafonítria*, where the monastery has a medieval tower and wall-paintings and the reputed cell of St Dionysos.—The road turns s. through *Maríes* and a series of upland villages often out of sight of the sea. Beyond (28¾ m.) *Ayios Nikólaos* the road winds down with views of the plain, the airport, and the Bay of Lagana.—At (34¾ m.) *Makhairádo* the church has a splendid interior with a fine carved iconostasis.—38 m. *Zákinthos*.

B. TO THE SOUTH-WEST, 12¾ m., asphalt. We leave the town by the Lithakiá road.—2 m. Turning to the Airport. We pass a succession of roads leading to *Lagana* (Zante Beach B), a beach c. 4 m. long with restaurants (crowded at summer week-ends).—At 10 m. we branch left and in ½ m. reach the shore of the Bay of Kerí, where are curious pitch springs (Pissa tou Keríou), a natural phenomenon known to Herodotus and Pliny, and used then as now for caulking ships. One may be seen at the base of the jetty.—12¾ m. *Kerí* has a 17C church and a beach with small cafés.

Over 30 m. to the s. of Zante lie the remote **Strophades**, visited only 2 or 3 times per year by caique from Zante. On the larger island stands a Byzantine fortress-monastery, once rich and populous until it succumbed to Saracen attack; it has a handful of monks, and in 1624–1716 guarded the relics of St Dionysios of Zante. The only other inhabitants keep the lighthouse on the N. point. The island is a breeding-place of shearwaters; in April wild doves on their migratory passage are decimated by hunters. The smaller island takes its name of *Artonisi* from a native species of gull.

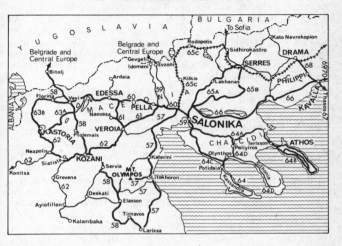

The provinces of Macedonia and Thrace, northernmost of modern Greece, are relatively recent acquisitions. Macedonia has been under Greek sovereignty since 1912, Thrace since 1920. Unknown before the First World War save to experienced Balkan travellers, and little visited as late as 1950, the region has great natural beauty and interest; it is now easily accessible, and increasingly fostering tourism, though remoter parts can still be remarkably primitive. The province of **Macedonia** (1,890,700 inhab.) is only part of the large but ill-defined area to which the name of Macedonia has been given since classical times; much of it is now within the territory of bordering states. The Greek province is shaped like a gigantic capital L, on its side, with the short arm extending N. from the Thessalian border and the long arm bounding the Aegean Sea on the N., as far as its junction with Thrace. This part of Macedonia is relatively narrow, varying in width from c. 30–60 m., with Yugoslavia and Bulgaria beyond the frontier. On the w. Macedonia marches with Albania. In the s. Mount Olympos rises on the Thessalian border and extends into both provinces. To the w. of Olympos the Kamvounian Mountains divide Macedonia from Thessaly.

Macedonia is divided politically into thirteen nomes and one autonomous region. These are: Florina; Kastoria; Grevena; Kozani; Emathia; Pella; Salonika; Pieria; Chalcidice; Kilkis; Serres; Drama; Kavalla; and the Ayion Oros (Athos). The regional capital is Salonika, second city of Greece and seat of the Minister for Northern Greece. Among the dozen most populous centres in the country are also Kavalla, Serres, and Drama. Of the great cities of ancient Macedonia that have no modern counterpart we may mention Pella, Pydna, Potidaia, Olynthos, Philippi, and Amphipolis.

Thrace, or *Western Thrace* (Dhitikí Thráki), as it is called to distinguish it from the region regained by Turkey, is the N.E. province of Greece. Extending from the Nestos to the Evros, which forms the frontier with Turkey it has a population of 329,600. The interior is largely covered by the Rhodope Mountains, which rise to 7474 ft and lie mainly in Bulgaria. The province is divided politically into the nomes of Xanthi; Rhodopi, with the chief town, Komotini; and Evros. Western Thrace was part of the Ottoman Empire before the Balkan Wars of 1912–13. The Treaty of Bucharest (1913) gave it to Bulgaria, but in 1920, after the Treaty of Neuilly (1919) it became Greek. From 1920 until the war of 1922 with Turkey, Eastern Thrace also was under Greek rule.

The original Thracians were Indo-European but not Hellenic; they came from the Carpathian region, and had fair or red hair and grey eyes. They spoke a language so far undeciphered. The whole area beyond the Strymon seems hardly to have been reached by the Bronze Age, and the ethnic and historical affinities of Thrace are with Bulgaria and Turkey rather than with Greece (comp. below).

The climate of the northern provinces is Balkan rather than Mediterranean, with extreme temperatures in summer and winter and a considerable rainfall. Their topography has few affinities with that of southern Greece. The coastline is little indented and safe anchorages are scarce. The larger rivers are perennial. The mountains are for the most part covered with dense forest or scrub. The interior is mountainous, the w. regions being traversed from N. to S. by part of the mountain backbone of Greece. The ranges are divided at intervals by valleys through which flow five important rivers. From w. to E. these are the Aliakmon (Bistritsa), the Axios (Vardar), the Strymon (Struma), marking the E. frontier of classical Macedonia, the Nestos (Mesta), marking the modern boundary between Macedonia and Thrace, and the Evros (Maritsa), dividing Western from Eastern Thrace. Mountain lakes are numerous on and near the N.W. frontiers and the formation of an additional forty by means of barrages is contemplated; the shallower marsh-lakes formed in the plains are slowly disappearing with the harnessing of the rivers. A noteworthy geographical feature of Macedonia is the Chalcidice Peninsula, with its three prongs—Cassandra, Longos, and Athos—projecting boldly into the Aegean and helping to form the Gulf of Salonika (ancient Thermaic Gulf) on one side and the Gulf of Orphani (Strymonic Gulf) on the other. Off the boundary with Thrace is the island of Thasos.

The argillaceous plains have not been cultivated to the extent that might have been expected; but this is largely due to the chequered history of the provinces. Important products are tobacco, rice, beans, sesame, and poppy seed; fruit and a wide variety of vegetables are grown in increasing quantity, and a sugar-beet industry, started in 1960, has proved highly successful. Manufactures include wine, cloth, macaroni, and soap. More important are the hydro-electric schemes in construction, and the development of Ptolemaïs as an industrial area: fertilizers are manufactured on an increased scale. Though rich in minerals (copper, chrome, gold, iron, lead, molybdenum, silver, magnesite, asbestos), Macedonian mines are not yet fully exploited. There is trade in timber, livestock, skins, furs, and wool. In Thrace sunflowers are grown for their seed oil.

During the long Middle Ages the population of Macedonia became very mixed. Slavs, chiefly Bulgarian, with a strong admixture of Bosnian and Serbian elements, and Turks were predominant inland while the coast from the Aliakmon to the Strymon including the Chalcidice trident was mainly Greek. A profound change was caused by the provisions of the Treaty of Lausanne (1923), whereby 348,000 Moslems living in Macedonia were exchanged for 538,600 Greeks from Asia Minor. As a result of the events of the Second World War and the Civil Wars the greater part of the Slav population retired or was exiled across the neighbouring frontiers. In Thrace, however, the Turkish population was not exchanged after 1922 but allowed to remain (as Greeks were allowed to remain in Constantinople). This fact gives to the province a special flavour, Turkish villages alternating with Greek; here Greeks and Turks still live together, yet separately, as they did all over the Ottoman Empire until 1922. The Moslem minority, comprises two-sevenths of the population; they enjoy full Greek citizenship and freedom of worship in their mosques. The N. provinces are still suffering depopulation by emigration, in recent years to Western Germany, Australia, and Canada.

The northern provinces are still rich in the variety of their flora and fauna, though excessive local hunting is rapidly exterminating many unique species, just as constant grazing of domestic goats is destroying many rare plants. The formation of national parks is still under consideration. Lions, which (according to Herodotus) troubled Xerxes in Macedonia, seem not to have survived into our era, and though the brown bear is protected on the Bulgarian side of the Rhodope Mountains, its appearance in Greece seems to be limited to the Pindus near the Albanian frontier. The jackal is still seen, wild cat and wild boar inhabit the Pindus, and wolves are not unknown. Roe deer and wild goat are much depleted since the war. Many of the larger European birds may be seen: vultures, hawks, and the golden eagle in the mountain regions, and storks, herons, cormorants, pelicans, and occasionally flamingoes in the coastal plains and marshes. Of the many reptiles, only two snakes are harmful: one, the adder, is common. The harmless lizards grow to a surprising size. Tortoises abound. The insect life is rich.

Communications now compare favourably with those elsewhere in Greece. The railways remain slow by reason of the terrain they traverse, but the main roads are mostly asphalted. The highway linking Yugoslavia with Turkey, which traverses the entire region, has been completely renewed. For much of its length in Greece it follows the course of the **Via Egnatia** (or Egnatia Odos), the great military road between the Adriatic and Byzantium, systematized by the Romans in the 2C B.C. to form, together with the Via Appia, a direct link from Rome viâ Brundusium with the East. Parts of it undoubtedly date from Macedonian times, at least the reign of Philip II. It had two branches starting from Apollonia (Avlona) and Dyrrachium (Durazzo), passed Lychidnus (near Lake Ochrida), Herakleia-Lynkestis (Bitolj), Edhessa, Pella, Thessalonica, Amphipolis, and Philippi. Neapolis (Kavalla) was the E. terminus until the conquest of Thrace in A.D. 46, ship being taken thence for the Troad. Later the road was extended through Thrace by Akontisma and Trajanopolis, to end at Byzantium (Istanbul). Its name may derive from its builder but not from Gnatia in Apulia. Augustus founded colonies along its route; Nero installed inns; Trajan repaired it in A.D. 107–112 (adding on the Italian side the Via Trajana as an alternative to the Via Appia). Milestones found on its route as far apart as Ocrid, Amphipolis, and Akontisma bear witness to repairs by Caracalla in 216–217. An epitaph discovered near the site of Ad Duodecimum, a staging post 12 Roman m. w. of Philippi, commemorates C. Lavus Faustus "institor tabernas". From the 4C A.D. the Via

Egnatia lost importance to the N. route viâ Sirmium, Belgrade, Naissus (Niš), Serdica (Sofia), Philippopolis (Plovdiv), and Hadrianopolis (Edirne), as Milan replaced Rome as the starting-point.—Good modern hotels are to be found in the larger towns, at recently exploited seaside resorts, and at some archaeological sites and beauty spots; elsewhere accommodation is still limited.

History. Archaeological research has suggested that in the earliest times Macedonia had affinities with the N.W., its short late-Neolithic culture (c. 2600 B.C.) stemming from the Danube. In Macedonia the Early and Middle Bronze Age (2500–1700) had Anatolian or Northern origins, and Aegean influences are felt only briefly in the Mycenean period, soon cut short by the so-called 'Lausitz Incursions' an Iron Age migration from Central Europe, of which the 'Dorian Invasion' was part. These people from the Hungarian plains swept all before their iron swords, passing onward to the S. A return wave from Thessaly founded the historical state of Macedonia about the 8C B.C.

The problem of whether Macedonians were Greeks has been endlessly debated from the time of Herodotus to the present day, usually to the accompaniment of political polemics. Some Greek tribes probably settled in the S. part of Macedonia. According to one tradition their leaders were the three sons of the Heraclid Temenos, who had fled from Argos. The youngest of the three, Perdikkas, is said to have founded the Macedonian monarchy and to have made his capital at Aigai, in Emathia. Another tradition makes an earlier Heraclid, Karanos, the founder of the dynasty and Perdikkas only the fourth of the line. It seems reasonably certain that by the 7C B.C. a kingdom was established at Aigai, from which the whole region was subdued and unified. Hence the poetic name of Emathia for the whole of Macedonia. The Greek settlers intermarried with the aborigines and spoke a dialect akin to the Doric, but with many barbarous words and forms; so much so that the Macedonians were never regarded as genuine Hellenes, though seldom actually called Barbarians. After the 6C B.C. Greek influence increasingly filtered N. from Thasos.

From written record little is known of Macedonia until the reign of Amyntas I (c. 540–505), under whom it was virtually a satrapy of Persia. His son Alexander I (d. c. 455 B.C.) was a secret philhellene despite the fact that he accompanied Xerxes on his invasion of Greece. He later extended his kingdom to the Strymon. The reign of Perdikkas II (454–414), coinciding with the period of Athenian expansion, is characterized by scheming but not very able vacillation between Athens and her enemies. Archelaus (413–399) was a patron of Greek art and literature and established cordial relations with Greece, which remained friendly until the advent of Philip II (359–336). That king, intent on universal conquest, began by seizing various Greek cities on the Macedonian coast, such as Amphipolis, Pydna, Potidaea, Methone, and Olynthos. The well-meaning but misdirected efforts of Demosthenes (comp. the Philippic and Olynthiac orations) to rouse the Athenians against the danger from Philip met with little response. The Athenians were not really aroused until Philip, invited by the Amphictyonic League (see Delphi), marched through the pass of Thermopylae on the pretext of punishing the Locrians of Amphissa. Through the influence of Demosthenes, the Athenians allied themselves with the Thebans, but the allies were defeated at Chaironeia in 338 and the independence of the Greek city states was lost. A congress held at Corinth after the victory decided on war against Persia; but, in the midst of his preparations, Philip was murdered. He was succeeded by his son Alexander the Great (336–323), who was destined to fulfil the ambition of world conquest that Philip had cherished.

On Alexander's death there was general upheaval. His regent in Macedonia, Antipater, won the Lamian War against the Greeks with the victory of Krannon. Antipater's son Cassander, who had been deprived by his father of the succession to the regency, proclaimed himself king of Macedonia in 306 and, after the battle of Ipsos (301), secured the possession of Macedonia and Greece. On his death in 297, his son Philip IV held the throne for a few months. In 294 Demetrios Poliorketes, son of Antigonus the One-Eyed, one of Alexander's generals who had become king of Asia and had been killed at Ipsos, was acknowledged king of Macedonia; but in 286 he was deserted by his own troops, who offered the throne to Pyrrhus, king of Epirus. Two years later Pyrrhus had to hand over Macedonia to Lysimachus, another of Alexander's generals, who had made himself king of Thrace in 306. In 277 Antigonus Gonatas, son of Demetrios Poliorketes, obtained the throne of Macedonia, though Pyrrhus contested it again in 273. Demetrios II (239–229), son of Antigonus Gonatas, and Antigonus Doson (229–220) tried to win the mastery over Greece. Now came the period of the three Macedonian Wars (214–205, 200–194, and 171–168), and of the last Macedonian kings. Philip V (220–179) was defeated by the Romans at Kynoskephalai in 197, and his son Perseus (178–168) at Pydna in 168. After Pydna Macedonia was divided into four republics with capitals at Thessalonica, Pella, Pelagonia (Herakleia Lynkestis), and Amphipolis. This arrangement did not last long, for in 148 Macedonia became a Roman province. In 27 B.C., as a senatorial province, Macedonia was separated from Achaia, and extended N. to the Danube, E. to the Hebros (Evros), and S. and S.W. to include Thessaly and Epirus. After the Roman subjugation of Thrace in A.D. 46, Macedonia, no longer a frontier province, recovered some of its prosperity, attracting the missionary zeal of St Paul.

The Goths invaded Macedonia in A.D. 252. In 269 Diocletian altered the province's boundaries by taking away Thessaly and Epirus. Constantine created the diocese of Macedonia, which took in Thessaly, Epirus, and Crete, the province becoming one of the first to receive the epithet 'Salutaris'. The Byzantine centuries saw incursions by Goths (378), Huns (434), Ostrogoths (478), Bulgars (500), Slavs (527), Huns again (540), and Goths again (558). In the 7C the Serbs reached the gates of Thessalonica. The 9C was marked by the invasions of Bulgars and Saracens who, at the beginning of the 10C, seized Thessalonica. In 1014 Macedonia came under the rule of Byzantium. In 1185 William of Sicily sacked Thessalonica. After the capture of Constantinople in 1204 by the army of the Fourth Crusade, the Latin kingdom of Thessalonica was given to Boniface of Montferrat; but his successor was expelled in 1223 by Theodore Angelus, despot of Epirus, who called himself Emperor of Thessalonica. He was defeated in 1230 by the Bulgarian Tsar Ivan Asen II, who incorporated N. and central Macedonia into the second Bulgarian or Bulgar-Vlach Empire, the remainder being absorbed in the Nicaean (Byzantine) Empire in 1246. On the extinction of the direct line of the house of Asen, the power of Bulgaria declined, and N.W. Macedonia again came under the despotate of Epirus. In the 14C Macedonia fell under the domination of the Serbs. Stefan Dušan (1331–55) conquered all Macedonia except Thessalonica, as well as Thessaly, Epirus, and part of Bulgaria. In 1364 Murad I, sultan of Turkey, routed the united Serbs, Hungarians, and Vlachs on the banks of the Maritsa and by 1375 the whole of the Balkan peninsula, with Macedonia, came under Turkish domination. The invasion of Timur (Tamerlane) reversed the trend of expansion. After the battle of Ankara in 1402, in which the Turks under Bayezid I were totally defeated, Timur reinstated the various principalities that had been suppressed, including the Christian ones in E. Europe. Under Murad II the Turks defeated the Christians at Varna in 1444 and established Ottoman domination in E. Europe. This survived till the Balkan Wars of 1912–13.

In 1900–08 the so-called 'Macedonian Struggle' took place, when armed bands (Greek 'andartes', Bulgarian 'comitajis', and Serb 'chetniks') contended for supremacy in various mountain regions. Greek Macedonia became a reality in 1912 (comp. below). The Treaty of Bucharest (1913) fixed the Mesta as the frontier with Bulgaria, which retained its seaboard on the Aegean until the end of the First World War. The treaties of St Germain (1919), of Neuilly (1919), and of Sèvres (1920) attempted to solve the problem of Macedonia. For some years until the war with Turkey in 1922 the whole of Thrace passed to Greece. The Treaty of Lausanne (1923) gave back Eastern Thrace to Turkey. In the Second World War Macedonia served in 1940 as the base for the successful Greek campaign against the Italians, but fell within a week to the German onslaught in 1941 (comp. below).

Campaigns. BALKAN WARS. In October 1912 the Balkan League (Bulgaria, Serbia, and Greece) rose against the Turks.

By the end of the month the Bulgarians had defeated the main Ottoman armies in Thrace, and the Serbs were in possession of the whole of old Serbia and most of Albania. The Greeks, under Crown Prince Constantine, advanced through the most difficult passes of Olympus, captured Elassona, defeated Hassim Tahsim Pasha at Servidje (Servia), and occupied Verria and Vodena (Edhessa), while the Turks retreated on Salonika and Monastir (Bitolj). On 1 Nov the Greeks won a victory at Yenidje Vardar (Yiannitsa); on 8 Nov (26 Oct O.S.; St Demetrius' Day) George I led his troops into Salonika. In Epirus a small column had captured Preveza and was besieging Ioannina.

An armistice was signed, but the Congress of London, meeting on 16 Dec, had no result except to show that the Bulgarians had not abated their claims to Macedonia and were intriguing against Serbia. On 6 March Ioannina surrendered; three weeks later the Bulgarians, assisted by the Serbs, took Adrianople. Meanwhile, the Greek Navy, under Adm. Koundouriotis, controlled the Aegean; Lesbos, Chios, and Samos were captured.

The First Balkan War ended with the Treaty of London (30 May 1913), and all territory West of the line Enos–Midia was ceded to the Balkan League as a whole. A Graeco-Serb treaty was ratified on 1 June after the Bulgarians had tried and failed to expel the Greek forces from the Mount Pangaion district to the east of the Struma mouth. Towards the end of June the Greeks were attacked by the 2nd Bulgarian Army under Gen. Ivanof on a wide front and lost Gevgeli. On 2 July the Greeks, their infantry attacking with dash and supported by mountain guns, recaptured the town; next day Lachanas was captured by bayonet assault. On 6 July they took the store-town of Doiran. Retreating to Strumnitsa and the Rupel Pass, the Bulgarians committed atrocities at Serres and Sidirokastron (Demirhisar). By the end of the month the Greeks had reached the Kresne Pass, the Rumanians were threatening Sofia and the Bulgarians had lost.

In the spring of 1916, during the FIRST WORLD WAR, the Bulgarians invaded Macedonia. In the previous autumn the Allies had landed an expeditionary force at Salonika, where Venizelos established a provisional Government. Until final victory in 1918 the inadequately equipped Allies (British, French, and Greek) could do no more than hold in check Austrians, Germans, and Bulgars on an almost static line along the N. frontier and the Struma. The main battle areas were in the Monastir Gap and round Doiran, but malaria and dysentery accounted for a great part of the casualties.

SECOND WORLD WAR. The Axis attack on Greece followed immediately upon the indefinite postponement of the invasion of Britain in favour of a drive for the Middle East. Mussolini, acting prematurely, and without Hitler's knowledge, delivered on 28 Oct 1940, an ultimatum to Gen. Metaxás demanding the passage of Italian forces, which provoked a terse ˚Οχι in reply. After the Italian attack, Greek forces soon moved forward from W. Macedonia into Albania, inflicting great losses on the Italians. British air units moved to Greece, but Greece, afraid of provoking German intervention, declined the aid of British land forces until February when it was obvious that such intervention was not only inevitable but imminent. The wavering attitude of Yugoslavia and the possible effects, both on Greek morale and Turkish participation, of withdrawing from E. Macedonia, had prevented any political decision being reached on which line should be defended. The available British force, commanded by Gen. Sir Maitland Wilson, consisted of the 1st British Armoured Brigade Group (Brig. H. V. S. Charrington), the New Zealand Division (Maj.-Gen. Sir Bernard Freyberg, V.C.), and the 6th Australian Division (Maj.-Gen. Sir Iven Mackey). The Australians were still arriving when the Germans invaded.

At 5.45 on the Sun morning of 6 April German forces in overwhelming strength were launched simultaneously against Yugoslavia and Greece. On 7 April, the Bulgarian Army occupied Alexandroupolis and Komotini, and Von List's 12th Army crossed the frontier at Doiran and Gevgeli. The Greek hope of holding the Metaxás Line in E. Macedonia was at once shown to be militarily impossible, but since the commanders in Albania could not be persuaded to give up their gains and retreat before the Italians, it was decided, against the judgement of the British commander, to try and hold the 'Aliakmon Line' (Kaimaktsalan–Vermion–Olympos). Salonika fell on the morning of 9 April and a small British armoured force held the Vevi pass for three days while Greek troops withdrew from northern frontier positions. The New Zealand brigades dug in athwart the Servia pass, the Petra pass, and the gap between Olympos and the sea. The collapse of Yugoslavia and a swift enemy advance in the N.W. from Kastoria to Grevena, driving towards the Meteora, cut off the Greek army in Albania and threatened to turn the Aliakmon Line even before preparations were complete. The 9th Panzer Div. reached the Aliakmon on 14 April and a fighting withdrawal and disengagement was ordered to Thermopylae. The Servia pass was held until 17 April when German troops were already penetrating the Vale of Tempe; rearguard actions were then fought in Tempe and at Elasson, and the New Zealand forces were extricated through the Larissa bottleneck by 19 April. In Athens Greek surrender and British evacuation were already under consideration and the campaign turned into a race for the southern beaches.

The Civil Wars of 1946–49 were waged with ideological intensity from beyond the Greek frontiers, the aim being Communist domination rather than acquisition of territory. Many civilians, particularly children, were kidnapped from frontier areas for indoctrination in Albania or Yugoslav Macedonia and though the bitterness has slowly healed and military control on movement has now been relaxed, depopulation is still characteristic of the N.W. frontier region.

57 FROM (ATHENS) LARISSA TO SALONIKA. MT OLYMPOS

ROAD, 96 m. (154 km.). This forms part of the main highway from Athens to Salonika (c. 313 m.), which by-passes Larissa to the E.; on the section through the Vale of Tempe a toll (car 40 dr.) is levied.—16¾ m. *Vale of Tempe.*—31½ m. *Pandeleimon.*—42 m. Turning to *Litókhoron* (3 m.) for the ascent of Mt Olympos.—54 m. **Katerini.**—74½ m. *Aiyínion.*—115 m. **Salonika.**—BUSES several times daily; through service from Athens by Pullman in 9 hrs.

RAILWAY, 106 m. (171 km.), the main State Rly. line from Athens (317 m.), 5 trains daily in c. 2½ hrs (fast through trains from Athens in c. 8 hrs; sleeping-cars on night trains).—*Plati* (83 m. from Larissa), where the line is a few miles N. of the road, is the junction for Veroia, etc. (Rte 61).

AIR SERVICE (Olympic Airways) from Athens to Salonika 6–8 times daily in 50 min. The route passes over Parnes and across the Euripos near Chalkis. Mt Dhirfis is seen on the right. As the aircraft passes over the strait separating Skiathos and Skopelos, the striking coastline of Magnesia and the Gulf of Volos are well seen. During the flight up the Thermaic Gulf, Pilion, Ossa, and Olympos appear successively to the left, while reaching out on the right are the three prongs of Chalkidiki, Kassandra in the foreground, Sithonia behind, and in the far distance Athos, the Holy Mountain.

Larissa, see Rte 48. We quit the town by the museum and join the by-pass. The road passes the first of the refineries for the sugar industry started in 1960, and runs parallel to the railway. Ahead (l.) we see the Olympos range, while the great cone of Ossa rises to the right above brown stony foothills (comp. Rte 48). We cross a flat cultivated plain, the bed of the classical *Nessonis,* one of the lakes left by the recession of the flood that once covered the Thessalian plain.—8¾ m. *Girtónis Station* (Restaurant).—17¾ m. Turning to *Ambelakia* (r.; 2 m.).

Ambelakia, beautifully sited amid oaks on Mt Kissavos, derives name from its vineyards. It was already known for its cotton and silk in the 17C, and became in 1780 the centre of a 'joint partnership' of spinners and dyers of red yarn, claimed as the world's first working 'co-operative', with branch offices as far away as London. The town was ruined in 1811 by the bravos of Ali Pasha, but the *Mansion of George Schwarz* (its president) and that of his brother, Demetrios, attest their prosperity; their rococo painted interiors have been splendidly restored. The village is now a summer resort (1968 ft).

At (18 m.) *Témbi,* formerly Baba, starts the toll road; the railway is seen across the river.

The **Vale of Tempe,* in Greek just *Témbi* (Τὰ Τέμπη), is a glen of surpassing beauty between Olympos and Ossa through which the Peneios, Thessaly's principal river, flows to the sea. The glen, called *Lykostoma* ('Wolf's Mouth') in the Middle Ages, is 6 m. long and only 30–55 yds wide; it is the most practicable way out of the Thessalian plain to the N.E. It was formed in the Quaternary Epoch by a convulsion that rent the mountains and, by providing the Larissan Lake with an outlet to the sea, allowed the Thessalian plain to emerge. The Thessalians, according to Herodotus (VII, 129), attributed the convulsion to Poseidon, the god of storms and earthquakes. This violent topographical distortion finds an echo in the legends of the War of the Gods and Giants (Gigantomachia).

The attraction of the glen is one of contrast. The stern, almost vertical cliffs, scarred by winter torrents and only partly clothed with ivy and other climbing plants, are offset by the peaceful river scenery below. The swift and turbid Peneios is overshadowed on either side by plane-trees and willows. The banks are fringed with lentisk, *agnus castus*, terebinth, and laurel.

Tempe, whose praises are sung by innumerable Roman and other poets, was a centre of the worship of Apollo. The god, having killed the serpent Python, purified himself in the waters of the Peneios, and cut a branch of laurel which he replanted by the Castalian Fountain at Delphi. In memory of this event, every eight years a mission of well-born youths was sent from Delphi to Tempe, to bring back cuttings of the sacred laurel. The Vale of Tempe was one of the gateways to the interior of Greece, but it could be turned by a narrow track to the N. viâ the Forest of Kallipeuke and the town of Gonnoi and by passes through the Olympos massif. In 480 B.C. a force of 10,000 Greeks occupied Tempe, to deny its passage to the Persians. However, hearing that Xerxes was already turning their position by the inland roads, they withdrew to Thermopylae, abandoning Thessaly to the invader. Herodotus (VII, 128, 173) tells us that the Persians came over the shoulder of Olympos and down on Gonnoi (as did the Germans in 1941). In 168 B.C. the Romans entered Thessaly by way of Gonnoi, but they established a military post in the Vale of Tempe.

Beyond the *Spring of Venus* we reach the Wolf's Mouth (see above). On a rocky hillock (r.) stand the ruins of the medieval *Kastro tis Oraias* (Castle 'of Oria', really 'of the beautiful maiden'), linked with a local legend and popular song; at the foot of the rock are the remains of an ancient fortress. At *Ayia Paraskevi* a graceful suspension bridge (for foot passengers only) crosses the river; it leads to a chapel and grotto on the opposite bank. The sea appears ahead.—22¾ m. The *Spring of Daphne* provides a cool and refreshing retreat.

A by-road continues on the right bank to *Omólion* (2 m.), which in ancient times had a Temple of Poseidon Petraios; a tomb near the river produced an exquisite hoard of Classical jewellery in 1961 (now in Larissa museum). Protogeometric tombs have yielded iron, bronze, and gold objects.—8 m. *Stómion* (Inn), formerly Tsagezi, is a peaceful seaside resort, with thermal springs, below the steepest face of Ossa.

We cross the river and the railway (23 m. *Station* for *Pirgetós*) and, with the mouths of the Pinios (fish hatcheries) on the right, thread the last low foothills of Kato Olympos. *Aigáni*, a post on the Turkish frontier of 1881–1912, can be seen on the hills c. 2 m. left. Soon afterwards we pass the *Spring of Diana*.—32½ m. (52 km.) **Pandeleímon** (*Maxim B*; *Artemis* C; others summer only), on the site of the ancient *Herakleia Platamona*, guards the narrows between Kato Olympos and the sea. Here is the splendid **CASTLE OF PLATAMÓNA*, built by Crusaders in 1204–22 to command the entrance to the Thermaic Gulf. It was taken by Theodore Angelos in 1218 when the Lombard followers of Roland Piche fell from the walls 'like birds from their nest'. Near by is a sandy beach, with two camp-sites. The *Spring of the Muses* is (l.) between the Xenia and the castle. Northwards is spreading coastal holiday development. We pass out of the toll road.—At (36 m.) *Skála Leptokariás* (Olympian Bay B) is the beginning of a bad road (comp. below) through the Olympos massif viâ *Leptokariá* (Galaxy C) to Elasson. To the left, row upon row of peaks rise to the crest of Olympos, usually snow-capped or shrouded in cloud.—39½ m. *Pláka Litokhórou* (Leto; Olympios Zeus, summer only, both B).—43¾ m. *Limín Litokhórou*, with the railway station of Litókhoron; the town (comp. below) is seen to the left.

The coastal plain broadens into the strip known to the ancients as PIERIA, birthplace of the Muses. Just beyond the station we cross the tiny Baphyras, a stream made navigable by the Macedonians to serve

Dion, the site of which lies 4 m. N.W. by a badly signposted and barely passable road. A better approach is from Katerini (see below).

We cross the Mavroneri, the *Aison* of Plutarch (comp. below), and skirt (54 m.) **Katerini** (*Olympion*; *Park*, by the highway, both **C**), a market town of 28,800 inhab., that commands a wonderful view of Olympos. Its *Paralia* (Alkyone, Akteion, Muse's Beach, all **C**) lies 4½ m. E. on the Thermaic Gulf.—To Elasson, see below.

Katerini is the best starting point for **Ancient Dion**. An asphalt road (10 m.; bus) runs S. to the modern village (formerly *Malathriá*). The site, a little to the s.w., is entered from the South Gate (during excavations the phylax conducts).

Dion rose to prominence under Archelaus (413–399), who built a temple to Zeus, a stadium for festival games, a theatre (to which Euripides contributed plays), and an enceinte wall. In Macedonian times the place was a troop concentration centre rather than a city. Here Philip II celebrated his triumph after the capture of Olynthos, and here Alexander sacrificed before invading Persia. With Dodona, the city was laid waste by the Aitolians in 220 B.C., Philip V taking revenge in 218 by destroying Thermon. Dion was quickly rebuilt, for Philip made it his base before Kynoskephalai as did Perseus his before the Third Macedonian War. After the Battle of Pydna (comp. below) the Romans established here the *Colonia Julia Diensis*. The town had a bishop in A.D. 346. It was sacked by Alaric and seems not to have recovered. Explorations undertaken in 1928–31 by Salonika University were renewed in 1962. The line of the walls has been traced but the remains appear to be later than the time of Archelaus. The Roman town measured c. 600 yds by 500.

The principal N.–S. **Street*, 14–17 ft wide, is exposed for its entire length, with side streets and part of the main E.–W. cross street, all with elaborate drainage systems. The s. end, of late Imperial date, is bordered with houses and baths having tesselated floors. A frieze of alternating corselets and shields marks an important monument. To the w. the *City Wall* with its towers is uncovered.

To the s. of the main site, but not usually open, the *Odeion* has been cleared and two superposed Christian *Basilicas* uncovered, the earlier having well-preserved mosaic floors. Outside the s.w. gate Macedonian 'Temple' tombs have been excavated. In the village a *Museum* (adm. free; standard hours) displays sculpture from the site.

At (62 m., 99 km.) *Kítros* (1980 inhab.; ½ m. w. of the road), a custom recalling Aristophanes survives, when, on 8 Jan (St Domenica), the women take control of the village, ejecting the men from the cafés; similar events occur at *Kolindrós* (3000 inhab.; c. 10 m. N.W.). At *Alikí*, 2 m. E. of Kítros, are the largest salt works in Greece. They surround the *Touzla Marsh* which corresponds to the ancient harbour of **Pydna**. Though some terraces have been observed and pottery found, there is nothing here to see but a pleasant beach (tavernas and rooms). Hammond places the Greek city on the kastro of Makriyialos much farther N., and Macedonian and Roman Pydna, transferred by Archelaus away from the sea, at Alonia, N.W. of Kitros. This was the place which gave name to the famous battle of 168 B.C.

When Lucius Aemilius Paullus took command of the Roman forces in 168, Perseus, the last king of Macedon, held an impregnable position S.E. of Dion. By a feigned attempt to turn the Macedonian position, the Roman general induced Perseus to retire to a point 7 m. S. of Pydna, near the Aison (comp. above), where the decisive *Battle of Pydna* took place between 38,000 Romans and 43,000 Macedonians. At first the Macedonian spearmen (in the centre) carried all before them;

but their close order was broken in their headlong drive over uneven ground. Then the Roman legions counter-attacked the Macedonian centre, while the two Roman wings threw themselves upon the Macedonian right wing. The Romans finally broke through the formidable phalanx. Some 20,000 Macedonians were killed and 11,000 captured; their king, who fled to Samothrace, was taken later and ended his life as a state-prisoner in Italy.

69 m. *Palaión Elevtherokhórion* (Arion **C**, on the shore, r.). Hereabouts was located ancient *Methone*, founded, according to Plutarch, from Eretria. The town was used on several occasions by the Athenians as a base against the Macedonians, and Philip II lost an eye besieging it.

The old road (19 m. longer) continues via *Aiyinion* (4500 inhab.) to join the Verria road at *Alexandreia*, see Rte 61.

The main highway branches right across the Pedhias Kampanias, crossing the Aliakmon and the Axios near their mouths, and joins the Verria road in the outskirts of (96 m.) **Salonika.**

Mt Olympos

OLYMPOS ("ΟΛΥΜΠΟΣ; in modern Greek *Ólimbos*), the highest mountain range in Greece, the traditional abode of the Gods, rises on the N.E. limit of Thessaly and falls away into Macedonia. The massif soars to 9570 ft and wears a crown of snow from early-Autumn to the end of April. On the seaward E. side is a line of vast precipices cleft by tree-filled ravines. To the s. the main range is separated by a depression from *Káto Ólimbos*, or LOW OLYMPOS, a region of wooded hills rising to 5205 ft in *Metamórfosis*. It is easy of access from *Kariá* on the Elasson–Leptokariá road (see below). To the N. rises HIGH OLYMPOS, with the highest peaks grouped round the centre of the massif in the form of an amphitheatre enclosing the deep Mavrolongos valley. Oak, chestnut, beech, and plane trees flourish at the lower elevations; higher up pine forests reach almost to the snow line. The principal summits are in three groups. To the s. are *Serai* (8870 ft), *Kaloyeros* (8860 ft), and *Palaiomanastri* (9235 ft). The central group comprises *Skolión* (9550 ft), from which fine precipices fall into the Tigania glen; *Skala* (9400 ft); *Mytikas* ('the needle'), highest of all (9570 ft; the Pantheon), more broken; and *Stefani*, the 'Throne of Zeus' (9545 ft), a majestic curve of limestone arête. Then, separated from the central group by the Col of Porta (8800 ft) come *Toumba* (9135 ft) and *Profitis Ilias* (9145 ft), an easy shale-covered peak on the top of which is a tiny chapel, which used to be visited once a year by monks; hence an arête called *Petróstrounga* descends towards the valley of the Varkos.

This range is the most famous with the name of Olympos, though there are mountains of that name in Euboea, Elis, Laconia, and Arcadia; also in Cyprus and in Asia Minor. In Greek mythology Olympos was the residence of the gods, whose life of pleasure there was imagined in human terms unencumbered with moral philosophy. Hesiod incorrectly reports Olympos as "never struck by the wind or touched by snow". Lions seem to have survived in the country about Olympos down to Classical times (Herod. VII, 126; Paus. VI, 5, 5). Evidence of a Sanctuary of Zeus of the Hellenistic period involving animal sacrifices was found in 1965.

The sultan Mehmet IV is said to have attempted the highest peak without success in 1669, and in 1780 a French naval officer, G. S. Sonnini, reached Ayios Dhionisios. Leake in 1806 and Pouqueville in 1810 toured the lower area. After 1821 it became a notorious haunt of nationalist bands and bandits. Heinrich Barth, in the wake of the medieval church builders, climbed Profitis Ilias in

1862 and in 1904 Tvigic, the Serbian geographer, did some geological work on the slopes, but the difficulty of the approach and the insecurity of the region deterred all but the keenest. As late as 1910 Edward Richter, on his third attempt at the climb, was captured and held to ransom after his escorting gendarmes had been killed. In 1912 the territory passed from Turkey to Greece and the following year two philhellene Swiss artists, Daniel Baud-Bovy and Frederic Boissonas, with Chr. Kakalos, a local guide, climbed the Throne of Zeus and Mytikas. In 1921 an official mission of two Swiss topographers, Marcel Kurz and Hans Bickel completed the exploration of the range and mapped it. A large international party explored the summits in 1927, and since the Greek Alpine Club established a shelter in 1931 the mountain has been explored by increasing numbers (508 in 1959). Col. John Hunt here held mountain training courses in 1945, and since 1961 the Greek Army has had a ski school on the slopes.

A. By Car from Larissa. From Larissa to (38 m.) *Elasson* and (43½ m.) *Mikró Elevtherokhórion*, see Rte 58. Here we turn right and shortly, at (47 m.) *Kallithéa*, the road divides; the left branch passes through the picturesque *Stená Pétras* between Olympos and Pieria to Katerini (81¼ m.). We take the right branch. Beyond (52 m.) *Olimbiáda* a military road (11 m. long) branches left through *Sparmos* to *Refuge B* (Vrissopoulos) below the Army Ski-Training Centre, which was moved here from Mt Vermion in 1961. The old road continues E. under High Olympos to (61½ m.) *Kariá*. Low Olympos rises to the right. The road passes below (72 m.) *Leptokariá* to join the Salonika highway at (74½ m.) *Skala Leptokariás* (comp. above), whence it is a further 36 m. to *Larissa*.

B. The Ascent from Litokhoron. **Litókhoron** (*Myrto* D; YH), a pleasant well-watered town of 5600 inhab. connected with its railway station (5 m.) by bus, stands nearly 1000 ft up on the E. flank of Olympos. Its people have long had a reputation as mariners and were prominent in the abortive uprising of 1878. The place developed in the 1920s as a health resort for the tubercular. Notwithstanding the provision of a military road up Olympos from the W. (comp. above), Litokhoron is the principal centre for climbing in the Olympos massif. Here from the office of the Greek Alpine Club (E.O.Σ.) information may be obtained, guides hired, and the keys of refuges borrowed. There are fixed charges for guides climbing, mules, and food.

The ascent (arduous rather than difficult for mountaineers) is made in two days, the night being spent at a refuge. July and August are the best months.

Route 1 (red marks). The dusty road (practicable for vehicles to the springs; 11 m.; see below) ascends N.W. passing the lower monastery of Ayios Dhionisios (the '*Metokhi*') and climbs steadily up the slopes of *Stavrós* (3115 ft) where there is abundant water.—1½ hr. Hut (refuge D) of the Alpine Club of Thessaloniki (3281 ft). We wind along the N. side of the *Mavrolongos Valley* shaded with pines, in which flows the Enippéas.—2½ hrs. We see below us the ruined Monastery of *Ayios Dhionisios* a building of c. 1500 visited by Sonnini in 1780, blown up by the Turks in 1828, but rebuilt before 1856. It was destroyed in 1943 by the Germans, who believed it to be used by guerrillas. The ruins may be reached in 20 min. by a path across a declivity, but we continue almost level on the main path (following the red marks).—At (3½ hrs) *Priónia* (c. 3300 ft), a primitive settlement of goat-herds with lean-to shelters, the springs of the Enippeas afford the last running water.

From this point the route rises fairly steeply amid thick beech woods in a region rich in botanic interest. We climb almost to the head of the Mavrolongos to reach (7 hrs) the **Katafiyio Spilios Agapitos** (6890 ft; 60 beds; rain-water reservoir), the A refuge of the Greek Alpine Club, on a spur facing E. towards the sea. The refuge can now be reached also from the Ski School of the Greek Army (comp. above). From the refuge the climb to one or other summit takes c. 2½ hrs;

the vegetation gives out after c. 1 hr. The mountain is usually shrouded in cloud at the mid-day hours in hot weather. The red marks continue to the summit of Mytikas.

ROUTE 2 (blue marks) diverges right a little beyond the Monastery.—5 hrs *Petróstrounga* (7395 ft). Here are a spring (Strangos) and, lower down, a cave. —8 hrs *Profítis Ilías*, with the King Paul Refuge (C; 18 beds) and a chapel. The traverse of the high summits from Profitis Ilias should be undertaken only by experienced mountaineers.

An alternative starting point for ascents is *Kokkinopló*, a village (site of ancient *Pythion*), 11 m. from Elasson on the Katerini road (comp. above).

58   FROM LARISSA TO KOZANI AND BITOLJ

ROAD, 154 m. (246 km.), one of the two international routes between Greece and Yugoslavia. We leave Larissa by the Pinios bridge.—10½ m. **Tírnavos**. Thence up the Titaríssios basin.—38 m. **Elassón**.—73m. **Servia**. We cross the Aliakmon.— 90½ m. **Kozáni** (turn right in the town).—108½ m. *Ptolemaΐs*.—129 m. *Vevi*.— 145 m. **Niki** (frontier post).—154 m. **Bitolj** (Monastir).—BUSES to *Elassón*, 10–12 times daily in 1½ hr; to *Kozáni*, 6 times daily in 4 hrs. From Kozani to *Ptolemaΐs* hourly; to *Flórina* 3–4 times daily.

RAILWAY from Kozani to Bitolj, 74½ m., once daily in 5 hrs (change at Amindaion).—AIR SERVICE from Larissa to Kozani, 3 times weekly in 30 min. The aircraft fly up the valley, affording many obvious glimpses of ancient occupation not seen from the ground.

We cross the Pinios and pass an Agricultural School of the Royal National Foundation.—3 m. *Yiánnouli*. The straight road runs N.W. across the plain.—10½ m. **Tírnavos** (ΤΥΡΝΑΒΟΣ; *Olympos* D) on the farther bank of the Titaríssios, is the chief town (10,450 inhab.) of an eparchy and a centre of ouzo production and of textile industries.— The road turns S.W. to enter the narrow gap between two hills, Tepes (l.) and Kladares (r.), through which the Titaríssios emerges to the Thessalian plain. A ruined tower guards the entrance. Before 1912 the Greco-Turkish frontier followed the ridge (which is crossed farther E. by an older road to Elassón, 12 m. shorter, in the *Pass of Melouna*; 1772 ft, view). We follow the river.

The **Titaríssios** has various other names, owing to uncertainty as to which affluent constitutes the main stream. In antiquity it was also called *Europos*, and today it is known as *Xeriás*, *Voulgára*, and *Sarandáporos*. The "lovely Titarissios", as Homer calls it (Il. II, 748) drains both Kato Olympos and the Kamvounia range, but its longest stream rises on Mt Titaros. In the Tertiary epoch the river fed the Larissan lake; it now joins the Pinios a few miles W. of the Vale of Tempe.

18 m. *Damásion*, reached by ford, lies on the other bank in the narrows. A ruined fortress crowning an isolated stony hill to the N. of the village is the *Mylas* that resisted the Macedonians in 171 B.C. The beautiful vale gradually broadens and the sandy river flows between thickly wooded banks.—28 m. *Doméniko* was identified by Leake with *Chyretiai* on the evidence of an inscription. *Verdikoússa* (3610 ft), 8 m. w. on the slopes of Antikhasia, with 2300 inhab., has abundant springs.— The road makes a long curving ascent away from the river, undulating through sheep pastures to the twin villages of (34 m.) *Galanóvrisi* (l.) and *Stefanóvouno*.

38 m. (62 km.) **Elassón** (ΕΛΑΣΣΩΝ; *Acropolis, Olympion,* D) stands at the mouth of a short gorge, through which flows the Elassonítikos. The town (7200 inhab.) has an annual fair on 20 August.

Elasson occupies the site of the 'white *Oloosson*' of Homer (Il. II, 739); its epithet derived no doubt from the limestone rocks in the neighbourhood. Chief town of the warlike Perrhaebi, it existed from the Bronze Age, but declined after the 5C B.C. It was made the Turkish base in 1897, and its capture by Greek forces in 1912 opened the way N.

A fine Byzantine *Bridge* spans the river. On a steep rock overlooking the gorge is the *Panayia Olimpiotissa*, a monastery with a Byzantine church resembling that of the Holy Apostles at Salonika. It has cushion capitals and a carved wooden door of 1296. Two classical tombstones are built into the gate. A little *Museum*, in a half-ruined mosque on the river bank, contains other relics of the past (police will locate key).

About 2½ m. E. of Elasson is **Tsarítsani** (2500 inhab.), a village founded, it is said, by a colony of Bulgarians in the 10C. Later the Slavs were replaced by Greeks, who preserved a kind of independence under the Turks. They manufactured silk and cotton, and practised agriculture, but their prosperity vanished with the plague of 1813.—About ¼ hr S.E. of the village is the *Monastery of St Athanasius*; about 1½ hr E. on a w. outlier of Kato Olympos is the *Monastery of Valetsiko* ('The Child'), founded by the Bulgarians, with a legend of a royal child miraculously healed.

We cross the Elassonítikos on a bridge (Restaurant) c. 1½ m. N. of the town. The road winds over a hill (1083 ft) used as a defensive position by the Turks in 1912.—At (43½ m.) *Mikró Elevtherokhórion* a road to Katerini and Olympos (Rte 57) diverges right. We cross several arms of the Sarandáporos ('Forty fords'), an affluent of the Titaríssios, mounting higher in the rolling country that characterizes its upper course. Away to the E. towers Mt Olympos. To the s.w. of the village of *Vouvála* (2 m. w. of our road) are ruins of ancient *Azoros*.—The road ascends towards the Kamvoúnia range and Títaros, which together form a natural barrier between Thessaly and Macedonia. It veers w. from its former line.

The difficult old road (now abandoned) passed through the STÉNA SARANDAPÓROU, or *Defile of Boloustana*, a natural cleft that opens between the two ranges. In the defile King Perseus is said by Livy to have stationed 10,000 men to deny its passage to the Romans; Hassim Tahsim Pasha failed to defend it against Prince Constantine's assault in 1912.

The new road bears w. past *Sarandáporon* to thread a gap in the Kamvounian range s. of Mt Dovrás. Metaxás is seen r. on its s. slope.—67½ m. *Polírrhakhon*. A steep descent takes the road through the jagged cleft of STÉNA PÓRTAS into the Aliakmon valley where the line of the old road is rejoined. In the gap two roads (see below) branch left; we turn right in the plain below the vertical cliffs of *Mt. Borsána* (2905 ft).

The **Aliakmon** rises in the Pindus on the Albanian frontier and flows for 109 miles entirely in Greek territory. Its upper course (comp. Rte 62) lies in gentle valleys, but in most of its middle reaches it threads narrow gorges, except for a few miles near Servia where its valley widens into a plain. This has been submerged since 1973 by the building of the Aliakmon Barrage some 10 m. downstream. Neolithic and Early Bronze Age settlements in the valley were investigated in 1971–73. Some finds from a mound excavated in 1931 by W. A. Heurtley are in Salonika museum. The mound was re-explored in 1971–73 before submersion and dated to c. 4930–4650 B.C. In its middle course the river is nowhere followed by a road, nor is it served with any continuity by tracks. In medieval times it was probably navigable to a point near Veroia; today its flat lower reaches are controlled by the Varvares Barrage (Rte 61). The mountains commanding the valley on the s. provide a natural defence line against invaders from the N., which can, however, be turned by the easy pass between Grevena and Kalambaka.

In the Stena Portas two roads branch s.w. The poor higher road winds through hilly country to the s.E. of the river. In a glen below (11 m.) *Mikrovalton* is the

Panayía Stanoú (or Zidaníou), a monastery founded in the 16C and rebuilt after destruction by the Turks in 1854.—12½ m. *Tranóvalton*.—Beyond (15½ m.) *Lazarádhes* bridle paths continue in 3 hrs round the steep N. side of *Vounása*, the highest peak (5300 ft) of the Kamvounia range, or over its E. spur, to Deskati (Makedonia D; comp. Rte 62). On the left bank of the Aliakmon, beneath Vounása (2 hrs from Lazarádhes), is the Monastery of *Osios Nikánoros Závorda*, where in 1959 was discovered a complete 13C MS. of the dictionary of the Patriarch Photios (c. 820–891), previously known only by an incomplete copy in Cambridge. It incorporates quotations from lost classics. The buildings date from 1534. Frescoes of the Raising of Lazarus, the Entry into Jerusalem, and the Crucifixion are thought from their similarity to those at Barlaam (Meteora) to be by Frangos Kastellanos.

The new lower road provides an alternative route to Kozani (c. 6 m. longer). It turns S.W. in the valley to *Rímnion* on the lakeside. Here it is carried across the lake by causeway and bridge to *Aianí*, whose several churches are decorated with 15–16C mural paintings. Here eight cist tombs have yielded grave goods of the 9C B.C.

73 m. (117 km.) **Sérvia** (ΣΕΡΒΙΑ; 1486 ft), a town of 3800 inhab., commands the only major route S. from the Aliakmon valley. It is situated, 4 m. from the river, between two sharp rocks and dominated by a Byzantine *Fortress*, which occupies a high hill behind the town. Within the Kastro is the ruined church of *Ayios Theodoros*.

Servia derives its name from a colony of Serbs, settled here in the 7C by Heraclius as a buffer to other invaders. By the 10C it was in the hands of the Bulgarians, who defended it valiantly but in vain against Basil II. In the 13C it was a frontier stronghold, and it has suffered in many wars. It was bombed on 14 Apr 1941, and occupied the following day by the Germans. The New Zealand 4th Brigade held a line behind the town from Kastanea to Rimnion until 17 April. Thirty German volunteers worked for a year in 1960–61 to make good war damage.—Some remains at *Palaiográtsano*, on the N. slope of Piéria 7 m. N.E. of Servia, probably represent the ancient *Phylakai*. At *Velvendós*, in the valley below (by-road from Servia), was born Stamatios Kleanthes (1802–62), the architect.

The Aliakmon hydro-electric lake is crossed by the longest bridge in Greece. Beyond the bridge a private road of the Electricity Authority (ΔΕΗ) branches N.E. in 10 m. to the Aliakmon Barrage (Fragma Aliakmonos). Above the road junction on the s.w. spur of *Patsoúra* is a fortress of uncertain date. We climb gradually. To the right is a series of isolated small hills (Skopós; Rte 62). Kozani can be by-passed to the E.

90½ m. (145 km.) **KOZANI** (KOZANH), though no longer astride the main Athens–Salonika road, remains the nodal point of communication between Macedonia and Epirus and the most important strategic centre for N.W. Greece. It is a clean and invigorating town (23,200 inhab.) with winding streets; the old houses are well kept, and many attractive timber-framed cottages are set off by walled gardens and cobbled courts. The capital of a nome and the seat of a metropolitan, it was a centre of Greek culture during the Turkish occupation. The inhabitants, who are notably good-looking, make textiles and agricultural tools.

Airport (see above) with service to Athens, viâ Larissa.—BOOKING OFFICE, 11 Triandafillidhou.
Railway Station, ¾ m. S. of centre; 3 good trains daily to Salonika in c. 4 hrs.
Hotels. Aliakmon, 54 El. Venizelou; Ermionion, in the main square; Metropolis, a little to the w., Anessis, Plat. Lassani, all C.—Xenia, on the outskirts, B.
Buses from Odhos Makedonomakhon, just off main square, hourly to *Salonika* and to *Ptolemáïs*; 6 times daily to *Larissa* and to *Grevena*; 4 times daily to *Siátista*, to *Kastoria*, and to *Flórina*; 3 times daily to *Sérvia* and to *Véroia*; twice daily to *Athens*; daily to *Kalambaka* and *Ioannina*.
Kozani was entered on 14 April 1941, by the 9th Panzer Division. As a centre of royalist sympathies, it was much harried by left-wing bands in 1944–45.

The centre of the town is the verdant PLATEIA NIKIS, with a tall clock-tower of 1855, whence all the principal roads of Western Macedonia radiate. *Ayios Nikólaos*, the metropolitan church, is a low, wide building of 1664–1721 lit by two lanterns. Built mainly of wood, it has ornate stalls and iconostasis, and a w. gallery on pillars. The frescoes are blackened with age. The *Museum* contains finds from a wide area and the *Library* has valuable 16C MSS. On a hill N.W. of the town, the park in front of the picturesque *Metamorfosis tou Sotiros* commands a good view of the town and over the plain of the Aliakmon to Sérvia.

From Kozani to *Salonika* and to *Kastoria*, see Rte 62.

From Kozani the road leads N.—88½ m. *Koíla*. We join the railway and skirt the w. side of Sarigkiol (see Rte 62), with low hills on our left.— 97½ m. *Kómanos*.—100½ m. *Proástion* lies (l.) in the *Stená Kománou*, a low 'pass' in which is situated the huge Ptolemáïs thermo-electric station, opened in 1959 and later linked with the Yugoslav grid.— 103½ m. **Ptolemáïs** (*George* C and others), a growing town (16,600 inhab.) on an upland plain, has become, since the exploitation of its lignite mines, an important industrial centre, producing low-grade coal, sulphuric acid, and nitrate fertilizers. It is the chief town of the eparchy of Eordaia.—Near (107 m.) *Perdikkas* a dam will provide further power.—At (115 m.) the *Mnemeia Pesonton Crossroads*, with a memorial to the fallen of the Balkan Wars, we cross the road from Kastoria to Amindaion (Rte 63).

117 m. *Xinón Nerón* (1¼ m. l.) has mineral waters. We keep company with the railway (gradient 1 in 40) in the gentle curving *Stená Kirli Derven*, crossing the line at (121 m.) *Kleidíon Station*. The pass was held for three days against the Germans in 1941 while railway installations were destroyed at Amindaion. We by-pass (123 m.) *Vévi* (Rte 63A) and leave the old Florina road on our left. Joining the course of the Via Egnatia, our road crosses an upland plain, watered by the Gieléska, leaves the new road viâ Florina on the left, and continues to (139 m.) **Níki** (*Tourist Pavilion*) where the Greco-Yugoslav frontier is marked by no natural barrier (the so-called 'Monastir Gap').—It is now more generally approached viâ Florina (comp. Rte 63). The road continues between the Peristeri Mountains (w.) and the marshy Tserna to (148 m.) **Bitolj** (*Makedonija* C), or *Monastir*, a Yugoslav provincial capital, the ancient *Herakleia Lynkestis* (site above main road to left).

59 SALONIKA

SALONIKA, in Greek **Thessaloníki** (ΘΕΣΣΑΛΟΝΙΚΗ), the Biblical *Thessalonica*, with 345,800 inhab., is the second city of Greece and the natural centre of communication with her Balkan neighbours. It is the residence of the Minister for Northern Greece, capital of the nome of Salonika, and a university city. Boasting a church of Apostolic foundation, it remains the seat of an Orthodox metropolitan and of a Roman Catholic bishop. In addition to being the headquarters of a Greek army corps, it has served as Advanced H.Q. (S.E. Europe) of NATO, with an armoured division. The city rises from the Bay of Salonika in the form of an amphitheatre on the slopes of Mt Khortiatis. Its citadel, the battlemented walls, and the huddled hillside houses of the upper town give to Salonika an appearance which remains characteristic despite its rapid transformation, since the devastating fire of 1917, into a modern city. Its monuments have re-emerged from the sordid but picturesque slums that hid them; though somewhat over-restored (and having no individual rival to the great churches of Ravenna), they are surpassed as an illustration of ten centuries of Byzantine architecture only by those of Istanbul. Outside the walls the huge grounds of the annual International Fair divide the old town from the new. Local industries are growing (fertilizers and animal foods, agricultural machinery, etc) and oil and sugar are refined. This is having an effect on the harbour, long rendered idle by the competition of Piraeus, and a few passenger shipping links have recently been restarted. The climate of Salonika runs to extremes: the winters are often severe, when the city is swept by the Vardarats, or Vardar wind from the N.W.; the summers can be oppressive.

Streets at right angles to the sea are numbered from the seaward end; those parallel to the sea from Axios Sq. (N.W.). Plan refs. refer to central plan.

Airport at *Mikra*, 7 m. S.E., with international services from London, Germany, etc.; also frequent domestic service to Athens; connecting buses from corner of Komninon and Vas. Konstandinou (Pl. 14).

Hotels. BETWEEN THE TSIMISKI AND THE WATERFRONT: Makedonia Palace, Leof. Megalou Alexandhrou, 295 R, L.—Electra Palace (p; Pl. 14), 5A Plat. Aristotelous 130 R, A.—Palace (d; Pl. 14), 12 Tsimiski; Astor (r; Pl. 13), 20 Tsimiski; City, 11 Komninon, these B.—Rhea, Komninon (Pl. 14), C.

IN OR NEAR EGNATIAS: El Greco (b; Pl. 9), 23 Egnatias; Egnatia (e; Pl. 9), 13 Leondos Sofou, 145 R, these B; Delta (j; Pl. 9), 13 Egnatias, 110 R; Esperia (k; Pl. 6), Olympia (j; Pl. 6), 58 and 65 Olimbou; Park (m; Pl. 10), 81 Ionos Dragoumi, these C.—Without restaurant: Olympic (f; Pl. 9), 25 Egnatias, B; Amalia, 33 Ermou (Pl. 10); Ariston (g; Pl. 9), 5 Dioikitiriou; Aighaion (a; Pl. 9), 19 Egnatias; Pella (o; Pl. 10), 65 Ionos Dragoumi, and others, C.

NEAR THE STATION: Capitol, 16 Monastiriou, 190 R., A; Capsis, 425 R., Rotonda, 28 and 97 Monastiriou; Victoria, 13 Langadha, all B—Without restaurant: Rex, 39 Monastiriou, C.

ELSEWHERE IN THE CENTRAL AREA: Telioni, 16 Ay. Dhimitriou, C.

NEAR OR BEYOND THE INTERNATIONAL FAIR: Metropolitan, 120 R., Queen Olga, 130 R., 65 and 44 Vasilissis Olgas, Philippeion, Antheon (beyond Meg. Alexandrou), all B; A.B.C., Plateia Sintrivaniou, 100 R., C.

In the Environs, see Rte 59D, below.

MOTEL. *Elissavet*, 283 Monastiriou.

YOUTH HOSTEL, 42 Od. Pringipos Nikolaou (Pl. 12).—Camping Sites at Nea Krini (comp. below).

Restaurants. *Olympos-Naousa*, *Stratis*, 5 and 27 Vas. Konstandinou; *Averof*, 17 Singrou; *Clochard*, *Riva*, Proxenou Koromila; *Payiantes*, Mitropoleos; *Nea Ilyssia*, 17 Leondos Sofou; *Perdika*, 40 Vas. Sofias; *Ivi*, *Kairon*, 63 and 54 Tsimiski. —TAVERNAS. *Krikelas*, 284 Vas. Olgas, on the way to the airport; *Fengaria*, *Xenophon*, Odhos Komninon; *Vlakhos*, Plat. Lefkou Pirgou; *Klimataria*, 10 Ay. Sofias; also by the sea at Aretsou (*Chez André*, *Paradeisos*) and Nea Krini (*Remvi*).

Post Office, 23 Tsimiski; Branch Office near the White Tower.—O.T.E. CENTRE, 55 Vas. Irakliou.—TOURIST POLICE, 10 Egnatias (Plat. Metaxa).—ALIENS OFFICE, 25 Tsimiski (W. end).

Information Offices. N.T.O., 8 Od. Aristotelous; E.L.P.A., 4 Kapetan Vanghelis (towards Airport).—TRAVEL AGENTS *Wagons-Lits/Cook*, 8 Tsimiski; *American Express*, 5 Plateia Aristotelous; *Olympic Airways*, 7 Vas. Konstandinou.

Buses. LOCAL SERVICES (KTEL 54): 1 (from the Rly. Stn.) and 2–7 traverse the Tsimiski or Vas. Konstandinou and Vasilissis Olgas; 4 terminates at *Mikro Karabournou*. 22, 23, and 24 serve Venizelou and terminate by the Ramparts in the upper town. To the *Agricultural School*, *Ayia Trias*, etc., from 23 Karolou Dil (Pl. 15); to *Asvestokhorion* from 22 Singrou.—COUNTRY BUSES from Plat Dikastirion or near by.—Long-distance Buses leave from various streets off the N.W. end of Odhos Egnatias: to *Veroia* and *Naousa* (KTEL 25 Imathias) from 26 Oktovriou; to *Kilkis* from 7 Perikleous; to *Drama*, to *Edessa*, to *Kozani*, to *Kastoria*, and to *Florina* from Antigonidhon; to *Serres*, to *Nea Apollonia* and *Stavros*, and to *Katerini* from Od. Dioikitiriou; to *Evzoni* (KTEL 41 Paionias) from Odysseus; to

Kavalla from 61 Ionos Dragoumi; to *Langadha* (KTEL 39 Thessalonikis) from 10 Frangon; to *Ierissos* and *Khalkidiki* from 3 Platonos); to *Ioannina* (KTEL 20) from 1 Od. Enotikon to *Athens* from Langadha.—O.S.E. 'PULLMAN' COACHES to *Athens* from the Railway Station.

Motor Launches in summer from quay (near White Tower) to *Aretsou, Peraia, Ayia Trias*, etc.—Taxis are painted blue and white.

Consulates. *British Cons.-General*, 39 Leof. Vas. Konstandinou; *American Consulate* 59 Leof. Vas. Konstandinou; *Yugoslav Consulate*, 98 Vassilissis Olgas. —BRITISH COUNCIL, 3 Leof. Vas Konstandinou.

Banks. *Bank of Greece*, 12 Tsimiski; *National, Ionian and Popular*, 3 and 7 Franklin Roosevelt; *Commercial*, 21 Ionos Dragoumi.

Clubs and Learned Organizations. *Inspectorate of Classical Antiquities* at the Museum; of *Byzantine Antiquities*, 114 Megalou Alexandrou; *Institute of Macedonian Studies*, opposite White Tower; *Greek Alpine Club*, 14 Venizelou.

Booksellers. *Molho*, 10 Tsimiski; *P. Zakharopoulou*, 23 Tsimiski; *Kaufmann*, 10 Aristotelous.

Theatres. *Vasilikon* (Royal), *Stratou* (Tekhnis), *Parkou* (Théâtre de l'atelier), *Makedonikon Spoudhon*, all near the White Tower.

Baths (Loutra). *Olympia*; *Nadir*, Aristotelous; *Paradeisos* (old-fashioned), Egnatias.—PUBLIC LAVATORIES in Plat. Aristotelous and by the White Tower.

Sports Centre between the University and the Kaftandzoglou Stadium.— TENNIS CLUB, *Astir*, Kiprou.

Festivals. *International Fair* in September. *St Demetrius* (26 Oct; religious processions) to *Okhi Day* (28 Oct; military parade) is a three-day holiday.

Churches are open to visitors 8–1.30 & 3.30–8.

History. The unimportant ancient town of *Therme* was incorporated with twenty-five others in 316 B.C. by Kassander and given the name of *Thessalonikeia* (in Strabo's spelling) after his wife, who was half-sister to Alexander the Great. It must soon have been fortified, for Antigonus Gonatas retired on it after his defeat in 274 by Pyrrhus, king of Epirus. In 146, when Macedonia became a Roman province, Thessalonica was made its capital. Its geographical position at the head of the gulf favoured its development, which was accelerated by the building of the Via Egnatia. Cicero spent part of his exile in 58 at Thessalonica; Pompey took refuge here in 49 from Caesar. Literary visitors included the Greek satirist Lucian and the historian Polyaenus. The city's support of Antony and Octavian before the Battle of Philippi assisted its fortunes. In A.D. 49–50 St Paul preached at Thessalonica, where he antagonized some of the Jews, who attacked the house in which he had been staying. His two letters to the church he founded here have come down to us as the Epistles to the Thessalonians; he revisited the city in 56. Thessalonica repelled repeated attacks by the Goths in the 3C. Galerius, who succeeded to the E. half of the Roman Empire on the retirement of Diocletian, dwelt in the city, where the persecution he instigated claimed as a victim St Demetrius, afterwards patron saint of the city. Constantine mustered his fleet here before his successful campaign against Licinius in 324. Under Theodosius the Great (379–395) Thessalonica became the seat of the prefecture of Illyricum, a metropolitan see, and the base of the Emperor's operations against the Goths. Here Theodosius himself, severely ill, was converted to Christianity and afterwards issued the Edict of Thessalonica (380), reversing Julian's toleration of pagan gods and condemning the Arian heresy held at Constantinople. In 390, after Botheric the Goth, military commander of the city, had been lynched for failing to control his soldiers' outrages, Theodosius invited the populace to a special performance in the circus and there had c. 7000 of them massacred. For this crime he was made to do penance by St Ambrose, Bp. of Milan.

Favoured by Justinian, Thessalonica rose to become the second city of the Byzantine Empire. Having endured further invasions of the Goths, and resisted five sieges by Avars and Slavs, it remained an enclave in Slav dominions until Justinian II's expedition of 689, and seems to have returned to direct Byzantine administration as a theme only after Stauricius' offensive c. 783. SS Cyril (d. 869) and Methodius (d. 885) the brothers who converted the Slavs to Christianity were natives of Thessalonica.

Thessalonica was stormed by the Saracens (led by the Greek renegade Leo of Tripoli) in 904, when 22,000 of its inhabitants were sold into slavery. It served Basil II as base against the Bulgars, who besieged it without success in 1041. When in 1185 the army and fleet of William II of Sicily, commanded by Tancred, captured the city, the celebrated Homeric scholar Eustathios, then Abp. of Thessalonica, left a detailed account of its barbarous sack. At the end of the Fourth Crusade, the city became the capital of the Latin kingdom of Thessalonica under Boniface of Montferrat (1204). Kalojan of Bulgaria was killed here in 1207 while attacking the walls, and Henry of Flanders died in the city in 1216, poisoned perhaps on the eve of marching against Theodore Angelus, despot of Epirus. Thessalonica fell to Epirus in 1222 (Theodore proclaiming himself Emperor), while the rest of Macedonia came under the sway of Ivan Asen II of Bulgaria; but in 1246 John Vatatzes reappropriated both to the Byzantine empire of Nicaea. In the 14C possession of Thessalonica was the recognized first goal of every usurper with his eyes on the Imperial throne. The Catalan Grand Company besieged the city unsuccessfully in 1308. Michael IX died here in 1320 and hence in 1328 his son Andronikos III launched his successful campaign against his grandfather. The same century witnesses the religious struggles of the Hesychasts, or Quietists, and the insurrection of the Zealots, a 'people's party' who murdered the nobles in 1342. The short period of reform before they were crushed coincided with the artistic Golden Age of the city. During a long period of anarchy Thessalonica fell to the Ottoman Turks in 1387 and again in 1394, but in 1403, after the Mongol Timur had crushed Bayezid I at Ankara, it was restored to the Byzantines. In 1423 Andronikos Palaeologus, son of the Emp. Manuel II, despairing of keeping back the Turks, placed Thessalonica under Venetian protection. However in 1430 Murad II stormed, sacked, and occupied the already depopulated city. Some churches were transformed into mosques.

The population was suddenly increased by the influx of 20,000 Jews banished from Spain by the Edict of the Alhambra (1492). They absorbed the Bavarian Jews who had arrived twenty years earlier. By the middle of the 16C they constituted the major part of the population, and had formed a small autonomous community speaking Ladino, a form of Castilian, which they wrote in Hebrew characters. Towards the end of the century the Greeks returned in some strength. The city suffered from fires in 1545 and 1617 and from the Jewish schism of 1659 when the sect of Donmeh broke away. In 1821, at the outbreak of the Greek War of Independence, a sympathetic movement at Salonika was savagely suppressed. During the 19C the Turks made a show of reforms; the Greeks improved their schools; the Jews increased their influence. In 1876 the French and German consuls were murdered by the mob; Pierre Loti, arriving in the frigate 'Couronne' in time to see the assassins hanged, found in Salonika's romantically squalid alleys the original of his 'Aziyadé'. In 1888 the railway link was forged with the rest of Europe, and in 1897–1903 a new harbour constructed.

Salonika (known to the Turks as *Selaïnik*) became a centre of intrigue against the misrule of Abdul Hamid. Here in 1906 was formed the Turkish Committee of Union and Progress (Ittihat ve Terakki Cemiyeti), which secretly organized the Macedonian revolt of 1908. In 1909 Abdul Hamid was deposed and exiled to Salonika. In the First Balkan War the Greek Army made a triumphal entry into Salonika on 8 Nov (26 Oct O.S.), 1912, and the city was ceded to Greece by the Treaty of Bucharest (1913). King George I was assassinated in Salonika on 18 March 1913. During the First World War the Entente landed an expeditionary force at Salonika on 12 Oct 1915, and here Venizelos set up his provisional government of National Defence. The railway link with Athens viâ Larissa was completed the following year. In the Second World War, German tanks, advancing down the Vardar, entered the city on 9 Apr 1941, three days after the start of the campaign, after Canadian engineers had destroyed installations during the night. During the occupation most of Salonika's Jewish population (c. 60,000) was deported to Poland, never to return.

The city was damaged by fires in 1890, 1898, and 1910, at which time it still had oil street lamps. Fire devastated the city on 5 Aug 1917, rendering 70,000 homeless, and the shanty town of refugees was swollen in 1923 by the exchange of population with Turkey. Replanning of the centre was put in hand in 1925–35, but the greatest transformation occurred after 1950. Since then Salonika has become a modern city, though the higher part of the city still retains some of the old atmosphere. In June 1978 severe earthquakes caused casualties and disruption. The early churches suffered worst and the old-established Mediterranean Palace hotel was wrecked, but serious damage to recent buildings was not widespread.

A. The Centre of the City

Despite many changes made since the fire of 1917, the ancient chess-board plan remains a feature of the town. The principal thorough-fares run roughly parallel to the sea, Ayiou Dhimitriou, Egnatias, and the Tsimiski effectively dividing the old city into four belts. The Egnatia Odhos extends from the Axios Gate in the N.W. to the Kassandreia Gate in the S.E. (though the actual gates are no more).

The street occupies an ancient course and, since it was spanned by two triumphal arches, was long assumed to represent the famous Via Egnatia. It is now supposed, however, on the evidence of milestones, that the Egnatian Way entered from Pella by the Axios Gate but left again by the Letaia Gate, also on the N.W., without passing through the city, rather as its successor does today.

Halfway along on the upper side opens the Plateia Dikastirion (Pl. 10), a vast square cleared by the fire of 1917. It served as the bus terminal until, in 1962, new courts were proposed. Immediate finds led to the identification of the Imperial Roman Forum, and systematic excavations were begun by the Greek Archaeological Service under Ph. Petsas. The *Odeion* and two stoas bounding the forum have been unearthed, and a long double *Cryptoporticus* explored. The courts have been abandoned and the area will remain the central square of Salonika. The lower part has been attractively planted with gardens. At the w. corner stands the **Panayia Khalkeon**, founded (as an inscription on the marble lintel of the w. entrance tells) in 1028 by Christophoros of Lombardy, and restored in 1934. The name *Our Lady 'of the Coppersmiths'* recalls the time from 1430 to 1912 when it served the Turkish smiths as a mosque (the Kazancilar-Cami). The brick church has the form of a Greek cross-in-square, extended to the E. by three apses and to the w. by a narthex. The central dome, with a straight cornice, is mounted on a lofty octagonal drum, and the arms of the cross have triangular pediments, which give a markedly angular appearance to the whole. On the façade, however, brick half-columns support deep round arches and the cornices of the two w. domes follow the rounded lines of the windows in the Athenian manner. The contrast suggests a later date for the upper stage of the narthex although the fresco of the Last Judgment inside is placed in the 11C. Within, the dome is supported by four marble columns. Contemporary frescoes in the dome (Ascension), round the drum, and in the apse, seem to derive from the mosaics of Ayia Sophia (see below). On the opposite corner the picturesque **Çifte Hamam*, a Turkish bath-house erected by Sultan Murad II in 1444, survives in use as the *Loutra Paradeisos*. It preserves its original dedicatory inscription. Beneath are remains of late Roman buildings.

Off the Egnatia Odhos, in Odhos Ayias Sofias (l.), is the **Panayia Akheiropoietos** (Pl. 11), one of the earliest Christian buildings still in use. It was probably dedicated to the Virgin soon after Her recognition by the Third Oecumenical Council (Ephesus, 431 A.D.) as Theotókos (Mother of God) and completed c. 470.

It took its name (Ἀχειροποίητος: 'Made without hands') at some time after the 12C from a celebrated ikon supposed to have been miraculously painted. A later popular name, *Ayia Paraskeví* (Good Friday), is said to come from a mistranslation of the Turkish name Eski Djuma, meaning 'old place of worship' (Djuma also meaning Friday since that was the Moslem day of worship). The church was converted into a mosque in 1430, not without detriment to its fabric. It was restored in 1910 but suffered further deterioration in 1923 when refugees were billeted in it. Reconsecrated, it has again been restored.

The church is a basilica of Syrian type with nave and two aisles. The atrium and exo-narthex have disappeared. The narthex opens into the nave by a 'trivilon' (τρίβηλον), a triple opening formed by two columns and closed by curtains. The arcades are formed by mono-lithic columns with 'Theodosian' capitals; the mosaics on the soffits, depicting birds, fruit, and flowers, show Alexandrian influence. Near the s. chapel (the former baptistery) are some brick walls of a Roman house and below the s. aisle have been unearthed two layers of Roman mosaic flooring.

Farther E. is *Ayios Pandeleimonos*, a pretty church with a central dome and a domed narthex, first mentioned in 1169 as a dependency of the Rossikon (Mt Athos). The cloister which surrounded it on three sides disappeared during its Turkish period as the *Issakié Mescid Cami*. It was transformed (c. 1500) by Kadi Ishak Çelebi, whose magnificent mosque is still the central feature of Bitolj. Damage in 1978 was severe.

Farther on, the realined Egnatia Odhos passes to the right of the **Arch of Galerius** (Pl. 12), beneath which the road in its narrower days made a slight angle. The great triumphal arch, erected to com-memorate the emperor's victories over the Persians in 297 A.D., was shown by the excavations of E. Dyggve, the Danish archaeologist, in 1939 to have formed part of a larger design, which included a Palace, Hippodrome, and Mausoleum. There survives of the arch part of its w. half; the entire E. half has disappeared. Two further piers to the s.E. carried a similar span, forming a double gate crowned by a central dome. The springers of the transverse arches can be seen above the cornice of the reliefs. Beneath them ran a lateral way, extended to the N.E. by a porticoed avenue leading to the rotunda (see below). The structure is of brick throughout, the piers being faced with *Reliefs in stone, in four zones separated by bands of sculptured garlands, and crowned by a cyma and cornice.

S. PIER. E. side. In the *Scene of Sacrifice* on the second zone from the bottom, Diocletian, Augustus of the East (l.), in the imperial purple, and Galerius (r.), his son-in-law and Caesar, in military uniform, celebrate the latter's victories. The altar is decorated with reliefs of Jupiter and Hercules, of whom respectively they claimed to be the reincarnation. The scene below represents the surrender of an Eastern town; those above, prisoners begging for clemency, and (top) Galerius addressing his troops. In the adjacent reliefs beneath the main arch, above a row of victories, Galerius is seen (top to bottom) riding in his chariot between two towns which receive him and bid him farewell; fighting on horseback (crowned by an eagle on the sculptured band); receiving the surrender of Mesopotamia and Armenia.—On the N. PIER the various scenes of combat, some with elephants, are less well preserved.

The line of the Roman avenue (comp. above), leads to **Ayios Yeoryios** (Pl. 12), the oldest as well as the most conspicuous intact monument in Salonika, with the only surviving minaret. The *Rotunda*, built of brick on the same axis as the triumphal arch, was probably erected in the lifetime of Galerius to serve as his mausoleum. The brick dome is protected by a low-pitched timber roof borne on the outer walls, one of the first known examples of this practice in Europe. After having served as church and mosque, the building is now preserved as an ancient monument (closed by earthquake damage).

Having died in Serdica (Sofia), Galerius was buried in near-by Romulianum, his birthplace, since Licinius would not permit his body to be moved to Thessalonica. The rotunda was transformed into a church before 400, when the S.E. recess was converted into an arch and the sanctuary constructed; the main entrance was moved from the S.W. to the N.W., and a narthex added. At the same time an ambulatory (now destroyed) was added round the outside and the recesses in the original wall opened into it. Some time after the 10C the upper part of the sanctuary fell and the dome was repaired. The buttresses date from this time. This is possibly the church known in the Middle Ages as the *Asomaton*, or Archangels, which gave its name to the quarter and its gate. For some time in the 15C the Asomaton served as the Metropolitan church of the Greeks. In 1591, the year of the Hegira 999 (when the end of the world was expected) the rotunda was turned into the *Mosque of Sinan Pasha*; later it was renamed after Hortaci Suleïman Effendi; his tomb (19C) stands in the courtyard (S.E. side). The elegant stelai surrounding the church date from the time of Mahmoud II (1807–39).

INTERIOR (closed at present). The marble stoup at the entrance is supported by columns of green Thessalian marble. The circular wall, 20 ft thick, has eight barrel-vaulted recesses. Over each recess is an arched window; above and between these are small lunettes; the dome is c. 26 yds across. *Mosaics, Hellenistic in feeling and dating from the end of the 4C, decorate the dome and the recesses. Eight compositions round the dome represent elaborate architectural façades with saints in prayer. Their vestments are varied and their features individual; all were martyred in the East, the majority under Diocletian. Of the middle zone, which probably represented the Apostles, only some sandalled feet survive. The central figure of Christ is lost, though some heads remain of the attendant angels. In the recesses (that to the S.E. restored in 1885) medallions with birds and fruit are displayed on a gold ground. In the apse, four truncated columns (of a ciborium?) show the original floor level, and fragments of 10C fresco decorate the lunette. Sculptural fragments and other Christian evidences have been gathered together in the building and a fine *Mosaic of St Andrew has been remounted.

Seaward of the Arch of Galerius, Od. Gounari leads to PLATEIA NAVARINOU, a large square formed by the excavations since 1970 in the **Palace of Galerius** (Pl. 16). A deep area is surrounded by a low wall so that the remains can be seen from various vantage points. Most impressive is an octagonal building, richly decorated within, perhaps the throne room.

A short walk N.W. takes us to **Ayia Sophia** (Pl. 11), conspicuously situated in a garden, planted with palms and Mediterranean pine, that occupies the site of its former atrium. The main façade closes the end of Odhos Ermou. The heavy exterior was not improved by the loss of the elegant Turkish portico, ruined by an Italian air raid in 1941, and the structure suffered severely in 1978.

The date of Ayia Sophia (the church of the Holy Wisdom) is disputed. Its imperfect pendentives and the style of its masonry led some scholars to think it older than its Justinianean namesake in Constantinople. More likely the building represents a transitional form between the domed basilica and the domed cruciform church and should be dated to the early 8C, perhaps to the reign of Leo III the Isaurian (717–40). It remained to the Christians until 1585 when it was transformed into a mosque by Raktoub Ibrahim Pasha. Damaged by fire in 1890, it was reconstructed in 1907–10 and restored to Christian worship in 1912. The Greeks used its minaret (since demolished) for a machine gun post in 1913 while subduing the Bulgarian garrison which had barricaded itself in a school nearby.

The spacious INTERIOR remains impressive despite being shored up with extensive wooden scaffolding. The drum, borne on pendentives, on which the dome rests, is a square with rounded corners rather than a circle. The dome, 33 ft in diameter, is decorated with mosaics of the Ascension. In the centre, in a circular medallion supported by two angels, the Almighty is seated on a rainbow throne; in the drum are the Virgin with an angel on either side, and figures of the Apostles divided by trees. Below the angels is a Greek inscription in four lines from Acts I, 11 (Ye men of Galilee, why stand ye gazing up into heaven?). The mosaics are now attributed to the 9C or 10C. In the apse are monograms of Constantine VI and of the Empress Irene, and the Virgin enthroned. The presence can be traced of an earlier mosaic of the cross, which during the iconoclastic period accompanied the liturgical inscription now interrupted by the Virgin's feet; the existing mosaics, therefore, are dated to 785–97.

To the s.e., across the road, is the entrance to a subterranean chapel, dedicated to St John the Baptist, that connects with the crypt of a Roman nymphaeum.— Excavations to the e. of the church in 1961 laid bare part of a basilica of the 4C a.d. adorned with mosaics and frescoes.

From the s. side of the church Odhos Skoleion Exadaktilon leads past a large school to the principal shopping street of the city, still known by its Byzantine name of Tsimiski (Pl. 14, 15). Its previous alternative name of Megalou Alexandhrou has now been transferred elsewhere. To the s. in Od. Ay. Sofias stands *Ayios Gregorios Palama*, built in 1912–13 to serve as the cathedral. Here is re-interred the body of Abp. Gregory Palamas (c. 1295–1359), champion of the Hesychasts. The Tsimiski crosses Odhos Karolou Dil, which honours Charles Diehl (1859–1944), the French Byzantinist, and Odhos Aristotelous (see below). On the left is the *Post Office*. Just beyond, on the right, the picturesque remains of the *Iaoudi Hamam* form part of a market. To the w. is Eleftherias Square. We now turn up the lively Odhos Eleftheriou Venizelou, with fashion shops. At its crossing with the Egnatia Odhos (lined to the w. with hotels) a cinema occupies the former *Hamza Beg Cami*, founded in 1468, enlarged before 1592 and partly rebuilt after a fire in 1620. It is the largest mosque on Greek soil. Behind rises the *Dhimarkhion*. Venizelou St. mounts to the *Dioikitirion* (Pl. 6), administrative centre of the Ministry of Northern Greece, which continues on the same site as the Turkish Konak. The square before its façade is laid out as a memorial to Prince Nicolas, first military governor of Macedonia (1912). Odhos Ayiou Dhimitriou follows an ancient course.

Ayios Dhimitrios (Pl. 6), a double-aisled basilica of the 5C, with transepts flanking the apse and projecting farther e., is the largest church in Greece. The building was reduced to a shell by the fire of 1917, though the main arcades stood and the sanctuary survived to roof level. It was reconstructed in 1926–48, where possible with surviving materials, more or less as it had been before the fire, save that the open timber roof has been replaced by one of reinforced concrete.

History. Local tradition makes St Demetrius a native of Thessalonica, though Sirmium, near Mitrovitsa, also claims him. He was martyred at the command of Galerius. The saint, as the city's guardian, defended it against enemy attacks. His tomb exuded a sacred oil with miraculous powers of healing. His cult fostered the opposition of Thessalonica to the 14C iconoclastic movement. A fair, of considerable importance in the Middle Ages, accompanied his festal days (20–26 Oct). Immediately after the edict of toleration the Christians built a small church on the site of the martyrdom. In A.D. 412–13 Leontius, prefect of Illyricum, miraculously healed of paralysis, founded "between the ruins of the Roman bath and the Stadium", a large church which was damaged by fire in the reign of Heraklius (c. 629–34) and shortly afterwards rebuilt by a Bp. Leo with the

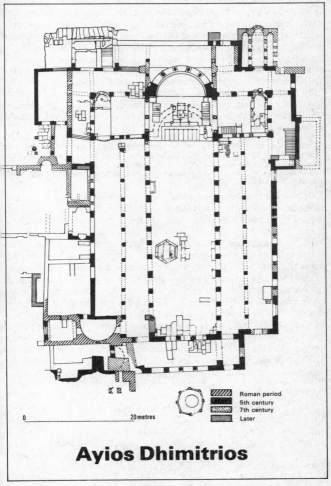

▨	Roman period
▬	5th century
▨	7th century
▨	Later

0   20 metres

Ayios Dhimitrios

addition of the E. transepts. The plan seems to have remained unaltered despite later repairs. Here in 688 the Emp. Justinian II celebrated his success against the Slavs. The church was pillaged in 1430 but left to the Christians until 1491 when, in the reign of Bayezid II (as shown by an inscription formerly above the W. door), it became the Kasimiye Cami. Between 1907 and 1912, when it was returned to Christian use, its wonderful mosaics were rediscovered, only to be largely destroyed in the fire of 1917. The rebuilding was achieved by architects Zachos (d. 1938) and Thanopoulos under the supervision of Ephor S. Pelekanides.

A cruciform appearance is given to the exterior by the transept roofs, which break the line of the aisles although they do not form a true crossing with the nave. Outside the w. front, which is flanked by two low towers, stands the great *Phiale*, a canopied immersion font. The usual entrance is by the s. door. The spacious **Interior**, 141 ft long, has been impressively restored, though the upper surfaces have only whitewashed plaster in place of the destroyed revetment of polychrome marble (traces above the arcade). The NAVE, 40 ft wide and ending in an apse, is flanked by double aisles, with round arches supported by columns of green, red, and white marble. The ancient shafts (some renewed) must have been replacements from elsewhere after the first fire for they have pedestals of uneven height. The carved *Capitals with their imposts repay detailed attention; many are Theodosian. The ancient marble revetment has been renewed on the piers, and the floor repaved in Thessalian marble.

At the w. end are a curious wall painting with a unicorn and a calendar of movable feasts for 1474–93. On the N. side is the marble tomb (1481) of Osios Loukas Spantounis, of Florentine workmanship most unusual in Greece. A domed chamber at the N.W. corner, survives from a Roman building and probably held the tomb of St Demetrius; it is poorly frescoed. At the entrance is a damaged mosaic of the saint.

On the floor of the nave remains of a hexagonal base mark the site of the silver ciborium of St Demetrius, burnt in 581. The great polygonal *Choros* is a noteworthy copy. On the first pier of the s. arcade a fresco depicts Abp. Palamas with the blessed Ioasaph (presumably John VI Cantacuzenos who took the habit under that name). The *Iconostasis* and the furnishings are replicas of Byzantine work in fretted marble, the *Ambo* to the left, the *Cathedra* to the right. On the pier behind the throne, fresco of Osios Loukas (d. 953). To the right and left of the iconostasis survive five *Mosaics, three contemporary with Leo's rebuilding. Right Pier. St Demetrius and the builders of the church, presumably the prefect Leontius and Bp. John, defender of the city in 617–619; St Sergius sumptuously attired as captain of the Imperial guard (a later work); St Demetrius with a deacon (discovered when a masking Turkish wall was removed). Left Pier. St Demetrius with two children; Virgin and (?) St Theodore (its date is still disputed).

In the outer s. aisle are frescoes of the Saint and of the miraculous defeat of a Barbarian invasion. At the S.E. corner stands the dark little *Chapel of St Euthymios*, with frescoes of 1303.

The CRYPT, brought to light by the fire, is entered from the s. transept. Here have been identified the *Martyrion* of the saint (early 4C), an adaptation perhaps of part of the *Roman Bath* in which St Demetrius was traditionally imprisoned. Beneath its apse was found a small cruciform reliquary-crypt containing a phial of blood-soaked earth. Parts of a fountain from a fish pond described by Abp. Eustathios (d. 1193) were also discovered. A stretch of paved Roman *Street* shows that the martyrion was above the ground level of that time.

To the N.W. of the church Byzantine walls, fragments of columns, and Hebrew tombstones lie in disorder. To the N. rise two domes of a Turkish bath. The trifoliate church of **Profitis Ilias** (Pl. 6), which served the 14C *Nea Moni*, occupies the site of a Byzantine palace, as its Turkish name (*Eski Sérai Camisi*) suggests. Converted to the Moslem rite by Fethi Murad, it was disfigured by massive external buttresses, the removal of which has revealed its fine brick decoration. The square narthex, with an upper story supported on pillars, is characteristic of the monastic Katholikon (much damaged mosaics and medieval graffiti). Internally the church needed such thorough restoration that its only original features are the four columns supporting the dome and fragmentary mosaics in the small window embrasures of the drum.

B. The Sea Front and the E. Quarter

From the centre Odhos Aristotelous, a broad flower-planted avenue, crosses Odhos Ermou and the Tsimiski and descends to the sea. At the seaward end is the British Consulate-General. Leoforos Vasileos Konstandinou (Pl. 14), a quayside esplanade with noted restaurants, replaces the 10C seaward rampart demolished in 1866–74. To the right it leads to Plateia Eleftherias, centre of banking, and to the *Harbour*.

The original port, constructed by Constantine the Great, was silted up in the middle ages. A new harbour was fashioned by a French company in the late 19C and in 1911 Salonika was the third port of Turkey. The competition of Piraeus and the through railway to Athens killed its passenger services and after the Second World War its commerce was virtually non-existent. Since 1960 new Macedonian industries have improved traffic to the extent that a new quay was begun in 1962. A Free Zone encourages Yugoslav use of the port.

We turn left along the promenade. On the shore at the far end ($\frac{1}{4}$ m.), set amid trees, is the famous **White Tower** (Pl. 16), or *Lefkós Pírgos* (Λευκός Πύργος), 105 ft high, which marked the s. angle of the ramparts. Built c. 1430 either by the Venetians or the Turks, it served in the 18–19C as a prison for the Janissaries. Their massacre in 1826 at the order of Mahmoud II gained for it the name of Bloody Tower, forgotten since the application of whitewash. The central chambers now form the headquarters of the four Sea Scout groups of Salonika and the summit affords a fine view of the city.

Grouped opposite the Tower, at the corners of Leoforos Vasilissis Sofias (Rte 59c), are the *Officers' Club* and the Society for Macedonian Studies (ΕΤΑΙΡΕΙΑ ΜΑΚΕΔΟΝΙΚΩΝ ΣΠΟΥΔΩΝ), with the adjacent *State Theatre* (1961), and by the sea the *National Theatre*. Beyond, a *Park* divides the old town from its huge E. extension. An avenue leads (l.) to the entrance of the Fair (see below).

Along the foreshore a broad Esplanade was laid out in 1961–62 on reclaimed land. This promenade, flanked by gardens, extends s. to ($2\frac{1}{2}$ m.) the new *Yacht Basin*. Beyond is the *Villa Allatini*, where the banished Abdul Hamid II, sultan of Turkey, lived in 1909–12; it is now a military hospital.—$3\frac{1}{2}$ m. **Mikro Karabournou;** on the point stands the *Kiverneion*, or Government House, a splendid Ionic building in white marble, which successfully adapts a pure classical style to modern use. A military encampment prevents access to the prominent *Tumulus* opposite.—Beyond the point are *Aretsou* (Okeanis C), a popular seaside resort with tavernas, N.T.O.G. beach, and yacht marina, and *Nea Krini* (camping sites). Both afford a fine view across the gulf to Mt Olympos.

Leoforos Vasileos Yeoryiou tou Protou continues E. to its crossing with Odhos Ayias Triados, on the corner of which a marble bust commemorates the assassination here in 1913 of George I. The road continues as Leoforos Vasilissis Olgas (comp. below), off which (l.) is the *Yeni Cami*, a large mosque which housed the archaeological museum in 1917–62. No. 68 houses the Museum of Popular Art (adm. free, 9–1.30; closed Tues), with traditional costumes of N. Greece. Leoforos Stratou leads back along the N. side of the park past the Army Headquarters to the permanent site of the **International Fair.** The commercial fair, held in the Middle Ages as part of the festivities of St Demetrius (Oct), was revived in 1926.

Inland, beyond the fair, rises the University (p. 518) and farther to the N.E. a new *Sports Centre*, with a covered *Swimming Pool*, and the *Kaftandzoglou Stadium*, erected from a bequest of Lysimachos Kaftandzoglou (1870–1937), the diplomat, and opened in 1960 by King Paul.

Across the road from the Fair entrance stands the *Archaeological Museum, opened in 1963. Admission 25 dr. (Sun and Thurs free); standard hours. The building forms a rectangle round a courtyard (Mosaic) with an outer and an inner series of rooms. Earthquake damage in 1978 was quickly repaired. The inner rooms were stripped in order to mount a temporary exhibition of Treasures of Ancient Macedonia (50 dr. extra). This consists of finds since 1977 from the Great Tumulus at Vergina, supported by material of the highest quality loaned from other museums in Greece, notably Larissa, Volos, Athens, Kozani, Pella, Kavalla, and Komotini (some items on loan will thus be missing from their normal location where we list them). The exhibition will be displayed here at least until September 1980 when it is hoped to augment it with borrowings from abroad and remount it in a new annexe. The finds from Vergina are certain to remain for some time. The permanent display (detailed below) will then be remounted with minor changes.

The OUTER ROOMS remain more or less as usual, except R. 1 (immediately l. of entrance) where the rich Dherveni finds are normally shown.— R. 2 (up steps from vestibule). Ionic capital and other fragments from a temple at Thermi (end 6C B.C.). A small head, which may be part of the frieze, is just inside R. 3. Here also are a draped kouros from Rhaedestos (6C); a fine grave relief from Pydna (late 5C); headless group of Demeter and Kore from Lete; sacred table from the sanctuary of Demeter and Kore at Dherveni (3C); votive relief from Potidaia (late 4C); grave stelai.—R. 4. Portrait head of a man from a grave relief of mid 1C, and other Hellenistic works.

ROOM 5, a long hall, partially arranged as a Roman courtyard with a central floor mosaic and wall mosaics, all from a villa in Salonika. The floor mosaics depict three legends: Dionysos and Ariadne at Naxos; Zeus and Ganymede; Apollo and Daphne (?). The wall mosaic of three spirited horses (r.) is attractive. Statuary includes a powerful Atlas, from the Agora of Salonika (1C B.C.); a dignified bust of Dionysos, from Drama; three headless Muses (late Roman copies of Hellenistic originals).—R. 6. Portrait statues and heads, mainly of 1C A.D., with two fine figures of Augustus and (headless) possibly Claudius.—R. 7. Later portrait heads: Girl, with pendant ear-rings, her fashionably dressed hair and petulant expression realistically caught; other fine female heads; statue of the Emp. Hadrian (?); *Bronze head of a man (the Emp. Gallienus ?) from Riakia (Pieria).— R. 8. Marble arch with rich relief decoration, part of the Palace of Galerius in Salonika, discovered in 1957 (early 4C A.D.): on the left is Thessalonica personified; on the right a portrait of the Emperor; on the sides Pan and a dancer. By the wall, to the right of the arch, are two fine busts of a man and a woman (late 4C A.D.).

We now descend steps to the vestibule, passing (l.) frames containing fragments of Roman fabric; also (in 1980) the reliquary casket and enamelled bracelets from the normal display (comp. below).

The normal display in the INNER ROOMS (occupied in 1980 by the Macedonian Treasures) is as follows:

Salonika
(Thessaloniki)

0   500 yards
0   500 metres

SIDE A. *Neolithic to Early Iron Age.* To the left, with an explanatory text in English, is a wall map showing location of finds in Macedonia. Neolithic and Bronze Age pottery from Paradimi; early and late Neolithic pottery from Servia, Olynthos, and Limnotopos; Early Bronze Age finds from various sites, including tools from Molivopirgos and Kritsana; imported Attic pottery found at Ankhialos. At the corner of the next side, under a glass case, is the outline body of a girl, with grave goods and jewellery as found (near Veroia, 12–10C B.C.).

SIDE B. *Classical Period.* Geometric pottery from Olynthos and other sites; Attic red-figured krater (Olynthos), showing the birth of Apollo at Delos. By the window, an Attic nuptial *Lekanis (4C B.C.; Peristerona); it shows the preparation of the bride by her women. Opposite in a wall-case is a fragmentary Attic krater representing Nereids bringing armour to Achilles (Olynthos).

SIDE C. *Classical to Byzantine.* Clay mould for terracottas of Cybele with her drum (Olynthos; 5C B.C.). On the right, three cases of terracottas, including a jug in the shape of a negro's head; silver *Hydria of 4C B.C. adorned with a Nike. Along the left wall, Roman glass; among gold, jewellery and metalwork from various sites, a gold diadem from Sedes tomb (4C); *Offerings from a young girl's tomb (Hellenistic) at Neapolis (N.W. of the city), with an exquisite pair of jewelled ear-rings with pendant Erotes; silver hydria from Yefira; case of armour and weapons, with three Illyrian style helmets (two 6C, one 7C). Far end of room, fine silver reliquary (4C) with O.T. scenes (the burning fiery furnace; Daniel in the lions' den; Moses receiving the tablets); Byzantine and later vases; 11C Byzantine jewellery and coins, found in 1956 near Axiou Sq., including ear-rings of pearls mounted in gold, rings, and two magnificent *Bracelets with 20 panels in enamel.

On the far corner stands Y.M.C.A. Headquarters, behind which the *Municipal Library* (open 8–1, 4–8) faces on to the beginning of the Tsimiski.

C. TOUR OF THE RAMPARTS

The Byzantine *Ramparts seem to have taken their present course in the reign of Theodosius (A.D. 379–395). Whether this perpetuates an enceinte of Kassander is uncertain, but here and there well-laid courses of Hellenistic masonry remain. Their 4C length was c. 5 miles, about half of which survives, with upwards of 40 towers, almost all square, spaced very irregularly at distances varying between 25 ft and 140 yds. The construction consists largely of rubble with courses of brick, though in places it is entirely of brick, sometimes with rows of brick arches to give added strength. This device (which enables the wall to remain standing even if the base is sapped) was not again revived in Europe until the 12–13C. Inscriptions survive from a number of rebuildings. The walls stand to a height of 25–50 ft, though the upper courses are largely 14C or 15C work with restorations. In places, 12–18 ft from the wall, can be traced an outwork (proteichisma) designed to deny access to enemy battering rams. All the major gates have now disappeared.

From the White Tower we take LEOFOROS VASILISSIS SOFIAS (Pl. 16). The ancient ramparts, here almost completely vanished, followed the line of the next street to the w. The Plateia Kalamarias occupies the site of the Kassandreia Gate on the Egnatia Odhos, one of four gates in the E. wall. It is known by an inscription to have been repaired by Abp. Eusebius in the 6C. To the left we catch a glimpse of the Arch of Galerius. Odhos Panepistimiou continues N.E. alongside gardens in which short sections of the wall are preserved. To the right extends the **Aristotelian University of Salonika** (Pl. 12), founded in 1925 and removed here in the following year to the building, the former *Turkish Military Academy*, that faces the road. The university now numbers 6000 students and occupies a huge precinct covering much of the former Jewish cemetery, systematically desecrated by the Germans in 1943. Among the more striking new buildings are the circular *Meteorological Observatory* and the huge *Polytechnic School*. The *Library* contains 300,000 books. Passing between the *Chemical Faculty* and the *Central Hospital* we bear left across a square where Odhos Ayiou Dhimitriou once threaded the walls by the Gate of the Archangels.

A little to the N. a red house in Odhos Apostolou Pavlou (next to the Turkish Consulate) is the *Birthplace of Mustafa Kemal* (Ataturk; 1881–1938), first President of Turkey. A plaque was placed here in 1933. Kemal, the son of a government clerk, spent his childhood in the city and attended the Military Cadet School. In 1907–11 he was posted to the Turkish Third Army (then in Salonika), and took part in the march to Constantinople that overthrew Abdul Hamid.—Near by is the 14C church of *Ayios Nikólaos Orfanós* where the contemporary frescoes were successfully cleaned in 1963.

From the road to the left of the *Evangelistria Cemetery* the first lane (l.) leads shortly to the walls, here partly hidden by popular occupation. We may follow the cobbled Odhos Athinas inside them or, better, the path outside, parallel to a new road that ascends past the grounds of the *Municipal Hospital* (Pl. 4). Here the walls become continuous with sections remaining to the battlements. Part of an inscription, 10 yds long in brick, high up on the *Hormisdas Tower* reads τείχεσιν αρρήκτοις Ὁρμίσδας ἐξετέλεσε τήνδε πόλιν (by indestructible walls Hormisdas completely fortified this town). Hormisdas the Younger held various offices in Salonika and Constantinople under Theodosius. The *Chain Tower* (Gingirli Koule), so called from the heavy stringcourse half way up, is a circular keep of the 15C, contemporary with the White Tower, and probably replaced a corner tower destroyed in 1430. To the left of its modern steps some regular masonry appears to be of classical date. We may pass inside the circuit through a gap in the wall or continue round the outside to the Acropolis.

The **Acropolis** still retains the greater part of its wall, though on the E. side it is largely Turkish. The long section facing N. is of greater interest. We may enter from within the city (see below), or from outside, beyond the Chain Tower, by the *Gate of Anna Palaeologus*, first opened in 1355 by the widow of Andronikos III. It preserves a Byzantine inscription. The triangle here, where the Acropolis wall meets the city wall, probably is to be identified with the *Trigonion* where the storming Turks gained entry in 1430. Within the Acropolis unremarkable suburban villas climb haphazard to the *Eptapirghion* (Yedi Koule), a fortress with seven towers, that crowns the summit. The massive central tower bears an Arabic inscription recording its construction in 1431 by Sungur Çauş Bey. The stronghold still serves as a prison (no adm.). Outside the Acropolis the barren countryside extends to the walls; in the cold winter of 1961 jackals were seen on the fringes of the city.

Odhos Eptapirghiou follows the excellently preserved *South Wall* of the Acropolis, which is also part of the main circuit of the city. Steps mount to the top, where the walk within the inner and outer parapets, accessible for c. 100 yds, commands the Acropolis; hence in 1345 the enraged mob hurled the nobles on to stakes below. The original towers face towards the Acropolis which, more vulnerable to an expected assault from the landward, might be invested first. In the 14C when the likelier danger had proven to be from the sea, four shallow

Salonika

0   300 yards

0   300 metres

1

2

ELIPIDOS

POLIORKITOU

SANTOURI

DHIMITRIOU

PRONOIAS

Ay. Ekaterini

Profit

STOURNARA

OLIMBIADHOS

5

6

KASSAN

Ay. Dhin

IFESTIONOS

Dioikitirion

AYIOU DHIMITRIOU

Ay. Apostoloi

OLIMBOU

l

PLAT

DIKASTIR

IRINIS

DIOIKITIRIOU

SINGROU

DRAGOUMI

VENIZELOU

IOUSTINIANOU

g

c

Dhimarkhion

10

Panayia Khalkeon

PLAT. METAXA (AXIOU)

j a b f

i

Cinema

EGNATIAS

IONOS

ELEFTHERIOU

DHODHEKANISOU

e

SOFOU

LEONDOS

R.C. Church

FRANGON

ERMOU

VASILEOS

IRAKLIOU

Bank

Ay. Minas

Hamam

LEOFOROS ARISTOTELOU

r

TSIMISK

Bank

d

PO

p

Bank

FRANKLIN

n

ROOSEVELT

13

KOUNDOURIOTOU

Bank

PLAT

14

PLAT

NAV

ELEFTHERIAS

Airways Office

ARISTOTEL

Brit. Cons. Gen.

LEOFORO

N

Custom House

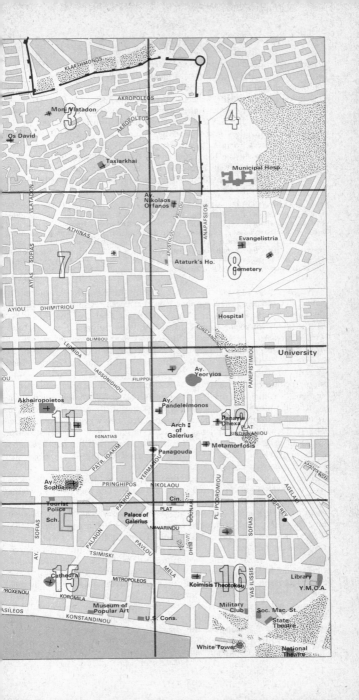

towers were added on the seaward side. The second one bears the device of Andronikos II Palaeologus. A small secret *Postern* survives between the second and third. A modern gate has been opened towards the w. end, nearly opposite which stands the *Moni Vlataion* (or Vlatadon; Pl. 3), a monastery which takes name from its foundation in the 14C by the Cretan brothers Vlatades. Since the church is dedicated to the Transfiguration, they were probably Hesychasts. Largely rebuilt in 1801, the church (originally on the plan of Ayia Ekaterini) preserves original frescoes in the bema and in the parecclesion to the right. The monastic buildings will house a Patriarchal Academy of Patristic Studies. Farther along Odhos Eptapirghiou, the wall is partly hidden by old houses.

A lane leads (l.) to **Osios David** (Pl. 2), a tiny church probably dating from the late 5C, though its foundation is attributed by tradition to Theodora, daughter of Galerius. In medieval times it served the Moni Latómou. Its plan, an inscribed cross of Syrian type and unusually early date, was mutilated when it became a mosque. In 1921 beneath plaster in the apse was discovered a *Mosaic, contemporary with the church, of Christ, depicted beardless, between Ezekiel and Habakkuk. It appears to interpret the visions of Ezekiel I and II in the spirit of the New Testament, for the two prophets can also represent SS Paul and Peter.

We may pass outside the walls again by the *Eski Delik*, an ancient gate, later blocked, then reopened by the Turks. The N. walls follow the rugged natural contour. The two abrupt angles of the salient w. of the gate are exceptionally furnished with polygonal towers, one with a postern. Just beyond the second is the triangular *Tower of Manuel Palaeologus* (c. 1230), on which (20 ft up) can be seen an inscription in four lines coupling his name with that of George Apokaukos, probably governor of the city. The ramparts facing N.E. and N., pierced by the Turkish *Yeni Delik* (New Gate), incorporate numerous vestiges of Hellenistic masonry and one section of Roman construction. A little distance from the wall is **Ayia Ekaterini** (Pl. 5), a pretty church of similar plan to the Dhodeka Apostoloi (see below) without a narthex. The outer walk has arcades, closed externally with glass, and surmounted by a wavy cornice. The church dates from the late 13C; the contemporary paintings were much spoiled during its time as the *Yakob Pasha Cami* after 1510.

The extreme N.W. corner of the ramparts is furnished with more frequent towers and protected by an outwork. The *Letaia Gate*, with a hexagonal barbican, has been reduced to ruin in this century; there remains some pseudo-isodomic masonry incorporating reused classical blocks. A few yards inside the gate is the *Dhodeka Apostoloi (Pl. 5), the least restored and perhaps the most charming of Salonika's churches. Founded by the Patriarch Niphou (1312–15), it was a monastic church until its conversion to the Mohammedan rite as the *Soouk Sou Cami*. The E. end has richly patterned brickwork. Round three sides of the central cross-in-square runs an outer aisle having four corner domes. The narthex has an arcaded façade. The inner dome is borne on four columns with capitals from an earlier edifice. The wall paintings, extensive but damaged, include a Tree of Jesse in the s. aisle. The four barrel vaults that support the drum have lively mosaics. S. Vault. Nativity, with a bucolic shepherd and soulful animals; the handmaiden Salome prepares a bath; the midwife tests the temperature of the water, while the Child apprehensively turns away. The Transfiguration is powerfully composed.

Just below are the *Loutra Phoenix* with an attractive dome.

We descend Odhos Irinis, where an animated fruit market largely masks the wall, to PLATEIA METAXA (Pl. 9), or *Axiou*, the busy w. entrance to the city. A *Statue of Constantine*, liberator of Salonika, occupies the site of the sculptured Golden Gate of the Flavian epoch, described and drawn by 19C travellers, but since totally demolished.

Here converge the two principal routes into the city. To the N. in Odhos Langadha stands a fine *Memorial* (1962) to the 50,000 Salonikan Jews who perished in the gas chambers of Auschwitz. The monument, a monolithic block of Pentelic marble, was designed by the Italian architect, Manfredo Portino.—To the N.W. Odhos Monasteriou leads shortly to the *Railway Station*.

From the square, Odhos Frangon follows the line of the early Byzantine walls, fragments of which survive in the derelict *Top Hane*, the Turkish fort and arsenal, and near the Roman Catholic Church. Between here and the modern harbour lay the classical port, silted up in the Middle Ages. Here now extends an interesting quarter of Turkish warehouses, threaded by streets paved with lava.

In the nearer suburbs of Salonika there are two British Military Cemeteries of the First World War. The *Zeitenlik* or *Lembet Road Cemetery*, off the w. side of the Serres road, contains 1648 British graves; the *Monastir Road Indian Cemetery*, 2 m. from the centre beyond the station, commemorates 520 fallen. Other cemeteries are situated at Mikra (see below; 1900 burials) and near Khortiatis (see below; 586 graves).

D. EXCURSIONS FROM SALONICA

I. TO AYIA TRIAS AND THE THERMAIC GULF. Road, 18 m. (29 km.), bus in summer; also by motor-boat. We leave the city by the long Leoforos Megalou Alexandhrou (once briefly renamed after John Kennedy) which, behind the water-front esplanade (p. 517), takes eastbound traffic (return by the older Leof. Vasilissis Olgas, parallel inland). Soon a turning goes off left for *Pilaía* (6900 inhab.) and *Panórama* (see below); between the two is *Anatolia College*, an American school for boys and girls. It was founded (as a boys' school) in 1886 in Asia Minor and removed to Salonika after the First World War.—The main road keeps inland of Aretsou and continues through lengthening ribbon development.—At 4¼ m. a road leads l. (½ m.) to the *American Farm School* (Amerikaniki Yeoryiki Skholí), founded in 1903 by John Henry House in order to introduce modern methods into Greece (c. 800 students; visit on application to the Director). We pass the *Army Staff College* and just touch the shore.—6¼ m. The Northern H.Q. of the Hellenic Air Force stands where the road for Poliyiros diverges left (Rte 64A).—7 m. Turning (r.) for the Airport (*Mikra*; Motel C); beside the road is the very prominent *Tsairi Toumba*. Other mounds can be seen as we skirt the airport.—At 9¾m. the road to Nea Moudhiana and Kassandra bears left.—We continue past turns to *Peraía* (Lena B, Aegli C), with a relay station of the American radio, and *Néoi Epivátai*, both popular beach resorts.—14½ m. (23 km.) Ayía Triás (*Sun Beach* B, *Galaxy* C, both summer only) has a large camp site and bathing beach of the N.T.O.G., and a Youth Hostel.—Beyond Ayía Triás is a turn (unpaved) for *Angelokhóri*, a centre of tomato and cucumber growing; before the village a track leads (r.) to Cape Megalo Karabournoú, site of ancient *Dinaion*. The main road continues to (18 m.) *Nea Mikhanióna*, a busy small fishing town on the open gulf, with many shaded restaurants just above the long beach.

II. Mt Khortiátis (3940 ft) rises to the E. of Salonika, and separates the Gulf of Salonika from Lake Langadha (Koronia). The summit is in a prohibited zone, but a height of 2500 ft may be reached by road. The approach road quits the N. suburbs of Salonika and rises to (5½ m.) *Asvestokhórion* (Philippion B), a popular summer resort (885 ft; 2600 inhab.) on the w. slope of Profitis Ilias (2520 ft).—8¾ m. Near quarries, roads descend (r.) to Panorama (see below) and, soon after (l.) to *Ayios Vasilios* on the Via Egnatia by the lake (Rte 66).—We pass the remains of an aqueduct and reach (11 m.) *Khortiátis*, facing N.W. on wooded slopes. Thence the road climbs a further 3 m. to the prohibited zone, affording a fine view over Salonika; there is also a signposted path from Khortiatis to (1¼ hr) a refuge of the Alpine Club.—We may return by taking the s. turn at the quarries to reach first *Nea Panorama* (with the option of bearing left and descending viâ Thermi, Rte 64), then **Panórama** (*Nephele* DPO, *Panorama*, both A; *Pefka* C) just above Anatolia College (comp. above).

III. FROM SALONIKA TO GHEVGELI, Road, 51 m. (82 km.) and railway (49 m. in 2 hrs). This is the main highway into Yugoslavia and the main railway route to Belgrade by the plain and valley of the Axios (Vardar). To (14¼ m.) *Yefira*, see Rte 60. The road turns N. and follows the left bank of the Axios. The river is largely controlled by irrigation and anti-flood works. From Yefira to the border the old road through the villages and the National Highway run parallel. From (24¼ m.) *Kastanás* the railway runs between the roads. To the E. are the American drainage works that reduced the former *Lake Amatovon*. At (33 m.) *Limnotopos*, we cross one of the sluices.—37¼ m. *Polykastron* (Olympion **D**), formerly *Karasouli*, has an international Military Cemetery with British graves. A large ammunition dump here was blown up in a German air raid in April 1917. The village is at the s.w. end of *Lake Ardzan*, also drained, on the N. shore of which the Iron Age site of *Chauchitsa* (Tsaoutsitza) was excavated by the British School in 1921. The railway now crosses to the w. of roads and river to follow the Vardar through the *Stena Tsingane Derven*, a defile 6 m. long at the E. foot of Païkon (with molybdenum mines in the foothills), to the frontier station of *Idoméni*. The roads remain E. of the isolated *Mt Skóli* (1160 ft), passing (43 m.) *Mikró Dhasos*, to (46 m.) Evzoni (*Evzoni* **B**), beyond which is the frontier post, still on the left bank of the river. The Vardar is crossed on Yugoslav soil.—51 m. Ghevgeli (*Vardar Motel*).

60   FROM SALONIKA TO EDHESSA

ROAD, Via Egnatia, 55¼ m. (89 km.), straight and level with a good surface; dual carriageway to Khalkidhon; bus hourly.—RAILWAY, see Rte 61.

We quit Salonika by the Plateia Axiou (Pl. 9) and the Railway Station, at first following the international line to Yugoslavia through industrial suburbs.—At (4¼ m.) *Dhiavatá*, road to Kilkis (23 m., r.). We cross the Serres railway and pass a memorial to French soldiers killed in the First World War. As we cross (7 m.) the Gallikos, from whose sandy bed small quantities of gold are extracted, the prehistoric mound of *Grademborion* can be seen to the N. A road branches left to Síndhos and into the central Pedhias Kampanias (comp. Rte 61).

Between (2½ m.) *Síndhos* and (7 m.) *Pírgos*, identified with the classical *Chalastra*, then on the coast, Xerxes' fleet lay waiting for the army to catch up.—9½ m. *Néa Málgara*, a huge refugee settlement amid rice-fields on the right bank of the Axios, is built on land reclaimed since ancient times.—15½ m. *Klidhíon* may represent ancient *Haloros*, where, following preclassical boundaries, the nome of Imathia pushes a narrow tongue to the sea.

8½ m. A large flat mound to the left is called *Trapezoeides*.—We cross over the National Highway to the frontier (comp. above) and over the railway to Yugoslavia.—15½ m. *Yéfira* (r.; Motel C), at the junction of the old road to Yugoslavia (spur to the Highway), is (as its name indicates) where the Axios was bridged before its diversion to its modern bed. A prehistoric table-mound and classical finds prove the antiquity of the site; here in 1912 was signed the agreement surrendering Salonika to Greece. About a mile farther on irrigation canals carry water from the *Axios River Barrage* (1954–58), situated 2 m. N. of the road (earth approach-road on top of dyke). We cross the Axios by a girder bridge (guard posts; traffic lights) of 14 spans, built by British sappers (228 Army Field Company) in 1945 (plaque, left at bridge entrance).

The Axios, or *Vardar*, the largest river in Macedonia, rises deep in Yugoslavia and flows for only 50 m. through Greece from the 'Iron Gates' to the sea. Before the flood and reclamation works, instituted by Venizelos in 1925, gave the river its present bed, the area was largely malarial marshes. Further irrigation works, jointly controlling the Axios and Aliakmon, undertaken in 1953–63 by C. Karamanlis, will bring the greater part under cultivation.

19 m. (31 km.) *Khalkidhón* (2900 inhab.; Restaurants) grew up after 1923 round the old timber-framed han at the junction where the Via Egnatia and the Veroia road, also of Roman origin or earlier, divided to pass Lake Loudias. We follow the Via Egnatia. About 1 m. farther on a road diverges to Idomeni. To the S. extends a fertile plain, drained by the Loudias, an artificial river that perpetuates the name of the classical LAKE LOUDIAS (later Lake Yiannitsa), drained in 1927–36. At an earlier era this was connected with the sea (comp. below). A series of funerary mounds, to the left of the road, marks the edge of the lake.—23½ m. (38 km.) *Pélla* (2100 inhab.).

PELLA (ΠΕΛΛΑ), capital of Macedonia at the height of its greatness and birthplace of Alexander the Great, was formerly connected by a shallow navigable lagoon with the Thermaic Gulf. Chance finds in 1957 located the exact site of the city, estimated to have occupied 1½ sq. miles; and excavations by Prof. Makaronas and Ph. Petsas in 1957–68 uncovered the celebrated mosaics of c. 300 B.C. which are the principal artistic attraction of the place so far.

An earlier settlement called *Bounomeia* by Stephanus Byzantius may have lain to the S., where prehistoric sherds have come to light. *Pella* is mentioned by Herodotus and has yielded coins from the mid-5C B.C. The Macedonian capital was transferred from Aigai to Pella by Archelaus (413–399 B.C.), whose artistic entourage included the painter Zeuxis, the poet Agathon, who died at the court in 400, and Euripides, who died here in 406. At Pella were born Philip II in 382 and Alexander the Great in 356. The city flourished especially under Antigonus Gonatas. It fell to Aemilius Paulus after the Battle of Pydna, and from 148 B.C. lost importance to Thessalonica. At one time the Romans called it *Diocletianopolis*; its site may then have been moved to the W.

The most spectacular finds have come from the N. part of three rectangular blocks, cut across by the main road. The richest of the houses, occupying the whole of 'Block 1' immediately behind the 'apotheke', is the **House of the Lion Hunt,** a building of the late 4C B.C., 165 ft wide and more than 300 ft long, having three open courts running N. and S. Three of its dozen rooms were decorated with mosaics now in the museum. Fragments of painted plaster, bronze bosses from the doors, and terracotta antefixes show it to have been a splendid edifice, and its stamped roof tiles suggest that it had an official function. The building is bordered by broad streets lined with clay water-pipes and stone sewers. Much of the central peristyle (six columns square) has been re-erected and the great patterned pebble mosaics of the main rooms restored.

Block 5 (two blocks to the w.) has yielded a further range of mosaics.

The Rape of Helen (Pl. D) and Stag Hunt (Pl. E), originally lifted, have been restored to position.

The ACROPOLIS occupied the more westerly hill behind but is scarcely worth visiting. Here foundations have been unearthed of an exedra and a large Hellenistic building with thick walls and Doric columns, possibly a sanctuary. It is unlikely to be the Palace of Archelaos, painted by Zeuxis, where in 356 B.C. Alexander was born. A second exedra was unearthed in 1970. So far no trace has been found of the Theatre where c. 408 B.C. the Bacchae of Euripides received its first performance.

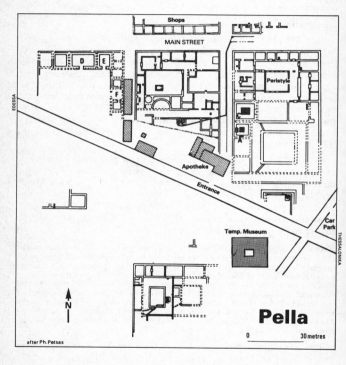

Among the finds temporarily displayed in a future Tourist Pavilion (open 9–1, 3.30–5.30; Sun and hol. 10–4; closed Tues) are the superb *Mosaics from Blocks 1 & 5. The life-size figures are fashioned with natural pebbles of various colours; special features are outlined with strips of lead or clay. The eyes (all missing) were probably semi-precious stones. The positions from which the mosaics came are indicated on the plan. Lion Hunt (Pl. C), perhaps the rescue of Alexander himself by Krateros near Susa; Dionysos on a leopard's back (Pl. B); Griffin attacking a deer (Pl. A); Amazonomachia (Pl. F). A well-preserved bronze statuette of Poseidon is a Hellenistic copy of the Lateran type. The marble Dog (460–450 B.C.) was found in 1954 in a cemetery to the E. Also notable are a marble measure for liquids, an inlaid table, and a marble statuette of a Horseman (Hellenistic). Ante-fixes and roof tiles are inscribed with the name of the city.

To the s. of the road, rising above the drained marsh, is a small green mound, originally the late-Helladic settlement of *Phacos*. On it was later built a fortified treasury that served the Macedonian kings and is described by Livy.

24½ m. *Nea Pella* (r.) is a refugee settlement. By the road are the so-called *Baths of Alexander*, a Hellenistic fountain, repaired by the Romans; here probably Aemilius Paulus pitched camp and a Roman settlement developed.—29¾ m. (48 km.) **Yiannitsá** (ΓΙΑΝΝΙΤΣΑ, or Γενιτσά; *Douvantzis* C), seat of an eparchy and the largest town (18,150 inhab.) in the nome of Pella, lies to the right of the road. As *Yeniceyi Vardar* it was a holy place of the Turks. In an ill-used mosque are the tombs of the Evrenos family (14–15C), descendants of the conqueror of Macedonia. A bronze *Monument* by the road com-memorates the Battle of Yiannitsa (1912), which ensured the liberation of Salonika. The battle actually took place at (33 m.) *Melíssi*, where the Turks fiercely contested the crossing of the Balítsa.—34¾ m. *Karió-tissa*. To the N., c. 6 m. away, *Meterizi* (5240 ft), the third highest peak of the *Páïkon Mts*, rises abruptly from the plain. Mt Páïkon itself (behind right) is 5410 ft. We cross two of the large flood canals that channel to the Aliakmon the waters of the Vodas, the Moglenitsa, and countless mountain streams from Vermion that once inundated the plain. Edhessa and its waterfalls are seen ahead.—We meet the railway from Veroia at (45¼ m.) *Skídhra* (Hero C), a fruit grading and canning centre (4000 inhab.). The road from Veroia (see below) is joined at the s. end of the bridge spanning the Vodas.—46¾ m. *Mav-rovoúnion* stands on the N. bank. Orchards of peaches and pears extend along the road. Beyond (51½ m.) *Rizárion* the valley becomes lush as we again cross the copious streams of the Vodas below Edhessa's falls. A short steep hill mounts to the ridge.

55¼ m. (89 km.) **EDHESSA** (*Xenia* B, DPO, above the falls; *Alpha*, *Pella*, both D; *Rest. Platanakia*, in the square, *Mitsos*, near the falls, and on the hill above the rly stn) is beautifully situated above a steep bluff, facing s.E., over which the waters of the Edhesseos fall into the Salonikan plain. The town itself occupies a semi-circular plateau (1150 ft), backed by the foothills of Mt Vermion. Through it flow numerous cascades which gave it its Slav name of *Vodena* (The Waters). Capital of the nome of Pella and seat of a metropolitan, the town (14,000 inhab.) is a favourite summer resort. Its commanding situation on the Via Egnatia has always given it strategic importance. Its industries include the manufacture of carpets, and it is a prominent trading and agricultural centre. The view from the town takes in the Pindos on the w., Olympos to the s.E., and the heights beyond Salonika to the E.

History. Until the discoveries in 1977 at Vergina (p. 532) *Edessa* was thought to be the site of ancient Aigai, a belief the local inhabitants are disinclined to relin-quish. It was a flourishing place in antiquity. During the temporary Bulgarian occupation it was called *Vodena*. In Oct 1912 the Greek army entered the town. It was re-occupied by Bulgarians in the Second World War.

The numerous streams that score the town unite on the E. to fall in cascades. To see them, we go to the cemetery and then turn right at the chapel. Thence a path leads direct to the **Falls*. The drop is 80 ft, after which the water descends steeply to the plain. The cliffs are covered with luxuriant vegetation, including vines, pomegranates, figs, and nut-trees. There are said to be crayfish in the waters. The volume of the cascades is diminished by hydro-electric works (p. 542). Under the falls is a cave with stalactites. Odhos Makedonomakhon has attractive old houses. From the terrace near the *Archbishop's Palace*, farther to the right, there is a splendid *View, with the attractive *Monastery of Kaisarianá* in the foreground. The church of *Koimisis tis Panayias*, now the archiepiscopal chapel, incorporates antique columns, probably from a temple on the site and has a good ikonostasis. In 1979 excavations were in progress within. Traces of the city's medieval walls can be seen in the lane descending to the right. At the N. end of the town is a fine single-span *Bridge*, of Roman or Byzantine date, which carried the Via Egnatia. Some Roman inscriptions and 5C mosaics found in 1963 are stored in an attractive 15C mosque, behind the Clock Tower.

The ancient circuit of the lower city was traced in 1968 in the 'Longos' area below the falls. The recent excavations (free; phylax on site) near Áyios Triádhos should not be missed. They are reached by taking the Salonika road for 3 m. and, at a sharp bend, turning left down a by-road. The site has a remarkable stretch of wall incorporating a cave shrine; a gate leads to a paved main street having an Ionic colonnade (inscriptions).—The road continues to the hydroelectric works (no adm.) but a right fork leads to the foot of the falls. By the huge pipe are remains of a marble Byzantine Church.

From Edhessa a road leads N., followed by a bus (6 times daily) to (15 m.) **Aridaía** (*Emborikon* D), or *Ardéa*, seat with 3600 inhab. of the eparchy of *Almopías*, in a low well-watered plain hemmed in by the magnificent crests of the Vóras range that form the Yugoslav frontier. Here are grown pimentos, tobacco, and silk. The French built a Decauville railway from Skidhra to serve the area in the First World War; this survived as a passenger line until 1935.—A road goes on W. to *Loutrá Aridaías* (7 m.), a large hydropathic establishment in a pretty glen with plane trees shading the tumbling waters.

To *Naousa* and *Veroia*, see Rte 61.

61 FROM SALONIKA TO VEROIA (AND EDHESSA)

ROAD, 46½ m. (75 km.), leaving the Via Egnatia (Rte 60) at (19 m.) *Khalkidhón*, and continuing, flat and monotonous, to (46½ m.) *Veroia*. BUS every ½ hr.

RAILWAY, 43 m. (69 km.), 6–8 trains daily in c. 70 min.; the line branches from the Athens line at (12 m.) *Platí* and runs 1–3 m. s. of the road most of the way to (43 m.) *Veroia*. Beyond Veroia the railway continues N. viâ Naousa to (69 m.) *Edhessa*.

From Salonika to (19 m.) *Khalkidhón*, see Rte 60. The road traverses the PEDHIAS KAMPANIAS, an exposed plain of exceptional flatness, that extends to the Gulf of Salonika; it was once a lagoon into which both the Axios and Aliakmon drained, and as late as classical times was navigable nearly to Pella. The settlement of *Adendron* ('without trees'), on the railway (l.), is aptly named. We cross the *Loudias*, an artificial river created in 1925 (comp. Rte 60), and enter the ancient district of *Emathia*, a monotonous country populated by herds of buffalo and goats, which gives name to the modern nome.—27 m. Turning for *Platí* (2 m. l.), an important railway junction (comp. above; 1930 inhab.) with a sugar refinery.—At 30½ m. the old road to Athens forks left through *Alexándhreia* (Manthos D), or *Yida*, a sprawling

agricultural town (8200 inhab.).—41 m. We cross the sluice by which
the waters of the Vodas are diverted to the Aliakmon. At **Néa Niko-
mídeia,** 2½ m. N., a neolithic settlement was laid bare in 1961–64 by a
combined team from the British and American Schools. Radio-carbon
tests have given a date of c. 6200 B.C., by far the earliest Neolithic
known on the Greek mainland though Palaeolithic sites have since been
located in Epirus. Houses of two periods were found, arranged round a
central structure which yielded female idols and serpentine axes. The
settlement was fortified.—At (44¾ m.) we pass close to *Véroia Station*
(r.), leave the Vergina road (see below) to the left, join that from
Edhessa, and enter Véroia from the North.

46½ m. (75 km.) **VEROIA** (ΒΕΡΟΙΑ), anciently Βέρροια, the *Berea*
of the New Testament, and nowadays pronounced *Vérria,* is the capital
of the nome of Imathia and the seat of a metropolitan. Situated on a
travertine terrace (615 ft) near the E. foot of Mt Vermion, it serves as a
base for skiers. Water from the Tripotamos, a tributary of the Aliakmon, runs through the streets. Cloth handicrafts are worked from
hemp and flax spun locally, and the town (29,500 inhab.) has a market
(Tuesday) for peaches and apples from the district. Its appearance is
changing rapidly from ramshackle vernacular to undistinguished
modernity.

Hotels. **Villa Ilia,** 16 Ilias; **Polytimi,** 35 Megalou Alexandhrou; **Vasilissa Vergina,** near Ay. Antonios; all C.—*Restaurant Ilia* (Tourist Pavilion).

Post Office, Leof. Mitropoleos.

Buses to *Vergina,* also to *Naousa* and *Edhessa* (3 times daily) from Ayios
Antonios; to *Salonika* and to *Kozani* (10 times daily) from the Plateia Orologiou.

History. *Beroea* emerges at the end of the 5C as the second city of Emathia,
known from an inscription to have been dedicated to Herakles Kynagidas. It
was the first Macedonian city to surrender after the Roman victory of Pydna
in 168 B.C. Pompey here spent the winter of 49–48 B.C. St Paul and Silas, having
experienced trouble at Thessalonika, withdrew to Beroea, where the Jews, more
noble than those of Thessalonika, searched the scriptures daily (Acts XVII,
10–12). At an early date Beroea became a bishopric. When Diocletian reorganized the Roman colonial empire, he made Beroea one of the two capitals of
Macedonia. About the end of the 10C it endured the Bulgar invasions, and in the
14C it was occupied by the Serbs. The Turks, who called the town *Karaferiye,*
established here a military colony.

At the top of the hill at the entrance to the town remnants of the
ramparts survive. A *Tower,* of pseudo-isodomic construction resembling
the Letaia Gate at Salonika has been dated to the 3C A.D.; among
reused blocks are incorporated grave reliefs and shield metopes. Odhos
Venizelou leads straight down to the centre, but it is pleasanter to take
the broad road to the left. This curves round to form an esplanade
where ramparts once overlooked the plain. Here the **Museum** (adm.
25 dr.; 9–1, 3.30–5.30; Sun 10–4) stands in a garden lined with inscribed
tombstones from Roman and later times. Displayed within are Geometric brooches, breast ornaments and weapons from tombs at Vergina
and Levkadhia; Neolithic finds from Nea Nikomidea; Roman portraits
and sculptural fragments found in Veroia; also a stele (2C B.C.) inscribed with the rules of the Gymnasion; and the painted roof from the
destroyed church of Ayia Fotini.

Farther on the garden suburb of ELIÁ has a belvedere and Tourist
Pavilion. The broad Leoforos Ilias runs up to meet Venizelou at the
centre of the town. Hence Mitropoleos rises gently past a Byzantine

church and the modern Cathedral (re-used capitals in the narthex) to the Plateia Orologiou, site of the Kastro, now partly occupied by law courts. Behind the Hawaii Rest. by the side of a mosque and minaret is the so-called *Bema* (a fanciful reconstruction of 1961) from which St Paul is said to have preached. From the w. corner of the square the narrow Odhos Kentrikos leads N. to the *Old Metropolis* (closed and decaying), with early Christian columns and a minaret, opposite which stands the *Plane-tree* from which the Turks hanged Abp. Kallimachos in 1436. Beyond are remnants of the old lower town.

The numerous churches of wattle and timber construction were the most unusual feature of the lower town. Built during the Turkish domination, they were sited inconspicuously behind houses and their appearance disguised. Formerly they were hard to find. Most of the ramshackle old houses have recently been replaced by modern blocks and the churches revealed. They have been over-restored but (though supposedly open at museum hours) are usually locked.

THE PRINCIPAL EXCURSIONS are to Mt Vermion and to the Macedonian tombs at Vergina and Levkadhia.

Royal and noble *Macedonian Tombs*, like those of Mycenae, were splendid subterranean structures, built of local poros stone, with a vaulted roof. Smaller tombs have a pediment or a simply sculptured cornice. Later and grander examples take the form of the classical temple having a complete façade with columns, entablature, and pediment. The doors were generally of marble and hung on metal hinges. The chamber within was furnished with marble couches or thrones; its walls were usually plastered and painted. The façade may also be frescoed. Some twenty or more tombs have so far been excavated in Macedonia, of which the most important and accessible are those near Veroia.

The road to Vergina (7 m.; bus 8 times daily) quits Véroia near the Tourist Pavilion, passing Lofos Vikellis, with the birthplace of the writer Konstantinos Vikelas (1808–86). The house is preserved.—3 m. *Ayía Varvára* has a spring and a café. The Piéria Mts stand out ahead. We descend to the *Aliakmon Barrage*, a graceful concrete structure, 350 yds long, whose 19 piers carry the road across the river. The curved approach on the N. side was made necessary by the discovery during construction of a *Temple Tomb* (visible left; no adm.) of the 3C B.C. The outer doorway has triglyphs, the inner doorway is white with a yellow moulding. The interior is plastered and painted in bands, white below, black and red above. At the end of the bridge we turn left.

7 m. **Vergína** (ΒΕΡΓΙΝΑ), a refugee village of 1923, named after a legendary queen of Beroia, replaces a city that existed from the beginning of the Iron Age to Classical times. This is now considered with some certainty to have been *Aigai*, which Perdikkas, founder of the Macedonian monarchy, made his capital.

The residence of the kings until the seat of government was transferred to Pella, it remained the national sanctuary and the royal burial-place. Here Philip II was assassinated in 336 B.C. A tradition that the Macedonian dynasty would perish as soon as one of the kings was buried elsewhere was given point by the chaos that followed the burial of Alexander the Great in Asia. The place was pillaged by Gaulish mercenaries left to guard it by Pyrrhus in 274/3 B.C.

The **Great Tumulus** may have been ordered by Antigonus Gonatas to protect his own tomb and cover the general damage by the Gauls. An exploratory trench from the s. edge dug by Prof. M. Andronikos in 1977 revealed foundations of a destroyed monument associated with an earlier mound covering a frescoed chamber-grave (pillaged) and an intact vaulted tomb with a painted façade, dated with some certainty both by the ritual remains of sacrifice and by the contents to 350–325 B.C. Within were found two marble sarcophagi containing larnakes of gold, and all the panoply of royal burial: purple and gold cloth shrouding the bones, gold wreaths, sceptre, ivory portraits from a throne or bier, weapons, and silver and bronze vessels. The **Finds have already been put on display in Salonika; the site of the Tomb itself is not accessible to visitors and excavations continue.

The so-called PALACE OF PALATITSA (named after the old village to the N.E. at its first discovery in 1861 by a French expedition) is situated on a low hill to the S.E. marked by a large oak-tree. Excavations of the Greek Archaeological Service in 1937–40 were resumed in 1954–61. The building, roughly 100 yds square, dates probably from the reign of Antigonus Gonatas and was destroyed by fire. The N. side, where the lower courses of the outer wall are well preserved, is littered with poros drums and capitals. A triple *Propylaia* leads through the E. wing to a central *Peristyle* of pilasters (16 by 16) having double engaged columns. On the s. side is a *Mosaic Floor* finely executed in polychrome pebbles.—Between the palace and the village extends a vast tumulus CEMETERY of the Early Iron Age (10–7C B.C.) excavated by Prof. M. Andronikos in 1952–61. Of the hundreds of mounds, many were disturbed in Hellenistic times, but intact burials have yielded iron swords, bronze ornaments (including a triple double-axe amulet), Lausitz ware, and Protogeometric pottery. We descend the right side of a ravine to the *Tomb of Vergina*, a Macedonian temple tomb with an Ionic façade closed by two pairs of marble doors. Within, a marble *Throne*, 6 ft high, with a footstool, has arms supported by carved sphinxes and a back with painted decoration.—Another tomb of this type has been found to the E. of Palatitsa.

FROM VEROIA TO EDHESSA, 29 m. (47 km.). From Ay. Antonios the road leads N. across the Tripotamos, then follows the railway.—8 m. *Náousa Station* lies off the road (r.). The flourishing town (17,400 inhab.) of Náousa (*Kioski Rest.*, good; bus from the station) stands 4 m. w. on a travertine terrace between two tributaries of the Arapitsa, one of which falls near by in a cascade. The town is renowned for its full red wine, its peaches, and its silk. Naousa is a corruption of *Nea Augousta* and has been known to the Turks as *Agustos*; it occupies an ancient site, perhaps that of *Mieza* (but comp. below). The town was destroyed in 1821 and again suffered in 1944–48 but its narrow streets remain on an old plan. In its carnival masked dancers with scimitars symbolize the oppression of the Janissaries. Near the modern church of *Ayia Paraskevi* a fine park looks out over the plain and there is a small military museum. The wooden *Ayios Dhimitrios* is built over an ancient edifice.

10 m. Levkádhia, a hamlet w. of the road, has given name to three Macedonian tombs, lying near the main road before we reach the village turn. The discovery of a building with mosaics s. of the village and another on a hill near the Arapitsa suggest that Levkadhia was a place of some importance, perhaps the ancient *Mieza* where Aristotle taught. Signposted (r., on a by-road crossing the railway) is the 'Great Tomb', protected by a concrete hangar (closed Mon morn. and Fri morn.). This is the largest *TEMPLE TOMB so far unearthed.

On the *Façade* two outer pilasters and four Doric fluted columns support an entablature with painted metopes and triglyphs and a frieze in bas-relief depicting a battle between Macedonians and Persians. A second (Ionic) story, rising above the vault, has seven false doors surmounted by a pediment (of which only fragments survive). Two life-size frescoes in vivid colours represent (l.) the deceased with Hermes Psychopompos and (r.) Aiakos and Rhadamanthys, the judges of the Underworld. An ante-chamber leads to a square barrel-vaulted *Chamber* with painted panels between engaged pilasters. Rows of nails remain *in situ* where presumably garlands were hung. The tomb is dated to the beginning of the 3C B.C.

Beside the main road, 200 yds farther N., is the '*Kinch*' *Tomb*, and 300 yds beyond this (l.; signposted) is a much smaller vaulted *Lyson Kallikles Tomb* of the early 2C B.C., plain without, which held the urn burials of three related families. Their names are inscribed on the niches inside, and the walls are painted with garlands and decorative panels. Another tomb found in 1971 has good paintings and ivory sculptures.

At (20 m.) *Skídhra* (see Rte 60) we join the Via Egnatia.—29 m. *Edhessa*.

Mt Vermion (6650 ft) is the most densely forested mountain in Greece, with beech, oak, chestnut, pine, hazel, whitethorn, cornel-cherry, and evergreen maquis, in which dwell roedeer, red deer, and wild pig. It is approached from Veroia (farther, but newer road) or from Naousa, whence a steep road mounts to (11¼ m.) *Seli* (Refuge, 18 beds), a village (4660 ft) on the N.E. slope. Here winter sports are held from mid-Jan to mid-March (Greek ski championship in late-Feb). Chair lifts rise to the ski slopes. In late spring and summer the mountain affords delightful walks.

62   FROM SALONIKA TO KOZANI AND KASTORIA

ROAD, 137 m. (221 km.). To (19 m.) *Khalkidhón*, see Rte 60; thence to (46½ m.) **Véroia**, see Rte 61. Beyond Veroia broad road through magnificent mountain scenery. 57¼ m. *Kastanéa*.—84 m. **Kozani**, thence through relatively flat upland country.—96½ m. *Siátista* turning.—111 m. *Neapolis*.—130 m. *Argos Orestikon*.—137 m. Kastoriá. BUS hourly to Kozani; 4 times daily from Kozani to Kastoria.

RAILWAY to *Kozani* (138 m.), 4 through trains daily in 4–5 hrs. The line follows the road to (43 m.) *Veroia* (see Rte 61), then turns N. to (69 m.) *Edhessa* (comp. Rte 61), whence it runs W. following the road described in Rte 63 to (100½ m.) *Amindaion*. Here the line divides, the s. branch following Rte 58 to *Kozani*.

From Salonika to (19 m.) *Khalkidhón*, see Rte 60; thence to (46½ m.) **Véroia**, see Rte 61. Beyond Véroia the road winds up past army depots, a reservoir, with a hydro-electric station, and a Restaurant with trout pools.—49¾ m. *Tripótamos*. Orchards clothe the rolling hills as we climb into the Tripotamos valley, which divides the outlying spur of *Máti Poulioú* (l.; 4060 ft) from the main Vermion range.—52 m. *Yeoryíanoi*. A turning (l.) crosses a ridge to *Lefkópetra* (3 m.), but the scanty remains of an ancient temple are hardly worth the diversion. The road clings to a shelf on the N. side of the narrowing valley, which is beautifully clothed with oak and beech woods.—55½ m. Spring.—57¼ m. **Kastanéa** is magnificently situated up the hillside (2960 ft) amid orchards of apples and nuts. Above the village stands the *Monastery of Panayia Soumela*, built by refugees who brought with them (c. 1930) from the Soumela monastery in Pontus an ikon of the Virgin attributed to St Luke. It is a scene of pilgrimage on 15 August.—As we cross the shoulder of Máti Poulioú, from a height of 3545 ft there bursts a tremendous **View** into the Aliakmon Valley; the river, just over 2 m. away, is more than 3000 ft below. Beyond it the jagged heights of *Piéria* tower to 7185 ft.—

We continue to climb and from the steep turns obtain a retrospective view towards Kastanéa before turning away from the Aliakmon to reach (62 m.) the road summit (4460 ft) on Diavasis Kadovas, a s. ridge of Vermion.—From (63 m.) *Zoodokhos Piyi* (4460 ft; Restaurant), which takes name from a small church built above a spring, Mt Olympos is seen to the E. behind Pieria. We descend by a spectacular ladder and vertiginous curves.—At (67½ m.) *Polímilos*, with water mills, we enter a gentle upland valley with the *Skopós Hills* to the s.; the villages lie off the road on their slopes. To the right extends a level plain, where the former *Sarigkiol* ('Yellow Marsh') has been drained.— 70 m. *Voskokhório*. Here a small Christian basilica (? early 6C) came to light in 1935; at *Akriní* (7 m. r.) another, with delightful animal mosaics, was uncovered in 1959.—The road descends gently with long straight stretches to (79 m.) *Dhrépanon*. Joining the railway from the N. (Rte 58) and the road from Larissa, it enters (84 m.) **Kozáni.**

Kozani and thence to *Larissa* and to the Yugoslav frontier (*Niki*), see Rte 58; to Grevena, see below.

Beyond Kozani the road maintains a fairly constant level just below 2000 ft all the way to Kastoria, keeping company with an unfinished railway planned to link Kozani with Kalambaka.—87½ m. *Vaterón*. A flat-bottomed pass opens between the *Voúrinos* and *Áskion* ranges, which extend to N. and s.—96¼ m. *Khani Bára*. Turning for Siátista (r.; 2 m.).

Siátista (*Arkhontikon* C) seems to have been settled in the 16C and to have become a caravan centre of merchants trading with Vienna. In the 18C as *Sisechte* it was noted for its wines, tanneries and for industry, but after 1821 it gradually declined. Since its vineyards were destroyed by phylloxera in 1928–35, it has reverted to the fur trade. The town (4850 inhab.), consisting of the two districts of *Khora* and *Yeraneia*, is (like Kastoria) noted for its 18C houses, timber-framed with jutting balconies and gabled roofs. The *Poulikos Mansion*, with an elaborately panelled and frescoed interior, was restored in 1962. The church of *Ayios Dhimitrios*, founded in 1647, was rebuilt after a fire in 1910; *Ayia Paraskevi* dates from 1677. The *Manousakis Library*, left to the town by the 19C scholar, contains local archaeological finds.

98¼ m. A *Restaurant* stands at the parting of the ways to Kastoria and Grevena.

FROM THE SIATISTA FORK TO GREVENA AND KALAMBAKA. Road, 61 m., mixed asphalt and gravel; bus from Kozani 6 times daily to Grevena, once to Kalambaka. We turn S. and cross the Aliakmon. The road continues sinuous and undulating below the foothills of the Pindus w. of the river.—Beyond (10 m.) *Vatólakkos* we enter the valley of the Greveniotikos.—17½ m. **Greven**á (1970 ft; *Anessis* C) is the chief town (8000 inhab.) of a mainly agricultural nome that corresponds roughly to the ancient district of *Elimeiotis*. It has a school of forestry. The town, at the confluence of two branches of the Greveniotikos, is the focal point of numerous mountain tracks. It was a centre of Greek learning in the Middle Ages and the headquarters of the Armatoles, an irregular militia of Byzantine times, kept up by the Turks, from whose ranks arose the patriotic brigand, or klepht. A comparable situation arose in 1944–49 with the German retreat, when ELAS supporters fought the established government. We descend into the curious eroded grey gorge of the Venetikos, which we cross; visible are the remains of two previous bridges. We now climb again into wooded uplands with views towards the Aliakmon.—37¼ m. Road to Deskati and Elasson (see Rte 58).— 44 m. *Ayiófillon* is on the low watershed that divides the Aliakmon basin from that of the Pinios. By-road (l.) to Deskati (comp. above).—At 54½ m. near the Meteora, we join the road from Ioannina (Rte 51B).—61 m. *Kalambaka*.

We turn N.W. into upland country, drained by the upper Aliakmon, where hamlets are frequent.—102½ m. *Mikrókastron*. Far to the w. is seen the distant *Smolíkas* (comp. below), usually snow capped.—104½ m. *Kalonérion* heralds, as its name suggests, a greener and more fertile countryside. We cross the Aliakmon and its tributaries by a series of Bailey bridges.—111 m. *Neápolis* (Galini C), with 1990 inhab., makes cheese.

The Kastoria road recrosses the Aliakmon and winds amid slopes clad with oak.—121 m. *Vogatsikón*, a pretty small town on seven low wooded hills, below the bluish-grey mountain (4465 ft) of the same name, is situated above a gorge. The road runs along the hillside above the beautiful valley.—Beyond (125 m.) *Kostarázion* where there is a military garrison, a concrete bridge crosses the emissary from Lake Kastoria that feeds the Aliakmon.—We bypass (130 m.) *Árgos Orestikón*, an important garrison town (5100 inhab.) with a military airfield on an ancient site. It is noted for the manufacture of 'flokkates' and 'kilimia', varieties of woollen carpet. The road surmounts a low rise and descends to (133½ m.) *Dispílion* (Tsamis B), on Lake Kastoria, meeting the road from Edhessa (Rte 63). Kastoria is seen across an arm of the lake. We pass a large military cemetery.

Lake Kastoria (*Limni Kastorias*), or *Lake Orestias*, 2035 ft above sea level, and measuring c. 4 m. long by 3 m. wide, is almost divided into two by the peninsula on the neck of which the town is built. The lake, which varies in depth from 25 to 50 ft, is fished for carp, tench, and eels. In summer the waters are hot, turbid, and often covered with a green film, and frogs keep up an incessant chorus; in winter the lake is often frozen. Birds abound and adders are not uncommon round the shores. Traces of a prehistoric lake dwelling were found on the s. shore in 1940. The circuit (road, 20 m., almost at lake level) can be made by car comfortably within an hour; it is interesting mainly for the surrounding mountains and for the apple orchards at the N. end.

137 m. (221 km.) **KASTORIA** (ΚΑΣΤΟΡΙΑ; accented Καστορία in official Greek but locally pronounced Kastoriá), the seat of a metropolitan and capital of a nome, is delightfully situated on the isthmus of a peninsula reaching into the lake from its w. shore. Many of its 15,400 inhabitants are occupied in the fur trade, being especially skilled in matching and joining rejected pieces of mink imported from abroad. Their large houses, many of the 17–18C ('arkhontika'), with workshops on the ground floor, are scattered amid trees and approached by narrow cobbled ways of the Turkish period when the town was known as *Kesriye*. Storks nest on the roofs. Of the 72 churches for which the town was noted, fifty-four survive; seven of the Byzantine period and about thirty others of medieval date were scheduled in 1924 as ancient monuments. With one exception the Kastorian churches are basilican, the earliest having two low aisles while the later ones are without. The naves are barrel-vaulted. Exteriors are either decorated with crude patternwork (including chi-rho symbols) in tile, or plastered and frescoed. The town is subject to sudden winds and changes of temperature.

Hotels. **Xenia Du Lac** (Pl. a), DPO, A.—**Kastoria** (Pl. b), by the lake; **Keletron, Orestion** (Pl. c), **Acropolis** (Pl. d), **Anessis** (Pl. e), these near the entrance to the town, without restaurant, C.

Restaurants near the Kato Agora.

Post Office, Mitropoleos; O.T.E. CENTRE, 19 Ay. Athanasiou.—TOURIST POLICE, 25 Grammon.—OLYMPIC AIRWAYS OFFICE, Komnenou; through bookings to Larissa and Athens (car connection Kastoria–Kozani).—*Banks* in the lower town. connection Kastoria–Kozani).—*Banks* in the lower town.

Buses hourly to *Argos Orestikon*; four times daily to *Kozani*; twice daily to

Amindaion; also to *Salonika*, viâ *Edhessa* (and once viâ *Kozani*); daily to *Florina*; to *Athens*, etc.

Carnival at Epiphany (6–8 Jan); Anniversary celebration of liberation from the Turks, 11 Nov.

History. The ancient *Keletron*, mentioned by Livy (xxxi, 40), probably occupied the hill Vigla above the shoreward suburb. It was captured in 200 B.C. after a siege by the Roman consul, P. Sulpicius Galba. Removed to the present site, the town was renamed *Justinianopolis*, according to the contemporary Procopius, after its refounder, but soon called *Kastoria* after the beavers that haunted the lake. The town was occupied by the Bulgars of Tsar Samuel in 990–1018 until freed by Basil II. It was surprised and captured in 1083 by Robert Guiscard from an English garrison of 300 men. Bohemond spent Christmas 1096 here, having crossed the Pindus by a route of his own. Disputed in the 12C between the despots of Epirus and emperors of Nicaea, Kastoria enjoyed a period of prosperity under Michael Paleologus. The town continued to thrive under the Serbs who held it in 1331–80. After five years of Albanian rule, it fell to the Turks in 1385 who remained its masters until 1912. A colony of Jews continued its trade with Vienna and Constantinople, and its fur industry has flourished for 500 years. It was the Greco-American base for the final campaign against the rebels of the Grammos and Vitsi Mts in the severe winter of 1949.

The *Bus Terminal* (Pl. 1) marks the entrance to the town. Some remains of the Byzantine *Ramparts* that guarded the neck of the isthmus can be seen from Plateia Davaki which is named after a hero of 1940 (statue). Odhos Mitropoleos, the main street of the town, runs S.E. past the Post Office. Steps on the left mount past the little *Taxiarkhis* (Pl. 7) by the Gymnasion to the *Panayia Koubelidiki*, an 11C triconchial church with a high central drum. Its frescoes date from the 13–16C. Farther along, off the triangular Plateia Omonoias, is *Ayios Nikólaos Kasnitsis* (Pl. 6), a rectangular church with a round apse. The 11C frescoes within are characterized by beauty of feature and contrasting light and shade. The left fork goes on to the Plateia Pavlou Mela. The *Taxiarkhai of the Metropolis* (Pl. 11), a crude aisled basilica of the late 11C, has external frescoes representing 15C persons buried in the church and a 13C Virgin and Child over the door. In the narthex is Mela's tomb. The internal frescoes (1359), by the monk Daniel, include a Dormition of the Virgin at the w. end of the nave. Beyond the ornate 19C Cathedral, with its detached belfry, is *Ayios Athanasios* (Pl. 10; key at No. 27, to the left), built in 1384–85 by Stoias and Theodore Musaki, members of the ruling Albanian family. In the contemporary frescoes the saints are depicted in Byzantine princely or military costume; above are scenes of the Life and Passion of Christ.

We return to Omonoia Sq. and take the right fork. *Odhos Mandakasi*, a pretty lane, to the right, descends to the unspoilt *Kariadi* quarter near the s. shore. Here three excellent examples of *Arkhontiká* lie to the S.E. of *Ayioi Anaryiroi* (Pl. 11), an over-restored church with an unusual w. gallery; its screen, carved and gilded, has panels of topographical scenes. The lakeside avenue leads to Ayios Ioannis Theologos, (Pl. 12) whence we follow the principal motor road through the town. *Ayioi Apostoloi* (Pl. 12) was frescoed by Onouphrios in 1545. Of the group of churches just to the N. (Pl. 8) *Ayios Nikolaos by Ay. Thomas* has been restored since it was hit by an Italian bomb in the Second World War; the frescoes date from 1663. *Ayios Stefanos*, an 11C basilica with a tall nave and a clumsy barrel vault, to the N.E., has a hexagonal apse and 12–14C frescoes and iconostasis. In the adjacent *Ayios Yeoryios* (rebuilt under the Turks) the Normans assembled to give themselves up to the Emp. Alexis in 1085. *Ayioi Anaryiroi Varlaam* (Pl. 4) an aisled basilica with a single apse, is the oldest church in Kastoria. Constructed soon after 1018 it has the earliest example of groined vaulting known in Greece. The frescoes date from the late 12C or 13C, save for an earlier St Basil and SS Constantine and Helena in the narthex. The scene of Jesus and Nathaniel is one rarely depicted in Byzantine art. Part of the w. front is also decorated with paintings. Below the Xenia Du Lac (Pl. 7) in a garden overlooking the lake,

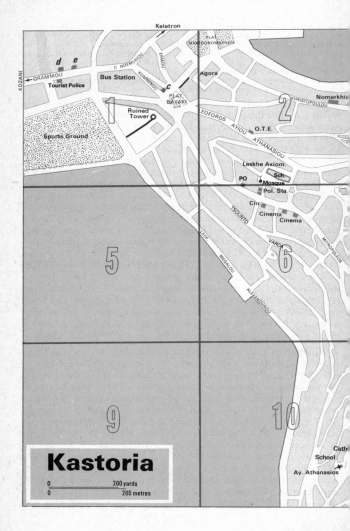

Kastoria

0   200 yards
0   200 metres

stands a statue of Athanasios Kristopoulos (1772–1847), a native poet. Odhos Ayiou Athanasiou returns to the Plateia Davaki, whence we skirt the *Byzantine Wall* to the Kato Agorá. The covered market faces the PLATEIA MAKEDONOMAKHON (Pl. 2), laid out to celebrate Gen. James Van Fleet, head of the U.S. Military Mission to the Greek Army (1948–50). At the little quay, with a fish market, can be seen the curious wooden boats peculiar to the lake, their primitive pattern unchanged, perhaps, since the earliest times.

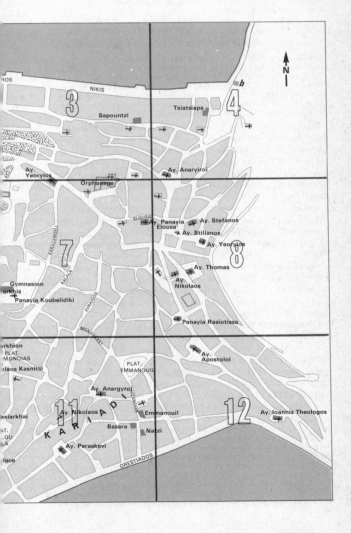

The lakeside walk is recommended for the *Views of the surrounding mountains. We leave the town on the N.E. and follow the Leoforos Stratigou Athanasiou Sougaridou. This leads in c. 1 hr to the *Moni Mavriotissa*, where the twin monastic churches have old doors. The 11–12C frescoes of the *Panayia* are among the most important of the region. *Ayios Ioannis Theologos* preserves its mid-16C paintings almost complete. The return (slightly longer) can be made by continuing round the rocky peninsula to the S.E. corner of the town.

At *Omorphoklissia*, formerly *Gallista*, 12 m. S.W. of Kastoria, is the church of Ayios Yeoryios, restored in 1955. A small rectangular edifice, built in the 11C, it was extended under Andronikos II (inscription). In the exo-narthex survive vigorous frescoes of seven saints from the beginning of the 14C, as well as an old wooden statue of St George.

63   FROM KASTORIA TO EDHESSA
A Viâ the Stena Kleisouras (Amíndaion)

ROAD, 78 m. (126 km.), crossing (18½ m.) the *Kleisoura Pass*, steep and tricky on the W. side, narrow and unsurfaced on the E.—38 m. (61 km.) *Mnemeia Pesonton Crossroads* (2½ m. W. of *Amíndaion*; the km. posts on this road show distance from Amíndaion). We turn left on to the main Kozani–Niki road (Rte 58).— 43 m. *Kírli Derven Pass* (easy).—At (46½ m.) *Vevi*, join the road from Florina (Rte 63B).—78 m. **Edhessa.**—BUS twice daily in 3½ hrs continuing to Salonika; to *Amíndaion* also twice daily (different times).

We quit Kastoria by the Kozani road (Rte 62) and bear left at (3½ m.) *Dispílion*, skirting the marshy confines of the lake. The road ascends the valley of the little Xeropotamos. Just short of (14¼ m.) *Vassileiás*, we climb out of the valley to the E. by a zigzag (retrospective *Views of Lake Kastoria), and the road becomes narrow and mountainous. Beyond (16¼ m.) *Vérga*, a grim alpine village, the hills are eroded by water-courses. Falls of rock may be encountered. The *Stena Kleisouras* is a steep and isolated saddle between Mt Vérbista (at the S. end of the Vernon range) and Mt Moríki (the N. extension of Askion).—18½ m. The summit (3870 ft) is marked by a stone arch. *Kleisoura*, where the church of Ayios Dhimitrios has a carved wooden templon of the 15C, stands a little higher to the right. The view into the Aspropotamos plain to the E. is not beautiful. The descent, less abrupt, follows the slopes of Vérbista, but as we enter the nome of Florina the road deteriorates. *Varikón* (reached viâ Kleisoura) is seen in a deep valley below.—A low saddle takes the road into the Mesikantítsa valley. The summit of Mt Vítsi, scene of much fighting in 1947–49, is seen to the left, while ahead the horizon is closed by the Vóras range, an enormous vista of mountains rising to 8000 ft on the Yugoslav frontier, 25 m. away.—24¼ m. *Lékhovon* enjoys cool springs on the oak-clad slope of Vérbista. A monument to Vanghelis (d. 1904), leader of a nationalist band, stands by the road near the village of *Aspróyia* (l.).—29 m. *Sklíthron*. The road, still shut in by hills, runs straight and level in the Stara valley to (33 m.) *Aetós*, from which a plain growing corn extends S.E. towards Perdikkas.—38 m. *Mnemeia Pesonton Crossroads* (Rte 58).

Aheaᴅ the road continues to **Amíndaion** (2¼ m.), a railway junction (3700 inhab.) and headquarters of an armoured group, that reputedly takes name from one of Alexander's generals. It is better known by its former name, *Sorovits*, for the battle fought here on 22–24 Oct 1912. In 1941 the railway was blown up before the advancing Germans by British irregular troops led by the author Peter Fleming. The local red wine has merit. A prehistoric cemetery (222 tombs) yielded valuable finds in 1900. Amindaion may be *Cellis* of the itineraries (comp. p. 539).—The road continues beside the railway along the shore of the little Lake Petron to (7 m.) *Ayios Pandeleimon* on Lake Vegoritis. The railway follows the W. shore of the lake to join the road just beyond *Ayios Spiridon* (comp. below).

We turn left on to the Ptolemais–Niki road (Rte 58), leaving it again (r.) after eight miles for (46½ m.) *Vévi*, where we join the road from Florina. Thence to (78 m.) **Edhessa**, see below.

B Viâ Florina

ROAD, 85 m. (136 km.), hilly and winding, passing within 6 m. of the Albanian frontier. (There are now no apparent restrictions on the main road, but on by-roads travellers may find police posts where they are discouraged from proceeding.) Gravel to (22 m.) *Trígounon*, then asphalt.—40½ m. **Flórina**.—54½ m. *Vévi*.—85 m. **Edhessa**.—BUS daily to Florina; also from Florina to Edhessa, several times daily.

RAILWAY from Florina to Edhessa (Salonika), 53 m. in 2 hr, three times daily (from Amindaion, 31½ m. in 70 m.), six times). The branch from Florina joins the line from Bitolj (Rte 58) at *Mesonision* in the plain N. of the road, passes S. of Vevi and traverses the Kirli Derven pass (Rte 58) to *Amindaion*. Thence it skirts Lake Vegoritis, passing through *Arnissa*.

From Kastoria we take the lakeshore road N. and quickly turn away left on gravel surface. We climb into bare hills and get a good retrospective view of Kastoria and its lake. Surmounting a ridge, the road descends to the oak-forested upper valley of the Aliakmon, which is crossed by Bailey bridge. In the river bed are stone breakwaters.—11¾ m. *Gavros Police Post*, and, immediately before it, road (r.) for *Melás* (9½ m.), formerly *Státistan tou Korestíon*, where the patriot Pavlos Mela was killed by the Turks in 1904.—At 15½ m. we cross the river again by a memorial of the civil war (1948–49) and, soon after, leave on our left the road to *Koritsa* (Korçë; 35 m.) in Albania (the frontier is closed).—At 18¼ m. we pass (r. of road) a bust of Christos Kota, a champion of Macedonian Hellenism, burnt alive by the Bulgarians; the near-by village is named after him.—The road, now asphalted, rises in the fertile small valley of the principal affluent of the Aliakmon, here called the Livadhopótamos.—Just beyond (22 m.) *Trígounon* is a Police Post, where a road (l.), signposted to *Laimós* (12 m.), climbs to a saddle overlooking the **Prespa Lakes**. *Megali Prespa* is shared between Albania, Yugoslavia, and Greece; *Mikra Prespa* between Albania and Greece only.—The road improves.—24 m. *Andartikón*. We continue to climb amid fine beech forests to (29¾ m.) the summit of the *Pisodhérion Pass* (4915 ft; inn) between the Varnoús (Peristéri) and Vérnon ranges. Here there is another Police Post. We descend, with a splendid vista down the wooded Lerínska valley to Florina and the plain beyond.

40½ m. (65 km.) **Flórina** (ΦΛΩPINA; 2165 ft; *Tottis*, on Ay. Kharalambos, *Lyngos*, both **B**, and others; *Oraia Hellas Rest.*, in square, good), with 11,200 inhab., is the capital of the nome of Florina. It has an important Agricultural School and a small Zoo. Near the entrance to the town is a statue of Kota (comp. above). Old Turkish houses, picturesque but mostly derelict, line the river. The church of *Ayios Yeoryios*, pleasantly situated outside the town, affords a view over the plain. Excavations on *Ay. Kharalambos*, a hill to the s., in 1931–34, uncovered the remains of a town built by Philip II (c. 352 B.C.) and burnt in 48 B.C. in the campaign that ended at Pharsala. This is not *Herakleia Lynkestis*, now surely placed by inscription at Bitolj. The finds are housed in a new *Museum* (adm. 8.30–12.30, 4–8; Sun 9–3; closed Tues) near the railway station.

Florina was a coveted objective of the guerilla rebels of the Civil War. They failed to take it in May 1947, and their assault on it using 4000 men and artillery, defeated in Feb 1949, was their last major effort.

We take the Salonika road E. across the Monastir plain. The road crosses the railway to Yugoslavia, then at 48¾ m. briefly joins the course of the ancient Via Egnatia which comes in on the left from Bitolj (Rte 58). The ancient road probably turned s. through the Kirli Derven pass (Rte 58) to Amindaion (p. 540) and crossed the valley now flooded by Lake Vegoritis to rejoin the modern road near Arnissa.—At 52 m., beside an unusual memorial (1917) from the Drina Division to their Serbian brothers, we fork left.—54½ m. *Vévi* (BEYH). The road traverses an upland plateau in a stony, desolate landscape. Ahead rise the massive outlying peaks of VÓRAS; behind the nearest (*Piperitsa*, 6550 ft) towers the snow-clad *Kaimaktsalán* (8280 ft).—60½ m. *Kélla* (3150 ft) is a stone-built town (1070 inhab.) reminiscent of the Scottish highlands; just beyond we have a view (r.) down to Lake Petron. The winding road undulates amid scrub covered hills. At a second summit level of 3150 ft, on the boundary between the nomes of Florina and Edhessa, sudden *View across the N. end of Lake Vegoritis to Arnissa. After an enclosed descent we join the gorge of a torrent that feeds the lake at Ayios Spiridon and descend to the lakeside.

Lake Vegoritis (1770 ft), or *Ostrovo*, is 12 m. long from N. to S.; its greatest width is 5 m. In places it is 160 ft deep. It is well stocked with fish, lake-trout having been successfully introduced from Switzerland in 1958. Off Arnissa, towards the N., is an island on which are the remains of a mosque which local tradition claims was once in the centre of a village now submerged. The level of the lake, which was formerly liable to periodic flooding, is controlled by an underground outflow that feeds the Vodas. In ancient times its area was considerably less.

70 m. Crossroads; Panayitsa lies 2½ m. N., *Árnissa* 1½ m. r. on the lake, where there is a trout hatchery. The main road passes behind the town, while the railway hugs the shore. Together they thread the almost level STENA EDHESSIS, joining the canalized *Vodas*, or Edhesseos, near its emergence from the marsh lake that feeds it.—At (83 m.) *Ágras* a hydro-electric station was opened in 1954; further works to harness the waters may diminish the famous Edhessa falls. Here is buried Tellos Agapinos, who fought under the name of Kapetan Agras in the Macedonian struggle and was killed while on a mission under truce to the Bulgarians in 1907. The valley broadens and becomes lush as we descend. The railway, seen intermittently across the river between its seven tunnels, crosses a viaduct.—85 m. (136 km.) **Edhessa**, see Rte 60.

64   CHALCIDICE AND MOUNT ATHOS

The peninsula of **Chalcidice**, in Greek **Khalkidhikí** (ΧΑΛΚΙΔΙΚΗ), received its name from the number of colonies planted there by the city of Khalkis in Euboea. Geographically it is the most prominent feature of Macedonia, projecting into the Aegean between the Gulf of Salonika on the w. and the Gulf of Orfani on the E. It branches into three smaller peninsulas: Kassandra (anciently *Pallene*), Sithonia or Longos, and Athos (Akte). The Gulf of Kassandra (Toronaios Kolpos) separates Kassandra and Sithonia, and the Singitic Gulf comes between Sithonia and Athos. Other than in the w., along the S. coastal plain, and in Kassandra, the interior is wooded and mountainous, the highest point Mt Athos, rising to 6670 ft. On the landward side the limit of Chalcidice is marked by the lakes E. of Salonika, though the nome boundary runs a few miles S. of them. Administratively the region is divided into the nome of KHALKIDHIKÍ, which comprises the greater part of the peninsula, and AYION OROS, coterminous with the territory of Athos, which has an autonomous constitution. The inhabitants are mainly engaged in agriculture, though the mines are important and tourism is playing a rapidly increasing role. Many miles of new road across the centre of the peninsula, with offshoots southwards into Kassandra and Sithonia, have recently been built to foster tourist holiday development of the coastal areas. The coasts in the remote past supported flourishing cities, some of them, notably Olynthos, of more than local importance. Finds from the many archaeological sites are in the Salonika and Poliyiros museums.

A From Salonika to Ouranópolis

ROAD, 89 m. (143 km.), asphalt.—BUS at least twice daily.

From Salonika to (6¼ m.) the Ay. Trias turn, see Rte 59D. We bear left and pass, soon afterwards, a turning (l.) to *Thermi*, a small place bearing the name of the predecessor of Salonika. The road runs in a cultivated plain dotted with factories.—12 m. *Loutrá Thermis*, a small spa with hot springs.—15½ m. *Vasiliká* (Tavernas). The village stands (r.) on a by-road to *Sourotí*, 3 m. s.w., with mineral waters. The plain changes to a wide valley as we cross the nome boundary and we climb along the N. side.—19 m. Crossroads, with (l.; 2 m.) the *Moní Ayía Anastasia Pharmakolitria*, founded c. 888 by Theophano, wife of Leo VI the Philosopher.—24½ m. *Galátista*, a mining centre (2300 inhab.), occupying the site of ancient *Anthemous*, was the scene of a Communist massacre in 1945.—30 m. *Áyios Pródromos* stands in pleasant upland country.—At 35 m. the road divides. To Poliyiros, see Rte 64D.

The road now climbs round the slopes of *Mt Kholomón* (3822 ft) amid chestnut woods, rising to 3300 ft on a ridge just below the summit before descending to (53½ m.) *Arnaía* (Inns), beautiful centre (2400 inhab.) of a fruit and wine-growing region.—At (56½ m.) *Palaiokhórion*, a good road runs s. to the equally delightfully situated *Megali Panayia* (5 m.) beyond which a bad road descends to the Singhitikos Gulf at *Pirgadhíkia* (17 m.). Another poor road diverges left at 59¾ m. to *Olympias Bay* (12 m.; Germany C), the ancient *Kapros Limen*, on the Strymonic Gulf, and thence along the shore N.W. to Stavrós (Rte 66).

At (61½ m.) *Stáyira* (Tourist Pavilion) a modern statue of Aristotle stands amid the ruins of a Byzantine fortress. In the village a Byzantine hall church has been restored. The remains of ancient *Stageira*, birthplace of Aristotle, lie on the by-road to Stratónion, see below. This, or (62½ m.) *Stratoníki*, represents the ancient Stratonike. In the hills to the s., gold and silver were mined in the 16C; probably the same mines provided the coinage of Akanthos in antiquity. Today iron and magnesite are worked. New forests have been planted on the coastal slopes.—70 m. By-road to *Stratónion* (¾ m. l.).

80 m. (129 km.) **Ierissos** (*Mount Athos* B, May–Oct; *Akanthos* E) is a straggling fishing village (2400 inhab.) on the shore of the bay of the

same name. The ruined medieval watch-tower outside the village to the N.W. has Hellenic foundations, and reused marbles. Ancient also are the remains of a mole still affording shelter to local boats. These vestiges of antiquity mark the site of *Akanthos*, passed through by Xerxes and seized by Brasidas in his Macedonian campaign. Akanthos was founded from Andros. Its Archaic and Classical cemetery is by the shore, with tombs in the sand. A part has been excavated and finds are in Poliyiros museum.—The road continues to (83 m.) *Néa Rhódha* (Xerxes Rest.), on the N. shore, and to the landing stage of (84½ m.) *Tripiti*, on the s. shore of the vale of *Provlaka*, as the narrowest part of the isthmus is called. The name is a contraction of Proaulax, the **Canal** (αὐλαξ).

In 480 B.C., aware of the disaster that had befallen Mardonius eleven years before, when he lost 300 ships and 20,000 men trying to round the promontory of Athos, Xerxes ordered a canal across the isthmus for the passage of his invasion fleet. The citizens of Akanthos awarded heroic honours to Artakhaies, who died while in charge of its cutting and was given a state funeral by Xerxes. The canal was dug in a hollow between low banks past the town of *Sane* (long since vanished). Several artificial mounds and substructions of walls can be traced along its course. Its width seems to have been 40–50 ft, and it is nearly filled up with soil. The isthmus is estimated to have risen 45 ft since the canal was cut.

Beyond Tripiti, with views towards the islet of *Amouliani*, we pass the Eagles Palace (Apr–Oct, **A**) and reach (89 m.) *Ouranópolis* (Xenia, DPO, May–Sept, **B**; Xenios Zeus **D**; Tavernas), known also as *Prosfori*, and from its tower as *Pirgos*. The fishing village (590 inhab.) built by refugees in 1922, has adopted the name of a lost town founded by Alexarchos, son of Antipater, in 316 B.C. though it is as likely to be ancient Dion. The inhabitants make knotted rugs to Byzantine patterns, a 'tradition' started by an Australian (Mrs J. N. Loch) in 1928. Beyond lies the territory of the Holy Mountain.

B   Mount Athos

The wild, roadless, and picturesque peninsula of **ATHOS** or Ayion Oros ('Holy Mountain'), anciently known also as *Akte*, easternmost of the three prongs of Chalcidice, is connected to the mainland by a low isthmus only 1½ m. across (see above). The length of the peninsula is c. 31 m. and its breadth varies between 3 and 6 miles. The area of the nome of Ayion Oros is 131 sq. miles. The population, exclusively male, is given by the 1971 census as 1732, though the last monograph on Athos puts the figure at "1163 of which only 518 are housed in monasteries, the remainder in dependencies". Our figures which include lay brethren are mainly from a Greek source of 1976. The ground rises abruptly from the isthmus to 300 ft and for the first dozen miles maintains a level of about 600 ft, for the most part beautifully wooded. Beyond the land becomes mountainous, rising immediately s. of *Kariaí*, the administrative capital, to 2000 ft; hence a rugged broken country, covered with dark forests, extends to the foot of *Mt Athos* (6670 ft), a cone of white limestone which rises in solitary magnificence from the sea. The jackal is still common.

The Holy Community, a kind of monastic republic (see below), is composed of 20 monasteries, of which 17 are Greek, one (Roussikon)

Russian, one (Zografos) Bulgarian, and one (Khiliandarion) Serb. There is also a Roumanian retreat, but the number of hermitages and cells has dwindled steadily along with the number of monks throughout the century. Divorced from distracting modernity, unaffected by hurry (the Julian Calendar, 13 days behind the rest of Europe, is still in use, and the day divided into Byzantine hours of variable length with sunset as 12 o'clock), the Holy Mountain affords to the devout a glimpse of life wholly dedicated to God, to the weary a welcome, if temporary, retreat from the world, and to the lover of nature and medieval art a treasury of beauty. That visitors are, in a sense, a contradiction of the reason for the community's existence should not be lost sight of by the traveller.

Formalities. The visitor, who must be male and (unless a theological student) over 21 years of age, must apply through his consul to the Foreign Ministry in Athens or to the Minister for Northern Greece in Salonika for a permit to visit Athos (fee). A letter of introduction from the Metropolitan of Athens or the Archbishop of Salonika is an additional advantage, and members of the clergy should have a written permit from the Patriarchate of Constantinople. The documents must be presented immediately upon arrival to the Nomarch at Kariai, who will issue a residence permit (*diamonitirion*), which has to be presented at each convent visited (take care to recover it when leaving). Members of conducted groups avoid personal formalities. A special permit is needed for photography. Cinematography and tape-recording are forbidden.

Mules are hired for the journey to the first convent, which will arrange for transport to the next, and so on. The gates of the monasteries are open only during the daytime. It is considered presumptuous to ride up to the gates; one should dismount and approach on foot. The visitor will everywhere be received with kindness and simple courtesy, lodged (for a maximum of four days), and entertained with fish, vegetables, rice dressed in various ways, cheese, sweetmeats, fruits, and very fair wine made on the mountain. He should not expect meat, which few of the monks ever taste. On 159 days in the year they have but one meal and then eggs, cheese, wine, fish, milk, and oil are forbidden; on the other days they are allowed only two meals. The visitor's contribution to monastic funds on leaving should be at least commensurate with the hospitality he has received. Supplementary rations and a supply of insecticide may not come amiss.

Organized tours of the Holy Mountain (advertised as "strenuous and austere") are arranged by Inter-Church Travel and other organizations; by this means the traveller is enabled to see more historical and artistic treasures than he could on his own, while inevitably substituting for the atmosphere of remote and timeless dedication something of the restless urgency of modern tourism. A better spiritual understanding of the unique nature of Athos is gained by a solitary stay in one or two monasteries.

Approaches. BY SEA either from *Ierissos* by caique down the E. coast to Vatopedi (uncertain owing to frequent rough seas), or by the regular motor-boat service from *Ouranópolis* down the W. coast to Daphni. There are two buses daily in summer from Salonika to the ports (comp. above). The morning bus connects three times weekly with the late-morning boat from Ouranópolis. At Vatopedi mules may be hired for Kariai. From Daphni a motor-road to Kariai (bus in 1 hr.) was constructed in 1962 for the millenary celebrations.—BY LAND Kariai may be reached on foot or muleback in c. 6 hours though this approach may lead to administrative difficulties.

History. Strabo, echoing Herodotus, says that Pelasgi from Lemnos came to the peninsula, where they founded five cities; Kleonai, Olophyxos, Akrothoon, Dion, and Thyssos. Colonies were also planted here by Eretria. On the isthmus stood the towns of Akanthos and Sane. Of all these only Akanthos is known by any remains. In 480 B.C. Xerxes dug his canal (see above), and in the time of Alexander the Great Deinokrates, architect of the Temple of Diana at Ephesus, proposed to fashion Mt Athos into a gigantic statue of the world-conqueror.

The fame of Athos rests entirely on its medieval monasteries. Legends of foundation by the Virgin Herself, by St Helena, or by one or other Roman emperor of the 4C or 5C, often supported by documents forged in the 18C, seem to have been tacitly abandoned with the official celebration in 1963 of the 1000th anniversary of the founding of the monastic community. It is likely that anchorites lived on the mountain at an earlier time, fugitives, perhaps, from iconoclastic persecution in 726–842; Peter the Athonite, the most famous of the early monks, is supposed to have lived for 50 years in a cave. Existing *lavras* (λαύρα, cloister or monk's cell) were organized by Athanasios the Athonite, friend and counsellor of the Emp. Nikephoros Phokas, the first historical benefactor of the Holy Mountain. He founded the monastery of the Great Lavra (963 or 961) and instituted the strict rule of the Abbot Theodore. Thereafter foundations multiplied under the protection of the emperors (especially Alexius I Comnenus, who placed them under imperial jurisdiction), until they reached the number of 40, with, it is said, 1000 monks in each. Andronikos II relinquished his authority to the Patriarch in 1312. The incursions of the Latins, Catalans (1307), Serbs (1346), and Turks caused the abandonment of a few outlying sites, but the importance of Mt Athos was not impaired. It reached its zenith in the 15C, after which a period of decadence set in, followed by reinvigorating reforms. After the fall of Constantinople in 1453 the monks kept on good terms with the sultans, one of whom, Selim I, paid a state visit to the peninsula. Thanks to this political dexterity, the Holy Mountain remained the spiritual centre of orthodoxy. It built its own schools, one of which, that of Vatopedi, had a famous headmaster, Eugene Bulgaris (1753–59). At the beginning of the War of Independence the community joined the insurgents, but sank defeated under the Turkish yoke.

Despite its seclusion, Mt Athos has always attracted the attention, not always disinterested, of the outside world. The Vatican has frequently, but without success, tried to exercise some influence. Russia was dominant here from 1830 to 1890. In 1912 the peninsula was occupied by Greek troops, and the Treaty of London (1913) proclaimed its independence and neutrality. During the First World War the Allies sent in a detachment and a cultural mission. In 1926 Mt Athos was formed into a theocratic republic under the suzerainty of Greece. During the Second World War a German antiquarian expedition visited the Holy Mountain.

Organization. By a decree of 16 Sept 1926 the peninsula forms part of Greece but enjoys administrative autonomy, while in church matters it depends on the Oecumenical Patriarch. All monks, of whatever race, become Greek subjects on retiring to Mt Athos; no heterodox or schismatics are admitted. Women are excluded. The Hellenic Republic is represented by a governor having the rank of nomarch, answerable to the Ministry for Foreign Affairs, and by a police force. The administrative autonomy is centred in the Synod, or Holy Council (*Hiera Synaxis*), with its seat at Kariaí, comprising 20 deputies (*Antiprósopoi*), one from each convent. The deputies are elected annually in January; and four of them, appointed in rotation, form the *Epistasia*, having executive powers. One of the four takes precedence as the First of Athos ('Ο πρῶτος τοῦ Ἀθωνος). The Holy Council exercises also financial and judicial authority.

The 20 convents are divided into two categories; *Coenobite* (κοινοβιακαὶ; 'living in common') and *Idiorrhythmic* ('ἰδιόρρυθμοι; 'eccentric', 'going their own way'). In the eleven coenobite convents all members are clothed alike, pool their resources, and live on the same meagre fare in the common hall or refectory (*Trápeza*). The monks of the nine idiorrhythmic convents enjoy a milder rule. They live apart from their fellows, though their convents may have refectories, and they have no property in common. Each monk provides his own clothes and obtains his food from his own resources. All of them attend services for at least 8 out of the 24 hours. These include Mass (*Leitourgia*), Vespers (*Hesperinón*), Compline (*Apódeipnon*), and Nocturnal Office (*Nykterninon*) which may on occasion last throughout the night and even exceptionally for 24 hours.—As well as the convents, there are *Anchorites*, who live apart in cells, some of them well-nigh inaccessible; *Sarabaites*, groups of two or three hermits living in hermitages or small houses; and *Gyrovakes*, mendicant and vagabond monks. The small retreats and cells have various names, such as *Sketai* (σκῆται) *Kellia*, *Kathismata*, etc.

Each convent is administered by an abbot (*Hegoumenos*), elected for life or for a definite period, assisted by two or three coadjutors (*Epítropoi*) and by a Council (*Synaxis*) of Elders (*Proistámenoi*). There is also a class of inferior monks (*Paramikroi*), who do manual labour. The monk begins as a novice (*Dókimos*, or *Rasophóros*, from the name of his black gown). In the next three years he becomes Crusader (*Stavrophóros*) or *Mikroschema* (wearer of short coat); then *Megaloschema* (wearer of long coat); this coat has elaborate symbolic embroidery). All the monks are bearded and wear their hair long, either hanging down or tucked into a bonnet known as a *skouphia*; their normal dress is the *zostikon*, a black gown with a leathern girdle.

Among the oldest and most strictly observed of the rules is that of Constantine Monomachus (1060), which forbids access to 'every woman, every female animal, every child, eunuch, and smooth-faced person'. This rule, relaxed in 1345, was confirmed in 1575, 1753, and 1780, and is still officially in force, save that it is no longer incumbent upon a visitor to be bearded. She-cats and hens are however now openly tolerated; some pig-breeding is indulged in; and the ban on young boys is not always strictly enforced.

The coenobitic monastery resembles "a compound of the walled town and the galleried inn" (Sherrard), having usually the form of a rectangle and being guarded by towers. The entrance is through a door at one of the four corners. The principal building in the middle of the enclosure, is the *Katholikón*, or communal church, cruciform with double narthex and several cupolas. Between the church and one of the short walls is the *Phiále*, a canopied stoup containing holy water. Built into the short wall beyond is the apsidal *Trápeza* (refectory), with an ambo from which a monk reads during meals, and, near the seat of the hegoumenos, a platter for the consecrated bread. Against the opposite short wall is the *Archontaría*, or guest-chamber. The monks' cells, adorned with porticoes and balconies, line the long walls.

Art. Though many treasures, particularly classical manuscripts, have been pillaged, burnt, neglected, or sold in the past, Athos is still rich in minor works of art. Little except charters and chrysobuls survive from the earliest times, but the archives (now jealously guarded) of Grand Lavra, Vatopedi, and Iveron, and the library of Vatopedi, are of the first importance. Reliquaries, chalices, and illuminated MSS. survive in quantity. In the major arts of architecture and painting, if there is not much of the first rank, there is sufficient of interest and merit to give a comprehensive picture of the late-Byzantine scene. The principal features in which Athonite churches diverge from general Byzantine practice are the apsidal ends to the transepts and the double narthex, divided into *lete* and *mesonyktikon*, often flanked by side chapels. Two schools of painting are represented. The *Macedonian School* skilfully adapts painting to architectural media. Its protagonists are Manuel Panselinos (early 14C), and his contemporaries. The *Cretan School*, affected by the art of Italy and S. Germany, was founded c. 1535 by Theophanes and continued by Frangos Kastellanos of Thebes. Some discoloured frescoes have been repainted from time to time.

Orthodox decoration, intended to illustrate Church doctrine, has become traditional and stereotyped. The Katholikon of Docheiarou is a complete example. In the top of the dome is the Almighty in glory, surrounded by the Virgin, John the Baptist, prophets, and angels. In the three apses and behind the ikonostasis are paintings illustrating the life of the saint commemorated. In the dome of the central apse are the Madonna and Child, with Christ below. In the left apse, Death and resurrection of the Saviour, with Old Testament figures; in the right apse, Christ and the Trinity, and similar figures. Above the altar, the Risen Christ. In the nave and choir are depicted the great church festivals, arranged in four parallel zones. In the narthex the cupolas glorify Christ; on the walls are Church councils, lives of the martyrs, and the Last Judgment. In the refectory (e.g. at Lavra) the subject of the frescoes is food. There may be local variations of the traditional style.—There are few ikons of importance.

The visitor arriving by sea at Daphne (Dhafni) takes the attractive road (bus) to Kariaí which at first runs close to the sea and then turns inland to the N.E. After ½ hr it passes the idiorrhythmic convent of **Xeropotamou** (40 monks), pleasantly situated c. 470 ft above the sea. It derives its name from a seasonal torrent. By forged documents the convent acquired in the 18C a 'traditional' foundation by Pulcheria, empress in 450–457. Its first genuine mention is in the 10C; it received privileges from Michael VIII in 1275 after an earthquake the previous year, and the Sultan Selim I (or, more probably, Selim II) rescued it from a period of decay. The earliest of the present buildings dates from 1763, when also the paintings in the katholikon were executed. Two ancient reliefs are built into the w. wall of the court; the 'Roman' inscriptions are 18C forgeries and the two busts on the clock-tower (said to be St Paul of Athos and Pulcheria) are of the 15C. The chief treasures are a piece of the Cross (13 in. long) and the so-called *Paten of St Pulcheria, depicting the Virgin at prayer standing adored by two angels with censers; in the first band is a procession of angels; in the second, the Apostles prostrate in worship. The paten was made in the 15C; the mounting showing the inscription, with the name, is an 18C addition. From the guest-chamber there is a fine view.

To St Pantaleimon and other w. coast monasteries, see below.

Farther on is the coenobite convent (50 monks) of **Koutloumousiou,** situated in the most fertile part of the peninsula, amid gardens, vineyards, olive plantations, and cornfields. This convent is first documented in 1169. It takes name from the princely Seljuk family of Kutlumush, of which its convent founder was a member. Bad fires in 1857 and 1870 wrought havoc with all but the *Katholikon,* rebuilt before 1540, and the arcaded E. range, which dates from 1767. The frescoes of the katholikon have been repainted. There is a fine view of Kariaí from the monastery.—2 hrs *Kariaí.*

Kariaí or *Karyes* (KAPYAI; two indifferent *Inns,* but visitors made welcome; post and telegraph office; telephone) is the capital of Mt Athos; hence its other names of *Protaton* ('Foremost') and *Mese* ('Middle'). It is a little town (300 inhab.) surrounded by vineyards and gardens, with a few shops kept by monks and lay brothers. Its monastery was reputedly founded by Constantine and destroyed by Julian the Apostate. The restored basilican Church of the **Protaton,** the oldest on Mt Athos, dates from the 10C. Various additions since 1508 were stripped away in 1955–57. The *Ikonostasis dates from 1607. In the *Chapel of St John the Baptist* are *Frescoes of the Nativity and of the Presentation in the Temple attributed to Manuel Panselinos (early 14C) and considered the finest in the peninsula; others, of a later date, are of admirable freshness and delicacy. There are also silver filigree crosses and a wonder-working ikon. The *Council House* has a chamber in which the 20 deputies deliberate sitting on divans. Each of the deputies has a lodge at Kariaí to accommodate himself and younger monks of his convent attending the school here. Visitors to any of the lodges are hospitably received. The *Athonite School for Novices* was established in 1950 for 60 boys.

The hazel (λεπτοκαρνα) from which the town derives its name, is common. Hazel nuts are exported.

FROM KARIAÍ TO VATOPEDI, 3 hrs. The track, passing the huge ruinous Russian church of *St Andrew,* goes N.—**Vatopédi** (Βατοπέδιον), one of the largest on Mt Athos and the most modern (with electric light, telephone, and motor-boats, and keeping European time), is an idiorrhythmic convent with 50 monks. The monastery, which somewhat resembles a country mansion, is built round a huge triangular court in a charming pastoral setting overlooking a little bay, with a highly picturesque harbour. The s.e. wing was destroyed by fire in Feb 1966.

Foundation traditions tell of Constantine as well as of Theodosius, the miraculous rescue of whose son Arcadius from the sea by the Virgin is supposedly commemorated by the name Vatopaidion (βατός, bramble, and παιδίον, child). The story tells of the boy being placed under a bramble for the hermits to find. The name is more likely Vatopedion (bramble-*ground*). The historical founders are Athanasius, Nicholas, and Antony from Adrianople (late 10C). The Emp. John VI Cantacuzenus retired here in 1355 under the name Ioasaph. The monastery was a cenobion in 1573–1661.

Most of the attractive buildings are of the 17C or later. The KATHO-LIKON (Annunciation), is an 11C basilica adapted to the plan of a Greek cross. It has a massive detached belfry and a double narthex. The 15C bronze doors, from St Sophia, Salonika, have panels in relief depicting the Annunciation. Over the second door is an 11C mosaic of Intercession (δέησις): centre, Christ in glory; at the sides, the Virgin and John the Baptist. The inner doors, inlaid with ivory, are dated 1567. The impressive interior, which has a polygonal apse, is decorated with frescoes of the Macedonian school (1312), restored in 1789 and 1819. Porphyry columns support the dome. In the *Chapel of St Demetrius* (N.) are ikons of St Peter and St Paul (16C), in a beautiful frame; of the Holy Conductress, in a 13–14C frame, with reliefs of Christian festivals; of St Anne; and of the Crucifixion (13C) in a 14C metal frame. The ikonostasis is a fine work of art. The *Chapel of the Holy Girdle* contains a good Nativity. The *Cup of Manuel Paleologos (early 15C) is made of a block of jasper 10 in. across, on a silver base decorated with enamel; the engraved handles are in the shape of dragons. There are some fine crosses with silver-gilt ornamentation. The most notable relic, the 'Girdle of the Virgin', was given to the monastery by Lazar I of Serbia (1372–89).

The *Library* contains 8000 volumes. Especially noteworthy are an Octateuch (first eight books of the Bible); a psalter (No. 610), autographed by Constantine IX Monomachos (1042–54); an evangelistary (No. 735), and a MS. of Ptolemy's *Geographia*, with which are 17 chapters of Strabo's *Geography*, the *Periplus* of Hadrian, and 42 maps in colour.

The monks' walk is an attractive promenade.—Not far from the convent are the ruins of the *Athonite Academy*, founded in 1749 with the aid of the learned Eugene Bulgaris of Corfù, but destroyed in the same century. Some arches of its aqueduct survive.

FROM VATOPEDI TO ESPHIGMENOU, 2½ hrs. The convent of **Esphig-menou** (coenobite; 40 monks) stands on the edge of the sea, at the mouth of a torrent in a little narrow valley (whence probably its name: 'εσφιγμένος, compressed). First mentioned in a document of 1034, it was restored in the 14C, but plundered by pirates in 1533. Except for short periods of revival, it lay abandoned till the end of the 18C. Its possession of the cave of the hermit Antony of Kiev (983–1073) assured it Russian support, but, though it was restored in the 19C, it has never been of the first importance. The *Church* (1808–11), overpoweringly ornate, has an ikonostasis carved with figures of Adam and Eve. It has a portable mosaic ikon of Christ (12C) and (in the library) an 11C Menologion (calendar).

About 1 hr away by track is **Khiliandárion** (31 monks; all Slavs), an idiorrhythmic Serbian convent, northernmost of the monasteries on the E. side of the peninsula. It is situated nearly a mile from the sea, in a vale watered by a torrent, and surrounded by thickly wooded hills. Its name is said to be derived from its having originally been built for 1000 monks (χίλιοι ἄνδρες). It was founded in 1197 by the Serbian prince Stefan Nemanja and his son Sava, and rebuilt in 1299 by Stefan Milutin, who eventually retired, after his abdication, to Vatopedi. Only the Katholikon was undamaged by a fire in 1722, and the cell of St Sava was destroyed by another in 1961. The convent has electric installations (disused) and a tractor, gifts from Yugoslavia. The court has a double arcade. The *Katholikon* (1293), built of brick of different colours arranged in patterns, has a richly decorated narthex of c. 1380. It contains frescoes of the 13–14C, restored in 1863–4 by artists of Galatista following the original style, a marble mosaic pavement (12C), and the cenotaph of Stefan Nemanja (the Monk Simeon). The little *Chapel of the Ascension* was decorated in 1302. The *Liti* is a rectangular hall in front of the church in which prayers are said on Saturdays. The *Refectory* has frescoes on its walls. Noteworthy are a mosaic ikon of the Virgin and Child (13–14C), another of the Panagia Tricherousa ('with three hands'; 14C), an altar cloth of 1399, with Christ standing between two angels blessing St Basil and St John Chrysostom.

The *Library* contains interesting MSS. in Slavonic tongues. In the *Muniment Room* of the library are four *Ikons depicting archangels from the ikonostasis presented by Stefan Dušan, charters and deeds of gift from Byzantine emperors and princes of Serbia and Bulgaria, as well as firmans promising protection and privileges from successive sultans and viziers.—The surrounding countryside affords delightful walks and the shore good bathing.

The northernmost part of the peninsula consists of hills intersected by deep valleys, down which torrents flow to the sea, the shore of which is indented with little bays. The hills are covered with the fragrant and feathery Isthmian pine, and with every variety of shrub and flower. The foliage of the N. and s. is blended in great variety, the olive with the oak, and the orange with the pine.

FROM VATOPEDI TO IVIRON, 4 hrs or by infrequent caique. The path runs S.E. and s., close to the E. coast of the peninsula. After 2½ hrs we reach **Pantokrátor** (20 monks), an idiorrhythmic convent founded c. 1357–63 by Alexios the Stratopedarch and John the Primicerius, whose inscribed tombs have been found in the narthex. The walls, repaired in 1536, have a massive tower. It is built on a sea-washed rock above a small cove and affords a fine view of Stavronikita. The old Katholikon has been often renovated (fragmentary 14C frescoes). The library has interesting 11C MSS.—An hour later we come to another idiorrhythmic convent, that of **Stavronikíta** (25 monks), perhaps founded in 1153 but refounded in 1542 by the Patriarch Jeremiah of Constantinople. The monastery, with its massive tower, crowns a precipitous rock at the edge of the sea. The *Katholikon* has frescoes of 1546 executed by monks. It has a mosaic ikon of St Nicholas and a psalter of the 12C.—After another hour we arrive at **Iviron** (Monastery of the Iberians), also idiorrhythmic, with 90 monks (Greeks, Russians, Roumanians, and Georgians). It was founded in 979 or 986 by three Iberians or Georgians under charter from Basil II the Bulgar-Slayer. Badly damaged by fire in 1865, it is a welter of buildings in an enclosed valley near the sea. The entrance opens into a vast court surrounded by heterogeneous buildings. In the middle is the *Katholikon*, with a pavement that dates from the foundation. In a little chapel (1680–83) adjoining is the miraculous 10C ikon of the Panagia Portaítissa which, found by one of the Georgians in the sea, enabled him to walk upon it. The *Library* is rich in MSS., particularly of the gospels including one

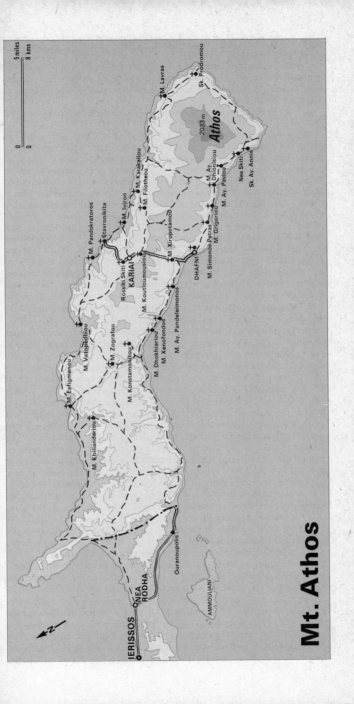

Mt. Athos

IERISSOS

NEA RODHA

Ouranoupolis

AMMOULIANI

M. Esfigmenou

M. Khiliandariou

M. Vatopadhiou

M. Zografou

M. Konstamonitou

M. Dhokhiariou

M. Xenofondos

M. Av. Pandeleimonos

Rossiki Skiti

KARIAI

M. Koutloumousiou

M. Pandokratoros

Stavronikita

M. Iviron

M. Karakalou

M. Filotheou

M. Xiropotamou

DHAFNI

M. Simonos Petras

M. Grigoriou

M. Av. Dhionisiou

M. Av. Pavlou

Nea Skiti

Sk. Av. Annis

M. Lavras

Sk. Prodromou

Athos

2033 m

5 miles

8 kms

the gift of Peter the Great. The Treasury (seldom shown) has a carved cross of 1607, another of carved wood (Raising of Lazarus), and remarkable vestments, including an embroidered tunic said to have belonged to the Emp. John Tsimiskis.

Near the convent is a former asylum for the mentally afflicted and lepers (good beach near by).—A road leads direct from Ivíron to Kariaí (1¼ hr).

FROM IVIRON TO THE GRAND LAVRA, 6½ hrs. The path runs s.e. along the coast to the end of the peninsula. After 1½ hr amid green meadows we reach the idiorrhythmic convent of **Philothéou** (35 monks), supposedly founded in the 9C by three monks of Olympus (Arsenius, Denys, and Philotheos), but first mentioned in the 12C. It numbered Stephan Dušan among its benefactors. The convent was rebuilt after a fire in 1781. Round its church are workshops where the monks employ themselves in wood carving. There is a fine view hence of the convents of Stavronikita and Pantokrator. About ½ hr farther on through rich and fertile country, or 40 min. direct from Iviron, is the coenobite convent of **Karakállou**, situated in hazel woods (1510 ft). It was founded in the 15C by Peter Raresch IV of Moldavia and dedicated to SS Peter and Paul by one John Karakallos. The convent, which has 30 monks, was restored in 1548. The mountainside falls abruptly to the sea and the view over the Aegean embraces Samothrace, Imbros, and Tenedos.

Some 4 hrs from Karakallou we reach the ***Grand Lavra** ('Η Μονή τῆς Μεγίστης Λαύρας), an idiorrhythmic convent, with 250 monks, including Russians, Rumanians, and Bulgarians (Lavra means cloister or monk's cell). The largest and perhaps the finest of all, partly because (alone of the 20) it has never suffered from fire, it is comparatively simple in plan, without the multiplicity of buildings characterizing some of the others. It was founded in the time of Nikephoros Phokas (963–4) by Athanasius of Trebizond. Resembling a fortified village, with a fine 10C *Tower*, it stands on a gently sloping spur (500 ft) overlooking a little harbour guarded by a fort. The entrance is by a long, winding and vaulted passage, with several massive iron gates. In the court are two ancient cypresses, said to have been planted at the foundation. The *Phiale*, erected in 1635, incorporates Byzantine relief panels between eight Turkish stalactite capitals. Paintings within the dome represent the Baptism of Christ. Below is an antique porphyry basin with a sculptured bronze fountain. The *Katholikon*, completed in 1004, which externally resembles a domed basilica, consists of a triconchal Greek cross extended to the w. and flanked by pareclesia in the form of two smaller cross-in-square churches. A hideous exo-narthex of 1814 now abuts the three w. fronts, occupying the site of St Athanasius's cell. Painted baroque doors of the Turkish period lead into the church, which was frescoed all over by Theophanes the Cretan in 1535–60. Representations of Nikephoros Phokas and his nephew, John I Tzimisces, benefactors of the church, dominate the nave. In the right pareclesia is the *Tomb of St Athanasius*. To the left the *Chapel of St Nicholas* has frescoes by Kastellanos. The cruciform *Refectory*, built by Gennadios, Abp. of Serres, in 1512, has *Frescoes by Theophanes the Cretan. Within the apse, Last Supper. Side walls (in three bands): below, SS Athanasius, Euthymus, and Gregory Palamas; middle, scenes of martyrdom; above, illustration of the hymn Ἅγιον ἐστύ. To the s., Life of St Solitarius, Council of Nicaea, scenes in the life of the Virgin.

To the N., Death of a just man, scenes in the life of St John. To the E., Last Judgment (centre, Second Coming; left, Paradise; right, Hell). The *Chapel of the Trinity (Ayias Trias)* has an ikonostasis of the 15–16C.

The treasures include the ikon of Koukouzelissa (12C), reliquary of Nicephoros Phokas (11C or earlier), and an enamelled ikon said to be that of John Tzinitzas (12C).—The *Library* has 5000 volumes and 2250 MSS., including a Bible of Nicephoros Phokas, set with precious stones; two leaves (from Galatians and 2 Corinthians) of the 6C 'Codex Euthalianus' are preserved.

Directly above the Grand Lavra rises the peak of **Mount Athos** (6670 ft), with its white cone and its precipices, in striking contrast to the dark foliage of the ridges below. The ascent can be made in one day from the convent viâ Kerassiá (see below; start in the early morning, return in the evening). It was climbed in 5 hrs from Nea Skiti by Sir John Hunt in 1948. On the summit is the little *Chapel of the Transfiguration*, in which a service is held annually (on 6 Aug). The peak was one of the stations of the fire-beacons that carried Agamemnon's signal to Klytemnestra (Aesch. *Agam.* 284). The ****VIEW** all round is unsurpassed, embracing the whole N. Aegean.

FROM THE GRAND LAVRA TO DAPHNE, 10 hrs, not counting halts. This itinerary follows the contour of the peninsula, rounding its extremity and going up the w. coast. Hereabouts are numerous hermit's cells (σκῆται), many of them almost inaccessible.—2 hrs *Kerassiá* is the principal halting-place (accommodation) and the closest point for the ascent of the Mountain (see above). A short distance away, on the coast, is *Kafsokalivia*, a colony of painters and woodcarvers who live in small groups.—3¾ hrs *St Anne's*, a retreat where 157 monks live in separate houses, clings in terraces to a steep mountainside. Here is a shrine with a relic of St Anne.

About 5 hrs from the Grand Lavra, the coenobite convent of **Ayiou Pavlou** (125 monks) is beautifully situated in an angle of stupendous cliff above a boulder-strewn torrent. Founded in the 11C by Serbs and Bulgars, it gets its name, not from the Apostle, but from a son of the Emp. Maurice, one of its chief benefactors. After a period of desertion, the buildings were renewed wing by wing in the 19–20C; the Katholikon of 1447 was replaced in 1844–50. The library was lost in a fire in 1905. The *Chapel of St George* has good frescoes in the Cretan style, dated 1423 but probably of the 16C: figures of saints and Apostles and, in the narthex, the Virgin as the source of life (Ζωοδόχος πηγή).—A difficult path leads hence in ¾ hr to the coenobite convent of **Dionysíou** (40 monks) founded in 1375 by Alexios III Emperor of Trebizond at the instance of Dionysios, brother of Theodosius, Abp. of Trebizond. The convent stands on a precipitous rock where a bleak gorge reaches the sea; it is approached from its little landing-stage by 420 steps. The huge *Tower* was built in 1520 and Peter IV Raresch of Moldavia restored the buildings (1547) after a fire in 1535. The *Katholikon* has frescoes of 1547 by Zorzis (Cretan school). In the refectory is a Last Judgment (1603). There are the silver reliquary of St Niphon and (in the library) a superb chrysobul and c. 600 MSS.—About 1 hr farther, just above the sea and shut in by rocky cliffs, is the compact and attractive Gregoríou (coenobite, with 36 monks), founded c. 1395 and rebuilt after a fire in 1762–83. Its katholikon has paintings of 1779.—About 1 hr farther on is the coenobite convent of **Simonópetra**, picturesquely situated over 1000 ft up on a rock isolated on all sides save the N.E., where a bridge of three superimposed arches joins it to the cliff. Its buildings, reconstructed on the old foundations in 1893–1902, with funds from Czar Nicholas II, are supported by heavy beams overhanging the precipice, recalling architecturally the Potala at Lhasa in Tibet. The view is magnificent.

The convent was founded in 1257 by St Simon and favoured by the Serbian Emp. John Ugleš. Fires took their usual toll in 1580 and 1625, and Turkish occupation in 1821–30, while the library and much else was destroyed in 1891. The convent has 32 monks.—From Simonopetra Daphne is 2 hrs walk.

OTHER CONVENTS ON THE WEST COAST. From Xeropotamos a path leads N.W. in ½ hr to **St Pantaleímon** or **Roussikon**, a huge coenobite convent once supporting 1500 Russian monks (now 20). It was founded in 1169 in an earlier abandoned building, burnt down by the Catalan Company in 1309, but re-endowed by Andronikos II two years later. It was occupied for about eighty years after 1735 by Greek monks, but rebuilt in 1812–14 in an exotic Russian style. It was swept by fire in 1968 when the assembly hall was destroyed. Above its scattered barrack-like blocks on the waterfront rise many towers and domes surmounted by golden crosses. It has a soapstone paten with a representation of the Virgin and Child, and an illuminated MS. of St Gregory of Nazianzen. The singing of its Russian choirs was famous.—About 1 hr farther, at the edge of the sea, is the coenobite convent of **Xenophóndos** (70 monks), founded at the end of the 10C by the monk Xenophon. The *Old Katholikon* has frescoes of the school of the Cretan Theophanes while the *New Katholikon* (1837) has two fine 14C mosaic panels of saints. In the refectory is a good Last Judgment.—Half an hour farther on, standing 150 ft above the sea, is the idiorrhythmic convent of **Docheiaríou**, with 25 monks, architecturally one of the most charming. It was founded at the beginning of the 10C by Euthymios, who had been Receiver (δοχειάρης) of the Grand Lavra. The *Katholikon* is one of the finest on Mt Athos; its frescoes, by an unknown artist of the Cretan school (1568) embody the traditional style of decoration in all its completeness. Count Alexander IV of Moldavia and his countess Roxandra are depicted as founders. The convent has an interesting ikon, an epitaphios of 1605, and 11–12C MSS.—The path now leads through wooded country to (1 hr farther) the little coenobite convent of **Konstamonítou** (21 monks), hidden in a deep defile. It was founded, according to the most probable account, in the 11C by someone from Kastamon, but tradition has altered the medieval spelling from Kastamonitou to accord with a legendary foundation by Constans, son of Constantine the Great. Its buildings are all of the 19C.—Finally, after another ½ hour, midway between the coasts we reach **Zográphou,** a coenobite convent of 15 Bulgarian monks founded by Slav nobles from Ochrid at the end of the 10C. The two churches date from 1764 and 1801 but the rest was largely rebuilt in 1860–96 in an ugly style.

Its miraculous ikon of St George (Italian style, 15C) is said to have come from Palestine without human aid, in the same way as the House of the Virgin at Loreto (see the 'Blue Guide to Northern Italy'). The monks declare that it was painted by divine will and not by man; hence the dedication to the Zographos or Painter. There is a small hole near the eyes of the painting made by an unbelieving bishop from Constantinople, who (it is said) inserted his finger in derision and could not withdraw it, so that it had to be cut off.

The ride from Zografou across the peninsula to Khiliandari is one of the finest on the Holy Mountain.

C Olynthos and Kassandra

ROAD TO PALIOURI, 72 m. (119 km.), fast highway to Nea Moudhaniá. 26 m. *Nea Kallikrateia.*—42 m. *Nea Moudhaniá,* for **Olynthos** (5 m.).—45 m. *Potidaia.*—57 m. *Kallithéa.*—72 m. Palioúri.

From Salonika we take the road past the airport (p. 525) and at 10 m. diverge left. The road passes through an open region of well-tended fields and skirts (26 m.) *Néa Kallikrátia* on the sea, only to turn inland again.—32 m. *Elaiokhória.* The Petralona Cavern (3 m. l.), where a Neanderthal skull came to light in 1960 and a full skeleton in 1976, may have been occupied in 500,000 B.C.—34½ m. *Néa Tríglia.*—42 m. *Néa Moudhaniá* (3100 inhab.; Kouvraki C; Glaros Rest.) has a small harbour. We skirt the town and reach a vast crossroads with traffic lights.

The road to the left runs through a flat cultivated plain across the base of the Gulf of Kassandra into Sithonia, joining Rte 64D at Paralia Yerakina (10 m.). We may diverge along this road to visit ancient Olynthos, turning left after 3½ m., by a mound, and at the beginning of the modern village (1 m. farther) taking a signed track (r.) for another ½ m. and fording the Retsinikia. The site of **Olynthos** (fenced; phylax; free) occupies twin flat-topped mounds running N. and S., overlooking the Retsinikia. In the 5C and 4C B.C. it was the most important of the Greek cities in this part of the Macedonian coast.

Neolithic dwellings occupied the S. spur of the hill in the early 3rd millennium B.C. The Bronze Age settlement was at Ayios Mamas (see below), but c. 800 B.C. the S. hill was reoccupied by a Macedonian tribe. It was settled by Bottiaians in the 7C. Xerxes here requisitioned troops and ships in 480 B.C. (Herod. VII, 122); meditating rebellion in the following year, it was burnt by Artabazus and the site given to the Chalcidians. Their city paid tribute to Athens until, in 432, Perdikkas II of Macedon moved many inhabitants of neighbouring Chalcidian towns into Olynthos and it became the head of the Chalcidian League. The population grew to c. 30,000 inhabitants, and the town spread to the N. hill. It maintained its independence except for a short period of submission to Sparta (379 B.C.). After first siding with Macedon, Olynthos was reconciled to Athens by Demosthenes, who, in his Olynthiac Orations, urged his countrymen to support the Olynthians against Philip. In 348, however, Philip took and destroyed Olynthos so thoroughly as to excite the comment of Demosthenes that a visitor to the place would never realize that there had been a city there (Phil. 3, 117). A Byzantine church later occupied part of the site.

The classical city was built on the Hippodamian system with insulae of uniform area, measuring 300 by 120 Greek feet. Its excavation by the American School in 1928–34 provided a knowledge of Greek town-planning and domestic building comparable with that gained by Roman scholars from Pompeii. Sculptural and architectural fragments, exactly dated by the historic destruction, clarified the relationship between Classical and Hellenistic styles. Its pebble mosaics, forerunners of those at Pella, have been covered over; some mosaics have been uncovered for display but these are not easy to find without help from the phylax and the site otherwise offers little to the layman. There are numerous open cisterns.

Returning to Nea Moudhaniá, we continue S. and traverse the narrow isthmus that joins Kassandra to the mainland; here in 1960 road-builders unearthed a tomb containing a laurel wreath of the 3C B.C., the first gold object found in the area. To the right, beyond the shallow canal cut across the isthmus in 1937 lies (45 m.) *Néa Potídaia* and its unremarkable remains.

Potídaia, a Dorian colony founded c. 600 B.C. from Corinth, soon minted its own coins. After Salamis the strongly fortified port led the Chalcidian revolt against the Persian lines of communication, resisting a siege by Artabazus. It became a member of the Delian Confederacy. Its revolt from Athens in 432 B.C. was one of the immediate causes of the Peloponnesian War (Thuc. I, 56). The city was subdued in 429 after a siege of two years; in the campaign Socrates saved the life of Alcibiades while serving as a hoplite. Potidaia remained an Athenian cleruchy until 404 when it passed to the Chalcidians. Recovered by Athens in 363–356, it fell to Philip of Macedon who gave it to the Olynthians. After destruction in the Olynthian War, the place was refounded by Kassander as *Kassandreia*, and became the most prosperous city in Macedonia. It repulsed the Roman fleet in the Third Macedonian War (171–168). It was destroyed by the Huns.

The peninsula of **Kassandra,** the ancient *Pallene*, is the most fertile of the three prongs of Chalkidike. Before the War of Independence it contained a population of cattle- and sheep-farmers. When news arrived in 1821 of the revolt of the Greeks in the S., the people of Kassandra decided at first to join in but, finding themselves unprepared, tried to back out. It was too late. The Pasha of Salonika, entering the peninsula, put all the inhabitants to the sword and razed all their houses. Kassandra was left untenanted for two years and only in the last few years has anything been done to restore its former prosperity.

From Nea Potidaia the road follows the E. side of the peninsula. *Saní*, with a bungalow hotel, lies 7 m. down the w. coast. 52 m. *Néa Fókaia* has a prominent medieval watch-tower.—55 m. *Áfitos* marks the site of ancient *Aphytis*, where in 380 B.C. Agesipolis of Sparta died of fever while campaigning against Olynthos. A sanctuary of Ammon Zeus (4C B.C.) with an associated Sanctuary of the Nymphs and Dionysos (Xen. Hell., 5, 3, 13) were found and excavated in 1969–71 (finds in Poliyiros museum).—At (57 m.) *Kallithéa* (Ammon Zeus B), with the huge Athos Palace and Pallini Beach hotels (both A, with bungalows), the road divides to form a circuit of 76 km. round the peninsula.

The pleasant E. coast road continues close to the shore through wooded hamlets.—3 m. *Kriopiyí* (Kassandra Palace A; Alexander Beach, open all year, B) has an N.T.O.G. camp site.—6¼ m. *Khaniótis* (Strand, May–Oct; Plaza, open all year, and others C). By the sea, 2 m. short of (18 m.) **Palioúri,** is a *Xenia Hotel* (June–Sept, DPO, B) and a large N.T.O.G. camp site. To the S.E. the peninsula ends in Cape Kalogriá, the ancient *Kanastraion*.

From Palioúri the road turns inland through *Ayía Paraskeví* to the w. coast at (25 m.) *Loutra* (Aphrodite, Apr–Sept, B) with hot springs.— At (29¼ m.) *Néa Skióni* (Skioni, small, D), chance finds in 1956 included coins and walls, relics presumably of *Skione*, once the chief town of Pallene.—Farther on is *Kalandra* (Mendi, May–Sept, A), the site of ancient *Mende*, noted for its wine and as the birthplace of the sculptor Paionios. At *Valta* some pottery of the 6C B.C. came to light in 1956; here or on Cape Poseidon to the s.w. may have lain ancient Kassandreia. The road recrosses the peninsula through (45 m.) *Kassándra*, properly Kassandreia, an unattractive little town (2130 inhab.), to (47½ m.) *Kallithéa*.

D Poliyiros and Sithonia

ROAD to *Nikítas*, 65 m. (104 km.), with, beyond, a circuit of 69½ m. (111 km.).

From Salonika to (35 m.) the Palaiókastro turn, see Rte 64A. We bear s. through the village (1750 ft), situated amid oak-woods, and wind through shaly hills.—40½ m. (65 km.) **Políyiros** (ΠΟΛΥΓΥΡΟΣ; 1755 ft), the chief town (3700 inhab.) of Khalkidhiki and seat of the Bp. of Kassandra. The ARCHAEOLOGICAL MUSEUM (adm. 5 dr.; standard hours) is to the right at the entrance to the town. Opened in 1970, it houses finds from all over Chalcidice. Of particular interest are those from the sanctuary of Ammon Zeus at Aphytis and a head of Dionysos from the associated sanctuary; early black-figure idols from Olynthos; and a late-Archaic Clazomenian larnax. Three silver coins displayed were found in the hand of a skeleton at Akanthos.

Beyond Poliyiros the road winds down through rounded hills, passes large quarries, and reaches (50½ m.) the coast at a T-junction. The road to the right leads past Ancient Olynthos (5 m.; see above) and joins Rte 64c at Néa Moudhaniá. We turn left and soon reach *Yerakina Beach Hotel* (**B**), with swimming pools and a conference centre.—53 m. *Psakoúdia* (Sermili, Apr–Oct, **B**). The site of ancient *Sermyle* is to be sought on the coast s. of Ormília or Vatopédi, inland villages served by by-roads (l.).—61 m. *Metamórfosis* (r.; Golden Beach **D**; Rest. Thessalonikis). Beyond a camp site we reach (65 m.) *Nikitas* (1800 inhab.) at the base of the Sithonia peninsula. About 1 m. farther on the road divides.

With its trees, sharp hills, and rocks, **Sithonia** is more attractive than Kassandra and still unspoilt though a coast road encircles the peninsula. The right branch follows the w. coast with occasional accessible but deserted coves.—10¾ m. *Néos Marmarás* is a pleasant village with good seaside restaurants (Panos). Beyond extend the estates (c. 7 sq. m.) of John C. Carras, run as a model farm to produce olives, citrus fruits, almonds, and excellent wines for **Porto Carras** (*Village Inn* **B**), a village expressly built in a modern Mediterranean idiom as a resort for 3000 guests and 1800 permanent residents. It has full sporting and cultural facilities, including a theatre for 4500 spectators, and a yacht marina. Its two vast hotels are expected to be fully open in 1981. Fine scenery with sandy coves and beaches extend below the wooded slopes of Melítonas (1620 ft).—26 m. *Toroni* (Taverna) has cheap rooms and a good beach. A small fishing fleet works from *Porto Koufo*, at the s. end of which are extensive ruins of ancient *Torone*. A joint Greek–Australian dig, begun in 1975, has shown that the site had three main periods. The peninsula ends in Cape Drepanon, the ancient Derrhis Promontory.

The road climbs over a spur with splendid views down towards (33¾ m.) *Kalamitsa*. Beyond (38¾ m.) the turning to *Sikea*, seen 1¼ m. l. in a bowl of hills, the road runs nearer sea level.—43¾ m. *Sarti* is a pleasant little place with seaside restaurants. The road runs en corniche with fine *Views up and down the coast and across to Mt Athos.—62½ m. *Bourbouras* lies on the sea.—At (66½ m.) *Ormos Panayías*, a tiny rock-strewn bay, a settlement of the 6 C A.D. has come to light with a basilican church. As we turn across the peninsula towards Nikitas, a road branches right to *Ayios Nikólaos* (2½ m.), whence a poor road continues to Pirgadhíkia (10 m.).

65 FROM SALONIKA TO SERRES
A By road viâ Lakhanás

ROAD, 59 m. (95 km.), the shortest route, coinciding for the first 56 m. with the main road to Bulgaria. Hilly winding road through varied upland country; careful driving necessary. In 1916 this was the main supply road for the right wing of the allied army and was remade by British engineers.—Buses hourly in 2¼ hrs.

We quit Salonika by its dreary N. suburbs. The busy highway carries traffic for Lakhanás, Nigrita, and Kavalla through a gap (950 ft) in the *Khortiatis* range that shuts in the town to N. and E.—7 m. *Dherveni* (signs to 'Macedonian Tomb' and 'Ancient Cemetery'). Burial mounds of the 4C B.C. covering cist graves were explored here in 1962; they yielded iron weapons, a pair of gilt bronze greaves, a unique embossed krater of gilt bronze, vases of silver and alabaster, and the burnt remains of a papyrus roll (4C B.C.), all now in Salonika Museum. To the right diverges first the Kavalla road (Rte 66), then that to Nigrita (see below), and c. 1 m. farther on we leave on our left a road to Kilkis (Rte 65c). We cross a cultivated plain. By the side of the road are (11½ m.) a spring and (12½ m.; l.) the *Toumba Assiros*, a prominent mound, excavated by the British School in 1975–77 and found to have been occupied probably continuously from c. 2000 B.C. to c. 800 B.C. The former Turkish name of (14 m.) *Ássiros* (r. of road) was Giovesnak. We begin the long climb into the foothills of the *Krousia Mts* (Turk.: Beşik Dağ), the ancient Dysoron, which separate the Axios basin from the Strymon. From the ridges fine views of the plain we have left take in Lakes Koronia and Volvi and the heights of Khalkidhiki. Beyond (21¾ m.) *Dorkás* (Taverna) we cross a declivity with pine clad slopes. At the top of the next rise, by-road (r.) to *Vertískos* (5 m.), which gives its name to the mountains to the S.E. The road undulates to (28 m.) *Xilópolis* at the head of another wooded valley.

32 m. (52 km.) **Lakhanás** was the farthest point reached by the Bulgarians in 1913. We pass first a *Memorial* of the bayonet charge that checked their advance, with a small *Museum*; then, at the road's summit level (2045 ft), ½ m. w. of the village a *British Military Cemetery*, in which are buried 270 soldiers who died on this front in 1916–17. The panorama extends to the Kerkini or Beles Mts (6665 ft; comp. below) on the Bulgarian frontier.—34¼ m. *Evangelístria* stands on an irregular spur projecting into the Strymon plain.—37 m. *Kefalokhórion* has wayside tavernas.

The **Strymon**, or *Struma* (155 m. long), called by the Turks Kara-Su, rises in the Bulgarian mountains, enters Greece through the Rupel Pass, and flows generally S.E. through a broad and fertile plain enclosed by parallel chains of mountains. Its upper reaches have been dammed to form a new lake (comp. Rte 65c). Its lower course has been controlled and the former *Lake Achinos*, anciently called *Prasias*, drained. At the S.E. end of the lake lay the city of *Myrkinos*, founded c. 510 by Histiaias. The river empties into the Kolpos Orfanou or Strymonic Gulf. At one time it formed the boundary between Macedonia and Thrace. In the First World War the river demarcated the static front line until the break-out of July 1918.

We descend gradually amid scrubby hills.—44½ m. *Kalókastron*, where in 1917 Stanley Casson recognized Byzantine walls and the remains of a Roman town, looks out from a low ridge towards Serres. To the left of the road is the *Struma Military Cemetery*, established in 1916 by the 40th Casualty Clearing Station; it contains the graves of 932 officers and men of the British, Indian, and Maltese forces who died on the Strymon front.—At 47½ m. we cross the artificially embanked Strymon by a long bridge.—50½ m. *Provatás* (1500 inhab.) produces ouzo. *Monokklissiá* (1½ m. s.) is notorious for its practices of 8 Jan (comp. Rte 57), when the women confine the men to domestic chores while they revel in street and tavern. The inhabitants brought the custom from E. Thrace in 1922; it may derive from the Dionysiac rites of ancient Thrace. Crossing the Belitsa, a tributary of the Strymon, and the railway, we pass (56 m.) the road to *Sidhirókastro* (12 m.; see below) and Bulgaria.

After Sidhirokastro, the road (Europabus twice weekly to Sofia in 8 hrs) and railway (daily to Sofia in 9 hrs from Salonika) to Bulgaria follow the river through the formidable RUPEL PASS, guarded by the conspicuous *Rupel Fort.*—25 m. *Koula* and (27 m.) *Kulata* are the frontier posts, beyond which the Bulgarian highway continues in the Struma valley.—95 m. **Sofia.**

We pass the huge Kolokotronis Barracks and enter (59 m.) Sérres.

Sérres or *Sérrai* (ΣΕΡΡΑΙ; *Xenia* **B**; *Galaxy, Park, Mitropolis*, these **C**; restaurants in the Plateia; P.O., O.T.E. Centre, and Nomarkhia, all in Od. Merarkhias Serron) is the capital of its nome and one of the most important commercial cities (39,900 inhab.) in Macedonia. Situated at a low elevation (165 ft) at the foot of mountainous country (to the N.E.), it overlooks the fertile plain to the s.w. through which the Strymon flows some 15 miles away. Serres is a pleasant town, with wide streets, surrounded by abundant woods and luxuriant gardens. It has a covered swimming-pool.

History. *Siris*, or *Serrhai*, was already chief town of its district in the time of Herodotus; in its plain Xerxes left the sacred mares of the Chariot of the Sun. It became the seat of a bishop and later of a metropolitan, and played a strategic role throughout the Middle Ages. It was ravaged in 1195–96 by the Bulgarians who defeated a Byzantine army and took prisoner Isaac Comnenus, the sebasto-crator. In 1205 the marauding Vlach, Johannica, besieged Serres; Hugues de Coligny was killed and the surrendered Frankish garrison slaughtered; Boniface de Montferrat, hastening from the Morea, recaptured and refortified the town. It resisted the attacks of Cantacuzenus but fell in 1345 to Dušan, who here promulgated his legal code (1354). Helen, his widow, retired here under the religious name of Elizabeth. Though Manuel recaptured Serres for the Byzantines in 1371, it attracted the attention of the Ottoman Turks the following year and in 1383 fell decisively into the hands of Lala Shahin. It remained Turkish (as *Siruz*) until 1913, when it was seized by the Bulgarians who set it on fire in their retreat. On 29 June the town celebrates its freedom from the Bulgarians.

The town, almost entirely rebuilt since the Bulgarian incendiarism, is best seen from the ruined 14C *Kastro* (Rfmts.) that crowns the round wooded hill to the N. To the N.E. is a pretty cypress-planted *Cemetery*; to the N.W. an ancient *Aqueduct* spans a gully. Immediately below lay the Christian quarter (Varoch), where two Byzantine churches have been completely restored since 1951. The *Old Metropolis*, dedicated to SS Theodore, is a large aisled basilica of the 11C, rather too high for its length, with a pretty domed chapel at one corner. In the apse is a huge mosaic of the Last Supper, still splendid in its decay. The neighbouring *Ayios Nikolaos* an attractive cross-in-square, has an exonarthex wider than the building. Its octagonal drum and small domes are ornamented with brick decoration. Two decayed *Mosques*, picturesque if unimportant, show where the former Turkish quarter lay. In the central square, opposite the Dhimarkhion, is a huge edifice with six domes which has seen Moslem and Christian worship in turn and is now an archaeological store.

Oinoussa, an attractive village with an old church, stands (3¾ m. E.) at the mouth of the Kazil Tsai valley, in which there are asbestos mines. Higher up the valley (7½ m.), in a cool wooded site, is the *Moni Timiou Prodromou* (1275), with the tombs of the founders and of Gennadios II Scholarios (d. 1472), first Patriarch of Byzantium under the Turk, and wall paintings.

From Serres a steep but beautiful mountain road crosses the pass between the Vrontous Mts and Menoikion to (30 m.) *Kato Nevrokópion* (Rte 68).

FROM SERRES TO DRAMA, 43¾ m. (70 km.), asphalt, bus. The road keeps to higher ground 1–3 m. N. of the railway, affording superb views of the mountain chains that ring the Strymon valley and the Drama plain.—18 m. *Néa Zíkhni* (850 ft) is the seat (3100 inhab.) of the small eparchy of Phyllis.—At (20½ m.) *Mesorrákhi* (620 ft) diverges the road to Amphipolis (Rte 66). Through the broad valley of the Angitis, for a short distance, road, river, and railway run close together, before the road climbs to (31 m.) *Alistráti* (855 ft), a village of 2700 inhab., once the seat of a bishop, on the easternmost spur of Menoikion. The descent commands a view N. to the Falakron range across the Drama plain. At 35 m. we cross the Angitis and see (r.) the Sitagroí tumulus excavated by the British School in 1968–69 (finds in Philippi museum).—37 m. *Sitagroí.*—At 41½ m. we join a road from Kato Nevrokopion.—43¾ m. **Drama** (Rte 68).

B   By road viâ Nigrita

Though this road is narrower and slightly longer, it has less traffic and the more varied scenery.

Leaving the Lakhanás road (see above) at (7 m.) Dhervéni, we turn E., passing (10 m.) between the *Saratse Toumba*, a Bronze and Iron Age tumulus, and the derelict *Perivolákion Station*, once the terminus of the Stavros Military Railway (comp. Rte 66).—12 m. **Langadhás** (*Olimpion Megaron Valkanion C*, summer only), the seat of an eparchy, with 6700 inhab., has alkaline warm springs (1½ m. S.E.). Here the Anastenaria, a ritual fire-walking ceremony, takes place on the feast of SS Constantine and Helen (21 May).

Tradition asserts that c. 1250 in the Thracian village of Kosti, the church of St Constantine caught fire. The sacred ikons were heard groaning in the flames, whereupon certain villagers dashed into the fire and rescued them without suffering harm. The ikons have been handed down by the families concerned from one generation to the next and the descendants honour their saints each year by walking barefoot on fire in a state of ecstasy carrying the ikons. The walkers are called Anastenarides from their imitative groaning (ἀναστενάξω). In 1914, when their territory was transferred from Turkish to Bulgarian rule, they fled with their ikons to Ayia Eleni (Serres), Mavrolefki (Drama), Meliki, and Langadhas, where, until 1948, their rituals were held in secret owing to opposition from the Greek Orthodox Church. Clerical objections in 1960 caused the ceremonies to be held that year only in Ayia Eleni. The orgiastic dance to drum and lyre with attendant chorus, together with the sacrifice of a bull decked with garlands, suggests an origin far earlier than the 13C, and the ceremony probably survives, shorn of attendant excesses, from the pre-Christian worship of Dionysos.

The road climbs into the wooded foothills of *Mt Vertískos*, passing close beneath the steep s. side of Kharvata (3620 ft). The chief town of the s. slopes is (30½ m.) *Sokhós.*—We skirt an upland plain with the marshy *Vromolimnai* ('stinking lakes'), a once notorious breeding-place of malaria; the Greek army began draining them in 1961. The road climbs the w. spur of Mt Kerdílion and makes a devious descent. To the N.E. extends the area once occupied by Lake Prasias (comp. above), the extent of which is betrayed by the prehistoric mounds that lined its shores.—50½ m. **Nigríta,** a town of 7300 inhab. and the seat of the eparch of *Visaltia*, overlooks the Strymon valley. It is a centre for tobacco. The Bulgarians took the town in April 1913 and destroyed it on retiring two months later.

At *Dimitrítsi*, 8 m. N.W., the Greek general Branas defeated the retreating Normans in 1185, putting an end to their expedition.

Crossing a long bridge over the Strymon, we enter (62 m.) **Serres** from the s. past the Railway Station.

C By Railway viâ Sidhirokastro

RAILWAY, 101 m. (162 km.), 6 trains daily in 2¾–6 hrs. This is part of the through route to Turkey (see Rte 69B). Between Salonika and Serres the line makes a wide detour to the N. viâ (26 m.) *Kilkis*, (60¼ m.) *Rodhopolis*, and (81 m.) *Sidhirokastro*, so that the distance covered is much greater than by road.

The roads that follow the course of the railway are mainly poor and local. From Salonika the best road to *Kilkis* (30 m.) branches left from the Serres road (comp. Rte 65A), though from the direction of Edhessa it is better to turn up the Gallikos at Dhiavata, following the railway. From Kilkis its continuation crosses the Krousia Mts to (55 m.) *Rodhopolis*. By road Sidhirokastro is better reached from the Lakhanas road (comp. Rte 65A) or visited from Serres.

The line runs N.W. but after 5 m. diverges from that to Ghevgheli and Central Europe.—Before (13¾ m.) *Filadelfianá* we cross from the left to the right bank of the Gallikos.—18½ m. *Gallikós*.—26 m. *Kilkis Station* (650 ft) is situated on the Salonika–Kilkis road by the village of *Krístoni*, 3 m. s.w. of the town. Just s.w. of the station is *Sarigöl Military Cemetery*, with the graves of 659 British soldiers who died here in 1917–18 of wounds received in the attacks on the Grand-Couronné and 'Pip' Ridge, the strongpoints of the Bulgarian defence of Doiran. **Kilkís** (*Evridiki* C), capital of the nome of the same name, with 10,500 inhab., was the scene of the defeat on 21 June 1913 of a Bulgarian attempt on Salonika. To the s. of the town a conspicuous monument crowns a wooded hill and a museum records the battle. The town's former name was *Avrathisari*. A small *Museum* (free 8–1, 3–6; Sun 10–1, 2–6, closed Tues), by the Nomarkhia at the far end of the town, houses the archaic kouros found at Evropós in the Axios Valley and bronzes from an Iron Age grave at Chauchitsa (p. 526).

We cross the road from Kilkis to Doïráni at (32¼ m.) *Metallikón*. An inscribed base for statues of Hadrian and Sabina erected by the city of *Bragylae*, found in 1952, gives for the first time the ancient name of the place. The railway descends the Ayák, or Doiránis, to the shore of Lake Doiran.—44 m. *Doiráni Station* is now separated by the Yugoslav frontier from the town whose name it bears. **Lake Doiran** (6 m. by 4), well stocked with fish, is shared between Greece and Yugoslavia. It formed part of the Vardar–Doiran front in various actions of the First World War.

On 'Colonial Hill' above the station (1 m. s.) is the *British Salonika Force Campaign Memorial*, an obelisk, 40 ft high, guarded by two carved couchant lions, with panels bearing the names of 2160 fallen who have no known grave. In the *Doiran Military Cemetery*, adjoining to the E., lie 1300 dead (875 British).

The railway-line follows the s.E. shore, then bears N.E. across the foothills of the KERKINI MOUNTAINS. Parallel, to the N., runs the main range, whose steep crest, rising in *Demir Kapon* to 6665 ft, forms the inhospitable frontier with Bulgaria; it is better known by the Slav name of *Belasica*.—Beyond (54 m.) *Kastanoússa* in the narrow *Dová Tepé* pass (886 ft), the views become extensive on all sides.—60¼ m.

Rodhópolis is the centre of the alpine area. The railway now veers E. through marshy country watered by the Koumoulis.—Beyond (69 m.) *Mandraki* we enter the valley of the Strymon, which to the s. has been transformed into *Lake Kerkinis* by a dam.—74½ m. *Viróneia*, a Greek headquarters during the war of 1913. Between here and the right bank of the Strymon were the silver mines of the Macedonian kings.—At 79½ m. the line crosses the Strymon on a long bridge near its emergence from the Rupel Pass, then turns s.E., leaving the line to Sofia (opened 1965).—83 m. *Sidhirokastro Town Station*, 2½ m. s. of the town.

Sidhirókastro ('Iron Castle'; *Thraki* D; cafés in the Plateia), a town of 6400 inhab., capital of the eparchy of Sintike, is picturesquely situated at the foot of a hill on which is a medieval Kastro. The town is better remembered by its Turkish name Demir Hisar and is improbably to be identified with the ancient *Herakleia Sintike.* It is watered by the Chrysovitikos, a tributary of the Strymon. The town carries on a brisk transit trade. The church of *Ayios Dhimitrios* incorporates the pedimental façade of a Macedonian tomb as its templon. On a hill to the E. is a monastery cut out of the rock. Road to Serres, see Rte 65A.

We traverse a bare region given over to cotton cultivation. Beyond (90½ m.) *Skotoúsa* we reach the broad valley of the Strymon.—101 m. (162 km.) **Sérres.** The station lies 1½ m. from the town centre.

66   FROM SALONIKA TO KAVALLA

ROAD, 103 m. (166 km.), in good condition throughout, on the course of the Via Egnatia to (63 m.) *Amphipolis.* Buses many times daily.

We quit Salonika as in Rte 65, and at (6 m.) *Dherveni* leave the Serres road on our left.—Beyond (8 m.) *Layiná*, with a spring, the road was paralleled by a railway (now derelict but visible a field's width left) of 60 cm. gauge, built by the Allies in 1916–17 from Sarakli (now Perivolákion; Rte 65B), just N. of (10¼ m.) *Kavallárion*, to Stavrós (see below). We approach LAKE KORONIA, 9 m. long but nowhere more than 20 ft deep, which is of great ornithological interest. Near the w. end of the lake a typical mound gives evidence of prehistoric occupation.—15 m. *Ayios Vasílios.* To the right rises Mt Khortiátis with its prominent observatory and radar station; we cross a series of torrent beds.—23¼ m. *Langadíkia.* We run above the s. shore of the much prettier LAKE VOLVI (12 m long) enclosed on its N. side by the Volves hills or *Mt Besikíon* (2160 ft).—At (31½ m.) *Loutrá Vólvis* (Aristotelis, June–Oct, C) are the hot sulphur springs of *Néa Apollonía* (1½ m. r.), a local spa. Beyond the Kotza Potamos and a tumulus (r.), (36½ m.) *Apollonía* preserves the name of a station on the Via Egnatia, perhaps founded by Chalcidians c. 432 B.C. on land given them by Perdikkas II of Macedon, and mentioned in the Acts of the Apostles (xvii, 1). The Roman character of the road remains. We pass several brick kilns.—44 m. *Rendína*, also with hot springs, lies at the E. end of the lake at the mouth of the *Stena Rendinas*, a pretty ravine sometimes called the 'Macedonian Tempe', which we traverse to the sea. Here stood *Arethousa*, where the 'Tomb of Euripides' became known to Roman travellers as a staging post. On the right rises a hillock with remains of a school whose foundation is attributed to Aristotle; opposite is the hot spring where Alexander the Great used to bathe when a student. A little farther on a cave (l.) faces the by-road to *Stavrós* (2¼ m. r.; Aristotelis, Poseidonion C, both small; Taverna O Yeoryios), a small bathing resort (1700 inhab.) and roadstead.

We reach the sea at the head of the GULF OF ORFANI, or Strymonic Gulf, one of the two great inlets bordering the Chalcidice peninsula. The foothills of *Mt Kerdhillion* (3580 ft) approach close to the sea.— 51½ m. *Asprováita* (Strymonikon **D**, tavernas) has a fine sandy beach and an N.T.O.G. camp site; the coast for the next ten miles is undergoing development.—At (61 m.) *Néa Kerdhíllia* a by-road runs inland to *Aïdonokhóri*, perhaps ancient Tragilos, where remains of a Heroön have been dug. Finds show this to have antedated Amphipolis.

Just after the turn the *Lion of Amphipolis* guards the long bridge over the Strymon. The colossal animal, reassembled from fragments in 1936–37, has been mounted on a pedestal built on the ancient foundation with blocks of the 2C B.C. dredged from the Strymon, where they may had been reused in a medieval dam. Originally the lion may have honoured Laomedon, the sailor of Mytilene who later became governor of Syria. Beyond the bridge, amid low hills (l.), are the scattered remains of ancient **Amphipolis**; the site is well worth the short diversion up the Drama road (½ m. farther on), though from the road itself nothing can be seen. The city was built on a commanding eminence (505 ft) above the E. bank of the Strymon, just below its egress from Lake Achinos, c. 3 m. from the sea. A loop of the river flowed round the w. half of the city walls.

The place, which belonged to the Edonians of Thrace, was originally called *Ennea Hodoi* ('Nine Ways'), for which reason, according to Herodotus (VII, 114), Xerxes on crossing its bridges buried alive nine local boys and nine girls. It was colonized as *Amphipolis* by the Athenians in 437 B.C. after an abortive attempt 28 years earlier. Deriving its wealth from the gold mines of Mt Pangaion, Amphipolis was one of their most important N. possessions: hence the consternation when it surrendered to the Spartan Brasidas in 424. The historian (and general) Thucydides saved its port of *Eion*, at the mouth of the Strymon, but, for failing to save Amphipolis as well, he was exiled for 20 years by his countrymen (Thuc., IV, 104–6; V, 26). In 421 the Athenians made an unsuccessful attempt to retake the city; in the cavalry battle both Kleon, the Athenian demagogue and general, and his opponent Brasidas were killed. Amphipolis was seized by Philip II of Macedon in 358. After the battle of Pydna (168) it became the capital of one of the four republics provisionally set up by the Romans (see p. 497). St Paul passed through Amphipolis on his way to Thessalonica ('Acts', XVII, 1). The city was a station on the Via Egnatia. Excavations have been made since 1956 by the Greek Archaeological Service. Visitors with limited time should go directly to the recently exposed walls (see below).

The Drama road climbs, and soon (l.) there is a small sign in Greek (*Macedonian Tomb*). Two tombs lie on the hill r. of the road: one had been plundered, but the other yielded precious articles now in Kavalla museum. Continuing up the road we reach (l.) the turning for the modern village. On the hill opposite this turn is a Hellenistic cemetery of rock-cut tombs. In the village a relief of Totoes, the Thracian equivalent of Hypnos, adorns the church. Beyond the village is the site of the ancient city, though the principal remains so far excavated are of four neighbouring Early Christian *Basilicas*, whose complete ground plans have been recovered; their *Mosaics, with fine and varied representations of birds, are at present covered, but it is planned to show them. A *Shrine of Clio* borders a deep ravine to the S.E.

Beyond the village turn, the next turning left from the Drama road leads in 400 yds to a derelict railway station below a ruined Byzantine tower. Here and farther on three long sections of the *CITY WALLS stand in places to a height of 23 feet. These have now been proved by soundings at 64 places to form a circuit of nearly 4½ m. with an inner acropolis wall of 1¼ m. Built in fine coursed masonry, with towers, gates, sluices for flood waters resembling archery embrasures, and walkways, the walls extend to guard a crossing of the Strymon. Fossilized wooden piles of the *Ancient Bridge* have been excavated.

At *Tsaghezi*, or Limin (the port of Amphipolis), 2 m, s., which has taken the place of Eion (comp. below), nitrate and phosphate fertilizers are made. The railway connecting it to the main line at Mirini (12 m.), completed in 1940, has not been used since the war.

FROM AMPHIPOLIS TO DRAMA, 33 m., new road. After 5 m. the road divides, the older road (l.) running N. to join the Serres–Drama road (18¾ m.; Rte 65A) at Mesorrákhi.—The right branch runs in upland country with views W. across the Strymon plain and with the mass of Pangaion to the E.—12½ m. *Rodholívos* (3160 inhab.) is the most populous village of the eparchy of *Phyllis*. Neolithic dwellings and remains of a Temple of Diana have been unearthed here.—15½ m. *Próti* (2160 inhab.).—33 m. *Drama*, see Rte 68.

As we continue towards Kavalla, the silted up harbour of *Eion* (comp. above), with some Byzantine walls beside it, is visible to the right between the road and the sea. Below (69 m.) Bournali, an isolated little hill, the road turns inland.

A by-road skirts the hill to (1¼ m.) *Orfánion*, the village that gives its name to the gulf; the prominent walls (not yet archaeologically explored) are Turkish and perhaps Byzantine.—Near (5 m.) *Karianí*, Gaïdhourókastro may represent the site of *Galepsos*, where Perseus of Macedon touched in his headlong flight to Samothrace after his defeat at Pydna (Livy, 44–5). The road continues along the inhospitable coast to (12½ m.) *Loutra Elevtherón* (Pangaion, July–Oct, C), a summer resort near the mouth of the pretty Marmara, with hot springs.

We enter the beautiful valley between Mt Pangaion on the N. and Mt Símvolon on the s., following the ancient road taken by Xerxes in 480 B.C.; by Roman times the Via Egnatia had been diverted round the N. of Pangaion in order to pass through both Amphipolis and Philippi.—76¼ m. *Podhokhórion* is connected by road with Karianí (see above). The villages are mostly to the left of the road on the s. slopes of Pangaion, where, near *Kiría*, a shrine of the rider-hero (Ἥρως Αὐλωνείτης) has been located.—89 m. Turning (asphalt) for Néa Péramos (8 m.), affording an alternative coastal run into Kavalla (comp. below).—91 m. **Elevtheroúpolis** or *Pravion*, a flourishing town of 4900 inhab., mainly engaged in tobacco culture, is the capital of the eparchy of Pangaios and the seat of a bishop. It is the usual base for the ascent of Mt Pangaion.

TOUR AND ASCENT OF MT PANGAION. A road (40 m., mostly unpaved; bus daily to Mesolakkia) traverses the bare N. side of the mountain, rejoining the main road near Bournali (see above).—4 m. *Andifílippoi. Palaiokhórion* lies in a valley to the left.—9½ m. **Nikísiani**, corresponding to the Byzantine *Aekisiane*, nestles in a broader valley 2 m. to the left. Traces of ancient gold workings have been observed. Hereabouts, according to some authorities, was *Skaptesyle*, where Thucydides had an estate incorporating gold mines, to which he retired in exile after the fiasco at Amphipolis. Here he collected materials for his history and here he died. Other scholars place the estate near Stavros or near Khrisoupolis. A large *Tumulus*, ¾ m. right of the road, was excavated in 1959–60 by D. Lazarides, when six shaft graves yielded vessels and coins (4C B.C.) now in Kavalla museum.—18 m. *Kormista*. For the ascent of Pangaion, see below.—26 m. *Rodholívos* stands on the Drama–Amphipolis road (comp. above).

Mules may be hired at Kormista for the ascent of the mountain. **Mount Pangaion** was celebrated for its oracle of Dionysos, for the roses that grew on its slopes, and for the gold and silver mines in its neighbourhood. Here the Maenads tore Orpheus to pieces for comparing Apollo with Dionysos. The higher slopes are of crystalline white marble so the metal deposits must have been lower down. Its riches attracted the cupidity of the ancient world and led to constant strife between neighbouring states until Philip II of Macedon gained control.

A climb of 2 hrs brings us to the **Monastery of the Ikosifoiníssis** (Μονὴ τῆς Εικοσιφοινίσσης), beautifully situated 2470 ft up in the midst of plane woods. The monks welcome visitors (donation expected). The monastery is said to have been founded in the time of Sozon, metropolitan of Philippi (443–54) but is probably not earlier than the 10C. It suffered much under the Turks, notably in 1823, when it was charged with having sheltered partisans in the War of Independence. The *Katholikon*, a fine Byzantine edifice restored in 1954, has good modern frescoes. The library is rich in treasures, including a MS. Gospel on vellum (1378), with a cover inlaid with precious stones.

The ascent is generally made early in the morning in order to see the sunrise. The route up is viâ the *Cavern of Asketótrypo*, past a secondary summit (5595 ft) to the highest peak, *Pilaf Tepe* (6425 ft). Above the tree line the path commands the whole Strymon valley.

At 98¾ m. we join the road from Drama (Rte 68) and wind up through the gap in the barrier ridge that separates Kavalla from its hinterland; the old Turkish paved road is clearly seen below (r.). From the summit (690 ft), with a sanatorium, a large Tourist Pavilion and post office, and the *Monastery of St Silas*, we get a superb sudden *View of the Bay of Kavalla, with the town framed between the hills and the sea; in the middle distance is the island of Thasos, and on a clear day Samothrace and even the Dardanelles can be seen. The road zigzags down to the town.

103 m. (166 km.) **KAVALLA** (ΚΑΒΑΛΑ), beautifully situated at the head of its bay and best seen from the sea, rises in a shallow amphitheatre on outlying slopes of Mandra Kari, one of the chain of hills that link Mt Simvilon with the Lekanis massif. The old citadel occupies a rocky promontory jutting into the sea. The second largest city (46,200 inhab.) of Macedonia, it is the chief town of the small *nome* of Kavalla, the seat since 1924 of the metropolitan of Philippi, Neapolis, and Thasos, and the headquarters of an army corps. Kavalla is the exporting centre of Macedonian tobacco. It is the best base for visiting Philippi and the main embarkation point for the island of Thasos.

Hotels. Galaxy (e; Pl. 7), 150 R.; Okeanis (k; Pl. 6), 170 R.; Philippi (b; Pl. 7), Olympion (f; Pl. 1), these B; Esperia (j; Pl. 5), 105 R.; Nepheli (g; Pl. 5), Panorama (h; Pl. 7), Acropolis (c; Pl. 7), these C, the last without restaurant; and others.
  Restaurants of good quality in the centre and by the old harbour.

Post Office (Pl. 3), Omonias.—O.T.E. CENTRE (Pl. 7), Megalou Alexandhrou/Mela.

Buses for local destinations from Plat. Karoali Dhimitriou; long-distance Bus Station at the quayside. Frequent services to all main towns in Macedonia and Thrace.

Ferry c. 6 times daily to Limen (Thasos); twice to Limenaria.—**Air Service** once or twice daily to Athens direct; terminal on quayside (Pl. 6).

Ancient Drama Festival in Aug at Philippi and Thasos.

History. Kavalla occupies the site of *Neapolis*, the port of Philippi and apparently of its predecessor, and is said to have been a colony of Thasos. At the time of the Battle of Philippi the fleet of Brutus was stationed here. Neapolis was the usual port of disembarkation for travellers to Europe from the Levant. St Paul landed here on his way to Philippi ('Acts', xvi, 11). In the Byzantine era the town seems to have adopted the name of *Christoupolis*. The burning of the town by the Normans on their march towards Constantinople in 1185 is recorded by an inscription from the kastro wall. Here Ramon Muntaner and the Catalan Grand Company landed from Gallipoli (1306) at the start of their march to Athens. Kavalla was Turkish until 1912, since when it has suffered three Bulgarian occupations in 1912–13, 1916–18, and 1942–44. Here was born Mehmet Ali (1769–1849), the son of an Albanian farmer, who became pasha of Egypt and founder of the dynasty that ended with King Fuad II in 1953.

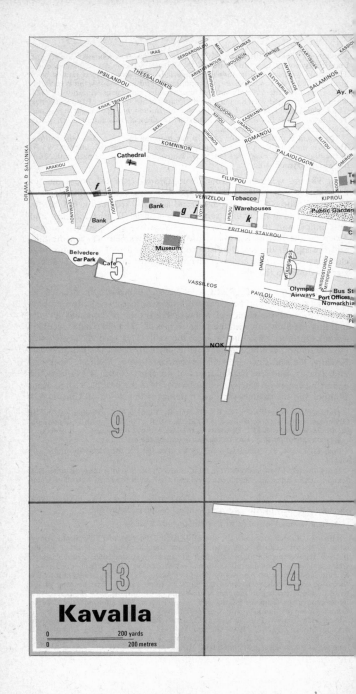

Kavalla

0 ————— 200 yards
0 ————— 200 metres

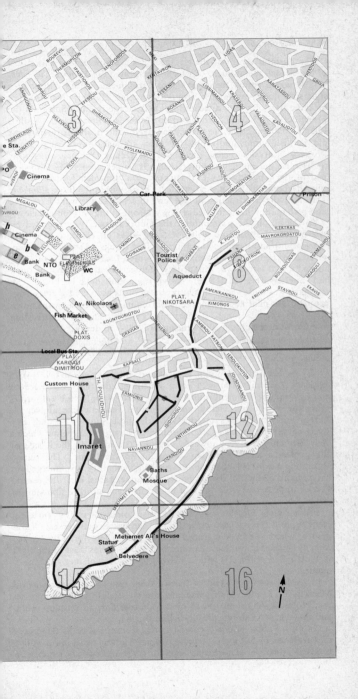

The business centre of the city occupies a depression to shoreward of the citadel, the accident of which necessitated the *Kamares Aqueduct* (Pl. 8) which forms the town's most prominent feature. Built in a style that derives ultimately from Roman models, this fine structure on three tiers of arches appears to date from the reign of Suleiman the Magnificent (1520–66), and carried water to the citadel. Odhos Ellenikis Dhimokratias, to the N., and neighbouring streets retain some old Turkish houses and shops, but these are fast disappearing. From PLATEIA NIKITARA, below the aqueduct, Odhos Omonias runs N.W. to become the main shopping street. It passes across the landward end of the long PLATEIA ELEVTHERIAS (Pl. 7), which extends to the inner harbour. This is a small artificial basin within the large *Harbour*, formed by the construction of two long moles since the war. Extensive land reclamation has provided a new seafront to the w. (comp. below).

To the E., on the promontory, the OLD CITADEL is surrounded by well-preserved Byzantine walls, restored after an earthquake in 926 (inscription) and again in the 16C; ancient blocks of stone are incorporated in them. The attractive multi-domed *Imaret* (Pl. 11), an alms-house for 300 softas, was founded by Mehmet Ali after his native town had unwisely rejected the alternative suggestion of a harbour. The seminary was endowed with the revenues of Thasos, and membership brought free pilaf and exemption from military service; it was known locally as Tembel-Haneh, the lazy man's home. The most interesting monument in the city, it is in a melancholy state of decay.

Excavations by Ephor Lazarides in 1959–61, N. of the Imaret, uncovered the peribolos of a *Sanctuary of the Parthenos* (6C B.C.); the pottery found included examples from all over the Aegean (see below).

In the Seraidaris Garden is *Mehmet Ali's Birthplace* (Pl. 15), a pleasant Turkish house with good panelling, admirably cared for by the Egyptian government until 1961 and since by the Greek authorities (ring for caretaker). Below are the stable and kitchen; above, the harem and the pasha's quarters. In the little square, beyond, is a lively equestrian *Statue of Ali* in bronze, by Dimitriades, below which a *Belvedere* affords a view towards Thasos. The rocks on the E. side of the peninsula afford excellent swimming to the locals. The ruined Byzantine *Kastro* (Pl. 12) that crowns the promontory is submerged on the E. flank of the hill by old houses (mosque, baths, etc); the central keep is approached from the E. side and its walls afford a fine view of the harbour.

From Plateia Elevtherias, Odhos Khrisostomou Smirnis (Venizelou) leads w. past the *Public Garden* (Pl. 6), then passes between tall *Warehouses*, where tobacco is graded and stored. These formerly backed directly on the shore. Kavalla once had 200 of them. Just to the right is the *Cathedral* (Pl. 1), with a marble iconostasis of many compartments.

In gardens at the w. end of the sea front stands the **Archaeological Museum** (Pl. 5; adm. 25 dr.; standard hours). Built in 1965 it comprises two ground-floor rooms linked by a wide corridor, an upstairs room, and courtyards. Exhibits are labelled in English.

GROUND FLOOR. ROOM I contains finds from the Kavalla Sanctuary of Parthenos (6–5C B.C.), including Ionic capitals, figurines, a votive naïskos in the form of a treasury, and pottery (both local and imported).

Along the CORRIDOR are displayed Late Neolithic and Early Bronze Age finds, mainly from Dikili Tach, though the best finds from this site are in the Philippi museum. At the far end, Metope (5C B.C.) from Aïdonokhóri (anc. Tragilos), showing a fight between two hoplites.

ROOM II, finds from the cemetery at Amphipolis: polychrome glass; gold wreaths and diadems, and *Jewellery; coloured busts of goddesses; grave stelai (one painted); figurines; and pottery, clearly from a local workshop, as yet undiscovered. At the end of the room: partial reconstruction of a double funeral chamber (3C B.C.) with paintings; its stele stands to the left. Near by are gold and other articles (male and female) from the same tomb, including a polished silver mirror in a folding case and a man's ring bearing the picture of a youth. Also here, but possibly to be moved to Philippi, is gold and jewellery from a tomb there.

The FIRST FLOOR ROOM (usually closed) houses finds of varied provenance, including pottery from Oisyme, a Dolphin mosaic from Abdera (3C B.C.); polychrome figurines, silverware, and coins of Philip II (gold staters) and Alexander the Great, all from Nikisianí; a lamp and chain in the form of a slave (Drama; 2C A.D.); a massive painted larnax (3C B.C.) from Aïdonokhóri.—In the COURTYARDS are marbles and inscriptions.

A new coast road runs w. from Kavalla to Néa Péramos (12½ m.; bus) and will eventually serve the whole of this developing coast back to Amphipolis.— At (2½ m.) *Kalamitsa* (Lucy B), site of ancient *Antisara*, of which a 4C Asklepieion and ane arlier wall have come to light, is the pleasant Batis beach; farther on a fine N.T.O.G. beach (Restaurant) and camp site, and the Tosca Beach (select and not cheap) backed by its hotel (A, summer only). The road continues past beaches and coves to (10 m.) *Iraklítsa* and (12½ m.) *Néa Péramos*, a small resort. To the right of the track leading s. from the village is the acropolis of ancient *Oisyme*; finds from its cemetery by the shore are in Kavalla museum. On the hill, on the opposite side of the track, is the fortress of the Byzantine city of *Anactoroupolis*.

67 THASOS

CAR FERRY from Kavalla 6 times daily to Prinó harbour; 3 times to Limen. Also from Keramoti (Rte 69A) 12 times daily to Limen.—The island deserves more than a day trip, Limen itself meriting at least a whole day's exploration.

Thasos, the northernmost of the islands of the Archipelago, is of volcanic origin, mountainous, and of great natural beauty. Situated close to the mainland, its nearest point is only 6 m. from the mouth of the Nestos, and it thus faces the boundary between Macedonia and Thrace. Politically the island forms an eparchy of the Macedonian nome of Kavalla. Its area is 154 sq. m.; almost circular in shape, it has a length from N. to S. of c. 15 m. and a width of c. 12 miles. Its highest point is *Mt Hypsarion* (3747 ft), nearly in the centre. The mountainsides are covered with forests, pines, planes, and chestnut trees predominating; the timber has always been in demand for ship-building.

The population of 13,300 is distributed between the capital and ten other villages, of which the most modern is *Limenária*, on the s.w. coast, where zinc workings are exploited. In the coastal areas tobacco and olives are cultivated. A road encircles the island: otherwise the only means of communication is by mule track. There is good water in the island. The marble quarries of Thàsos have always been famous; the gold mines earned in antiquity for the island the epithet of 'golden'. Minerals worked today include silver, antimony, and zinc.

History. The tradition of an early Phoenician occupation, recounted by Herodotus (VI, 47), is not confirmed by excavation, though the Parian colonists of c. 710–680 B.C. seem to have had commerce with Tyre. The Parians, among whom was the poet Archilochos, excused their annexation of the island by calling it the command of Herakles, and the Phoenician myth probably dates from the time of Theogenes (mid-5C), the boxer-politician who claimed Herakles as his father. The colonists prospered by exploiting the Thasian gold mines and later took control of Skaptesyle on the mainland. Their zenith of prosperity was in the 6C B.C. Early in the 5C Histiaios, tyrant of Miletus, unsuccessfully besieged the island. In the Persian wars, despite the famous walls of their city, the Thasians submitted tamely to the invader. A dispute with Athens about the mainland mines led to the reduction of the island in 463, but in 446 Thasos seems to have taken over again the mineral wealth of Galepsos. From Thasos in 424 Thucydides set out on his unsuccessful attempt to break the Spartan siege of Amphipolis. Lysander massacred its Athenian partisans in 404, but Thasos again allied with Athens in 389 and became a permanent member of the second Athenian league. About 340 the island was seized by Philip II and it remained Macedonian until the Romans arrived in 196 B.C. During this period it developed a flourishing export of wine, and Thasian merchants carried on the trade between Thrace and S. Greece. Under the Empire Thasian marble and oil enjoyed an international reputation. The medieval history of Thasos is obscure; the capital was removed to the interior because of pirates. Before passing under Turkish domination in 1455, the island was a fief of the Genoese Gattilusi. In 1760 it was given by Mahmud II to the family of Mehmet Ali, and became in consequence in 1813–1920 a quasi-independent appanage of Egypt, having its own president. In 1770–74 it was occupied by a Russian fleet which made great inroads into its timber. In Oct 1912 it was occupied by the Greek army, in 1916 by the Allies, and in 1941 by the Bulgars.

Thasos was the birthplace of Polygnotos, the painter, of the rhapsodist Stesimbrotos, and of Theogenes, son of Timoxenos, who is said by Pausanias to have carried off no fewer than 1400 athletic crowns. The physician Hippocrates lived for three years in Thasos, whose climatic variations he recorded. Excavations since 1910 have been undertaken by the French School, which publishes an excellent detailed guide.

The island capital is **Limen** ('The Harbour'), or **Thásos,** on the N. coast, on the site of the ancient city of Thasos. As well as being the administrative headquarters with 2050 inhab., Limen is the seat of a bishop and popular as a summer holiday centre with Greeks and Yugoslavs.

Hotels. Xenia, Timoleaon, both B, Glyfada C, all closed in winter.—Angelika, Lido, both C, open all year; and others.

*TOUR OF THE WALLS, 2 hrs. The earliest circuit was demolished by order of Darius (492–1), the second by Kimon (464–3); the existing wall, on the old foundations throughout, dates mainly from a reconstruction in 412–411 B.C. Two styles of masonry, polygonal and ashlar, can be distinguished. From the modern landing-place at Limen we first visit the ancient *Naval Harbour*, which, although silted up, still shelters small caiques. The two moles, once protected by walls forming a marine extension of the enceinte, have been raised to the level of the water, in which can be seen the foundations of a large round tower at the angle of the s. mole.

From this harbour a path, following the line of the walls, leads N. We soon reach two ancient gateways which afforded access to the shore between the two harbours. Each gate is adorned with an Archaic bas-relief, contemporary with the date of the circumvallation (494 B.C.), after which they have been called the *Chariot Gate* and the *Gate of Semele-Thyone*. The first relief represents Artemis in her chariot, the horses of which are held by Hermes; the second is a mutilated group of Hermes and the Graces.

Inland of the gate an ancient quarter has been uncovered by removing most of the Roman remains to show the growth of the town between the 8C and 5C B.C.

The path ascends gradually inland (E.) and we see, submerged in the sea, the remains of the moles of the *Commercial Harbour*. The constructions on the promontory are of medieval date. *Thasopoula*, the small island to the N., now inhabited only by birds and snakes, has slight ancient and medieval remains. The path, now bears S. along the walls, here of admirable polygonal blocks, to a wood of holm oaks, amid which (below, r.) is the cavea of the *Greek Theatre*. The remains were tidied up in 1957 to show the surviving architectural members of the 4C B.C., recovered from the late remodelling of the orchestra (by the Romans for wild beast shows).

We continue to climb, following the scarp (the wall here has been destroyed) to the **Acropolis**, a ridge with three summits. The first is known by inscriptions to have held a *Sanctuary of Pythian Apollo* (the god who told the Parians to colonize Thasos). The existing remains except for parts of the foundations are of the *Genoese Citadel*, dating partly from a reconstruction by Tedisio Zaccaria (c. 1310) and in part from the Gattalusi era. At the s. angle is the guard-room, built of ancient materials; near by, in the outer wall, is an elegant relief of a funeral feast (5C or 4C B.C.).—The wall now runs s.w. through remains of a medieval village to a high terrace of fine construction on which are the foundations (all that survives) of the 5C *Temple of Athena*, identified in 1958 by the discovery of sherds dedicated to Athena Poliouchos. The path now descends to a little col where there is a rock-hewn *Sanctuary of Pan*, with a worn Hellenistic bas-relief of the god piping to his goats. Just beyond this a high rock forming the third summit commands an extensive *View of Samothrace and the mainland.

We descend steeply to the s.w. by a secret *Stairway* hewn from the rock in the 6C B.C., until we regain the line of the walls. Having passed a tower, we note a large stone on which is carved an *Apotropaion*, two enormous eyes to protect the enceinte from the Evil Eye. Just before reaching a sharp bend in the wall to the w., we come to the *Gate of Parmenon*, with its lintel still in place; near by is a block signed with the name of the craftsman: 'Parmenon made me'. We pass through the gate and descend. On reaching level ground we turn away from the town to see the *Gate of Silenus*, an unusual oblique postern, with a colossal mutilated *Bas-relief of Silenus holding a kantharos; below is a niche for votive offerings. The sculpture, which is of Ionian workmanship and unique for its style and size, survives from the earliest circuit. Beyond a tower with embrasures is the *Gate of Dionysos and Herakles*. An archaic inscription still in place records that these two gods were the patron divinities of Thasos. The relief of the archer Herakles is in Istanbul; that of Dionysos is missing. We go on to the *Gate of Zeus and Hera*, which has 5C bas-reliefs in the Archaic manner: before the seated Hera stands Iris; before Zeus, Hermes. A few yards away, in the midst of olive trees through which we glimpse the sea, is the fine Roman *Sarcophagus of Poliades.* The line of the walls continues N.W., crossing the village square (see below) to reach the harbour.

THE LOWER TOWN, 1 hr. A few yards E. of the two gates near the naval harbour (see above) is a group of ruins, the chief of which is the *Sanctuary of Poseidon* entered by a path between gardens. This is a large quadrangular terrace, with the remains of a circular and a square altar. At the gate of the sanctuary are two bases with inscriptions (beginning of 4C); a little in front, almost intact, is the *Monumental Altar to Hera Epilimenia* (Protectress of Harbours), which had an inscription (now in the Museum) reciting the sacred law forbidding the sacrifice of she-goats.—To the S. is the *Sanctuary of Dionysos,* a triangular temenos, re-explored in 1957–58, and covered again except for the remains of a 3C choragic monument. On its semicircular base are engraved the names of victors in a theatrical competition; the categories in which they competed were represented by statues; the statue of comedy is in the museum together with the colossal head of Dionysos from the centrepiece of the group.

The **Agora** (entered from the square by the Museum; key from the caretaker; adm. 5 dr. incl. museum) is bordered by porticoes. Its layout has been clarified by judicious restoration of the foundations since 1955. The place was entered from the harbour by *Propylaia* in the N.W. corner, and from the town side by several passageways which led into the *South West Stoa,* a Doric colonnade of 33 columns (1C A.D.). In the S. angle of the square is a monumental *Altar.* The *South East Stoa,* also of the 1C A.D., had 31 columns of which three have been re-erected at the E. end. This fronted a long hypostyle gallery, entered by four doors; the wall which they pierced still stands to a height of six feet. Beneath the E. end is the base of a *Monument of Glaukos* (7C B.C.). In the centre of the Agora the excavators have unearthed a *Heroön of Lucius Caesar* and another of *Theogenes;* and in the N. angle a *Sanctuary of Zeus Agoraios* surrounded by a balustrade, later interrupted by a *Tholos* (3–2C B.C.). On the N.E. side, next to the Propylaia, is a building with projecting wings (c. 330 B.C.), similar to the Stoa of Zeus at Athens; this survived to the 5C A.D. when it gave place to a Christian *Basilica.*

Outside the E. angle is the unexplained flagged *Passage of the Theoria* (c. 470 B.C.) from which came reliefs now in the Louvre, and inscriptions with lists of magistrates (in the museum). Farther to the E. is the *Artemision;* ex-voto objects dedicated to Artemis have been recovered dating from the 7C B.C. The Hellenistic sanctuary had a square temenos, traced in 1959, though most of its statuary was carried off to Istanbul in 1909.

The **Museum** is generally opened on request by the caretaker. In the CENTRAL HALL (I). Colossal Kriophoros (early 6C; unfinished), found in the acropolis wall; Head of Pegasus, part of the architectural decoration of the Herakleion; Torso of a kouros, found in the sea off Cape Pachys; Funerary stele (late 6C); painted terracotta plaques and heads, including a frieze of riders; Head of Silenus (c. 525 B.C.); Kouros of the school of Pythagoras from the Herakleion; Head of a horse from the same (c. 460 B.C.), much less archaic in style.—ROOM II (behind) contains finds from the Temple of Artemis, including a bronze statuette of the goddess and an exquisite lion's head in ivory (6C B.C.);

boustrophedon funerary inscription of Glaukos, son of Leptine, of Paros (companion of Archilochos); fine silver coins; Archaic pottery.— In the small R. III off the main hall: beautiful Attic kylix, shining as new.—Room IV (front). Architectonic fragments; metope carved between triglyphs in one piece; statues of Dionysos and Comedy; inscriptions.—Room V (opposite): Two heads, school of Skopas; Relief decoration of an altar to Cybele (2C A.D.); head of young Dionysos (3C B.C.); Aphrodite on a dolphin with Eros clinging to its tail; reliefs; beautiful but mutilated reclining youth; Roman imperial *Heads, among them a negroid head and portraits of Claudius, Julius Caesar, and Lucius Caesar.

Outside the s. corner of the Agora a paved street, uncovered for 50 yds, leads s.w., passing a well-preserved *Exedra* (1C A.D.), the remains of an *Odeion* (l.), and the so-called *Court of 100 Flagstones*. Continuing, we reach the remains of the *Triumphal Arch of Caracalla*, identified by its inscription, and the **Herakleion,** or *Sanctuary of Herakles*.

The monumental entrance to the sanctuary was a Propylon, with a staircase, leading to the Court. On the N. side is an *Ionic Temple*, a peripteral edifice with 6 by 8 columns surrounding a single chamber (early 5C). In front of it is a ruinous *Altar*. To the s., partly covered by the modern road leading to the Silenus Gate, is a building divided into rooms, which incorporated or replaced a 6C Temple in polygonal masonry. In the s. corner is a *Triangular Court*, which had a circular monument.—Farther to the s. an empty site marks the *Monument of Thersilochos* (excavated in 1913 and filled in again).

In the village square are a few fragments of an early Christian *Basilica* (?6C), probably ruined in 904 when Leo of Tripoli occupied the island. To the E. of the apse is a mosaic belonging to a building of the age of Hadrian; the caretaker of the museum will remove the protective cover.

An asphalt road leads in 35 min. past a classical cemetery to *Makri Ammos* (Hotel A, summer only), a pleasant beach with two small tavernas.

An easy excursion may be made to two delightful inland villages. The road rises through pine-woods, and, crossing a ridge, emerges on a ledge (*View of the beautiful bay of Potamia).—3 m. *Panayía* (Inn) has a square with two gushing fountains, shaded by plane-trees.—4 m. *Potamiá*, slightly larger, with steep stone streets and old Turkish houses, is a starting-point for the ascent of Ipsarion (Hypsarion; 3745 ft) in 2–3 hrs.

The road, now part of the island round (57 m.), continues down the E. coast. The island abounds in unexcavated Hellenic and medieval remains (an account of which in J.H.S., vol. 29, 1909 is supplemented in B.C.H., 1930). On *Cape Pirgos*, in the N.E., are some remains of an ancient lighthouse inscribed as his own tomb and memorial by one Akeratos. Vestiges of ancient *Koinyra* may be found farther s. At *Alikí* are ancient marble quarries, an Archaic sanctuary, and two excavated basilican churches. The best preserved of many Hellenic Towers is near *Thimoniá*, the greatest concentration of them near *Astrís*; they were probably for defence against pirates. Beyond Astris the road passes the Theologos turn before reaching (33½ m.) *Limenaria* (Inns), a centre (1500 inhab.) of cadmium mining. *Theologos*, in the Dipotamos valley below the s. slope of Ipsarion, was the medieval capital. The house of Mehmet Ali's youth survives. Remains of a castle (*Kouphókastro*) crown a hill to the south-east.

From Limenaria the road follows the w. coast passing many small pensions and camping places amid the pines.—*Órmos Prínou*, incorrectly but more usually called *Prinó* (Leto D), is c. 10 m. short of Limen (bus).

Acropolis

Temple

Artem

Theatre

Dionysion

Dimitriadis
Quarter

Poseidonion

Gate

Chariot Gate

Harbour

HARBOU

Sanctuary

Thasos

0   150 metres

68 FROM KAVALLA TO PHILIPPI AND DRAMA

ROAD, 23 m. (37 km.), passing (9½ m.) *Philippi*. Bus every 20 min. (20 min. ride to Philippi).

We quit Kavalla by the Salonika road (Rte 66) and beyond the coastal range take the right fork. The road passes the airfield of Kavalla.—5 m. *Daton*, a village on the edge of the marshy plain of Philippi (l.), bears the name held by the district even before the foundation of Philippi. The ensuing straightness of the modern road (Rest. o Yeoryios at 7½ m.) is deceptive, for the Roman road ran farther E. On it, ¾m. before it rejoins our course at the approach to Philippi, is the *Khan of Dikili Tach*, where a monument erected by a Roman officer, C. Vibius, has Latin inscriptions on each face. Opposite, on the s. side of the Roman road, is a hill where the French School has unearthed an important prehistoric settlement. Its neolithic and Early Bronze Age pottery is dated to the period of the foundation of Troy. Finds are in the Philippi and Kavalla museums. Where the two roads meet, ancient stone fragments strewn about the tobacco fields show that a large suburb extended to the E. of Philippi.

9½ m. **Philippi** guarded the narrow gap between hill and marsh through which the Via Egnatia has to pass. The highway formed the *decumanus* of the city and the modern road, on the selfsame course, passes through the excavations; the bus stops at the entrances (adm. daily, 5 dr.). To the left lies the larger area with the forum of the Roman city; to the right at the beginning of the ruins is the theatre, with a large car park and tourist pavilion for the festival. Dominating the plain, the Greek acropolis with its prominent medieval towers, occupies the last outcrop of the Lekanis range which extends E. to the Nestos. In general visible remains are Roman or early Christian.

History. The ancient town of *Krenides* ('Fountains'), colonized by Thasos in the 6C B.C. but lost to local tribes, was refounded in 361 B.C. by Thasians led by the exiled Athenian Kallistratos, only to be taken over in 356 by Philip II of Macedon, who renamed it *Philippi* after himself. The place was of little importance until the establishment of the Via Egnatia as a military road. After the momentous battle of 42 B.C. (see below), the city was refounded with veterans of the battle by Octavian and from 27 B.C. bore the name *Colonia Julia Augusta Philippensis*. Philippi was the first stage on the journey westwards from its port, Neapolis (Kavalla). In A.D. 49 St Paul, having sailed from the Troad to Neapolis, spent some time at Philippi, where he first preached the gospel in Europe and where, with Silas, he was cast into prison ('Acts', xvi, 9–40). Six years later St Paul again visited Philippi ('Acts', xx, 6). From his prison in Rome in 64, or possibly earlier from Ephesus, he wrote his Epistle to the Philippians, for whom he seems to have had a special affection. Christianity throve at Philippi, which had a large basilica as early as the 5C. It was occupied by the Goths in 473. It gave the title to a Byzantine metropolitan and (though the city was deserted by c. 950) remained his seat until, in 1619, the see, renamed 'Philippi and Drama' was transferred to Drama. Since 1924 the title has passed to the Metropolitan residing at Kavalla.— The site has been excavated by the French School (1920–24 and since 1927).

Battle of Philippi. Following the assassination of Julius Caesar in 44 B.C., the republicans Brutus and Cassius made for the East. By the time Antony and Octavian, great-nephew of Julius, had temporarily assuaged their own rivalry by the device of the triumvirate (43), Brutus, who has seized Macedonia, and Cassius, who had secured Syria, were in control of all the Roman provinces E. of the Adriatic, and commanded 19 legions and numerous cavalry. Leaving Lepidus behind to rule Italy, Antony and Octavian, with an equivalent force marched against Brutus and Cassius. The armies met in the plain of Philippi in October 42. The republicans were encamped to the w. of the town athwart the main road (where traces of their field works have been noted). In the ensuing two battles Brutus and Cassius made the same mistakes as Pompey had at Pharsalus. Having command of the sea at Neapolis and shorter communications, their obvious policy was to exhaust the enemy by avoiding action. A hazardous frontal attack by Antony forced a pitched battle, and muddled generalship contributed to the defeat of Cassius, who committed suicide. Brutus, who had been victorious over Octavian, was three weeks later forced against his better judge-

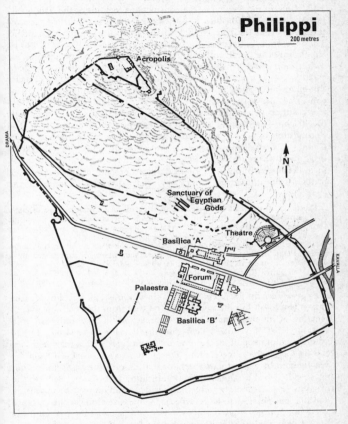

ment to fight again in the same place, where the legions of the Triumvirate were executing a dangerous infiltration between his troops and the marsh. The outcome was disastrous and Brutus, too, killed himself. The poet Horace fought on the republican side and joined in the 'headlong rout, his poor shield ingloriously left behind' ('Odes', II, 7).

The FORUM, a paved rectangle 108 yds by 55, had uniform porticoes on three sides approached by steps. The plan is quite clear, though the remains do not stand much above the foundations. On the N. side monumental *Fountains* flanked a *Tribune* and monuments to citizens and emperors; the decumanus passed along and above its rear wall (remains parallel with and below the modern road), leaving a view towards the Acropolis. The rear walls of all four sides make an enclosing rectangle, and this replanning of the general ensemble can be dated by inscriptions to the reign of Marcus Aurelius. At the N.E. and N.W. angles stood two *Temples*; on the E. side a *Library*. The S. side replaced houses of the Augustan period.

To the S. of the forum rise the conspicuous remains of the 'DIREKLER' (Turk: 'Pillars') or **Basilica B,** one of the failures that marked the slow transition from the true basilica to the cruciform church with dome. The 6C architect attempted to cover the E. end of a basilica with a brick cupola. The E. wall collapsed under the weight before the altar or synthronon could be assembled, so that the sanctuary was never dedicated. The W. end, still standing in 837 when the invading Bulgars carved an inscription in it, fell in turn, leaving only the narthex to be converted into a small church in the 10C by the addition of an apse made out of reused materials. The pillars, formed of reused antique blocks, have interesting capitals with acanthus-leaf decoration. The central arch of the W. wall shows the springing of the narthex vault. Chunks of the fallen dome survive and a fine *Capital. The Bulgarian inscription was removed in 1943. Two contemporary annexes to the N. form the *Baptistery*; two to the S., designed perhaps as the diakonikon, probably constituted the sanctuary itself after the collapse of the chancel.

The remains, particularly interesting to students of architecture, are exhaustively discussed by Paul Lemerle in 'Philippes et la Macédoine orientale à l'époque chrétienne et byzantine' (1945). To make way for the basilica a covered market and the greater part of a *Palaestra* were levelled; much of the material went into the church. The most interesting part surviving (below the S.E. corner) is a monumental *Public Latrine*, almost perfectly preserved, which is approached by a descending flight of steps and a double portal. Many of the 50 marble seats are still in place.—Farther over are *Roman Baths*, built c. A.D. 250 and destroyed by fire soon afterwards (mosaics destroyed by the Bulgarians in 1941–45).

Excavations by Prof. Pelekanides since 1960 E. of the Forum (the area is fenced off but the remains can be seen from the road) uncovered remains of an octagonal **Church,** comparable in size and plan with San Vitale at Ravenna, except that the octagon is squared. It had an inner colonnade of 20 columns on seven sides with a marble screen closing the bema on the eighth. The church was approached from the Via Egnatia by a great gate (perhaps that described by Eusebius). On the N. side it had a *Baptistery* communicating with *Baths*. Beneath the octagon a Macedonian tomb has yielded gold finds (at present in Kavalla, but possibly to be returned): the massive stone at the entrance is still in position. More recent excavation has shown that a 4C basilican church dedicated to St Paul preceded the octagon.

On the N. side of the road is **Basilica A,** erected c. A.D. 500 on a prepared terrace. It was probably ruined in an earthquake in the same century, then used as a quarry. Its plan was recovered before 1939 and its N. walls stand to a considerable height.

The terrace is reached by Propylaea and a broad *Stairway* (to the left of the modern entrance). Half-way up on the right was a *Crypt* of Roman date, taken by the 5C to be the prison of St Paul and later frescoed with scenes from his life and crowned by a chapel. On the terrace the foundations of a Hellenistic temple were converted into a *Cistern*. A huge paved *Atrium*, having a W. façade with fountains and three porticoes, extended E. to the CHURCH, which is entered by three doors. The *Narthex* gave access at the N. end to a separate *Baptistery* (well preserved, with mosaic floor) and by three openings to the church itself. This is an aisled basilica with E. transepts and semi-circular apse, comparable in size with Ayios Demetrios at Salonika. Within can be traced the position of an *Ambo* and the *Screen*. The E. wall, unusually, had two doors.—Farther w., close to the museum, a third basilica was located in 1963.

The MUSEUM (adm. 5 dr.; standard hours), stands above the road w. of the entrances. Exhibits are labelled in English. The vestibule houses the French School's neolithic finds at Dikili Tach. The two main rooms are devoted to Philippi, with the Early Christian material (good capitals) downstairs. The main part of the upper room (Roman) includes three Nike figures and an Athena from the Forum. A smaller section devoted to earlier periods includes a fragmentary inscription of a plan for the city of Philippi by Alexander the Great.—In a further ground-floor room are British School neolithic finds from Sitagroí.

From the museum an easy path ascends to the ACROPOLIS (1020 ft) with its three massive medieval towers built on the ruins of the Macedonian walls. The climb is recommended more for the view of the forum, the battlefield, and the plain than for the remains, though the hill is remarkable also for the variety of its insect life (butterflies, dragonflies, etc.). On the way up are some Christian evidences, carved in the rock, and the ruins of a *Sanctuary of Egyptian Deities* (Isis, Serapis, Harpocrates), comprising a terrace on substructions of various buildings.

Returning to the basilica and continuing E. round the base of the rocks, we encounter a series of *Rock Sanctuaries*. Farther on are numerous lengthy Latin inscriptions (2–3C) recording benefactors of a religious college, dedicated to Silvanus. There are also scores of reliefs cut in the rock (extending above the theatre), mainly dedicated to Bendis, the Thracian equivalent of Artemis. We descend to the **Theatre,** built against the slope of the hill, which dates back to the foundation of Philippi. Of the original building there survives some well-built masonry of the analemma and parodoi. In the Roman era (2C A.D.) the theatre was remodelled; the orchestra was paved, the parodoi vaulted. Remains of the Roman *Frons Scenae* show it to have resembled the type of Asia Minor, with its rubble wall pierced by five doors. The Roman stage disappeared in the last alterations (3C) into an arena. To this period belong three bas-reliefs of Nemesis, Mars, and Victory, found in the w. parodos. The building remained virtually whole till the 16C. The seating of the cavea was restored in 1957–59 to allow the staging of dramatic performances.

To regain the road, we follow the Byzantine enceinte, which was built on the top of the 4C walls. Although ruinous, its line can be traced along the slope of the Acropolis and for most of its course in the plain. It is equipped with towers and redans. No trace remains of the arch which early travellers describe as bestriding the road.

We by-pass (15¼ m.) *Dhoxáto* (375 ft), a deme of 3400 inhab., engaged in tobacco cultivation. We join the road from Paranestion (comp. below) on a low plateau and cross the railway. The isolated *Korílovo* (2045 ft) stands out on the right, while *Bóz Dág* (7320 ft), the summit of the Falakron range, towers to the N.

23 m. (37 km.) **Drama** (ΔPAMA; 345 ft; *Xenia* B; *Emborikon, Apollo*, both C), a thriving town of 29,700 inhab., is the capital of the nome of Drama, the seat of a metropolitan, and the headquarters of

an army corps. It is ringed but not overshadowed to the N. by the heights of Falakron, and commands the 'golden plain', the tobacco from which provides its livelihood. The town has a *Tobacco Research Station*, but the processing of timber affords a secondary occupation. Though it holds no particular interest for the tourist, its large shaded squares and restaurants make it a pleasant place to pause.

History. *Drama* is thought to occupy the site of an Edonian town called *Drabeskos* by Thucydides (I, 100), where the Athenians in 465 B.C. were cut to pieces in their first and unsuccessful attempt to colonize Amphipolis. The Edonians, a Thracian people who dwelt between the Strymon and the Nestos, were notorious for their orgiastic worship of Dionysos. Drama was of some importance in the late-Byzantine era. Boniface de Montferrat fortified the town in 1205 and here in 1317 died Irène de Montferrat, second wife of Andronikos II. The Turks occupied it in c. 1371. Briefly in the 14C Drama (previously in the see of Philippi) was raised to the status of metropolitan see, only to be incorporated with Serres. In 1619 the see of Philippi (which already included Kavalla) was removed to Drama, the metropolitan taking the dual title 'Philippi and Drama'. In 1924 this see was divided, the title of Philippi passing to the new see at Kavalla.

FROM DRAMA TO XANTHI BY THE INLAND ROAD, 55 m. (88 km:), asphalt except for c. 1 m. near the Plovdiv turn. We quit the town by the Kavalla road (Rte 68), but turn left at (3 m.) *Khoristí*, and follow the course of the railway all the way to Stavroúpolis.—Beyond (10 m.) *Nikifóros*, a centre of tobacco cultivation, are remains of an aqueduct. The road traverses rugged country with wild mountain views all round as we cross the watershed between the Angistis and the Nestos. Just before (22½ m.) *Paranéstion*, the railway crosses the Nestos by Bailey bridge to the left of the road bridge. Keeping to the left bank, we follow the river valley to the S.E., passing through the most attractive country of the route.

The Nestos, or *Mesta*, rises in the Rhodope Mts in Bulgaria and divides Macedonia geographically from Thrace, though the modern nome boundaries rather reflect local convenience. Under the Treaty of Bucharest (1913), the river formed the frontier with Bulgaria, which for two or three years enjoyed an Aegean seaboard extending from the Mesta to Dedeagatch and beyond. Above Paranestion the river is enclosed in inaccessible gorges that rival in wildness that between Stavroupolis and Toxotai, and the whole of its basin N. to the Bulgarian frontier is hemmed in by the Rhodope chain, the rolling heights of which, swathed in beech forests, constitute much of the nome of Drama. The area, which has a good climate and fertile soil, has not found favour with Anatolian Greeks, and since 1923 has remained practically uninhabited. The lower course of the Nestos lies through the alluvial plain of Chrysopolis.

At (38 m.) *Stavroúpolis* (Inn at the Rly Stn), a deme of 1280 inhab., in the fairest part of the Nestos valley, a kafenion in the attractive little plateia has an interesting collection of bygones. To the S.E., reached from the station by minor road (turn after 2 m. towards Komniná, then take signposted motorable track left for 1 m.), is a remarkable vaulted tomb, excavated in 1953. The chamber is 10 ft square and the vaulted dromos 16 ft long. The tomb was constructed in local marbles with paintings done directly on to the marble surface (a technique unusual in Macedonia). Within are two handsome marble funerary couches.— From Stavroúpolis the road turns E., climbing through a low pass to the N. of Akhlat Tsal (4595 ft).—At (49½ m.) the junction of two predominantly Moslem valleys we meet the road from Plovdiv, guarded by police-post.—55 m. **Xánthi,** see Rte 69.

FROM DRAMA TO KATO NEVROKOPION, 28 m. The road at first goes N.W. as far as (15 m.) *Prosotáni* (3800 inhab.), the ancient Pyrsopolis, which it leaves on the left. It then turns N. into the Falakron Mts, climbing the *Stena Granitou*, a defile between Mavro Longos (4605 ft) and Vothlitsi (3940 ft). The valley broadens and divides, the main road following the w. opening in thick woods (the right branch goes on to the Bartiseva refuge from which Boz Dag is climbed).—From (20½ m.) *Granítis* (2600 ft) we descend into an intensely cultivated flat depression, where (28 m.) *Káto Nevrokópion* (Akritas **D**) guards the road to the Bulgarian frontier (no crossing), 7 m. to the N.—To the E. of this road, between Drama and the frontier, live the nomadic Sarakatzanai who wear a picturesque costume.

From Drama to *Serres* see Rte 65A.

69   FROM SALONIKA TO ALEXANDROUPOLIS AND THE TURKISH FRONTIER (ISTANBUL)

A   By road

ROAD, 457 m. (735 km.), of international standard all the way. To (103 m.) **Kavalla,** see Rte 66.—138 m. **Xánthi.**—180 m. **Komotiní.**—220½ m. **Alexandroupolis.** —241½ m. *Ardánion*. Here the main highway into Turkey diverges viâ Ipsala and Keşan (Istanbul, 164 m.; *Gallipoli–Çanakkale* ferry, 101 m., for Izmir).—282 m. **Dhidhimotikhon.**—307 m. *Kastaneai* (frontier).—313 m. Edirne, whence 144 m. to *Istanbul*.

From Salonika to (103 m.) **Kaválla,** see Rte 66. We quit Kaválla by its E. suburbs passing a huge stadium. Beyond (109½ m.) *Néa Karváli*, where scanty remains of a large enceinte have been equated with ancient *Akontisma*, we turn away from the coast and at 114 m. pass (r.) a square (?) Roman fort.—116 m. *Pondolívadhon* is to become an industrial dependency of Kavalla. An ancient site (r.) may be *Pistyros*, a point on Xerxes' march mentioned by Herodotus. To the left the indented foothills of the *Lakanis Mts* (home of the Edoni) rise to 4260 ft; to the right the flat Pedhias Khrisoupoleos extends to the Nestos.— 118¾ m. *Gravoúna*.

About 1 m. beyond the village a by-road runs S. to (2½ m.) **Khrisoúpolis** (ΧΡΥΣΟΥΠΟΛΙΣ), seat (5780 inhab.) of the eparchy of Nestos and in Byzantine times a town of some importance on the high road. It was known to the Turks as Sari Saban, meaning Yellow Plain.—11½ m. **Keramotí** (*Evropi* **D**; N.T.O. Campsite; Taverna) is linked by frequent car-ferry with Thasos, 3 m. offshore. The successful culture of oysters was started in 1959 in the little inlet on which the harbour stands, and the bird life is varied.

The villages lie off the road in the foothills to the left.—126 m. *Kríni* has a small medieval fortress.—128 m. *Parádeisos*, a prettily terraced village, overlooks the tree-grown banks of the Nestos (p. 574). The river is crossed by a barrage which controls the irrigation of the whole delta. The Via Egnatia appears to have crossed the river nearer its mouth, and the Topiros and Roumbodona of the itineraries must be sought to the S. of our road. We join the railway (comp. p. 581), and enter Thrace.—130½ m. *Toxótai* (l.), with a minaret, and *Tímbano*, with wooden balconies, are typical villages of the S. slope of Akhlat Tsal (l.), where Turkish growers still produce the prized Xanthíyaka, the finest quality of Turkish tobacco. The picturesque irregularity of these villages with their gardens and decaying mosques is emphasized by neighbouring Greek refugee settlements, planned in rigid lines with churches in the functional style of the 1920s. A huge sugar factory epitomizes a more recent agricultural direction.

138 m. (222 km.) **Xánthi** (ΞΑΝΘΗ; *Xenia* **B**; *Democritus, Sissy*, both **C**; and others), seat of a metropolitan and the prosperous capital (24,900 inhab.) of the nome of Rhodopis, stands at the opening of the

narrow upper valley of the Esketze, the ancient Kosintos. The main road by-passes the town, which is, however, worth a visit for its pleasant squares and restaurants. Like the river, it was called Eski-je by the Turks, corrupted to Skatchia during the brief Bulgarian occupation of 1913. Byzantine *Xanthea* grew up beneath a *Fortress*, built on a crag to the N. to defend the defile from Bulgar incursions. A mere summer resort under the Turks, Xánthi has, since the coming of the railway, superseded Yenije (see below) as the centre of the fine tobacco-growing area. A brand of cigarettes (kiretsiler), obtainable only locally, is much prized. Below the Kastro are some pleasantly sited monasteries.

FROM XANTHI TO ABDERA, 16 m. (26 km.), bus. From the Porto Lagos road (see below) we take the right fork at (5 m.) *Vaféïka*.—7 m. *Yeniséa*, long the centre of the tobacco trade and the local Turkish capital (Yenije), has declined in importance. Continuing beyond the modern village of (12 m.) *Ávdira*, reach the sea at (17 m.) *Ayios Pandeleimon*. A little to the E. Akti Avdiris or Cape Baloustra is the site of **Abdera** (Ἄβδηρα; *Tourist Pavilion*), a city traditionally founded by Herakles on the spot where Abderos was killed by Diomede's horses, but in fact colonized c. 656 B.C. from Klazomenai. Refounded c. 500 B.C. by refugees from a Persian occupation of Teos (S.W. of Smyrna), it became a prominent member of the Delian League and famous for the beauty of its coinage. Democritus, the 5C philosopher who expounded an atomic theory, Protagoras (c. 481–411), the first of the Sophists, and Anaxarchos, the counsellor of Alexander the Great, were all born here, but despite the celebrity of its school of philosophy, the inhabitants generally were proverbial for their dullness. Hippocrates and Juvenal inveigh against its sickly air. Abdera shared the fortunes of Macedonia and, despite a sack in 170 B.C. by an over-zealous general, remained nominally free of Rome down to Imperial times, when the city apparently succumbed to its climate. Systematic excavations were begun in 1950 by the Greek Archaeological Service under D. Lazarides. The complete outline of the walls has been established; considerable tracts remain, especially of the W. wall and gate (4C B.C.). The city was built on a chessboard plan. A Hellenistic building of two courts and 26 rooms has come to light, probably part of the commercial *Agora*, and traces of a *Theatre* have been found.—To the W. are some remains of *Polystylon*, Abdera's medieval successor.

The road to Plovdiv in Bulgaria is closed at the frontier. A permit is required to go beyond (5 m.) the Stavroupolis fork, and there is little of interest between there and (30½ m.) the frontier post.

From Xanthi there is a choice of two routes: the main road leading S.E. to Lagos on the coast or the Via Egnatia, which, though here a secondary road, is an adequate and rather more interesting alternative for the antiquary; it is also c. 6 m. shorter.

FROM XANTHI TO KOMOTINI BY THE VIA EGNATIA, 30 m. (48 km.). The road strikes due E., followed by the railway (Rte 69B). About 1 m. beyond (11½ m.) *Amaxádhes*, a track (r.) follows the arches of an aqueduct for 3 m. to the ruins of *Anastasioupolis*.—Beyond (17½ m.) *Íasmos*, we cross the Kourou a little above the railway, and, farther on just before crossing the railway, pass just S. of Sóstis. In the hills, 1½ hr N. of Sostis, is *Keraséa* with a 10C Byzantine cemetery.—26 m. Track (l.; signposted) to the site of medieval *Mosynopolis*, the limit of Norman penetration in 1185. Originally Porsula, the town was granted city rank by Diocletian with the name *Maximianopolis*, and sent a metropolitan to the Council of Ephesus. Geoffroy de Villehardouin, chronicler of the 4th Crusade, accepted it as his fief. The ruinous walls of cement and small stones, which barely rise above the tobacco fields, enclose a considerable area. *Paradhimí*, to the S., is known for its prehistoric tomb (signposted; finds in both Kaválla and Komotini museums).—At 27½ m. we join the main road, comp. below.

The main road leaves Xànthi to the s.e., crossing the railway. The well-watered country to the right grows excellent tobacco.—At (143 m.) *Vaféïka*, by-road (r.; see above) to Abdera.—154 m. (248 km.) **Porto Lagos** (Inn), the port of Komotiní, stands on a tongue of land separating the Vistonian Gulf from Lake Vistonis. Here was an early Christian settlement, probably *Peritheorion*, to which a see was transferred from Trajanopolis in the 14C. The remains of a Byzantine basilica lie r. of the road (sign) just beyond the town. The place still has a bishop. Worth a glance are the old Genoese fort and an attractive church. Beyond the channel through which the lake drains into the sea, the road is carried on a causeway with a marshy lagoon on the right. Fish and eels are caught in great numbers and the area is celebrated for the variety of its water-birds. The eels are almost exclusively exported live in tanks to Germany and Central Europe. The fish traps can be visited.

A low hill rising to the s.e. (off the by-road to Fanarion) may be the site of ancient *Dikaia*. Graves have been excavated (1977). Near the village is an N.T.O.G. camp site.—Some ruins, identified with *Stryme*, once famed for its wine, were explored by Salonika University (1957–59) on the remote coast c. 10 m. farther e. A city wall was traced with houses, which yielded a hoard of Maroneian tetradrachms of the 4C b.c.

At (173 m.) *Messoúni* is the airport of Komotiní. We join the direct road from Xànthi (see above) between Paradhimí and Maximianoupolis, then cross the Akmar.—180 m. (289 km.) **Komotiní** (KOMOTHNH; *Orpheus*, *Xenia* B; *Democritus*, *Astoria*, C), a garrison town only 14 m. from the Bulgarian frontier, and the capital of Greek Thrace, has pleasant broad streets and squares. It is a flourishing market centre (28,900 inhab.) for tobacco, cattle, hides, and agricultural goods (annual livestock fair in Holy Week). About half of the inhabitants are Turks, who know the town as *Gümülcüne*, and many are Bulgarian speaking (Pomaks). Here are the University of Thrace and a Moslem secondary college. The city is linked by bus with Istanbul. The seasonal Boukloutza on which Komotiní stands has been diverted since the town was flooded in 1960. The walls of a Byzantine fortress are to our left on entering the town. The *Archaeological Museum* (adm. 25 dr.), opened in 1976, on the s. side of the inner ring road (Od. N. Zoidou) houses finds from all Thrace. Outstanding is the unique gold imperial *Bust (? of Marcus Aurelius) found at Plotinoupolis. Also displayed are a remarkable phallic altar; a Klazomenian sarcophagus from Abdera; Archaic pottery and a grave stele from Dikaia (part formerly in Athens); votive plaques from Mesambria; finds from the Paradhimí tomb and from tombs at Ardanion and Orestiadha; honorific decrees from Doriskos and Maroneia (4C b.c.); an inscribed marble block (3C b.c.) with impressions of feet, from Maroneia; and ground plans of Stryme, Mesambria, and Maroneia.

The principal archaeological sites of this region, the ancient KIKONES, lie to the s.e. of Komotini on the coast. They are cut off from the hinterland by barren limestone hills scored by ravines and torrents. A road (bus from Komotini) crosses the railway and the Filiouri to (11¼ m.) *Xilayani* and to (19½ m.) *Maroneia* on the w. slope of *Mt Ismaros*. The site of **Maroneia**, a city of importance from Homeric times to the Genoese period, which in the classical era had a noted cult of Bacchus, is marked by the church of *Ayios Kharalambos*, on the coast 2¼ m. s. of the modern village. The extensive ruins, visited by Reinach in 1880 when the walls were still 40 ft high, have been partially explored since 1973. The Acropolis is a huge enceinte of the 13–12C b.c.

188 m. *Áratos* has an attractive minaret.—At (190½ m.) *Arísvi*, to
the left of the road are six arches of a Roman bridge that carried the
Via Egnatia over the Filiouri. The road turns s.w. at (197 m.) *Sápai*, a
pleasant town of 2500 inhab., where the fez and the veil linger on.—
Beyond (201 m.) *Vélkion* we cross a stream and the railway by a double
bridge (1961) and climb amid scrub-covered hills noted for quail,
woodcock, and snipe.—210½ m. By-road to Mesambria.

The by-road diverges (r.) to *Dhikella* (1 m.), from which a poor but motorable
track continues to the site of **Mesambria** (phylax), 5 m. farther w. The visible
remains (mainly Roman), excavated since 1966, are not impressive, though blocks
of the Greek wall (4C B.C.) survive. The place is mentioned by Herodotus and is
not to be confused with Mesembria on the Euxine. There is a good beach and a
fine view w. to the mountain spur that hides Maroneia (path; 3½ hrs).

The road descends to the coast amid the dense vineyards of (213 m.)
Mákri.—217 m. *Néa Khilí* (Aphrodite, Dionysos C).

220½ m. (355 km.) **ALEXANDROUPOLIS** (ΑΛΕΞΑΝΔΡΟΥ-
ΠΟΛΙΣ, often written abbreviated to ΑΛΕΞ/ΠΟΛΙΣ), the pleasant
chief town (23,000 inhab.) of the nome of Evrou, was known to the
Turks as *Dedeagaç*. It was renamed after King Alexander in 1919.
With air services to Athens and Salonika, a station on the Salonika–
Istanbul railway, and a sea connection with Samothrace, it is the best
centre from which to explore Thrace. It is noted for its fish; caviare
and mussels are specialities.

Airport, 4 m. E., with services to Athens and Salonika.—AIR TERMINAL on sea
front E. of lighthouse.
Railway Station, E. of centre of town.
Hotels. Astir Motel, on w. edge of town, A; Egnatia Motel, 100 R., adjacent to
Astir, B; Alkyon, Galaxy, Alex, Olympion, all C, in or near the main street.—
N.T.O.G. Camping Site, w. of town.
Restaurants. *Panellinion*, near the hotels; also near the Dhimarkhion and near
the lighthouse.
Post Office on the sea front w. of the Harbour.—TOURIST POLICE, Od. Karaïs-
kaki.
Buses to *Xanthi*, *Kavalla*, and *Salonika* daily; to *Dhidhimotikhon* and *Orestias*,
7 times daily; to *Makri*, 5 times daily.
Steamer to Piraeus (weekly) viâ Samothrace and Lemnos.—Caique service to
Samothrace daily in summer.
Wine Festival in July–Sept.
The Turkish name (Dede-ağaç; Tree of the holy man) derives from a colony
of dervishes established in the 15C. The place remained a fishing village until
reached in 1872 by the railway from Edirne, after which it rapidly usurped the
importance of Ainos. The Greek archbishopric was transferred in 1889. Ancient
Zone is placed hereabouts.

The main road, parallel with the sea, forms the principal boulevard
of the town, the Leoforos Vasileos Yeoryios B′, venue of the 'volta'
which necessitates the evening diversion of traffic. On the shore facing
the large artificial harbour is a conspicuous lighthouse, to the w. of
which a broad promenade has been laid out above the beach. The
huge modern cathedral farther inland is prominent from the sea.

Beyond Alexandroupolis road and railway continue E. together,
passing the airport.—229 m. We cross the Tsáï. On the far bank are
some ruins of the Roman and Byzantine staging-post of **Trajanopolis**,
which succeeded *Doriskos* (see below). It was the scene in A.D. 161 under
Marcus Aurelius of the spectacular miracles of St Glyceria, a Roman
maiden later martyred in the Propontis. After a long period as a Metro-

politan see, the town seems to have been ruined in the wars of 1205 and lost importance to Demotika; the see was removed c. 1353 to Peritheorion. The adjacent thermal springs are efficacious against kidney ailments. The hills visible to the s. are across the Turkish frontier.— 235½ m. Turning (r.) for ancient *Doriskos*, a Persian fortress town established in 512 B.C. by Darius I, where Xerxes numbered his armies in 480 (modern scholarship suggests that Herodotus' inflated figures be reduced to 200,000). Some remains (not so far identified as earlier than 4C B.C.) stand on the flat-topped hill of Saraiya (c. 1 m. l.) overlooking the railway. The by-road goes on into the Evros delta (comp. below; permit necessary).—237¾ m. *Férai* (ΦΕΡΑΙ), with 4400 inhab., was known to the Turks as Farecik. It has a Byzantine monastic church of 1152 with frescoes, remains of fortifications, and a picturesque water-gate.—At (241½ m.) *Ardánion*, we quit the main highway to Turkey which follows the ancient course of the Via Egnatia, crossing the Evros by a long bridge (1962) to *Ipsala* (7 m.; anc. Kypsela), the Turkish frontier town (Motel).

The ancient *Kypsela*, greatest city of the Thracians, lost importance by the 4C B.C. and in Livy's time was only a fort. Returning towards Thessalonika from his meeting here with Henry of Flanders in 1207, Boniface of Montferrat was intercepted and decapitated by a Bulgarian ambush.

The Evros (Ἕβρος, anc. *Hebros*; Turk., Meriç; Bulg., Maritza), of which we have periodic glimpses, rises in Bulgaria s. of Sofia and, after a course of c. 300 m., enters the Aegean opposite the island of Samothrace through a delta 7 m. wide. Since 1923 its lower course through the flat Thracian plain has formed the boundary between Greece and Turkey, save where the suburbs of Edirne make a Turkish enclave w. of the river. It is navigable for small boats as far as Edirne, below which it is crossed by bridges only at Pithion and Ipsala. Its waters abound in fish and water fowl; rare geese and eagles may be seen. Round its twin mouths, noted by Strabo, are several swamps and lakes, of which the largest is Gala-Gölu, the ancient *Stentoris* of Herodotus, on the Turkish side. Some way s.w. of this lake is the town of Enos, familiar to diplomats as one end of the Enos–Midia line and the ancient *Ainos*, the foundation of which Virgil ascribes to Aeneas.— The river has given its name to the nome of Evrou whose capital is Alexandroupolis. The hill slopes that rise in the w. of the province to 3000 ft are clothed with oak forests; cereals, vines and tobacco are cultivated in the plain.

247 m. *Provatón* is a local communication centre, with (1¼ m. beyond the village) a memorial to Gen. Asimakópoulos.—261½ m. *Soufli* (ΣΟΥΦΛΙΟΝ; inns) is a pleasant town (5600 inhab.), engaged in the cultivation of vines and silkworms.—At (268¼ m.) *Mándhra* we meet a by-road that descends a wooded valley from Mikrón Déreion (14 m. N.W.), a group of villages near the Bulgarian frontier.

282 m. (454 km.) **Dhidhimótikhon** (ΔΙΔΥΜΟΤΕΙΧΟΝ; *Hellas*, *Ameriki*, both D; *Taverna* in Odhos Venizelou; *Cafés* and *Nat. Bank* in the Plateia; *Public Lavatory* facing the Dhimarkhion), a market town (8400 inhab.) of Turkish timber-framed houses, clusters round an abrupt hill overlooking the Erithropotamos or Kizil Remma. An inscription, found in 1937, identifies the site with *Plotinoupolis*, founded by Trajan in honour of his wife, Plotina.

History. The fortress-town of *Demotika* played an important part in Byzantine history. In 1189 during the Third Crusade Frederick Barbarossa held the town hostage while negotiating with the Emp. Isaac II Angelos. Hither the wounded Michael IX fled after his defeat by the Catalan Grand Company at Aprus (1305), and here in 1341 John VI Cantacuzene had himself proclaimed emperor. The town fell to the Turks in 1361 and Murad I made it his capital for four years before transferring to Adrianople; his son Bayezid was born here. Charles XII of Sweden lay at Demotika in 1713–14, a virtual prisoner of Ahmed III, to whose dominions he had fled after the Battle of Poltava.

A new bridge, taking the main road E. of the town, replaces the medieval *Bridge* farther W. whose many arches were ruined in the Second World War. In the Plateia is a huge disused *Mosque*, square in plan with a pyramidal roof; its attractive Minaret has two fretted balconies. The hill is crowned by the **Kastro** which popular occupation has brought to ruin. Byzantine or late-Roman gateways on the S.W. side apparently incorporate classical masonry. Within, a medieval stone road leads to a church, below which, masked by a Byzantine wall, is a rock-cut *Cavern*, perhaps a cistern, popularly supposed to have been the prison of Charles XII, who more likely lived in some comfort. The *Walls* afford good views of the valley of the Evros, but the summit of the hill is occupied by the military.

From Dhidhimotikhon a road diverges E. viâ (6 m.) *Petrádhes*, the frontier village, to (12½ m.) *Uzunköprü* in Turkey. Another leads w. up the Erithropotamos valley to (19½ m.) *Zoni*, on the Bulgarian frontier, whence it continues viâ (30 m.) *Filakion* and down the right bank of the Arda to (38½ m.) *Kastaneai* (see below). From Zoni an old Ottoman road (now in Bulgarian territory) traverses the mountains to Komotiní (66½ m.). These roads are generally subject to military control and permit on both sides of the frontier.

The highway continues N., rejoining the railway (which makes a wide loop to the E. through Pithion) at (288½ m.) *Thoúrion*.—At (295 m.) *Orestiás* (Vienni, Selini, **C**, and others), seat of an eparchy (10,700 inhab.) and the only refugee settlement in the North to be founded as a town, sugar is refined. The minarets of Edirne can be seen in the distance (r.) from the road into (307 m.) **Kastaneai** (Custom House).

The small triangle of Greek soil lying between the Arda and the Evros is served by a road from Kastaneai and by railway to *Orménion*, its principal village.

313 m. (503 km.) **EDIRNE** (Hotels), formerly *Adrianople*, both names being successive corruptions of *Hadrianopolis*, a city which has lost its former importance, stands beyond the frontier. Refounded by Hadrian in A.D. 125 from *Uscudama*, chief town of the Bessi, it remained a strategic stronghold until the decline of the Ottoman Empire. The period of its zenith in 1367–1458 as the Ottoman capital left many fine buildings though the later Selimiye Cami by Sinan is its masterpiece. It remains the market town (30,000 inhab.) of the area.

B By Railway

RAILWAY to *Alexandroupolis*, 274 m. (442 km.), two trains daily in 7½–8¾ hrs and Pithion, 344 m. (555 km.) in 10–11½ hrs, one (the daily through train from Piraeus to Istanbul) continuing viâ Uzunköprü to (518 m., 834 km.) *Istanbul* in 35 hrs from Athens.—To *Serres*, see Rte 65; to *Drama*, 5 trains daily in 4–7 hrs. One extra train daily between Drama and Alexandroupolis (in c. 4¾ hrs) and two from Alexandroupolis to *Pithion* (2½ hrs), continuing to *Edirne* (3½ hrs) and *Ormenion* (4 hrs); or to *Dikaia* and *Svilengrad*.

The railway was designed in Turkish times as a strategic route and built by a French company in 1892–95. It was deliberately laid at least 12 m. from the coast so as to be beyond the range of naval bombardment, and at the two ports where for convenience it approached the coast (Dedeagatch and Salonika) was provided with inland by-passes (now abandoned). The section E. from Alexandroupolis dates from 1869–72.

From Salonika to (100½ m.) *Serres*, see Rte 65. The railway now follows the N. limit of the former Lake Prasias, winding across the plain. The landscape is peppered with tumuli. Many of the settlements were established after 1923 as refugee colonies. For some distance the only interest is provided by the changing perspective of the Menoikion range to the N. and the more distant views, to the S., of Kerdilion. Between (116 m.) *Tholós* and (120½ m.) *Mirrínis*, where the line crosses the Amphipolis road, a branch line (no passenger service) diverges to Tzagezi. We keep company with the Serres–Drama road through the Angitis valley, and beyond (128 m.) *Angístis*, where a fine but looted Macedonian tomb near the station was excavated in 1972, thread the *Tasliki Stena*, the narrow gorge by which the river forces its way out of the Drama plain between Menoikion and Pangaion. We cross the 'golden plain' of Drama, extensively cultivated with tobacco.—144 m. (232 km.) **Drama**, see Rte 68; the station lies ½ m. S. of the centre. Beyond Drama the line runs E., followed closely as far as Stavroúpolis by a secondary road described in Rte 68. We ascend the valley of the Xeropotamos (maximum gradient 1 in 40) to reach, at (160 m.) *Plataniás*, the watershed (1056 ft) between the Angitis and the Nestos. The line descends equally steeply the Stena Korpilón and at (167 m.) *Paranéstion* crosses the Nestos and follows it.—Beyond (181¼ m.) *Stavroúpolis* it threads a spectacular defile passing through numerous tunnels.—At (194¼ m.) *Toxótai* we cross the Kavalla–Xanthi road.—203 m. **Xánthi,** see Rte 69A. Beyond Xanthi the line runs E., following the low ground to the S. of the Via Egnatia. The railway passes S.W. of (232 m.) **Komotiní** (Rte 69A), the station of which is 1½ m. from the centre. For a while the railway keeps well S. of the road to Alexandroúpolis, then, at (252 m.) *Méstis*, just S. of Vélkion, crosses it at right angles, continuing E. to a summit of 912 ft and (261 m.) *Kírki* in the valley of the little Iren. The hills to the N. have tin and silver mines. The railway descends the stream to (274 m.) **Alexandroúpolis** (Rte 69A).

Hence to (335 m.) *Dhidhimótikhon* the line is never more than 2 m. E. of the road (see Rte 69A); in places they run together.—344 m. **Píthion** (ΠΥΘΙΟΝ), on a loop to the E. of the road, is an important frontier junction where the Hellenic and Turkish State Railways meet. The little town occupies the site of an ancient fortified city with an acropolis. To the S.E. the line crosses into Turkey.—350 m. *Uzunköprü.* —518 m. Istanbul.

The W. branch from Pithion, which once linked with the international line from Turkey into Bulgaria, is now virtually defunct since the Turks have built a new connecting line entirely on their own territory.

70   SAMOTHRACE AND LEMNOS

These two islands, which geographically form part of the Eastern Sporades (Rte 74), are described here as they are more easily reached from the Thracian coast.

A   Samothrace

Motor caique from Alexandroupolis (21 m. in 5 hrs) daily in summer, twice or 3 times weekly in winter. The island is also visited by occasional steamer services which tend to change each year. Accommodation at the *Xenia* (23 R., closed in winter, B), or in private houses (primitive) in the village.

The island of **Samothráki** (ΣΑΜΟΘΡΑΚΗ), in English *Samothrace,* lies some 20 m. s.w. of Alexandroupolis and almost equidistant from the Gallipoli peninsula. The surrounding sea, swept by the prevailing N. winds, is usually rough and stormy, making access difficult. There is only one anchorage. Save for a narrow coastal plain in the N. and a region of rolling hills to the s.w., the island, elliptical in shape and only 68 sq. m. in area, consists of eroded granite mountains, rising in Mt Fengari to 5250 feet. Wild goats roam the mountainsides. Winters are hard, with heavy rains and thick snow. The island enjoys copious springs, and in classical times was probably much more fertile. Fruit is abundant. Politically the island belongs to Thrace as an eparchy of the nome of Evros. More than one third of the population (3000 inhab.) is concentrated in Khora.

History. In the Neolithic and Bronze Ages Samothrace was occupied by people of Thracian stock. From 'the topmost peak of wooded Samothrace' Poseidon watched the fighting on the plains of Troy (Iliad, xiii, 12), a city supposedly founded from the island though in fact more likely founded from Lemnos (comp. below). The non-Greek Thracian language and religion survived the arrival of Greek colonists c. 700 and in cult ritual to the 1C B.C. Archaeological evidence contradicts the classical tradition that the colonists were earlier and came from Samos; Strabo indeed suggests that the Samians invented the story for their own glory. The colonists' dialect has been shown by inscription to have been Aeolian rather than Ionian, and probably derived from Lesbos or the Troad. In the 6C Samothrace had a silver coinage, the city reached its greatest extent, and colonies were established on the mainland. The Samothracian navy was represented at Salamis. In the 5C her power declined, though the fame of her cult increased until the island became the chief centre of religious life in the N. Aegean. At the Sanctuary of the Great Gods Herodotus and King Lysander of Sparta were initiated. Aristophanes and Plato refer to its Mysteries. Here Philip of Macedon met and fell in love with his wife Olympias of Epirus, mother of Alexander the Great. The Macedonian dynasty continued to adorn the sanctuary until their downfall. Though the presence of the sanctuary assured the independence of the city, the island was used as a naval base by the Second Athenian League, by King Lysimachos of Thrace, and by the Ptolemies, Seleucids, and Macedonians in turn. After the Battle of Pydna, Perseus, the last king of Macedon, sought refuge in the island, only to be taken prisoner by the Romans. Aristarchus (fl. 155–143 B.C.), editor of Homer, was a native. In 84 B.C. the sanctuary was pillaged by Corsairs, but soon revived under Roman patronage. The legend that Dardanos the legendary founder of Troy, had come from Samothrace and that his descendant, Aeneas, had brought the cult to Rome, gave Samothrace a particular interest to the Romans. Varro and Piso (father-in-law of Julius Caesar) were initiates. The island, a natural port of call between the Troad and Neapolis, saw St Paul on his way to Philippi. Hadrian visited Samothrace and though an earthquake c. A.D. 200 began its decline, the ancient religion survived to the 4C. In 1419 the island was visited by Buondelmonte, and in 1444, when it had passed into the hands of the Genoese Gattilusi, princes of Enos and Samothrace, by Cyriacus of Ancona. It was taken by the Turks in 1457, passed to Greece after the First World War, and suffered a Bulgarian occupation in 1941–44.

The landing-place of *Kamariótissa*, on the w. coast, is close to the promontory of Akrotiri. In a craggy fold of the mountains above is the village of *Khóra*, or Samothrace, with 1210 inhab. and a medieval castle. On the N. coast, reached by road from Kamariótissa, is the ancient *Palaiópolis*, marked on the w. by a grove of plane-trees and the Tourist Hotel (comp. above). The ancient city, now a confusion of rocks and wild olive trees, occupies the shoulder of Ayios Yeóryios, a ridge extending N. towards the sea from the central massif of Phengari. From the Acropolis on the ridge the colossal *City Wall*, archaic (polygonal) and Hellenistic, runs w. across a ravine and takes in a smaller hill before reaching the shore by a small chapel. Two ruined medieval *Towers*, built of antique materials by the Gattilusi in 1431–34, command the sea, beneath which lie remains of the harbour mole and of a Byzantine church. Between the w. hill and the Tourist Hotel a river descends to the sea, and between its three streams stood the **Sanctuary of the Great Gods.** A path leads past the museum (see below) to the site.

The religion of the Great Gods was a pre-Greek Chthonic cult. The Great Gods

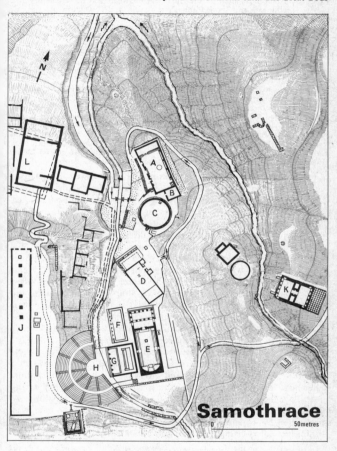

comprised the Great Mother or Axieros (related to Cybele and later identified with Demeter), an ithyphallic fertility god called Kadmilos (later identified with Hermes), the powerful Kabeiroi (Dardanos and Aetion), twin demons later fused with the Dioskouroi, and Axiokersos and Axiokersa (Hades and Persephone). In later times Hekate, Aphrodite, and Kadmos and Harmonia were added by assimilation or confusion. Ancient writers fought shy of saying much about the Kabeiroi, whose wrath was considered implacable. They were Anatolian in origin and, save at Thebes, hardly known in mainland Greece. Towards the end of the Archaic period Samothrace overtook Lemnos in importance as their principal place of worship.

The sanctuary had an extra-territorial character, apparently independent of the city-state that adjoined it, since at festivals this sent envoys like any other polis. Initiation into the mysteries, which was not essential for attendance at the sanctuary (unlike Eleusis), was open to anyone, regardless of nationality, sex, age, or social status. Initiation could be obtained at any time, and its two degrees (myesis and epotiae) could be taken without interval. A moral standard seems to have been required for the higher degree (which was not obligatory but, rather, exceptional) and some form of confession and absolution preceded it. Ceremonies apparently took place by torchlight.

The early sanctuary, approached from the w., occupied the promontory between the E. and central streams; a nucleus of sacred rock and precinct was established before the 7C B.C. The temple area, which grew piecemeal in Archaic and Classical times, was lavishly renewed in marble by the Ptolemies. A new access from the town side was provided by Ptolemy II Philadelphus, after which the site was extended to a typically Hellenistic planned design on the promontory between the central and w. streams.

Excavations were begun in 1863 by Champoiseau, French consul at Adrianople, who discovered the famous Victory now in the Louvre in Paris. A French mission mapped the site in 1866. Austrian expeditions, directed by A. Conze in 1873 and 1875, uncovered the Ptolemaion; its marbles were divided between Austria and Turkey, but only a few of those shipped to Gallipoli arrived at Istanbul. A Swedish team worked on the site in 1923–25. In 1938 systematic exploration was begun by New York University and excavations have been continued each year since 1948 under Karl and Phyllis Williams Lehmann. Admission 25 dr. Guide in English to the Excavations and Museum, by the excavators.

To the left of the path, the **Anaktoron** (Pl. A) served as a hall of initiation into the Mysteries (myesis). Built of good polygonal masonry it was long held to date from the 6C B.C. but has recently been redated to early Imperial times (the repercussions of which are yet to be felt); its walls still stand in places to a height of 12 feet. The interior ($88\frac{1}{2}$ ft by $37\frac{1}{2}$ ft), reached by three doors, from the w. terrace, was divided by a partition into a main hall and an inner sanctum (on the N.). This was guarded by bronze statues and marked by a warning stele. Limestone bases show where a wooden grandstand occupied the E. and part of the N. wall of the hall. In the centre was a circular wooden platform; in the S.E. corner a libation pit.—Built on to the s. end of the Anaktoron was a *Sacristy* (Pl. B; Iera Oikia), dating in its existing plan from 289–281 B.C. (but replacing an earlier structure) and repaired in the 3C and 4C A.D. Here, it seems, the novice was vested and hither he returned to receive a document certifying his initiation.

The *Rotunda* (Pl. C), the largest circular building known in Greek architecture (more than 65 ft across), was dedicated to the Great Gods by Queen Arsinoe between 289 and 281 B.C., whence its appellation **Arsinoeion**. Numerous marbles that survived the destroying earthquake have been arranged to show the structure of the building. A marble wall, interrupted by a beautiful moulded stringcourse, was surmounted by a gallery of pilasters supporting a Doric entablature. Within, the gallery had Corinthian half-columns with an Ionic cornice.

In the interior of the rotunda are some walls of the '*Double Precinct*' of the early 4C B.C. The rock *Altar* and its terrace here are the earliest preserved remains of the sanctuary.

Farther s. (Pl. x; reached from the path) a *Sacred Rock* of blue-green porphyry has a yellow tufa pavement from which libations were poured. This had already been buried by the 6C B.C.—In the cliff below the N.W. corner of the Temenos is another archaic altar (Pl. y) by a spring; this originally stood in a partly artificial glade, perhaps to be identified with the *Cave of Hekate Kerynthia*, mentioned by ancient authors.

The **Temenos** (Pl. D) is a rectangular precinct, open to the sky;

surviving courses of masonry represent only the foundations of its latest state in the 4C B.C. It was entered on the N.E. side by an Ionic *Propylon* of Thasian marble, of which many fragments can be seen both here and in the museum. Within the precinct probably stood a famous statue of Aphrodite and Pothos by Skopas. Abutting is an artificial terrace with a good view towards the sea.

To the S. are the imposing remains of the **Hieron** (Pl. E; the Sanctuary), a Doric edifice used for the Epopteia, or higher initiation ceremonies. Begun in the last quarter of the 4C B.C., it was not finished until c. 170 years later and was extensively restored in the 3C A.D. The limestone foundations are complete and most of the euthynteria in Thasian marble still in situ. The *Façade* consisted of a double porch of 14 columns standing before antae; five columns and one architrave block were re-erected in 1956 and the steps restored with modern blocks. The capital on the corner column was returned from Vienna, where the pedimental statues still remain.

A marble ceiling beam is preserved in the pronaos. The marble floor has disappeared, leaving the limestone under-pavement exposed. The spectators' benches on either side date from the Roman restoration, as does the marble floor of the apse. Here foundations of limestone blocks and irregular fieldstones (5C and 6C B.C. respectively) show that the building had precursors.—Outside the foundations, on the E. side, two sacred stones flank a torch-holder; here it is conjectured the hierophant heard the candidate's confession before admission.

Along the W. side of the Hieron were two buildings. That to the N., dubbed the *Hall of Votive Gifts* (Pl. F), took the form of a rectangular stoa with a Doric limestone colonnade of 6 columns between antae. Built c. 540 B.C., it survived with minor repairs for close on a thousand years. Adjacent, to the S., is the better-preserved substructure of the *Altar Court* (Pl. G), a hypaethral enclosure entered through a colonnade, the unequal spacing of whose columns is indicated by the surviving drums. Fragments of the architrave bear a dedicatory inscription by (?) Arrhidaios, half-brother of Alexander the Great.

The outline of the *Theatre* (Pl. H) is recognizable though all but two of its seats of white limestone and red porphyry vanished in 1927–37. The river is channelled under the orchestra in a late-Roman concrete culvert (restored).

A path following the line of an ancient pebble road, winds up to the WESTERN HILL. The N. part of this is occupied by the so-called '*Ruinenviereck*' (Pl. L), a medieval structure probably a fortification, built entirely of antique material from the sanctuary. Along the ridge above the theatre was a *Stoa*. Its foundations (Pl. J), 100 yds long, laid bare by the Austrian expedition were examined in 1963–64. Hundreds of blocks with elements of Doric and Ionic orders from outer and inner colonnades survive. It was probably of the early 3C B.C. Farther on is the *Nike Fountain* (Pl. I) with a shallow upper and a deep lower basin; in places the clay pipelines that fed and drained it can be traced.

The Parian marble 'Winged Victory', that formed the centrepiece of the fountain, was removed to Paris in 1863 and the ship's prow on which it stands in 1891. The right hand, recovered in 1950, is on permanent loan to the Louvre.

The path leads across the river and over the hill where the crowded *South Necropolis* (6C B.C.–2C A.D.) was excavated in 1957 to the E. ravine, beyond which stood the **Ptolemaion** (Pl. K), a monumental gateway to the sanctuary, dedicated to the Great Gods by Ptolemy II Philadelphus. The sub-structure is pierced by a barrel-vaulted tunnel through which at that time the river was channelled. The foundations carried a double Ionic portico. The Austrians carried off many decorative elements of its two pediments; other blocks lie in the ravine. Abutments for a wooden bridge (with a span of c. 60 ft) that crossed the river after its course had been altered by an earthquake can still be seen. Immediately opposite are a flagged circular Area and a later Doric structure dedicated by Philip and Alexander, successors to Alexander the Great.

The **Museum**, (25 dr. extra), is arranged as an aid to the understanding of the site. In HALL A typical sections of each building have been reconstructed from available fragments, though these are not necessarily in their original juxtaposition. Also in this room are two Stelai, from the Anaktoron and the Hieron, prohibiting entry to the uninitiated.—HALL B is devoted to SCULPTURE. Fragments from the Propylon of the Temenos (c. 340 B.C.): monolithic Ionic column of Thasian marble; necking with anthemion ornament and fragmentary capital; portions of the frieze of over 80 dancing maidens and musicians, probably depicting the wedding of Kadmos and Harmonia (in deliberately archaistic style). Two figures retrieved from the central river bed of the sanctuary, probably parts of a pedimental group (c. 460–450 B.C.): Bust of the blind seer Tieresias, which owing to a misidentification by Cyriac of Ancona became a model for Renaissance portraits of Aristotle; the eyes were recut in the 19C when the bust was used as an ikon on a house in Khora. Headless statue of (?) Persephone.

Case 1 contains religious and votive objects, including iron finger rings (one of the outward signs of initiation commented upon by Pliny); *Case* 2, coins and stamped roof tiles; in *Case* 3 are small architectural fragments; water-spouts, antefixes, mouldings, sections of floor, ceiling, etc. *Case* 4 displays sculptural pieces (4C B.C.–1C A.D.), including a marble portrait head of Queen Arsinoe III; bronze statuette of Herakles; fragments in high relief representing Centaurs.

HALL C. Acroterial Victory from the Hieron (c. 130 B.C.), reconstituted in 1950 from fragments buried after the statue fell in the earthquake c. A.D. 200. Cases on the right side of the hall contain finds from the Sanctuary (the pottery reflects its long history and the cosmopolitan origins of its pilgrims); those on the left side objects from tombs round the city. *Case* 2. Bronze decorations from the Propylon of the Temenos; votive gifts, including fragments of an iron chain-mail cuirass of the 3C B.C. (?Gaulish La Tene workmanship). *Case* 3. Local ware of the 7C B.C. *Case* 10. Terracotta statuette of a young winged god (3C B.C.) from the S. necropolis; fine blown glassware; complete contents of a Roman tomb chamber of A.D. 135; terracotta figurine of a girl (early 1C B.C.). *Case* 11. Stele of c. 400 B.C. with an inscription in Greek characters but in an undeciphered (presumably Thracian) language. Further inscriptions, set up in the courtyard, include lists of initiates, dedications, etc.—HALL D. Grave goods, pottery, and jewellery from the cemeteries.

ASCENT OF MT SAOS, 5–6 hrs from *Khora*, or (preferable) in 4 hrs from *Therma*, a place on the N. coast with hot sulphur springs, 2 hrs E. of Palaeopolis. **Mount Saos**, *Saoce* or *Phengari* (5249 ft) was the peak from which Poseidon gazed upon the plains of Troy; the modern traveller can do the same. The *View is all-embracing. N. to W., the coast of Thrace and Macedonia as far as the Chalkidike peninsula and Mt Athos, with the island of Thasos in between; S., the islands of Imbros and Lemnos; E., the Dardanelles, the plain of Troy, and Mt Ida in the far distance.

B Lemnos

Approaches. BY AIR, from Athens once or twice daily, in 45–65 min.; also twice weekly in c. 40 min. from Salonika.

BY SEA. From Piraeus a weekly mail boat ('Lemnos') departs at noon on Mon, calling at Skyros, Ayios Evstratios, and *Lemnos* (Tues noon), continuing to Alexandroupolis and Kavalla, whence it returns viâ Lemnos to Piraeus. Local connection (motor-boat) from Lesbos.

The island of **Lemnos** (ΛΗΜΝΟΣ; *Limnos*) is situated in the middle of the N. Aegean, midway between Mt Athos and Asia Minor. Intervening on the Asian side are the Turkish islands of Imbros and Tenedos. To the N. rises Samothrace; to the S.E. is Lesbos, to the nome of which Lemnos belongs, together with the islet of Ayios Evstratios (p. 595), which lies due S. Lemnos, with a population of 17,400 and an area of 175 sq. m., is almost bisected by two deep inlets of the sea—the Gulf of Moudhros in the S. and the Bay of Pournia in the N.—the isthmus between them being only 2 m. across. Valerius Flaccus ('Argonautica', II, 431) calls the island 'tenuis Lemnos', though the W. half is rugged and hilly, rising in the N.W. corner to 1410 ft. The bare plains of the E. yield small quantities of cereals, sesame, cotton, and tobacco. Numerous hot springs attest to the island's volcanic origin.

History. According to Homer the inhabitants of Lemnos were of Thracian stock; Herodotus and Thucydides, however, call them Pelasgi or Tirrheni (the same Tyrrhenian pirates that Dionysos transformed into dolphins). This may well represent two stages of pre-Greek history. Recent archaeological evidence shows that Lemnos had the most advanced Neolithic civilization in the Aegean, and a Bronze Age culture of Minoan–Mycenean type, connected with Troy and Lesbos, which continued without a sharp break into the Geometric period. In the 8–6C the island seems to have had contact with the Greeks, though it is certain from inscriptions that before the 6C the inhabitants were not Greek; their language is undeciphered and their burial customs show affinities with Villanovan (Etruscan) burials in Italy. The island is said by Polybius to have borne the more ancient name of *Aithaleia*; it possibly took the name Lemnos from a goddess identifiable with the Great Mother. The principal cults, however, were those of Hephaistos (said to have been thrown down to Lemnos from Olympos for intervening in a quarrel between Zeus and Hera, his parents) and of the Kabiroi.

Among many legends is that of the curse of Aphrodite upon the Lemnians for impugning her virtue. This alienated the men from their wives, who murdered their husbands. Only king Thoas escaped, saved by his daughter Hypsipyle. When the Argonauts put in at Lemnos, some of their number stayed behind to marry the Lemnian widows, becoming by them the fathers of the Minyans. The Minyans were driven out by the Pelasgians to Elis Tryphilia in the Peloponnesos. Homer tells of Philoktetes, the most celebrated archer of the Trojan War, who spent ten years on Lemnos with a wounded foot. The proverbial expression 'Lemnian deeds' for atrocities is attributed by Herodotus (VI, 138) to an episode in the Persian Wars. The Lemnians carried off some Athenian women from Brauron. The children of this enterprise looked down on their Lemnian half-brothers, whereupon the Lemnians slaughtered both them and their Athenian mothers.

Lemnos fell to Persia c. 513 B.C. and changed hands more than once before the end of the Persian wars. Here Hippias is said to have died after Marathon. From 477 B.C. the island formed part of the Delian League, and later received cleruchies from Athens (they dedicated the famous Lemnian Athena of Pheidias on the Acropolis of Athens). Lemnian troops fought for Athens at Sphakteria (425) at Amphipolis (422) and at Syracuse (413). Save for brief periods of domination by Sparta (404–393), by the Macedonians, and by the Seleucid Antiochus the Great, Lemnos remained under Athenian influence to the time of Septimius Severus. The island was twice visited (A.D. 162 and 165) by Dioskorides. In the 2C and 3C the Lemnian Philostratus family achieved fame in Rome as sophists. The island was plundered by the Heruli and later passed to Byzantium. It had a bishop in the 4C and became a metropolitan see in the reign of Leo VI. In 924 the Saracens under Leo of Tripoli were defeated by a Byzantine fleet off the island. Venetian merchants settled in the 11C and 12C, establishing sovereignty after 1204 under the Navigaiosa grand dukes. In the 13–15C the island was disputed between Venetians, Genoese, and Byzantines, and after 1462 between Venetians and Turks. John of Selymbria spent some years in exile here after 1344 and Gregory Palamas took refuge here in 1349. After 1670 the Turks in their turn used it as a place of exile for disgraced notables. Orloff's Russians occupied the island in the war of 1770, only to be driven out by Hassan Bey. Lemnos became Greek for a few months in 1829 before being exchanged with the Turks for Euboea. It fell to Greece in 1912, and was the British base for the Gallipoli campaign. Its connection with Turkey ended by treaty in 1920.

The island capital and chief port *Mírina* or **Kastron** (*Akti Mirinis*, bungalows, 125 R., May–Oct, DPO, L; *Sevdalis, Lemnos,* C) is situated on the w. coast. The verdant town (4000 inhab.) is the seat of the Metropolitan of Lemnos. Its two good anchorages are divided by a rocky promontory on which, in commanding position, stood the ancient *Myrina.* The conspicuous Turkish walls rise on ancient foundations; houses and streets can be traced; and inscriptions attest a sanctuary to Artemis. The MUSEUM (adm. 5 dr.; standard hours) is arranged for the purposes of study and labelled in Greek and Italian. Finds from Hephaisteia and Poliochni are well displayed in ten rooms.

Two roads lead towards Mudros, the inland one to the N. passing near a *Bath-House,* built by Hassan Bey. The shorter way, more southerly, which touches the coast, passes *Kondiá,* to the s.E. of which, at *Vriokastron* and *Trochaliá,* are some Bronze Age remains. The roads join at *Livadhokhórion* and continue to **Moúdhros,** or *Mudros.*

The *Gulf of Mudros,* one of the best natural harbours in the Aegean, became the base, in the First World War, of the Mediterranean Expeditionary Force. Hence Sir Ian Hamilton launched his attack on the Dardanelles (25 April 1915). In the same harbour the armistice with Turkey was concluded on 30 Oct 1918 on board H.M.S. 'Agamemnon'.—*East Mudros Military Cemetery,* to the N.E. of the town, with c. 900 British Commonwealth dead, contains also a French memorial, though the French graves were removed in 1922. At *Portianos,* on the w. side of the inner harbour, lie a further 350 dead of the Gallipoli campaign.

The most important archaeological remains of Lemnos are at **Poliochni** on the E. coast below Cape Voroskópos (anc. *Droskopos*). This presumably represents the Homeric 'Lemnos'. Excavations in 1931–36, by Alessandro della Seta of the Italian School, uncovered four superposed settlements, the latest an unfortified town of the Early Bronze Age (c. 1500–1000 B.C.). Beneath lay a city of the Copper Age (pre-Mycenean and probably earlier than Troy VI), and beneath that again remains of two Neolithic cities. The later of these was equipped with stone baths, the earliest found in the Aegean. The *Town Walls* (c. 2000 B.C.), with towers and gates, stand in places to a height of 16 ft. The city seems to have been destroyed by an earthquake. The main street and a number of houses were explored. The earliest city (4th millennium B.C.) is believed to be more ancient than Troy I.

A third road runs from Mudros to the N.E. tip of the island. *Komi,* between Mudros and Kondopoúlion, is known from an inscription to have had a sanctuary of Herakles, but only slight Byzantine remains are visible today. The *Bay of Pournia,* to the N. of the road, has yielded several sites to the excavator's spade. The medieval castle of KOKKINO, or *Kotchinos,* rose to importance with the decline of Hephaistia (see below). Here in 1442 the Empress of Constantine XI Palaeologus died in childbirth while under siege by the Turks; the castle was successfully defended by the Venetians against the Turks in 1476. Between the castle and the village of *Repanidhion* lay *Mosychlos*, famous in antiquity and in the Middle Ages for Lemnian Earth, a red bole containing a large percentage of silica, used as a tonic and astringent medicine. It was extracted on only one day in the year (latterly 6 Aug) to the accompaniment of religious ceremonies and exported (anciently under the seal of Artemis; 'terra sigillata') right up to the 19C.—The hamlet of *Palaiópolis*, on a rocky peninsula above the sea, occupies the site of **Hephaistia** ('Ηφαιστία), in Classical times the principal city of Lemnos, paying the larger tribute to Athens. It had pre-Greek origins. It became seat of a Byzantine bishop, fell to the Venetians in 1204, and c. 1395 was wrecked by a landslide and abandoned. Excavations in 1926–30 and 1937–39 by the Italian School uncovered a necropolis (8C B.C.) and a sanctuary destroyed in the last years of the 6C B.C. The local pottery carries Minoan–Mycenean traditions into the Geometric period; imported ware proves a lively trade with Macedonia, Corinth, and Athens. Among traces of later Greek occupation are a *Theatre*, remodelled in Roman times, and Byzantine churches.—On the opposite side of the bay (at *Khloi*) is the **Kabeirion**, excavated in 1937–39 by the Italian School. The sanctuary goes back to the Pelasgian epoch, when it had precedence over that of Samothrace. It occupies two level tracts divided by a rocky spur. Archaic foundations have been ascribed to an *Anaktoron*, a *Telesterion*, and a *Stoa*. The N. level is occupied by a huge edifice, probably the Hellenistic *Telesterion*, with a façade of 12 Doric columns. Among many inscriptions listing officials of the cult was found a letter from Philip V requesting initiation as epoptes.—*Cape Hermaeon*, on the N.E. coast, was, according to Aeschylus, one of the series of hills on which fire-beacons were lit at the instance of Agamemnon to signal to his wife Klytemnestra at Mycenae the fall of Troy (*Agamemnon*, 283), possibly an anachronism suggested by a similar system used in the opposite direction by Xerxes during the invasion of Greece (?).

Submarine research in 1960 in the *Charos Reef*, 10 m. offshore, located blocks of marble belonging to an Archaic Temple of Apollo that once stood in the ancient town of *Chryse*. One of the prehistoric centres of the island, Chryse is mentioned by Herodotus as having been engulfed by the sea as the result of an earthquake. Here (according to the Iliad) died Philoktetes, the exiled Achaean general.

About 20 m. s. of Lemnos is the small island of **Ayios Evstratios** or **Aistrates** (17 sq. m.) used periodically as a deportation settlement for political offenders. Its highest point is Mt Semadi (972 ft). Small quantities of iron, coal, and oil are found. The island village, *Ayios Evstratios*, lies on the N.W. coast. The site of the ancient city, on a hill between two streams, shows traces of Mycenean, Greek, Roman, and Byzantine occupation. The inhabitants cultivate cereals, grow fruit, and fish in local waters.

The Cyclades

0 ————————————— 25 miles
0 ————————————— 40 kilometres

IKARIA

AKRA
PAPAS

AKRA
EVROS

Mikonos
MIKONOS

DILOS

AKRA
STAVROS

Apollona

Koronis

Naxos   Koronos

Enkarai

DENOUSSA

Apiranthos

NAXOS

AKRA
PRASINO

OS

AKRA
KATOMERI   KOUFONISIA

KAROS

AMORGOS

Katápola

Amorgós

SKHOINOUSSA   ANDIKAROS

IRAKLEIA   DHRIMA

Arkesini

AKRA
KORAX

Ios

IOS

AKRA
AKHLADHI

ANIDHROS

AKRA
MAVROPETRA

SANTORINI

THIRASIA   **Thira**

Karterádhos

ANAFI

Akrotirion   Emborion   Anáfi

N

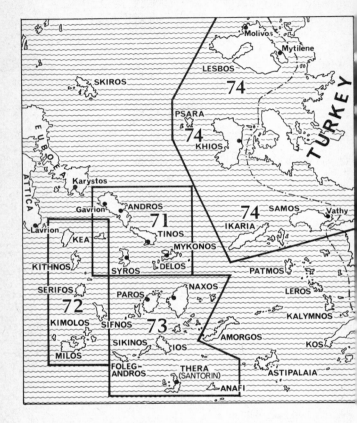

The **Aegean Sea** is bounded on the N. by Macedonia and Thrace, on the W. by the mainland of Greece, on the E. by Asia Minor and on the S. by Crete. Ancient writers divided it into the *Thracian Sea*, in the N.; the *Myrtoan Sea*, in the S.W., so called after Myrtos, an obscure island off the coast of Argolis; the *Ikarian Sea*, in the E., named after the island of Ikaria; and the *Cretan Sea*, in the S. The derivation of the word Aegean (AIΓAION) is uncertain; it may be from αἰγίς, in its secondary meaning of squall, in reference to the sudden gales that affect the area. The Byzantines and Venetians called it the *Archipelago*, and the Turks, the *White Sea*.

In the centre of the Aegean are the **Cyclades** (KYKΛAΔEΣ), a group of islands forming a rough circle (κύκλος) round Delos. In antiquity only twelve or fifteen islands were regarded as belonging to the Cyclades

(Strabo, X), and they depended on Delos. Today some thirty islands and islets are comprised within the nome of the Cyclades (*Kikládon*), with its capital at Ermoúpolis (Syros). This political division, which includes Delos and the S. Sporades, as well as the Cyclades proper, is divided into eight eparchies and has just over 86,000 inhabitants. The **Sporades** are three island groups 'scattered' in the Aegean, to the N., S., and E. of the Cyclades. The Southern Sporades are described with Delos and the Cyclades in the first three routes of this section; the Eastern Sporades, excluding the Dodecanese, in the remaining route. The Northern Sporades are described for convenience in Rte 43; the Dodecanese are described in a separate section (IX) and Amorgos with them; Crete, which partly closes the Aegean on the S. occupies the last section of the book.

The Aegean islands are the peaks of a submerged plateau now 300–650 ft below the surface and bounded by deeps of 2000–3000 ft. In the N. they are formed of limestone, gneiss, schist, and marble; in the S. of volcanic rock, lava, basalt, and trachyte. The highest point is in the island of Naxos. These mountainous and largely arid islands have lost their once luxuriant forests, but the larger ones produce olives, figs, and vines. The wines of Santorini and Naxos are renowned. The marble of Paros and Tinos is famed. Milos has long been noted for obsidian. Iron is found in Serifos, Kithnos, and Andros. The limpid air and the equable climate are a great attraction and the heat of summer is alleviated by the periodic N. winds (Tramontana; anc. Boreas) and later by the more predictable Etesian winds (Meltémi), which, blowing also from the N., prevail from early July to mid-September, sometimes reaching gusts of great violence.

The little seaside villages, with their clean white houses and their sparkling streets paved with marble, vary widely in atmosphere from island to island as the temperament of the islanders varies with the resources of the islands. They often contrast markedly with the villages inland, where terraced cultivation is a feature of the landscape. Windmills, another characteristic feature, usually have a dozen sails of canvas furled to tiny triangles. The inhabitants, partly Roman Catholic, claim a purer Greek strain than those of the mainland: they have, perhaps, been more influenced in the past by contact with the Italian peninsula and less by contact with the Turks. They are hospitable to strangers and generally intelligent.

The islands are increasingly tending to diverge into two categories: those 'earmarked for tourist development' on which for half the year modern mainly characterless hotels and souvenir shops superimpose an alien sophistication, but give some sort of prosperity; and those where the slow rhythm of island life continues, free from the stresses of modern technology but equally free from its benefits. Tiny 'unspoilt' islands subject to increasing depopulation do without mains electricity, hot water, the international telephone, and wide choices of menu; they may have days without transport and be two islands away from medical aid. Visitors should remember that it is pointless to opt for the simple life and then be irked by its simplicity. The larger islands are in fact better able to absorb tourists without losing their individuality.

COMMUNICATIONS. Most of the islands may be reached by regular steamer services (increasingly being replaced by vehicle ferries), which serve the islands in groups, travelling outward one day and returning in inverse order next day. Two of the Cycladic routes make the return voyage in the day every day with a common port-of-call in Syros and on some days Mykonos provides a further interchange point between the Cyclades and the Dodecanese. Apart from this, to reach an island on a different round it is usually necessary to return to Piraeus. Services are most frequent on Mon and Sat, least frequent on Tues and Sunday. Those outlined in the route headings were those in force in summer 1979; they are less frequent in winter and subject to change. Sailing times should always be checked on day of sailing (tel. 143). Mykonos and the Eastern Sporades are individually linked by air with Athens.

CRUISE SHIPS operating from Piraeus usually combine the most popular islands into a round trip of 5–7 days, calling nearly always at Mykonos, Delos, Rhodes, Heraklion (Crete), and Santorin. Additional calls may be made at Patmos and Kos. More ambitious rounds include Istanbul, Troy, Izmir, Ephesos, and Halicarnassos in Turkey.

The traveller who wishes to go from island to island according to his fancy must hire a caique, an expensive and often arduous business, or a yacht, which (though not less expensive) is more easily arranged. Details of the many yacht brokers in Athens and Piraeus may be had from the Greek Yacht Brokers and Consultants Association, 25 Loukianou, Athens. Of the eighty-one Greek harbours and anchorages now equipped with facilities for servicing of yachts, some twenty-five are in the Aegean island area. The Aegean is an uncertain and capricious sea and should be sailed only by yachtsmen of experience; excellent pilots may be found among the sailors of Mykonos, Skyros, and Milos.

History. At some remote period the Cyclades were populated by Carians. Thucydides tells us that (I, 4) that King Minos conquered the Cyclades and expelled the Carians. Herodotus (I, 171) says that in ancient times the Carians, who went by the name of Leleges, were subjects of Minos and served in the ships of his navy; and that, long after the time of Minos, they were driven from the islands by Ionians and Dorians and settled on the mainland of Asia Minor.

So far there have been few discoveries of the Neolithic Age in the Cyclades. They enjoyed a flourishing Bronze Age civilization which had affinities at first with Crete and later with Mycenae. For ease of reference, the Cycladic Bronze Age has been divided into Early, Middle, and Late Cycladic, each division being subdivided into three. These nine periods, roughly corresponding to those into which Sir Arthur Evans divided the Minoan civilization in Crete, cover c. fifteen centuries from 2600 to 1100 B.C. Perhaps the most important single evidence of the spread of Cycladic civilization is the volcanic mineral obsidian. The principal though not the only place in the Aegean where obsidian is found is Melos, which abounds in it. This mineral was of great importance before the discovery of copper and bronze and even for some time after they had come into use. The prehistoric trade in obsidian from Melos was considerable, and it has been found in Crete and other Aegean islands, on the mainland of Greece, in Thessaly, and on the coast of Asia Minor. This dispersal proved the early existence of sea communications even before the discovery of the 'Libyan' fresco in Thera, where civilization seems to have been on a par with Crete.

Before the end of the Early Cycladic Period people lived in houses often grouped in villages. Some of the pottery had elaborate designs of spirals and glaze paint was introduced. Melos made pottery with white designs on a dark ground, inspired by Early Minoan examples. Model boats of lead prove not only the use of this metal but the commonplace of navigation. Primitive marble figurines were imported into Crete. In the Middle Cycladic Period there was considerable progress. The second city at Phylakope had larger and better-built houses, and it was protected by a wall. Pottery designs showed a naturalistic tendency, flowers and animals being freely represented. During this period Middle Minoan pottery of the best style was imported into Melos, and Melian vases imitated the Cretan polychrome designs on a black ground (Kamares ware). Contemporary Melian vases have been found in the Temple Repositories at Knossos. Intercourse with the mainland is proved by the discovery in Melos of Minyan ware of the Middle Helladic Period. Before the end of the Middle Cycladic Period (c. 1600 B.C.) the Cyclades appear to have been completely under the domination of Crete, thus confirming the tradition that they were conquered by Minos (comp. above). This view is borne out by the fact that in Melos there was a script resembling and probably derived from the Minoan, and by the discovery on Thera of Middle Minoan vases imported from Crete. The Flying Fish fresco found in the Palace at Phylakope and the frescoes on Thera may have been the work of Cretan artists. Cycladic pottery imitating Cretan and small objects in bronze, ivory, and stone show that the culture of the islands was now a reflection of the Minoan. After the volcanic explosion of Thera the influence of the mainland became stronger and Mycenean imports rivalled Minoan. At the end of the 15C, when the centre of Aegean civilization passed from Knossos to Mycenae, both native pottery and imported ware declined in quality. As the use of metal spread, the demand for Melian obsidian fell off and the island's fortunes waned. In the third period of Late Cycladic the imports from Crete stopped altogether and the only source of supply was the mainland. At the end of this phase the culture shaded off into that of the Protogeometric Period.

In the 10C and 9C Ionians colonized the islands and Delos became the religious centre of the Greek world. The islands were overrun by the Persians in the invasion of 490 B.C. In 478/7 they were included in the Delian League and so imperceptibly became incorporated in the Athenian Empire. They remained tributary to Athens till 404, after which they had a few years of independence. In 378 they joined the Second Athenian League and again came under the influence of Athens. In the Social War (357–355) they revolted, only to become subject to Macedon. In 308 they passed to Antigonus, who founded the League of Islanders; then to the Ptolemies who, vanquished at Andros in 228, were supplanted by the Macedonian, Antigonus Doson. He was succeeded by Philip V. After Philip's defeat at Cynoscephalae in 197, the Cyclades passed to the Rhodians, and later to the Romans. Temporarily conquered by Mithridates in 88, they were returned to Rome. They were abandoned by the Eastern Empire to the raids of the Goths, Saracens, and Slavs.

In 1204 the islands were given by the Crusaders to Venice, who handed them over to adventurers as hereditary fiefs of the Republic. The result was twenty small vassal states. Members of the Ghizi family held Tenos, Mykonos, Skyros, Skopelos, Skiathos, and Astypalaea, as well as parts of Keos and Seriphos, of which the Giustianini and Michieti had the remainder. The Sanudi held Naxos and Paros, with many smaller islands, and called themselves dukes of Naxos; the Navigajosi aspired to the title of grand dukes of Lemnos; the Venier were marquesses of Cerigo (Kythera); the Viari had Cerigotto; the Barozzi, Santorini (Thera); the Dandoli, Andros; the Quirini, Amorgos, and the Foscoli, Anaphe. Most of these island dynasties were suppressed by the Turks after the fall of Constantinople in 1453; but some survived for another century. Among them were the dukes of Naxos, who had almost from the start broken with Venice and gone over to her enemies. In 1210 Marco Sanudi, first Duke of Naxos, took an oath of fealty to the Latin emperor Henry of Flanders and, as a reward, was made feudal superior of the other Aegean barons, with the grandiose title of Duke of the Archipelago and Sovereign of the Dodecanese.

Early in the 17C the islands were ransacked by English adventurers looking for antiquities. Admiral Sir Kenelm Digby acted as the agent of Charles I, who is said to have amassed 400 pieces of sculpture. The rival collection of the Duke of Buckingham was enriched by the efforts of Sir Thomas Roe, ambassador to the Porte. More successful than either was the Rev. William Petty, chaplain to the second Earl of Arundel (1580–1646), whose daring adventures in the pursuit of the antique became a byword. The famous Parian Chronicle was one of his prizes. Lord Arundel is regarded as the founder of classical archaeology in England; his collection of ancient sculptures was presented in 1667 to the University of Oxford by his grandson Henry Howard, afterwards sixth Duke of Norfolk. It is now in the Ashmolean Museum, Oxford.

The Civil War brought these archaeological forays to an end. In the month that Naseby was fought (June 1645) the Turks invaded Crete. During the 24 years of the Candian War the islands were alternately occupied by Turks and Venetians. On its termination in 1669 the Archipelago enjoyed a century of comparative peace, broken by the outbreak in 1770 of war between Turkey and Russia. The Russian fleet spent the winter of 1770–71 at Paros and annexed eighteen of the Cyclades to the Russian Empire. The Russian domination lasted however, for only four or five years. Thereafter no event of importance disturbed the tranquility of the islands till the Revolution of 1821.

In both world wars the Aegean was tragically prominent. In 1915, during the first, the natural harbour of Moudros, on the island of Lemnos, was made the Allied base, and the island of Imbros the G.H.Q. of the ill-fated Dardanelles Expedition. In the Second World War the Germans had for a time air and local naval superiority which enabled them to occupy Crete after Greece had been over-run and, later, to thwart the British landings at Kos and Leros.

71 NORTHERN CYCLADES
A Syros

STEAMER from Piraeus, 79 m. in 3½–5½ hrs at least twice daily, continuing either viâ Tinos to Mykonos, or viâ Paros to Naxos. Additional services: 3 times weekly, continuing to Samos; twice weekly, continuing to Ios, Santorini, Sikinos, and Folegandros; less frequently to some other islands.

Síros (ΣΥΡΟΣ, more usually in English spelled **SYROS** or **Syra**), situated in the centre of the Cyclades, owes its development to its port and its manufactures. The island, 14 m. long with a maximum width of 5½ m., is pleasant but not spectacular and no longer deserves the eulogy of Homer, who calls it rich in herds and flocks and having plenty of wine and corn. It does, however, produce barley, wine, oil, figs, and green vegetables. Syros is the nursery of Roman Catholicism in Greece; about half the population of its capital and nearly all the inhabitants outside it are Catholic.

Ermoupolis (*Hermes*, on the quayside, B; *Nissaki*, Ep. Papadam; *Europe*, 74 Stam. Proeon; *Kykladikon*, in Plateia Miaoulis, these **C**; Restaurants on the quay), capital of the island and of the nome of the Cyclades (Kikládon), is situated on the E. coast. The clean town, with well-built 19C mansions adorned with wrought-iron balconies, has 13,500 inhab., two-thirds of the island population. It is the seat of a Greek archbishop and of a Roman Catholic bishop. The older quarters are built on two conical hills, that to the S., crowned by the R.C. cathedral, being the medieval *Ano Siros*, still a separate deme of 1300 inhabitants. The hill of Vrontado, to the N., is the Orthodox quarter. The port is the traffic centre of the Cyclades, with steamer services to many islands and the possibility of caiques to others.

History. Nothing survives of the ancient city of *Syria*. In the middle ages the inhabitants, in fear of pirates, withdrew from their seaside town to a lofty hill about 1 m. inland, where they built Ano (Upper) or Old Syros. This became the quarter of the Roman Catholics, descendants of the Genoese and Venetian settlers who, during the Turkish rule after 1566, were under the protection of the King of France. The inhabitants took no active part in the War of Greek Independence, but took refugees from Psara and Chios, who founded Ermoupolis. The port became the coal-bunkering station for packet ships of the E. Mediterranean and the chief port of Greece, but declined when oil-burning became general to its present role as mercantile junction of the Aegean. Syros is one of the most highly industrialized towns in Greece with cotton mills and tanneries.

Protected by the Asses' Isle (Gaidouronisi) and by a long breakwater, and bounded on the s. by the old *Lazareta*, or quarantine station, the port is generally crowded with cargo ships laid up or under repair. It has a hydraulic slip capable of lifting large vessels. Round the outer harbour are ironworks and tanneries. The lower town is built round the inner or *Commercial Harbour*. To the left, behind the waterfront, is the conspicuous belfry of the church of the *Koimisis*.

The *Quay*, bustling and animated, is lined with cafés, tavernas, and shops selling loukoumi (Turkish delight), and farther w. enlivened by caiques and fish markets. Odhos Ermou, or Od. Khiou (the fruit and grocery market) farther on, lead to PLATEIA MIAOULIS, the town centre. This dignified square, paved with marble and shaded by trees, contains a bandstand and an obelisk to Andreas Miaoulis (1768–1835), the admiral and patriot. It is dominated by the *Town Hall*, an elegant building of c.

1870, and round the square are grouped arcaded çafés, clubs, and the Public Library. Behind this is the Apollo Theatre. In the side street to the left of the Town Hall, below the *Clock Tower*, is the entrance to the small *Museum* (9.30–1, 3–6, free). Here three rooms contain prehistoric antiquities from Paros, casual finds from Syros (including a phallic idol similar to those on Delos), and a small relief of a boar hunt from Amorgos. To the w. is the Orthodox *Cathedral* (Metamorfoseos), with the tomb of Anthimos Gazis (1758–1828), the Thessalian patriot.

Hence, partly by 800 steps (stiff climb; c. 1 hr), Odhos Omirou passes between the French *École des Frères* (r.) and *St Sebastian* (l.), and mounts to **Ano Síros** (590 ft), which may be reached by bus or taxi viâ the fashionable quarter of *Neapolis*. Halfway up is the *French Hospital*, served by sisters of mercy. In the upper town are many Catholic churches and the cathedral of St George, *Ayiou Nikoláou* of the Orthodox faith, and tier upon tier of whitewashed houses. Next to Ayios Yeoryios and shaded by pepper-trees is the *British Military Cemetery* where lie 108 British and other dead from the Aegean Is., more than half of whom were drowned when the transport ship 'Arcadian' was torpedoed on its way from Salonika to Alexandria on 15 Apr 1917. The view of the port and of neighbouring islands is striking.—Another splendid viewpoint is the church of the *Anastasis* on the hill of *Vrontado*.

The favourite summer evening promenade is the E. wall of the commercial harbour.—In the Vaporia quarter, with its elegant villas, is the church of *Ayios Nikolaos*, adorned with a blue dome, and higher up the *Trion Ierarkhon* and its orphanage. A road leads N. from the first along the cliffs in 30 min. to *Ayios Dhimitrios*, a fair example of modern 'Byzantine' style (1936).

Kíni (6¾ m.) on the w. shore and *Galessás* (7 m.), farther s. on the slopes above the coast, are pleasant villages served by buses (from Custom House). A frequent service plies on the asphalted road viâ (2½ m.) *Mánna* to **Poseidonía** (*Dellagrazia* B, *Poseidonion* C, both Apr–Oct); and *Fínikas* (ΦΟΙΝΙΚΑΣ), situated a mile apart on an inlet of the s.w. coast. They bear the names of the two cities ruled, according to the Odyssey, by Ktesios, father of Eumaeus the swineherd (Od. xv, 406); minor finds have been unearthed in both places. Poseidonía, better known by its popular name *Dellagrázia* (ΝΤΕΛΛΑΓΡΑΤΣΙΑ), is the favourite summer resort of the islanders, with attractive villas and small tavernas. Beyond Manna a by-road leads s. to *Vari* (6 m.; Alexandra C and others), a developing resort on a pretty bay, whence Dellagrazia may be pleasantly reached on foot in 2 hrs round the s. coast.

The N. quarter of the island, rising in Mt Pirgos to 1476 ft, is accessible only on foot or muleback. Here is the so-called *Cave of Pherekydes*, recalling the teacher of Pythagoras (fl. c. 544 B.C.). Farther N. near *Khalandriani* tombs of the Cycladic era, excavated by the Greek Archaeological Service, yielded vases and other finds.

B Andros and Tinos

A FERRY plies daily in the afternoon from Rafina (50 min. from Athens by hourly bus; comp. Rte 21) to *Gavrion* and *Batsi* (2½ and 3 hrs) the s. harbours of **Andros**, then continues to *Tinos* (c. 6 hrs), returning early the following morning.

Tinos is better served from Piraeus (morning) direct in 4¾ hrs or viâ Syros in 5¼–6½ hrs on the lines to Mykonos.

ANDROS (10,450 inhab.), or *Ándhros* (ΑΝΔΡΟΣ), the northernmost and one of the largest of the Cyclades, is 21 m. long and 8 m. wide with an area of 117 sq. miles. It is separated from Euboea by the dangerous Doro Passage and from Tinos by a strait only 5 furlongs wide. The well-wooded island produces figs, oranges, lemons, oil, silk, and wine. Andros was sacred to Dionysos and there was a tradition that during the festival of the god a fountain in his sanctuary flowed with wine. It has little antiquarian interest and is not much visited by foreigners. Apart from a short 'season' (July–Aug), when the island is thronged with Athenian holiday-makers, Andros is a good choice for a restful stay. Characteristic of the island are the stone field-walls, which are given rhythm and visual interest by triangular orthostats set at intervals, and the medieval dovecotes, square towers ornamented in patterned tilework. The latter are also found on Tinos, and seem to have marked a Venetian craze for dove-keeping combined with the competitive mania for tower building which swept Italy (comp. Bologna, San Gimignano, etc.).

History. The island is said to have been settled by Andreus, a general of Rhadamanthos of Crete, and later colonized by Ionians. Andros joined the fleet of Xerxes in 480 B.C., for which Themistokles attempted to impose a heavy fine on the islanders; on their refusal to pay, he laid siege unsuccessfully to their city (Herod. viii, 111). Later Andros became subject to Athens and then to Macedon. In 200 B.C. the Romans captured it and handed it over to Attalos I of Pergamon. In the Byzantine era it suffered from piratical raids. From 1207 the Dandoli held it under Venice as a hereditary fief. It was seized by the Turks in 1556 and ceded to Greece after the War of Independence.

The steamers call first at *Gavrion* (Aphrodite B), an unprepossessing village on a sheltered bay (sandy beach to the N.W.), from which the connecting bus plies to the capital (1¼ hr).

About ¾ hr inland at Ay. Petros is a fine round *Hellenic Tower*, of five floors, c. 65 ft high. It is built on a base of large stones 13 ft high and has an inner hall 18 ft in diameter with a corbelled dome pierced by lunettes. A shaft dug into the wall above the entrance gave access by means of ladders to the upper stories, served also by a winding staircase. In the walls are windows with stone shields and loopholes.

5 m. *Batsí* (ΜΠΑΤΣΙΟΝ; Lykion B; Chryssi Akti C; Avra D), a seaside village farther along the coast, is attractively grouped round its little harbour, the steamers' other port-of-call. The road rises steadily along the s. slope of Mt Petalon (3260 ft), the central culmination of the island, with views toward the unimportant island of *Gyaros*. We pass above (10 m.) *Palaiópolis*, whose scattered habitations drop amid steep cultivated terraces to a wide bay. Near the shore remains (wall, gateway, mole) of the ancient city of *Andros* have been identified, but are scarcely worth the effort entailed in locating them. The road divides, the right branch continuing to *Kórthion* (10 m.; Korthion C), a small landing-place on a deep bay near the s.E. corner of the island.

On the promontory of *Zagorá*, c. 1½ m. beyond the fork, a late-Geometric settlement was excavated by the Univ. of Sydney in 1967–69 and since. Fortification walls were uncovered and remains of a 6C temple probably built after the settlement was abandoned.

Our road turns inland on the slopes of Pétalon to run high above the beautiful valley of *Mésaria*, which divides the island into two unequal parts. The villages multiply, fig-trees abound, and the countryside is dotted with dovecotes.—15 m. *Ménites*. A stiff climb of 1 hr in the direction of Phállika (s.E.) leads to the *Moní Panakhrántou* supposed to have been visited by Nikephoros Phokas.—16¾ m. *Mesariá* has a Byzantine church (1158). We descend through *Lámira* to (20 m.) the 'Khora' or chief town.

The town of **Andros** (*Xenia, Paradisos*, both B, summer only; *Aegli* C), seat of a bishop with 1830 inhab., is situated on the E. coast and subject to cool winds even in summer. It occupies a low eminence between two exposed beaches and extends picturesquely along the rocky tongue of land that juts out between them. The poor anchorage is on the

N. side. The main street (no motors), paved in marble and overhung by little balconies, descends past the *Post Office* (within is a large-scale map of the island) to the little *Plateia Kaïris* overlooking the sandy S. beach. Beyond it continues along the spine of the promontory in the *Kato Kastro* past the Metropolis to terminate before the little maritime *Museum* in the windswept Plateia Riva. Here a modern bronze to the Unknown Sailor faces the eroded ruins of a Venetian castle, built on a detached outcrop of rock joined by a narrow bridge.

On the slopes, 2 m. N.W., stands *Apoíkia* (Sariza, June–Sept, D) with mineral springs, the water of which is celebrated throughout Greece. The road passes the medieval tower of Montelos.

TINOS (ΤΗΝΟΣ), lying between Andros and Mykonos and N.E. of Syros, is 17 m. long and 7½ m. wide. The port and capital lies on the S. coast; there is also an anchorage at Panormos on the N. coast. Elsewhere the island rises abruptly from the sea, especially in the N.E. where Mt Tsiknia attains 2340 ft. In the centre it is peppered with villages, compactly built on the hillsides. Their characteristic churches have an Italianate look with many-storied open-worked belfries, attractive W. façades, and lateral arcades. Conspicuous also in the green and pleasant landscape are the medieval dovecotes (comp. Andros). Tiny terraces are intensely cultivated with vines, figs, and vegetables. The wine of Tinos, famous in antiquity, is still esteemed, both the retsina and the sweet un-resinated vintage. The Tinians are skilful workers in marble.

History. The island was anciently called *Ophiousa*, as it was said to abound in snakes; for the same reason the name *Tenos* may derive from the Phœnician word tenok. A celebrated temple was dedicated to Poseidon who was credited with sending storks to exterminate the snakes. In 480 B.C. the Tenians were forced to serve in the fleet of Xerxes against Greece, but one of their ships deserted to the Greeks before the battle of Salamis with news of the Persian intentions. For this service the name of Tenos was inscribed on the Tripod of Delphi (Hdt. VIII, 82). Tenos was captured by the Venetians under Andrea Ghisi in 1207. It withstood assaults for over 500 years, not falling to the Turks till 1714. The long Venetian domi-nation made Tenos the most Catholic of the Cyclades. In the War of Greek Independence, while the Orthodox inhabitants took an active part, the Catholics held aloof. Today they have their own bishop and their churches, convents, and schools. The Ursulines have a noteworthy girls' school at Loutra (see below). In 1822 the discovery of a wonder-working ikon of the Virgin made Tenos into a place of pilgrimage. On 15 Aug 1940, before the port of Tenos, during the celebration of the Feast of the Assumption (see below), the Greek cruiser *Helle* was torpedoed by a submarine of unknown nationality, on the eve of the outbreak of the war between Greece and Italy.

Tinos (*Tinos Beach*, 1½ m. w., A; *Tinion, Theoxenia*, DPO, both B, *Asteria, Avra*, C, these closed in winter; *Meltemi, Poseidonion, Oceanis, Delfinia, Flisvos*, all C, open all year), the capital, is an attractive town of 3400 inhab., with houses of dazzling whiteness, dominated by the great pilgrims' church. The cheerful waterfront abounds with hotels, restaurants, and cafés, which, while modest, are of a standard to encourage a stay. A broad avenue leads in 5 min. to the church of PANAYIA EVANGHELISTRIA (Our Lady of Good Tidings), which, with its conventual buildings, forms a picturesque group. The white marble, of which it is built, includes reused material from the Temple of Apollo at Delos, as well as local and Parian stone. A gateway with an ogee arch, preceded by a floor of pebble mosaic, admits to the great *Court*, shaded by trees and surrounded by porticoes. A monumental staircase mounts to the *Church*, where, surrounded by innumerable gold and silver ex-votos, is displayed the celebrated ikon discovered in 1822. Twice a year, on the feasts of the Annunciation (25 March) and of the Assumption (15 Aug), thousands of halt and sick pilgrims from all over Greece flock hither in hope of a cure.

On the right on the descent from the church is the **Museum**, built in 1969 in the island's dovecote style. It contains a colossal pithos of the 7C B.C. with five bands of frieze figures in relief; another (8 ft high) with geometric designs; sculpture of various periods; and a sundial attributed to Andronikos Kyrrhestes. In a room above are modern paintings and sculpture.

At *Kionia*, ½ hr w. along the shore, just before the Tinos Beach hotel, is a *Sanctuary of Poseidon and Amphitrite*, first dug by Belgian archaeologists in 1900. Since 1975 the French School have established the limits of the sanctuary, founded in the 4C and destroyed in the mid-1C, and exposed foundations of a portico 550 ft long.

Excursions. Buses from the quay to most of the island villages.

1. TO XÓMBOURGO AND KÓMI. The road runs N. to (4 m.) *Tripotamos*, where we turn left, then right (leaving the Isternia road) to skirt the w. side of **Xómbourgo**, a hill (1854 ft) crowned by the ruins of a Venetian castle commanding a fine *View of the Cyclades. The ascent (1½ hr) is best started from (8 m.) *Xynara*, where the catholic archbishop resides. Below the Kastro lie the remains of the ancient city of *Tenos*, which flourished from the 8C to the 4C. Excavations in 1958–59 uncovered part of the fortification wall (7C B.C.), a huge public building, and a Geometric temple. At (8¾ m.) *Loutrá* in a beautiful situation, is the girls' school run by Ursuline nuns. The road continues to (10¾ m.) *Kómi* and (12 m.) *Kalloní*, whence a rough descent may be made to the N. coast at the shallow bay of *Kolimvíthras*.

2. TO ISTERNIA AND PANORMOS, 21¾ m. (35 km.), the most attractive excursion but poor road. We take the left fork at Tripotamos (comp. above) and run along the s. flank of the hills with views seaward to Syros.—8¾ m. *Kardianí*.—At (15½ m.) *Istérnia* the church has a dome incorporating pottery tiles.—18½ m. *Pánormos*, locally called *Pirgos*, the largest village (512 inhab.) on the island, has celebrated quarries of white, black, and green marble. The old grammar school, built by Capodistrias in 1830, houses a School of Fine Arts.—21¾ m. *Ormos Panormou*, its small harbour, has a fine beach.

3. *Moní Kekhrovouvíou*, with eighty nuns, is reached by bus in 30 min. on the road to Falatados to the N.E. of Tinos.

C   Mykonos and Delos

STEAMERS from Piraeus 2–4 times daily in 5½–7½ hrs. The return journey is made in the afternoon or overnight. A round trip (allowing a view of Tinos and Mykonos) can be made in a long day.—From Tinos twice daily in c. 1 hr. From Syros in c. 3 hrs.—Steamers continue 3 times weekly from Mykonos to Kalymnos, Kos, and Rhodes (twice weekly calling intermediately at Patmos and Leros). The larger ships disembark passengers by lighter; in calm weather smaller vessels can moor alongside.

Míkonos, more familiarly in English **MYKONOS**, is a rocky island of 23 sq. m. producing manganese and a little barley, wine, and figs. Four-fifths of the 3900 inhabitants live in or around the capital, which, from being solely the point of departure for Delos, has developed into the most popular tourist centre of the Cyclades, welcoming cruise ships daily.

History. In antiquity the island had two cities, *Mykonos*, on the w. coast, and *Panormos*, on the N. coast. Strabo notes that baldness was prevalent here so that bald men were sometimes called Mykonians. The Persian commander Datis touched at Mykonos in 490 B.C. on his way to Greece. After the Persian wars the island became an Athenian colony. In the middle ages it belonged to the dukes of Naxos and later was incorporated in the Venetian province of Tenos. In 1822, under the leadership of the heroine Manto Mavrogeneous, the islanders repulsed an attack by the Turks. Mykonos now forms part of the eparchy of Syros.

The town and port of **Mykonos** (*Leto*, DPO, A; *Manto* C, both open all year; *Theoxenia, Rhenia, Kouneni*, B; *Mykonos Beach* C, all closed in winter; *Apollo Rest.*, good, with R.; rooms available in private houses) is situated on the w. coast on the site of the ancient city, a curving bay ending in a low promontory and backed by an amphitheatre of hills. Its small churches and chapels, and its glittering white houses, with their arcades and marble staircases, give it a special charm, and its narrow lanes seemingly inexhaustable scope for losing one's way (a deliberate defence against pirates). The less attractive ESPLANADE, lined with cafés, is a favourite promenade and the pelican, which has become in the last two decades the mascot of the island, a constant curiosity. In summer artists from all countries frequent the *Skholís Kalón Tekhnón*, a branch of the Athens school of fine art. The locally woven linens are colourful.

Of the many little churches erected from the proceeds of fishing and piracy, the *Paraportiani*, near the quay, is typically picturesque. Near by is the *Local Museum* with a floor of black Tinos marble and bygones from demolished houses. The Metropolis and the Roman Catholic church, bearing the Ghizi escutcheon, are on the way to the promontory where three celebrated windmills catch the wind in their small triangular sails. Below them picturesque houses rise straight from the sea.

At the other end of the bay, beyond the Leto hotel, the *Archaeological Museum* contains important finds from the necropolis of Rheneia, used in 425 B.C. during the purification of Delos. Notable are a statue of Herakles in Parian marble; cinerary urns, ossuaries in lead, and a quantity of pottery from all parts of the Aegean found on Delos. Of unusual interest is a fine 7C *Pithos (found in Mykonos in 1961; restored) showing relief scenes of the Trojan horse and the massacre at Troy.

To N. and S. of the town paths lead to several beaches in 20–40 min.; *Ayios Stéfanos* has a bungalow hotel (Alkystis B); the farther ones, reached by bus, afford better bathing.

Excursions. These are of minor interest but may be combined with visits to more distant beaches. Boats may be hired in the harbour and taxis (fixed charges displayed) from the square.

1. *Garden of Raphaki*, ¾ hr E. This garden, with its fine trees, was bequeathed by the patriot sailor Sourmales, who ran the blockade of Crete in 1862.—2. *Mt Ayios Ilias*, 2 hrs N. on mule-back. This hill (1195 ft), the highest point of the island, is supposed to be the *Dimastos* of Pliny. The return may be made viâ the sandy bay of *Panormos*. At Palaiokastro, near by, the ruined medieval castle of *Darga* occupies the site of the ancient city of Panormos.—3. *Lenos*, 1 hr S.E., has the remains of a round Hellenic tower and of a gatehouse.—4. *Tourliani*, or Ano Merà, 2½ m. E., has a convent. On the sea beyond is *Kalafáti Beach* (Aphrodite B). About 1 m. out to sea is the islet of *Dragonísi*, with remarkable caves haunted by seals, and crumbling cliffs.

FROM MYKONOS TO DELOS, caique c. 8.30–9, returning from 12. The crossing (c. ½ hr) is often choppy and cold; in rough weather (not infrequent when the N. wind blows) it cannot be made. On leaving Mykonos we pass the islets of Ayios Yeoryios and Kavouronisi and head for Cape Kako, the N. point of Delos. On a clear day Tinos stands up grey and black to starboard with the Panayia Evanghelistria white above the town and the villages prominent below Xombourgo. Syros is seen for a time ahead (beyond Rheneia) and, far to port, Paros. The cloud effects above the islands are often enchanting. We double C. Kako and enter the strait separating Delos from Rhenia.

The island of **DELOS** (ΔΗΛΟΣ), or Lesser Dílos (ἡ Μικρὰ Δῆλος), is 3½ m. long and ¾ m. wide, and has an area of only 2 sq. miles. It is separated from Rheneia or Greater Dílos by a channel 1000 yds wide, running from N. to s. Two rocky islets, Little Rhevmataria and Great Rhevmataria (ancient Isle of Hecate), rise from the middle of the channel. The w. coast is indented by three small havens—the Bay of Skardana; the Little Harbour, the ancient Sacred Harbour, adjoined by the ancient Commercial Harbour; and the Bay of Phourne. On the other side of the island, on the N.E. coast, is the anchorage of Gourna, used by caiques in rough weather. The interior of the island is sharply undulating, reaching a height of 370 ft in the bare conical Mt Kynthos. To the s.w. is the dry gorge of the Inopos.

Delos, though the smallest of the Cyclades, was once the political and religious centre of the Aegean, with a teeming population. Birthplace of Apollo and Artemis, it boasted an oracle second only to that of Delphi and a famous temple of Apollo, raised by the common contribution of the Greek states. Today it is virtually uninhabited save by members of the French School and their staff, whose houses and offices are clustered near the ruins of the Sanctuary of Apollo. The unremitting exertions of the French School, begun in 1873 and still in progress, have revealed a complex of buildings that bear comparison with those of Delphi and Olympia. The archaeologists have unearthed the great Panhellenic Sanctuary and the area of the Sacred Lake; the maritime and commercial city, with its docks, harbours, and warehouses; and finally a town of the 3C B.C., the streets of which invite comparison with those of Pompeii. The ****Ruins** extend for nearly ¾ m.; to explore the site thoroughly more than one visit is necessary. There is a *Tourist Pavilion* (Xenia **B**) on the site with a restaurant and bar; it has only four rooms but camping is permitted.

History. *Delos* was anciently called *Ortygia*, or Quail Island. The remains of a prehistoric settlement on the top of Mt Kynthos prove that Delos was inhabited at the end of the 3rd millennium B.C. From a very early period it was a religious centre and a busy port. The Ionians who colonized the Cyclades in the 10–9C brought to Delos the cult of Leto, who here was said to have given birth to Artemis and Apollo. By the 7C the sacred island, under the protection of Naxos, became the headquarters of a league of Aegean Ionians, who held a great festival, the *Delia* (see below) in honour of Apollo, celebrated in the Homeric Hymn. The Athenians took advantage of their kinship with the Ionians to enter the league, of which they became the ruling spirit. They sent religious embassies annually to Delos (see below) and purified the sanctuary on more than one occasion. The first purification was by Peisistratos in 543 B.C. Polykrates, tyrant of Samos (d. 522 B.C.), having conquered the Cyclades, attached Rheneia to Delos with chains and dedicated the larger island to Apollo.

In 490 B.C., the Delians fled from their island to Tenos, but the Persian commander Datis, who had sent his fleet to Rheneia, left Delos inviolate. Delos was the centre of the *Delian* or *First 'Athenian' Confederacy*, the maritime league founded in 478 B.C. under the leadership of Athens, and its treasury was established in the island until its transference to Athens in 454.

In 426 the Athenians ordered a second purification of Delos. They removed to Rhenia all the coffins of the dead which were in Delos and passed a decree that thenceforward no one should die or give birth in the sacred island, and that all who were near the time of either should be carried across to Rheneia. After the purification the Athenians restored the Delian Festival, which had lapsed in the course of years (see below) and instituted the Delian Games. In 422 the Athenians banished the remaining Delians on the pretext that they were impure and unworthy of the sacred island. Later, however, at the bidding of the Delphic oracle, they let the Delians return. Athenian overseers called *Amphictiones*, administered the temple, with the nominal concurrence of the Delians. Plutarch tells us that in 417 Nikias, head of the Athenian embassy, disembarked in Rheneia and crossed to Delos in procession on a temporary wooden bridge that he had brought with him.

After the defeat of Athens at Aegospotami in 404, Delos appealed to Sparta and from 401 to 394 enjoyed a short independence until the Athenians regained possession. In 378 they instituted the *Second Athenian Confederacy*, notably different from the first, as it was purely defensive and not an instrument of imperialism. The Delians were not satisfied, as only two years later they attempted to regain control of the sanctuary, and the Athenians had to reassert their authority.

By 315 B.C. the command of the Aegean had passed to Egypt. Delos, again independent, became the centre of an island confederacy, and entered on the most prosperous period of its history. Rich offerings flowed into the sanctuary. Honours decreed to foreign benefactors attest to the variety and importance of the island's diplomatic and commercial relations. From the mass of contemporary inscriptions that have survived we may obtain a detailed picture of the temple administration and of the island economy. Delos was a democracy with an archon, a senate and an assembly. The care of the sanctuary was in the hands of four *Hieropes* elected annually, each of whom combined the office of priest and administrator.

By 250 B.C. the first Romans had settled in Delos, and Roman merchants soon predominated over other foreign immigrants. In 166 the Roman senate allowed the Athenians to reoccupy the island and in order to counterbalance the commercial power of Rhodes made Delos into a free port. The Delians were expelled, never to return and the island became a cleruchy under the control of an Athenian *Epimeletes*. The Romans, however, remained the true masters of the island. In 146 the importers of Corinth moved from their devastated city to Delos. Strabo says that the great religious festival was now in essence a trade fair on a heroic scale, and reminds us that Delos acquired the grim reputation of being the slave-market of Greece, as many as 10,000 slaves changing hands in a single day. The sanctuary continued to attract its devotees, but it was trade that filled the island coffers. An association of Italian merchants, with the backing of Rome, was formed under the title of *Hermaists*, and made itself prominent. Commercial houses and syndicates of merchants from Tyre, Beyrout, Alexandria, and elsewhere formed trade associations. The town was embellished with monuments of every kind.

In 88 B.C., during the First Mithridatic War, in which Athens had supported Mithridates and Delos repudiated Athens in favour of Rome, Menophanes, a general of Mithridates, descended on the island. He killed natives and foreigners alike, enslaved the women and children, seized the sanctuary treasure, looted the merchandise, and razed the city to the ground. Regained the following year by Sulla, Delos was returned to the Athenians and partly rebuilt with Roman aid. In 69 the island was sacked by Athenodoros. About 66 B.C. the Roman legate Triarius built a wall round the city to protect it from further piratical attacks. But its day was done. In the 2C A.D. we find Pausanias observing that, were the temple guard withdrawn, Delos would be uninhabitable. Philostratus (3C) says that the Athenians put the island up for sale but there were no offers. The emperor Julian is said to have consulted the Delian oracle. Ravaged by successive masters of the Cyclades—barbarians, pirates, Knights of St John of Jerusalem; used as a marble quarry by Venetians and Turks, and even by the inhabitants of Mykonos and Tenos; the sacred island sank into insignificance.

In the 17C Sir Kenelm Digby removed marbles from Delos for the collection of Charles I.

The Delian Festivals. Festivals called *Delia* in honour of Apollo and Artemis and their mother Leto were celebrated in Delos from remote antiquity. The Athenians took part, sending ambassadors called *Deliastae* and later *Theoroi*. The sacred vessel, called *Theoris*, in which they sailed, was said to be the one which Theseus had sent after his adventures in Crete. In the course of time the ancient festival ceased to be held, and it was not till 426 B.C. that the Athenians revived it (see above). They not only restored the *Delia* but instituted the Delian Games. Festival and games were held every four years. In virtue of their leadership of the Delian Confederacy, the Athenians took the most prominent part in the ceremonies. Though the islanders shared in providing choruses and victims for the sacrifices, the leader, *Architheoros*, was an Athenian. On arrival in the island, the embassy from Athens marched in procession to the temple, singing the *Prosodion*, the hymn recounting the story of Leto and the birth of the divine twins, and intoning chants in honour of Apollo. The procession then made a solemn tour of the sanctuary. After that, the victims were sacrificed, and the games began. The games comprised athletic sports, horse-racing, and musical contests. The *Geranos*, or sacred dance, was performed before the altar of Apollo. Proceedings ended with theatrical plays and banquets.—The *Lesser Delia* were less elaborate but an annual festival. For this the Athenians sent the Theoris every year to Delos. Before embarking, they offered sacrifice in the Delion at Marathon, to ensure a happy voyage. During the absence of the sacred vessel, the city of Athens was purified and it was forbidden to execute criminals.

Plan. The numbered references on our plan correspond with those in the definitive Guide of the French School, though not every building is described in our text.

I. HARBOUR AREA

We disembark at a mole (made of debris removed during the excavations) at a point between the Sacred Harbour (l.) and the Commercial Harbour (r.). If we have come ashore at Gourna, the rough-weather landing-place on the N.E. coast, we take a path across the island to the Sacred Harbour, past the Stadium, the Gymnasium, and the Museum. The **Sacred Harbour,** which by the 2C B.C. was also used as a commercial port, was protected on the N. by a breakwater of granite blocks, 165 yds long built in Archaic times. Most of its remains are underwater and the harbour is sanded up. From the 2C B.C. the *Commercial Harbour* extended s. for ½ m., being divided by moles into five basins. Some mooring stones are visible.

At the base of the modern mole is an open space called the **Agora of the Competialists** (Pl. 2), which divides the maritime and residential quarters to the s. (see below) from the Sanctuary to the N. The Competialists were the heads of associations of freedmen and slaves who celebrated annually the Roman festivals of the Lares Compitales, gods of the crossroads. In the centre are parts of a circular shrine, and a larger square base, both offerings of the Hermaists to Hermes and his mother Maia. They probably also built c. 150 B.C. the *Ionic Naiskos* (l.) before which stands a marble offertory box, adorned with a relief of two snakes.

We turn left into a paved road, 42 ft wide, known as the DROMOS, or *Sacred Way*. It is lined with exedrae and statue bases, notably, at its commencement (r.), that of an equestrian statue of Epigenes of Teos, a general of Attalos I of Pergamon (241–197 B.C.). On the seaward side are the remains of the **Stoa of Philip** (Pl. 3), dedicated to Apollo by Philip V of Macedon, who was master of the Cyclades until his defeat at Kynoskephalai in 197 B.C. The dedicatory inscription on the architrave is clearly seen. The stoa in grey marble, 234 ft by 36 ft, had sixteen Doric columns, fluted on the upper part only, of which one remains standing. The building was doubled on the w. some thirty years later by a stoa with twenty-five columns that faced the sea. To the right of the Sacred Way is the so-called *South Stoa* (Pl. 4), built in the 3C B.C.

A passage through this portico led into the **Agora of the Delians** (Pl. 84), which before the three stoas were built had direct access to the shore. It is bounded N. and E. by an angled 2C portico, over which is an Ionic story, and s. by another portico (3C), set obliquely. A white mosaic survives from the Imperial epoch when Roman baths were installed here.—To the s. and E. of the Agora are the ruins of houses; one of them has been called the *House of Kerdon*, from a sepulchral stele now in the Museum. Near the s.E. corner of the Agora, at a crossroads, is the *Shrine of Tritopator*, ancestor of the Attic family of Pyrrhakides. This is a little circular enclosure, with an opening to the N.W. Behind it, reached by a few steps, are the ruins of the BASILICA OF ST QUIRICUS (Pl. 86), a 5C Byzantine apsidal church.

II. THE HIERON OF APOLLO

At the end of the Dromos in a little square (r.) are a small sanctuary, and the marble *Exedra of Soteles*. Three marble steps lead up to the *South-West Propylaia* (Pl. 5), erected in the mid-2C B.C. by the Athenians to form the main entrance to the sanctuary of Apollo. It had three doorways and four Doric columns. A statue of Hermes was erected in front of its predecessor in 341 B.C. We enter the **Hieron of Apollo**, a huge precinct enclosing temples, altars, votive offerings, and remains from a thousand years of worship. Within we see on the right the *Oikos of the Naxians* (Pl. 6), a 7–6C building with a central colonnade. It replaced a Geometric structure and may take its orientation from 'Building Γ' (Pl. 7), the most ancient temple (perhaps of Mycenean date), respected throughout antiquity; the remains of this lie 6 yds E. Against the N. wall of the Oikos is the rectangular base of the colossal **Statue of Apollo** (Pl. 9), made of Naxian marble. It bears the celebrated inscription in Archaic letters (7C B.C.) "I am of the same marble, statue and pedestal"; a 4C dedication "The Naxians to Apollo"; and numerous graffiti of Venetian and 17C travellers.

The god was represented as a kouros in characteristic Archaic posture, nude, standing, with hands on thighs; he wore a metal belt. Plutarch relates that Nikias, sent in 417 B.C. from Athens in charge of the sacred embassy brought with him a bronze palm-tree among the votive offerings (the base of which survives; comp. below). A gust of wind blew over the palm-tree, which carried with it the statue of Apollo. It was then probably re-erected in the present position. Two fragments of the statue that the Venetians tried in vain to remove (part of the trunk and part of the thighs) are now behind the Temple of Artemis (see below); a hand is in the museum; part of a foot is in the British Museum.

On the right of the Sacred Way are three important temples. The first is the **'Great' Temple of Apollo** (Pl. 13), begun at the time of the foundation of the Delian Confederacy in 477 B.C. Construction languished after the transfer to Athens of the treasury in 454, and was not resumed until the 3C B.C. Erected on a high base of granite blocks, and approached by steps of Delian marble, it was a Doric hexastyle peripteral edifice (97 ft by 44 ft) having thirteen columns at the sides. The columns were fluted only at the base and at the neck of the capitals. The metopes were plain and the architrave was decorated with palm leaves and lion-mask spouts placed above each triglyph. The cella had pronaos and opisthodomos.

Adjoining is the **Temple of the Athenians** (Pl. 12), a Doric amphiprostyle building of 425–417 B.C. with six columns in front. It measures 58½ ft by 37½ ft, and had a *Prodromos* with four columns in antis. In the *Cella* were the statues, probably chryselephantine, which gave the temple its alternative name of 'House of the Seven'. They were placed on a semicircular pedestal of Eleusinian marble, the base of which has been reconstituted behind the temple. The roof sloped to a ridge presumably to accommodate the Archaic statue of Apollo, by the Naxian sculptors Tektaios and Angelion, previously in the Porinos. Fragments of the corner acroteria are now in the Museum.

The third temple, in poros and dating from the 6C, is the **Porinos Naos**

(Pl. 11) of the inscriptions. It is 51½ ft long and 32¾ ft wide. Here was originally deposited the treasure of the Delian Confederacy.

In front, on the Sacred Way, a long base bears a 3C inscription in honour of Philetairos, first King of Pergamon (280–263 B.C.). An adjacent base has a Doric frieze with roses and bullheads alternating with metopes.—The buildings arranged in an arc to the N. have been given the name of *Treasuries* on the analogy with similar structures at Olympia and Delphi. Beneath this group are remains of a Mycenean settlement.

To the w. of the Sacred Way, in a paved square, is the angled *Stoa of the Naxians* (Pl. 36). In its s.w. corner are the granite foundations, with a cylindrical hollow in the middle, of the *Bronze Palm-Tree* (see above) dedicated by Nikias. On one of the fragments (replaced) of the lower marble course of the monument can be read the name of Nikias, beginning the dedicatory inscription. Near by have been set up some courses of a column on which was a statue of Antiochus the Great (223–187 B.C.). —To the N.W. of the column are two late 6C houses (Pl. 43, 44) called the *Hieropoion* and the *Oikos of Andros*.—To the N. of the houses, near a portico, three of whose columns have been replaced, is a *Temple* (Pl. 42) preceded by a colonnade, perhaps the *Keraton* built by the Athenians. Portions of its sculptured frieze have been set up on a neighbouring wall. Close by are the foundations of an apsidal building (Pl. 39) which may have enclosed an altar.

The **Artemision** or *Sanctuary of Artemis*, farther N., is bounded by Ionic porticoes on the E. and N. To the left is a semicircular platform hewn in the rock, which seems to have been a cult object from the Late Helladic II period, perhaps the *Sema* or tomb of the two Hyperborean maidens who brought the first offerings to Apollo. The Ionic *Temple of Artemis* (Pl. 46), on a high granite base, was rebuilt c. 179 B.C. on the site of an Archaic predecessor, itself orientated to a Mycenean forerunner. Behind it are two fragments of the kouros (comp. above) abandoned here by 17C collectors. Many statues of Artemis have been found here (now in the museum), including that dedicated by Nikandra now in Athens.

To the E. and s. of the Apollo temples was an open space bounded by an Archaic building with a central colonnade, perhaps the *Bouleuterion*, and the *Prytaneion*, where a votive herm has been re-erected. Farther E. is the '**Monument of the Bulls**' (Pl. 24), a misnomer derived from its decoration. It is an oblong building, 220 ft long and 29 ft wide, of Hellenistic date and unusual design, which had a granite peribolos. The foundations, all that remains, are in gneiss and granite. A Pronaos, at the s. end, led into a long gallery with a hollow floor placed over a partitioned framework and surrounded by a pavement 18 in. above it. It probably housed a trireme dedicated after a naval victory, perhaps by Demetrios Poliorketes, and is therefore to be identified with the *Neorion* named in inscriptions. A cella at the N. end has a trapezoidal base or altar.

The Hieron is bounded on the E. by a late enceinte wall (Pl. 26), with an entrance gateway (Pl. 27) through which we may quickly reach the Museum (see below). Just outside the gate, vestiges of a small *Sanctuary of Dionysos* are characterized by several choregic monuments in the form of a huge phallus with Dionysiac reliefs on the pedestal, one erected by Karystos c. 300 B.C.

Extending westwards to form the N. boundary of the Hieron is the **Stoa of Antigonus** (Pl. 29), dedicated, according to its mutilated inscription, by a king of Macedon, son of Demetrios (supposedly, therefore, by Antigonus Gonatas). The portico, 136 yds long, has two longitudinal galleries with a salient wing at either end. On the s. side were forty-seven columns; within nineteen. The triglyphs of the frieze are decorated with bulls' heads. In the E. wing a statue of C. Billienus has been replaced on its base. In front of the stoa are two parallel lines of statue bases, including the *Base of the Progones*, on which stood some twenty statues of the ancestors, real and mythical, of Gonatas. This may have been modelled on the Monument of the Eponymous Heroes in the Agora at Athens.

Near by in a circular abaton (Pl. 32) is a Mycenean ossuary, comprising small chamber tombs, reached by a dromos, in which were found skeletons and Mycenean and earlier vases. This may be the *Theke*, where Arge and Opis, two of the Hyperborean maidens, were buried and where some curious sacrificial rites were performed (according to Herodotus) by the women of the island.—In the street outside the Hieron, behind the stoa, is the *Minoe Fountain* of the inscriptions. Farther on, adjoining the s. end of the Stoa of Antigonus, is an *Oikos* (Pl. 47) of 402–394 B.C. The gap beyond was a passage admitting to the Hieron, beyond which are some remains of the *Ekklesiasterion* (Pl. 47), several times enlarged, and of a 5C edifice comprising two hypostyle halls with a peristyle court between, doubtfully identified as the *Thesmophorion* (Pl. 48).

III. REGION OF THE SACRED LAKE

The **Agora of Theophrastos** (Pl. 49; often muddy), raised on an embankment and dating from c. 166 B.C., is named after the Epimelete Theophrastos, whose statue-base survives. Another base commemorates L. Cornelius Sulla. To the N. is the little *Sanctuary of Poseidon Nauklarios*, identified by an inscription on its 4C altar. Adjacent is a large hypostyle hall (Pl. 50), which resembles in form the Telesterion at Eleusis and has been given the name '**Stoa of Poseidon**'; it seems, however, to have been built c. 208 B.C. as an exchange or merchants' hall. The original inscription 'The Delians to Apollo' was altered in 166 B.C. to read "The Athenians to Apollo". Doric and Ionic columns, forty-four in number, supported a roof sloping to a ridge with a central lantern. The s. side comprised an open Doric colonnade.

Returning E. past the phylax's house we see the foundations of the *Dodekatheon* (Pl. 51), a small hexastyle Doric temple of the 4C B.C., dedicated to the Twelve Gods. Turning left we have (r.) the remains of a small *Temple of Leto* (Pl. 53) of the 6C, and (l.) a granite building with a double court. The ground floor was divided into small rooms, perhaps sculptors' workshops, while above was an assembly room. A ruined Doric *Propylon* leads to the **Agora of the Italians**, a huge open court, 110 yds by 75 yds, surrounded by a Doric peristyle of white marble columns on red bases with an Ionic colonnaded gallery above.

The Agora was built by Italian residents of Delos; the peristyle by individuals or trade groups known as Hermaists (see above). Begun c. 110 B.C., it was repaired after Mithridates' sack, but abandoned before 50 B.C. On the inner side is a series of cells or exedrae containing votive monuments, statues, and mosaics. Noteworthy cells on the w. side are those of *L. Orbius, O. Cluvius*, and *C. Ofellius*, the last with a fine nude statue by the Athenian sculptors Dionysios and Timarchides, now lying overturned by its base; the cell of P. Satricanius, on the N. side has a good mosaic. In a cell on the E. side was found a statue of a fighting Gaul. Outside, on the E., s., and w. sides, are lines of shops opening into the street.

The avenue leading N. is bordered on the left by the **Terrace of the Lions.** Here at least nine lions in Naxian marble of the 7C B.C. guarded the sacred area. Five remain *in situ*; at least one more, removed in the 17C, adorns the Arsenal at Venice. The lean animals are represented 'sejant', that is, sitting on their haunches with their front legs upright, and face the Sacred Lake.

The **Sacred Lake**, dry since 1926, is an oval depression surrounded by a modern wall, which represents its extent in Hellenistic times. This is the lake called 'The Hoop' (Τροχοειδής) of which Herodotus was reminded when describing the Sacred Lake of Sais in Egypt (II, 170). In it were kept the sacred swans and geese of Apollo. The marshy ground that extended to the s. before the construction of the Agora of the Italians was probably part of the domain of Leto. This lake, possibly formed by an overflow of the Inopos which, a little to the N., fell into the Bay of Skardana, was closely associated with the cult of Apollo. A palm-tree has been planted in the centre in memory of the sacred palm to which Leto clung when giving birth to Apollo (comp. *Odyssey* IV).

Beyond the Lion Terrace a street ascends to the **Institution of the Poseidoniasts of Berytos** (Pl. 57), an association of Syrian shipowners and merchants from Beirut, who worshipped Baal, a god they identified with Poseidon.

The vestibule leads into a court bounded w. by a portico into which opened four chapels. One of these, later than the others, was dedicated to the goddess Roma and contains her statue. On the E. side a colonnade leads to a peristyle court, with a cistern. To the w. of this court is another court, with a mosaic pavement, which was probably used as a meeting-place. To the s. were reception rooms and, in the basement below them, a series of shops. Statues found in this building included the 'Slipper-slapper' group of Aphrodite and Pan.

Beyond the Institution a road runs N.–S. alongside four houses bearing apotropaic symbols. To the N. the **House of the Comedians** was excavated, with the adjacent two houses, in 1964. It had an unusual peristyle of two stories, Doric and Ionic, in marble.

To the w., situated on the promontory overlooking the Bay of Skardana, is *Hill House* (Pl. 60), well-preserved but unremarkable.

Returning along the N. flank of the Institution in the direction of the Sacred Lake, we reach the **House of the Diadumenos** (Pl. 61), so called from the discovery here of a replica of the celebrated statue of Polykleitos. The house had an elaborate water-supply system. Turning E. and leaving on the left a Hellenistic altar, we next enter the *Lake House* (Pl. 64), which occupies a trapezoidal island with doors on streets to E. and w. On the other side of the farther street is the *Granite Palaestra* (Pl. 66), built partly of granite blocks some time after 166 B.C. In the middle of this building is a large cistern of four compartments, with a poros roof; it is surrounded by a Doric peristyle. To the N. was a granite colonnade.—To the E. is a granite retaining wall, between which and the city wall, is the *Well of the Maltese*, the only known well in Delos before the excavations. Adjoining is the *Lake Palaestra*, ruined when the city wall was built.

The **City Wall** (Pl. 69), called also the *Wall of Triarius*, was built by the Roman legate Triarius c. 66 B.C. to protect Delos from the attacks of the pirate Atheno-doros. It was partly built over houses and shops which were demolished and filled with rubble to form a foundation. The s. part of the wall was demolished in 1925–26. It skirted the E. side of the Sacred Lake and of the Agora of the Italians. On a bastion of the wall, a little to the s., was found a small *Prostyle Temple* (Pl. 68), with four columns, open to the E. and with an altar in front.

Hence the *Tourist Pavilion* and the *Museum* are conveniently reached.

Enthusiasts who wish to explore farther to the N.E. will come shortly to the *Archegesion* (Pl. 74), sacred to the worship of Apollo in the guise of the legendary king Anios. The latest part of the structure dates from the 6C B.C. Farther on are the square Ionic peristyle of the *Gymnasium*, and the *Stadium*, both built before the *Xystos* (covered track) was added (c. 200 B.C.) between them. Beyond the Stadium is a cluster of ancient houses and near the E. shore the remains of a *Synagogue*.

IV. THE MUSEUM

The **Museum** contains most of the finds from the island except the finest sculpture which is in Athens. In the CENTRAL HALL, kouroi and korai of the 6C; in the centre, Triangular Base, in white marble, one of its corners decorated with a ram's head, the other two with gorgon masks. This base carried a statue of Apollo by the Naxian sculptor Eutychartides (end of 7C B.C.). Archaic Sphinx from Naxos, replaced on its capital. Archaistic Bas-Relief in marble, depicting a procession of four gods.—To the left, by the wall, two marble Stelai from the Temple of Good Fortune; in each of them was set a bronze relief. The surviving one, replaced, shows Artemis, with a torch in each hand, lighting the fire on an altar; the satyrs on either side indicated a connection with the cult of Dionysos.

FIRST ROOM TO THE LEFT. In the centre, Fragments of paintings, mainly from the Stadium quarter, which decorated the houses and domestic altars. To the right, on a bench, two Heads of Gauls.—Seated statue of Dionysos; two statues of actors dressed as Silenus, one of them with a wine-skin and a tambourine; Roman portrait-statues; statue of pensive Muses and of Artemis with a hind. Sepulchral relief of a seated woman holding a leaf-shaped fan.—To the left, Fragments of corner Acroteria (Victories) and of the ridge of the Temple of the Athenians showing Boreas carrying off Orithyia and Aurora with Kephalos. Colossal Head; numerous Herms.—In front, Sepulchral Steles, including that of Kerdon, representing him falling off a ship. Two kneeling Satyrs wearing shorts made of ivy-leaves, from an altar of Dionysos. Relief of a coiled Serpent with bearded head above a platform covered with drapery; personification of the Agathodaemon. Above, Omphalos surrounded by a coiled serpent.

SECOND ROOM TO THE LEFT. In glass cases, from the left. Objects from the Sanctuary of Apollo. Figurines, terracottas and vases. The vases include examples of Corinthian, Attic, and Cycladic ware; among them, 152. Aryballos, 546. Lekythos. Numerous perfume bottles; Orientalizing Geometric vases mainly from the Sanctuary; Hellenistic vases and figurines found in various houses.—In the middle of the room are articles of furniture.

THE ROOMS TO THE RIGHT contain sculpture fragments and inscriptions.

V. THE THEATRE QUARTER AND MT KYNTHOS

From the Museum we return towards our starting point and turn s. into the **Ancient Town**. Here is the quarter where Delos is comparable with Pompeii. In sharp contrast with the spacious sanctuaries and public buildings, the crowded residential area, with twisting narrow streets, huddles behind the shore establishments on rising ground. With the increase of population it spread right up to the sanctuaries.

The **Delian House** of the Hellenistic and Roman period had its rooms grouped round a central courtyard which was reached from the street by a corridor. Richer homes had a peristyle round the court, with marble columns, and the walls plastered and painted. The court had a mosaic floor serving as an impluvium, beneath which a cistern stored rainwater. The RHODIAN PERISTYLE is also found on Delos; a large hall fronted by a taller colonnade occupied one side, and one or two stories of rooms the others.

The ROAD OF THE THEATRE, paved and drained, ascends between houses and shops giving directly on to the street. Here and there niches show that the street was lit by lamps. To the right is a house with a stove and built-in basins, probably a *Dyer's Workshop*. A small passage and

Delos

0   100 metres

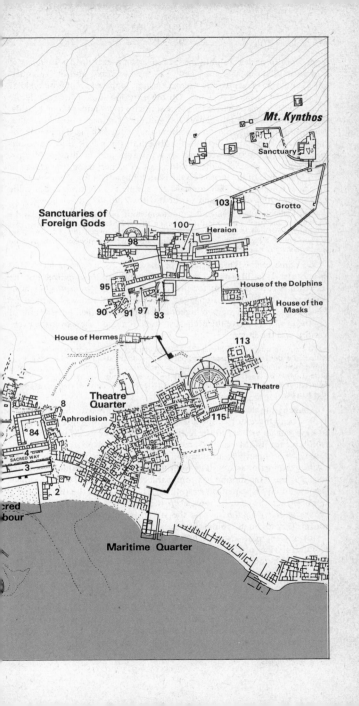

Mt. Kynthos

Sanctuary

103 Grotto

**Sanctuaries of
Foreign Gods**

100

Heraion

98

House of the Dolphins

95

House of the
Masks

90 91 97 93

House of Hermes

113

Theatre

**Theatre
Quarter**

8

Aphrodision

115

84

4
SACRED WAY

3

2

cred
bour

Maritime Quarter

steps lead up past a dolphin mosaic covering a cistern to the *House of Cleopatra*. The marble colonnade has been restored and in the court-yard stand two elegant statues representing Cleopatra and Dioscourides, the Athenian owners (2C B.C.). On the opposite side of the road is the *House of Dionysos*, where part of the staircase to an upper floor remains. In one room the rough plaster has graffiti (triremes, horseman, etc.), perhaps done by the plasterers before they added the surface layer for the painted marbling. The courtyard contains a mosaic in opus vermi-culatum of Dionysos, wreathed in ivy leaves and holding a thyrsos, mounted on a panther wreathed in vines. Farther along, the *House of the Trident*, one of the largest on the island, has a 'Rhodian' peristyle and an elegant well-head. The mosaics are simple but striking, and include an anchor with a dolphin and a trident with a ribbon tied in a bow.

Prof. Lallemand has pointed out the resemblance between this design and the trademarks on amphorae found in a sunken ship off Marseille, and suggests that the house belonged to the Delian wine-merchant who owned the ship. Another mosaic depicts a Panathenaic amphora suggesting that a member of the household had won a victory in a chariot-race.

We come to the **Theatre**, built in the early 3C B.C. to hold c. 5500 spectators. It is surrounded by a fine analemma of local marble but the theatron is ruinous except for the lower tiers. The *Orchestra* has been restored. The *Skene* had engaged Doric columns and was flanked by Paraskenia, each having two higher columns. From the highest point of the theatre, 55 ft above the orchestra, there is a fine *View over the exca-vations and the shore.

To the w. is a huge *Dexamene* (Pl. 115), or cistern, of nine compartments, which collected water from the theatre and partly supplied the town. Near by is the great foundation which supported the Altar of Dionysos, with, behind it, remains of a little *Temple of Apollo* in antis, dated by an inscription to 110–109 B.C. Two adjacent temenoi were dedicated to Artemis-Hekate (w.) and Dionysos, Hermes, and Pan (E.).

Abutting the theatre on the s.E. is a building known as the '*Hotel*' (Pl. 113). It had three stories and a large cistern, from which it is conjectured to have put up visitors to the festival. The **House of the Masks** (Pl. 112) is notable for its *Mosaic pavements with designs inspired by the cult of Dionysos or directly by the drama. It may have been used as a hostel by visiting troupes of actors. The walls were plastered and painted to repre-sent marble. One mosaic has comic and satyric masks. The best known depicts Dionysos seated on a panther. The god holds the thyrsos and a tambourine; the detail shows even the whiskers of the animal.—The *House of the Dolphins*, across the street, is named from another fine mosaic (Erotes on dolphins) signed by the artist.

An ancient path ascends **Mt Kynthos** (368 ft) which commands a wonderful view of the Cyclades. The height furnished a surname for both Apollo and Artemis, who must have been worshipped here in the 7C B.C. The site has yielded remains of Cycladic dwellings of the 3rd millennium, but it was abandoned for long periods and became an important sanctuary only in 281–267 B.C. when existing buildings were rebuilt and the peribolos constructed. On the flattened summit stood the *Sanctuary of Kynthian Zeus and Athena*; here niches for votive offerings, statue bases, and a dedicatory mosaic were found. The little distyle vestibule of 208 B.C. was replaced in 94 B.C. by a marble propylon.

Near by, on the s. summit, are the remains of a little *Sanctuary to Zeus Hypsistos*

and other gods.—To the E., on a barely accessible terrace (190 ft) has been excavated a *Sanctuary of Artemis Locheia*, with the foundations of a temple having a
doorway in the middle of the long s. side.—On the way down to the N. (traces of an
ancient road) are the ruins of several other sanctuaries.

We descend by the Sacred Way, pausing to look at the **Grotto of
Herakles** which is roofed to a peak with inclined slabs of granite in a
Cyclopean fashion reminiscent of the Sybil's Cave at Cumae, though
probably of Hellenistic date. On a platform outside stands a circular
marble altar of the Hellenistic period, while within is the pedestal that
bore a statue of the hero. Farther down is a sanctuary attributed by the
Athenians to Agatha Tyche (good fortune), in reality the *Philadelpheion*
(Pl. 103) dedicated to the cult of Arsinoë, sister and wife of Ptolemy II
Philadelphos, who was deified after her death in 270 B.C. We reach the
terrace of the Heraion.

The **Heraion** is firmly identified by the dedication to Hera of vases and
terracotta figurines found beneath the imposing marble *Altar* to the s.
The *Temple*, of the early 5C, was also of marble and had a Pronaos of
two columns in antis. It replaced a 7C edifice in poros of which foundations are visible below the later pavement.

Below to the left extend the **Sanctuaries of the Foreign Gods**, which
occupy a long terrace; the s. section is reserved for Egyptian, the N. for
Syrian divinities. Against the granite retaining wall of the Heraion
terrace is the E. portico of an enclosure having in the centre an *Avenue*
bordered by alternating little sphinxes and massive altars. To the N. is
Serapeion C (Pl. 100), the most important of the three Egyptian sanctuaries at Delos. The main entrance was on the s. side. Serapis had powers
of healing and of foretelling the future.

The paved court was bounded on the s. and partly on the w. by an angular Ionic
portico. To the N. is the little *Temple of Serapis* (first half of 2C B.C.), revealing
careful construction. We note a course of bluish marble and, behind, a poros wall
coated with stucco. To the E., on a higher level, is the marble façade of the *Temple
of Isis*. At the end of the cella is a statue of the goddess, on a rocky bench serving
as a base. In front of the temple, lower down, is a *Perfume Altar*, the upper part of
which is decorated in front with four slabs of marble in the form of horns.

From the Sanctuary Court we approach the great **Sanctuary of the
Syrian Gods** (Pl. 98), whose cult started c. 128 B.C. Here were worshipped
Adad and Atargatis, introduced from Bambyke-Hierapolis, and after
ten years regularized under an Athenian high priest. Atargatis was then
identified with Holy Aphrodite and the worst orgiastic rites of the fertility cult abandoned. The *Theatre* (400–500 spectators) in which its rites
were performed was protected from view by walls which surrounded the
precinct. This was entered by a portal with Ionic columns. Sacred fish
were kept in a tank in the sanctuary.

From the s. end of the terrace a long flight of steps descends to the bed of the
Inopos, a torrent only a few hundred yards long which even in ancient times must
have had a long dry season. It flowed from a source on Mt Kynthos past the
Sacred Lake into the Bay of Skardana, and is mentioned in the Homeric Hymn.
The Delians imagined that its waters came from the Nile, an association perhaps
endorsed by the resemblance of the local lizards to baby crocodiles. A *Reservoir*
(Pl. 97) in white marble, provided with a staircase, sluice-gates, and outlet channels,
collected the waters. Today terrapins inhabit it.

On the farther bank, s. of the reservoir, are the ruins of the **Samothra-
keion** (Pl. 93), dedicated to the Kabeiroi, built on two terraces. The
upper level bore a *Temple* of the 4C B.C. with a Doric portico, and the

lower level a circular shrine (2C B.C.) for the reception of offerings to the Chthonic divinities, together with a monument to Mithridates (120–63 B.C.) having two Ionic columns and a frieze of medallions depicting his generals and allies.

Turning N. we enter a street running between the Reservoir (l.) and a row of shops. Between two of the shops is an alley, with a bench (l.) carved with dedicatory inscriptions to Serapis, Isis, and Anubis. At the end of the alley is a staircase leading to the ruins of **Serapeion B**. The court of this sanctuary is bounded on the E. by a covered portico, under which is a rectangular crypt. The little *Temple*, placed in the N.W. corner of the court, faces S.

The street bears left in front of the *House of the Inopos* (Pl. 95). Beyond the reservoir, on our left, are the *Shrine of the Nymphs of Pyrrhakides*, a little circular building, and **Serapeion A** (Pl. 91), the oldest sanctuary of Serapis on the island. Its temple stands on a stepped basement in a paved court; under its cella is a rectangular crypt, reached by a staircase and supplied with water by a conduit. Descending the ancient road we pass the **House of Hermes** with three stories built against the hill. The colonnades of the ground and first floors have been restored. Here were found a number of Herms. Farther on is a small *Temple of Aphrodite*, built of irregular marble blocks in the 4C B.C. We pass behind it and descend to the Agora of the Competialists (Pl. 2).

VI. The Maritime Quarter

Along the seashore, s. of the landing-place, a series of *Magazines* or *Warehouses*, have their backs to the Theatre Quarter. They opened on to a quay bordering one of the four basins of the Commercial Harbour. —Continuing s., we cross the line of the City Wall (comp. above), which here ran down to the sea, and reach a second group of Magazines.

There was no communication between these warehouses and the Theatre Quarter behind them, an indication that the trade of Delos was essentially a transit trade between E. and W. Island blocks, divided by streets running parallel to the sea or at right angles to it, each had a central court surrounded by large structures used as bonded warehouses. A typical example is the *Magazine of the Columns*. The building adjoining it has a fine marble basin in a vestibule.

About ½ m. farther s. is the **Bay of Phourne**, sheltered from the N. winds by a rocky promontory on which are the ruins of a *Sanctuary of Asklepios*, with three buildings in line. The northernmost is a prostyle Doric temple with four columns, measuring c. 50 ft by c. 20 ft. Beyond it is a large hall of granite with a door on its E. side; and finally the Propylaia to the sanctuary, paved in white marble.

Rheneia, or **Greater Delos**, now uninhabited, on the w. side of the Channel of Delos, is 6 m. long and has a maximum width of c. 2½ miles. It is almost divided into two by a narrow isthmus about its middle. It has a ruined *Lazaret* for ships in quarantine bound for Syros, with an anchorage facing Delos (25 min. by caique). That part of the shore which faces the Rhevmataria islets (10 min. from the Sacred Harbour) was reserved as a birthplace for pregnant, and as a necropolis for dying Delians expelled from their island by the Athenians. Rheneia was the landfall of Nikias in 417 B.C., when he crossed in state to Delos on the bridge that he had brought with him. The island town was on the w. coast, facing Syros.

In the area for expectant and dying Delians is a series of tombs, circular sepulchral altars and sarcophagi with holes for the insertion of steles, and numerous ruined little houses, probably for the reception of the evicted people.

In the village of *Herakleion* a sanctuary was discovered, with a well and a portico. —Opposite Great Rhevmataria, on the seashore below the chapel of *Ayia Kiriaki*, is the **Necropolis**, discovered in 1898, in which the Athenians during the purification of 426 B.C., placed the coffins exhumed from Delos. This is a walled enclosure

c. 70 yds' square, divided into small rectangular sections. It contained a mass of human bones and vase fragments of every period down to the 5C.—A little to the s., in the small bay of *Porto Generale*, is a curious Greek columbarium. This is a rectangular vault, reached by a staircase, and containing on either side two tiers of niches for coffins, closed by stone slabs.

72   WESTERN CYCLADES

Despite its proximity to Attica, this is the least visited group of the Aegean islands.

A Kea

STEAMER daily but at varying times and places: 5 days a week from *Lavrion* (comp. Rte 17) in 2 hrs, the remaining days from *Rafina* (Rte 22).

KEA, the ancient Keos, locally known as *Tziá* (1680 inhab.), is the nearest of the Cyclades to Attica, being only 13 m. from Cape Sounion and 40 m. from Piraeus. Oval in shape, 12 m. long from N. to s. and 6 m. wide, the island which has a hilly interior rises to 1862 ft. It is well watered (hence its early name of *Hydroussa*) and has always been one of the most fertile of the Cyclades (comp. Virgil, 'Georgics', I, 14). The eparchy of Kea includes the islands of Kithnos, Serifos, and Makrónisos.

History. At an early date *Keos* was populated by Ionians. Kean ships fought on the Greek side at Artemision and Salamis (Hdt. VIII, 1, 46). The island had four cities: Ioulis, with its port Koressia, Karthaia, and Poiëessa. Ioulis was the birthplace of the lyric poets Simonides (556–468) and Bacchylides (481–431), of the sophist Prodikos, of the physician Erasistratos, and of the peripatetic philosopher Ariston. The Keans, unlike the Chians, were noted for their modesty and sobriety: hence the adage οὐ Χῖος ἀλλὰ Κεῖος (Aristophanes, Ran. 970).

Landing is made at Livádhi (*I Tziá mas* B; *Karthea* C), officially *Korissía*, pleasantly situated amid trees on the bay of Ayios Nikolaos in the N.W. of the island. Ancient *Koressia* occupied a site a little to the w., with a temple of Apollo Sminthios, from which the kouros in the National Museum was recovered in 1930. About 1 m. E. round the bay is *Vourkári*, a fishing hamlet which attracts summer visitors. On the near-by promontory of Ayia Irini excavations by the Univ. of Cincinnati under John Caskey since 1960 have proved occupation as early as Early Helladic II, and uncovered a large walled settlement of the Bronze Age. Its deposits of imported and Cycladic pottery are helping to clarify the temporal interrelationship of Cycladic, Minoan, and Mycenean styles; with its central position, Keos experienced all three influences. A 'Palace' of the Late Minoan II period has been explored. A large *Temple* of the Middle Bronze Age, several times rebuilt, with an adjacent roadway may both have continued in use beyond the end of the Mycenean era. Inscribed letters of Linear A script and potters' marks of the Phylakope type have been found, also an incised representation of a warrior (apparently Mycenean).

An earth road continues N.E. to the delightful bay of (3 m.). *Otziás*, then turns E. to (6¼ m.) the monastery of *Panayia Kastriani* (18C; accommodation).

A road (bus) climbs to the depopulated town of Khora (*Ioulis* B), the island capital with 690 inhab., on a hill (1145 ft) once occupied by the ancient city of *Ioulis*. The Kastro of Domenico Michelli (1210), demolished in 1865, incorporated material from a Temple of Apollo situated on its acropolis. A small *Museum* displays fragments from past ages. About 15 min. E. of the town is a colossal *Lion* carved out of the rock, 20 ft long and 9 ft high—a rude but vigorous piece of sculpture.

The extensive ruins of ancient *Poiëessa* (Ποιήεσσα) on the w. coast may be reached in c. 2 hrs from Khóra, viâ *Astra* and *Káto Meriá*. The bays of Písses and *Koundouros* (Kea Beach, DPO, **B**), to the s., afford good bathing. The return may be made viâ the ruined monastery of *Ayía Marína*, built round a Hellenic *Tower, probably the finest of its kind in Greece. It is c. 25 ft square, and built of rectangular blocks of schist, admirably joined without mortar. There are three stories supported by stone joists.

On the opposite coast, c. 1½ hr s.e. of Káto Meriá is *Póles*, where the ruins of ancient *Karthaia* include a Doric Temple of Apollo and two other buildings, one of them conjectured to have been the choragic school of Simonides. Considerable remains of the enceinte wall can be traced.

B   From Piraeus to Milos

STEAMER, daily, calling at *Kithnos*, *Serifos*, *Sifnos*, and *Kimolos*. Serifos and Sifnos are served by every boat, Kithnos and Kimolos less frequently. Sifnos and Milos have a weekly connection to Santorini (comp. Rte 73); and Kithnos once weekly has connection with Syros.

KITHNOS (ΚΥΘΝΟΣ), separated from Keos by a strait 5 m. wide, owes its alternative name *Thermia* to its hot springs. A low-lying island with an area of 29 sq. m., it has a steadily declining population. Since 1940, when the iron mines went bankrupt, the Thermiots (1590 inhab.), all but a handful of whom are divided between two villages, have made a precarious living by farming, fishing, and latterly fruit-growing.

Kythnos supplied two ships to the Greek fleet at Salamis. It was a member of the Delian Confederacy and became tributary to Athens. After the death of Nero in A.D. 68, an imposter claiming to be the emperor was driven ashore at Kythnos in a storm; he was seized and put to death by Calpurnius Asprenas, the proconsul of Galba. Pliny notes that the island produced excellent cheese; it still does, other products being barley, wine, figs, and almonds.

According to the weather the boat puts in at Loutrá on the N.E. coast or at Mérikhas on the w. The tiny harbour of Loutrá (*Anayénnisis* C, June–Oct) has warm iron-bearing springs which cover the ground with a reddish deposit. The Turks used them for bathing and King Otho built a *Hydro* for invalid visitors. One spring (37° C.) is used for drinking; another is hot (52°). The waters are used in the cure of eczema, gout, sciatica, and nervous complaints.—On Cape Kephalos (505 ft), the N.E. point of the island (45 min. walk), stands the *Kastro tou Kataképhalou*, the medieval citadel, abandoned c. 1650; the ruins include towers, monasteries, and the Byzantine church of Our Lady of Compassion with wall-paintings.—The site of ancient Kythnos has been located at *Rigókastro* in the N.W. of the island.

A road leads from Loutrá to (2½ m.) **Kíthnos** (Inn), known also as *Messariá* or just *Khora*, the little capital (740 inhab.), where several churches have ikons by Skordili (c. 1700). *Ayía Saba* (1613) bears the arms of Ant. Gozzadini, a descendant of the Italian medieval governors. The road continues s. to (5¼ m.) *Síllaka*, officially Dhriopís (ΔΡΥΟΠΙΣ), the other village (790 inhab.) and former capital. Near by is Katafíki, the best known of the island's many caves.—A longer return (8½ m.) may be made to Khora viâ the hamlets of *Mérikhas* (Poseidonion C) and *Episkopí*, each on a sheltered inlet of the w. coast.

On a headland of the s.e. coast (1 hr by mule from Dhriopis) stands the *Panayia tin Kanála*, a monstery with a holy ikon of St Luke.

SERIFOS (ΣΕΡΙΦΟΣ), a small rocky island (25 sq. m.), with 1080 inhab., lies almost equidistant between Kithnos and Sifnos and c. 8 m. from either. Lighters land passengers at *Livádhi*, the hot little land-locked harbour from which the road rises through market gardens to (1 m.) **Khora** (490 inhab.), a white village built precipitously on a com-manding spur. Accommodation must be found in private houses. *Psilí Ammos*, 20 min. walk to the N.E., is the best sandy beach.—A road runs w. across the island to (4 m.) *Megálo Khorió*, said to be the site of ancient *Seriphos*; in 1880–1912 it was the centre of a mining district, with outlets to the sea at *Megálo Livádhi* (Perseus **B**, open June–Sept) and Koutalá on the s.w. coast. A little iron ore is still shipped.

On ancient Seriphos Perseus and Danaë were washed ashore, and here later Perseus turned King Polydeuces to stone with Medusa's head. The Roman emperors used the island as a place of exile for political prisoners.

A path from Khora leads N.E. in 1 hr to *Kallítsos*, a pretty village, and (15 min. more) to *Moní Taxiarkhón*, an interesting building of late medieval date. The return can be made in 1 hr viâ *Galaní*, farther w.—*Panayía*, to the N.W. of Khora, is called after its 10C church.

SIFNOS (ΣΙΦΝΟΣ), lying S.E. of Sérifos, is a fertile island with a delightful climate and an abundance of excellent water. The interior is mountainous, rising to 2936 ft in Mt Profítis Ilías. In the time of Herodotus it was famous for its gold-mines, which gave out in classical times. The deceitfulness and greed of the islanders had become a byword, and Pausanias tells a characteristic tale about the destruction of the mines by Apollo after the Siphniacs had offered a gilt egg at Delphi in place of their customary gold one. The island is distinguished by the remains of nearly forty towers of the classical period and dotted with monasteries which afford shelter for the night. New hotels are in construction.

The ship anchors between high cliffs in the *Bay of Kamáres* on the less attractive w. coast and passengers are taken off by motor-boat. On the slopes above are two monasteries. A bus ascends under the steep cliffs of Profítis Ilías to (3 m.) **Apollonía** (*Apollonía*, open all year, small, B; Rest. *Kentron*), the island capital (880 inhab.). Its flat-roofed white houses rise in an amphitheatre on three terraced hills. In Stavrí, the principal quarter, are the library and the cultural centre built in 1961. In the N. quarter of Péra Geitoniá are the house of Kleanthis Triandaphillou-Rabaga (1849–89), the poet, and the church of Panayia Yeraniofóra, where the external figure of St George was restored in 1767. The frescoed church of the Sotiros has a carved wooden ikonostasis.—About 1 m. to the N. is *Artemón* (815 inhab.; Artemon, Apr–Oct, C), the only other sizeable village; hence the N. part of the island may be explored by mule path.

To the S. of Apollonía paths lead past Ay. Andréas, where a L.H. IIIB and Geometric settlement has been dug since 1969, to Vathí on the S.W. coast, better reached by boat.—A road runs S.E. viâ *Exámbela* (1½ m.) to *Platí Yialós* (Hotel, June–Sept, DPO, B), on a sandy bay at the S. end of the island. Nearer to Exambela (path) is *Fáros*, another bathing place.

Below Apollonia to the E. lies the hamlet of *Káto Petáli*, whence a path descends towards the E. coast. On the way is the nunnery of *Khrisostómou*, built in 1550; it was adorned by the Bavarians and used as a school in 1834–44.—25 min. *Kastro*, a delightful but decaying medieval village on the E. coast, occupies the site of **Ancient Siphnos**. Part of the 14C wall built by the Venetian Corogna family survives and there are many old churches. One on the hill may mark the site of a Temple of the 7C B.C., the votive deposit of which has been unearthed. Beneath the ruins of the Venetian fortress are houses of the Geometric period, and a section of marble walling of the 4C B.C. was discovered by the British School.

KIMOLOS (ΚΙΜΩΛΟΣ), an island barely 5 m. across with 1090 inhab., lies between Sífnos and Mílos, from which it is separated by a strait only ½ m. wide. Pliny says that it was once called *Echinousa*, from echinus, a sea-urchin; it owed its Italian name, *Argentiera*, to the silver mines formerly worked here. The island has long been noted for its Fullers' earth, used in the preparation of cloth and in barbers' shops in Athens (Aristophanes, *Ran.*, 713). Kímolos was incorporated by Marco

Sanudi into the duchy of Naxos; it later became a notorious pirates' nest. Its olive trees were felled by the Venetians during the Turkish wars and it is now barren, but given colour by the variety of its rocks.

Kímolos, the only village, crowns a hill ½ m. from *Psáthi*, its harbour, which is on the S.E. coast (landing by lighter). The little houses open on to an inner court. The church of the *Evanghelistria* dates from 1614. *Prássa*, 15 min. N. by boat, has radio-active springs. On the W. coast *Palaiókastro*, on a steep rock 1300 ft high, has remains of strong fortifications.—Excavations in 1937 on the islet of *Ayios Andréas*, off the S.W. shore, revealed remains of an ancient settlement which, with its *Necropolis* (on the mainland opposite) lasted from Mycenean to early-Christian times.
    The barely inhabited islet of *Políaigos* lies off to the S.E. extremity of Kímolos.

MILOS (ΜΗΛΟΣ), or *Melos*, the S.W. outpost of the Cyclades, with 4500 inhab., is divided almost in two by an arm of the sea forming a spacious natural harbour, the entrance to which is on the N. The coast is much indented. The island has an area of 59 sq. m. and is roughly 13 m. long by 8 m. wide. Mt Profítis Ilias (2465 ft) rises to the S.W. of the harbour, but the rest of the island is arid low hills, much gashed by mines and quarries. The volcanic nature of the soil is expressed in the hot springs, the mines of sulphur and alum, and the obsidian that gave the island its importance in prehistoric times. Bensonite, barium, perlite, and kaolin are also mined. Melos early yielded information about the Cycladic civilization, the site of Phylakope having been especially prolific. From the island came the celebrated Vénus de Milo, now in the Louvre, Paris. The eparchy of Mílos includes the islands of Sifnos, Kimolos, Sikinos, and Folegandros. Outside Adamas rooms and meals are difficult to find and transport scanty, but the recent start of a daily air service from Athens presages change.

History. *Melos* was a centre of the Bronze Age civilization that flourished in the Cyclades contemporaneously with, and at first independently of, the Minoan civilization of Crete. Before the end of the Middle Cycladic Period (c. 1600 B.C.) Melos, with the rest of the Cyclades, seems to have been absorbed in the Cretan empire associated with King Minos. When the sceptre passed from Knossos to Mycenae, the Cretan colonial possessions passed also. After the Dorian invasion (c. 1100 B.C.) Melos was colonized by Dorian Lacedaemonians. In the Peloponnesian War it declared itself neutral, but, provoked by Athens, it inclined towards Sparta. Athens, having command of the sea, determined to coerce the Melians into submission (416 B.C.). Before taking action, the Athenians sent envoys to Melos. Thucydides has preserved in his 'Melian dialogue' (V, 85–111) the gist of the speeches made on either side. The Melians declined the Athenian terms and the Athenians besieged their city. After several months the Melians surrendered unconditionally. The Athenians killed all the males of military age, enslaved the women and children, and repopulated the island with 500 Athenian colonists. In the middle ages the island was under the Franks. During the Turkish domination (here very lightly felt) and afterwards, the Melians acquired and kept a reputation for intrepid seamanship which they still enjoy. Here in 1628 Sir Kenelm Digby began his memoirs. From Melos in the 1680s a party under Abp Georgirenes migrated to London where they built the first Greek church there on a site assigned to them by James, duke of York. The memory of this survives in 'Greek St.', Soho. During the First World War the island harbour was an Allied naval base.

The port of Mílos is *Adámas* (Venus Village, Adamas, **B**; Corali **C**, and others), founded on the E. side of the harbour by Cretan refugees fleeing Turkish reprisals (1912). Their ikons can be seen in the small church of Ayía Triádha. Both this and a larger church at the top of the town have pebble mosaics. On the shore to the W. of the town stands a small monument to French soldiers and sailors who died on Milos in 1897.

A winding road ascends N.W. to (2¼ m.) **Plaka,** officially *Mílos* (850 inhab.), the island capital with a 10C church and two small museums. Below the town is a stadium (1971), built to serve the needs of all the Cyclades. Above rises the *Kastro* (920 ft) whose Frankish remains enclose the 13C church of Thalassítras. The view is of surprising clarity and brilliance. The hill on which Plaka stands was probably the Acropolis of the ANCIENT CITY, which extended mainly s. towards the modern hamlet of Klima lying on the shore at the foot of a steep valley below the village of Tripití. The site was excavated by the British School in 1896–99; a kouros and some important Archaic vases are in the National Museum at Athens. On the slopes of this valley (easily accessible by road) survive tracts of *City Wall*, in particular a well-preserved polygonal section adjoining a round bastion of regular Hellenic masonry close to the site where the Venus was discovered; the Roman *Theatre*, excavated in 1917 and now somewhat restored; and an early Christian *Baptistery*. Across to the s.e. are extensive early Christian *Catacombs*, discreetly lit (adm. 25 dr.). The long narrow entrance leads into a low-pitched room, beyond which run tunnels, lined with tombs, some of which show remains of frescoes.

A road leads E. to follow the N. coast to (4½ m.; beside the road, l.) the remains of ancient **Phylakope**, or *Phlakopí*, excavated by the British School in 1896–99. The remains of three successive prehistoric cities have been uncovered. The *First City* dates from the Early Cycladic Period. The *Second City*, built during the Middle Cycladic Period, had houses decorated with frescoes, including the noted Flying Fish fresco. The *Third City*, showing Mycenean influence had an enceinte wall round its palace. During renewed work in 1974–77 a Mycenean shrine (L.H. IIIA–c) yielded a terracotta female figure possibly of mainland manufacture. A Linear A tablet was found in the context of both Minoan and Mycenean sherds, and the site remains a key one in Cycladic prehistory. Interesting also are the natural hexagonal basalt pillars, originating from the Glaronisia (see below).—The road continues to (6 m.) *Pollónia*, a fishing village facing the island of Kimolos.

To the N.W. (boat from Pollonia) are the curious volcanic islets known as the *Glaronisia* (Gull Is.). They have remarkable caves and crystalline rocks.

From Adámas a road runs s.e. along the shore. After 2 m. a by-road branches left past the electricity works to Palaiokhori (1 m.), site of ancient *Zephyria*, occupied from the 8C to 1793, when the survivors of an epidemic moved to the Plaka area. The by-road continues to (2½ m. more) an excellent beach, backed by multicoloured rocks.—Immediately beyond the fork, small rings of bubbles can be seen a few yards out to sea. These mark the eruption of hot springs. The road passes salt-pans, then continues viâ Provatá to the monastery of Ayia Marina on the slopes of Mt Profitis Ilias. Beyond here the road serves mines and quarries in the s. and w. of the island.

To the N.W. of Milos is the uninhabited island of *Andímilos*, kept as a reserve for a rare species of chamois.

73 SOUTHERN CYCLADES AND SOUTHERN SPORADES

STEAMER, direct or viâ Syros, 2–3 times daily to *Paros* and *Naxos*, continuing at least once daily to *Ios* and *Santorin*, and returning in reverse order. Twice weekly the boat calls at *Sikinos* and *Folégandhros*, and once weekly at *Anáfi*. Santorin can also be reached once a week from Milos by a boat that continues to Rhodes and Crete, and once weekly from Paros on the way to Herakleion. Amorgos, the most easterly of the S. Sporades included in the nome of the Cyclades is served by steamers to the Dodecanese and is described with them; comp. Rte 75.

PAROS (ΠΑΡΟΣ), one of the most attractive of the Cyclades, with

6800 inhab., has an area of 64 sq. m. and is oval in shape. The interior is almost entirely taken up by *Mt Profitis Ilias* (2530 ft), on the slopes of which are the famous marble quarries. The mountain slopes evenly down to the maritime plain which surrounds it on every side. Barley and wheat are grown and the red wine is full and palatable, but there are few trees. Sheep, oxen, goats, and asses are numerous. Paros was the birthplace of the lyric poet Archilochos (fl. 714–676 B.C.), inventor of Iambic verse. The island had a bishop before 431; the present joint see with Naxos dates from 1683.

History. *Paros* was colonized by Ionians. In the 7C it sent a colony to Thasos, the poet Archilochos accompanying the expedition (comp. Rte 67). In 490 B.C. Paros sent a trireme with the Persian fleet. After Marathon Miltiades led a retaliatory expedition against the island but failed to take it, receiving an injury that, becoming gangrenous, proved fatal (Hdt. vi, 133). After the defeat of Xerxes, in 480, Paros became subject to Athens.

In the middle ages Paros formed part of the duchy of Naxos until 1389. In 1537 it passed to the Turks, who held it until the War of Greek Independence. In the early 17C the 'Parian Chronicle' was discovered in the island by Wm. Petty, chaplain to the Earl of Arundel. This is a chronological account of the principal events in Greek history (biased on the side of art rather than politics), from Kekrops (traditional date 1582 B.C.) to the archonship of Diognetos (264 B.C.). The greater part of this inscription is in the Ashmolean Museum at Oxford. Hugues Creveliers, the original of Byron's 'Corsair' operated from Paros in the 1670s (he was eventually blown up in his flagship by an offended servant). The Russian fleet spent the winter of 1770–71 at Paros.—Excavations on the island have been the care of the German School.

Backed by distant hills beyond the coastal plain **Paroikía** (*Xenia*, DPO, **B**; *Paros* C, both Apr–Oct; *Kontes, Oasis*, open all year, **D**), or *Paros*, the capital (1950 inhab.), lies on the w. coast. The town extends along the shore in a restful horizontal fashion, the line of its white flat-roofed houses broken only by the blue domes of churches. The ship moors alongside a small mole.

The **Panayia 'Ekatontapiliani'**, traditionally the cathedral church of Our Lady 'with a hundred doors', a corruption probably of *Katapoliani* ('below the town'), was greatly altered externally, some may think not for the better, by its restoration in 1960–63 under Prof. Orlandos from Venetian Baroque to a primitive Byzantine style. The church had needed attention since the earthquake of 1733. Said to have been founded by St Helena, mother of Constantine, while she was on her way to the Holy Land in search of the True Cross, it occupies the site of a secular Roman edifice of c. 300 (mosaics of the Labours of Hercules). Altered in the 10C after an earthquake, it has the form of a Greek cross, sombre and impressive, with an unusual triforium and a dome borne on pendentives. The apse is flanked by 'parekklisia', of which one at any rate antedates the main building, for *Ayios Nikolaos* (l.) dates at least from the time of Justinian I; it has Doric column shafts and a marble ikonostasis of 1611. The *Baptistery*, off the s. transept, has a sunken immersion font, cruciform in plan.—In the *Archaeological Museum* (near the Gymnasion) are a winged victory of the school of Skopas, an inscription relating to Archilochos, and part of the 'Parian Chronicle'.

The narrow main street, or the parallel shore promenade, leads to a hillock, crowned by the ruined Venetian *Castle* built in 1260 with material from a Temple of Demeter. The temple site is occupied by the church of *Ayiou Konstandinou*. Near the school a bust commemorates Panayiotis Kallierou (1861–1937), the Pestalozzi of Greece, who taught here for 30 years. Farther on, the hill of Ayia Anna, with windmills, affords a pleasant sea view.

To the s. of Paroikia, just beyond the Xenia hotel, are a *Grotto of the Nymphs* and, on the terrace of a small hill (l.), some remains of an *Asklepieion*. Farther s. are the site of the *Pytheion* and the *Moni Khristos Dhasous*, attractively surrounded by trees. The road, not very interesting, continues with views of Andíparos to the villages at the s. end of the island. Near (6 m.) *Piskopianá* the Grávari estate is known as *Petaloudhes* from the migratory butterflies seen there (comp. Rhodes).

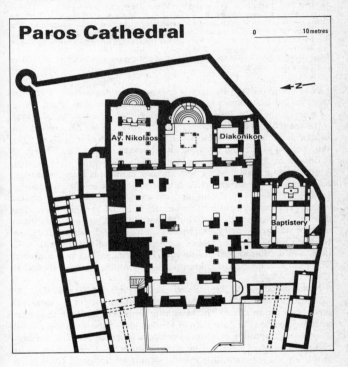

Paros Cathedral

0   10 metres

Ay. Nikolaos

Diakonikon

Baptistery

To Náoussa, 6½ m. (10½ km.), motor-bus. The road leads N.E. past the park. At 1¼ m. Track (r.; 2 m.) to the *Monasteri Zoodokhos Piyi Longobárdas* (women not admitted) with a library and wall-paintitgs. At the next fork we bear left and cross the little Helytas, c. 200 yds beyond which we see (l.) the excavated remains of a 7C basilican church on the site of the *Heroon of Archilochos* (4C B.C.). There are vestiges of a *Sanctuary of Delian Apollo* on the hill called Kastro to our left. The road passes small churches to right and left in a pleasant valley between rolling green hills.—6½ m. *Náoussa* (Naoussa B, Hippokambos C, both Apr–Oct; tavernas), a pretty fishing village with 1150 inhab., has a small caique harbour, interesting churches, and a half-submerged Venetian fortress. Remains of an early Geometric fortified site lie on Oikonomos headland to the E.

To reach the famous **Parian Marble Quarries**, we take the Naoussa road and fork right beyond the park up the Helytas valley. On the other side of the valley (l.) rises Profitis Ilias with a Cave of Eileithyia and a sanctuary of Aphrodite. We continue to (3 m.) *Maráthi*. The quarries lie near the deserted monastery of Ayios Minas. The numerous excavations are underground. The largest is 100 yds long and nearly 30 ft wide with a chamber on either side of the central passage. The marks of the wedges used by the ancient quarrymen are visible everywhere; also to be seen is a sculptured tablet. The quarries had lain idle for centuries until 1844 when marble was required for the tomb of Napoleon. The road goes on to (10½ m.) *Marpissa* (Marpissa, May–Sept, B).

The 540 inhab. of **Andiparos** (ΑΝΤΙΠΑΡΟΣ) are served by a daily mail boat from Paroikia (1½ hr). The island, now separated from Paros by the 'Fourteen-foot Channel', was joined to it in prehistoric times. Its ancient name was *Oliaros*. The principal attraction is the stalactite *Cavern* at the s. end of the island (excursions in summer from Paroikia). The Anaryiros Hotel (**D**) opens July–Sept.

In 1964–65 excavations by the British School on the islet of *Saliagos* (between Paros and Andiparos) uncovered a Neolithic site, the first to be excavated in the Cyclades. Stone building foundations, obsidian arrow-heads, a 'fiddle' idol, and a marble figurine of a fertility cult were found, the relics of a sheep-farming people of the 4th millennium B.C.—On *Dhespotikó*, an islet to the w. of Andiparos, the *Prepesinthos* of ancient times, early Cycladic cist-graves were explored in 1960 by the Greek Archaeological Service.

NAXOS (ΝΑΞΟΣ), the largest and most beautiful of the Cyclades, made an indelible impression on the youthful Byron. The island, 18 m. long and 12 m. wide, forms a complete eparchy. The interior of Naxos is traversed by a mountain range, rising to 3295 ft in Mt Zévs, or Ziá, the highest summit in the Cyclades. Other peaks are Kóronos (3280 ft) in the N. of the island, and Fanári (3050 ft) between it and Zia. The island is divided by fertile and well-watered valleys. Groves of olive, orange, lemon, pomegranate, and fig trees abound, bamboo is grown, and fruit, oil, corn, and wine are exported. Naxian white wine enjoys considerable repute, the honey is excellent, and the cheeses varied. Citron, a local liqueur, is distilled from lemons. Emery is found in abundance. The marble of Naxos, scarcely inferior to that of Paros, was anciently much used for statuary. The 14,200 inhabitants are Orthodox except for a few Roman Catholic descendants of medieval Venetian settlers, who have their own archbishop (of Naxos-with-Tinos) as well as two convents. There are a number of little-known small Byzantine churches (see AJA, 1968).

Naxos (*Ariadne* **B**; *Apollon, Hermes, Koronis* **C**; *Okeanis* **D**), the *Khora*, with 2900 inhab., perpetuates the site of the ancient and medieval capitals on the w. coast. The Mycenean settlement has been shown by recent excavations to have been at Grotta, just to the N. Not the most immediately appealing of island towns, partly on account of its claustrophobic labyrinth of lanes, narrow, steep, and enclosed, partly because its people are less spontaneously friendly than is general in the Cyclades, it has so far avoided the excesses of tourism.

History. *Naxos* is perhaps best known in myth as the place where Theseus deserted Ariadne on his way back to Athens from Crete, a story celebrated in one of the most accomplished poems of Catullus and an opera by Richard Strauss. Herodotus says that the Naxians were Ionians of Athenian stock. In 501 B.C. Naxian exiles, living in Miletus, enlisted Persian aid against the island's ruler. The failure of the Persian expedition precipitated the Ionian revolt (Hdt. v, 30). The Persians sacked the island in 490. The Naxiots sent four ships to join the Greek fleet at Salamis, and in 471 were the first of the allied states to come under the dominion of Athens. At the battle of Naxos in 376 B.C. the Athenians routed a Lacedaemonian fleet. In 1207 Naxos was seized by Marco Sanudi, who founded a Venetian duchy. Breaking with Venice, he put himself under the protection of Henry of Flanders, the Latin emperor, and was rewarded in 1210 with the titles of Duke of the Archipelago and Sovereign of the Dodecanese, making him feudal superior of the other Aegean barons. His house, and the succeeding dynasty of the Crispi, ruled over much of the Cyclades for 360 years. The island was ravaged by the Turkish corsair Amur in 1344. Naxos fell to the Turks in 1566 but became a seat of Greek learning. In 1770–74 it was occupied by the Russians.

On the quay is a statue, erected in 1963, of Petros Protopapadakis (1858–1922), the politician, a native of Apíranthos. A causeway crosses to the islet of *Palatia* where the huge doorway of the *Temple of Apollo* stands on a partially restored stylobate amid remnants of shattered columns. The temple may date from the days of Lygdamis, tyrant c. 530 B.C. The harbour mole, rebuilt by Marco Sanudi, corresponds with an ancient breakwater.

The walls of the town have mostly disappeared. From the little square, lanes climb to the outer enceinte of the **Kastro**, within which are picturesque but decayed houses of Venetian character, many bearing coats of arms. The *Panayia Theoskepastos* preserves a remarkable 14C ikon of the Crucifixion. The Latin *Cathedral*, founded in the 13C, is paved with heraldic tombstones, many still claiming pretentious titles centuries after the Duchy of the Archipelago had fallen to the Turks. Near by are the French Ursuline convent and a house, at one time a school at which Nikos Khatzandakis was a pupil for 2 years, now the *Museum*. It contains Cycladic idols and bead jewellery; Mycenean pottery, including fragments of a large pithos decorated in relief with chariots and riders (note the Homeric figure-of-eight shields), from sites within the town, from tombs on Aplómata and from Kamini and Koufonisi; small Classical torsos and sculptures, fragmentary kouroi from Sangri, and a Roman mosaic.

Excursions. To ENKARES (5 m.). Just outside the town to the N. rises the hill of *Aplómata*, with Mycenean chamber-tombs (on the very edge of the cliff) and a memorial to a local resistance hero of 1944. Here was the ancient fort of *Delion*, where occurred the events in the Naxo-Milesian war, related by Plutarch. We pass a Turkish fountain erected by Ishmael Kasan Aga in 1759. The *Moní Khrisostómou*, above, was built about the same time by Bp. Anthimou. We turn inland to (5 m.) *Mitriá* in the fruit-growing Enkarés valley, whence in 1½ hr we may reach the *Faneromeni*, a monastery (1606) farther along the coast to the N. From Mitriá a track runs N.E. to Komianí (see below).

To APIRANTHOS, 17½ m. (28 km.). The main road of the island leads S.E. across the fertile plain of *Livadion*. At 1¼ m. we leave on our left a road to *Mélanes* (5¼ m.) and the quarries of *Flerio* (7½ m.) where two unfinished Kouroi of the 7C lie abandoned.—3 m. *Galanádon*. To the right of the road is a cluster of villages, of which *Trípodes* is the most important. An hour's walk from it towards the sea are towers of various periods.—5 m. We reach a col, from which a mule-path descends (l.) to *Ayios Mámas* (8C), once the cathedral of Naxos.—6¾ m. *Sangrí*, which we leave on our right, has many relics of the middle ages in its vicinity (towers, churches, monasteries), together with the site of ancient *Aulonos*, where a temple of Demeter and Kore has been superseded by a Byzantine church. We enter the olive-growing plain of *Tragaías*, of which **Khalkí** is the principal village in a group. Its Byzantine churches have wall-paintings; of the Venetian tower-houses the Pirgos Frangopoulou is the most striking; and above stands Epano Kastro, built by Marco Sanudi II (1244–63). At *Tsikkalarió*, just below, there is a Geometric site.—12 m. *Filóti* (Inn), the island's largest village (1475 inhab.), a former Frankish fief, stands on the N. flank of Zia (3290 ft), the highest point of the Cyclades.—17½ m. **Apíranthos** (ΑΠΥ-ΡΑΝΘΟΣ; inn, post office), called locally *Aperáthou*, a decaying village (950 inhab.), was rebuilt by the Sommaripa and Crispi in the 14C on an ancient site.

From Khalki a bus serves the villages in the N. of the island, notably (8 m.) *Koronís* (690 inhab.) centre for the rich emery quarries (to the E.), which are linked by aerial ropeway with a bay on the E. coast; and (13 m.) *Komiaki*, a pretty village, from which the bus goes on to (13 m.) *Apóllona*, on the N.E. coast. Here there is a colossal *Kouros, broken and unfinished; it is, however, more easily approachable by sea from *Ayios Ioannis*, a fishing hamlet with a pleasant beach.

The Hellenistic *Tower of Kheimárrou* in the S.E. (due S. of Zevs) can be reached in 3½ hrs on foot from Filoti. It stands to 45 courses of masonry.

The four islets to the E. and S.E. of Naxos (but in the eparchy of Thera) are served by mail boat once a week. *Donoussa*, or Denoussa, has a Geometric fortified settlement explored in 1969–72. In a bay off the island on 9–10 Aug 1914 S.M.S. 'Goeben' and 'Breslau' coaled during their successful flight to Constantinople.

IOS or **Nio** (46 sq. m.), lying E. of Sikinos (see below) and between Paros (N.) and Santorin (S.), belongs to the eparchy of Thera. As the name implies, this beautiful little island was Ionian. An apochryphal Life of Homer relates that, during a voyage from Samos to Athens, the poet was driven ashore on Ios, died there and was buried on the seashore. Ios was a fief of the Venetian Pisani, but was captured by the Turks in 1537. The hilly interior has twin peaks—Pirgos (2368 ft) and Megalo Vouni (2342 ft). The island yields corn, dairy produce, and oil. The oak forests of Ios were once a considerable source of wealth. Landing is made by small boat to *Ormos Iou* (Chryssi Akti **B**, Armadoros **C**, both summer only; Actaeon **D**, open all year), an excellent harbour, on the W. coast, with a good beach (Yialós) near by and a better one in Milopóta bay to the S. The island capital, **Ios** (1270 inhab.), lies ½ m. inland near the site of the ancient city. Ios is remarkable for the large number of its attractive chapels, said to amount to 400; *Ayia Ekaterini* incorporates fragments of classical sculpture. Behind the town windmills grind the corn. The ruined *Palaiokastro*, built by the Crispi in the 15C, stands on a commanding height 2½ hrs E. At the N. tip of the island (2 hrs walk) is the creek of *Plakotós*, where the Dutch traveller Paasch van Krienen claimed to have discovered the tomb of Homer in 1770; all he did was to open some prehistoric graves. At the S. end of the island is the sandy bay of *Manganari* (Hotel, DPO, summer only, **B**).

THIRA (ΘΗΡΑ), or **SANTORINI** (ΣΑΝΤΟΡΙΝΗ), is the most important of the Southern Sporades and the most southerly of the islands included in the nome of the Cyclades. It owes its alternative name to its patron, St Irene of Salonika, who died here in exile in 304; officially it has readopted the ancient name *Thera*. The island, one of the great natural curiosities of Greece, is a huge volcano, the centre of which disappeared in a terrific explosion in prehistoric times. Today it has the form of a crescent of area 29 sq. m., the horns projecting westward, with an intrusion of the sea now forming a roadstead where once the crater rose. In the middle of this lagoon, which is 208 fathoms deep, are the Kaimeni ('Burnt') Islands still actively volcanic. On its N.W. side the island of *Therasia* partly continues the circular outline. Between its S. coast and the S. horn of Thira is an opening of the sea, in the middle of which is the tiny islet of Aspronisi.

The inner (w.) side of the crescent of Thira has weirdly shaped precipitous cliffs up to 1000 ft high. Thence to the E., the ground, covered with lava and pumice, slopes down gradually to the sea, the surface being interrupted by conical hillocks and by a few hills, the highest being Megalos Ayios Ilias (1857 ft), Mikros Ayios Ilias (1105 ft), and Mesa Vouno (1110 ft) all, in the S.E. and Megalo Vouno (1092 ft) in the N. On the volcanic soil only vines and tomatoes are cultivated, but an experiment is being made with growing pistachios. The potent Santorini wine has a great reputation. The mining of pumice ash is the island's main industry. Apart from one or two wells, the island is waterless, and rainwater is collected in cisterns. The light is famous for its intensity. The ships call first at *Oia* at the N.W. horn of the island, where disembarkation is by motor-boat.

By Air the island can be reached directly from Athens twice daily in 55 minutes.

Geology. The island, originally a volcano of marble and metamorphic schist with its main crater in the middle of what is now the roadstead, has from earliest times changed its shape as the result of eruptions. One, analogous to that of Krakatoa in 1889 and placed c. 1500 B.C., caused the middle of the island to sink, so that a circular depression 6 m. wide came into being, into which the sea poured. In the s.w., the islet of Aspronisi is the only surviving land remnant. In 236 B.C. another eruption separated *Therasia* from the N.W. of Thera. In 196 B.C. the islet of *Hiera* or *Old Kaimeni* made its appearance. In A.D. 46 another islet, *Thia* appeared and vanished. In 1570 the s. coast of Thera, with the port of Eleusis, collapsed beneath the sea. Three years later *Mikra Kaimeni* appeared, and in 1711–12 *Nea* or *Great Kaimeni*. In Jan 1866 there began a violent eruption that lasted two years, observed by Fouqué, the French geologist and archaeologist. This eruption produced the George I Volcano, in the s. of Great Kaimeni, and the islet of *Aphtoessa*, which disappeared in 1868. Another eruption began in July 1925, and lasted till May 1926; this joined Nikra and Nea Kaimeni. Further disturbances occurred in 1928. An earthquake in July 1956 caused great damage; over half the buildings on the w. coast were destroyed.

History. *Thera*, anciently known as *Kalliste* ('most beautiful') was populated before 2000 B.C. and its colonists are said to have founded the African city of Cyrene. The great eruption that transformed its shape and which, together with the preceding earthquakes, destroyed its settlements may have been the catastrophe that overwhelmed the Cretan palaces but there are many chronological problems still unsolved. Thera has been suggested as the site of Metropolis, the destroyed capital of the lost 'continent' of Atlantis. In legend it was colonized by Cadmus who had stopped at the island during his search for Europa. In the Peloponnesian War Thera and Melos were the only two of the Cyclades that declined alliance with Athens, but Thera escaped the fate of Melos. It was eventually, however, absorbed in the Athenian empire. The Ptolemys made the island into a naval base. In 1207–1335 it was held by the Barotsi as a fief of the Sanudo, and was thereafter included (till 1537) in the duchy of Naxos. The ancient city of Thera was situated in the S.E. of the island; the medieval capital *Skoros* to the N.W. of the modern capital. The island has been used in the present century as a place of exile for political prisoners. Vampires were once said to be especially prevalent in Thera.

Excavation. In 1869 the French School discovered on the s. coast of Therasia the ruins of a prehistoric city overwhelmed by the great eruption of c. 1600 B.C. and covered with pumice thrown up by it. This discovery proved that Thera, like Melos, was a centre of Cycladic civilization.—In 1896–1903 the German archaeologist Baron Hiller von Gärtringen excavated the ruins of Thera city; the neighbouring necropolis is still being excavated.—In 1867 the French started investigations near Akrotiri; current Greek excavations on this site were begun in 1967.

In favourable weather ships berth at *Órmos Athiniós*, a tiny haven beneath towering volcanic cliffs on the inner side of the crescent; a bus and taxis take passengers to Fira, the island's capital. In unfavourable weather, ships anchor offshore below Fira, whose dazzling white houses and domes extend along the clifftop nearly 700 ft above. Motor-boats take passengers to *Skala Fira*, whence Fira is reached by mule up a steep, zigzagging, paved track. Most cruise ships use Skala Fira. Transport on the island is by bus (infrequent), taxi, or mule (not necessarily cheaper than taxi).

Firá, officially *Thíra* (1320 inhab.; *Atlantis* B, *Kavalari* C, both Apr-Oct; *Panorama*, open all year, C; many rooms to let) has an Orthodox and a Roman Catholic cathedral, French schools, and a Dominican convent. From the terraces there is a magnificent view of the Kaimeni islets and Thirasia. The damage of 1956 has been made good with modern variations in new materials on the traditional barrel-vaulted style of building. At the Orthodox Cathedral is a Byzantine Museum. Immediately to the s. of the town are the pumice mines, with ship-loading chutes. In the N. part of the town, near the R.C. Cathedral, is a school founded by Queen Frederika where local girls are trained in carpet weaving. Near by is a small factory making spectacle frames. Just below is the MUSEUM (closed Tues), founded in 1902 and moved to the present new building in 1970. (Another museum is projected near the Orthodox Cathedral to house all prehistoric material. The Classical exhibits will remain in the present building.)

VESTIBULE. L.M. 1A jars from the French excavations at Akrotiri in 1867; case of Early Cycladic figurines and small objects from the pumice mines; vases from recent excavations at Akrotiri.—L-SHAPED HALL. In the long arm: Geometric and Archaic finds, mainly pottery; 'Santorini Vases'. On a pedestal is an outstanding 7C Archaic *Vessel, with relief decoration including a pelican and charioteers with Pegasus. Four Archaic kouroi; statuette of a woman combing her hair. In the shorter arm: pottery (6C and later), including three intact Attic black-figure vases; case of small figurines and animals; Hellenistic and Roman sculpture, continued in the SMALL ROOM, beyond, and in the COURTYARD. Here are also inscriptions, Archaic to Roman.—BASEMENT. Late-Roman and Early-Christian glass, lamps, etc.

FROM FIRA TO AYIOS ILIAS AND ANCIENT THERA. By taxi (100 dr.) direct to Ayios Ilias and on to Ancient Thera. By bus to Pirgos, thence on foot to Ayios Ilias (45 min.) and Ancient Thera (30 min. more); or by bus (morn.) to Kamari, thence on foot with a steep climb of c. 2½ m. up the road to the ruins. By mule, c. 3 hrs, with visit to Ay. Ilias.

ROAD, 7½ m. (12 km.). We run s.e. through vineyards. 3 m. Turning (l.) to *Monolithos*, a conspicuous isolated outcrop by the shore.—Soon after a road forks right to *Pírgos*, with picturesque old houses and a Venetian fort. Hence a road ascends to the top of *Megalos Ayios Ilias*, the highest point on the island (1857 ft). The *View is magnificent, extending to the mountains of Crete. On the summit are a radar station and a small monastery of 1711, with a museum of ikons, MSS., and vestments.—Our road continues s.e., passing *Episkopí* (r.), a Byzantine church of the 11C; there are two chapels, at one time used simultaneously by the Orthodox and R.C. faiths.—Beyond *Kamári* (Kamari C), with its black beach, we climb in steep zigzags to (7½ m.) the *Sellada*, the high saddle where the road ends. A short way up a path (l.) is the entrance to the ancient city.

Before entering the ruins we may see near the top of the road the Classical and Archaic cemeteries, being excavated; also, left of the road, a section of ancient paved road. Below the Sellada, to the s.w., is the Geometric necropolis: here were found some of the famous 'Santorini Vases'; fine pottery and bronze tripods continue to come to light.

Ancient Thera, covering an area 875 yds long from N.W. to S.E. and 150 yds wide, occupies a rocky spine of Mesa Vouno and was built on a terrace supported by massive foundations. In the Byzantine era it was surrounded by a wall. The main street, crossed by numerous side streets, ran along its entire length.

Archaic tombs show that *Thera* was in existence before the 9C B.C. The ruins, however, largely date from the time of the Ptolemies (300–145 B.C.), who made Thera into an advanced naval base from which they could control the Aegean, and

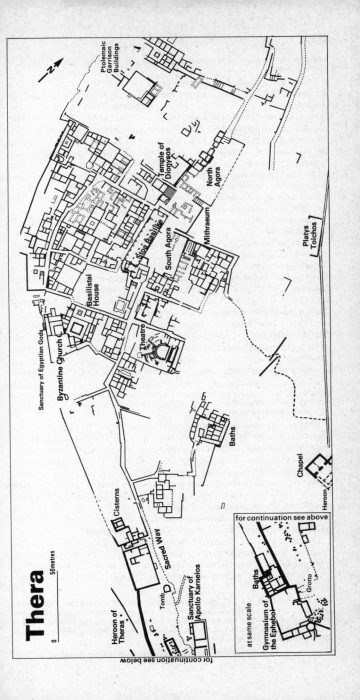

Thera

0   50 metres

Ptolemaic Garrison Buildings

Temple of Dionysos

North Agora

Mithraeum

South Agora

Stoa Basilike

Basilistai House

Byzantine Church

Sanctuary of Egyptian Gods

Theatre

Baths

Platys Toichos

Chapel

Heroon

for continuation see above

at same scale

Gymnasium of the Epheboi

Baths

Grotto

Cisterns

Sacred Way

Tomb

Heroon of Theras

Sanctuary of Apollo Karneios

for continuation see below

from the Byzantine era. The port of Thera, *Oia*, was situated at Kamári at the foot of Mesa Vouno.

From the entrance gate the path leads up to the tiny chapel of *Ayios Stefanos*. This was built over the ruins of the Byzantine *Basilica of the Archangel Michael* (4C or 5C). About 200 yds farther on we come to the *Temenos of Artemidoros of Perge* (r.), an admiral of the Ptolemies. The enclosure, with a black lava floor, has an Altar of Concord and, in relief on the wall, the Eagle of Zeus, the Lion of Apollo Stephanephoros, the Medallion of Artemidoros, and the Dolphin of Poseidon. We reach a narrow stepped road leading up to the Ptolemaic Garrison buildings, with the *Gymnasium* and the *Governor's Palace*. Back from these towards the N. is a little grotto converted into a Chapel of Christ, and N. again, the *Votive Niche of Demeter and Kore*, with a throne carved out of the rock, at the entrance to a large cave called Pitaros.

The main street enters the **Agora**, 120 yds long by 18–33 wide and divided in two. The N. part, with a row of shops, overlooks the *Platys Teichos* ('broad wall'), a fine quadrangular bastion of unknown purpose. Beyond (r.) are the *Altar of Ptolemy Philometer* and the terrace of the *Temple of Dionysos*. The s. part of the Agora is bordered by the STOA BASILIKE, or *Royal Portico* (44 yds by 11 wide) with an interior Doric colonnade and rows of columns against the walls. It was probably founded by one of the Ptolemies. The roof was restored in the time of Trajan, and further alterations were made in A.D. 150. Above and behind it are four blocks of Hellenistic houses, decorated with mosaics and provided with cisterns and lavatories. Each block stands in a little square. One of the houses has a wall-medallion in relief bearing a phallus inscribed "To my friends". Beyond the Agora are (r.) *Roman Baths*, complete with well, wood oven, and water conduits, and (l.) the *Theatre*.

A track leads up w. past the *Basilistai House*, or Residence of Ptolemaios the Benefactor, to the ruins of Byzantine churches (earlier the Temple of Pythian Apollo). Just beyond is the *Sanctuary of the Egyptian Deities* (Isis, Anubis, Serapis) with small niches carved in the rock.

We descend towards the promontory, following the SACRED WAY past the small *Temple of Ptolemy III* and the *Column of Artemis*, partly engaged in the rock, to the Temple of Apollo Karneios. This dates from the 6C B.C. and occupies a rectangle 105 ft by 33 ft. The gate, on the s.w., opens into a square court with a cistern. On the E. side is a room; on the w. are the paved *Pronaos* and the *Cella*, flanked on the s.w. side by two little rooms with walls and doors intact.—On the w. side of the temple are the foundations of the *Heroon of Theras*, the eponymous colonizer from Sparta. Below, to the N., is the *Chapel of the Annunciation*, near which are remains of a Heroon and a Rotunda,

We reach next the **Terrace of the Festivals,** with a fine view across the beach of Perissa to the promontory of Akrotiri. This terrace, dating from the 6C B.C., has impressive retaining walls in two styles (best seen from below at the end of the promontory) and it overlooks further Roman Baths.

This terrace was the religious centre of the oldest Dorian cults. On it were celebrated the *Gymnopaediai*, dances of nude boys in honour of Apollo Karneios. Scratched on the rocks are names of the gods inscribed by the faithful, and of favourite dancers, with erotic appreciations by their admirers. Some of these graffiti are as early as the 7C B.C.

At the extreme s. of the city is the **Gymnasium of the Epheboi,** with a spacious court and many more graffiti, including numerous outlines of feet. Off the court are a staircase, a rotunda, and numerous rooms; and, in the N. corner, the Grotto of *Hermes and Hercules*, the gods of the epheboi.

On foot or by mule, instead of returning the same way, we may descend from the Sellada to ($\frac{1}{2}$ hr) *Périssa* (Christina C) on the coast (buses to Fira in summer). A white church, built in the 19C as a result of the miraculous vision of a peasant, occupies the site of a Byzantine basilica. The flying buttresses were added after an earthquake. In the s. corner are the foundations of a circular *Heroon* converted in the 1C A.D. into the tomb of a certain Herasikleia.—We turn inland.—$2\frac{1}{2}$ m. **Emboreion** (*Archaea Elefsina* D), or *Nimporio*, a village of 1050 inhab., situated on the foothills of Mesa Vouno, has a regular bus to Fira. In the cemetery is a statue of Polyhymnia surrounded by a wall. Beyond Emboreion, beside the road (r.), is the chapel of *Ayios Nikólaos Marmarinos*, converted from a marble *Temple of Thea Basilica* (the Mother of the Gods) of the 3C B.C. (note the coffered ceiling). Near the s. tip of the island (30 min. s. of Emboreion) are some remains of ancient *Eleusinos*.—We pass the turning (l.) for Akrotiri (see below) and, following the road N., passing Pirgos (r.), reach (10 m.) Fira.

FROM FIRA TO AKROTIRI, $7\frac{1}{2}$ m. to the village (bus twice weekly), thence $\frac{1}{2}$ m. to the site; taxi to the site; or by mule in 2 hrs. The road runs high above the bay, passing turnings (r.) to Ormos Athinós and (l.) to Pírgos and Périssa.—$7\frac{1}{2}$ m. (12 km.) **Akrotíri** (220 inhab.) has a ruined medieval castle. At the entrance to the village a road leads left in $\frac{1}{2}$ m. to the excavations, begun in 1967 by the late Prof. Sp. Marinatos (who died at work here in 1974). The site may be compared with Herculaneum, alike for the similarity of complete burial beneath layers of pumice by a great eruption, and for the magnitude of the discoveries.

The site is in a small ravine. Excavation has revealed Late Minoan IA houses and streets, destroyed by the earthquakes that preceded the great eruption. One house was three stories high and there are unusually intact doors and windows, with evidence of wooden frames. Particularly fine frescoes have been found and detached; these have been put on display in Athens, but will return to Thíra when the new museum is completed. In the upper part of the site are rooms with large storage jars.

There is evidence that 'squatters' returned to the ruins after the earthquake. They removed debris, opened up entrances, and shored up ruins against collapse. But they undertook no serious repairs, staying probably 2–3 years at most, possibly the period between the earthquake and the great eruption.

FROM FIRA TO OIA, 8 m., bus (twice weekly) or taxi. By mule or on foot in c. $2\frac{1}{2}$ hrs. As far as Foinikia the road runs inland of the path. The path leaves Fira on the N. and follows the cliffs through white hamlets.— $\frac{1}{2}$ hr. *Merovígli* (taverna), a village on a height; its name 'Ημεροβίγλι means 'Watch Tower'. On the left is a promontory (997 ft) bearing the ruins of **Skaros**, the medieval capital of the island, with a castle of the Crispi.—The path continues to skirt the shore as far as (1 hr) a track fork on the slopes of *Megalo Vouno* (1092 ft). The turning to the right leads in $\frac{1}{2}$ hr to *Cape Koloumbos*, on the N.E. coast, near which some rock-hewn tombs have been discovered.—Keeping left, we reach ($1\frac{3}{4}$ hr) the hamlet of *Foinikiá*, near here joining the road.—$2\frac{1}{2}$ hrs. *Oía* (300 inhab.), the official but incorrect name adopted by Apáno Meriá; for ancient Oia, see above. The village was ruined by the 1956 earthquake. Below the village, to the s. is the little port of *Ayios Nikolaos*, facing the island of Thirasia (boats available).

Thirasia, once part of the island of Thera before the great prehistoric eruption, is now an island c. 3 m. long and 1½ m. wide. It has a landing-place at *Manolas*, in the middle of the E. coast. The ancient city of *Therasia* was in the N. of the island. In the s., between Capes Kimina and Tripiti, are pumice ash quarries, which supplied much of the material for building the banks of the Suez Canal. In these quarries a Middle Cycladic settlement was accidentally discovered in 1869. Nothing remains to be seen.

EXCURSION TO NEA (GREAT) KAIMENE. A motor-boat from Skala Fira crosses in 20 min. to the island. From the landing stage a walk across cinder leads in 30 min. to the Metaxa Crater where gases and hot vapours issue from fissures.

Anaphe (ΑΝΑΦΗ), or *Anáfi*, is a small island (14½ sq. m.) to the E. of Santorin, to which politically it belongs. It was celebrated in legend as having been raised out of the sea by Apollo as a refuge for the Argonauts when overwhelmed by a storm. Landing is made at *Ayios Nikolaos* in the centre of the s. shore. *Anáfi*, or Khora (350 inhab.), the only village, lies 15 min. inland. Paths lead E. to (80 min.) *Katelimátsa*, where there are ancient ruins, and on to (100 min.) the attractive monastery of the *Kalamiótissa*, site of a temple of Apollo of which there are remains. Other traces of ancient habitation can be seen to the N. of Katelimátsa, at *Kastélli* (20 min. walk). Many antiquities were removed by the Russians in 1770–74 to St Petersburg.

Síkinos and Folégandhros lie between Ios and Milos and belong to the eparchy of Milos. **Síkinos** (ΣΙΚΙΝΟΣ; 14½ sq. m.; 330 inhab.) is said to have once been called *Oinoe* ('Wine I.') from the fertility of its vines. The s. coast is rocky and barren, but elsewhere the island produces wine, figs, and wheat. The Skala at *Aloprónoia*, on the S.E. coast, is exposed and often inaccessible. About 1 hr inland, in the middle of the island, is the village capital, called *Kástro* or *Khóra*, at the foot of a rock crowned by a fortified monastery (Zoodókhos Piyí), now ruinous. To the s.w. (1¾ hr), at *Episkopí*, stands a Heroon, or temple-tomb (3C A.D.), converted in the (?) 7C into the church of Koimisis Theotokou, and remodelled after earthquake damage shortly before 1673. At the N.E. tip of the island (1½ hr from Kastro) is *Palaiókastro* with ruins of another ancient sanctuary.

Folégandhros (ΦΟΛΕΓΑΝΔΡΟΣ) is one of the smallest of the Cyclades (13½ sq. m.; 650 inhab.). From *Karavostásis*, the harbour, a mule path leads in 40 min. to Khora (240 inhab.), with a medieval portion called *Kástro*. The ancient city crowned the hill above. The beautiful church of *Panayía* stands on a headland to the N. *Apáno Meriá* (390 inhab.), a scattered village, lies 1 hr to the N.W. of Khora; from the windmills on the way a wide view embraces Sifnos and Kímolos and the coast of Crete.

74   THE EASTERN SPORADES

The **Eastern Sporades** lie off the coast of Asia Minor. Imbros and Tenedos belong to Turkey; most of the remainder, which extend s. to the Dodecanese, are under Greek sovereignty. Samothrace and Lemnos, the most northerly, are described for convenience with Thrace (from which they are most easily accessible; see Rte 70). The islands generally are more fertile and greener than the Cyclades, and if they have been less exploited for relics of antiquity, they had till recently preserved more of the customs and traditions of the more immediate past.

A Ikaria and Samos

STEAMERS from Piraeus ply five times weekly (once direct, 3 times viâ Syros, once viâ Syros–Tinos) to Ikaria (in 8½–11 hrs) and to Samos (Vathy in 9½–15 hrs; Karlóvasi in 12–17 hrs), where arrival may be very early in the morning. At Ikaria the usual port-of-call is Ayios Kirikos, but some steamers call also at Armenistí and Évdilos. Samos is also connected weekly with Khios, Lemnos, and Salonika, and with the Dodecanese.—Occasional connections to Kuşadası on the Turkish mainland.

BY AIR daily in 45–65 min. (fare approximates to 1st class boat ticket). The airfield lies between Pithagorion and the Heraion.

Ikaria (IKAPIA), a green, well-watered island with many scattered hamlets among the orchards and vineyards, is noted for its honey as well as for its radioactive hot springs. With *Foúrnoi* it forms an eparchy (9000 inhab.) of the nome of Samos. The name, perhaps deriving from the Phoenician 'ikor' in reference to an abundance of fish, attracted to itself a legendary past in which Ikaros and Daedalus figure prominently. In antiquity it had other names, notably *Doliche*. The s. coast rises in a line of steep cliffs to a ridge (*Athéras*), the highest point of which (3415 ft), s.w. of the capital, was known to the ancients as Pramnos or Drakanon.

The little capital, *Áyios Kirikos* (Ilios D), with 1080 inhab., lies on the s.e. shore. Neighbouring to the E. is **Therma** (*Toula* A; *Apollon* C; *Ikarion*, *Radion*, D, all summer only), the principal spa, whose name and fame were similar in antiquity. Some ancient remains can be seen. An unidentified Archaic acropolis and Classical tombs have been noted at *Katafíyion*, c. 4 m. E. Remains of *Drakanon*, another Classical town, lie near Faro at the E. end of the island (1 hr by boat). Most impressive here is the circular *Tower of the 3 C. Some finds are on view in the Gymnasion of Ayios Kirikos.

The N. coast of the island is best reached by boat. *Évdilos* (ΕΥΔΗΛΟΣ), a pretty village in the middle of the N. coast, with an inn, can be used as a base for the w. half of the island. At *Kámbos* (1¾ m. w.), with a museum, are the remains of ancient *Oinoe*. The Byzantine town on this site readopted the name of Doliche, and left the ruins called 'Palatia' and an 11C church (Ay. Irini).—*Armenistí* lies farther w. Inland the most interesting excursion is to *Kosoíkia* (45 min. s. of Evdilos) where the Kastro tis Nikariás dates from the 10C.

SAMOS (ΣΑΜΟΣ) lies closest of all Greek islands to the coast of Asia Minor, to which it was connected in prehistoric times, being separated from Cape Mykale by a strait under 2 m. wide. A range of mountains (a continuation of the mainland chain) runs through the island from E. to w., rising to peaks at Karvouni or Ampelos (3740 ft) in the centre and Kerkis (4740 ft) in the extreme w. Samos, with an area of 190 sq. m., supports 41,700 inhabitants. The N. coast, on which lies the capital Vathy (in the bay of the same name) is precipitous and rocky, while the s. coast opens on little plains and beaches admirably suited for bathing. The island is thickly wooded and abounds in springs and winter torrents. At all times it has been known for its fertility, which gave rise to many of the names by which it was known in antiquity (Anthemousa, Phyllas, Dryousa, etc.), and which led Menander to claim it could produce even birds' milk (Strabo xiv). The main products are wine (the Samian Moschato, a sweet red wine, is widely exported and has a high reputation), tobacco, shipbuilding timber, and olive oil. The mean winter temperature is warmer than that of Athens.

History. That *Samos* was inhabited at least as early as the 3rd millennium B.C. is proved by neolithic finds at Pithagorion. The island's name is said to derive from a Phoenician word meaning 'high'. Pelasgians introduced the cult of Hera, and the Classical writers endowed the island with an eponymous hero, son of an Arogonaut colonist. Later Samos was settled by Ionians. In the 8C or 7C Samos came into the possession of territory on the opposing mainland, which gave rise to continual boundary disputes with Priene. About 650 B.C. the Samian Kolaios voyaged through the Pillars of Hercules and returned with wealth that soon become proverbial. After the overthrow of the tyrant Demoteles during the 6C Samos was ruled by a landed aristocracy (the Geomoroi).

About 540, Polycrates and his brothers Pantagnotus and Syloson became tyrants (it is possible that the dynasty was established earlier by their father Aeaces). Polycrates soon ousted his brothers and ruled alone, bringing Samos to the height of its prosperity. He built up a great naval force, annexed many of the neighbouring islands and concluded alliances with Cyrene and with Amasis of Egypt. His court attracted many eminent artists and poets, among them Anacreon of Teos, and Polycrates was responsible for what Herodotus describes as the three greatest works to be seen in any Greek land—the aqueduct constructed by Eupalinos, the mole of the harbour, and the temple of Hera (the largest known to Herodotus) built by the architects Rhoikos and Theodoros. During this century, Samos founded many colonies, especially in the Propontis, and as far afield as Zancle in Sicily. In 522 B.C. Polycrates was tricked and captured by the Persian satrap Orontes and crucified on the mainland opposite.

Syloson, Polycrates' brother now became tyrant with Persian support, although anti-Persian feeling in the island led to Samian participation in the Ionian revolt against Persia. In the battle of Lade however, in 494, the Samian fleet deserted to the Persians. Samos fought on the Persian side at Salamis, but finally turned against Xerxes at the battle of Mycale. In 479–440, Samos was an independent member of the Athenian League, contributing ships instead of tribute. Following a revolt, Samos was crushed by Pericles after a nine-month siege—a feat which received favourable comparison with the capture of Troy. A democratic régime was installed, though in 424–412 this was overthrown by the oligarchs. The island was faithful to Athens during the Peloponnesian War, and was captured by the Spartan Lysander in 404 B.C. In 394 B.C. the Athenian admiral Konon recaptured Samos, which seceded from Athens in 390 B.C. The Athenians recaptured the island in 365 and replaced the entire native population with colonists. The Samians returned from exile only in 321 B.C. as the result of an edict of Alexander the Great, put into effect after his death by his regent Perdikkas. In the same year Antigonus Monophthalmus gained control of Ionia, and probably of Samos which he certainly controlled some time before 306. After his death Samos fell to Lysimachus of Thrace, and when he was defeated and killed in the battle of Corupedion in 281, passed under the influence of the Ptolemies of Egypt who used the island as a naval base. Later in the century Kallikrates of Samos became Ptolemy's admiral, a position amounting to viceroy of the sea. Ptolemaic control of the island lasted until 197 B.C., with a short interruption in 259–246 when Samos came under the rule of Antiochus II. After a brief occupation by Philip V of Macedon, Samos came under the influence of the Pergamene dynasts, and became part of the Roman province of Asia in 129 B.C. The works of art of the city and sanctuary were plundered by Verres in 82 B.C. and further suffered from pirates' raids between c. 70–67 B.C. It recovered somewhat under the pro-consulship of Cicero in 62 B.C., but was plundered again by Antony, who with Cleopatra visited the island in 39 B.C. Relations between Augustus and Samos were more friendly—he restored the island's autonomy (19 B.C.), preserved until A.D. 70 when Vespasian removed it. Augustus also restored many works of art to Samos.

In the Byzantine era Samos belonged to the eparchy of the Cyclades. It was from here that Nikephoros Phokas embarked on his expedition against Crete in 960. This period marks the rapid decline of Samos. After the invasion of the Turks in 1453 it was depopulated until the 17C, when it was re-occupied and ruled by an archbishop. Samos was occupied by the Russians in 1772–74. In 1821 the island played a leading part in the uprising and proved such a valiant adversary that 'to go to Samos' became the proverbial expression used by the Turks to mean certain death. The Samians won a series of victories, but the island was restored to the Turks at the end of the war. They were, however, accorded special privileges amounting to autonomy. They were governed by a Greek prince, the first being Stephanos Bogoridas (1834–59). In 1912 the Turkish fleet at Vathy was bombarded by two Italian warships, and Samos was re-united with Greece. In 1943 Samos was temporarily occupied by the British, and heavily bombarded by the Germans, who later seized it. After the war it was plagued by partisans.

Vathy (ΒΑΘΥ; *Xenia* B; *Samos* C; *Hera* D), the capital of the island, consists of the port of **Samos** (or *Limín Vathéos*), with 5100 inhab., situated in a deep bay on the N. coast, and the attractive suburb of *Ano Vathí* (2500 inhab.) on a hill to the s. of the bay. This affords a wonderful view of the port itself, the bay, and the coast of Asia Minor. The town dates from the 19C when it was named *Stephanoupolis* after the first autonomous governor. The best local bathing is to be found in sandy coves c. 3–5 m. W.

The *Museum* (temporarily closed in 1976) lies behind the Public Garden, next to the Town Hall and the Post Office. Housed in it are finds mostly of the 6C B.C. from the ancient city of Samos and the Heraion. These include sculptures (among which are the three remaining statues of the Archaic group by Geneleos) and grave reliefs, votive bronzes, with a large collection of griffin-heads; pottery and ivories; and inscriptions.

SHORTER EXCURSIONS. The monastery of *Zoödokhos Piyi*, founded in 1756 on the hill Pabaidoni, is 4½ m. from Vathy to the E. It is noted for its wood-carving, its hospitality, and for the spectacular view it affords of the strait of Mykale. A visit to *Ayia Zoni* (1695), another monastery, in the plain of Vlamari, c. 2 m. from Vathy, can easily be combined in the excursion.

A visit may be paid to the lighthouse of *Kotsikas* c. 3 m. N. of Vathy at the mouth of the bay (fine view).

About 1½ m. S. of the town, off the Pithagorion road (see below) by-roads lead to *Palaiókastro* (3¾ m. from Vathy) and to (7½ m.) the Strait of Mykale (Stenon Kouzantazi) close by the bathing-beach of Psili Ammos.

Regular STEAMER excursion weekly to *Patmos*; Caiques to Kuşadası, the Turkish port opposite Samos which is close to the ruins of Ephesos.

THE PRINCIPAL EXCURSIONS on the island are to Ancient Samos and the Heraion and to Karlovasi. By car they can be combined into a round TOUR OF THE ISLAND, 53 m. (85 km.), in a day.

TAXIS for hire (legally fixed prices displayed in Plateia); BUSES 2–3 times daily to *Karlovasi*, either direct or viâ Pithagorion but inconveniently timed; 5–6 times daily to *Pithagórion*, either by the main road or viâ Mytilini and Khora.

The road leads s. over a ridge affording a splendid view of the Strait of Mykale and of the islands of the Dodecanese. The modern town of (8¾ m.) **Pithagório** (ΠΥΘΑΓΟΡΕΙΟΝ; *Evpalinion, Pithagorion, Damo*, all **C**) lies on the s. coast of the island. Formerly called *Tigáni*, it was given its present name in 1955 in honour of Pythagoras. It has 1320 inhabitants and occupies the site of **Ancient Samos**. A small *Museum* contains sculptures, among them an Archaic statue of Aiakes; Archaic grave stelai bearing anthemia; Hellenistic grave reliefs; and Roman remains. A new museum is planned to house these objects, together with a further collection (inaccessible to the public) now in the Kastro of Logothetes.

The *Castle of Logothetes*, built in 1824, and the church of the *Transfiguration* occupy the hill to the W. of the harbour which is shown by the discovery of neolithic pottery to have been the site of the prehistoric town of *Astypalaia*, later incorporated into the town of Samos.

The mole of the harbour is built on the foundations of the ancient mole of the era of Polycrates, described by Herodotus (3, 60) as one of the greatest works of any Greek land. There are three miles of good pebble and sand beaches to the w.

A short way out of the town on the main road to Vathy a track branches (l.) to the traces of the ancient *Theatre*. Here the path divides, the right branch leading to the small monastery of Panayia Spilianí which hides the mouth of a series of underground caves and cisterns used as a place of refuge during the Turkish occupation and during more recent wars. The left branch continues to the Eupalineion (Evpalínion), or *Tunnel of Eupalinos*, completed during the tyranny of Polycrates in 524 B.C.

The tunnel may have been started during the tyranny of Aiakes and probably took fifteen years to complete. It was hewn through the mountain, under the direction of Eupalinos of Megara, its architect, from the N. side (outside the walls) to a point within the walls, work being begun from both ends. Besides assuring the water supply during time of siege, the tunnel provided an escape route in emergency. It was so used by Maeandrius during Darius' attack. The visitor needs a torch. A low and narrow entrance from a small white building gives place in the tunnel proper to a ledge beside the deep water channel.

Beyond the tunnel we may continue w. for 2 or 3 min. across a field to reach the *City Wall*. This wall runs spectacularly up the side of the mountain, turns E. along the top and returns towards the sea at a point E. of the Panayia Spilianí. Its whole extent of 4¼ m. with 35 towers has been traced. It is excellently preserved at the top, and the views over Mykale and over the inland plain are superb.

From Pithagorion to the Heraion, 5 m. asphalt; taxi, no convenient return bus. From the Khora road we take the left fork, pass the airfield on our left and at 3¾ m. again take the left fork.

The **Heraion**, or *Sanctuary of Hera*, lies on the coast at a place called *Kolonna* after the one surviving column of the great temple. It is close by the torrent Imbrasos, which is said to have seen the birth of Hera, and is a few minutes walk on the Pithagorion side of its small village, frequented as a bathing resort. Few Greek sanctuaries can boast a history of such length that can be traced in such detail. Adm. 25 dr., daily.

Excavations undertaken by the German Archaeological Institute in 1910–14, 1925–39, and since 1952 have revealed that the history of the site begins in the Bronze Age. Among buildings uncovered is a tholos tomb of the late-Mycenean period. The continuous history of the sanctuary during the next centuries is attested by two temples earlier than the first great temple. The early 8C structure was developed into the first true Greek temple by the addition of a peristyle (7 × 17); after its destruction c. 670 B.C., it was replaced by another (6 × 18 columns). During the 6C the sanctuary was widely extended, activity beginning probably a generation before Polycrates and being continued by him. To this period belongs the great temple. Further buildings belong to the Hellenistic and Roman periods and include a Christian basilica of the 5C A.D.

The first GREAT TEMPLE was built about the middle of the 6C by the celebrated Samian artist Rhoikos, in association (according to some authorities) with the architect Theodoros. Herodotus claims it was the largest temple of its day. Built in the Ionic order, 320 ft long by 160 ft wide, it was a dipteron, having 8 columns by 20 (rectangle on Plan). This temple was destroyed by fire c. 525 B.C. and many of its parts, notably the column-bases were reused in a larger replacement. The second temple (Pl. 1), probably begun under Polycrates, extended farther to the w.; the *Pronaos*. on the E., had three rows of eight columns, while the *Opisthodomos*, on the w., had three rows of nine. Its construction, suspended at the death of Polycrates, was resumed during the early 5C and again in the 3C but was never completed. A single column, itself incomplete, stands at the present time.

The complex of buildings immediately to the E. includes an *Altar* (Pl.

2), a late building having butresses (Pl. 3), a small *Bath* (Pl. 4), a peripteral *Temple* (Pl. 5) belonging to the Roman era, a second Roman *Temple* (Pl. 6), dating from the 2C A.D., and a *Basilica* of the early Christian era. All that remains of the last today is the N. aisle with the foundations of the nave, and the apse (Pl. 7). To the s. lies the base (Pl. 8) on which stood statues of the orator Cicero and his brother Quintus. Beyond this group, to the E., is the large *Altar* (Pl. 9) which is said to have been erected by Rhoikos. This was constructed on the site of a cult area of the 2nd millennium B.C. above a more recent altar which had been restored in the Geometric period.

To the N. of this group of buildings lies another complex of constructions dating from various periods. These include two small *Temples* in antis (Pl. 10, 11), the second of which overlies a peripteral temple, and a third Temple (Pl. 12) of late date. To the W. of this group are the foun-

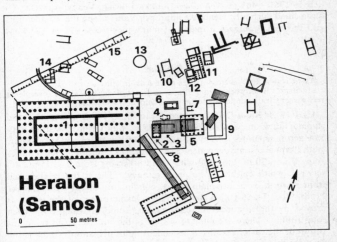

Heraion (Samos)

0   50 metres

dations of a circular building (Pl. 13), and farther to the W. an Archaic *Stoa* (Pl. 14). A number of members of the temple of Rhoikos were found beneath this stoa, where they were buried after the fire, thus proving it to belong to the late Archaic period. Between this stoa and the great temple is a *Stoa* (Pl. 15) of the Hellenistic period.

In the extreme E. area of the site have been uncovered the foundations of a number of buildings, including treasuries, temples, and administrative offices. Also, four wells were discovered here full of vases dating from the Geometric period to the 7C. A late-Mycenean wall and the remains of several Mycenean buildings were also found in this area,

About 1 m. W. of the site and 10 min. walk from the village is the Pirgos Sarakini, a tower dating from the Turkish occupation (late 16C).

Our round tour continues by the right fork (comp. above) to (13½ m.) *Khóra* (1090 inhab.), before 1821 the island capital, then winds across the rugged centre of the island.—21¾ m. *Pírgos* (920 inhab.; Koutsi D). —31¾ m. (51 km.) **Karlóvasi** (ΚΑΡΛΟΒΑΣΙ; *Merope* B; *Morpheus, Samion,* D) is a small port (4400 inhab.) on the N. coast (2 hrs from Vathy), at which all boats to and from Piraeus call. The area inland of the town is rich in vines which contribute to the reputation of the Samian wines. From Karlovasi the visitor can make many walks on *Mt Kerkis*, from the summit of which a magnificent view of the Aegean and the neighbouring islands may be obtained. Hence too the villages of Léka, Kastanéa, and *Marathókambos* (Chrysopetro D) may be visited, the last offering a splendid view of the s. coast of the island.

The road from Karlovasi to Vathy skirts the coast all the way, offering spectacular views of the rocky coastline. Beyond the huge plane-tree of *Ayios. Dhimítrios*, it runs high along the cliffs.—40 m. *Ayios Konstandínos* is a fishing hamlet. Just beyond is a Tourist Pavilion (*Ta Plantanákia*) and a branch road through woods to Manolates in an area growing cherries and nuts.—43 m. Turning to *Vourliótes*, a centre of vine-growing, from which may be visited the monastery of *Vrondianí*, the oldest on the island, founded in 1566. Tombs of the 3–4C A.D. were discovered here in 1961.—46½ m. *Kokkárion* (Kokkari Beach, Venus, Apr–Oct, C) has a small harbour. Hence we approach Vathy along the w. side of its gulf through *Malagari*, a region of many pine-trees.—52 m. (85 km.) *Vathy*.

B   Chios

APPROACHES. BY AIR from Athens twice daily in 1 hr.
STEAMERS 5 times weekly from Piraeus to Chios direct in 9–11 hrs (overnight; very early arrival), continuing to Lesbos (comp. also Rte 74c).

CHIOS, or **Khíos** (XIOΣ), famed for its fertility and with a delightful climate, lies 40 m. N.W. of Samos and 35 m. s. of Lesbos. A strait only 5 m. across separates it from the peninsula of Karaburnu in Asia Minor. With Psarà and some dependent islets it forms a nome of 53,900 inhabitants. Chios, 30 m. long and with a width varying from 8 to 15 m., deserves Homer's epithet Παιπαλόεσσα (craggy). The island is traversed from N. to s. by a mountain range, culminating in Mt Pelinaíon, or Profítis Ilias (4255 ft), in the N. The volcanic origin of the island is proved by the frequency of earthquakes, some of which have been catastrophic. There are numerous springs but no rivers and the cultivation of the eastern plains is dependent upon irrigation. Chios is the chief source of mastic, a resin of the lentisk tree, once used in making picture-varnish, but now almost entirely in the flavouring of a favourite Levantine liqueur and in the manufacture of chewing-gum. The villages where the tree is 'milked' are called Mastikhokhoria. Lemons, oranges, and tangerines are exported; olives and almonds are grown. Chian wine, famous in antiquity, is produced on the N.W. coast. The Chians of the Classical era were overfond of it, according to Aristophanes, who contrasted them with the sober inhabitants of Keos (comp. Rte 72A).

History. According to some authorities the name Chios is of Phoenician origin and means mastic. That the island was occupied at the beginning of the Bronze Age has been proved by excavation (see below). Whoever may have been the earliest settlers, Chios was by tradition colonized by the Ionians. Neleus and Androklos, younger sons of Kodros, King of Athens, after a dispute about the succession to the throne, crossed the Aegean in search of a new home 140 years after the fall of Troy. They settled on the w. coast of Asia Minor between the rivers Hermus and Maeander and in Chios and Samos, the two islands off this coastal strip. In historical times we find twelve cities united into the IONIC CONFEDERACY. These cities were, from N. to s. Phokaea, Erythrae, Klazomenae, on the Gulf of Smyrna (Izmir), the city and island of Chios, Teos, Lebedos, Kolophon, Ephesus, the city and island of Samos, Priene, Myus, and Miletus. Smyrna, which was situated in this district but was of Aeolic origin, was added c. 700 B.C. to the confederacy. Its common sanctuary was the Panionion, on the promontory of Mykale, opposite Samos; here was held the *Panionia*, or great national assembly of the confederacy.

These cities soon attained a high degree of civilized prosperity. In them, as nowhere else in the Greek world save at Athens, the arts and literature throve exuberantly. Out of the lengthy list of artists and authors after Homer (claimed as a native of Chios) we may mention the philosophers Thales of Miletus, one of the Seven Sages, and Pythagoras of Samos, and the poet Anacreon of Teos, and the painters Apelles of Kolophon, Zeuxis of Herakleia (Miletus), and Parrhasius of Ephesus. Other natives of Chios were the tragic poet Ion, the historian Theopompos (b. c. 378 B.C.), and the sophist Theocritus (4C B.C.). The chief cities of Ionia had an international reputation, which endured into our era, and they occupied a special place in the early history of Christianity: witness the Acts of the Apostles, the Epistles of St Paul to the Ephesians, and the Revelation of St John to the Seven Churches of Asia, two of which were Ephesus and Smyrna.

In the 6C and 5C B.C. Chios had a celebrated school of sculpture. One of its artisans, Glaucus (fl. 490 B.C.) invented the art of soldering metals. Chios was the first Greek city to engage in the slave trade, later so profitable in Delos. Towards the end of the 5C the Chians had more domestic slaves than any other Greek state except Sparta.

The Ionians were first conquered by Croesus, king of Lydia (reigned 560–546 B.C.), and then in 545 by Harpagus, a general of Cyrus, king of Persia. In 499 B.C., instigated by the wayward Aristagoras, Governor of Miletus, the Ionians revolted against Persian domination. Aristagoras canvassed help for the rebels from Athens and Eretria. Athens sent twenty ships "the beginning of mischief both to the Greeks and to the barbarians" (Herod, V, 97). At the Battle of Lade in 494, the Greek fleet was worsted, despite the valour of the Chiot Squadron, and Miletus sacked.

In 477, after the defeat of the Persian invasions, Chios joined the Delian Confederacy and remained a member till 412. Thucydides says (III, 10) that Chios and Lesbos were the only free allies of Athens, the remainder being subordinate in lesser or greater degree. In 412 Chios revolted against Athens. Though she was joined by other Ionian cities, including Miletus, Teos, and Mytilene, the Athenians defeated the Chiots and ravaged their country. In 378 Chios joined the Second Athenian Confederacy; in 354 she revolted again and her independence was recognized. In 333 the island was captured by a general of Alexander the Great. In the 3C B.C. Chios joined in alliance with Aetolia. Later, as an ally of Rome, she took part in the war with Antiochus. Her wealth excited the cupidity of the legionaries and the island was pillaged by Verres and by the forces of Mithridates. In 86 B.C., after its recapture by Sulla, it regained its independence, which was at first respected by the Roman emperors. After the earthquake of 17 B.C. Tiberius contributed towards its rehabilitation. Vespasian incorporated it in the province of the Islands.

From now on the history of the island becomes obscure. St Paul "sailed over against Chios on his way to Miletus" (Acts XX, 15). A Christian church was established in the island. In the 8C it was ravaged by Saracens. Occupied by Zachas, a pirate chief, it was freed in 1092 by Alexander Comnenus. In 1172 it was captured by Doge Vital Michialli; and in 1204, occupied by Venetians. They were replaced in 1261 by the Genoese. There followed incursions of Franks, Catalans, and Turks. By the middle of the 14C, however, Genoese domination was secure under the aegis of the Giustianini. In 1344 they formed a kind of chartered company, the *Maona*, which administered the island and was responsible for its defence. Chios again became prosperous. As early as 1513 a consul for the English was appointed to look after the affairs of the Levant Company who were engaged in trading cloth for wine. In 1566 the Turks under Piali Pasha captured the island. Thereafter, until 1821, despite several risings, it enjoyed under the Turks a measure of semi-independence. At the beginning of the War of Greek Independence in 1821 the Samians induced the Chians to join them in their revolt. In 1822 the Turks inflicted dreadful vengeance. They massacred 25,000 and enslaved 47,000. Only the mastic towns were spared. In the same year the Greek admiral Kanaris avenged his compatriots by destroying with fireships the Turkish flagship, with its commander Kara Ali; but his was a hollow victory. Those Chiots who had escaped the massacre had fled abroad. The more fortunate of the Chian refugees later made a name for themselves as merchants in London (the Rallis brothers), Liverpool, Manchester, Paris, Marseilles, Leghorn, Palermo, Odessa, Alexandria, and India. Chios never fully recovered from the events of 1822. The earthquake of 1881 did great damage; over 3500 of the islanders perished. In 1912 the island was liberated by the Greek fleet. Many of the best known shipping families are Chiot.—From Chios came Leo Allatius (1586–1669), scholar and librarian of the Vatican.

Khíos, or *Khóra*, the capital of the island and a seaport with 24,100 inhab., is situated in the middle of the E. coast, facing Asia Minor, and is known to the Turks as *Sakiz*. It occupies the site of the ancient city. The town lies within a fertile coastal strip; behind are wooded hills, with the bare mountains of the interior beyond.

Airport, 2½ m. s.

Hotels. Xenia, on the beach at Bellavista, to the s., Apr–Oct, DPO, B; Chandris Chios, 155 R, DPO, B; Kyma, in the town, open all year, C; and others.

Post Office, behind quay, near s. end.

Buses from Od. F. de Coulans to most villages.

Ferry daily to Çeşme in 1 hr (May–Oct); weekly in winter.

The *Harbour* is smaller than in antiquity, as landward building has encroached upon it. From it we quickly reach *Plateia Vounaki*, the town centre, laid out on the w. with gardens containing a statue of Kanaris, by Tobros, and vestiges of a 16C church. On the opposite side of the square is a former Turkish mosque converted into a small *Museum* (adm. 5 dr., standard hours). It contains vases in local style, yields from local excavations, an inscribed letter to the Chiots from Alexander the Great, and an indifferent copy of Delacroix's famous canvas of 1824 (original in the Louvre). To the N. rises the ruined 14C **Frourio** which commanded the harbour. There survive a few towers, gates, and case-mates, some bearing the arms of the Giustianini. Within is the old Turk-ish quarter, established in the 16C over the ruins of Genoese houses, and the marble tomb of Kara Ali.

The *Gymnasion* dates from 1792. The *Library* was founded in 1817 by Adamantios Koraï (1748–1833), the great scholar, who bequeathed to it his own collections, including works on Egypt given to him by Napoleon. It was further enriched in 1962 by the collections of Dr Philip Argenti, well known in London as scholar and philatelist. Above is a museum of local costume (closed Sun).

Though swamped by modern building, scanty remains of walls and of a theatre may be traced on a hill to the N. of the town. Outside the town (N.) are the *Tabakika* behind which are remains of an early-Christian basilica, and an imposing *Leper Hospital* founded in the 16C.

EXCURSION TO NEA MONÍ, 8½ m., asphalt (bus on Sun; daily as far as Karies then 5 m. mountain walk). The convent of *Nea Moni was founded between 1042 and 1054 by the Emp. Constantine IX Monomachos after the discovery by a peasant of a miraculous ikon. The 11C church, which has a marble pavement, was badly damaged in the earthquake of 1881, when the main dome fell, but has been restored. The contemporary *Mosaics include a Dormition of the Virgin, Raising of Lazarus, a Deposition from the Cross, the only known mosaic example in Greece, etc.

TO KARDAMILA, 17½ m. N., asphalt. The road (signposted) quits Plateia Vounaki, passing (r.) a bronze *Memorial to the Unknown Sailor* by Apartis.—2½ m. *Vrontádos*, a town of 4300 inhab., straggles along the coast. On its N. outskirts is the Stone of Homer, or Dhaskalópetra, an enormous block of dressed stone on a spur, probably a country shrine connected with the cult of Rhea or Cybele.—4½ m. (r.; on a pro-montory) Tomb of Yianni Psychares (1932), son-in-law of Renan.—Beyond (6½ m.) the little bay of *Milinka*, with a spring, the road zigzags up, then descends again to the sea. View across to the five Oinoussai Is. (see below).—10 m. *Langádha*, a fishing village (simple restaurants).—The road passes the Plain of Delphinion. In antiquity the city of *Delphinion* was a strong point with more than one harbour. The Athenians fortified it in 412. The site of the harbours was explored by the British School in 1954.—17½ m. **Kardámila** (ΚΑΡΔΑΜΥΛΑ; *Kardamyla* B) is made up of the picturesque upper town (915 inhab.) and *Mármaro* (1655 inhab.), especi-ally noted for the skill and daring of its sailors. Nagós and Vlikhádha, on the shore to the N., are noted for their beaches and tavernas (excellent fish and local fruit).

TO VOLISSOS, 25 m. N.W., asphalt. We leave Khora by the Kardamila road, but diverge left after a mile. The road climbs round Mt Aipos.—5½ m. *Memorial* to the fallen of 1912.—11½ m. *Ayios Isídoros.* The view opens out over the w. coast to Psará.—25 m. (40 km.) *Volissós* was once the home of the Homeridai, a clan that claimed descent from Homer. The so-called Castle of Belisarius was probably built by the Genoese. Beyond Volissos the road continues w. to the *Moní Ayías Markéllas,* named after a local 16C saint.

To PIRGI AND MESTA, 22 m. (35 km.), asphalt to Pirgí. We leave by the inland southern road, passing a turning (r.) for *Lithí,* a fishing village on the w. coast, birthplace of the philanthropist, Andreas Singros.—5 m. We skirt (r.) *Váviloi,* a village with a church frescoed in 1963 by a Hawaiian artist; beyond Vaviloi is *Sklaviá* (1¼ m.) with Byzantine and medieval remains, and, farther N., the *Panayía tis Krínis,* a church of 1287.—6¼ m. Small col, with two windmills. Ahead (l.) on its hill can be seen *Naós tis Sikeliás,* a church of the 13C with characteristic tile ornament.—12½ m. *Armólia,* with turning (l.) for Kalamotí (see below). Soon after is a kastro on a hill (r.).—14½ m. Road (l.) to Emborio (3 m.; see below).—15½ m. **Pirgí** (ΠΥΡΓΙΟΝ), a medieval fortress *Town of 1455 inhab., is the most interesting and attractive place on Khios, with churches and houses having curious sgraffito decoration. Good examples surround the main square, off one side of which is the tiny church of *Ayioi Apostoloi,* with 12C frescoes. The narrow streets have many round-roofed houses, and arches span the streets as a protection against earthquakes. Today Pirgí is the principal mastic town.—19½ m. *Olímboi;* turning (l.) for Kato Fana (see below).—22 m. *Mestá,* formerly the principal mastic centre, has ramparts and tortuous streets; some of the women still wear traditional costume.

At **Emborió,** on a promontory of the S.E. coast, an Early Bronze Age settlement was unearthed near and at sea-level, which had four stages of existence and was destroyed in a great fire. It has been equated with *Leukonion,* a rival to Troy. The town survived the fire and in the Middle and Late Bronze Ages spread up the hill, later crowned by a late-Roman fortress which was ruined c. A.D. 660. A Greek city of the 8–6C B.C. was discovered on the higher hill (Profitis Ilias), N. of the harbour. Traces of fifty houses were revealed, as well as a megaron and a temple of Athena. Nearer the harbour an Archaic temple (6C) was discovered, replaced in the 5C by a Classical building; both were used in the 6C A.D. as quarries for the building of a Christian basilica. A votive deposit yielded a kylix signed by the potter Nikesermos. —The black pebble beach offers good bathing. Underwater exploration brought to light numerous amphorae not only of Chian origin but also from Attica, Rhodes, Kos, and Thasos, an indication of the extent and importance of the wine trade to Chios.

At Kato Fana some ruins of a Temple of Apollo (late 6C) mark the site of ancient *Phanai,* which existed as early as the 9C. Both this site and Emborió were excavated by the British School in 1951–54.

The return to Khóra may be made by branching right at Armolia through Kalamotí, then continuing N. along the road closer to the coast (asphalt except for 2 m.). We pass *Ayios Minas* (c. 1590), where in 1822 the Turks massacred 3000 Chiots (ossuary), then cross the Kambos plain, a rich citrus-growing area, with (r.) *Kondári,* where the liberators disembarked in 1912.

Off the N.E. coast of Chios, in the strait separating it from Asia Minor, are the five small *Oinoussai Is.* (daily boat from Khora; inn; post office; good bathing). The inhabitants (975) are renowned sailors and fishermen and have produced some leading shipowners. The Navtikó Gymnásio is the only nautical boarding school of Greece.—In the bay of Çeşme in 1770 a Roman squadron destroyed a huge Turkish fleet.

About 12 m. w. of the N.W. coast of Chios lies the island of **Psará**

(ΨAPA), whose inhabitants won renown in the War of Greek Independence. It is reached by caique three times weekly from Volissos or by the Aegean mail boat approx. every 10 days. Rocky and mountainous it has an area of 16 sq. m. and a population of 487, all, save a few monks, in one town. There is no electricity and no telephone and accommodation must be sought privately. At 'Arkhontikí' in 1962 Mycenean tombs of the 13C B.C. were uncovered together with traces of a settlement.

After the fall of Constantinople in 1453 the islanders fled to Chios, whence some of their descendants returned to mingle with refugees from Euboea and Thessaly. In the Russo-Turkish war Psarian ships harried the Turks. The Psarians escaped reprisals because the Turkish governor was prevented from landing by bad weather, and after the Treaty of Kutchuk Kainardji achieved a certain protection and prosperity by sailing under the Russian flag. Psara was the birthplace of Konstantinos Kanaris (1785–1877) and many other noted sailors. In the war that began in 1821, Psara (with Hydra and Spetsai) was among the first to revolt, Psara in particular causing the Turks great annoyance. In 1823 the Psarians raided the coast of Asia Minor. In revenge the Turks under Hosref Pasha attacked the island from Mytilene in June 1824. Influx of refugees from Chios, Lesbos, and Smyrna had swollen the population to 20,000. The Turks silenced the batteries of Kanalos on the N. side of the island, and stormed the island with 14,000 Janissaries. The islanders blew up their own powder magazines at Ftelia and Palaiokastro, and only 3000 souls escaped the subsequent massacre by the Turks. Ruined houses, a simple white memorial (1956), and six famous lines by Solomos bear witness to the event. The refugees fled to Monemvasia and later founded Nea Psará in Euboea. In 1844 Psara was given special electoral privileges, but the island has never recovered.

C Lesbos

APPROACHES. BY AIR: from Athens, three times daily in 45 min.

STEAMERS from Piraeus daily exc. Sat, overnight viâ Khios, including ferry boat every other day in 14 hrs. Once weekly a freighter connects Mitilini with Lemnos and Salonika to the N., and Khios, Samos, and Rhodes to the s.

Caique service daily in summer round the island; twice weekly from Molivos, viâ Mitilini, to *Ayvalik* on the Turkish mainland (c. 35 m. to Pergamon).

LESBOS (ΛΕΣΒΟΣ, in modern pronunciation *Lésvos*; more generally called **Mitilíni** after its capital) is after Crete and Euboea the largest of the Aegean islands, with a maximum length of 43½ m., a width extending to 28 m., and an area of 630 sq. miles. It lies close to Asia Minor, its N.E. coast facing the Gulf of Edremit (Adramyti), and is 187 m. from Athens. To the N. is Lemnos and to the s. Khios. Oval in shape, Lesbos is deeply indented by two arms of the sea: the Gulf of Kalloni in the s. and the Gulf of Yera in the S.E. The interior is mountainous, fertile with dense olive plantations in the E., bare in the w., where much of its former vegetation has been petrified in a remarkable manner. The climate is temperate, with mild winters and cool summers, especially at Molivos, where the temperature tends to drop heavily at night; in Mytilene it is usually warmer and sometimes humid. The island is subject to earthquakes and there are numerous hot springs. The population (97,000 inhab.), still diminishing by emigration, is mainly occupied in producing the olives and olive-oil for which the island has long been celebrated; there are over 100 refineries. The vineyards also are productive though less famed than they were in antiquity. The chief manufacture is soap; there are also tanneries and textile mills, and in the w. tobacco is cultivated. The roads were built during the Turkish occupation by an English engineer. The island's fauna include the rare star shrew, called locally 'blind mice', and a species of salamander. Notable also are the herds of horses that graze round the Gulf of Kalloni, connected perhaps with the ancient horse-breeding traditions of the Troad. Though there is little of great archaeological importance, the cultural associations, both ancient and modern, and beautiful scenery and beaches of the island are increasingly attracting visitors.

History. Its geographical situation and its many harbours made *Lesbos* a centre for trade and communications from the earliest times and it is only recently that the division between Greece and Turkey has, by severing its connections with Asia Minor, frustrated its natural role as an intermediary between the mainland and the Aegean. Prehistoric remains indicating occupation from c. 3300 B.C. until destruction by fire at the end of the Mycenean period relate closely to those at ancient Troy. According to Homer, Lesbos, siding with Troy, was invaded by both Achilles and Odysseus. The inhabitants were probably Pelasgian, but in the 10C B.C. the island and the mainland opposite were colonized by Aeolians under the leadership of the Penthelides, the last of whom was murdered in 659 B.C. A struggle developed between Methymna and Mytilene for the leadership of the island, and although Mytilene won and has remained the capital, a tradition of independent resistance was fostered in the w. part of the island, which was to recur at critical moments. Lesbos was governed oligarchically with increasing chaos until Pittacus, one of the Seven Sages (589–579), calmed the island and as Aesymnetes (dictator) gave it its period of greatest prosperity and cultural importance. A large fleet and wide mercantile interests (especially in Egypt) were combined with a high standard of education and a comparative freedom for women, two traditions still noticeable today. Terpander, the father of Greek music, and Arion, who invented dithyrambic poetry, had already made Lesbos famous in the 7C, but it was with Alcaeus and Sappho, both aristocrats and enemies of Pittacus, that the island reached its cultural climax. In 527 Lesbos fell under Persian domination and was not freed until 479, when it joined the Athenian League.

In 428 soon after the Peloponnesian War started, Mytilene tried to break away with Spartan help, but the plan was betrayed by Methymna to Athens. The Mytileneans were severely punished (Thuc. III, 36–50). This was the dramatic occasion when a second galley with a reprieve was sent after the first had left with orders for wholesale massacre, and arrived in time. In 405 Lesbos fell to the Spartans and thereafter changed hands frequently, being ruled by Persia, Macedonia, and the Ptolemies until Mithridates occupied it (in 88–79 B.C.) only to be ousted by the Romans. According to Suetonius, Julius Caesar "won his spurs" during the Roman storming of Mytilene. It was much favoured by Pompey. St Paul, on his way back to Jersualem from Greece (c. A.D. 52), spent a night at Mytilene before passing by Chios and Samos. By the 5C Lesbos had many fine basilicas.

As a Byzantine dominion, the island was used as a place of exile, notably for the Empress Irene in 809. It suffered Saracen invasions in 821, 881, and 1055, which prompted the inhabitants to quit the coast for the mountains. In 1085 it fell to Tzachas, the Seljuk conqueror of Izmir, although Alexius Comnenus retook the island which remained under Byzantine control until 1128, when it passed for a time to the Venetians. In 1204 Lesbos became part of the Latin empire, but fell to the Greeks of Nicaea in 1247. At the end of the 13C it was devastated by Catalan mercenaries and in 1334 Dom. Cataneo made an attempt on it. In 1354 it was given to Francesco Gattelusio, a Genoese adventurer who had helped John Paleologus regain the Byzantine throne, as a dowry for John's sister Maria, who married Francesco; the island then enjoyed a century's untroubled prosperity under the Gattelusi who established an important trading principality in the N. Aegean. Lesbos fell to the Turks in 1462 and, despite attempts to free it by Orsano Giustiniano in 1464, by Pesaro in 1499, and by a Franco-Rhodian fleet in 1501, remained under Turkish domination till 1912, though enjoying considerable privileges and prosperity in the 19C (despite a revolt in 1821). Large numbers of refugees from Asia Minor were absorbed after 1912. In 1941–44 the island was occupied by German forces.

The chief town, near the S.E. corner of the island, is **Mytilene** (MYTI-ΛHNH), pronounced *Mitilíni*, capital of the nome of Lesbos, which includes the islands of Lemnos and Ayios Evatratios. It is the seat of a metropolitan. The modern town (23,400 inhab.) is spread over the slopes overlooking the harbour and the isthmus that joins to the mainland the wooded promontory on which the kastro stands. Still retaining much of its Levantine flavour, Mytilene is a bustling entrepôt port without particular interest and need not long detain the visitor from an exploration of the island.

Airport, 6 m. s. of the town.
Hotels. Lesvion B; **Blue Sea,** DPO, B; **Sappho, Rex,** C.—**Xenia** to the s. of the town, with swimming pool, DPO, Apr–Oct only, **B.**
Post and Telegraph Offices, on the quay (24 hrs telephone service).—Tourist Company of Lesvos (Delfinia hotel), on the N. quay.
Market Buses from near s. quay (once daily to most villages).

In antiquity the castle hill, with the Classical town, was separated from the mainland by a channel joining the N. and s. ports. Later the city overflowed from the island and the channel was crossed by marble bridges. The new town was built on the Hippodamian (grid) plan, a fact Vitruvius deplored since the streets caught the full blast of the N. and s. winds. Mytilene disputes with Eressos the honour of being the birthplace of Sappho. Alcaeus and Pittacus were both natives, as were also the two renegade Greek brothers, Horuk Barbarossa (d. 1518) and Khair-ed-din Barbarossa (d. 1546), who became Turkish corsairs and terrorized the Mediterranean. A modern worthy is Theophilos Hadjimichalis (d. 1934), the primitive painter.

The ancient s. port has become the main *Harbour* with the boat agencies and post office distributed along the N. and E. quay, the hotels, restaurants, cafés, and Dhimarkhion on the w. quay with the main shopping street, or *Agora*, running parallel behind it. The *Gymnasion* houses a small museum of local costume, pottery, etc. *Ayios Therapon*, near by, has a 15C ikon of St John the Evangelist.

In a villa on the front below the Kastro are housed the Khorafa mosaics and other antiquities, including a rare example of an Aeolian capital, but most of the collection has been in store for some years pending the construction of a new museum. Included are an inscribed marble throne from the theatre, mosaics from early-Christian basilicas, and prehistoric finds from Thermi. During the summer season the villa opens to display small items of archaeological interest, but the main collection cannot be seen. Beyond this villa by the pinewood below the Kastro there is a small beach with cafés.

The **Kastro,** which affords a fine view over the town and across to Turkey, was constructed by the Gattelusi in 1373 on the site of a Byzantine castle of which there are remains on the w. side. The Turks built a Medresse, or theological college inside the upper bailey and added surrounding walls to the N. down to the seashore, where can be seen traces of an ancient breakwater.

The main entrance through three gates is on the s. side, whence we pass through the upper bailey to the Gattelusi keep, dominating a steep cliff at the s.e. corner. Near by to the s. is a small entrance with a plaque depicting the Palaeologue eagle, the Gattelusi scales, and the monogram of Maria and Francesco, which are also to be seen on the wall of the keep (together with carvings of armed men and lion fights) and on the middle w. gate.

The ancient *Theatre* lies on the side of a hill to the left of the road leading out of the town to Thermi. Excavations in 1958 revealed the orchestra, the stage, and some seats, which were restored in 1968. The original plan was altered in Roman times for animal-combats and gladiatorial shows and also served as a model for the Theatre of Pompey in Rome. To the N. of the theatre above Ayia Kyriakí cemetery are remains of the city *Walls* in polygonal masonry of the 5C B.C., which ran from the N. breakwater of the N. port (Maloeis) to the s. end of the s. port, encompassing all the theatre hill. Lower down was the site of a late-Roman *Villa*, where were found the Khorafa mosaics (4C), depicting scenes from the comedies of Menander.

To the s. of Mytilene a road runs along the coastal plain.—At (2½ m.) *Vareiá* a track leads inland to Akrotíri (1 m.), where there is a museum of paintings by Theophilos. Just to the s. of (3¾ m.) *Neápolis* are remains of the early-Christian basilica of Argala. Beyond the airport and (6½ m.) *Krátigos* the road, no longer asphalted, continues round Cape Argiliós at the s.e. corner of the island. At 12½ m. a lane branches left to Cape Ermouyenis (¾ m.) at the entrance to the gulf of Yera (chapel, café, and beach); keeping right, we reach (13½ m.) the site of the early-Christian basilica of Loutra with a mosaic.—15½ m. *Loutrá* is an old thermal station. Hence an asphalt road returns to Mytilene (5¼ m.) over a saddle of Mt Amali, affording superb views both e. and w., or (if we keep left) another descends to Skala Loutrón and Koundouroudhiá on an inlet of the gulf of Yera, across which a regular passenger ferry plies to Pérama (see below).—For the n. outskirts of Mytilene, see below.

To YERA AND PLOMARI, 25½ m. (41 km.). The island's (asphalted) main road runs w. from Mytilene and crosses a low ridge. Soon after reaching the shore of the Gulf of Yera we pass the hot springs of (5½ m.) *Thérmai Yéras* (below the road, l., down a short unsignposted track). About 1 km. farther on Pelasgic walls can be found on a steep hill.—At 7½ m. we turn off to the left through a region thickly populated in antiquity. Soon after a river bridge and before the big olive refinery at (8¾ m.) *Dipi* (ΝΤΙΠΙ) are some remains of an ancient harbour (partly submerged).—Near (9½ m.) *Káto Trítos* (½ m. r.) are ruins of ancient houses. We cross a ridge and descend to (14¼ m.) *Palaiókipos*, with an underground church (Taxiarkhon).—From (15½ m.) *Pappádhos* (Inn) a road leads (r.; 1 m.) to *Mesagró* and the remains of the medieval Castle of Yera. At the far end of Pappádhos are turnings to Pérama (1 m.) and to Skópelos (½ m. r.).

Pérama, with a tannery and oil refineries, stands on the Gulf of Yera, near the site of ancient *Hiera*, said by Pliny to have been destroyed by earthquake. *Skópelos* (2400 inhab.) has catacombs (Lagoúmis tis Ayías Magdalinís) and a Turkish fountain.

Our road winds across the e. shoulder of Mt Olympos, then descends through a narrow valley to Ayios Isidoros on the shore.—25½ m. **Plomári** (ΠΛΩΜΑΡΙ; *Oceanis* C), a centre (4400 inhab.) created as *Bilmar* in the 19C when the inland villagers returned to the s. coast, is now the second town in size of the island, famed for its ouzo, with a small port. Hence a poor road leads n. to *Megalokhóri* (5½ m.) and through chestnut forests round the slopes of Olympos to Ayiassos (see below).

To AYIASSOS AND POLIKHNITOS, 28 m. (45 km.). We follow the main road w. (see above), pass the turn to Plomári, then after another mile turn left.—Just beyond (9¼ m.) *Keramía*, turning (l.; 1 m.) for *Ippeion* (ruins of ancient houses near by).—13¾ m. Fork l. for Ayiassos (2½ m.).

Ayiássos (ΑΓΙΑΣΟΣ; inn), a shaded and well-watered hill-town of 3800 inhab., stands on a by-road under Mt Olympos (3170 ft). It is noted for weaving and pottery. The monastery of the *Koimiseos tis Theotókou*, of Byzantine foundation, has a good collection of ikons and a big festival on 14–15 Aug. On *Kastelli*, a pine-clad hill to the n.w. are strong walls of a medieval castle. The remains of *Penthile*, 2½ m. s. on the Plomari road, now ploughed out, are fabled to date from the Aeolic migration.

The major road continues w. through beautiful pine woods with views of Mt Olympos to (24½ m.) *Vasiliká*, supposed place of exile of the Empress Irene.—26¾ m. *Lisvórion* has thermal springs.—28 m. *Polikhnítos* (ΠΟΛΥΧΝΙΤΟΣ; inn), a little town (4150 inhab.) with hot saline springs. A road goes through the town w. to *Skala Polikhnitou* and the salt flats on the Gulf of Kalloni; another road (l.) goes s. to *Vríssa* (3 m.; inn), with a Genoese tower near by, and down to *Vaterá* (5 m.), a long beach with cafés ending to the w. in Cape Phokas, site of a Temple of Dionysos and probably of the ancient city of *Brisa*, earlier known as *Lyrnessos*.

FROM MYTILENE TO MANDAMADHOS (and Molivos), 23 m. (37½ km.). Coast road asphalted to Makriyialou Bay, then unsurfaced inland. The road runs N.W.—At (2½ m.) *Kourtzes* the hot baths (Thermakiás) date from Roman times. About ¾ m. farther on a road branches (l.) to *Mória* (1 m.), a village, w. of which stand several impressive arches of a Roman aqueduct that brought water to Mytilene.—5 m. *Pámfilla*. We cross the base of a small promontory.—6¼ m. *Pírgoi Thermís*, 17C Turkish towers, just beyond which a track leads (l.) to the *Panayía Tourlotí*, a Byzantine church of the 15C or earlier.—7¾ m. **Loutrá Thermís** (*Motel Votsala* B, on the sea). We arrive opposite the *Sarlitza Hotel* (E), immediately left of the entrance to which are the baths. The therapeutic qualities of the hot saline and chalybeate springs (49° C). were recommended by Claudius Galen. By the modern spring is the site of an ancient temple to Artemis and an adjoining complex of baths.

The prehistoric site of **Thermi**, to the E. of the road, was excavated in 1929–33 by the British School under Miss Winifred Lamb. It was first occupied at the beginning of the Bronze Age (c. 2750 B.C.) evidently by colonists from the Troad since there is a close resemblance between the black pottery found here and that of Troy I. Cycladic influences then began to outweigh those from Asia Minor and c. 2000 B.C. the city was depopulated, despite the construction of considerable fortifications. The site was reoccupied c. 1400 until its destruction by fire some two hundred years later (by Greek armies in the Trojan War?).

Beyond (10¼ m.) *Mistegná*, where are traces of ancient *Aigeiros*, a by-road ascends (l.) to *Neai Kidoníai* with a ruined medieval castle.—15½ m. *Vatíka* (cafés) has a good beach.—20 m. *Aspropotamos* lies to the right of the road, on the Bay of Makriyialos. We turn inland to (23 m.) *Mandamádhos* (Lesbos, small, E), a village (1800 inhab.) set amid low hills, where the church of the Taxiarkhon, ½ m. N., possesses a remarkable black ikon of St Michael, carved in wood and smelling of spring flowers. At a festival soon after Easter bulls are sacrificed and eaten, a rite suggestive of a pagan origin (comp. below).

The dirt road continues to (26¾ m.) *Kápi*, where it divides to pass either side of *Mt Lepédimnos* (3180 ft). To the s. a passable road leads viâ (32½ m.) *Ipsilométopo*, where (30 min. s.) an early-Christian basilica of c. 550, with columns, mosaic, and tombs, was excavated in 1925 (Greek Archaeological Service), to (34½ m.) *Stipsi* (ΣΤΥΨΗ) and then joins the main Kalloni–Petra road (comp. below).—On the N. road is (28 m.) *Klió*, whence a track leads down to the Gulf of Tsonia (good beach; cafés); a wooded hill in this area bears remains of a fort, perhaps the historic castle of *Ayios Theodoros*, where Giustiniano encountered the Turks in 1464. A very difficult road continues w. of *Klió* to (30½ m.) *Sikamiá*, the beautiful little port of which (reached by track; 2½ m. r.) is known locally as 'Little Egypt' because of its warmth in winter.—32¼ m. *Argennos*.—38½ m. (62 km.) *Molivos* (comp. below).

FROM MYTILENE TO KALLONI AND MOLIVOS, 38½ m. (62 km.), by the main (asphalt) road. To the Plomari and Ayiassos turns, see above. Keeping to the right we cross pine-wooded hills.—18½ m. Kakadélli bridge, ½ m. N. of which, at a locality called *Mesa*, are remains of an Ionic pseudo-dipteral temple of Aphrodite (8 by 14 columns).—We reach the *Gulf of Kalloni* at (20½ m.) the turning (l.; 2 m.) for ancient

Pyrra, or Pyrrha, set in a little valley. The remains of an earlier Pyrra (destroyed by earthquake c. 231 B.C.) are believed to have been located some 5 m. S.W. beneath the gulf. Near the first site has been excavated the early-Christian basilica of 'Akhladeris'. The by-road continues to Vasiliká (p. 649) on the Ayiássos–Políkhnitos road—The main Kalloni road now skirts salt-flats.—22½ m. Turning (r.; asphalted) to Ayía Paraskeví.

About ½ m. up this turning some vestiges of ancient *Gerna* are marked by a chapel.—2 m. *Ayía Paraskeví* (Inn), a large village (3000 inhab.) is noted for its festival of St Charalambos soon after Easter. A bull sacrifice is followed by an equestrian parade and races.

There are many attractive excursions in the district. About 45 min. E. is the early-Christian basilica of *Khalinados*, built in the 6C on the Syriac plan; columns and capitals have been restored to place and other columns have been observed in a chapel on the hill of Tsiknía overlooking the Kalloni–Molivos road. About the same distance N.W. on the road to Stipsi is the *Packhorse Bridge*, built by the Gattelusi, with a fine arch across the two affluents of the Tsiknias; 3 m. W. of Ayia Paraskevi on a track which leads to the main Kalloni–Petra road, near *Klopedi*, ruins of two archaic temples, one to Apollo Napaios, yielded numerous Aeolian capitals of the 6C B.C. now in the Archaeological museum at Mytilene.

We cross the Tsikniás.—24½ m. *Arisvi*; vestiges of ancient *Arisbe*, ruined by earthquake in 321 B.C., can be reached by track to the right; on its acropolis are remains of the Byzantine castle of Kalloni, rebuilt by the Turks but abandoned in 1757.—24¾ m. **Kalloni** (ΚΑΛΛΟΝΗ; Inns; 1650 inhab.) stands at an important crossroads. Its *Skala*, 1¼ m. S. on the gulf, is the centre of the sardine-fishing and a good red wine is also locally produced.

We turn N., leaving the Antissa road (see below) and shortly pass the track to (15 min., l.) the Byzantine *Moní Myrsiniótissas*, with the tomb of Bp. Ignatius (d. 1568); the nuns do embroidery. We climb out of the Plain of Kalloni, meet at 30½ m. the road from Stipsi (comp. above) and, topping a rise, descend to **Petra** (*Petra* C) on the N.W. coast. It is notable for the church of the *Panayia Glykofiloussa* (1747) built on top of a high rock near the fine beach. The 16C church of *Ayios Nikolaos* is frescoed; festival 15 Aug. The road meets the shore at *Khiliopigádha*, supposedly the landfall of Achilles.

38½ m. (62 km.) **Mólivos** (*Delfinia* B with swimming pool; Rooms to let; *Rest. Kokhili, Neon*; tourist office by the bus stop) has officially resumed its ancient name **Methymna** (ΜΗΘΥΜΝΑ), pronounced Míthimna, a word of pre-Greek derivation. Picturesque tower-houses face S. over a small fishing harbour and a long beach. On a steep hill above the maze of narrow stepped streets, a Genoese *Castle* of the Gattelusi dominates the town and commands a fine view N. across the strait to Cape Baba in Turkey. Remains of polygonal walls (8C B.C.), of an Archaic temple, and of a Roman aqueduct are visible.

Methymna, the second city of Lesbos, was the birthplace of the poet Arion (fl. 625 B.C.) and the historian Hellanicus (c. 496–411 B.C.). The celebrated Lesbian wine grew in the neighbourhood. The city refused to join the great Lesbian revolt (428 B.C.); in 406 it was sacked by the Spartans.

Along the coast, 2 m. E., is *Eftalous*, with radio-active springs and good bathing. From this his native village Kleanthes Michaelides, the 19C short-story writer who died in Hull, took his pen name Argyris Eftaliotis.

THE W. PART OF THE ISLAND is best approached from Kalloni (see above). The road has long, rough unpaved stretches beyond Vadoússa.

We bear left outside Kalloni.—3 m. The monastery of *Leimónos* (l.), built in 1523 by St Ignatius, metropolitan of Methymna, has a library with 450 MSS., including an 8C evangelistery; festival 14 Oct. On 'Tyrannída' hill (2265 ft), to the right of the road, took place the Turkish last stand in 1912 (memorial). The terrain is rough and volcanic. As we climb there are fine retrospective views over the Gulf of Kalloni and its salt pans.—5½ m. Col; we descend above the little plain of *Fília*. The road passes just above (9¾ m.) *Skalokhóri* (religious festival on 23 Aug). From here a track leads down to the coast near ancient Antissa (see below). Soon after we see the N.W. coast.—15½ m. *Vadoússa.*—18¾ m. (r.; just below the road) the Byzantine *Perivoli* monastery (1590, restored 1962) has good frescoes of the Second Coming.—20 m. Turning to *Gavatha* (r.) with a fine beach (cafés).—21¼ m. *Ándissa* (1800 inhab.; inn).

The remains of ancient **Antissa** (comp. above) lie on the coast near a ruined Genoese castle. The ancient acropolis was excavated by the British School in 1931; its life extended from the Bronze Age until the Romans destroyed it for harbouring the Macedonian admiral Antinora in 168 B.C.

Beyond modern Antissa the road divides. The left branch turns s. to Erossos (see below). The right branch continues w., passing (24¾ m.) a stepped pathway (l.) up to the Ipsilon monastery on Mt Ordimnos (view). Just beyond is a track (l.) signposted to the Petrified Forest (comp. below).—32½ m. (52 km.) *Sigri* (ΣΙΓΡΙ; *Nisiopi* B; Village G.H.), lies at the w. end of the island. The red-roofed village has a small Turkish castle of 1757 on a low rocky promontory and a fine beach. The region of Sigri is famous for the *Petrified Forest (ΑΠΟΛΙΘΩΜΕΝΟΝ ΔΑΣΟΣ), well seen on the rough track that leads S.E. to Eressos. This unique phenomenon was caused by various trees (mainly conifers and sequoia) being buried in volcanic ash (when is not certain) and then petrified by the action of hot waters containing silicic acid and iron pyrites.

30½ m. **Eressós** (ΕΡΕΣΟΣ), known to the Turks as *Herse*, has 1800 inhab. and a local archaeological museum (adm. 5dr., standard hours) with sculpture and mosaics. The modern inhabitants, as in many other villages, migrate down to the coastal plain in summer, where (2 m. s.) *Skala Eressou* (Sappho Eressia C) occupies the site of *Ancient Eressos*, birthplace of Sappho and of the philosopher Theophrastos (d. 287 B.C.). The village lies at the E. end of a long beach underneath a rocky acropolis (Vigla) on the E. side of which are to be seen the remains of a Byzantine-Genoese castle, some Roman cisterns, and a fine example of Archaic polygonal walling. In the village are the ruins of a large 5C basilica of St Andrew with mosaics; along the beach by the mouth of the Khalandras, remains of a similar basilica of Aphendélli (also 5C) in the Syriac style.

To the S.E. of Lesbos, near the Asiatic shore, are the three islets of *Arginusae*, off which in 406 B.C. the Athenians won a naval victory over the Lacedaemonians. The Spartan admiral Kallikratidas was killed and seventy of his ships sunk or captured. The Athenians lost twenty-five ships and were prevented by the weather from rescuing the crews. For this omission eight of the Athenian commanders in the battle were recalled to Athens, tried, and six of them executed. This drastic action was a major factor in the Athenian annihilation at Aegospotami.

IX THE DODECANESE

The **DODECANESE** (ΔΩΔΕΚΑΝΗΣΑ; 'Twelve Islands') are politically a group of islands, lying in the S.E. Aegean, off the coast of Asia Minor, of which they are geographically a part. Their name is a misnomer, for 14 islands have independent local government status and a few of their dependent islets are inhabited. The nome is divided into four eparchies: that of Kalymnos includes also Patmos, Lipsos, Leros, and Astypalaia; that of Karpathos includes Kasos; that of Kos includes Nisiros; and that of Rhodes includes Telos, Syme, Chalki, and Megisti, the last lying some way to the E. of Rhodes. They are strictly the S.E. continuation of the Eastern Sporades, and are sometimes rather confusingly called Southern Sporades. Their total population is about 121,000.

The somewhat misleading term Dodecanese for this group is of relatively recent date. It came into use in 1908, when 12 'privileged' islands of the Eastern Aegean, excluding Rhodes, Kos, and Lipsos, but including an intruder, Ikaria (see Rte 74), united in protest against the deprivation by Turkey of the special privileges that they had enjoyed since the 16C under Suleiman the Magnificent (1495-1566). In the course of years the term has come to include the island of Rhodes and other islands not on the list of 1908: so much so that Rhodes is now regarded as the chief of the Dodecanese and its city is their capital.

During the Italo-Turkish war of 1911-12 the islands were seized by Italy and were retained by her as a pledge for the fulfilment of the first Treaty of Lausanne (1912). After the First World War the Treaty of Sévres (1920) gave the islands to Italy but, by an agreement between Italy and Greece, they were all to be passed on to Greece. This agreement was repudiated by Italy after the disastrous Greek campaign of 1922. The second Treaty of Lausanne (1923) gave the Dodecanese to Italy. In 1944–45 the islands were occupied as opportunity occurred and put under British Military Administration. On 7 March 1947 they were officially united to Greece. By far the largest of the islands is Rhodes.

Approaches. By Air from Athens to *Rhodes*, 3–5 times daily in 55 min.; also in summer from Herakleion several times weekly. To *Kos* 4 days weekly in 50 min.—Rhodes is also served in summer by direct flights (mainly charter) from Britain, Germany, Sweden, etc.

By Sea. From Piraeus the departure is usually made in the afternoon, and the voyage takes 19–27 hrs according to route and ports of call. There are c. 10 services weekly. They may be divided into those taking the long s. route (Rte 75B), twice weekly, calling at either Ios or Folegandhros, Thira, Ayios Nikolaos and Siteia in Crete, *Kasos, Karpathos,* and *Khalki*; and those which take the N. route (Rte 75A). These in general call at Mykonos or *Patmos* (sometimes both), *Leros, Kalymnos,* and *Kos* (also, once weekly only, at *Nisyros, Tilos,* and *Symi*). One service weekly substitutes for Patmos and Leros *Amorgos* and *Astipalaia*. Many of the services carry cars.

From Salonika a steamer does a weekly round viâ the Eastern Sporades and Ikaria to Patmos, Leros, Kalymnos, Kos, and Rhodes and return.

A local steamer (once weekly) connects all the W. Dodecanese in a round voyage from Rhodes.—Kastellorizo, see Rte 76.

The Dodecanese enjoy special exemptions from customs duties and returning visitors must clear customs before leaving even for destinations in Greece.

75 FROM PIRAEUS TO RHODES

A The Northern Route

STEAMERS from Piraeus, see above.

The alternative route, viâ the Cyclades, calls at Amorgos and Astipalaia.

AMORGOS (ΑΜΟΡΓΟΣ), the most easterly of the Cyclades, and part of the eparchy of Thira, is a narrow island, 11 m. long, extending from s.w. to N.E., with 1360 inhabitants. It has three mountain peaks: Krikelas (2560 ft) in the N.E., Profitis Ilias (2410 ft) in the centre, and Korax (1890 ft) in the s.w. Krikelas lost its forest in 1835 in a fire that lasted three weeks. The cliffs on the s. coast are scenically magnificent. In antiquity there were three cities, Aigiale, Minoa, and Arkesine, all situated on the N. coast. Amorgos was the home of Semonides (fl. 664 B.C.), who came here from Samos. The local waters were the scene of the decisive defeat of the Athenian fleet in the Lamian War, from which Athenian naval power never recovered.

The landing-place is *Katápola* (Psakis Rest. with R), on the w. coast, about the middle of the island. On a hill above it are the considerable remains of *Minoa*, including a gymnasium, a stadium, and a temple of Apollo, excavated by the French School in 1888. A track leads in 50 min. to **Amorgós** (1184 ft), or *Khora* (Inn), the little capital. About ½ hr N.E. of Khora, at the base of a precipitous rock, is the celebrated *Khozoviotíssa*, or Convent of the Presentation of the Virgin, founded by the Emp. Alexis Comnenus. It contains an ikon of the Virgin 'miraculously' conveyed hither from Cyprus.

About 3 hrs s.w. of Khora, at *Sto Khorio*, is a well-preserved Hellenic tower, from which a path leads in 1 hr to the scanty ruins of *Arkesine*.—If we go N. from

Khora, we reach in 3 hrs *Aigiali* (290 inhab.; *Miki's* C, July–Sept), near which is the church of *Exokhoriani*, incorporating a temple of Athena. Near here was found in 1906 a tablet on which were inscribed 134 verses relating to the laws of Amorgós (now in the Epigraphical Museum in Athens).—At the N.E. extremity of Amorgós are the ruins of *Aegiale*, best visited by sailing-boat from Katápola. The tombs excavated here have yielded pottery and other objects dating from the Early Cycladic period.

ASTIPALAIA (ΑΣΤΥΠΑΛΑΙΑ; the accent is impartially placed on any of the last three syllables, and in local dialect the name becomes *Astropaliá*), the westernmost of the Dodecanese, is said to be the only Aegean island without snakes. It lies 25 m. S.E. of Amorgos and about the same distance w. of Kos. By the Venetians in the Middle Ages and again during the later Italian occupation it was called *Stampália*. The island consists of two peninsulas connected by a long slender isthmus and has a length of 11 miles. The coastline is much indented and has high cliffs. The hilly interior rises to 1660 ft on the w. peninsula and to 1100 ft on the E. The women's traditional costumes are of great variety and elaboration. The long Venetian occupation has left its mark on the dialect and outlook of the inhabitants, who number 1140.

History. The island, which had some importance in antiquity, was called Ichthyoessa from its abundance of fish and the 'Table of the Gods' because of its flowers and its fertility—today not much in evidence. After a Cretan period, it received colonists from Epidauros. The most colourful Astipalaian was the strong-man Kleomedes, who killed his opponent Ikkos of Epidauros in a boxing match during the 71st Olympiad and was disqualified. He returned mad with rage and grief to Astipalaia and pulled down the local school about its children's ears, killing them all. The Romans used the island bays in their operations against Aegean pirates. From 1207 to 1522 Astipalaia was ruled by the Venetian family of Quirini, who introduced settlers from Mykonos and Tinos. In 1522 it fell to the Turks who slightly altered its name to *Ustrupalia*. Except during the Cretan War (1648–68) and during 1821–28, they held it until 1912, when it became the first of the Dodecanese to be occupied by the Italians and the springboard of their expedition to Rhodes.

The port of *Periyialo* (Astynea D), situated on the w. side of the Bay of Malte-sana, virtually forms one commune with the island capital **Kastello** (263 ft), named after its Venetian castle. The streets of the town are steep and narrow and many of the houses have wooden balconies. The **Castle**, built by John Quirini in the 13C, has its entrance on the w. Over the vaulted entrance, which bears the Quirini arms, is the restored Church of the *Madonna of the Castle*; on the outer wall of the apse the Quirini arms are repeated. On one occasion the defenders of the castle are said to have repelled assailants who were milling round the gate by throwing down on to them beehives full of previously maddened bees. The interior of the castle is a complex of narrow lanes, dilapidated houses and covered passage-ways, among which is another church, *St George's*.

Of the many attractive seaside hamlets, linked by dirt roads or mule paths, the prettiest is *Livádi*, just s.w. of the town.

The steamers on the more direct services leave Cape Sounion to port, and round the s. point of Kea (light-house) close inshore. Kithnos is seen to starboard and Siros, farther on, to port.

PATMOS (ΠΑΤΜΟΣ), where St John the Divine received his Revelation, is the northernmost of the Dodecanese. Though its area is only 15 sq. m., a most irregular shape gives the island a long coastline with many little bays. Its three sections are joined by two narrow isthmuses, of which that nearest the centre forms the focal point of the island. Here was the ancient city, here is the modern port, Skala, dominated from the s. by Patmos Town and its fortified monastic crag. The rocky and volcanic soil is moderately hilly, rising to 885 ft. The climate is healthy, but the arid soil yields only a small quantity of cereals, vegetables, and wine, not sufficient for the needs of the 2500 inhabitants, who live mainly by sponge-fishing. The water is brackish.

History. *Patmos* receives passing mention by Thucydides, Strabo, and Pliny. Its early inhabitants were Dorians, who later received Ionian colonists. The

Romans made it a place of exile for political prisoners. Here, in A.D. 95, during the reign of Domitian, was banished St John the Divine, by tradition identified with the Apostle John, though the identification has been disputed. For centuries the island was deserted owing to incursions of Saracen pirates. In 1088, the blessed Christodoulos, a Bithynian abbot, obtained permission from Alexis I Comnenus to found a monastery at Patmos in honour of St John. The island was captured by the Venetians in 1207. In 1461 Pope Pius II took both island and monastery under his protection. The Turks captured Patmos in 1537, and exacted from the monks an annual tribute. In 1669 the island received Venetian refugees from Candia (Crete).

Landing is made at **Skala** (*Patmion* B; *Astoria* C; *Rex* D; rooms in private houses), the commercial centre (1180 inhab.) of the island, situated in a sheltered bay that opens to the E. The animated Plateia, with arcaded buildings in the Italian colonial style, opens directly from the quay. Near by on the shore is a pleasant church with twin domes. A motor-road (1¼ m.; taxis) has all but superseded the ancient paved mule-path (20 min.) to Patmos Town. On the ascent there are fine *Views of the surrounding islands and rocks. Half-way up are the new buildings of the *Theological College*, founded in 1669 and attended by students from all Greece, and the CONVENT OF THE APOCALYPSE (Μονὴ τῆς Ἀποκαλύψεως), a cell of the monastery. Here are three small churches, and the *Cave of St Anne*, where by tradition St John dictated the Revelation to his disciple Prochoros.

Patmos, or *Khora* (850 inhab.), has pleasant 16–17C houses spread round the foot of the monastery, 500 ft above the sea. The fortified ***Monastery of St John,** founded in 1088 by the Blessed Christodoulos, has the appearance of a great polygonal castle, with towers and battlements. It is visited by the faithful on 21 May, the saint's day, and celebrates Easter week with some pomp. Visit, daily 8 or 8.30–12 & 3–6 (winter 2–4), closed Sun aft; 10 dr. An excellent illustrated guide (1964; 60 dr.) is available in English. To the left, as we enter by the fortified gate, is the tomb of Gregory of Kos, Bp. of Dhidhimotikon (d. 1693). The *Entrance Court*, built in 1698, is attractive. Its E. side forms the exo-narthex of the church, which incorporates elements from an earlier chapel and perhaps from a Temple of Artemis. Between the arches hangs a huge wooden simantron.

We enter the CHURCH by the right-hand door, which admits to the *Founder's Chapel*; his marble sarcophagus is surmounted by a reliquary covered with repoussé scenes in silver-gilt (1796). We pass into the *Narthex* by a low doorway having an ancient lintel and a medieval door, and thence into the church proper, a Greek cross-in-square. The floor, of grey and white marble, dates back to the foundation. The Ikonostasis (1820) is heavy and ornate, and some of the furniture has inlaid work in a Saracen style. Above the door of the Outer Treasury is an ikon on a gold ground, signed by Emmanuel Tzanes (1674). The 12C *Chapel of the Theotokos*, to the s., contains near-contemporary *Frescoes, brought to light in 1958, when later paintings were stripped away. Behind the altar, the Holy Trinity, represented as three angels being given hospitality by Abraham; below, the Virgin, flanked by the archangels, Michael and Gabriel, wearing Byzantine imperial robes.

Leaving by the s. door, we find ourselves in the *Inner Courtyard*, from which opens the *Refectory*, a modified 11C edifice equipped with long stone tables. The walls have remains of 12C frescoes representing scenes of the Passion, miracle of the loaves, etc.—A stair leads up to the *LIBRARY (c. 2000 printed books) in which are displayed a selection from the collection of 890 MSS. The greatest treasure, since the 9C Plato codex was removed in 1803 (now in Oxford), is 33 leaves of the *Codex Porphyrius*, comprising most of St Mark's gospel. The greater part of the book (182 ff) is in Leningrad. It was written in the early 6C on purple vellum, in uncials of silver and the holy names in gold. Important textually also are an 8C Book of Job, with commentaries drawn from 19 scholars; and the Discourses of St Gregory, written in 941 in Calabria. This is one of the works listed in 1201 in a surviving Catalogue of the Library. Some exquisite illumination in the Byzantine tradition can be seen in various Gospels and Cartularies (12–14C). Also displayed are charters and deeds from the *Monastic Archives* (13,000 documents), including the foundation chrysobul of Alexis Comnenus.

The *TREASURY, the most important monastic collection in Greece outside Mt. Athos, contains embroidered stoles (15–18C); ikons, notably a miniature mosaic framed in silver of St Nicholas (11C) and a celebrated St Theodore (13C); church furniture, including a handsome chalice of 1679, a superb crozier (1677) with gold relief decoration and pale blue enamel work, ornamented with diamonds; benediction crosses in wooden filigree; pendant model ships (16C) in enamelled silver set with precious stones, worn by the wives of rich ship-owners. The windows command a fine view of Skala and the w. roof terrace the finest *Panorama of the greater part of the Aegean.

Some vestiges of *Ancient Patmos* crown the hill *Kastelli* behind Skala to the N.W.—Launches depart at frequent intervals in July–Aug for various beaches, of which *Grikou* (Xenia **B**) lies to the S.E.; *Kambos* (taverna) to the N.E. (25 min.); and *Lampi*, bright with coloured stones, on the N. coast.

Arkoí, to the N.E. of Patmos and N. of Lipsoi, is a dependent islet with under 50 inhabitants.

Lipsoi (ΛΕΙΨΟΙ), situated E. of Patmos and N. of Leros and surrounded by numerous islets, is one of the smallest of the Dodecanese with an area of 6 sq. miles. Its outline is irregular and indented, especially on the S.E. coast, in which is the little harbour. The only centre of population is the village (590 inhab.) of *Lipsoi* (Kalypso **D**) above the harbour. A little food is produced; fishing has some importance.

LEROS (ΛΕΡΟΣ), like Patmos, consists of three peninsulas joined by two isthmuses, its irregular shape being caused by deep indentations of the sea. The largest of these, affording safe anchorage, are the Bay of Alinda on the E. coast, on which is the island capital, and the bays of Gourna and Porto Lago, on the w. coast. The island is well wooded and its hills accessible by Italian military roads. The fertile valleys in the centre yield olives, figs, carobs, tobacco, fruit, and wine.

History. *Leros* and *Kalymnos* are believed to have been the Kalydnian Isles mentioned by Homer. Leros is said to have been colonized by Miletus. The inhabitants had a reputation for being unprincipled. The island was famed for its honey and for a Temple of Artemis, associated with the story of Meleager and his sisters. Leros shared the medieval history of its neighbours. In 1916 the Royal Navy set up a base at Porto Lago, which was greatly developed by the Italians after 1923. Here on 3 Feb 1926 Adm. de Pinedo ended his pioneer flight from Australia. In the Second World War British forces temporarily occupied Leros. In more recent times of political stress it has known internee camps.

Island Customs. During the Carnival men and women compose satirical verses which children, in the garb of monks, recite at parties given in houses where a marriage has taken place during the previous year. This custom seems to derive from the ceremonies in honour of Dionysos at Eleusis. A peculiarity of local law is that all real property passes in the female line, with the result that virtually all the houses and landed property belong to women.

The ship enters Porto Lago bay (comp. above) and landing is made at **Lakki** (*Leros* C), a busy place of 2400 inhabitants. An asphalt road mounts to (2 m.) **Platanos** which, with *Ayía Marína* (Alindon **B**), its other port on the Bay of Alinda, 2 m. N.E., forms the capital, with 2450 inhabitants. The houses rise on the hillside below the *Kastro*, which is situated on a height inaccessible from the E. and precipitous on the other sides. The castle, originally Byzantine, was rebuilt by the Knights of St John. A cross on the hillside marks the *British Military Cemetery*, where lie the casualties of the battle in November 1943.

From Platanos a road leads round the bay to the summer resort of *Álinda*, while a mule path descends to *Panteli*, a beach 500 yds S.E. of the castle.

Leros is surrounded by numerous islets. About 12 m. E. is *Pharmáko*, or Pharmakousa, where Julius Caesar, returning from his notorious sojourn in Bithynia, was captured by pirates and detained for 38 days until his ransom arrived; he later caught and crucified his captors.

KALYMNOS (ΚΑΛΥΜΝΟΣ) lies immediately s. of Leros and w. of the Asiatic peninsula of Bodrum (Halicarnassus). The island is approximately rectangular in shape, with a peninsular extension to the N.W. separated by a channel of only $1\frac{1}{2}$ m. from Leros. Its greatest length is 13 m. and its width 8 m., giving an area of 42 sq. miles. The surface is mountainous and barren, except in the valleys. A range extending along the peninsula joins the northernmost of three transverse ranges in the main part of the island. The central range is the highest, with Mt Profitis Ilias (2250 ft); it is continued to the w. by the hills of the islet of Telendos. These three ranges are separated by two fertile valleys, that of Vathy between the N. and the central range, and that of Pothia and Brosta between the central and s. range. The coastline is much indented, with precipitous cliffs and small coves. The population of 13,300 is mainly concentrated in the island capital *Pothia*. The chief industry now as in ancient times is the fishing and marketing of sponges. The produce includes figs, oranges, olives, grapes, and cereals. Kalymnos was once famed for its honey, which rivalled that of Attica.

History. *Kalymnos* is believed to be one of the Kalydnian Isles of the Homeric Catalogue of Ships, the other being Leros. The earliest inhabitants were probably Carians; later the island was colonized by Dorians from the Argolid. In antiquity its fortunes tended to follow those of Kos, and in the Middle Ages it underwent the usual Venetian, Rhodian, and Turkish periods. It was most actively opposed to Italian rule, using blue and white paint everywhere to simulate the Greek national colours, and in 1935 rioting against an attempt to suppress Greek in schools and to set up an autocephalous Church of the Dodecanese. In the Second World War most of the Kalymnians took refuge in the Asiatic peninsula opposite the island, whence they dispersed to various places, including Gaza in Israel.

The capital **Pothia** (*Olympic*, *Thermai* **C**), or *Kalymnos*, is also the chief port and the industrial and commercial centre of the island, a town (9500 inhab.) comparable in size with Ermoupolis in Syra. It is situated at the head of a bay of the s. coast. Lively in autumn and winter when the sponge-divers are home, it is less gay after Easter-tide when they depart *en masse* for the North African coast. To the S.E. of the town, which holds little interest for visitors, is a small thermal establishment. There is a small *Archaeological Museum*.

A motor-boat may be taken in 35 min. to the *Cave of Kefalas*, near the s.w. promontory of the island. The cave (adm. fee) was explored in 1961 and discovered to have been a sanctuary of Olympian Zeus.

A road (bus; cars for hire at Pothia) leads up the fertile and beautiful valley. Soon after leaving the town, we pass on the left a hill with three disused windmills on its slopes and on its summit a ruined *Castle of the Knights*, with a little church.—2 m. *Khorío* (2300 inhab.) is the former capital of Kalymnos, built below a *Castle* which served as a refuge in the Middle Ages. Farther on the valley narrows.—Near (2½ m.) *Damos* we pass a ruined church, of which only the apse remains, near which are the remains of a Temple of Apollo, of a theatre, and of many rock-hewn tombs of the Mycenean Age.—The road now bears s.w. and descends.—3½ m. *Pánormos* (Drosos **C**), on the w. coast, and *Mirtées* (Delfini **C**), 1 m. farther on, are summer resorts.

To the N., close to the shore, is the islet of **Telendos**, with Greek and Roman remains and the ruins of the *Monastery of Ayios Vasileios*, dominated by a medieval castle. Since the Middle Ages the coastline has receded; for about a mile from the shore the remains of medieval houses can be seen under water.

FROM POTHIA TO VATHY, poor coast-road. Just beyond the entrance to the inlet is seen the mouth of the *Grotto of Daskaleios*, the most considerable of the caves in the island. It is accessible only from the sea and difficult to reach. Immediately inside is a chamber 82 ft long, from which opens on the right another chamber, at a lower level, with stalactites and stalagmites and a cavity full of brackish water. Here many prehistoric objects were found, ranging from the Neolithic to the Bronze Age.—At the head of the inlet we reach the district of **Vathy**, comprising three villages, *Rhina*, the little port, *Platanos*, named after a huge plane tree, and *Metokhi*, farther inland. The VALLEY OF VATHY is the most delectable part of the island, its luxuriant vegetation thriving on the volcanic and well-watered soil. At its mouth are orange and tangerine orchards and occasional olive groves; farther inland are figs and vineyards. The barrenness of the enclosing hills is in sharp contrast to the fertility of the valley. It is rich in antiquities. At Rhina is a rock-hewn throne; near Platanos are cyclopean walls and a little chapel in an enclosure of Hellenic walls.

Between Kalymnos and Kos is the islet of *Pserimos* (4 sq. m.), with a monastery and a hundred inhabitants.

The island of **KOS** (ΚΩΣ), or *Cos* (16,650 inhab.) is the second most visited of the Dodecanese, though, with an area of 109 sq. m., it is only one-fifth the size of Rhodes. It is a long narrow island, with a length of 28 m. from N.E. to s.w., and a width varying from 7 to 1 m., its narrowest part being the isthmus leading to the Peninsula of Kephalos at its s.w. end. It is situated at the entrance to the deeply indented Gulf of Kos, the Ceramic Gulf of antiquity, between the Asiatic Peninsula of Bodrum (Halicarnassus) on the N., from which it is separated by only 3 m., and the Peninsula of Knidos on the s., which is 10 m. away. A long mountain chain runs near the s. of the island from Cape Phoka, at its E. end, to the neighbourhood of Pylae, in the centre. Its highest point is Mt Oromedon or Dikaios (2780 ft), gently sloping on the N., precipitous on the s. In the N.W. there is a plateau, whence the ground slopes towards the sea. The Peninsula of Kephalos is moderately hilly, with Mt Latra rising to 1404 ft, the hills sloping down to Cape Krikhelos, the southernmost point of the island. The coastline is scarcely indented, and there is only one real harbour, Mandraki, at the city and port of Kos, which is situated at the N.E. end of the island. The inhabitants are mainly engaged in agriculture. Kos produces an abundance of juicy grapes, as well as fine water melons and oil, cereals, vegetables and tobacco. Among local wines are Glafkos (white) and Apellis (red).

The island is better watered than any other of the Dodecanese. It is especially rich in warm and tepid ferruginous springs celebrated even before the time of Hippocrates, the greatest physician of antiquity, who was born at Kos c. 460 B.C. and is said to have died in 357 at the age of 104. Another native was the poet Philetas, a contemporary of Ptolemy II Philadelphos (285–247 B.C.). The bucolic poet Theocritus, born at Syracuse c. 310 B.C., lived for a time in Kos as a disciple of Philetas. His 7th Idyll has a Coan setting. The painter Apelles, whose Aphrodite Anadyomene adorned the Asklepieion, is claimed as a native of Kos, though he may have been born in Ionia at Kolophon or Ephesus. He flourished in the time of Alexander the Great (336–323 B.C.).

History. The island has had several names. Thucydides and Strabo called it *Kos Meropis*, Pliny *Nymphaea*, and Stephanos of Byzantium *Karis*. In the Middle Ages it was known as *Lango*, perhaps because of its length, and later as *Stanchio*, a corruption of 'stin Ko', whence the Turkish *Istanköy*. Kos was inhabited in Neolithic times, as is proved by discoveries in the Cave of Aspropetro, near Kephalos. It was colonized by Carians and, in the Homeric Age, by Dorians from Epidauros. In the Persian wars it was under the sway of Artemisia, queen of Caria, and so fought on the losing side. Kos was at first a member of the Dorian hexapolis and of little importance. Its city (later remembered as Astypalaia, 'old city') was situated in the S.W. of the island and was destroyed by the Lacedaemonians in the Peloponnesian War. The new city of Kos was founded in 366 B.C. and rapidly prospered to become one of the greatest maritime centres of the Aegean. Its sanctuary of Asklepios and school of medicine made it famous all over the ancient world. The city was adorned with a plethora of artistic monuments. Its wines and silks had a great reputation; the light silk dresses called *Coae vestes* were well known to the Romans for their transparency.

Kos was occupied by Alexander the Great in 336 B.C., and on his death in 323 passed to the Ptolemies. Ptolemy II Philadelphos was born in the island in 309. Cleopatra is said to have used the island as a store for some of her treasures. Later Kos was allied to Rome before becoming part of the pro-consular Province of Asia. In the Byzantine era Kos was the seat of a bishop and many early Christian basilicas (5–6C) have been uncovered. In the 11C Kos was ravaged by Saracens. Later it passed to the Genoese, becoming in 1304 a fief of the Zaccharia family. Two years later it was ceded to the Knights of St John, who did not take possession till 1315. The Knights made it into a strong-point. It was attacked by the Turks in 1457 and 1477, and fell to them, with Rhodes, in 1522. Hadji Ali Haseki, voivode and tyrant of Athens, was finally exiled to Kos and there on 23 Dec 1795 beheaded. In 1912, after nearly four centuries of Turkish domination, it was occupied by the Italians in the course of their war with Turkey. In the Second World War British forces temporarily occupied the island until driven out by the Germans.

The city of **Kos** is situated in a plain at the N.E. end of the island, just s. of the Kos Channel (here at its narrowest; 3 m.), which separates it from the Anatolian coast. Despite undistinguished modern buildings it is a pleasant town with tidy open streets, resplendent gardens and orchards, and extensive Classical and Roman remains. The climate is somewhat relaxing but there are numerous springs. Of the 7800 inhabitants, about half are Muslims and most of the remainder of the Orthodox faith. Kos has some importance as a trading port, and has given name in English to a variety of lettuce introduced from its shores.

Airport, 16 m. w. near Andimákhia; daily service to Athens in 50 min., to Rhodes in 45 min.; also to Frankfurt, and (by charter) elsewhere.

Hotels. Continental Palace, Atlantis, both A; **Alexandra** (Pl. a); **Theoxenia** (Pl. b), **Kos** (Pl. c), **DPO,** these Apr–Oct, B; **Elli** (Pl. d), **Oscar** (Pl. f), **Milva** (Pl. g), **Koulias** (Pl. h), **Elizabeth** (Pl. i), these open all year; **Zephyros** (Pl. e), closed Dec–Mar, all these C, and others.—**Dimitra Beach B,** 5 m. s.e. at Ay. Fokas.

Restaurants on the waterfront.

Tourist Police in Town Hall.—**Post Office,** 2 Leof. Vas. Pavlou.—**OTE Centre,** 8 Vironos.

Bus Station, Kleopatras/Pisandhron.—Bicycles for hire by the hour.

Admission to *Museum, Castle,* and *Roman House* at standard museum hours (except that only the museum closes Tues and is free Thurs & Sat); to the *Asklepieion* at standard site hours; each 25 dr.

History. A number of Minoan-type tombs have been discovered s.w. of the town, and Protogeometric and Geometric graves within its walls. The ancient city, founded in 366 b.c., had a perimeter of c. 2½ miles. Devastated by earthquakes c. 5 b.c., in a.d. 142, and again in 469, it was virtually destroyed in 554. The old materials were largely reused in each new rebuilding and later pillaged for the medieval defences. The City of the Knights, bounded by an enceinte, erected in 1391–96 to counter the menace of Bayezid, occupied only the agora and harbour quarter of the old city. Vestiges remain opposite the castle, whence the course of the wall may be traced to the s.w. tower (see below). The Schlegelholz Bastion, adorned with arms of the bailiff and of Grand Master Heredia, survives at the s.e. corner; within the walls remain three small Byzantine chapels and a house bearing the arms of Bailiff Francesco Sans (1514). Archaeological explorations, begun in 1900 by Rudolf Herzog, were undertaken after 1928 by Luciano Lorenzi of the Italian School, and given impetus by the havoc caused on 23 April 1933 by a severe earthquake. The most important digs were in 1935–43. Many of the mosaics recovered were removed to adorn the castle in Rhodes.

The picturesque harbour of *Mandraki* has the same name as its counterpart in Rhodes. It is well equipped as a yacht station. Opposite the landing-place the former *Palace of the Regent,* by F. di Fausto (1928), houses the Town Hall, Custom House, and Port Offices. We turn left and mount to the terreplein of the castle, now Plateia Platanou. In the centre grows the so-called *Plane-tree of Hippocrates,* a gigantic tree with a trunk 45 ft in diameter and branches propped up by antique marble fragments. Inevitably tradition insists that Hippocrates taught under its shade, though it is not more than 500 years old. To the right stands the *Mosque of Gazi Hassan Pasha,* or *of the Loggia,* a three-storied building of 1786, entered on the first floor by a graceful staircase with a double portico or loggia. An elegant *Minaret* stands at the corner. Beneath the tree a *Fountain* has for basin an antique sarcophagus. A little grove shades the cemetery.

From the terreplein a stone bridge leads across the outer moat (now a palm-shaded avenue) to the **Castle of the Knights,** the city's principal monument. The fortress has two enceintes, one within the other. We enter by a drawbridge and a gateway in the s. curtain wall of the outer enceinte. Above the gate are a Hellenic frieze and the quartered arms of Amboise and the Order.

The original castle, roughly rectangular in plan, was begun in 1450 by the Venetian Fantino Guerini, governor of Kos (1436–53), and completed in 1478 by the Genoese Edoardo de Carmadino (governor 1471–95). After the unsuccessful Turkish assault of 1480, an outer enceinte was begin in 1495 by Grand Master Pierre d'Aubusson and completed in 1514 by G. M. Fabrizio Del Carretto. In its construction Italian architects and craftsmen were employed. Both enceintes incorporate masonry from the Asklepieion and other ancient Greek buildings. There is a deep fosse between the two lines of walls.

A passage-way leads to the s. terrace, from which a flight of steps gives access to the *Antiquarium*, containing Coan marbles, inscriptions, sculptural fragments, sepulchral monuments, and a number of fine knightly escutcheons carved in marble. One of the inscriptions commemorates the physician Xenophon, who helped to poison the Emp. Claudius (Tacitus, 'Annals', xii, 67, 2).

The heavy cylindrical *Bastion Del Carretto*, at the s.w. angle of the Outer Enceinte, resembles the bastion of the same name in the walls of Rhodes. The corresponding *North-East Tower*, which projects somewhat, commands a good view over the sea towards Anatolia. The n.w. tower, or *Tower of Aubusson*, overlooking the harbour, is polygonal. It bears the arms of Aubusson quartered with those of the Order, and an Italian inscription of 1503.

From the terrace we descend a staircase to the left of the Antiquarium and reach a horseshoe ravelin in front of the Inner Enceinte. On its right is the entrance. All four angles of the Inner Enceinte have cylindrical towers, with battlements

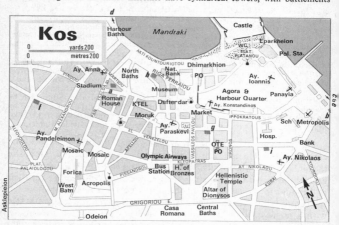

and embrasures, and appropriate escutcheons. The inner curtain wall is similarly adorned. On the *Inner South-West Tower* are the fleurs-de-lis of France.

We turn s. again and enter the partially walled area of the Chora, or city of the Knights (comp. above), excavated since the earthquake of 1933 to show Roman levels of the AGORA AND HARBOUR QUARTER.

The n. sector of the excavations lay outside the Hellenistic city walls. From e. to w. may be distinguished a Hellenistic sanctuary, orientated to the n.; next, a *Stoa* (4–3C), of which 8 columns with acanthus capitals have been re-erected. These were recovered from the foundations of the *Harbour Basilica*, built on the remains of the Stoa in the 5C A.D. Its ruins lie immediately s. of the Mosque of the Loggia. Farther w. are scanty but extensive vestiges of the *Sanctuary of the Port Quarter*, probably an Aphrodision. The s. sector of the area represents the n. extremity of the ancient city proper, which is divided by a broad road running N.–S. To the e. are insulae of houses and shops. To the w. lies the **Agora,** just within the Knights' w. gate, which bore through the Middle Ages the name 'Porta tou Forou'. A fine stretch of rusticated ashlar masonry marks its e. boundary and some columns have been re-erected.

We quit the site by the gate leading to PLATEIA ELEFTHERIAS, the main square of the town. The **Museum** contains sculpture of the Hellenistic and Roman periods, notably a small Aphrodite and Eros, figures of Diana of Ephesus, and a statue of Hippocrates. Across the square is the 18C *Defterdar Mosque*. Odhos Vas. Pavlou leads to another area of excavations in which are a large *Roman House* (rebuilt by the Italians to protect its many mosaics) and the *Central Baths*. Hence we may turn right to visit the **Odeion**, approached by an avenue of cypresses; of its 14 rows of marble seats, seven are original. The near-by church of *Ayios Ioannis Prodromos* is the baptistery of the largest early Christian church of Kos.

Opposite are the *WESTERN EXCAVATIONS, a huge L-shaped area below the Acropolis, a low hill crowned by a minaret. A section of the *Decumanus Maximus* is exposed with the houses on its N. side, many of which retain mosaics (3C A.D.) and frescoes. The large *House of the Europa Mosaic* is the best preserved, and yielded many complete statues. The *Cardo*, beautifully paved and recalling the streets of Pompeii, leads N. To the left are extensive *Roman Baths*. The calidarium is well preserved; the frigidarium was transformed into a Christian *Basilica* at a later date. The marble immersion font and much of the mosaic door survives of the baptistery, the marble door-way of which has been re-erected. Farther w. the colonnade of the *Xystos* of a Hellenistic gymnasium (2C B.C.) has been restored. To the right of the road, beyond a row of antique taverns, stands the restored *Forica* of the Baths, a sumptuous latrine built round a peristyle court. Beyond, a shelter protects a large mosaic showing gladiatorial scenes.

A flight of steps by the Forica leads up to the Acropolis, whence the picturesque Odhos Apellou, an old street of the Turkish quarter, returns N.E. Farther N.W. are some remains of the *Stadium*, principally the curious aphesis, or starting-gate.

THE PRINCIPAL EXCURSION is to the Asklepieion, 2½ m. by road. We take the Kephalos road and, beyond the town, fork left.—2 m. *Ghermi*, or Khermetes, a Muslim village, officially *Platánion*. By an avenue of cypresses we approach the **Asklepieion**, or *Sanctuary of Asklepios*. It occupies the site of a grove sacred to Apollo Kyparessios, mentioned in the 4C, but it was not built until after the death of Hippocrates (357 B.C.) and dates from the Hellenistic period.

The sanctuary was one of the main seats of the Asklepiadai, supposed descendants of Asklepios, who were a hereditary close order of priests, jealous guardians of the secrets of medicine. The technique of healing differed from that at Epidauros and elsewhere, where cures were effected by suggestion. At Kos, as is revealed by inscriptions, patients underwent positive treatment at the hands of physicians on lines laid down by Hippocrates. Herondas in his fourth mime describes a sacrifice at the Asklepieion. The sanctuary had the right of asylum. It throve in the days of the Ptolemies and later under Nero. The rich court physician Xenophon (see above), on his return to Kos, lavished on the sanctuary the statues he had amassed in Rome. Even in the late-Imperial period great baths were built. In the 6C A.D. all was overwhelmed, either by an earthquake or in 554 when Anatolian hordes ravaged the island. The Knights of St John used the ruins as a quarry. A local antiquary, G. E. Zaraphtis, identified the site; in 1902 the German Herzog began systematic excavation, and the work was completed by the Italians with their customary extensive restoration. An International School of Medicine is planned near by.

We pass (l.) remains of *Roman Baths* (1C A.D.), where the hypocaust and plunge bath are well preserved, and ascend to the LOWER TERRACE of the sanctuary. This was surrounded on three sides by porticoes. On the fourth side was a retaining wall of massive proportions, part of which survives. Near the middle of the wall are a fountain, which still plays, the staircase leading to the Middle Terrace, and several reservoirs fed by conduits from ferruginous and sulphurous springs and drawn upon by invalids taking the cure. Between the reservoirs and the staircase are the remains of a small *Temple*, with the pedestal of a statue of Nero as Asklepios (the inscription records its dedication by the physician Xenophon). On this terrace were probably held the Asklepian

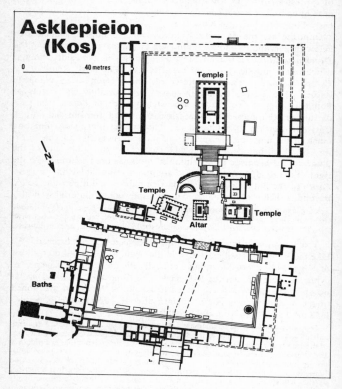

Festivals, which, on the evidence of inscriptions, included athletic games and other contests.

We ascend to the MIDDLE TERRACE. On the right is an Ionic *Temple in Antis*, dating from the late 4C or early 3C B.C., and so the oldest temple in the Sanctuary. The capitals, of painted marble, are exceptionally fine; the rest of the building was in white or black marble. In the floor of the cella was a coffer of marble slabs for the reception of votive offerings. The temple was adorned with paintings by Apelles, including the celebrated Aphrodite Anadyomene, removed by Augustus to Rome. Behind the temple is a *Roman House* on a Greek foundation, probably the priest's dwelling. In front of the temple, to the left, is the *Great Altar*, similar to that at Pergamon; it is in the form of the Greek letter Π, with a central staircase. Its ceiling, partly surviving, was coffered; between the columns of the portico were statues of Asklepios, Hygieia, and members of their family, attributed to the sons of Praxiteles. To the left of the altar is a *Roman Temple*, orientated aslant. It is a peripteral Ionic building, with half-fluted columns and a magnificent entablature with floral decoration, part of which remains. In the wall at the end of the terrace is a *Monumental Staircase*, to the left of which is an *Exedra*, with niches for statues.

The UPPER TERRACE occupies the site of the Sacred Wood. On it is the great Doric **Temple of Asklepios**. This is peripteral, with six columns by eleven. It stands on a base of three carved steps, the lowest of which is of black marble. The well-preserved *Pronaos* is in antis; its threshold is a black limestone monolith. In it was installed in the Christian era a chapel of the *Panayia tou Tarsou*, the altar of which survives. Three sides of the terrace were lined with porticoes, on which houses were later built.

From the Upper Terrace there is a magnificent *View. Below is the town of Kos, with its harbour, surrounded by gardens and orchards. In the distance, across the sea, are the Peninsula of Knidos to the s.e., the deeply indented Gulf of Kos to the e., the Promontory of Bodrum (Halicarnassus) to the n.e., and the islands of Pserimos and Kalymnos to the n.w.

The Asklepieion is situated near the foot of **Mt Oromedon**, the highest peak of which is *Dikaíos* (2780 ft). The mountain has many springs, one of which, ¾ hr distant, supplies the town of Kos with water by means of an aqueduct. This is the ancient *Vourina*, the Sacred Spring of Theocritus. It is enclosed in a domed building approached by a corridor. Another fountain has the name of *Kokkinero*, or 'Red Water'.

FROM KOS TO KEFALOS, road, 27 m., traversing the island lengthwise. We leave on the left the turning for the Asklepieion, which we see on our left ½ m. farther on, with Mt Dikaíos behind it. To the right, reaching to the sea, extends an agricultural plain. At (5½ m.) *Zipári*, which had an early basilica dedicated to St Paul (mosaics and early font) a road leads left for *Asfendioú* (2 m.; 800 ft), on the slopes of Dikaíos, where a Byzantine basilica and a small temple of Demeter and Kore were explored by the Italians. Dikaíos can be ascended in 1 hour.—On the left is the mountain ridge forming the backbone of the island; on the right, over the sea, are the islands of Pserimos and Kalymnos. We pass a ruined Roman aqueduct. From (9½ m.) **Pilí** (1500 inhab.) a mule-track leads to **Old Pylai** (2½ m.), a ruined village dominated by a hill (1050 ft) on which are the remains of a concentric Byzantine *Castle*. Within the lowest enceinte is the church of the *Purification of the B.V.M.*, incorporating ancient masonry and decorated with well-preserved 14C frescoes.

From Pilí a winding road descends to *Kardámaina* (Stelios, Panorama, C), on the s. coast, where pottery and tomato-juice are made. There are remains of a Hellenistic theatre and of an early-Christian basilica (Ayia Theotis). It has an infrequent caique service to Nisyros.

After passing a large windmill, the road rises to a plateau and begins to descend. —At (15½ m.) **Andimákhia** (420 ft), a straggling village of 1260 inhab., is the airport of Kos. A track leads left in 2 m. to the battlemented *Castle of Antimachia* (472 ft), dating from the time of the Knights. It is triangular in plan and has a drawbridge in front of its only gate, which bears the quartered arms of Amboise and of the Order. Inside are ruins of houses, cisterns, and two churches.

As we proceed, we obtain a view of the curving end of the island, dominated by Mt Latra (1404 ft), and known as the Peninsula of Kephalos. The road, unsurfaced beyond the airport, gradually descends to cross a stream and then rises steeply to a bare plain, where the island contracts into an isthmus only 1 mile across. The road approaches the n. coast and then descends to (21 m.) the shore of the Bay of Kamares, on the s. coast. In the bay is the picturesque *St Nicholas Rock*. The ruins of two Christian basilicas are exposed. The ancient capital city of *Astypalaia* was in the neighbourhood, but its exact location is unknown.—27 m.

Képhalos (347 ft; 2100 inhab.; *Sidney* D) dominates the Bay of Kamares. On a neighbouring height is a ruined *Castle*. About 20 min. s. are the remains of a Hellenistic Doric *Temple* in antis; its stylobate and some column drums remain. About 10 min. farther are another Temple in antis and a *Theatre*. The rock-hewn *Cave of Aspropetro*, farther s.e., has yielded Neolithic objects.

Nisyros (ΝΙΣΥΡΟΣ), a small pentagonal island of 16 sq. m., is an extinct volcano, whose hot sulphurous springs have been celebrated since antiquity. The population of 1290 souls is divided among four places linked by one road, 5 m. long. *Mandráki* (820 inhab.; Inns), on the n. coast, has a ruined castle of the Knights and a subterranean church; its little spa (*Loutrá*) is 1 m. to the e. Farther on is *Páloi*, a fishing hamlet, with more baths. The other villages, *Emboriós* and *Nikiá* (prettier of the two with an extraordinary view), are on the rim of the central depression, which is 2½ m. across. The central cone, within, rises to 2270 ft.—In summer there are daily excursions from Kos (boat 2¼ hrs and bus).

Tilos (ΤΗΛΟΣ), lying between Nisyros on the n. and Khalki on the s., is accurately described by Strabo as long, high, and narrow. The Italians, reviving a medieval name of uncertain origin, called it *Piscopi*. Apart from a coastal plain in the n., the interior is hilly, rising in the n.w. to 2145 ft. Most of the 350 inhabitants are engaged in agriculture. The women wear traditional costume. The rugged coastline is indented with bays. *Livadia*, the island landing-place, on a bay of the n.e. coast, is connected with *Mikro Khorió*, a hamlet just below a central saddle, by a dirt road c. 1 m. long. The road continues n. to (4½ m.) *Megalo Khorió*, which through the ages has been the island capital. There are remains of Pelasgic walls; the church of the Archangel Michael is on the foundations of a Greek temple of the Acropolis; and the whole site is crowned by a ruined Venetian castle built of ancient masonry and incorporating a Classical gateway.

Syme (ΣΥΜΗ), or *Sími*, is situated at the mouth of the Doridis Gulf, between two Asiatic peninsulas—that of Knidos on the n. and that of Dorakis on the s. It is only 6 m. from the latter, which was called Cynossema Promontory in antiquity. The island is 15 m. n. of Rhodes across the Strait of Marmara. Of irregular shape, it has an area of 26 sq. miles. The arid interior is hilly, but the once deficient water supply is now augmented by a solar still. The coasts have high cliffs and are difficult of access, but there are inlets in which small ships can find shelter. Except in the fertile valley of Pédhi and Panaidakia and on the plateaux, the soil is allergic to cultivation. The climate is mild except in the height of summer, when the temperature may exceed 100°F. The population (23,000 in 1912; 6300 in 1937), much reduced by emigration, is 2500, all but a few in the capital. Small quantities of cereals, wine, olives, honey and tobacco are produced. The main industry is sponge-fishing. Symian divers are the ablest in the Aegean; they recovered the Ephebos of Antikythera. Their ships pass by inheritance in the male line, houses in the female line with the dowry.

History. The Homeric Catalogue of Ships records a contribution of three vessels from Syme to the Trojan expedition. Later Syme was colonized by the Carians, who abandoned it during a drought. In 411 b.c. the Lacedaemonians, after a successful engagement off Knidos with an Athenian naval detachment, set up a trophy on Syme. This action led to the revolt of Rhodes from the Athenian Confederacy. The islanders have always been renowned shipbuilders. They built fast skiffs for the Knights of St John and were employed in the same capacity by the Turks, under whom they enjoyed numerous privileges and extensive estates on the mainland. Much of their timber was used up during the War of Independence.

The town of **Syme** (*Nireus* **B**), in the N. of the island, is divided into *Yialós*, on its bay, and *Khorió*, above. Most of the inhabitants live in the upper town, where there is a small *Museum*. On a height above the town is a *Castle of the Knights*, partly built of blocks from the walls of the ancient Acropolis which once surrounded the hill. Over the entrance gate are the arms of Aubusson quartered with those of the Order (1507). Inside the castle are the *Church of the Panaya*, and the remains of a Temple of Athena. Below the houses of Upper Syme is the ancient Greek necropolis.

The *Bay of Emborio*, 1½ m. N.W. of lower Syme, once the island's commercial harbour, is now a summer resort.—In the *Bay of Pédhi*, 1½ m. E., is an isolated village normally occupied by farm labourers and fishermen and frequented by summer visitors. In the vicinity are Greek and Roman remains.

The *Monastery of St Michael Panormitis* (motor-boat in 1¾ hr), is situated on the Bay of Panormitis at the S. extremity of the island. It was built in the 18C, and used as a staging camp in 1945 for refugees returning from Turkey. The church has fine frescoes and an ikon of St Michael. The sanctuary contains offerings from Symians all over the world. The chief festival, on 7–9 Nov, attracts pilgrims from far and wide. In the church is a magnificent ikonostatis by Mastro Diaco Tagliaduro of Kos.

B The Southern Route

STEAMERS, see above. By this route a visit to the Dodecanese can be conveniently combined with a tour of Crete.

Kasos (ΚΑΣΟΣ) is the most southerly of the Dodecanese. It lies c. 30 m. E. of Zakro in Crete, across the Kasos Channel, and is separated from Karpathos by a channel of 7 miles. The island, elliptical in shape and with an area of 19 sq. m., has an overall length of 11 m. with precipitous and inaccessible coasts, save on the N.W. side where the few villages are scattered. The sea is often rough. The hilly interior rises in Mt Priona to 1800 ft. The population (1350) has been greatly reduced by emigration, in the past particularly to Egypt. More than 5000 Kasiots are said to have helped build the Suez Canal.

Kasos is mentioned in the Homeric Catalogue of Ships. It was made subject to the Venetian family of Cornaro in 1306, when they acquired Karpathos, and was lost to the Turks only in 1537. In 1824 the Egyptians ravaged the island, an event remembered as 'the Holocaust' by the Kasiots, and for some years afterwards the island was deserted.

Emboreió (Anagenissis **C**), the port, midway along the N. coast, lies just E. of the capital, *Frí* (ΦΡΥ), an abbreviated form of *Othrys*. It has many abandoned houses and is uninteresting save for the fine view of Karpathos to the E. Inland is *Póli*, the former capital, on the site of the acropolis of the ancient city.

KARPATHOS (ΚΑΡΠΑΘΟΣ), better known by its medieval name *Scarpanto*, is the chief of the group midway between Crete and Rhodes. Long and narrow, it is 30 m. from end to end with a maximum width of 7 m. and has about the same area as Kos. The coastline is steep but little indented: there are bays, but only the Bay of Tristoma at the N. end affords much protection from the prevailing winds. A mountain range traverses the island from N. to S., rising to Mt Profitis Ilias (3325 ft) and Mt Kalolimni (Lastros; 3675 ft), the twin peaks in the centre which virtually divide the island in two, isolating one part from the other. The long N. section, covered with stunted pine trees on the E. and bare on the W., is sparsely populated, preserves many ancient customs, and has few springs; the more populous s. section (known as 'European' Karpathos) is well watered and its valleys are productive. The 5400 inhabitants are mostly engaged in agriculture and pasture. There are said to be more Karpathiots in Piraeus than in Scarpanto. A great concourse of emigré islanders assembled in 1966 to discuss the island's future economy.

History. In antiquity, as officially today, the island was called *Karpathos*, though Homer has it as *Krapathos*. Its medieval name of *Scarpanto* was revived by the Italians and is still in common use. The Turks called it *Kerpe*. Despite its size, Karpathos has had an uneventful existence. The Latin Empire gave it in fief to the Genoese Andrea and Lodovico Moresco. In 1306 it was acquired by the Venetian family of Cornaro, who yielded it to the Turks in 1538. In 1835 Sultan Mahmoud II gave it certain financial privileges.

The chief port and 'capital' is **Pigádhia** (*Porphyris* C; *Karpathos*, *Anessis*, D), or *Kárpathos*, a modern town (1360 inhab.) on the wide sandy bay of *Vrónti* in the s.e. of the island. Gardens and olive-groves fringe it on the n.w. The rocky citadel to the e. is the site of Classical *Potidaion* and equally of a Mycenean settlement (tombs near by).

Tour of the s. part of the island, $21\frac{1}{2}$ m. ($34\frac{1}{2}$ km.). The road leads n.w. to ($4\frac{1}{2}$ m.) **Apéri** (490 ft), the former capital (600 inhab.), divided into two by a stream. It is the seat of the Metropolitan of Karpathos and Kasos. The streets are steep and narrow, many of them in steps.—The road ascends s.w. to ($5\frac{3}{4}$ m.) *Voláda* (1475 ft), with a castle on a prominent hill.—7 m. *Óthos* (2295 ft), starting-point of the overland route to the n. half of the island (comp. below).—$8\frac{3}{4}$ m. *Pilés* (1310 ft), with pleasant gardens, looks towards the w. coast, to which we descend and turn s.—12 m. *Finíki* is a little fishing harbour in a fertile region growing citrus fruits and vegetables. At the s. end of the same bay is ($13\frac{1}{2}$ m.) *Arkássa*, a picturesque village, with fruit orchards. It has remains of a 5C Byzantine church (Ayia Anastasia), the mosaic pavement of which is in Rhodes museum. On a steep-sided promontory to the s.w. are some remains of Classical *Arkaseia*.—A road, less good, climbs inland to ($17\frac{1}{2}$ m.) *Menetés*, a village served by bus (20 min.) from ($21\frac{1}{2}$ m.) Pigádhia (comp. above).

The centre of the island is reached by a mule-track from Othos (comp. above) round the w. side of Mt Kalolimni.—$8\frac{1}{2}$ m. *Mesokhório* is built on a precipitous rock on the w. coast. Here a stream gushes out of the pavement of a church. In the environs is the church of *Ayia Irini*, with frescoes, and many Byzantine ruins. On the islet of *Sokastro*, close inshore, is a ruined Frankish castle. From Mesokhorio a mule-track leads across the island to *Spóa* (1150 ft) above the little e. coast harbour of Ayios Nikólaos. From Spóa, where the pine forests are bent double by the wind, a mule-path goes along the mountain crest in 6 hrs to Olimbos (see below).

The n. part of the island is reached more easily (in 2 hrs) by hired launch from Pigádhia. Landing is made at *Dhiafáni* on the n.e. coast, whence a mule-path ascends to ($5\frac{1}{2}$ m.) **Ólimbos** (535 inhab.), perched on the flank of Profitis Ilias, overlooking the w. coast. On the slopes of the mountain are more than 40 windmills. Olimbos is supposed to be the oldest settlement in Karpathos. The inhabitants wear traditional costume, not merely on special occasions, but for everyday use. Their dialect retains many ancient Doric words. The well-built houses are in three sections and have handsome doors with wooden locks and keys said to be of a pattern dating back to Homeric times. The Byzantine village church has some frescoes. In the vicinity are the remains of an ancient temple.—About 3 hrs N. is *Trístoma*, with a landing-place on a relatively sheltered bay. A headland about half-way to Trístoma is taken as the site of *Brykoús*.

Immediately N. of Kárpathos and separated by a channel only 30 yds wide is the islet of *Sariá* (4 sq. m.), inhabited in summer only by shepherds. On it are the ruins of a Byzantine church.

The island of **Khalki** (ΧΑΛΚΗ), the ancient *Chalke* and medieval *Charki*, lies 10 m. w. of Rhodes. The bare and hilly interior culminates in Mt Merovigli (1955 ft). There are no springs and few wells. The population (390 inhab.) has been greatly reduced by emigration. The landing-place *Nimboreió*, or Skala, at the N.E. corner of the island, is served by daily boat from Kameiros Skala. A mule-path climbs inland in 30 min. to the villiage of *Khorió* (900 ft), now virtually abandoned. Its church is partly built of Hellenic materials. One mile inland, on top of a bare hill, formerly a Greek acropolis, is the Castle of the Knights, built on Greek foundations and incorporating much ancient masonry. Inside is the church of Ayios Nikolaos. with late Byzantine frescoes.

76 RHODES

The island of **RHODES** (ΡΟΔΟΣ), in Greek *Rhódhos*, with 66,600 inhab., is separated from the s.w. coast of Asia Minor by the Strait of Marmara, about 7 m. wide. By far the largest of the Dodecanese with an area of 540 sq. m., Rhodes is diamond-shaped, 48 m. long from N. to s. and with a maximum width of 22 miles. It is traversed from N. to s. by a range of hills rising from either end towards the w. centre, where Mt Ataviros shoots up to 3985 ft. The other summits do not exceed 2700 feet. Much of the island is very fertile, with a wide variety of plants and trees; vegetation grows to some of the mountain-tops. There are oranges, lemons, figs, pears, pistachio, and olives. Broom, myrtle, heath, spurge, and laurel grow in profusion, as well as aromatic plants such as lavender, sage, marjoram, and styrax. The rock-rose is so exuberant that Rhodes is often called the 'Island of Roses'. The fauna include deer (reintroduced by the Italians), foxes, hares, badgers, martens, and hedgehogs; partridges, vultures, jackdaws, and jays. In antiquity the island was infested with snakes (its name may derive from 'erod' a Phoenician word for snake), and farmers still wear leather boots to the knee as protection against a small species which is poisonous. The larger snakes are harmless. Some of the lizards are large: the 'Rhodes dragon' (*Agama stellio*) grows to 14 inches. There are so many butterflies that Rhodes has been called 'Butterfly Island'.

The climate of Rhodes resembles that of eastern Sicily. The temperature varies from 50°F. in winter to 86–90°F. in summer. The winds are constant and occasionally violent, though the E. side of the island is usually sheltered. Their force is put to use in the numerous windmills that are a feature of the landscape. The year is equally divided into a dry season, from April to the end of October, and a wet season, from November to the end of March. The best months for a visit are April–May and September–October. From spring to autumn the island is crowded with tourists from every country in Europe and hotel accommodation is at a premium.

History. In antiquity the island was called *Aithrea, Ophioussa* (from its snakes), *Telchinia* and several other names. The name of *Rhodes* is of uncertain etymology, but is probably not derived (as so often stated) from the Greek word for rose, ῥόδον. In one of his Odes, Pindar tells us of the birth of Rhodes, offspring of the love of Helios, the Sun God, for the nymph Rhoda. In the prehistoric era the island shared the culture of Crete and later of Mycenae Homer mentions three cities in Rhodes—Lindos, Ialysos, and Kameiros ('Iliad', II, 656). These three cities, with Kos, Knidos, and Halicarnassus, formed the Dorian hexapolis in the s.w. corner of Asia Minor.

The three Dorian cities of Rhodes attained a high degree of prosperity, with trade routes throughout the Mediterranean, and founded colonies in the neighbouring islands and on the coasts of Asia Minor and Europe. In the 6C B.C. they were governed by tyrants. Having submitted to the Persians in 490, in 478 the Rhodians joined the Delian Confederacy as subject-allies of Athens, but in 411, late in the Peloponnesian War, they revolted in favour of Sparta. In 408 the three cities united to found the capital *City of Rhodes*, which they populated with their own citizens. This was planned by Hippodamos of Miletus, the most famous architect of his age.

The new city, whose planning Strabo praises extravagantly, immediately became prominent. At first it had an oligarchic government and in 396 submitted to Sparta. Later its citizens acquired a democratic constitution and went over to the Athenians, whom they helped, in conjunction with the Persian fleet, to defeat the Spartans at the battle of Knidos (394). In 378 Rhodes joined the Second Athenian Confederacy, but in 357 she revolted again, this time at the instigation of Mausolus, king of Caria, who placed a Carian garrison in the island. As allies of Persia the Rhodians gave help to the city of Tyre when it was besieged by Alexander the Great. In 332 they had to suffer a Macedonian garrison, which they expelled after the death of Alexander. In the wars that followed, they allied themselves with Ptolemy I, who assisted them in 305 when their city was besieged by Demetrios Poliorketes. When, after a year, Demetrios was compelled to raise the siege, he was so impressed by the defenders' valour that he left them his siege artillery, from the sale of which they defrayed the cost of the Colossus. The Rhodians accorded divine honours to Ptolemy as their saviour: hence his name Soter.

Soon afterwards with heightened prestige, Rhodes attained the zenith of her prosperity. Her port became the centre of trade between Italy, Greece and Macedonia, and Asia and Africa. She became the first naval Power in the Aegean, with ships well built, efficiently manned and skilfully manoeuvred. Her currency was everywhere accepted. Rhodian law, the earliest code of marine law, was universally esteemed: Augustus adopted it as a model, an example followed by Justinian, and its provisions are still quoted today. With a population of 60,000–80,000, the city was lavishly equipped and adorned and began its artistic golden age. The devastation wrought by the great earthquake of 222 B.C. inspired an international programme of aid in money and talent. Even as late as the 1C A.D., when the city had been despoiled of most of its treasures, Pliny counted no fewer than 2000 statues, many of them colossal. The Rhodians were enthusiastic admirers of athletics, music, and oratory. The orator Aeschines (389–314 B.C.), after his discomfiture at the hands of Demosthenes, founded at Rhodes a school of rhetoric, which was later to be attended by famous Romans, including Cato, Cicero, Julius Caesar, and Lucretius. Apollonius (fl. 222–181 B.C.), a native of Alexandria, taught rhetoric at Rhodes with so much success that the Rhodians awarded him the cognomen Rhodius.

By the 2C B.C. the Rhodians were allies of Rome. Their help against Philip V of Macedon, which led to his defeat at Cynoscephalae in 197, gained them the Cyclades, and the participation of their fleet in the war against Antiochus the Great, king of Syria, won them in 188 B.C. the former Syrian possession of S. Caria, where they had from an early period made numerous settlements. The Rhodian espousal of the cause of Persius brought swift Roman retribution. After Pydna Rhodes had to surrender her possessions on the mainland of Asia Minor and, in 166, found her trade injured when the Romans declared Delos a free port. In the Mithridatic wars Rhodes recovered the favour of Rome. Mithridates unsuccessfully besieged the city. Sulla restored to Rhodes her lost Asiatic possessions. In the civil war Rhodes sided with Julius Caesar and suffered in consequence at the hands of Cassius, who plundered the city in 43 B.C. and destroyed or captured the Rhodian fleet. This was a fatal blow to the naval power of Rhodes.

Augustus accorded to Rhodes the title of Allied City. Vespasian (emperor A.D. 70–79) incorporated it in the empire. Reattached to the province of Asia, it became under Diocletian (284–305) capital of the province of the Islands. It was visited by St Paul during his second or third journey (Acts, xxi, 1) and it had a bishop at a very early date. In the 4C the bishops of Rhodes were granted the title of Metropolitan, with jurisdiction over 12 of the dioceses of the Archipelago.

In the 9C the Rhodians deserted the Roman church. In 1274, however, we find the Metropolitan of Rhodes attending the Council of Lyons and a signatory of the short-lived reunion of the Eastern and Latin churches.

After the division of the Empire in 395, Rhodes naturally became part of the Eastern Empire and followed its destiny. From 654 it was frequently pillaged and for a time occupied by the Saracens. In 1082 Alexander Comnenus gave the Venetians important privileges in the island. In the Crusades Christian ships used the ports of Rhodes as a convenient stopping-place. During the Fourth Crusade, which established the Latin empire of Constantinople, the Greek Governor of Rhodes, Leo Gavalas, declared the independence of the island. Later the Genoese obtained control of it and in 1306 received as refugees the Knights of St John of Jerusalem. The refugees soon became the masters of Rhodes.

The *Knights of St John of Jerusalem*, otherwise Knights of Rhodes and later Knights of Malta, were originally *Hospitallers*, charitable brotherhoods founded for the care in hospital of the poor and sick. They originated c. 1048 in a hospital which merchants of Amalfi had built in Jerusalem for pilgrims to the Holy Sepulchre. Their first rector, Gerard, formed them into a strictly constituted religious body subject to the jurisdiction of the Patriarch of Jerusalem. The Order soon became predominantly military and the Hospitallers were sworn to defend the Holy Sepulchre to the last drop of their blood and to make war on infidels wherever met. In 1191, after Saladin had captured Jerusalem, they retired to Acre. Bitter rivalry arose between them and the Knights Templars, ending in hostilities in which the Templars got the upper hand. Clinging to Acre, the Hospitallers were driven out in 1291 after a terrible siege, and they sailed to Cyprus. In 1306 they fled from Cyprus to Rhodes. Having in vain demanded from the emperor the fief of Rhodes, they took it by force in 1309, after a two years' siege.

The brethren were divided into three classes—knights, chaplains, and serving brothers or fighting squires who followed the knights into action. In the 12C the Order was divided into seven 'Tongues' or Languages—Provence, Auvergne, France, Italy, Spain (later subdivided into Aragon and Castile), England and Germany. Each 'Tongue' had a Bailiff, and the Bailiffs, under the presidency of the Grand Master, elected for life by the Knights, formed the chapter of the Order. The modern British Order of St John of Jerusalem, founded in 1827, may be regarded as a revival of the 'Language' of England.

Having conquered Rhodes, the Knights of St John built a powerful fleet which protected the island's trade. Pope Clement V assigned to them part of the property of the Templars who had been suppressed in 1312. For two centuries the Knights of St John defied the Turks. For his assistance to the Knights during the siege of 1313, Amadeus V, count of Savoy, was rewarded by a grant of the arms of the Order with a collar bearing the letters F.E.R.T. (Fortitudo ejus Rhodum tenuit). The Knights took part in the capture and later in the defence of Smyrna, and withstood two great sieges—in 1444 by the Sultan of Egypt, and in 1480 by Mehmet II, at which time their infantry general ('turcopolier') was an Englishman, John Kendal. At last, in June 1522 Suleiman I, having captured Belgrade, attacked Rhodes with a force said to have numbered 100,000 men. The Knights mustered only 650, with the addition of 200 Genoese sailors, 50 Venetians, 400 Cretans and 600 of the inhabitants. Pope Adrian VI vainly implored the Christian princes to come to their aid. The Turks had the city blockaded by sea. They eventually secured the heights above it and thence shelled the fortifications. Several times the besieged repaired the breaches in the walls, but their numbers daily diminished. They had spent their strength and traitors had infiltrated into their ranks. In December the Turks made another and final breach in the walls. The Knights capitulated on honourable terms. On 1 Jan 1523, the Grand Master, Villiers de l'Isle Adam, with 180 surviving brethren, left the island. They first retired to Candia (Herakleion), Crete, and in 1530 to Malta.

After their departure the churches were converted into mosques. Not till 1660 were the Fathers of the Mission able to return to Rhodes and administer to the Christian slaves. In 1719 they were placed under the protection of the Apostolic Prefecture of Constantinople. In 1873 French Franciscan Sisters established schools and in 1889 the Brothers of the Christian Doctrine founded the College of St John. In 1877 the island was created an apostolic prefecture.

In 1912, during their war with Turkey, the Italians captured Rhodes after a short siege. In the latter part of the Second World War the Germans took over from the Italians. In 1945 the island was freed by British and Greek commandos, and in 1947 it was officially awarded to Greece.

Rhodian Art. Rhodian artefacts of the 2nd millennium B.C. show marked influences of Crete and Mycenae. No palaces have been discovered, but chamber tombs have yielded sepulchral furniture, notably pottery, women's ornaments, and weapons. The vases are of pinkish yellow, with marine and floral decoration in relief, and are thought, because of certain peculiarities of design, to be of local origin. The women's ornaments include articles of glass paste (from Egypt), gold jewellery engraved with the burin, filigree work, enamel, precious stones and incised scarabs. Among the weapons are bronze swords and daggers.

As elsewhere in the Aegean, the Mycenean Age was succeeded by the Geometric and Orientalizing Periods (1100–650 B.C.). The excavations at Lindos, Ialysos, Kameiros, and Vrulia have given rich yields of pottery. Rhodian vases of the 7C and 6C are decorated with animal figures, including goats and fugitive hares, palm, and vine leaves, and geometric designs (roses, circles, and swastikas). With the native ware are found vases from Corinth, Attica, Cyprus, and the Orient. The votive clay and porcelain statuettes, scarabs, and engraved stones found in the Temple of Athena at Lindos and at Ialysos are of Phoenician origin.

The foundation in 408 B.C. of the city of Rhodes brought an influx of famous artists. Lysippos of Sikyon, the sculptor attached to the court of Alexander the Great, produced at Rhodes his famous Chariot of the Sun. Under the influence of Lysippos was founded the *School of Rhodes*, which flourished for three centuries and of which Pliny gives an account. Leaders of the school included Protogenes, the painter from Caria who lived in poverty until acclaimed by Apelles, Chares of Lindos, creator of the Colossus of Rhodes, and Bryaxis, responsible for at least five statues of note. These were followed by a host of other artists, both native and immigrant, of whom little is known save their names, many of which appear on statue bases uncovered on the Acropolis of Lindos. The sculptors, from Chares downwards, worked chiefly in bronze. We know something about Philiskos, author of a group of the Muses, which was carried off to Rome, perhaps by Crassus, and placed in the Porticus of Octavia. Inspired by Lysippos, Philiskos was especially skilled in the treatment of drapery. Heliodoros of Rhodes produced a group of Pan and Olympus, now believed to be in the Museum at Naples.

The loss of her independence did not halt the artistic activity of Rhodes. One of her sculptors made a Colossus 40 ft high, dedicated to the Roman people and placed in the Temple of Athena Polias and Zeus Polieos on the Acropolis of Rhodes. There followed Boïthos of Chalcedon, and Apollonios and Tauriskos of Tralles, who made a group of Dirce which was found in the Baths of Caracalla in Rome and is now at Naples. Pliny mentions Aristonidas, who executed a statue of Atamos bewailing the death of his son Learchos. The group of Menelaus and Patroclus, a fragment of which is now in Rome under the name of Pasquino, came from Rhodes. Best known of all is the Laocoön, found in 1506 in the Golden House of Nero in Rome; this group was produced in the 1C B.C. by the Rhodian sculptors Agesander, Polydorus, and Athenodorus. After the creation of this masterpiece Rhodian art declined.—Such ancient monuments as remain in the island prove that in the Hellenistic age the Doric style prevailed.

The Byzantine era contributed little of note that has survived. With the arrival of the Knights of St John the art of Rhodes becomes westernized. The Grand Masters, most of whom came from France or from Spain, naturally favoured the style of their native countries, and French or Spanish Gothic predominated. We may distinguish two periods: from 1309 to 1480, and from 1480 to 1522. In the earlier period the Knights depended on local labour unfamiliar with the Gothic style, and the work was heavy and maladroit, with intrusive Byzantine elements. In the second period, which was inspired by d'Aubusson (1476–1503), one of the most eminent of the Grand Masters, we see the hand of the Western craftsman. The Gothic character of the work remains, but the forms are more harmonious, the execution more accurate, and the decoration natural or cleverly stylized. Towards the end of the period a few Renaissance motives were introduced, alleviating the severity of the monastic Gothic. These included marble cornices to doors and windows, elaborate escutcheons, and inscriptions carved in superb Latin characters. Here and there are forms deriving from Sicily and southern Italy.

The walls of Rhodes, with their succession of towers, bastions, lunettes, ravelins, and barbicans, are a magnificent example of military architecture of the 14C, 15C, and 16C. The inscriptions and escutcheons that adorn the walls enable us to follow the history of their development. Up to the time of the siege of 1480 the emphasis was on the architectural aspect; later building and modification relied less on the architect than on the engineer. Many Italian engineers were employed on the work.

Gothic influences persisted into the Turkish period, which added little but an Oriental veneer, some elegant minarets and fountains, and the introduction of pottery from Anatolia. The brief Italian period left a mixed legacy of bombastic architecture, over-restoration, and well-engineered roads.

The **City of Rhodes** (32,100 inhab.), situated at the N. end of the island, today consists of two distinct parts. The *Old City*, hemmed in by walls built by the Knights, is clustered round the Central or Commercial Harbour, and is itself divided into two. In the N.W. is a walled enclosure called the *Castle of the Knights* or *Collachium*. The rest of the city is known as the *Chora*. The *New Town*, built since the Italian occupation of 1912, and consisting largely of hotels, extends to the N. of the Old City as far as the N. extremity of the island, and westwards to the foot of the Acropolis of ancient Rhodes. It includes two quarters of the Greek city, Marasi and Neochori. On its E. side is Mandraki, the second and smaller harbour of Rhodes, generally used by yachts and caiques calling at the island. The gardens of Rhodes are noted for their oleanders, bougainvilleas, and hibiscus. The city has suffered greatly from earthquakes. That of 225 B.C. overthrew the Colossus. Others occurred in A.D. 157, 515, 1364, 1481, 1851, and 1863. Of the ancient city few traces remain, though much of its street plan has been plotted under the present town.

Airport, 10 m. s.w.

Hotels. There are c. 100 all in the new town (see Plan, where many are named). At most pension-terms are obligatory: among the best, with swimming pool or private beach, are **Grand Hotel Astir Palace** L; **Hibiscus, Mediterranean, Chevaliers' Palace,** DPO, these A, above open all year; also **Park, Belvedere,** both DPO, **Blue Sky, Siravast,** all A, closed in winter (mostly Nov–Feb).

Open all year, with restaurant, DP not obligatory: **Plaza, Spartalis,** both B; **Pavlides, Isabella, Astoria, Savoy,** all C.—Closed in winter: **Imperial, Kamiros, Regina,** A; **Athena** (closed Jan), **Cactus, Anglia, Amphitryon, Despo, Thermai,** all B; and many others.

Post Office (Pl. 7), opposite the cathedral.—OLYMPIC AIRWAYS, 9 Ierou Lokhou.

Buses from Od. Papagou, behind the Agora to the island villages, *Lindos* etc. Also Excursions to *Lindos, Kameiros,* etc.

The MODERN CITY is laid out along the waterfront of **Mandraki** (Pl. 7), the northern of the two natural harbours, now equipped as a yacht anchorage. The harbour entrance is guarded by two bronze deer (that to seaward replacing the former Italian she-wolf). On the mole protecting the E. side of the basin stand three windmills and Fort St Nicholas, a cylindrical tower dating from 1464–67, topped by a lighthouse (view).

The word Mandraki, used elsewhere in the area for small enclosed harbours, means a small sheepfold. The alternative name *Harbour of the Galleys*, is a misnomer; Mandraki was always secondary to the equally misnamed Commercial Harbour, and under the Knights was occupied by small boat builders. Here probably stood the **Colossus of Rhodes,** a bronze statue of Helios, the Sun-god, set up by Chares of Lindos c. 290 B.C. and considered one of the seven wonders of the world. Its erection was financed by the sale of the siege artillery that Demetrios Poliorketes had presented to the city at the end of his unsuccessful siege (305–304 B.C.). It was 60 cubits (c. 90 ft) high. Helios, the protector of the city of Rhodes, was represented with his head framed in sunrays and dressed in a chlamys; in his right hand he held a torch, which served as a beacon to mariners. The tradition that the statue bestrode the harbour entrance and that ships passed beneath it is without foundation. The earthquakes of 225 B.C. overthrew the statue. For eight centuries its huge fragments lay undisturbed, respected by the superstitious reverence of the Rhodians. At last, in 653 Saracen corsairs collected them and brought them to Tyre. There they were sold to Jewish merchants of Emesa, who carried them away on 900 camels to be melted down and resold.

The public buildings lining the waterfront all date from the Italian occupation and were designed in various monumental styles by Florestano di Fausto. Dominating the harbour mouth is the square campanile of the **Cathedral** (Pl. 7), or *Church of the Evangelist*, built in 1925 on the model of the church of St John in the Old City, destroyed in 1856. The *Fountain* outside the w. end is a copy of the 13C Fontana Grande at Viterbo; the main *Post Office* stands opposite. Linked to the Cathedral is the *Nomarkhia*, or Prefecture, formerly the Governor's Palace, the most considerable monument of the Italian period, built in a Venetian Gothic style. Its picturesque arcaded façade, with marble decoration, closing the seaward side of the Plateia, is set off by the severity of the *Dhimarkhion* and the *Theatre*. To the N. is a popular public beach (fee).

Beyond the Theatre rises the elegant minaret of the *Mosque of Murad Reis* (Pl. 3). In front stands a circular turbeh enclosing the tomb of Murad Reis, admiral of the Turkish fleet during the siege of Rhodes. In the cemetery flanking the mosque are the tombs of many noble Turks who died in exile in Rhodes, including a Shah of Persia and a prince of the Crimea. Farther on, beyond the Hotel des Roses (1927), the road follows the shore to *Akrotiri Ammou* (Sandy Point), the N. extremity of the island. Here the HYDROBIOLOGICAL INSTITUTE (Pl. 2; 10 dr.) houses a remarkable collection of preserved marine creatures caught in local waters (sharks, sun-fish, manta, sword-fish, etc.) and an *Aquarium* unusually rich in octopods, molluscs, crustacea, etc.

The w. shore, overlooked by many hotels, is still freely accessible.

Returning s. along Mandraki, here fronted by gardens, we pass in succession the *Law Courts*, a popular café under a neo-Gothic loggia, and the *Bank of Greece*. Contrasting with their golden stone is the flat whiteness of the NEA AGORA (Pl. 7), a huge polygonal market in a Turkish style, which is the focal-point of the modern town. Beneath the N. wall of the medieval city extends the *Garden of the Deer*, ablaze with sub-tropical flowers.

We enter the ****Old City** by the *New Gate*, or *Gate of Liberty*, opened in 1924, and enter the Plateia Symi or Arsenal Square. We are now in the **Collachium**, or *Castle of the Knights*, the preserve of the Knights of St John, divided from the remainder of the city by an inner wall. In it are the Palace of the Grand Master and the 'Inns' or residences of the 'Tongues' (see above). In Arsenal Square, which communicates with the commercial harbour (see below) by Arsenal Gate, are the remains, discovered in 1922, of a *Temple of Aphrodite* (Pl. 11) dating from the 3C B.C. They include foundations, bases, and shafts of columns, and fragments of the entablature. To the right is the *Municipal Gallery*, while behind the temple is the INN OF THE TONGUE OF AUVERGNE (Pl. 11), a 15C building restored in 1919, the side of which overlooks the attractive Plateia Argirokastrou. In the centre of this square a Byzantine font serves as fountain; the heaps of cannon-balls were amassed during the siege of 1522. On the right the Institute of History and Archaeology (with the ephorate of antiquities) occupies the *Palace of the Armeria*, built in the 14C under Roger de Pinsot and used as the first hospital of the Order. Also in this square is the *Museum of Decorative Arts* (Mon, Wed, Fri, 9–1). We pass beneath an arch. Beyond (l.) is the 13C Byzantine *Church of St Mary* which became the first Cathedral of the Knights. After 1522 the Turks converted it into a mosque called *Enderoum*, and it now serves as a *Byzantine Museum*.

In the courtyard of the building opposite is an amusing modern mosaic of black and white pebbles in a style that has survived unchanged in Rhodes from Byzantine times.

Leaving on our right the Street of the Knights (see below) we enter Hospital Square. Here on the left is the INN OF THE TONGUE OF ENGLAND (3; Pl. 11), built in 1482, despoiled and almost destroyed in 1850, rebuilt on the original plan by Colonel Sir Vivian Gabriel, and repaired by the British in 1949. Opposite stands the **Hospital of the Knights** (Pl. 11), begun in 1440 over the remains of a Roman building and completed in 1481–89. During the War of Greek Independence the Turks used it for their sick and wounded, but later degraded it into barracks. It was skilfully restored under Amedeo Maiuri in 1913–18. Bomb damage sustained to the s. side in the Second World War has again been made good. The FAÇADE, set forward from the plain E. wall above, consists of eight deep arches of unadorned severity. Seven, surmounted by a wall relieved by two string-courses lead into open magazines, while the one to the right of centre shelters the main gateway and supports a projecting apsidal chapel (comp. below). By skilful use of vertical moulding this arrangement is given the appearance of a gate-tower. The *Portal* is decorated with a rope design. The original door of cypress was presented by Sultan Mahmoud to Louis-Philippe in 1836 and now reposes at Versailles.

Since 1916 the building has housed the *Archaeological Museum (adm. 25 dr.; standard hours, exc. June–mid-Oct when 8–7 daily; closed Tues). The GREAT COURT is enclosed by a double portico, of which the lower story is vaulted. Beneath the lower colonnade are various fragments; in the centre crouches a marble lion (1C B.C.); in the corners are cannon balls and catapult shot. An outside stair leads to the upper gallery where are ranged funerary stelai and altar-bases. The entire E. wing is occupied by the INFIRMARY WARD, a rectangular hall divided lengthways by an arcade borne on seven columns; its ogee arches support a ceiling of cypress-wood.

The ward held 32 beds with brocaded canopies, and the patients ate from silver plate. Two surgeons were on duty at all times. The dark cubicles that open from the hall have been variously explained as confessionals, isolation wards, and wardrobes.

Beneath a flamboyant arch in the long wall opens the vaulted exedra, with three Gothic windows, that projects above the main gate. This held an altar where mass was said daily. Round the walls of the hall are ranged *Memorials* of the Knights from the destroyed church of St John. Notable are a classical marble sarcophagus used in 1355 as the tomb of Grand Master Pierre de Corneillan (lid in the Cluny Museum, Paris; copy here) and tomb-slabs of Thomas Newport (1502), of Nicholas de Montmirel (1511), commandant of the Hospital, of Tomaso Provena (1499), and of Fernando de Heredia (1493). Heraldic devices include the royal arms of England.

Beyond the Infirmary Ward is a Small Hall, with reliefs on the walls, once the refectory for the hospital staff, and beyond this three rooms of **Sculpture.** *First Room:* Head of Helios; head of Menander (after Praxiteles). *Second Room:* small headless Nymph, seated on a rock; bearded Dionysos (Hellenistic); Zeus; Asklepios and Hygieia (2C A.D.); *Aphrodite of Rhodes, kneeling and separating the strands of her hair, after emerging from the waves (1C B.C.). *Third Room:* Head of Bacchus, in porphyry; stooping Nymph (headless) where the vertical folds of the himation emphasize the soft round form of the body; the famous *Aphrodite 'Thalassia' of the 3C B.C., also called Venus Pudica, found in the sea off Sandy Point.

Still at first-floor level we enter a garden that overlooks the *Little Court*, excavated in 1907, with a 6C mosaic pavement from Arkassa in Karpathos.

We cross to two further rooms. In the first, funerary stele of young Timarista taking her last farewell of Crito, her mother, a work of the 5C B.C.; Crito's hair was recut after damage in antiquity. In the second, two headless Kouroi (6C B.C.) found at Kamiros, but which appear to come from Paros and Naxos; two fragmentary heads; sculptured perirrhantirion stand of the 7C B.C.—We return to the gallery to visit its surrounding rooms (not always open): on the first side three containing pottery from excavations at Kamiros and Ialysos; then three interlinked rooms containing jewellery from Mycenean tombs in Ialysos, and a hoard of 75 silver coins from Kremasti; on the last side, four rooms of which the last contains Mycenean pottery from Karpathos and Astypalaia.

Leaving the museum we turn left from Hospital Square to ascend the cobbled *Street of the Knights (Odhos Ipoton; Pl. 11), the main thoroughfare of the Collachium which it traverses from E. to w., rising towards the Palace. Its noble buildings, plentifully adorned with coats-of-arms, were restored with care and accuracy in 1913–16, so that the street provides a faithful picture of late medieval architecture, though the overall effect is perhaps too tidy to evoke the full spirit of the Middle Ages.

The knightly houses and inns follow the same general pattern, having two stories with a flat ornamental façade and a terrace roof. Vaulted store-houses, or stables (?), occupied the lower floor while the upper story was reached by an open stair and gallery from a central court. The rounded arches, the horizontal emphasis given by string-courses, and the large square windows suggest that the Renaissance was already affecting even a military order of medieval chivalry.

On our left is the N. façade of the Hospital (see below) with a good portal at the far end. Opposite is the *Inn of the Tongue of Italy* (4; Pl. 11) rebuilt in 1519 when Del Carretto was Grand Master. Beyond a house bearing the arms of de l'Isle Adam quartered with those of his mother (d. 1462) is the *INN OF THE TONGUE OF FRANCE (5; Pl. 11), architecturally the most harmonious building in the street. It was built in 1492–1509, disfigured by the Turks, and carefully restored at the expense of Maurice Bompard, French ambassador to the Porte. The escutcheons include that of Pierre d'Aubusson (Grand Master 1476–1503). The crocodile gargoyles recall the legend of Gozon (comp. below). The building opposite, with an Aragonese portal and an attractive garden court, bears the Spanish arms of Villaraguts. Next to it is a charming building with an upper floor in the Turkish style.

In a side street (r.) is the so-called *Palace of Zizim* (6; Pl. 11), pretender brother of Bayezid II, given asylum here for a short time in 1482 before being conveyed to France.

Farther on (r.) the small *Chapel of the Tongue of France* (8; Pl. 11) bears a statue of the Virgin and Child and the lilies of France. The adjacent *Chaplain's House*, dated by the arms of Béranger (Grand Master 1365–74) on the façade, is occupied by the Italian consulate. An arch spans the road. Two buildings, to the left of the street, before and beyond the arch, constitute the *Inn of the Tongue of Spain* (7; Pl. 11); the first (Aragon and Castile) dates from the mid-15C, the second from c. 50 years later. The *Inn of the Tongue of Provence* (9; Pl. 11) of 1518, to the right, has an elegant portal surmounted by four coats-of-arms set in a cross-shaped niche.

At the top of the street we enter Citadel Square beneath the *Loggia of St Peter* (10; Pl. 11), a modern reconstruction of a portico of unknown purpose. Already in ruins before the explosion of 1856, it used to join the entrance-court of the Palace to the *Conventual Church of St John* which lay parallel to the palace. A fragment of wall is all that remains of the church, and a Turkish school now occupies the site.

Built in a plain 14C style, more or less faithfully copied in the church on Mandraki, it contained the tombs of the Knights. After 1522 it was turned into a mosque. In 1856 it was destroyed when lightning struck the minaret and exploded beneath it a forgotten underground cache of gunpowder, killing c. 800 people.

On the N. side of the square in the highest part of the Collachium stands the **Palace of the Grand Masters** (Pl. 11; adm. 25 dr.; weekdays, summer 9.30–1, 3.30–7, winter 9.30–1, 2.30–5; Sun and hol. from 10; closed Tues), rebuilt in 1939–43 from old drawings of the original 14C building.

Son et Lumière in English, French, German, and Swedish (entrance from municipal garden outside the walls).—The tour of the walls (see below) begins from the main entrance of the Palace.

The Palace stands on the site of an ancient temple of Apollo. Begun soon after the arrival in Rhodes of the Knights, and completed at the end of the 14C, it was a superb building on a rectangular plan, 260 ft by 245, and was in effect an independent fortress designed with underground store-rooms to withstand a siege. It served in time of peace as the residence of the Grand Master and the place of assembly of the Order. Repaired after the earthquake of 1481, it suffered little damage in the siege of 1522. The Turks turned it into a prison. It was badly damaged by the earthquake of 1851 and the remains were further shattered by the explosion of 1856. Some of the material was used by the Turks to build a military hospital (since razed) in the grounds. The Italians, intending it as a summer residence for Victor Emmanuel III and Mussolini, rebuilt the exterior as far as possible in the old style, but redesigned the interior for modern occupation, including central heating, disguised lifts, and electric chandeliers. The preparations were barely completed when Italy relinquished the island.

The *Courtyard* is decorated with Roman statuary. The **Interior** achieves grandeur though sometimes at the expense of taste. The spacious halls have timber ceilings supported on Roman and Byzantine columns and are paved in coloured marbles or with vast antique *Mosaics brought from Kos. Some are lit by alabaster windows. The furniture, of many styles and periods, includes good Renaissance woodwork from Italian churches. The windows afford charming views of the city and sea. The garden contains sarcophagi of Masters, and a bronze she-wolf of Rome that once adorned the E. mole of Mandraki.

At the w. end of the square we pass through the Collachium wall by a

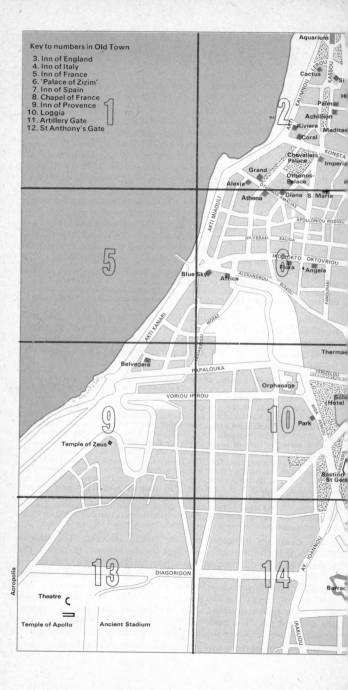

Key to numbers in Old Town

3. Inn of England
4. Inn of Italy
5. Inn of France
6. 'Palace of Zizim'
7. Inn of Spain
8. Chapel of France
9. Inn of Provence
10. Loggia
11. Artillery Gate
12. St Anthony's Gate

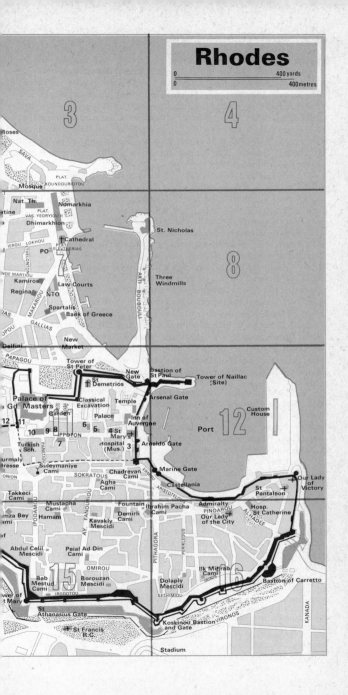

Rhodes

0   400 yards
0   400metres

3

4

Roses

SAVA

PLAT.
KOUNDOURIOTOU
Mosque

Nat. Th
PLAT.
VAS. YEORYIOU
Dhimarkhion

Nomarkhia

St. Nicholas

tine
a

IEROU   LOKHOU
ETHELONTON
PO   PLAT.
ELEFTHERIAS
Cathedral

8

NDE MARTIOU
Kamiros
Regina
NTO
Law Courts

Three
Windmills

Spartalis
Bank of Greece

IAS
MAKARIOU
GALLIAS

PPOU   GALLIAS

Delfini

PAPAGOU

New Market

New
Market

Tower of
St Peter

New
Gate

Bastion of
St Paul

Tower of Naillac
(Site)

Palace of
e Gd. Masters

St
Demetrios

Classical
Excavation

Arsenal Gate

Garden

Temple

Palace

Custom
House

12

11

10   9 8
7
PANEPO
IPPOTON

6

5

4 St
Mary's
Hospital
(Mus.)

Inn of
Auvergne

3

Arnaldo Gate

Port

12

Turkish
Sch.

urmaly
dresse

Suleymaniye
Cami

SOKRATOUS

Chadrevan
Cami

Marine Gate

Castellania

ERMOU

Our Lady
of
Victory

ONION
Takkeci
Cami

Agha
Cami

ARISTOTELOUS

St
Pantaleon

mza Bey
ami
of
Mustapha
Cami
Hamam

Fountain

Ibrahim Pacha
Cami

Admiralty
PINDAROU
Our Lady
of the City

Hosp.
St Catherine

ALIFADEF

Demirli
Cami

Kavakly
Mescidi

PODAMOU

AY FANOURIOU

Abdul Celil
Mescidi

Peial Ad Din
Cami

PITHAGORA

PERIKLEOUS

Ilk Mihrab
Cami

OMIROU

IRINIS

Bab
Mestud
Cami
wer of
t Mary

Borouzan
Mescidi

15

IRODOTOU

St
Athanasius Gate

Dolaply
Mescidi

EFTHIMIOU

16

Bastion of Carretto

KANADA

St Francis
R.C.

Koskinou Bastion
and Gate

VIRONOS

Stadium

double arch to Plateia Kleovoulou, a long tree-lined 'piazza' with small shops and cafés. To the right an arch and a shaded walk (comp. below) lead to the Amboise Gate and then over the moats (deer in the outer moat) out to the new town. We turn left towards the ugly *Clock Tower*, which replaced a 15C tower (overthrown in 1851) at the s.w. corner of the Collachium. A few yards farther on Odhos Apollonion leads (r.) to the *Kurmale Medresses* (Pl. 11; 'College of the Date-Palm'), called locally *St George's*, a derelict Turkish adaptation of a Byzantine conventual church. The dome, set on a drum of 21 blind arches, preserves its ancient tiles.

The **Mosque of Suleiman** (Pl. 11), erected soon after 1522 on the site of a Church of the Apostles and rebuilt in 1808, is preceded by the customary court with a fountain. It has a double portico, a portal in a Venetian Renaissance style, and an elegant minaret with a double balcony. Opposite is the *Turkish Library* (1793) with illuminated 15–16C Koran. Hence we descend ODHOS SOKRATOUS, the former *Bazar*, whose balconied houses, open shops and coffee-houses still preserve a Turkish atmosphere. Beyond the *Mosque of Aga* (Pl. 11), curiously raised on wooden pillars, we reach Plateia Ippokratous. Here the Municipal library and Island Archives occupy the so-called *Palace of the Castellan* (Pl. 12), a square building of 1507 bearing the arms of Amboise. It was probably the commercial court of the Knights and was restored by the Italians after use as a mosque (above) and a fish-market (below). The upper hall, supported by an arcaded loggia, is reached by an external stair and a sculptured marble portal; the windows are delicately moulded. To the E. of Od. Pithagora, the long street that runs s. towards the Koskinou Gate, lies the former Jewish quarter, once noted for its animation compared with the Turkish streets.

Odhos Aristotelous continues E. past houses with Turkish wooden balconies to *Martyrs' Square*, damaged in the Second World War. A fountain adorned with bronze sea-horses, stands in front of the misnamed *Admiralty* (Pl. 16), whose inscriptions in Latin and Greek suggest that it was the palace of either the Orthodox metropolitan or the Latin archbishop. Odhos Pindarou passes (r.) the ruins of the Gothic church of Our Lady of the Bourg, now split in two by a road with an arched exit to the waterfront, and ends before the *Hospice of St Catherine* (Pl. 16), founded by Fra Domenico d'Alemagna in 1392 to shelter Italian pilgrims travelling to the Holy Land; it was enlarged in 1516. At the N.E. corner of the town is the small church of Ayios Phanourios, beyond which, on the ramparts (l.) stood the church of *Our Lady of Victory* (Pl. 12), built to commemorate the heroic defence of this rampart in 1480 and destroyed c. 1522. To the left *St Catherine's Gate* leads to the **Commercial Harbour,** the larger of the two harbours of Rhodes.

This, the 'Grand Harbour', was protected by two moles, defended with artillery, between which was stretched a chain. The N. mole bore the *Tower of Naillac*, a key-point during the siege, but overthrown in 1863 (reconstruction planned); that to the E., separating the harbour from the Bay of Akandia and once adorned with 15 windmills, has been enlarged to form the modern quay where inter-island steamers moor. The defences round the harbour consist of a high curtain-wall with a *Marine Gate* (1478; sometimes by confusion called St Catherine's Gate, see above) that recalls the Fort St André at Villeneuve-lès-Avignon in Provence; it figured prominently in the film 'Guns of Navarone'. Following the wall we may re-enter the old city by the *Arsenal Gate*, or reach Mandraki by traversing the N.E. salient by the *Bastion of St Paul*.

The interest of the old city has by no means been exhausted, and visitors staying in the city may explore the confined alleys that thread its s. sector at their leisure. The small houses and occasional churches, the unexpected archways and courtyards, and the mosques (for the most part derelict and stripped) present a colourful mixture of medieval and eastern styles.

We may begin in the S.E. with two former churches, the *Ilk Mihrab Cami*, whose name marks it as the first shrine at which Allah was worshipped in 1522, and the neighbouring *Dolapli Mescidi*, or Oratory of the Well; both are decorated with frescoes. Farther W., beyond a characteristic windmill, is the *Redjeb Pasha Cami* (1588), the most notable mosque built by the Turks on Rhodes, with Persian faience decoration. The *Peial ad Din Mescid* has returned to the Greek rite; the frescoes were restored by the Italians in 1938.

Grouped near the centre of the town are the **Ibrahim Pasha Cami**, a spacious mosque of 1531, whose plane-tree is said to have provided a place of execution for the Turks, the ruined *Demirli Cami*, once a Gothic church, and the disused *Kavakli Mescidi*, a small Byzantine church provided with a minaret. In the square of the *Mustapha Cami* are the *Turkish Baths* (1765, rebuilt), whence the Mosque of Suleiman (see above) may be regained viâ the disused *Takkeci Cami* (once the Greek church of Ay. Sotira). In the s.w. corner of the town is the *Abdul Djelil Mescid*, a medieval church with cable ornament and vaulting, damaged in the Second World War.

TOUR OF THE WALLS

No visitor should omit the tour of the walls, which is conducted on Mon and Sat at 4, in winter 3 (adm. 10 dr.) from the courtyard of the Palace (see above). A complete circuit takes 1½ hr—generally the guided tour ends at the Italian Tower, reached in ¾ hr. From the top a good defender's view is obtained; a visitor who has already seen the harbour defences is well advised to return (mostly by shaded walks) along the outside of the same section to obtain an attacker's view.

The ***Walls of Rhodes**, a masterpiece of 15–16C military architecture, are well preserved throughout their extent of 2½ miles, having successfully withstood the siege of 1480 and for a long time that of 1522. They bear 151 escutcheons of Grand Masters and knights.

In places the walls have ancient or Byzantine foundation blocks, but little is known of the Byzantine enceinte save that it resisted the Knights for three years. The remaining towers probably date in part from before 1330, as does the moat. Reconstruction began under Grand Masters Heredia (1377–96) and de Naillac (1396–1421), who built a massive tower on the N. mole of the main harbour. In 1437–71 the walls were rebuilt to incorporate a number of detached towers. After the siege of 1480 and the earthquake of 1481, Pierre d'Aubusson (1476–1503) began a systematic and thoroughgoing reconstruction: the curtain-walls were thickened, parapets widened, the gates reduced in number from five to three and made more difficult of access, and the ditches doubled in width. The work was completed by Del Carretto (1513–21), with the technical help of Italian architects. In 1522 Villiers de l'Isle Adam, again with Italian help, organized the final defences. In 1465 the enceinte had been divided into eight sectors, each allotted to one of the 'Tongues',and this arrangement was in force at the time of the final siege.

The fortifications, strongest on the landward side, comprise a continuous vertical or scarped wall, on which is a platform or walk, 45 ft wide, also continuous, protected by battlements and embrasures sited for firing in any direction. In many sectors there is also a lower walk. This circumvallation is surrounded by an external fosse, 35–50 yds wide and 50–65 ft deep, provided with scarp and counterscarp.

We quit Citadel Square by the *Artillery Gate* and *St Anthony's Gate* and cross the dry moats of the Palace to reach the wide parapet above

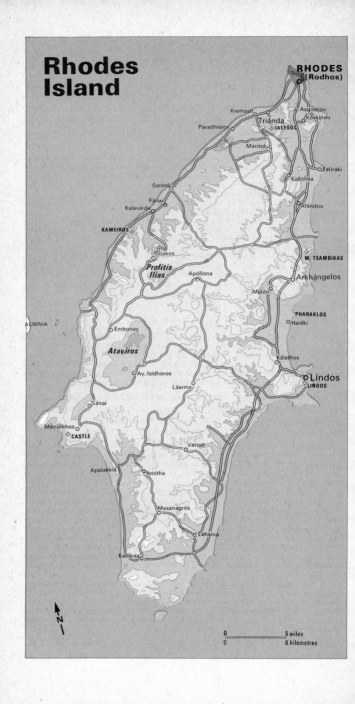

Rhodes Island

RHODES
(Rodhos)

Kremasti
Asgoúrou
Koskinoú
Triánda
IALYSOS
Paradhísion

Maritsá

Faliráki

Soroni
Kallithéa

Fánai
Kalá-várda
Afándou

KAMEIROS

Salakos
M. TSAMBIKAS

Profítis
Ilías
Apóllona
Arkhángelos

Malón

ALIMNIA
PHARAKLOS
Haráki

Embonas

Atáviros
Kálathos

Ay. Isídhoros
Láerma
Líndos
LINDOS

Sánai

Monólithos
CASTLE

Vation

Apolakkiá
Arnitha

Mesanagrós

Lahaniá

Kattavía

| 0 | | 5 miles |
| 0 | | 8 kilometres |

N

the **Gate of Amboise** (1512). A bridge of three arches spans the outer moat. The main gate, which bears the arms of the Order and of Amboise, opens below us between massive cylindrical towers. In the thickness of the wall the vaulted road makes an S-bend, then passes beneath a second gate, over an inner moat, and through a third gate to a *Terreplein*, now a shaded avenue (comp. above). This was exposed to fire on all sides and still separated from the Palace and the town by a third moat with further bridges and gates.

We follow to the s. the short sector of the TONGUE OF GERMANY, the least numerous defensive group. On the left we see Suleiman Square, the Clock Tower, and the mosques of Hurmale and of Suleiman. The *Bastion of St George* has a relief of St George on the original square tower, with the arms of Pope Martin V, of the Order, and of Grand Master Antonio Fluvian (1421–37). A polygonal bulwark was added later, and in 1496 the roadway through it was closed when the final bastion was erected. The next sector is that of the TONGUE OF AUVERGNE, ending at the circular *Tower of Spain*.

Beyond the tower is the sector of the TONGUE OF ARAGON, one of the most picturesque, which bears s.e. and then s. From it there is a comprehensive view, taking in the mosques of Suleiman, of Mustapha, of Ibrahim Pasha, and of Redjeb Pasha, the Tower of the Windmills, the Commercial Harbour, the Tower of St Nicholas, the port of Mandraki, the new town and the coast of Anatolia. The ravelin was completed in 1522 which did not prevent the Turks in December making here the breach that enabled them to capture the city.

The *Tower of St Mary* bears a relief of the Virgin and Child and an inscription dated 1441. Round the tower in 1487 a great polygonal bastion was added for the protection of the *Gate of St Athan* by d'Aubusson; later he closed the gate. Reopened for a sortie in 1522, it was closed again by Suleiman in 1531 and remained so until 1922. The wall turns e. to one of its most striking sectors, that of the TONGUE OF ENGLAND. Along it we see numerous windmills, one of them, all white, being predominant. The *Gate of Koskinou*, or Gate of St John, shows clearly the difference between early and later military architecture. The earlier wall has a square tower with small embrasures and battlements, while the additions of c. 1480 take the form of a huge bastion of horseshoe plan with ravelins and embrasures for larger artillery. Its defence was shared between the Tongues of England and PROVENCE, whose sector follows a zigzag line marked by three towers.

The large *Bastion del Carretto*, or of Italy, is a blend of an older tower and a semicircular bastion of 1515, 165 ft in diameter and of three stories. The sector skirting the Bay of Akandia, fronted by a ravelin, was defended by the TONGUE OF ITALY. Nearing the mole on which is the Tower of the Windmills the wall makes a right-angled turn to the left. Just beyond the tower is the Gate of St Catherine. The new sector, that of the TONGUE OF CASTILE, skirts the Commercial Harbour (described above). Half-way is the picturesque *Marine Gate*, with large guardrooms. Beyond it the wall coincides for a time with the e. wall of the Collachium. Beyond a square tower with a chapel (frescoes), the *Arnaldo Gate* leads into Hospital Square. Passing *Arsenal Gate* we arrive at the *Gate of St Paul*, where the wall runs both w. and e. along the mole. This is commanded by a tower and protected without by a low triangular curtain with a parapet. At a late period the defence of the Naillac mole was allotted to the Captain of the Port.

From the Gate of St Paul to the Gate of Amboise (where we began) is the sector of the TONGUE OF FRANCE. This runs in a general E.–W. direction, passing above the Gate of Liberty. At the circular *Tower of St Peter*, which bears a figure of St Peter and the arms of Pope Pius II, the wall turns abruptly s. and then again w. Skirting the Palace of the Grand Master, we gain Citadel Square.

To THE ACROPOLIS, 20 min. We take Odhos Ethnarkhou (Arkhiepiskopou) Makariou and pass the Soleil Hotel, in the grounds of which excavations (1960) revealed a cellar containing more than 100 intact amphorae, possibly buried in the earthquake of 227–226 B.C. From Leoforos Vasilissis Frederikis we take the right fork, whence Odhos Diagoridón (r.) rises towards *Mt Ayios Stefanos* (364 ft), a ridge called also *Mt Smith* after Adm. Sir Sidney Smith (1764–1840), who occupied a house here in 1802 while keeping watch on the French fleet. The **Acropolis**, identified in 1916 and partly excavated in 1924–29, occupies its gentle E. slope. Amid olive groves (l.) are a *Stadium* (restored) and a small *Theatre*, of unusual square plan (only the orchestra and three seats are original work). A massive retaining wall supports a higher terrace where the stylobate of a *Temple of Pythian Apollo* bears three corner columns tastelessly fabricated from fragments. A small fountain-house, below, has a plaster-lined cistern and feed channel with draw-basin behind. At the N. end of the ridge is the site of a *Temple of Athena Polias*, marked now only by some foundations and a few column drums. Odhos Vorion Ipíron winds back down into the town.

Excursions in the Island

ROAD CONDITIONS. The road down the w. coast to Ancient Kamiros and then inland almost to Embona is asphalted. On the E. coast there is asphalt to Lindos and Lardhos. The unpaved roads, however, are generally much superior to those on the mainland. To those who enjoy leisurely motoring through sparsely in-habited country with varying scenery, the island offers a reasonable network of roads leading to Kattavia in the s. and linking the two coasts. Below are described only excursions to places of particular interest.

To RHODINI, 2 m. s. on the Lindos road. This is a pleasant ancient park, where, it is said, was once the School of Rhetoric of Aeschines. The park, frequented by peacocks, is shaded by plane-trees and has a stream and ponds. There are remains of a Roman aqueduct, and about 20 min. walk s.w. is the so-called *Tomb of the Ptolemies*, a Hellenistic rock tomb with a decorated façade (restored 1924).

To IALYSOS AND MT PHILAREMOS, 9¼ m. s.w. From the Nea Agora we take any road leading w. and on reaching the sea turn left and follow Leoforos Triandon, the coast road, past the huge Rodos Palace (L) and a succession of other hotels (Oceanis, Rodos Bay, Bel-Air, Metropolitan Capsis, Avra Beach, all A).— 2 m. Turning (l.) to *Malpasos*. On the right of this road is the *Cave of the Dragon* with a cypress in front. The legend concerning the dragon said to have been killed here by Dieudonné de Gozon, a Provençal knight who later became Grand Master (1346–53), was convincingly exploded by F. W. Hasluck ('BSA', Vol. XX).—3 m. *Ixia* (Miramare Beach L).—5½ m. *Trianda* (Golden Beach, Electra Palace, A), with 3500 inhabitants, has an interesting little church. A good road rises to the left to (9½ m.) *Mt Phileremos*, an isolated wooded hill (875 ft) whose level summit (*View) was the site of *Ialysos*, one of the three ancient cities of Rhodes. The strategic value of this hill, dominating the plain, has been recognized from Phoenician times; John Cantacuzene was besieged here by the Genoese in 1248, and hence Suleiman directed the siege of Rhodes in 1522. It was contended in 1943 between the Germans and Italians. Of the classical Acropolis there remain the foundations of a 3C *Temple of Athena Ialysia*. Later remains include some ruins of a Byzantine church. Imposing, though over-restored in 1931 and given a new tower, is the Knights' church of *Our Lady of Phileremos*, with Catholic (l.) and Orthodox altars. Above is the restored *Monastery*, from which a path leads N. to a ruined castle of the Knights. Lower down are a *Fountain* of the 4C B.C., reconstructed in 1926, and the *Necropolis* where c. 500 tombs have been excavated in Late Mycenean, Geometric, Archaic, and Classical cemeteries.

To KALLITHÉA, 6½ m. (11 km.). From Arsenal Gate we follow the shore road, then, by a large cemetery (l.), turn left over a bridge. Soon after, we see (r.) the caves of the Hellenistic and Roman necropolis (1C B.C.–1C A.D.).—4 m. *Reni Koskinou* (Eden Roc, Paradise, A).—6½m. *Kallithéa* (Sunwing A), a strange hydropathic establishment comprising mock-Moorish buildings, gardens, and grottoes, all placed amid the natural shore rocks. The waters are recommended for various internal ailments.

FROM RHODES TO LINDOS, 35 m. (55 km.), bus 5 times daily, also ex-cursion coaches daily.—2 m. *Rhodini* (see above). The road passes through varied scenery of hills interspersed with fertile plains and orange groves. White cubic houses and date palms give the villages a Saharan appearance.—8 m. *Faliraki* (Apollo Beach, Faliraki Beach, A). Several roads lead down to beaches.—13 m. *Afándou* (Xenia B), the first 'Saharan' village (2300 inhab.). Near by is a U.S. transmitter that broadcasts the 'Voice of America'. To the S.E., near the coast, is *Katholikí*, where the church has elements from Classical times.—16¼ m. Immediately after a river bridge, turning (r.) to *Eleoússa*, passing (2 m.) the *Eptá Píyes*, seven springs which form a little lake in a gorge of pine-trees.—Our road now threads a narrow gap with *Mt Tsambíka* (1070 ft) to the left. *Moní Tsambíkas* (signposted) has an ancient tree in the courtyard and a good carved screen in the church.—We cross a ridge (765 ft) and descend to *Arkhángelos* (ΑΡΧΑΓΓΕΛΟΣ), another village (3020 inhabitants) of African appearance, dominated by a Castle. Near by the church of Ayioi Theodoroi (1377) has wall paintings. The road turns inland, then descends steeply to a fertile valley with nut and orange groves.—24 m. *Malóna*, from which a road (3 m.) descends to the coast and a promontory where stands the *Castle of Pharaklos*, one of the strongest built by the Knights. It is well seen from our road as we continue S.—Just beyond (31 m.) *Kálathos* the road divides, the right branch continuing to the S. of the island. We turn left; from the top of a low but rocky pass we gain a sudden *View of Lindos as we descend to the village.

*Lindos (ΛΙΝΔΟΣ), now a village of 700 inhab., was the chief of the three cities before the foundation of Rhodes, and in the Middle Ages was the most important place in the island after Rhodes itself. Its delightful situation, with a beautiful beach (*Lindos Bay* A; restaurants), its old houses and trafficless streets, and its superb acropolis give it a charm altogether unique.

History. The site was occupied in the 3rd millennium and a temple to Athena existed from at least the 10C B.C. Thanks to a geographical position between two harbours it became the most important of the three ancient cities of Rhodes. Colonists from Lindos founded Parthenopea (forerunner of Naples) and Gela, in Sicily, during the 7C. In the 6C Lindos was governed by tyrants, the most celebrated of whom was Kleoboulos (fl. 580 B.C.), one of the 'Seven Sages', who had a weakness for setting and solving riddles. After the foundation of the city of Rhodes, Lindos remained the religious centre of the island. St Paul is said to have landed at Lindos on his way to Rome. In the Byzantine era the acropolis was turned into a fortress, which the Knights of St John made into the headquarters of a castellany, with twelve knights and a Greek garrison. In 1317 Grand Master Foulques de Villaret took refuge in the castle after the Knights had deposed him. The Turks continued to use the acropolis as a fortress. In 1902–14 and in 1952 a

Danish mission excavated the acropolis, but the restorations were done by the Italians before 1938.

DOMESTIC ARCHITECTURE. In Lindos there are numerous 15C houses built in a style derived from the Gothic of the Knights with Byzantine and Oriental decoration. They have a gatehouse, a courtyard with staircase, and the main building, usually with doorways and windows elaborately carved with rope designs, doves, roses, etc. The floors are paved in black and white pebble mosaic. The reception room usually contains Lindos ware, either medieval or in modern reproduction. The ceilings are often painted.

Lindos Pottery. There is a story, without foundation, that in the 14C a Grand Master captured a Levantine ship in which some Persian potters were travelling, and that he forced the potters to work for him at Lindos: this is supposed to have been the origin of the Lindos dishes. Manufacture of the ware is supposed to have stopped after the Turkish occupation. In fact there were no native potteries, and all the dishes and vases came from the mainland of Asia Minor. Instead, however, of the stylized Persian decoration, the Lindos ware had floral motives, such as tulips, carnation, hyacinths, and roses in bud or in bloom, with a green background picked out in red. Since the Second World War very attractive copies of this ware have been made in Rhodes itself.

At the w. end of the village is the small PLATEIA, shaded by mulberry trees, with an old fountain and two restaurants. Here, or in the road (l.) towards the beach, may be found parking space. Near the Plateia donkeys may be hired for the Acropolis. In the village most of the streets are only just wide enough to take a donkey with panniers. We follow the arrows for the Acropolis, leaving on our left the Church of the Panayia (see below), and running the gauntlet of many souvenir shops. The path climbs steeply.

The **Acropolis** occupies a triangular outcrop of rock (380 ft) accessible only from the N. side. From below it presents the aspect of a huge medieval *CASTLE remodelled and enlarged by the Knights from an earlier stronghold. Passing under the outer gate we come to a terrace, where hewn out of the rock, is an exedra with a *Relief, 15 ft long and 18 ft high, of the stern of a ship, with its lateral rudder and the helmsman's seat; the deck served as the base of a statue of a priest of Poseidon called Hagesandros (inscription). To the right of the relief are the remains of the ancient *Sacred Way*. A long staircase leads to the main gate (adm. 25 dr.; standard hours) by which we enter a vaulted passage. Above (spiral stair) is a medieval chamber, which formed part of the *Governor's Palace*. Within the battlemented enceinte is the ruined Byzantine chapel of *St John*.

The SANCTUARY OF ATHENA LINDIA occupies the greater part of the area to the S., which is strewn with bases of statues inscribed with the names of local artists. From a huge double-winged Stoa (added c. 208 B.C.) a monumental staircase leads to a higher terrace with foundations of the *Propylaea* built after 407 B.C. The small *Temple* (75 ft by 25) beyond, stands at the edge of the cliff near the S. point of the Acropolis. The existing remains, including the w. wall of the cella, date from a rebuilding after a fire in 348 B.C. They overlook the smaller rock-girt harbour associated by tradition with the supposed visit of St Paul. The S.E. end of the Stoa affords a splendid *View of the *Great Harbour*, with the two islets at its entrance and the promontory beyond.

THE VILLAGE. Descending from the Acropolis and entering the village, we pass (r.) the *House of Phaedra Moschorides*, with a doorway of 1642. We may now quit the main street and explore the maze of unspoilt streets to the s., with their many old houses, courtyards, and staircases. Particular houses are not necessarily marked nor easily identified, but worth seeking out are the *House of Ioannis*

Krekas, for its wooden ceiling, and the **House of Papas Konstandinos*, the most elaborately decorated of the Lindos houses. Its gatehouse has an ogival doorway and the courtyard an elegant staircase, while the main façade is pierced by ogival and rectangular windows. At the s. end of the village we see (l.) an ancient wall of well-made limestone blocks, part of the peribolos of a *Temple* of the 2–1C B.C. Alongside, set in the hill, is the *Theatre*. Its cavea is divided into two by a landing and into five cunei by four staircases; some 27 steps remain. Returning towards the Plateia we may visit the church of the *Panayia*, bearing the dates 1484–90 but probably earlier. It has the form of a Latin cross, with an octagonal drum and cupola. The interior has frescoes executed in 1779 by Gregory of Syme (restored 1927) and the floor is of black and white sea pebbles.

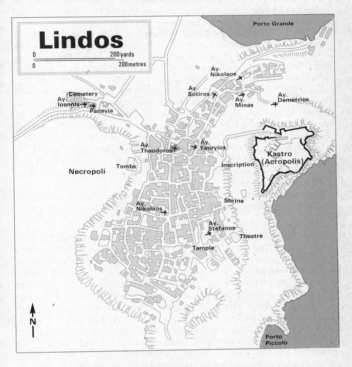

On the promontory of Ayios Aemilianos, near the N.E. end of the Great Harbour, is the so called *Tomb of Kleoboulos*, a pre-Hellenic cylindrical structure formed of square blocks of masonry, recalling the Lelego-Carian tombs on the mainland. The sepulchral chamber is approached by a dromos. In the Middle Ages the tomb was converted into the church of St Aemilianos.

FROM RHODES TO KAMEIROS (22½ m.; bus 4 times daily) AND MONO-LITHOS (c. 50 m.). This excursion may be combined with that to Ialysos (comp. above). Beyond (5½ m.) Trianda we continue along the coast with views across the sea to the coast of Turkey.—7½ m. *Kremasti* (ΚΡΕΜΑΣΤΗ; 2300 inhab.) is noted for its annual festival held on 14–23 Aug, which, like those of antiquity, combines religious cere-monies (here centred on a miraculous ikon of the Virgin) with athletic games, music, and dancing. To the s. (1¼ m.) is *Maritsés*, the airport of Rhodes. Beyond, close to the shore, was found a collection of amphorae of the 2C B.C., nearly all with the craftsman's name and mark, stacked and awaiting shipment.—At 11 m. (18 km.), just after a long ford, is a turning (l.) to the wooded area of Kalamon with a Cattle Breeding Station and an Agricultural School. Beyond a Boy Scout village extends the VALLEY OF BUTTERFLIES (*Petaloudhes*). The myriad butterflies, best seen in July–August, are attracted by the thick growth of storax with its pungent scent.—The main road continues through fig orchards and past numerous wind pumps. On the outskirts of (18½ m.) *Kalavarda*, we bear r. along the coast.

21 m. Turning (l., signposted) to **Kameiros** (½ m.), the third of the ancient cities of Rhodes, called 'chalky' by Homer. It was rediscovered in 1859 after centuries of oblivion and excavated in 1929. The extensive REMAINS (weekdays, standard hours 25 dr.; closed Sun), undisturbed in the Middle Ages, occupy a gentle slope overlooking the sea. The city had neither fortifications nor acropolis. We come first to an imposing *Temenos*, or court, of the 3C B.C., with scanty remains of a Doric temple, beyond which rises the main street of the town. Here a number of houses have come to light including one with a peristyle court. Above, the *Agora* consists of a long row of shops bordered by a Doric *Stoa* (3C) of which 6 columns with their entablature have been well restored. It covered a 6–5C *Cistern* made redundant by a new system of wells, a row of which may be seen behind. A few traces remain among the trees higher up of a peripteral *Temple of Athena*.

Leaving Kameiros, we may either continue along the coast road or return to the Kalavarda fork and take the asphalted inland road.

———

THE COAST ROAD. We pass the ruins of *Kretinae*, a city said to have been founded by Althaemenes from Crete. Pottery found bears a strong resemblance to that of the Early Minoan period of Crete.— 26 m. *Mandriko*.—28 m. *Kameiros Skala*. About 4 m. out to sea is a group of islets, of which the largest is *Alimnia* (3 sq. m.), with a ruined castle of Greek origin, rebuilt by the Knights. To the s.w. of Alimnia is Khalki (p. 664).—Near (32 m.) *Kritinia* is **Kastellos,** an important castle of the Knights, perched on a rock (425 ft) and dominating the sea. Probably built in 1480, it is on three levels, each assigned to a different Grand Master. It is ruinous on the precipitous N.E. side (*View). We turn inland.—38 m. *Embona* (1427 ft), a village growing wine and tobacco, is the starting-point for the ascent of *Mt Ataviros*, the highest mountain in the island (3986 ft).

The ascent takes 2 hrs, and the descent about the same time. The mountain is bare of vegetation and has no springs. From the summit the whole of the island of Rhodes can be seen. On it are the scanty remains of the *Temple of Zeus Atabyros*, said to have been built by Althaemenes, founder of Kretinae (see above). It is certainly one of the oldest temples in Rhodes. It was adapted in the Byzantine era into the Church of St John the Baptist. The site was excavated in 1927 but the cella could not be found. About 100 yards N.E. are the remains of a stoa or propylaeum. Votive offerings found on the site and now in the Rhodes Museum include bronze, lead, and terracotta statuettes of oxen, goats, and other domestic animals.

About ½ m. farther on we rejoin the inland road.

———

THE INLAND ROAD. From the Kalavarda fork we ascend the lower slopes of Mt Profítis Ilías and at 28 m. reach a road leading to the left up the mountainside.

This well-engineered but steep and winding road ascends continually, with fine retrospective views of the sea. It soon enters the Wood of the Prophet, luxuriant thanks to a local superstition that the prophet will slay anyone cutting down a tree. The trees are mainly pines, including umbrella pines and cypresses. 4 m. *Hotels Elaphos, Elaphina* A, in a wonderful situation 2300 ft above the sea. The hotels are appropriately named ('Stag' and 'Doe') because of the number of deer in the neighbourhood. A path leads to the summit of Mt Prophet Elias (2620 ft).—The road continues to Eleoúsa and the E. coast.

Just short of (32½ m.) *Embona* (comp. above) we meet the coast road. We now make a wide sweep round the foothills of Atáviros, on the E. side of which is the *Monastery of Artamiti* (1247 ft).—We continue through sparsely inhabited hills to (c. 50 m.) *Siana* (1453 ft). A steep track, ending in a dangerous descent, leads to the *Castle of Monolithos, situated on the top of a precipitous rock called *Monopetra* (775 ft) and accessible only by a single path. Inside it are two cisterns and the modernized church of *Ayios Pantaleonos*, with another edifice beside it. There is a magnificent *View over the sea towards Khalki and another landwards of Mt Akramytes.

Kastellorizo

STEAMER ('Panormitis') from Rhodes, twice weekly in 6–8 hours.

Kastellorizo, officially *Megísti*, the Italian *Castelrosso*, once celebrated for its medieval castle, belongs to the Dodecanese on ethnological rather than geographical grounds, for it is in the E. Mediterranean rather than the Aegean. It is 72 m. E. of Rhodes. Largest of a miniature archipelago lying close to the coast of Lycia, Asia Minor, it is a small triangular island 4 m. long by 2 m. wide, with an area of 3½ sq. miles and thus the smallest of the 14 islands of the Dodecanese. Of its 11 dependent islets only two, *Rhó* and *Strongilí*, are inhabited—by lighthouse-keepers. The coastline is precipitous and inaccessible save on the E. side, where it forms a bay on which is the only centre of population. The interior is hilly. Cape Ayios Stefanos, at the N. end of the island, is only 1½ m. from the Anatolian coast. The inhabitants depend on tanks of rainwater collected during the winter rains. The chalky soil yields only olives, grapes, and vegetables in insignificant quantities.

The 270 inhabitants are mainly concentrated in the little port and village of *Kastellórizo*, or *Megísti*, on the E. coast. Many thousands of Castellorizans, however, live abroad, and the island is largely supported by the remittances of its emigrants who retire here when their fortunes have been made. The port of Kastellorizo provides the only safe shelter on or near the Asiatic coast between Makri and Beirut, and the island's caiques do a lively transit trade.

History. In antiquity the island was called *Megiste*, that is, the largest of the small archipelago. Another name for it appears to have been *Kisthene*. The Turks called it *Meis*. In 1306 it was occupied by the Knights of St John, who strengthened the existing castle and used it as a place of detention for recalcitrant knights. The island was captured in 1440 by Djemal ed Din, Sultan of Egypt, who destroyed the castle. In 1450 Alfonso I of Aragon, king of Naples, reconquered the island and rebuilt the castle. Kastellorizo remained in possession of Naples, except for short intervals, until it was captured in 1512 by the Turks. It was temporarily occupied by the Venetians in 1570 and again in 1659, when the castle was again destroyed. From 1828 to 1833 it was held by the Greeks. During the First World War it was bombarded from the Anatolian coast. Since 1920 it has shared the fortunes of the Dodecanese.

Steamer passengers land at *Mandraki*, the port of the island capital **Kastellorizo.** The Plateia is the centre of the small town. From it ascend narrow lanes, in which are houses with characteristic wooden balconies, and windows of Anatolian type. In another square is the modern church of Ayios Yeoryios and, near it, the *Cathedral* of SS Constantine and Helena. The cathedral is divided into nave and aisles by monolithic granite columns from the Temple of Apollo at Patara, in Lycia; the columns support ogival arches. From the end of this square is a good view of Mandraki and the Anatolian coast.—From a small square near Mandraki we may take the Street of the Knights, which follows the line of the promontory guarding the harbour. Leaving the street, we turn right into a steep and partly stepped path, which leads to the *Lycian Tomb*. This is cut out of the rock and has a Doric façade and a rectangular interior. Many similar but less elaborate tombs are to be found on the Anatolian coast opposite (see below).— Higher up are the ruins of the **Castle of the Knights.** This was built by Juan Fernando Heredia, 8th Grand Master of the Knights of St John. Its vicissitudes up to its second destruction are noted above. There survive parts of the curtain wall, and of three towers. A Doric inscription found on the site proves that a fort existed here in classical times.

A path on the right of the harbour leads to the *Palaiokastro*, on the top of Mt Viglo (885 ft). This is an ancient Greek stronghold built on a rectangular plan (265 ft by 200). Inside are numerous cisterns and an ancient tower of squared blocks. To the E. are the remains of propylaea, with a Doric inscription of the 3C or 2C B.C. on which is recorded the name Megiste and its dependence on Rhodes. There is a good view of the town and of the Anatolian coast.

To THE BLUE GROTTO, 3 hours by boat. This is the most attractive excursion in the island; the best time for a visit is late afternoon. Leaving the harbour, we bear S.E. and follow the inaccessible coast until we come to a slight curvature of the coastline, in which is the narrow mouth of the grotto. The *Blue Grotto, locally known as *Phokeale* ('Refuge of Seals'), recalls the Blue Grotto of Capri, but it is more extensive. Its length is 130–165 ft, its breadth 80–98 ft, and its height 65–80 ft. As at Capri, the gorgeous colouring is said to be caused by the reflection and refraction of the sun's rays through the water. The roof on the left side has collapsed, the debris forming a little island. At the end of the cave, on the right, is another grotto.

On the Anatolian coast, opposite Kastellorizo, is the town of *Antiphilo*, with a Roman theatre, numerous Lycian tombs and other ancient remains.

X CRETE

Among the islands of the Aegean **CRETE**, in Greek *Kríti* (KPHTH), because of its position and size has always been of paramount importance. Lying across the southern Aegean basin, it forms a link in the chain through Kythera to the mainland of Greece, through Kasos and Karpathos to Rhodes and Turkey, while to the s. the coast of Africa is but 200 m. away. The island, 160 m. long and 36 m. wide, is dominated by its great mountain backbone: in the w. the White Mountains (Lefka Ori, 8045 ft), the massif of Mt Ida (Psilorites, 8060 ft) in the centre, to the E. of which are the Lasithi Mountains (Spathi, 7045 ft), and at the eastern end the Thripte range (4840 ft) guarding the narrow isthmus of Ierapetra. These mountains are mainly limestones of all periods from Tertiary to Carboniferous set on a schist, phyllite or crystalline bed. The schists have obtruded in many places at the western end and there is much dolomite in the E.; other areas are considerably metamorphosed, outcrops of serpentines, chlorites, talc, and gypsum occurring in the foothills of the main ranges. These slope gently to the N. and very sharply on the southern coast. This has meant that habitation is concentrated on the N. coast around and behind the great bays of Kastelli, Khania, Soudha, Rethymno, Herakleion, and Mirabello. By contrast the southern coast cannot support much of a population and there is only one town, Ierapetra. The large and fertile Mesara plain, watered by the Ieropotamos stream, is the only cultivable area of any size in the south. An interesting geographical feature is the incidence of high upland plains enclosed by a ring of mountains. Such are the Lasithi plain, that of Nidha on Mt Ida and the Omalo in the White Mountains.

The favourable climate enables olives, grapes, carobs (Crete produces most of the world's crop), bananas, melons, peaches, and numerous other fruits to be grown in the lower regions and potatoes, onions, and apples on the higher plains. Cretan oranges are said locally (with some justification) to be the best in the world. Tomatoes, with some forcing, are produced all the year round. The climate and position are responsible for the island's astonishing variety of wild plants and flowers. There are many hundreds of known species including over 130 peculiar to Crete. In particular many varieties of orchid and ophrys are to be found in the spring. The only wild animals now found are the Cretan ibex (kri-kri), badger, wild cat, and weasel. The bird life is varied. Reptiles are less widepread than on the mainland, though the viper is known. Scorpions are not uncommon and there is a dangerous species of poisonous spider, the rogalidha, though this is rarely seen.

There is little industry, apart from a few small factories in or near the main towns and a number of gypsum quarries and limestone workings for cement. The greatest concentration of the total population (456,000 inhab.) is in the centre of the island. Above a quarter lives and works in the main towns, Herakleion, Khania, and Rethymno, the remainder in the villages, where most of the work is concerned with the vines and olives. In some areas, especially in the s., rural depopulation is distressingly noticeable.

Crete is, however, now very conscious of the tourist potential of scenery and archaeology. The E.–W. highway has fostered development of the N. coast and a similar project approaches fruition in the s.

To the intelligent visitor the material remains of the island's history will always be the chief objects of interest, especially the Minoan palaces, towns, and villas, the Classical and Roman cities of Gortyn, Lato, and Aptera, and the products of these former civilizations, chiefly in the Archaeological Museum of Herakleion. Nor should the evidences of more recent history be neglected, notably the large number of churches with fresco paintings (Crete was the home of a brilliant late Byzantine school) and Venetian buildings in the large towns. But the direct and always generously offered friendship of the Cretan people also enables anyone who will to enjoy the modern life of the island, especially at the local church festivals (panayiri).

The island is here described for the traveller making a short visit: those planning an extended stay are referred to the separate 'Blue Guide to Crete'.

History. NEOLITHIC PERIOD (6000–3000 B.C.). The first inhabitants of Crete lived in caves and open settlements, as at Knossos and Phaistos. They arrived about 6000 B.C. (according to a recent radiocarbon date from Knossos), perhaps from Anatolia (Asia Minor). These first inhabitants did not use pottery (though theirs was probably not a true pre-pottery culture) but soon the characteristically Neolithic dark burnished wares came in. Stone axes and perforated maceheads and bone tools are characteristic artefacts while clay and stone female figurines, some with pronounced steatopygy, perhaps indicate the cult of a great mother goddess. Obsidian from Melos is used for small tools. Houses are simple rectangular constructions with fixed hearths.

MINOAN PERIOD (3000/2800–1100 B.C.). The Cretan Bronze Age was divided by Sir Arthur Evans into three main periods, Early, Middle, and Late Minoan (named after the legendary king Minos), and each of these has three subdivisions (I, II, III).

The transition from Neolithic to Early Minoan, accompanied by an influx of new people, perhaps from Anatolia, is marked by the occupation of many new sites and by three distinct pottery styles, grey and brown wares with dark burnished patterns, the red on buff and white on red painted wares, and red monochrome wares. Gradually copper replaces stone for artefacts; by E.M. II flat leaf-shaped copper daggers are common, stone vessels and primitive sealstones begin and there is very high competence in the making of jewellery. The houses, with rectangular rooms, are of more complex plan, as at Vasilike in East Crete. It is from this site that the brilliant black and orange pottery characteristic of E.M. II is best known. There is considerable variety in burial practice; already in E.M. I the circular stone-built communal ossuaries (tholos tombs) occur, especially in the Mesara, while rectangular ossuaries and chamber tombs are found in East Crete and clay coffins were used at Pyrgos on the N. coast.

In Middle Minoan I the first Palaces, witness to the presence of kings, were founded c. 1950–1900 B.C. There is fuller evidence of town life on the main sites and individual villas were built at Mallia and Khamaizi. Peak sanctuaries as on Iuktas above Knossos, Petsofa above Palaikastro and at Koumasa are established. The Early Minoan tombs continue in use everywhere, but in many places a new method of burial, in clay storage jars (pithoi) is introduced. Examples of this are the cemetery at Pakhyammos near Gournia and in the Mesara tholos tomb at Voroi. In the Palaces the M.M. I style of pottery is succeeded by brilliant thin-walled polychrome vases, M.M. II Kamares Ware. Metal techniques are more developed: daggers and swords have medial ribs, jewellery has granulation and filigree decoration, seals have elaborate patterns on the torsional principle whereby the designs find their equilibrium through revolution about a centre rather than symmetry about an axis. A hieroglyphic system of writing is invented and used on seals, clay bars, and labels. Foreign contacts are wide; Egyptian scarabs appear in Crete and M.M. II pottery in Egypt and the Near East. A few stone vessels reach the mainland and the islands. Then, c. 1700 B.C., comes a great catastrophe, probably due to earthquakes, which laid the Palaces in ruins. The same disaster doubtless overcame the town sites though it is not so easy to identify 'destruction horizons' in view of the rebuilding and adaptation of the houses.

After this great disaster the Palaces are rebuilt (in M.M. III) and the island enters on its greatest age, from soon after 1700 to c. 1450 B.C. In this period most of the Minoan buildings which survive today were constructed, notably the great villas in the country and those around the Palaces. In architecture limestone and gypsum masonry in ashlar construction is used in the Palaces and some of the villas. Open planning with courts and columned porticos was favoured; large rooms were divided by partitions and light was introduced by light wells in internal parts of buildings. Fresco paintings decorated the walls of major rooms; highly elaborate plumbing and drainage systems were installed. The extensive space devoted to magazines filled with great storage jars bears witness to the great prosperity of the age. Town sites such as Gournia, Palaikastro, and Zakro are fully developed. Foreign contacts are wide, extending to mainland Greece, where a strong artistic influence is exercised, the islands, on which several colonies are settled, Troy, Miletus, Cyprus, Rhodes, Syria, Egypt, and the Lipari Islands in the west. To these places went Late Minoan I clay and stone vessels while Crete received fine stones like Egyptian alabaster, Spartan basalt, antico rosso and obsidian for the manufacture of stone vases and sealstones. In the island a script known as Linear A is used to write an as yet undeciphered language; tablets for domestic inventories are known from Ayia Triadha, Palaikastro, Tylissos and Zakro; inscriptions appear on large clay pithoi, on a potter's wheel and on a number of offering tables. These last are often from sacred caves or sanctuaries and their inscriptions are doubtless religious. At this time clay and stone vases, sealstones and bronzes reach their acme. Then, c. 1450 B.C., there is a total destruction involving all the major sites of the island. Its cause is not known for certain but it may well be the result of the great volcanic explosion of Thera (Santorini) to the north. Such explosions are regularly accompanied by earthquakes.

Only at Knossos was there immediate recovery and the Palace now enters on its final phase, c. 1450–1400/1380 B.C. Taking note of the presence of Linear B tablets, found only here in Crete but regularly on the mainland at Pylos, Mycenae, and Thebes, and the formalized pottery patterns known as the Palace Style, most archaeologists accept that the rulers of Knossos in this last phase were Myceneans, though from where on the mainland is not known.

After the great destruction some of the sites were not reoccupied, for example Mochlos, Pseira, and the large villas at Nirou Khani, Sklavokampos and Vathypetro. At other places there was reoccupation in the 14C and 13C on a reduced scale, as at Gournia, Knossos, Mallia, Palaikastro, Tylissos, and Zakro; on these sites individual houses or rooms were cleared and re-used; there was some building on a bigger scale, as at Ayia Triadha, and at least one new site, Khondros Kephala, s. of Viannos, was established. The settlement at Khania is at its most flourishing, with pottery imported from Cyprus. Shrines characterized by snake tubes and clay figures with raised arms are found, such as those at Ayia Triadha, Gortyn Mitropolis, Gournia, and Knossos. A new and distinct method of burial is introduced, with rectangular painted clay chests (larnakes), placed in chamber tombs. The pottery shows some similarities with the Mycenean wares now being spread from Italy to Syria, but in the main it goes its own independent way, no longer exercising external influences, except perhaps through Close Style octopus-decorated, stirrup vases towards the end of the Bronze Age in the 12C.

Life at this time was troubled for there was a movement of population to refuge cities on high inaccessible mountains such as Karphi above Lasithi. Knowledge about this period is still slight, but two things are noticeable: there is a continuity of cult from the Late Bronze Age to the Iron Age, as shown by the deposit of objects in sacred caves, notably the Idaian Cave on Mt Ida and the Diktaian Cave above Psykhro; and a number of Iron Age settlements have traces of Late Minoan III occupation. Gortyn, Praisos, and Vrokastro are examples. A rich cemetery at Prinias in central Crete is in continuous use from late Minoan times to the Iron Age.

GEOMETRIC AND ARCHAIC PERIODS. By the 8C Crete is a flourishing Dorian island. It is possible that Greeks speaking the Doric dialect had entered during the disturbed conditions of the early Iron Age. Homer ('Odyssey', XIX, 177) speaks of a mixed population including Dorians. The older Minoan population might have survived in the Eteocretans whose language, known from inscriptions found at Dreros and Praisos, is in a Greek script using pre-Hellenic words. Artistically the island now flourishes to a remarkable extent: in bronze it produces the decorated shields from the Idaian Cave and the hammered statuettes from Dreros; the Dedalic school with its formal statues and statuettes with wig-like hair plays a leading part in the beginnings of Greek sculpture; the Geometric pottery, especially the polychrome amphoras from Fortetsa, is distinctive; somewhat later come the Archaic relief pithoi. Fine jewellery is also produced and there are interesting clay votive relief plaques. Settlements are of all kinds, on high peaks like Vrokastro, on acropolis hills like Dreros and Prinias or on low hills like Knossos and Phaistos. Burials in tholos tombs continue from Protogeometric, if not L.M. III, into the Geometric period. Cremation is now universal.

CLASSICAL, HELLENISTIC, AND ROMAN PERIODS. From the 5C until the Roman conquest in 67 B.C. Crete is divided into many small cities, regularly on defensible hills with a saddle between two summits. Defence walls are usual, as for example at Aptera and Eleutherna. Many cities mint their own coins. There is frequent inter-city warfare. The social structure is dominated by aristocratic families. The island had Dorian institutions like those of Sparta, and the Cretan Kosmoi, like the Spartan Ephors, exercised so much control over public and private life as to draw from Aristotle the criticism that it was overdone ('Politics', II, 10). Culturally the island offers nothing distinct from the Classical and Hellenistic world. Life cannot have been everywhere as easy or comfortable as in the Roman period when more peaceful conditions produced large spreading settlements in the low-lying or coastal areas, as with Gortyn, Knossos, or Stavromenos on the coast E. of Rethymno. Sites like Mochlos are inhabited for the first time since the Bronze Age. After the brutal conquest by Q. Metellus Creticus in 67 B.C. Gortyn became the capital of the new province of Crete and Cyrenaica and as such the residence of the governor. Villas are built, such as the Villa Dionysus at Knossos, and there is extensive public building at Aptera, Gortyn, Knossos, and Lyttos.

MEDIEVAL AND MODERN PERIODS. That Crete continued to flourish in the early Byzantine period (5–9C), is shown by the large number of basilican churches, often with mosaics and columns made from imported stones. Examples of such churches are at Gortyn (Ayios Titos), Khersonesos between Herakleion and Mallia, at Knossos, and at Vizari in the Amari valley. Then for over 100 years, c. 823–961, the Saracen Arabs conquered and held the island, though little survives from their occupation save for their coinage. The liberation was achieved by the Emperor Nikephoros Phokas, who catapulted the heads of his Mussulman prisoners into the town of Herakleion, or Kandak as it was then called. After the Fourth Crusade the Genoese ruled for the early years of the 13C until the island was sold by Boniface of Montferrat to Venice who held it for over 400 years (1210–1669). Cretan malmsey was drunk in England in the Lancastrian era and the early Tudors employed a consul to ensure its supply. Under the Venetians and after the fall of Constantinople in 1453 there was a late renaissance of Byzantine art resulting in the fresco paintings of many Cretan churches; Crete also produced many notable icon painters, Tzanfournares, Dhamaskinos, Klotzas, the famous Theotokopoulos (El Greco), who moved to Venice and Spain and, in the 18C, Kornaros who painted the great icon in the monastery of Toplou. Three notable Cretan painters, Theophanes, Anthony, and Tzortzis, worked on the Greek mainland. In the field of literature the poetic drama, the Sacrifice of Abraham, appeared and another Kornaros produced the epic rhymed romance, Erotokritos. Khania, Rethymno, Herakleion, Ierapetra, and Siteia had their walls built or were fortified; Spinalonga, N. of Ayios Nikolaos, received a fortress to guard the natural harbour. Numerous public buildings were erected in the cities, and docks, harbours, and wharves were constructed.

The Turkish occupation (1669, the fall of Herakleion, to 1898) was exacting, and life reached the lowest level since the end of the Bronze Age. The Sublime Porte was not so much harsh as indifferent to the economic condition of the island. Pashley in 1837 describes the poverty of life. After the insurrection of 1821 an Egyptian viceroy, Mehmet Ali, was put in charge and he had reconquered most of the island by 1840. This whole period is punctuated by revolutions of which that of 1866 is the best known.

From 1898 to 1913 Crete was independent under a High Commissioner, Prince George, appointed by the Great Powers, Britain, France, and Russia. In 1913 the island became part of Greece and in 1922–23 took part in the interchange of populations whereby the Turkish element left and Greek refugees from Asia Minor came in, making settlements on the outskirts of the main towns. The Germans occupied the island in 1941–44 after a successful but costly airborne invasion under Gen. Student, and during this time burnt a number of villages as reprisals. Since the war tourism, attracted by the climate and splendid remains of the Minoan civilization, has brought rapid prosperity to the towns without effecting much change in the life of the villages.

Approaches to Crete. By Air. From Athens to *Herakleion*, 6 or more times daily in c. 1 hr; to *Khania* 3 or more times daily in ¾ hr. From Rhodes to *Herakleion* daily.

By Sea from Piraeus in 11–12 hrs. To *Herakleion*, car ferry (two services) daily overnight; also twice weekly by day; to *Soudha* (Khania), car ferry daily (overnight exc. Sun); to *Ayios Nikolaos* and *Siteia* on Sun.

From Herakleion to *Ios, Mykonos, Santorini,* and *Tinos* twice weekly.—From Siteia to *Khalki, Karpathos, Kasos, Folegandros, Rhodes, Santorini,* and *Sikinos* weekly.

Communications. Roads between main towns and to most places of tourist interest are asphalted. Few villages are not reached by bus once a day. Cars may be hired from agencies in the main towns and there are organized trips by car or coach from Herakleion and Ay. Nikólaos to the main archaeological sites. Taxis may also be hired by the day, the itinerary and price being agreed beforehand.

77   HERAKLEION

HERAKLEION, or **Iráklion** (HPAKΛEION), known also by its medieval name of *Candia*, lies midway along the N. coast of Crete, of which it is the most considerable city. By population (77,500 inhab.) it ranks fifth among the cities of Greece (after Athens, Salonika, Piraeus, and Patras). Enjoying a central position, good communications with the mainland, and a high standard of accommodation, it provides the obvious centre for a first exploration of the island; and, though the town itself is of no great interest, its splendid museum and the proximity of Knossos make it for the visitor one of the most important objectives in the Aegean.

Airport, just E. of the city; services, see above.

Hotels. With restaurant, but DPO: **Astoria** (Pl. b), 145 R.; **Atlantis** (Pl. e), 135 R.; **Xenia** (Pl. f), all with swimming pool; **Astir** (Pl. a), these A. **Mediterranean** (Pl. k) B.

Without restaurant and less expensive: **Castro** (Pl. i), **Esperia** (Pl. j), **Cosmopolite** (Pl. c), all B, **Daedalus** (Pl. p), **El Greco** (Pl. m), **Olympic** (Pl. o), **Park** (Pl. h), **Selena** (Pl. g), **Domenico** (Pl. l), **Herakleion** (Pl. n), **Knossos** (Pl. d), all C.

Outside the city: **Galini, Poseidon, Pasiphae,** in suburban Poros, to the E., C. **Youth Hostel** (120 beds), 24 Khandakos.

Restaurants and Tavernas in the street linking Od. Evans and Od. 1866; *Maxim*, next to Park Hotel; also *Minos, Klimataria,* in Od. Daidalou; *Caprice, Knossos,* opp. Morosini fountain; *Psaria,* at foot of Od. 25 Avgoustou; and others on quay w. of harbour; also at the hotels.—Good Cafés in Elevtherias Sq. and Zakharoplasteia in Dikaiossinis.

Post Office, Plat. Daskaloyiannis.—O.T.E. Centre, overlooking El Greco Park; Olympic Airways Office, Plat. Elevtherias; Shipping Offices, Banks, in Od.

25 Avgoustou.—N.T.O.G. REGIONAL INFORMATION BUREAU, 1 Od. Xanthidhidhou, near the Arch. Museum.

Buses through the town and to *Knossos* (No. 2) from the Harbour. To *Rethimno* and *Khania*; to *Ayios Nikólaos, Ierapetra,* and *Siteia*; and to *Mallia,* from Bus Station on quay below Leoforos Beaufort (see plan); to *Phaistos* from Pantokrator Gate.—COACH EXCURSIONS by Creta Tours and others.

History. In the prehistoric period there was a Minoan harbour town and cemetery in the Poros suburb on the E. side of the modern city. On the heights to the s., of this, above the Kairatos stream bed, a Neolithic settlement existed. Much later in Roman times, *Heracleium* was the harbour of Knossos. After the Saracen conquest c. 823–8 the town was named *Kandak* from the great ditch dug round it. It became a centre of piracy and the chief slave market of the Mediterranean. Nikephoros Phokas liberated it in 961 and during the second Byzantine period (961–1205) its name was corrupted to Khandax. When Crete passed to the Venetians in 1210 they made the city their capital, calling it and the island *Candia*. The impressive walls, gates, bastions, and fortifications were built over a long period (14–17C) to make Candia one of the leading seaports of the East Mediterranean. In 1538 the military engineer Michele Sammicheli came to take charge of their construction and here in 1570 Fr. Laparelli da Cortona (the architect of Valletta) died of plague. Venice appointed a governor, known as the Duke of Crete. To develop the city it was enacted that the Venetian nobility and Greek aristocracy must build houses in it and reside there for part of the year.

Discontent with Venetian rule brought a series of revolts from within the island but in 1648 an external oppressor, the Turk, began the great siege of the city. This was to last more than 21 years. The Turkish camp lay on the hill of Fortetsa, c. 3 m. s., whence their cannons operated against the town. In the siege it is said that the Venetians and their allies lost 30,000 men, the Turks 118,000. Relief forces were sent out by Louis XIV in 1668 and 1669 under the Dukes of Beaufort and of Navailles. A sortie involved the destruction of Beaufort and his force and the remaining French withdrew. On 5 Sept 1669 the Venetian commander, Francesco Morosini, surrendered and the Venetians were allowed to leave Crete unharmed. Under the Turks the town, known now as *Megalo Kastro,* was the seat of a Pashalik. It was renamed *Herakleion* after Turkish rule ended in 1898. Though Khania was then made the capital, Herakleion, because of its central position, grew rapidly to become the chief commercial city.

In the centre of the town is Plateia Venizelou with the **Morosini Fountain,** constructed in 1626–28 by the Venetian Governor, Francesco Morosini the elder. The lions are older (14C); below the basins are reliefs with marine scenes. Opposite the fountain is *St Mark's Hall,* formerly the Venetian church of St Mark, now restored and used for lectures and concerts. It was rebuilt after earthquakes in 1303 and 1508; in Turkish times it was converted into a mosque and the base of the minaret may still be seen to one side of it.

From the fountain ODHOS IKOSIPENDE AVGOUSTOU (25 Aug), the principal commercial street, runs down to the harbour. On the right is the newly constructed copy of the 16C Venetian *Loggia,* finally destroyed during the last war. This backs on to the Venetian Armoury, now used as the *Dhimarkhion.* On the N. side of this building is the *Sagredo Fountain,* also Venetian. Just beyond the loggia we reach the church of *Ayios Titos.* The original Byzantine church underwent many reconstructions before its destruction by earthquake in 1856. The present building was designed as a mosque in 1872. The head of St Titus, which the Venetians took with them in 1669, was returned from St Mark's in 1966.

The small inner *Harbour* is guarded by a Venetian *Fortress* of 1523–40 (adm. fee), with interesting interior and defaced Lions of St Mark. The well-preserved vaulted *Arsenals,* also 16C, opposite the Port Offices of the modern harbour, are used as warehouses. Other Venetian buildings along Leof. Koundouriotou have been restored. Above the Bus Station the Duke of Beaufort Avenue ('Leoforos Dhoukos Bofor') ascends to PLATEIA ELEVTHERIAS and the **Archaeological Museum** (see below). In the huge square the town takes the air in the early evening and the city band plays on Sunday. Opposite the museum the road for E. Crete descends through the walls where stood St George's Gate (Porta del Lazzareto), built in 1565. An old fountain survives in the wall on the left of the road.

From the Plateia, Leoforos Dikaiossinis passes down to the town centre. This avenue approximately follows the southern limit of the Saracen and Byzantine town; the digging of foundations for modern houses revealed traces of the rampart of this period. The government offices on the left of the avenue occupy Turkish buildings on the site of Venetian barracks. On reaching PLATEIA NIKEPHOROU PHOKA, we may turn left into Odhos 1866, the lively food market of the town. The first street off this on the left consists of small tavernas. At the top, beyond the market, stands the *Bembo Fountain* built in 1588 of antique fragments. It stands behind a polygonal kiosk, now a shop, adapted from a Turkish fountain. We are now at the N. side of PLATEIA KORNAROU. From the square, Evans St. continues up to pass through the walls at the *Kainouria Porta* (New Gate), dated 1567–87. The passage through the gate shows the walls to be 45 yds thick. The s. sections of the **City Walls**, if reclaimed from neglect and misuse, could be the city's principal attraction. The road to the right within the walls leads to the *Martinengo Bastion* on which is the tomb of Nikos Kazantzakis, the the author, who died in 1957.

From Plateia Nikephorou Phoka (see above) a main shopping street, Kalokairinou, runs out to the *Porta Khanion* (Khania or Panigra Gate), built c. 1570 (now restored); beyond it are the Phaistos and Tylissos bus terminals. A short way along Kalokairinou any of the little streets to the left leads to Plateia Ayia Aikaterini (St Catherine's Square), named after the church of *Ayia Aikaterini*, which was built in 1555 but altered in the 17C. The Mt Sinai monastery of St Catherine had a centre here in the adjacent Ayioi Dheka during the Cretan renaissance (16–17C). The Basilica (open 10–1, 5–7; 10 dr.) contains the six *Ikons by Dhamaskinos (c. 1580) from Valsamonero. Just below stands the smaller church of *Ayios Minas*, built in the 18C.

The *Historical Museum of Crete, near the Xenia Hotel, occupies the family house of Andreas Kalokairinos, a notable benefactor of Herakleion, who gave it for the collection.

ADMISSION 9–1, 3–5.30 or 6, 20 dr.; closed Sunday. There are two entrances, the front giving on to the main floor, the back into the basement. A gradual rearrangement is to be expected.

BASEMENT. ROOM 1. Early Christian and Byzantine Period. 6C sculptures from the basilica of Ayios Titos at Gortyn; Byzantine stone well-heads; relief plaques; 6–9C Byzantine tombstones. The doorway to Room 2 is from a Venetian building of Candia (Herakleion).

ROOM 2. Venetian Period. Above the doorway is a relief plaque with the Lion of St Mark (comp. that on the Harbour Fortress). Left: tombstone dated 1605; along the wall are architectural fragments from the loggia (1626–28), now rebuilt in the town; doorway with double arches from a Venetian house; above the doorway a Venetian frieze and a coat of arms with a lion and a Hebrew inscription of a Jewish family living in Crete in 16C; in front of the doorway is an elaborate fountain from a Venetian palace and between the two windows the arms of the Venetian family of Capello. Along the right-hand wall are other Venetian arms: one of the 15C with a tower, a cross, and a griffin and an inscription in Latin and Armenian (used as a tombstone in the Armenian Church of Candia). The doorway with double arches leads to a small room containing fragments from the Venetian Church of St Francis, destroyed in the earthquake of 1856: part of a Gothic rose-window and a relief representing an angel.—ROOM 4. Turkish Period. Inscriptions, tombstones, and glazed porcelain tiles from an 18C mosque in the town.

FIRST FLOOR. ENTRANCE HALL. Fresco painting from the Venetian church of the Madonna dei Crociferi in Herakleion; prow of a Venetian galley. In the corridor (Room 3) from the hall are tombstones and inscriptions in Greek and Latin from the Venetian period.—ROOM 5. Early Christian and Byzantine Antiquities. Oil lamps, bronze crucifixes, candlesticks, bronze objects (6C) from the basilica of Ayios Titos at Gortyn and 14C and 15C fresco fragments from Cretan churches.— ROOM 6. Left: icons of 1655 from the monastery of Savathiana, including the Virgin and the Prophets and St Peter and St Paul, the descent from the Cross and the Virgin between two angels (the latter from the Armenian Church of St John). At the end of the room is a painted crucifix from the Church of the Panayia Gouverniotissa. On the wall to the right of the entrance: late 16C to early 17C fresco fragments from the Church of the Gouverniotissa Pedhiadhos and the Potamies monastery. Note also the remains of a 16C wooden iconostasis. On each side of the entrance are glass cases with 16–17C pottery. Two other cases contain exhibits from the Asomatos Monastery (Rethymno Province), vestments, crucifixes, Gospels, and other liturgical objects. Other cases contain coins from the Byzantine, Venetian, and Turkish periods and Byzantine and Venetian jewellery and seals.—ROOM 7. Documents and other objects relating to Cretan insurrections during the Turkish period. Also on this floor is a reconstructed Byzantine *Chapel.*

SECOND FLOOR. ROOM 8. Manuscripts (10–19C) including Venetian maps and plans.—ROOM 9 is furnished as the study of Nikos Kazantzakis (1883–1957). It contains his desk, his library, editions and translations of his novels, photographs, and various personal possessions.— ROOM 10 represents the living-room in the house of a Cretan peasant of about 1900.—ROOM 11. Exhibition of Cretan and Island dresses and woven fabrics. A large room displays material concerning the Cretan statesman M. Tsouderos (1817–77), and another shows photographs of the Battle of Crete (1941).

The **Archaeological Museum,** off Plateia Eleftherias, contains a vast collection of material of all periods of Cretan history from Neolithic to Roman. At least two visits should be made, preferably before and after the sites have been seen.

ADMISSION 50 dr.; 9–3.30, Sun & hol. 10–4.30, closed Monday.
Detailed catalogues and illustrated souvenirs are available in English.—Qualified guides may be hired to conduct parties or individuals round (charge agreed beforehand).

A detailed Guide Book in English by S. Alexiou, with an introduction by N. Platon (1968), is available.—Qualified guides may be hired to conduct parties or individuals round (charge agreed beforehand).

The case-numbering of the lower floor rooms starts with the right-hand wall as you enter, goes round the room anti-clockwise and ends in the centre. Our description sometimes diverges from exact case order.

GALLERY I. NEOLITHIC AND MINOAN PREPALATIAL CIVILIZATION (Early Minoan). Cases 1 & 2 contain Neolithic and Sub-neolithic pottery, violin-shaped and steatopygous idols, and bone and stone implements.—Case 3 illustrates the various styles of Early Minoan I (3000–2400 B.C.) with grey wares and pattern-burnished vases and red on buff painted wares.—Case 6 contains E.M. II Vasilike mottled ware, in particular jugs and long spouted teapots. In Case 7 the finest of the early stone vases come from Mochlos (E.M. II–III, 2400–2100 B.C.). The vases were made by hand, the inside being cut out with a reed or copper drill with an abrasive powder to do the cutting.—Case 8 displays Early Minoan III vases from Vasilike and Mochlos. A style with white decoration on a dark ground now replaces the Vasilike mottled ware but many of the earlier shapes continue. Cases 9 & 10 contain vases from the Mesara tombs, and E.M.–M.M. I vases from Palaikastro in E. Crete. Note the four-wheeled cart, the earliest evidence for wheeled transport from Crete.—Case 11. Early and Middle Minoan I sealstones.—In Cases 16–18 are displayed elegant gold, rock crystal, and carnelian jewellery and necklaces, among them gold chains with minute links, from Mochlos and the Mesara tombs.

GALLERY II. MINOAN PROTOPALATIAL CIVILIZATION (M.M. I–II). This room is devoted mainly to finds of this period from **Knossos** and **Mallia**. Cases 22 & 23. Pottery from houses below the West Court at Knossos, then fine Middle Minoan I–II vases from Knossos. Between these cases are several clay burial chests (larnakes). Case 24 contains M.M. I figurines from the peak sanctuary of Petsofa, above Palaikastro at the eastern end of Crete. Note the elaborate headdresses of the female figures and the daggers worn in their belts by the males. Clay model shrine with doves perched on the pillars, from Knossos. The central case (25) nearest the entrance to the room contains the polychrome faience plaques from Knossos, known as the Town Mosaic since they are models of Middle Minoan house façades, sometimes three storeys high. This case also contains tablets, labels, and bars in the M.M. Hieroglyphic script.

GALLERY III. Same period. Here (Case 30) are the polychrome vases from the Kamares cave, which gave Kamares ware its name, and the remainder of the room is devoted to the astonishing collection of *Vases and other objects from the **First Palace of Phaistos**. Some of the smaller vases are known as eggshell ware because of the incredible thinness of their walls. Of the larger vessels a tall vase with attached white flowers and a fruitstand or bowl with elaborately painted interior (both in Case 43) are noteworthy. The central case (42) displays the contents of a shrine from a room bordering the W. Court at Phaistos. Notice the great red-burnished clay libation table with border decoration of oxen and spiral designs. In Case 41 is the famous *Phaistos Disk, with stamped characters in an unknown Hieroglyphic script. The words are divided by incised lines and the inscription runs from the outside to the centre. The disk was found in a room of M.M. III date (17C B.C.).

GALLERY IV. NEOPALATIAL CIVILIZATION (Middle Minoan III to Late Minoan I). In Case 44 from **Knossos** are two conical clay cups with ink inscriptions in the Linear A script. From Knossos also (in Case 45) come the vases with spiral decoration and others with white lilies on the dark ground. Case 46. Vessels used in worship of the Sacred Snake. On the opposite side of the room, in Cases 47–48, finds from the Palace and houses of **Mallia**, notably the brown schist sceptre, one end a leopard, the other an axe, a series of domestic vessels and lamps in clay and stone, and several bronze utensils. The finds from the final destruction of the Palace of **Phaistos** in Late Minoan I B, c. 1450 B.C., were few, but notice the graceful jug with grasses all over and a rhyton decorated with argonauts.—Case 50 contains the smaller finds from the M.M. III Temple Repositories at Knossos: the Snake Goddess and her votaries, the flying fish and other decorative plaques, all these in faience, banded limestone and marble libation vases, a rock crystal rosette for inlay, and painted shells.

The central cases contain some of the finest products of the Minoan civilization. Case 51. The **Bull's Head Rhyton (so called because of the holes in the mouth and head through which sacred libations were poured) is from the Little Palace at Knossos. It is made of serpentine, the eyes inlaid with jasper, rock crystal, and white tridacna shell, the horns (restored) of gilded wood. In Case 57 is the royal *Draughtboard or gaming table, inlaid with ivory, rock crystal, faience, lapis lazuli and gold and silver foil. It was found in a corridor of the Palace at Knossos and is dated c. 1600 B.C. Case 56. Ivory acrobats, probably covered with gold leaf originally. The main figure is in the act of leaping over a bull. Of the other cases, 55 contains bronze scales or balances, and lead and stone weights from various sites, on one side, and on the other faience reliefs, including a very naturalistic cow suckling her calf and a marble cross from the Knossos Temple Repositories; Case 54 contains the large vases from the Repositories including the bird amphoras imported from the Cycladic Islands; adjacent in Case 58 are the stone ritual vessels from the Shrine Treasury of the Palace at Knossos. These are mostly rhytons in alabaster, banded limestones, and other variegated stones.—From the same Treasury came the Lioness Head Rhyton made of a white marble-like limestone. This has Case 59 to itself.—A splendid series of bronzes from houses at Knossos is displayed in Case 53. These include a large saw, a tripod cauldron and bowls with chased decoration of leaves round the rims.

Beside the bronzes is Case 52 with a ceremonial *Sword and other weapons from Mallia, of Middle Minoan date. The sword, nearly a metre long, has a pommel of rock crystal on an ivory hilt.

GALLERY V. KNOSSOS. THE FINAL PALACE PERIOD (Late Minoan II–IIIA, 1450–1400 B.C.). Around the walls are a series of Palace Style amphoras, some from the Palace, others from the Little Palace and Royal Villa. It may be noticed how a formal element has entered into the decoration, in contrast to the naturalism of the Late Minoan I vases. On the right as we enter is a giant unfinished stone amphora from the Palace with a decoration of shallow spirals. Cases 60 & 61 contain Late Minoan vases from the recent Knossos excavations, architectural fragments from the Palace, stone friezes with split rosettes and spirals in relief, a large stone jug in banded limestone and a ewer of breccia imitating basketwork, clay vases from the Little Palace and silver vessels from the S. House.—Case 62 contains several fine large stone vases and lamps from Knossos made from a reddish marble, antico rosso, imported from the southern Peloponnese. Above are Egyptian finds from Knossos, including an alabaster lid with a cartouche of the Hyksos king Khyan, a large Pre-dynastic or early Dynastic bowl, carinated bowls (Fourth Dynasty) of diorite with a Minoan obsidian imitation, and a diorite statuette of an Egyptian, perhaps an ambassador, called User (Twelfth or early Thirteenth Dynasty).

In the central cases are (Case 69) Linear A tablets from Ayia Triadha, Tylissos, Phaistos, Zakro, Palaikastro, and Gournia; Linear B tablets from the Knossos archives; (Case 65) some exquisite Late Minoan sealstones; (Case 66) stone vases from the Palace including the big flat gypsum alabastrons found in the Throne Room; (Case 70) various ivories of very fine workmanship; and (Cases 67 & 68) Palace Style octopus amphoras and one of Late Minoan Ib date, c. 1450 B.C., for contrast (naturalistic, not degenerate like the others) from the recent Knossos excavations.

GALLERY VI. NEOPALATIAL CEMETERIES (Middle Minoan III–Late Minoan III, c. 1650–1350 B.C.). Case 71 contains Late Minoan vases from the tholos tomb, used uninterruptedly from Middle Minoan I, at Kamilari s.w. of Phaistos. With them is a most interesting clay shrine with divinities and worshippers. The bird alabastrons are painted in a lively style. Case 72. Material from the Temple Tomb at Knossos and the Royal Tomb at Isopata. From the latter is the splendid series of Egyptian Eighteenth Dynasty alabaster *Vases and an Old Kingdom bowl in porphyry. Vases of clay and stone from the Knossian cemeteries of Mavro Spelio and Zapher Papoura follow in Case 73, with a Kourotrophos figurine; then Case 74 for a chamber tomb from the rich cemetery at Katsamba, the harbour town of Knossos on the eastern side of Herakleion. The tomb group includes an ivory *Pyxis with a bull-catching scene akin to that on the gold cups from Vapheio (Athens, National Museum); there is also an early Dynastic diorite bowl with a Minoan lid. Next comes Case 75 with bronze vessels and utensils from tombs at Zapher Papoura, and Arkhanes.

Beyond, wall cases (76 & 77) display clay and stone vases from tombs at Isopata, including the Tomb of the Double Axes, from the Late Minoan II Warrior Graves under the Sanatorium N. of Knossos and from another tomb of this date from Knossos. In Case 78, a reconstructed boar's tusk *Helmet from the Zapher Papoura cemetery (a Mycenean import?).

The central cases contain amphoras from the Royal Tomb at Isopata; (Case 82) large stone vessels from the Katsamba cemetery including an Egyptian alabaster vase with a cartouche of Thutmosis III (1504–1450 B.C.), the great king of the Eighteenth Dynasty, and a Late Minoan II amphora showing helmets with cheekpieces. Case 80. Libation jug from Katsamba with stylized argonauts and spiked decoration. Cases

81, 86 & 87 contain jewellery and ivory toilet articles from the Phaistos and Knossos cemeteries, and from various other tombs. Particularly fine (in Case 87) is the gold *Ring with a dancing divinity and worshippers from Isopata, and ear-rings in the shape of bulls' heads, done in the granulation technique. Case 88 contains finds from Mycenean tholos tombs at Arkhanes, including jewellery, a bronze mirror with an ivory handle and a pyxis lid in ivory with figure-eight shield handles. Cases 84 & 85 contain weapons from Mycenean warrior graves near Knossos with a bronze *Helmet equipped with cheek-pieces.

GALLERY VII. NEOPALATIAL SETTLEMENTS OF CENTRAL AND SOUTH CRETE (Late Minoan I, c. 1550–1450 B.C.). The first objects on the right are large bronze double axes set up on restored poles and painted bases. These are from the megaron of Nirou Khani on the coast E. of Herakleion. Case 89. Bronze figurines of male worshippers, vases, and stone lamps, from Nirou Khani and finds from the villas at Tylissos, including a rhyton of dark grey imported obsidian. In Case 90 vases from the villas at Amnisos, Sklavokambos, and Vathypetro. Notice the fine bridge-spouted jug with zig-zag patterns and the stone conical rhyton from Sklavokambos. The opposite wall cases (91 & 93) contain vases from Prasa, a little E. of Herakleion, and from Ayia Triadha. Carbonized beans, barley, millet, and figs from Phaistos and Palaikastro are also shown. In between, Case 92, bronze figurines and small votive animals from the Dictaean Cave and other cave sites.

Separately displayed in the small central cases are the three famous serpentine relief vases from Ayia Triadha, the *Chieftain Cup (95), the *Boxer Vase (96), and the **Harvester Vase (94), often considered the finest product of Minoan art. Each portrays scenes from the daily life of the Minoans. The other cases contain (97) bronze weapons from the votive cave at Arkalokhori, two thin ivory figurines from Nirou Khani, and bronze discs or dumps, perhaps a form of money; and (98) the hoard of votive double axes from the Arkalokhori cave. Case 99. Copper talents or ox-hide ingots (weight 64 lb.), incised in Cypriot script, and copper hammers from Ayia Triadha; (102) human and animal votive offerings from the same site, stone vases, including a beautiful dolium shell of white-spotted obsidian and a Hittite sphinx; (100) bronze tools, utensils and jewellery, all from Ayia Triadha, two potter's wheels from Vathypetro and seals from various sites. Along one wall are three huge bronze cauldrons from Tylissos.

Standing on their own are various large vessels, including a huge stone basin from Ayia Triadha. Two coarse limestone thrones are from Katsamba and Prinias. In the central Case 101, gold and silver jewellery from Central and E. Crete. There are several examples with granulation. Here also is one of the great treasures of Minoan art, the gold *Pendant of M.M. I date from the Khrysolakkos cemetery at Mallia. It consists of two conjoined bees (or wasps or hornets) around a golden ball with a smaller ball within, covered with granulation.

GALLERY VIII. THE PALACE OF ZAKRO (Late Minoan I, c. 1550–1450 B.C.). The wall cases (103–110) are mainly devoted to clay vases found in the Palace. These include a series of plain flower vases with high curving handles, a fruitstand with spiral decoration, Marine Style vases, and a large ritual jug; (109) an exquisite rock crystal *Rhyton with a handle of beads turned green by the bronze wire on which they are threaded. There are also white limestone libation tables and a stone column capital. Case 111 contains the *Peak Sanctuary Rhyton, a magnificent vase showing in relief a mountain shrine with wild goats, plants, and flowers. A few traces survive of the gold leaf which once covered it. Case 116 holds a bull's head rhyton, made of chlorite. It is smaller than that from Knossos but of equally fine workmanship. Other cases display (117) objects of faience, including a large argonaut and butterflies; (112) a large double axe with chased decoration (see the restored drawing on the wall); (113) a huge burnt ivory tusk said to be imported from Syria, bronze ingots, and several very fine Late Minoan I$_B$ vases; (115) bronzes including long swords and a huge saw; and, in two cases (114 & 118) the magnificent series of *Stone vessels, mostly from the Shrine Treasury.

GALLERY IX. NEOPALATIAL SETTLEMENTS OF EAST CRETE (Late Minoan I, c. 1700–1450 B.C.). The finds are from the settlements of Palaikastro, Mochlos, Gournia, Pseira, and Zakro. Cases 119 & 120 on the right are devoted to Palaikastro. The first contains stone vases and lamps, one of antico rosso with ivy scrolls on the column. Notice also a clay bull rhyton and bronze figurines, the large one from Praisos. The second case contains three fine L.M. I$_B$ vases including an octopus flask and a jug with papyrus decoration, and two clay cat's heads. The central case (125) opposite has Marine Style rhytons, a gabbro rhyton and stone libation tables from Palaikastro. In Case 121 (opposite wall) are a series of L.M. I vases from Gournia (an octopus stirrup vase in its own case), a small bull's head rhyton, and a bronze figurine, and, in Case 122, clay and stone vases and lamps from Pseira, with a magnificent rhyton of breccia. The remaining wall-case (123) contains, from the M.M.–L.M. I peak sanctuary at Piskokephalo near Siteia, clay votives, human and animal, beetles (rhinoceros oryctes) being the most common. Sometimes they have climbed on to the human figures.

In the central cases are (124) clay sealings from Knossos, Ayia Triadha, Zakro, and Sklavokambos, one from Knossos showing two personages with a Hieroglyphic inscription, perhaps a title, beside them, together with small objects, notably ivories and inlays, from Palaikastro and other E. Cretan sites; (128) an unparalleled collection of Late Minoan *Sealstones in agate, carnelian, chalcedony, jasper, lapis Lacedaemonius, lapis lazuli, rock crystal, and other stones, from many sites. The main shapes are the lentoid, amygdaloid (almond shape), and flattened cylinder.

Beyond stands Case 129 with finds from Mochlos, clay vases, bull rhytons, a stone lamp with foliate band decoration, and bronze vessels including a cup with chased ivy decoration, closely similar in shape to the gold cups from Vapheio in Athens.

GALLERY X. POSTPALATIAL PERIOD (Late Minoan III, c. 1350–1100 B.C.). The decline in the Minoan culture is reflected in the remains of the postpalatial age. It is noticeable how vase-painting has lost its vitality. Fine stonework no longer occurs. Most of the material exhibited is from tombs for there has as yet been little preserved from settlements of this period. Wall cases (130 & 131) on the right exhibit L.M. III pottery from Phoinikia, Katsamba, Phaistos, Gournia, and Palaikastro. Popular shapes are the high-stemmed kylix, tankard, ladle krater, and stirrup vase. The earlier L.M. patterns have now become stylized, but the bird decoration of the first part of L.M. III is interesting.—Case 132. From Palaikastro comes the group of figures dancing round a musician playing the lyre. The single wall case (133) contains large clay idols with raised arms from Gazi, w. of Herakleion. The central figure may be a goddess since she has a head-dress of poppies.

The central cases contain the following objects: (139) bead necklaces, mostly of glass paste, some of semi-precious stones, from the tombs at Gournes, Episkope and Stamnioi, Pedhiadha, and Milatos, together with stone moulds for ornaments; (140) finds from L.M. III shrines at Knossos (Shrine of the Double Axes), Phaistos and Gournia, with clay huts also from the first two sites; (141) large vases, especially kraters, from Mouliana (one with a warrior on horseback), Phaistos and Knossos; (142) contents of shrines from Gournia, Prinias (Sub-Minoan), Koumasa in the Mesara and Kalo Khorio Pedhiadha (the head of a large idol); (143) clay idols, animals and human, from sanctuaries at Ayia Triadha (notice especially the figure on a swing) and the cave of Hermes in the gorge of Patsos; (144) tools and weapons of all kinds in bronze, the main series from the two L.M. IIIc tombs at Mouliana in E. Crete.

GALLERY XI. SUB-MINOAN AND GEOMETRIC PERIOD. 1100–650 B.C. The wall cases on the right (145, 146, 147) contain, in the first, Proto-geometric and Geometric vases from Phaistos (upper shelf) and from the large cemetery at Kourtes, including a kernos with alternating cups and figurines; in the second, vases of this period from Kavousi and Vrokastro in E. Crete with a basket vase (kalathos), a horse figurine and a bronze tripod; and in the third, Geometric vases and bronze figurines from sites in Central and E. Crete, Psykhro, Ay. Triadha, Ay. Syllas, Amnisos, Kavousi, and Vrokastro. In the adjacent central case (154) are clay vases and ritual objects, including clay huts, from the L.M. IIIc mountain refuge settlement at Karphi above Lasithi. The model of a house sanctuary is from a Protogeometric tomb at Teke, between Herakleion and Knossos. The large clay idols from Karphi are exhibited in the single wall case (148). The one with sacred symbols on her head may be a goddess. With these is a peculiar rhyton in the form of a charioteer drawn by bulls, of which only the heads are shown. Continuing round, we find in Case 149 objects from the cave of Eileithyia at Inatos on the s. coast. These include clay figurines suggestive of fertility (Eileithyia was the goddess of child-birth), model boats and double axes. Case 150 and the two adjacent central cases (156 & 157) contain a large series of vases from Geometric tombs at Teke.

GALLERY XII. GEOMETRIC AND ARCHAIC PERIODS. 8–7C B.C. In this room is a large series of Geometric burial urns from tombs in the Knossos area, especially near Fortetsa, and from the Arkadhes (Aphrati) cemetery in Central Crete. Note the unusual polychrome decoration of the Knossian vases, with patterns of lilies, papyri, and rosettes. The miniature vases on the lids of some urns were for offerings for the dead. Smaller vases show Orientalizing and Protocorinthian influence. The vases from the Arkadhes cemetery (Case 168) are also Geometric and Orientalizing. Human and mythical figures and scenes are shown and there is also a series of plastic figures, human and animal. Imported vases are from Rhodes and Corinth. In the central case (170) is a magnificent collection of 8–7C *Jewellery, mainly from a tomb at Teke.

THE GALLERY OF THE SARCOPHAGI. The Minoans often used clay chests or larnakes for burial purposes. Those displayed here are of two periods: Middle Minoan tub-shaped examples, painted with abstract designs, from various sites including Voros in the Mesara. Late Minoan III rectangular chests on four feet, often with gabled lids.

GALLERY XIV. HALL OF THE FRESCOES. This is reached by the stairs from the Gallery of the Sarcophagi. Here and in XV and XVI are displayed the **Minoan Frescoes**. Though only fragments of the original wall-paintings and sometimes much burnt, they vividly illustrate the life of the Minoans, especially their interest in animals, plants, and flowers.

Among the most celebrated are the Procession Fresco and the Cup Bearer; the Priest King or Prince of the Lilies; the *Toreador Fresco, a vivid representation of bull-leaping; and the Madonna lilies from Amnisos.

In the centre (Case 171) stands the famous painted limestone *Sarcophagus (c. 1400 B.C.) from Ayia Triadha.

GALLERIES XV & XVI open off the main fresco hall. Most of the pieces are from Knossos; those in XV include 'La Parisienne', probably a priestess because of the Sacral Knot over her neck; while in XVI, opposite, are restorations of the Saffron Gatherer, originally incorrectly as a boy, and more recently as a blue monkey. There are also the Blue Bird and Monkey frescoes from the House of the Frescoes.

GALLERY XVII. THE *GIAMALAKIS COLLECTION. The collection formed over a period of forty years by the late Dr S. Giamalakis, a surgeon of Herakleion, is now displayed in this room. There are many objects of outstanding interest but not all of them were found in Crete: (175) Early and Middle Minoan pottery and a Cycladic 'frying-pan' with incised decoration; a steatopygous burnished Neolithic figurine from Apano Khorio near Ierapetra; (176) over fifty stone vases including some of banded marble like those from Mochlos; a case (187) of Minoan and later seals; another (189) of non-Minoan seals, including cylinder seals and Sassanid bullas made of chalcedony; (178) a bronze figure bearing a ram over its shoulders; (191) a gold treasure from Zakro which includes a diadem with the Mistress of Animals, a gold cup and a bull's head; several bronzes; (182) Archaic and Classical Greek terracottas and vases and some very fine Venetian jewellery.

GALLERY XVIII. ARCHAIC TO GRECO-ROMAN ANTIQUITIES. The exhibits in this room consist mainly of terracottas, bronzes and coins from the Archaic, Classical, Hellenistic, and Roman cities of the island.

Beside the door to the Study Collection is a bronze *Statue of a youth from Ierapetra. It is a most sensitive portrayal of the 1C B.C.

GROUND FLOOR. GALLERY XIX. ARCHAIC SCULPTURES AND BRONZES. 700–550 B.C. Above the entrance is a 7C Gorgoneion from Dreros. In the corner to the left there is a lion head in poros from Phaistos and up on the wall to the left a frieze of horsemen from one of the two mid-7C temples at Prinias (ancient Ryzenia). Below this frieze are two groups of Archaic sculpture from the acropolis of Gortyn, one representing a god embracing two goddesses, the other three goddesses. Also on this side are two funerary stelai from Gortyn, a warrior and a lady spinning. Above the door to Gallery XX are the seated goddesses from the doorway leading into the cella of one of the Prinias temples. Their thrones are placed over a frieze of lions and deer, suggesting that the divinity may be the Cretan Britomartis (Artemis), Mistress of Animals.

On the other side of the room are cases (207) with hammered and riveted bronze statuettes of the 7C B.C. from Dreros (a god, perhaps Apollo Delphinios, for this was the name of the sanctuary, between two other figures), and (208 & 209) the famous bronze shields from the Idaian cave. These have lion's head bosses and repoussé decoration showing battle and hunting scenes, an eagle gripping a sphinx, and the Mistress of Animals. Other shields are from Palaikastro and Arkadhes. A bronze tympanon from the Idaian cave shows a god or hero overthrowing wild animals to the beating of drums.

From Praisos comes a crouching clay lion, c. 600 B.C., in the centre of the room. Beside the bronze statuettes are architectural members from the 6C temple of Zeus at Palaikastro, showing running chariots and dogs, and Archaic relief pithoi. Against the wall on the right of the entrance are lion's head water spouts from the Palaikastro temple, a head from Axos (mid-6C), a Roman copy of the Archaic Hymn to Zeus Cretagenes from Palaikastro, and a black stone stele from Dreros with a winged human figure holding a bird.

GALLERY XX. CLASSICAL, HELLENISTIC, AND ROMAN SCULPTURES. Only the

78 THE ENVIRONS OF HERAKLEION
A Knossos

We quit Herakleion by Plateia Eleftherias and beyond the walls turn s.—At 2½ m. a road forks right for *Fortetsa*, the site of the Turkish encampment from which Herakleion was bombarded in the great siege.

Beyond the fork are the site of the Medical Faculty of the University of Crete and the Venezelion Hospital, a former Sanatorium, in digging the foundations for which Late Minoan II warrior graves with rich finds (Herakleion Museum) were discovered in 1952. In the field above the main road opposite and beyond the Sanatorium was part of the Geometric cemetery of Knossos, while below the Sanatorium on the Knossos side are the remains of an early Christian basilica. In the right bank of the main road are the remains of the Roman *Amphitheatre* and a little farther on, in the field opposite, left of the road, of the *Roman Basilica*. Above the road on the right is (3 m.) the *Villa Dionysus* a Roman building with fine mosaics of 2–3C A.D., depicting the Dionysiac cult. Just beyond this a short drive leads off right to the *Villa Ariadne* (formerly the house of Sir Arthur Evans and in 1926–52 the property of the British School at Athens). It now has adjacent a stratigraphical museum (no adm.). A hundred yards farther on steps lead up from the main road on the right to the Little Palace (see below).—3¼ m. *Knossos* (car park on left beyond village tavernas).

KNOSSOS, the Minoan capital with its vast Palace and surrounding villas, dependent buildings and cemeteries, was excavated by Sir Arthur Evans and his assistant Dr Duncan Mackenzie from 1900, after 1951 (extensively in 1957–61) by M. S. F. Hood and since 1967 by other members of the British School at Athens.

Admission, 50 dr.; times of opening should be checked in Herakleion. The best detailed description of the site is J. D. S. Pendlebury's 'A Handbook to the Palace of Minos, Knossos' (London, 1954). The Royal Villa, the Little Palace, and Royal Temple Tomb cannot normally be visited.

Chronology of the site. *Knossos* was first inhabited at the beginning of the New Stone Age c. 6000 B.C. Gradually through the Neolithic period the mound of occupation debris accumulated here so that by the beginning of the Bronze Age, c. 3000 B.C., the Neolithic strata were up to 7 metres thick. Simple houses, roughly rectangular, were built, with walls, probably of mud brick, on a stone socle, and fixed hearths. Occupation continued through the Early Minoan period: of E.M. I date is a well, over 30 ft deep, in the N.E. Quarter of the Palace. Houses of E.M. II date were found on the s. edge of the Palace below the West

Court and (1972–73) alongside the Royal Road N.W. of the Palace. E.M. III pottery has been recovered in recent excavations.

The first Palace seems, like that at Phaistos, to have been built late in or at the end of Middle Minoan IA, c. 1950–1900 B.C. Of this period, before the foundation, are extensive deposits of pottery below the earliest palace floors, notably the Vat Room deposit under the entrance leading N. out of the E. Pillar Crypt (Pl. 21), the Monolithic Pillars Basement deposit in the S.E. part of the Palace (Pl. 52), and under the West Court, where two houses of this period were excavated. The first Palace lasted from this foundation to the great earthquake destruction at the close of M.M. II, c. 1700 B.C. For the initial layout the earlier buildings on the top of the hill were erased and much of their material was dumped on the N.W. part of the site. From this unstratified pre-palatial material have come fragments of imported Pre-dynastic and early dynastic Egyptian stone vessels, important for demonstrating Minoan links with Egypt before the Palace was founded. There is evidence that at its beginning the first Palace consisted of a series of blocks, or *insulae*, the rounded corner of one of which can be seen on the N.E. corner of the Throne Room complex (Pl. 12). By the close of M.M. II there was considerable architectural unity: the great West Magazines had been constructed, as well as the N. Entrance Passage (Pl. 31), the Royal Pottery Stores and Magazine of the Giant Pithoi in the N.E. Quarter (Pl. 38), the complex on the E. side of the Central Court N. of the later East–West corridor (Pl. 41, 42), and a great cutting had been made on the E. side in which were rooms later remodelled into the Domestic Quarter. Tombs of this period and the next, M.M. III, lay on the slopes of Ailias hill opposite the Palace on the E., and others on the Acropolis hill to the West.

After the great earthquake destruction the Palace was rebuilt in M.M. III and it is the building of this period, with various modifications, which survives today. The main construction was in the Domestic Quarter with the building of the Grand Staircase, the Hall of the Double Axes, the Hall below it and the complex of rooms to the S. (Queen's Megaron). The N. Pillar Hall (Pl. 30) was built on to the remodelled N. Entrance Passage (Pl. 31). Modifications in the W. Magazines were made through the sinking of rectangular cists, or kasellas, into the floors of magazines 3–10 and in the Long Corridor beside them. Towards the close of M.M. III, c. 1600–1580 B.C., a severe earthquake necessitated some rebuilding and restoration of the W. Façade and S. Propylaeum (Pl. 3). At this time too the W. Porch (Pl. 1) was built and both the W. and Central Courts paved. In the W. Court this meant the covering of the great circular stone-lined rubbish pits (koulouras). Also in this period a new development took place, the building of a series of great houses around the Palace, the N.W. Treasure House and the House of the Frescoes, the S. House, House of the Chancel Screen and S.E. House being the main ones. Now also the Little Palace, the Royal Villa, and the Temple Tomb were constructed. These great dependent buildings correspond to the M.M. III–L.M. I villas and towns throughout the rest of Crete.

In Late Minoan I there were further slight modifications, including a good deal of fresco painting and in Late Minoan II the Throne Room complex as it now survives was built. The Palace was finally destroyed in a great conflagration c. 1400–1380 B.C. (This is the destruction date assigned by Evans and, though recently criticized, accepted by nearly all archaeologists, although there is disagreement about the nature and characterization of the period after c. 1400–1380.)

From the destruction debris of the Palace came large numbers of Linear B tablets. Most philologists have accepted the decipherment of this script as an early form of Greek. Knossos is the only place in Crete where Linear B tablets have been found, whereas Linear A, the Minoan language from which many of the Linear B signs were taken, is found at many places, notably the L.M. sites of Ayia Triadha and Zakro and on stone offering tables. Linear B tablets are of course well known from Pylos and Mycenae on the Mainland, in Late Helladic IIIB contexts, c. 1200 B.C. The presence of these tablets at Knossos together with a development in pottery decoration known as the Palace Style (Late Minoan II–IIIAi), a formalized and stylistic adaptation of the very naturalistic L.M. I vase painting and closely akin to mainland vase painting of this period, has led most archaeologists to accept that in its final phase, Late Minoan II-IIIAi, c. 1450–1400/1380 B.C., Knossos was inhabited by Mycenean Greek mainlanders.

After the destruction of the Palace there seems to have been some later reoccupation in Late Minoan IIIB, c. 1200 B.C., most notably in the Shrine of the Double Axes (Pl. 48) and in the Little Palace. After this date the Palace site was never again inhabited apart from a simple rectangular building, probably a Classical Greek temple lying between the staircase of the S. Propylaeum and the s.w. corner of the Central Court. Later ancient remains lie thick all over the Knossos region, but it seems that a tradition of sacred ground pervaded the Palace area, perhaps fostered by the idea of the Minotaur and labyrinth (perhaps from 'labrys' and meaning the House of the Double Axe), standard symbols of the coins of later Knossos.

A cemetery of L.M. IIIA date, contemporary for the most part with the final years of the Palace, lay at Zapher Papoura, the rising ground $\frac{1}{2}$ m. due N. of the Palace. A richer and possibly royal cemetery of this time was situated at Katsamba, the harbour town of Knossos. Here a number of rich chamber tombs, reached by long dromoi, have produced L.M. II–IIIA vases in clay and stone and several Egyptian stone vessels. The (now destroyed) Royal Tomb at Isopata, built in M.M. III, had its main burials in this period. Slightly later, L.M. IIIA–B, is a cemetery with 18 tombs recently excavated on Gypsadhes Hill, immediately s. of the Palace. There were a number of clay burial chests (larnakes) and the burial goods included a clay rhyton and stirrup vase and a bronze mirror, knives, and razor. Other L.M. III tombs have been found on the Ailias hill to the E. and elsewhere in the area. At *Sellopoulo*, c. 2 m. N.E. of Knossos, the L.M. IIIA tombs are contemporary with much of Zapher Papoura but much richer.

Later History. That there was a flourishing settlement in the Geometric period is shown by the contents of the cemetery to the N. of the site. Later Knossos became, with Gortyn and Kydonia (Khania), the leading city of Crete. Of 4C date are the remains of a temple recently traced on Gypsadhes Hill; here was found a large votive deposit of terracottas. In the 3C B.C., the city was a member of the Cretan Koinon, a loose federation of cities. After the war with Lyttos in 220 B.C., it lost the leadership of the island to Gortyn. During the 2C B.C., it was engaged in further conflict, first with Gortyn, then with Kydonia. It passed under Roman control after the conquest in 67 B.C., becoming in 36 B.C. a colony, Colonia Julia Nobilis, with veterans of Augustus. The Roman city was vast, stretching at least from the Vlychia stream w. of the main road (see Plan) to the area of the Villa Dionysus, the amphitheatre and the basilica on the N. (see above). Strabo (10, IV, 7) gives the original circuit of the city as 30 stades (over 3¼ m.). Though the 3C A.D. saw troubles and possibly a temporary break in life, habitation continued into the early Byzantine period, to which the 6C basilica s. of the Sanatorium and the adjacent early Christian cemetery bear witness. The bishop of Knossos was present at early Councils of the Church, in A.D. 431, 451, and 787.

The ****Palace** is reached from the paved *West Court*. Note the large circular Middle Minoan rubbish pits below the court and at the bottom of one remains of Middle Minoan I houses, also the raised paved ways across the court and the altar bases in front of the *West Façade* of the Palace (see Plan). The well-cut limestone masonry in ashlar construction and the revetments of the walls, a characteristic feature of Minoan architecture, are very noticeable along the façade.

We enter by the *West Porch* with its column base preserved and inner room, perhaps for those awaiting entrance and for guards (Pl. 1). To the right of the porch are remains of later house constructions. The porch leads into the *Corridor of the Procession* (Pl. 2), so called because the walls were lined with frescoes depicting a procession of people bearing offerings. The Cup Bearer fresco (Herakleion Museum) is the best preserved of these figures, which resemble the Keftiu (Minoans) bearing their tribute on the walls of Eighteenth Dynasty Egyptian tombs. The Corridor originally went s. and turned l. to the *South Propylaeum* (Pl. 3). From the end of the Corridor as it is now we obtain a fine view of the southern dependencies of the palace with the South House immediately below. To reach the Propylaeum now we turn left before the end of the Corridor. The Procession Fresco continued round to the Propylaeum and restored figures are now displayed on its wall. Also here are the large horns of consecration from the S. Front of the palace. Immediately to the right of the monumental staircase was the small rectangular Greek temple, of which all traces have now been removed.

Ascending the staircase we come to the *Upper Propylaeum* (Upper Floor Pl. 4). This floor was restored by Sir Arthur Evans on the evidence of column bases, door jambs, paving slabs, and steps which had fallen through on to the remains below. The walls of the lower story also helped to indicate where the upper walls stood. We pass to a tricolumnar hall (Pl. 5), off which was a small treasury (Pl. 6), filled with a great hoard of stone rhytons and other ritual vessels (Herakleion Museum). Thus the large hall may have been a shrine. From here the *Upper Long Corridor* (Pl. 7) runs N. with magazines (Pl. 8) and halls opening off it on the left (Pl. 9). On the right it opens on to a series of rooms (above the Throne Room complex) in one of which (Pl. 10) are modern copies of some of the palace frescoes. This room looks down on to the lustral basin beside the Throne Room. From the upper floor we may descend either to the *Central Court* by the monumental staircase with its column bases (Pl. 11; note at the top the marks of steps for an ascending staircase from the upper floor to a further story), or by a small private staircase (Pl. 12) to reach the Throne Room complex. The outer wall of this staircase at the bottom has its rounded corner dating from the First Palace.

The Throne Room is preceded by its *Antechamber* (Main Pl. 13) in which is a fine purple limestone basin, found in the passage immediately N. of this room. The **Throne Room** (Pl. 14) contains the gypsum throne with its guardian griffins (copies, originals in Herakleion Mus.) painted on each side. Benches line the walls, seats for those participating in ritual ceremonies, and opposite is the *Lustral Basin* entered by a descending staircase. Evans found dramatic evidence of the final moments of the Palace here in the Throne Room: overturned jars and the great flat gympsum alabastrons lying on the floor. Beyond the Throne Room was a small shrine which contained cult objects (Pl. 15).

Coming out into the *Central Court* (58 yds by 29 yds) we turn right past the traces of a tripartite shrine (Pl. 16), like one portrayed on the Miniature Frescoes (Herakleion Museum), into the *Lobby of the Stone Seat* (Pl. 17), the *Room of the Tall Pithos* (Pl. 18) and the room beyond (Pl. 19) in the floor of which were two large Middle Minoan III cists, the Temple Repositories, containing the faience snake goddess, her votaries, faience flying fishes, and all the other furniture of a shrine. In the floor one of the later (L.M. I–II) cists is visible. From the Lobby of the Stone Seat the two *Pillar Crypts* are reached (Pl. 20). Note the double axe signs on the pillars and the channel at their base for liquid offerings. Under the entrance on the N. side of the first crypt was found the *Vat Room Deposit* (Pl. 21), of pre-Palatial, M.M. IA, date, c. 2000 B.C. From the crypts are reached the *Long Corridor* (Pl. 22) with the eighteen magazines opening off it (Pl. 23). Note the cists in the floors of some of these and the vast numbers of large clay pithoi, indicating the enormous storage capacity of the Palace. Marks of burning are clearly visible on the walls at the entrance to some of the magazines. In the corridor are several pyramidal stone stands for double axes on poles.

Proceeding to the top of the corridor and passing a narrow magazine where the Middle Minoan Hieroglyphic Deposit of clay sealings, labels, and bars was discovered (Pl. 24), we reach a complex of rooms (Pl. 25) in which the Saffron Gatherer and Miniature Frescoes were found. Below these are the M.M. I stone-lined pits, perhaps granaries or dungeons, as Evans thought. Beyond here is the N.W. Portico and N.W. *Lustral Basin* (Pl. 26), now restored. Outside and below this on the w. was found the alabaster lid with a cartouche of the Egyptian Hyksos king Khyan. From here can be seen the *Theatral Area* (Pl. 27) with its 'royal box' or loggia (Pl. 28).

The paved *Royal Road* (Pl. 29), leads out w. towards the Little Palace. On the left of the road are Minoan houses, including the Late Minoan I HOUSE OF THE FRESCOES, and on the right was the ARSENAL, or Armoury. Beside the Armoury further excavations were made in 1957–61 and produced pottery deposits from Early Minoan II to Late Minoan III, as well as a fine series of ivories of L.M. IB, c. 1500–1450 B.C. Excavations (1971–73) to the left of the road have revealed building remains from E.M. II (c. 2600 B.C.) to the 4C A.D. At the far end, on the left, a newly found road, precisely like the Royal Road in construction, leads off southwards. This and the Royal Road were built at the same time as the first Palace, c. 1950–1900 B.C.

Returning to the Palace, we pass through the *North Pillar Hall* (Pl. 30) and up the *North Entrance Passage*, in which was found a large deposit of Linear B tablets, and flanking which is the great stucco relief (modern copy) of the charging bull (Pl. 31).

We now cross the Central Court to descend the **Grand Staircase* (Pl. 32) with its five flights of easy, shallow steps to the light well and *Hall of the Colonnades* at the bottom (Pl. 33). From here we continue along the lower *East–West Corridor* (Pl. 34) and turn left at the end to the *East Portico* (Pl. 35), behind which is a small storeroom with blocks of Spartan basalt (lapis Lacedaemonius) imported from the sole source, near Sparta, for making stone vases and gems (Pl. 36). Beyond these rooms are what may have been a potter's workshop (Pl. 37), the *Court of the Stone Spout* (Pl. 38) and *Magazines of the Giant Pithoi* (Pl. 39), mighty vases dating from the first Palace, M.M. II. Beyond these to the N. are the remains of the Royal Pottery Stores also dating from M.M. II. A staircase descends from here to the *East Bastion* (Pl. 40). Walking down to the bastion, note the stone water channel descending a series of parabolic curves to break the flow of the water down the steep slope; this shows a remarkable perception of hydrodynamics. Ascending the stairway past the Giant Pithoi we reach the *Corridor of the Draught-board* (Pl. 41) where the magnificent inlaid gaming board was found (Herakleion Museum). Below the corridor the clay pipes of the Palace's elaborate drainage system (or fresh water system) are visible: notice how they taper (to produce a greater head of water to be driven through) and are carefully fitted together. From the corridor we pass the stone drain (which goes into the Court of the Stone Spout) to enter the magazine of the Medallion Pithoi, so-called from their decoration (Pl. 42). A similar pithos in stone was found in the Tomb of Klytemnestra at Mycenae. From here we return to the Grand Staircase along the *Corridor of the Bays* (Pl. 43), the thick walls of which must have supported spacious rooms above.

Before descending to visit the lower floor of the Domestic Quarter we may go along the Upper East–West Corridor past the Shield Fresco, into the restored *Upper Hall of the Double Axes*. Part of a Late Minoan II fresco with a bull's foot has been preserved here. Returning to the

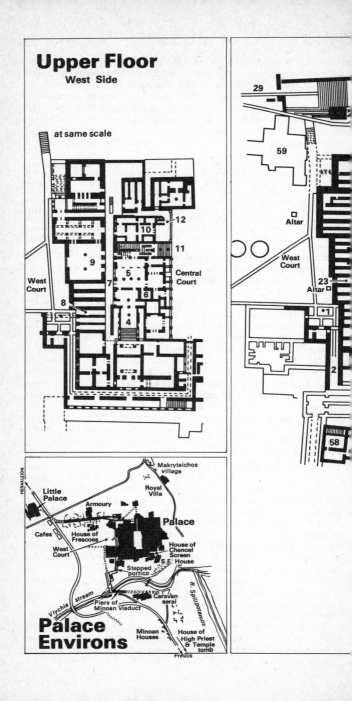

Upper Floor
West Side

at same scale

West Court

9

7

8

5

4

6

10

12

11

Central Court

29

59

Altar

West Court

23
Altar

1

2

58

Palace Environs

HERAKLION

Makryteichos village

Little Palace

Royal Villa

Armoury

Cafes

House of Frescoes

West Court

Palace

House of Chancel Screen

S.E. House

Stepped portico

Vlychia stream

Piers of Minoan viaduct

Caravan serai

R. Spiliopotamos

Minoan Houses

House of High Priest & Temple tomb

PYRGOS

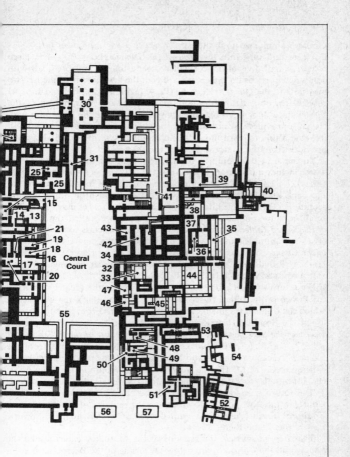

Palace of Knossos

0 _____ 50 metres

Grand Staircase we go to the bottom again, along the Lower East–West Corridor and turn into the *Hall of the Double Axes* (Pl. 44), a large reception hall divisible into smaller compartments and provided with columned porticos on the E. and S. From the S.W. corner of the hall we may pass to the *Queen's Megaron* (Pl. 45) with its Dolphin and L.M. II rosette frescoes. Below the floor part of the irregular paving of the First Palace floor is visible. Beside the megaron is the bathroom with clay tub provided. A corridor now leads us to the Queen's toilet with its remarkably modern fitments and drainage system (Pl. 46). Light is provided from the adjacent *Court of the Distaffs* (Pl. 47).

To the S. of this complex the S.E. rooms of the Palace can be seen. These include a bathroom (Pl. 48) and the tiny *Shrine of the Double Axes* (Pl. 49), of Late Minoan IIIb date, in which were found on a ledge at the back little idols with drum-shaped bases and little horns of consecration. On a pebble floor before these was a series of clay vases. The small corridor immediately W. of the shrine was called the *Corridor of the Sword Tablets*, since Linear B tablets of this class were found here (Pl. 50). Before leaving this part of the Palace we may visit the *House of the Chancel Screen* (Pl. 51), the *South East House* (Pl. 52), both M.M. III–L.M. I buildings, the M.M. IA Monolithic Pillar basement (Pl. 53) and a Minoan (L.M. I–II) kiln (Pl. 54).

We return to the Central Court in order to see the great Priest King (or Prince of the Lilies) fresco, set up in restoration on the wall below which the original fragments were found (Pl. 55). From here by passing along the Southern Corridor, which looks on to the remains of the *House of the Sacrificed Oxen* (Pl. 56) and the *House of the Fallen Blocks* (Pl. 57; named after the blocks of masonry that fell into it from the Palace), we can descend to another great building constructed after the earthquake in M.M. III, the *South House* or *House of the High Priest* (Pl. 58) with its several stories and pillar crypt remarkably well preserved.

The return is made by the Corridor of the Procession to the West Court, in the N.W. corner of which are the remains of the *North West Treasure House* (Pl. 59), so named because a rich hoard of bronze vessels was found there.

The *Stepped Portico*, the remains of the Minoan *Viaduct* across the valley, and the *Caravanserai*, below the S. side of the Palace, all merit a visit.

The great dependent buildings are never open to the public, but can sometimes be seen by visiting specialists and are in part visible from outside the fences. To the S. of the Palace a small path leads down from the main road to the *Caravanserai* with its partridge and hoopoe fresco and adjacent Spring Chamber. This was the stopping-place for those coming from the S. before they went across the great viaduct, dating from the Middle Minoan I, and up the ramp and stepped portico to the Palace. Proceeding S. along the main road, we find the *House of the High Priest* below the road on the left. It is designated thus because of its stone altar set behind a columnar balustrade, with stands for double axes on either side.

To the N.E. of the Palace lies the **Royal Villa**. The main hall, fronted by a portico with two columns, has a gypsum balustrade at its inner end and a throne set in the wall behind the balustrade. A fine purple stone lamp stood in the opening.

Finally there is the **Little Palace**, just off the main road before Knossos is reached. This building is the largest explored at Knossos after the Palace.

Since 1967 new excavations behind the Little Palace have revealed another large mansion with magnificent walls and a pillared hall of ashlar masonry. Scores of fine painted clay vases of L.M. II have been recovered from the destruction debris of this, the 'Unexplored Mansion' of Evans.

B Tylissos

ROAD, 8¼ m. (13 km.). We leave Herakleion by the Pantokrator Gate, taking the main road for Rethimno and Khania. At 6½ m. (10 km.) we turn left off the main road along an asphalt road for (8½ m.) *Tílissos* (ΤΥΛΙΣΟΣ), a picturesque village (1170 inhab.). The Minoan villas (open all day, 15 dr.) are signposted (1.) in the village.

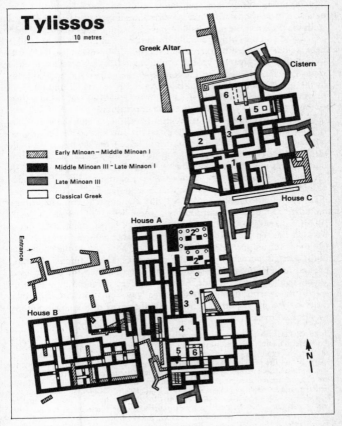

TYLISSOS was inhabited in Early Minoan times, while in several places beside and under the later villas are traces of Middle Minoan constructions. The three large villas, of L.M. I date, are typical examples of fine Minoan country houses of this great age. They were destroyed about 1450 B.C. The finds in them were numerous and included many large clay storage jars, a fine bronze statuette of a man with a paunch, and pieces of miniature frescoes, one with boxers. The early, E.M.–M.M. I, buildings also produced quantities of pottery.

Afterwards, as at Knossos and Ayia Triadha, there was considerable reoccupation of the site (L.M. III), including the building of a large circular cistern on the N.E. corner. There was also later Greek occupation and Tylissos at this time had its own coins.

House A, the central of the three houses, had its entrance on the E. (Pl. 1). Before it are traces of M.M. and L.M. III buildings. The northern part of the house contained two large magazines (Pl. 2) with a number of big storage jars, their bases set in the floor.' The rectangular pillars in these rooms will have supported an upper story, reached by a staircase (Pl. 3) off the main hall. A paved corridor leads to the southern part of the house which contains other magazines (Pl. 4, 5), and a light well surrounded by three columns (Pl. 6). In one magazine (Pl. 5) were found the gigantic bronze cauldrons (Herakleion Museum) and some Linear A tablets. In the S.W. corner another staircase ascends to the upper floor.—**House B** lies to the W. It is smaller and less well preserved but below several of its rooms are walls of earlier buildings. In the N.E. corner was a staircase to the upper floor.

House C, like House A, is entered from the E. and there are also L.M. III walls at this point. In the eastern rooms a good deal of original paving survives. On the S. side a corridor leads from the paved vestibule to a staircase (Pl. 1). The rooms on the W. were magazines. In one of these (Pl. 2) is a column base dating from the rebuilding in L.M. III. The northern corridor (Pl. 3) has remains of the paving of this later period built over it. Off this corridor is a staircase of which the lower flight dates from the original L.M. I villa, the upper from a later Greek building. Opposite the corridor is a room with well preserved walls (Pl. 4); beyond is another room with a Greek block, probably a statue base (Pl. 5). To the N. of these rooms is a large hall with two columns (Pl. 6) having an open court on its W. side. To the N.E. of the house and built over its corner is a circular cistern of Late Minoan III date, entered by a staircase from the N. The water reached the cistern by a stone channel on the W. side, having first been decanted in a basin or trap at the W. end of this channel. Finally we may notice remains of a large early construction of E.M.–M.M. I date, N. of the house, among which is a Greek altar.

FROM TYLISSOS TO AXOS AND RETHYMNO, 53½ m. (86 km.), distances cumulated from Herakleion. The road (asphalt) climbs to cross through a narrow pass into the long valley at the head of which stands Gonies.—At 13 m., on the left side of the road are the remains of the large Minoan villa of *Sklavokambos*. It is not so well built as the Tylissos houses and has walls of large, partly worked boulders. Of Late Minoan I date, it produced some clay sealings with impressions of fine gems, a stone rhyton and clay vases.—15¾ m. (25½ km.) *Gonies*, situated on a hill of chloritic and serpentine rock.—20¼ m. *Anóyia*, a mountain village straggling along a saddle (2390 ft) destroyed as a reprisal by the Germans in the last war, has been rebuilt. It is noted for its weaving, many of the houses having their own looms. From the village the ascent can be made in 4–6 hrs to the **Idaian Cave** near the upland plain of Nidha on Mt Ida (Psiloritis). There is also a rough car track. The sacred cave (excavated by the Italian Mission) contained many rich finds of Iron Age date, 9C B.C., including the famous bronze shields depicting scenes of conflict in relief (Herakleion Museum). Descent to the S., see Rte 79.— 26 m. (42 km.) *Axos*, a perched village with orange trees. Above (path signposted), on a steep acropolis, is the ancient city of the same name. There was a Late Minoan III settlement here but the city was fully established in the 8C B.C. (Geometric Period). Its walls survive in part and it has produced many relics, including its own coins and some bronzes.—The road descends on a ridge between two valleys to (31 m.) *Garazon* and (33 m.) the old Herakleion–Rethimno road (Rte 81).

C Arkhanes, Vathypetro

Road, 11¾ m. (19 km.), asphalt to *Arkhanes*.

We take the Knossos road out of Herakleion and beyond Knossos pass (4½ m.) the fine Venetian aqueduct which brought water to Herakleion.—At 6¾ m. we branch right for (8 m.) *Káto Arkhánes* and (9¼ m.) *Epáno Arkhánes*. **Arkhánes** (*Hotel Dias* B, s. of the village), as the latter is more simply known, is the leading grape-producing centre (3500 inhab.) of the island. Best known are its table grapes, rozakia (ροζάκια). In the village Sir Arthur Evans discovered a Minoan circular well-house. Recent excavations (I. Sakellarakis) near this have revealed Minoan buildings contemporary with the last Palace at Knossos, and built in the finest style of masonry. Evidence of human sacrifice has come to light. Minoan walls standing several yards high have been incorporated in some of the neighbouring houses. A water channel leads from the well-house and it may be that water was led to the Palace at Knossos from here. The church of *Ayía Triádha* in the village has early 14C frescoes, and that of the *Panayía* Byzantine ikons.— Near Arkhánes the church of the *Asomatos* also has early 14C frescoes, by Mikhail Patsidiotis, including a remarkable Crucifixion and a Capture of Jericho in which Joshua is depicted in Frankish armour.

New excavations, in 1966–67, uncovered a Minoan cemetery on the hill of Phourni just N.W. of the village. The principal discoveries were an ossuary of c. 2500 B.C., and tholos tombs of c. 1400 B.C., one containing the first unplundered royal burial found in Crete. The sealed larnax held 140 gold pieces of jewellery of a Priestess-Queen, now displayed in Herakleion museum. More recent finds include a group of marble idols of Cycladic type, and a Mycenean-type grave circle having seven shaft graves.

From the village it is a climb of c. 1 hr to the summit of *Mt Juktas* (2660 ft) on the w., now crowned by a radio transmitter, and affording a wide panorama of all this part of the island. On the summit a little N. of that with the church of Afendes Khristos, Evans discovered the remains of a Minoan peak sanctuary with a massive temenos wall, first built in M.M. I.

Beyond Arkhánes the road continues to (11¾ m.) **Vathypetro**, a Minoan villa, a short distance below the road on the right, overlooking the broad valley. The *Villa*, of the Late Minoan I date, is one of the largest known, and of particular interest in that remains of various industries and handicrafts are preserved, including a wine-press, oil-press, weaving rooms, and potters' workshops (the latter on the N. side). On the E. is a court with traces of a tripartite shrine of lighter construction than the villa walls. A long East–West corridor across the s. part, the well-built West façade with its cult niche, a main hall with three columns off the central court, and a great magazine for large storage jars on the s. side comprise other noteworthy parts of the building.

A poor road goes on from Vathypetro through *Khoudhétsi* and *Ayios Vasileios* to rejoin the main road which was left when forking off for Arkhanes.

The main road beyond the Arkhanes turn continues s. on a picturesque run through *Arkalokhóri* (22¼ m. from Herakleion), near which is a sacred cave used from Early Minoan I to Late Minoan times. It contained E.M. I vases with black pattern burnish, M.M.–L.M. I swords and a series of small votive double axes in gold, silver, and bronze, many of those in gold bearing chased decoration and one or two with Linear A inscriptions. L.M. III tombs have since been found

in the area.—From Arkalokhóri the road continues. In the w. foothills
of Mt Díktis to (40½ m.) *Áno Viánnos* (ancient *Biennos*), a large and
picturesque village, on the highest part of which is the little church
of Ayia Pelayia with frescoes of 1360. About 3 m. before Viannos is
reached, a road turns off right (s.) from the main road and in 2½ m.
comes to *Khóndros*. About 10 min. walk from the village is an important
Late Minoan III settlement, excavated by N. Platon. It covers a flat-
topped hill called Kephala and has extensive remains of houses.—
Árvi (Inn, June–Oct), on the s. coast c. 6 m. s.e. of Viannos, has a
spectacular gorge and good bathing.

79   THE MESARA: GORTYN, PHAISTOS, AYIA TRIADHA

ROAD, 38 m. (61 km.), asphalt throughout.—28 m. (45 km.) **Gortyn**.—38 m.
Phaistos and Ayia Triadha.

The road leaves Herakleion by the Pantokrator Gate, and after 2 m.
bears left for Phaistos.—3¾ m. By-road for *Ayios Myron* (11¼ m.), near
which was ancient *Raukos*, an independent city which minted its own
coins. The 13C Venetian church in the village has naves and aisles.
—18 m. *Ayía Varvára.*

In the village a by-road turns right for *Prinias* (3½ m.) near which on the
acropolis, called Patela, is ancient *Ryzenia.* There are two Archaic temples,
7–6C, and, at the w. end of the hill, a square Hellenistic fortress with corner
bastions. The temple sculptures (Herakleion Museum) include figures of a seated
goddess and friezes of horses with their riders and lions.

At the end of the long Ay. Varvara village, a road to Kamares (asphalt to Zarós)
turns right to run along the s. foothills of the Ida massif.—8½ m. *Zarós*, a pleasant
village with good water.—10½ m. Turning (r.) for the monastery of *Vrondisi*
up on the hillside. The church has 14C frescoes. There is also a 16C Venetian
fountain with worn statues of Adam and Eve. The church of **Valsamonero** lies
below the road, a little beyond the turning for Vrondisi. It may be reached by a
path from (13¼ m.) *Vorizia*, the next village. The italianate exterior of the church
is notable for its architectural details (14–15C). The 14C frescoes, ascribed to
Konstandinos Rikos, are among the finest in Crete and include scenes from the
life of the Virgin and a scene with John the Baptist in the desert. There is a fine
wooden iconostasis. The Damaskinos icons in Ay. Aikaterini, Herakleion, came
from Valsamonero.—At (15½ m.) *Kamáres* mules and guides may be hired for the
4 hr climb to the Kamares cave (4985 ft) on Mt Ida. This was the first place where
the superlative Middle Minoan IB–II polychrome pottery was discovered and so
gave it its name, Kamares Ware. The ascent to the summit of **Mt Ida** (Idhi Oros;
8058 ft), or *Psilorítis*, takes about 5 hrs from the cave. This should not be attempted
without a guide. From the summit it is a further 4–5 hrs to the famous Idaian
Cave, on the edge of the Nidha Plain to the N.E. From this cave the descent to
Vorizia takes c. 4 hours.

We cross (20 m.) the watershed and the whole **Mesara Plain** is revealed below. Its size, fertility, and favourable climate have caused it
to be densely populated from Minoan times to the present day.—27½ m.
Ayioi Dheka is named after ten martyrs of the persecution of Decius
(A.D. 250). The aisled Byzantine church incorporates reused material
from Gortyn.

28 m. **GORTYN,** the capital of the Roman province of Crete and
Cyrenaica, was the largest ancient city in the island. The main road
goes through the middle of the city, our stopping-place being before the
basilica of Ayios Titos just off the road on the right.

The Acropolis, inhabited in Neolithic and again in Sub-Minoan times at the
end of the Bronze Age, had a rectangular temple in the Geometric to Archaic

periods (8–7C B.C.). Homer ('Iliad', II, 646) refers to this city as walled, though no walls survive today. The city in the plain below must have been flourishing by 500 B.C., for this is approximately the date of the famous Code of Laws (see below). In the Hellenistic period it was one of the group of allied cities in the Cretan Koinon. Its harbours were at Matala and Lebena on the s. coast. In 220 B.C. it joined with Knossos against Lyttos; it is said to have received Hannibal in 189 B.C. After the Roman conquest (67 B.C.) Gortyn was made the capital of the province and it is from the imperial period, particularly the 2C A.D., that many of the great buildings date. The importance of the city was maintained in early Christian times, for it received Titus as first bishop, commissioned by St Paul to convert Crete. It continued as a religious centre in the early Byzantine period before the Saracen conquest c. A.D. 823–8.

Gortyn was excavated in the 1880s by the Italian Mission under F. Halbherr, and in 1954–61 by the Italian School, when the temple and altar on the acropolis were investigated. The whole area is littered with ploughed-out stones and pottery and systematic excavation has been undertaken only in a few places.

The basilica of *Ayios Titos*, 7C and later, has its apse preserved and traces of its early frescoes remain in one of the side chapels. Some of the original contents are in the Herakleion Historical Museum. Beyond the church we pass through the Agora, a Greco-Roman market area, to the Roman *Odeum*, rebuilt by Trajan in A.D. 100. Into the back of this the Romans incorporated the Law Code of Gortyn. The code, inscribed, probably by 500 B.C., in a form of the Dorian dialect, is concerned with different classes of individuals and with civil and criminal offences including land tenure and inheritance, assault, adultery, and divorce. The 17,000 letters are written boustrophedon i.e. one line from left to right, the next right to left and so on alternately. The Odeum was built on the site of earlier structures, including a 1C B.C. round building, itself made with material from an earlier round structure which originally bore the Archaic laws. A final restoration was effected in the 3–4C A.D.

Opposite the Odeum across the stream are the remains of a *Theatre*, built into the slope of the Acropolis hill. On the **Acropolis** is a rectangular *Temple* with its central bothros or circular pit (8–7C B.C.) on the site of the Late Minoan III–Sub-Minoan settlement. The temple contained a stone cult statue of three naked female figures (Herakleion Museum). Below the temple on the E. slope of the hill are remains of an altar of sacrifice, 14 yds long, near which was found a rich votive deposit with terracotta figurines, painted clay plaques with figures in relief and bronze objects of all periods from Late Minoan III to Roman. On the lower slopes of the hill on this E. side and across the stream on the opposite hill are remains of the aqueducts which brought water to the city from the region of Zaros (see above).

We return to the main road to explore the remains on the s. side of it. These may be reached by a path from the main road about 500 yds back in the direction of Herakleion. The path, which is signposted, brings us first to the Temple of Isis and Serapis. Another path (see Plan) leads off E. from the Mitropolis road.

The Roman *Temple of Isis and Serapis* has a rectangular cella and annexes. The architrave records the construction of the building by Flavia Philyra and her two sons. Beyond is the apsidal **Temple of Pythian Apollo**, the main sanctuary of the city. It was built in the Archaic period on the site of a Minoan building of which there are traces of walls and gypsum paving inside the Hellenistic pronaos by the N. wall. The Archaic temple consisted of the rectangular cella and

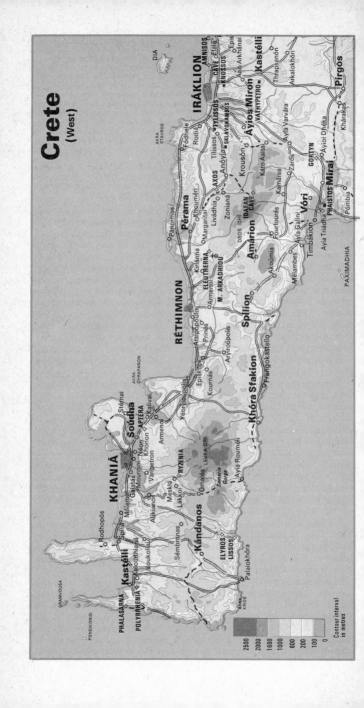

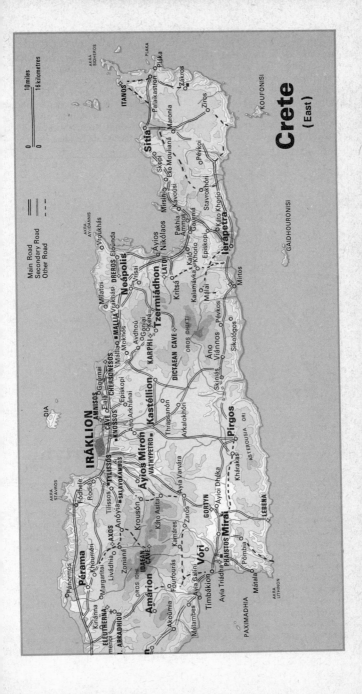

Crete
(East)

Main Road
Secondary Road
Other Road

0 10 miles
0 16 kilometres

treasury at its N.E. corner. In the Hellenistic period the pronaos with six columns was added; four stelai between the intercolumniations were used to record treaties of Gortyn with other cities and with Eumenes II of Pergamon. In the 2C A.D. the apse and the internal Corinthian columns of the cella were added. The altar before the temple and *Heroon* to the N. of the altar are Roman. A little distance s.w. of the temple are the remains of the brick-built Roman theatre and s.w. of this, across the E.–W. path, those of a Byzantine basilica church.

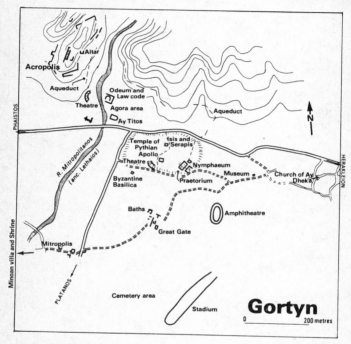

To the E. of the temple (but also reached by another signposted path off the main road) is the *Praetorium*, the residence of the Roman governor of the Province. Like the rebuilt Odeum, this is of Trajanic date, extended in the 4C with a great paved basilican hall. Along the w. side are bases of statues of prominent citizens. The *Nymphaeum* was built towards the end of the 2C A.D. and transformed into a public fountain in Byzantine times. About 150 yds S.E. of the Praetorium are the remains of the *Amphitheatre* (2C A.D.) and about 200 yds s. of this are traces of the *Stadium*. To the w. of the amphitheatre is what survives of the *Great Gate*, a vast structure of Roman brick. Within are remains of the *Baths*.

A small local MUSEUM to be opened near Ay. Titos will contain inscriptions and sculptures from the city. One inscription is of A. Larius Lepidus Sulpicianus, quaestor of Crete and one of Vespasian's commanders in the siege of Jerusalem in A.D. 70. Another inscription records Trajan's rebuilding of the Odeum. The sculptures include a head of Caracalla and a headless statue of Hermes-Anubis.

FROM GORTYN TO LEBENA, 17 m. (27 km.). From the main Herakleion–Phaistos road, a little before the Basilica of Ay. Titos is reached, a side road branches off for *Mitropolis*, ¼ m. along, where some remains of an early Christian church may explain the name. Near here at *Kannia* is a Late Minoan I villa or farm with a shrine which contained clay figures of goddesses with raised arms. The road now crosses the Mesara plain to (3½ m.) *Plátanos*. About 150 yds w. of the village are remains of three tholos tombs, circular stone-built communal burial-chambers dating from Early Minoan to Middle Minoan I. There are many such throughout the Mesara but Tombs A and B at Platanos are the largest. From Tomb B came the significant Babylonian haematite cylinder seal of the period of Hammurabi. At Platanos we take the road left for (4½ m.) *Plora*, near which lay ancient Pyloros. We turn left on entering Plora and right soon afterwards to climb to (12 m.) *Miamou*, and over the mountain to (17 m.) *Lenda* (ancient Lebena). The therapeutic springs made this a great sanctuary for healing. The temple of Asklepios (Asklepieion) dates from the 4C B.C. and the settlement flourished in Roman times, the temple being restored in the 2C A.D., the great building period at Gortyn, of which this was the harbour. The temple walls are of conglomerate blocks covered with brick and marble facings. The interior sides of the cella have mosaic pavements. The base for the cult statue of Asklepios by Xenion survives in the S.W. corner of the cella. Immediately N.E. of the temple is a Classical treasury which has fine mosaics of the Hellenistic period. Farther N. are porticoes separated by a marble staircase. Lying E. of the temple and S.E. of the E. end of the northern portico was the fountain built for the therapeutic springs. On the hillside a little below the temple are two great basins, perhaps for the total immersion of the sick. The large building to the S.W. of the sanctuary complex is probably a hostel. Bounding the bay of Lebena on the w. is Cape Lion and N. of this is the Minoan settlement. S. Alexiou has excavated five Early–Middle Minoan tholos tombs E., S., and W. of the settlement. One of these, at *Yerokambos*, has produced a great deposit of vases of Early Minoan I date and from the whole group of tombs have come three Egyptian scarabs (Twelfth Dynasty).

From Lenda a fair but not asphalt road leads W. to *Kaloí Liménes*, the Fair Havens of St Paul (Acts, xxvii, 8). This is equated with the *Lasaia* of late antiquity and is connected with Mires by an asphalt road (14½ m.).

At (33½ m.) *Mires* (2900 inhab.) a colourful market is held each Saturday morning. Here a minor road left may be taken for Petrokephalo and *Mátala* (10 m.), another harbour of Gortyn, with ancient rock-cut tombs in the cliffs and a fine beach.—At 36½ m. a road turns left for the climb up to (38 m.) **PHAISTOS**. The bus stop and car park are just below the *Tourist Pavilion*, which is reached by a short paved path. The Palace has a superlative **Situation on a low, flat-topped hill, the easternmost of a chain which extends to Ayia Triadha; to the N. is the Ida massif, snow-capped for most of the year, while away to the E. stretches the Mesara plain, bounded on its S. side by the Asterousia mountains. More open, rolling country stretches on the s.w. to the sea.

The *Palace of Phaistos* and the surrounding area were excavated in 1900 and the following years for the Italian School of Archaeology at Athens, chiefly by L. Pernier. Since 1952 D. Levi, Director of the Italian School, has made further extensive excavations on the w. side revealing many rooms of the First Palace. The site was inhabited in Neolithic and Early Minoan times since pottery deposits of these periods are found beneath the earliest Palace floors. The first Palace was built in Middle Minoan I. The excavations of D. Levi have revealed three distinct phases for this building before it was destroyed, like Knossos, c. 1700 B.C. Over this first Palace a thick cement-like fill was laid and upon this was built the second Palace, which is mainly what is to be seen today. On the w. side the rooms of the first, M.M. I–II, Palace are preserved. The second Palace was destroyed, like all the other major sites, c. 1450 B.C. in Late Minoan IB. There was some reoccupation in L.M. III at the end of the Bronze Age, and in the Geometric period (8C). Of the Classical–Hellenistic period are remains of a temple (first built in the 8C) and some fine houses. The city, mentioned in the Linear B tablets and by Homer ('Iliad', II, 648) was important in the later periods and minted its own coins, before it was destroyed by Gortyn.

The planning of the surviving *Palace is akin to that of Knossos and Mallia, the rooms being grouped round the large, paved central court (51 yds by 24), with a West Court across which ran raised paved ways. Certain areas had special purposes, religious and cult rooms being in the s.w. part, the store-rooms N. of these, while the principal domestic apartments lay N. and, probably, E. of the Central Court. There is

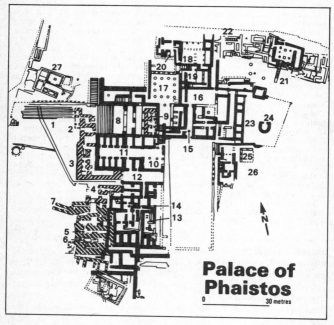

Palace of Phaistos

0   30 metres

some evidence that the N.E. area contained workshops. Features distinctive to Phaistos are the tiered rows backing the Theatral area on the N., the monumental Grand Staircase, and the peristyle court. Also noticeable is that the w. façade of the Second Palace is set back from the rooms of the earlier building, making the Palace considerably smaller on this side, but giving it a larger West Court.

The visit begins in this **West Court** or *Theatral Area* (Pl. 1), where tiered rows provided seats for such events or ceremonies that took place here. In the N.E. corner at the foot of the Grand Staircase are a group of small rooms, a shrine complex of the First Palace (Pl. 2). In these were found a large clay offerings table, stone vases, and cult objects (Herakleion Museum). To the s. of these rooms and below the level of the court are the recently excavated rooms of the First Palace with their West Façade (Pl. 3).

The N. group of rooms (at present within a fenced area) was built (Phase I B, Middle Minoan IIA) after the s. group (Phase I A, Middle Minoan IB) and terminates in a corridor (Pl. 4) which provided a monumental entrance on the N. side. The s. rooms include a group of small magazines (Pl. 5) and a room with benches round the walls, perhaps a waiting room, entered by a staircase on the w. in the final state of the First Palace (Pl. 6). Attached to these s. rooms on the w. side is a ramp (Pl. 7). Overlying the same complex but set well back from it is the West Façade of the Second Palace.

To the w. of the wall bounding the Theatral Area, beyond a Minoan paved road, lies a part of the town. Excavations since 1965 have brought to light more rooms of the First Palace period to the w. of those shown on the plan and below the Tourist Pavilion. These (fenced off) belong to important houses that perished with the First Palace. From the whole complex has come an astonishing number of polychrome 'Kamares' vases, displayed in Herakleion Museum.

From the West Court the monumental *Grand Staircase* leads up the *Propylaion* (Pl. 8). Below this are magazines of the First Palace which contained large clay pithoi with polychrome decoration (Pl. 9). From the Propylaion we descend by another staircase (r.) to the huge Central Court. Off this on the w. is an almost square pillared hall (Pl. 10). Beneath the floor and from the earlier Palace came an archive of clay sealings bearing seal-impressions of great variety. The hall leads directly to the double line of *Magazines* (Pl. 11), their heavy construction and the central pillars suggesting one if not more stories above. In one of the magazines on the right were gypsum slabs, dadoes, and variegated column bases fallen from above. To the s. of the magazines is a Corridor (Pl. 12) forming a monumental entrance on the w. side. Farther to the s. several of the rooms were for cult purposes: there is a pillar crypt (Pl. 13), as at Knossos, and a lustral basin (Pl. 14).

In the s.w. corner of the Palace at an oblique angle to its walls are the remains of a *Classical Temple*, founded in the 8C and perhaps dedicated to the Great Mother, Rhea.

From the Central Court a corridor (Pl. 15) leads N. to an internal court (Pl. 16). In the Central Court on each side of the entrance to this corridor are fresco decorations with a dark zigzag pattern on a light ground. A staircase from the N.w. corner of the Central Court ascends to a large peristyle hall (Pl. 17). From its N.E. corner a further staircase leads down to the northern apartments which are fenced. They can all be well seen from the farther (E.) side. One was very possibly that of the king (Pl. 18), with door jambs indicating that it could be partitioned, and another of the queen (Pl. 19). A lustral basin (Pl. 20) stands adjacent to the king's room. This basin has been newly paved with gypsum slabs from near-by quarries at Ayia Triadha. On the N.E. edge of the hill lies a further complex of rooms reached by a staircase (Pl. 21). These are of First Palace date with much rebuilding in the Second Palace period. From one of them (Pl. 22), came the famous Phaistos Disk (Herakleion Museum). Returning to the Palace s. of this complex we pass workshops (Pl. 23) with an open court E. of them. In this court metal-working took place for there are remains of a large furnace in the middle (Pl. 24).

To the s. are further domestic apartments which produced fine Late Minoan I vases, an offerings table, and some bronze double axes. These rooms include a portico with columns on two sides (Pl. 25) and a hall divided by internal doors (Pl. 26). As we pass into the Central Court we may note the pillared façade (comp. Mallia).

Below the Tourist Pavilion and on the platform above the N. wall of the theatral area are remains of Hellenistic buildings, including an exedra (Pl. 27). On the s. slope of the hill Levi has excavated Middle and Late Minoan and Geometric (8C) to Hellenistic houses.

FROM PHAISTOS TO MATALA (7½ m.), good road, bus 5 times daily. From the car park the road continues s. and w.—4 m. *Pitsídhia* (Restaurants). At *Kommos*, 2½ m. s., excavations on a hill above the seashore by the American School since 1976 have suggested a large and prosperous town with occupation in MM II-LM III. Considerable structural remains have been uncovered of a Classical and Hellenistic sanctuary.—7 m. **Màtala** (*Matala Bay* C; good Restaurants), another harbour of Gortyn, has ancient rock-cut tombs in the cliffs. There is good swimming.

To AYIA TRIADHA. From Phaistos the motor road continues to Ayía Triádha (2 m.); alternatively on foot the pleasant path takes 45 min.

Ayía Triádha (named after the double-nave Venetian church 250 yds s.w. of the site) is beautifully situated just below the road's end amid pomegranates and orange groves overlooking the plain and the sea. The place had some slight occupation in the Neolithic and Early Minoan periods. Middle Minoan I house remains were found under the Late Minoan I villa and town and a small group of rooms of this date is still visible (Pl. 18). The large villa (perhaps a small palace) and several houses are L.M. I (black on Plan). The site is notable for extensive L.M. III reoccupation after the destruction of the palaces and main sites in Crete (unshaded on Plan). In the Geometric period the central part of the large villa seems to have been a place of cult, for clay and bronze figurines of this date were found there. In Hellenistic and Roman times there was slight occupation. The church on the site, *Ay. Yeóryios Galatas*, is Venetian (1302) and has notable fresco remains. The Minoan cemetery area lay to the N.E. of the site.

On entering the open, partly paved *Court* we see first, in the S.E. corner, a rectangular *Shrine* (Pl. 1), built in M.M. III–L.M. I, the floor of which was decorated with painted marine scenes (originals in Her. Mus.). The shrine was used in L.M. III and clay tubes with snake handles, like those from the Gournia shrine, were found in it. Beside the shrine are the remains of a large L.M. I *House* (Pl. 2) in which was found a fine bronze double axe with incised decoration.

The main rooms of the N. wing of the **Villa** or *Small Palace* consist, at the E. end, of residential or reception rooms (Pl. 3), w. of which are magazines with large clay pithoi (Pl. 4). Over these rooms were erected two large rectangular buildings on different axes from the L.M. I constructions (Pl. 5 and 6). Abutting the first of these later buildings and on the same axis is a kind of loggia (Pl. 7). Immediately w. of the main magazines is a small room with a channel for collecting liquids (Pl. 8). The residential apartments of the villa were in the w. wing. Here is a large hall with door jambs for partitions to divide it into smaller units (Pl. 9). A small chamber had a triple opening and benches round its walls, which were covered with a gypsum façade (now restored) with red stucco filling between the slabs (Pl. 10). This room leads on the left to a smaller chamber with a huge, slightly raised gypsum slab in its floor. Both rooms were lit by tall pedestal lamps (originals in Herakleion Museum).

From here we move to the archives room (Pl. 11), in which was found a deposit of clay sealings bearing impressions of numerous sealstones, and used to secure string-tied papyrus rolls and bundles. Next to this room is another (Pl. 12) the walls of which were covered with exquisite frescoes (Her. Mus.), including a seated lady in a garden and a cat stalking a pheasant. Immediately N. is a portico with a central bowl for rain-water (Pl. 13). On the stucco plaster of the walls were scored graffiti in the Linear A script. From one of the rooms to the S. of this complex (Pl. 14) came the famous serpentine relief cup with a band of soldiers and their captain. Bordering the w. wing and running N.–S. was a paved road (Pl. 15). From the main court we can also see the small narrow treasury (Pl. 16) from which came the 19 bronze 'talents' or ox-hide ingots in Herakleion. In the court at the foot of a small stairway were found the fragments of the famous relief rhyton with boxing scenes (Pl. 17).

From the N.E. corner of the court a staircase descends to the '*Rampa del Mare*', a main way which runs along the N. side of the villa, leading w. towards the sea. On the N. side of this are traces of Middle Minoan *Houses* (Pl. 18) and farther on an L.M. III staircase adapted to the re-entrant façade of the villa (Pl. 19). Returning along the 'Rampa del Mare' we pass to a large L.M. I house, rebuilt in L.M. III, from which an L.M. III stairway descends to the **Town** area. Much of this is of L.M. III date, 14–13C B.C., a number of houses being built over or adapted from L.M. I buildings. On the right, opposite the town houses, is a row of magazines or shops fronted by a columned portico, an L.M. III building, unique in Minoan architecture (Pl. 20).

We leave this area at the N. end to visit the *Cemeteries*, a minute or so along the path to the N.E. Above the path are the remains of the two circular stone-built tholos tombs of Ayia Triadha, in use in E.M.–M.M. I. From them and the annexes outside them came many small clay and stone vases. Above the western of the two tombs was the Late Minoan cemetery area from which came the famous painted sarcophagus in Herakleion Museum.

From Ayía Triádha an unpaved road descends to join the main Mesara road c. 1 m. s. of the Phaistos turn.

Beyond the turning for Phaistos the main Mesara road continues w. to (40 m.) *Timbáki* (3200 inhab.), beyond which it divides, left to (46¼ m.) Ayía Galíni (Rte 81) and Spili, right for Amari.

80 FROM HERAKLEION TO AYIOS NIKOLAOS AND SITEIA

ROAD (asphalt), 85¼ m. (137 km.), bus. 23 m. (37 km.) Palace of **Mallia**.— 42¼ m. (68 km.) **Ayios Nikólaos** (by-pass).—53 m. (86 km.) **Gournia**.—85¼ m. **Siteia**.

The NEW ROAD, which most through travellers will take, duplicates the Old Road a little farther from the coast. The section by-passing Herakleion was not complete in 1979 and does not supersede the old road for the beaches or for visitors to Amnisos. In the area of Mallia its alinement is that of the old road. Farther on it keeps to the valley of the Gorge of Selenari, traversing a tunnel at the far end to avoid the pass, resulting in a shorter journey where some loss of scenery has to be balanced against a safer, smoother, and less arduous drive.

The old road (very busy on Sundays) leaves Herakleion below the Archaeological Museum and passes through the suburb of *Póros* where, on the right at *Katsamba*, a Neolithic house and a Minoan cemetery contemporary with the last years of the Palace of Knossos (c. 1450–1380 B.C.) have been excavated by S. Alexiou. At Poros in 1971 in an LM IIIB building was found a scarab of Ankhesenamun, wife of Tutankhamun. We pass in succession an Army Officers' Training School (r.), the Airport (l.), a small cave church, and a number of organized bathing beaches (NTO, Tobrouk, etc.).—At 4¼ m. a road branches right (for Episkopi) and in 1 m. reaches the **Cave of Eileithyia**, goddess of childbirth (below the road, on the left). The cave, mentioned by Homer ('Odyssey', XIX, 188), has stalactites (torch necessary) in connection with which the cult ritual took place. Pottery remains show that the cave was used from the beginning of the bronze age (E.M. I), if not from Neolithic, through to Roman times.

5 m. **Amnisos** (*Minoa Palace* A; *Xenia Karterou, Amnisos Beach* B, both w. of the site and closed in winter; the better beach lies to the E.). The low hill (*Palaiokhóra*) which rises from the sea-shore has Minoan remains at its base on each side (the ruins on the summit appear to be of a 16C Venetian village though on earlier foundations). On the w. are remains of substantial constructions (L.M. I), perhaps harbour works, for this was a port of Knossos; and on the E. the villa of the same date which produced the graceful frescoes of white Madonna lilies (Herakleion Museum). The Archaic Sanctuary of Zeus Thenatas, excavated by S. Marinatos, is at the foot of the hill near the shore on the

w. side. Hence Idomeneus is supposed to have sailed for the Trojan War. Farther w., on the site of the motel buildings, and below the shore line are the remains of the Late Minoan settlement. Amnisos, like Knossos, Phaistos, and Tylissos, is mentioned in the Linear B tablets.

The road continues along a coast where hotel development proceeds apace.—8 m. *Nirou Khani* (Arena, Knossos Beach A, just to the w.), conspicuous by its protective shelter (gate generally locked) at the landward side of the old road, is a fine large Minoan villa (L.M. I) with a paved front court. The rooms contained a store of religious furniture, including large, flat, bronze double axes and painted plaster altars.— 9¼ m. *Goúrnes* (America B), where in the little valley to the right of the road Late Minoan III rock cut tombs yielded jewellery, seals, and clay and bronze vessels. We pass a large base of the U.S. Air Force. The old and new roads come together just before (12 m.) the turning (l.) to the Candia Beach Hotel (A).—14¼ m. Turning (r.) for Lasithi (signposted Kastellon).

Lasithi. The excursion is much recommended, both for the dramatic climb to the top of the pass which cuts through the girdle of mountains round the Lasithi plain, for the plain itself with its thousands of wind pumps, and for the Dictaean Cave, a traditional birthplace of Zeus, near Psykhro.

3½ m. The road forks (right for Kastelli); we keep left, and skirt *Potamiés*, where the church of the Panayia has frescoes of the 14C (Christ Pantokrator in the cupola), and 15C.—10 m. *Avdhóu* has been a centre of Cretan revolts. In the village is a church of Ay. Antonios with 14C frescoes, and there are paintings in two other near-by churches.

A road runs from Avdhou to *Kastelli* through Askoús. Off this route before *Xidás* is the site of *Lyttos*, an important Classical city which minted its own coins. It was destroyed by Knossos in 220 B.C. Inhabited again in the Byzantine period it had a large early Christian basilica with mosaics which are in part preserved under a church of more recent date.

We start to climb.—14¼ m. (24 km.). Turning (l.) to *Krási* (½ m.; 2035 ft). Near by is an Early Minoan circular stone-built tholos tomb discovered by Evans and excavated by S. Marinatos in 1929. In the village, opposite the fountain, stands an enormous plane tree which twelve men cannot girdle.—16 m. *Kerá*, just below which, by the road, is the monastery of the *Kardiótissa* (12C), with frescoes. The road now climbs steeply by the Seli Ambelou pass (2950 ft; marked by a remarkable row of 26 derelict stone windmills) into the upland **Plain of Lasithi,** filled with countless wind-pumps. The stream which irrigates it is drained off by a swallow-hole at this western end. The plain, too high for olive cultivation, but fertile in apples, potatoes, and other vegetables, is encircled by dominating mountains: Selena to the N., Aphendes to the w., Katharo and Varsami to the E., all about 5000 ft, while to the s. rises Spathi (7050 ft).—23 m. *Tzermiádhon* (1130 inhab.) is the principal village of the eparchy. To the N. the summit of *Karphi* held a Minoan refuge city dating from the very end of the Bronze Age (c. 1100 B.C.). From this came some of the large clay goddesses with raised arms in Herakleion Museum. In the hills immediately E. of the village are the

Cave of Trapeza, with remains from Neolithic to Middle Minoan I, and the site of *Kastellos*, a Middle Minoan settlement.—After Tzermiadhon one road branches left to Neapolis and Ay. Nikolaos. This is a fine scenic drive of 27½ m. reaching 3600 ft. After a col, with a cluster of derelict stone windmills, the road descends.

Our road continues round the plain through several villages (*Ayios Yeoryios* has a small hotel and there is a Byzantine site on the rocky knoll a short way off in the centre of the plain).—28½ m. *Psikhró*. At the end of the village, a turning (l.; signposted Spileon) leads up to a Tourist Pavilion, from which a stepped path ascends (15 min.) to the *Cave of Psykhro*, which may be the **Diktaean Cave** where the Hymn of the Kouretes says Zeus was born. An oracle had decreed that Kronos would be dethroned by his son, so his mother Rhea, to protect the child from his father, gave him to the Kouretes to conceal in the cave. That Kronos might not hear Zeus' cries, the Kouretes beat their shields. The cave, excavated by D. G. Hogarth (B.S.A. 1899–1900), produced remains from Middle Minoan to Archaic Greek times. Notable are stone tables of offering, one (in Oxford) inscribed with Linear A signs, and a series of small bronzes. The descent into the cave is steep but with a torch not difficult (guides available at Tourist Pavilion). The upper part of the cave contained remains of a temenos, or sacred enclosure, with an altar; to the s. is the entrance to the main cavern, which descends 210 feet. There are fine stalactites. Water lies in this lower part for most of the year.

Excursions to the summit of *Mt Diktys* (7045 ft) can be made in summer.

---

16 m. *Limín Khersonísou* (Creta Maris **A**, to the w.; Belvedere **A**; Nora **B**, to the E.; Rest. Rodanthi), a growing resort. The ancient city of **Chersonesos** (see below) extends from the village westwards for a considerable distance, but to the layman offers little of interest. It was the harbour town of Lyttos (comp. above) but was independent and minted its own coins, through which its ancient name is known.

A road (l.) in the village soon passes (l.) a much restored pyramidal Roman fountain decorated with spirited mosaics showing expeditions to catch various kinds of fish. A concrete path leads to the church of Ayia Paraskevi on the promontory. From the E. side of the point, when the sea is calm, the Roman quays may be seen with their stone bollards, slightly submerged in the bay below; this demonstrates the rise in sea level here since ancient times. On the summit of the promontory hill are the remains of an early Christian basilican church (6C) with curvilinear mosaics. The form of the apse is well preserved; it is unusual, being included in a rectangle. Below the church at the N. point of the promontory, rectangular Roman fish tanks are cut in the rock at sea level. Vestiges of the theatre survive. The remains of another basilica church with mosaics are preserved on the edge of the sea, c. ½ m. E. of Khersonesos village.

18¾ m. *Stalís* (Anthousa Beach **A**; Blue Sea **B**).—21 m. (34 km.) *Mállia* is an undistinguished village (Pensions), from which a road leads through wind-pumps and banana groves to the sea (Grammatikakis **C**), where large new holiday hotels line the sandy beach.— At 23 m. we turn left from the main highway for the Palace. The site called **Mallia** lies at the foot of the hill of Ayios Ilias, the seaward spur of Seléna (5114 ft). The ancient name of the place is not known.

The **Palace of Mallia** and the surrounding villas and cemeteries have been systematically excavated by the French School of Archaeology since 1922 after the Greek archaeologist, J. Hatzidhakis, had discovered it and made some preliminary investigations. Mallia is somewhat larger in area than Phaistos though poorer architecturally.

The Palace, like those of Knossos and Phaistos, was founded in Middle Minoan I, c. 1900 B.C., and suffered a great destruction contemporary with that of the other palaces, c. 1700 B.C. The rebuilt Second Palace lasted until Late Minoan Ib, c. 1450 B.C., when it was destroyed, like the surrounding houses and the other major sites

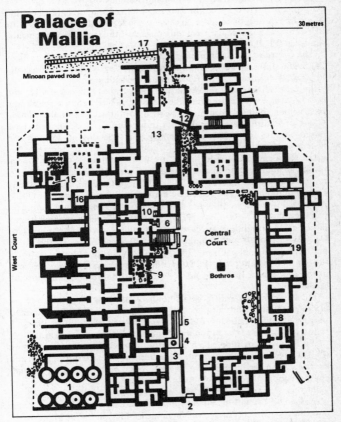

of the island. A few parts of the Mallia site, notably House E, were reoccupied in L.M. III. after the Palatial Age, while one building within the Palace (Pl. 12) appears to be later because its walls have a different alinement. The surviving remains of the Palace and Houses are almost entirely those of the Second Palace Period, M.M. III–L.M. I.—In its general plan, with rooms, magazines, staircases, and corridors disposed round the rectangular central court, Mallia resembles the other great Palaces, but it has a number of individual features.

The Palace is approached from the *West Court* with its paved ways; one of these serves the North Entrance (see below), another runs parallel with the w. front. At the s. end, and contemporary with the First Palace, is a group of eight circular structures, each c. 17 ft across, which were used as granaries (Pl. 1). We follow the s. front just inside the fence, passing the narrow opening to a shrine, to the main *Entrance* (Pl. 2), a flagged passage between walls. This was probably cut off from the main court by an extension of the wall at the end, so that entry was made by turning left through a door into an antechamber (Pl. 3), which gave on to a paved terrace (Pl. 4) opening directly by two steps on to the central court. Here, set in the floor, a circular stone table (kernos) has 34 small depressions round a large central one; its function seems more likely to have been secular than religious. Just to the N. is a Monumental Staircase (Pl. 5).

The CENTRAL COURT, more than twice as long as it is wide (52 yds by 24), had a different elevation on each side, and each wing differs greatly in plan. In the exact centre is a *Bothros*, or shallow pit.

To the E. of the Central Court are the E. entrance corridor (Pl. 18) and the *Magazines* (Pl. 19) behind the portico of alternating circular and rectangular columns (comp. the portico on the E. side of the Central Court of Phaistos). The magazines (now within a locked shed) have raised benches for vessels and channels for collecting liquid. Oil and wine were presumably stored here.

Off the Central Court to the w. are what seem to be cult or official rooms, including a raised platform (Pl. 6), perhaps for ceremonial purposes, and a *Grand Staircase* (Pl. 7). Between this and the more southerly stair (comp. above), and served by many doors from a Corridor (Pl. 8) running down the w. side, are a number of interconnecting rooms including a flagged *Pillar Crypt* (Pl. 9) like that at Knossos opening from a large hall. Cult symbols are carved on the pillars. From the w. corridor we may return through storage rooms with huge pithoi to the raised platform (comp. above) and its associated suite of rooms. Of these the 'Hall of the Leopard' (Pl. 10) yielded to the excavators an axe-head in the shape of a leopard, and a sword, both in Herakleion Museum (gallery IV).

The N. Wing was fronted by a colonnade, the bases for which remain *in situ*. Behind extends a large *Hall* (Pl. 11) with 6 rectangular pillars to support a suite, presumably of large rooms, on the upper floor. Part of a staircase remains to the E. and another exists farther N.

We follow a corridor which is partly obstructed by a later building (Pl. 12) on an oblique alinement. This faces the North Court (Pl. 13) and its orientation has been shown to correspond with certain exceptional appearances of the full moon above Mt Seléna.

Farther w. open the principal apartments of the palace, including the *Megaron* (Pl. 14) with its antechamber and a *Lustral Basin* (Pl. 15) and the palace *Archives* (Pl. 16), which yielded tablets in hieroglyphic script as well as in Linear A. To the N. extended the garden of the Second Palace which covered the foundations of the First Palace (Middle Minoan I). We return to the North Court in order to leave the palace by its *North Entrance* (Pl. 17). A fine paved way still leads up to the gateway; near by stand two huge pithoi.

Around the Palace and of the same period as its surviving remains are a series of large houses, part of a town of considerable size which remains to be explored. Immediately to the N. lies the *Agora*, subject of recent excavations. To the w. of the Palace and N. of the Excavation House is the so-called *Hypostyle Crypt* (conspicuous by its protective cover) below ground level and approached by a staircase. The building consists of a series of stores and two interconnected halls with benches round three sides. The purpose of the building may have been to provide a place for refreshment and deliberation of the city fathers.

The old and the new roads merge for a while. Continuing eastwards we suddenly enter the *Gorge of Selenári*. The holy ikon of St George of Selenári has been given a new and more sumptuous setting above the junction of the old and new roads where bus passengers can still dismount to pay their homage. The new road now keeps lower without further access to the Neapolis or Elounda roads and avoids the pass by a tunnel.

The old road remains narrow and awkward.—28½ m. *Vrakhásion* stands near the head of the pass. Beyond the summit (1310 ft) the views are spectacular towards the S.E. *Latsídha* stands on the old road to the E. of the new.—33 m. (53 km.) Neápolis (*Neapolis* D), a market town (3100 inhab.) and the seat of the eparchy of Mirabello, has a large plateia shaded by Mediterranean pine, round which are grouped the bus station, town hall, and post office. There is a small *Museum* (key from the Gymnasion) with antiquities from the Minoan cemetery at Elounda (comp. below), several sealstones and a clay potter's wheel with a Linear A inscription. There are also finds from the Archaic city of Dreros.

Dreros is reached by leaving Neapolis on the Ay. Nikolaos road, turning left at *Nikithianó* (1½ m.) for *Kastélli* (3¾ m.; asphalt). Here a minor road leads left and the site lies a ¾ hr's walk farther on the hill Ayios Antonios. Remains preserved on the hill with two peaks separated by a saddle include walls on the E. and W., houses on the slopes, supported by retaining walls, the Archaic *Agora*, to the S. of which is a Geometric temple, the *Delphinion*, consecrated to Apollo Delphinios, and a large cistern of the Hellenistic period. From the Delphinion came important Archaic statuettes of hammered bronze (Herakleion Museum). A much ruined building, S. of the Delphinion, is evidently the *Prytaneion*, the public hall for the magistrates and for the reception of official visitors. The cemetery lay to the N. of the eastern of the two summits. The ancient name is known by an inscription found in 1855 but removed to Constantinople.—From Kastelli this road continues to Elounda (see below), then down the coast to Ayios Nikolaos.

Farther on an asphalted loop road to the right (followed by the bus) serves the village of *Khoumeriákos*. On the tedious descent through scrubby hills we join the road from Lasithi.

42¼ m. (68 km.) **Ayios Nikólaos**, a little harbour town (5000 inhab.), pleasantly situated on the w. side of the Gulf of Mirabello, developed into a fashionable resort of Crete and is now also one of the most popular. It has the unusual distinction of being the chief town of the nome (Lasithi) but not of the eparchy (Mirabello) in which it is situated. The town is conveniently placed for excursions and has boat connections with Karpathos and Rhodes.

Hotels. On the coast N. of the town: **Minos Beach**, 105 chalets, DPO, L; **Mirabello**, 175 R, air conditioned, A (also 130 chalets L), both these with private beach, swimming pool, tennis, etc.

In the town: **Hermes** (Pl. a), 200 R, swimming pool, A; **Coral** (Pl. b), 135 R, DPO, B; **Creta** (Pl. g), small and good; **Akratos** (Pl. d), **Alcestis** (Pl. e), **Du Lac** (Pl. f), **Rhea** (Pl. c), 110 R, **Delta** (Pl. h), these all C.

Youth Hostel (60 beds), 3 Stratigou Koraka.

Restaurants. *Cretan* (Vassilis); *Charis*, on the harbour; also on the shore at N. end of Akti Koundourou.—Cafés round the harbour and by the lake.

The town has a *Museum* (on the road leaving for Herakleion from the harbour) housing finds from Myrtos, Mokhlos, and Kritsa (Late Minoan III tombs) together with Classical or Greco-Roman objects, notably terracottas. The inner harbour and the aviary in its surrounding cliff should also be visited.

From Ayios Nikolaos to Elounda, 7½ m. (12 km.), asphalt road. At (2 m.) *Sta Lenika* are remains of a 2C B.C. temple dedicated to Aphrodite and Ares and excavated by the French School in 1937. After crossing a headland the road drops down towards the modern village of *Elounda* (Astir Palace, 200 R, Elounda Beach, 300 R., DPO, L; Aristea C). Before the village, where the road reaches sea level, tracks lead (r.) to salt pans (largely disused). Dating from the Venetian period, these were fed latterly by a canal cut through the isthmus of Poros which joins the Spinalonga peninsula to the mainland. A causeway and bridge lead to a restored mill. The unexcavated site of ancient **Olous**, the port of Dreros, is strewn with pottery, and near the canal ancient walls can be seen below the surface of the sea. In a field to the N.W. of a small church is an excavated *Basilica* with lively fish mosaics, almost the only remains visible above ground of a city that had temples of Zeus Talaios and Britomartis. It was often in conflict with Lato (see below), especially in the 2C B.C. Towards 200 B.C. it concluded a treaty with Rhodes. The stone walls surrounding the carob orchards are doubtless witness to much destruction by plough. A Late Minoan III cemetery lay at *Stous Traphous* on the mainland immediately s. of Olous. At the N. end of Spinalonga the Venetians built a fortress in 1579 (see the inscription of the Provveditore over the Main Gate on the w. side) and separated it from the isle by cutting a channel. It thus controlled the large natural harbour between Spinalonga and the mainland. The Turks did not gain the fortress till as late as 1715. After they left in 1904 it became a leper colony but is now uninhabited. Inside the melancholy *Fortress Venetian and Turkish buildings may be seen, including vaulted cisterns on the w. side. The name Spinalonga, probably a Venetian misinterpretation of 'stin Elounda', survives an absurd official attempt in 1954 to change it to Kalydon.

From Ayios Nikolaos to Kritsa (7 m.; asphalt) and Lato. We take the Siteia road and after 1 m. bear right.—5¼ m. The *Church of the Panayía Kéra*, to the right of the road, is usually considered the finest church with fresco paintings in Crete and dates from the early years of the Venetian occupation. The s. aisle has scenes from the life of St Anne, the Virgin's mother, St Joachim, and the infant Mary, the N. aisle scenes from Paradise, while the central paintings are devoted to the life of Christ, the Last Judgment and the punishment of the damned. Other frescoed churches in the district should be seen, especially Ay. Georgios Kavousiotis (14C).

At the village of (7 m.) *Kritsa* is the motorable track (3 m. farther; c. 1 hr on foot) for ancient Lato, now known as *Goulas*.—We keep to the right at two forks to reach the site which, as usual, covers two acropolis peaks and the saddle between. *Lato was founded in the Archaic period (7C B.C.) and is of interest for its early town plan, but is principally to be enjoyed for the beauty of the situation. Excavations of the French School started in 1967. Four terraces are approached by a broad staircase (suggesting an affinity with the traditional Minoan 'theatral area'). On one long terrace with a rustic polygonal retaining wall, well preserved, stands a small rectangular *Temple* of pronaos and cella. On the N. side of the pentagonal Agora is the *Prytaneion* (Hellenistic).

The road to Siteia continues round the *Gulf of Mirabello amid outstanding scenery.—54½ m. **Gourniá**, the most completely preserved Minoan *Town, was excavated in 1901–04 by the American archaeologist, Harriet Boyd Hawes. It was founded in Early Minoan times but most of the surviving remains are L.M. I, with one or two houses reoccupied in Late Minoan III. Features to be noticed are the narrow streets and connecting stairways, a Middle Minoan I house on the N.E.

corner of the site (Pl. 1), the Palace (Pl. 2), or residence of the local ruler, with its magazines (Pl. 3) reached by a staircase from the open court (Pl. 4), houses of the Reoccupation Period (L.M. III, 14–13C B.C.; Pl. 5), and a little shrine (Pl. 6) in which were found clay tubes with snakes modelled in relief, an offerings table and a clay goddess with raised arms. Among the best preserved houses are those of the

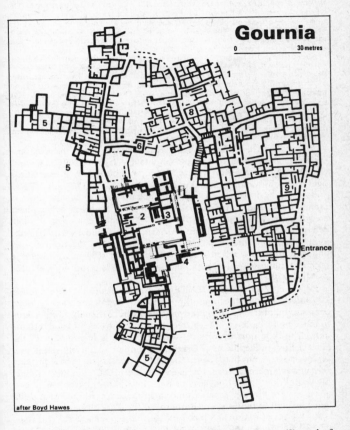

Carpenter (7), where sets of saws were found, of the Potter (8), and of the Smith (9). On the shore are remains of Minoan houses, associated with the port (now submerged).

56 m. *Pakhyammos*, officially *Pakhía Ámmos* (cafés). A Middle Minoan cemetery with burials in clay jars (pithoi) was excavated on the beach by the American archaeologist R. B. Seager. Just beyond, the w. face of the eroded mountain falls sheer to the sea.

FROM PAKHYAMMOS TO IERAPETRA, 9½ m. (15 km.); asphalt road across the isthmus, the narrowest point of Crete. To the left is the massive Thripte range with a dramatic gorge opening into the mountain; off the road to the right lies *Vasilikí* with its important Early Minoan settlement.—3¾ m. *Episkópi.*—9½ m. **Ierápetra** (IEPAΠETPA; *Kreta* C, and others more modest) is the only large town (6600 inhab.) on the s. coast of Crete and a favoured summer resort. The *Museum* (next to the Dimarkheíon, where the key is kept) has the finest Minoan clay larnax in the island, from near-by Episkopi. It is of Late Minoan III date and is painted with amusing hunting scenes. There are also antiquities from the Roman city, *Hierapytna*. This lies just outside the modern town on both sides of the coastal road to Viannos. On the seaward side traces of the theatre survive. The city made a treaty with Rhodes in 201 B.C. but did not reach its acme until Roman times. The fortress was built by the Genoese on a small promontory at the beginning of the 13C. The near-by minaret and Turkish fountain are worth seeing and a house near these is said without much evidence to have been occupied by Napoleon on his way to Egypt on the night of 26 June 1798.

About 10 m. w. of Ierapetra, reached by a good new road (completed to Viannos; in construction to Gortyn), on the steep-sided hill of Fournou Korifí, 2¼ m. before the modern village is the Early Minoan settlement of *Myrtos*. This was excavated by the British School in 1967–68, when c. 90 rooms were uncovered. These represent two periods of urban occupation of E.M. II date, c. 2500 and c. 2170 B.C. Many evidences were found of the manufacture of pottery and textiles. Just before Myrtos village, on a hill (r.), is another site called **Pyrgos** by the British School who excavated here in 1970–73. This was a Minoan settlement of long duration, dominated (M.M. III–L.M. I) by a large country house facing the sea. Notable are the floors of variegated stone.

59½ m. *Kavoúsi.* From here the road climbs high above the coast and turns inland through the verdant mountain villages of (69½ m.) *Sfaka* (turning left for *Mokhlos* village, 4¼ m., from where one can take a boat across to Mokhlos island in a few minutes), and (72½ m.) *Mirsíni*. Near here, on the slopes of Aspropilia hill, an Early to Middle Minoan tholos tomb and Late Minoan III rock-cut chamber tombs have recently been excavated by N. Platon. The road continues through *Mesa Moulianá* near which, at *Selládhes*, were found L.M. III tombs with swords and fibulae dating from the very end of the Bronze Age; and *Exo Moulianá*, noted for its red wine.—At (80¾ m.) *Khamaízi* a prehistoric house, oval in plan, had several phases of use in E.M. III– M.M. I (2200–1700 B.C.).

85½ m. (137 km.) **Siteía** (ΣHTEIA; *Siteian Beach* A; *Siteia, Alice, Crystal* C; boat connections for Karpathos and Rhodes) seat of an eparchy and of the Bp. of Hierapytna and Siteia, a friendly town of 6200 inhab., has a pleasant frontage, tree-lined and with several good restaurants. The little port exports raisins. The town is identified with the ancient *Eteia* of Stephanus of Byzantium, though no ancient site is preserved. Myson, one of the Seven Sages of Greece, is said to be from here, as also was Vincenzo Kornaros, author of the 17C Cretan literary epic, the Erotokritos. *Sitia* (formerly La Stia, hence Lasithi) was walled and given a fortress by the Venetians but suffered from earthquakes in 1303 and 1508 and at the hands of Barbarossa, the Turkish pirate, in 1539.

FROM SITEIA TO PRAISOS AND IERAPETRA, road, 40 m. (64 km.). The road (sign-posted Lithines) runs s. overlooking an open valley. A little out of Siteia, at a spot called *Manares*, is the first of a series of country villas of Late Minoan I date (1550–1450 B.C.) excavated by N. Platon. Note the staircase of two flights, the magazines, and, to the E. of the villa, a raised bank or dike, perhaps to protect the building from floods.—2½ m. *Piskokéfalo*. Here there has been excavated a Minoan sanctuary which contained many clay figurines, animal and human. We may turn left at Piskokefalo for *Zoú* (2½ m.) where there is another large Minoan villa. It lies a little outside the village, to the s. By turning right in Piskokefalo we reach the village of *Akhládhia* (3¾ m.) where, at *Platyskinos*, stands a completely preserved Late Minoan III tholos tomb. About half an hour's walk N.E. of the village, at *Riza*, are two more Late Minoan I villas.—The main road continues s. through (6¼ m.) *Maronía*, rising gradually with wide views to the left.

From an E.M. cave near here came a beautifully carved green stone pyxis with spirals (Her. Mus. case 7).—At (7½ m.) *Epáno Episkopí* we may diverge left to *Praisós* (3 m.). Ancient **Praisos**, capital of the Eteocretans (perhaps the descendants of the Minoan population) lies N. of the village, spread over three acropolis hills and the area between them. The remains, excavated by the British School at Athens at the beginning of this century, date from Late Minoan III to Hellenistic times and include tholos tombs of L.M. III and Geometric date to the S. of the acropolis, and rock-cut houses with a fine large Hellenistic one on the main, easternmost acropolis. The city was destroyed by Hierapytna in 155 B.C. (Strabo, X, 479, 12). Finds from the site include a fine L.M. III larnax, Archaic terracottas, small bronze models of armour and inscriptions in the Eteocretan language (6C–3C B.C.) in the Greek script but an unknown tongue, perhaps descended from Minoan Linear A (comp. B.S.A. 1901–02). A poor road rejoins the main road at Sikéa.—The main road rises gradually amid rolling country to the island's watershed between *Sikéa* and *Pappayiannádhes*, then descends through (15½ m.) *Lithínai*. There are long straight stretches of new road in the Andromilos valley. As we round the last bend to the coast, range upon range of the Siteia Mountains extend to the W. rising to the heights of Thriptis. We keep at low level near the coast in plains devoted to the forcing of tomatoes.—40 m. **Ierápetra**.

From Siteia to Zakro (village 23¾ m., Palace 28¾ m.). The road rounds the bay eastwards from Siteia, then turns inland. The road left for the isolated monastery of **Toploú**, or *Panayia Akrotiriani* (1¼ m.). The monastery, founded in 1365 (though there was an earlier church), was called Our Lady of the Cape in Venetian times and Toplou ('cannon-ball') from the Turkish period. It has a long tradition of hospitality to refugees and wayfarers and as a resistance centre. In addition to its architecture it has several objects of interest, a Hellenistic inscription (c. 138–132 B.C.) found at Itanos and describing the relations of Itanos and Heirapytna with Magnesia in Asia Minor, one of the earliest editions of Suidas (10C A.D.), and the famous ikon 'Lord, Thou Art Great', painted by Ioannes Kornaros in 1770, one of the great masterpieces of Cretan art.

The main road continues to (11 m.) **Palaíkastro** (*Itanos*, small) near the base of Cape Plaka. The Minoan town lies about 20 min. E. of the village through the olives towards the sea. It has become overgrown and there is now little to see. The site was occupied from the beginning of the Bronze Age (Early Minoan II) but the preserved remains are, as at Gournia, Late Minoan I. A typical house, excavated by the British School in 1962–63, lies to the right of the main street. On the E. part of the site remains of a temple of Dictaean Zeus were found. The prominent hill *Kastri*, N. of the town, was occupied in Early Minoan times and then again at the end of the Bronze Age (Late Minoan III C). To the S. a Middle Minoan I peak-sanctuary with many human clay figurines was found on Mt Petsofa.

A new road runs to (2¼ m.) *Váï*, where a remarkable grove of tall palm trees (despite the local legends about Arabs, probably *phoenix Theophrasti Greuter*, a wild date-palm indigenous to Crete) fringes a fine sandy beach (taverna). The road continues to (4 m.) *Erimoúpolis* (Itanos C) at the base of Cape Sidheros. Here ancient **Itanos** (r.) occupied the usual double acropolis; the plan is best understood from the W. height. There are remains from the Geometric period to the Hellenistic, when this was a Ptolemaic naval station, while lower down was a Byzantine town. In the cemetery N. of the site is a fine Hellenistic stone-built tomb.

The road leaves the sea and winds through defiles and hills.—23¾ m. *Áno Zákro* (Zakro C). A Late Minoan villa here yielded a wine press in 1965 and a pithos inscribed in Linear A (now in Herakleion). We continue through arid hills, pass the top of an impressive gorge, then wind down to the sea.—28¾ m. *Káto Zákro*, a hamlet on a small bay, has a good shingle beach. Simple rooms are let at the café (Stelios Vassilakis). At the entrance to the hamlet (l.) is the **Palace of Zakro.** The site was partially investigated by D. G. Hogarth at the beginning of the century, and has been more thoroughly excavated by N. Platon since 1962. It consists of a terraced town with narrow streets, stepped and cobbled as at Gournia, and overlain by larger villas or palace

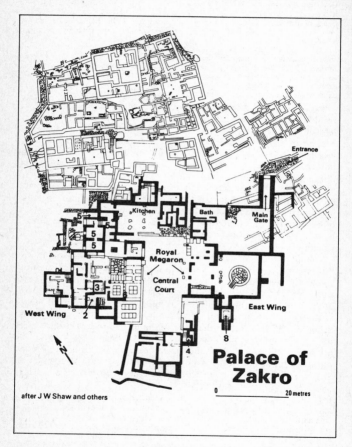

Palace of Zakro

after J W Shaw and others

0   20 metres

dependencies, and below it a *Palace* of Late Minoan I period. This is often in part under water. It is similar in plan to the others, though smaller, and itself covers earlier remains (also probably Palatial). The palace seems to have suffered a sudden and terrible catastrophe.

We enter by the remains of a Minoan road (Pl. 1) which came up from the harbour to the main entrance at the N.E. corner. Thence it is easiest to start from the *Central Court*, c. 33 yds by 13, which was surrounded by façades in ashlar masonry (pseudo-isodomic) with timber beams. The squared blocks came from a quarry at Pelekita, c. 3 m. to the N. The WEST WING provided the cult centre, the walls being inscribed with double-axes. Here six ingots of bronze from Cyprus and three elephant tusks from Syria had fallen from the upper floor. Next to the small *Central Shrine* is a *Lustral Basin* (Pl. 3). The *Treasury* (Pl. 2) of the shrine yielded a remarkable collection of vessels in porphyry, alabaster, and basalt, now displayed in Herakleion (Arch. Mus. Gallery VIII). The *Archive Room* contained record tablets on shelves; most had been crushed but thirteen in Linear A were recovered. The *Magazines* (Pl. 5) should be noted. To the s. lies the so-called Hall of Ceremonies (Pl. 6) lit by a colonnaded light-well, and connecting with a *Banquet Hall* which was decorated with a frieze of painted stucco and yielded many drinking vessels.

The EAST WING, damaged by farming and by flooding and not completely uncovered, contained the private apartments, equipped with a bathroom (Pl. 7). A unique feature is the circular *Cistern* in a large hall served by a spring. The *Well of the Fountain* (Pl. 8), in an open court behind, formed the main water supply of the palace, and there is another well (Pl. 4) farther w.

81   FROM HERAKLEION TO RETHYMNO AND KHANIA

ROAD, 85 m. (137 km.), a modern coastal highway (few petrol stations) except for c. 15 m. still in construction.—49 m. (79 km.) **Rethymno.**—75 m. *Aptera.*— 81 m. *Soudha.*—85 m. **Khania.**

Between Herakleion and Rethymno the OLD ROAD provides the only access to many places of interest in the area and is followed by most buses. The road quits Herakleion by the Pantokrator Gate. At 2 m. diverge left the road to Phaistos and the Mesara (Rte 79) and the access road to the new highway (see below). At 6¾ m. the road to Tylissos (Rte 78B) and Anoyia diverges left, and at 26 m. a road from Anoyia comes in from the left. On this section of the way are many pleasant shady villages.—34½ m. *Pérama.* Turning for Pánormos (4¼ m.; see below). Off this road, at *Melidhóni* is a celebrated stalactite cave where 370 Christians were smoked to death by the Turks in 1824.—35½ m. Turning (l.) for *Margarítes* (3 m.), a delightful potting village where all stages of the manufacture of clay vessels can be studied, and *Prinés* (4½ m.). After Margarites the road is unpaved and rough.

From Prinés ancient **Eleutherna** can be reached in ten minutes' walk by a path from the centre of the village. The acropolis stands at the end of a sharp, precipitous ridge, and is reached by a narrow rock causeway, guarded by a Byzantine tower. The acropolis fell to the Roman conqueror, Metellus Creticus (67 B.C.), only after a strong tower had been drenched with vinegar (Dio Cassius, XXXVI, 18, 2). Around the sides of the ridge are remains of the classical walls. In the W. side are vast Roman cisterns, while on the E. side a connecting conduit can be explored (torch advised). The cistern and conduit are not easy to find, and it is worth arranging for a guide in the village. From the site came an important Archaic statue (Herakleion Museum). Below the Acropolis to the N.W. (c. 15 min. walk) in the stream valley a remarkably fine and possibly Classical bridge can be seen, still in use. The road, still poor, continues through modern Eleutherna to join the main road at Viran Episkopi (9½ m. from Prinés).

40½ m. *Virán Episkopí.* Here are a 16C Latin church and a 10C or early 11C Byzantine basilica, partly covered by a modern church, which also overlies the remains of a Hellenistic sanctuary (perhaps that of Artemis Diktynna). The basilica may have succeeded Sybrita as the seat of the medieval bishopric of Agrion after Sybrita was destroyed by the Saracens.

We soon reach the coast at Stavroménos and keep just inland of the new highway until it joins in from the right.

The new Highway may be joined 2 m. s.w. of Herakleion and for the most part runs level with good coastal scenery along a still deserted shore.—Beyond (15 m.) the *Capsis Beach* hotel (on headland, r.), it passes just seaward of *Fódhele*, the village where El Greco (Domenikos Theotokopoulos; c. 1541–1614) is thought on scanty evidence to have been born. The tradition was crystallized in 1934 when the University of Valladolid erected in his honour a bilingual inscription carved on slate from Toledo. The village lies amid orange groves and the church has two books with copies of his works.

At 21¼ m. (34 km.) a turning, signposted *Sisai*, provides a link to the old road. *Balion*, farther on, is a developing bathing resort, named from the Bali café. We cross an approach road from Perama (see above) just inland of *Pánormos* (Lavrys **B**), where, a little to the N.W., are the remains of an early Christian aisled basilica (5C) with an atrium, at the N. end of which is a baptistery. The church was perhaps the seat of the bishopric of Eleutherna at this period.—Just before (38½ m.) the *Yeropotamos Bridge* the White Mountains come into view.—New hotels are being built near the point (at 42½ m.) where the highway provisionally joins the line of the old road. Beyond the turn for Moni Arseniou (l.) is the El Greco Bungalow Hotel (**A**).

45¼ m. *Plataniés* (Rithymna **A**). Here a road goes left through great groves of ancient olives for *Amnátos* and up a rocky gorge to the monastery of **Arkádhi** (9¼ m.; *Arcadi*, 3R, **B**). Traditionally founded in the 11C, the *Monastery* today (mainly late 17C) has as its chief architectural interest the w. front of the Church (1587) in which elements of Classical, Corinthian, and Baroque are extraordinarily well combined. The fame of the place dates from November 1866 when it housed the powder magazine of the insurgent Gen. Panos Koroneos. It was attacked by Mustafa Kyrtli Pasha, the Turkish commissioner. After two days' siege, the Abbot Gabriel blew up part of the building rather than surrender, so that defendants and assailants alike perished (829 in all). In three of the rooms in the gallery the relics of this event, including the Abbot's vestments, are preserved. Today there are only 9 monks. The old refectory is a melancholy place.—46¾ m. Road (signposted for Prassies) for the Amari valley (see below). Several camping sites lie to seaward of the main road.

49 m. **RETHYMNO** (ΡΕΘΥΜΝΟ; *Idaion, Xenia*, DPO, **B**; *Valari, Park*, both without restaurant, **C**), or **Réthimnon**, a pleasant town (15,000 inhab.), the capital of its nome as it was formerly of a Venetian province, is considered by its inhabitants as the intellectual capital of the island; the University of Crete will have its main faculties here. It is built round a splendid sandy beach, dominated by the eccentric lighthouse that guards the old Harbour. The relics of its medieval past are being restored and a new harbour is under construction. As an important market centre it is connected by bus with the villages in the nome.

Minoan occupation is attested by Late Minoan III tombs at Mastaba, s.e. of the main square. The Classical city was called *Rithymna*. The town flourished in the Venetian period but was pillaged and burnt by Uluc-Ali Pasha's Turkish corsairs in 1571. The Venetians then built the surrounding walls and fortress (overlooking the sea on the N.E. of the town) but the Turks took it in 1645.

Just off the large main square is the *Public Garden*, formerly a Turkish cemetery, where the varieties of trees and shrubs are labelled. Each year in the last week of July the Cretan Wine Festival is held here.

A walk through the town will reveal many charming Venetian house façades and doorways. The houses with wooden balconies supported by angular stays date from Turkish times; there are also several minarets. From the N.W. corner of the square we pass down the narrow main street. The 'Odeion' or concert hall has a 17C portal in the style of Seb. Serlio from its Venetian days as the church (Santa Maria) of a religious house. At the foot of the main street to the left is the *Arimondi Fountain*, to the right the *Loggia*, one of the best Venetian buildings in Crete. Once the army club, it is now the **Museum** (adm. fee; closed Mon and at midday). The contents, from sites all over the province of Rethymnon, are arranged as nearly as possible chronologically clockwise. Notable in the wall-cases (l.) are goddess idols (L.M. III) from Sakhtouria and Pangalokhori, and archaic heads and figurines from Axos. The central cases, between good clay larnakes with octopus decoration, display fine jewellery from Axos; Minoan necklaces; bronze axes from Amari and a huge mirror from the Cave of Ida. Within the central columns, between cases of good Minoan pottery from Mastaba and provincial red-figure from various sites, is a remarkable case of coins, Classical to very late Imperial, from various mints, Cretan and mainland. Behind a column, unfinished statue, half-worked with chisel marks; on the wall opposite the door, tympanum of 1531 in a very debased style. On the right side of the room an unexpected case of Egyptian statues, cartouches, and scarabs (not found in Crete); also Roman bronze finds from the Ay. Galini shipwreck, and some crude medieval sculpture.

The **Frourion** (adm. 7–3, free), or *Fortetza*, reached by steps alongside the modern prison, is imposing both in size and for the extent of the remains within. In the lower ward (l.) a deep well is reached by a sloping subterranean passage. Notable within the main enceinte are a little church, the Mosque with a fine dome, a lone date palm, and the battlemented or loop-holed ramparts. Judicious excavation and renovation are uncovering much interesting detail in the Venetian governor's quarters.

FROM RETHYMNO TO THE AMARI VALLEY, an excursion recommended for the beauty of the scenery in this valley between the Ida massif on the E. and Mt Kédros on the W. and for the innumerable little frescoed churches mostly off the beaten track (comp. the 'Blue Guide to Crete'). The road leads S. from just E. of Rethymno to (5½ m.) *Prasses*.—8¾ m. Road (r.) for Mirthios and *Gouledhiana* (3 m.) to the S. of which, at *Onithe* (possibly ancient *Phalanna*) N. Platon has excavated two Archaic houses (7–6C B.C.) and beyond which, at *Kare*, there is an early Christian basilica with mosaic pavements in the narthex. The apse of the nave has been restored.—Continuing on the road to the Amari valley we reach (17½ m.) *Apostoloi*, at the head of the valley. Here we turn left to reach *Thronos* with its frescoed Church of the Dormition overlying a basilica with mosaics; close by is the hill of ancient *Sybrita*, with fine walling and a gateway on the Thronos side. From Thronos we return to the valley road and pass between Yénna and Kalóyeros, both with frescoed churches.—25½ m. *Vizari*. Among the olives 5 min. W. of the village are the remains of a large Roman town where there is a mosaic floor (A.D. 250–300) and an early Christian basilica with the foundations well preserved. Two Arab (Saracen) coins were found in its destruction debris. From Vizari we may continue viâ (31½ m.) *Nithavris* to Apodhoulou and down to *Ay. Galini* (Astoria, Acropolis, C), a little resort on the S. coast.—The Amari valley can also be traversed on the W. side, keeping right at Apostoloi and passing *Meronas* and Ano Meros to *Ay. Ioannis*. Here a road goes E. to Nithavris (comp. above) or we can continue S. to join the eastern valley road about 3 m. above *Ayia Galini* (ancient *Soulia*).

From Ay. Galini, an alternative return may be made by taking the main asphalt road through (6¼ m.) *Melambes*, and the lovely village of (19¼ m.) *Spili*.—From (21 m.) *Myxorrouma* there is a minor road to *Labini* (1 m.), with its interesting frescoed church.—At 24¼ m. a road branches left through *Koxare* (½ m.) and the magnificent gorge of the Megapotamos to *Preveli* monastery (8 m.), finely situated on the sea.—31 m. *Armeni.*—38 m. *Rethymno.*

Beyond Rethymno the highway at first follows the coast. We cross the Yerani bridge and round a bend to see the White Mountains ahead. There are frequent lay-bys for the (deserted) beaches. Beyond the nome boundary the old and new roads coincide for some miles. Off to the left (c. 3 m.) is *Lake Kournás,* the only lake in Crete, set at the foot of Mt Trypali.—61½ m. *Yeoryioúpolis* (on the old road; r.) occupies the site of ancient *Amphimalla,* a port of Lappa, the powerful city in the hills to the s.w.—We follow an inland valley dotted with villages and cypress clumps, through which runs the Tris Almirí river.—67 m. *Vríses* (ΒΡΥΣΕΣ; l.; junction unfinished and not well marked in 1973), a delightful stopping-place beneath tall plane trees, has a memorial of the 1898 rising. Here diverges the road to Khóra Sfakíon (25 m.).

The road (tarmac to Khóra Sfakíon) climbs into the eastern end of the White Mountains and passes the upland villages of (11¼ m.) *Askyphou,* and (15 m.) *Imbros,* before descending to (23 m.) a road fork. The right branch leads down into (25 m.) *Khóra Sfakíon* (Xenia, small, C). From this, the capital of the Sphakiots, famed for their independence through all periods of Cretan history, excursions can be made by boat, E. to *Ay. Galini* or w. to *Loutro* and *Ay. Roúmeli* for the Gorge of Samaria.—The left branch goes to *Komitadhes* (½ m.; church with fine frescoes, 1313), and *Kapsodhasos* (5½ m.). From here there is a track s. (20 min.) to the great fortress of *Frangokastello,* built by the Venetians in 1371. It is square in plan with towers at the corners. It is claimed that at dawn on 17–18 May each year phantoms dance round the fort representing the army of Khatzimikhalis which was overwhelmed here by the Turks in 1828.

The bare cuttings of the new highway resemble pale chocolate layer cake, argillaceous bands alternating with rock. We leave the peninsula of Vamos on our right, running between the White Mountains and the sea, which we approach near (74 m.) *Kalíves.* The road passes between two large Turkish fortresses (see below). The approach road to Aptera (l.) climbs and after 1¼ m. divides: left for the deserted Turkish fort (*View) and right for the abandoned monastery that marks the ancient city. **Aptera,** one of the largest ancient cities of Crete, is said to take its name (Wingless Ones) from the Sirens who were defeated in a musical contest by the Muses, plucked off their wings and, drowning in the bay below, formed the little islets visible there. The city flourished in Classical and Roman times (its coins are common) and was the seat of a bishopric in the early Christian period. Remains of monuments to be seen include a small Doric *Temple of Apollo* near the Roman *Theatre,* a Hellenistic *Temple of Demeter,* a double temple or *Treasury,* and fine Classical defence *Walls* in the valley on the N.E. of the site. The vast underground Roman cisterns, having three great vaulted arcades of five bays, are comparable with those at Pleuron in N.W. Greece.

On the promontory of (75½ m.) *Kalámi,* below the fortress of Aptera, is a Venetian fortress, taken by the Turks in 1715 and used, together with another fort on the islet opposite, to guard the entrance to Soudha Bay. Still called *Itzedin,* it is now a prison. The main road continues along the s. shore of Soudha Bay, passing the attractive modern Naval Hospital.—81 m. **Soúdha** (*Parthenon, Knossos,* both **D**), a major Greek naval base and a NATO harbour, is also the port of Khania. The great *Bay* will take the largest ships and is well protected. Just off the main road (r.) is the large main square with many cafés, and beyond, a spacious waterfront. Near the head of the bays is a *British Military Cemetery* containing graves (mostly Commonwealth) of 1497 men who fell in May 1941 during the Battle of Crete. Among them is that of John Pendlebury, the English archaeologist, shot by the Germans as a member of British Intelligence. Hither in 1963 were transferred from the Consular cemetery 19 graves from the First World War and 51 other graves dating back to 1897.—85 m. (137 km.) Khaniá.

82 KHANIA AND WESTERN CRETE

KHANIÁ (ΧΑΝΙΑ), officially *Ta Khania*, the capital of Crete, with 40,600 inhab., is a pleasant town, well provided with squares and gardens, and preserving many features of its Venetian and Turkish past. It has a museum with finds from various parts of Western Crete and is a good centre for excursions to the sites from which they came.

Airport at Akrotiri (*Sternes*), 10 m. E.; services to Athens 3 times daily.
Car Ferry services from *Soudha*, 4 m. E., to Piraeus. Shipping Offices in Khatzimikhaili Yiannari and Khalidhon.
Hotels. Kidon (Pl. a), Plat. E. Venizelou, 110 R.; Xenia (Pl. b), by the sea, with swimming pool, both DPO, A. Doma (Pl. i), small, in a restored historic mansion 124 El. Venizelou; Porto Veneziano (Pl. j), on the old harbour; Lissos (Pl. e), 68 Vas. Konstandinou, without rest., B. Lucia (Pl. k), Akti Koundourioti; Kriti (Pl. f), Foka/Kiprou; Diktynna (Pl. g), Plat. 1866; Khania (Pl. h), 18 Plat. 1866; Cyprus (Pl. d), 17 Tzanakaki; Hellenis (Pl. n), 68 Tzanakaki, these C.
Restaurants. *Faros, Delfini, Kavouria* on the harbour; and in Plateia 1866 and 1897; also in Khalépa near the shore.
Post Office, Stratigou Tsanakaki.—O.T.E. CENTRE adjacent.
Buses from Bus Station to *Rethymno* and *Herakleion*; from Plateia 1866 to local villages.

History. This was the site of ancient *Kydonia*, a place-name found in the Linear B tablets of Knossos. Minoan occupation is attested by the settlement discovered on the Kastelli, dating right through from Neolithic times to Classical, with the L.M. IIIB period representing the zenith. Late Minoan III tombs have been found in the area of the Law Courts, Kydonia in post-Minoan times was one of the three leading cities of Crete (with Knossos and Gortyn). The Venetians occupied it in 1252 (calling it La Canea) and, apart from a short period when it fell to the Genoese (1267–90), held it until 1645. Under them a notable building programme was executed, at first on the Kastelli with a Cathedral and the Palace of the Rector, which area was walled around between 1320 and 1366. The raids of Barbarossa, the corsair Turk, in 1537, compelled Venice to fortify the whole town. The walls and bastions were fronted by a great moat up to 50 yds wide. On its S. side this moat ran approximately along the line of Skalidhi and Khatzimikhaili Yiannari Streets. After a siege the city fell to the Turks in 1645. It became the seat of the Pashalik and in the 19C the old Kastelli was the capital of the island. There were several Cretan insurrections in this period but it was not until 1898 that Turkish rule was ended. Prince George of Crete entered the city and governed the island as High Commissioner under the Allied Powers (Britain, France, and Russia). During this period of Crete's independence (until 1913) and since, Khania has remained the island's capital. It was captured by the Germans after the Battle of Crete in May 1941 and liberated in 1945.

The focal point of the town is the large open space in front of the cruciform covered *Market* together with the *Plateia 1897* to the W., whence Odhos Khatsimikhaili Yiannari (with a fine minaret) leads W. to the other important square, *Plateia 1866* (good view of the White Mountains). To the N. lies the Venetian walled town with its dilapidated streets. Odhos Khalkidhon leads N. towards the harbour. On the left is the Venetian church of *San Francesco*, which has a vaulted nave and narrow aisles, with side chapels on the S. A Turkish fountain in the

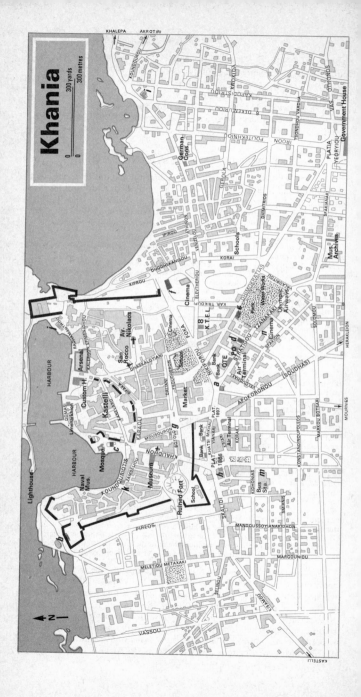

adjoining garden survives from its days as the Mosque of Yusuf Pasha. Since 1962 the church has housed the **Archaeological Museum** (adm. 25 dr.). We enter by the 'West' Door (the church in fact has a reverse orientation).

To the left of the door, Cases 1–3 display fine Early Minoan pottery from the Platyvola cave, excavated since 1966. Note the inscription of 1617 above Case 2. The next group (Cases 4–7 & 9) continues the ceramic ware from Platyvola, from Perivolia, and from the Kastelli excavations in Khania. Case 8 contains Neolithic pottery from the Kumarospilio, a cave on Akrotiri, also Cycladic vases from the Tsivourakis collection. Farther on, in the left aisle, Cases 10, 11 & 13 contain Minoan vases and imported Cypriot ware from Kastelli Khania, while Case 14 (in front) holds necklaces from various sites.

In the centre the clay *Larnakes include magnificent polychrome examples from the cemetery near Armenoi, s. of Rethymno. One with double axes has bulls of cartoon aspect. In the s.w. corner are further cases of fine Minoan ware: Case 15 includes a large painted krater from Soudha; Case 16, bronze mirrors, swords, and axes from tombs in the town and from near-by Samona. In Cases 17–21 recent pottery finds include very fine L.M. III vases from a tomb at Kalami, particularly a pyxis with a man playing a lyre to birds. An unnumbered case by the s.w. door contains the Linear A tablets found in Kastelli.

Returning to the n. aisle: Cases 22–23, Protogeometric pottery from tombs at Nokhia (Modi), and (24) from Kavoussi. The Sanctuary contains 'the Philosopher of Elyros', a heroic Roman copy of a Greek orator, and a vigorous Roman mosaic portraying Neptune and Amymone. On the s. side, Colossal head of Hadrian from the Diktynnaion. Returning along the s. side: Cases 26–27. Archaic figurines from Axos. Case 31, Black-figure vases from Phalasarna. On a pillar: plaque, Nymph and Satyr, with Erotes, from Polyrrhenia. Case 32, Bronze mirrors. Beyond the Renaissance S. portal, Case 37 contains good Roman glass from Kissamos and from various tombs.

In the body of the Nave, Sculpture, mainly Classical: *Youth with delicate features from the Asklepieion at Lissos; opposite, Pan from Hyrtakina; well-preserved obese figure of Herakles from Hydramias; Artemis from the Diktynnaion; Asklepios; Hygieia from Aptera; Aphrodite from Kydonia, several charming marble statues of children and a table from Lissos.

We reach the peaceful OUTER HARBOUR, protected by a long Venetian mole with a Turkish lighthouse, but now largely deserted for Soudha. To the left stands the *Naval Museum of Crete* (daily 10–12 & 5–8; fee), in which episodes of Greek naval history are illustrated by ship models and photographs; there are few genuine relics.

On the quay to the right are the Plaza hotel, the external staircase of which incorporates a Venetian/Turkish fountain, and the *Mosque of the Janissaries*, built in 1645, now restored as a tourist pavilion (information bureau and restaurant). Continuing round the foot of Kastelli hill (comp. below) we come to the INNER HARBOUR, fronting which is the vaulted *Arsenal*, constructed towards 1600. A Yacht Marina is under construction. Part of the *Sabbionara Bastion*, to the n.e., and the *East Wall* are preserved. In the quarter behind stands AYIOS NIKOLAOS, a Dominican church of the Venetians, transformed by the Turks into the Imperial Mosque of Sultan Ibrahim when its tower became a minaret; the Orthodox church claimed it in 1918. The galleried nave has a coffered ceiling. The great plane-tree in the square is a Turkish survival as the inevitable plaque recording 1821 recalls. The maze of tiny streets to the e. forms the most picturesque corner of the town. *Ayioi Anargyroi* (16C) contrived to remain an Orthodox church under both Venetians and Turks. The little church of *San Rocco*, farther w., bears a Latin inscription of 1630.

Stretches of the *Inner Wall*, the original 14C rampart, may be seen between Sfaka and Kanevaro streets. The Castello itself (or Kastelli) has suffered from bombing and military occupation and little remains on the hill; at 37 Lithinoi the doorway of the Venetian *Archives* survives, with an inscription of 1623. Greco-Swedish excavations since 1966 on the hill in and around Plat. Ay. Aikaterini brought to light houses dated to Late Minoan IIIB; a scarab of Thothmes III was found out of stratigraphical context, and there were pieces of pottery imported from Cyprus. Clay tablets bearing Linear A inscriptions were found in 1972–73. Off Zampeliou is a *Gate* bearing the arms of the Venieri family, dated 1608. To the N.W., on and behind the waterfront of the Outer Harbour, picturesque Venetian houses extend to the Bastion of *San Salvatore*. The church of the same name lies behind. From the Xenia Hotel we may follow the *Western Wall* to the *Bastion of San Demetrio*, backed by the great circular mound of the *Lando Bastion*. These were all constructed by 1549.

From the centre Odhos Stratigou Tzanakaki leads s.e. past the Post Office and the *Public Gardens* to the interesting **Historical Museum and Archives** in a quarter of 19C villas and fashionable apartments. Hence we may reach the former *Palace of the Governor* and the *House of Eleutherios Venizelos* in the pleasant KHALÉPA quarter on the E. edge of the town. This ends, beyond the Doma hotel and a taverna, in a quaint waterside village with tanneries, a cottage industry producing sheep and goat skins and chamois-leather.

Behind Khalépa runs the road to the **Akrotíri**, the limestone peninsula on the N.E. of Khaniá that protects Soudha Bay.—3 m. Road (l.) for *Profitis Ilias*, the hill where the Greek standard was raised by insurgents in 1897 in the teeth of an international naval bombardment. A statue of Eleutheria (Liberty) commemorating the event has been destroyed by lightning, but the tomb of Eleutherios Venizelos (1864–1936) is impressive in its simplicity. Three popular restaurants command a fine view over the Bay.—A little beyond this fork is another where we keep left, leaving the Stérnes (airport) road. At (5 m.) *Kounoupidhianá* we keep right for *Kabáni* and (10¼ m.) the monastery of *Ayía Triádha*. Erected in the early 17C and sometimes called after its Venetian founder Tzangarol, it has a fine gateway (1632) and a church built in Renaissance style (1632), the campanile being a little later. A walk of c. 1 hr to the N. will bring us to the Monastery of *St John of Gouverneto*, whose cave is near by (festival on 7 Oct).

EXCURSIONS

FROM KHANIA TO LAKKOI AND THE GORGE OF SAMARIA. This excursion may be made by car, or by bus (twice daily), to the Tourist Pavilion on the Omaló Plain, whence the descent on foot through the Gorge to Ayia Roúmeli on the coast takes about 7 hrs. From Ayia Roúmeli, where the Kapheneion on the beach offers accommodation, three boats a day in summer ply E. to Loutro and Khora Sphakion (whence there is a morning bus viâ Vryses to Khania or w. to Palaiókhora).

We leave Khania by the main Kastelli road to the w., and after 1 m. turn left (signposted Omalo).—5½ m. *Ayiá*, with a 14C church with three naves.—At (9½ m.) *Fournés* the road forks. The right branch goes direct to (15¼ m.) *Lákkoi*, or we may take the left fork to visit *Mesklá* (12¾ m.), where the Byzantine church of the Metamorphosis (Transfiguration) has frescoes of 1303, while mosaics from an ancient Temple of Venus underlie another church at the s. end of the village. Another fine church with Byzantine frescoes is that of Christ the Saviour. From the village there is a steep path (c. 1 hr) up to Lákkoi. From Lakkoi the road winds up to (24¼ m.) the *Omaló Plain* where wheat and vegetables are grown in the spring and summer, though it is too high for the olive (3610 ft). We enter the plain from the E.; the top of the gorge is at the S., at which point is the *Tourist Pavilion*. The descent into the gorge is called *Xyloskala* (Wooden Staircase). The ***Gorge of Samaria** (Φαράγγι) is said to be the longest true gorge in Europe (c. 11 m.) and throughout is a region of outstanding beauty. In parts the walls come very close together, rising sheer for nearly 1000 feet. The walk itself presents no problems, for there is a footpath all through and four guards patrol the gorge. It is not possible in winter. This is the only region where the Cretan agrimi or wild goat is to be found in its natural habitat. About half-way through is *Samaria*; the village is now deserted though some houses still stand. Farther down are the 'Iron Gates', where the walls of the gorge are only a few yards wide. We emerge at *Ayía Roúmeli*, the site of ancient *Tarrha*, which has produced fine Roman glass. The ancient temple on the site of the Church of the *Panayía* was probably that of Artemis.

FROM KHANIA TO SOÚIA (ΣΟΥΓΙΑ), 43½ m. (70 km.). From Khaniá to Ayia, see above. Beyond Ayia, at 6¾ m. we turn right for (7½ m.) *Alikianoú*, but before reaching the village turn off left. The village church (Ay. Yeoryios) has frescoes of 1430 by Paul Probatus.—16 m. *Nea Roúmata*. The road climbs over the White Mountains, passing a string of mountain villages on the descent.—37¾ m. *Rhodhováni*. About 500 yds E. of Rhodhováni are the ruins of **Elyros**, the most important ancient city of S.W. Crete. It flourished under the Romans and Byzantines (when it was the seat of a bishop) but was destroyed in the 9C Saracen invasions. Traces of walls, a theatre, and an aqueduct may be seen.—43½ m. (70 km.) *Soúia*, where is ancient *Syia* (Σύια), the port of Elyros; remains of an aqueduct and baths survive and in the village church there is a mosaic pavement of a 6C basilica with representations of deer, peacocks, and interwoven vines. A little W. of Soúia at *Ayios Kyrkos* is ancient **Lissos**, the port of Hyrtakina to the N.; a good deal of the *Asklepieion* is preserved, including mosaics inside the temple. The ancient water supply for the building passed under the floor to feed a fountain. On a terrace to the N.E. are remains of baths; other buildings, including perhaps a waiting place for the sick, lie to the N. In excavations in the temple, important finds were made, including statuettes of the 3C B.C. and, more recently, a Theatre has come to light.

FROM KHANIA TO KASTELLI KISSAMOU, 26 m. (42 km.). The road runs W. along the coast over which the German airborne invasion of 1941 swept in from bases in Attica.—1¼ m. *Aptera Beach* (Bungalow Hotel C). To the left of the road the German monument to their 2nd Parachute Regiment takes the aggressive form of a diving eagle. *Glaros Beach* and *Kalamáki Beach* are passed amid haphazard development along the sandy Khaniá Bay. The bathing is not always safe. The island of *Ayión Theodóron*, prominent off the coast, is one of several reserves for the Cretan wild goat.—6½ m. *Plataniás* (taverna). We cross the Kerítis amid groves of bamboo and wind through small orange groves, each protected by high bamboo windbreaks against the meltémi. —10 m. *Máleme* (Maleme Beach B) has a German military cemetery (l.).

A new bridge over another torrent has superseded two Bailey bridges (r.) that did service for thirty years. At (12½ m.) *Tavronítis* (cafés) a road branches left for Palaiokhóra (see below). Beyond *Kamisianá* (tavernas) we cut across the base of the RHODOPOÚ PENINSULA, on which *Kolimvári*, the first village, with its monastery is prominent. The Moní Goniás, or Hodegetria, was founded in 1618, though the buildings date from 1662 and later. There are fine 17C icons, including one signed by the Cretan artist, Konstandinos Palaiokapas (1637).—14¾ m. The Rose Marie Hotel (D, small, Apr–Oct) stands at the turn.

The main road threads a natural gap in the hills. Suddenly the Gulf of Kissamou, with the plain of Kastelli, bursts on the view (superb *Pano-rama in the evening). To the s., as we descend, craggy dolomitic moun-tains fill the sky, and ahead the long line of Gramvousa rears out of the sea. We pass the turning (r.) for *Nopígia* on the coast, near which was ancient *Mithmyna*.—23 m. *Kaloudhianá*; by-road for Topolia, see below. The plain is densely planted with olives.

26 m. (42 km.) **Kastélli Kissámou** (*Kastell* C) lies to seaward of the road, a long straggle of buildings, set back from its fine sandy beach. Here was ancient *Kissamos*, the port of Polyrrhenia. Kastelli was a thriving Venetian town, fortified in the 16C. The *Museum*, not much more than an Apotheke, situated below the Post Office in the main square, contains local finds, notably a good grave relief and a marble satyr. Two small fishing harbours lie isolated to the w. of the town; one of these has been developed to accommodate passenger boats ply-ing from Piraeus viâ Yithion, providing in summer a direct link between Crete and the Peloponnese.

The village of **Polyrrhenia**, 4 m. s. of the town, is built on the site of the ancient city of the same name. Classical, Roman, and Byzantine walling is preserved on the N. and E. sides of the hill, and there are the remains of public buildings. The coins show the worship of several deities, including Diktynnaian Artemis.

On the coast w. of Castelli is ancient *Phalasarna*, where walling and a rock cut throne are preserved. The city was independent and had a temple to Diktynnaian Artemis. Its cemetery has started to yield black-figured pottery, some of Corinthian origin, of the 6C B.C. Here best of all in West Crete, the rising of the land since ancient times is demonstrated, the old sea line being up to 28 ft higher than the present one. This tilting has brought the ancient harbour remains 150 yds inland.

To PALAIOKHORA, 48 m. (77 km.). To (12½ m.) *Tavronítis*, on the Kastelli road, see above. The road follows a wide wooded valley before climbing into the foothills on the White Mountains.—27 m. Rocky col (c. 1600 ft) with fine retrospective view towards N.W. We descend, soon reaching a widened and realined road.—36¼ m. *Kándanos* (1892 ft), the chief place of the eparchy of Selino, was destroyed by the Germans in 1941. At the entrance to the town (l.) are the waterworks given by a German group as an act of atonement (plaque). There are excellent frescoes in the churches of the Panayia and Ayia Anna.—Soon after Kándanos the road becomes rough.—40½ m. Track (l.) to Kadros and ancient Kandanos.—48 m. **Palaiokhora** (*Livikon* D), the *Castel Selino* of the Venetians, who built a fort on the promontory in 1279, is now a sizeable village straddling the base of the peninsula. There is a large sandy beach, backed by trees. Tourist rooms can be arranged. Boats may be hired to visit ancient Lissos (c. 1 hr), Souia (c. 1¼ hr), Ayía Roúmeli (c. 3 hrs), etc.

INDEX

Topographical names are printed in **bold type** (modern names) or SMALL CAPS (ancient or medieval names); names of eminent persons in *italics*; other entries (including sub-indexes) in Roman type. Note on transliteration, see p. 56.

Printed by Fletcher & Son Ltd, Norwich

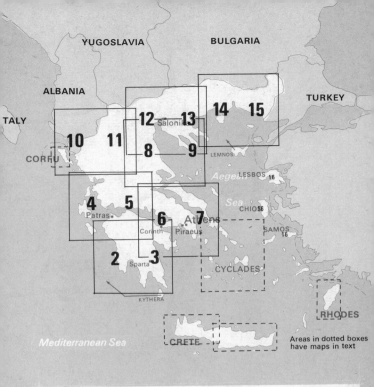

key page to Map numbers

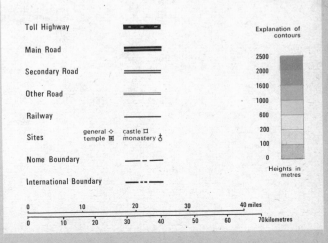

Toll Highway			Explanation of contours
Main Road			
Secondary Road			
Other Road			
Railway			
Sites	general ◇ temple ▥	castle ☐ monastery ⚲	
Nome Boundary			
International Boundary			

Heights in metres

0	10	20	30	40 miles
0	10	20	30	40	50	60	70 kilometres